HISTORY OF A FREE PEOPLE

HISTORY OF A FREE PEOPLE

Henry W. Bragdon
Samuel P. McCutchen

Macmillan Publishing Co., Inc.
New York

Collier Macmillan Publishers
London

About the Authors

HENRY BRAGDON was for many years a much-admired teacher at the Phillips Exeter Academy in Exeter, N.H., winding up his career there as Cowles Professor in the Humanities Emeritus. In addition to his work on this textbook, he was the author of a biography of President Woodrow Wilson, *Woodrow Wilson: The Academic Years,* which was nominated for a National Book Award. He also served as president of the New England History Teachers' Association, chief examiner in Social Studies for the College Entrance Examination Board, and lecturer at Harvard College.

SAMUEL P. McCUTCHEN spent a long career as teacher of high school social studies and as a teacher of teachers of social studies. He was professor of education at New York University. On the high school level he taught at Fayette (Mississippi) High School and was chairperson of the social studies department of the John Burroughs School, St. Louis, Mo. He also served as president of the National Council for the Social Studies.

Verna Fancett, who prepared the section on history study skills and the part-end study materials of this textbook, has long been interested in helping students broaden their understanding of history. She is an editor of the periodical *The Social Studies* and served for many years as chairperson of the Social Studies Department of the Jamesville-Dewitt (New York) Central Schools.

Donald A. Ritchie, who prepared the new text material for this edition of *History of a Free People,* pursues his profession as Associate Historian with the Senate Historical Office. Previously, he taught history at the University of Maryland and at George Mason University. He has also taught at the high school level.

Special thanks are due to Leon Hellerman, Chairman of the Social Studies Department, George W. Hewlett High School, Hewlett, New York, for his work on the Data Labs.

Macmillan Publishing Co., Inc.
866 Third Avenue, New York, New York 10022
Collier Macmillan Canada, Ltd.

Printed in the United States of America

Pupil's Edition: ISBN 0-02-115380-9
Teacher's Annotated Edition: ISBN 0-02-115390-6

9 8 7 6 5 4 3 2

Contents

Part Three • The Nation and the Sections

Part Four • Division and Reunion

Maps

Vital American Documents

Data Labs

Charts, Graphs, and Tables

Vignettes

Prologue

The American Experiment

In terms of size and natural resources, the United States is one of the great nations of the world. It covers 3,000,000 square miles from sea to sea, plus Alaska and Hawaii. Immense productive capacity has given its people a very high standard of living.

But the true greatness of a nation may have relatively little to do with its size or its ability to produce goods. The lasting greatness of the United States rests on something more than material things. What ideals has this country preached and tried to practice? What in American life, in addition to mere abundance, has made this country such a desirable place to live?

Outstanding characteristics of the American way of life have varied from period to period and section to section, but the following can be traced from colonial times to the present.

(1) **Economic opportunity.** There has generally been a chance for individuals to improve themselves by their own efforts. For over two centuries there was abundant cheap land, and even now the United States contains untapped wealth. Americans have prized willingness to work as a primary virtue and have been skilled in turning natural resources into food, clothing, houses, luxuries, and gadgets.

Furthermore, Americans have found means to see that wealth is widely shared. Americans have used the power of government to promote general prosperity. However, they have seldom done this by sharing wealth through state-owned enterprise. Instead, Americans have used government to regulate private enterprise, and often to aid it. They have used taxation and social legislation to try to equalize wealth.

(2) **Wide participation in politics.** From colonial times to the present, there has been widening opportunity for Americans to have a share in government. The United States was the first large nation to attempt "government of the people, by the people." In the twentieth century, while many countries have fallen under the control of oppressive one-party governments or military rulers, we in the United States have managed to maintain democracy.

(3) **Belief in reform rather than revolution.** The United States has now embarked on the third century of its existence. Since its beginning, there has been only one major armed conflict within the country. In general, Americans have agreed to settle even the most bitter disputes by ballots rather than bullets.

(4) **A mobile population.** Families in this country have been continuously on the move.

Americans have usually been ready to "pull up stakes" and move to other sections of the country. Witness the van and motor home. The American people have also been socially mobile. They are not fixed in one social class or occupation. Although in fact there have always been the rich and the poor, Americans have cherished the ideal of a "middle class" society.

(5) Relatively high position and freedom for women. American women have not yet achieved social, economic, or political equality. From the first, however, they obtained greater freedom and opportunity than existed in most other lands.

(6) Belief in education and widespread educational opportunity. From the Massachusetts School Law of 1647, which required that all children be taught to read and write, until the present, there has been ever-increasing educational opportunity. Without schooling for all, there cannot be effective democracy. No other major country provides its citizens with as many years of formal schooling as the United States, or as varied educational opportunities.

(7) Concern for the welfare of others. When Americans lived under frontier conditions, they had to cooperate in order to survive. Today, concern for others is shown by innumerable private organizations such as the Red Cross and the United Fund. On an international scale the same concerns are revealed by the Marshall Plan, which restored Western European prosperity after World War II, and by the Peace Corps, which sent thousands of Americans to developing countries to aid in raising living standards.

(8) Toleration of differences. The United States is home to people of different races, with different national backgrounds, speaking different languages, practicing different religions. To pull together these diverse people into a nation, Americans have had to learn tolerance. The first clause of the Bill of Rights in the Constitution protects the right of all to speak, write, and worship freely. And recent years have brought progress in the treatment of minority groups.

(9) Respect for the rights and abilities of the individual. This is the most fundamental characteristic of all, and to some degree includes all the others. Free public education is based on the idea that people have the right to an equal start in the race of life. Freedom of speech and press are based on both the right of persons to speak their minds and the faith that people have enough intelligence to choose wisely between voices urging different courses of action.

(10) World-wide responsibility. At the time they declared their independence, in 1776, American political philosophers had a sense of responsibility to the world. They thought it their mission to show people everywhere something new: a free society governed by reason and law. But until the twentieth century the people of the United States hoped to be isolated politically from Europe; their foreign policy was generally confined to the Western Hemisphere. In the twentieth century they have come to realize that they cannot isolate themselves from a world that has rapidly shrunk as communication and transportation have improved. The United States has been suddenly thrust into a position of world leadership. Americans have accepted—although sometimes reluctantly—this world-wide responsibility.

While these characteristics have helped to form our system of values, it must be remembered that they are not exclusive to the United States. Participation in politics is wider in several other countries. Belief in the ballot box is just as strong in England. Technical skill, toleration of differences, belief in education, respect for the individual—none of these is exclusive to us. Taken together, however, they represent a distinct national character and a general perspective unique to the American people.

History Study Skills

Success in your study of American history depends to a great extent on your ability to handle certain special skills in the subject. This section of your textbook is designed to help you acquire and apply these skills. It also provides an opportunity to strengthen those history study skills you already have developed.

You will find that careful study of this history skills section will be a useful preparation for reading *History of a Free People*. In addition, you will want to use it from time to time throughout the course to review or brush up on these skills. Here is a list of the history study skills covered in this special section:

Understanding Historical Maps

Historical maps are visual ways of showing and explaining events in history. Such maps help to describe the geographical setting of historical events during a specific time period.

Historical maps are special-purpose maps. They differ from other kinds of maps like road maps or maps showing climate, rainfall, or natural resources. Historical maps may include some of the features of those maps, but only if these features help to explain history.

All historical maps do the following:
- focus on a **specific topic, event,** or **development** in history
- deal with the subject in a **specific time period**
- place the subject in a **specific location** on the earth

On these two pages, we will study two historical maps that deal with population changes in the United States. By examining them carefully and answering the questions that follow, you will learn much that applies to all historical maps.

THE COLONIAL PERIOD

The historical map below clearly illustrates a stage of development that took place in several locations during a specific period.

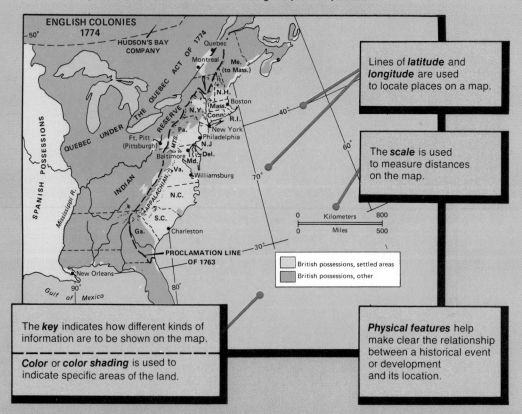

Lines of **latitude** and **longitude** are used to locate places on a map.

The **scale** is used to measure distances on the map.

The **key** indicates how different kinds of information are to be shown on the map.

Color or **color shading** is used to indicate specific areas of the land.

Physical features help make clear the relationship between a historical event or development and its location.

THE MOVEMENT WEST

A common purpose of historical maps is to show change in a particular place over a period of time. Note that this map shows an important development occurring in three locations in the United States during three different time periods.

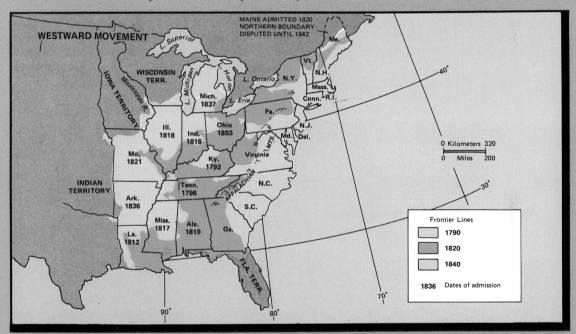

Keeping Track of Time and Chronology

History is the study of what happened in past *time*. Many questions that are asked in the study of history are related to time: When did something happen? How long did it last? How long ago did it take place? In what time sequence did certain events happen? That is, which event happened first, which event happened next, which event happened after that, etc.?

The following materials will help you become familiar with the vocabulary of time, and the time sequence of events.

THE VOCABULARY OF TIME

- *decade*—10 years. (Give your age three decades from now.)
- *score*—20 years. (In 1863, Lincoln began his Gettysburg Address with the words, "Fourscore and seven years ago...." Name that year.)
- *generation*—about 30 years, the time it takes a person to mature and raise a family. (What does "second-generation" American mean?)
- *century*—100 years. Note that a century may be dated in two ways: 1600's = 17th century; 1700's = 18th century; 1800's = 19th century; 1900's = 20th century. (In which century is the year 1607? Name a year in the second half of the 18th century.)

Here are some other words that also refer to time: *era, period, age.* These words have similar meanings: They describe time spans during which certain related events or developments took place. An era, period, or age may be fairly short or last for many years. Here are some examples of these time words in American history: the Age of Jackson—12 years (about 1829-1841); the Progressive Era—about 20 years (around 1900-1917); the Colonial Period—over 175 years (about 1607-1783). (Think of a time span in the life of someone you admire. Name it: *era, period,* or *age.*)

CHRONOLOGY—ONE THING AFTER ANOTHER

Chronology is the arrangement of events in time. Chronology puts historical events in the order in which they occurred. Historical relationships, trends, and developments can often be better understood if they are placed in chronological order.

One way to show chronological order is with a table. For example:

TERRITORIAL EXPANSION OF THE CONTINENTAL U.S. IN THE 1800's.	
Area Acquired	*Date of Acquisition*
Louisiana Purchase	1803
Purchase of Florida	1819
Annexation of Texas	1845
Oregon boundary settlement	1846
Mexican Cession	1848
Gadsden Purchase	1853
Purchase of Alaska	1867

While a table can be used to show time relationships of events, chronology is more easily visualized with a *time line.* On a time line, events are arranged in chronological order, with each event placed in its proper position on a scale of years. Here is a time line showing the same events that are given in the table on the previous page:

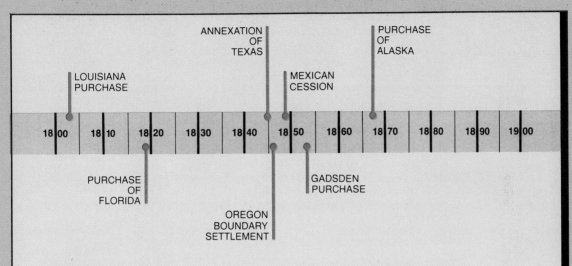

This time line is a *topical time line* because it deals with one particular topic—the territorial expansion of the United States. The information on a topical time line is often more meaningful when it is expanded to include other events.
Copy the above time line on a sheet of paper and add the following major events in American history that occurred in the 19th century:

1812-1814—War with Great Britain

1820—Missouri Compromise

1846-1848—War with Mexico

1861-1865—Civil War

1869—First transcontinental railroad

1898—Spanish-American War

QUESTIONS

1. Name the one area acquired by the United States after the Civil War.

2. How many years after the Louisiana Purchase did the Missouri Compromise take place?

3. Which territories were acquired during the five years before and after the end of the war with Mexico?

4. Prepare a table and a time line of events in the life of a person you know or admire. Add presidential elections and other important events you can think of.

Studying Historical Pictures

You can learn much about the past by studying historical pictures. Paintings, drawings, prints, and photographs often give us more of a sense of an event or a period than is possible in words.

Here are some things to be aware of in studying a picture:

- **subject**—what person, event, or subject does the picture deal with?
- **time and place**—when and where is the subject taking place? What details tell you this?
- **point of view**—is the artist or photographer trying to tell you how he or she feels about the subject?
- **emotional impact**—what general impression does the picture make? How does the picture make you feel about the subject?
- **form of expression**—what kind of picture is it (drawing, photograph, etc.?) and how does this affect the content of the picture?

LOOKING AT TWO HISTORICAL PICTURES

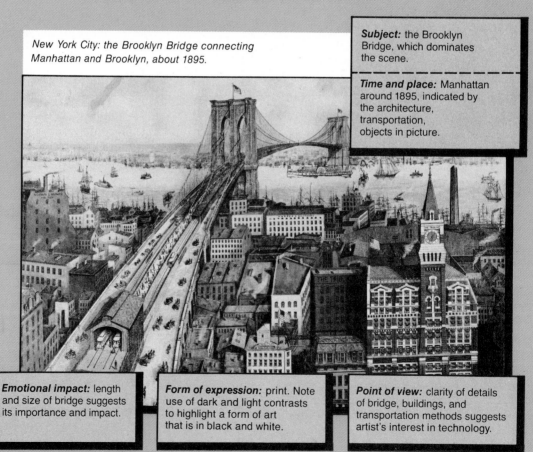

New York City: the Brooklyn Bridge connecting Manhattan and Brooklyn, about 1895.

Subject: the Brooklyn Bridge, which dominates the scene.

Time and place: Manhattan around 1895, indicated by the architecture, transportation, objects in picture.

Emotional impact: length and size of bridge suggests its importance and impact.

Form of expression: print. Note use of dark and light contrasts to highlight a form of art that is in black and white.

Point of view: clarity of details of bridge, buildings, and transportation methods suggests artist's interest in technology.

QUESTIONS

1. What impression does the picture of the Brooklyn Bridge make on you? How do you feel about the treatment of the subject?

2. List all the types of transportation you see in the picture. What kinds of buildings are shown?

3. Using only what you see in this picture, describe life in New York City at the time of the picture.

4. Compare this picture with the one of Orchard Street below. Using the guidelines above, in what ways are the two pictures similar? different?

New York City: Orchard Street on the Lower East Side, about 1910.

QUESTIONS

1. Compose a title for this picture that identifies its subject and form.

2. What details help you identify the time and place of this picture?

3. From this picture, what impression do you get of life in this part of New York City? What do you think is the photographer's point of view on this subject?

4. Using this textbook's pictures, find examples to support each of the following statements:
    a. Interpretation of historical pictures may change with time.
    b. Any picture is only one possible view of the subject.
    c. Pictures in any form vary in accuracy, purpose, and effect.
    d. Pictures can be a powerful means of shaping the viewer's opinion, attitudes, and feelings.

Interpreting Historical Cartoons

A cartoon is a drawing that deals with a topic of the day, often in humorous or satirical ways. Most of the cartoons you will see in a history textbook appeared originally in newspapers or magazines. Like written editorials, they express a point of view or state an opinion. Therefore, they are known as *editorial cartoons.*

Editorial cartoons, like many other kinds of pictures, present ideas very directly and, often, powerfully. For this reason it is important to be able to understand them and to analyze how they achieve their effect. Ask yourself these questions when you look at a cartoon:

- Who are the characters in the cartoon? Are they drawn realistically or in an exaggerated way to express the cartoonist's opinion?
- Does the cartoonist use any symbols, such as Uncle Sam or the American flag? What function do these symbols perform?
- What idea is the cartoonist presenting? What is his or her point of view? If the cartoon is on a current topic, do you agree with it?

UNDERSTANDING A CARTOONIST'S TECHNIQUES

Symbols: The American flag indicates the setting. The spectators represent the American people.

Exaggeration: Note the overweight bodies, skinny legs, anxiety on the faces of runners in foreground. Compare this look with how the runner labeled "Inflation" is drawn.

Labels: Each character has a label that identifies him.

Caption: This sentence or phrase helps sum up the meaning of the cartoon.

'ARE WE STILL CATCHING UP WITH HIM OR IS HE CATCHING UP WITH US?'

ONE SUBJECT—TWO POINTS OF VIEW

Since a cartoon often expresses a point of view, you will not be surprised to find two cartoons on the same subject taking different sides. Study these cartoons about President Franklin D. Roosevelt's New Deal in the 1930's.

"YES, YOU REMEMBERED ME"

Labels: each item is clearly identified.

Exaggeration: smallness of the man on a narrow ledge against a big cliff.

Symbols: FDR stands for Franklin Delano Roosevelt.

Notice the **appeal to emotion** in both cartoons.

Caption: indicates the response of the character on the left.

QUESTIONS

1. What is the main idea of each cartoon? What criticism of the New Deal is made in the first cartoon? What does the other cartoon find praiseworthy about the New Deal? In this cartoon, who is the speaker?

2. What symbols do the cartoonists use and what do they stand for?

3. How does each cartoonist's special techniques help get across his point of view?

4. What emotions does each cartoonist try to arouse in the viewer?

Getting the Most from Graphs

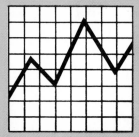

One way to present historical information that deals with quantities is by means of graphs. A graph is a kind of diagram that uses lines, bars, or circles to show statistical data. Graphs can present historical information more vividly and dramatically than lists of numbers on the same topic. In history books, graphs are often used to show changes over a period of time and other kinds of comparisons.

Three basic kinds of graphs are used in history books:

- *circle or pie graph*
- *bar graph*
- *line graph*

On these two pages, the same information on the U.S. population is shown on these three different kinds of graphs. Study each of them. Which type of graph do you think most clearly presents the information?

CIRCLE OR PIE GRAPH

The *title* indicates the subject of the graph.

Each circle represents the total *quantity*, in this case 100% of the nation's population.

Notice the *date* of what each circle covers.

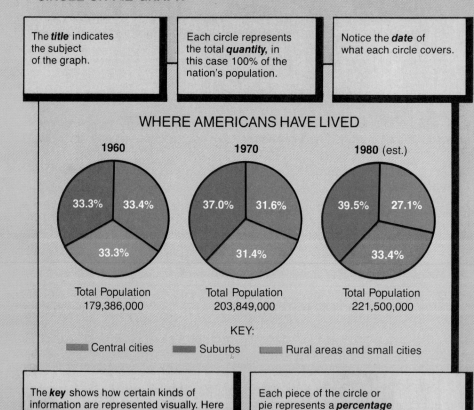

WHERE AMERICANS HAVE LIVED

1960

33.3% 33.4%
33.3%

Total Population
179,386,000

1970

37.0% 31.6%
31.4%

Total Population
203,849,000

1980 (est.)

39.5% 27.1%
33.4%

Total Population
221,500,000

KEY:

▬ Central cities   ▬ Suburbs   ▬ Rural areas and small cities

The *key* shows how certain kinds of information are represented visually. Here the key distinguishes between the three kinds of places in which Americans live.

Each piece of the circle or pie represents a *percentage* of the total population.

BAR GRAPH

The horizontal axis shows *time* periods.

The vertical axis represents *percentages*, or *quantity*.

Each bar is drawn to *scale*. It indicates the size of each population group.

LINE GRAPH

The vertical axis represents *percentages*, or *quantity*.

The horizontal axis shows *time*.

The lines represent the changing population *percentages*. Note that the *scale* shows percentages for *all* years between 1960 and 1980.

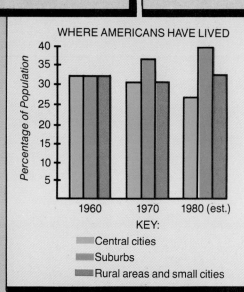

WHERE AMERICANS HAVE LIVED

KEY:
- Central cities
- Suburbs
- Rural areas and small cities

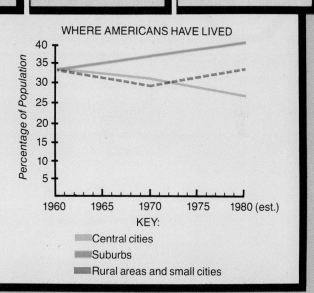

WHERE AMERICANS HAVE LIVED

KEY:
- Central cities
- Suburbs
- Rural areas and small cities

QUESTIONS

1. What percentage of the population lived in the suburbs in 1970? Which graph or graphs did you use to find this information?

2. What percentage of the population lived in central cities in 1975? Name the one graph that contains this information.

3. Which kind of graph would you use to show the following information? Explain your choice.
   a. A comparison of age groups in the U.S. today.
   b. High school enrollment at the start of each decade, 1950-1980.

4. Using the information from the graphs shown, write a summary entitled "Changes in Places in Which Americans Lived, 1960-1980."

5. Examine the statistical information about the U.S. in 1790 on page 80 of this book. Use any portion of the data you wish and draw it by means of a graph.

Working with Diagrams and Flowcharts

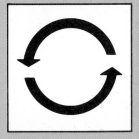

Diagrams and flowcharts are visual ways of presenting complex ideas so that they can be readily understood. Their main purpose is to summarize an important idea and to show how the idea is made up of many parts, each related to the others.

In studying a diagram or a flowchart, first discover the subject being presented—this is often given in the title. Then examine the flowchart or diagram as a whole to get a general impression of what it contains. Finally, examine each part of it to see how the parts help you understand the main idea of the material.

STUDYING A DIAGRAM

In 1785 a law was passed that provided for a new way of dividing up land to be sold in the Northwest Territory. Study the two diagrams below to help you understand the effect of this law.

The **title** indicates the topic being analyzed.

The purpose of the diagram is to show change in types of land settlement.

Labels define the parts of the diagram, or its organization.

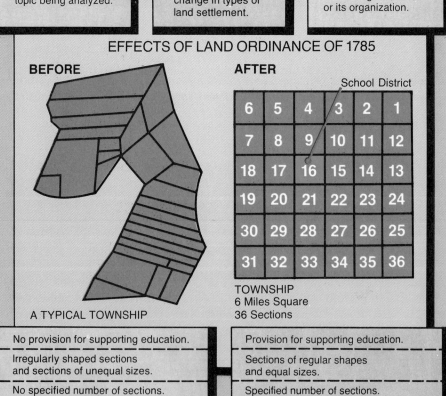

EFFECTS OF LAND ORDINANCE OF 1785

BEFORE

A TYPICAL TOWNSHIP

AFTER

School District

6	5	4	3	2	1
7	8	9	10	11	12
18	17	16	15	14	13
19	20	21	22	23	24
30	29	28	27	26	25
31	32	33	34	35	36

TOWNSHIP
6 Miles Square
36 Sections

No provision for supporting education.

Irregularly shaped sections and sections of unequal sizes.

No specified number of sections.

Provision for supporting education.

Sections of regular shapes and equal sizes.

Specified number of sections.

STUDYING A FLOWCHART

A flowchart's purpose is to show stages in a process or event. The flowchart below shows how the United States went from prosperity to depression in the late 1920's and '30's, and the main factors that caused this change.

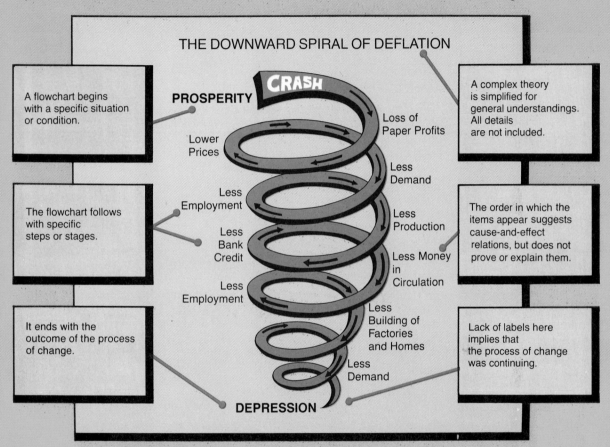

THE DOWNWARD SPIRAL OF DEFLATION

A flowchart begins with a specific situation or condition.

The flowchart follows with specific steps or stages.

It ends with the outcome of the process of change.

A complex theory is simplified for general understandings. All details are not included.

The order in which the items appear suggests cause-and-effect relations, but does not prove or explain them.

Lack of labels here implies that the process of change was continuing.

PROSPERITY

CRASH

Lower Prices

Less Employment

Less Bank Credit

Less Employment

Loss of Paper Profits

Less Demand

Less Production

Less Money in Circulation

Less Building of Factories and Homes

Less Demand

DEPRESSION

QUESTIONS

1. What is the subject of the diagram on the left on page S-12?

2. What is the main idea of this diagram? of the flowchart?

3. From the flowchart, name four factors that were important as the United States moved from prosperity to depression.

4. By what means does the diagram show change?

5. Draw a diagram illustrating the organization of your school, the layout of your classroom, or some other subject you choose.

Practicing Study and Review Skills

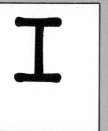

BEFORE YOU BEGIN YOUR ASSIGNMENT

Studying an assignment in a textbook is achieved most effectively when you plan what to do. Here are some suggestions for that plan. You may, of course, modify any part of it to best suit your own study needs. But you will get the most out of an assignment if you try to accomplish each of these steps before you start to read the lesson.

• *Skim the assigned pages.* This will give you a general idea of the content you are going to study. Pay special attention to the *headings* and *subheadings,* or the words in dark type, which are used as labels to describe each of the topics you are going to study.

Before you begin to read, make a list of the headings and subheadings in the lesson. For example, turn to page 3. The main heading is "The Indians of North America." The first subheading is "Eastern Woodland Indians: The Iroquois." What are the next subheads? These headings will help you see how the chapter is organized. They also will help you decide how best to take notes on the lesson (see below).

• *Examine the pictures, maps, charts, and other features.* These are included in the textbook to present additional information about the subject. In the "Indians of North America" section (pages 3-11), there is a map showing some of the main Indian tribes of North America as well as a topographical map of the United States. There also are pictures of Indian villages. As you can see, examining the maps and illustrations ahead of time helps prepare you to understand the information you will read in the assignment.

AS YOU STUDY YOUR ASSIGNMENT

Taking notes as you read the textbook is one of the best ways to help you learn more efficiently. Moreover, as you will see, these notes will come in handy later on when you go to review the lesson.

Here are some suggestions for taking notes on any assignment:

• *Outline the text.* Below is a "blank" outline. It can be filled in by using the content of your assignment. (Because the textbook content varies, you will find that sometimes certain parts of the outline may not be needed.)

A. INTRODUCTION
B. MAIN TOPIC
   1. Supporting detail
   2. Supporting detail . . .
   3. Topic conclusion

C. MAIN TOPIC
   1. Supporting detail
   2. Supporting detail . . .
   3. Topic conclusion
D. CONCLUSION

In the Introduction, you can use your own words or use words and phrases from the textbook to describe the main subject you will be studying in the lesson. In the Main Topic, you can state the main idea of each part of the lesson. There usually are several topics in each lesson. And each of these topics contain supporting details, or information that explains the topic. Topics often have a conclusion, which sums up the topic. The final Conclusion wraps up the discussion, often by summarizing or giving the significance of these topics.

Here is an example of how you might make such an outline when you read pages 31-32 of your textbook. You will notice, for example, how the outline form has been modified in taking notes on this section about English Colonial Government.

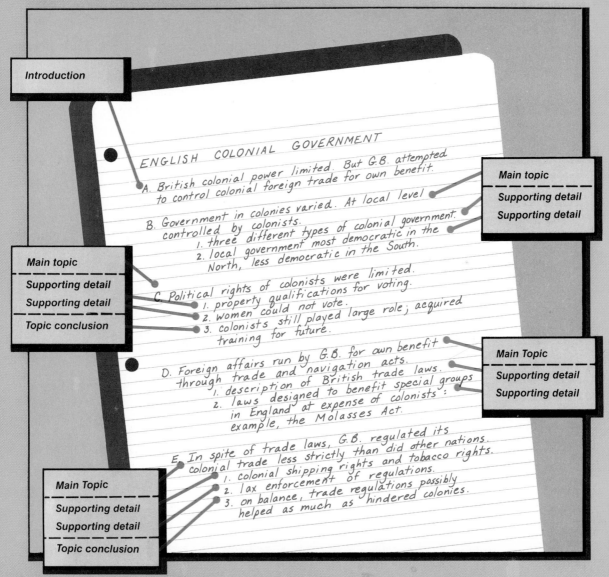

Introduction

ENGLISH COLONIAL GOVERNMENT

A. British colonial power limited. But G.B. attempted to control colonial foreign trade for own benefit.

Main topic
Supporting detail
Supporting detail

B. Government in colonies varied. At local level controlled by colonists.
   1. three different types of colonial government.
   2. local government most democratic in the North, less democratic in the South.

Main topic
Supporting detail
Supporting detail
Topic conclusion

C. Political rights of colonists were limited.
   1. property qualifications for voting.
   2. women could not vote.
   3. colonists still played large role; acquired training for future.

D. Foreign affairs run by G.B. for own benefit through trade and navigation acts.
   1. description of British trade laws.
   2. laws designed to benefit special groups in England at expense of colonists: example, the Molasses Act.

Main Topic
Supporting detail
Supporting detail

E. In spite of trade laws, G.B. regulated its colonial trade less strictly than did other nations.
   1. colonial shipping rights and tobacco rights.
   2. lax enforcement of regulations.
   3. on balance, trade regulations possibly helped as much as hindered colonies.

Main Topic
Supporting detail
Supporting detail
Topic conclusion

• *Make an outline with notes.* Another way of taking notes is to organize your notes by using outline headings and filling in information under each heading. You can use the headings given in the text or you can make up your own headings. Then under each heading, you can write phrases or short sentences telling about the subjects that each of them includes. For example, here is an outline with notes for the first heading of the text on p. 31:

ENGLISH COLONIAL GOVERNMENT

    British power varied from colony to colony / always limited / examples from charter, proprietary, royal colonies over governorship.

    Local government in colonists' hands / NE town meeting most democratic / middle and southern colonies less so.

    Political rights limited by property and religious qualifications / nevertheless wider political participation in colonies than in Europe / training for future.

Hints for Taking Notes

Here are some hints that may save you time when you take notes as you study the lesson.

• *Develop your own shorthand.* Here are examples of such shorthand notes:

    G.B. = Great Britain
    NE = New England
    WW II = World War II.
    X = Very important idea or information
    ? = Not sure what this means; find out

• *Omit unnecessary words* like "a," "an," "the," and "it."

• *Use phrases* rather than complete sentences.

• *Underline important points,* but don't overdo this.

• *List items* like major causes of a war or key terms of a treaty.

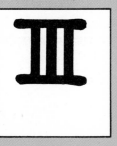

REVIEWING THE LESSON

Reviewing helps you to refresh your memory. It means taking a second look and rethinking what you have studied. Reviewing helps you organize facts and information in order to make sure that you understand the main ideas of the lesson. Reviewing brings together everything you have just read so that you comprehend the assignment as a whole. Here are some useful techniques to use in reviewing an assignment.

• *Study your notes on the text.* Read through the notes you took on each assignment. Clear, accurate notes increase your comprehension and save you time. Check with the text discussion to fill in any gaps in your information or to clarify anything you don't understand.

• *Look at the headings.* Leaf through the pages of the textbook, concentrating on the headings. Without reading the text itself, try to recall the main ideas and some important supporting details. Then reread some of the text to see if you remembered it correctly.

• *Look for text clues.* Look for details about a topic that are listed 1, 2, 3. Look for definitions of words given in *italics,* or slanted type. Look for synonyms of words, often given in parentheses. Look for word clues like "because," "as a result," "in this way." These word clues tell you about the relationship between events or the effects of an event or action.

• *Study the illustrations.* Glance at each of the pictures, graphs, charts, and cartoons. Ask yourself, "What does this illustration tell me about the subject of the text?"

- *Reread the special features.* Look at the quotation at the beginnning of the chapter. Study the vignette, data bank, and vital documents in the chapter. Check over each of these special features for the information they contain, which supplements that in the text and often offers points of view on the text.

- *Study the chapter study aids.* Use these aids to check on what you have learned. Notice the ways in which they help you review.
  - Identify . . .
  - Give the significance of . . .
  - Define . . .
  - Complete these statements . . .
  - Locate . . .
  - Compare . . .
  - List the causes . . .
  - Describe the effects of . . .
  - Explain how . . . or why . . .
  - Evaluate the influence of . . .
  - Summarize . . .

- *Study the Part "Summing Up."* Use these study aids to test your recall and understanding of the facts and ideas you studied in *several* chapters. In addition, use other review techniques such as those suggested in the list above.

Hints for Reviewing

Here are some hints that may save you time when you review the lesson.

- *Develop your own reviewing style.* Base it on those methods that seem to produce the best results for you.

- *Use flash cards or note cards,* with questions written on one side and the answers on the other, for dates and events, people and their contributions, key words and definitions.

- *Focus on important topics and supporting details* like these:
  - stages in a process or event (the coming of the Civil War, for example)
  - key features of a development (inflation, for example)
  - or a movement (women's rights, for example)

culture (when jazz became popular in the "roaring twenties," for example)

- *Form your own ideas and conclusions.* Ask yourself questions like these:
  - "Do I have all the information I need to make a valid conclusion?"
  - "Have I weighed all the evidence fairly?"
  - "How and why might new information cause me to change or modify my conclusion?"

Establishing your own plan for study and review, then using it throughout the year, is one of the most effective ways of helping you get the most out of your American history course. It will help you remember information, understand ideas more clearly, and use your time more efficiently.

Part

1

The Dutch Gallery, Museum of the City of New York

A Free Country in a New World

Chapters in this Part

Nieuw Amsterdam, the view up Broadway, 1661

The Land and the People

There was a time when our [ancestors] owned this great island, their seats extended from the rising to the setting sun. The Great Spirit had made it for the use of the Indians. . . . But an evil day came upon us. Your ancestors crossed the great water, and landed upon this island.

—RED JACKET (A SENECA CHIEF), 1805

The human race probably developed in Asia or Africa. Modern people were present in Europe 50,000 years ago, and they may have been there 75,000 years before that. It is now believed that the first human beings reached America at least 15,000—possibly more than 25,000—years ago. There is general agreement that they came via the Bering Strait. Today the Strait is only fifty-six miles across with three islands. The water is very shallow. It may have been possible at one time to cross from Siberia to Alaska on dry land. The wandering newcomers could then have worked their way south.

It is probable that people came to America in small groups over very long periods. It is hard otherwise to account for the amazing number of different languages. In 1500 A.D. there were something like five hundred distinct Indian languages north of Panama and three times that many in South America. Some of the languages are related to each other, as French is to Spanish. But many groups of languages are utterly unconnected with others.

The first people to reach America looked rather unlike modern American Indians, but later arrivals had much the same physical characteristics as the Indians of today. They came with very little in the way of skills or tools. They lived by gathering fruit, nuts, edible plants, shellfish, and the like. But gradually they developed hunting skills. Their spear points are found by archaeologists with the bones of many animals now extinct in America: mammoths, mastodons, tapirs, camels, giant bison. These gatherers and hunters spread over both continents from Alaska to the Straits of Magellan, which they reached almost 9,000 years ago.

Faced by new and sometimes harsh environments, the American Indians developed their diverse cultures.

CULTURE

In anthropology (the study of the development of people), the word *culture* has a very definite and special meaning. It signifies *the whole way of life of a people;* its language, art, religion, literature, and music. But just as clearly included are the methods of securing food, organizing families, settling disputes, fighting, gov-

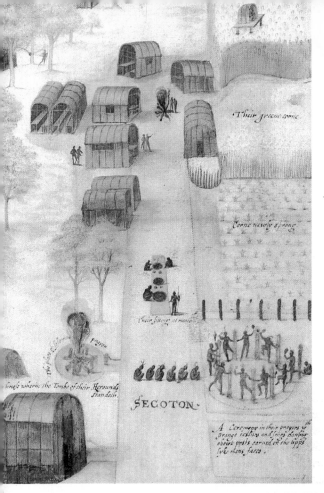

The commonly held image of the Indian is of a nomad, following game and living in tipis — tents that they carried with them. But this early picture-diagram of an Indian village in what is now Virginia shows highly developed agriculture and a settled community.

a very complex one, involving elaborate kinship arrangements, a rich folklore, and remarkable hunting techniques.

The peoples who settled the Americas had, by 1500 A.D., created a very large number of distinct cultures. A few of them are described in the following pages to indicate how widely they varied from one another and from those of the European peoples.

While many Indians in 1500 A.D. were living in tiny groups as hunters and food gatherers, others had developed elaborate civilizations and achieved many advances, especially in agriculture. Two of the crops first raised by Indians, maize (corn) and white potatoes, are now among the four most important food crops on earth. (The others are wheat and rice.) Corn itself was a remarkable creation, for it took hundreds of years of selection, cultivation, and crossing to develop this staple food from its wild plant ancestors. Some of the Indian peoples built long roads, great cities, complicated irrigation works, and mighty temples. Others made textiles, jewelry, and pottery still admired for their beauty. It has been estimated that north of Mexico there were, in 1500 A.D., somewhat over a million Indians as against 8 or 9 million or more in Mexico and several million in Peru.

THE INDIANS OF NORTH AMERICA

Northern Indians had less-developed cultures than some of those to the south. But to show the wide differences among the northern people and their many achievements, a brief look will be taken at those living in several areas. Let us start with the famous northeast woodland Indians, the Iroquois.

Eastern Woodland Indians: The Iroquois

The Mohawk, Seneca, Oneida, Onondaga, and Cayuga tribes were the Five Nations of

erning people, owning or not owning property, playing games, and interpreting dreams. Clothes, styles of hair dressing, table manners, jewelry, pots and pans, furniture, and food—all are part of a culture.

A culture is a social inheritance handed down from parents to children and is often reinforced through some system of education of young people by their elders. The word, in this sense, has no implication of advancement or refinement. Just as have people in France or Britain, a tribe that lives without clothes and subsists on wild food has a culture, and perhaps the Iroquois who, in turn, were part of a much larger family of related groups. In New York State the Iroquois occupied a territory that they called their "Longhouse." Its eastern "door" was at Albany on the Hudson, its western "door" at Niagara Falls.

The way of life of the Iroquois was much like that of other Indian tribes that inhabited the forested area east of the Mississippi and north into Canada. The Iroquois were good farmers. The men cleared the land but the women did all the other work: raising corn of five colors as well as sixty varieties of beans and eight of squash planted between the rows.

The women owned the corn fields and passed them on to their daughters. They owned the dwellings too—the longhouses of poles and bark, each of which was the home of eight or ten families. When a woman married, her husband moved into the longhouse where she lived with her mother and sisters. A village might contain fifty or more longhouses. The men did the hunting and fighting, using bows, flint-pointed arrows, and war clubs. People wore deerskin clothes decorated with dyed porcupine quills. In winter they traveled on snowshoes, in summer in canoes of elm or birchbark.

Each tribe was organized in a number of clans. The Mohawks had only three (Bear, Wolf, Turtle), while others had as many as eight. The clan animals had religious significance, and so did other animals, for the Iroquois gave them human qualities. The Iroquois also thought that stones, trees, and the forces of nature, such as storms, had spirits. There was an invisible force in the world, they said, which they called "Orenda." It was in spirits and in people. Usually, a person made contact with this force in dreams. So important were dreams to them that a war party would turn back if one of its members dreamed that the expedition was going to fail.

In all these things the Iroquois were not very different from their Indian neighbors. Nor were they originally outstanding in warfare, for they were driven away from the St. Lawrence by the Algonquin Indians. What made the Five Nations strong and famous was their political organization, a federation to enforce peace among themselves and at the same time to make them a power for war by firmly uniting their forces. It was probably founded in the sixteenth century when two semi-mythical leaders, Dekanawida and Hiawatha, brought together the five tribes that had previously warred on each other.

The federation of the Iroquois had an elaborate organization of fifty chiefs, some from each tribe. The position of chief was inherited in cer-

A village of the Algonquin Indians. The houses are built of mats, bark, and poles. The fence around the village is built of saplings too light to be of much use for defense. The Algonquins were typical woods Indians of northeastern United States and southern Canada. They lived by hunting.

tain families, and descent and membership in the family group came through the mother, not the father. Chosen by the women of the group, the chiefs could also be replaced by them. Each tribe ran its own internal affairs, but foreign affairs—especially war—were decided by the League. Some scholars think the elaborate and balanced organization of the Iroquois League provided ideas for the constitution of the United States.

Because the League was designed to stop bloodshed and violence among the Five Nations, Dekanawida called it the Great Peace. Other tribes were invited to join, as the quotation below from the "Great Binding Law" of the five tribes shows. There were to be peaceful negotiations at two meetings. Then:

At the third council the War Chief of the Five Nations shall address the chief of the foreign nation and request him to accept the Great Peace. If refusal steadfastly follows, the War Chief shall let the bunch of white lake shells drop from his outstretched hand to the ground and shall bound quickly forward and club the offending chief to death. War shall thereby be declared and . . . must continue . . . until won by the Five Nations.

The Iroquois probably never numbered more than 16,000, even in the seventeenth century when they could muster war parties of 1,000 men. But their League made them so strong and successful that they wiped out, conquered, or dominated all the nearby people, and they were feared from Virginia to the St. Lawrence and from the Atlantic to Illinois. A Jesuit missionary wrote of them: "They approach like foxes, fight like lions, and fly away like birds." Their hostility slowed the advance of the French and their friendship helped the English. The League suffered great losses in its many wars, but kept up its strength by absorbing the remnants of conquered tribes and adopting likely youths into its own families and clans. In 1712–1715 it also took in, as the sixth nation, the Tuscaroras, who had been driven out of North Carolina.

So impressive was the success of the League that the Iroquois keep alive its traditions generation after generation. Each of the fifty chiefs who rules the League has as his title the name of one of the founders of the confederacy, and the list of these founding fathers is chanted as a roll call at every council meeting. The second name on the list is that of Hiawatha.

California Indians

In 1500, California was, as it is now, a pleasant place to live. It was the most heavily populated area north of Mexico and an astonishing variety of Indian peoples lived there, including the tallest in North America (Mohave) and the shortest (Yuki). These tribes spoke more than a hundred separate dialects and languages belonging to six distinct language families.

Most of the California Indians had a culture suited to the area. Their clothes were scanty. The men usually had none at all, while the women wore a short double apron of bark or fiber. They lived in simple brush-covered huts in family groups or small villages, with little or no tribal organization. They were essentially food gatherers without agriculture. They moved around with the seasons collecting seeds, fruits, roots, and shellfish. Mostly, they ate acorns, which were processed by pouring water again and again through acorn meal in a sieve-like basket. The acorns had to be gathered and cracked; the kernels had to be pounded, boiled, and dried. The whole process required six or eight baskets, each specially made for its purpose. These baskets are masterpieces of art. Some are so fine that a magnifying glass is needed to count the number of stitches.

The California people were later called "Diggers" or "Mission Indians." They got the later

TOPOGRAPHICAL MAP OF THE UNITED STATES

To understand the history of the United States it is necessary to understand the way it has been affected by land formation and climate. Examine the map below carefully, making special note of the following:

(1) The Atlantic Coast. There were many good harbors, although more above Chesapeake Bay than below, and the numerous rivers flowing into the Atlantic provided the early "highways" into the coastal plain. Most European settlements were made at or near the points where rivers entered the sea. These settlers could adjust themselves to life in America because the climate was similar to that of Europe, except that winters here are generally colder and the summers hotter.

(2) The Fall Line. This marks the boundary between the flat Atlantic coastal plain and the piedmont, a gently rolling plateau which slopes up to the Appalachians. Where eastward-flowing rivers cross the fall line, there are rapids and waterfalls blocking navigation from the sea. In colonial times the great plantations lay in the tidewater area, while the piedmont was an area of small farms. Many early towns grew on the fall line because on it were the points of transshipment from ships to land transportation or canals. Water power also furnished the basis for industry and further urban growth.

(3) The Appalachian Mountains. For over one hundred and fifty years after the founding of the first English colonies along the Atlantic Coast, these mountains were a barrier to westward settlement. When settlement of the region west of the mountains did begin, in the late eighteenth century, the Appalachians made communication between East and West so difficult that there was fear the Union would be split apart. The Hudson-Mohawk route to the West was the only natural break in that barrier, but in the nineteenth century canals and railroads cut through the Appalachians and linked the sections together.

(4) The Mississippi-Missouri River System. This is the third largest drainage basin in the world. Nearly all of it is fertile, and for many years it has sent out more grain and meat than any other agricultural region in the world. Rivers were the early means of transportation. Until canals and railways were built, the sole outlet for the produce of this area was through New Orleans at the mouth of the Mississippi.

(5) The Area with 210 or More Days Free of Frost. Here is "the land of cotton." It is not practicable to raise most varieties of cotton north of this line, so it has become a sectional crop. In this region slavery was concentrated.

(6) The Great Plains. The eastern half of the United States has sufficient rainfall so that streams are abundant and drought unusual.

West of a line running roughly along 98 degrees west longitude, however, rainfall averages less than 20 inches a year. Here lie the Great Plains, which slope gently upward from an elevation of 1,000 to 2,000 feet on their eastern edge to 5,000 to 6,000 feet at the base of the Rockies. Almost without trees, this vast natural grazing area was formerly the principal home of the buffalo. Inhabited by warlike Indians and thought to be infertile, it was once a barrier to the westward march of the frontier. Now the region contains valuable farming lands, although the lack of rainfall presents special problems.

(7) The Rocky Mountains and Great Basin. This great highland, most of which is more than a mile above sea level, is generally unsuitable for cultivation, because of either lack of rainfall or the steepness of mountain slopes. It contains abundant mineral wealth, however, and large grazing areas. It is the most sparsely settled portion of the country.

(8) The Pacific Coastal Region. The attractions of this narrow strip along the Pacific brought newcomers to the region long before it was part of the United States. All except the southerly portions are well-watered because winds from the Pacific rise when they come to the mountains and discharge their moisture in the form of rain or snow. Where it is at its heaviest, this moisture so encourages tree growth that the Pacific Northwest is today our most important source of timber. Several excellent harbors along the coast are among the distinctive geographic features.

Basic facts about the geography of the United States *not* shown on the map are:

(1) *The area covered by the United States contains vast natural resources.* The few hundred thousand Indians who occupied this area before the Europeans scarcely touched its resources. So far as is known, no other region of equal size on the globe is so well endowed with fertile soil and mineral wealth. "From almost any point of view the United States is the outstanding mineral country. . . . It is the only country in the world possessing adequate quantities of nearly all the principal industrial minerals, and leads the world in the production of coal, oil, natural gas, iron, copper, lead, zinc, aluminum metal, phosphates, gypsum, and sulphur."

(2) *The United States is isolated.* For nearly nine hundred years the English Channel, 20 miles wide at its narrowest point, protected England from invasion. The United States, protected east and west by great oceans, and north and south by relatively unpopulated countries, has not had to fear invasion until the twentieth century. Its people thought themselves isolated from the problems of the rest of the world.

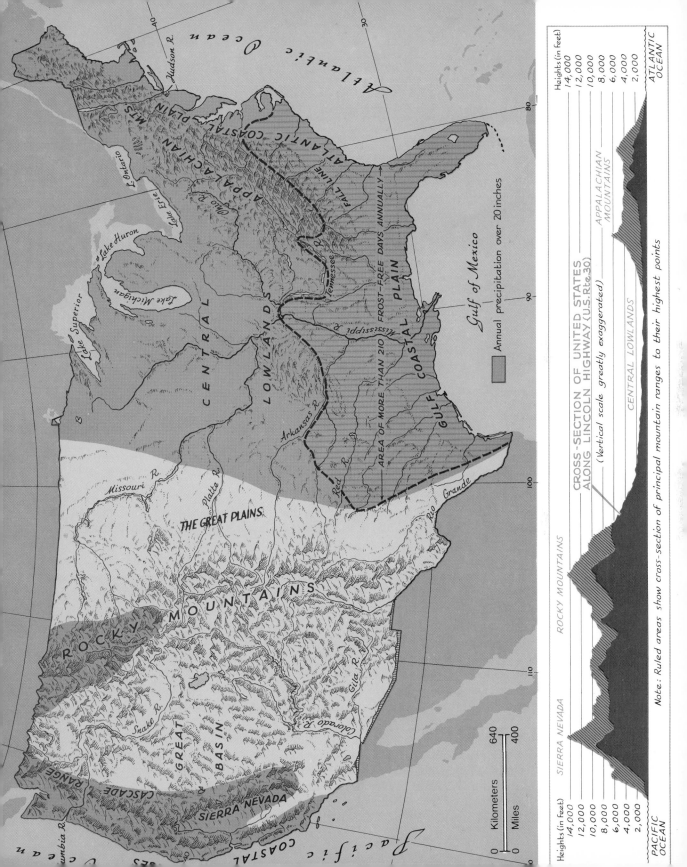

Atlantic Ocean

Hudson R.

40

30

L. Ontario

Lake Erie

Lake Huron

Lake Michigan

Lake Superior

APPALACHIAN MTS.

ATLANTIC COASTAL PLAIN

Ohio R.

Tennessee R.

FALL LINE

Mississippi R.

AREA OF MORE THAN 210 FROST-FREE DAYS ANNUALLY

GULF COASTAL PLAIN

Gulf of Mexico

Annual precipitation over 20 inches

80

90

CENTRAL

LOWLANDS

Arkansas R.

Red R.

Missouri R.

Platte R.

THE GREAT PLAINS

Rio Grande

100

ROCKY MOUNTAINS

Gila R.

Colorado R.

110

GREAT

BASIN

Snake R.

Columbia R.

CASCADE RANGE

SIERRA NEVADA

COASTAL RANGES

Pacific Ocean

Kilometers

Miles

640

400

0

0

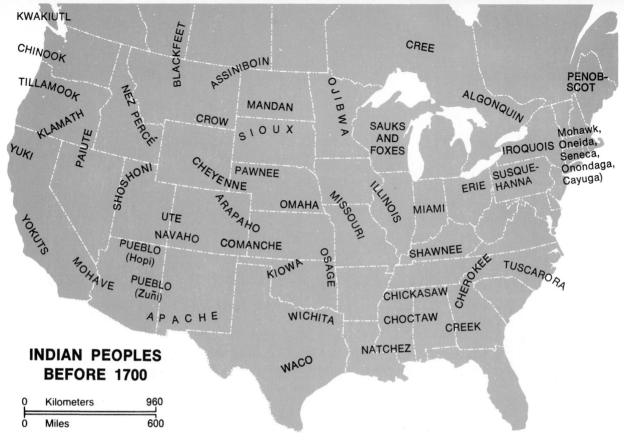

**INDIAN PEOPLES
BEFORE 1700**

0 Kilometers 960
0 Miles 600

The major Indian tribes of what is now the United States are shown on this map. Many more tribes are shown than are mentioned in the text. The present state boundaries are shown here to help locate these people.

name because when the Spanish came, the priests founded missions (from San Diego, 1769, to San Francisco, 1832) and tried to convert the inhabitants and settle them in farming villages. The priests had some success, though the Indians preferred a wandering life and hated the heavy clothes the missionaries wanted them to wear. When the Americans flooded in with the gold rush in 1849, the Indians were exploited and badly treated. But today there are about 40,000 people of Indian descent in California, some on small reservations and some living alongside other Americans.

The Northwest Indians

In contrast to the peaceful California Indians, there were nearby tribes with very different and much more warlike cultures. They lived on the coast, from northern California all the way up into Alaska. Here the Indians were well off, for they had an unfailing source of food in the five species of salmon that came back each year by the millions to spawn in the rivers. Some tribes of the Washington coast went out to sea for fish and seals in great dugout canoes, thirty feet long or more. They even dared to pursue and capture whales. The tribes farther north, in British Columbia, were extremely venturesome and warlike. They made long raids to the south to capture loot and slaves. These northwest Indians built houses of posts and planks (split with wooden wedges) so large and well-constructed that the first white men could not believe that they were put together without nails. The women of the Puget Sound tribes wove blankets on looms using mountain goat hair, milkweed fiber, and the wool of small white dogs kept for this purpose.

With the tools of wood, bone, shell, and stone the northwest Indians made the most elaborate carvings, among them the great totem poles with which we are familiar. The art style of these tribes is extremely distinctive. In the north, especially, an animal was depicted as split in two so as to show both profiles at once. On carved and painted posts, housefronts, canoes, and wooden boxes, animals or monsters were portrayed: spirits which had revealed themselves to ancestors in visions. The carvings had religious meaning and also were related to a man's forebears, so that they at the same time displayed his famous ancestry and his own importance.

QUESTION • *Would you consider the Iroquois or the Indians of the Pacific Northwest more able to fend off European culture?*

An even more characteristic and unusual way of indicating one's wealth and one's importance were the potlatches. These were great feasts at which a chief or rich man gave away all his wealth: blankets, canoes, baskets, furs, dried fish, copper plates, shells, and slaves. He might hope to get back even more wealth when others in turn gave their potlatches. Since almost everybody except slaves could get invited to potlatches, and since they were frequent (for births, marriages, deaths, a baby's first tooth, and so on), they formed a way of redistributing wealth, supporting the poor, and reducing envy and hatred of the rich. A rich man could even, in this culture, gain prestige by destroying his wealth: killing slaves or breaking up copper plates and throwing them into the sea.

Southwest Indians: Pueblos and Navahos

Very different was the way of life in Arizona and New Mexico. Here there was no easy source of food like the salmon and the seals. Instead, people lived by agriculture and won their crops by hard work and careful use of the scanty water supplies. A stable and complicated culture developed. Along the streams and rivers lived peaceable agricultural tribes. They depended primarily on the corn, squash, and beans they raised. But they also grew cotton, wove blankets with bright colors and intricate designs, and made beautiful pottery. When the first Spaniards arrived they found people living in compact communities, often with multi-story houses of stone and adobe. The Spaniards called them *pueblos* (villages) and these Indians are still known by that name.

Two of the Pueblo tribes are the Hopi of Arizona and the Zuñi of New Mexico. Since the area in which the Hopi and the Zuñi live is arid, the sun, rain, and clouds play a great role in their religious ceremonies. Many of the pueblos were built on top of mesas (flat-topped mountains) or in cliffs, so as to be easily defended. And there was a good reason for this, since the ancestors of the Pueblo Indians had been driven south and west by more warlike tribes.

One group, the Navahos, settled near the Pueblos, learned how to farm and weave, and eventually became less warlike, though they were still raiding and plundering in the mid-nineteenth century. Today they are the most numerous Indian people in the States, famous for their blankets, their silver work, and their ability to learn new ways. The Apaches (the name means "strangers" or "enemies") came from the same people as the Navahos, but they never settled down. They remained nomadic hunters and fighters with inaccessible retreats in the mountain fortresses. They became renowned for their bravery, cleverness, and cruelty. Not until 1886 did the last of the Apaches give in to the United States army after long and bloody campaigns in which most of them perished.

The Plains Indians

In the vast area stretching from the Rocky Mountains to the Mississippi River and from central Texas to southern Canada, lived tribes that hunted buffalo, wore elaborate headdresses of feathers, and lived in conical-shaped houses called tipis. These people, the Plains Indians tribes, are the people whose dress and way of life became that of *the* Indian to non-Indian people.

There were many different tribes of the plains, but they may be divided into two sub-groups. The more eastern peoples such as the Osage, Omahas, Mandans, and Pawnees lived in settled villages. Like their eastern neighbors, the Woodland Indians, the women tended fields of corn, squash, and beans. The men fished. But they also hunted the buffalos which roamed in vast herds on the grassy plains. Further to the west were tribes that did not fish or farm, among them the Crows, the Sioux, the Cheyennes, the Comanches. These tribes followed the buffalo herds throughout the year. The buffalo gave them all they needed: food, material for clothes —decorated by both sexes with porcupine quills and later, beads from the traders—and the skins that along with grass and mats covered their tipis.

In the sixteenth century, the Spanish got horses to Mexico. By the 1750's, horses were found all the way to Canada. Guns were brought to the Indians by Canadian and French traders. These two possessions enabled the Plains peoples to go further and hunt better when they chased buffalos. Before having horses, such a hunt took days. The men traveled with their possessions carried in a bag slung between two trailing poles hauled by a dog. To catch the buffalo, the hunters might put on a skin disguise and creep up on their prey. Or they would surround the animals or stampede them off a cliff.

In later times, warriors raided each other for horses and guns. Before going out on a raid, a war dance would inspire the men towards feats of personal bravery. One of the most admired was to "count coup"—to touch a live enemy without being harmed. While warfare was common, the raids were usually short and swift, often planned by an individual seeking personal glory.

Most tribes had clubs open to men only, with rituals that the women and children were forbidden to see. To everyone, spiritual visions were very important. They were sought through dreams and personal quests. Doctors and priests, called shamans, were people especially gifted with spiritual powers.

The Plains peoples spoke many different languages. For periods of truce when they traded and counseled with each other, they developed a universal sign language of gestures. They also sent messages long distances by smoke signals understood by all.

Having acquired guns and horses, the Plains peoples became the toughest fighters the newcomers had to face. Plains Indians defended their territory until the end of the nineteenth century. They were finally conquered only when the buffalo herds on which their lives depended were destroyed.

THE INDIAN HERITAGE

When the first non-Indian people landed on the coasts of North America, they found many different kinds of people living here. These people were lumped together as one group—"Indians"—whose ways of life, manners, and customs were strange. The differences among Indian people did not appear as great to the Europeans as their differences from themselves. To the Europeans, the way the Indians worshipped the Great Spirit appeared wild at times and crude. The Indian view that land was a gift of the Great Spirit, that it could not be owned individually, seemed impossible to people whose rank in society was based on land ownership. The simplicity of certain Indian material things: houses, farming tools, clothing, seemed primitive.

In a word, the way of life, or culture, of the Europeans and the Indians appeared to be so different that only great understanding could bridge the gaps that separated each from the other. This understanding took place among individuals on both sides. It did not take place among non-Indians generally. By the end of the nineteenth century, the Indian way of life had been nearly destroyed.

Today, this way of life is being reasserted, and the importance of the Indian heritage is clearer. It is not that we are more aware of the many Indian names and terms in everyday life: Connecticut, Wabash, Yosemite; walking Indian file, burying the hatchet. Nor is it in the realization of the things the Indians contributed to the Europeans: the canoe, the hammock, the snowshoe, and foods: tobacco, hominy, succotash. Rather, it is in an understanding of what Indian people valued in life. We see that they lived close to the land and water and sky, and that they respected the things of the earth. We find that they had a sense of sharing and of being related to each other and the land in a way that must not be broken. And so, we are beginning to understand that what the Indians believed to be good and true and beautiful had universal meaning, that it should not be lost, and that it has a place and a purpose in the world today.

The Land and the People: SUMMING UP

I. CHECKING THE FACTS

To which Indian group does each of the descriptions below apply?

a. A purpose of accumulating wealth was to give it away.
b. The corn fields and the longhouses belonged to the women.
c. The acorn was their staple food and they were expert basket makers.
d. The buffalo supplied them with all their needs.

II. INTERPRETING THE FACTS

Use the map and the reference material on pages 6–7 to decide which of the statements below are *true* and which are *false*.

a. A "fall line" is a geographic boundary of falls and rapids between a plain and an upland area.
b. The Southern cotton belt is the only area with nearly two-thirds of the year frost-free.
c. The Great Plains, today a vast farming area, is blessed with abundant rainfall.
d. The Indians lived in a variety of geographic environments.

III. APPLYING YOUR KNOWLEDGE

How would you interpret this Indian prayer? *Oh, Great Spirit, help me not to judge my neighbors until I have walked a mile in their moccasins.*

DON'T FORGET THE "BACK TIER"!

We tend to think of the early American colonists as frontiers people, hewing farms out of the wilderness, building houses, gradually establishing a relatively prosperous and comfortable society "from Europe's woes and wars remote." But we must also remember that behind this frontier was a "back tier." The ancestors of all the non-Indian peoples came from far across the seas, bringing with them technical skills, art, music, language, literature, and religious beliefs. They brought social and political skills as well, as can be seen by the way the Pilgrims organized their community before they disembarked from the *Mayflower*. The first eight amendments to the Constitution, on pp. 138 and 140, are rights of Americans that the federal government is forbidden to invade. They are rights for which Americans fought the Revolutionary War. But every one of these was previously one of the "rights of Englishmen" whose every phrase was hammered out in nearly five hundred years of struggle between the British people and their monarchs. To carry the point further, the court procedures in all but one of our fifty states come from the common law of England.

Furthermore, the thirteen colonies were very much part of what we have recently come to call the "Atlantic community." What they gathered or produced was what Europe or Africa or the West Indies would buy, whether tobacco from Virginia, cod and lumber from Massachusetts, rum from Rhode Island, or furs from New York. A complex web of trade tied together the Atlantic Ocean and the Mediterranean. The books the Americans read, their costume, their architecture, were dictated by Europe. And whenever England and France went to war, the English and French colonists dutifully enlisted Indian allies and fought each other.

And yet—something unique was also developing in the thirteen colonies. The French settler, Crèvecoeur, writing at the time of the American Revolution, maintained that the American was "a new man" living in "a new society," a society in which there was far greater chance than in Europe for average people to make their own way by their own efforts. And the American Revolution owes its enduring importance to the fact that it was much more than a rebellion against England. It was also, as Lincoln said in the Gettysburg Address, an attempt to found "a new nation . . . dedicated to the proposition that all men are created equal."

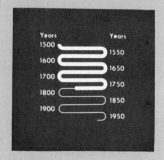

Years	Years
1500	1550
1600	1650
1700	1750
1800	1850
1900	1950

Chapter 1

The Heritage of the Colonial Period

Here, individuals of all nations are melted into a new race of people whose labor and posterity will one day cause great changes in the world.
—MICHEL-GUILLAUME JEAN de CRÈVECOEUR, 1782

The first European colonies in America were established during the so-called Age of Exploration, which lasted from about 1450 to about 1550, and which saw the greatest increase in geographical knowledge in European history. Like the twentieth century, it was a "space age," although the space involved was the surface of the earth, not that outside it.

The people who performed almost incredible feats of heroism and endurance in making the great voyages of discovery were driven by powerful motives. The hope of immense wealth lured both the discoverers of the sea routes to the Far East and the men who first explored the east coasts of America. Missionaries dared innumerable hardships in hope of bringing Christianity to the peoples of Asia, Africa, and America. This was the period of the Renaissance in Europe, when people were intensely curious about the world about them. Excited by fabulous reports of the first voyages, adventurers flocked to new lands in search of more marvels.

The Age of Exploration would not have taken place except for the rise in Western Europe of the new middle class of bankers and merchants who were gaining wealth at the expense of the landowning nobility. From this class came many of those most eager to find new sources of wealth. They financed many of the explorers and established trading posts throughout the known world.

In Europe central governments were increasing their power and seeking new sources of revenue. On the Atlantic seaboard no less than six countries—Portugal, Spain, France, the Netherlands, Sweden, and England—undertook voyages of discovery. At first they were intent on breaking the monopoly of eastward trade held by Genoa and Venice, but later they engaged in bitter rivalry to establish colonies and control the new trade routes.

A number of technical discoveries enabled Europeans to sail the great oceans for the first time. Previously, sailors had to depend on landmarks. Now the compass, the astrolabe (for determining latitude), and the development of

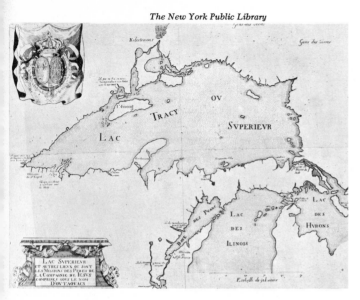

Jesuit missionaries drew an amazingly accurate map of Lake Superior in 1670–1671, revealing how carefully they had explored in their zeal to convert the Indians. No map as accurate as this appeared until after 1850.

more accurate mapmaking enabled them to navigate the open seas with at least a rough idea of where they were, although it was not until the invention of the chronometer (for measuring time) in the eighteenth century that really accurate navigation was possible.

In less than a hundred years, European explorers traced the outlines of all the major continents except Australia and Antarctica. This was done in ships as small as fifty tons. The propellers of a modern liner like the *Queen Elizabeth II* weigh as much as Columbus' flagship, the *Santa Maria*. These early vessels were so slow, and so little was known of prevailing wings, that a journey across the Atlantic often took three months. Seamen regularly suffered from scurvy, a terrible disease caused by lack of vitamin C that sometimes carried off whole crews.

From Obstacles to Goal

At first the Europeans thought North America to be part of Asia. Columbus believed that Haiti was part of Japan and died not knowing he had sailed to new continents. When it was realized that North America barred the way to the Far East, explorers sought a way around it to the north. On a map of Canada today, the names Davis Strait, Hudson's Bay, and Baffin Bay commemorate men who took part in these fruitless explorations. Even after gold was discovered in Mexico and Peru, the search for a northwest passage went on.

During the two centuries after Columbus, Spain, France, and Great Britain gained control over large portions of North America and started colonies. Thus they determined how people have lived on this continent ever since. One must go back to colonial times to explain the different ways of living of today's French Canadians, Mexicans, and people of the United States.

The carry-over of patterns of life inherited from Europe is understandable when you realize the length of the colonial period. It was almost as many years from the founding of the first permanent English colony at Jamestown in 1607 to the winning of the independence of the United States in 1783, as from the latter event to the present. And the Spanish colonies were founded more than a century earlier than the English.

THE SPANISH COLONIES

The Spanish were the first to find wealth in the Americas, and the first to establish colonies. In the century after Columbus, the Spanish founded an empire that was larger than the United States today and that lasted for over three centuries. The Spanish empire-builders were called *conquistadors*. Their accomplish-

A Spanish mission in California. The missions were established as a means of converting Indians to Christianity. Each one was a self-supporting community.

ments point to great achievements and great failings. On the one hand, they looted the lands they discovered. They wiped out some of the people they conquered and enslaved others. On the other hand, they built aqueducts, theatres, bookshops, a university, great cathedrals and churches. They introduced European crops such as wheat and alfalfa, fruits such as oranges, figs, and pears; and livestock such as cattle, sheep, and horses. Their attitudes to the Indians were that of a superior people who had come to save the ignorant and to suppress those who opposed them. In these points of view they were similar to other European peoples of their day. But unlike either the French or the English, the Spanish found mineral wealth that was the envy of all Europe. From Peruvian and Mexican mines flowed so much precious metal that ships returning to Spain were sometimes ballasted with silver. Many Spaniards had become farmers on great estates worked by Indian or Negro labor, producing grain, livestock, and sugar.

The Indians, the Africans, and the Church

Although the Indians were subdued and put to work for their conquerors, their interests were guarded by the Roman Catholic Church. As worthy of remembrance as any conquistador was the Spanish priest Bartolomé de Las Casas, who devoted most of his ninety-two years to defending Indians from other Spaniards. Las Casas was only one among thousands of missionaries who regarded the Indians primarily as souls to be saved. The missionaries influenced the kings of Spain to issue orders defending Indians from oppression. They taught the Indians agriculture and handicrafts. Both the Church and the Spanish government approved of marriage between whites and Indians, so that the distinction between the races was gradually reduced. In the United States today probably less than 1 per cent of the population has any Indian ancestry.

Almost from the first, the Spanish imported enslaved people from West Africa to work in plantations and mines. That the lot of the slaves was hard was demonstrated by several desperate insurrections against their owners. As in the case of the Indians, the Catholic Church tried to better the lot of the black slaves whose souls were as worth saving as those of their white masters. The Church taught that "Slavery is not to be understood as conferring on one man the same power over another that men have over cattle. . . . For slavery does not abolish the natural equality of man." Church authorities therefore insisted that slaves be baptized, that they marry, and that they be granted holidays when they might work for themselves and earn money to buy their freedom. Both the Spanish government and the Church encouraged owners to free slaves. Slavery as an institution was not abolished, however, until the nineteenth century and usually only after the colonies had gained independence.

Weaknesses of the Spanish Empire

The founding of the Spanish Empire was one of the great achievements of history. But after the first century of conquest, growth and economic development slackened. There are several reasons for this:

(1) Spain tried to do too much in the "Spanish century." In addition to founding an empire in America and in the Philippines, Spain led the fight against the Turks in the Mediterranean, was embroiled in costly wars in Italy, tried to put down the revolt of the Dutch, and attempted the conquest of England. After the defeat of the great Spanish Armada by the English in the year 1588, Spanish power declined.

(2) The Spanish kept colonial trade in a strait jacket. Until 1713, goods could be legally imported to Spain only in Spanish ships, and only at a few ports. Any colonist trading with a foreigner was liable to the death penalty. Although these rules were poorly enforced, such excessive control stifled commerce and industry.

(3) Society in the Spanish colonies became fixed in a pyramid. There were a few wealthy landowners and officials at the top, while the mass of the people lived in poverty. Many of the latter were *peóns,* tied to the soil they cultivated. Such a society kept down initiative and ability.

Despite these drawbacks, the Spanish extended their culture over an area many times larger than their own, and kept control for three centuries or more. Furthermore, the influence of the Catholic religion helped to lessen the cruelty and worst forms of oppression against the native population.

THE FRENCH COLONIES

Compared to that of Spain, French colonization in North America was late and feeble. France had sent early explorers such as Giovanni da Verrazano and Jacques Cartier to the New World, and her fishermen had been on the Grand Bank since about 1500, but there was no serious attempt at colonization until after 1600.

The colonies established by France in North America were little more than a long string of outposts, extending from Biloxi and New Orleans on the Gulf of Mexico to Nova Scotia by way of the Mississippi River system, the Great Lakes, and the St. Lawrence River (see map, p. 37). Only Acadia (now Nova Scotia) and the shores of the St. Lawrence were settled.

Obstacles to French Colonization

The French did not consider their holdings on the continent of North America as valuable as their West Indian "sugar islands"—Guadeloupe, Martinique, and what is now Haiti. Furthermore, the monarchs of France were far more interested in extending their dominions in Europe than in settling the North American wilderness.

The French government had great difficulty in recruiting colonists, and was even reduced to such dishonest practices as ordering regiments of soldiers to Canada and disbanding them there without means of transportation home. The French missed an opportunity to gain an energetic group of settlers when they forbade French Protestants, called Huguenots, to settle in America. Denied the right to practice their religion at home, many Huguenots would have been glad to come over to the New World. They were mostly well-to-do merchants and craft-workers whose industry and organizing ability would have greatly increased the prosperity and strength of the French colonies.

Government and Society

The government of the French colonies resembled that of the Spanish in that the colonists enjoyed almost no self-government. Political power centered in the person of the royal governor. As in the Spanish colonies, land was often parceled out to great landlords, called *seigneurs.* They were supported by fees from the peasants, who were called *habitants.* The society that developed, like that in the Spanish colonies, was aristocratic. The habitants were, however, considerably more independent than the Mexican peons. The influence of the Roman Catholic Church was, as in the Spanish colonies, very great, the bishop wielding practically as much power as the royal governor. The descendants of the habitants are today among the most devout Catholics in the world.

In the French colonies, as in the Spanish, trade was strictly controlled by the government. The greatest efforts to colonize North America were made in the reign of King Louis XIV under the direction of Jean Colbert, finance minister from 1661 to 1683. Colbert was a defender of the economic theory known as mercantilism. According to this theory, a nation should make itself wealthy by taking in more specie (gold and silver) from exporting goods abroad than it spends abroad for imports. It should make itself secure by becoming self-sufficient, depending on no other country for vital imports. A colony, therefore, existed for the good of the mother country. If the colony lacked deposits of precious metals, it should furnish commodities such as sugar and tobacco that were readily salable in other countries. Or it should produce goods the mother country would otherwise have to buy elsewhere—especially those of military importance, such as masts and ship timber. The industry of a colony should not compete with that of the mother country because the colony was supposed to provide a market for goods produced at home.

Putting mercantilism into practice demanded state regulation at every turn. In France, Colbert raised tariffs on foreign goods, paid foreigners to come and start new industries, and forbade skilled workers to leave the country on pain of death. In the colonies the government required that furs, lumber, and fish be sent only to France or to other French colonies. Fur traders had to swear not to trade with the Dutch or British. Colonists might import only French goods carried in French ships.

Two French trappers (known as *coureurs de bois*) meet an Indian friend. Note the Frenchmen use an Indian canoe.

The French and the Indians

The French were usually friendly to the Indians who were allies in war and suppliers of furs. French missionaries, like those of Spain, devoted their lives to the conversion of Indians to Christianity. Undaunted by starvation and torture, Jesuit priests made heroic journeys far into the middle of the continent. The French made one serious mistake, however. In 1608, Samuel de Champlain, founder of French Canada, joined a war party of Algonquins and Hurons in a raid against their enemies, the Iroquois. From then on the Iroquois, the most formidable warriors in eastern North America, were the sworn enemies of the French and the allies of the British. Occupying rich lands south of Lake Ontario, the Iroquois protected the colonies of New York and Pennsylvania from invasion and forced the French to use a roundabout route to the Ohio and Mississippi valleys. (See map, p. 37.)

As a result of mistakes in policy and lack of interest at home, the French colonies grew very slowly. By 1750, after nearly a century and a half of colonization, only about 80,000 whites

Father Jogues, a Jesuit priest, preaching to the Iroquois in one of their "long houses." Jogues was later tortured and put to death.

inhabited the huge area claimed by France. Meanwhile, the English had started colonies which grew so rapidly that by 1750 their population approached two million.

THE FOUNDING OF THE ENGLISH COLONIES

England, like France, participated in the early voyages of discovery, but then failed to establish colonies for more than a century. In 1497 the merchants of the city of Bristol sent the Venetian seaman John Cabot westward in order to discover a route to the Far East. Cabot explored the shores of Nova Scotia, Newfoundland, and Labrador. Like Columbus, he believed he had found Japan. But when a second expedition found only the barren coasts of Labrador and Greenland, English interest in westward exploration and settlement waned. The great Tudor monarchs—Henry VII, Henry VIII, and Elizabeth I—had little money to spend on colonization, their country being disturbed first by religious difficulties and later by the threat of war with Spain.

Rivalry Between England and Spain

Rivalry between England and Spain was one reason why the English became interested in colonization. English buccaneers, such as Francis Drake, cruised the shores of Spanish America, capturing treasure ships and looting towns. But a better way to strike at Spain was obviously to attempt to seize the Spanish colonies, or at least to set up permanent English bases in America. As long as Spain seemed the strongest power in Europe, founding colonies in America appeared a risky business.

The way for English colonization was cleared by the defeat of the Spanish Armada that sailed against England in 1588. Comprising 130 ships manned by 27,000 men, this was the greatest naval expedition the world had ever seen. The English fleet sent out to meet it had a new idea of naval warfare: that a warship should be a floating platform for artillery. The Spanish had the older idea that it should carry soldiers who would board the enemy ships. The English ships were also far easier to handle than the Spanish galleons. Able to choose its point of attack and pound Spanish ships to pieces without coming close enough to allow them to grapple, the English fleet harried the Armada up the English Channel and out into the North Sea. Most of the surviving Spanish ships were later destroyed in a storm north of Scotland. Disheartened by this disaster, Spain was no longer a serious threat to settlement of North America. The English gained new faith in their ability to undertake great enterprises.

Motives and Methods of English Colonization

Rivalry with Spain was only one of several reasons for English colonization in America. Clergymen hoped to bring "savages from the Devill to Christ." Colonies would provide an outlet for "idle women and sturdy beggars." American fisheries and trade would strengthen English naval power by increasing the number of ships and sailors. Above all, there was the hope of wealth.

Although they started late, the English had certain advantages in the race to establish colonies in America. England's island position, her good harbors, her fisheries, and her extensive trade with Europe all encouraged seafaring. Her people enjoyed a relatively high level of prosperity, and there was capital available for investment in the expensive business of planting new settlements.

English society was aristocratic; it was dominated by a few great lords and ladies and many more "gentlefolk," who boasted coats of arms and were considered to be above the common people. But by the standards of most other European countries the society of Elizabethan England was remarkably mobile. Among men, an apprentice might become a rich man and marry his daughter to a nobleman, and in turn the penniless younger son of a noble might himself become an apprentice or hire himself out as a soldier in foreign wars. Changes in agriculture drove some farmers off their holdings, and they were ready to go anywhere they could make a living. English women were less restrained by social taboos than the women on the Continent. They were free to come and go and marry as they pleased. Many of them

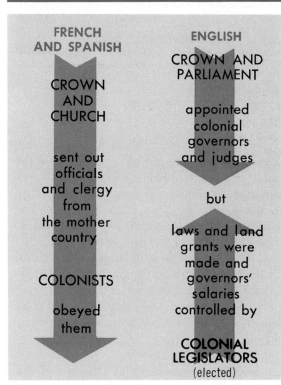

TYPES OF COLONIAL GOVERNMENTS

FRENCH AND SPANISH

CROWN AND CHURCH

sent out officials and clergy from the mother country

COLONISTS

obeyed them

ENGLISH

CROWN AND PARLIAMENT

appointed colonial governors and judges

but

laws and land grants were made and governors' salaries controlled by

COLONIAL LEGISLATORS
(elected)

An examination of colonial governments in the New World reveals how English limited monarchy differed from French and Spanish absolutism.

A nineteenth-century engraving presents a sentimental picture of the Pilgrims' first Sunday in New England. Not allowed freedom to worship as they pleased in England, the Pilgrims fled first to the Netherlands and then to America.

worked at trades, and some owned their own businesses. Thus of all the countries in Europe, England probably had the highest proportion of men and women ready to travel to a new and strange environment and to survive on arrival.

The first permanent English colony was started at Jamestown, Virginia, in 1607. By 1640, the English had made several more settlements on the Atlantic seaboard (see map, p. 44). English methods of planting colonies differed from the Spanish and French in three major respects.

(1) *The English colonies were founded by private enterprise instead of by the government.* The expense and risk of founding the English colonies were borne by individual proprietors such as George Calvert in Maryland, or by joint-stock companies such as the London Company, which founded Virginia. These companies were organized by business people who shared in the profits and losses resulting from the company's trading, according to the number of shares they owned.

(2) *The English permitted religious dissenters to settle in their colonies.* Avoiding the mistake of the French in excluding the Huguenots, the English government let people worship in the colonies in ways forbidden at home. Most of the settlements made before 1640 were led by those who came to America to worship as they pleased.

(3) *The English colonies enjoyed a large measure of self-government.* The English settlers enjoyed personal freedom and rights of self-government unknown in other colonies. Ever since Magna Carta in 1215, the idea had been

developing that there were certain "rights of Englishmen" which even the king was bound to respect. The charter granted to Sir Walter Raleigh before he established the ill-fated colony on Roanoke Island stated that the settlers and their descendants "shall and may have all the privileges of free denizens and persons native of England." Even before they landed at Plymouth in 1620, the Pilgrims signed the Mayflower Compact whereby they agreed to be bound by such laws as they themselves should make. In 1619 the settlers in Virginia first elected their own legislature, the House of Burgesses, to manage local affairs. In 1639 the towns of Hartford, Windsor, and Wethersfield drew up the Fundamental Orders of Connecticut, the first written constitution in modern times that actually worked.

QUESTION • *If a modern American corporation secured a land concession in Africa or South America and sent some people there to develop the natural resources, would a colonial government such as that of Virginia develop?*

"A Newe Englishe Nation"

A generation after the first settlement of Massachusetts, a Salem clergyman could exult about the success of the young colony as follows:

Look on your habitations, shops, and ships and behold your numerous posterity and great increase of blessings of land and sea. . . . Lord thou has been a gracious God, and exceedingly good to thy servants. . . . We live in a more comfortable and plentiful manner than ever we did expect.

By 1700 all but one of the English colonies later to become the thirteen original states had been founded, and all were growing rapidly due to immigration and the natural increase of the population. "A newe Englishe nation" was beginning to appear.

ECONOMIC DEVELOPMENT IN THE ENGLISH COLONIES

Captain John Smith complained of the first settlers at Jamestown that they thought of nothing but to "dig gold, wash gold, refine gold, load gold." But the hope of finding quick and easy wealth proved to be a mirage; it turned out that the two great sources of wealth in the thirteen colonies were land and labor. Colonial proprietors learned that the kind of settlers they most wanted were those described by William Penn in a prospectus for Pennsylvania: "industrious Husbandmen and day Laborers . . . Carpenters, Masons, Smiths, Weavers, Taylors, Tanners, Shoemakers, Shipwrights, etc." The great attraction of America for such people was the opportunity to own land, and the cheap land available in the English colonies acted like a magnet drawing poor men and women with the ambition to better themselves. Eventually perhaps 90 per cent of the colonists made their living by farming.

Although agriculture was everywhere the main pursuit, differences in geography and climate produced different ways of making a living in the various colonies. Three distinct regions appeared: New England, the middle colonies, and the southern colonies.

The Southern Colonies: The Plantation System and the Piedmont

The chief products of the southern colonies—rice, indigo, turpentine, and above all tobacco—either commanded a ready market in Europe or were needed by the mother country. Except for turpentine, these products were best grown on large estates worked by cheap labor. As a result, a plantation system of agriculture grew up, similar to that in the sugar island of the West Indies. The large-scale farming of the plantations was limited, however, to the tidewater area, where crops could be loaded

With abundant supplies of oak for beams and pine and spruce for planks and masts, the New England Yankees built sturdy ships that sailed all over the world. Shipbuilding was long a major New England industry. Nearly a quarter of the ships in the British merchant marine were built in New England.

directly on ships instead of being hauled long distances overland.

Upstream from the tidewater lay the piedmont (see map, p. 32), where the land was tilled by small farmers. Here was that characteristic American phenomenon "the frontier," a region where people were pushing back the wilderness, living partly by farming and partly by hunting and trapping, in frequent danger from Indian attacks. The people of the piedmont, poor for the most part, tended to resent the aristocratic planters of the coastal areas.

The "Bread Colonies"

The middle colonies, blessed with rich soil and navigable rivers, were sometimes called the "bread colonies." Their principal exports were grain and livestock. These were produced on family-type farms, except in the Hudson Valley, where there were large estates. Pennsylvania attracted some excellent German farmers, the "Pennsylvania Dutch," many of whom have kept their language and traditional ways to this day. To send produce to market, the Ger-

mans invented the Conestoga wagon, a roomy, high-wheeled vehicle which horses or oxen could pull over rough roads; it was the ancestor of the "prairie schooner" which later carried pioneers to California and Oregon.

The back country of nearly all the colonies produced furs and other pelts that were not only used here but provided an important export to Europe. The great center of the fur trade was Albany, New York, where pelts were obtained from French smugglers and from the Iroquois Indians.

New England: Fisheries and Shipping

New England, with thin soil and a harsh climate, had the scantiest natural resources; the region's only important native product was lumber. But the inhabitants developed qualities of thrift, industry, and practical ingenuity that made the term "Yankee" synonymous with these qualities. From the first, New Englanders took to the sea. They exported great quantities of salted fish to the West Indies and to the Mediterranean. By the close of the colonial period, 30 per cent of the ships in the British merchant marine were American, and most of these sailed from New England ports. New Englanders carried on a large share of the African slave trade. They were the first to hunt whales in the Antarctic; in 1774, 360 whaling ships sailed from the island of Nantucket alone.

In these activities New England became a formidable competitor of the mother country. In no colony, however, did the colonists offer much competition to the British in manufacturing. They usually obtained from Britain any manufactured goods not homemade.

As transplanted Europeans, the colonists demanded European goods—fine clothing, books, wine, cutlery. But to pay for them they had to produce staples that Europeans wanted or to send gold or silver. They acquired the latter mostly through trade with the West Indies. There the Spanish dollar was the common currency, and this explains why the United States today uses the dollar instead of the pound as its monetary unit.

COLONIAL SOCIETY

In each of the thirteen colonies there was an upper class whose superior position was fixed by law or custom. In New England this class was composed of merchants, shipowners, and clergymen. In the South and along the Hudson River in New York, the great landowners made up an aristocracy who aped the country gentry of England. Early colonial laws forbade any but upper class men to wear silver buttons, and any but upper class women and daughters to wear silk dresses. Social rank was indicated in college catalogues and marriage certificates, and even on tombstones. By modern standards, therefore, life in the English colonies might appear undemocratic. It was, however, an even more mobile society than that of England, one in which a person could move up or down according to ambition, ability, and energy, or lack of such qualities.

At the bottom of the scale were "indentured servants," people bound by contract to serve someone for a number of years in return for nothing more than their keep and the cost of passage to America. When the contract expired, the servant was a free person able to sell his or her labor for what could be got. Since labor was scarce, wages in the colonies were two or three times those in England. In some colonies an indentured servant received as much as fifty acres of land on achieving freedom. So a person who started life in America practically a slave might end it an independent landowner.

Spanish dollars circulated widely in the English colonies. Divisible into eight parts, or bits, they were known as "pieces of eight." Hence the modern phrase "two bits," meaning a quarter dollar.

Shortly after 1660, thirteen of the twenty-eight members of the Virginia House of Burgesses were men who had originally come to the colony as indentured servants.

The Position of Women

A reason for rapid growth of white population in the English colonies was that proportionately more women came to them than to the Spanish and French colonies. The only respectable career for women was thought to be marriage. Colonial women were considered fortunate because they easily found husbands.

As in all European societies of the time, women were denied higher education. Their principal task was rearing children. Most of them died during the child-bearing years.

Most women were married to farmers, and here they were full partners in their husbands' business. A farm could not carry on without the skills of women in making cloth, garments, candles, soap, and breadstuffs.

Life on the frontier also made women more self-reliant. A visitor to the North Carolina–Virginia backcountry in 1710 gave this description of a frontierswoman:

> . . . she is a very civil woman and shows nothing of ruggedness or Immodesty in her carriage, yett she will carry a gunn in the woods and kill deer, turkeys, etc., shoot down wild cattle, catch and tye hoggs, knock down beeves with an axe and perform the most manful exercises.

And what was true of women on the frontier was true elsewhere. Women had more freedom of action and more chance to take part in life outside the home than in England. Colonial laws gave them more protection. In England, for instance, the common law allowed a husband to beat his wife with any "reasonable instrument"; according to Massachusetts law, he could beat her only in self-defense. Widespread home manufacturing allowed wives as well as their husbands to learn trades. In the South the mistress of a plantation was a full partner in directing the working force. When seafaring New England husbands left their wives, sometimes for years at a time, women were successful as merchants or storekeepers. Still other women were printers, newspaper publishers, druggists, and doctors.

Widespread Prosperity

During the first half century or so of colonization, life in English America was hard. A high proportion of those who sailed for these shores died within the first year because of the hardships of the voyage. Settlements were prey to Indian attacks, to starvation from crop failures, to disastrous fires, and to epidemics of smallpox, dysentery, malaria, diphtheria, and yellow fever.

By the eighteenth century, conditions were much improved. Epidemics were still common and human life was therefore uncertain, but this was also true in Europe. There was widespread prosperity—a product of cheap land, a ready market for colonial exports, and hard work. Idleness was generally regarded as a sin akin to drunkenness or gluttony. There were no beggars and few paupers. Organized crime was almost unknown, except for occasional piracy on the high seas and banditry on the frontier. It was a society of mixed origins. At first most of the settlers, except for the Dutch and the Negroes, came from England. From about the time of the founding of Pennsylvania in 1681, American prosperity began to attract people of different nationalities and religions—Scots, Irish, Huguenots, Jews, and Germans.

Just as there was no class of beggars at the bottom, there was no class of idle rich at the top. Even the wealthiest people, whether New England merchants, Hudson Valley patroons, or Virginia plantation owners, habitually arose at dawn and worked until dark.

Black Slavery

One group of settlers must be omitted from this happy picture—the Negro slaves. By the time of the American Revolution they were numerous in all the colonies, the proportion being highest in the southern colonies because slave labor proved most profitable on rice and tobacco plantations. In South Carolina three-quarters of the population were Negroes. About 20 per cent of the total colonial population were of African descent.

At first it was not clear that the blacks were to be treated differently from white indentured servants, who were temporary slaves. The white servants had usually chosen to migrate to America, however, and the Americans wanted to persuade more to come. They inherited the rights of English people and so had the protection of the law. The Africans, on the other hand, had been totally uprooted; they were protected by no law or tradition and by no powerful institution like the Catholic Church in the Spanish colonies. Thus white indentured servants gained freedom and even wealth, while methods were found to rivet the Negro into hopeless bondage.

Slave labor was especially well adapted to the southern plantation system, where much of the work demanded simple tools and was done in gangs so that it could be easily overseen. Slavery came to be considered necessary to the prosperity of the South, and slaves came to compose a high proportion of the population in the tidewater areas. The laws of the southern colonies declared Negroes to be slaves for life, and their children after them; they even forbade owners to teach Negroes to read for fear that they might acquire dangerous ideas. Whereas in the Spanish colonies slaves were obliged to marry and the integrity of the family was protected,

QUESTION • How much of their former rich African culture did the Negroes retain in America?

A coffle (from an Arabic word meaning "caravan") of slaves being driven from the interior of Africa to the coast. From there they were carried to America by ship.

in the English plantation colonies slave marriages had no standing in law and children might be sold away from their mothers. Slaves could own no property and had slight legal protection against irresponsible or cruel owners. In brief, Negroes were treated as cattle. Their only protection was that they were such a valuable commodity that it was to the interest of the owner to keep them reasonably healthy and reasonably provided with food, clothing, and shelter.

In the North, where slavery was less profitable and slaves less numerous, and where

The slave trade that furnished Africans to American markets was a horrible example of inhumanity. It has been estimated that about 30 per cent of the blacks put on shipboard in Africa died crossing the Atlantic, it being a common practice to throw the sick overboard. Probably half the survivors died soon after reaching America because of strange food and disease for which they had built up no immunity.

New York Public Library

religious convictions sometimes operated against slavery, Negro slaves were treated less harshly. In New England they were not only allowed but required to marry; they could acquire property and testify in court. They might be punished by their owners, but an owner who killed a slave was held guilty of murder. There was also increasing feeling that slavery was a moral wrong. In 1700 Samuel Sewall, a famous Massachusetts judge, published *The Selling of Joseph*, a pamphlet that maintained that slavery was contrary to the Bible. In Pennsylvania the institution was denounced by both the Quakers and the Mennonites, a German religious sect. The number of free blacks increased, and a few even became prosperous. In Jaffrey, New Hampshire, Amos Fortune bought other Negroes out of slavery and left money for the town school. Even when free, however, blacks were not permitted equality with whites in the northern colonies. Custom kept them usually in menial positions, and the laws denied them the right to vote or hold office.

In the South, there were owners who disapproved of slavery, but hesitated to free their Negroes because the lot of the freed person was not a happy one. Since their color marked them as different, free blacks were kept in an inferior position, lacking the security of the slave, who was at least clothed and fed. Freed people were feared as possible leaders of slave insurrections. Most southern colonies therefore had laws that made it difficult or impossible to give the slaves their freedom.

The English and the Indians

The coming of the English was a disaster for the Indians. A few colonial leaders, notably Roger Williams and William Penn, tried to treat them fairly, and some Protestant ministers regarded the Indians principally as souls to be brought to knowledge of Christ. The Iroquois were so valuable as allies in war and as a source

Although the over-all English policy toward the Indians was harsh (below), some settlers did treat the Indians favorably. Above is Edward Hick's painting of William Penn's treaty with the Indians, 1682, which provided for purchase of their land and proclaimed "that the Indians and the English must live and Love as long as the Sun gave light."

of furs that they were not molested. But the overall English policy was one of expulsion and extermination, and various reasons were put forth to justify it. It was held that since the Indians did not have settled dwellings, but were on the move like "the foxes and wild beasts ... so it is lawful now to take a land which none useth; and make use of it." Some Puritan ministers held that the Indians were children of the devil, in the same category as witches; they therefore might be killed in good conscience.

Man for man, the Indians were better fighters than the white man—more skillful, more inured to hardship, more self-reliant, more daring. But they were divided into scores of

QUESTION •
*Now we live in a land
    of plenty,
But where would we be if
    in 1620,
Indians, fired with
    a racist notion,
Had tossed our fathers into
    the ocean?*

tribes and never united for long. The Indian warrior was often unreliable. He might or might not fight on a particular day according to his mood, or omens, or dreams; he did not cooperate easily with others. The whites had the advantages of far better organization and larger numbers. They also had grim allies in diseases such as smallpox, which sometimes wiped out whole Indian communities. Rum, which white traders exchanged for furs, destroyed Indian character and self-respect.

In any case, the English lived in compact settlements, and constantly pushed inland. The historian James Truslow Adams wrote:

When a French trader or trapper plunged into the forest, and the green leaves closed behind him, it was to mingle with the life of the natives, which, in its main aspects, flowed on unaltered by his presence. When, on the other hand ... the English frontier crept ever farther and farther inland, and town succeeded town, it was as if, adding stone to stone, great dykes were being built, which more and more dammed up the waters of native life.

Religion

The variety of religious beliefs in the English colonies was almost as great as in western Europe. In the South the planter aristocracy usually belonged to the Church of England, but there were also Roman Catholics, Methodists, Baptists, and Presbyterians. In New England the great majority of the people were Congregationalists, but there were small groups of other Protestant sects. The middle colonies had the greatest variety—Dutch and German Lutherans, Mennonites, Quakers, Presbyterians, and members of the Church of England. In most colonies a single official church was "established"—that is, supported by taxes.

Although many people came to America to worship as they pleased, this did not imply that they were ready to grant others the same privilege. Thus the Massachusetts Puritans believed that religious toleration was a weakness inspired by the devil and that one who favored it must be "either an atheist or a heretic or a hypocrite or at best a captive of some lust." They banished both Roger Williams and Anne Hutchinson for preaching what Puritans considered dangerous doctrines, and they hanged Quakers on Boston Common. Virginia, on the other hand, expelled ministers who came from Massachusetts to preach. In time, however, toleration of religious differences developed.

Anne Hutchinson

Anne Hutchinson was the daughter of a famous Puritan preacher from Lincolnshire, England. She gained a taste for religious discussion as a girl. She married William Hutchinson, a prosperous merchant. The Hutchinsons had 14 children in 22 years. One of their sons migrated to Massachusetts and sent back such favorable reports that Anne and her husband followed him. They settled in Boston.

A constant student of the Bible, Anne Hutchinson formed her own ideas about its meaning. She started to hold meetings to discuss the sermons preached Thursdays and Sundays. Soon 70 or 80 people came to hear her. This was bad enough, since Anne was taking on a role reserved for men. What was even worse, she taught that there was no need for ministers or for a church. Each individual might know the truth and gain salvation by direct contact with God. Thus each person was a law unto himself or herself. This was revolution.

Mrs. Hutchinson was called before the highest officials and accused of undermining the authority of the ministers. The trial shocked the new colony to its foundations because Anne had won wide support. Some of her friends were exiled. Others were frightened into silence. Anne was found guilty and banished. Governor Winthrop of Massachusetts wrote a pamphlet in which he rejoiced in the departure of this female leper sent by Satan to infect the good people of Boston.

Anne fled first to Rhode Island and later to Long Island, taking her younger children—two more had been born in America. In 1643 a band of Mohican Indians attacked her home, killing her and all but one child. Pious Puritans hailed Anne's unhappy ending as proof that her unwomanly and poisonous ideas offended God.

Roger Williams claimed that it was "the will and command of God... that a permission of the most Paganish, Jewish, Turkish, or Antichristian consciences and worships be granted to *all* men," and his colony of Rhode Island followed this principle. In the seventeenth century no other colony went as far as that, but in Catholic Maryland the Toleration Act of 1649 granted liberty of worship to Christians, and later Pennsylvania welcomed people of all Christian sects. By the eighteenth century, religious persecution in the colonies was a thing of the past, although all religious groups were not equal before the law. Foreigners were especially struck by the freedom granted Jews, who still suffered severe penalties in most European countries. A foreign traveler to New York about 1750 was astonished to find that Jews owned prosperous shops, farms, and trading vessels. In Newport, Rhode Island, another prosperous Jewish community built a handsome synagogue.

Schools and Colleges

The New England Puritans believed that citizens should learn enough English to read the Bible and understand the laws of the country. The famous Massachusetts General School Act of 1647 stated two principles of American education today: local communities have a duty to set up schools, and this duty is enforced by law.

In the middle colonies, schooling was not as universal as in New England, but it was widespread nevertheless.

In the southern colonies, book learning was generally limited to children of large landowners and professional men, and there was some feeling that education should be reserved for the few. Governor Berkeley of Virginia expressed this sentiment in a letter to England:

...there are no free schools, or printing, and I hope we shall not have them these hundred years, for learning has brought disobedience and heresy and sects into the world ... God keep us from both!

Even where there was a will to establish schools, the widely separated plantations and farms of the South made them impractical, as compared to the close-knit communities of New England.

By modern standards colonial schools were primitive. One New England teacher wrote of his schoolhouse, "one might as well nigh as good keep school in a hog stie." There were few books, and instruction was given only two or three months a year. Most girls received no instruction at all. Two-thirds of the women whose names appear on Massachusetts legal documents in the early 1700's could not write their signatures. In spite of all shortcomings, however, colonial schools taught so many children that in no other region of equal size in the world could such a high proportion of the population read and write.

Religion was the principal force behind the founding of most institutions of higher learning in the English colonies. Harvard, William and Mary, Yale, Rhode Island College (later Brown), the College of New Jersey (later Princeton), and Rutgers were founded principally to train young men for the ministry. Colleges were also attended, however, by sons of wealthy families and by ambitious poor boys anxious to improve their situation in life.

By the middle of the eighteenth century, college curriculums began to change because there was a growing interest in science and a demand for practical subjects. Thus when King's College (later Columbia) was opened in New York City in 1754, it was announced that the "comprehensive scheme of studies" would include not only the traditional Latin, Greek, and Hebrew, but also "Surveying and Navigation,

Geography, History, Husbandry, Commerce, Government, the Knowledge of All Nature in the Heavens above us and in the Air, Water, and Earth Around us, Meteors, Stones, Mines and Minerals, Plants and Animals, and of everything *useful* for the Comfort, Convenience and Elegance of Life."

This interest in science produced in America, as in Europe, a new confidence in human reason which came to be known as the Enlightenment. Characteristic works of the Enlightenment widely read in America were those by the English philosopher John Locke, a friend of Newton. In *An Essay Concerning Human Understanding,* Locke maintained that people could best gain knowledge of and power over the universe by observation of the world around them and by experiment. In the second of two *Treatises on Government,* Locke taught that people were born with certain "natural rights" to life, liberty, and property; that people formed governments to protect these rights; and that a government interfering with these might rightfully be overthrown. Practical Americans readily accepted his idea that government was the agent of the people, not their ruler.

Newspapers and Almanacs

Schools and colleges were not the only educational influences in the colonies. Newspapers, almanacs, books, and circulating libraries all helped to raise the level of public information. Since paper and type were expensive and the reading public in America small, most books came from England. But by 1750 there were twenty-five or thirty newspapers, mostly four-page sheets, printed weekly. The subscription lists were never more than a few thousand, but readers were more numerous. Printed on tough rag paper, these newspapers were passed from

Harvard University about 1740. The first college in the thirteen colonies, it was founded in 1636, principally to train men for the ministry. The brick and stone buildings shown here were built in 1675, 1695, and 1720. Professors pastured cows in the "yard" enclosed by the fence.

Library of Congress

hand to hand until half the men in a village often read a single copy at the local tavern.

Colonial editors occasionally criticized British laws or officials. In 1735, Peter Zenger of the New York *Weekly Journal* accused the royal governor of corruption. As a result, copies of the paper were publicly burnt by the sheriff, and Zenger was brought to trial on a charge of libel. His lawyer, Andrew Hamilton, argued that the editor was not guilty, since the charges against the governor were true, and since free speech was one of the rights of the English. Zenger was acquitted. Later, the case came to be regarded as a landmark in the development of a free press in America, but at the time it was of less importance.

Almanacs attracted as many readers as newspapers. In addition to a calendar, dates of holidays, and times of sunset and sunrise, almanacs published advice on farming, accounts of scientific discoveries, poems, jokes, news of the year, and practical advice.

European travelers in America were amazed to find that political discussions in public inns were joined intelligently by everybody from college-educated gentlemen to stableboys.

ENGLISH COLONIAL GOVERNMENT

The degree of power that was exercised by British officials varied from colony to colony, but it was limited everywhere. In all colonies the voters elected their own legislature, and in "charter" colonies, such as Connecticut, their governor as well. In "proprietary" colonies, such as Pennsylvania, the governor was appointed by the proprietor or by his heirs to whom the colony had been granted; in "royal" or "crown" colonies, such as Virginia, the governor was chosen by the king. The governor of a proprietary or crown colony had wide powers, such as a veto over the legislature and control of land grants. Yet he was often at the mercy of the legislature which might refuse to vote him his salary. (See chart, p. 19.)

Government at the town and county levels was run entirely by the colonists themselves. In New England, the important local unit was the township, and all major decisions were in the hands of the town meeting, which most heads of families had a right to attend. The town meeting was (and is) one of the most democratic types of government ever devised. In the southern and middle colonies, local government was usually less democratic, but nevertheless entirely independent of British control.

None of the colonies was so democratic as to allow full political rights to all men or to *any* women. Active citizenship and the right to vote and hold office were everywhere limited to adult males owning property, who usually had to be members of the established church. In spite of these limitations, a higher proportion of people was involved in government in the English colonies than anywhere in the European world. This wide participation gave Americans the idea that governments existed to serve them rather than to rule them. It also gave training that was valuable when the colonies later declared independence.

The Acts of Trade and Navigation

While allowing her colonies to run local affairs pretty much as they pleased, Britain attempted to control their foreign trade in the interest of the British Empire as a whole. Here the basic idea was the same mercantile theory which Colbert put into effect in France (see p. 17). The Acts of Trade and Navigation, passed by Parliament in 1651 and repeatedly amended, ruled that certain "enumerated commodities," all of them goods that Britain lacked or produced in small quantity, must be sent to England. Among these were tobacco, cotton, indigo, and sugar. This was a profitable arrangement for British merchants, who resold many of the enumerated commodities outside their own country. American ships returning from European ports were required to make a "broken voyage," stopping at a British port on the way home to pay duty on goods acquired on the Continent before returning to America. By raising the price of non-British goods, this widened the colonial market for British products. The Navigation Acts said that all trade within the British Empire should be carried in British ships. This helped colonial shippers, however, because in this case they were given the same rights as inhabitants of the British Isles.

A number of British laws were clearly designed to help special groups at the expense of the thirteen colonies. The Molasses Act of 1733 was designed to help the owners of sugar plantations in the British West Indies, by putting a heavy tax on the import of sugar and molasses from any other source. To protect the farmers of the mother country from competition, the export of grain from the colonies to England was forbidden. Large-scale manufacturing in the colonies was prohibited in order to prevent competition with British manufacturers. One British law forbade the export of hats from the colonies; another, the construction of steel and iron works. Benjamin Franklin expressed himself sarcastically on this kind of legislation:

> A colonist cannot make a button, a horse shoe, nor a hobnail but some sooty ironmonger or respectable buttonmaker of Britain shall bawl and squall that his honor's worship is . . . maltreated, injured, cheated and robbed by the rascally Americans.

In spite of all these laws, Britain regulated colonial trade much less strictly than did other European nations. The English colonies might ship their fish, lumber, grain, and furs wherever they could find a market. Certain laws

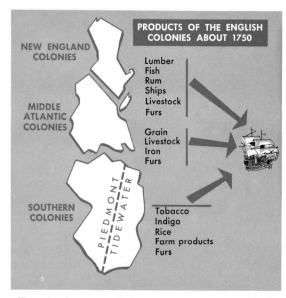

Even in the self-sufficient economy of colonial life, each section produced some staple that it could export. Common to all sections were furs, for which there was a constant demand in Europe.

were designed to help the colonists, such as the one ruling that no British merchant could buy tobacco except in the colonies, and that tobacco might not be grown in England itself.

British regulations were seldom strictly enforced. Revenue officers, receiving their positions through political pull, often did not bother to go to America, but hired deputies. In regard to the Molasses Act, the British pursued a policy of "salutary neglect," and did not provoke colonial resistance by trying to enforce the law. The colonists naturally got into the habit of evading British legislation, and smuggling assumed the position of a long-established right. When smugglers were occasionally brought to court, colonial juries seldom found them guilty, no matter how strong the evidence.

Although British trade regulations were deliberately designed to subordinate the colonies to the mother country, on balance they may have helped as much as they hindered. The colonists benefited from those regulations that favored them and evaded those that hurt them. But if ever the latter should be enforced, there were certain to be outcries in America.

Activities: Chapter 1

For Mastery and Review

1. What were major reasons for the Age of Discovery? Explain each.

2. In three parallel columns, list reasons for the limited success of Spanish and French colonies in America and for the greater success of the English colonies.

3. Give as many reasons as you can why the English colonies were established and why settlers went to them.

4. Describe the various social classes and groups in the English colonies in America. Which groups found in Europe were missing?

5. Describe and explain the differing treatment of Negro slaves in the Spanish and English colonies.

6. Describe and explain the differing treatment of Indians in the Spanish, French, and English colonies.

7. Why were schools and colleges founded? Explain the variations between the New England, middle, and southern colonies in the amount of schooling available. What was the importance of newspapers and almanacs?

8. What were the main features of British colonial government? Of trade policy?

Who, What, and Why Important?

middle class	Anne Hutchinson
Las Casas	aristocracy
mercantilism	bread colonies
Samuel de Champlain	indentured servants
John Cabot	Negro slavery
Spanish Armada	frontier
Jamestown	Amos Fortune
Mayflower Compact	Roger Williams
House of Burgesses	Maryland Toleration Act
Fundamental Orders of Connecticut	Massachusetts General School Act of 1647
John Locke	triangular trade
Peter Zenger	Acts of Trade and Navigation
colonial governments	igation
town meeting	salutary neglect

Unrolling the Map

1. On an outline map of the eastern United States locate the thirteen colonies. Indicate also Maine (then part of Massachusetts) and Vermont.

2. On the map of the thirteen colonies locate the following cities and towns: Portsmouth, Salem, Boston, New Haven, Providence, New York, Albany, Philadelphia, Annapolis, Williamsburg, Jamestown, Wilmington, Charleston, and Savannah. What is the common feature of all these cities, and what does this indicate about the economy of the thirteen colonies?

To Pursue the Matter

1. How did the French establish a claim to the Mississippi Valley? See "Sieur La Salle and the Mississippi," in Arnof, *A Sense of the Past*, pp. 12–16.

2. How did the Spanish, with mere handfuls of men, overthrow the great kingdoms of the Incas and the Aztecs? See Wellman, *Glory, God, and Gold*.

3. What qualities and points of view did the early English settlers bring to America? See Notestein, *The English People on the Eve of Colonization*.

4. Prepare a report, with maps, pictures, and diagrams, on the African slave trade. Possible sources: prelude to Benét, *John Brown's Body;* Cowley, *Black Cargoes*.

Chapter 2

Road to Revolution

The Revolution was effected before the war commenced. The Revolution was in the minds and hearts of the people.
—JOHN ADAMS

The American Revolution was an unforeseen event. The people of the thirteen colonies had prospered under the mild rule of Britain and had seemed devoted to George III, who came to the British throne in 1760 and who was known to his affectionate subjects as "farmer George." Benjamin Franklin, who knew as much as anyone about colonial opinion, later wrote, "I never heard in any Conversation from any person drunk or sober the least Expression of a wish for Separation or Hint that such a thing would be advantageous to America." Two centuries later historians still argue why the freest colonies of any European nation were the first to rebel. In any case, the revolution had its origins far back in the colonial period.

By the mid-1700's most Americans of English descent were three to six generations removed from their immigrant ancestors. The original settlers themselves had not been the most loyal English subjects, since many came here to escape poverty, or imprisonment. Other settlers, such as the Dutch, the Irish, and the Germans, had been either indifferent or anti-British from the first.

The colonies had been founded with little help from the British government and had developed their prosperous agriculture and extensive trade on their own initiative. In a fertile area many times larger than the mother country, they were doubling their population every twenty-five or thirty years. They had learned to govern themselves. Above all, they had developed a sense that they were different from Europeans—more free, more able to rise in the world by their own exertions. Ten years before the Americans declared their independence, John Adams wrote, "I always consider the settlement of America as the opening of a grand scheme and design in Providence for the illumination of the ignorant and the emancipation of the slavish part of mankind all over the earth."

One great tie holding the Americans to the mother country was the need for protection. Without aid from Great Britain they had difficulty defending themselves from the French in Canada. Not until France was expelled from North America did the thirteen colonies take the road to revolution.

THE STRUGGLE BETWEEN
FRANCE AND ENGLAND

In 1689 England and France began a contest that went on for generations with only short intervals of peace. It was on a world-wide scale, with active military operations in Europe and the Mediterranean, in the East Indies and India, in the Caribbean and North America. The long rivalry for the control of North America was a drama full of excitement and horror played against the romantic background of a vast wilderness.

Francis Parkman, Historian

The heroism of the people who engaged in the struggle for a continent was hardly greater than that of the man who best described it. As a sophomore in college, Francis Parkman (1823–1893) made it is his life's aim to tell the story of the rise and fall of the French empire in America. He achieved his ambition—although it took him fifty years—in spite of eyesight so poor that he could only read through a magnifying glass and such a fragile physique that he could sometimes write only five or six lines a day. To learn about Indian life, he went west and lived with a party of Sioux Indians along the Oregon Trail. The ten books resulting from this courageous life of effort are still read because Parkman was both a great historian and a great storyteller.

Comparative Strength of
Britain and France

The Anglo-French contest for North America had two phases. Between 1689 and 1713 occurred wars known in the thirteen colonies as King William's War and Queen Anne's War, in Europe as the War of the League of Augsburg and the War of the Spanish Succession. At the close of this first phase, Great Britain gained Nova Scotia, Newfoundland, and Hudson's Bay Territory (see map, p. 37). The second phase, from 1742 to 1763, included the wars known in the colonies as King George's War (1742–1748) and the French and Indian War (1754–1763); in Europe they were called the War of the Austrian Succession and the Seven Years' War. This ended in complete victory for Britain, with the French giving up all their holdings on the mainland of North America.

It is not as difficult to see why Great Britain won the war in America as it is to understand why France was able to hold out so long. The British colonies were many times more populous than the French, and the British navy generally had control of the sea, over which supplies and troops were sent to America. The French, however, had the great advantage of a unified command; on the other hand the thirteen colonies were highly independent of one another.

In 1754, on the eve of the Seven Years' War, delegates from seven northern colonies met at Albany to find some means of union. Benjamin Franklin presented to the conference a remarkable document, the so-called Albany Plan of Union. Franklin proposed that the colonies form a Grand Council to deal with Indian relations, new settlements, raising troops, and taxes for defense. The actions of this intercolonial legislature would be subject to the veto of the British crown. The plan never went through because both the colonial and British governments feared loss of power. The resulting lack of cooperation handicapped the war effort. American militiamen would seldom consent to serve outside their own colony. Colonies evaded taxes imposed by Britain for their own defense, nor would they tax themselves. Colonial merchants and ship captains continued illegal trade with the French West Indies.

The French and Indian War

The final round of the great struggle began in the Ohio Valley. In the mid-eighteenth century the French, determined to possess this rich and beautiful area, drove out English fur traders. In 1753 they built Fort Duquesne at the point where the Monongahela and Allegheny rivers meet to form the Ohio River. Fort Duquesne, in territory claimed by both Virginia and Pennsylvania, was a threat to these colonies and a barrier to their expansion westward. In 1754 a force of 150 Virginia militiamen under the command of young Major George Washington advanced on the fort and ambushed a party of French troops sent out to scout them. But later, the French captured Washington's entire force at Fort Necessity. Thus hostilities began without a declaration of war. In the next year, the English General Edward Braddock, commanding 1,300 men, advanced again only to suffer a defeat even more disastrous than Washington's. Two-thirds of Braddock's force were killed or wounded, and he himself was mortally wounded. He was buried on the line of march; the survivors with their baggage trains passed over his grave, obliterating all traces of it, so that the Indian allies of the French might not find the body and mutilate it.

Disasters continued after Great Britain and France formally declared war in 1756. French Canada had a great military commander in General Louis Montcalm, while British generals were poorly chosen. Utter failure met British expeditions seeking to advance on Montreal by way of Lake George and Lake Champlain and to take the French fort of Louisburg on Cape Breton Island (see map, p. 37). These setbacks coincided with equally severe defeats elsewhere. All along the frontier the Indian allies of the French attacked outlying settlements, massacring men, women, and children. They even wiped out a settlement only sixty miles from Philadelphia.

In the midst of disaster, William Pitt, England's greatest war minister before Winston Churchill, came to power. Pitt's supreme self-confidence was expressed in the famous sentence, "I know that I can save this country and that no one else can." Immediately he instilled new vigor into the British war effort. By the end of the year 1758, Louisburg and Fort Duquesne were in British hands; and in June 1759, a British army of 9,000 men was encamped on the St. Lawrence River a few miles below the great fortress of Quebec.

The Fall of Quebec, 1759

The British forces at Quebec were commanded by James Wolfe, an able young officer whom Pitt had advanced from lieutenant colonel to temporary major general in less than two years. For over two months, Wolfe tried in vain to find a weak spot in the defenses of "the Gibraltar of America." Time was running short, for winter would soon set in. Finally the English commander hit upon a plan so daring that his staff refused to approve of it. This was to land at night and scale a wooded cliff almost under the guns of the fortress. Wolfe gambled on surprise, suspecting that the French would not have a strong guard at a point considered completely safe from attack. As Wolfe sat with his officers the night before the assault, he perhaps foresaw his death the next day, for he read them Thomas Gray's recently published poem, "Elegy Written in a Country Churchyard," emphasizing the verse:

> The boast of heraldry, the pomp of power,
> And all that beauty, all that wealth e'er gave,
> Await alike th' inevitable hour:
> The paths of glory lead but to the grave.

Led by Scottish Highlanders wearing kilts, Wolfe's soldiers clambered up the cliffs and overpowered the few guards. Before daybreak 4,500 men were drawn up for battle on open

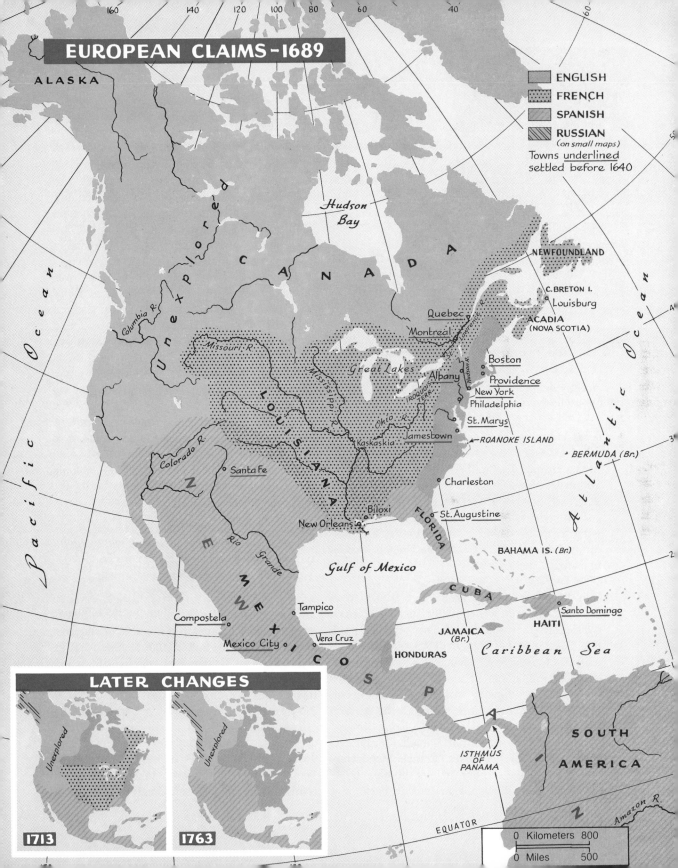

EUROPEAN CLAIMS - 1689

ENGLISH
FRENCH
SPANISH
RUSSIAN (on small maps)
Towns underlined settled before 1640

ALASKA

Hudson Bay

C A N A D A

NEWFOUNDLAND

C. BRETON I.
Louisburg

ACADIA (NOVA SCOTIA)

Unexplored

Columbia R.

Missouri R.

Mississippi R.

Great Lakes

St. Lawrence R.

Quebec
Montreal

Boston
Providence
New York
Philadelphia

Albany
IROQUOIS TERR.
Hudson R.

LOUISIANA

Ohio R.

St. Marys
Jamestown
→ ROANOKE ISLAND

Kaskaskia

● BERMUDA (Br.)

Colorado R.

N E W

Santa Fe

Charleston

Biloxi
New Orleans

FLORIDA

St. Augustine

M E X I C O S P A I N

Rio Grande

Gulf of Mexico

BAHAMA IS. (Br.)

CUBA

Compostela

Tampico

JAMAICA (Br.)

Santo Domingo
HAITI

Mexico City

Vera Cruz

HONDURAS

Caribbean Sea

Pacific Ocean

Atlantic Ocean

SOUTH
AMERICA

ISTHMUS OF PANAMA

EQUATOR

Amazon R.

0 Kilometers 800
0 Miles 500

LATER CHANGES

Unexplored

1713

Unexplored

1763

Wolfe's army, including kilted Highlanders (in the far background), scaled the cliffs at Quebec and fought the battle that ended French rule.

fields known as the Plains of Abraham. Montcalm was quick to gather a force to meet them. In the ensuing battle, the volleys of the British infantry mowed down the French and Canadians, who were driven back into the town and forced to surrender. Both commanders were mortally wounded in the battle. The fall of Quebec meant the end of the French empire in North America.

The Peace of Paris, 1763

Great Britain was equally successful elsewhere, and by the Peace of Paris, which ended the Seven Years' War in 1763, she secured control of the largest amount of territory ever gained by a single nation in a single treaty. From France, Great Britain obtained all of Canada not yielded earlier, and all the eastern watershed of the Mississippi. From Spain, France's ally, Great Britain gained Florida. To repay Spain for her losses, France transferred the Louisiana Territory to her at this time, although in 1800 Napoleon took it back, just

before selling it to the United States. On the other side of the globe, Britain gained a dominant position in India. It is no wonder that the British were dazzled by the brilliance of their triumph. "Burn up your Greek and Roman books, histories of little people!" exulted the English author Horace Walpole. From this time dated England's sense of being a great imperial power with a mission to hold "dominion over palm and pine."

The French defeat was as bitter as the British victory was exciting. One hundred and fifty years of colonization, all the enterprise and heroism of her great pioneers, missionaries, and soldiers had proved utterly fruitless. There was only one small crumb of comfort—the thirteen colonies might revolt. A French statesman likened them to a "ripe fruit," ready to drop off the bough. Within two years after the Peace of Paris, secret agents of the French government were traveling through the English colonies to investigate the chances of a revolution.

With the coming of peace in 1763, Benjamin Franklin wrote verses to celebrate the loyalty of the colonies:

Know ye, bad neighbors, who aim to divide
The sons from the mother, that she's still our pride,
And if ye attack her, we're all on her side,
     Which nobody can deny, deny,
     Which nobody can deny.

Thirteen years later Franklin had completely reversed himself: he was a member of the Continental Congress that declared America's independence of Britain and was fighting a war to make it good. He had been caught up in a revolution. Ask anyone today what comes to mind when you say the words, "American Revolution," and you will usually get some such answer as "redcoats," "Yorktown," or "Don't fire until you see the whites of their eyes." People naturally think of the Revolution in terms of the war against Great Britain. Yet in the words of John Adams, who played a large part in it, "The Revolution was effected before the war commenced. The Revolution was in the minds and hearts of the people."

Although it was not immediately apparent, the Seven Years' War had caused a change in the relationship between colonies and mother country. Freed from the French menace, the Americans no longer depended on British regiments and warships for their very lives. The British had a new sense that they must rule their colonies. The former slipshod practice of leaving them pretty much alone should be replaced by strict and efficient control. British taxpayers, furthermore, felt that the Americans should pay a fair share of the immense cost of the victory over France.

QUESTION • *The Spanish colonies were held down much more than the English colonies. Why didn't they revolt first?*

ENGLAND TIGHTENS CONTROL

The new British attitude was apparent as soon as the Seven Years' War came to an end. It showed itself in stricter enforcement of existing laws, in attempts to tax the colonies, in an effort to take over control of the West, and in attacks on colonial rights of self-government.

Stricter Enforcement of Laws

George Grenville, British minister of finance from 1763 until 1765, was an energetic administrator who believed that existing laws should be enforced. He was said to be the first minister in a generation who read the dispatches from American revenue collectors and so was really aware of the degree to which the Americans had become habitual smugglers. The revenue service in the thirteen colonies was costing the British government four times as much as it collected in customs duties!

During Grenville's term of office, customs men were required to go to their posts in America rather than stay in England and hire deputies. They were armed with Writs of Assistance—general search warrants allowing them to seek smuggled goods without swearing out a particular warrant for every building they entered. British warships helped in the suppression of smuggling, and alleged smugglers were tried in Admiralty Courts, where the accused person had no right of trial by jury and the judges pocketed five per cent of the fines they imposed.

New Taxation

Between the years 1764 and 1767, the Parliament levied new taxes designed to shift part of the burden of the war debt from British landowners to the colonists. Never before had the British government seriously tried to raise revenue in America. The idea of previous taxes had not been so much to collect money as to steer colonial trade into channels that would make it profitable to England or to other portions of her empire.

Grenville increased the number of enumerated commodities that had to be shipped to the mother country; this reduced the profits of colonial trade with Europe. He persuaded Parliament to pass laws levying new duties on colonial imports, the most important of these being the Sugar Act of 1764. This law cut in half the rates of the Molasses Act of 1733 (see p. 32). The British government had winked at evasions of the earlier act; the appalling thing about the new one was that it was likely to be enforced. It would reduce the profits of the trade with the Spanish and French West Indies that brought much-needed specie (gold and silver) into the colonies. In the same year as the Sugar Act, Parliament forbade colonial governments to issue paper money, so that specie became scarcer than ever. Caught in a "two-way squeeze" of lower profits and scarcity of money, many colonial merchants faced bankruptcy.

In 1765 Parliament, on Grenville's advice, passed the famous Stamp Act designed to raise revenue *within the colonies themselves* instead of through customs duties collected at the ports. It required that stamps be affixed to 54 kinds of articles and documents, including wills, playing cards, newspapers, dice, almanacs, and licenses. Duties ranged from 1 cent on newspapers to $10 for college diplomas. Payment was to be made in specie. Whereas the previous laws devised by Grenville affected principally those engaged in foreign trade, especially in New England, the Stamp Act angered colonists everywhere. It especially affected those best able to stir up feeling against it: lawyers, newspaper editors, and ministers. On the day it was supposed to go into effect, men and women wore mourning, and church bells tolled in towns all the way from Portsmouth, New Hampshire, to Savannah, Georgia.

For reasons shortly to be described, the Stamp Act proved to be unenforceable and was repealed in 1766. In 1767 the so-called Townshend Act attempted to raise revenue by import duties on tea, paper, glass, and paint. These could not be collected either, and all the Townshend duties except the tax on tea were repealed in 1770.

British Attempt to Control the West

In 1763 the violent Indian uprising known as Pontiac's Rebellion broke out in the West. Pontiac, one of the greatest Indian leaders, had foreseen that the defeat of France by Britain meant a hard fate for his people. The French had traded with the Indians, protected them, intermarried with them; the ever-advancing settlers of the British colonies threatened to wipe them out. Pontiac's Rebellion began with simultaneous surprise attacks on the English posts beyond the Appalachians, destroying eight of eleven. It was suppressed by British regulars, specially trained in wilderness fighting, after nearly two years of warfare.

To pacify the frontier and prevent American pioneers from being massacred, the British government issued the Proclamation of 1763, whereby all settlement west of a line running along the crest of the Appalachian Mountains should cease (see map, p. 44). The entire western region was to be reserved for Indians. Although this was alleged to be a temporary measure, some members of the British government hoped it would be permanent. It would divert settlers to Georgia or Nova Scotia "where they could be useful to their Mother Country instead of planting themselves in the Heart of America out of reach of Government where, from the great difficulty of procuring European commodities, they would be compelled to engage in commerce and manufactures to the infinite prejudice of Britain." Although the Americans at first accepted the Proclamation of 1763 as a means of averting bloodshed, they later resented it. They claimed that it deprived them of land rightfully theirs for settlement and interfered with the charter rights of colonies whose grants extended "from sea to sea." American interests, it appeared, were being sacrificed in order to fill the pockets of British fur traders who wished to see the Indians undisturbed.

Threats to Colonial Self-Government

There could be no question that the British government now pursued a deliberate policy of increasing its power within the thirteen colonies. Grenville's new customs collectors and admiralty judges were followed by ten thousand British regulars, for whom the colonists were required to provide barracks and supplies. These troops were sent, it was said, to protect the

Americans. But to protect them from whom? The French had been defeated and the Indians pacified. The redcoats, furthermore, were not stationed in frontier posts, but in towns such as Boston and New York, where there was no more danger from Indians than in London or Paris. The British motive for sending the redcoats may have been simply to find a way of taking care of veterans, but they also served to strengthen the hand of colonial governors and to overawe colonial legislatures.

That the British were eager to free royal officials from colonial control could be seen by the shifting of customs cases to the Admiralty Courts. In 1767 the Townshend Acts provided that British judges and governors were to be paid out of customs revenues collected by British revenue officers. No longer could colonial legislatures restrain royal governors by holding up their salaries.

When colonial legislatures became centers of resistance to British measures, royal governors prevented them from meeting. Thus the New York legislature was suspended in 1767 for protesting against the quartering of redcoats in the colony, and the Massachusetts legislature suffered the same fate in 1768 for issuing a Circular Letter which asked other colonies to join with Massachusetts in resisting the Townshend Act. Such actions denied the Americans' long-established rights of self-government.

AMERICAN RESISTANCE

The efforts of the British government to tighten control met resistance so determined that it surprised even the Americans themselves. It took a variety of forms, including simple disobedience of British laws, formal protests against British violations of American rights, increased cooperation among the thirteen colonies, boycotts, and violence.

The New York Public Library

Revere's depiction of the landing of British troops in Boston harbor in 1768. The caption says the troops "Marched with insolent Parade, Drums beating, Fifes playing, and Colours flying, up to King Street."

Disobedience of British Laws

The Americans, long used to evading British revenue laws, did not hesitate to evade the new ones. In spite of a more vigorous customs service, smuggling went on much as usual. The coast of America was so long that revenue officers could not inspect all ships landing, especially when the local inhabitants were constantly working to thwart them.

When the ten thousand redcoats were sent to America, Parliament passed the Mutiny Act of 1765, which directed the colonies to provide the soldiers with barracks and supplies. The New York and Massachusetts legislatures flatly

George III faced opposition in England as well as in the new United States. Here a British cartoon shows him drawn by obstinacy and pride into a chasm.

refused to vote the necessary money, regarding the act as a concealed means of taxation, and most other colonies found means of evading it.

The Proclamation of 1763, forbidding trans-Appalachian settlement, was flouted by the Americans. In the long years of bitter Indian warfare that started with the struggle for the Ohio Valley, there had developed a new breed of frontiersmen, as familiar with the wilderness as the Indians they had fought, as brave and as wily in warfare, and as contemptuous of all direction from above. Governor Dunmore of Virginia wrote to England of the impossibility of controlling these people.

I have learnt from experience that the established authority of any government in America, and the policy of government at home, are both insufficient to restrain the Americans. . . . They acquire no attachment to place; But wandering about seems engrafted in their nature; and it is a weakness incident to it, that they should forever immagine the Lands farther off are still better than those upon which they are already Settled. . . . impressed from earliest infancy with Sentiments and habits, very different from those acquired by persons of a Similar condition in England, they do not conceive that Government has any right to forbid their taking possession of a Vast Tract of Country, either uninhabited, or which serves as a shelter to a few scattered tribes of Indians.

It was in this period, when the Proclamation of 1763 supposedly forbade them, that the colonists made their first settlements across the Appalachians (see map, p. 44).

Formal Protests Against British Violations of American Rights

Simple disobedience was not enough to meet the crisis presented by Britain's measures. Again and again the colonists protested that they could not submit to the new policies without surrendering their rights as English people. Protesting the Stamp Act, the Virginia House of Burgesses declared, in a set of resolutions drawn up by Patrick Henry:

Resolved, That the first adventurers and settlers of this His Majesty's Colony and Dominion of Virginia brought with them, and transmitted to their posterity, . . . all the liberties, privileges, franchises, and immunities, that have at any time been held, enjoyed, and possessed by the people of Great Britain.

The principle to which the Americans appealed most frequently was that of "no taxation without representation." Great Britain, they said, had no right to tax the colonies, since the Americans elected no members to the British

Parliament. The colonists could be rightfully taxed only by their own legislatures. Such arguments appeared again and again in resolutions by town meetings by colonial legislatures, and by the Stamp Act Congress, a meeting of colonial representatives in New York in 1765. The colonists revealed extraordinary awareness of the tradition of English liberties as embodied in such documents as Magna Carta (1215) and the Bill of Rights (1689). How strongly they felt is suggested by a resolution voted by the town meeting of Newburyport, Mass. Although professing loyalty to George III, it flatly repudiated the Stamp Act in these terms:

QUESTION • *Young people who have not reached voting age are subject to sales taxes, excise taxes, and income taxes. Have they a legitimate grievance under the principle of "no taxation without representation"?*

That a People should be taxed at the Will of another, whether of one man or many, without their own Consent is Rank Slavery. For if their Superior sees fit, they may be deprived of their whole Property, upon any frivolous Pretext, or without any Pretext at all.

Intercolonial Cooperation

Hitherto there had been very little cooperation among the thirteen colonies. The first time they ever seriously united on anything was in resisting the Stamp Act. A committee of the Massachusetts legislature sent letters to leaders of the other colonial legislatures urging that all send delegates to a convention of all the colonies to decide on a common policy toward the British government. As a result, the Stamp Act Congress met in New York in October 1765. Nine state legislatures were represented, and the others sent word that they approved of the venture. The delegates drew up a set of resolutions and organized a general boycott of British-made goods. Unity was promoted in *Letters from a Farmer in Pennsylvania,* by John Dickinson, published in the *Pennsylvania Gazette* in 1767 and 1768. Dickinson argued that the people of the thirteen colonies, "separated from the rest of the world, and firmly bound together by the same rights, interests, and dangers," formed "one political body of which each colony is a member." In 1768 the Massachusetts legislature helped to get common action against the Townshend Act by issuing a Circular Letter calling on all the other state legislatures to join with them in protest against the measure.

The new spirit of cooperation was accompanied and given strength by a rising spirit of patriotism. In a speech to the Stamp Act Congress, Christopher Gadsden of South Carolina declared, "There ought to be no New England Man, no New Yorker, known on the continent, but all of us Americans." At the Princeton College commencement in 1771, Philip Freneau delivered a poem, "The Rising Glory of America," that revealed his optimistic faith in:

The rising glory of this western world,
Where now the dawning light of science spreads
Her orient ray, and wakes the muse's song;
Where freedom holds her sacred standard high,
And commerce rolls her golden tides profuse
Of elegance and ev'ry joy of life.

An American nation was coming into being.

Boycotts and Violence

Colonial protests against the Stamp Act were given real bite because they were accompanied by an effective boycott of English goods. Men and women made solemn promises to wear homespun instead of British woolens, and merchants signed agreements to buy nothing from England until the unpopular law

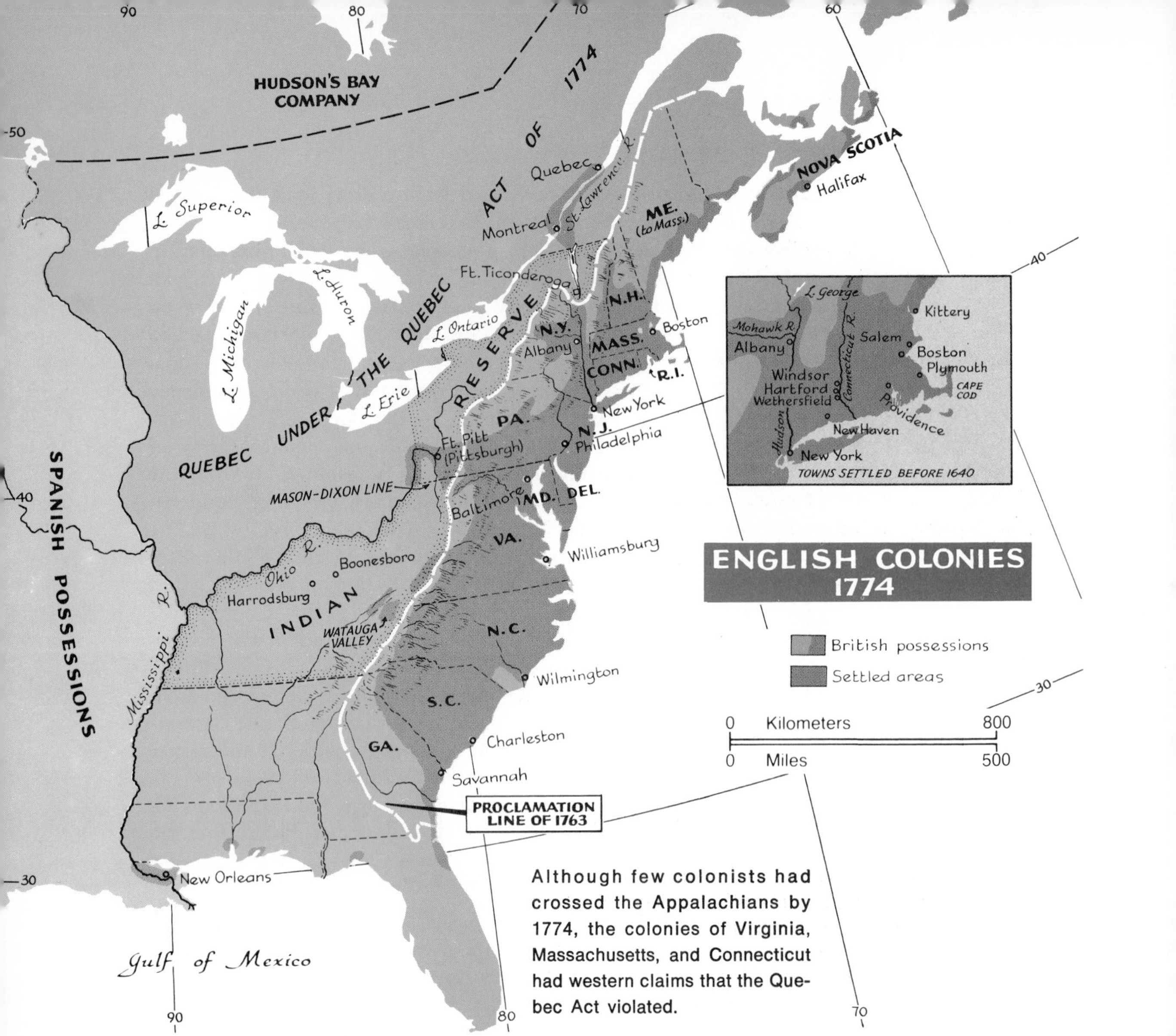
ENGLISH COLONIES
1774
HUDSON'S BAY COMPANY
QUEBEC UNDER THE QUEBEC ACT OF 1774
SPANISH POSSESSIONS
INDIAN RESERVE
NOVA SCOTIA
Halifax
Quebec
Montreal
St. Lawrence R.
ME. (to Mass.)
N.H.
MASS.
CONN.
R.I.
N.Y.
PA.
N.J.
MD.
DEL.
VA.
N.C.
S.C.
GA.
L. Superior
L. Michigan
L. Huron
L. Ontario
L. Erie
Ft. Ticonderoga
Albany
Boston
New York
Philadelphia
Ft. Pitt (Pittsburgh)
MASON-DIXON LINE
Baltimore
Williamsburg
Ohio R.
Boonesboro
Harrodsburg
WATAUGA VALLEY
Mississippi R.
Wilmington
Charleston
Savannah
PROCLAMATION LINE OF 1763
New Orleans
Gulf of Mexico
British possessions
Settled areas
0 Kilometers 800
0 Miles 500
L. George
Mohawk R.
Kittery
Salem
Plymouth
CAPE COD
Windsor
Hartford
Wethersfield
Connecticut R.
Hudson
Providence
New Haven
TOWNS SETTLED BEFORE 1640
90
80
70
60
50
40
30

Although few colonists had crossed the Appalachians by 1774, the colonies of Virginia, Massachusetts, and Connecticut had western claims that the Quebec Act violated.

should be repealed. Soon imports from England dropped to the lowest point in a generation, and British merchants, saying that they were faced with "utter ruin," besieged Parliament with petitions against the Stamp Act. Under such pressure, Parliament repealed the law in 1766.

Although most of the leaders of colonial resistance to the measures of the British Parliament were members of the colonial upper classes, they received assistance from an organization of small shopkeepers, clerks, and artisans known as the Sons of Liberty, with a female auxiliary, the Daughters of Liberty. The Sons of Liberty, who formed the "action wing" of the organized resistance, kept watch on shopkeepers suspected of selling British goods and publicly denounced those they caught or threatened them with bodily harm. Their activities were sometimes accompanied by displays of violence. Because Thomas Hutchinson, a wealthy Bostonian, was suspected of favoring the Stamp Act, a mob attacked his home and destroyed the finest collection of books and documents in the thirteen colonies. In New York a crowd of three thousand men wrecked the house of an unpopular British officer. Such actions succeeded in cowing British sympathizers into silence, but they also frightened many who favored the American cause. Colonial leaders attempted to prevent their recurrence.

At the time that Parliament repealed the Stamp Act, it passed the so-called Declaratory Act, by which it claimed full power "to bind the colonies and people of America, subjects of the crown of Great Britain, in all cases whatsoever."

Parliament was following the principle of this law when it passed the Townshend Act in 1767. The Townshend duties differed from the stamp duties in being *external* taxes on imports which, it was hoped, would irritate the Americans less than an *internal* tax. But the colonists argued that any law designed to raise revenue from them without their consent was a violation of their liberties. Again they voted non-importation agreements. Again the Sons of Liberty patrolled docks where English goods might be landed and shops where they might be sold. The Daughters of Liberty foreswore imported finery, made tea out of local herbs, and pro-

Sam Adams, Agitator

Some men have a genius for agitation. Eager for unrest and controversy, they search for incidents that can be blown up into conflicts.

Sam Adams was such a man—and as such became one of the architects of the American Revolution. Just possibly, without his constant efforts, there would have been no break with Britain. Why did this Harvard-trained provincial lawyer keep agitating against England even after the Stamp Act and Townshend duties were no longer in effect?

To be sure, he had personal reasons for disliking the British. His father had been a principal stockholder of the Land Bank organized in Massachusetts in 1740; when Parliament destroyed the bank, the family's fortunes were ruined. This seemed to flavor Sam's entire career, for, as Machiavelli wrote, "It is better to kill a man's father than to destroy his inheritance." Certainly Sam hated the tyranny of an aristocratic government of privilege. And, just as ardently, he believed in liberty.

Adams was perhaps the first American to fully understand the power of publicity. Using many pen names, he wrote untiringly against the government. He organized committees to take advantage of widespread colonial discontent. He stirred up the committees to write tracts and pamphlets on colonial rights to appeal to the educated. In town meetings he whipped up inflammatory debates and resolutions. The Sons of Liberty organized the artisans and craftsmen; the minutemen pledged instant action when needed. Constantly alert, this "Bostonian in homespun" was an instigator of it all. Considering his social class, Sam Adams might have been expected to be a conservative, even a Loyalist. But he was not, and the American Revolution perhaps came when and as it did because he was not.

duced homespun cloth. New England ministers organized the women of their congregations in great spinning contests. On one occasion, over a hundred Daughters of Liberty ran spinning wheels all day, while hundreds of spectators cheered them on. Perhaps never before in history had so many women taken an active role in politics. In 1770 Parliament gave in a second time, retaining only the tea duty as a symbol that it was not giving up the right to tax the colonies.

In 1770 the first clash between Americans and British troops took place. Two regiments of redcoats had been sent to Boston to support the governor and to overawe the radicals who, led by Samuel Adams, were making Massachusetts a center of opposition to Britain. One evening a squad of soldiers, commanded by a Captain Preston, was set upon by 50 or 60 men and boys, among them Crispus Attucks, a black. Without orders, the British soldiers opened fire, killing five men, including Attucks. Later a colonial jury acquitted Captain Preston and all but two of the soldiers, who were found guilty of manslaughter. It is ironic that a member of a race deprived of freedom became the first martyr of the American Revolution. The event became known as the "Boston Massacre" and has come down in history as the first physical resistance to the British.

CALM FOLLOWED BY STORM

From 1770 to 1773 there was a lull in the controversy between Great Britain and the thirteen colonies. Having won relief from some taxes, the Americans allowed the British to collect others. The colonial boycott on tea was retained, but was widely violated. Imports of British goods rose from 8 million dollars in 1768 to 21 million dollars in 1771. The basic issues had not, however, been settled. The British still held that Parliament had the right to legislate for the colonies "in all cases whatsoever." The Americans, while admitting some vague parliamentary right to regulate their trade, continued to insist that they were no more obliged to pay taxes levied by Parliament than the British had to pay those levied by the Virginia House of Burgesses.

That the calm would not last indefinitely was indicated by occasional acts of violence. In 1771 a British customs schooner that had taken a smugglers' ship into custody was attacked at night. The captive ship was released, the customs men locked into their own hold, and their schooner badly damaged. When another British revenue boat, the *Gaspée*, ran aground off Rhode Island, "persons unknown" attacked and burned it.

Meanwhile the men who led the resistance to British measures were improving their organization. Starting in Virginia and Massachusetts, under the leadership of such able agitators as Patrick Henry and Samuel Adams, they formed "committees of correspondence" in towns throughout the colonies. In forming this network, they were greatly assisted by the efficiency of the British intercolonial postal service that Franklin had organized. By keeping in constant touch with each other, these committees enabled the radicals to work out common policies and common lines of action.

The Boston Tea Party, 1773

The three-year truce came to an end with the so-called Boston Tea Party. This started a chain of events leading directly to war and a breaking of the tie between England and the colonies.

In 1773 the British East India Company was in difficulties for several reasons, among them being a terrible famine in the Indian province of Bengal, shrinking of the American tea market, and mismanagement. Bankruptcy

The Library of Congress

"The Repeal, or The Funeral Procession of Miss America Stamp." The Sons of Liberty expressed protest through political cartoons that often epitomized many of their grievances at once. Here the Stamp Act (see page 40) is being carried to a tomb for burial alongside such other affronts as the Star Chamber and excises, "which tended to alienate the Affections of Englishmen to their Country."

for the company would be another disaster, because the savings of many individuals were invested in it, and government funds as well.

To save the East India Company, Parliament voted to relieve it of all taxes on tea at home and to grant it a monopoly of the American market. At the insistence of Lord North, the prime minister, the three-penny per pound tax on tea imported into the colonies was retained. Even so, the company would be able to undersell tea smuggled in from France or Holland. The move would thus be a blow to colonial tea merchants.

The announcement of the new plan produced an immediate outcry in America. It was argued that if Parliament could give the East India Company a monopoly of trade in tea, it could arrange for monopolizing other commodities as well. Old religious fears came into the controversy. There had been rumors that the English government would appoint a bishop to preside over the Anglican churches in America, and that then the other Christian sects would be placed in the subordinate place they held in England. Once submit to Parliamentary taxation, went the argument, and you lay yourselves open to its tyranny over you in religion. Above all, objection to the arrangements for selling the East India Company's tea centered on the idea that they were designed to bribe the colonies into accepting Parliament's claim that it had the right to tax. "The baneful chests [of tea] contain a slow poison . . . ," wrote Benjamin Rush of Philadelphia, "something worse than death—the seeds of SLAVERY."

The excellent organization of the radicals was revealed when the East India Company tea reached America. At none of the four ports where it was to be landed—Charleston, Philadelphia, New York, and Boston—did the company sell a pound. At New York and Philadelphia the tea ships were forced to turn back. At Charleston the tea was kept in a warehouse until after the Revolutionary War broke out. In Boston a great protest meeting in the Old South Meeting House was followed by the famous "tea party." Radicals disguised as Indians boarded the tea ships and threw 342 chests of tea, valued at $75,000, into the harbor.

The Intolerable Acts

Benjamin Franklin called the Boston Tea Party "an act of violent injustice," and some Boston merchants were willing to take up a subscription to pay for the damage. To the British government, it was an act of lawlessness that had to be severely punished. Thomas Gage, an officer with long service in the colonies, told George III, "They will be Lions whilst we are Lambs, but if we take the resolute part they will undoubtedly prove very meek." Acting on this advice, in March 1774, Parliament passed what the colonists called the Intolerable Acts. They provided (1) that the port of Boston should be closed to shipping until the tea was paid for; (2) that British officials accused of violence in carrying out their duties should be tried in English courts rather than American; (3) that troops might be quartered in any town in Massachusetts— even in private homes; and (4) that the Massachusetts charter should be so amended as to greatly reduce the colony's right of self-gov-

ernment. Town meetings, for instance, could not be held more than once a year without special permission from the royal governor. Thus, the city of Boston and the whole colony of Massachusetts were to suffer severely for the actions of a handful of unknown men.

Passed at the same time, and considered by the colonists one of the Intolerable Acts, was the Quebec Act. This allowed the French inhabitants to use their own legal system (which did not include trial by jury) and to practice freely the Roman Catholic religion. It also extended the boundaries of the Province of Quebec to the Ohio River. In the excited state of American opinion the first two provisions seemed to prophesy abolition of jury trials and of the Protestant religion in the thirteen colonies unless the power of Parliament was checked. The change of boundaries seemed an attempt to exclude American settlers permanently from western lands; it also violated charter claims of Massachusetts, Connecticut, and Virginia. The Intolerable Acts revealed that the British government now intended once and for all to show the Americans who had authority. This was partly because of the attitude of George III.

QUESTION • What action should the British government have taken in regard to the Boston Tea Party?

George III Tries to "Be a King"

During the reigns of George III's predecessors, George I and George II, the direction of English affairs had been taken over by the leaders of Parliament. During George III's childhood, however, his mother had urged him, "George, be a king!" When he ascended the throne he tried to carry out his mother's advice. "Farmer George" was a popular king and a good family man. He had some ability and a strong will. As monarch he could appoint men to office; he used this power of patronage to influence Parliament. Members who voted as the king wished received government jobs with large salaries and few duties. By 1770 the king's power had become so great that Lord North, his personal nominee, became prime minister.

George III did not begin the quarrel between the British government and the colonies, but he intensified it because he came to believe that they must be ruled with a strong hand. After the Boston Tea Party he refused any compromise. "The colonies," he said, "must submit or triumph."

THE FIRST CONTINENTAL CONGRESS

The British Parliament had passed the Intolerable Acts in the expectation that the other American colonies would agree to Massachusetts being justly punished. William Pitt (now Lord Chatham) had warned, however, that the acts would give the colonies new reason to unite. Chatham proved to be right. The Intolerable Acts convinced many Americans that the men who ruled Britain were engaged in a conspiracy to extinguish their liberties. What happened to Massachusetts could easily happen elsewhere. Other colonies came to her aid, and hundreds of cartloads of food were sent to Boston to enable the city to hold out. All the colonies except Georgia sent delegates to the First Continental Congress, which held its first session in Philadelphia in September 1774. The Congress acted much as the Americans had done before in resisting the Stamp Act and the Townshend Act. It petitioned the king for relief from the Intolerable Acts, and cut off trade with England until they should be repealed. A Declaration of Rights and Grievances was designed to appeal to moderate men in that its tone was reasonable and it expressed devotion to George III. But it denounced every

step taken by Britain since 1763 to raise revenue or to tighten control as violating colonial charters or the colonists' rights as Englishmen.

"The Association"

The new boycott established by the First Continental Congress proposed to cut off exports to Britain as well as imports. To make the colonies able to bear such a self-inflicted blow to their commerce, the Congress urged Americans to set up local manufactures. Appealing to the spirit of self-sacrifice, the Congress also resolved to "discourage every species of extravagance and dissipation, especially all horse-racing, and all kinds of gambling, cockfighting, exhibitions of shows, plays and other extensive diversions and entertainments." For the enforcement of its rules the Congress tried to set up "in every county, city, and town," an organization known as "the Association." By the very nature of its task the Association exerted a surprising degree of control over Americans, telling them what they should eat, drink, and wear, as well as how they should behave in public. The Association was extraordinarily effective; imports of British goods into New York, for instance, dropped from over two million dollars in 1774 to six thousand dollars in 1775.

Meanwhile in every colony a volunteer army was organizing, and military stores were being collected. In New England, minutemen assembled to drill on village greens, while the town officials gathered powder, ball, uniforms, and food. In Philadelphia a group of young men formed a company called "the Quaker Blues" and were "read out of meeting" for violation of the Quaker stand against war. In the southern colonies, wealthy planters undertook to recruit and equip companies of men at their own expense. It began to appear that the dispute between Great Britain and her colonies would be settled only by force of arms.

Activities: Chapter 2

For Mastery and Review

1. Summarize reasons for the weakening of Americans' ties to England.

2. Explain the eighteenth-century victory of England over France in America.

3. What were the major elements of the British program to tighten control over the colonies? How did specific acts carry out this program?

4. In what ways did Americans resist the British program of tightening control? Describe each briefly.

5. For a protest to become a revolution, an organization is needed. Describe each of the following organizations: Stamp Act Congress, Sons and Daughters of Liberty, Committees of Correspondence, the Continental Congress, the Association, minutemen.

6. Outline (a) the causes of the Intolerable Acts; (b) their provisions; and (c) their results.

7. Make a time line, showing important events of the period 1763–1775.

Unrolling the Map

1. Study the map on page 43. Then explain why and where the Proclamation of 1763 was violated, and why the Quebec Act of 1774 was resented.

Who, What, and Why Important?

Francis Parkman
Albany Plan of Union
French and Indian War
Fort Duquesne
Pitt
Wolfe
Quebec
Peace of Paris, 1763
Grenville
Writs of Assistance
Sugar Act, 1764
Stamp Act

Townshend Acts
Pontiac
Proclamation of 1763
Stamp Act Congress
Declaratory Act
"Boston Massacre"
Sam Adams
Sons of Liberty
committees of correspondence
First Continental Congress

Quebec Act
George III
Boston Tea Party

the Association
minutemen
Intolerable Acts

To Pursue the Matter

1. What did the members of the First Continental Congress agree on? On what matters did they disagree? See Arnof, *A Sense of the Past*, "The First Continental Congress," pp. 30–33.

2. Assume that George Grenville, Charles Townshend, Lord North, and George III must each appear before the bar of history and justify the course of action he took toward the thirteen colonies during the decade before the Revolutionary War. Write their speeches in defense of their actions. For data consult Labaree, *The Road to Independence, 1763–1776*.

3. What were the "liberties, privileges, franchises, and immunities" to which the Virginia House of Burgesses referred? (See p. 42.) Study, in English history, Magna Carta, the Petition of Right, and the Bill of Rights to find some of the "rights of Englishmen" which the colonists claimed to be defending.

4. Was the "Boston Massacre" a massacre? See Forbes, *Paul Revere and the World He Lived In.*

5. How did the period of the Seven Years' War and afterward breed a new kind of frontiersman? How were the first English settlements established beyond the Appalachians? Questions such as these are answered in a highly readable book, Van Every, *Forth to the Wilderness: The First American Frontier, 1754–1774.*

6. By what means did Wolfe take Quebec? See Arnof, *A Sense of the Past*, for Parkman's classic account, and "The Battle That Won an Empire," *American Heritage*, December 1959, for a modern description.

7. How was resistance to British measures organized in American cities, and why were British authorities helpless to suppress it? See Gipson, *Coming of the Revolution, 1763–1775.*

Chapter 3

The Struggle for Independence

By the rude bridge that arched the flood,
Their flag to April's breeze unfurled,
Here once the embattled farmers stood
And fired the shot heard round the world.
—RALPH WALDO EMERSON

Hostilities between the Americans and the British broke out near Boston, which had been occupied in 1774 by a British army under General Thomas Gage. Early in the morning of April 19, 1775, a detachment of 700 British regulars was secretly sent from the city to destroy American military stores collected in Concord. Even though the minutemen had been alerted by William Dawes and Paul Revere, the British were at first successful. They easily dispersed a small force of Americans collected at Lexington; at Concord, they held off a sharp attack by three or four hundred minutemen. As the redcoats marched back toward Boston, however, they were attacked by an ever-increasing number of Americans, firing at them from behind trees, buildings, and stone walls. What started as an orderly retreat might have become a rout had it not been for the extraordinary discipline of the redcoats, or had the American force been anything but a disorganized crowd of individuals acting without direction. As it was, a brigade sent out from Boston saved the British from annihilation,

but about 250 of them were killed or wounded, as against less than 100 Americans.

THE COLONISTS MOBILIZE

The news of Lexington and Concord, carried by swift-riding horsemen, electrified the colonies. The Massachusetts Committee of Public Safety, which directed the Patriot organizations in the colony, called for an army of 30,000 men "to defend our wives and children from the butchering hands of an inhuman soldiery." Militiamen from all over New England marched toward Boston, one New Hampshire company covering 54 miles in 18 hours. Gage suddenly found himself besieged.

On June 17 the British discovered that the Americans had occupied Breed's Hill on a peninsula overlooking Boston from the north. The American army could easily have been trapped from behind, but the British commander decided to make a frontal attack uphill. The redcoats advanced in close order, each man carrying a heavy pack in addition to his

15-pound musket. Since the effective range of a musket of this period was scarcely more than 50 yards, the Americans were ordered to hold their fire until they could see the whites of their enemies' eyes. They repulsed two attacks with heavy slaughter, but were finally driven back to the mainland when they ran out of ammunition. The Battle of Bunker Hill, as it came to be called, was a moral victory for the Americans because their militiamen had stood up to professional troops. The British, whose casualties in the battle were over 40 per cent of those engaged, henceforth made no attempt to attack the besieging Americans.

QUESTION • How near must people be for you to be able to see the whites of their eyes?

Meanwhile, in May 1775, a handful of Green Mountain Boys from Vermont had overcome the little garrisons guarding the fortresses of Crown Point and Ticonderoga on the vital Lake George–Lake Champlain route. The Americans thus gained much-needed artillery.

The Second Continental Congress

On the day Ticonderoga fell, a Second Continental Congress met in Philadelphia. Called merely to devise further protests against British actions, it immediately assumed the powers of a central government and took steps to prosecute the war that had begun on the village green at Lexington. It voted to ask the colonies for war supplies and troops, to send agents to France for financial assistance, to encourage rebellion among the French Canadians, and to

Ethan Allen and the Green Mountain Boys

On May 10, 1775, Ethan Allen surprised Fort Ticonderoga and told the sleepy British commander he must surrender. Asked by what authority he made such a demand, he replied, "In the name of the Great Jehovah and the Continental Congress." So says his own account; other sources hint that his language could not have been repeated in polite society.

Ticonderoga's conqueror was a real adventurer. A man of gargantuan strength, with showy manners and a taste for fine clothes, he was a frequent speechmaker and a natural leader. He had gone into the back country of New England with his brothers to speculate in land. There, he was made the "commander" of the local militia—the Green Mountain Boys.

Vermont, lying between New Hampshire and New York, was claimed by both colonies, but the residents rejected all outside rule. Rough pioneers, they resented any decisions they had not helped to make. They insisted that Vermont be separate from any other colony—and, after independence, from any other state. They defied the British Privy Council, the Continental Congress, Governor Clinton, and General Washington. Stoutly, they fought the British at Ticonderoga and at Saratoga. Just as stoutly, they prepared to be a separate nation rather than accept New York authority. This was the way frontiersmen played politics, a heritage still traceable in local political dog fights. The Vermonters were successful: New York gave up her claims in 1790, a convention at Bennington ratified the United States Constitution, and Vermont became the fourteenth state of the Union on February 18, 1791.

dignify the motley array of militia besieging Boston with the name Continental Army. For commander in chief it chose George Washington, not only because of his experience and ability, but also because the fact that he was a Virginian would help to keep the southern and middle colonies from thinking of the struggle with Britain as "New England's War."

MOVING TOWARD SEPARATION

In spite of warlike measures, the majority of the Continental Congress did not at first favor separation from England. Instead, they wanted union with the mother country through common loyalty to the king, but with the right to rule themselves and not submit to Parliament. In a petition to George III, the Americans blamed all their troubles on his ministers, "those artful and cruel enemies who abuse your royal confidence and authority for the purpose of effecting our destruction." Congress appealed to the king for relief from Parliament and continued to open its meetings with prayers for his health. The Americans were careful to refer to the British armies they were fighting as "ministerial" troops.

No matter what Congress might have intended, events were driving them toward separation. First, there was the great fact of continuing war. Not content with bottling up Gage in Boston, the Americans invaded Canada —a possible base for British operations. One force under General Richard Montgomery, starting from Ticonderoga, took Montreal and advanced on Quebec by way of the St. Lawrence. Another little army under General Benedict Arnold also reached the great stronghold after an amazing march through the wilderness of Maine. When in December the two armies joined on the Plains of Abraham outside Quebec, they did not number more than 1,200. Yet the commanders attempted to surprise the defending garrison by an early morning assault. The attack failed when Montgomery was killed

and Arnold wounded; as a result, Canada remained in British hands.

George III's Inflexible Attitude

Meanwhile, the British government adopted a more and more inflexible attitude. George III refused even to read a conciliatory petition from the Continental Congress, but instead denounced the "diverse wicked and desperate persons" leading the Americans. He called on loyal subjects to bring the American leaders to justice as traitors. At this time the British punishment for treason was as follows:

... that the offender be drawn on a hurdle to the place of execution, that there he be hanged by the neck but not till he be dead, that while yet alive he be disembowelled and that then his body be divided into four quarters, the head and each quarter to be at the disposal of the crown.

In October a British naval force burned to the ground the defenseless port of Falmouth, Maine. Finally, in December, George III declared the thirteen colonies entirely outside his protection and all their ports under blockade by the British fleet. Unable to raise troops in England, because the war against the Americans was so unpopular there, the king hired soldiers from the rulers of small German states. They were generally known as "Hessians," because a large contingent was supplied by the Prince of Hesse, who was paid $500,000 a year plus $35 for each soldier killed and $12 for each one wounded. It was increasingly obvious that compromise between Great Britain and the thirteen colonies was impossible. Yet the Americans still held back, unwilling to cut their ties with the mother country.

"Common Sense"

At this critical moment, there appeared one of the most persuasive and widely read pamphlets in the world. Entitled *Common Sense*, and published in January 1776, it was written by Tom Paine, an English radical recently arrived in America. Paine hit directly at the strongest bond still keeping America tied to Britain—the sentiment of loyalty to the king, which was as ingrained an attitude as is respect for the Stars and Stripes in the United States today. Paine ruthlessly attacked monarchy in general and George III in particular. Hereditary kingship, he wrote, was a superstition that had been sold to the ignorant by means of lies and fables. A king was usually "the principal ruffian of some ruthless gang," and George III, "the royal brute of Great Britain," was typical of his breed. Paine added to the effect of this by explaining the advantages the Americans might gain when rid of English commercial restrictions and when no longer involved in England's quarrels with her European neighbors. Above all, Paine appealed to the Americans' sense that they were a chosen people, pioneers of liberty. "Freedom hath been hunted around the globe," he wrote. "Asia and Africa have long expelled her. Europe regards her like a stranger, and England hath given her warning to depart. O receive the fugitive, and prepare in time an asylum for mankind!"

Common Sense had an amazing circulation and helped to convince thousands of Americans that it was "time to part." Its arguments were more persuasive because American arms were extraordinarily successful. In Virginia the royal governor and the soldiers defending him were expelled; in North Carolina the militia repulsed an attempted landing of redcoats; in South Carolina a full-scale British attack on Charleston was brilliantly driven back. The greatest victory was in Boston. At first Washington had almost no artillery, but during the winter over fifty cannon from Fort Ticonderoga, weighing two to six tons apiece, were lashed to sledges and dragged by oxen 200 miles over snowy trails and frozen rivers. This amazing feat was followed up by bold action. On the night of March 4, 1776, about 2,000 men set batteries of these guns on Dorchester Heights,

Museum of Fine Arts, Boston

Although most famous for his ride to arouse the countryside against the British, as depicted in Grant Wood's famous painting (right), Paul Revere was a noted silversmith, artist, and political agitator. The above portrait by John Copley commemorates Revere as an outstanding silversmith in Colonial America.

overlooking Boston, and protected them with ingenious prefabricated fortifications. General William Howe (who had replaced Gage as commander of the British force) had no choice but to abandon the city. On March 17, he sailed for Halifax, carrying with him a thousand Loyalists who preferred exile to rebellion against George III.

A strong argument for independence was the need for military supplies and for reopening foreign trade. The Americans lacked guns, gunpowder, ammunition, uniforms, tents, and medical supplies, and did not have the facilities to make them in quantity. The stoppage of trade with the British Empire caused acute distress among American shippers and mer-

image caption*Metropolitan Museum of Art, New York*

chants. New markets were needed, and to get them commercial treaties with other nations had to be arranged. Such treaties could not be written by rebellious colonies, but only by independent states. Furthermore, the members of the Continental Congress hoped for aid from France. Ever since 1763 the French had been planning revenge on Great Britain for the terrible defeat suffered in the Seven Years' War (see p. 35). As early as November 1775, a French secret agent conferred with members of the Continental Congress. A few months afterward the French government started to smuggle arms to the Americans. But it was made clear that no alliance was possible and no commercial treaty guaranteeing American ships the right to trade with French ports until the Americans declared themselves an independent nation.

Colony after colony, starting with North Carolina in April 1776, advised its delegates in Congress to vote for independence. On June 7, Richard Henry Lee of Virginia introduced a resolution calling for independence and foreign alliances. The Continental Congress debated this for nearly a month while the moderates made a last stand for further attempts at reconciliation. By July 2 twelve states had approved Lee's motion, and on July 4 Congress agreed to accept the public statement of American rights and grievances known as the Declaration of Independence.

A Declaration by the Representatives of the UNITED STATES OF AMERICA, in General Congress assembled.

When in the course of human events it becomes necessary for one people to dissolve the political bands which have connected them with another, and to assume among the powers of the earth the separate and equal station to which the laws of nature & of nature's god entitle them, a decent respect to the opinions of mankind requires that they should declare the causes which impel them to the separation.

We hold these truths to be self-evident; that all men are created equal, that they are endowed by their creator with equal rights, that among these are life, & liberty, & the pursuit of happiness; that to secure these rights, governments are instituted among men, deriving their just powers from the consent of the governed; that whenever any form of government becomes destructive of these ends, it is the right of the people to alter or to abolish it, & to institute new government, laying it's foundation on such principles & organising it's powers in such form, as to them shall seem most likely to effect their safety & happiness. prudence indeed will dictate that governments long established should not be changed for light & transient causes: and accordingly all experience hath shewn that mankind are more disposed to suffer while evils are sufferable, than to right themselves by abolishing the forms to which they are accustomed. but when a long train of abuses & usurpations [begun at a distinguished period, &] pursuing invariably the same object, evinces a design to reduce them under absolute Despotism, it is their right, it is their duty, to throw off such government & to provide new guards for their future security. such has been the patient sufferance of these colonies: & such is now the necessity which constrains them to expunge their former systems of government. the history of the present king of Great Britain is a history of unremitting injuries and usurpations, [among which appears no solitary fact] to contradict the uniform tenor of the rest, all of which have in direct object the establishment of an absolute tyranny over these states. to prove this, let facts be submitted to a candid world, [for the truth of which we pledge a faith yet unsullied by falsehood.]

Thomas Jefferson made the rough draft at left of the Declaration of Independence. The changes, mostly by Benjamin Franklin, were few, but each made the Declaration more forceful. On July 2, 1776, Washington wrote, "The time is now near at hand which must probably determine whether Americans are to be Freemen or Slaves." Two days later, the Congress voted for independence. The scene is shown above in a painting by Robert Edge Pine and Edward Savage, done in 1785.

THE DECLARATION OF INDEPENDENCE

The Declaration of Independence was principally the work of Thomas Jefferson, a young Virginian who had been a rather inconspicuous member of Congress. Shy, a poor speaker in public, Jefferson was nevertheless known to be an able writer of pamphlets, so that when a committee was appointed to draw up a public statement justifying independence, he was included. Of the five members of the committee, two took no part in the work, and the other two, Benjamin Franklin and John Adams, more prominent and busier than Jefferson, were glad to leave to him the rather routine task of drawing up the statement of a decision already made.

Since Jefferson was busy and time was short, he did not compose an entirely new document. Instead, he did a scissors-and-paste editorial job of piecing together fragments from a declaration of grievances he had written earlier, from the new Virginia Bill of Rights (written by George Mason), and from Lee's resolutions. He then took his draft to Franklin who, wearing bifocal glasses of his own invention, made a few changes, each one of which made the Declaration more effective. Finally, it went to Congress, where additional changes were made in it before its final acceptance.

QUESTION • Look carefully at the corrections made in Jefferson's original longhand copy of the preamble of the Declaration of Independence. Did the corrections strengthen the first draft?

When the Declaration is examined in detail, it falls into three parts: first, the preamble, which states the general ideas upon which the

No American, not even Washington, made quite such an impact on eighteenth-century Europe as did Benjamin Franklin. This was partly because of his versatility: he was eminent as a scientist, a journalist, and a statesman. Also, his rise to fame from humble beginnings made him a symbol of a free and mobile society. This portrait by Charles Willson Peale was made when Franklin was 81 years old and a member of the Constitutional Convention.

American Revolution was founded; second, a long list of grievances against George III; and finally, the formal resolution of independence itself. (The text of the Declaration of Independence is found on pp. 814–815.)

The Preamble

Of the three sections, the preamble is the most important. It sets forth a philosophy of human rights and of democracy that has affected men's behavior ever since. This was by no means Jefferson's own invention, but was especially derived from the *Second Treatise on Government* written by John Locke to justify the right of the English to overthrow James II in the "Glorious Revolution" of 1688.

After a statement that the Americans are publishing the Declaration out of "a decent respect to the opinions of mankind," comes this famous sentence, the basis for all that follows:

We hold these truths to be self-evident, that all men are created equal, that they are endowed by their Creator with certain inalienable Rights, that among these are Life, Liberty, and the pursuit of Happiness.

Few sentences in all human history have been so debated. It has been endlessly pointed out that it is self-evident that human beings are created *un*equal: no two are exactly equal in physique, ability, circumstances, or character. Rights are not "inalienable": they are taken away by tyrants and surrendered by those unwilling to defend them. Such criticisms are based on misunderstanding of Jefferson's meaning. "Equal" does not mean "equal in abilities" nor "equal in circumstances," but simply "equal in rights." As all persons are equal before God, so they are *equal in God-given rights.* Therefore society should see that people are *equal before the law* and that they should have *equal opportunities.* "Inalienable" does not mean that tyrants are unable to take the rights of people away, but simply that they may not do so without violating divine law. A contract to sell yourself into slavery is null and void from the first, because your God-given rights are not yours to abandon.

Government as the agent of the people. Out of the idea of natural rights flow the following "self-evident truths" about the relation of the people to government:

That to secure these rights, Governments are instituted among men, deriving their just powers from the consent of the governed, that whenever any form of Government becomes destructive of these ends, it is the right of the people to alter or to abolish it, and to institute new Government, laying its foundation on such principles and organizing its powers in such form, as to them shall seem most likely to effect their Safety and Happiness.

Thus the origin of government is traced to a *contract* in which the people grant power to the rulers and in exchange are promised protection of their rights. It may be pointed out that most eighteenth century governments had their origin in conquest or seizure of power by strong men in the distant past, surely not in any agreement by the people to set up a right-protecting agency. This passage, however, insists only that the *rightful* aim of government is to protect the individual, and that *government is the agent of the people, not their master.* Obviously, then, a rightful government is one in which the people continually and freely consent to the rule of the state because all officials are their servants. In 1776 this idea was stated in contrast to the notion that a king had a divine right to govern. It has had force in the twentieth century in contrast to the Fascist idea that people exist to serve the state or to the Communist tendency to sacrifice individual wants to the alleged needs of society as a whole.

The rights of revolution and self-determination. The idea that a just government rests on popular consent leads to the idea that the people may refuse their consent to an unjust government, may "alter or abolish it," and may set up a government of their own. This passage, then, is a statement of a right of revolution. It is also a statement of what has been called in modern times the right of "self-determination," meaning the right of a people to be free from foreign rule. When the Philippines gained their independence from the United States on July 4, 1946, it was an expression of this right. The United States was also acting in accordance with its principles in freely granting independence to the Philippines.

From the expression of the right of revolution, the Declaration turns to showing that the government of Great Britain had been attempting to put the Americans under an "absolute despotism," that is, to put them completely under the power of the king. An early version blamed British misdeeds on Parliament, but this was altered to "the present King of Great Britain." This change increased the effectiveness of the Declaration by helping to destroy that loyalty to the monarch already mentioned.

A Listing of Grievances

The greater portion of the Declaration is taken up with a list of grievances against "the present King of Great Britain" (note the hint that he may not be on the throne much longer). Relentlessly, Jefferson piles wrong on wrong. Note the effectiveness of the monotonous, dirge-like repetition: "He has refused ... He has forbidden ... He has utterly neglected ... He has obstructed ... He has plundered ... He has ... He has ... He has. ..." There was a measure of unfairness in these charges. George III did not begin the quarrel with the thirteen colonies, nor did he play any important role in shaping policy toward America until 1774. From then on, to be sure, he resisted all concessions and so helped to bring on the Revolutionary War. But sole blame cannot be truthfully laid at his door.

Jefferson, however, was not writing a cool appraisal of the causes of the Revolution. He was appealing to world opinion in the heat of battle. Write about the unwarrantable actions of the majority in Parliament and you have to explain the workings of the British constitution. How much easier, how much more effective it is to blame everything on George III and add him to the long roll of tyrants who have written their names in blood—Xerxes, Herod, Nero, King John, Genghis Khan, Ivan the Terrible!

Independence

The Declaration of Independence closes by maintaining that the Americans have done everything possible to preserve peace with "our British brethren" and have been spurned. There is nothing left for them but to declare that "these United Colonies are, and of right ought to be, Free and Independent States." To defend this action, the Americans pledged their lives, their fortunes, and their sacred honor. Then come the signatures of the members of the Continental Congress, each man now a traitor in the eyes of the British government.

Widespread Influence of the Declaration

However casually it may seem to have been produced, the Declaration of Independence is one of the two or three most important documents of modern times. By it the Americans made a commitment, as Lincoln said in the Gettysburg Address, "to the proposition that all men are created equal." As a result, the Declaration has been a continual lever for change in American society, in the direction of equal rights, equal opportunities, and equal voice in government. At different times in our history, it has operated toward ending Negro slavery, giving women the right to vote, enlarging job opportunities, and extending the chances for education. With a genius for simple and eloquent prose, Jefferson managed to express the democratic faith in such a form that ideals of equality and self-government, while not yet fully realized, are embedded in the American tradition.

Up to 1776 the colonists based their claims to self-government within the British Empire on colonial charters and on their traditional "rights of Englishmen." Now they demanded independence from Britain on the basis of the natural, inborn rights of all persons. Thus the Declaration of Independence acquired worldwide significance. When Lafayette went back to France after fighting on our side in the Revolutionary War, he hung a copy of the Declaration in a niche in his dining room, with an empty niche beside it awaiting a similar French declaration of human rights. When the Spanish-American colonies revolted in the early nineteenth century, several of them drew up declarations modeled on ours. And in the twentieth century, the late Jawaharlal Nehru, who was the first prime minister of India, called the Declaration of Independence a "landmark in human freedom."

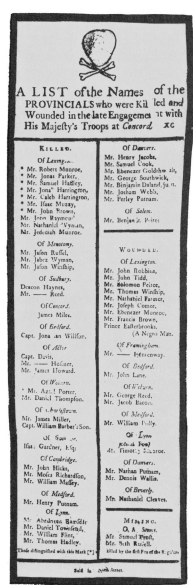

A LIST of the Names of the PROVINCIALS who were Killed and Wounded in the late Engagement with His Majesty's Troops at *Concord* &c.

KILLED.

Of Lexington.
* Mr. Robert Munroe,
* Mr. Jonas Parker,
* Mr. Samuel Hadley,
* Mr. Jona Harrington,
* Mr. Caleb Harrington,
* Mr. Isaac Muzzy,
* Mr. John Brown,
Mr. John Raymond,
Mr. Nathaniel Wyman,
Mr. Jedediah Munroe.

Of Menotomy.
Mr. Jason Russel,
Mr. Jabez Wyman,
Mr. Jason Winship,

Of Sudbury.
Deacon Haynes,
Mr. —— Reed.

Of Concord.
James Miles,

Of Bedford.
Capt. Jonathan Willson.

Of Acton.
Capt. Davis,
Mr. —— Hosmer,
Mr. James Howard.

Of Woburn.
* Mr. Asahel Porter,
Mr. Daniel Thompson.

Of Charlestown.
Mr. James Miller,
Capt. William Barber's Son.

Of Spencer.
Isaac Gardner, Esq:

Of Cambridge.
Mr. John Hicks,
Mr. Moses Richardson,
Mr. William Massey.

Of Medford.
Mr. Henry Putnam.

Of Lynn.
Mr. Abednego Ramsdle
Mr. Daniel Townsend,
Mr. William Flint,
Mr. Thomas Hadley.

Those distinguished with this Mark [*]

Of Danvers.
Mr. Henry Jacobs,
Mr. Samuel Cook,
Mr. Ebenezer Goldthwait,
Mr. George Southwick,
Mr. Benjamin Daland, jun.
Mr. Jotham Webb,
Mr. Perley Putnam.

Of Salem.
Mr. Benjamin Peirce.

WOUNDED.

Of Lexington.
Mr. John Robbins,
Mr. John Tidd,
Mr. Solomon Peirce,
Mr. Thomas Winship,
Mr. Nathaniel Farmer,
Mr. Joseph Comee,
Mr. Ebenezer Munroe,
Mr. Francis Brown,
Prince Easterbrooks,
(A Negro Man.

Of Framingham.
Mr. —— Hemenway.

Of Bedford.
Mr. John Lane.

Of Woburn.
Mr. George Reed,
Mr. Jacob Bacon.

Of Medford.
Mr. William Polly.

Of Lynn.
Joshua Felt,
Mr. Timothy Munroe.

Of Danvers.
Mr. Nathan Putnam,
Mr. Dennis Wallis.

Of Beverly.
Mr. Nathaniel Cleaves.

MISSING.
Of Lynn,
Mr. Samuel Frost,
Mr. Seth Russell.

killed by the first Fire of the Regulars

Sold in North Street.

The engagement between British redcoats and the American minutemen at Lexington was a skirmish rather than a battle. The minutemen fled before the British fire. Real resistance to the British began at Concord Bridge.

WHICH SIDE WOULD WIN?

The Declaration of Independence made all-out war a certainty. The Americans had taken a step that made reconciliation impossible. For the leaders of the rebellion, now branded as traitors to their king, failure would mean disgrace and death. As Franklin said, "We must all hang together now, or assuredly we shall all hang separately."

What Favored a British Victory?

In the coming struggle there were so many reasons to predict victory for England that a historian of the war has written, "The British should have won the Revolution handily." The following factors favored Britain:

(1) The British government, even though corrupt and inefficient by modern standards, was probably the most powerful in the world, while the United States hardly had a government worth the name. When the Declaration of Independence referred to the United States as "one people," it expressed a hope rather than a fact. The fact was that the Continental Congress exerted no real power over the thirteen

Connecticut Historical Society

states. Furthermore, only a minority of the American people actively supported the war. Most of them were indifferent to the Patriot cause except when fighting reached their doorsteps. There were portions of the country, too, where the Loyalists were in control, and thousands of Loyalists enlisted in the British army.

(2) The strength of the British government and the weakness of the Continental Congress meant that the British had the larger purse. The British paid their troops in hard cash and could always buy food for them in America. The Continental Congress, lacking the power to tax, printed paper money called "Continental Currency" which became so worthless that the phrase "not worth a Continental" has been part of American slang to this day. American soldiers starved, deserted, and sometimes mutinied because Congress could not pay them.

(3) The British had more disciplined troops and more trained officers. The easy victories won by American militia in 1775 were seldom repeated. The American cause, in fact, suffered from "the myth starting with the day of Concord and Lexington that amateur, half-disciplined militia were fully the equal of trained troops under any circumstances provided they possessed the ability to shoot." The fact was that militiamen were sometimes worse than useless. They were often unruly and mutinous. They were likely to run away in the face of danger, or to desert before danger was near. The only trustworthy force the United States possessed was the Continental Army, seldom numbering as many as 5,000.

(4) During most of the war, Great Britain had command of the sea. This gave British armies the choice of where to strike along the Atlantic coast and enabled them to supply their armies with ease. At one time or another the British held most of the principal ports of the United States—Boston, Newport, New York, Philadelphia, Wilmington (North Carolina), Charleston, and Savannah.

What Favored An American Victory?

There were a number of reasons why the Americans overcame the advantages of the British and ultimately won the War for Independence:

(1) The United States had only to hold out to win, while the British had to utterly destroy American resistance. In this latter task they had to "conquer a map." Distances were so great in America and the people, living mostly on self-sufficient farms, were so scattered that Great Britain could not win the war just by taking the principal cities. When British forces ventured into the country, they could often march in any direction they pleased without meeting American forces strong enough to resist them, but they suffered continual losses from guerrilla attacks.

(2) The British had to carry on war across the Atlantic. It took whole fleets to transport as many troops as a single great liner could ferry across the ocean today. Sailing vessels were so uncertain that a British commander sometimes went six months without receiving dispatches from home. It was difficult, sometimes impossible, to keep in touch with commanders in the field. Because of this, the British lost a whole army at Saratoga.

(3) The war was not popular in Britain. The British could fill their regiments only by recruiting criminals and vagrants, as well as 30,000 Hessians. Many of these German troops deserted and some even joined the Continental Army. Although untrained "embattled farmers" were not to be relied on, when the Americans were disciplined, as in the Continental Army, they proved to be excellent troops—active, enterprising, inventive. Thousands of Negroes served in the Continental Army, generally receiving freedom as the reward for enlistment. "For great patience under privations, fatigue, and wounds," it was reported, "the Negro, trained in the hardest of schools, was not to

Although to Americans Washington seemed the embodiment of an aristocrat and his home at Mount Vernon quite a grand house, Europeans who met him were impressed by the simplicity of his manners and the lack of great style at Mount Vernon, which he used to call "my farm."

be surpassed." American troops were more skillful in the use of firearms than European soldiers, and some of them were equipped with the "Pennsylvania rifle," a far more effective weapon than "Brown Bess," the British musket. The Americans might not have been perfectly united, but a far higher proportion of them than of the English people believed in their cause and were willing to risk their lives for it.

QUESTION • What is the difference between the musket and the rifle? Why is one superior?

(4) American leadership was superior to that of Britain. In spite of its weakness, the American Congress displayed more statesmanship and devotion to duty than did the British Parliament. Favoritism and bribery were an accepted part of British politics. There was graft and self-seeking on the American side too, but there were also men like Nathan Hale, who regretted that he had but one life to give for

his country, and leaders like John Adams and Benjamin Franklin, who freely gave their services to the Patriot cause. It has been estimated that nearly a third of the graduates of American colleges served as members of American state governments, as members of the Continental Congress, or as army officers.

Although handicapped at the start, the Americans eventually found able commanders. Some were men with little training but great natural ability, such as Nathanael Greene, Daniel Morgan, and George Rogers Clark. Others were foreigners such as Karl von Steuben, Thaddeus Kosciusko, Casimir Pulaski, and Marquis de Lafayette. In terms of leadership, Washington was undoubtedly the greatest American asset, even though he lost more battles than he won. He may have been mistaken in training his army on strictly European lines. He sometimes annoyed his men by his stiff manner and by a tendency to talk as though all were lost. But no man did more to win the war. While British commanders often returned to England for the winter, Washington's devotion to duty was such that he saw his home at Mount Vernon only once during the war, and then only for a few hours. He alone commanded sufficient respect to keep the Continental Army in being. Often soldiers remained with the army, even when they were unpaid and their enlistments were up, because, as one of them used to tell his grandchildren, "He was a fine man, General Washington—he was everything a man should be."

(5) Finally, the United States was able to win the Revolutionary War because of foreign help. It is hard to see how the Americans could have held out without the aid of France. In the latter years of the war, when money raised by the Americans Haym Salomon and Robert Morris had been exhausted, the French government provided more money as well as trained troops. The French navy briefly wrested control of the

sea from Great Britain. Also, the struggle gradually developed into a general European war in which Great Britain was fighting a ring of enemies in the West Indies, the Mediterranean, and India, as well as in the United States.

THE REVOLUTIONARY WAR: PRINCIPAL CAMPAIGNS

The Declaration of Independence had been signed during a period when there were no British armies on our soil. But in August 1776, perhaps the largest single military force ever sent from Europe to America appeared off New York—over 400 transports bearing 32,000 troops, guarded by 30 warships, under the command of Sir William Howe. Easily defeating 20,000 ill-trained militia under Washington's command, the British took New York City and held it until the war was over, seven years later. They followed Washington up the Hudson and, when he crossed to New Jersey, pursued him southward to the Delaware River. The American army was now reduced to 5,000 men and the Continental Congress fled from Philadelphia to Baltimore.

Washington's Victories at Trenton and Princeton

Then, when all seemed lost, Washington won brilliant victories in New Jersey at Trenton and Princeton. Trenton was held by three regiments of Hessians under the command of a Colonel Ralls, who regarded the Americans as "country clowns." Ralls took few precautions against attack. Washington, knowing that these German troops would be likely to celebrate Christmas by getting thoroughly drunk, took a chance on surprising them the morning after. He recrossed the Delaware River and attacked the Hessian force just at dawn on December 26. In only three-quarters of an hour, over 1,000 of about 1,300 Hessians were killed or cap-

American victory at Princeton, where British forces were caught offguard, boosted colonial morale at a critical juncture in the war. British surrender at Yorktown, (below), was idealized by painter John Turnbull. Actually, Cornwallis stayed in his quarters, and a staff member carried his sword to Washington.

tured, with a loss of only two American lives. Ralls was killed in the battle; on his body was found an unopened note from a Loyalist who had warned him the night before that Washington was coming. Had Ralls read this note, he might have ambushed Washington instead of the reverse, and the course of history might have been changed.

When General Howe heard of the defeat at Trenton, he sent General Charles Cornwallis from New York with 6,000 men to capture Washington's force. Washington, whose troops numbered only 1,500, pretended to be trapped, then slipped away and successfully attacked a surprised British force at Princeton on January 3, 1777. He then moved his army into the highlands of New Jersey out of reach of Cornwallis.

These victories saved the American cause. There were great celebrations at Philadelphia when the Hessians captured at Trenton were paraded through the streets. Because of his repeated failures, Washington had been in danger of being removed from command. Now a hero again, he was given more power by Congress, and new enlistments filled the ranks of his army.

British Attack from Canada

Although the American attempt to conquer Canada in 1776 had been a failure, it forced the British to divert to Canada troops who might have been better used in New York and New Jersey. In 1777 the British government planned to bring these forces into the war, as part of a great three-pronged attack which would cut the colonies in half along the line of Lake Champlain and the Hudson Valley. While Howe moved up the Hudson from New York City, an army under General John Burgoyne was to come south from Montreal, and a lesser force under Barry St. Leger was to invade by way of Lake Ontario and the Mohawk River (see map, p. 68). The three armies were eventually supposed to meet near Albany.

Because the British war office could not keep in touch with him, Howe's army never participated in the plan at all. Instead Howe made the fatal mistake of leading an expedition to Philadelphia, leaving Burgoyne in the lurch. He took the city in September, overcoming Washington's forces at the Battle of Brandywine and inflicting a further defeat on the Americans at Germantown in October. Congress fled to York, Pennsylvania.

Meanwhile, Burgoyne's force of 8,000 men had started south. Claude Van Tyne in *The War of Independence* described the spectacle as the army came down Lake Champlain:

As the great fleet pushed out into the lake, the Indian forces were first, in great birchbark canoes. Then came the British advance guard, followed by the flotilla which had beaten Arnold, and the bulk of the army, in row galleys, forming the rear. Into the still blue of the lake, and against the varied greens of the wooded shore, came a rainbow of color such as the wilds had seldom seen. There were, in the combined British and German troops, companies and regiments in blue coats, others in red or in green with cuffs of red. The breeches might be of yellow buff, or of white, or even the leather of the dismounted dragoons. In headdress there were little caps of black leather, plumed cocked hats, and the high hats of the grenadiers. . . . In footwear the most notable things were the high-spurred jackboots of the German dragoons, whose whole outfit was far too heavy for forest warfare. Finally, as if to clog the dragoon still further, he carried a broadsword with a three-pound scabbard. Swelling this riot of color were the varied regimental flags flaunting in the breeze.

Opposed to Burgoyne's army were ill-trained, ill-equipped American soldiers, commanded by officers who employed so much energy quarreling among themselves they could scarcely control their men. Burgoyne easily took Ticonderoga in midsummer and moved toward Albany, where he expected to meet Howe. But then his troubles began. A force of 1,000 American axmen felled trees across the only road, so that Burgoyne's army could move only about a mile a day. A British force sent toward Bennington was surrounded by Vermonters under John Stark. Soon came news that St. Leger's advance from Lake Ontario had been stopped at the bloody battle of Oriskany, and that Howe had gone south to take Philadelphia instead of north to meet Burgoyne.

QUESTION • How might later history have been different if Ralls had read the message from the Loyalist? If Howe had gone to Albany instead of to Philadelphia?

Saratoga—Turning Point of the War, 1777

In spite of his own difficulties near Philadelphia, Washington sent some of his best troops to General Horatio Gates, the American commander opposing Burgoyne. Meanwhile, with their homes actually threatened by the British advance and Burgoyne's Indian allies scalping civilians, New York and New England militia began to gather. Eventually, Burgoyne was surrounded by a force nearly twice as large as his own. He was unable to get food, to retreat to Ticonderoga, or to advance on Albany. After making one unsuccessful attempt to cut through the American lines, the entire British army surrendered at Saratoga in October 1777.

Saratoga proved to be the turning point of the war because it brought France into the war. Although the French had been providing so much secret aid that most of the guns and half the powder used at Saratoga had come from them, they had refrained from full support until the United States had proved that it could carry on effective war. Saratoga offered this proof. Furthermore, England now offered to grant the Americans generous rights of self-government within the British Empire, and the French were afraid the offer might be accepted. In February 1778, the French signed two treaties with the United States: the first recognized American independence and granted commercial privileges; the second offered an alliance on generous terms.

The French alliance proved absolutely invaluable to the American cause. From then on, the Continental Army was largely supplied and paid with French gifts and loans, and was reenforced by disciplined French regiments. The French navy interfered with the ability of the British to move troops as they pleased up and down the Atlantic coast. Following the lead of France, Spain and the Netherlands entered the war against England, while Russia, Prussia, Denmark, Sweden, and Portugal formed a League of Armed Neutrality to resist British sea power.

Benjamin Franklin in Paris

One reason why French aid came so generously was that Benjamin Franklin was America's principal envoy to France. Perhaps no foreign diplomat in all history enjoyed such popularity as did Franklin in Paris. His homely face appeared everywhere, not only in books and pamphlets, but on rings, watches, brooches, and snuffboxes. Women even did their hair in a *"coiffure à la Franklin,"* designed to imitate his beaver hat. The middle class admired him because of his successful business career and the sayings of Poor Richard. Intellectuals admired him as a scientist. To radicals and liberals, he represented the way a free society allowed a man to rise by his own talents. The French officials whom he pressed for more troops, money, and supplies to America were won over to his cause by his ability, courage, cheerfulness, and tact.

American Fortunes at Low Ebb

French aid did not win the war at once. When the militia returned to their farms after Saratoga, the American military effort again

REVOLUTIONARY WAR, 1775-1781

Map 1: 1775-1777

0 Kilometers 160
0 Miles 100

BURGOYNE May 1776

MONTGOMERY Dec. '75–May '76

Quebec

St. Lawrence R.

Montreal

Ft. St. John

CARLETON Oct. 1776

L. Champlain

ARNOLD Dec. 1775

MAINE (Part of Mass.)

VALCOUR I.

MONTGOMERY Aug.–Sept. 1775

Crown Pt.

Ft. Ticonderoga

ARNOLD Oct. 1776

ETHAN ALLEN May 1775

Falmouth

Ft. Oswego

Ft. Schuyler

Mohawk R.

N.H.

Bennington

Br. to Halifax, Mar. 1776

Albany

Lexington Concord Apr. 1775

BUNKER HILL, June 1775

Boston **(BRITISH)**

West Point

Hudson R.

White Plains, Oct. '76

MASS.

CONN. R.I.

WASHINGTON Nov. '76–Jan. '77

New York, Aug.–Sept. 1776

British from Halifax, July–Aug. 1776

Morristown Winter Hq.

Princeton, Jan. 1777

Trenton, Dec. '76–Jan. '77

PA.

N.J.

1775–1777

Map 2: 1777-1778

0 Kilometers 160
0 Miles 100

Montreal

ST. LEGER June–Aug. 1777

St. Lawrence R.

L. Champlain

MAINE (Part of Mass.)

L. Ontario

Ft. Oswego

Crown Pt.

Ft. Ticonderoga

BURGOYNE June–Oct. 1777

Ft. Schuyler

Oriskany

Mohawk R.

Saratoga

N.H.

Bennington

GATES Oct. 1777

Boston

HERKIMER-ARNOLD Aug. 1777

Albany

MASS.

PROCLAMATION LINE OF 1763

N.Y.

West Point

Hudson R.

CONN.

R.I.

Newport

PA.

WASHINGTON Winter Hq. Oct. '77–June '78

Valley Forge

Germantown, Oct. '77

Brandywine Sept. 1777

Delaware R.

N.J.

New York (held by Br.)

Monmouth, June 1778

Philadelphia, Sept. 1777

Baltimore

MD.

DEL.

VA.

HOWE from N.Y. to Philadelphia, Sept. 1777

Chesapeake Bay

1777–1778

Map 3: 1778-1781

0 Kilometers 320
0 Miles 200

→ Principal American moves
→ Principal British moves

HAMILTON 1778

Wabash R.

GEORGE ROGERS CLARK 1778–1779

Ft. Pitt

Redstone

PA.

Philadelphia

N.J.

New York (held by Br.)

St. Louis

Cahokia

Vincennes Feb. 1779

Ohio R.

Baltimore

MD.

DEL.

WASHINGTON ROCHAMBEAU Sept. 1781

Kaskaskia July 1778

OF 1763

Ohio R.

Boonesborough

Harrodsburg

KENTUCKY

LAFAYETTE June–Sept. 1781

VA.

GRAVES from N.Y.

Mississippi R.

Charlottesville June 1781

James R.

Richmond

Williamsburg July 1781

Yorktown – Surrender, Oct. 19, 1781

REPULSE OF BR. FLEET Sept. 5–9, 1781

DE BARRAS from Newport, R.I.

Watauga Settlements

PROCLAMATION LINE

Guilford C.H. Mar. 1781

CORNWALLIS Apr.–May 1781

CORNWALLIS Jan.–Mar. 1781

Charlotte

N.C.

DE GRASSE from West Indies

Cowpens Jan. 1781

GREENE Jan.–Mar. 1781

Cheraw

Winnsboro

Camden

Wilmington

Ninety-Six

S.C.

Augusta

Savannah R.

GA.

Charleston

1778–1781

Map 4: 1778-1780

from Watauga

Charlotte

GATES Aug. 1780

N.C.

KINGS MT. Oct. 1780

Cheraw

Ninety-Six

Winnsboro

Camden Aug. 1780

S.C.

CORNWALLIS Mar.–May 1780

Augusta

Savannah R.

GA.

BRITISH Dec. 1778

Charleston

1778–1780

One of the persistent myths of American history is that the American Revolutionary War was won by militiamen — "Yankee Doodles." Actually, militia were very poor troops, and the only really effective American forces were the trained regiments of the Continental Army. Much of their training was under the direction of veteran European officers. The Prussian drillmaster Baron von Steuben is shown here at Valley Forge.

slackened off. It was only with the utmost difficulty that Washington held a starving army together at Valley Forge, outside Philadelphia, during the winter of 1777–1778, while the British inside the city lived well on food bought from American farmers.

In 1778 the British evacuated Philadelphia and marched across New Jersey toward New York. While they were on their way, Washington attacked their 12-mile baggage train at Monmouth, New Jersey, but a mistaken order and possible treachery prevented an American victory. This was the last major battle in the north, although New York City remained in British hands and Washington kept his headquarters in New Jersey.

From 1778 on, the British made their major military effort in the South, partly because they had the idea that the region was a stronghold of Loyalists and partly because the southern colonies were considered more valuable, since they fitted better into the mercantile system. For three years the redcoats marched almost at will through Georgia, the Carolinas, and Virginia, their main forces never suffering defeat.

The year 1780 was one of gloom for the American cause. British armies were victorious in the South. A French army of 6,000 men landed at Newport, Rhode Island, but was promptly blockaded by a British fleet. Benedict Arnold turned traitor and attempted to turn over the important fortress of West Point, New

York, to the English. The unpaid Continental Army was mutinous. There was great suffering among civilians because of high prices; tea sold at $90 a pound in the paper money with which the Continental Congress and the new state governments had flooded the country.

Military Victory: Yorktown, 1781

The British were having their troubles too. Ireland was in a state of rebellion and there were pro-American riots in London. The British armies could not keep their conquests in the south because they could not win the loyalty of the inhabitants. A British officer likened the force in which he served to a ship at sea: it moved in any direction at will, but left no trace behind. The British were also harassed by guerrilla fighters under the leadership of Francis Marion, "the Swamp Fox." Sometimes commanding as few as 30 men, sometimes as many as 900, Marion repeatedly surprised and defeated small British forces.

The worst aspect of the British position in 1780 and 1781 was that they suffered naval defeats at the hands of the French and so lost command of the sea. This made possible the capture of the principal British force in the South, under Lord Cornwallis, who was stationed at Yorktown, Virginia. At the urging of General Jean Baptiste Rochambeau, commander of the French troops in America, Washington agreed to a remarkable combined operation against Cornwallis. A French fleet sailed north from the West Indies and blocked the entrance of Chesapeake Bay, beating off a British fleet sent to relieve Cornwallis. Meanwhile, a French army sailed from Rhode Island to Virginia, and Washington went south with most of his best troops from the New York area. Besieged on land and hemmed in by sea, Cornwallis was forced to surrender in October 1781. After this disaster, and defeats elsewhere at the hands of Spain and France, the British government was finally ready to make peace, even if it meant recognizing American independence.

Diplomatic Victory: The Treaty of Paris, 1783

The peace treaties ending the Revolutionary War were not finally signed until 1783, because it took some time for France and her ally Spain to stop fighting. Spain, more or less backed by France, was not eager to see the United States extend its boundaries beyond the Appalachians and become a threat to the Spanish control of Louisiana and Florida. This situation allowed Great Britain to drive a wedge between the United States and France by offering the former thirteen colonies generous terms.

According to the Treaty of Paris between Great Britain and the United States (not to be confused with the Peace of Paris, 1763), the United States gained independence and land from the Atlantic to the Mississippi. This resulted partly from the British effort to bribe its way out of war, partly from the ability of the American peace commissioners John Adams and Benjamin Franklin, and partly from a brilliant expedition of 180 Virginia soldiers under George Rogers Clark in 1778. Clark's capture of the British posts of Kaskaskia and Vincennes (see map, p. 68) gave the United States a claim to the trans-Appalachian West.

Although several provisions of the Treaty of Paris led to later disputes, it was a great diplomatic victory. The United States gained an area four times that of France and nearly ten times that of the British Isles, so that from the first they had the natural resources to become a great power. (See map, p. 84.)

THE REVOLUTION WITHIN AMERICA

The American Revolution involved a civil war as well as a war against Great Britain. In every one of the thirteen states there were Loyalists who refused to abandon allegiance to King George III. Antagonism between them

One of the ablest delegations the United States ever sent to a diplomatic conference: (left to right) John Jay, John Adams, and Benjamin Franklin. Henry Laurens, the fourth delegate, did not reach the conference until it was almost over. The man on the right is Franklin's grandson. The British delegates refused to sit for this portrait by Benjamin West, so it remained unfinished.

and the Patriots was even more bitter than that between the Patriots and the English, since the Loyalists were regarded as traitors to the American cause. John Adams said that if his own brother became a Loyalist, he would not hesitate to have him hanged. Loyalists tended to belong to the wealthier classes, but this was by no means universal. In some southern states, for instance, backcountry farmers became Loyalists because they disliked the Patriot merchants and planters of the coastal areas. Sometimes the division between the two groups involved religious differences.

Many women actively served the patriot cause. As secret agents they supplied Washington and other American generals with information about British positions and plans. They raised money to equip troops. They ran farms and businesses while husbands were away. The John Adamses would have gone bankrupt had not Abigail managed their farm in Braintree, Mass. so well. A few women fought in the ranks, the most famous being Mary Ludwig Hays, better known as Molly Pitcher. Carrying water to the artillerymen during the battle of Monmouth in 1778, she saw her husband fall. She ran to take his place at the cannon. For her services, she received a pension of $50 a year from the government when she was 68 years old.

In most areas, known Loyalists lost their property and were banished. It is estimated that a hundred thousand people fled to Canada, where their descendants still live. Many Loyalists who remained were tarred and feathered, not a few killed by angry mobs. Their confiscated estates were put up to public auction. Since these were often divided and sold to small owners, a wider distribution of property among the people resulted.

Trends Toward Greater Equality and Democracy

The division of Loyalist estates was only one example of a general trend toward greater equality. State laws promoted more equal property division by abolishing primogeniture, a legal arrangement whereby property was inherited entirely by the eldest son. Following the principles of the Declaration of Independence, most of the thirteen states solemnly proclaimed bills of rights, spelling out in detail the equal rights of citizens that it was the duty of government to protect.

A result of the war was an increase in religious freedom. Throughout the southern states, the Church of England was disestablished, that is, it was no longer supported by taxation. The state of Virginia passed a bill for religious freedom written by Thomas Jefferson. It asserted:

... that no man shall be compelled to frequent or support any religious worship, place or ministry whatsoever, ... nor shall otherwise suffer on account of his religious opinions or belief; but that all men shall be free to profess, and by argument to maintain, their opinion in matters of religion.

In New England, although religious differences were tolerated, the Congregational Church continued to be supported by taxation, and only Protestants were allowed to vote.

There was no way to square the proposition that all people were created equal with black slavery. One important result of the American Revolution was that nearly all the northern states arranged to free their slaves. In some states this was done by "compensated emancipation," that is, by paying off the masters; in others by declaring that children of slaves born after such and such a date would be free. In two states the courts held that provisions in the state constitutions that "all men are born free and equal" meant the end of slavery.

In the South there were many slave owners who felt that slavery was a terrible wrong. In 1782 the Virginia legislature passed a law allowing slave owners to free their slaves, and 10,000 Negroes were granted freedom within eight years. Little was done elsewhere. The slaves represented a large proportion of the wealth of the South, and the plantation system was dependent on their labor. Thomas Jefferson hated slavery and wrote, "I tremble for my country when I reflect that God is just; that His justice cannot sleep forever. . . ." Yet Jefferson, and others like him, could see no immediate way to end the institution of slavery in the southern states.

The break with England made it necessary to set up new governments to take the place of the former colonial administration. The only exceptions were Connecticut and Rhode Island, formerly self-governing colonies, where the old charters continued to operate. The new constitutions revealed the influence of John Locke in their insistence that government existed to protect individual rights and that it was the agent of the people. They also revealed a distrust of strong executive power, the result of experience with the former royal governors and with George III. Most state governors were elected for only one year at a time and had no power to veto bills passed by the legislature.

Although the new governments were supposed to represent the people as a whole, there was a question as to who should be allowed to vote. According to John Locke, a major purpose of government was to protect property, and so in every state the right to vote depended on the possession of a certain amount of property, such as fifty acres of land. Qualifications for office-holding were often more restrictive. There was also some debate in northern states as to whether the franchise should be limited to whites. In 1778 the town meeting of

Sutton, Massachusetts, protested a proposed provision of the state constitution that denied the franchise to Negroes and Indians:

This [provision] is manifestly adding to the already accumulated burden of guilt lying upon the Land in supporting the Slave Trade, when the poor innocent Africans who never hurt or offered any Injury or Insult to this country have been . . . cruelly brought from their Land, and sold here like Beasts, and yet now by this Constitution, if by any good Providence, any of their Posterity gained their Freedom and a handsome Estate they must be excluded from the Privileges of men! This must be the *bringing or incurring more Wrath upon us.* And it must be thought more insulting tho not so cruel, to deprive the original Natives of the land the Privileges of Men.

This protest was not heeded, and Massachusetts, along with the other states, limited the franchise to white males.

Although the American Revolution did not immediately bring the full equality and democracy that a literal reading of the Declaration of Independence would indicate, it did push American society in that direction.

When John Adams was serving in the Continental Congress, he received a message from his wife, Abigail:

Remember the Laidies, be more generous and favorable to them. Do not put such unlimited power into the hands of Husbands. Remember all men would be Tyrants if they could. If perticular care is not paid to Laidies, we are determined to foment a Revolution, and we will not hold ourselves bound by any laws in which we have no voice or representation.

Abigail Adams' words went unheeded. The American Revolution did very little to change the position of women as it existed in the eighteenth century. State bills of rights declared all people equal, but they reserved full privileges of citizenship for white males.

WIDE INFLUENCE OF THE AMERICAN REVOLUTION

When the British troops marched out of Yorktown to lay down their arms, their band played a tune called "The World Turn'd Upside Down." The defeat of England, a strong, established nation, by a raw, new country was considered amazing. The success of the United States promoted ideas of freedom and equality. It gave new hope to the friends of the oppressed in Europe, and endangered the old system of monarchy and a privileged upper class.

France was the country most immediately affected by the American Revolution. The ideas found in the preamble of the Declaration had already been popularized by famous writers such as Jean Jacques Rousseau. The contention of these authors that a free society made men virtuous seemed borne out by the honesty and patriotism of American diplomats such as John Adams, Jefferson, and Franklin. It was even more impressive when Washington quietly returned to Mount Vernon, instead of using his position as head of the army to make himself a dictator or a king. The French watched Americans establish successful state governments; they read state bills of rights; they marveled at the reports of widespread prosperity, so unlike the unequal distribution of wealth in France. The example of America was a trump card in the hands of those who planned revolution in both society and government.

The amount of money France poured into the Revolutionary War brought the government to the verge of bankruptcy. When in 1788 the king's ministers proposed new loans or taxes to balance the budget, Frenchmen raised the familiar cry of "no taxation without representation" and forced King Louis XVI to call representatives of the people together in a body known as the Estates-General. In the summer of 1789, the French Revolution began. The Estates-General set itself up as a national assembly to make over French government and law, according to the principles of equality and self-government; French peasants seized the land of the nobles; and a Paris mob took the great royal fortress and prison called the Bastille. That the French revolutionaries fully realized their debt to America was shown when they sent Washington the key to the Bastille and when they decreed three days of national mourning on hearing of the death of Franklin in 1790.

In Great Britain, the British defeat in the Revolutionary War discredited George III and put an end to his attempt to "be a king" by buying control of Parliament. After the news of Yorktown, Lord North, George III's personal choice as prime minister, was voted out of office, and Parliament took steps to see that in the future no king could corrupt and control its members as George III had done. Thus the American Revolution helped to make the king of England the figurehead he is today. In the long run, it also persuaded the British to allow their colonies more self-government. The idea expressed by the colonists before the Revolutionary War was that they were tied to Great Britain only by loyalty to the crown and not by subjection to the British Parliament. This is essentially the arrangement by which Canada, Australia, and New Zealand are tied to Britain today.

Emerson did not exaggerate when he wrote in the "Concord Hymn" that the shot fired by the minutemen on April 19, 1775, was "heard round the world."

Activities: Chapter 3

For Mastery and Review

1. What influences caused the Americans to fight for independence instead of rights within the British Empire?

2. Trace step by step the argument of the preamble to the Declaration of Independence. This might be done in the form of a geometrical proof: "Given: That all men are endowed by their Creator with certain unalienable rights. To prove . . ." What has been the influence of the preamble? (For text, see Appendix, p. 814.)

3. Study the portion of the Declaration that lists the grievances against George III. Wherever you can, note for each grievance the specific act to which the Americans objected. (See Appendix, pp. 814-815.)

4. Contrast the conditions during the Revolutionary War favorable to the British with those favorable to the Americans. This might be done by a written summary in parallel columns.

5. What were the consequences of the American victory at Trenton? At Saratoga? At Yorktown?

6. Why was the French monarchy willing to help the American revolutionists? How did French aid influence the decision of the colonies to declare independence? What was the importance of French aid to the American cause?

7. Why may the Treaty of Paris (1783) be regarded as an American diplomatic victory?

8. Sum up the contributions of the Revolution to American democracy.

9. How did the Revolution affect France and Great Britain?

Unrolling the Map

1. On an outline map of eastern United States show the Burgoyne-St. Leger campaign from the north and the Howe campaign against Philadelphia. Bring out the failure to coordinate the attack. On the same map, show the Yorktown campaign, emphasizing the successful coordination of land and sea forces.

2. On a map of eastern United States, show the boundaries of the United States as established by the Treaty of 1783, bringing out which portions were unresolved or disputed.

Who, What, and Why Important?

Lexington and Concord	Sir William Howe
Bunker Hill	Trenton
Second Continental Congress	Burgoyne
	Saratoga
George Washington	Valley Forge
treason	Benedict Arnold
Common Sense	Francis Marion
Dorchester Heights	Yorktown
Thomas Jefferson	George Rogers Clark
preamble to the Declaration of Independence	Treaty of Paris, 1783
	Loyalists
	Bill of Rights
Hessians	primogeniture
Lafayette	disestablishment
	French Revolution

To Pursue the Matter

1. How did the battles of Lexington and Concord appear to a British officer? See Arnof, *A Sense of the Past,* pp. 34–35.

2. Who was more responsible for persuading the Americans to demand independence, Tom Paine or George III? Just what *was* the cause of the American Revolution? See Labaree, *The Road to Independence, 1763–1776.*

3. How and why did Negroes get to be enrolled in the Continental army? See Ginsberg and Eichner, *The Troublesome Presence: American Democracy and the Negro.*

4. Washington takes command, 1775–1776 — why, how, to what effect? For contemporary accounts see Scheer and Franklin, *Rebels and Redcoats.*

5. What made the Declaration of Independence effective propaganda at the time it was written? See Bragdon *et al., Frame of Government.*

6. What did Benjamin Franklin contribute to American success in the Revolution? See Carl Van Doren's biography of him, and Bailey, *A Diplomatic History of the American People.*

7. Was Washington at fault in failing to prevent Sir William Howe from taking Philadelphia? See Alden, *The American Revolution.*

8. How did the British take their defeat at Yorktown? See Arnof, *A Sense of the Past,* pp. 49–50.

Chapter 4

Trials of
a New Nation

The thirteen colonies, which simultaneously threw off the yoke of England ... had ... the same religion, the same language, the same customs, and almost the same laws; they were struggling against a common enemy; and these reasons were sufficiently strong to unite them to one another and to consolidate them into one nation. But as each of them had always had a separate existence and a government within its reach, separate interests and peculiar customs had sprung up which were opposed to such a compact and intimate union as would have absorbed the individual importance of each in the general importance of all. Hence arose two opposite tendencies, the one prompting the Anglo-Americans to unite, the other to divide, their strength.
—ALEXIS DE TOCQUEVILLE

The United States was the first "new nation" in modern history, the first of many colonies to throw off the yoke of European domination. Its example was followed in the nineteenth century by the colonies in Latin America and in the mid-twentieth century by scores of colonies in Asia and Africa. It is instructive to compare the situation of the United States when it had first won its independence with that of the new nations of today.

Take Nigeria, for example, the most populous state of Africa, which gained independence from Great Britain in 1960. In establishing a unified nation, the Nigerians have certain advantages from the very fact of living in the twentieth century. It is easier for modern governments to keep in touch with large areas because there is instantaneous communication by telephone and radio, and rapid travel and transportation by steamship, railroad, automobile, and airplane. In eighteenth-century Amer-

ica, a message could go no faster than a man on horseback or a sailing vessel. The fastest travelers could seldom average more than 50 miles per day. In winter and spring, roads were impassable because of snows and floods. Nigeria today is also more fortunate than the United States was in the 1780's because its separation from Great Britain was amicable. The British government has poured millions of dollars into Nigerian education and economic development; it has granted Nigerian products a privileged position in her markets. The United States, on the other hand, were at first handicapped because Britain showed an unfriendly attitude toward them. The British deliberately hampered American trade and refused to evacuate territory that had been granted to the United States by the Treaty of Paris.

In other important respects, however, the position of the United States was far better than that of Nigeria. The nearly sixty million

Nigerians occupying 350,000 square miles of land are relatively well off by African standards, but they are not so fortunate as were the four million Americans who had hardly begun to tap the rich resources of a land which contained close to 900,000 square miles. Nigeria's difficulty—and in this she resembles many other new nations—is that her people speak many different languages, practice several different religions, and observe quite different traditions and customs. The Nigerians have adopted English as their official language. They attempted to set up an English form of government and English guarantees of personal liberty, but before gaining independence they had had only thirteen years of practice in limited self-government. It is not surprising, therefore, that elections were marked by violence and that early in 1966 a military clique ousted the civilian government in a coup in which the prime minister lost his life. And in 1967 the Ibos in the East seceded, proclaiming themselves the independent Republic of Biafra. Civil war followed. Compare this situation to the young United States, where nearly all the people spoke one language, practiced forms of the same religion, inherited the same system of government, and where they had been governing themselves in all local matters for over a century.

QUESTION • Is it fair to make a comparison of present-day Nigeria and the United States in the eighteenth century?

Yet with all their blessings, the Americans had a difficult time in establishing a nation. Many intelligent people thought that the union of thirteen states would certainly break apart. It was a common opinion that countries in which the people had a voice were too changeable, too unmilitary, and too slow-moving to govern large areas. Republics could be successful, according to eighteenth-century notions, only in small, defensible countries such as the Netherlands or Switzerland. An English clergyman, Josiah Tucker, who was not unfriendly to America, reflected the ideas of his time when he wrote of the United States:

As to the future Grandeur of *America,* and its being a rising Empire under *one Head,* whether Republican, or Monarchical, it is one of the idlest and most visionary Notions, that ever was conceived even by Writers of Romance. . . . the *Americans* will have no *Center of Union* among them, and no *Common Interest* to pursue, when the Power and Government of England are finally removed. Moreover, when the Intersections and Divisions of their Country by great Bays of the Sea, and by vast Rivers, Lakes, and Ridges of Mountains:—and above all, when those immense inland Regions, beyond the Back Settlements, which are still unexplored, are taken into the Account, they form the highest Probability that the *Americans* never can be united . . . under any species of Government whatever. Their fate seems to be—A DISUNITED PEOPLE, till the End of Time.

THE ARTICLES OF CONFEDERATION

Although the Continental Congress had taken on most of the functions of a central government in carrying on the Revolutionary War, it had not been formally granted the right to do so. Congress therefore drew up the Articles of Confederation, designed to set up a formal union of the thirteen states. In 1777 it asked the states to accept the plan, which would go into effect only when all thirteen states had ratified it.

Not until 1781 did all the states agree to ratify the Articles. The reason for delay was the claim of seven states to immense tracts of western land (see map, p. 84). These claims mostly went back to colonial charters granting land "from sea to sea." Virginia's claim included all of what is now Kentucky, West Virginia, Ohio, Indiana, Illinois, Michigan, and Wisconsin. States without western lands were faced with the prospect of being completely overshadowed by their neighbors. Maryland insisted that the western claims be abandoned as a condition of ratifying the Articles of Confederation. Fortunately, the states with western lands valued the long-time benefits of union more than their short-time selfish interests. In 1781 Virginia and other states agreed to cede their claims to the central government and Maryland finally ratified.

The authors of the Articles of Confederation were wary of a strong central government. Having thrown off one master, the British Parliament, they did not intend to put themselves under another. They also feared that a national government would be too far removed from the people; self-government could be successful, they thought, only at the local level. And yet, the Articles of Confederation granted considerable power to a Congress of the United States. The Congress could wage war and make treaties, which the states were forbidden to do. It might raise armies and navies, borrow money, establish a postal system, manage affairs with the Indians, and coin its own money. The states furthermore agreed to "give full faith and credit to the public acts of other states," such as wills and legal decisions, so that citizens of one state could easily do business in another. Each state agreed to return escaped criminals and runaway slaves. There was freedom of movement across state lines: no passports were required for travelers from one state to another and there were no barriers to immigration. Finally, the states agreed that differences between them should be settled not by war, but by arbitration.

In spite of the foregoing features, the government of the United States under the Articles proved too weak to operate effectively. There was no separate executive department to carry out laws. There were no federal courts. Congress had no control over foreign commerce or commerce between states. Worst of all, it had no power to collect taxes, but had to ask the

states for most of its money. During the years 1781–1789, the states gave Congress only about one-sixth of the money it requested.

Without money or real power, the Confederation Congress commanded so little respect that its members often did not bother to attend sessions. In 1783 it was difficult to get a quorum to ratify the Treaty of Paris ending the Revolutionary War. In the same year, the threats of a few hundred unpaid soldiers drove Congress out of Philadelphia. For a time it wandered from place to place, like a troupe of actors, finally settling in New York.

FOREIGN AFFAIRS UNDER THE CONFEDERATION

One of the blessings of independence that Tom Paine had predicted in *Common Sense* was that America would at last be free of European rivalries that had dragged her again and again into war. Even before the Treaty of Paris was ratified, the Confederation Congress passed a resolution saying that "the true interest of these states requires that they should be as little as possible entangled in the politics and controversies of European nations." The governments of Europe were quite willing to ignore the upstart new republic; only six of them recognized the United States in the 1780's, and only two, France and Spain, bothered to send ministers to this country.

But total isolation from Europe was impossible. The prosperity of the United States depended, after the Revolution as before, on trade with Europe and the Caribbean colonies. Satisfactory trading arrangements demanded that the United States make commercial treaties. There were also unsolved problems connected with British Canada to the north and Spanish Florida and New Orleans to the south, and these could be settled only by diplomacy.

It was in its foreign relations that the United States suffered most from the defects of the government set up by the Articles of Confederation. A government unable to control commerce or force states to do its bidding could neither make binding treaties nor carry out existing ones. Unable to tax, it could not pay back the money owed its former allies nor keep up an army and navy to protect its interests.

Relations with Great Britain

As was predictable, the new government did not enjoy happy relations with its recent foe, Great Britain. The British did consent to receive John Adams as minister from the United States, even though during the war he had been one of the rebels singled out for special punishment. They refused, however, to send a minister to the United States, explaining that they did not know whether to send one envoy or thirteen. Neither country carried out in full the terms of the Treaty of Paris. The United States had agreed that British creditors could recover pre-war debts by suing in American courts, and that Congress would recommend to the states that persecution of Loyalists cease. But when British merchants sued American debtors in American courts, they were seldom able to collect a penny from unfriendly juries and judges. The states also ignored the recommendation of Congress as to treatment of Loyalists, who for a time continued to suffer exile, confiscation of property, and sometimes even lynching. The British government used the treatment of Loyalists and British merchants as an excuse to hold some forts inside the northern border of the United States (see map, p. 84). These "fur posts" were the centers of trade with the Indians of the Great Lakes region and the Ohio Valley. This trade was worth more than a million dollars a year, and Great Britain was resolved to keep it for herself.

American trade suffered because the United States were now outside the British Empire. American tobacco and naval stores no longer enjoyed a preferred position in British markets. American ships were banned from the British West Indies, and they were allowed to enter English ports only with the products of their home states. Thus a Massachusetts ship might not carry Rhode Island whale oil, New York furs, or North Carolina turpentine to London. John Adams had been sent to England principally to write a commercial treaty, but the last thing the members of the English government wanted was to grant economic privileges to their former colonies. Instead, they planned a trade war against the United States. One British politician wrote:

> Our great national object is to raise as many sailors and as much shipping as possible. Parliament should endeavour to divert the whole Anglo-American trade to British bottoms. The Americans cannot retaliate. It will not be an easy matter to bring the Americans to act as a nation. They are not to be feared as such by us.

Difficulties with Spain

During the Confederation period, the United States had difficulties with Spain as serious as those with Great Britain, even though Spain as an ally of France had been on the American side in the recent war. The Spanish were not happy about the immense domain beyond the Appalachians which the United States acquired in the Treaty of Paris. They correctly foresaw that the future expansion of the United States would be a threat to the Spanish empire in America. Spain insisted that the southern boundary of the United States from the Appalachians to the Mississippi was not the 31st parallel described in the Treaty of Paris, but a line nearly 100 miles to the north, or even the Tennessee River (see map, p. 84). The Spanish made alliances with the Cherokee, Creek, and Chickasaw Indians and supplied them with arms. They also found citizens of the United States who were willing, for a price, to act as Spanish secret agents.

A "New Nation"
Factors Favoring Unity and Disunity

As is pointed out on pages 76-77, the United States after the Declaration of Independence was the first "new nation" in modern times. There were those who predicted that the new nation could not long endure, but must inevitably break up—because the Americans could not establish an effective central government, or because different groups of Americans would quarrel, or because the country was too big.

In 1790 the new federal government established by the Constitution made the first decennial (once-every-ten-years) census in U.S. history. Below is shown some of the data the census takers collected. Examine these figures—and also the map entitled "The United States in 1800" on pages 174-175. Then see if you can find evidence that helps you to answer the following questions:

- What factors shown here would have served to unify the United States? To weaken or prevent unity?
- How would you define a "typical" American of 1790?

THE UNITED STATES IN 1790

Total Population	4,730,000		**Black Population**	759,000
			(692,000 slaves, 67,000 free)	

Urban Population
(People living in towns of 2,500 or more) — 5.5%

Rural Population — 94.5%

Religion (approximate)

Protestant (various sects)	85%
Catholic	10
Jewish and other	5

Ethnic Origins

English	60.1%
African	20.0
Scots and Scotch-Irish	8.2
German	5.3
Catholic Irish	3.1
Dutch	2.1
Other	1.2

Population by States

	White	Black
New Hampshire	238,000	1,000
Massachusetts	379,000	5,000
Rhode Island	69,000	4,000
Connecticut	238,000	6,000
New York	380,000	26,000
New Jersey	184,000	14,000
Pennsylvania	434,000	10,000
Delaware	59,000	13,000
Maryland	320,000	111,000
Virginia	748,000	306,000
North Carolina	394,000	106,000
South Carolina	249,000	109,000
Georgia	83,000	30,000

Note: In 1790 Maine was still part of Massachusetts. Vermont, Kentucky, Tennessee, and Ohio were not yet admitted as states.

By her control of the mouth of the Mississippi, Spain was in a position to throttle the entire export trade of the West. The bulky goods of the Westerners—lumber, grain, deerskins—could not profitably be carried over the mountains to the Atlantic coast, but had to go down the Ohio and Mississippi rivers by means of rafts and flatboats. The Westerners asked the Spanish to grant them the "right of deposit" whereby they might put their goods ashore at New Orleans or some other Spanish port for transfer to ocean-going ships without payment of duty. The Spanish generally refused this privilege except to certain Americans whom they hoped to use as agents. The Westerners demanded that Congress make a treaty by which Spain would grant free navigation of the Mississippi.

Meanwhile, the shippers and merchants of the northeastern states wanted Spain to open to them the trade of the Spanish West Indies, which would make up for the loss of markets in the British Empire. The influence of the populous states of the Northeast on the Confederation government was much stronger than that of the far-off, thinly settled West. In 1785 a Spanish envoy, Diego de Gardoqui, negotiated with the U.S. secretary of foreign affairs, John Jay, a treaty whereby the United States gave up a claim to the right of deposit at the mouths of the Mississippi and other rivers emptying into the Gulf of Mexico, in return for which Spain opened her own ports to American ships. The Jay-Gardoqui Treaty so obviously sacrificed the West to the Northeast that Congress was unwilling to ratify it, but even so, Westerners were thoroughly angry.

Relations with France

Relations with France were not so difficult as those with Great Britain and Spain, but neither were they entirely happy. During the latter years of the Revolutionary War, the United States had been able to keep armies in the field only with money given or loaned by France. Yet now the United States were unable to pay back even the interest on their debts, and this at a time when the French monarchy was going bankrupt. It is no wonder that Jefferson, who replaced Franklin as minister to France, wrote a friend that American diplomats were "the lowest and most obscure of the whole diplomatic tribe."

The French were also disappointed by the commercial opportunities opened to them by American independence. Franklin had predicted that with the end of British trade regulations the valuable commerce of the thirteen states would be largely transferred from Britain to France. The French did reap some benefits: the French West Indies found more of a market in the United States; a number of Frenchmen invested in American lands; and the French could get American products such as tobacco more cheaply than before. In general, however, trade tended to fall back into the old grooves. By 1789 the British were exporting as much to the United States as ever before, while the French share of the American market had increased only slightly.

The Barbary Pirates

The most humiliating evidence of the weakness of the United States during the Confederation period was the treatment at the hands of the Barbary Pirates. The four North African states of Morocco, Tunis, Tripoli, and Algiers made a regular practice of capturing the ships and crews of all nations not paying them annual tribute. Now that the United States were outside the protection of the British fleet and the British treasury, American ships were subject to brutal attack. Lacking either funds for tribute or a fleet for defense, Congress was unable to prevent American shipping from being driven from the Mediterranean.

American artists were at their best when portraying American life, even if in somewhat sentimental terms, as shown in these two pictures by George Caleb Bingham. Fertile land tempted Americans to pull up stakes and go West. Daniel Boone (below) leads a group of pioneers through the Cumberland Gap, which became a part of the Wilderness Road to the Kentucky River. Meanwhile, river traffic on flatboats (above) expanded America's commercial boundaries. Flatboats like these were in use when the right of deposit was a pressing issue to Westerners.

THE WEST HANGS BY A HAIR

Until the end of the nineteenth century, "the West" in the United States was not a fixed tract of land, but a continually shifting area of new exploitation of natural resources and new settlement. It was the region where at any particular time white pioneers were driving back Indians; where cultivation was replacing hunting, trapping, and grazing; and where settled ways of living were replacing Indian warfare and lynch law. First to arrive were hunters and trappers. They were followed by a restless population who built temporary homesteads, planted corn or wheat, and raised a few hogs. This second wave of pioneers was apt to be always on the move, ever in search of greener pastures. Abraham Lincoln's father was a typical example of this breed. Born in Virginia, he moved in the course of his lifetime to Kentucky, on to Indiana, and finally to Illinois.

Close behind the pioneers of legend came others who built flour mills and stores and started to manufacture brick, harness, shoes, barrels, and carts. They congregated at natural points of trade, such as Pittsburgh at the head of the Ohio River, and in areas where the soil was rich, such as Lexington in the bluegrass region of Kentucky. Soon these town dwellers built schools and churches and laid the foundations for a more settled society like that of the East or of Europe from which they had originally come.

During the Confederation period, the West lay just beyond the Appalachians. Only three roads connected the region with the East. Yet on foot and on horseback, so many settlers crossed the mountains between 1780 and 1790 that the white population grew from about 2,000 to perhaps as many as 100,000. Life was hard in the western settlements. So many men and women died of starvation, accident, disease, and Indian attacks that it has been said that the sight of "a man dying of natural causes in his bed was regarded with special solemnity because it seemed so uncommon."

As a result of the cession of the state land claims, the trans-Appalachian West became the common possession of the United States, under the direct control of Congress. But the powerless Confederation Congress was unable to meet the Westerners' needs. It could not dislodge the British from the fur posts to the north or persuade the Spaniards to grant the right of deposit to the south. It could prevent neither the Spanish nor the British from furnishing the Indians with arms. In Kentucky alone, 1,500 settlers were killed by Indians between 1788 and 1790. Without money, Congress could neither purchase land from the Indians nor provide troops to protect settlers from them.

The Westerners had other grievances in addition to the failure of Congress to aid them. Many of them resented the way eastern speculators had laid claim to large tracts of land. In 1785 a convention of Kentucky settlers declared:

That to grant any Person a larger quantity of land than he designs Bona Fide to seat himself or his Family on, is a greevance, Because it is subversive of the fundamental Principles of a free republican Government to allow any individual, or Company or Body of Men to possess such large tracts of Country in their own right as may at a future Day give them undue influence.

As we have seen, Westerners were also incensed when they heard of the Jay-Gardoqui Treaty. In 1784, George Washington made a journey to the West, and on his return he reported the West was hanging by a hair. In eastern Tennessee settlers had created a short-lived government called the State of Franklin, paying the governor in whiskey and deerskins. Unable to get recognition from Congress, some of the leaders talked of seceding from the Union. Later, Kentucky talked of secession.

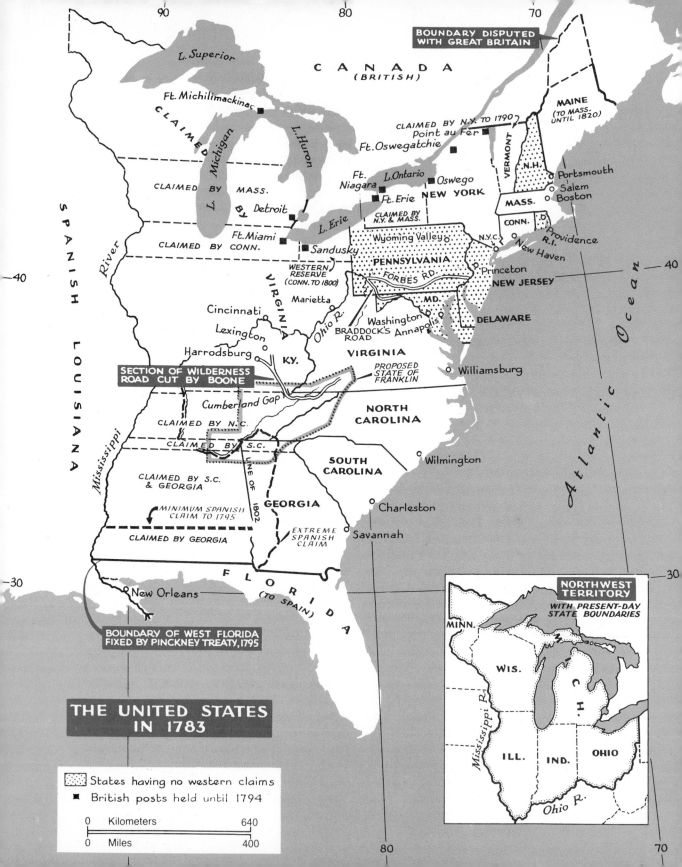

THE UNITED STATES IN 1783

90 · 80 · 70

BOUNDARY DISPUTED WITH GREAT BRITAIN

C A N A D A
(BRITISH)

L. Superior

Ft. Michilimackinac

CLAIMED

L. Michigan

L. Huron

CLAIMED BY MASS.

Detroit

BY

CLAIMED BY CONN.

Ft. Miami

Sandusky

CLAIMED BY N.Y. TO 1790
Point au Fer

Ft. Oswegatchie

Ft. Niagara

L. Ontario

Oswego

Ft. Erie

L. Erie

NEW YORK

CLAIMED BY N.Y. & MASS.

MAINE
(TO MASS. UNTIL 1820)

VERMONT

N.H.

Portsmouth

Salem
Boston

MASS.

CONN.

Providence
R.I.

N.Y.C.
New Haven

Wyoming Valley

PENNSYLVANIA

FORBES RD.

Princeton

NEW JERSEY

WESTERN RESERVE
(CONN. TO 1800)

VIRGINIA

Marietta

MD.

DELAWARE

Cincinnati

Ohio R.

Washington
BRADDOCK'S ROAD

Annapolis

Lexington

Harrodsburg

KY.

VIRGINIA

Williamsburg

SECTION OF WILDERNESS ROAD CUT BY BOONE

PROPOSED STATE OF FRANKLIN

Cumberland Gap

CLAIMED BY N.C.

NORTH CAROLINA

CLAIMED BY S.C.

LINE OF 1802

CLAIMED BY S.C. & GEORGIA

SOUTH CAROLINA

Wilmington

Mississippi

MINIMUM SPANISH CLAIM TO 1795

GEORGIA

Charleston

EXTREME SPANISH CLAIM

CLAIMED BY GEORGIA

Savannah

F L O R I D A
(TO SPAIN)

New Orleans

BOUNDARY OF WEST FLORIDA FIXED BY PINCKNEY TREATY, 1795

S P A N I S H   L O U I S I A N A

River

A t l a n t i c   O c e a n

40

30

━━━ States having no western claims

■ British posts held until 1794

0   Kilometers   640

0   Miles   400

NORTHWEST TERRITORY
WITH PRESENT-DAY STATE BOUNDARIES

MINN.

WIS.

Mississippi R.

ILL.

IND.

OHIO

M.I.C.H.

Ohio R.

Although unable to solve the immediate problems of the West, the Confederation Congress passed two laws of immense importance for the future—the Ordinances of 1785 and 1787.

The Land Ordinance of 1785

During the colonial period, there had developed two distinct methods of surveying and allotting land. New England had developed a system whereby land was granted to individuals only after new townships had been surveyed, and settlement proceeded township by township. This resulted in orderly, compact settlement and prevented conflicting land claims. In the South, and especially in Virginia, there developed a system of allotting new lands whereby individuals were granted a certain number of acres and then went out and selected the best land they could find. The result was chaos. Claims often conflicted, causing quarrels which sometimes resulted in loss of life. Large blocks of land were left unclaimed, so that settlements were often scattered, making it difficult to establish communities or to ward off Indian attacks.

When Congress was planning to dispose of the first pieces of the lands it controlled north of the Ohio River, it passed the Land Ordinance of 1785 to provide for an orderly method of survey and sale. This law provided for an adaptation of the New England system. The land was divided into townships 6 miles square, each of which contained 36 sections of one square mile each. These sections could in turn be subdivided into smaller rectangular tracts. This arrangement was continued in later surveys. From an airplane over the Middle West today, one can see in the checkerboard arrangement of farms

QUESTION • What practical objections can you see to the system of survey established by the Land Ordinance of 1785?

In the older states, irregular property lines led to constant disputes. The Ordinance of 1785 laid out regular patterns. The rectangular design apparent as one flies over the Midwest today is a result of the early survey system.

the permanent influence of the system set up in 1785.

The Land Ordinance of 1785 was also designed to promote the sale of western lands and so to increase the slender revenues of the Confederation government. To make the land attractive to speculators, purchasers were obliged to buy at least a whole section, 640 acres, and the minimum price was low, a dollar per acre. The ordinance also provided the first federal subsidy to education. Proceeds from the sale of one section in each township were to be used for establishing schools.

The Northwest Ordinance, 1787

The so-called Northwest Ordinance of 1787 was even more important than that of 1785. It provided for future political development of the entire territory bounded by the Ohio River, the Great Lakes, and the Mississippi (see map, p. 84). The region was to be divided into not

Rights for the People of the Frontier
The Northwest Ordinance, 1787

How would new territories be governed and what rights would the people there have? These are the questions the Northwest Ordinance addressed. To what area did the Ordinance apply? See map, pages 174-175. What states were carved out of it? See map, pages 320-321.

The latter part of the Northwest Ordinance is a solemn contract between the original states and the people of the Northwest Territory, then on the frontier. This contract contains six articles:

Article I. Religious Freedom. No person, demeaning himself in a peaceable and orderly manner, shall ever be molested on account of his mode of worship or religious sentiments . . . .

Article II. Individual Rights. The inhabitants of the said territory shall always be entitled to the benefits of the writs of *habeas corpus* and of Trial by Jury. All fines shall be moderate; and no cruel or unusual punishment shall be inflicted. No man shall be deprived of his liberty or his property, but by the judgment of his peers, or the law of the land . . . .

Article III. Education, Indians. Religion, Morality, and Knowledge being necessary to good government, and the happiness of mankind, schools and the means of education shall be forever encouraged. The utmost good faith shall always be observed towards the Indians . . . their lands and property shall never be taken from them without their consent . . . .

Article IV. Duties. The said territory and the states which may be formed therein, shall forever remain a part of the confederacy of the United States of America . . . .

Article V. New States. There shall be formed in the said territory not less than three or more than five States. . . And whenever any of the said States shall have sixty thousand free inhabitants therein, such State shall be admitted to the United States, on an equal footing, in all respects . . .

Article VI. Slavery banned. There shall be neither slavery nor involuntary servitude in the said territory otherwise than in the punishment of crimes, whereof the party shall have been duly convicted . . .

•In what specific ways does the Northwest Ordinance carry out ideas expressed in the Declaration of Independence?

•Compare the purposes and the contents of these articles with the first ten amendments of the U.S. Constitution, known as the Bill of Rights, on pages 138-141.

•Why were Southerners willing in 1787 to accept Article VI, excluding slavery from territories of the U.S., when later they raised violent objections to such exclusion? See pages 72, 333-334.

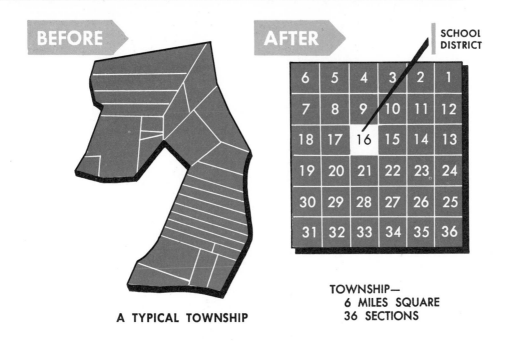

BEFORE

AFTER

SCHOOL DISTRICT

6	5	4	3	2	1
7	8	9	10	11	12
18	17	16	15	14	13
19	20	21	22	23	24
30	29	28	27	26	25
31	32	33	34	35	36

A TYPICAL TOWNSHIP

**TOWNSHIP—
6 MILES SQUARE
36 SECTIONS**

less than three nor more than five states. Whenever the adult male citizens reached 5,000, there was to be set up a territorial government modeled on the former royal colony (see p. 31). The citizens of the new territory were to elect their legislature, while the federal government appointed judges and a governor with the power of absolute veto of the laws passed by the territorial legislature. To make sure the judges and governor would be beyond the control of the citizens of the territory, they were paid by the federal government.

So far it might seem that the United States intended to control their territories in the West as tightly as Great Britain had tried to govern the thirteen colonies. *But* the Northwest Ordinance provided that when the population of a territory reached 60,000, the people might organize a new state, and that it should be admitted to the Union on terms of *full equality*

with the original states. This was something new; never before had a country formally promised full political equality to its colonies or territories or set up machinery for carrying out such a promise.

The Northwest Ordinance provided a model for territorial government that has been followed down to the present. It started the practice of admitting new states to the Union on equal terms. This was in line with the principles of the Declaration of Independence, as were two other provisions of the ordinance: (1) that all citizens of the region were guaranteed personal rights, such as freedom of religion and freedom of speech, and (2) that slavery was forbidden. The last provision had been suggested by Thomas Jefferson and was supported by Southerners as well as Northerners. As has been shown, many slaveholders deplored the institution of slavery and were quite willing

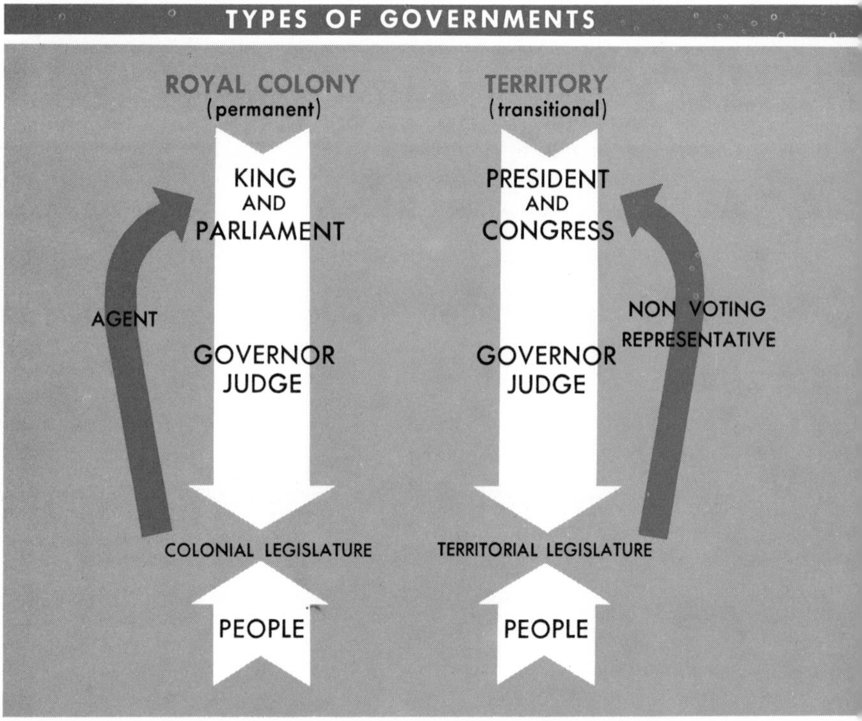

ROYAL COLONY
(permanent)

TERRITORY
(transitional)

KING
AND
PARLIAMENT

PRESIDENT
AND
CONGRESS

AGENT

NON VOTING
REPRESENTATIVE

GOVERNOR
JUDGE

GOVERNOR
JUDGE

COLONIAL LEGISLATURE

TERRITORIAL LEGISLATURE

PEOPLE

PEOPLE

Government of the territories, as set up by the Ordinance of 1787, was similar to that of the royal colonies (see chart, p. 19). Territorial governors were, moreover, to be paid by Congress rather than by local legislatures. The territories differed from royal colonies in that they were only a transitional stage on the way to statehood.

to see it forbidden in future settlements. This antislavery prohibition of the Northwest Ordinance profoundly affected the political geography of the United States by making the Ohio River a boundary between slave and free territory.

DISPUTES BETWEEN STATES AND ECONOMIC GROUPS

During the Confederation period, several of the thirteen states engaged in disputes with each other, while within some states there were struggles between different economic groups. These difficulties resulted from interstate suspicion and rivalry, from the usual postwar depression, and from the weakness of the central government.

Each state was free to pass tariff laws taxing goods from other states. New York, for instance,

taxed firewood from New Jersey. Since these interstate tariffs were lower than those on goods from outside the United States and since there was little interstate trade anyway, state tariff laws were a less serious cause of ill feeling than might be expected.

Much more serious were disputes over boundaries. The majority of the thirteen states were engaged in boundary disputes with their neighbors during this period. Disagreement between Connecticut and Pennsylvania over the possession of lands in the Wyoming Valley (see map, p. 84) almost resulted in war. In the spring of 1784, Connecticut settlers in the valley were driven from their homes by Pennsylvania militia, with loss of life to men, women, and children. Parts of the region now Vermont were disputed among Massachusetts, New Hampshire, and New York. The Vermonters wanted to set up a state of their own and extend its borders eastward into New Hampshire and westward into New York. Some Vermont leaders even considered rejoining the British Empire, and carried on correspondence with the British governor of Canada.

Controversy Over "Cheap Money"

Another source of disunion was the fact that there was no national currency, the "continentals" issued by Congress during the war having lost all value. Since there was little gold and silver in the country, all the states were forced to issue paper money. These currencies differed in value from state to state and were often worthless outside the borders of the states issuing them. This obviously made it difficult to carry on interstate trade.

In Rhode Island and North Carolina, state paper money was worth almost nothing because so much was printed. This was a result of pressure from debt-ridden farmers. With the closing of the usual markets in the West Indies and Britain, farmers were often unable to pay off their debts and faced the loss of their lands and homes. If the currency could be inflated, however, they could pay their creditors with cheap or worthless paper money. Getting control of both the North Carolina and Rhode Island legislatures, the debtors simply ran the printing presses. In Rhode Island, the legislature passed laws forcing creditors to accept the valueless currency in the payment of all debts.

Shays's Rebellion, 1786

In Massachusetts wealthy creditors gained control of the state government in 1784. The legislature levied very heavy taxes to pay off the state debts, putting a great burden on small farmers, in addition to their normal load of debt. The farmer began to threaten the courts when the property of persons unable to pay taxes was confiscated, and when people were sent to jail or deprived of their land because

Public unrest and disorder increased in intensity until Daniel Shays, formerly an officer in the Revolutionary War, led a rebellion aimed at overthrowing the government of Massachusetts. His followers were mainly small farmers and other debtors.

of inability to pay private debts. In 1786 mobs prevented the courts from sitting in three Massachusetts towns. Finally, Daniel Shays, a veteran of the Revolutionary War, enlisting nearly 1,000 men, tried to seize the lightly guarded federal arsenal at Springfield, and started a rebellion against the state government. Only by getting private subscriptions from wealthy merchants was the state able to raise a military force strong enough to meet Shays.

Shays, a reluctant rebel, proved to be a very poor leader. His main force was easily defeated early in February 1787, and within a few weeks the rebels were wholly dispersed. Only ten men were killed on both sides, and two rebels were later hanged. So Shays's Rebellion proved to be one of the mildest in history. But it caused great alarm throughout the United States. Even Samuel Adams, a professional friend of the people, had been for fierce measures against the Shaysites. Throughout the colonies, men who believed in orderly government were fearful. In the crisis Massachusetts might have expected help from the central government, but Congress had neither troops nor money. Even the federal arsenal in Springfield had been saved from seizure only by the Massachusetts militia. Here was just one more example of the feebleness of the government that had been set up by the Articles of Confederation.

Gloomy Prospects

By the year 1787, it seemed as though the prophecies of those who said that the United States, or any other large republic, could not form an effective government were being fulfilled. The British held the fur posts and controlled the Indians of the Northwest; the Spanish closed the mouth of the Mississippi and controlled the Indians of the Southwest; feeling between creditors and debtors had reached the point of civil war; the West threatened secession; foreign commerce, handicapped by the weakness of the Confederation Congress, was still below what it was in 1774, the year before the Revolutionary War began. There was serious talk that the United States might divide into three or four smaller confederacies. These were some of the difficulties which led Washington to write his friend Henry Lee a gloomy letter:

They [the difficulties of the United States] exhibit a melancholy proof of what our transatlantic foe has predicted; and of another thing, perhaps, which is still more to be regretted, and is yet more unaccountable, that mankind, when left to themselves, are unfit for their own government. I am mortified beyond expression when I view the clouds that have spread over the brightest morn that ever dawned on any country.

THE CONSTITUTIONAL CONVENTION

Washington did not content himself with writing letters. At this time he was much interested in a project to build a canal by way of the Potomac River toward the Ohio River system. He saw this venture as a means both of enriching Virginia and of keeping the western settlements in the Union. He was one of those who felt strongly, however, that it was fruitless to build canals to overcome natural barriers while there remained political barriers such as tariffs and varying currencies. In 1785, representatives of Virginia and Maryland met at Washington's home in Mt. Vernon to discuss common problems relating to such matters as the navigation of Chesapeake Bay and the Potomac. The conference worked out an agreement between the two states providing for joint control of currencies, import duties, and navigation. It also issued an invitation to all the states asking them to send delegates to Annapolis, Maryland, for a discussion of better commercial relations.

The Annapolis Convention

When the Annapolis Convention met in 1786, only five states were represented, so it was powerless. One of the twelve delegates, however, was Alexander Hamilton of New York, who ardently desired a powerful central government. Hamilton persuaded his fellow delegates to send a memorial to the thirteen states and to Congress calling for a new convention which should devise a uniform system of controlling commerce and propose measures to make the federal government more effective. Congress acted on this suggestion and summoned representatives of the states to a meeting in Philadelphia, "for the sole and express purpose of revising the Articles of Confederation."

Opening of the Constitutional Convention

The date set for the opening of the Constitutional Convention was May 14, 1787, but it was not until ten days later that enough delegates had gathered to do business. Eventually twelve states were represented, although some state delegates did not arrive until midsummer. Of the 73 men chosen as delegates, only 55 ever attended. The average number at sessions of the convention was about 30. In spite of the discouraging start and small attendance, the members settled down to hard work at once. They were in session almost every weekday for sixteen weeks, usually meeting both morning and afternoon. George Washington, who represented Virginia, was elected presiding officer. To insure good order, the rules of the convention said, "That every member, rising to speak, shall address the President; and whilst he shall be speaking, none shall pass between them, or hold discourse with another, or read a book, pamphlet, or paper...." It was also agreed that the meetings should be private, and members were forbidden to let the public know what went on in the debates. This secrecy aroused suspicion, but it had the advantage of making compromise easier by preventing disputes within the convention from exciting people outside.

The convention was fortunate in its membership, which included many of the ablest political leaders in the United States. The majority were college graduates, and their study of Greek and Latin had familiarized them with the political writings of Aristotle and Cicero. Nearly all of them had had practical experience in government. More than half had sat either in the Continental Congress or the Confederation Congress and so had seen for themselves the unhappy consequences of weakness at the center. The delegates were mostly young men, their average age being 42. They were vigorous, bold, imaginative, and ambitious. They were obsessed with a vision of a great continental republic that would teach the world that people were capable of governing themselves.

Motives of the Founding Fathers

The members of the Constitutional Convention were hardheaded as well as visionary. They were, for the most part, lawyers, merchants, and plantation owners. Such people would benefit from a stronger central government. Landowners wanted the better markets for their produce that would come with the commercial treaties a stronger government could arrange. Merchants wanted better protection for American shipping and a national currency that would promote interstate commerce. Owners of western lands wanted protection from the Indians. Creditors wanted more severe bankruptcy laws, an end to inflation of currency by the states, and a government that paid its debts.

Because the propertied classes wanted a stronger union and would benefit from it, the work of the Philadelphia Convention has been portrayed as a sort of plot whereby the wealthy created a government for their own selfish purposes. This "rich people's plot" theory overlooks the fact that the Constitution was designed to benefit the poor as well as the rich and that if a stronger government had not been created, the United States might have broken up. A new government could have been formed only by the relatively well-to-do, since at the time the Constitution was created, they alone had the necessary knowledge, political experience, and training to see the needs of the whole country.

Human motives are always mixed. The men who spent a long, hot summer working six days a week at Philadelphia were certainly aware that a more powerful federal government might benefit some of them personally. They were also

This is the famous orrery by David Rittenhouse owned by Princeton University. An eighteenth-century planetarium of ingenious workmanship, it shows not only the movements of the planets around the sun, but of the moons of Earth, Jupiter, and Mars around their planets. It was thus meant to demonstrate the new astronomy of Copernicus and Newton. Newtonian astronomy, with its concept of an eternal balance between gravity and centrifugal force, affected the framing of the Constitution, in which nationalism, represented by the central government, is balanced by federalism, represented by the states.

Princeton University

performing, at considerable cost to themselves, what they conceived to be their public duty. The more one studies their work, the more one is likely to agree with one of their number, James Madison, who later wrote:

> ...there never was an assembly of men, charged with a great and obvious trust, who were more pure in their motives, or more exclusively and anxiously devoted to the object committed to them than were the members of the Federal Convention of 1787.

Prominent Members

The convention probably owed most to two members from Virginia, Washington and Madison. Washington was so universally trusted that his presence alone helped to make the work of the convention acceptable to the country. His dignity and fairness as presiding officer also helped to keep the debates orderly and in good temper. Madison, thirty-six years old, was the first delegate to arrive in Philadelphia, and he came better prepared than any other. He had made a special study of confederations and leagues, ancient and modern, and he brought with him a plan for a new government of the United States. His ideas were embodied in the so-called Virginia Plan, presented to the convention by Edmund Randolph. The Virginia Plan became the basis for discussion in the convention and provided the main ideas for the government as finally set up.

Benjamin Franklin represented Pennsylvania. Over eighty years old, often in pain, and so weak that he had to be carried to the meetings in a sedan chair, Franklin took no prominent part in the debates. His tact and cheerfulness, along with his ability to tell a good story, helped to keep the convention from breaking up when disagreements developed and tempers rose. Furthermore, he was so popular that, like Washington, he helped to make the convention a success by his mere presence.

From New York came Hamilton, one of the youngest men in the convention and perhaps the most brilliant. Hamilton was not particularly influential, however, because his attendance was irregular and his views were extreme. He proposed a government in which the states would be reduced to mere provinces under governors appointed by the president of the United States, who was to hold office for life. Hamilton's attitude perhaps had a certain usefulness, since it made other plans to strengthen the union seem mild by comparison.

CONCORD, CONFLICT, COMPROMISE

Historians have sometimes emphasized the differences of opinion and the resulting controversies that divided the members of the Philadelphia Convention. When one considers, however, the varying interests of the states they represented, the remarkable fact is that the delegates were in concord about so many aspects of their common task.

(1) Most of them were "nationalists," who believed that the highest loyalty of Americans should be to the country as a whole rather than to the separate states. The Virginia Plan frankly called the three branches of the government it proposed the "National Legislature," the "National Executive," and the "National Judiciary." The members of the convention believed that the Articles of Confederation were so hopelessly inadequate for the needs of the country that they decided to create an entirely new

James Madison as portrayed by Gilbert Stuart. Although a man of great ability, Madison was overshadowed by his great friend and political colleague, Thomas Jefferson. With Hamilton and Jay, Madison wrote the articles in *The Federalist*.

frame of government. Here, they agreed with Washington, who urged them to create a government they believed in even if it meant violating their instructions, which said they were to do no more than amend the Articles.

(2) As good children of the eighteenth-century Enlightenment, the convention members believed that there were "Laws of Nature and of Nature's God" that governed human beings, akin to those that governed the physical universe. Madison had been much impressed by the orrery, an intricate and extraordinarily accurate mechanical model of the solar system, that Princeton College had bought from David Rittenhouse of Philadelphia (see photo). Just as Newton had revealed that the solar system was a wonderful mechanism held in its pre-

dictable course by balancing centrifugal force and the power of gravity, so Madison and his colleagues believed that political scientists could discover means to balance such opposing forces as liberty and authority. It was in keeping with this point of view that one member of the Philadelphia Convention spoke of how "the general government was to be likened to the sun, the center, and the state governments to the other planets revolving around it. Virginia was the Earth and Kentucky her moon." The two political scientists who carried the most weight were John Locke, some of whose ideas we have already encountered in the Declaration of Independence, and Baron Charles de Montesquieu, a Frenchman whose most important work, *The Spirit of Laws,* was published in 1748. Montesquieu's writings, taken as political gospel by the makers of the American Constitution, insisted on the necessity of separating the

Montesquieu, Political Philosopher

It is difficult to get something out of nothing. And the men at Philadelphia were political practitioners, not philosophers. Where did they get the Constitution? Primarily, they drew on the British constitution. Their view of that unwritten document, however, was colored by an analysis of it written by Charles Louis de Secondat, Baron de la Brède et de Montesquieu.

And who was he? A judge, legal scholar, satirist, and above all, political philosopher. He was an eighteenth-century Frenchman, a provincial noble who looked so like a peasant as to be mistaken for one as he worked on his lands at La Brede, near Bordeaux. He spent over twenty years analyzing the nature of man and the nature of government. His witty, bitingly accurate *Persian Letters* surveyed the Parisian court scene through the eyes of two incredulous Persians. But he reserved his best writing, with its "gaiety, . . . balance, . . . level-headedness, [and] simplicity of style," for the monumental *De l'esprit des lois*—in English, *The Spirit of Laws.* In that work he described free government in terms that the Founding Fathers of the American republic could appreciate and use. He said that he found in the British constitution the doctrines of the "separation of powers" and of "checks and balances." Although modern political writers feel that he was mistaken in some details, he felt that in England people's liberties were protected from arbitrary government because legislative, executive, and judicial powers were "separated," that is, held by different people. Parliament made the laws, the executive (in England, the king) carried them out, and an independent judiciary enforced them. While these ideas were not original with him, his reputation helped to elevate them into "laws" of politics, considered by eighteenth-century students of government to be as fixed as the law of gravity. They also accorded with American colonial experience, since the governors of the thirteen colonies had been appointed by the crown and the legislatures elected by the colonists themselves.

The book, published in 1748, was known and used by such diverse Americans as Sam Adams, James Madison, and Alexander Hamilton. The last two, for instance, cited it in their *Federalist* papers as an authority beyond all others on the nature of republican government, a position now often accorded *The Federalist* itself.

executive, legislative, and judicial powers as a means of averting tyranny.

(3) Although familiar with political theory, the delegates were practical politicians who thought constantly in terms of what would work. In attempting to create a federal government and to define its powers, they were guided by their experiences with British and colonial government. In many important features, the government they set up was simply an adaptation of the government of England.

(4) The convention was unanimous in wanting to protect property rights from such assaults as Shays's Rebellion and the Rhode Island paper money laws. They saw these attacks as resulting from an "excess of democracy." Here they found support in the works of Locke, who saw protection of property as the principal task of government, and in the writings of Aristotle, the Greek philosopher, who saw extreme democracy as leading first to chaos and then to tyranny.

(5) Although the convention feared that too great a dose of democracy made societies turbulent and changeable, they nevertheless believed that the ultimate source of government must be the people. They attempted to devise means of slowing down and filtering the popular will, rather than to try to frustrate it. And when they had finished their handiwork, they directed that it be judged by a democratic means—conventions elected by the voters specifically to ratify the Constitution or to reject it.

QUESTION • How far should democracy go in a school? In a family? In a business concern? On a merchant ship? On an athletic team?

There were two serious conflicts in the convention for which it proved difficult to find compromises: that between the large states and the small states over the basis of representation in Congress, and that between the northern and southern states arising from differing economic interests and from slavery.

The Conflict
Between Big and Small States

The dispute between the large and small states almost broke up the convention. The large states demanded that the representation of each state in both houses of Congress be based on population. By what possible right, they asked, could Delaware's 40,000 inhabitants demand permanent equality with Virginia's 750,000? The small states were just as insistent that they would never part with the equal power they enjoyed under the Articles of Confederation. If representation in the new Congress was to be on the basis of population, they feared to be swallowed up. William Paterson of New Jersey said his state would "rather submit to a monarch, to a despot, than to such a fate."

There was also disagreement as to the very nature of the new federal government. As a basis for the Constitution, the large state delegates generally favored Madison's Virginia Plan. This proposed a government with separate executive, legislative, and judicial departments and with the states reduced to a clearly subordinate position. The small state delegates tended to favor the New Jersey Plan, the work of Paterson, which provided only for strengthening the Articles of Confederation.

Over this conflict the Constitutional Convention came to "a full stop," as one delegate described it. Washington wrote a friend that he despaired of the convention and repented having had anything to do with it. For a week, during a spell of hot weather, there was bitter debate, while flies buzzed over the delegates' heads and settled on legs exposed by knee breeches. There seemed no middle ground between the demands of the large and the small states. Franklin proposed that each session be opened with prayer, to invoke divine aid in finding an acceptable compromise.

The jam was broken when the delegates took a day off to celebrate the Fourth of July.

During the recess, a committee worked out what has since been called "the Great Compromise." According to this arrangement in the lower house of Congress, the House of Representatives, the number of members would be based on population; in the upper house, the Senate, each state would have an equal vote. This was accepted by a vote of 5 states to 4, with one state evenly divided and the others not represented. So today Nevada sends but one representative to Congress and the adjoining state of California sends thirty-eight, but each is represented by two senators. Equal representation in the Senate is a provision of the Constitution that may not be changed unless a state agrees to give up the right.

On the whole, the Great Compromise was a victory for the small states, since they gained the right to be perpetually represented in the Senate beyond their population. On other matters, however, the convention tended to follow the Virginia Plan, favored by the big states, which provided for a strong and effective central government.

Compromises
Between North and South

Once the dispute between small and big states was settled, the other dangerous conflict was that which eventually led to the Civil War —that between the commercial interests of the North and the plantation interests of the South. The Southerners wanted to count slaves in the population for determining representation to Congress, but not for direct taxation; the North wanted to count slaves for taxation but not for representation. This disagreement was settled by the three-fifths ratio, according to which five slaves were counted as equal to three free people in determining both a state's representation and taxation.

The delegates from South Carolina and Georgia, the only states where slavery was profitable in the 1780's, were afraid that a national government might deprive them of their supply of slaves by putting an end to the slave trade. They insisted that the Constitution should forbid any interference with the slave trade and made this a condition of joining the Union. It was arranged that for twenty years the federal government might not prevent the importation of slaves or charge an import duty of more than $10 a head.

The other point of dispute between North and South concerned commerce. Northern merchants and shippers wanted a government with ample powers to pass navigation laws to protect shipping from foreign competition. Southern planters, fearing that they would be forced to pay more for shipping their produce abroad, insisted that a two-thirds vote of both houses of Congress should be required to pass navigation laws. Such a provision would give the South practically a veto on such legislation. The South also feared that the federal government would try to raise money by duties on exports such as tobacco. As the great exporting region, the South would then pay more than its share of taxes. A compromise was arranged whereby navigation laws might be passed by a simple majority in Congress, while the federal government was forbidden to levy taxes of any kind on exports.

THE NEW FEDERAL GOVERNMENT

These compromises cleared the way for the two essential jobs of the Philadelphia Convention: to give the federal government more power and to provide a workable machinery of government.

The new Constitution clearly granted to the federal government the powers it had most needed under the Articles of Confederation:

(1) It could levy and collect taxes, except duties on exports, provided such taxes were

"uniform throughout the United States." The new government would be able to pay its own way rather than beg from the states.

(2) It could regulate commerce with foreign nations and between the states. Thus it could write and enforce commercial treaties which would increase foreign trade, and it could keep trade among the states free of barriers.

(3) It had the sole right to coin money and regulate its value, so there would be only one national standard of money instead of state currencies with differing values.

Many of the powers granted the central government were not new but were simply carried over from the Articles of Confederation. For instance, the Articles had granted power to Congress to raise armies and navies and borrow money. But since the Confederation Congress could not raise money by taxation, such powers existed only on paper. Now the federal government could carry out all the powers granted to it. This was especially true because *it could exert its power directly on individuals and compel them to obey.* Under the Confederation, the central government had generally been able to act only through the states. Now it could carry out its laws through its own agents, such as revenue collectors, and enforce its laws in federal courts.

In certain matters the states were put under federal control. No longer might state legislatures relieve debtors by scaling down debts or issuing paper money. No state might levy tariffs on goods from another state. Moreover, all state officials had to swear to support the Constitution of the United States, as well as federal laws and treaties. This made all of them, from governors to constables, agents of the federal government as well as of their own states. The state militias were also put under control of Congress, so that they might be used in the future for defense of the nation or for the suppression of uprisings like Shays's Rebellion.

THE STRUGGLE OVER RATIFICATION

On September 17, 1787, the Founding Fathers, as the members of the Philadelphia Convention came to be called, held their last meeting and signed the document they had written. In the evening they held a farewell dinner. Their work, however, was not yet over. It remained to be seen whether the states would agree to accept the new Constitution. The authors of the Constitution provided that it would go into effect when ratified by nine of the states. It was impossible to propose unanimous acceptance, as provided in the Articles of Confederation, because Rhode Island was certain not to ratify and other states were doubtful. Ratification was to be carried out by conventions called for the purpose, a democratic process following out the idea of the Declaration of Independence that governments "derive their just powers from the consent of the governed."

To get even nine states to ratify the Constitution was no small task. Opposition was widespread, and there was suspicion of any sort of strong central government. Why revolt from Great Britain, it was asked, simply to fall under a new kind of tyranny? Debtors and paper-money advocates were opposed to any plan forcing full payment of debts and restoring sound currency. Popular leaders, including Patrick Henry and Richard Henry Lee of Virginia, George Clinton of New York, and Samuel Adams and John Hancock of Massachusetts, maintained that a federal government as powerful as that provided in the Constitution would eventually suppress the liberties of the people.

"Federalists" and "Anti-Federalists"

Those who favored the new plan of government, most of whom should rightly have been called "nationalists," called themselves "Federalists" to emphasize the fact that under the new

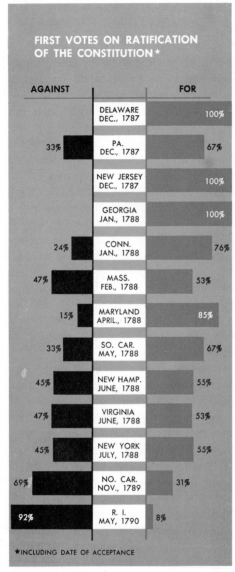

FIRST VOTES ON RATIFICATION OF THE CONSTITUTION *

AGAINST		FOR
	DELAWARE DEC., 1787	100%
33%	PA. DEC., 1787	67%
	NEW JERSEY DEC., 1787	100%
	GEORGIA JAN., 1788	100%
24%	CONN. JAN., 1788	76%
47%	MASS. FEB., 1788	53%
15%	MARYLAND APRIL., 1788	85%
33%	SO. CAR. MAY, 1788	67%
45%	NEW HAMP. JUNE, 1788	55%
47%	VIRGINIA JUNE, 1788	53%
45%	NEW YORK JULY, 1788	55%
69%	NO. CAR. NOV., 1789	31%
92%	R. I. MAY, 1790	8%

*INCLUDING DATE OF ACCEPTANCE

Enthusiasm for the Constitution varied greatly among the several states. The percentages shown in this chart refer to the votes in conventions called to ratify the Constitution. The two key states were New York and Virginia, which voted for ratification 30 to 27 and 88 to 78 respectively. Two states, controlled by farmer-debtors, did not join the Union until after Washington had been inaugurated.

constitution the states would retain many of their powers. This tactic pushed the opposition, who were really "federalists" in the sense of favoring a league of states over a centralized government, into being tagged by the meaningless label "Anti-Federalists." There has been much dispute, by no means ended, as to just what sort of people composed the two groups. It was once asserted that the Federalists in general represented the propertied interests—merchants, creditors, professional men, big planters, and the governing class in the coastal regions. The Anti-Federalists were said to be composed of debtors, small farmers, and people in backcountry areas. Recent historical research has shown that such a clear-cut division did not exist, and that the basis for joining one side or the other varied from state to state. As a loose generalization, it can be said that those who gained their living by some form of commerce —this including merchants, shipowners, city artisans, and farmers near navigable waters— tended to favor the Constitution, while the large class of subsistence farmers tended to oppose it. But even so there are many exceptions. Thus the small farmers of backcountry Georgia, Virginia, and Pennsylvania voted Federalist because they wanted a government strong enough to drive back the Indians. On the other hand, in New York State the Anti-Federalists included a number of great landowners with estates bordering the Hudson; they were apparently motivated by local political squabbles having little to do with economic advantages or disadvantages offered by the new constitution.

Advantages of the Federalists

The two parties were quite equally divided, but several facts operated in favor of the Federalists:

(1) They were united and they supported a definite program to meet the difficulties facing the country. The Anti-Federalists were nowhere near so well organized, and they had nothing

to offer other than to continue with the hapless Confederation or to call a new constitutional convention.

(2) In the election districts of the time, the more recently settled backcountry, which tended to be Anti-Federalist, was under-represented. Therefore, the votes of the Federalist coastal districts counted more heavily than their actual numbers warranted.

(3) The Federalists were supported by men commanding great popularity and respect, especially Franklin and Washington. They were supported by most of the newspapers of the country. They usually had the better of the argument in pamphlets, sermons, and debates in state ratifying conventions. The electioneering over ratification produced, in fact, one of the finest pieces of political writing of all time. This was a collection of eighty-five articles, called the *Federalist*, written by Hamilton, Madison, and John Jay to explain how the Constitution would benefit the people. The articles were originally published under a pen name in a newspaper, the New York *Journal*. The very first paragraph contains a passage that reveals the great importance the Founding Fathers attached to the success of the American union, not only for this country, but for the world:

It has been frequently remarked that it seems to have been reserved to the people of this country, by their conduct and example, to decide the important question, whether societies of men are really capable or not of establishing good government from reflection and choice, or whether they are forever destined to depend for their political constitutions on accident and force.

Although written for the needs of the moment, the *Federalist* papers contain so much political wisdom that they are still widely read and have had a continuing influence not only in this country, but in South America and in Europe.

(4) The Federalists succeeded in getting the Constitution ratified not merely because they were politically wise, but also because they were politically shrewd. In states where there was strong opposition, they were able to outmaneuver their opponents. In Pennsylvania, the Federalists managed to call an election to the state convention before the Anti-Federalists had a chance to organize. In Massachusetts, a slight majority against the Constitution was changed to a slight margin in its favor by suggestions to the influential John Hancock that he might be elected the first president under the new government. In New York two-thirds of the State Convention were Anti-Federalists. But the persuasiveness of John Jay and the news that ten states had already ratified induced enough Anti-Federalists to change sides so that New York became the "eleventh pillar" of the new federal roof.

Ratification Completed

The vote in various key states was extremely close: in Massachusetts it was 187 in favor of the Constitution to 168 opposed, in Virginia 88 to 78, and in New York 30 to 27. By July 1788, however, all the states except Rhode Island and North Carolina had ratified, and preparations were made to start the new government the next year.

As the news of the state ratifications came in, there were great Federalist celebrations in the cities. These culminated in an Independence Day procession in Philadelphia in which there were eighty-eight separate parts and about five thousand participants. The displays included elaborate floats drawn by as many as ten horses. Various craft workers took part, many of them giving demonstrations of their art. Shoemakers made shoes; cabinetmakers made chairs; and a pair of blacksmiths made plow irons out of old swords. Following the craft workers came city and state officials, the students at the University of Pennsylvania, the lawyers and law students, military companies, and "the clergy of the different denominations, and the Rabbi of the Jews, walking arm in arm." The

Federalists evidently knew how to enlist public opinion.

The framing and adoption of the Constitution were indeed events worthy of celebration. The Constitution was a unique document whose influence on the course of world history cannot yet be estimated. It gave a new meaning to the word "federal" by creating a new type of government, one which attempts to combine a powerful national government with vigorous local governments, and thus meets the needs both of the nation as a whole and of particular regions. It has provided a pattern for uniting other large areas, such as Canada and Australia. It is especially adapted today for meeting the needs of new nations containing peoples of different languages and cultures, such as India and Nigeria. Advocates of a union of the free nations have recommended it as a model.

It was an impressive fact that this new, strong government was formed not by military leaders bent on conquest, nor by a seizure of power by a strong man or clique, but by citizens acting for the good of the country and submitting their work to their fellow countrymen. As the French student of America, Alexis de Tocqueville observed, "It is new in the history of a society to see a great people turn a calm and scrutinizing eye upon itself... when the wheels of its government are stopped."

Activities: Chapter 4

For Mastery and Review

1. What were some advantages and disadvantages of the United States as a "new nation"?

2. What powers did the Articles of Confederation give to the central government, and what powers of government were left to the states?

3. Summarize (a) the causes and (b) the terms of the Ordinances of 1785 and 1787. In what ways did the Northwest Ordinance carry out the principles of the Declaration of Independence?

4. List events occurring between 1783 and 1787 that revealed the weaknesses of the central government.

5. What difficulties did the Confederation government have with Spain and England?

6. In parallel columns headed Mount Vernon Conference, Annapolis Convention, and Philadelphia Convention, summarize (a) the reasons for the meeting, (b) the authority, and (c) the accomplishments of the meeting.

7. What were the areas of agreement among the delegates at the Philadelphia Convention?

8. What serious conflicts did the Convention face? How was each settled?

9. What new powers were given to the central government by the Constitution? What powers held by Congress in the Confederation were strengthened? How were the powers of the individual states restricted?

10. How was the Constitution to be ratified? Why was this method chosen? Who composed the Federalist group? The Anti-Federalists? Account for the success of the Federalists.

11. Describe the grievances of the western frontiersmen against the central government. Why was the right of deposit at New Orleans important to the West?

Unrolling the Map

1. On a map of eastern United States, locate (a) the major rivers and mountain ranges, (b) the areas of difficulty with Spain, (c) the fur posts held by the British, (d) the major routes taken by settlers moving into the West, and (e) the Northwest Territory.

2. On a world map, locate the points of origin of things which you and members of your family ate, used, or wore yesterday. Compare this global interdependence with the self-sufficiency of the eighteenth-century farmer.

Who, What, and Why Important?

Articles of Confederation
western land claims
John Adams
fur posts
right of deposit
Annapolis Convention
George Washington
James Madison
Benjamin Franklin
Alexander Hamilton
Thomas Jefferson
Barbary pirates

State of Franklin
Land Ordinance of 1785
Northwest Ordinance
Wyoming Valley
Shays's Rebellion
William Paterson
Great Compromise
ratification
Patrick Henry
Federalists
Anti-Federalists
The Federalist

To Pursue the Matter

1. What was it like to undergo an Indian raid? See the chapter entitled "War in the Dooryard" in Van Every, *Ark of Empire: The American Frontier, 1784–1803.*

2. Make a diagrammatic comparison of the Articles of Confederation and the United Nations Charter. Which provides for stronger bonds of union? See Bragdon *et al., Frame of Government.*

3. How did John Adams, recently thought a damnable traitor in England, and George III, recently denounced by the Americans as a damnable tyrant, behave when they met shortly after the close of the Revolutionary War? See Arnof, *A Sense of the Past,* pp. 52–55.

4. How did the Founding Fathers go about their work? What motivated them? See Broderick, *The Origins of the Constitution, 1776–1789.*

5. How did Spain attempt to detach western settlements from the United States after the Revolution? See Bailey, *A Diplomatic History of the American People.*

6. One of the most disputed questions among American historians has been whether the period after the Revolutionary War was a "critical period." The question is touched on in Broderick, *The Origins of the Constitution, 1776–1789,* and in Morgan, *The Birth of the Republic, 1763–1789.*

READINGS FOR PART ONE

Fiction and Drama

Edmonds, W. D. *Drums Along the Mohawk.* Dramatic tale of the Revolution on the New York frontier.

Fast, H. *April Morning.* Vivid picture of the Lexington and Concord campaigns through a boy's eyes.

Miller, A. *The Crucible.* A gripping play that deals with the Salem witch trials.

Hawthorne, N. *The Scarlet Letter.* A famous and chilling story about the Puritans.

Richter, C. *A Light in the Forest.* The story of an Indian captive and divided loyalties.

Seton, A. *The Winthrop Woman.* The adventures of a spirited woman of the Massachusetts Bay Colony.

Non-fiction

Crèvecoeur, M. G. J. *Letters from an American Farmer.* A primary source classic.

Driver, H. *Indians of North America.* An excellent overview.

Forbes, E. *Paul Revere and the World He Lived In.* A popular, colorful, and sympathetic account.

Franklin, B. *Autobiography.* A beautifully written, amusing, and revealing book.

Haley, A. *Roots.* Part literature, part fact: the author's search for his ancestral roots from Africa to America, and the story of an "ancestor."

Mannix, D. and Cowley, M. *Black Cargoes.* An account of the African slave trade.

Miller, J. C. *The First Frontier: Life in Colonial America.* Good social history; easy reading.

Niethammer, C. *Daughters of the Earth, The Lives and Legends of American Indian Women.* An illuminating and absorbing chronology of life from the female perspective.

PART ONE: SUMMING UP
Chapters 1–4

I. CHECKING THE FACTS

1. *Distinguishing Between Fact and Opinion*
Which of the sentences below are *statements of fact* (they can be proved true or false) and which are *statements of opinion?*
  a. The French controlled more territory in the New World than did the English.
  b. The colonial culture inherited from Europe was superior to that of the native American people.
  c. Most English colonies were founded by private enterprise.
  d. The Boston Tea Party was actually a very foolish form of protest.
  e. After 1763, English control of the colonies became more strict.
  f. Thomas Paine was right when he criticized the English monarchy.
  g. The *Declaration of Independence* has been called a "landmark in human freedom."
  h. The main cause of the American Revolution was the desire for political freedom.
  i. Most of the Founders were landholders.
  j. The most serious weakness in the Constitution was the lack of power given to the Supreme Court.

2. *Judging Sources*
If you were researching the status of women during the colonial period, which of these sources would you consider *primary* (first-hand) and which would you consider *secondary* (second-hand, interpretive)?
  a. the diary of a farmer's wife.
  b. a record of home ownership in Boston.
  c. a painting of the governor of Virginia, his wife and children.
  d. An ad in a London newspaper describing working conditions for women in the New World.
  e. Your textbook.
  f. a television "special" directed and produced by the American Historical Society.
  g. a village storekeeper's inventory of women's clothing and accessories.
  h. a list of candidates for public office in Salem, Massachusetts, 1650–1775.
  i. a list of graduates from colonial colleges.

3. *What and When: Putting Things in Order*
In each of the pairs below, tell which *occurred first*. Defend your decision by giving either dates or a logical explanation.
  a. mercantilism/Navigation Acts
  b. cotton cultivation/corn cultivation
  c. "salutary neglect"/French and Indian War
  d. First Continental Congress/Intolerable Acts

e. American Revolution/French Revolution
f. adoption of the Constitution/Northwest Ordinance
g. Shays's Rebellion/Articles of Confederation
h. Federalist Party/Constitutional Convention

4. MAP WORK

Select the number on the map that most accurately locates each of the areas or sites below.

a. Area with the largest coastal plain.
b. Section that produced grains and food products.
c. Section most involved in triangular trade.
d. City where Crispus Attucks was killed while leading a protest group against the British.
e. Area of refuge for persecuted loyalists.
f. Decisive battle of the Revolution.
g. Western United States boundary, 1783.
h. Two areas held by Spain in 1783.
i. Area most affected by the Land Ordinance, 1785.
j. Southern boundary of the Northwest Territory.
k. Site of Constitutional Convention.

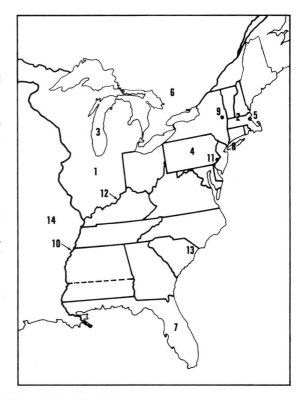

II. INTERPRETING THE FACTS

1. *Drawing Inferences*

Reread the quotation from the Declaration of Independence in column 1 on page 59. Basing your answers *only* on that quotation, decide which of the statements listed here (1) can be inferred as *true,* (2) can be inferred as *false,* (3) cannot be inferred from the reading.

a. All monarchs at that time were unjust.
b. Revolutions were sometimes justified.
c. There was no need for an army in the colonies.
d. No government at all was better than unjust government.
e. Minority groups, such as Indians, women, and eighteen-year-olds, should be able to vote.
f. The voice of the people should be heard by government leaders.
g. Government exists because people give it birth.
h. Government need have no responsibility to the governed.

III. APPLYING YOUR KNOWLEDGE

1. During the first years of independence under the Articles of Confederation, conflicts arose over several issues. Copy the table below on your answer sheet of paper. In the appropriate place, explain how each of the items at the left was a source of conflict at that time. Then, illustrate how each item is a source of conflict among nations of the world today.

Source Of Conflict	U.S. Then	World Today
Population distribution		
Scarce Resources		
Divided loyalties		
Government power		
Commercial policies		
Economic system		

A PUZZLE

Fill in the letter blanks below after you have read each clue. The completed puzzle will reveal the *key word,* outlined, which is one of the ideals for which the colonists fought the Revolution.

```
 1.  — — — — —  ▯  — — — — — —
 2.      — — —  ▯  — — — — —
 3.  — — — — —  ▯  — — — — — — —
 4.  — — — — —  ▯  — — — — — —
 5.      — — —  ▯  — — — —
 6.      — — —  ▯  — — — — —
 7.  — — — — —  ▯  — — — — —
 8.      — — —  ▯  — — — —
 9.      — — —  ▯  — — — — —
10.       — —   ▯  — — — —
11.           ▯  — — — — — — — —
12.      — — —  ▯  — — — — —
```

Clues

1. Approval of the Constitution by states.
2. British advocate of strict colonial controls.
3. Our form of government, 1783–1789.
4. First son's inheritance rights.
5. A "right" disputed with Spain.
6. Name adopted by those who favored ratification of the Constitution.
7. An economic system of the 17th and 18th centuries.
8. Area of small farms beyond the tidewater.
9. A servant under contract.
10. Indian leader who resisted British control.
11. How the Philadelphia Convention settled major disputes.
12. What people called Shays's protest.

SUGGESTED READINGS FOR THE ENTIRE COURSE

The following bibliography contains suggested readings for the entire course. Usually hardback publishers are given, though many of these books also come in paperback editions. When books are out of print but available in many libraries, no publisher is given.

Special Supplements

The books listed here have been specially prepared to provide supplementary material geared to the organization and emphases of this text. All are in paperback, published by Macmillan, New York.

Arnof, Dorothy S., *A Sense of the Past: Readings in American History*, rev. ed. The readings are arranged chapter for chapter and Part for Part to coincide with *History of a Free People*.

Black in White America. A series of four books documenting the historical and contemporary experience of black people. Cassette recordings accompany Books 3 and 4.

Cole, D. B. (ed.), *New Perspectives in American History*. A series of paperbacks to give depth to the text.

Documents and Sources

Commager, Henry S. (ed.), *America in Perspective, the United States Through Foreign Eyes.* Selections from European writers concerning their American travels.

Rothman, David and Sheila (eds.), *Sources of the American Social Tradition* (2 vols.). New York: Basic Books, 1975. A rich mine of highly interesting documents from early and modern American social history.

Ver Steeg, Clarence L. and Hofstadter, Richard (eds.), *Great Issues in American History: A Documentary Record, 1765–1969* (2 vols.). New York: Vintage, 1969 (paper).

Pictorials and Graphics

Andrews, Wayne, *Architecture in America: Photographic History.* New York, Atheneum, 1969.

Hughes, Langston and Meltzer, Milton, *A Pictorial History of the Negro in America.*

Josephy, Alvin (ed.), *The Indian Heritage of America.* New York: Knopf, 1968.

Atlases and Almanacs

The American Heritage Pictorial Atlas of United States History. New York: American Heritage, 1960.

Information Please Almanac. Published annually.

Historical Statistics of the United States (colonial times to 1957). U.S. Bureau of the Census.

Statistical Abstract of the United States (1878 to present). Published annually.

World Almanac. Published annually.

Basic Books

Bailey, Thomas A., *A Diplomatic History of the American People.* New York: Appleton, 1958.

Baxandall, Roselyn et al., *America's Working Women, A Documentary History.* New York: Vintage, 1976.

Franklin, John H., *From Slavery to Freedom: A History of Negro Americans.* 4th ed. New York: Knopf, 1974.

Garraty, John and James, E. (eds.), *The Dictionary of American Biography.* 10 vols., and supplements. New York: Scribner, 1974.

Morris, Richard B. (ed.), *Encyclopedia of American History,* rev. ed. New York: Harper, 1970.

Smith, Page, *Daughters of the Promised Land: Women in American History.* Boston: Little, Brown, 1976.

Watts, Jim and Davis, Allen F., *Generations: Your Family in Modern American History.* New York: Knopf, 1974.

Part

2

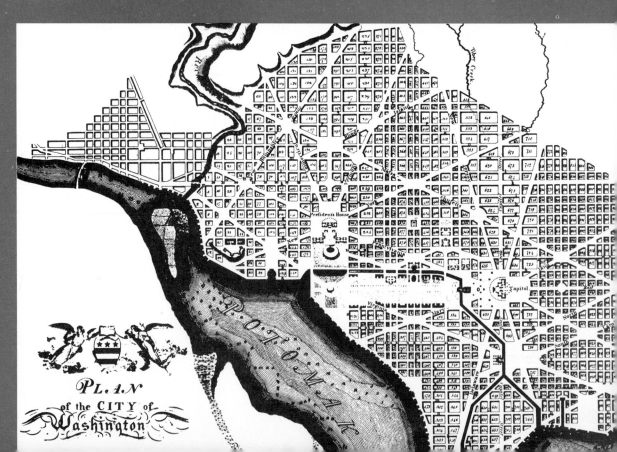

PLAN
of the CITY of
Washington

Launching
the Republic

Chapters in this Part

Plan for Washington, D.C., 1800

COMPLETING A REVOLUTION

Revolutions have a way of getting out of hand. What starts with a few street riots or demands for a new constitution escalates into full-scale social upheaval, mass violence, and civil war and ends in dictatorship as the only apparent alternative to anarchy. This was the course pursued, for instance, by two of the great revolutions of modern times, the French Revolution that started in 1789 and the Russian Revolution of 1917. Usually, the moderate leaders of the early phase are imprisoned, exiled, or executed by later extremists.

The American Revolution was unusual in that it ran its course with little domestic violence, and the same men who led the revolutionary movement at the first also guided the destinies of the new nation. As previous chapters have shown, the Americans set up local governments with little difficulty and, after a period of uncertainty, wrote a new constitution to bind the thirteen states together.

The great English statesman William E. Gladstone once called the Constitution of the United States "the most wonderful work ever struck off at one time by the brain and purpose of man." While people interested in fields other than politics, such as literature, music, art, or science, may dispute Gladstone's opinion, there can be little doubt that the Constitution is one of the most important documents in the history of the world. It is the oldest written frame of government used by any major country, and most constitutions adopted since 1789 have been influenced by it.

But it is one thing to write a constitution and another to make it work. The United States Constitution was a success not merely because the Founding Fathers at Philadelphia were able, informed, moderate, and persuasive. The new government needed men of the highest ability, and fortunately they were available. For the most part, the same men who led the thirteen states through the War of Independence and the troubled period that followed it now helped to set up the new national government. The first three Presidents were George Washington, commander of the Continental Army, John Adams, leader of the independence movement in the Second Continental Congress, and Thomas Jefferson, author of the Declaration of Independence. They did their work well, and the American Revolution brought nationhood and self-government along with independence.

In another sense the American Revolution is not yet over: the principle of equal opportunity for all, expressed in the Declaration of Independence, has never been achieved, in spite of immense advances during the nearly two centuries since it was written. And the Revolution goes on, as Americans continue to crusade for equality.

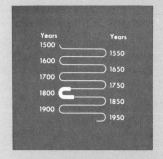

Chapter 5

The Constitution of the United States

*It will be the pattern for all future constitutions
and the admiration of all future ages.*
—WILLIAM PITT

Every American citizen should have a thorough knowledge of the Constitution. To understand the Constitution requires that the student know the different ways in which it has been applied and interpreted in the course of nearly two centuries. To encourage frequent reference, the pages on which it is printed are edged in brown.

In studying the following pages the reader should note that:

(1) *Description of general features* of the federal government and the Constitution is placed at the top of the right-hand pages in double column.

(2) *Explanatory notes on particular clauses, phrases, or terms* are printed on the bottom part of the right-hand page.

(3) Portions of the Constitution that are no longer in operation are printed in light-face type.

(4) The descriptive headings on Articles, Sections, and clauses of the Constitution are not part of the document itself, but these have been added for the convenience of the readers.

One way to study this chapter systematically is as follows:

(1) Read through an article, rather rapidly, simply to get the over-all sense of what it is about.

(2) Read the relevant sections of the general discussion on the top right-hand pages, referring constantly to the document itself.

(3) Read the explanatory notes of the article, again referring to the actual text.

(4) Go on to subsequent articles and do the same thing, but do not attempt to do too much at one sitting.

(5) When you have finished, use the questions under the heading "For Mastery and Review" on pp. 154–155 to test yourself.

(6) Throughout the Constitution, the term "man" is used to refer to people in general. When you read, therefore, keep in mind that the Founding Fathers intended to include all persons in this usage, not just males.

109

The Constitution of the United States

THE PREAMBLE

We the People of the United States, in Order to form a more perfect Union, establish Justice, insure domestic Tranquility, provide for the common defence, promote the general Welfare, and secure the Blessings of Liberty to ourselves and our Posterity, do ordain and establish this Constitution for the United States of America.

THE PREAMBLE

"The preamble is not, strictly speaking, a part of the Constitution, but 'walks before it.'" It explains the *source* of the Constitution and its *purposes*. When the preamble states, "We the People of the United States . . . do ordain and establish this Constitution . . ." it follows the principle expressed in the Declaration of Independence: that governments derive "their just powers from the consent of the governed." The Constitution was drawn up by representatives of the people and ratified in conventions elected by them.

In 1789, however, "We the People" did not mean *all* the people, but only the minority possessing political rights. The right to vote was limited to white adult males with a certain amount of property. The proportion of voters varied from state to state. We do not know just how many voted in elections, but in any case it was certainly a minority. In the many years since the Constitution went into effect, however, the advance of democracy has broadened the meaning of "We the People" so much that today it means "nearly all adults."

For many years there was dispute as to whether "We the People of the United States" meant "We the people of the different states" or "We the people of an American Nation." In 1789 the former meaning was more accurate: the delegates to the Philadelphia Convention were chosen by states, the Constitution was ratified state by state, and a person's first loyalty was to their state. The meaning of the phrase changed, however, as the loyalty of the American people to the nation became stronger than that to the states. (See, for instance, the account of Daniel Webster's "Second Reply to Hayne," pp. 264–265.)

Each purpose of the Constitution described in the preamble had a special meaning in 1789. The authors of the Constitution were trying to create "a more perfect Union" than the Articles of Confederation. They sought to "establish Justice" for creditors, to "insure domestic Tranquility" by suppressing disorders such as Shays's Rebellion, and to "provide for the common defence" against Indians and Barbary pirates. They hoped the new government would "promote the general Welfare" by increasing interstate and foreign commerce. Finally, the purpose of the Constitution was to "secure the Blessings of Liberty" by creating a stronger government to protect people in their rights. This was different from the purpose of the Declaration of Independence which had been to obtain liberty by freeing the United States from the strong government of England.

Since the establishment of the Constitution, its purposes have become wider. Today, for instance, the federal government tries to "establish Justice" in ways not dreamed of in 1789. It defines the rights and duties of labor unions. It fixes "fair" rates for railroads. It protects women and blacks from job discrimination, and consumers from misbranded products. When Americans "provide for the common defence" in this century, they may be defending not merely the shores of America, but allies all over the globe. Provision for the "general welfare" now includes federal aid to the needy and unfortunate, such as medical care and support for elderly people.

Today, then, the preamble to the Constitution has a far broader meaning than in 1789. Then a minority set up the federal government to provide for the simple needs of a small rural population living on the edge of an isolated continent. Now the federal government represents the great majority of the people, and the Constitution must provide for the complex needs of a great industrial nation in a world made small by instantaneous communication and rapid transportation.

ARTICLE I. LEGISLATIVE DEPARTMENT

SECTION 1. CONGRESS

The Two Houses of Congress. All legislative Powers herein granted shall be vested in a Congress of the United States, which shall consist of a Senate and House of Representatives.

SECTION 2. HOUSE OF REPRESENTATIVES

1. *House Members Elected by the People.* The House of Representatives shall be composed of Members chosen every second Year by the People of the several States, and the Electors in each State shall have the Qualifications requisite for Electors of the most numerous Branch of the State Legislature.

2. *Qualifications of Representatives.* No Person shall be a Representative who shall not have attained to the Age of twenty five Years, and been seven Years a Citizen of the United States, and who shall not, when elected, be an Inhabitant of that State in which he shall be chosen.

3. *House Membership Based on State Populations.* Representatives and direct Taxes shall be apportioned among the several States which may be included within this Union, according to their respective Numbers, [which shall be determined by adding to the whole Number of free Persons, including those bound to Service for a Term of Years, and excluding Indians not taxed, three fifths of all other Persons.] The actual Enumeration shall be made within three Years after the first Meeting of the Congress of the United States, and within every subsequent Term of ten Years, in such Manner as they shall by Law direct. The Number of Representatives shall not exceed one for every thirty Thousand, but each State shall have at Least one Representative; [and until such enumeration shall be made, the State of New Hampshire shall be entitled to chuse three, Massachusetts eight, Rhode-Island and Providence Plantations one, Connecticut five, New-York six, New Jersey four, Pennsylvania eight, Delaware one, Maryland six, Virginia ten, North Carolina five, South Carolina five, and Georgia three.]

4. *Election for Vacancies in the House.* When vacancies happen in the Representation from any State, the Executive Authority thereof shall issue Writs of Election to fill such Vacancies.

5. *Election of Speaker of the House, Impeachment.* The House of Representatives shall chuse their Speaker and other Officers; and shall have the sole Power of Impeachment.

HOW CONGRESS IS ORGANIZED AND CONDUCTS BUSINESS

The Congress under the Constitution differed from that under the Articles of Confederation in being bicameral, that is, having two chambers. This was a return to the English system whereby Parliament is divided into a House of Lords and a House of Commons. The Senate was originally designed to resemble the House of Lords in being somewhat removed from popular control, and the House of Representatives to resemble the Commons in being more democratic. In the American system, a further difference between the two branches of Congress resulted from the Great Compromise (see p. 96). The House, chosen on a basis of population, represented the idea of a nation. The Senate, in which each state is equally represented, retained the idea of a league.

Usually in a bicameral legislature one house or the other becomes dominant, and it is usually the house more directly responsible to the people that gains the upper hand. The culmination of this process can be seen most clearly in Great Britain where nearly all legislative power is now lodged in the House of Commons, and the House of Lords has become little more than a ceremonial body.

In the United States neither the House nor the Senate has gained ascendancy over the other, although individual senators generally enjoy more prestige than individual representatives, if only because the senators are fewer in number and serve longer terms. But the two bodies retain practically equal powers of legislation. Since every law must be passed by both houses, each acts as a check on the other. Each house judges the qualifications of its own members and enjoys the same privileges of free debate and freedom from arrest during session. On the other hand, each branch of Congress has certain special powers. The House has the right to impeach members of the executive and judicial departments for "high crimes and misdemeanors," and it first proposes bills which involve raising money. The Senate acts as a court to try impeachments brought by the House, and it has the right to accept or reject the President's appointments. The most famous special power of the Senate lies in the field of foreign affairs. The President must submit treaties to the Senate before they go into operation. A vote of two-thirds of the sen-

(*Continued on page 115.*)

EXPLANATORY NOTES

Article I, Section 2, clause 1. "Electors" here means simply "voters."

Article I, Section 2, clause 3. "Those bound to Service for a Term of Years" means "indentured servants and apprentices." "Other Persons" means "slaves." Note that the latter were formerly counted for representation in the House at three-fifths of their number.

Article I, Section 2, clause 5. The Speaker is chosen from the majority party in the House. This is in contrast to the British Parliament where the Speaker is an impartial umpire "above party." The American Speakership is a powerful office, second only to the presidency. (See p. 513.)

"Impeachment" means "indictment," "bringing charges against." Thus President Andrew Johnson was impeached by the House in 1868, but when the Senate failed to convict him, he remained in office. (See p. 371.)

In 1974 the Judiciary Committee of the House recommended the impeachment of President Nixon. The whole House did not vote impeachment, however, because Nixon resigned. (See p. 789).

SECTION 3. SENATE

1. *Number of Senators, Election, Term of Office.* The Senate of the United States shall be composed of two Senators from each State, [chosen by the Legislature thereof,] for six Years; and each Senator shall have one Vote.

2. *One-Third Senate Chosen Every Two Years.* Immediately after they shall be assembled in Consequence of the first Election, they shall be divided as equally as may be into three Classes. [The Seats of the Senators of the first Class shall be vacated at the Expiration of the second Year, of the second Class at the Expiration of the fourth Year, and of the third Class at the Expiration of the sixth Year,] so that one third may be chosen every second Year; [and if Vacancies happen by Resignation, or otherwise, during the Recess of the Legislature of any State, the Executive thereof may make temporary Appointments until the next Meeting of the Legislature, which shall then fill such Vacancies.]

3. *Qualifications of Senators.* No Person shall be a Senator who shall not have attained to the Age of thirty Years, and been nine Years a Citizen of the United States, and who shall not, when elected, be an Inhabitant of that State for which he shall be chosen.

4. *Vice-President Presides over Senate.* The Vice President of the United States shall be President of the Senate, but shall have no Vote, unless they be equally divided.

5. *Other Officers.* The Senate shall chuse their other Officers, and also a President pro tempore, in the Absence of the Vice President, or when he shall exercise the Office of President of the United States.

6. *Senate a Court in Cases of Impeachment.* The Senate shall have the sole Power to try all Impeachments. When sitting for that Purpose, they shall be on Oath or Affirmation. When the President of the United States is tried the Chief Justice shall preside: And no Person shall be convicted without the Concurrence of two thirds of the Members present.

7. *Punishment for Officials Convicted in Cases of Impeachment.* Judgment in Cases of Impeachment shall not extend further than to removal from Office, and disqualification to hold and enjoy any Office of honor, Trust or Profit under the United States: but the Party convicted shall nevertheless be liable and subject to Indictment, Trial, Judgment and Punishment, according to Law.

SECTION 4. ELECTION AND MEETING OF CONGRESS

1. *Regulation of Elections.* The Times, Places and Manner of holding Elections for Senators and Representatives, shall be prescribed in each State by the Legislature thereof; but the Congress may at any time by Law make or alter such Regulations, except as to the Places of chusing Senators.

(Continued from page 113.)
ators is required to ratify a treaty. This provision was inserted to make sure that no treaty would sacrifice the interests of one section to those of another, as the 1785 Jay-Gardoqui Treaty (see p. 83) had sacrificed western interests to those of the Northeast.

The two branches of Congress have developed different ways of doing business. The House of Representatives became so unwieldy in size (435 members) that debate had to be severely restricted to get anything done at all. Nearly all the work of the House is done by committees dealing with particular problems, such as agriculture, government finances, foreign affairs, military affairs, commerce, education, and labor. The chairmen of these immensely powerful committees reach their position by seniority, and their average age is generally close to seventy years. Debate and the order of business in the House is strictly controlled by the Speaker and a 15-person Committee on Rules.

The Senate, because of its smaller size (it now contains 100 members), has been able to retain "freedom of debate," which means that any senator may speak on any motion. This leads to the practice of "filibustering," whereby a few senators, or even a single one, may block legislation they dislike by unlimited talk. A cloture rule to prevent this practice is rarely applied. Full-scale debate in the Senate, on the other hand, often educates the public on

(Continued on page 117.)

EXPLANATORY NOTES

Article I, Section 3, clause 4. The Constitution does not give the Vice-President enough to do. His only stated function is to preside over the Senate, his only power to cast the deciding vote in case of a tie. Prominent people have avoided an office regarded as a "political graveyard." The office has sometimes gone to persons who were hardly more than political hacks. Presidents have traditionally ignored their Vice-Presidents. Franklin Roosevelt met Truman only three times in the three months they were in office together.

The sudden death of Franklin Roosevelt in 1945, the assassination of John F. Kennedy in 1963, and the resignation of Richard Nixon in 1974 all pointed to the danger of treating the Vice-President like a spare tire. In the presidential campaign of 1976, Jimmy Carter chose a man of stature, Walter F. Mondale, as his running mate. Once in office, Carter attempted to upgrade the vice-presidency by drawing Mondale into his closest circle of advisers with an office in the White House. He also sent Mondale on important missions to foreign governments.

Article I, Section 3, clause 6. When trying a case of impeachment brought by the House, the Senate becomes a court. The two-thirds vote necessary to convict officials under impeachment and remove them from office is one of several cases where the Constitution demands a two-thirds majority of either or both houses of Congress. Actions demanding a two-thirds vote involve matters of more than ordinary importance, or ones in which a simple majority vote might be unfair to individuals or minority groups. The complete list is as follows: (1) *trial of impeachments*—Article I, Section 3, clause 6 (two-thirds of the Senate); (2) *expulsion of members from either house of Congress*—Article I, Section 5, clause 2 (two-thirds of the house in which the member holds a seat); (3) *passing a bill over the President's veto*—Article I, Section 7, clause 2 (two-thirds of both houses); (4) *ratification of treaties*—Article II, Section 2, clause 2 (two-thirds of the Senate); (5) *proposing amendments to the Constitution* (two-thirds of both houses of Congress, or a constitutional convention proposed by two-thirds of the state legislatures).

2. *Sessions of Congress.* [The Congress shall assemble at least once in every Year, and such Meeting shall be on the first Monday in December, unless they shall by Law appoint a different Day.]

SECTION 5. ORGANIZATION AND RULES OF EACH HOUSE

1. *Power over Membership and Sittings.* Each House shall be the Judge of the Elections, Returns and Qualifications of its own Members, and a Majority of each shall constitute a Quorum to do Business; but a smaller Number may adjourn from day to day, and may be authorized to compel the Attendance of absent Members, in such Manner, and under such Penalties as each House may provide.

2. *Power over Rules and Behavior.* Each House may determine the Rules of its Proceedings, punish its Members for disorderly Behaviour, and, with the Concurrence of two thirds, expel a Member.

3. *Keeping a Record of Proceedings.* Each House shall keep a Journal of its Proceedings, and from time to time publish the same, excepting such Parts as may in their Judgment require Secrecy; and the Yeas and Nays of the Members of either House on any question shall, at the Desire of one fifth of those Present, be entered on the Journal.

4. *Adjournment.* Neither House, during the Session of Congress, shall, without the Consent of the other, adjourn for more than three days, nor to any other Place than that in which the two Houses shall be sitting.

SECTION 6. CONGRESSIONAL PRIVILEGES AND RESTRAINTS

1. *Payment and Privileges.* The Senators and Representatives shall receive a Compensation for their Services, to be ascertained by Law, and paid out of the Treasury of the United States. They shall in all Cases, except Treason, Felony and Breach of the Peace, be privileged from Arrest during their Attendance at the Session of their respective Houses, and in going to and returning from the same; and for any Speech or Debate in either House, they shall not be questioned in any other Place.

2. *Congress Members not to Hold Other Federal Offices.* No Senator or Representative shall, during the Time for which he was elected, be appointed to any civil Office under the Authority of the United States, which shall have been created, or the Emoluments whereof shall have been encreased during such time; and no Person holding any Office under the United States, shall be a Member of either House during his Continuance in Office.

(*Continued from page 115.*)
major issues. It also often insures thorough consideration of legislation which might otherwise be passed hurriedly. In general, however, the Senate, like the House, transacts most of its business in committee.

SEPARATION OF POWERS

The authors of the Constitution feared unlimited political power, no matter who wielded it. Concentration of power in the hands of a few people (oligarchy) or in one person (monarchy) was likely to result, they knew, in the oppression of the people as a whole. The members of the Philadelphia Convention also distrusted a government dominated by the unrestrained will of the people. They were convinced that such a complete democracy would be weak and changeable, and that it would enable the poor to rob the rich. Finally, there was always danger that office holders would try to seize more power than the people wanted to grant them.

In order to avert what they regarded as the triple dangers of tyranny, mob rule, and seizure of power, the Founding Fathers created a government based on the principle of "separation of powers." According to this principle —which stemmed both from American colonial experience and from the writings of Montesquieu—the major powers of government should be divided among different officials. So in the American Constitution the first three Articles are devoted to defining the powers of the legislative, executive, and judicial branches of the federal government, *each branch being administered by different people.* How careful the authorites of the Constitution were to preserve

(*Continued on page 119.*)

EXPLANATORY NOTES

Article I, Section 4, clause 2. The Twentieth Amendment, ratified in 1933, has changed the date of the opening of the regular session of Congress to January 3.

Article I, Section 5, clauses 1 and 2. The power enjoyed by each house of Congress to judge the qualifications of its members is absolute; there is no appeal from it to any court or other governmental agency. Very seldom, however, is a member of Congress excluded or expelled, for such action robs the people of his or her district or state of their right to be represented in the national legislature.

Among the reasons why individual members of the House or Senate have been excluded or expelled have been the following: practicing polygamy, using corruption and fraud in elections, advocating a socialist revolution, and bribing fellow members of Congress to vote generous land grants to railroads.

Article I, Section 6, clause 1. Members of Congress now receive a salary of $57,500 plus a tax-free expense account and staff assistance in proportion to the size of their constituency and load of committee work. Very few members of Congress can more than break even on their salary because their expenses are heavy.

The privileges of members of Congress—freedom from arrest during session and freedom of speech within the halls of Congress—are taken from the practice of the British Parliament. These were won by the House of Commons during a long struggle with the Stuart kings of England in the seventeenth century. Such privileges may be abused, as when members recklessly accuse defenseless individuals. Congressional immunity is necessary, however, if members are to act independently and speak freely on public questions.

Article I, Section 6, clause 2. The purpose of this clause is to prevent the President from influencing members of Congress by promising or giving them jobs.

SECTION 7. HOW BILLS BECOME LAWS

1. *Revenue Bills.* All Bills for raising Revenue shall originate in the House of Representatives; but the Senate may propose or concur with Amendments as on other Bills.

2. *President's Veto.* Every Bill which shall have passed the House of Representatives and the Senate, shall, before it becomes a Law, be presented to the President of the United States; If he approve he shall sign it, but if not he shall return it, with his Objections to that House in which it shall have originated, who shall enter the Objections at large on their Journal, and proceed to reconsider it. If after such Reconsideration two thirds of that House shall agree to pass the Bill, it shall be sent, together with the Objections, to the other House, by which it shall likewise be reconsidered, and if approved by two thirds of that House, it shall become a Law. But in all such Cases the Votes of both Houses shall be determined by yeas and Nays, and the Names of the Persons voting for and against the Bill shall be entered on the Journal of each House respectively. If any Bill shall not be returned by the President within ten Days (Sundays excepted) after it shall have been presented to him, the Same shall be a Law, in like Manner as if he had signed it, unless the Congress by their Adjournment prevent its Return, in which Case it shall not be a Law.

3. *Veto Power Extended to Resolutions.* Every Order, Resolution, or Vote to which the Concurrence of the Senate and House of Representatives may be necessary (except on a question of Adjournment) shall be presented to the President of the United States; and before the Same shall take Effect, shall be approved by him, or being disapproved by him, shall be repassed by two thirds of the Senate and House of Representatives, according to the Rules and Limitations prescribed in the Case of a Bill.

SECTION 8. POWERS GRANTED CONGRESS

1. *Taxation.* The Congress shall have Power To lay and collect Taxes, Duties, Imposts and Excises, to pay the Debts and provide for the common Defence and general Welfare of the United States; but all Duties, Imposts and Excises shall be uniform throughout the United States;

2. *Borrowing.* To borrow Money on the credit of the United States;

3. *Regulation of Commerce.* To regulate Commerce with foreign Nations, and among the several States, and with the Indian Tribes;

4. *Naturalization and Bankruptcies.* To establish an uniform Rule of Naturalization, and uniform Laws on the subject of Bankruptcies throughout the United States;

(*Continued from page 117.*)
separation of powers can be seen by Article I, Section 6, clause 2, this forbids any person to hold both an executive or judicial office and a seat in Congress at the same time.

This system of separation of powers is in contrast to the British system of "parliamentary" or "cabinet" government. In Britain the real heads of the government, the prime minister and the cabinet, are chosen from the legislature itself. They represent the party that commands a majority in the House of Commons. Thus, instead of being separated, the British executive and legislative powers are merged.

CHECKS AND BALANCES

To prevent any branch of the federal government from overstepping its powers, the Constitution sets up an elaborate system of "checks and balances" whereby each branch of government is given some power to oversee or interfere in the work of the others. Thus the lawmaking power of Congress is checked by the President's veto, which is a negative power of legislation. While it is the President's job as chief executive to appoint civil servants and judges, the Senate shares in this executive power since it must ratify all major appointments. Although it is the function of the federal judiciary to try persons accused of crime, the President has the judicial power of granting pardons and reprieves.

Separation of powers plus checks and balances have received criticism. If any two branches of the federal government disagree, decisive action may be difficult, even impossible. Especially if the President and Congress are in opposition, the government tends to go into "dead center," with Congress unwilling to take action recommended by the President, and the President vetoing bills passed by Congress. In any case, checks and balances tend to slow up federal action to such a degree that one

(*Continued on page 121.*)

EXPLANATORY NOTES

Article I, Section 7, clause 2. The President has a "suspensive veto"; it suspends action until Congress has a chance to try to "override" the veto by a two-thirds vote. The President within less than ten days of the end of a congressional sitting may also use the "pocket veto." In such case, the President ignores a bill ("puts it in his pocket"), and it automatically fails to become a law.

Article I, Section 8, clauses 1 and 3. These clauses contain the most important new powers: taxation and control over interstate and foreign commerce.

The taxing power has been used for other purposes than raising money. Protective tariffs have always been levied in order to promote American industry. Since "the power to tax is the power to destroy," heavy taxation has been used to prevent the use of certain products, such as sulphur matches, by raising their price so high that no one would buy them. Congress has attempted to discourage gambling by a special tax on professional gamblers.

Article I, Section 8, clause 3. The exact meaning of "commerce" has caused controversy for many years (see *Gibbons v. Ogden*, p. 233). The tendency has been constantly to expand the meaning and the application of the word. Under the "commerce clause" the federal government now fixes railroad rates, establishes frequencies for radio stations, protects migratory birds, establishes safety regulations for airplanes, and forbids racial discrimination in public facilities, such as motels and restaurants.

5. *Coinage.* **To coin Money, regulate the Value thereof, and of foreign Coin, and fix the Standard of Weights and Measures;**

6. *Punishing Counterfeiters.* **To provide for the Punishment of counterfeiting the Securities and current Coin of the United States;**

7. *Postal Service.* **To establish Post Offices and post Roads;**

8. *Copyrights and Patents.* **To promote the Progress of Science and useful Arts, by securing for limited Times to Authors and Inventors the exclusive Right to their respective Writings and Discoveries;**

9. *Lower Courts.* **To constitute Tribunals inferior to the supreme Court;**

10. *Punishing Piracy.* **To define and punish Piracies and Felonies committed on the high Seas, and Offences against the Law of Nations;**

11. *Declaring War.* **To declare War, grant Letters of Marque and Reprisal, and make Rules concerning Captures on Land and Water;**

12. *Army.* **To raise and support Armies, but no Appropriation of Money to that Use shall be for a longer Term than two Years;**

13. *Navy.* **To provide and maintain a Navy;**

14. *Regulating the Armed Forces.* **To make Rules for the Government and Regulation of the land and naval Forces;**

15. *Calling Out Militia.* **To provide for calling forth the Militia to execute the Laws of the Union, suppress Insurrections and repel Invasions;**

16. *Regulating Militia.* **To provide for organizing, arming, and disciplining, the Militia, and for governing such Part of them as may be employed in the Service of the United States reserving to the States respectively, the Appointment of the Officers, and the Authority of training the Militia according to the discipline prescribed by Congress;**

17. *Areas under Exclusive Control of Congress.* **To exercise exclusive Legislation in all Cases whatsoever, over such District (not exceeding ten Miles square) as may, by Cession of particular States, and the Acceptance of Congress, become the Seat of the Government of the United States, and to exercise like Authority over all Places purchased by the Consent of the Legislature of the State in which the Same shall be, for the Erection of Forts, Magazines, Arsenals, dock-Yards, and other needful Buildings; —And**

18. *The "Elastic Clause."* **To make all Laws which shall be necessary and proper for carrying into Execution the foregoing Powers, and all other Powers vested by this Constitution in the Government of the United States, or in any Department or Officer thereof.**

(*Continued from page 119.*)
authority has written, "The time element in the American Constitution makes it a luxury the United States cannot afford in the modern world."

On the other hand, checks and balances and separation of powers are an insurance against seizure of power of the federal government by an individual or an organized group. They are a protection against rash, ill-considered action. These advantages more than outweigh the apparent inefficiency of the system.

THE FEDERAL SYSTEM

Article I, Section 8, has been called "the heart of the Constitution." It grants the federal government the great powers needed to govern the United States effectively. In the many years since the Constitution went into effect, it has been found necessary to add very few new powers to the original list.

The authors of the Constitution attempted to set up a system of "divided sovereignty," whereby the federal government was to control interstate and foreign relations, while the states controlled local affairs. This arrangement was probably a result of the fact that during the colonial period Americans had become used to a similar scheme. To try to prevent such an increase in the powers of the central government as had caused the American Revolution, the Founding Fathers made the federal government one of "enumerated powers." This meant that the actions of the government of the United States were restricted to the powers specifically granted in the Constitution. All other power remained in the hands of the states.

In the course of time federal powers expanded with the needs of a growing country. Until recently this was in part accomplished by interpretation of the so-called "elastic clause" (Article I, Section 8, clause 18). This states that Congress may make all laws "necessary and proper" for putting into effect its stated powers. Just what "necessary and proper" meant was a matter of bitter dispute. Those who wished to restrain the power of the federal government emphasized the word "necessary." They were known as "strict constructionists," because they wished to interpret the Constitution strictly and so limit the federal

(*Continued on page 123.*)

EXPLANATORY NOTES

Article I, Section 8, clause 5. Control over money is an exclusive federal power since the states are forbidden to issue currency (Article I, Section 10 clause 1). This arrangement was designed to end the confusion which resulted when each state had its own currency.

Article I, Section 8, clause 11. The Founding Fathers probably intended that the power to declare war should lie exclusively with Congress. From the very first, however, the President, as commander in chief of the armed forces, carried on warfare without a formal declaration by Congress. The United States carried on undeclared war with France in 1798–1800 during the presidency of John Adams and with Tripoli in 1801–1805 under Thomas Jefferson. In modern times the Korean and Vietnam wars are examples of hostilities engaged in without a formal congressional declaration, although the war effort in both cases received congressional support.

Article I, Section 8, clause 12. The condition that money may be voted for the armed forces for only two years reveals fear of a standing army. The Constitution endeavors to see that the military forces of the United States shall be servant of the people, not their master.

SECTION 9. POWERS DENIED TO THE UNITED STATES

1. *May Not Interfere with Slave Trade Before 1808.* [The Migration or Importation of such Persons as any of the States now existing shall think proper to admit, shall not be prohibited by the Congress prior to the Year one thousand eight hundred and eight, but a Tax or duty may be imposed on such Importation, not exceeding ten dollars for each Person.]

2. *May Not Suspend* Habeas Corpus *Except in Crisis.* The Privilege of the Writ of Habeas Corpus shall not be suspended, unless when in Cases of Rebellion or Invasion the public Safety may require it.

3. *May Not Pass Bills of Attainder or* Ex Post Facto *Laws.* No Bill of Attainder or ex post facto Law shall be passed.

4. *May Not Levy Taxes Except in Proportion to Population.* No Capitation, or other direct, Tax shall be laid, unless in Proportion to the Census or Enumeration herein before directed to be taken.

5. *May Not Levy Export Taxes.* No Tax or Duty shall be laid on Articles exported from any State.

6. *May Not Favor One Port over Another.* No Preference shall be given by any Regulation of Commerce or Revenue to the Ports of one State over those of another: nor shall Vessels bound to, or from, one State, be obliged to enter, clear, or pay Duties in another.

7. *May Not Spend Money without Appropriations or Maintain Secrecy in Finances.* No Money shall be drawn from the Treasury, but in Consequence of Appropriations made by Law; and a regular Statement and Account of the Receipts and Expenditures of all public Money shall be published from time to time.

8. *May Not Grant Titles of Nobility.* No Title of Nobility shall be granted by the United States: And no Person holding any Office of Profit or Trust under them, shall, without the Consent of the Congress, accept of any present, Emolument, Office, or Title, of any kind whatever, from any King, Prince, or foreign State.

SECTION 10. POWERS DENIED TO THE STATES

1. *Various Actions Forbidden to the States.* No State shall enter into any Treaty, Alliance, or Confederation; grant Letters of Marque and Reprisal; coin Money; emit Bills of Credit; make any Thing but gold and silver Coin a Tender in Payment of Debts; pass any Bill of Attainder, ex post facto Law, or Law impairing the Obligations of Contracts, or grant any Title of Nobility.

2. *May Not Levy Import or Export Duties.* No State shall, without the Consent of the Congress, lay any Imposts or Duties on Imports or Exports, except what may be absolutely necessary for executing its inspection Laws: and the net Produce of all Duties and Imposts, laid by any State on Imports or Exports, shall be for the Use of the Treasury of the United States; and all such Laws shall be subject to the Revision and Controul of the Congress.

(*Continued from page 121.*)

government to the powers *enumerated* or *specified* in the document itself. Those who desired to expand federal power stressed the word "proper." They were known as "loose constructionists" because they wished to allow the federal government to exercise power *implied* in the document. Loose constructionists argued, for instance, that the enumerated power to build post roads implied the right to dig canals.

No matter how much the "elastic clause" might be stretched, federal power was theoretically limited to the purposes stated in the Constitution. According to the Tenth Amendment:

The powers not delegated to the United States by the Constitution, nor prohibited by it to the States, are reserved to the States respectively, or to the people.

The twentieth century has seen such immense expansion of federal power that the idea that certain matters are exclusively reserved for local jurisdiction is breaking down. This was dramatized by the establishment of cabinet-level Departments of Health, Education and Welfare in 1953 and of Housing and Urban Development in 1965. Local governments lacked revenues to provide relief for the unemployed or decent schools, so the federal government provided funds, at the same time having a say in how they should be spent. When states allowed or even promoted discrimination against minority groups, Congress passed laws whereby the federal government guaranteed the right to vote and to use public facilities such as buses and restaurants. In the years since World War II, defense spending has become a seemingly permanent part of the economy, and where defense contracts are awarded may determine whether an urban area will be prosperous or poor.

(*Continued on page 125.*)

EXPLANATORY NOTES

Article I, Section 9, clause 2. *Habeas corpus* was a legal concept developed in England to protect individuals from arbitrary arrest and imprisonment. A writ of *habeas corpus,* issued by a judge, requires a sheriff or other jailer to bring a prisoner to court and to show cause why he or she should be detained.

Article I, Section 9, clause 3. A bill of attainder was a means whereby the British Parliament formerly punished officials and private individuals without a trial. An *ex post facto* law is one passed after an act has been committed, making that act a crime and prescribing punishment for it.

Article I, Section 9, clauses 4, 5, 6, and 7. The taxing and spending powers of the federal government are limited in order to prevent taxation falling more heavily on one part of the country than on another and to discourage misuse of public funds. The Sixteenth Amendment was needed to legalize a federal income tax.

Article I, Section 10. Much of this section is designed to reinforce the powers granted to the federal government in Article I, Section 8. The states are prohibited from taking any part in control of foreign affairs, war, and control of interstate and foreign commerce.

Article I, Section 10, clause 1. Several phrases in this clause protect creditors from state laws designed to make it easier for debtors to repay what they have borrowed. The states are forbidden to "emit Bills of Credit"—that is, to print paper money which would reduce the value of the currency. The prohibitions on making "any Thing but gold and silver Coin a Tender in Payment of Debts" and on passing any "Law impairing the Obligations of Contracts" were both designed to prevent the states from scaling down debts.

3. *May Not Wage War Unless Invaded.* No State shall, without the Consent of Congress, lay any Duty of Tonnage, keep Troops, or Ships of War in time of Peace, enter into any Agreement or Compact with another State, or with a foreign Power, or engage in War, unless actually invaded, or in such imminent Danger as will not admit of delay.

ARTICLE II. EXECUTIVE DEPARTMENT

SECTION 1. PRESIDENT AND VICE PRESIDENT

1. *Term of Office.* The executive Power shall be vested in a President of the United States of America. He shall hold his Office during the Term of four Years, and, together with the Vice President, chosen for the same Term, be elected, as follows:

2. *Number of Electors.* Each State shall appoint, in such Manner as the Legislature thereof may direct, a Number of Electors, equal to the whole Number of Senators and Representatives to which the State may be entitled in the Congress: but no Senator or Representative, or Person holding an Office of Trust or Profit under the United States, shall be appointed an Elector.

3. *Election of President and Vice-President.* [The Electors shall meet in their respective States, and vote by Ballot for two Persons, of whom one at least shall not be an Inhabitant of the same State with themselves. And they shall make a List of all the Persons voted for, and of the Number of Votes for each; which List they shall sign and certify, and transmit sealed to the Seat of the Government of the United States, directed to the President of the Senate. The President of the Senate shall, in the Presence of the Senate and House of Representatives, open all the Certificates, and the Votes shall then be counted. The Person having the greatest Number of Votes shall be the President, if such Number be a Majority of the whole Number of Electors appointed; and if there be more than one who have such Majority, and have an equal Number of Votes, then the House of Representatives shall immediately chuse by Ballot one of them for President; and if no Person have a Majority, then from the five highest on the List the said House shall in like Manner chuse the President. But in chusing the President, the Votes shall be taken by States, the Representation from each State having one Vote: A quorum for this Purpose shall consist of a Member or Members from two thirds of the States, and a Majority of all the States shall be necessary to a Choice. In every Case, after the Choice of the President, the Person having the greatest Number of Votes of the Electors shall be the Vice President. But if there should remain two or more who have equal Votes, the Senate shall chuse from them by Ballot the Vice President.]

(*Continued from page 123.*)

In spite of the growth of federal power, local governments still have the major share in controlling matters that concern the day-to-day lives of people most closely—health, schooling, water supply, police and fire protection. This promotes democracy by encouraging people to take an active interest in local politics. States and cities often serve as "political laboratories" where new attempts to solve the ever-changing problems of an industrial civilization may be worked out. They are schools of politics for many people who later hold federal office.

The federal system thus retains vigor, even though the strict division between the sovereignty of the national and state governments has become a thing of the past. Ques.

THE PRESIDENCY

No branch of the federal government gave the authors of the Constitution so much difficulty as the executive department. The Founding Fathers knew that a strong President was needed, but they also had to reckon with widespread fear of a strong executive. This was a carry-over from the struggles with royal governors in colonial times and from the dislike of George III during the Revolution.

Under the circumstances it is surprising how much power the President was granted. He has been called "an elective monarch," and historically this is an accurate description. The President's major powers are those formerly enjoyed by the monarch of England. They are, briefly, (1) conduct of foreign affairs, (2) supreme command of the army and navy, (3) appointment of executive and judicial officers, (4) the right to reprieve or pardon those accused of crime, and (5) a veto on legislation. In addition to these great powers, the President had a four-year term and was allowed to succeed himself in office. Contrast this to the position of many state governors, who in the 1780's were allowed to hold office for only one year, had no veto power, and were not allowed to succeed themselves. It is no wonder that during the fight over ratification in 1787 and 1788 the Anti-

(*Continued on page 127.*)

EXPLANATORY NOTES

Article II, Section 1, clause 2. The Philadelphia Convention had trouble deciding how the President was to be chosen. A proposal to have him selected by Congress was voted down because it would violate the principle of separation of powers. Direct election was rejected because of fear that a President with a great popular following might seize power. Choice by state legislatures, each state having one vote, was considered, but the large states were naturally opposed. The system finally agreed upon was indirect election by "electors" chosen for the purpose. The presidential electors are collectively called the "electoral college." During the early years of the republic, the presidential electors were, like the senators, chosen by state legislatures rather than by vote of the people. For further discussion, see notes on the Twelfth Amendment (p. 143).

Article II, Section 1, clause 3. This clause has been largely replaced by the Twelfth Amendment. In the original Constitution each elector had two votes, and the person with the highest number of votes became President and the next highest became Vice-President. If there was no majority, the election was thrown into the House of Representatives. The House, with each state having one vote, would make a choice from the highest five candidates. It was expected that this would happen frequently, on the assumption that electors would vote for "favored persons" from their own states or regions. The House has elected the President only twice, in 1800 and 1824.

4. *Time for Choosing Electors.* The Congress may determine the Time of chusing the Electors, and the Day on which they shall give their Votes; which Day shall be the same throughout the United States.

5. *Qualifications for President.* No Person except a natural born Citizen, [or a Citizen of the United States, at the time of the Adoption of this Constitution,] shall be eligible to the Office of President; neither shall any Person be eligible to that Office who shall not have attained to the Age of thirty five Years, and been fourteen Years a Resident within the United States.

6. *Presidential Succession in Case of Vacancy.* In Case of the Removal of the President from Office, or of his Death, Resignation, or Inability to discharge the Powers and Duties of the said Office, the same shall devolve on the Vice President, and the Congress may by Law provide for the Case of Removal, Death, Resignation or Inability, both of the President and Vice President, declaring what Officer shall then act as President, and such Officer shall act accordingly, until the Disability be removed, or a President shall be elected.

7. *Presidential Salary.* The President shall, at stated Times, receive for his Services, a Compensation, which shall neither be encreased nor diminished during the Period for which he shall have been elected, and he shall not receive within that Period any other Emolument from the United States, or any of them.

8. *Presidential Oath.* Before he enter on the Execution of his Office, he shall take the following Oath or Affirmation:—"I do solemnly swear (or affirm) that I will faithfully execute the Office of President of the United States, and will to the best of my Ability, preserve, protect and defend the Constitution of the United States."

SECTION 2. POWERS OF THE PRESIDENT

1. *Military Power; Executive Departments; Reprieves and Pardons.* The President shall be Commander in Chief of the Army and Navy of the United States, and of the Militia of the several States, when called into the actual Service of the United States; he may require the Opinion, in writing, of the principal Officer in each of the executive Departments, upon any Subject relating to the Duties of their respective Offices, and he shall have Power to grant Reprieves and Pardons for Offences against the United States, except in Cases of Impeachment.

2. *Treaties and Appointments.* He shall have Power, by and with the Advice and Consent of the Senate, to make Treaties, provided two thirds of the Senators present concur; and he shall nominate, and by and with the Advice and Consent of the Senate, shall appoint Ambassadors, other public Ministers and Consuls, Judges of the supreme Court, and all other

(Continued from page 125.)

Federalists made the presidency one of the principal points of attack in their criticism of the Constitution.

Nearly every one of the President's stated powers has been expanded since the Constitution first went in effect. At first, for instance, the veto power was used sparingly, but since Andrew Jackson's time Presidents have used the veto to hold up any legislation they disliked. Lincoln used his power as commander in chief as the basis for issuing the Emancipation Proclamation which declared slaves free in the South. Recently, as in Nixon's extension of the Vietnam War into Cambodia in 1970, Presidents have assumed an almost independent power of carrying on war.

Much of the President's power comes from the fact that he is head of one or the other of the two great political parties. The members of his party in Congress are under pressure to support legislation which he recommends. The presidential office has also gained strength because, as Grover Cleveland said, "The presidency is the people's office." While members of Congress represent particular states, he represents the whole country. His every action attracts nation-wide attention. No one can rival him in his ability to appeal to public opinion—especially since the invention of radio broadcasting and television.

In time of crisis, as in wartime or a depression, when quick, decisive action is called for, Congress may turn over many of its powers to the President "for the duration." On such an occasion he may come close to being a temporary dictator.

The influence of the presidency varies according to the personality and purpose of those *(Continued on page 129.)*

EXPLANATORY NOTES

Article II, Section 1, clause 6. Congress has made various provisions for succession to the presidency in case of the death or removal of both the President and Vice-President. As of 1966 the law provides that the speaker of the House of Representatives shall succeed to the presidency, followed by the president *pro tem* of the Senate.

A question never satisfactorily answered until 1967 was: who decides if a President is unable to discharge the duties of his office, and in such case, who takes over? In 1919 and 1920 the country was almost leaderless when President Wilson fell seriously ill and yet failed to give others authority to act for him. The problem reappeared in less acute form when President Eisenhower suffered serious illness three times during his presidency. Both Presidents Kennedy and Johnson had written agreements with their Vice-Presidents on the disability question. These did not, of course, have the force of law. Such informal agreements were only interim attempts to solve a serious problem.

The other question, brought back once again by the assassination of President Kennedy, was the lack of a way to fill the office of Vice-President when it became vacant. This lack had been noticed on previous occasions when the Vice-Presidency was vacant, but the shock of the Kennedy assassination finally forced a constitutional amendment. Both questions were settled once and for all in 1967 with Amendment XXV (see p. 152).

Article II, Section 2, clause 1. Mention of "the principal Officer in each of the executive Departments" is the only suggestion of the President's cabinet to be found in the Constitution. President Washington started the cabinet by asking the heads of government departments to meet with him for discussion of public questions. The cabinet is a purely advisory body, and its power depends on the President.

Officers of the United States, whose Appointments are not herein otherwise provided for, and which shall be established by Law: but the Congress may by Law vest the Appointment of such inferior Officers, as they think proper, in the President alone, in the Courts of Law, or in the Heads of Departments.

3. *Recess Appointments.* The President shall have Power to fill up all Vacancies that may happen during the Recess of the Senate, by granting Commissions which shall expire at the End of their next Session.

SECTION 3. PRESIDENTIAL DUTIES

Presidential Messages; Congressional Sessions; Executing Laws. He shall from time to time give to the Congress Information of the State of the Union, and recommend to their Consideration such Measures as he shall judge necessary and expedient; he may, on extraordinary Occasions, convene both Houses, or either of them, and in Case of Disagreement between them, with Respect to the Time of Adjournment, he may adjourn them to such Time as he shall think proper; he shall receive Ambassadors and other public Ministers; he shall take Care that the Laws be faithfully executed, and shall Commission all the Officers of the United States.

SECTION 4. IMPEACHMENT

Removal of Executive Officers. The President, Vice President and all Civil Officers of the United States, shall be removed from Office on Impeachment for, and Conviction of, Treason, Bribery, or other high Crimes and Misdemeanors.

ARTICLE III. JUDICIAL DEPARTMENT

SECTION 1. FEDERAL COURTS

Supreme and Lower Courts; Term and Salary of Judges. The judicial Power of the United States, shall be vested in one supreme Court, and in such inferior Courts as the Congress may from time to time ordain and establish. The Judges, both of the supreme and inferior Courts, shall hold their Offices during good Behaviour, and shall, at stated Times, receive for their Services, a Compensation, which shall not be diminished during their Continuance in Office.

who hold the office. Andrew Jackson and Theodore Roosevelt increased their power by sheer force of personality. A President like Woodrow Wilson, with a program of legislation that he wants to put through Congress, is likely to exert more power than a "stand-patter" like Calvin Coolidge.

From 1941 until the early 1970's, Presidents governed a country at war. First it was the desperate struggle against the Axis, then the Cold War against communism (which also involved "hot war" in Korea and Southeast Asia). During this long period, the powers of the chief executive vastly expanded and those of Congress declined, especially in the sphere of foreign affairs. This "imperial presidency" reached its climax with President Nixon. Even before Nixon's resignation in 1974, Congress attempted to regain the right to decide when the United States should engage in war. Both Presidents Ford and Carter have been at pains to consult leaders of Congress. Carter has also reduced the pomp and ceremony of the White House. He has tried to make the President less isolated, more accessible.

THE FEDERAL JUDICIARY

Of the three branches of government, the judicial department is the one most sketchily described in the Constitution. It was simply stated that there was to be a Supreme Court and inferior courts. Other details were left for later decision by Congress. Soon after the first Congress met, during the administration of George Washington, it passed the Judiciary Act of 1789 which set up the federal courts on a plan which has been followed ever since. The lowest courts are the district courts, each presided over by a district judge. Most cases involving federal laws are tried here. Above the district courts are the circuit courts. Their principal business is to hear cases which have been appealed from district courts on the ground that there was an error or injustice in the original decision. (*Continued on page 131.*)

EXPLANATORY NOTES

Article II, Section 3. By delivering special messages urging particular laws or by calling special sessions for Congress to consider some particular problem, the President can focus public attention on legislation which he wants passed. When a crisis comes up while Congress is not in session, the President may attempt to keep matters in his own hands by failing to call Congress into session before the regular time.

The President's duty to receive foreign diplomats carries with it the power to ask a foreign country to withdraw its diplomatic officials from this country. This is called breaking diplomatic relations, and often carries with it the threat of war. The President likewise has the power of deciding whether or not to recognize a new foreign government. Thus in 1913 President Wilson refused to recognize a Mexican government headed by Victoriano Huerta, because Huerta had gained power by violence. Presidents Truman, Eisenhower, Kennedy, and Johnson have all refused to recognize the Communist government of China.

The President's duty to faithfully execute the laws carries with it a power to interpret laws according to his judgment. A President must decide what to do when two laws contradict each other—as they sometimes do. Or Presidents may vary in the degree to which they carry out a law. Thus the Sherman Antitrust Act was almost a dead letter until Theodore Roosevelt chose to enforce it more vigorously than his three predecessors (see p. 505).

Article II, Section 4. Remember that "impeachment" means merely to "bring charges against" not "to remove from office." Removal takes place *after* the accused officer has been convicted of the offense for which he or she was impeached.

SECTION 2. JURISDICTION OF FEDERAL COURTS

1. *Kinds of Cases Tried in Federal Courts.* The Judicial Power shall extend to all Cases, in Law and Equity, arising under this Constitution, the Laws of the United States, and Treaties made, or which shall be made, under their Authority;—to all Cases affecting Ambassadors, other public Ministers and Consuls;—to all Cases of admiralty and maritime Jurisdiction;—to Controversies to which the United States shall be a Party;—to Controversies between two or more States; [—between a State and Citizens of another State;] —between Citizens of different States;—between Citizens of the same State claiming Lands under Grants of different States, and between a State, or the Citizens thereof, and foreign States, Citizens or Subjects.

2. *Original and Appellate Jurisdiction of Supreme Court.* In all Cases affecting Ambassadors, other public Ministers and Consuls, and those in which a State shall be Party, the supreme Court shall have original Jurisdiction. In all the other Cases before mentioned, the supreme Court shall have appellate Jurisdiction, both as to Law and Fact, with such Exceptions, and under such Regulations as the Congress shall make.

3. *Jury Trial Guaranteed; Place of Trial.* The Trial of all Crimes, except in Cases of Impeachment, shall be by Jury; and such Trial shall be held in the State where the said Crimes shall have been committed; but when not committed within any State, the Trial shall be at such Place or Places as the Congress may by Law have directed.

SECTION 3. TREASON

1. *Definition of Treason.* Treason against the United States, shall consist only in levying War against them, or in adhering to their Enemies, giving them Aid and Comfort. No Person shall be convicted of Treason unless on the Testimony of two Witnesses to the same overt Act, or on Confession in open Court.

2. *Punishment for Treason; How Limited.* The Congress shall have Power to declare the Punishment of Treason, but no Attainder of Treason shall work Corruption of Blood, or Forfeiture except during the Life of the Person attainted.

(*Continued from page 129.*)
The Constitution was more precise about the types of cases which should go to federal courts than about how the courts should be set up. The principal function of the federal judiciary under the Constitution is plain: to try offenses against federal laws and treaties. Thus the new federal government differed from that established by the Articles of Confederation because *it could compel individual citizens to obey it.*

A most vital power of the federal judiciary is not stated in the Constitution. This is the practice of "judicial review." In the course of deciding cases brought before them, the courts must sometimes decide whether a state or federal law accords with the Constitution. If the judiciary finds that a law is unconstitutional, it ceases to have effect. Thus the courts, and especially the Supreme Court, exert a veto power. This veto also extends beyond legislation to the actions of state and federal executives (see p. 196) and to state court decisions. Only in West Germany and Japan does the judiciary enjoy this power.

Whether the Founding Fathers meant to grant the federal courts such authority is not clear, but judicial review was an obvious corollary of Article VI, clause 2, which states that the Constitution, federal laws, and treaties are the "supreme Law of the Land."

Today almost the only business of the Court is to deal with constitutional questions. In the performance of its task the Supreme Court not merely decides the law, but may also issue orders (called injunctions) demanding compliance with its decisions. One way to override a Supreme Court decision is by the difficult process of amending the Constitution. For example, Amendment XVI permitted Congress to levy an income tax after the Supreme Court had declared such a tax unconstitutional. Another way of controlling the Court is by Congressional action. Thus the "crime control" Act of 1968 eliminated some restrictions the court had placed on criminal confessions to the police. Furthermore, the court is cautious in declaring state or federal actions illegal. Nor does it pass

(*Continued on page 133.*)

EXPLANATORY NOTES

Article III, Section 2, clause 1. The phrase "in Law and Equity" reflects the fact that American courts took over two kinds of traditional law from England. The basic law was the "common law" which was based on over five centuries of judicial decisions. "Equity" was a special branch of law developed to take care of cases where common law did not apply, or to prevent an injustice from being done. Federal courts deal mostly in "statute law"— legislation passed by Congress, treaties, or the Constitution itself. "Admiralty and maritime jurisdiction" is a branch of law inherited from Great Britain. It covers all sorts of cases involving ships and shipping on the high seas and on navigable waters such as rivers, canals, and the Great Lakes.

The meaning of the phrase "between a state and citizens of another state" has been altered by the Eleventh Amendment (see pp. 142–143).

Article III, Section 2, clause 2. When a court has "original jurisdiction" over certain types of cases, it means that such cases are referred to it first. A court with "appellate jurisdiction" tries cases which have been appealed from lower courts.

Article III, Section 3, clause 1. The charge of treason had been used by tyrants as a means of getting rid of people who opposed them. To prevent this abuse the authors of the Constitution defined it carefully, insisted that it be clearly proved, and limited punishment for it.

SECTION 1. OFFICIAL ACTS

Reciprocal Recognition. Full Faith and Credit shall be given in each State to the Public Acts, Records, and judicial Proceedings of every other State. And the Congress may by general Laws prescribe the Manner in which such Acts, Records and Proceedings shall be proved, and the Effect thereof.

SECTION 2. MUTUAL DUTIES OF STATES

1. *Exchange of Privileges of Citizenship.* The Citizens of each State shall be entitled to all Privileges and Immunities of Citizens in the several States.
2. *Extradition.* A Person charged in any State with Treason, Felony, or other Crime, who shall flee from Justice, and be found in another State, shall on Demand of the executive Authority of the State from which he fled, be delivered up, to be removed to the State having Jurisdiction of the Crime.
3. *Fugitive Slaves, Apprentices, and Indentured Servants.* [No Person held to Service or Labour in one State, under the Laws thereof, escaping into another, shall, in Consequence of any Law or Regulation therein, be discharged from such Service or Labour, but shall be delivered up on Claim of the Party to whom such Service or Labour may be due.]

SECTION 3. NEW STATES AND TERRITORIES

1. *Admission of New States.* New States may be admitted by the Congress into this Union; but no new State shall be formed or erected within the Jurisdiction of any other State; nor any State be formed by the Junction of two or more States, or Parts of States, without the Consent of the Legislatures of the States concerned as well as of the Congress.
2. *Control over Territory and Property of the United States.* The Congress shall have Power to dispose of and make all needful Rules and Regulations respecting the Territory or other Property belonging to the United States; and nothing in this Constitution shall be so construed as to Prejudice any Claims of the United States, or of any particular State.

SECTION 4. FEDERAL PROTECTION FOR STATES

Guarantees Against Invasion, Despotism, and Domestic Violence. The United States shall guarantee to every State in this Union a Republican Form of Government, and shall protect each of them against Invasion; and on Application of the Legislature or of the Executive (when the Legislature cannot be convened) against domestic Violence.

(Continued from page 131.)

on all laws, only on those brought before it. And while the justices do not face the people at election time, and so feel free to oppose the popular will, actually the court sooner or later usually "follows the election returns"—in other words, it goes along with public opinion as expressed through the actions of state governments, of Congress, and of the federal executive. As old justices die or resign, new men are chosen by the party in power. Sometimes justices simply change their minds. The Supreme Court, in short, acts as a balance wheel rather than as a brake.

Federal judges hold office "during good behavior," which means for life or until they choose to resign. Combined with the provision that judges' salaries may not be reduced, this is designed to make the federal courts independent. As long as they are not guilty of "high crimes or misdemeanors" (for which they may be impeached), federal judges are free of popular, presidential, or congressional control. The idea of an independent judiciary originated in England in the seventeenth century in order to prevent judges from being controlled by the monarch. The idea was carried over into the United States Constitution to prevent judges from being controlled by anybody.

While the wisdom of the federal judiciary has often been questioned, the Supreme Court has never been touched by corruption, and it has always behaved with the dignity fitting its high position as guardian of the Constitution.

INTERSTATE AND FEDERAL-STATE COOPERATION

The Constitution provides for cooperation between the states and between the states and the federal government. Article IV declares that the states shall respect each other's laws and court actions, shall aid each other in bringing persons accused of crime to justice, and

(Continued on page 135.)

EXPLANATORY NOTES

Article IV, Section 1. The "full faith and credit clause" was carried over from the Articles of Confederation. It means that court judgments and legal actions such as contracts, wills, marriages, partnerships, and corporation charters should be valid throughout the United States. "Full faith and credit" does not extend, however, to matters that fall within what is called the "police power" of the states. It does not extend, for instance, to licenses to practice medicine, law, or engineering.

Article IV, Section 2, clause 1. The "privileges and immunities" guaranteed by each state to citizens of other states do not include privileges that demand residential qualifications such as the right to vote, to run a restaurant, or to sell drugs. By the so-called "insular decisions" in the early twentieth century, the Supreme Court decided that this provision of the Constitution did not extend to inhabitants of the overseas territories of the United States. Such people became citizens only when Congress granted them the privilege by legislation (see p. 483).

Article IV, Section 2, clause 3. During the early nineteenth century, fixed labor contracts of apprentices and indentured servants were abandoned. In 1865 slavery was abolished. This clause thus became a dead letter.

Article IV, Section 3. Neither in this section where one might logically expect it, nor anywhere else in the Constitution is there any statement that the federal government may acquire new territory, whether by conquest or purchase. This omission embarrassed Jefferson when he negotiated the Louisiana Purchase in 1803.

ARTICLE V. THE AMENDING PROCESS

How Amendments Are Proposed and Ratified. The Congress, whenever two thirds of both Houses shall deem it necessary, shall propose Amendments to this Constitution, or, on the Application of the Legislatures of two thirds of the several States, shall call a Convention for proposing Amendments, which, in either Case, shall be valid to all Intents and Purposes, as Part of this Constitution, when ratified by the Legislatures of three fourths of the several States, or by Conventions in three fourths thereof, as the one or the other Mode of Ratification may be proposed by the Congress; Provided [that no Amendment which may be made prior to the Year One thousand eight hundred and eight shall in any Manner affect the first and fourth Clauses in the Ninth Section of the first Article; and] that no State, without its Consent, shall be deprived of its equal Suffrage in the Senate.

ARTICLE VI. FEDERAL CREDIT
AND FEDERAL SUPREMACY

1. *Prior Debts of the United States.* All Debts contracted and Engagements entered into, before the Adoption of this Constitution, shall be as valid against the United States under this Constitution, as under the Confederation.

2. *The Supreme Law of the Land.* This Constitution, and the Laws of the United States which shall be made in Pursuance thereof; and all Treaties made, or which shall be made, under the Authority of the United States, shall be the supreme Law of the Land; and the Judges in every State shall be bound thereby, any Thing in the Constitution or Laws of any State to the Contrary notwithstanding.

3. *Official Oath: No Religious Test.* The Senators and Representatives before mentioned, and the Members of the several State Legislatures, and all executive and judicial Officers, both of the United States and of the several States, shall be bound by Oath or Affirmation, to support this Constitution; but no religious Test shall ever be required as a Qualification to any Office or public Trust under the United States.

(*Continued from page 133.*)

shall return runaway apprentices, indentured servants, and slaves to their masters. It also says that the federal government shall aid states in preserving rights of self-government, in repelling invasion, and in keeping order.

In the twentieth century the area of interstate cooperation has been widened. Since state lines often cut across natural geographical regions, a single state may be incompetent to deal with important problems. With the approval of Congress, states may make compacts for cooperative action. New Jersey and New York jointly established the Port of New York and New Jersey Authority. It controls shipping and docking in the Hudson River. Before it was worthwhile to build the Hoover Dam on the Colorado River, seven states had to make an agreement about the control and use of its water.

Cooperation between the federal and state governments also extends far beyond what is specified in the Constitution. In certain fields, such as conservation and control of aviation, federal and state governments have arranged similar laws and joint enforcement. It is a federal offense to carry across a state line game killed in violation of local law. The federal government also provides financial aid for state activities such as road building, public health, control of insect pests, and education.

THE AMENDING PROCESS

If amendments to the Articles of Confederation had not required unanimous consent of the states, the Confederation might have lasted much longer than it did. Twice during that period, a single state blocked a proposal to give Congress the power it most needed—the right to levy taxes. The authors of the Constitution made the amending process easier by arranging (1) that amendments be *proposed* either by a two-thirds vote of Congress or

(*Continued on page 137.*)

EXPLANATORY NOTES

Article V. One of the two methods for proposing amendments—through a convention called on request of two-thirds of the states—has never been used. In the 1960's there was a movement, however, to call for such a convention with a view to overriding a Supreme Court decision that electoral districts for elections to state legislatures must be approximately equal in population.

Only one amendment, the twenty-first, has been ratified by state conventions.

Article VI, clause 2. The "supremacy clause" is one of the most important in the entire Constitution. It was principally on the basis of this clause that Chief Justice John Marshall wrote his classic statement of loose construction in *Marbury v. Madison* (see p. 196). The Judiciary Act of 1789 and the Fourteenth Amendment reinforced this supremacy of federal law over state law.

Article VI, clause 3. Notice that state as well as federal officials must solemnly agree to support the Constitution. This makes local officers, from town clerks to governors, federal officials as well. Also, the Constitution put many duties on the states, such as arranging elections to federal office.

The fact that the Constitution forbids a religious test as a qualification for office reveals that its authors thought that church and state should not mix. How or if a person worships God should be, they felt, a private affair. This principle of "separation of church and state" is also found in the First Amendment, which forbids Congress to set up a state church or to interfere with religious freedom.

ARTICLE VII. RATIFICATION OF
THE CONSTITUTION

Nine States Necessary for Ratification. The Ratification of the Conventions of nine States, shall be sufficient for the Establishment of this Constitution between the States so ratifying the Same. Done in Convention by the Unanimous Consent of the States present the Seventeenth Day of September in the Year of our Lord one thousand seven hundred and Eighty seven and of the Independance of the United States of America the Twelfth. In witness whereof We have hereunto subscribed our Names, G^o Washington—Presid^t

and deputy from
Virginia

New Hampshire	John Langdon Nicholas Gilman	Delaware	Geo: Read Gunning Bedford jun John Dickinson Richard Bassett Jaco: Broom
Massachusetts	Nathaniel Gorham Rufus King		
Connecticut	Wm Saml Johnson Roger Sherman	Maryland	James McHenry Dan of St Thos Jenifer Danl Carroll
New York	Alexander Hamilton		
New Jersey	Wil: Livingston David Brearley Wm Paterson. Jona: Dayton	Virginia	John Blair— James Madison Jr.
		North Carolina	Wm Blount Richd Dobbs Spaight Hu Williamson
Pennsylvania	B Franklin Thomas Mifflin Robt Morris Geo. Clymer Thos FitzSimons Jared Ingersoll James Wilson Gouv Morris	South Carolina	J. Rutledge Charles Cotesworth Pinckney Charles Pinckney Pierce Butler.
		Georgia	William Few Abr Baldwin

(*Continued from page 135.*)

through a convention called by Congress on request of two-thirds of the state legislatures; and (2) that amendments be *ratified* by three-quarters of the states. Ratification might be either by state legislatures or by state conventions called for the purpose. Although these provisions made altering the Constitution easier than changing the Articles, the process of amendment was still so difficult and slow that the original Constitution has undergone few alterations.

How is it possible that a Constitution devised in the eighteenth century to meet the needs of a sparsely settled, isolated, agricultural country is still used by a great industrial nation with world-wide interests? As has already been suggested, the Constitution has been greatly altered by *interpretation* and by *usage*. It has changed its meaning from generation to generation. New demands on government have tended to widen its sphere and to alter its methods. The Supreme Court, by its power of judicial review, generally controls how far and how fast this change in meaning may go. Ultimately, though, the power of modifying the Constitution rests with the people and the officials whom they elect.

RATIFICATION OF THE CONSTITUTION

The authors of the Constitution arranged that it should go into effect when ratified by special conventions in nine states. This carried out the idea expressed in the Declaration of Independence that governments "derive their just powers from the consent of the governed." As has already been pointed out, *all* the people did not have an opportunity to say whether or not they would accept the Constitution because in the 1780's voting rights were limited to men of property. At the time it was ratified, however, the new federal Union came nearer to expressing the will of the people than did the governments of any other country in the world. As Jefferson said at the time, the United States had given an example to the world in altering its government "by assembling the

(*Continued on page 139.*)

EXPLANATORY NOTES

Article VII. "The Unanimous Consent of the States present" does not mean "the unanimous consent of delegates from all the states," because Rhode Island was not represented. Nor does this mean that all the delegates sent to the Convention approved of the Constitution. A few people were so much opposed to what was going on in Philadelphia that they went home.

The Signers. The signers were young men for the most part; only eleven had passed their fiftieth birthday. Of the 55 delegates who attended the Constitutional Convention, 42 remained to the end. Three of these were opposed, however, and George Mason of Virginia said that he would sooner chop off his right hand than sign the Constitution. But more common was the attitude of Benjamin Franklin, who said that he did not approve of every feature of the document, but was still astonished to find it as good as it was. Thirty-nine signed it. (Six delegates—Benjamin Franklin, Robert Morris, Roger Sherman, George Read, George Clymer, and James Wilson—signed both the Declaration of Independence and the Constitution.) Historians who have studied the work of the Founding Fathers generally agree with the judgment of Charles and Mary Beard, who wrote, "Among the many historic assemblies which have wrought revolutions in the affairs of mankind, it seems safe to say that there never has been one that commanded more political talent, practical experience, and sound substance than the Philadelphia Convention of 1787."

AMENDMENT I. FREEDOM OF OPINION (1791)

Religion, Speech, Press, Assembly, Petition. Congress shall make no law respecting an establishment of religion, or prohibiting the free exercise thereof; or abridging the freedom of speech, or of the press; or the right of the people peaceably to assemble, and to petition the Government for a redress of grievances.

AMENDMENT II. RIGHT TO BEAR ARMS (1791)

Maintaining a Militia. A well regulated Militia, being necessary to the security of a free State, the right of the people to keep and bear Arms, shall not be infringed.

AMENDMENT III. QUARTERING TROOPS (1791)

No Soldiers in Private Homes in Peace Time. No Soldier shall, in time of peace be quartered in any house, without the consent of the Owner, nor in time of war, but in a manner to be prescribed by law.

AMENDMENT IV. SEARCHES AND SEIZURES (1791)

No General Search Warrants. The right of the people to be secure in their persons, houses, papers, and effects, against unreasonable searches and seizures, shall not be violated, and no Warrants shall issue, but upon probable cause, supported by Oath or affirmation, and particularly describing the place to be searched, and the persons or things to be seized.

AMENDMENT V. RIGHTS OF ACCUSED PERSONS (1791)

Protection of Individual Rights. No person shall be held to answer for a capital, or otherwise infamous crime, unless on a presentment or indictment of a Grand Jury, except in cases arising in the land or naval forces, or in the Militia, when in actual service in time of War or public danger;

(*Continued from page 137.*)
wise men of the state, instead of assembling armies."

The Articles of Confederation had insisted on the unanimous consent of the states for amendment. Opponents of the Constitution therefore claimed that the Founding Fathers had been guilty of exceeding their powers by providing for ratification by only nine out of thirteen states. In fact, however, the Constitution was not an amendment to the Articles of Confederation, but an entirely new frame of government.

For many years it was not clear whether once a state had joined the Union it had the right to withdraw. The Constitution itself is silent on the point. The question was put to the ultimate test when in 1861 eleven southern states attempted to form a separate union of their own, the Confederate States of America. Northern victory in the war that followed decided that problem: once having joined the Union, a state may not leave it. (See Chapter 14.)

THE BILL OF RIGHTS

One of the principal objections to the Constitution when it was presented for ratification in 1787 was that it contained no section spelling out the rights and liberties of American citizens. Several states were persuaded to ratify only on the assurance that such a statement would be added immediately. The first ten amendments, ratified in 1791, are known as the Bill of Rights. They were designed to make sure that the new federal government would not abuse its great powers by oppressing the people or the states. They underline the basic principle of the Declaration of Independence: that the purpose of government is to protect individual rights.

The rights of the individual stated here are not unlimited. In general, a citizen's rights end where abuse of them hurts other individuals or threatens public safety. Freedom of speech does not include the right to utter slander (defaming a person by word of mouth) or to pub-

(*Continued on page 141.*)

EXPLANATORY NOTES

Amendment II. This provision is designed solely to guarantee to states the right to maintain a militia. It does not restrict the power of federal and state governments to regulate private ownership of weapons, unless such regulation interferes with the militia.

Amendments III and IV. These are based on a principle of English law that "a man's house is his castle." They also reflect grievance against the British government before the Revolution. The British had quartered redcoats in private houses and had used "writs of assistance" (general search warrants) to seek out smuggled goods.

Amendments IV–VIII. These amendments carefully protect the rights of the person most at the mercy of society: an individual suspected of crime. They reflect two principles of Anglo-Saxon justice: that a person is assumed to be innocent until proved guilty, and that it is better to let the guilty go free than to punish the innocent.

To bring "a presentment or indictment" means to bring formal charges against a person. It is the function of a "Grand Jury" to see whether there appears to be enough evidence against a man or woman to warrant his or her being brought to trial.

"The land and naval forces" and "Militia" are, while in actual service, subject to "military law," breaches of which may be tried in a "court martial." In times of emergency, such as invasion or natural disasters, civilians may temporarily be controlled by the armed forces under martial law.

nor shall any person be subject for the same offence to be twice put in jeopardy of life or limb; nor shall be compelled in any criminal case to be a witness against himself, nor be deprived of life, liberty, or property, without due process of law; nor shall private property be taken for public use, without just compensation.

AMENDMENT VI. RIGHTS OF ACCUSED PERSONS (continued) (1791)

Conduct of Trials. In all criminal prosecutions, the accused shall enjoy the right to a speedy and public trial, by an impartial jury of the State and district wherein the crime shall have been committed, which district shall have been previously ascertained by law, and to be informed of the nature and cause of the accusation; to be confronted with the witnesses against him; to have compulsory process for obtaining witnesses in his favor, and to have the Assistance of Counsel for his defence.

AMENDMENT VII. SUITS AT COMMON LAW (1791)

Right to Trial by Jury. In Suits at common law, where the value in controversy shall exceed twenty dollars, the right of trial by jury shall be preserved, and no fact tried by a jury, shall be otherwise reexamined in any Court of the United States, than according to the rules of the common law.

AMENDMENT VIII. BAILS, PUNISHMENTS (1791)

Moderation in Bails, Fines, Punishments. Excessive bail shall not be required, nor excessive fines imposed, nor cruel and unusual punishments inflicted.

AMENDMENT IX. RIGHTS NOT ENUMERATED (1791)

People Retain Rights Not Stated in Constitution. The enumeration in the Constitution, of certain rights, shall not be construed to deny or disparage others retained by the people.

AMENDMENT X. POWERS NOT DELEGATED (1791)

Powers Reserved to State and People. The powers not delegated to the United States by the Constitution, nor prohibited by it to the States, are reserved to the States respectively, or to the people.

(*Continued from page 143.*)
Such periods of excitement reveal the advantage of putting judges beyond direct popular control by allowing them to hold office "during good Behavior" (Article III, Section 1). Less swayed than most citizens by the emotions of the moment, the federal judiciary usually protects liberties the Constitution grants to suspects and fanatics as much as to people whose loyalty is unquestioned and whose opinions are those of the majority.

THE NATIONAL SUPREMACY AMENDMENTS

During the Reconstruction period that followed the Civil War (see Chapter 14, pp. 365–376), three amendments were added to the Constitution. All of them attempted to define the position of the blacks of the South. The Thirteenth Amendment declared all slaves free; the Fourteenth Amendment granted them citizenship, and the Fifteenth Amendment was intended to give black men the vote.

The Civil War resulted not only in the freeing of the slaves, but decided once and for all the supremacy of the nation over the states. Until the war, supporters of "states' rights" insisted that the federal government was simply an agent of the states, that states might nullify (ignore) federal laws they considered unconstitutional, and that states might secede from the Union. The victory of the North marked the defeat for such ideas. Furthermore, these "National Supremacy Amendments" limited state action and deprived states of powers they formerly claimed.

Of these amendments, the most important is the Fourteenth. Through its first clause, which says that a state may not "deprive any person of life, liberty, or property without due process of law," the federal courts have gained a general power to oversee state legislation. Thus a New York law that fixed a 10-hour day for employees of bakeries was declared unconstitutional; the Supreme Court said that it deprived workers of their "liberty" to make their own contracts with employers as to how long they might work (*Lochner v. New York*, 1905). A Minnesota law that set up a commission to fix railroad rates was declared unconstitutional on the ground that it deprived railroad corporations (which are "persons" under the law) of property by lowering rates. Since the late 1930's, the federal judiciary has reversed itself, however, and no longer opposes state regulatory legislation which it formerly found unconstitutional. Recently its major emphasis in interpreting the Fourteenth Amendment has been in the direction of protecting individuals from unfair trial by state courts and from violations

(*Continued on page 147.*)

EXPLANATORY NOTES

Amendment XIII. This was only the final act in freeing the slaves. Other slaves had been freed earlier by state legislation, and by Lincoln's Emancipation Proclamation of January 1, 1863 (see p. 367).

Amendment XIV, clauses 2, 3, and 4. The authors of this amendment were Radical Republicans (see p. 367.) who wanted to make sure that the South accepted defeat of the Civil War. Clauses 2, 3, and 4 are designed to penalize southern states not granting blacks the vote, to keep former Confederate leaders out of politics, to forbid payment of the Confederate debt, and to insure payment of the war debt of the Union. Southern states were obliged to ratify this amendment before their political powers, such as representation in Congress, were fully restored.

4. *Confederate Debt Declared Void.* [The validity of the public debt of the United States, authorized by law, including debts incurred for payment of pensions and bounties for services in suppressing insurrection or rebellion, shall not be questioned. But neither the United States or any State shall assume or pay any debt or obligation incurred in aid of insurrection or rebellion against the United States, or any claim for the loss or emancipation of any slave; but all such debts, obligations and claims shall be held illegal and void.]

5. *Enforcement.* [The Congress shall have power to enforce, by appropriate legislation, the provisions of this article.]

AMENDMENT XV. BLACK SUFFRAGE (1870)

1. *Blacks Made Voters.* The right of citizens of the United States to vote shall not be denied or abridged by the United States or by any State on account of race, color, or previous condition of servitude.

2. *Enforcement.* The Congress shall have power to enforce this article by appropriate legislation.

AMENDMENT XVI. INCOME TAX (1913)

Congress Given Power to Levy Income Taxes. The Congress shall have power to lay and collect taxes on incomes, from whatever source derived, without apportionment among the several States, and without regard to any census or enumeration.

AMENDMENT XVII. DIRECT ELECTION OF SENATORS (1913)

1. *Qualifications of Voters in Senatorial Elections.* The Senate of the United States shall be composed of two Senators from each State, elected by the people thereof, for six years; and each Senator shall have one vote. The electors in each State shall have the qualifications requisite for electors of the most numerous branch of the State legislatures.

2. *Vacancies; Interim Appointments.* When vacancies happen in the representation of any State in the Senate, the executive authority of such State shall issue writs of election to fill such vacancies: *Provided,* That the legislature of any State, may empower the executive thereof to make temporary appointments until the people fill the vacancies by election as the legislature may direct.

3. *Not Applied to Senators Already in Office.* [This amendment shall not be so construed as to affect the election or term of any Senator chosen before it becomes valid as part of the Constitution.]

(Continued from page 145.)

of fundamental liberties of speech and religion. In *Brown v. Board of Education* (1954), the Supreme Court declared that to segregate school children by race was a denial of "the equal protection of the laws." More recent cases under the Fourteenth Amendment have protected black rights to equality and peaceful protest against grievances.

THE PROGRESSIVE AMENDMENTS

Following passage of the three National Supremacy Amendments of 1865–1870, it was forty years before others were added to the Constitution. Then there occurred a period, 1913–1920, when four amendments were ratified within a space of seven years. These may be called the "Progressive Amendments" because they reflect the reforming spirit of the progressive move-

ment of the early twentieth century (see Chapters 21-22).

The Sixteenth, Seventeenth, Eighteenth, and Nineteenth Amendments are characteristic of their period. It was a time when there was feeling against persons of great wealth, and the Sixteenth (income tax) Amendment gave the federal government power to make them pay a larger share of taxes. It was a time when there was increasing belief that government should actively intervene to make people's lives better. By the Eighteenth (prohibition) Amendment the federal government was given power to interfere with the personal habits of American citizens. It was a time when there was widespread belief that "the cure for the evils of democracy is more democracy." The Seventeenth Amendment made the federal

(Continued on page 149.)

EXPLANATORY NOTES

Amendment XV. From the end of the period of Radical Reconstruction (see pp. 367–373) until recently, the Fifteenth Amendment, purporting to guarantee blacks the right to vote, was widely evaded throughout the former slave states. Starting in 1957, however, Congress passed successively stronger laws designed to end racial discrimination in voting rights.

Amendment XVI. The demand for this amendment went back to 1895 when the Supreme Court declared that a federal income tax was unconstitutional. Such a tax, said a majority of the Court, violated Article I, Section 9, clause 4, which states that the federal government may levy no direct tax unless in proportion to population. The only lawful way to overrule a Supreme Court decision on the Constitution is to pass an amendment.

Amendment XVII. In clause 1 of this amendment, as in Article I, Section 2, clause 1, of the original Constitution, "electors" means simply "voters."

The Seventeenth Amendment had been urged for many years before it was finally passed. It was designed not only to make the choice of senators more democratic, but also to reduce corruption and to improve state government. When choosing senators, state legislatures had been too often influenced by bribery or by political bosses. The task of electing senators was an extra burden on the states; the proper business of a legislature is to pass laws for the good of the state, not to choose federal officials.

In the latter part of Section 2, it is provided that states may empower their governors to appoint others to fill unexpired terms of senators when vacancies occur. But in the House of Representatives vacancies can only be filled by new elections (Article I, Section 2, clause 4). This difference results from the theory that the senators represented the separate states, as did the Confederation Congress, while the members of the House represented the people as a whole, the nation.

AMENDMENT XVIII. PROHIBITION (1919)

1. *No Intoxicating Beverages in United States.* [After one year from the ratification of this article the manufacture, sale, or transportation of intoxicating liquors within, the importation thereof into, or the exportation thereof from the United States and all territory subject to the jurisdiction thereof for beverage purposes is hereby prohibited.]

2. *Enforcement.* [The Congress and the several States shall have concurrent power to enforce this article by appropriate legislation.]

3. *Must Be Ratified in Seven Years.* [This article shall be inoperative unless it shall have been ratified as an amendment to the Constitution by the legislatures of the several States, as provided in the Constitution, within seven years from the date of the submission hereof to the States by the Congress.]

AMENDMENT XIX. WOMAN SUFFRAGE (1920)

1. *Women Made Voters.* The right of citizens of the United States to vote shall not be denied or abridged by the United States or by any State on account of sex.

2. *Enforcement.* Congress shall have power to enforce this article by appropriate legislation.

AMENDMENT XX. ABOLITION OF "LAME DUCK" SESSIONS (1933)

1. *Beginning of Terms of Federal Elective Officers.* The terms of the President and Vice President shall end at noon on the 20th day of January, and the terms of Senators and Representatives at noon on the 3rd day of January, of the years in which such terms would have ended if this article had not been ratified, and the terms of their successors shall then begin.

2. *Regular Congressional Sessions.* The Congress shall assemble at least once in every year, and such meeting shall begin at noon on the 3rd day of January, unless they shall by law appoint a different day.

3. *Election of President in Unusual Circumstances.* If, at the time fixed for the beginning of the term of the President, the President elect shall have died, the Vice President elect shall become President. If a President shall not have been chosen before the time fixed for the beginning of his term, or if the President elect shall have failed to qualify, then the Vice President elect shall act as President until a President shall have qualified; and the Congress may by law provide for the case wherein neither a President elect nor a Vice President elect shall have qualified, declaring who shall then act as President, or the manner in which one who is to act shall be selected, and such person shall act accordingly until a President or Vice President shall have qualified.

(Continued from page 147.)

government more democratic by declaring that senators should be elected directly by the voters. The Nineteenth Amendment gave women the right to vote.

World War I helped to promote the passages of the Eighteenth and Nineteenth Amendments. The enactment of nation-wide prohibition was aided by the fact that the American people were in a self-denying mood as a result of war sacrifices. Women's contributions to the war effort caused many who had opposed woman suffrage to change their minds and hastened the passage of the Nineteenth Amendment. The opponents of the amendment had included President Wilson, but he, too, now joined its supporters.

EXPLANATORY NOTES

Amendment XVIII. This amendment was repealed by the passage of the Twenty-first Amendment in 1933. In providing for the enforcement of this amendment, Congress in 1919 passed the Volstead Act, which defined intoxicating beverages as those having an alcoholic content of more than one half of one per cent. One reason why this amendment was widely violated was that some states, especially those with a large urban population, made little effort to aid the federal authorities in enforcing prohibition.

Amendments XVIII and XIX. These amendments marked the triumph of reform movements which had been demanding prohibition and woman suffrage for many years. The temperance movement, which started in the 1820's and 1830's, had won its first great triumph in 1851 when Maine passed a state prohibition law (see p. 289). The women's rights movement, dating from the same time, first gained full voting rights for women in four western states before 1900 (see pp. 282-283, 532).

Amendment XX. This amendment had two major purposes: (1) to abolish the "lame duck" session of Congress, and (2) to shorten the time between a President's election and his inauguration. Lame duck sessions took place every other December, after the November congressional elections. The Congress which met in December of an election year was *not* the newly elected Congress but that which had been elected over two years before. It therefore contained many "lame ducks"—members who had failed to be reelected. In order to make Congress more responsive to the will of the people, the Twentieth Amendment abolished the lame duck session and provided that Congress hold its first session soon after election.

When the Constitution first went into effect, means of transportation and communication were slow and uncertain. It was necessary to arrange for quite a long period, November to March, between the President's election and his inauguration. With the development of rapid travel and instant communication, however, such a prolonged gap between election and taking office was unnecessary. In a time of crisis it was also dangerous. Between Lincoln's election in November 1860, and his inauguration in March 1861, seven southern states left the Union and nothing was done to prevent it. Buchanan, the outgoing President, was unable to act because he had lost the confidence of the people. Lincoln, the President-elect, could take no action because he was not yet in office. Between the election of Franklin Roosevelt in November 1932, and his inauguration in March 1933, there was a similar crisis. The country was in the grip of the Great Depression, yet President Hoover could do nothing; although still in office, he had been repudiated by the electorate. Roosevelt could not act until in office.

Clauses 3 and 4 of the Twentieth Amendment provide for various situations where choice of a President or of his successor might be difficult.

4. *Provision for Death of Minority Candidates for President and Vice-President.* The Congress may by law provide for the case of the death of any of the persons from whom the House of Representatives may choose a President whenever the right of choice shall have devolved upon them, and for the case of death of any of the persons from whom the Senate may choose a Vice President whenever the right of choice shall have devolved upon them.

5. *When Amendment Goes into Effect.* [Sections 1 and 2 shall take effect on the 15th day of October following the ratification of this article.]

6. *Must Be Ratified in Seven Years.* [This article shall be inoperative unless it shall have been ratified as an amendment to the Constitution by the legislatures of three-fourths of the several States within seven years from the date of its submission.]

AMENDMENT XXI. REPEAL OF PROHIBITION (1933)

1. *Eighteenth Amendment Repealed.* The eighteenth article of amendment to the Constitution of the United States is hereby repealed.

2. *Federal Guarantee of Local "Dry" Laws.* The transportation or importation into any State, Territory, or possession of the United States for delivery or use therein of intoxicating liquors, in violation of the laws thereof, is hereby prohibited.

3. *Must be Ratified in Seven Years by State Convention.* [This article shall be inoperative unless it shall have been ratified as an amendment to the Constitution by conventions in the several States, as provided in the Constitution, within seven years from the date of the submission hereof to the States by the Congress.]

AMENDMENT XXII. LIMIT ON PRESIDENTIAL TERMS (1951)

1. *Number of Terms.* No person shall be elected to the office of the President more than twice, and no person who has held the office of President, or acted as President, for more than two years of a term to which some other person was elected President shall be elected to the office of the President more than once. But this Article shall not apply to any person holding the office of President when this Article was proposed by the Congress, and shall not prevent any person who may be holding the office of President, or acting as President, during the term within which this Article becomes operative from holding the office of President or acting as President during the remainder of such term.

2. *Must Be Ratified in Seven Years.* [This article shall be inoperative unless it shall have been ratified as an amendment to the Constitution by the legislatures of three-fourths of the several States within seven years from the date of its submission to the States by the Congress.]

AMENDMENT XXIII. VOTING IN DISTRICT OF COLUMBIA (1961)

1. *Presidential Electors for the District of Columbia.* The District constituting the seat of Government of the United States shall appoint in such manner as the Congress may direct:

LOOSE ENDS

The authors of the Constitution left some loose ends that later caused difficulty. They neglected, for instance, to grant Congress the power to acquire new territory. This caused embarrassment at the time of the Louisiana Purchase (see pp. 199–200). Another omission that later caused difficulty was that although the Senate was given power to ratify the President's appointments to office, nothing was said about whether there should be senatorial approval when the President wanted to remove someone from office. Beginning with Washington, Presidents insisted that they had the sole power of removal. For many years the senators grumbled at this without taking action. In 1867, however, Congress passed a Tenure-of-Office Act that forbade removals without senatorial approval. When President Andrew Johnson defied the law, he was impeached and came within one vote of being expelled from office (see p. 371). The Tenure-of-Office Act was repealed in 1887, and now it is agreed that Presidents need not consult the Senate before firing a subordinate official. But a century of dispute would have been averted if the Constitution had been clear in the first place.

The Twentieth Amendment attempts to tie up some loose ends by providing for various situations in which the choice of a President or his successor may be difficult. Even so, it cannot provide for every possible future contingency. To fit an eighteenth-century constitution to twentieth-century needs means constant new adaptations and new interpretation—see the discussion of the "unwritten constitution" on page 153.

EXPLANATORY NOTES

Amendment XXI, clause 3. The Twenty-first Amendment was the only one ever submitted to special ratifying conventions; all others have been ratified by state legislatures. The convention method is considered to be more democratic because the voters express their opinion of a proposed amendment in choosing the convention members.

Amendment XXII. This amendment wrote into the Constitution a custom started by Washington, Jefferson, and Madison whereby Presidents limited themselves to two terms in office. Although both Ulysses S. Grant and Theodore Roosevelt sought third terms, the precedent was not broken until Franklin D. Roosevelt was elected to a third term in 1940 and a fourth in 1944. The passage of the Twenty-second Amendment was therefore in effect a posthumous rebuke to F.D.R. It has received criticism by authorities on American politics to the effect that it is unwise for the United States to deny itself in advance the continued services of some future President of great ability after only eight years of service, when some Congress members and Supreme Court justices hold office usefully for several decades. On the other hand it serves notice that no President is to be considered indispensable.

A number of electors of President and Vice President equal to the whole number of Senators and Representatives in Congress to which the District would be entitled if it were a State, but in no event more than the least populous State; they shall be in addition to those appointed by the States, but they shall be considered, for the purposes of the election of President and Vice President, to be electors appointed by a State; and they shall meet in the District and perform such duties as provided by the twelfth article of amendment.

2. *Enforcement.* The Congress shall have power to enforce this article by appropriate legislation.

AMENDMENT XXIV. VOTER QUALIFICATIONS IN FEDERAL ELECTIONS (1964)

1. *Barring Poll Tax in Federal Elections.* The right of citizens of the United States to vote in any primary or other election for President or Vice President, for electors for President or Vice President, or for Senator or Representative in Congress, shall not be denied or abridged by the United States or any State by reason of failure to pay any poll tax or other tax.

2. *Enforcement.* The Congress shall have the power to enforce this article by appropriate legislation.

AMENDMENT XXV. PRESIDENTIAL DISABILITY AND SUCCESSION (1967)

1. *Succession of Vice President to Presidency.* In case of the removal of the President from office or of his death or resignation, the Vice President shall become President.

2. *Vacancy in office of Vice President.* Whenever there is a vacancy in the office of the Vice President, the President shall nominate a Vice President who shall take office upon confirmation by a majority vote of both houses of Congress.

3. *Vice President as Acting President.* Whenever the President transmits to the President pro tempore of the Senate and the Speaker of the House of Representatives his written declaration that he is unable to discharge the powers and duties of his office, and until he transmits to them a written declaration to the contrary, such powers and duties shall be discharged by the Vice President as Acting President.

4. *Vice President as Acting President.* Whenever the Vice President and a majority of either the principal officers of the executive departments or of such other body as Congress may by law provide, transmit to the President pro tempore of the Senate and the Speaker of the House of Representatives their written declaration that the President is unable to discharge the powers and duties of his office, the Vice President shall immediately assume the powers and duties of the office as Acting President.

THE UNWRITTEN CONSTITUTION

Containing only 7,500 words, the Constitution of the United States is remarkably brief. Most state constitutions are much longer, that of Louisiana running to 200,000 words. By its very brevity the Constitution left a great deal to be filled in later, either by legislation or by custom. This legislation and custom may be called the "Unwritten Constitution." The Unwritten Constitution includes the power of the Supreme Court to decide on the constitutionality of state and federal laws, and the practice whereby the President calls the heads of executive departments together to form an advisory body known as the cabinet. Institutions never dreamed of by the Founding Fathers have been added to the governmental system. Among these are the commissions which regulate much of the nation's economic life, such as the Interstate Commerce Commission and the National Labor Relations Board. Others include the two-party system and such institutions as primary elections and national conventions.

The Twenty-second Amendment, forbidding the President to serve more than two terms, is an example of a part of what was formerly part of the Unwritten Constitution being written into the document itself (see Explanatory Notes on p. 151).

A most important element in the Unwritten Constitution is the loyalty of Americans to the system established by the Founding Fathers. For its successful operation it demands self-discipline, patience, and tolerance. In office, a majority must be willing to try to achieve its ends without violating the rights of the minority. Out of office a minority must be willing to wait until it is able to gain its ends by peaceful victory at the polls.

The very success of the Constitution has, of course, helped to make citizens willing to practice the discipline and self-restraint necessary to make it work.

EXPLANATORY NOTES

Amendment XXIII. This grant of the vote in presidential elections goes only a short way to meet the charge that the people of the District of Columbia are second-class citizens. At one time the city of Washington had an elective mayor, but since 1874 the District has been under the direct control of Congress and elected none of its officials. In 1965 Congress rejected a proposal to give the District local self-government. In 1967 President Johnson gave day-to-day control of the city to a 9-person commission of appointed residents, and gave one of them—Walter E. Washington, a black—the title, "Mayor." But the city's taxes and budget were still under the control of Congress, and no officials are as yet elective, except the Board of Education.

Amendment XXIV. The poll tax as a condition of being registered as a voter was a way that states kept poor people, especially blacks, from the polls. Usually the poll tax was cumulative—that is, in order to get a name on the voting list a citizen had to pay all back taxes for the years since coming of voting age. Passage of Amendment XXIV was the climax of years of agitation to abolish this barrier to equal political rights.

Amendment XXV. The text of this amendment is so unusually precise and detailed that the student must read it carefully to learn how a critical constitutional problem was solved. For some of the historical background, see the Explanatory Note on Article II on p. 127.

Thereafter, when the President transmits to the President pro tempore of the Senate and the Speaker of the House of Representatives his written declaration that no inability exists, he shall resume the powers and duties of his office unless the Vice President and a majority of either the principal officers of the executive departments or of such other body as Congress may by law provide, transmit within four days to the President pro tempore of the Senate and the Speaker of the House of Representatives their written declaration that the President is unable to discharge the powers and duties of his office. Thereupon Congress shall decide the issue, assembling within 48 hours for that purpose if not in session. If the Congress, within 21 days after receipt of the latter written declaration, or, if Congress is not in session, within 21 days after Congress is required to assemble, determines by two-thirds vote of both houses that the President is unable to discharge the powers and duties of his office, the Vice President shall continue to discharge the same as Acting President; otherwise, the President shall resume the powers and duties of his office.

AMENDMENT XXVI. EIGHTEEN-YEAR-OLD VOTE (1971)

1. The right of citizens of the United States, who are eighteen years of age or older, to vote shall not be denied or abridged by the United States or by any State on account of age.

2. The Congress shall have power to enforce this article by appropriate legislation.

Activities: Chapter 5

For Mastery and Review

1. Explain briefly the meaning of these key phrases of the Constitution *at the time it was written:* (a) "We the People of the United States"; (b) "a more perfect Union"; (c) "establish Justice"; (d) "insure domestic Tranquility"; (e) "provide for the common defense"; (f) "promote the general welfare." How, in general, have the meanings of these phrases changed since 1787?

2. In parallel columns, describe the qualifications for membership, the structure, and the powers of the House of Representatives and Senate, noting similarities and differences.

3. Define "separation of powers." What was its purpose? How do "checks and balances" reinforce "separation of powers"? What are advantages and disadvantages of these features of the Constitution?

4. What powers are granted to the President by the Constitution? What powers has the President gained since the Constitution was written? Why? What method of electing the President was first used? How was this method altered by the Twelfth Amendment?

5. What powers did the Constitution grant to the federal courts? How has judicial review made the courts the guardians of the Constitution? How can court decisions be changed?

6. What relations between states are prescribed by the Constitution? Why have new types of interstate cooperation been developed in the twentieth century?

7. By what methods may the Constitution be amended?

154

8. List ten rights guaranteed to you by the Bill of Rights. How are such rights limited and defined?

9. Why have Amendments XIII, XIV, and XV been called the "National Supremacy" amendments? What change in governmental structure or power was made by each of Amendments XVI through **XXV?**

10. What change in governmental structure or power was made by each of Amendments XVI through XXV?

11. What effects will Amendment XVI have on the nation?

Who, What, and Why Important?

preamble to the Constitution	judicial review
	appellate jurisdiction
Speaker of the House	Judiciary Act of 1789
congressional privileges	statute law
filibustering	martial law
cloture	treason
interstate commerce	full faith and credit
elastic clause	eminent domain
loose construction	self-incrimination
strict construction	grand and petit juries
writ of *habeas corpus*	National Supremacy
electoral college	amendments
cabinet	Progressive amendments
supreme law of the land	"Unwritten Constitution"

To Pursue the Matter

1. Woodrow Wilson was a professor of political science before he entered politics. In Arnof, *A Sense of the Past*, pp. 77–79, you will find his analysis of the office of President, written several years before he entered the office. On the basis of the opinions he expresses here, how would you expect him to act as President? If you want the answer, look ahead in the text to Chapters 22 and 23.

2. Because of what they knew of English politics, why did the framers of the Constitution:

a) forbid bills of attainder?

b) set limits on the punishment for treason?

c) grant congressmen immunity from punishment for statements made during sessions of the legislature?

d) forbid congressmen to hold positions in the executive department?

e) limit military appropriations to two years?

f) forbid suspension of the writ of *habeas corpus,* except in extraordinary emergency?

g) provide that judges should hold office "during good behavior"?

3. Groups of students might prepare debates or panel discussions on one or more of the following proposals that have been made for changes in the Constitution:

a) that the President should be given power to veto separate items of bills. (See Bragdon *et al., Frame of Government,* p. 215, for the reason that this provision was included in the Confederate Constitution.)

b) that equal representation of states in the Senate should be abolished.

c) that the President should be elected by direct popular vote.

d) that treaties should be ratified by a simple majority of the Senate.

4. The Bill of Rights is constantly being reinterpreted in the light of present-day conditions and needs, and the courts must settle difficult questions. How do you think the following should be decided?

a) A person swallowed incriminating evidence in the presence of the police. The latter got it back by using a stomach pump. Was this an "unreasonable search" under the Fourth Amendment?

b) A child of atheist parents sat alone in a high school room while other students were given religious instruction by priests, ministers, and rabbis in the high school building, according to the desires of their parents. Was this a violation of the part of the First Amendment regarding an "establishment of religion"?

c) May an extremist be punished for attacking Quakers in an open meeting, thus causing a riot, under a Chicago ordinance forbidding speech that "stirs the public to anger (or) brings about a condition of unrest"?

d) May the federal government be forced to pay damages to a chicken farmer whose hens were severely frightened by the noise of low-flying military planes?

5. In what ways did the framers of the Confederate Constitution seek to remedy mistakes or omissions in the original document? See Bragdon *et al., Frame of Government,* pp. 200–243.

Chapter 6

The Washington Administration

The preservation of the sacred fire of liberty and the destiny of the republican model of government are justly considered, perhaps, as deeply, as finally, staked on the experiment intrusted to the hands of the American people.
—GEORGE WASHINGTON, 1789

The Confederation had come to an end, leaving behind it 70 unpaid clerks, an "army" of 672 men, and millions of dollars of debts. Before it disbanded, the Confederation Congress had arranged for elections under the new Constitution in November 1788, and for starting the new government on March 4, 1789. When March arrived, however, only a third of the senators and less than a quarter of the representatives had reached New York, the temporary capital. This delay was partly the result of bad roads and bad weather, but it was a discouraging way to have things start. "The people will forget the new government before it is born," lamented a senator from Massachusetts. It was not until April that the houses of Congress had enough members to do business. Their first action was to send word to George Washington at Mount Vernon that the electoral college had unanimously chosen him to be the first President.

THE FIRST PRESIDENT

Washington accepted the presidency unwillingly. On the day he set off for his inauguration, he confided to his diary:

About ten o'clock I bade adieu to Mt. Vernon, to private life, and to domestic felicity, and with a mind oppressed with more anxious and painful sensations than I care to express, set out for New York.

Washington's practical training had been in agriculture and military service. Because of lack of experience in government and limited knowledge of political science and history, he felt himself unfitted to be chief magistrate.

Although Washington doubted his own capacities, fellow Americans regarded him with admiration bordering on awe. No sooner had he won his first victories at Trenton and Princeton than a Philadelphia newspaper wrote of him: "If there are any spots in his character they are like the spots on the sun, only discernible through a telescope. Had he lived in the days of idolatry he would have been worshipped as a god." This hero worship continued, and it had its uses for the new government. As a visible symbol of the unity and power of the new government, Washington provided a focus for loyalty to the nation. It is not far-fetched to say that he filled a psychological void that had been left when the concept of George III was suddenly altered from that of the beloved father of his people to that of a detested tyrant.

156

In addition to the tumultuous salute in New York harbor (see page 158), Washington received a tremendous ovation at his inauguration. When he kissed the Bible after taking the oath of office, bells were rung, cannon boomed, and a great crowd shouted enthusiastic approval of their first President. The building on Wall Street where Washington was inaugurated still stands today.

As President, he was far more than a symbolic figurehead. He knew the United States as well as any person alive, having traveled in every state except Georgia and having met or exchanged letters with most of the prominent men of the country. From the time he took over the army in 1775, he had worked, as he said, to "discourage all local attachments" and to substitute "the greater name of American." Washington's mind moved with deliberation; he studied public questions with great care and reached decisions only after consulting others with differing points of view. After making a decision, he often turned over the job of expressing his ideas to men with abler pens than his own, such as Madison or Hamilton. But no one dictated his conclusions, and one of his greatest personal qualities was good judgment, both of people and of courses of action.

Although Washington's reputation is that of a man of action, and he was surely not a political philosopher, he was devoted to the principles of the American Revolution. In the course of the Revolution, for instance, he had changed his opinion of slavery. Whereas in his early life he had accepted the institution unthinkingly, he now believed that it was a terrible evil. He saw its continuance as leading to national disaster. "Not only," he wrote a British friend, "do I pray for it [the abolition of slavery] on the score of human dignity, but I can clearly foresee that nothing but the rooting out of slavery can perpetuate the existence of our union, by consolidating it in a common bond

157

of principle." In his will, Washington freed all the slaves he owned and provided that they should be educated at the expense of his estate. As the excerpt from his inaugural address at the head of this chapter reveals, Washington was one of those who thought that the American experiment in trying to found a government based on popular will was of vital importance for the whole world.

At almost every town and village on the way to New York, where he was to be inaugurated, Washington was met by cheering crowds, troops of cavalry, and addresses of welcome. When he reached the capital on April 22, he was rowed across the Hudson River on a barge built especially for the occasion, manned by thirteen harbor pilots in white uniforms. Practically the whole population of New York lined the wharves and cheered as he neared the shore. On April 30, 1789, he took the oath of office and gave the first inaugural address, an event celebrated by the ringing of church bells and the firing of cannon. The public rejoicing over Washington's taking office was fully justified. He was perhaps the only indispensable man in the history of the United States.

Administration and Finances

Even with Washington in office and Congress in session, the Constitution was still only a book of directions, and it was months before the government was really functioning. Laws had to be passed to establish the administrative departments such as the treasury and the post office. One of the most important actions taken by Congress was to pass the Judiciary Act of 1789, which filled a gap in the Constitution (see p. 129).

Once offices had been established, hundreds of men had to be found who were willing to give up their regular employment to serve as judges, tax collectors, and postmasters. In staffing the new federal government, Washington's wide acquaintance and the respect he com-

manded were invaluable, since he was able to find competent men to serve the new government. Once the executive departments were set up, Washington proved himself to be a first-rate administrator. He kept in touch with his subordinates and insisted on being consulted in all important matters, but he knew how to delegate authority and did not interfere in matters of detail. When seeking counsel on important matters, he asked the heads of departments to meet with him. Thus, the cabinet was created as it remains to this day: an advisory body with only such influence as the President gives it.

The creation of the cabinet was only one of several ways in which Washington set precedents in areas where the Constitution was silent or not clear. Thus he insisted that the Senate's power to accept or reject appointments did not extend to removal from office. Partly because the Senate refused to cooperate with him, he took the active direction of foreign affairs entirely into his own hands, leaving it to the Senate to ratify (or reject) treaties after they were made. In regard to legislation, Washington was much more than a mere executive. Both directly through messages to Congress, and indirectly through reports prepared by his Secretary of the Treasury, Alexander Hamilton, he took the initiative in urging that Congress pass laws that he thought to be in the public interest. Congress almost invariably followed his lead. So the President became what the political scientist Clinton Rossiter calls him today: "the chief legislator."

The Tariff of 1789

Finances were the most important problem facing the country. The new government had to be able to pay its way if it were to survive. Even before Washington took office, Congress had discussed taxation. All members of both houses agreed that as soon as possible the federal government should begin to collect taxes on imports.

A tariff law was not passed until July 1789. This delay was caused because certain interests wanted to make tariff duties high enough to protect them from foreign competition. Different sections wanted protection for their own products while they opposed it for goods produced elsewhere. Thus, Pennsylvania iron manufacturers had a hard time competing with Britain. But the rest of the country preferred buying cheap British iron to paying more for Pennsylvania iron. Similarly, the South wanted a high tariff on hemp, which was used in making rope, but New England was opposed because it would cost more to rig ships. New England, in turn, wanted a high tariff to protect its rum distilleries, while the South wanted to import rum direct from Jamaica.

QUESTION • When a government taxes imports, who pays?

The settlement of these intersectional differences in Congress was managed by what has since been called "logrolling." Logrolling means "I will vote for what you want, if you will vote for what I want," or sometimes "I will abandon my demands, if you will give up yours." In making the first tariff law, the second type of logrolling was followed. On the whole, the duties were set low, averaging about 8 per cent of the value of the goods. The primary purpose of the tariff was to bring in revenue.

The greater part of the money raised by federal taxation was needed to pay off the $54,000,000 owed by the United States. This debt was of two kinds: (1) about $12,000,000 owed to France and the Netherlands for loans made during and after the Revolutionary War and (2) about $42,000,000 in domestic bonds, also a result of the war. The Continental Congress, unable to tax, had borrowed from individual Americans. Also, when unable to pay off veterans and army contractors in cash, Congress had given them promises to pay in the future. In addition to the money the United States owed, there were state debts, estimated at $25,000,000.

Alexander Hamilton, Secretary of the Treasury

In the debate over federal finances, the dominating figure was Alexander Hamilton, the relatively young man whom Washington had chosen as Secretary of the Treasury. Born in the West Indies in 1757, Hamilton had shown extraordinary ability from boyhood. At the age of thirteen, he had been left in sole charge of a merchant's business. At fifteen he wrote an account of a hurricane which was considered so remarkable that a group of men raised enough money to send him to New York for further education. Hamilton entered King's College (later Columbia) in 1774, but left college to fight in the Revolutionary War. Before reaching the age of nineteen he was a captain, and before twenty-one he was a member of Washington's staff with the rank of lieutenant colonel. He later became a successful lawyer and married into the Hudson River aristocracy.

During the Confederation period, Hamilton favored the interests of the wealthy merchants and large landowners over those of the small farmers and laborers. Believing in a strong central government, he wrote many of the *Federalist* papers in support of the Constitution and was the strongest leader of the pro-ratification forces in New York. He was, however, by no means pleased with the Constitution and called it "a frail and worthless fabric" because it allowed too much power to the states and to the people.

Asked by Congress to recommend action on federal finances, Hamilton produced two "Reports on Public Credit" and a "Report on Manufactures." Not only did these become the basis for a series of laws passed in 1790 and 1791, but they had a continuing influence both in this country and abroad. Hamilton was a brilliant financier and a writer of great clarity and force.

Hamilton's Financial Program

The essentials of Hamilton's program were:

(1) *There should be sufficient revenue to meet the running expense of the government, to pay interest on the debt, and gradually to reduce the principal of the debt itself.* In addition to the tariff law already described, Hamilton proposed an excise tax on whiskey produced in the United States. In 1791 Congress passed a law establishing the whiskey tax.

(2) *The debt owed foreign nations should be paid off at once.* As long, said Hamilton, as we owed money to any foreign nation, we were not truly independent. The debts of the United States to France and the Netherlands were entirely paid back by 1796.

(3) *The domestic debt should be funded at par.* By this Hamilton meant that new federal bonds should be issued to take the place of the old, and that the amount paid back should be the original face value plus interest. This was treating the bondholders generously, because the original bonds had seldom or never been worth their face value and sometimes had gone as low as 10 cents on the dollar. Hamilton argued that in paying its debts at par, the United States would give notice to its citizens and to the world that its promises were good. Hamilton's ideas were followed out in the Funding Bill of 1790.

(4) *The federal government should take over the state debts.* Hamilton argued that since the state debts had resulted from state efforts to help the nation as a whole in the Revolution, they should be paid back by the national government. This assumption of state debts would also reduce state taxes and thus make it easier for the federal government to tax. This was accomplished by the Assumption Act of 1790.

(5) *The federal government should establish a central bank.* Hamilton proposed that there should be a federal bank on the model of the Bank of England. Such an institution would have many useful functions. Its central office

FUNCTIONS OF THE BANK OF THE UNITED STATES

BANK OF THE UNITED STATES

Aided the Federal Government
Collected taxes
Depository for government funds
Made short-term loans to it
Agent in selling its bonds

Promoted Interstate Commerce
Transferred funds from city to city by drafts
Provided a sound paper money
Increased the money in circulation

Regulated state banks
Required their bank notes to be sufficiently backed by specie
Prevented excessive lending beyond their resources

Served individual banking needs
Accepted deposits
Made loans
Transferred funds from place to place

The Bank of the United States was really a private institution, since the government owned only one-fifth of its stock. It served as an agent of government and gave the country a sound currency. It also faced strong opposition from those who considered the B.U.S. an overextension of federal power.

and branches would provide places where taxes could be paid and where the government could deposit its money. When the government needed money to tide it over a temporary deficit, it could borrow from the central bank for a short term. If it wished to borrow and pay back slowly (long-term borrowing), the bank could act as the selling agent for federal bonds.

Furthermore—and this was most important—the central bank would promote interstate commerce. It could move large sums of money for either the government or individuals. If a businessman or treasury official wanted to send funds, say, from Massachusetts to South Carolina, he would ask that money deposited in the Boston branch be paid in Charleston. The Boston branch then would issue a "transfer draft" asking the Charleston branch to deliver the amount to anyone named by the sender.

Although the authors of the Constitution hoped to establish a "hard" currency, meaning one based on gold and silver, there was an insufficient amount of these precious metals in the country. To attempt to carry on commerce with only the specie (gold and silver coin) actually minted would be like playing a poker game with too few chips. To remedy this situation, Hamilton proposed that the new bank issue bank notes. These notes, which would come into circulation when the bank loaned money, were to be limited in amount, in order to prevent anything like the runaway inflation that occurred during the Revolutionary War. As an additional safeguard, they were to be "backed" by specie. The central bank might issue notes for a greater amount than its gold or silver on hand, but there was to be enough specie on deposit so that holders of banknotes could at any time exchange them for coin. The notes of the central bank, circulating freely throughout the country, would furnish a national currency, as good in New Hampshire as in Georgia. This

would be in contrast to the situation a few years earlier when each state had its own money, as we saw on page 89.

The notes of state banks were often used to pay taxes. In receiving these state bank notes, the central bank would become the creditor of other banks. Thus it could require that state-chartered banks pay their notes in specie and curtail their loans to individuals.

The central bank was to be privately owned and managed, 80 per cent of its stock being reserved for private individuals, the federal government taking the remaining 20 per cent. But the Secretary of the Treasury had the right to investigate the management of the central bank at any time, thus providing for public control.

Congress followed Hamilton's recommendations, and in 1791 established a central bank, the Bank of the United States, with a 20-year charter and a capital of $10,000,000.

(6) *The federal government should encourage the development of home industries.* In December 1791, Hamilton sent to the House of Representatives a "Report on Manufactures." In it he argued that the federal government should encourage home industries. He maintained that increase in industry would make the country more wealthy, since capital applied to manufactures often yielded a higher return than capital invested in agriculture. Industrial growth would also encourage the immigration of skilled labor. Factories would put idle women and children to productive work. Furthermore, Hamilton argued that the United States would be neither truly independent nor safe in war until it ceased to depend on Europe for many essential goods.

Hamilton proposed a variety of measures to promote manufacturing. Bounties should be paid to producers of certain products which the country greatly needed, and premiums for goods of especially high quality. Above all, there should be higher tariffs to protect "infant industries" until they could compete with foreign producers. All import duties should be removed, however, on much-needed raw materials. Thus Hamilton proposed a tariff on gunpowder, but none at all on sulphur and saltpeter, two of its principal ingredients.

Although the "Report on Manufactures" later became one of the most influential state papers in American history, its proposals comprised the one portion of Hamilton's program that did not go through at once. Most of the American people were farmers, and a high proportion of the rest were engaged in foreign trade and shipping. Farmers feared that protection would raise the price of goods they had to buy; shippers feared it would reduce the volume of foreign trade. Congress refused to act on Hamilton's plans, and duties on imports remained low.

Hamilton's program was an immediate success in restoring the credit of the United States. In 1788, United States bonds were selling at 15 to 20 per cent of face value. By 1792 they were selling for 120 to 125 per cent, even in foreign cities such as London and Amsterdam. Eight million dollars' worth of shares in the Bank of the United States were sold to private investors in two hours.

There was another purpose in addition to sound finance behind Hamilton's policies. He believed in government by the wealthy, and distrusted the people. All his measures were designed to attract men of property to the support of the federal government, because they then would be selfishly interested in its survival. Funding the domestic debt at par put millions of dollars into the pockets of speculators who had sent agents throughout the country buying the old bonds from people ignorant of their value. The Assumption Act turned the attention of investors from the states to the federal government. The federal government received no interest on the money it deposited in the Bank of the United States, even though the B.U.S. charged interest when it lent this money to borrowers. This was one of the reasons why the B.U.S. shareholders received high returns. These annual returns averaged over 8 per cent on their investment.

Opposition to Hamilton

It was no wonder that the Hamilton program met with bitter opposition. The Funding Bill was attacked as unfair to the original holders—"the warworn soldiers" and their "widows and orphans," to quote an anti-Hamilton newspaper. The Assumption Act was opposed not merely by those states which had paid off most of their debts, but by those who did not want to see all financial power centered in the federal government.

When the bill to establish the Bank of the United States was before Congress, James Madison, then a representative from Virginia, attacked it on the ground that the federal government had no right to establish a bank. Such a power is not found among the enumerated powers of Congress (Article I, Section 8, clauses 1–17, pp. 118, 120). Nor, argued Madison, is it an "implied power" allowed by the "elastic clause" (Article I, Section 8, clause 18, p. 120). The elastic clause gives Congress such powers as are "necessary and proper" for putting its stated powers into effect.

A central bank, said Madison, might be *useful* in collecting taxes, borrowing money, and regulating interstate commerce, but it was *not necessary*. The federal government must be denied a power which was neither stated nor implied in the Constitution. The Tenth Amendment stated clearly that "the powers not delegated to the United States by the Constitution . . . are reserved to the States respectively, or to the people." If the federal government were allowed to set up the Bank of the United States,

The Old House of Representatives, painted by Samuel F. B. Morse. Sixty-five members composed the House in 1789, as contrasted with 435 today. Designed to be more responsive to the people than the Senate, it was so especially before the direct election of senators. It was in the House that Jefferson gained victory, with Hamiltonian support and after 35 ballots, in the disputed election of 1800 (see pages 185-186).

reasoned Madison, there would be no limits to federal power.

Congress passed the Bank bill by an almost two-to-one majority, but Washington hesitated to sign it. He realized that whichever way he acted—whether he signed the bill or vetoed it—he would be creating an important precedent. He asked the Attorney General, Edmund Randolph, and the Secretary of State, Thomas Jefferson, for written opinions on the constitutionality of the Bank. Both opposed it on essentially the same grounds as Madison: that it was an over-extension of federal power. Washington passed on Jefferson's and Randolph's opinions to Alexander Hamilton. Working day and night,

Hamilton composed a reply that convinced Washington that he should sign. Hamilton argued that since the purposes of the Bank were constitutional, as everyone admitted, the federal government had the right to choose any obvious means to carry out those purposes. Hamilton's communication to Washington on the Bank was a classic statement of loose construction and implied powers (see p. 123). According to a recent historian it was "perhaps the most brilliant and influential one-man effort in the long history of American constitutional law."

Gradually, there grew up a well-organized opposition to almost everything Hamilton stood

Jefferson and Hamilton: A Comparison

The opposition to Hamilton was led by Jefferson. The struggle between the two men has affected American politics ever since. Hamilton, a self-made man, distrusted the people and called democracy a "poison." He thought that people are naturally selfish, unreasonable, violent. Jefferson, born to wealth and social position, thought that if people are given the opportunity, they are naturally decent and reasonable. Hamilton believed in a highly centralized government as a means of keeping *order*. While the people must be given some share in choosing their rulers, government should be as far removed from them as possible. This in Hamilton's opinion meant strengthening the federal government and reducing the powers of the states. It also meant a strong executive department, strong courts, and a standing army.

Disagreement over the extension of federal power led Jefferson to resign from a Hamilton-dominated cabinet. Jefferson's strong actions as President, however, indicate that their conflict went deeper than the issue of state vs. federal government. Jefferson's portrait (above) is by Charles Willson Peale; John Trumbull painted Hamilton from a sculpture.

for. Where Hamilton's policies favored merchants, bankers, and speculators, his opponents spoke for the interests of the farmers and laborers. When Hamilton favored increasing the power of the federal government, his opponents sought to limit it. Whereas Hamilton's following was chiefly in the North, where shipping and commerce were centered, his opponents were strongest in the South, which was dominated by the planters, and in the frontier democracy of the West.

Jefferson, defender of human *liberty,* believed in a minimum of government, with that minimum as close to the people as possible. Therefore, he favored local government over national, and Congress over the other branches of the federal government because he thought it best reflected the popular will. He was much opposed to standing armies because he feared that a military leader might seize control of the government. Hamilton was considered a conservative, yet his policies looked forward to the time when the United States would become a great industrial nation. Jefferson was thought a radical, yet he wished to keep American society in much the same condition it was in his own day.

QUESTION • Thomas Jefferson regarded Francis Bacon, Isaac Newton, and John Locke as the three greatest men who ever lived. Alexander Hamilton admired Julius Caesar. What does this reveal about the two men?

The contrast between Hamilton and Jefferson can be overdone. Neither man was an extremist. While Hamilton despised "this thing of a republic," he worked loyally to make it a success. While Jefferson professed to fear the power of the federal government, he spent sixteen years of his life holding federal office. While Hamilton believed in a government as much like that of Great Britain as possible, he thought that those who wanted to introduce a king and nobility into America were "visionary." Jefferson believed in self-government, but he had been in France when the Paris mob looted, burned, and carried heads on pikes. He therefore favored putting political power in the hands of men with some education and property (especially in land). Finally, while Hamilton favored centralized power, he realized that state powers and state interests could not be ignored. And while Jefferson favored local government, as ambassador to France he had come to realize how much the United States had suffered because the government was despised by European nations. He therefore favored the new Constitution. Although one of the least military of men, he also favored the creation of an American navy as the best means of persuading Europe to respect our shipping.

While the two great antagonists carried on bitter and often unfair political warfare against each other, they played the game of politics within the rules that democratic government requires. They strove to win their battles by winning elections or by persuading congressmen to "vote right" rather than by resorting to violence.

THE WEST

The West presented the Washington administration several difficult problems left over from the Confederation period. It was fortunate that the President had an extensive and sympathetic knowledge of the people of the region and their difficulties. The most immediate cause for alarm was the Indian menace, to which Washington devoted most of his first message to Congress in 1789. Made bold by the weakness of the Confederation government and armed and egged on by the British and Spanish, the Indians were raiding the entire frontier, killing thousands of men, women, and children.

Once the new federal government had money to raise armies, Washington sent a force to defend the new settlements north of the Ohio River. In 1790 an expedition destroyed a few Indian villages, but suffered heavy losses. The next year General Arthur St. Clair advanced into Indian country with the largest military force the trans-Appalachian West had ever seen—2,300 regular troops, plus several companies of militia. Because of desertion and disease, the force dwindled, and it numbered no more than 1,400 when Indians ambushed

In 1795 Anthony Wayne made a treaty with Indians at Greenville, in the Ohio wilderness. By it the Indians gave up half of what became the state of Ohio.

it near Fort Wayne. Only 600 of St. Clair's command escaped, and they fled so fast that they covered nearly thirty miles in a single November day. It was the worst defeat that Indians had ever inflicted on an organized force of white men.

Finally, Washington gave the command to General Anthony Wayne, who had distinguished himself in the Revolutionary War. Wayne had little use for militia and took time to give thorough training to a force of regulars he called the American Legion. Superior discipline enabled his army to defeat a large force of Indians at the battle of Fallen Timbers in August 1794. Wayne pursued his foes to the very walls of Fort Miami, a British fur post where the Indians had been furnished weapons. In 1795 the Indians agreed to the Treaty of Greenville, whereby they gave up about half the present state of Ohio and promised to stay off the warpath. Two other treaties in the same year, the Jay Treaty with England and the Pinckney Treaty with Spain, also helped to reduce the Indian danger. By the former, England gave up the fur posts inside the United States boundaries and retreated beyond the Great Lakes. By the latter, Spain accepted the United States claim to the boundary of West Florida and agreed to stop giving military aid to Indians within the United States. (See map, p. 175.)

The Whiskey Rebellion, 1794

Washington was aware that the western settlers had been discontented in the 1780's, and he feared that they might attempt to secede. An uprising did in fact take place at the time that Wayne was defeating the Indians. Known as the Whiskey Rebellion, this was a violent protest against Hamilton's excise tax. In a day before canals and railroads, Westerners could not sell their grain in the East because the cost of transportation by wagon was prohibitive. Western grain was therefore distilled into whiskey which, with its small bulk and high value, could pay the cost of transportation. Whiskey was even used as currency in the West, where there were few gold and silver coins or bank notes.

In these circumstances, Westerners thought that the excise tax on whiskey, first levied in 1791, was aimed directly at them. There may have been some truth in this idea. Hamilton had welcomed the excise tax as a means of getting the interior of the country used to recognizing the authority of the new federal government.

Feeling against the excise tax was especially strong in western Pennsylvania, where the citizens refused to pay the tax, attacked revenue officers, and burned the barns of neighbors who informed where stills were located. They even raised a military force and defied the federal government. The Whiskey Rebellion was as plain a challenge to law and order as Shays's Rebellion eight years before. The outcome, however, was very different. Massachusetts had suppressed the Shaysites entirely by her own effort, without help from the near-bankrupt Confederation government. When the Governor of Pennsylvania hesitated to take action against the Whiskey Rebellion, the federal government stepped in and crushed it with ease. Washington called out over 12,000 militia from four states, a force so overwhelming that when it reached western Pennsylvania the "Whiskey boys" had dispersed. Some of their leaders were taken to Philadelphia for trial and two were found guilty of treason. Washington pardoned both of them. The new government, he felt, had shown itself so strong that it could afford to be merciful.

Settlement of the West

Even before the new government was organized, a great migration to the West had begun. In the spring of 1788 it was reported that 308 boats carrying 6,320 people, 2,824 horses, 515 cattle, 600 sheep, and 150 wagons had passed a single point on the Ohio River. Once the Indians had been pacified, the bluegrass meadows of Kentucky and the rich bottom lands along the rivers of Tennessee drew over 300,000 settlers into the region south of the Ohio between 1790 and 1800. With this great increase in population, Kentucky and Tennessee demanded admission to the Union. The Northwest Ordinance, which had been re-enacted by the new federal government, legally applied only to territory north of the Ohio River, but it had established the principle that new states should be admitted on terms of equality with the old. Accordingly, Kentucky became a state in 1792 and Tennessee in 1796. Meanwhile, Vermont had won her claim to independence and had been taken into the Union in 1791.

Settlers float down the Ohio River on flatboats steered by long oars as a boy fishes from the stern. Such boats took hundreds of settlers into the new territory.

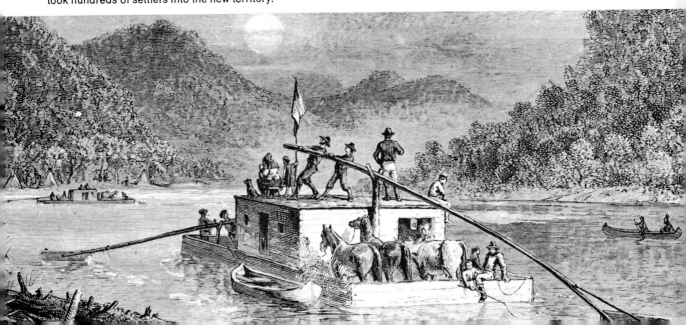

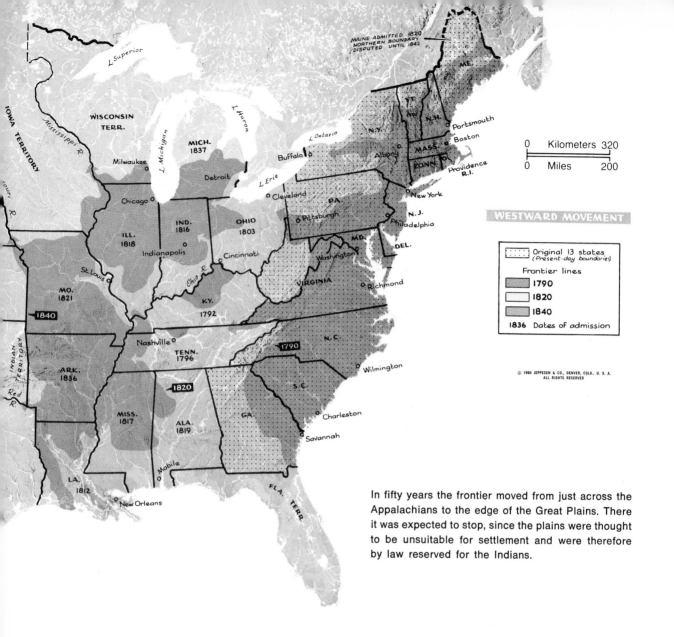

In fifty years the frontier moved from just across the Appalachians to the edge of the Great Plains. There it was expected to stop, since the plains were thought to be unsuitable for settlement and were therefore by law reserved for the Indians.

A New England migration to the Northwest Territory began in 1788, when General Rufus Putnam and 48 Massachusetts settlers came down the Ohio River on a flatboat fittingly named *The Mayflower* and established a town they called Marietta. Another center of New England settlement was the Western Reserve on Lake Erie—land which Connecticut had retained to pay off veterans of the Revolution. By 1800 the region north of the Ohio contained over 50,000 settlers. (See map, pp. 174–175.)

One reason why the Northwest Territory was settled less rapidly than Kentucky and Tennessee was the opening of western New York. For many years this fertile and accessible region was closed to white settlement by the powerful League of the Iroquois. When the majority of the Iroquois took the British side in

An Indian village in the Mississippi Valley. Note the extensive use of bark for building purposes. A council meeting may be under way in the foreground. Indians of the Mississippi region were driven entirely west of the river after the defeat of the Sauk chieftain Black Hawk in 1832.

American Museum of Natural History

the Revolutionary War, the United States sent an overwhelming military force against them and deprived them of their lands. Eventually, much of the former Iroquois territory fell into the hands of two Massachusetts speculators. These men sent agents through New England with accounts of the marvelous fertility of the Genesee Valley, where there were no rocks in the fields and farms did not "lie edgeways." Such salesmanship started a mass movement, called the "Genesee fever," which almost depopulated some New England villages. On a single winter day in 1795, five hundred sleighs full of New Englanders and their baggage were counted going westward through Albany on their way toward the Genesee.

This rapid filling in of the West had a great effect on politics. Reflecting the spirit of the frontier, the new states were more democratic than those in the East. The constitutions of Kentucky and Tennessee required no property qualifications for voting; all white men over 21 years of age had the franchise. A good frontier argument for manhood suffrage was that any man who helped to clear land and fight Indians had a right to a say in the government. The Westerners tended to throw their

weight on the side of Jefferson, who believed in the people, and against Hamilton and his followers, who distrusted them.

Nothing better revealed the effectiveness of the Washington administration than the success of its policies in the West. The Indians had been pacified; the Spanish and English had been persuaded to draw back and cease meddling; and all danger of secession had passed.

FOREIGN AFFAIRS

Shortly after Washington was inaugurated in 1789, the French Revolution began. At first all Americans sympathized with the Revolution, because the French were demanding the same rights as those won by the United States a few years earlier. The French "Declaration of the Rights of Man and the Citizen" stated that henceforth all Frenchmen were to be equal before the law, were to have the right to a fair and open trial, and were to be taxed only by their elected representatives. As has been pointed out, the French revolutionaries were fully aware of their debt to the United States (see pp. 60, 73–74).

169

In this country, popular enthusiasm for France became for a time almost a madness. Americans sang French revolutionary songs such as the "Marseillaise," erected "liberty poles" and wore "liberty caps," and even took to calling each other Citizen and Citizeness instead of Mr. and Mrs. In New York, King Street was renamed Liberty Street, and in Boston, Royal Exchange Alley became Equality Lane.

Cheers for France were often joined with damnation of Britain. Not only was the memory of the American Revolution still strong, but there was resentment because of the British refusal to give up the fur posts and to stop arming the Indians of the Northwest.

Anglo-French Hostilities Create a Difficult Situation

When war broke out between France and Great Britain in 1793, the French expected American aid. According to a literal reading of the Treaty of Alliance of 1778, they might have been justified in asking for active military assistance. They did not go that far, but they did hope to enlist soldiers and sailors in the United States and to use American ports as bases for French privateers.

QUESTION • *Did the French government have the right to expect assistance from the United States in its war against Britain?*

This placed the United States in an extremely difficult position. To be dragged into hostilities with Great Britain, whatever our sentiment for France, would have been a disaster. Three-quarters of American trade was with Britain and tariff duties on British goods provided the greater part of the revenue of the federal government. Since the British fleet controlled the seas, war would have meant a cessation of foreign trade and bankruptcy for the newly established government.

On hearing of the outbreak of the Anglo-French war, Washington called a cabinet meeting and presented a series of questions, the most pressing of which was whether the President should issue a declaration of neutrality. The cabinet members, including both Jefferson and Hamilton, thought he should, and accordingly, in April 1793, Washington issued a Proclamation of Neutrality. This declared that the conduct of the United States toward the warring powers was to be "friendly and impartial." It warned that American citizens who helped either side would be denied the protection of the government and would be subject to punishment.

The arrival of a new French minister, Citizen Edmond Genêt, put the neutrality proclamation to the test. Disembarking in South Carolina, Genêt went overland to Philadelphia, capital of the United States from 1790 to 1800. He was invited to so many dinners and pro-French celebrations that his journey was a triumphal progress. Along the way, he made arrangements to man French privateers with American crews and offered George Rogers Clark a commission in the French army. On arriving in Philadelphia, Genêt demanded that the United States advance him money to pay his new recruits.

The French minister's efforts to involve this country in war were soon checked. Washington received him with icy politeness. Hamilton, who hated the French Revolution, used all his influence against Genêt. Even Jefferson, a friend of France, lectured Genêt on international law and flatly refused his demands.

Genêt ignored the warnings issued him, went on fitting out privateers, and even threatened to appeal to the American people against Washington. Finally, our government demanded that he be recalled to France. Genêt lost his post, but he begged to remain in this country, for he feared his enemies might kill him if he

On October 18, 1794, Washington and his staff reviewed the American troops at Fort Cumberland, at a time when war with Britain seemed imminent. (A contemporary artist, A. Kemmelmeyer, portrayed the occasion.) In an effort to avert the war, Washington sent Jay to England and the Jay Treaty of 1795 resulted. Although the treaty was generally resented, Washington urged the Senate to ratify it.

went home. His request was granted. After his marriage to a daughter of Governor Clinton, he spent the rest of his life in obscurity.

Growing Tension with Great Britain

When the British realized that the new government under the Constitution was much more powerful than that under the Articles of Confederation, they at last consented to send a minister to the United States. But once the European war began, they issued a series of Orders in Council that forbade neutral ships to trade with the French West Indies, to carry any French West Indian produce, or to carry arms, munitions, or even food to France. These restrictions fell most heavily on the United States which had the largest neutral merchant marine. English warships seized hundreds of American vessels, often without serious inquiry as to their destination, and confiscated their cargoes. This was a clear violation of the rights of neutrals. Meanwhile, the British governor of Canada made a speech to a delegation of Indians from the Northwest Territory and promised them aid in driving white settlers out of the region. Public opinion was aroused to the point where Congress began preparations for a war against England. In the spring of 1794, Congress embargoed American exports for two months with the idea of hurting British commerce. Washington decided to make one last effort to keep the peace. He sent John Jay, Chief Justice of the United States, as a special envoy to London to try to settle the outstanding disputes between the United States and Great Britain.

The British were willing to sign a treaty because an American war would divert them from prosecuting hostilities with France and because the United States was their best market. Jay got rather poor terms, however, partly because Alexander Hamilton committed the serious indiscretion of letting the British know the American envoy's instructions. The so-called Jay Treaty was completed late in 1794 and presented by Washington to the Senate the next year. By it the British at last agreed to evacuate the fur posts on American soil. American ships were allowed into ports in the British Isles on the same terms as British ships in American ports. The treaty permitted a very limited trade with the British West Indies, but none at all with British ports on the mainland of North America, such as Halifax and Quebec. Some matters, notably the debts owed to British merchants from before the Revolution and losses by American ships at the hands of the British fleet, were to be submitted

John Jay, Conservative

"Those who own the country ought to govern it" was the sentiment of the Federalist party; the words were John Jay's.

Jay was surely one of the most conservative of the men who urged the revolution against Great Britain and molded the new republic into stable form. He was twenty-nine, with a substantial law practice, when he became a member of the Continental Congress in 1774. Before the Declaration of Independence, he was among the moderates who tried to check extremists such as Sam Adams and Patrick Henry. When the revolutionary movement started to roll, however, Jay supported it energetically, though the moderates gave it a relatively conservative direction. After the Constitution was written, he was responsible for five of the *Federalist* papers—on foreign affairs and the treaty-making power of the Senate— urging ratification by New York State.

A man of distinguished appearance, with a prominent nose, a strong chin, and a brow which was heightened by partial baldness, Jay was wholly self-assured. He was often suspicious of others; his lack of trust in the French minister, Vergennes, led the American commissioners to deal separately with the British in negotiating the treaty of independence in 1783.

It is unfortunate for John Jay's reputation that he is remembered chiefly as the negotiator of the unpopular Jay Treaty, in regard to which he was accused of being hoodwinked by the British. Even here he has been dealt with unfairly, and for the rest the roster of his services to his country is impressive: he was chief justice of New York, minister to Spain, Secretary for Foreign Affairs in the Confederation government (see the Jay-Gardoqui Treaty, p. 83), the first Chief Justice of the Supreme Court (1789–1795), and, at the same time, acting Secretary of State while Thomas Jefferson was in France. After negotiating the Jay Treaty, he served as governor of New York. In 1801 he went into retirement. Jay lived to be eighty-four, a Federalist and a conservative to the end.

A Republican caricature: while Washington and armed volunteers rush to keep "cannibal" French revolutionaries off America's shores, Gallatin, Citizen Genêt and Jefferson try to slow them down. The volunteers trample heedlessly on the editor of the anti-Federalist "Aurora."

to later arbitration by commissions of Americans and Englishmen. On the whole, the British gave fewer concessions than they received There was no assurance that the violation of American neutral rights by the Orders in Council would cease. Nor was there any promise that British agents would stop giving weapons to Indians living within the territory of the United States.

Outcry Against Jay Treaty

When the news of the Jay Treaty became known, there was a tremendous outcry against it. Dummies representing "the arch-traitor, Sir John Jay," were hanged, burned, and guillotined in city squares. Hamilton, speaking for the treaty in New York City, was stoned by a mob. In spite of adverse opinion, the Senate ratified the treaty by an exact two-thirds vote, 20 to 10. Washington, although dissatisfied with the terms and with British disregard of American rights, finally signed the treaty after he was presented evidence that a French agent had attempted to bribe Edmund Randolph (now Secretary of State, Jefferson having re-

signed) to work against ratification. Later there was a struggle in the House of Representatives, where opponents of the treaty, led by Madison, attempted to hold it up by refusing to vote funds necessary to put it into effect. But a growing fear that the alternative to a not wholly satisfactory treaty was war with Britain finally resulted in the House voting the necessary funds by a vote of 50 to 49.

Pinckney Treaty with Spain

Jay's treaty helped the United States to win concessions from Spain. It was so much in Britain's favor that the Spanish government suspected a secret agreement whereby Britain would support the United States in an attack on New Orleans and Florida. When Thomas Pinckney was sent to Spain to settle outstanding difficulties with the United States, the Spanish granted far more than they had been willing to concede at the time of the Jay-Gardoqui negotiations a decade earlier (see p. 83). In 1795, by the Treaty of San Lorenzo, known in this country as the Pinckney Treaty, the United States was granted two demands it had been

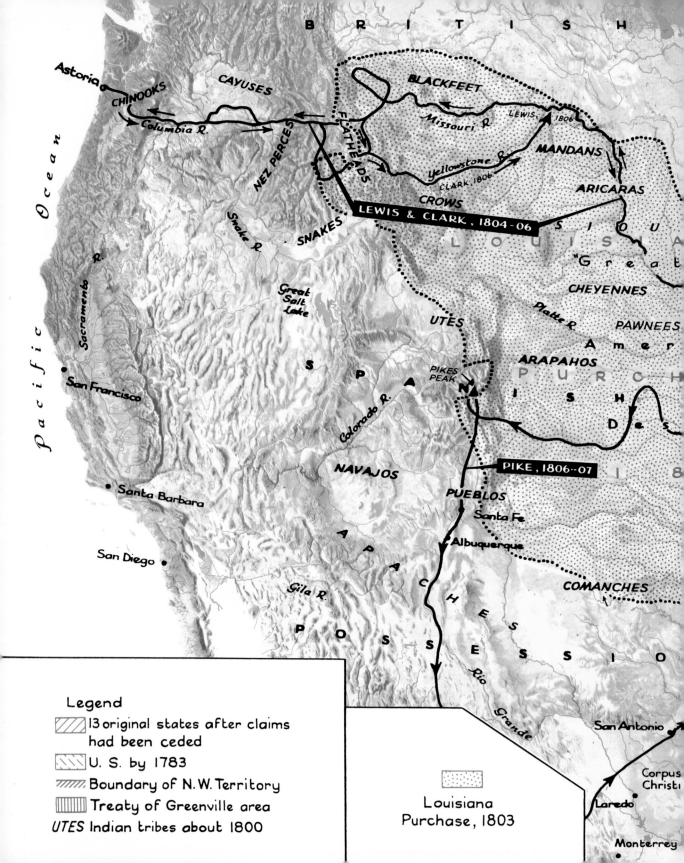

B R I T I S H

Astoria
CHINOOKS
CAYUSES
Columbia R.
NEZ PERCES
FLATHEADS
SNAKES
Snake R.
Sacramento R.

Pacific Ocean

San Francisco

Santa Barbara

San Diego

Great Salt Lake

S P A

Colorado R.

NAVAJOS

Gila R.

A P A C H E S   P O S S E S S I O

BLACKFEET
Missouri R.
LEWIS, 1806
Yellowstone R.
CLARK, 1806
CROWS
LEWIS & CLARK, 1804-06

MANDANS
ARICARAS

S I O U

L O U I S I A
Great
CHEYENNES
Platte R.
PAWNEES
Amer
ARAPAHOS
P U R C H
PIKES PEAK
N
PIKE, 1806-07
I S H   D e s
I 8
UTES

PUEBLOS
Santa Fe
Albuquerque
COMANCHES

Rio Grande

San Antonio

Corpus Christi

Laredo

Monterrey

Legend

/// 13 original states after claims had been ceded
\\\ U. S. by 1783
/// Boundary of N. W. Territory
||| Treaty of Greenville area
UTES Indian tribes about 1800

Louisiana Purchase, 1803

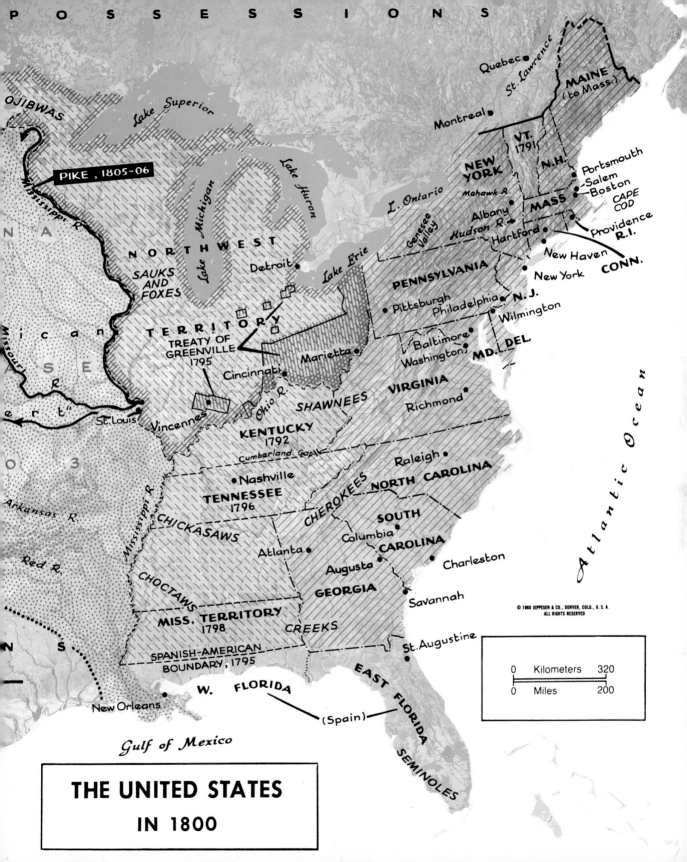

POSSESSIONS

OJIBWAS

Lake Superior

PIKE, 1805-06

Lake Huron

Lake Michigan

Quebec
St. Lawrence

Montreal

MAINE
(to Mass.)

VT.
1791

NEW
YORK

N.H.

Portsmouth
Salem
Boston
CAPE
COD

L. Ontario

Mohawk R.

Albany

MASS

Genesee
Valley

Hudson R.

Hartford

Providence
R.I.

New Haven

CONN.

N A

NORTHWEST

Detroit

Lake Erie

PENNSYLVANIA

New York

SAUKS
AND
FOXES

Pittsburgh

Philadelphia

N.J.

Wilmington

ican

Missouri R.

TERRITORY
TREATY OF
GREENVILLE
1795

Marietta

Baltimore

MD.

DEL.

SE

Cincinnati

Washington

Ohio R.

SHAWNEES

VIRGINIA

O 3

St. Louis

Vincennes

KENTUCKY
1792

Richmond

ert"

Cumberland Gap

Arkansas R.

Nashville

Raleigh

Red R.

TENNESSEE
1796

NORTH CAROLINA

CHEROKEES

Mississippi R.

CHICKASAWS

SOUTH

Columbia

N S

Atlanta

CAROLINA

Charleston

CHOCTAWS

Augusta

GEORGIA

© 1960 JEPPESEN & CO., DENVER, COLO., U.S.A.
ALL RIGHTS RESERVED

Savannah

MISS. TERRITORY
1798

CREEKS

St. Augustine

Atlantic Ocean

SPANISH-AMERICAN
BOUNDARY, 1795

EAST FLORIDA

New Orleans

W. FLORIDA

(Spain)

0   Kilometers   320

0   Miles   200

Gulf of Mexico

SEMINOLES

THE UNITED STATES

IN 1800

making ever since the end of the Revolutionary War: the right of deposit at the mouth of the Mississippi, and the establishment of the 31st parallel as the southern boundary of the United States (see map, p. 175). Each country also agreed to restrain Indian attacks against the territory of the other.

WASHINGTON STEPS DOWN

Washington had wanted to retire to private life after his first term as President, saying he would rather dig ditches than go on. He consented to run for a second term only after prominent politicians, including both Jefferson and Hamilton, urged him to do so as a patriotic duty. In 1793, as in 1789, he received no opposition vote in the electoral college. He enjoyed his second term even less than his first. Forced to choose between Hamiltonian and Jeffersonian policies, he increasingly leaned toward the former and thus opened himself to the attacks of Jeffersonian orators and newspaper editors. He was accused of trying to make himself king and of selling out to Great Britain. When he left office, the Philadelphia *Aurora,* a leading anti-administration newspaper edited by Benjamin Franklin's grandson, exulted:

If ever there was a period for rejoicing this is the moment. Every heart in unison with the freedom and happiness of the people ought to beat high with exultation that the name of Washington from this day ceases to give a currency to political iniquity and legalized corruption.

Washington was more sensitive than is generally realized. He confessed that he wished to escape attacks on him written "in such exaggerated and indecent terms as could scarce be applied to a Nero, a notorious defaulter, or even a common pickpocket."

On returning to his beloved Mount Vernon, Washington had every reason to feel proud of the achievements of the federal government

during his eight years as President. Most of the major difficulties of the Confederation period had been met successfully. As a result of Hamilton's financial program, the credit of the United States was as high as that of any nation in Europe. The easy suppression of the Whiskey Rebellion revealed the power of the new government. The major demands of the West had been fulfilled. In the difficult situation presented by war between France and Britain, Washington had steered a course which kept the United States prosperous and at peace.

Farewell Address, 1796

As the last important act of his presidency, Washington published his famous Farewell Address. After explaining that he felt he had fulfilled his duty in acting as President for two terms and therefore did not propose to serve a third, Washington went on to give advice to the young republic. The best known portion of his address is that which relates to foreign affairs. Washington warned the American people against permanent dislike of some nations and passionate affection for others. "The nation," he said, "which indulges toward an habitual hatred or an habitual fondness is in some degree a slave." Such a nation will be too quick to resent the actions of the country it dislikes, and too apt to make concessions to the country it likes.

"Europe," wrote Washington, "has a set of primary interests which to us have none or a very remote relation." The United States should therefore avoid "the insidious wiles of foreign influence" and "steer clear of permanent alliances with any portion of the foreign world." He did, however, favor temporary alliances for particular situations as well as commercial treaties to open up "the streams of trade." His advice to practice a policy that today would be called "neutralism" was directed to the particular conditions of 1796, when the Anglo-

French rivalry was a threat to the very existence of the United States. British and French agents had actually lobbied in the halls of Congress, and the treaty of alliance with France had threatened to involve us in a disastrous war with Britain. The Farewell Address also fitted into a general tradition of attempted isolation from European politics that can be traced back to the Revolution and that became the dominant note in United States foreign policy until well into the twentieth century.

The Farewell Address warned not only against permanent alliances, but against the formation of permanent political parties. Washington feared that "the baneful effects of the spirit of party" might lead to "riot and insurrection . . . foreign influence and corruption," and even to the destruction of the Union. The President was referring to the bitter struggle that had developed between the followers of Hamilton and Jefferson. The Hamiltonians had crystallized into a party called the Federalists and the opposition to Hamilton had been organized by Madison and Jefferson into a party called the Republicans. (See footnote on page 180 for different meanings of "Republican.")

Activities: Chapter 6

For Mastery and Review

1. Summarize Washington's major accomplishments in war and peace.

2. What were the main elements in Hamilton's financial program? In what ways did his measures favor the commercial classes? Why and how did his "Report on Manufactures" propose to encourage industry?

3. What were the functions and services of the federal bank that Hamilton proposed? Summarize Madison's constitutional objections to it. What arguments persuaded Washington to approve the Bank of the United States?

4. Compare Hamilton's and Jefferson's beliefs concerning politics, economics, and society. On what did they agree?

5. What troubles with Indians developed during Washington's administrations? How were these situations handled?

6. What were the causes and results of the Whiskey Rebellion? Compare it to Shays's Rebellion.

7. Describe the westward movement of settlers into (a) Kentucky and Tennessee, (b) the Northwest Territory, and (c) the Genesee Valley. What were the effects on national politics?

8. Explain Americans' early enthusiasm for the French Revolution. Why did this sentiment change?

9. What were the circumstances leading to the Jay Treaty? Its terms? The reactions to it in the United States? How did it affect the Pinckney Treaty? What were the terms of the latter?

10. Contrast the accomplishments of Washington's administrations (1789–1797) with the failures of the Confederation Congress (1781–1789).

Unrolling the Map

1. On an outline map of eastern United States, locate: the Spanish possessions and the British posts (see map, p. 85) as sources of arms for the Indians; New Orleans and the 31st parallel; the states of Vermont, Kentucky, and Tennessee, with dates of admission to the Union; western settlements such as Nashville, Cincinnati, Marietta, the Genesee Valley, and the Western Reserve.

2. Study carefully the map on pp. 174–175. What was the size of the United States at that time compared with those of the leading nations of Europe (consult a historical atlas)? What boundary of the United States had recently been settled? What factors promoted or retarded the settlement of the trans-Appalachian region?

Who, What, and Why Important?

Alexander Hamilton

Thomas Jefferson

cabinet

Judiciary Act, 1789

Tariff of 1789

excise tax

Assumption Act

Bank of the United States

Report on Manufactures

James Madison

loose construction

Anthony Wayne

Treaty of Greenville

Whiskey Rebellion

Genesee fever

Citizen Genêt

Neutrality Proclamation, 1793

Jay Treaty

Pinckney Treaty

Washington's Farewell Address

To Pursue the Matter

1. What did Hamilton and Jefferson have against each other? See Arnof, *A Sense of the Past*, pp. 85–87.

2. How did the Judiciary Act of 1789 provide for the organization and powers of the federal judiciary? What did it leave unsettled? See Bragdon *et al., Frame of Government*, pp. 161–169.

3. How did the Jay Treaty become a political football? See Allis, *Government Through Opposition*, pp. 31–55.

4. Compare the reasons for St. Clair's terrible **defeat** at the hands of the Northwest Indians with those for Anthony Wayne's later victory. See Van Every, *Ark of Empire*. Accounts of these battles would make effective class reports.

5. How can Alexander Hamilton's immense power over President Washington and over Congress be explained? See Miller, *The Federalist Era,* and Cunliffe, *The Nation Takes Shape.*

6. What qualities and practices made Washington a first-rate administrator? See White, *The Federalists.*

7. Matters for reflection, discussion, investigation:

a) Is "logrolling" a desirable practice? Can it be prevented or controlled?

b) Why did Hamilton and Jefferson not make themselves leaders of military factions and fight for control of the central government?

c) Why did some editors and political orators heap bitter and unfair abuse on Washington as President?

Chapter 7

Federalists
and Republicans

For Nature always does contrive . . .
That every boy and every gal
That's born into the world alive,
Is either a little Liberal
Or else a little Conservative.
—WILLIAM S. GILBERT

There was nothing in the Constitution of the United States to suggest rival political parties. When in his Farewell Address Washington deplored the fact that parties had arisen, he simply reflected the general feeling of the founders of the republic about them. Vice-President John Adams had said in 1792, "There is nothing I dread so much as the division of the Republic into two parties, each under its own leader." And yet political parties soon appeared in the young republic and have been a characteristic feature of American politics ever since.

THE FORMATION OF PARTIES

Throughout the revolutionary period there had been a tendency for people who differed on major issues to divide into rival groupings such as the Patriots and the Loyalists, who fought over the question of separation from Britain, or the Federalists and the Anti-Federalists, who fought over ratification of the Constitution. But these groupings broke up as soon as the issues they were connected with were settled. During the debates over Hamilton's financial program, rival combinations again appeared, and those who supported his measures gradually organized into the first American political party—the Federalists. They included not merely those who obviously benefited from Hamilton's program, such as creditors, merchants, and bondholders, but people of a generally conservative cast, such as Congregational ministers in New England, Episcopalian clergymen in the South, tidewater plantation owners, and members of the Society of the Cincinnati (an organization of former officers of the Revolutionary War). The Federalists also gained mass support from wage earners in the shipping industry, from small farmers who stood to gain from export of agricultural products, and from people in states that had benefited when the federal government assumed the state debts.

This complicated web of sentiment and self-interest was held together and given direction by Hamilton himself, assisted by prominent Federalists holding federal and state offices, by newspaper editors, preachers, and local organizations. Reflecting Hamilton's distrust of the people, the Federalist party hoped to put the direction of government into the hands of the "rich, well-born, and able." They favored a strong central government, a strong executive department, and a standing army to keep "the swinish multitude" in control. President Washington, who tried to stand above party but favored Federalist policies, became a sort of patron saint of the new party.

Gradually there developed a party opposed to the Federalists, led at first by Madison, with Jefferson as a later recruit. It found its strength chiefly among the agricultural classes—southern planters, subsistence farmers of the backcountry, and "mechanics" such as carpenters, shoemakers, and masons. None of these groups gained immediate benefit from Hamilton's measures, although they were taxed to pay for them. The people of Madison's and Jefferson's party called themselves Republicans to suggest that they were defending American self-government, freedom, and equality against the aristocratic and monarchical tendencies of the Federalists. The Republicans professed to believe in limiting the power of the central government and reducing that of the President, as well as in preserving the maximum of individual liberty.[1]

The French Revolution widened the division between the parties. The conservatives who led the Federalist party were appalled by the mob violence accompanying the revolution, as well as by its threat to property and religion. Starting by reducing the power of the Roman Catholic Church and taking away its property, the French revolutionaries went on to abandon Christianity in favor of the worship of the "Goddess of Reason." When war broke out between France and Britain, the Federalists sided with the British as defenders of stability and sanity against chaos. Furthermore, the merchants and shippers supporting the Federalists felt they would be ruined by a war with Britain, because American commerce would be driven from the seas. By pushing the federal government into bankruptcy, war would also injure those Federalists who owned 45 million dollars' worth of United States bonds.

The Republicans tended to dismiss the violence of the French Revolution as a passing phase in a great crusade for human rights. Jefferson sorrowed over French friends who were guillotined, but thought that the shedding of "a little innocent blood" might be a necessary price for the righting of ancient wrongs. If French aristocrats suffered, so had American Loyalists. The Republicans regarded the French struggle with Britain as a counterpart of the American War of Independence.

The early enthusiasm for the French Revolution caused the formation of a network of Democratic Societies, rather like the Sons of Liberty of the 1770's. They organized public demonstrations and festivals, such as the one held in Boston in January 1793. Proceedings began at daybreak with the discharge of cannon. An ox was roasted whole and dragged through the streets, accompanied by wagons containing hogsheads of rum punch and hundreds of loaves of bread. These were distributed free to the crowds. Schoolchildren received cakes stamped with the words "Liberty and Equality." Money collected from spectators bought debtors out of the city jail. There were two balloon ascensions and finally a great dinner at Faneuil Hall. The Democratic Societies did not last very long, but they organized and stirred

---

[1] The labels of the two parties may cause confusion. "Federalist" took on three different meanings in a short time. Just before the formation of the Constitution, the "federalists" were those who preferred a loose union of states, like that under the Articles of Confederation, to a "national" government. In 1787 and 1788, the "Federalists" were those who supported ratification of the Constitution, as against the "Anti-Federalists" who opposed it. Finally, in the 1790's the label was applied, as explained above, to a political party.

The Republican party of Jefferson's time is the direct ancestor of the present Democratic party. The modern Republican party was founded in 1854 (see p. 338).

The difficulties of the new nation were portrayed in the cartoons of the day. Above, the five-headed French Directory was demanding money, money, money from the American representatives (see p. 184), who replied, "Cease bawling monster, we will not give you sixpence." Left, Republican Matthew Lyon (see p. 185) and Federalist Roger Griswold involved in a brawl in Congress.

up voters who later joined the Republican party.

The party struggle, which reached a climax in the debate over ratification of the Jay Treaty, was one of great bitterness. Federalists called their opponents "filthy Jacobins" (after members of the most extreme party in France), who were bent on destroying all morality, abolishing property rights, throwing the Bible into the fire, and erecting guillotines on street corners. The Republicans called the Federalists "Tories" (after members of the reactionary party in Great Britain), who were resolved to establish an aristocracy and a monarchy and to trample on the rights of the people. "May all Tories have a perpetual itching," went one Republican toast, "and never the gratification of scratching."

The Election of 1796

As the presidential election of 1796 drew near, both sides increased their activities, since Washington had refused to run again. Jefferson was the Republican candidate for President. The Federalists put up Vice-President John Adams, who was highly respected in the country at large and had solid support from his native New England. Each party began a practice which has been followed ever since, known as "balancing the ticket." With a northern candidate for President, the Federalists nominated Thomas Pinckney of South Carolina for the vice-presidency. The Republicans balanced Jefferson, the Virginian, with Aaron Burr of New York. This first party election saw widespread abandonment of the idea that members of the electoral college should make up their own minds. Instead, each side put up its own slate of electors, pledged in advance to support its party candidates.

The election was somewhat confused by intersectional differences within the Federalist party. Some New England Federalist electors left Pinckney off their ballots in order to make sure that Adams would get the highest vote. The result was that Adams was elected President with 71 electoral votes, while Jefferson, his opponent, became Vice-President with 68 electoral votes.

In his Farewell Address, Washington had warned above all against parties formed on

This map suggests why, in his Farewell Address, Washington expressed alarm over parties based on sectional divisions. Just such a clearcut division in 1860 presaged disaster (see p. 341).

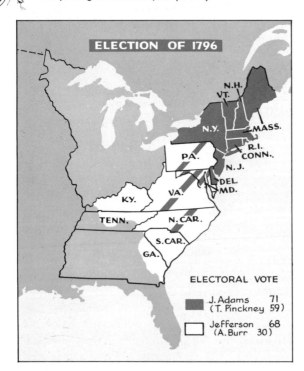

ELECTION OF 1796

ELECTORAL VOTE

J. Adams   71
(T. Pinckney 59)

Jefferson   68
(A. Burr   30)

sectional lines; the voting in 1796 seemed to justify his fears. Adams received only 2 of the 52 electoral votes of states south of the Potomac, while Jefferson received not one of the 51 votes of New York and New England. Thus was revealed the sectional division which eventually led to the Civil War.

PRESIDENT JOHN ADAMS

John Adams had spent most of his life in public service. An early leader of the revolutionary movement in Massachusetts, he was a prominent member of the First and Second Continental Congresses. Jefferson considered him the most effective speaker in favor of declaring independence. During the Revolutionary War, he was an envoy to France and Holland, as well as one of the commissioners to make peace. During the Confederation period, he acted as our first minister to Great Britain. During Washington's two terms as President, Adams served as Vice-President.

In all these positions Adams had revealed ability and honesty. He was a man of great moral courage, as he showed early in his career when he acted as lawyer for the defense of Captain Preston, who had been in command of the British troops in the Boston Massacre. A modern historian writes of this action:

Not only physical courage was here demanded, for he invited personal attack, but moral courage at its highest. He was dependent for his clientage on the Boston public and the victims of the massacre were Bostonians. He was an American and he was standing between a hated redcoat and American revenge. He gambled with his career, for he armed his enemies with ammunition, and he was charged with selling his country for an enormous fee. The fact that he received but eighteen guineas would have been the answer, but he maintained a dignified silence. There is nothing finer or more courageous in the records of any politician.

Adams was the founder of the most distinguished family in the history of American politics. His son, John Quincy Adams, also became President. A grandson, Charles Francis Adams, was United States minister to Great Britain during the Civil War. A great-grandson, Henry Adams, was one of the best American historians, and a great-great-grandson, Charles Francis Adams, served as Secretary of the Navy under President Hoover.

In spite of his talents and character, Adams was not a complete success as President. For one thing, he was too aware of his own virtues. During the Revolution he had written of himself: "At such times as this there are many dangerous things to be done which nobody else will do, and therefore I cannot help attempting them." Enemies satirized both his love of ceremony and his roly-poly figure by nicknaming him "His Rotundity." He was difficult to deal with, because compromise was foreign to his nature and because he was often as suspicious of others' motives as he was proud of his own.

Even without these handicaps, Adams's position as President would have been difficult. He kept the members of Washington's cabinet in office, and this proved to be a mistake because these men did not feel they owed their first loyalty to the new President. Although Hamilton had resigned as Secretary of the Treasury in 1795, the cabinet members were in the habit of consulting him on important matters. When Hamilton and Adams were in disagreement, as they often were, the cabinet followed the lead of their former colleague instead of that of the President.

Difficulties with France

Adams inherited the dispute with France. From the beginning of the Anglo-French war in 1793, the French, as was shown by the activities of Citizen Genêt, had expected aid from the United States. The French disappoint-

John Adams, from his portrait by Gilbert Stuart. The picture indicates why Adams was nicknamed "His Rotundity." He was a man of great courage and personal integrity. (See also page 71.)

ment following the Neutrality Proclamation of 1793 turned to active hostility after the Jay Treaty. During the election of 1796, the French minister to the United States actively campaigned against Adams. When Charles C. Pinckney was sent as minister to France in 1796, he was ordered out of the country. Meanwhile, the French navy started to prey on American shipping.

Adams was anxious to make peace; immediately after taking office he sent a three-man commission to Paris to negotiate a treaty. France was now governed by the Directory, one of the most corrupt governments in her history. When the Americans arrived, they were approached by secret agents of Charles Maurice de Talleyrand, French foreign minister, and told they would be received only if they paid bribes to the Directors. Unwilling and unable to produce the money, our commissioners broke off negotiations. When the news of this incident reached the United States, Adams sent an account to Congress, labeling Talleyrand's agents X, Y, and Z. The XYZ Affair produced an outburst of popular anger against France. Adams was cheered when he declared to Congress that he would "never send another minister to France without assurances that he will be received, respected, and honored as the representative of a great, free, powerful, and independent nation." The slogan of the day was a toast by C. C. Pinckney, one of the commissioners: "Millions for defense, but not one cent for tribute."

Undeclared War

At the beginning of his presidency, Adams had called Congress into special session to strengthen American defenses. A navy department was created. Soon fourteen warships and two hundred privateers were carrying on an undeclared naval war with France. The United States even entered into a sort of unofficial alliance with Great Britain. The British gave the American fleet their system of signals and "lent" it guns and ammunition. When Washington died in 1799, British warships flew the Union Jack at half-mast.

The war fever suited many of the leaders of the Federalist party, including Hamilton. It strengthened the power of the central government, made the Federalists popular, and discredited the pro-French Republicans. If war continued, the Federalists could count on winning the election of 1800.

Federalists who wished to use the war for partisan advantage failed to reckon with John Adams. The President absolutely refused to subordinate American foreign policy to winning re-election for himself and for his party. As soon as he had word that Talleyrand was willing to receive Amercian diplomats properly, Adams

sent to the Senate the nomination of a minister to France. Federalist senators, engaged in a debate over war preparations, were furious, but they could not long oppose an effort to make peace. Eventually, another three-man commission was sent to France, where it was honorably received. The United States demanded $20,000,000 for damages to American shipping and an end to the Treaty of Alliance of 1778. A compromise was reached in 1800 whereby the United States gave up its claim to damages while France agreed to give up the alliance. Thus the United States bought its way out of the only long-time alliance it has ever made with a single nation. Adams's action in making peace against the wishes of most of his party was an act as courageous as his defense of Captain Preston. With understandable pride, he later wrote that he wished no other inscription on his gravestone than, "Here lies John Adams who took upon himself the responsibility of the peace with France in the year 1800."

Partisan Legislation

Many Federalists had convinced themselves that prominent Republicans were actively and treasonably in league with France, and that the United States was crawling with French "apostles of sedition" who threatened, as one Federalist editor put it, "to burn all our cities and cut the throats of all our inhabitants." In 1798 the Federalist majority in Congress pushed through three laws designed to hurt the Republican party—a Naturalization Act, an Alien Act, and a Sedition Act. Many French and Irish refugees had recently come to America; being anti-British, they usually joined the Republicans. Therefore, the Naturalization Act extended the time necessary for a foreigner to become a citizen from five to fourteen years. The Alien Act reflected the almost hysterical fear of French agents who were thought to be using the Republicans as dupes. It required all foreigners

Avoid Permanent Alliances—
Stay Out of European Politics
George Washington's Farewell Address, 1796

VITAL AMERICAN DOCUMENTS

Relations with foreign countries—especially with the warring nations of Europe—brought grief to each one of the first four Presidents of the United States. In his Farewell Address (mostly written by Alexander Hamilton), George Washington faced the problem and issued a solemn warning, which American leaders tried to heed from then on. (Note, for instance, that Jefferson says much the same thing in his Inaugural Address, p. 194.) Read this excerpt from the Farewell Address and answer the questions that follow it:

Observe good faith and justice toward all nations. Cultivate peace and harmony with all. . . .

In the execution of such a plan nothing is more essential than that permanent, inveterate antipathies against particular nations and passionate attachments for others should be excluded. . . . The nation which indulges toward another an habitual hatred or an habitual fondness is in some degree a slave. It is a slave to its animosity or its affection, either of which is sufficient to lead it astray from its duty and its interest. . . .

The great rule of conduct for us in regard to foreign nations is, in extending our commercial relations, to have with them as little *political* connection as possible. So far as we have already formed engagements let them be fulfilled with perfect good faith. Here let us stop.

Europe has a set of primary interests which to us have none or a very remote relation. Hence she must be engaged in frequent controversies, the causes of which are essentially foreign to our concerns. . . .

Why quit our own to stand upon foreign ground? Why, by interweaving our destine with any part of Europe, entangle our peace and prosperity in the toils of European ambition, rivalship, interest, humor or caprice?

It is our true policy to steer clear of permanent alliances with any portion of the foreign world.

Taking care always to keep ourselves by suitable establishments on a respectable defensive posture, we may safely trust to temporary alliances for extraordinary emergencies.

•What great statement of U.S. foreign policy in 1823 reinforced Washington's advice? See pages 237-240.

•When and why did the U.S. abandon Washington's advice as to European politics and permanent alliances? See Chapter 30, "The Cold War Begins," especially references to the Truman Doctrine and NATO, pages 698-701.

•To what extent is Washington's advice still valid today?

vanians, who had expected the capital to be in their state, Philadelphia was made the capital from 1790 to 1800.

To design the new city, Washington chose Pierre L'Enfant, a Frenchman who had served in the American army during the Revolutionary War. L'Enfant's plans for a vast metropolis with great avenues radiating from key points were so ambitious and expensive, and he was so difficult to work with, that he was dismissed. L'Enfant took his maps and designs with him, but they were partly reconstructed from memory by one of his surveyors, Benjamin Banneker, a free Negro from Maryland, who was also noted as a self-taught astronomer and editor of a popular almanac.

At the time the federal government moved to Washington, the plans for a great city had not proceeded far. The President's house, with Mrs. Adams' laundry sometimes hanging in the unfinished East Room, stood in an open field with two boxlike buildings for executive offices

Benjamin Banneker, Man of Many Talents

The group meeting in Philadelphia was perplexed. A new city was to be built on the banks of the Potomac, designed expressly to be the capital of the United States. Commissioners had been named by President Washington, and they had chosen Major Pierre L'Enfant to draw the city plans. Now that irascible genius had stormed away in a rage, taking the plans with him. The Commission met to examine their plight.

Thomas Jefferson, presiding, asked for suggestions. Every eye turned to Benjamin Banneker as he stood up.

"May I ask, sir," he hesitated a little, "if the plans we had were satisfactory?"

Jefferson frowned slightly. "How can I say? I never saw them. Why?" The single word was like a pistol shot.

"Because, sir," responded Banneker evenly, "I have the plans in my head."

Benjamin Banneker was a "free Negro from Maryland," and free Negroes in the late eighteenth century faced difficult problems. American slaves had security even though the price was the absence of freedom. They knew where they stood in the social order; indeed, they had their own social lines, which placed house servant "aristocracy" above the artisan "middle class" and both above the field workers. But the free black was a displaced person, on the fringe of society.

Banneker, however, was extraordinary. Through hard work and study, he had become a skilled draftsman and surveyor. He used his brilliant mind to become a notable mathematician. His professional ability enabled him to work with Major L'Enfant, and his phenomenal memory reproduced the plans on which they had worked. From L'Enfant's plans come the immense vistas and formal design. And the often-remarked position of the Capitol, which faces away from the center of Washington, is a reminder of L'Enfant's wish that it face the rising sun.

near-by. Across a swamp over a mile away, stood the Capitol, of which only one wing was completed. There were as yet no churches, no shops, and no places of amusement. Congressmen had to live "like bears" in a few crowded boarding houses. The avenues were as yet mere muddy wagon tracks, bordered with the stumps of recently felled trees. As late as 1809, a British diplomat noted a covey of partridges within a quarter of a mile of the Capitol.

Thomas Jefferson, Scientist

If Washington, D.C., was an odd sort of capital in 1801, the first President inaugurated there was in many ways an odd sort of man to be the founder of a political party and head of a state. Thomas Jefferson hated crowds, avoided making speeches, and disliked the rough-and-tumble of politics. Like Washington, he infinitely preferred farming to public office. The Marquis de Chastellux, who met Jefferson shortly after the Revolutionary War, was amazed at finding in backcountry Virginia "an American, who without ever having quitted his own country, is at once a musician, skilled in drawing, a geometrician, an astronomer,

The Library of Congress

In its early days Washington, D. C., was an uncomfortable place. Its streets were knee-deep in mud, the government buildings were inadequate, and officials were crowded into crude boarding houses. Today the city is one of the most beautiful in the world. As this air view shows (below), it was carefully planned with circles and tree-lined boulevards. The public buildings, many with classic architectural lines, dominate the city mall from Capitol Hill to the Potomac Basin.

Monticello:
A National Shrine

One of America's hallowed shrines, Monticello (above) was the home of Jefferson. Jefferson's bedroom (right) shows his love of gadgets. On the table near the bed is an optique which Jefferson used to read maps and papers in fine print. Nearby is a combination revolving chair, work table, and chaise longue. Facing page, a view of the entrance hall shows a seven-day calendar clock operated by cannon balls on either side. As the clock ticks, the cannon balls move past the names of the days on the right-hand wall.

a natural philosopher, legislator, and statesman." Chastellux did not begin to exhaust the list of his accomplishments. Jefferson's interest in agriculture led him to import hundreds of foreign plants into this country and to send hundreds of American plants abroad. One of the foremost architects of his day, he designed not merely his own beautiful home, Monticello, in Char-lottesville, and homes for his friends, but also the Virginia Capitol and a wonderful complex of buildings for the University of Virginia. His many inventions included an improved plow, a swivel chair, and a folding buggy top. A lover of English, French, and classical literature, he collected a fine library that eventually became the nucleus of the Library of Congress.

192

Although the variety of Jefferson's interests was amazing, his life was dominated by one central theme. He was a scientist. It was fitting that he was elected president of the American Philosophical Society in 1796 and re-elected annually for nearly twenty years. He had a passion to assist in extending the boundaries of knowledge and by doing so to increase the happiness of life. His interest in government was part of his purpose: he wanted to apply organized reasoning to the problems of society in such a way as to benefit individual human beings.

In appearance and manner Jefferson had little of Washington's dignity. He deliberately tried to reduce the ceremony surrounding the office of President because he felt his predecessors had acted too much like monarchs. He walked to his inauguration instead of being drawn by a coach-and-six, and sent written messages to Congress instead of appearing before that body in person. It amazed foreigners to see him riding through the dusty streets of Washington on horseback, dressed in faded corduroy overalls, with a bag of clover seed in front of the saddle. A British diplomat described him as follows:

He was a tall man, with a very red freckled face, and gray neglected hair; his manners good-natured, frank and rather friendly, though he had somewhat of a cynical expression of countenance. He wore a blue coat, a thick gray-colored hair waistcoat, with a red underwaistcoat lapped over it, green velveteen breeches with pearl buttons, yarn stockings, and slippers down at the heels,—his appearance being very much like that of a tall, large-boned farmer.

Jefferson's Inaugural Address

Jefferson's Inaugural Address was in its day almost as famous as Washington's Farewell Address or the Declaration of Independence. In relatively few words it explained his philosophy of government.

After declaring that the task before him was beyond his talents, Jefferson asked for national harmony after the bitterness of the election of 1800. "Let us," he said, "restore to social intercourse that harmony and affection without which liberty and even life itself are but dreary things. . . . We are all Republicans," he went on, "we are all Federalists." By this he meant that in spite of their distrust of democracy, the Federalists recognized the republican principle that decisions are finally settled by the will of the people, and that in spite of their distrust of centralized power, the Republicans did not propose to destroy the federal government.

Jefferson then took up three problems still much discussed in the twentieth century:

(1) *What is to be done with those "who would wish to dissolve this Union or to change its republican form"?* Should such people be jailed, exiled, or forced to register with the police, as the Alien and Sedition acts had provided? There was genuine and widespread fear of disloyalty and foreign influence. Jefferson, however, had such a belief in human freedom and such faith in human reason that he refused to be seriously alarmed. Of those who wished to alter or destroy the Union he said, "Let them stand undisturbed as monuments of the safety with which error of opinion may be tolerated where reason is left free to combat it."

(2) *Can a government by the people be sufficiently strong to meet crises?* Many feared that because the federal government lacked a strong police system and a big standing army, it was too weak to last. Jefferson answered that he thought the government of the United States was on the contrary the strongest in the world because each citizen had a personal interest in defending it.

(3) *Can human beings be trusted to govern themselves?* Jefferson countered this question by asking who is good enough to govern someone else. "Or have we," he asked sarcastically, "found angels in the form of kings to govern him?" "King" in Jefferson's time had much the meaning that "dictator" has today.

Jefferson then went on, as thousands of speakers have done since, to describe the peculiar good fortune of Americans, isolated from "the exterminating havoc" of European wars, possessing land enough for "the thousandth and thousandth generation," nearly all professing some form of religion designed to make them honest, truthful, and friendly.

Jeffersonian Principles of Government

Jefferson described in some detail what he thought to be the right principles of "wise and frugal government." In contrast to Hamilton's idea that the federal government should actively promote banking, commerce, and industry (pp. 160–165), he expressed his belief in what economists called *laissez-faire*—"leave people alone." Government should not control the way businessmen or farmers carry on their affairs, but should simply "restrain men from injuring each other, and . . . leave them otherwise free to regulate their own pursuits." Jefferson urged the preservation of personal freedom and the rights of the states. He asked that all accept the decisions of the majority or face the prospect of civil war. He proposed to reduce the regular army to an absolute minimum and to trust the militia to defend the country. This was partly an economy measure designed to reduce taxes, but even more it reflected the fear that a strong army was a threat to popular liberty.

Jefferson followed completely in Washington's footsteps in his definition of the foreign policy of the United States; he advocated "honest friendship with all nations, entangling alliances with none."

While expressing his belief in democracy and individual freedom, Jefferson said much that made the Federalists breathe easier. He proposed "the preservation of the General Government in its whole constitutional vigor," which surely did not suggest the idea of nullification presented in the Kentucky and Virginia resolutions of 1798 and 1799. He spoke of "the honest payment of our debts." This was a great relief to owners of federal bonds who feared that as an opponent of Hamilton's financial policies Jefferson would prevent repayment to the bond-holders.

THE REPUBLICANS IN OFFICE

Jefferson liked to speak of his election to the presidency in 1800 as a "revolution." It was perhaps a revolution in the sense that men who distrusted democracy were replaced by those who believed in it, but it was surely one of the mildest revolutions in all history. Not only was there no violence, but surprisingly little Federalist legislation was repealed. The Alien and Sedition acts had already run out and were not renewed; the period necessary for naturalization was reduced from fourteen years to five. The excise tax on whiskey was abolished. The major features, however, of Hamilton's financial program remained untouched: the Bank of the United States, the Funding Act, and the assumption of state debts. Jefferson hoped to do away with the federal debt not by canceling it but by paying it off rapidly. The money to do this was found by practicing the strictest economy in government. The regular army was reduced to 3,000 men, and it was proposed to put almost the entire navy in dry dock.

Once in control of the federal administration, the Republican leaders found that their new role of being in power instead of in opposition pushed them toward modifying or even violating some of their previously expressed principles of government. Jefferson, for instance, professed to fear executive power, and in his Inaugural Address hinted that he would allow Congress to guide policy. He reduced the symbolic dignity of the presidency. He made gestures toward giving Congress more detailed control of the executive departments, but he soon found that if he did not give leadership, his party would break into factions. He therefore used his position as party leader to influence congressional legislation. By consultation with Republican leaders in Congress, and by

seeing that his supporters gained key positions, Jefferson became just as much "chief legislator" as Washington had been. Similarly, Jefferson professed to fear extension of the power of the federal government, but, as the next chapter will show, when he felt he had to choose between the welfare of the nation and his principles, he chose the former. Thus he illustrated the fact that the "outs" tend to be strict constructionists, because they want to prevent action by their opponents who control the federal government, while the "ins" are apt to be loose constructionists, because they are in power and wish to act.

Attack on the Federal Judiciary

The congressional elections of 1800 gave the Republicans safe majorities in both the House and Senate, and they were thus in a position to repeal any Federalist legislation they disliked. But the only point at which they made a major attempt to undo the work of their predecessors was in trying to reduce the power of the federal judiciary and to drive some judges from office. The Republicans feared the judiciary for a number of reasons: (1) Federal judges, holding their positions "during good behavior" (which meant for life), were beyond the control of the people. (2) The federal courts had declared several state laws unconstitutional and so were a means of strengthening the power of the federal government and reducing that of the states. (3) During their last month in office, the Federalists had "packed" the judiciary. They increased the number of federal judges by the Judiciary Act of 1801, and Adams promptly filled 67 positions with members of his party. These new judges were known as "midnight judges," because the story went that Adams signed appointments until midnight of his last day in office.

One of the first acts of Congress after Jefferson came into office was to repeal the Judiciary Act of 1801. After doing away with the "midnight judges" by abolishing their offices, the victorious Republicans went on to try to remove other Federalists from the judiciary by impeachment. In 1804 a Federalist district judge, John Pickering, was impeached by the House and convicted by the Senate for actions that indicated that he had gone insane. The House then impeached Justice Samuel Chase of the Supreme Court. Chase had attacked democracy in general and Jefferson in particular while addressing a Baltimore jury. The Senate, however, refused to convict Chase because it was not convinced that he had been proved guilty of "treason, bribery, or other high crimes and misdemeanors." (See Article II, Section 4, p. 128.) The failure to remove Chase reduced the use of impeachment in the future to serious wrongdoing. Only once again, in the case of President Andrew Johnson in 1868, was it used simply as a political weapon.

John Marshall and Judicial Review

In 1801, shortly before leaving office, President Adams appointed John Marshall as Chief Justice of the United States. Marshall was an ardent Federalist and detested his cousin and fellow-Virginian, Thomas Jefferson. In one of the first cases to come before him, *Marbury v. Madison* (1803), Marshall claimed for the federal judiciary the power of judicial review of acts of Congress. In his opinion, Marshall declared illegal a portion of the Judiciary Act of 1789, by which Congress first set up the federal courts. He argued that since the courts exist to enforce the law, and since the Constitution is "the supreme law of the land" (see Article 6, clause 2, p. 134), it is for federal judges to decide, when cases come before them, whether or not laws passed by Congress are constitutional. This decision greatly angered the Republicans because it gave a veto on federal laws to judges who were neither chosen by the people directly nor made accountable to them by periodic elections. It was in fact not the first

time that the federal judiciary had declared federal laws unconstitutional, and judicial review of state legislation had been established in the Judiciary Act of 1789, but *Marbury v. Madison* was in the long run of immense importance. The relentless logic with which Marshall showed that the federal courts *must* interpret the Constitution in order to obey it impressed itself on men's minds. The power of the federal judiciary, and especially of the Supreme Court, to exercise the great power of judicial review became as much a fact as the President's veto. In only two other countries, West Germany and Japan, does the judiciary exert such unrestricted power.

Jefferson's Re-election, 1804

Jefferson's first term was a success. "The vessel in which we are all embarked amidst the conflicting elements of a troubled world," as he metaphorically called the federal government in his Inaugural Address, had been successfully steered on a new course. The national honor had been redeemed by the Tripolitan War, and the national domain increased by the Louisiana Purchase, both of which will be described in Chapter 8. War had broken out in Europe, but its first effect in this country was only to increase foreign trade and to enrich shipowners. Although taxes had been reduced, the income of the federal government from the tariff was sufficient not merely to pay running expenses but also to reduce the national debt. This good management and good fortune resulted in a great Republican victory when Jefferson ran for a second term in 1804. He received 162 out of 176 electoral votes, carrying every state except Connecticut and Delaware. Only Washington before him, and James Monroe in 1820, Franklin D. Roosevelt in 1936, Lyndon Johnson in 1964, and Richard Nixon in 1972, gained such overwhelming triumphs. Jefferson's second term was to be far less successful than his first.

Activities: Chapter 7

For Mastery and Review

1. Explain the three different political meanings of "Federalist."

2. Compare the Federalist and Republican parties with regard to (a) leaders and candidates, (b) purposes and principles, (c) social groups from which each drew, (d) economic programs, and (e) other differences. Parallel columns might help here.

3. Summarize relations between the United States and France during Adams's administration.

4. What were the terms of the Alien and Sedition Acts? Why were they passed? What were the reactions to them?

5. Describe the presidential campaign of 1800. Why did the Republicans win? Why was the election decided in the House of Representatives?

6. Summarize the major ideas of Jefferson's First Inaugural Address. Why did he say, "We are all Republicans; we are all Federalists"? Why did he think a republic is a strong form of government? What did he want done with those who would change the form of government? What foreign policy did he advocate? How would he have divided governmental powers between the states and the central government?

7. What were the major accomplishments of the Federalist party? Why did it lose power? What parts of the Federalists' program were retained by the Republicans? What parts were changed? For what reasons did the Republicans attack the federal judiciary?

8. Outline the decision given in the case of *Marbury v. Madison* and the importance of that decision to American history.

Unrolling the Map

1. Study the election maps of 1796 and 1800 (pp. 182, 187). What differences do you see? How do you account for the differences?

2. Prepare a display of the city of Washington. Include a map showing the location of the District of Columbia.

Who, What, and Why Important?

Federalists
Republicans
French Revolution
Thomas Jefferson
John Adams
Aaron Burr
XYZ Affair
Naturalization Act
Alien and Sedition acts

Virginia and Kentucky
   Resolutions
Twelfth Amendment
Major L'Enfant
Benjamin Banneker
laissez-faire
"midnight judges"
John Marshall
Marbury v. Madison

To Pursue the Matter

1. How close did Aaron Burr come to being elected President? See Arnof, *A Sense of the Past*, pp. 102–105, and/or Allis, *Government Through Opposition: Party Politics in the 1890's*, pp. 79–81.

2. What were the actual effects of the Alien and Sedition acts? Did their enforcement cause a "reign of terror," as the Republicans insisted? See Miller, *The Federalist Era, 1789–1801*.

3. For reflection, discussion, investigation:

a) If the capital of the United States were to be relocated today, where should it be placed? Should it be created out of nothing, as was Washington, D.C., or should it be placed in an existing city? For a contemporary example of a country's building a capital from scratch, see Peterson, *Latin America*, pp. 88–89.

b) "The major American political parties have tended to be bundles of local interests, loosely tied together for the purpose of winning elections." To what extent does this statement apply to the two major parties today?

4. By what means did Jefferson exercise control over Congress? See Cunningham, *The Jeffersonian Republicans in Power: Party Operations, 1801–1809*.

5. Thomas Jefferson considered David Rittenhouse, builder of the famous orrery (see p. 92), one of the three greatest Americans, along with Washington and Franklin. Why? See Boorstin, *The Lost World of Thomas Jefferson*.

Chapter 8

Foreign Entanglements

If you wish to avoid future collision,
you had better abandon the ocean.
——HENRY CLAY, 1812

Jefferson hoped that "nature and a wide ocean" would keep the United States entirely isolated from European rivalries. "Peace," he wrote to an English friend, "is our passion." As has been seen, he proposed to lay up the navy and to trust the defense of the United States to militia instead of a standing army. Unarmed isolation, however, proved impossible.

TROUBLE WITH TRIPOLI

The first threat to peace came not from one of the great powers of Europe, but from Tripoli, a small country on the north coast of Africa. Piracy was a principal business of Tripoli and the other Barbary Coast states of Morocco, Algiers, and Tunis. The ships of countries not paying them tribute were subject to capture and their crews to enslavement. In the Confederation period, American shipping had been driven from the Mediterranean because the United States lacked money to pay tribute. During the Federalist period, however, the United States treasury could afford the demands of the Barbary pirates. Between 1789 and 1801 the United States paid over $2,000,000 in "protection" for our ships. At the time of the XYZ Affair, when Americans were cheering the

toast, "Millions for defense, but not one cent for tribute!" a United States warship carried twenty-six barrels of silver dollars to Algiers.

Thinking the United States as weak as it was distant, the Barbary Coast states increased their demands. In 1801, just two months after Jefferson's inauguration, the ruler of Tripoli cut down the flagpole of the American consulate in his capital to show his dissatisfaction with the amount of American tribute.

Although peace might have been Jefferson's passion, he did not propose that the United States should be perpetually subject to organized robbery. He therefore carried on a four-year war with Tripoli. Eventually the commander of the American naval force in the Mediterranean had fourteen ships under his command. In Egypt an American consul, William Eaton, organized a small force of Americans, Greeks, Arabs, and Tripolitans. Crossing 500 miles of the desolate Sahara, he invaded Tripoli and captured a strong fortress. The ruler of Tripoli then made peace on payment of $60,000 ransom for American sailors captured in the course of the war. The vigor of the American forces for a time discouraged the other Barbary Coast states from asking additional tribute. In 1807 Jefferson withdrew the American naval squadron from the Mediterranean and attacks on American shipping were resumed. The piracy of the Barbary states did not end until 1815, when an American flotilla under Stephen Decatur, joined by warships of European nations, once and for all put an end to the nuisance.

Although the Tripolitan War thus was not, as is sometimes thought, especially decisive, it did save the American navy from being disbanded and gave American officers training which proved valuable in the War of 1812. The war also revealed the power of the President. There was never a congressional declaration of war. Jefferson as commander in chief simply ordered American ships to the Mediterranean to defend American interests.

THE LOUISIANA PURCHASE, 1803

A far more serious threat to the United States than any possible demands of the Barbary pirates came with the news that in 1800 Spain had secretly ceded Louisiana, including New Orleans, back to France. The French were now ruled by Napoleon Bonaparte, whose devotion to conquest and war kept Europe in turmoil for many years. Napoleon made France stronger in Europe than ever before, and he intended to create a new French empire in America.

The prospect of seeing New Orleans taken over by French officials and garrisoned with French troops greatly alarmed Jefferson. Although regarded as a friend of France, he wrote Robert Livingston, our minister in Paris, as follows:

There is on the globe one single spot, the possessor of which is our national and habitual enemy. It is New Orleans, through which the produce of three-eighths of our territory must pass to market.

If France took possession of New Orleans, wrote Jefferson, "we must marry ourselves to the British fleet and nation." Thus, to keep a strong power from controlling the mouth of the Mississippi, Jefferson was willing to abandon his opposition to "entangling alliances." Before tying up with Britain, he authorized Livingston to offer France $10,000,000 for New Orleans and West Florida, and sent James Monroe as a special envoy to Paris to help put across the purchase.

It is unlikely that American arguments, threats, or dollars would have moved Napoleon if his plans for a French empire had not suffered a terrible defeat. The most valuable of the French colonies in the Americas was Sainte Domingue (later called Haiti). In the eighteenth century its exports of sugar, indigo, coffee, and cotton almost equaled in value those of the entire thirteen colonies. In 1791 its half-million Negro slaves, inspired by the French Revolution, threw off the yoke of their white masters. Under the leadership of a remarkable general, Pierre Toussaint L'Ouverture, "the black Napoleon," the Haitian Negroes attempted to make their island an independent state.

In 1801 Napoleon sent an army under his brother-in-law, General Charles LeClerc, to subdue the Haitians. Toussaint L'Ouverture organized such effective resistance, however, that the French expedition failed, although he himself was captured. The warfare and yellow fever killed 50,000 French troops, including LeClerc himself. The disaster was so complete that Napoleon was induced to abandon his American ambitions completely.

Meanwhile, Livingston for many months had been urging the French to sell New Orleans. One day in April 1803, Talleyrand, French foreign minister, astounded him by asking how much the United States would give for the whole of Louisiana. At just this time Livingston was joined by Monroe, and it took only a few days to reach an agreement by which the United States was to pay about $15,000,000 for a region which would double the size of the United States.

Was the Purchase Constitutional?

When news of French willingness to sell this vast territory reached the United States, Jefferson was torn between joy over a magnificent bargain and worry over the constitutional powers of the federal government. Although the right to acquire new territory is nowhere stated in the Constitution, Jefferson had already convinced himself that the federal government possessed such a power. What really worried him was a provision in the Louisiana Purchase treaty which stated that Louisiana was to be "incorporated into the Union" and its inhabitants were to become citizens of the United States. If the treaty were carried out, it meant that the executive department, with the consent of the Senate, assumed the right to admit aliens to citizenship. Yet under the Constitution the powers of admitting new states and naturalizing foreigners were clearly reserved to Congress.

Jefferson urged a constitutional amendment to remove any doubts about the legality of the Louisiana Purchase treaty. His followers in the cabinet and Congress pointed out that time was pressing and that Napoleon might change his mind. Waiting for the slow processes of a constitutional amendment might lose Louisiana altogether. Jefferson therefore agreed to submit the treaty to the Senate. His strict-constructionist principles were thus sacrificed to the immense benefits which the Louisiana Purchase brought to the farmers of the West by acquiring the mouth of the Mississippi, and to the whole nation by averting difficulties with France.

The Senate approved the greatest real estate bargain in history in October 1803, and Amer-ican officials took over from the French in December. Just what territory the United States had acquired was still, however, not clear. Did the purchase include "West Florida" (see map, p. 175)? Did it include Texas? No one knew for sure. These uncertainties were likely to cause difficulty later. None could doubt the tremendous significance of the Louisiana Purchase in spite of its vague boundaries. The annexation of this vast area made the United States master of one of the largest and most fertile river valleys in the world. There could no longer be much doubt that, if it could remain united, the United States would dominate North America and expand to the Pacific. (See U.S. in 1850, pp. 320–321.)

QUESTION • *Suppose Jefferson had refused to buy Louisiana. Would it have reverted to Spain? Become a new French empire? Been captured by the British and added to Canada? Later have been acquired by the United States?*

Exploratory Expeditions, 1804–1806

Very little was known about the area west of the Mississippi, and it excited Jefferson's curiosity. The first scientific project to receive federal funds was the expedition sent up the Missouri River under Meriwether Lewis and William Clark, officers in the United States Army. Jefferson himself drew up their instructions. He told them to find the sources of the Missouri, to try to find a practicable route across the Rockies to the Pacific, to observe the customs of the Indians they met, and to make detailed zoological, mineralogical, geological, and meteorological observations. The expedition, numbering 29 "robust healthy hardy young men," as Clark described them, started from St. Louis in May 1804, in three boats. They returned over two years later with their mission accomplished, having surmounted hardships ranging from "ticks and musquiters" to near-starvation, floods, attacks by Indians, and pursuit by immense grizzly bears as yet unafraid of man. Amazingly, only one man was lost, and he through a sudden attack of illness that was probably appendicitis. The expedition added immensely to the knowledge of the vast area it traversed, and it helped the United States to lay claim to the region beyond the Rockies known as Oregon.

In 1805 another expedition, under Lieutenant Zebulon M. Pike, was sent up the Mississippi to seek its source. Although he failed to find the exact spot where the great river began, Pike made good maps and brought back valuable information. The next year he journeyed westward across the Great Plains to the Rockies, within sight of the great peak that bears his name. When he ventured southward toward Santa Fe, he was captured and for a time held prisoner by the Spanish, who feared he was a spy, but was later freed.

INTERNAL DISSENSIONS

Jefferson's great majority in the election of 1804 might seem to show that the United States was becoming completely united. But two plots, in both of which Aaron Burr was implicated, revealed that the federal union was still in danger of breaking apart.

The Louisiana Purchase drove some New England Federalists to plan for secession of the northeastern states. They feared that the expansion of the West would submerge New England as a force in politics and would subordinate its commercial interests to the agricultural interests of the South and West. "The people of the East," said a prominent Federalist, "cannot reconcile their habits, views, and interests with those of the South and West."

It was felt essential that New York should join the new federation. The plotters found a tool in Aaron Burr, who was willing to desert

Missouri Historical Society

William Clark's journal of the expedition he and Meriwether Lewis led to the Pacific contained careful descriptions of flora and fauna. Hence his drawing of a Pacific salmon caught in the Columbia River.

the Republican party and run for governor of New York as Federalist candidate in 1804. Once elected, he apparently hoped to detach his state from the Union.

Burr's plans were thwarted in part by Alexander Hamilton, who in 1800 had helped to prevent his being elected President over Jefferson. Some of Hamilton's criticisms of Burr were quoted in an Albany newspaper and had a wide circulation. Burr demanded that Hamilton either back up or deny what he had said, putting his demands in such a form that they might be regarded as a challenge to a duel.

Aaron Burr, whose character is still a matter of dispute among historians, narrowly missed both election to the presidency and conviction for treason. The portrait above was done in 1809.

It is strange that Hamilton should have finally agreed to fight. He had a wife and several young children; he was burdened with debts; and his eldest son had recently been killed in a duel. Apparently, he believed he must observe the code of military men of the day so that he might later be available for command. He foresaw a situation in which he might be needed as an American Napoleon to suppress an uprising of the people and restore order.

Early on a July morning in 1804, Hamilton, Burr, their seconds, and a physician rowed across the Hudson to a little shelf of rock at the foot of the Palisades. At the signal to fire Burr, an excellent shot, sent a bullet into Hamilton's body. Hamilton died the next day. Thus he went to his death in part because he had tried to protect the Union from dismemberment and in part because he lacked faith in government by the people. When a New York coroner's jury indicted Burr for murder, he slipped out of New York, but this was not the end of his troubles.

Burr's Conspiracy, 1805–1806

In 1805 and 1806, Burr was in the West arranging a conspiracy of which the details are even now obscure. He tried to draw a number of influential men into his schemes, as partners or as dupes. These included a senator from Ohio, the British and Spanish ministers to the United States, the commander of the federal troops in the West, and leaders of the former French colony in New Orleans. Sometimes Burr talked of secession of the western states, sometimes of the conquest of Mexico (with himself as emperor). He collected arms, bought flatboats on the Ohio, and floated down toward New Orleans with fifty or sixty men. His movements became so widely known, however, that the federal government had ample time to prepare for anything he might do. Eventually, Burr fled in disguise, but he was caught and taken to Richmond to face trial for treason before Chief Justice Marshall.

At the trial Marshall followed the letter of the Constitution in protecting the rights of a person accused of treason. The Chief Justice insisted that the prosecution produce two witnesses to an "overt act" on Burr's part (see Article III, Section 3, p. 130). Since Burr had had little chance to do more than talk, and since there were no trustworthy witnesses against him, he was acquitted. He went into exile for four years and then returned to New York.

CONFLICTS WITH THE INDIANS

During Jefferson's administration and that of James Madison which followed it, the ever-advancing white settlers, hunters, and land speculators pressed hard on the Indians. Jefferson favored a policy of forcing the Indians from east of the Mississippi and settling them in unoccupied lands in the Louisiana Territory. He insisted that the Chickasaws and Cherokees give up their lands in what is now Alabama and Georgia and move to what is now Arkansas. North of the Ohio, the Treaty of Greenville had not satisfied the whites' desire for land. By persuasion, force, and fraud, Indian chiefs were induced to give up more and more land. In spite of solemn treaty promises that were to run "as long as the sun shall climb the heavens or the waters shall run in the streams," whites persisted in hunting in areas reserved for Indians, thus destroying their principal source of livelihood. Mere contact with white people degraded the Indians. William Henry Harrison, long governor of the Northwest Territory, wrote as follows:

I can tell at once upon looking at an Indian whom I may chance to meet, whether he belongs to a neighboring or more distant tribe. The latter is generally well-clothed, healthy, and vigorous; the former half-naked, filthy, and enfeebled by intoxication.

Harrison, who has been described as "the most talented American at depriving the Indians from their ancestral lands," wrote fifteen treaties whereby Indians gave up nearly all of modern Indiana and Illinois, plus other territories.

At this time of crisis for the Indians, there appeared a remarkable leader, Tecumseh, chief of the Shawnees. He hoped to unite all the tribes, north and south, into a great federation to resist the ever-encroaching whites. He and his brother persuaded his people to avoid alcohol and to refrain from fighting white people except in self-defense. He went to Harrison and urged that the United States give up some recently "purchased" territory on the ground that the chiefs who signed the treaty had no authority. Harrison replied that only the President of the United States could comply with the request. Tecumseh answered:

Well, as the great chief is to decide the matter, I hope the Great Spirit will put sense enough into his head to induce him to give up this land. It is true, he is so far off he will not be injured by the war; he may sit still in his town and drink his wine, while you and I will have to fight it out.

This prediction came true. In 1811 Harrison started a preventive war against Tecumseh's followers at a time when he knew the great Indian leader was absent. Invading the Indian lands, he fought a rather inconclusive battle at Tippecanoe in modern Indiana. The Indian braves were armed with guns received from British fur traders. Westerners believed that Tecumseh was a hired British agent, and that the British government egged on the Indians and paid them handsomely for the scalps of white settlers.

DEFENDING AMERICAN NEUTRAL RIGHTS AT SEA

Jefferson's presidency saw a renewal of war in Europe. In 1803 Great Britain and France went to war, after a truce of less than two years. Again the United States as the neutral nation possessing the largest merchant marine benefited greatly because of the wartime demand for goods. As in the period from 1793 to 1801, the warring countries again violated American rights.

In 1805 Napoleon won the great battle of Austerlitz, which made him master of most of western Europe. In the same year, Admiral Horatio Nelson's victory at Trafalgar gave Great Britain undisputed command of the sea. Thus the war became one "between the tiger and the shark." Unable to strike directly at Great Britain, Napoleon resolved to ruin the trade of "the nation of shopkeepers." By the Berlin and Milan Decrees in 1806 and 1807, the emperor forbade any country under his control to import British goods or to allow British ships to enter its harbors. Neutral ships bringing British goods, stopping at British ports, or even submitting to search by British naval vessels were to be confiscated.

Great Britain answered the Napoleonic decrees by Orders in Council directed especially at the United States. British traders were already alarmed by the great increase in the American merchant marine. If American ships now took over the trade with Europe forbidden to the British by the French decrees, the United States might displace Britain as the greatest trading nation in the world. Therefore, Orders in Council of 1807 forbade neutral ships to trade with Europe unless they stopped in England first, and in any case to carry no products of the French colonies and nothing of military value.

American Shipping in Difficulties

If thoroughly enforced, the Napoleonic decrees and the Orders in Council might have put

Tecumseh, the Great Shawnee

History is too often written by the winners, about the successful. The United States, however, sometimes honors the greatness of a loser and a failure. Such was Tecumseh, chief of the Shawnees.

A tall, handsome man, with proud bearing, Tecumseh had little reason to feel friendly toward the whites—his father had been brutally murdered by frontiersmen—but he sternly opposed the savagery of Indian retaliation against white captives.

Learning English from the daughter of a pioneer farmer, he tried to understand Americans in order to deal with them. Someone had to deal with them: white settlers were flooding into the Old Northwest. Tecumseh tried to stop them by uniting the Indian tribes into a single, strong nation. Traveling constantly, he spoke eloquently at tribal meetings from Florida to Michigan and west to Iowa. Young braves, anxious for adventure, shouted approval, but the older leaders shook their heads. Not for them any union with old enemies!

Tecumseh's greatest wrath fell on the common white practice of "lickering up" the Indians and persuading them to sign treaties ceding tribal lands. In conference with General William Henry Harrison, he challenged the rights of a drunken chief: "Sell a country? Why not sell the air, the clouds and the great sea as well as the earth? Did not the Great Spirit make them all for the use of his children?"

Alarmed at Tecumseh's activities, General Harrison wiped out the town of the Prophet, Tecumseh's brother and ally, on the Tippecanoe River. But the chief was not there. As the American-Indian warfare merged into the War of 1812, he joined his British allies against American forces near Detroit, on the Thames River. Deserted by the British, the Shawnees fought gallantly until Tecumseh fell. Then they fled, carrying his body—and all hope of Indian unity—with them.

an end to American trade with Europe. If an American ship visited a British port, it was liable to seizure by the French; if it sailed direct to the Continent, the British might confiscate it. British warships cruised outside American harbors to search our ships and learn their destinations. French officials confiscated hundreds of American ships in European ports. Neither blockade, however, was complete, and the profits from successful evasion were so great that the American merchant marine prospered.

Even more humiliating than the attempt to cut off our trade was the British practice of "impressing" sailors from American ships. Discipline in the British navy was so strict, and the pay so low, that it was impossible to man the British navy with volunteers. For centuries, Britain had secured sailors for its navy by a legalized form of kidnaping known as impressment. Sailors might be not merely impressed in port, but even taken off merchant ships at sea. British sailors frequently deserted their country's service and signed on American vessels, where the conditions and pay were better. Sometimes a British warship calling in an American port found it difficult to sail away because so many of the crew deserted. Therefore, Britain claimed the right to stop our ships, search for former British subjects, and force them back into service.

The United States had protested about this practice ever since 1794, when John Jay had gone to England with instructions to persuade the British to give it up. No British government, however, would abandon impressment off American ships for fear it might become impossible to man the Royal Navy. In the course of the Napoleonic Wars, it has been estimated that about 9,000 American citizens were forced to serve under the Union Jack; many of them lost their lives in the king's service.

In June 1807, an American warship, the *Chesapeake*, was just leaving this country for a voyage to the Mediterranean when she was hailed by a British naval vessel, the *Leopard*. The commander of the *Leopard* demanded that he be allowed to search the *Chesapeake* for British deserters. When he was refused, the British ship fired three broadsides at the wholly unprepared *Chesapeake*, killing three Americans and wounding eighteen. After the American ship surrendered, the British carried off four sailors.

Like the later sinkings of the *Maine* in 1898 and the *Lusitania* in 1915, the attack on the *Chesapeake* caused tremendous indignation in this country. Jefferson, however, delayed calling Congress until passion had time to cool. The President did not intend to accept humiliation at British hands, but sought some alternative to war.

Embargo Act, 1807

Jefferson thought he had found a substitute for war in the use of an economic boycott. Before the Revolutionary War, stopping trade with Great Britain had been successful in forcing repeal of the Stamp Act and modification of the Townshend acts. Now Jefferson assumed that both Britain and France were so dependent upon American exports that if the United States cut off trade with them, they would stop violating American neutral rights. Under the President's urging, Congress in December 1807 passed the Embargo Act which forbade American ships to sail for foreign ports anywhere in the world.

The Embargo Act proved to be a disastrous failure. It caused some suffering in Britain, but hurt France very little. Its worst results were in the United States. Thousands of sailors were put out of work and many had to beg. Ships rotted at the docks. Merchants were ruined. Stores of wheat, cotton, and tobacco piled up on the wharves while prices dropped. Success of the embargo depended upon popular support,

D—n it, how he nicks 'em

Oh! this cursed Ograbme

A cartoon criticizing Jefferson and protesting the Embargo (Ograbme spelled backwards). Jefferson, at left, watches goods being smuggled from a British ship. Many vessels tried to evade the Embargo; freight rates were so high that one successful trip might pay for the cost of the entire ship.

but it became intensely unpopular, especially in New England, where it was widely evaded and where town meetings condemned Jefferson in language similar to that used against George III a generation earlier. The Jefferson administration resorted to such "un-Republican" measures as an increase in the regular army to control smuggling into Canada and powers of search and seizure that went beyond anything attempted by British customs officers before the American Revolution. "No peacetime President," it has been observed, "ever sought, or received, such a vast concentration of power as did Jefferson, and at the expense of provisions in the Bill of Rights which he himself once advocated as necessary checks against tyranny."

Madison Elected President, 1808

Jefferson was glad to step down as President after two terms and retire to Monticello. For the rest of his life he carried on an immense correspondence and busied himself with founding the University of Virginia. He did not look back on his years as chief magistrate with pleasure. He had felt driven by the requirements of the office into violating his oft-expressed principles of individual freedom and limited federal power. In the epitaph he wrote for himself he asked to be remembered only as the author of the Declaration of Independence and the Virginia Bill for Religious Freedom, and as father of the University of Virginia.

Jefferson's refusal to run for a third term as President helped to fix the two-term tradition that continued until Franklin D. Roosevelt's election for a third term in 1940, and that the Twenty-second Amendment made part of the Constitution in 1951. Jefferson used his influence to pass the Republican nomination on to his close friend and Secretary of State, James Madison. Madison defeated his Federalist opponent, Charles C. Pinckney, by an electoral vote of 122 to 47. Because of opposition to the Embargo Act, all of New England except Vermont went Federalist.

Fruitless Efforts to Defend Neutral Rights

Even before Jefferson left office in March 1809, Congress repealed the unpopular Embargo Act. In its place was substituted the Nonintercourse Act, which banned trade with ports under British or French control but allowed it with the rest of the world. Although less disastrous in its effects on American trade than the Embargo Act, the Nonintercourse Act was no more successful in forcing the warring countries to respect American rights. In 1810 it was replaced by a strange piece of legislation known as Macon's Bill No. 2. Macon's Bill temporarily dropped all restrictions on foreign trade, but provided that if France would abandon her decrees, the United States would revive nonintercourse against Britain, and that if Britain would drop the Orders in Council, the United States would revive nonintercourse against France. Napoleon saw in Macon's Bill a chance to trick the United States into action against Britain. In August 1810, his foreign minister sent a letter to the United States minister to France offering to repeal the Napoleonic decrees if the United States forced England to respect American rights.

Madison failed to see that the condition attached to the French offer made it worthless. Not even waiting for the actual repeal of the French decrees, Madison cut off trade with Great Britain in February 1811. Napoleon shortly revealed how little his offer meant when his officials continued to seize American ships trading from Britain to the Continent.

Drifting Into War

In May 1811, tension between the United States and Great Britain broke out into actual hostilities. An American frigate, the *President,* cruising off New York, attacked and defeated a small British warship, the *Little Belt.* American opinion applauded this action as a deserved revenge for the attack on the *Chesapeake,* while British opinion considered it an act of unprovoked aggression. Popular feelings were reflected in diplomacy. The American minister to England left London in disgust and returned to this country. A British minister to the United States continued to serve in Washington, but he was not empowered by his government to offer the United States the slightest concession. The two governments had reached the point where they were, in effect, no longer on speaking terms.

Neither the British nor the Americans really wanted war. Hostilities with the United States would distract Britain from fighting its primary enemy, Napoleon, and Canada might be lost. The United States was almost wholly unprepared militarily, and in the process of carrying on an extended war, the federal government might go bankrupt. Why a useless and unwanted war nevertheless broke out in 1812 is a matter of continuing debate among historians.

In the nineteenth century the common view was that the War of 1812 was fought for "seamen's rights," brought on because the British Orders in Council and her impressment of American seamen were intolerable invasions of American rights on the high seas. The difficulty with this interpretation was that the war was most strongly opposed in New England, where the shipping industry was concentrated. The people who had suffered most at the hands of the British were the least anxious to retaliate. The most outright support for the war came from the agrarian West and South. This fact led to a theory that the nation was impelled toward war by Westerners eager to end the Indian menace in the Northwest and to satisfy their insatiable land hunger by annexing Canada, allied with Southerners anxious to drive the Spanish out of Florida.

Those who called the most loudly for a showdown with Britain were a group of young western and southern congressmen, nicknamed the "War Hawks," led by Henry Clay of Kentucky and John C. Calhoun of South Carolina. But the Westerners and Southerners together did not have enough votes in Congress to bring a declaration of war. The most votes in favor of war came from Pennsylvania, a state that had no fear of Indian raids and nothing to gain from annexing Canada or Florida. So recently the wheel has come full circle, and historians are coming back to the original idea that the War of 1812 was caused primarily by British impressment and by Orders in Council. Americans had become increasingly exasperated by the fact that British cruisers were taking young men off American coasting vessels and seizing ships in sight of our shores. The policy of commercial coercion had apparently failed, so there seemed to be just two choices left: submit or fight. Further submission would be galling to the sensitive pride of a new nation. It would also be confirmation of the opinion we have met before: that republics were by their nature too weak and vacillating to survive in the jungle world of international politics. If the United States continued to accept humiliation, therefore, it would not only be a blot on the national honor, but it would hurt the cause of free government everywhere. Led by the War Hawks, the Republican majority in Congress finally decided, rather hesitantly, that the country must accept the appalling risks of war rather than allow itself to be pushed around.

Declaration of War, June 19, 1812

The War of 1812 would never have been fought had there existed any means of instantaneous communication, such as the Atlantic cable or wireless. On June 23, 1812, the British government formally revoked the Orders in Council. British harvests had been bad and British manufacturers had bombarded Parliament with statements that they faced utter ruin unless the American market was reopened. Jefferson's and Madison's policy of commercial coercion was at last effective—but too late. The United States had declared war four days earlier. The vote on the war resolution was 79 to 49 in the House of Representatives, 19 to 13 in the Senate. Thus in neither branch of Congress was the declaration supported by two-thirds of the members. Even the members of Congress who voted for war did so with little enthusiasm, and only because they saw no alternative. Knowledge that the British were even thinking of abandoning the Orders in Council would have held up the vote, and their revocation would have averted war. The declaration of war against Great Britain did not suggest any sort of alliance with France. A proposal to include France in the declaration of war was defeated in the Senate by the close vote of 18 to 14.

QUESTION • A two-thirds vote in the Senate is needed to make peace, only a majority of Congress to declare war. Should the latter provision be changed?

Madison's Re-election, 1812

In the presidential election of 1812, Madison was opposed by De Witt Clinton of New York, a Republican who broke the New York-Virginia alliance and gained support from the New England Federalists. Issues were confused because Clinton made appeals to both those who wanted to end the War of 1812 and those who wanted to prosecute it more vigorously. The voting, however, revealed the same pattern as that on the declaration of war itself. Clinton carried most of the northeastern states, but lost in the electoral college 89 to 128. Had he carried Pennsylvania, which he lost by a narrow margin, he would have won the election.

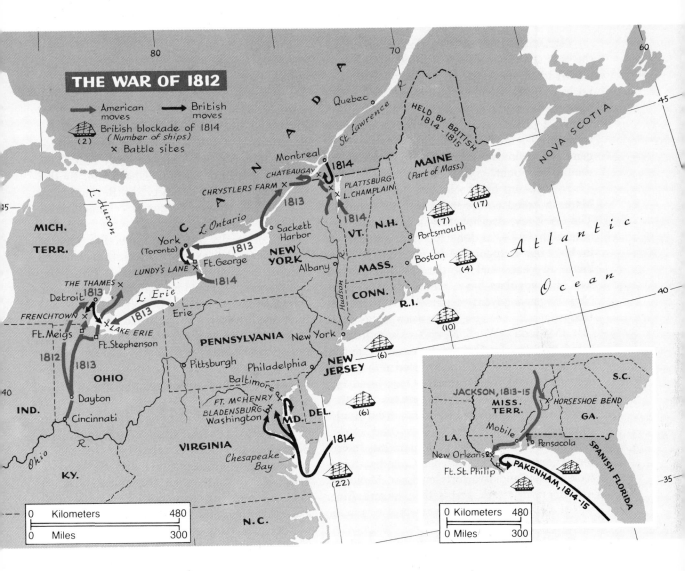

THE WAR OF 1812

Map Legend

THE WAR OF 1812

→ American moves
→ British moves
🚢 British blockade of 1814 (Number of ships)
(2)
× Battle sites

Battle sites and locations shown on the map:
Quebec, Montreal, CHATEAUGAY 1814, CHRYSTLERS FARM ×, PLATTSBURG L. CHAMPLAIN ×, HELD BY BRITISH 1814-1815, MAINE (Part of Mass.), NOVA SCOTIA, St. Lawrence R., L. Ontario, York (Toronto), Sackett Harbor, Ft. George, LUNDY'S LANE ×, 1813, 1814, N.H., VT., NEW YORK, Albany, Portsmouth (7), (17), Boston (4), MASS., CONN., R.I., Hudson R., Atlantic Ocean

MICH. TERR., L. Huron, L. Erie, THE THAMES × 1813, Detroit 1813, FRENCHTOWN ×, LAKE ERIE ×, Ft. Meigs, Ft. Stephenson, 1812, 1813, OHIO, Dayton, Cincinnati, IND., KY., Ohio R., Erie, PENNSYLVANIA, Pittsburgh, Philadelphia, New York (6), NEW JERSEY, Baltimore, FT. McHENRY ×, BLADENSBURG ×, Washington, MD., DEL. (6), VIRGINIA, Chesapeake Bay, 1814, N.C. (22), (10)

0 Kilometers 480
0 Miles 300

Inset map (Southern theater)

JACKSON, 1813-15, MISS. TERR., S.C., × HORSESHOE BEND, GA., LA., Mobile, New Orleans ×, Pensacola, Ft. St. Philip, PAKENHAM, 1814-15, SPANISH FLORIDA

0 Kilometers 480
0 Miles 300

THE WAR OF 1812

Andrew Jackson was expressing a widely-held opinion when he predicted that the conquest of Canada by the United States would be a "mere military promenade." There were indeed a number of reasons why an attack northward promised well. Canada was sparsely populated, and the French Canadians were lukewarm toward their British rulers. The narrow strip of settlement running up the St. Lawrence and north of Lake Ontario was so close to the United States that it was everywhere subject to attack. Montreal, the strategic center of Canada, was only thirty miles from New York State.

Yet Canada did not fall, principally because the military forces of the United States were almost totally unprepared. The regular army of perhaps 6,000 men was scattered throughout the frontier posts. The top commanders, veterans of the Revolution, were too old for warfare. There was no single commanding general and no over-all plan as to how the war should be fought.

To make up for the lack of regular troops, Madison called on the states to furnish militia. The result revealed how false was the idea that militia could be, as Jefferson had called them in his First Inaugural Address, "our best reliance in peace and for the first moments of war, till regulars may relieve them." Some New England governors refused to furnish any troops at all, because they were opposed to "Mr. Madison's War." New York's militia refused to cross the Niagara River into Canada, maintaining that they had enlisted only to defend their state from invasion. Once lured into battle, militiamen were apt to flee, because they lacked the discipline which comes from proper training.

The results of this unpreparedness were seen at once. Small but ably led Canadian forces took Detroit and two forts on Lake Michigan. An American attack across the Niagara River was turned back. No serious attempt was made to take Montreal.

In 1813 matters improved at the western end of the war zone. Commodore Oliver H. Perry built a small fleet on Lake Erie and won a brilliant victory over a similar British squadron. This forced the British to abandon Detroit. A force of Kentucky volunteers under William Henry Harrison then advanced into Canada and defeated a British army at the battle of the Thames. In the East, however, incompetent American commanders failed dismally in attempted invasions of Canada from Sackett Harbor and Lake Champlain.

In 1814 Napoleon was defeated and forced into exile, so the British were able to send much stronger forces to America. From Montreal, in late summer, an army of over 10,000 British veterans advanced southward under Sir John Prevost. This was a stronger force than the Burgoyne expedition of 1777, and was three times as big as the American army barring its way at Plattsburg on Lake Champlain. By this time, however, the relics of the Revolutionary War had been weeded out of command positions. In their place were younger men who had risen to the top by sheer ability. One of these, General Alexander Macomb, was at the head of the American land forces at Plattsburg, and another, Commodore Thomas Macdonough, commanded a small fleet. Both men handled their smaller forces so well that they repulsed British attacks, inflicting heavy losses. Prevost retreated to Montreal.

Attacks on Washington, Baltimore, and New Orleans

In 1814 the British sent two other expeditions to America: one to attack Washington and Baltimore, the other to take New Orleans. In August British transports landed an army of about 4,000 soldiers at Chesapeake Bay; it marched overland and took the capital with ease. Five thousand American militia, in a position to defend the city, ran away after only ten of their number had been killed. The British burned the public buildings of Washington in revenge for similar destruction by American troops at York (now Toronto) in a raid across Lake Ontario in 1813. From the capital the British went on to attack Baltimore, but were repulsed by the forts guarding the city.

The British expedition to capture New Orleans did not reach the mouth of the Mississippi until December 1814. To oppose the 6,000 veteran redcoats, there were gathered an equal number of Americans commanded by

Loss of a Capital — the Birth of a National Anthem

The British cartoon suggests that Madison will flee "to Elba to his bosom friend," following the burning of Washington, D.C. The picture on the right commemorates the British bombardment of Fort McHenry in September 1814, during which time Francis Scott Key wrote the "Star Spangled Banner."

Maryland Historical Society

Andrew Jackson, a Tennessee Indian fighter. The American force consisted mostly of militia, with a few pirates recruited for their ability to handle artillery. Jackson was a man of such extraordinary qualities of leadership that he was able to instill discipline into his ill-trained soldiers.

When the final British attack came on January 8, 1815, the American troops were sheltered behind a barricade of cotton bales. The British advanced in the open, as they had at Bunker Hill forty years before, and as at Bunker Hill they suffered terrible losses. After more than a third of their number had been killed or wounded, the invaders gave up the

Both the American and British forces burned and plundered during the War of 1812. Above, British troops burn and plunder Havre de Grace, Maryland. Below, an American fleet under Commodore Perry decisively defeats the British on Lake Erie. Although the Americans achieved notable success in individual engagements with the British, the naval superiority of the British fleet was soon felt and most American ships were bottled up in port.

Courtesy of the Chicago Historical Society

assault, and New Orleans was safe from capture. The battle of New Orleans, greatest American victory of the War of 1812, was a useless slaughter, for it occurred two weeks after peace had been signed. Again the lack of a transatlantic cable affected the course of history.

The War at Sea

The American navy had not been expected to take much part in the War of 1812. Only five ships were ready for service when hostilities began. Jefferson and Madison had no interest in the navy, and the only vessels built during their administrations were four small ships for the Tripolitan War, plus a number of small gunboats designed for coastal defense. These gunboats were so unseaworthy they had to stow their guns in the holds except in calm weather. The United States had no ships of the line, the counterparts of the modern battleship. In John Adams's administration, however, there had been completed half a dozen excellent frigates, such as the famous *Constitution*. A frigate was the sailing ship counterpart of the modern cruiser. The American frigates were specially designed to have more fire power than any European ships of the same class and to be fast enough to escape from ships of the line. The Tripolitan War had trained a number of excellent officers, and American crews were composed of volunteers rather than men impressed into service. They were especially skillful at gunnery.

When war broke out, the American frigates put to sea and within a few months had won an uninterrupted series of victories in duels with individual British vessels. These triumphs had no noticeable effect in weakening British sea power, because the British navy outnumbered that of the United States at least twenty to one. But the British had ruled the sea so long that even a few defeats came as a shock. After reporting one of the American victories, a British newspaper of the day lamented as follows:

Can this be true? Will the English people read this unmoved? Any man who foretold such disasters this day last year would have been treated as a madman or a traitor. He would have been told that ere seven months had gone by the American flag would have been swept from the ocean. . . . Yet not one of the American frigates has struck. They leave their ports when they choose and return when it suits their convenience. . . . Nothing chases them; nothing interrupts them—nay—nothing engages them but to yield in triumph.

On this side of the Atlantic, the naval victories helped to make up for the dismal failure of the war on the northern frontier.

In addition to naval vessels, the United States sent to sea more than 500 privateers; they took 1,330 British vessels and made captures within sight of the British coast. Like the frigate victories, their success served to raise American morale and alarm Britain.

As the war went on, American success at sea diminished. The British rejoiced when one of their frigates, the *Shannon,* won a duel with an American frigate, the *Chesapeake.* What was even more important was that, with overwhelmingly superior numbers, the British fleet was able to lay a tight blockade on the entire Atlantic coast. American foreign trade ceased almost entirely, and the American navy was bottled up in port. While the war on land started with disaster and ended in success, the war at sea started with victories and ended in failure.

The Hartford Convention, 1814

New England opposed the War of 1812 from the first. The opposition took the form of refusal to send militia to the Canadian borders, of failure to purchase United States bonds issued to cover the cost of the war, and of protests by individuals and public meetings. Typical of

The naval battle between the *U.S.S. Constitution* and the British *Guerrière* (right) was one of the single-ship engagements that demonstrated the fighting ability of the American frigates and their superior gunnery. This picture is by Thomas Chambers.

the latter was a "Memorial to the President of the United States" issued by the town meeting of Brewster, Massachusetts, in July 1812. The people of Brewster, hoping that no "suspicion of treason" would fall upon them for exercising "the privilege and duty of free citizens to inquire and judge of publick proceedings," declared that the war created an "awful crisis." They saw no navy sufficient to protect them, and disliked fighting on the same side as "the monster" Napoleon. Above all, they foresaw that the war would be ruinous to themselves:

We ask leave in conclusion to state that about three fourths of our townsmen depend on the sea for the means of subsistence for themselves and their families. By the recent declaration of war more than one half of that proportion is liable to fall into the hands of the enemy with a large part of their prop-

erty, and many of their wives and children may thereby be reduced to extreme poverty. . . . We feel it therefore most strongly incumbent upon us by all lawful and constitutional methods to seek for a speedy termination of the present war.

By 1814, prominent New England leaders were ready to discuss separation from the Union. Not only were trade and shipping at a standstill, but a British force had invaded Maine and occupied several eastern counties. In December 1814, delegates from the New England states met at Hartford, Connecticut, to confer on their grievances and recommended action. These sessions were secret.

The Hartford Convention did not go so far as to recommend that New England leave the Union at once, but it did demand seven amendments to the Constitution to increase the po-

Hartford Convention delegates (right) are mocked as trade and title seekers who are timid to boot. Below is the Battle of New Orleans as designed on the scene by an artist. The slaughter of British soldiers charging the American breastworks (in left foreground) was needless, as a peace treaty had already been signed.

litical power of the New England states and to protect their interests. The Convention insisted, for instance, that southern states no longer be allowed to count three-fifths of their slaves in determining representation in Congress. It urged a two-thirds vote of both houses of Congress for admitting new states and for declaring war.

The resolutions passed by the Hartford Convention expressed the hope that the Union should be preserved "if possible," but there was a strong suggestion that if the war continued and New England's demands were not met, the next step might be an attempt to secede.

The Hartford Convention sent commissioners to Washington, D.C., to present its demands to the President and Congress in person. They arrived at the capital at exactly the time when word came that Jackson had won a great victory at New Orleans and that a peace treaty had been signed. Amidst the great celebrations attending these events, the commissioners had no choice but to return to their homes.

The Treaty of Ghent, 1814

A curious fact about the War of 1812 was that almost from the moment it began, both sides tried to end it. Great Britain had no wish to be diverted from fighting Napoleon. The United States would have stopped fighting at once if Great Britain had agreed to stop impressment. Partly through the efforts of Alexander I, czar of Russia, commissioners representing the two nations met at Ghent, Belgium, in July 1814. The American delegation included three very able men—John Quincy Adams, Henry Clay, and Albert Gallatin. It was well that this was so because it was something of a

QUESTION • If the War of 1812 had not been fought, what would have been different in American history?

diplomatic triumph for them to persuade the British to accept a peace treaty that simply restored the situation before the war. The Treaty of Ghent contained not a word about neutral rights or impressment. Not a square mile of territory changed hands. The warring nations simply agreed to stop fighting, to restore previous boundaries, and to put other problems off to future settlement. Signed on Christmas Eve, 1814, the treaty was unanimously ratified by the Senate when it reached Washington, D.C., in January 1815.

On the face of it, the War of 1812 was a useless and foolhardy adventure. The Americans risked foreign invasion, loss of territory, bankruptcy, and disunion, but failed to gain any of the purposes for which they fought. Yet the war also brought benefits. When in 1816 Henry Clay was challenged in Congress to say what the United States had gained by it, he replied:

What is our present situation? Respectability and character abroad—security and confidence at home. If we have not obtained in the opinion of some the full measure of retribution, our character and Constitution are placed on a solid basis, never to be shaken.

The Americans had regained confidence and self-respect. They soon forgot their dissensions and defeats and remembered only their victories. The disgraceful flight of the militia entrusted to defend Washington was forgotten, while the successful defense of Baltimore is celebrated in our national anthem, "The Star-Spangled Banner." Probably a hundred people know of "Old Ironsides" to one who knows of the successful British blockade. Perry's victory on Lake Erie and Jackson's at New Orleans were added to Bunker Hill, Saratoga, and Yorktown as stimulants to American patriotism. It is not surprising that the War of 1812 was followed by a period in which men consciously strove to strengthen the American nation.

Activities: Chapter 8

For Mastery and Review

1. Why did the United States pay tribute to the Barbary States? How was the problem finally dealt with?

2. Why did France regain Louisiana? What were Jefferson's reasons for seeking the purchase of New Orleans? Why was Napoleon willing to sell all Louisiana? What was Jefferson's concern over the constitutionality of the Purchase? Why did he not wait for an amendment?

3. What were the instructions to and the importance of the Lewis and Clark expedition?

4. Describe the conspiracies in which Burr was accused of taking part. What did he attempt to do in each? What were the results?

5. Show how the Berlin and Milan Decrees, the Orders in Council, and impressment injured American commerce.

6. What conditions, including Jefferson's reasoning, led to the Embargo Act? What were its effects at home and abroad?

7. Trace the steps in our foreign policy as a neutral from the Embargo to the break with England in 1812. What are some of the explanations of why the United States declared war on Great Britain? Would better communications have prevented war?

8. Outline the course of the War of 1812 (a) on land and (b) on sea. What were the terms of the Treaty of Ghent?

9. Why did the Hartford Convention meet? Explain its demands.

Unrolling the Map

1. In a modern atlas study the Mediterranean region. Locate places which were once part of the Barbary Coast: Tripoli, Morocco, Algiers, Tunis. Study the patterns and kinds of trade that took American shipping into the Mediterranean. What commodities were involved in that triangular trade?

2. On an outline map of the United States, show the Louisiana Purchase, with its indefinite boundaries. Show the Mississippi River system and New Orleans, to indicate the commerce situation. Locate West Florida and the part of Texas claimed by the United States. Trace the routes of (a) the Lewis and Clark expedition and (b) the Pike explorations.

3. Study the map on p. 209 in preparation for a class discussion of the War of 1812. Note the blockade and the battle sites. Where did the Americans succeed and where did they fail?

Who, What, and Why Important?

Tripolitan War
Louisiana Purchase
Toussaint L'Ouverture
Lewis and Clark
Aaron Burr
Tecumseh
Berlin and Milan Decrees
Orders in Council
impressment
the Embargo Act
James Madison
the Nonintercourse Act
War Hawks
battle of the Thames
Plattsburg
capture of Washington
battle of New Orleans
frigate
British blockade
Hartford Convention
Treaty of Ghent
The "Star-Spangled Banner"

To Pursue the Matter

1. How did John Marshall extricate himself from a difficult position in *Marbury v. Madison*? See Bragdon *et al., Frame of Government,* pp. 175–183.

2. Did Burr's conspiracy actually threaten the safety of the federal union? See Abernathy, *The Burr Conspiracy.*

3. Explain Tecumseh's effectiveness in uniting the Northwest Indians and why he failed eventually. See Van Every, *The Final Challenge: The American Frontier, 1803–1845.*

4. How do you define the difference between a politician and a statesman? When you have formulated a definition, apply it to Washington, Hamilton, Burr, Jefferson, and John Adams.

5. The German statesman Bismarck remarked that there seemed to be a special providence watching over idiots, children, drunkards, and the United States of America. Assess this remark as applied to the Louisiana Purchase and the War of 1812. For a useful source of information see Bailey, *A Diplomatic History of the American People.*

PART TWO: SUMMING UP
Chapters 5–8

I. CHECKING THE FACTS

1. *What and When:* Putting Things in Order
Each sentence below describes an event, a fact, or what is in a document. After each sentence, tell (1) what the sentence refers to, and (2) during which time period it occurred, by letter.

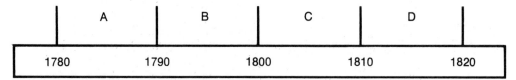

	A	B	C	D	
1780	1790		1800	1810	1820

a. A sectional convention threatened secession from the union.
b. Amendments to the Constitution guaranteed basic American rights.
c. The British government agreed to give up the fur posts.
d. The territory of the United States doubled in size.
e. Armed conflict with England ended. (There are two possible answers here).
f. The Indians were suppressed in what is now Indiana.
g. Finances were put on a sound basis.
h. First presidential election in which rival candidates represented political parties.
i. The first President steps down.

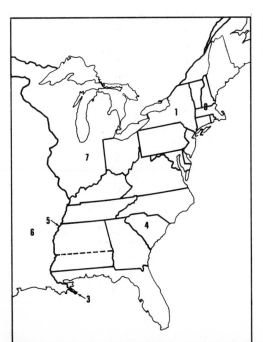

2. MAP WORK
Select the number on the map that most accurately locates each of these areas:
a. Site of "deposit rights" gained from Spain.
b. Part of the Northwest Territory.
c. Section most opposed to the Embargo Act.
d. Western boundary in Washington's time.
e. Land reserved for Indians by Jefferson.
f. Home of the powerful Iroquois.

II. INTERPRETING THE FACTS

1. *Establishing Relationships*
    A. In each of these pairs, tell whether the first item *encouraged* or *discouraged* the second. Support your decision, orally or in writing.
        a. the Constitution—Louisiana Purchase
        b. Genêt mission—neutrality
        c. Greenville Treaty—minority rights
        d. elastic clause—federal powers
        e. Jay Treaty—nationalism

    B. Three of the items in each group below are related. One is not. First, decide which item is *not related.* Then, tell what the other three *have in common.*
        a. Whiskey Rebellion, Canada, War Hawks, Congress
        b. impressment, embargo, right of deposit, blockade
        c. coin money, make treaties, pass laws, declare war

III. APPLYING YOUR KNOWLEDGE

1. Develop your own qualifications for the office of the President of the United States.
    a. List those qualities you think are necessary for the "ideal" President.
    b. Now, rate Washington, Adams, Jefferson, and Madison on each of your qualifications.
    c. Do the same for our current President.
Go a few steps further . . .
    d. Is it possible to define the "ideal" President? Defend your answer.
    e. What problems do you see in judging the performance of a President?
    f. What can the "average voter" do to make the best judgments about the quality of presidential candidates and their performance?

2. Washington warned against the dangers of political factions (parties). In your opinion, which would be best for our country: (1) one party, (2) two major parties, (3) two major and some minor parties, (4) a multitude of special-interest parties? Defend your choice.

READINGS FOR PART TWO

Fiction

Hale, E. E. *The Man Without a Country.* A powerful and moving story about the different facets of patriotism.

Hepburn, A. *Letter of Marque.* A fast-moving story of the War of 1812.

Roberts, K. *The Lively Lady.* A novel about the War of 1812.

Vidal, G. *Burr.* A fictionalized account of the life of Aaron Burr.

Non-fiction

Bakeless, J. (ed.). *The Journals of Lewis and Clark.* Fascinating reading about an intriguing journey.

Boorstin, D. *The Lost World of Thomas Jefferson.* The attitudes and values of Jefferson's times as reflected in his thinking.

Chinard, G. *Honest John Adams.* A sympathetic biography.

Part

3

The Nation and the Sections

(Detail)
"Fur Traders on the Missouri" by George Caleb Bingham

HISTORY AS FABLE

History, it has often been remarked, is but a fable agreed upon. In American history, a generally accepted part of the fable has been that 1815 marked a turning point. But what, it may be asked, was so special about the year 1815? Did Americans suddenly and collectively turn their backs on Europe? Were they ever in fact "free of foreign entanglements"? Were they not still part of an Atlantic community being drawn ever closer together as steamships replaced sailing ships, as wheat from the Dakotas and pork from Indiana began to feed Liverpool and London, and as an ever-increasing flood of European immigrants poured into American ports?

And yet the fable that a great change had started in 1815 was itself a fact. Americans thought they were isolated from Europe; indeed, they congratulated themselves upon it. The millions of immigrants seeking a new life in America often strengthened American isolationism because they sought to escape from their past. It took two world wars in the twentieth century to shock Americans out of the belief that with the close of the Napoleonic Wars the United States had no further need to concern itself with European politics.

Or consider the myth that men make history while women wash the dishes. History books have so consistently left half the human race out of account that Henry Adams remarked, "History is useful to the historian by teaching him his ignorance of women." Notice that to Adams himself *historian* meant "he."

The very word "pioneer" conjures up the picture of a man in coonskin cap and leather jacket armed with a rifle. But as you trace the march of the frontier from the Appalachians to the Pacific, we now see that there were women pioneers too. Left to himself, the man on the frontier often left behind his usual customs and way of life. It was the women who turned cabins into homesteads, planted flowers outside the doors, and put curtains in the windows. It was usually the mothers and schoolteachers who transmitted to the next generation the heritage of the past.

It was, nevertheless, a man's world insofar as men could make it so. By law, the husband legally ruled the wife. Rigid taboos dictated women's clothing and freedom of action. Small wonder, then, that some brave women demanded equal rights with men and started a revolution that continues to the present (see p. 282). The embattled feminists who met at Seneca Falls, New York, in 1848 appealed to the principles and used the phrases of 1776. Thus, each generation must find new uses for the Declaration of Independence, or it too could become a fable.

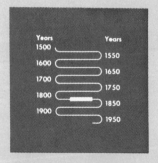

Years
1500
1600
1700
1800
1900

Years
1550
1650
1750
1850
1950

Chapter 9

Forces for Union and Disunion

*In war we are one people. In making peace we are
one people. In all commercial relations we are one and the same
people. In many other respects the American people are one.*
—JOHN MARSHALL

*Always the free range and diversity—always the continent of
    Democracy—*
Always the prairies, pastures, forests, vast cities, travelers . . .
—WALT WHITMAN

The year 1815 saw the beginning of a century of peace in Europe that lasted with few interruptions until the outbreak of World War I in 1914. For nearly a century no warring nations preyed on the foreign commerce of the United States or violated our neutral rights. Apparently free of foreign entanglements, Americans turned their backs on Europe. "The continent lay before them," wrote the historian Henry Adams, "like an uncovered ore-bed." The conquest of the continent was for the most part not a matter of military force, although it involved us in numerous Indian wars and a war with Mexico. Instead, it was a struggle between people and their environment—the conquest of eastern forests by the axe, of the prairies by the plow, of vast distances by canals, steamboats, and railroads. Lured by the promise of a better life, millions of Europeans came to America, and within America the people were on the move. Helping to promote these developments

came the greatest technological change in the history of humankind—the industrial revolution.

The expansion of the United States created political problems, of which the most obvious was that of holding the Union together. In all history such a huge area as the United States had seldom been ruled effectively by a single government—*never* by a government of the people.

THE SPIRIT OF NATIONALISM

The survival of the United States as one country was a product of many forces. The Americans were fortunate to inherit a common language and common institutions. The territory they inhabited was immense, but at least from the Atlantic coast to the Rocky Mountains it is one of the most unified geographical areas in the world. Much of it lies within the flat watershed of the Mississippi and Missouri rivers, the world's third largest river system. East of the Rockies, the Appalachians are the only mountain barrier, and they are far easier to penetrate than European ranges such as the Alps, the Pyrenees, or the Carpathians.

By 1815 the economic unity of the United States was not far advanced. Most Americans traded with people of their own localities or with foreign nations. But during the nineteenth century, various developments growing out of the industrial revolution tended to tie the United States together economically. As manufacturing cities grew, they had to find both markets and sources of raw materials throughout the country, and a great web of transportation was developed to carry goods back and forth.

The most important binding force of all was the development of American nationalism. Nationalism has been one of the powerful forces in the modern world. At the time of the French Revolution, it inspired the French not only to resist foreign invaders, but to embark on a career of conquest that subsided only when Napoleon lost an army in the snows of Russia in 1812. In the nineteenth century, it was the spirit that turned Germany and Italy from geographical expressions into nations. In the twentieth century, nationalism has inspired scores of colonies to break the bonds of imperialism and to declare their independence. Nationalism is not easy to define, because it is a complex matter and its characteristics vary from country to country. More a matter of emotion than of reason, it is a compound of beliefs, loyalties, and traditions. It expresses itself in literature and song, as well as in symbols such as the Statue of Liberty and the Stars and Stripes. It expresses itself in action: "To have done great things in the past and to wish to do more of them are the essential conditions of being a people." Nationalism in the United States is bound up with the idea expressed in the Declaration of Independence that people can create for themselves a great society based on freedom, equality, and human brotherhood.

The "Era of Good Feelings"

The War of 1812 provided a stimulus to American nationalism. It revealed the dangers of disunion and at the same time promoted a sense of self-confidence and pride. Albert Gallatin, a former member of Jefferson's cabinet who had been one of the commissioners at the Ghent peace conference, described the new spirit in a letter written only a few months after the close of hostilities:

The war had renewed & reinstated the National feelings & character, which the Revolution had given, & which were daily lessened. The people . . . are more American: they feel & act more as a Nation, and I hope that the permanency of the Union is thereby better secured.

For four or five years after the Treaty of Ghent, national sentiment was so much stronger than before that the period is commonly called the "Era of Good Feelings." The leaders of the Federalist party had never overcome their scorn for the mass of people, and the people in turn were less and less disposed to choose Federalists for public office. Now the party was so discredited by its connection with the New England secession movement that it disappeared from the national scene. In 1816 James Monroe, Republican candidate for President, was elected over Rufus King, his Federalist opponent, by 183 votes to 34. In 1820 Monroe was re-elected with only one opposing vote, since there was no longer a Federalist candidate in the field. "The demon of party for a time departed," said a newspaper of the period, "and gave place to a general outburst of national feeling."

The Country Fair, 1824, by John A. Woodside, suggests the prosperity of American farmers at a time when growing cities and better transportation were expanding the market for agricultural products.

NATIONALIST LEGISLATION

Postwar nationalism was revealed not only in election results but in legislation. The war had shown that the Jeffersonian ideal of a central government with strictly limited functions failed to meet the needs of the country in crisis. The result was that during the two years after the close of hostilities a Congress dominated by Jefferson's Republican party passed a series of laws that might have been written by Alexander Hamilton.

Republicans had consistently opposed the first Bank of the United States. They let its charter run out in 1811 and substituted nothing for it. The results were disastrous. The notes of the B.U.S. had been a universally accepted national currency. Now the country, lacking sufficient specie for metallic currency, had to fall back on notes issued by banks chartered by the different states. These state bank notes were generally accepted only in the locality where they were issued. Thus it was almost impossible for a citizen of Kentucky, say, to send money to Boston.

Meanwhile, hundreds of new banks were started, many of them without sufficient capital and some of them downright dishonest. With-out a central bank, the federal government had a hard time borrowing during the War of 1812 and sometimes could not pay its troops. "More than once the paymaster of the army was unable to meet demands for sums so trifling as thirty dollars."

Under these circumstances the very men who in 1811 had opposed the recharter of the Bank of the United States now supported the creation of a new bank modeled on the old. In 1816 Congress passed a law to establish a second Bank of the United States. It was signed without argument by President Madison, who in 1791 had argued that the first Bank of the United States was unconstitutional. The new Bank had a capital of $35,000,000, 80 per cent owned by private individuals, 20 per cent by the government. Five of the twenty-five directors were appointed by the President; the rest were elected by private individuals who owned the stock. The Bank could issue notes which served as a national currency. It also acted in a number of ways to provide federal control of state banks and to prevent their issuing worthless notes.

During the War of 1812 it was impossible for Americans to obtain British manufactures, and this situation provided a stimulus to American industry. Once the war was over, goods from Britain flooded the American market at prices so low that they threatened to put American manufacturers out of business. Congressmen now reread Hamilton's "Report on Manufactures" and found its arguments more persuasive than they had been in 1791. Although protection would mean that American consumers would pay more for clothing, pots, pans, and plates, this seemed simply the price of securing economic independence from Great Britain.

Although there was opposition to protection, especially from northeastern shipping interests and southern agriculturalists, support for higher tariffs came from all sections of the country. The tariff was expected to bind the country together, for the manufacturing sections would sell their goods to the agricultural sections and buy food from them. Also, every section still had hopes of becoming a manufacturing area. In 1816 a tariff law was passed, levying duties averaging over 20 per cent on foreign manufactures.

The War of 1812 had revealed the need for a better transportation system, since it had proved extremely difficult to move armies, with their baggage and cannon, from one place to another. There were many who felt it was the duty of the federal government to improve transportation. In 1816 John C. Calhoun of South Carolina presented to the House of Representatives a bill to set aside for the building of roads and canals the $1,500,000 that the private owners of the Bank of the United States had paid for their charter. In a speech in support of the so-called Bonus Bill, Calhoun said,

QUESTION • *The governor of Georgia in 1827 complained that wheat from central New York sold for less in Savannah than wheat from central Georgia. How could this be so?*

Let it not be forgotten, let it be forever kept in mind, that the extent of our republic exposes us to the greatest of all calamities, next to the loss of liberty, and even to that in its consequences,—*disunion*. We are . . . rapidly—I was about to say fearfully—growing. . . . Let us, then, bind the republic together with a perfect system of roads and canals. Let us conquer space.

The Bonus Bill passed both houses of Congress, but President Madison vetoed it. He argued that to spend money improving transportation was an unconstitutional extension of federal power.

ROADS AND WATERWAYS

Calhoun was undoubtedly correct when he argued that the United States had a crying need for better transportation. There was as yet no way in which the agricultural products of the West or bulky manufactures from the East could be shipped across the Appalachians. With the steamboat in its infancy, the Mississippi River was still a "one-way street." Goods could be floated downriver, but very little could be brought upstream.

The National Road and Private Turnpikes

The first great step toward the creation of a national system of transportation was the building of the Cumberland or National Road. Starting from Cumberland, Maryland, on the Potomac River this road reached the Ohio River at Wheeling, Virginia, in 1817 (see map, p. 229). It spanned the Ohio River on what was in its time the longest suspension bridge in the world; it measured 1,010 feet in length and was hung from towers rising 153 feet above the river. The National Road went westward as far as Vandalia, Illinois. The older portion was built with great care. It cut a path 80 feet wide through the wilderness, the center 30 feet being "macadamized" with crushed stone. Along this

Travel by stagecoach on the new turnpikes was apt to be an uncomfortable experience. The roads were usually rough. They were dusty in summer and muddy in winter. Travel by canalboat or steamboat was much more pleasant.

route went great Conestoga wagons drawn by teams of four, six, or eight horses.

The National Road was the only great federal transportation project. Madison's veto of the Bonus Bill set a precedent for discouraging the use of federal funds for building roads and canals. In general, improvements in transportation were undertaken by states or by private enterprise.

The so-called turnpike era lasted from about 1790 to 1820. During this period, hundreds of miles of roads were constructed by state-chartered private companies that charged tolls. These toll roads were called turnpikes because they were barricaded at intervals by piked poles which held up the traveler until he paid his fee. They turned out to be profitable only in the East, where traffic was heavy, or on main routes such as that from Albany to Lake Erie. Western highways were therefore generally constructed by the states themselves, at times with the aid of federal funds.

Although by 1840 the country was crisscrossed with roads, they were in many ways an unsatisfactory means of transportation. Except in the East, few of them were surfaced or had adequate bridges. In woods, the stumps were likely to be cut low to 12 or 18 inches but not removed. In swampy places, there was "corduroy" (logs laid sidewise), which hurt horses' legs and jolted wagons to pieces. Roads were vitally useful for those on horseback, for families traveling west with their belongings, and for people who herded cattle and hogs to market. But bulky goods could not be profitably transported long distances by land.

Inland Waterways and Steamboats

Far more important for moving products such as grain, coal, dressed beef, barrels of pork, and bales of cotton were inland waterways. Throughout much of the nineteenth century, rivers were used for transporting goods to an extent which today seems almost unbelievable. This was true not merely on great rivers like the Ohio but on quite small streams. When in 1840 Henry Thoreau and his brother went off camping on the Concord and Merrimac

Transportation: Pre-Civil War

The natural outlet for the surplus produce of the "Old Northwest" was down the Mississippi River system. The picture of the harbor at New Orleans in 1850 (below) indicates the volume of this traffic. But the amazing Erie Canal opened an East-West water route. The canal was carried over the Genesee River by a remarkable stone aqueduct, here portrayed (left) on a plate made in Staffordshire, England.

MAIN TRANSPORTATION SYSTEM, 1840

Canals (under construction)
Main highways (west of N.Y.)
Rivers navigable for steamboats
U.S. Population, 1840
17,100,000

0 Kilometers 320
0 Miles 200

Canals (like the Erie, shown on p. 228) and highways created eastward routes to markets in the 1830's and 1840's, helping to lay the groundwork for the economic "take-off" of the 1850's (see p. 322). As the cost of transport by road was high, waterways were the preferred routes. But by the 1850's the "canal craze" was over, as railroads assumed supremacy. (See also maps p. 324).

rivers, the Merrimac was alive with small barges carrying bricks, hay, and cordwood.

It was the invention of the steamboat, however, which really made American rivers, especially the Mississippi system, into national highways. The steamboat era began with Robert Fulton's famous vessel the *Clermont,* which made its first voyage on the Hudson River in 1807. The *Clermont* had no feature in it that had not been seen in still earlier steam-

boats. What made it unique was that it became a commercial success, Robert Fulton's business sense being just as good as his inventiveness.

The first steamboat in western waters was the *New Orleans,* built at Pittsburgh, which in 1811 went down the Ohio to New Orleans and then steamed upriver as far as Louisville. By 1850 there were about 800 steamboats on the Mississippi system—more than in the entire British merchant marine!

River steamboats navigated the Mississippi and nearly all its tributaries, sometimes for hundreds of miles. Flat-bottomed steamboats were developed which, it was claimed, could navigate on a heavy dew. Actually, some of them drew less than two feet of water. Profits were high, but risks were great. The average life of a river steamboat has been variously estimated as from three to six years. The high mortality is not surprising when one takes into account the danger from snags, ice, bursting boilers, collisions, fires, and sand bars. So great were these dangers that many boats were deliberately built to last only a short time—which, of course, increased the risks.

Almost as important in their day as the river systems were the thousands of miles of canals built during the first part of the nineteenth century. For the purpose of moving heavy goods, canals were far more efficient than even the best roads. On a good road it took four horses to haul a payload weighing

DeWitt Clinton and the Erie Canal

DeWitt Clinton was a politician who had his downs as well as his ups, partly through faults in his own character. He was inconsistent in his principles; he was overbearing in manner; he sometimes failed to show gratitude to his supporters; and he was an intriguer who often made the mistake of being found out. Yet he was also a great public servant. His principal claim to fame is that both as a private citizen and as governor of New York he was the man most responsible for persuading the people of his state to undertake the digging of the Erie Canal.

Clinton had a true and prophetic vision of what the canal would mean to the nation and to his city. In 1825, as the great work was nearing completion, he wrote:

As an organ of communication between the Hudson, the Mississippi, and the St. Lawrence, it will create the greatest inland trade ever witnessed. The most fertile and extensive regions of America will avail themselves of its facilities for a market. All their surplus productions, whether of the soil, the forest, the mines, or the water, their fabrics of art and their supplies of foreign commodities will concentrate in the city of New York, for transportation abroad and for consumption at home.... And, before the revolution of a century, the whole island of Manhattan, covered with habitations and replenished with a dense population, will constitute one vast city.

Along the great waterway there developed other prosperous cities, although less huge than Manhattan: Buffalo, Syracuse, Rochester, Albany, Utica, Rome. Life on the canal became the subject of many songs. The verse of one of them, sung in a minor key, gives a sense of the slow pace of the mules hauling the boats:

I've got a mule and her name is Sal,
Fifteen miles on the Erie Canal.
She's a good old worker and a good old pal,
Fifteen miles on the Erie Canal.
We've hauled some barges in our day,
Filled with lumber, coal, and hay,
And we know every inch of the way
From Albany to Buffalo.

a ton and a half. A single pair of horses or mules could draw a canalboat with a load of fifty tons.

The Erie Canal, 1825

Before 1815 a number of short canals had been built, most of them around rapids and falls in rivers or connecting nearby natural waterways. Yet the canal craze did not really begin until the completion of the Erie Canal. At the time it was dug, the Erie Canal was the greatest engineering feat in the history of the Western Hemisphere. Built by New York State between 1817 and 1825, it cost what was then considered a huge sum—$7,000,000. Running from Albany on the Hudson River to Buffalo on Lake Erie, the canal was 363 miles long. It averaged 40 feet wide and 4 feet deep. In an age when concrete, dynamite, and structural steel had not yet been invented, the labor that went into the canal was prodigious. The "big ditch" itself had to be dug entirely by men with shovels and scoops drawn by draft animals. The stone to face the 83 locks had to be cut and set by hand. At Rochester, the canal was carried across the Genesee River by an aqueduct over 800 feet long. Several reservoirs and many miles of feeder canals were needed to insure a steady supply of water.

The Erie Canal was an immediate success. It lowered from $100 to $8 the cost of carrying a ton of goods from Buffalo to New York City. It made New York the greatest port in the country and upstate New York for a time America's most prosperous agricultural region.

The Erie Canal started a craze for canal-building. Faced with competition from New York, Pennsylvania completed in 1834 an extraordinary system of canals and portage railways connecting Philadelphia and Pittsburgh. At the highest point in this route, canalboats were hauled over a ridge 2,326 feet above sea level! Ohio went deeply into debt to build over 500 miles of canals connecting the Ohio River

and Lake Erie. Before the canal boom collapsed in the late 1830's, it saw at least 10,000 miles of canals either built or being built. (See map, p. 229.)

In terms of the nation, the most important effect of the Erie Canal was that it connected the Northeast and the "Old Northwest" (see map, pp. 174–175). The natural geographical connection of the Northwest was with the South by way of the Mississippi. The natural market for the farm products of the Northwest, however, was the industrial Northeast. The Erie Canal by opening this market helped to create an economic alliance between the two sections (see maps, p. 324). Later, this became a political alliance.

THE NATIONALIST DECISIONS OF JOHN MARSHALL

The nationalism of the period after the War of 1812 was also revealed in a series of decisions by Chief Justice John Marshall interpreting the Constitution. Marshall, appointed by the last Federalist President, John Adams, had always stood for the basic Federalist ideas—defense of the rights of men of property, distrust of democracy, and strengthening the power of the federal government. Although by 1815 the majority of the Supreme Court justices had been appointed by Republican Presidents, Marshall still dominated the Supreme Court. He was a man not only of strong convictions but of such great friendliness and persuasiveness that, according to one historian, he "moulded his fellow judges like putty." During his 34 years as Chief Justice, Marshall found himself in a minority on only one case. He composed the majority of the decisions, and they were written with such clarity that any non-lawyer could understand them. Marshall was a magnificent debater. Once admit his premises and you were lost. Jefferson once said that when conversing with Marshall he

John Marshall, through his judicial decisions, played a greater part in shaping American government than any other man, with the possible exceptions of Washington and Madison. Marshall served as Chief Justice of the Supreme Court for thirty-four years.

never admitted anything for fear it would be turned against him. "Why if he were to ask me if it were daylight or not," said Jefferson, "I'd reply: 'Sir, I don't know. I can't tell.'"

Implied Powers and Loose Construction

McCulloch v. Maryland (1819) involved an attempt by Maryland to tax the Baltimore branch of the Bank of the United States. The case brought out basic questions about the origins and powers of the federal government.

Was the Constitution created by the states or by the people of the United States? Marshall argued that "the people" acting collectively had created the federal government. It is, he wrote, "the government of all; its powers are delegated by all; it represents all, and acts for all." It is thus a national government and in no way subordinate to the states within its sphere. But what was its sphere? This brings up the next question:

Was the federal government to be held strictly to its enumerated powers? In answering this question Marshall simply paraphrased Hamilton's argument in favor of the constitutionality of the first Bank of the United States (see p. 160). As long as the purposes of a law are constitutional, he wrote, it is the right of the federal government to choose any obvious means. The purposes of a central bank—to control currency, to assist in borrowing money and collecting taxes—are stated in the Constitution. The Bank was clearly adapted to carry out these purposes. Therefore the Bank was constitutional. This was an eloquent statement of implied powers and loose construction (see pp. 121–123).

Having established the constitutionality of the B.U.S., Marshall finally considered whether Maryland had the right to tax its operations. Arguing that "the power to tax is the power to destroy," he said no. If a state could tax one agency of the federal government, it could tax any other—the mails, the courts, the custom houses—and so make it impossible to carry on government at all. This was the weakest part of the decision. The Chief Justice's comparison of the B.U.S. to the post office was not accurate. The former was a profit-making corporation, mostly owned by private individuals; the latter was part of the executive department. The true issue was not the fact that Maryland taxed the Bank, but the degree—was the tax so unreasonably high as to put the Bank out of business? This part of the *McCulloch v. Maryland* decision has been overridden by the Supreme Court in the twentieth century.

Protection of Property Rights

Dartmouth College v. Woodward (1819) was one of several cases in which Marshall laid down decisions protecting property rights from interference by state legislatures. In 1815 the New Hampshire legislature had attempted to alter a charter granted to Dartmouth College by George III in 1769. Under the new charter a new set of trustees was elected, and the college was put under stricter state control. The old trustees, however, did not resign, and the former officials refused to turn over the college records and funds. When the case came before the Supreme Court, Marshall wrote a decision in which he supported the original charter. He argued that a charter was a contract with which a state had no right to interfere (see Article I, Section 10, clause 1, p. 122). Much of American business is carried on by corporations receiving charters from state legislatures. The Dartmouth College case, called the "Magna Carta of the corporation," helped to free business from attempts by state legislatures to alter the terms under which it might operate.

Expansion of Commerce Clause

Gibbons v. Ogden (1824) involved an attempt by New York to grant Robert Fulton and others associated with him a monopoly of all steamboat traffic on the Hudson River and other New York State waters. Marshall declared this monopoly unconstitutional. He argued that in granting such a monopoly New York invaded the power of the federal government over interstate commerce. In the course of this decision, he produced definitions of interstate commerce which have been of great importance in increasing federal power, especially in the twentieth century. Marshall said that interstate commerce was not just the exchange of goods but included a wide variety of interstate relations.

It is under this interpretation that the federal government has come to exert control over all sorts of activities which seem remote from commerce—radio, television, kidnaping, the protection of migratory birds, and so forth. Marshall maintained that whatever affects interstate commerce may come under federal control. Thus the federal government may exert control over a dam on a stream which runs into a navigable river which eventually crosses a state line.

Criticism of Marshall; His Influence

In the three cases mentioned, and in a number of others, the Supreme Court overrode the actions of state legislatures, and also the decisions of state courts. Thus the Court became a means whereby the federal government increased its power over the states. Marshall was naturally attacked by defenders of states' rights. He was also branded as an enemy of democracy. It was pointed out that the state legislatures which taxed the Bank of the United States, altered the Dartmouth College charter, and granted Fulton a monopoly were all elected by the people of their states and presumably acted in accordance with what the people wanted. Marshall had been appointed in 1801 by a President already repudiated by the voters. When Andrew Jackson was President, he once simply refused to carry out one of Marshall's decisions.

Yet in the long run Marshall triumphed. His great decisions became the law of the land. His nationalist, loose constructionist point of view, written into constitutional law, made the Constitution flexible enough to meet the ever-changing needs of a growing country in its passage from the horse-and-buggy age to the twentieth century.

FOREIGN AFFAIRS, 1815–1825

Although peace with Great Britain had been declared in 1815, bitter feelings continued. For many years a standard feature of Fourth of July celebrations—along with firing of cannon, balloon ascensions, and parades of militia—were

James Monroe, portrayed by Gilbert Stuart. Monroe was twice elected President, exercising the office during a period of strong national sentiment known as the "Era of Good Feeling." The famous Doctrine that bears his name was actually a policy originated by his Secretary of State, John Quincy Adams.

speeches damning the country that had impressed our seamen and burned our capital. Britain's true character, said a typical Independence Day orator, is "vain-glorious, haughty, mean, profligate, unjust; uniting the barbarities of savage life to the more refined cruelties of civilized man." The Treaty of Ghent was widely regarded as a mere truce. "That man must be blind to the indications of the future," declared Henry Clay in 1816, "who cannot see that we are destined to have war after war with Great Britain." Disputes over fishing rights at the mouth of the St. Lawrence River led to acts of violence between Canadian and New England fishermen. There was a naval race on the Great Lakes. On Lake Ontario the British built a vessel carrying the amazing total of 112 guns, and in answer the United States started to build

two ships of the line. From Maine to Oregon the boundary between the United States and Canada was unsettled.

Fortunately, there were influences that worked for peace. Each country was the other's best customer: industrial Britain provided a market for American raw materials, and agrarian America was an outlet for British manufactured goods. Neither country had anything to gain by renewed hostilities. The British foreign minister, Lord Castlereagh, was of the opinion that there were no two states "whose friendly relations are of more practical value to each other, or whose hostility so inevitably and so immediately entails upon both the most serious mischiefs." Under Castlereagh's leadership, Britain again and again took action to smooth out Anglo-American relations. For instance, the British ended all assistance to Indian tribes in United States territory south of the Great Lakes, and they allowed Stephen Decatur to use Gibraltar as a naval base for his ships operating against the Barbary pirates.

Secretary of State
John Quincy Adams

It was fortunate, too, that John Quincy Adams served as United States minister to Britain in 1815–1817 and as Secretary of State under President Monroe from 1817 to 1825. Son of John Adams, he had already spent eighteen years abroad in the diplomatic service. From the time he started his college studies at the University of Leyden in Holland at the age of thirteen, he had shown great ability and an amazing capacity for work. He knew five foreign languages. An intense patriot and strong nationalist, Adams looked forward to the day when the United States would dominate the entire North American continent.

As minister to England, Adams started negotiations leading to the famous Rush-Bagot Agreement of 1817. By this the United States

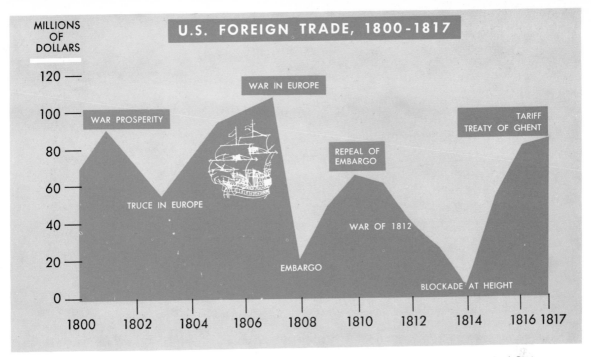

MILLIONS OF DOLLARS

U.S. FOREIGN TRADE, 1800-1817

WAR IN EUROPE

WAR PROSPERITY

TARIFF
TREATY OF GHENT

REPEAL OF EMBARGO

TRUCE IN EUROPE

WAR OF 1812

EMBARGO

BLOCKADE AT HEIGHT

120 — 100 — 80 — 60 — 40 — 20 — 0 —

1800   1802   1804   1806   1808   1810   1812   1814   1816 1817

American foreign trade reflected both conditions in Europe and the foreign policy of the United States. Note the decline that came with a brief truce in Europe in 1801-1803, and the sharp drop accompanying the Embargo Act and the War of 1812. On the other hand, foreign trade boomed when the goods of the United States, a neutral, were in demand in warring Europe.

and Britain agreed to lay up all armed ships on the Great Lakes, built or building, except for a few small vessels to control smuggling. Its importance should not be overemphasized, since it did not end fortification of the border and either party could withdraw from the agreement at any time. It was, however, the first example of mutual naval disarmament in history, and eventually the United States and Canada removed all fortifications along the 3,000 mile boundary from the Bay of Fundy to the Strait of Juan de Fuca.

Convention of 1818

A year after the Rush-Bagot Agreement came the Convention of 1818, dealing with fisheries, the northern boundary of the Louisiana Purchase, and Oregon (see map, p. 236). In regard to the St. Lawrence, this treaty tried to specify where United States fishermen might sink their lines and nets, and on what shores crews might land to dry and cure their catch. It fixed the northern boundary of the Louisiana Purchase by running the 49th parallel from the Lake of the Woods to the Rocky Mountains. Beyond the Rockies, the treaty provided "joint occupation" of Oregon for ten years. This meant that each country was free to carry on the fur trade and make settlements without interference from the other. Thus the Oregon question was not settled but deferred for later decision.

It was an achievement to make these treaties with Britain within three years of the close of the War of 1812, at a time when public opinion in each country was antagonistic to the other. The Rush-Bagot Agreement and Convention of 1818 did not settle all disputes. The Maine boundary, for instance, was still unclear. But when there is tension between nations it often clears the air to agree on *anything*.

235

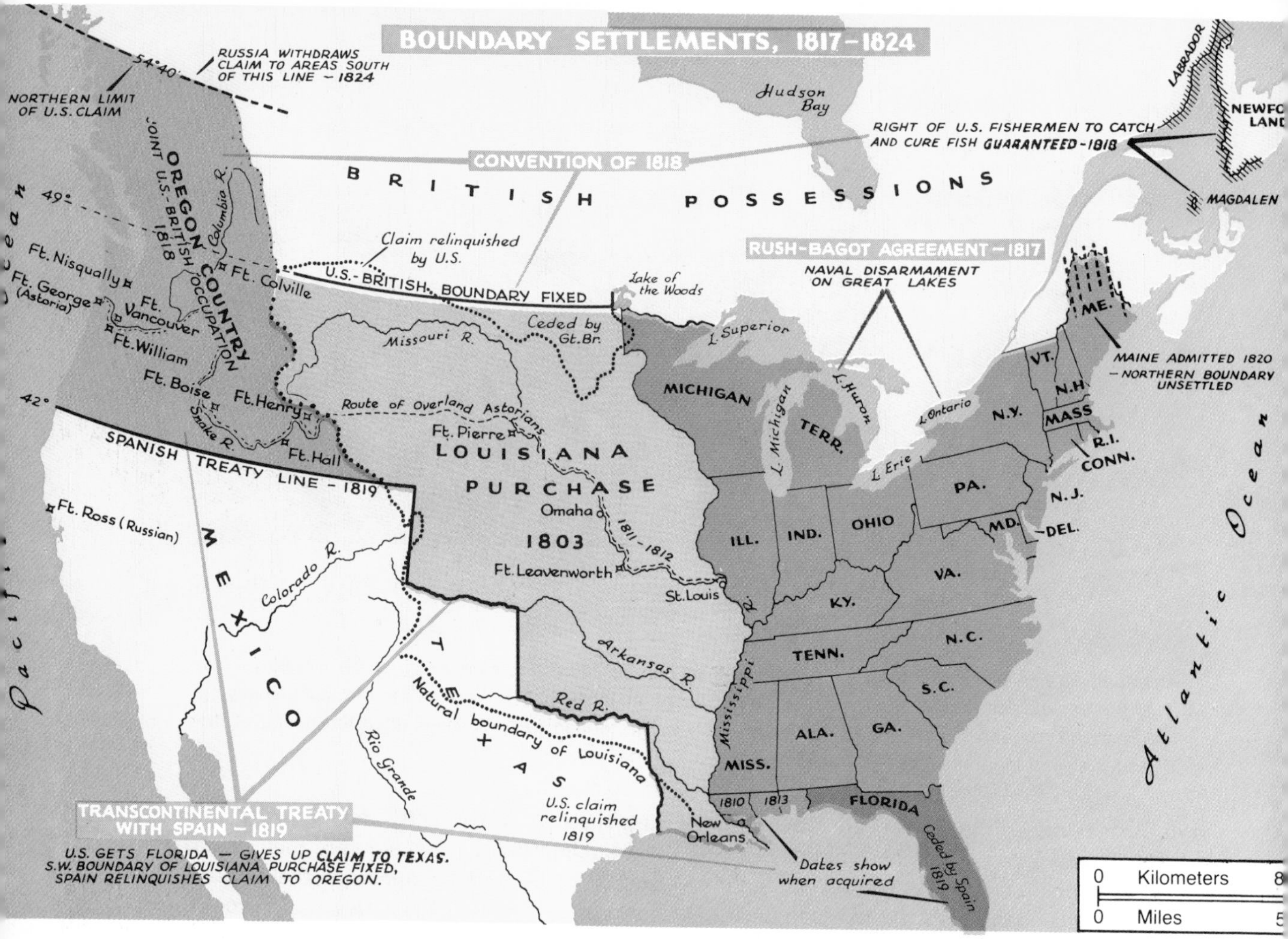
BOUNDARY SETTLEMENTS, 1817–1824
RUSSIA WITHDRAWS CLAIM TO AREAS SOUTH OF THIS LINE – 1824
54°40'
NORTHERN LIMIT OF U.S. CLAIM
Hudson Bay
RIGHT OF U.S. FISHERMEN TO CATCH AND CURE FISH GUARANTEED–1818
LABRADOR
NEWFO LAN
MAGDALEN
CONVENTION OF 1818
BRITISH POSSESSIONS
OREGON COUNTRY
JOINT U.S.-BRITISH OCCUPATION 1818
Columbia R.
49°
Ft. Nisqually
Ft. George (Astoria)
Ft. Vancouver
Ft. William
Ft. Colville
Claim relinquished by U.S.
U.S.-BRITISH BOUNDARY FIXED
Lake of the Woods
Ceded by Gt. Br.
RUSH-BAGOT AGREEMENT – 1817
NAVAL DISARMAMENT ON GREAT LAKES
L. Superior
L. Huron
L. Michigan
L. Ontario
L. Erie
ME.
MAINE ADMITTED 1820 – NORTHERN BOUNDARY UNSETTLED
VT.
N.H.
MASS.
N.Y.
R.I.
CONN.
N.J.
DEL.
MD.
PA.
OHIO
IND.
ILL.
MICHIGAN TERR.
VA.
KY.
N.C.
TENN.
S.C.
GA.
ALA.
MISS.
FLORIDA
Ceded by Spain 1819
1810
1813
New Orleans
Dates show when acquired
Missouri R.
Ft. Boise
Ft. Henry
Snake R.
Ft. Hall
Route of Overland Astorians
Ft. Pierre
LOUISIANA PURCHASE 1803
Omaha
1811–1812
Ft. Leavenworth
St. Louis
Mississippi R.
Arkansas R.
Red R.
42°
SPANISH TREATY LINE – 1819
Ft. Ross (Russian)
MEXICO
Colorado R.
TEXAS
Natural boundary of Louisiana
Rio Grande
U.S. claim relinquished 1819
TRANSCONTINENTAL TREATY WITH SPAIN – 1819
U.S. GETS FLORIDA – GIVES UP CLAIM TO TEXAS.
S.W. BOUNDARY OF LOUISIANA PURCHASE FIXED,
SPAIN RELINQUISHES CLAIM TO OREGON.
Pacific Ocean
Atlantic Ocean
Kilometers
Miles

John Quincy Adams, a great Secretary of State, arranged the "transcontinental treaty" whereby Spain agreed to cede Florida, fix the boundary of Louisiana, and give up claim to Oregon. With Great Britain he arranged the Convention of 1818, dealing with Oregon, the Canadian-U.S. boundary, and fishing rights. He also induced Russia to withdraw from Oregon to the 54° 40′ line.

The Florida Question and the "Transcontinental Treaty," 1819

Florida had been a cause of friction between the United States and Spain ever since the purchase of Louisiana in 1803. Spain claimed that the western boundary of Florida was the Mississippi River, while the United States maintained that it was the Perdido River, 200 miles farther east. By 1813 the United States had seized the disputed territory.

During the War of 1812, Spain was an ally of Great Britain. Florida therefore became a base of British and Indian operations against the United States. Even after the war, it remained a base for Creek and Seminole Indians who were on the warpath against the whites in Georgia and Tennessee.

In 1818 Andrew Jackson, in command of a force of Tennessee militia, pursued a force of Seminoles into Florida. Jackson not only ignored the boundary between the United States and Spanish territory but also seized Spanish posts at Pensacola and at St. Marks. (See pp. 320–321.)

Angry protests from Spain followed. The Spanish government demanded an indemnity for the "outrage" and punishment for Jackson. A majority of Monroe's cabinet at first thought Jackson should at least be censured, but John Quincy Adams defended him, saying his actions were a result of Spanish failure to keep order in Florida. Spain must either govern it efficiently or cede it to the United States.

Too weak to police or to defend Florida, Spain gave in. In 1819, by the Adams-Onis Treaty, the United States gained Florida and in return agreed to pay claims of American citizens against Spain, up to $5,000,000. Also called the "Transcontinental Treaty," this agreement fixed the "step boundary" from the Gulf of Mexico northwest to the 42nd parallel and along that line to the Pacific. This meant that the United States abandoned a shadowy claim to Texas, while Spain gave up a claim to Oregon as strong as our own. The Adams-Onis Treaty has been called with justice "the greatest diplomatic victory won by a single individual in the history of the United States."

THE MONROE DOCTRINE

The last great event of John Quincy Adams's term as Secretary of State was the issuance of the Monroe Doctrine in 1823. This famous statement of foreign policy had a rather complex background. It involved events in Latin America, in Europe, and on the Pacific coast of North America.

Between 1814 and 1824, many of Spain's South American colonies declared independence under the leadership of two great heroes, Simón Bolívar, "the Liberator of the North," and José de San Martín, "the Liberator of the South."

"Spectacular as were George Rogers Clark's expedition to the West and Washington's march to Yorktown," it has been observed, "they represent but short walks compared to Bolívar's slow advance to Peru through more than two thousand miles of towering mountains." Even more amazing was San Martín's expedition across the Andes from the Argentine, when he led an army of 5,000 across mountain passes over 12,000 feet high. By 1823 Mexico and Central America had also declared independence from Spain. The people of the United States were enthusiastically on the side of the revolutionaries, who declared their right to rule themselves as Americans had done in 1776.

Sympathy for the Spanish Americans was increased by European events. After Napoleon's defeat, Europe was dominated by the monarchs of Russia, Austria, Prussia, and Britain, who were united in the Quadruple Alliance, popularly although mistakenly called the "Holy Alliance." Gradually Britain withdrew, but since the king of France was admitted in 1818, the foursome remained. A purpose of this alliance was to suppress democracy. In the words of Klemens von Metternich, the Austrian prime minister, democracy was "the disease which must be cured, the volcano which must be extinguished, the gangrene which must be burned out with the hot iron." The rulers declared the right to intervene in other countries to suppress liberal revolutions. In 1821, Austrian soldiers put down revolutions in Italy. In 1823 a French army crossed the Pyrenees into Spain and quelled a rebellion there.

Fear of European Intervention

After their success in crushing democratic movements in Europe, some leaders of the Quadruple Alliance talked of attempting the same thing in the Western Hemisphere. Although in fact there was never any likelihood that the project would be adopted, rumors that it was being considered caused alarm in the United States.

Once relieved of Spanish commercial restrictions, the new Latin-American republics threw open their ports. This was an advantage to Britain, which had the largest merchant marine in the world and the cheapest manufactured goods. If the Quadruple Alliance returned these republics to Spanish rule, Britain would suffer loss. George Canning, successor to Castlereagh as British foreign minister, also feared that France might take advantage of an opportunity to re-establish a colonial empire in America. He therefore hoped to discourage intervention to suppress the young republics. He also desired to promote better relations between the United States and Britain. In August 1823, he suggested to Richard Rush, United States minister in London, that they issue a joint statement to the effect that they thought Spain could not recover her colonies, that they opposed acquisition of them by any other power, and that the United States and Great Britain would not acquire any portion for themselves. The extraordinary proposition almost amounted to setting up an Anglo-American alliance, and Rush referred the question to Washington for decision.

Greek Rebellion;
Russian Expansion in North America

At the time of these events, there also arose two other situations that disturbed relations between the United States and European powers. In 1821 the Greeks rebelled against their Turkish masters, demanding independence. For eight years they carried on a heroic war against their oppressors. The Greeks won great sympathy in this country, because they were Christians and because they claimed descent from the heroes of classical times. Throughout the United States, churches collected money and arms for Greece. Some young Americans talked of raising a volunteer army to fight the Turks.

There were demands that the federal government aid the rebels. This helped to promote popular enthusiasm for ancient Greece, with significant effect on American culture. This was seen in the Greek revival movement in American architecture, in the founding of Greek letter fraternities in colleges, and in literature (see Edgar Allan Poe's poem "To Helen").

In 1821 Russia, already in possession of Alaska, made an aggressive move on the Pacific coast. The czar proclaimed that his dominions extended south to the 51st parallel, far into Oregon. He warned all non-Russian ships to stay over a hundred miles away from the region he claimed.

In the latter part of 1823, therefore, the United States was faced with a number of difficult decisions in foreign policy. Should the United States allow Russia to expand her holdings in North America? Should the United States aid the Greeks? How should the United States meet the threat of intervention in America by the Quadruple Alliance? Should the United States accept Canning's offer of co-operation or act alone?

Monroe discussed these questions with his cabinet and consulted his fellow Virginians, Jefferson and Madison. The former Presidents favored Canning's proposal for a joint statement with Britain. But John Quincy Adams remarked that it would look ridiculous for the United States "to come in as a cock-boat in the wake of the British man-of-war." He urged that the United States act independently, and his view prevailed.

Principles of the
Monroe Doctrine

Out of these discussions came the Monroe Doctrine. This landmark in foreign policy was presented to the world in an undramatic way. It appeared in two widely separated passages in Monroe's annual message to Congress on December 2, 1823. It contained four essential provisions—two warnings and two reassurances.

(1) *Hands off the American republics.*

The political system of the allied powers is essentially different . . . from that of America. . . . We . . . should consider any attempt on their part to extend their system to any portion of this hemisphere as dangerous to our peace and safety.

"The political system of the allied powers" means the system whereby countries are dominated by kings and noblemen. "That of America" refers to self-governing republics, like the United States and most of the new Latin-American countries. This statement denies to European countries any right of intervention in the Western Hemisphere.

(2) *No new colonization in the Americas.*

. . . the American continents . . . are henceforth not to be considered as subjects for future colonization by any European powers.

This was directed at Russian expansion into Oregon. This "no colonization" principle, as applied to the whole Western Hemisphere, originated with John Quincy Adams. It is now broadened, so that it forbids transfer of colonies in the Western Hemisphere from one European power to another. When in 1940 Germany conquered Denmark, for instance, the principle was invoked to prevent the Danish territory of Greenland from coming under German rule.

(3) *Existing European colonies are in no danger from the United States.*

With the existing colonies or dependencies of any European power we have not interfered and shall not interfere.

While objecting to *new* colonization, the United States reassured European countries as to their existing colonies. This applied especially to the fertile island of Cuba, still under Spanish rule. Many Americans, with John Quincy Adams, expected Cuba to fall into the hands of the United States eventually, "like a ripe apple," but this statement was designed to allay British fears that immediate annexation was planned.

(4) *No participation by the United States in purely European affairs.*

In the wars of European powers in matters relating to themselves we have never taken any part, nor does it comport with our policy so to do. It is only when our rights are invaded or seriously menaced that we resent injuries or make preparations for our defense. . . .

Our policy in regard to Europe, which was adopted at an early stage of the wars which have so long agitated that quarter of the globe, . . . remains the same, which is not to interfere in the internal concerns of any of its powers.

This meant specifically that the United States would send no aid to the Greeks in their war with the Turks and that the United States would take no action to prevent intervention by the Quadruple Alliance in European countries. These sentences have a far wider significance, however, than their particular meaning in 1823. They are a restatement of the isolation and nonentanglement principles laid down in Washington's Neutrality Proclamation of 1793 and in his Farewell Address, as well as in Jefferson's First Inaugural Address. Not until the twentieth century, when the United States had become a world power, were these principles altered.

Importance of the Monroe Doctrine

Monroe's message had no special influence at the time it was issued. If the statesmen of the Quadruple Alliance ever seriously contemplated intervention in America, it was the British navy, not Monroe's warning, that made them back down. In 1824 the Russians, already in possession of more

QUESTION • *Was the Monroe Doctrine a "bluff"?*

Sectionalism: Different Ways of Life

Fogg Museum of Art, Cambridge, Mass.

"Flax Scutching Bee" (detail) by Linton Park. National Gallery of Art, Washington D.C. Gift of Edgar William and Bernice Chrysler Garbisch.

By 1853, Studebaker had established a wagon factory in Hangtown, California, as depicted by H. M. T. Powell, top. At right, a "scutching bee" on a farm in the North, with men and women beating flax as well as each other. Bottom, a cotton market in New Orleans, painted by the French impressionist Degas.

land than they could efficiently govern, agreed to withdraw from Oregon and to make 54° 40′ the southern boundary of Alaska. The Greeks managed to gain independence without American aid.

Obviously, then, the Monroe Doctrine owes its importance to later developments. Its bold warnings to European powers became important only when the United States was able to back them up without reliance on British sea power.

Latin-American nations have never shown much enthusiasm for the Monroe Doctrine. This may seem odd when the doctrine was apparently designed to protect them. But in fact the doctrine was *unilateral*—it was a one-sided statement of the interests of the United States. While it asserted that Latin-American countries were to be protected from European aggression, they were not consulted. Furthermore, the doctrine did not protect our southern neighbors from intervention or expansion by the United States itself.

SECTIONALISM

In most countries there are centrifugal or divisive forces working against the spirit of nationalism. They take a variety of forms: tribalism and language differences that handicap many African states; antagonism between classes, such as that between the bourgeoisie, the peasants, and the proletariat in nineteenth-century France; or religious strife, such as that between Hindus and Muslims in India, or between Roman Catholics and Buddhists in Vietnam. During the early years of the United States, the most obvious counter to nationalism was sectional rivalry.

By the 1820's it was clear that the three major sections—the Northeast, the South, and the "Old Northwest"—were following different lines of development. Manufacturing plants were multiplying in the Northeast. The South was doubling its production of cotton every ten years. The Northwest was the home of independent farmers who raised crops on land they themselves cleared and put under the plow. Regional differences led to regional loyalties. A recent historian claims, perhaps with some exaggeration, that these loyalties were stronger than national patriotism:

By the close of the 1830's every one-horse planter in the cotton belt, every coonskin-clad farmer along the western waters, every shopkeeper in the smoky mill towns of New England, was blindly loyal to the region where he lived. This spirit of sectional patriotism alone allowed Americans to place regional interests above those of the nation.

Manufacturing in the Northeast

In the long history of civilization from the building of the Egyptian pyramids three thousand years before the birth of Christ until the eighteenth century, there was little important change in tools used or sources of power. Then came the industrial revolution. This has changed the way people live, especially in Europe and America, more in 200 years than it changed in the previous 5,000. Basically, the industrial revolution has consisted of three developments: (1) the substitution of complicated machines for simple hand tools; (2) the substitution of artificial sources of power, such as the steam engine and electric motor, for natural sources of power such as draft animals and falling water; and (3) the invention of faster, more efficient means of transportation and communication.

The industrial revolution began in England. Between 1730 and 1800, new machines transformed the cotton industry. So great was the efficiency of mechanical means of spinning and weaving that cotton cloth, formerly a luxury, became the cheapest textile the world had ever seen. With the great improvements made by James Watt, the steam engine began to supply a tremendous new source of power for industry and transportation. For a time the industrial revolution was almost a British monopoly. Britain enjoyed certain advantages over the rest of the world: among them were established markets, mechanical skills, and surplus capital to build factories. British laws, furthermore, forbade the export of textile machinery or the emigration of skilled workers.

The Textile Industry

The new technology reached America with the arrival of the Englishman Samuel Slater in 1789. Before coming here, Slater had memorized the details of the best English textile machinery. Within a year he built machines that were set up in a factory in Pawtucket, Rhode Island. This was but the first of many mills that Slater equipped with his machinery.

The textile industry centered in New England for a number of reasons. The region contained available water power and an abundant water supply. There were funds available for

The Union Manufactories of Maryland, about 1812. Not all of America's early textile factories were in New England. This Maryland plant was established during the Embargo, when it was necessary to produce at home many goods previously obtained abroad. Here 600 employees tended 80,000 spindles driven by 16 water wheels.

investment in new enterprises. But New England's principal resource was human. In over two centuries of wresting a living from an unpromising environment in a harsh climate, New Englanders had developed traits that made the term "Yankee" a synonym for ingenuity, thrift, and hard work. Unable to meet the competition from newly cleared, more fertile farm regions in the West, many Yankees moved to factory towns. By 1840, some 700 cotton mills and 500 woolen mills in New England employed about 50,000 workers. There were also many small factories turning out products such as shoes, clocks, carriages, and paper. All this was, however, just a beginning. There were in the region as many people engaged in shipping as in manufacturing, and even more engaged in farming.

In the Middle Atlantic states—Pennsylvania, New Jersey, and New York—manufacturing took hold even more than in New England. The new transportation system opened western markets, and European immigrants supplied much cheap labor. There were textile factories in this region, although not as many as in New England. The area was the great center of the iron industry and of the manufacture of machinery.

Early Effects of the Industrial Revolution

The beginnings of the industrial revolution had several important effects: (1) Existing cities, such as New York and Philadelphia, grew rapidly; at power sites new cities appeared, such as Lowell and Lawrence at falls and rapids on the Merrimac River. (2) There was a great demand for better transportation to carry food and raw materials to the cities and manufactured goods to markets. (3) The cities provided new markets for farm products. (4) There appeared two new classes of people—the industrial capitalists and the industrial laborers—those who built and owned the factories and those who worked in them. In the handicraft age, the master worker who owned a shop sat at the same bench as his journeymen and apprentices and dressed as they did. Now owners and workers performed distinctly different functions; they no longer worked together daily; they led dissimilar lives. Their differences in dress became symbols that are still understood today: a top hat and frock coat designate a capitalist; a cap and overalls, a factory worker. (See also p. 286.)

The profits from manufacturing and shipping in the Northeast were great. Much of the money went back into the businesses, but much of it also went into banks in the larger cities. The bankers of Boston, Philadelphia, and New York in turn made investments all over the country. They lent money to speculators in western lands, to companies building Mississippi River steamboats, and to Alabama cotton producers. Thus the country began to be tied together by a web of credit.

Cotton Culture in the South

The British industrial revolution affected the South even more than New England, although in a different way. As British cotton mills produced cheaper and cheaper goods for a worldwide market, they demanded more and more raw cotton, most of which came from the southern states.

It was the cotton gin, invented by Eli Whitney in 1793, which made it possible to produce cotton cheaply in the South. In cotton as it is harvested from the fields, the fibers are so tightly fastened to the seeds that a hand laborer could get rid of the seeds in only one pound of cotton per day. Whitney's machine, operated by hand, could clean fifty pounds a day; with water power, a thousand pounds.

Change in the Southern Attitude Toward Slavery

British demands for cotton and the invention of the cotton gin changed the southern attitude toward slavery. In the late eighteenth century the only part of the South where slave labor paid its way was in the rice fields of South Carolina and Georgia. Elsewhere, planters were "slave poor" because they owned slaves but could make little profit from their labor. Slaves were usually less efficient than free laborers. Having no incentive to work hard, they required continual supervision. They had to be fed and clothed in seasons when there was no work to do.

As we have seen, many Southerners, including Jefferson, Washington, and Patrick Henry, publicly condemned slavery. In 1787 Southerners supported the Northwest Ordinance, which prohibited slavery north of the Ohio River. In 1808 they supported the abolition of the slave trade at the earliest date allowed by the Constitution.

Southern planters were perplexed, however, as to what to do with slaves after they were freed. Many of the Negroes would be helpless, particularly if not given land, tools, and training in how to live on their own. To meet this situation, slaveowners in Virginia, Maryland, and Kentucky founded the American Colonization Society to send freed slaves back to Africa. Among the early members were James Madison, Andrew Jackson, and Henry Clay. In 1819 Congress appropriated $100,000 to support the project, and in 1822 the society founded the republic of Liberia ("land of freedom") on the west coast of Africa as a haven for American Negroes. But the society lacked funds to send more than a few thousand people back to the continent from which their ancestors came. The project was impractical in any case, because long residence in America made it difficult for them to adapt themselves to conditions in

In the heyday of river traffic on the Mississippi, from about 1840 until the Civil War broke out in 1861, the volume of traffic through New Orleans was exceeded only by that through New York. Following the harvest season, the levee and the streets behind them were piled high with the staples of the vast region drained by the Mississippi River and its tributaries — sugar, molasses, rice, tobacco, corn, pork, barrel staves, wheat, oats, flour, and, above all, cotton.

Africa, and few had any desire to leave this country.

Meanwhile, cotton culture proved ideally suited to the use of slave labor. The operations—planting, hoeing, picking, and ginning—were simple and required little training. Most of the work was done in gangs and so could be easily supervised. Cotton growing occupied the Negroes more continually than other crops, such as wheat or tobacco, so they did not have to be supported through any long periods of idleness. Thus slavery became profitable. Southerners began to change their attitude and to defend slavery. Criticism of the institution died out. In 1827 there were over a hundred antislavery societies in the South; ten years later all had disbanded.

Since the climate of the upper South was unsuited to cotton growing (see map, p. 7), cotton first was a major crop in South Carolina and Georgia. Cotton plantations moved rapidly west into the fertile "black belt" of Mississippi and Alabama and then into the rich bottom lands along the Mississippi River and its tributaries. The admission into the Union of the states of Mississippi in 1817, Alabama in 1819, and Arkansas in 1836 revealed this migration. The rapid expansion of cotton culture was not merely the result of the increased demands of British mills. It also came from the fact that planters often sowed one cotton crop after another until they had "mined" the fertility from the soil and had to move on. It was cheaper to migrate than to restore fertility.

Cotton was not the only important southern crop. Virginia, Kentucky, and North Carolina produced tobacco. Louisiana produced sugar. Everywhere farmers raised corn, wheat, hogs, and cattle. Still, "Cotton is king" was a common southern saying; it was the greatest export, not only of the South, but of the nation.

The institution of slavery, which had been abolished in the North, made southern society unique. The characteristics and effects of slavery in the South will be discussed in a later chapter (see pp. 331–334). Suffice it to say now that the South developed something like a caste system. At the top were a few great planters, owning 50 to 200 or more slaves and cultivating the best land. Below the great owners was a class of small planters who generally made a rather poor living. Then there was a large group of small farmers raising diversified crops. This group often fared rather well, especially in regions unsuited to cotton growing. At the bottom of the white social scale was a class of impoverished white people, some of them on the move and others just managing to live on exhausted soils for which cotton growers had no use. At the bottom were the Negroes. All but a few were slaves, and nearly all performed heavy labor or menial tasks.

There was little manufacturing in the South. There was no such readily available labor supply as in the Northeast because whites disliked factory labor and blacks were not thought to be fitted for it. Furthermore, the money and credit of wealthy people were tied up in land and slaves, so there was little surplus capital available for building factories or buying expensive machinery.

Rapid Settlement of the Northwest

"All America is moving westward," wrote a British traveler who passed through Pittsburgh in 1816. The census of 1820 revealed that one-quarter of the population of the United States lived west of the Appalachians. Even more rapid than the settlement of the Gulf states was that of the Northwest.

Settlement of this region had been slowed up until after the War of 1812 because of the danger from Indians. The result of the war had been to break up Tecumseh's Indian league and to put an end to British support of the northern tribes. After the defeat of the Sauk chieftain Black Hawk in 1832, the Indians were driven west of the Mississippi.

Many who first came to the Northwest described it as a paradise on earth. The Ohio, they wrote, was truly "the beautiful river" if only because of the magnificent hardwood trees—oak, maple, ash, chestnut—along its shores. The forest was occasionally broken by clearings where the grass grew four and five feet high in the rich soil. The amount of game was almost unbelievable. There was an abundance of deer, bear, duck, turkey, goose, and partridge. A single flock of pigeons might take four or five hours to fly over a spot, and when they alighted they were so tame they could be slaughtered easily using only a club. Fish were no less plentiful. A party fishing at a waterfall on the Maumee River in Ohio in the 1830's filled 850 barrels with walleyed pike and bass.

Cheap Land

But the greatest lure of the Northwest was vacant land. According to the English economist and novelist Harriet Martineau, who made an extended tour of the United States in the years 1834 to 1836:

The possession of land is the aim of all actions, generally speaking, and a cure for all social evils, among men in the United States. If a man is disappointed in politics or love, he goes and buys land. If he disgraces himself, he betakes himself to a lot in the West. If the demand for any article of manufacture slackens, the operatives drop into the unsettled lands. If a citizen's neighbours rise above

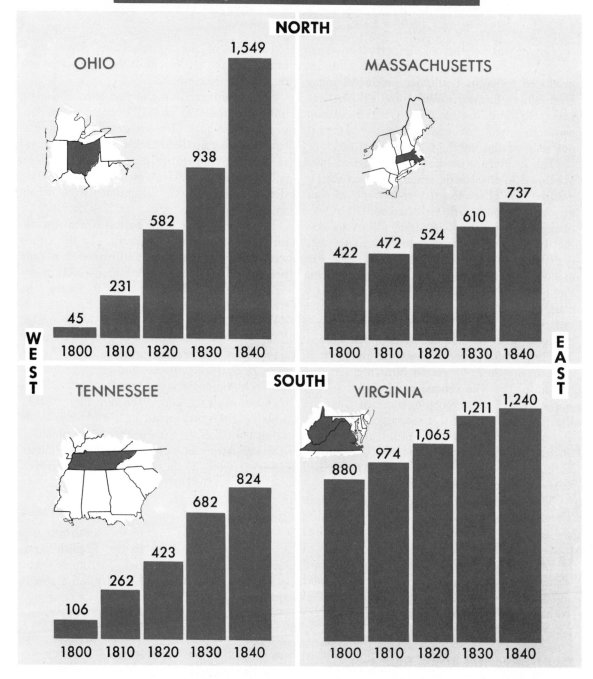

GROWTH OF POPULATION (in thousands) 1800—1840

NORTH

OHIO

1800	1810	1820	1830	1840
45	231	582	938	1,549

MASSACHUSETTS

1800	1810	1820	1830	1840
422	472	524	610	737

WEST

SOUTH

EAST

TENNESSEE

1800	1810	1820	1830	1840
106	262	423	682	824

VIRGINIA

1800	1810	1820	1830	1840
880	974	1,065	1,211	1,240

Can the rapid growth of two typical western states be explained by the attraction of cheap land? Does the fact that Massachusetts expanded more rapidly than Virginia, and Ohio more rapidly than Tennessee, suggest the superiority of a free labor system over one based on slave labor? What other information would you need to draw this conclusion? What other conclusions can you draw from the above charts?

him in the towns, he betakes himself where he can be monarch of all he surveys.

Land was everywhere cheap. Many settlers did not even bother about survey lines and "squatted" on whatever unoccupied acres they could find.

So the settlers poured into the Northwest. From the South came independent farmers and impoverished whites anxious to get away from slavery and the plantation system. From the northeastern states came farmers lured by tales of the almost unbelievable fertility of the western lands. Eventually, Europe supplied a third stream of immigrants, who often landed at New York and traveled west by the Erie Canal.

Typical citizens of the northwestern states lived on their own farms, which were cultivated by themselves and their family. On the very edge of the frontier, they might live in an open-sided lean-to. Killing the trees by "girdling" (cutting the bark all around at the base in order to let in the sun), they would plant a crop of corn. They might also raise a few razorback hogs, which would be allowed to run practically wild in the woods. For the rest, they lived on game. In longer-settled areas, farmers would probably build a frame house. They would then raise more varied crops and acquire cash by sending their products to market.

Growth of Towns and Cities

But farmers alone did not develop the West. They could not prosper entirely by their own efforts. They needed sawmills for lumber and flour mills for grain. They needed barges and wagons to carry produce to market, merchants to buy it, and storekeepers to provide the goods they could not make themselves, such as glassware, shoes, lamps, and iron tools. These people, as has been pointed out earlier (p. 86), gathered in towns usually situated at points of transshipment. Among these were Cincinnati (near where three tributaries pour into the

Ohio River), Louisville (at the Falls of the Ohio), and Nashville (at the head of steam navigation on the Cumberland River).

Manufacturing sprang up in such cities. The showpiece of Cincinnati at one time was a combined flour and textile mill run by a steam engine. This "stupendous pile" of stone and brick reached the then amazing height of nine stories. The largest manufacturing center, however, was Pittsburgh. Here were glass factories, which in 1815 produced glassware worth $235,000. Even more important were Pittsburgh's iron works.

In western towns, people could often make money more rapidly than on the farms. Skilled workers such as masons and wheelwrights were so scarce that they demanded, and got, high wages. Manufacturers could charge high prices because the demand for their articles was always increasing and because the cost of transporting goods across or around the Appalachians acted as a sort of tariff, raising the price of eastern goods. Western towns offered such prospects of wealth that selling lots in future cities became a standard way for speculators to fleece suckers. Glowing descriptions of town sites were satirized in a southern editor's imaginary prospectus of the "City of Skunksburgh":

This charming place . . . is situated . . . not far from the junction of Pitt's main branch, and a Western fork called the Slough, which runs in the rainy season, and washes the confines of Farnsworth's lower hog pens. . . . A noble bluff of 18 inches commands the harbor. . . . Commodious and picturesque positions will be reserved for the Exchange and City Hall, a church, one Gymnastic and one Polytechnic foundation, one Olympic and two Dramatic theatres, an Equestrian circus, an observatory, two marine and two Foundling Hospitals, and in the most commercial part of the city will be a reservation for seventeen banks, to each of which may be attached a lunatic Hospital. . . .

A line of Velocipede stages will be immediately established from Skunksburgh straight through the

Women Demand Independence
The Seneca Falls Declaration, 1848

The women's rights movement in the United States was formally launched at a convention at Seneca Falls, N.Y. in July 1848 (see pages 282-283). Its principal leaders, Elizabeth Cady Stanton and Lucretia Coffin Mott, had resented being denied full membership in abolitionist societies or the right to speak at abolitionist meetings. The convention published a declaration, closely modeled—as these excerpts show—on the Declaration of Independence:

We hold these truths to be self-evident: that all men and women are created equal; that they are endowed by their Creator with certain inalienable rights; that among these are life, liberty and the pursuit of happiness . . .

The history of mankind is a history of repeated injuries and usurpations on the part of man toward woman, having in direct object the establishment of an absolute tyranny over her. To prove this, let facts be submitted to a candid world.

He has never permitted her to exercise her inalienable right to the elective franchise. . . .

He has monopolized nearly all the profitable employments . . . .

He has denied her facilities for obtaining a thorough education, all colleges being closed to her.

He allows her in Church as well as State but a subordinate position . . .

He has endeavored to destroy her confidence in her own powers, to lessen her self-respect, and to make her willing to lead a dependent and abject life.

Resolved, That the objection of indelicacy and impropriety, which is so often brought against women when she addresses a public audience, comes with very ill grace from those who encourage, by their attendance, her appearance on the stage, the concert, or feats at the circus.

Resolved, That it is the duty of the women of this country to secure to themselves the sacred right of the elective franchise.

Resolved, that the speedy success of our cause depends upon the zealous and untiring efforts of both men and women, for the overthrow of the monopoly of the pulpit, and for securing to women an equal participation with men in the various trades, professions, and commerce.

- What grievances did the declaration set forth?

- To what extent have these grievances been eliminated? When and how? For references, consult the index, under "Women."

- What other instances of unequal treatment might the declaration have set forth?

- Have women achieved equality with men in the U.S. today?

O-ke-fin-o-cau Swamp, . . . and, as soon as a canal shall be cut through the Rocky Mountains, there will be a direct communication with the Columbia River, and then to the Pacific Ocean. Then opens a theatre of trade bounded only by the Universe.

Western Democracy

A western man was proud of his self-reliance and independence. A man was judged by what he could do for himself—how well he could handle an axe, slaughter a hog, or plow a furrow. Equality was not a theory stated by philosophers, but a fact of life. "Into all activities was carried the practice of democracy, whether politics, law, military, or religious life. The judge could leave his bench, and return to his plow; the preacher from pulpit to stable work."

With equality went democracy. Whereas in the original thirteen states voting rights had depended on ownership of a certain amount of property, in the West this was replaced by manhood suffrage—the right of all adult males to vote. In the older states, voters had usually chosen for office their "betters"—men of wealth and social position; in the West, they elected men like themselves. When young Abe Lincoln started making his way in Illinois politics in the 1830's, part of his success as a vote-getter was the result of his skill in wrestling, handling a scythe, and splitting rails.

QUESTION • *What might western women have prided themselves on?*

Points of Sectional Conflict

Of the different sections here described, each had its own prevailing attitude on four major issues—public land policy, a protective tariff, internal improvements at federal expense, and the extension of slavery into the territories. The questions involved in these issues and the attitudes of the sections may be summarized as follows:

(1) **Public land policy.** Should lands be offered to settlers at a low price or a high one?

Should they be opened to settlement rapidly or slowly? Should "squatters," who occupied lands before they were opened for sale, have any rights to the land they farmed? Western frontier farmers naturally favored cheap land, rapid settlement, and "squatters' rights." Eastern manufacturers were opposed to such policies for fear the West would draw off their labor supply. Eastern farmers were often opposed to cheap western lands for fear of western competition. Southerners were divided on this issue. Plantation owners wanted lands opened rapidly to sale, but were opposed to "squatters' rights" because the squatters might get to the best lands first.

(2) **A protective tariff.** Should there be high tariffs to protect United States industries? Or should there be a low tariff which would allow foreign goods to come in cheaply in exchange for American agricultural products? Northeastern manufacturers and laborers naturally favored protective tariffs that would keep out foreign goods, or at least raise the prices for the consumer, so that American factories could compete successfully in the American market. As Southerners came to realize that their section was not to become a manufacturing region, they turned more and more against the system of protection. The high tariff caused them to pay more for manufactured goods, but they received no benefit from it. Furthermore, they felt they would get a better price for their cotton from Britain if the British could sell more goods in this country. Surprisingly, the Northwest, a farming region, was the section most completely in favor of protection. The explanation for this apparent contradiction is that the Westerners thought that the growth of industrial cities would increase the market for farm products. Protection might encourage manufacturing west of the Appalachians, and revenue from the tariff might be used for building much-needed roads and canals. The American protective system also included high tariffs on cer-

tain staples grown in the West, such as wool from Ohio and hemp from Kentucky.

(3) **Internal improvements.** Should the federal government spend money to build roads and canals, or at least help states and private companies to build them? The Northwest was overwhelmingly in favor of using federal money for such purposes because it needed roads and canals to get its goods to market and yet had very little cash. The South, with a fine river system, was opposed. Southerners also feared that such schemes would be used as an argument to keep up tariffs in order to obtain more money for the federal government. The Northeast generally favored internal improvements at federal expense, partly because the tariff might have to be kept high to pay for them.

(4) **Extension of slavery into territories.** Should the territories be closed to slavery on the model of the Northwest Ordinance? Or should slaveowners have the right to take slaves with them into the territories, just as they might take cattle or horses? Since cotton culture demanded the expansion of the plantation system into new lands and apparently depended on slave labor, Southerners insisted that they be allowed to take their slaves with them anywhere but into the free states. Opposed to the southern attitude were northern convictions equally determined. Many Northerners felt that slavery was a moral wrong. While agreeing that southern states had a right to maintain slavery where it already existed, they felt it should not be allowed to expand. Another argument against extending slavery, especially strong in the Northwest, was that the territories should be reserved as an area where poor people could go and establish farms for themselves. Wherever slavery existed, the free laborer and small farmer did not fare well. Plantation owners took the best lands, and manual labor was scorned as the occupation of slaves.

These conflicting sectional interests became the major problem of national politics. It was the task of politicians to find means of compromise in order to save the Union.

Activities: Chapter 9

For Mastery and Review

1. What are basic elements of nationalism? In what ways did it express itself in federal politics?

2. What was the National Road? How did turnpikes differ from it? In what ways were the roads of the day unsatisfactory? Describe the Erie Canal. What were some of its economic and political effects?

3. For four of John Marshall's decisions (see pp. 196, 231–233), explain (a) the factors involved in each case, (b) the opinions themselves, and (c) their importance. On what grounds were Marshall's decisions attacked?

4. Outline the terms of the agreements made between the United States and Great Britain while John Quincy Adams was Secretary of State. What were the causes of friction between the United States and Spain over Florida? What were the terms of the Adams-Onís Treaty? Why was it called the "transcontinental treaty"?

5. What was the Quadruple Alliance? What were its purposes? How did these purposes apparently affect Latin America? What was the United States' interest in the situation? How was England affected? Explain the specific meaning and application of each part of the Monroe Doctrine as of 1823. Explain the Latin-American reaction.

6. Describe the geographical concentration of industry. Why did the textile industry settle in New England? What manufacturing developed in the Middle Atlantic states? Why? What were the effects of the beginning of the industrial revolution?

7. Trace the developments by which cotton became "King" in the South. What were the main social classes in southern society? Why was there little manufacturing there?

8. What factors led to the rapid settlement of the West? Describe the life of the "independent farmer." Where and why did cities develop in the West? Why did the West lead the manhood suffrage movement?

9. Make a chart comparing in three parallel columns the stands of the Northeast, the Northwest, and the South on (a) the policy of public land, (b) a protective tariff, (c) internal improvements at federal expense, and (d) the extension of slavery into the territories. Indicate divided opinion within the sections.

Unrolling the Map

1. On an outline map of the eastern half of the United States, trace and name the major rivers, showing the head of navigation of each. Draw in the National Road and other major highways. Show the major canals. Place on the map cities that owe their importance to transportation: those at important points of canals, those at heads of navigation of rivers, and those located on the National Road.

2. On an outline map of the United States, trace the boundaries settled while John Quincy Adams was Secretary of State (1817–1825). Emphasize the element of compromise by shading the territorial claims relinquished by the United States and cross-hatching its gains.

Who, What, and Why Important?

nationalism	National Road
"Era of Good Feeling"	turnpike
James Monroe	Robert Fulton
second B.U.S.	Erie Canal
Tariff of 1816	John Marshall
John C. Calhoun	John Quincy Adams

Rush-Bagot Agreement
Convention of 1818
Adams-Onis Treaty
Latin-American independence
Quadruple Alliance
Monroe Doctrine
Greek Revolution
sectionalism

Samuel Slater
Eli Whitney
American Colonization Society
plantation system
"independent farmer"
public lands
internal improvements

To Pursue the Matter

1. For opinions of English ladies about travel in America and the people they met see Arnof, *A Sense of the Past*, pp. 128–134.

2. For texts and analyses of some of John Marshall's great constitutional decisions see Bragdon et al., *Frame of Government*, pp. 171–199.

3. What hardships of frontier life so shortened people's lives that few men and women lived to old age? See Clark, *Frontier America*, ch. 9.

4. What was it like to travel on Mississippi River steamboats? See Mark Twain, *Life on the Mississippi*, or "Heyday of the Floating Palace," *American Heritage*, October 1957.

5. Who should get credit for the Monroe Doctrine? See Fine and Brown, *The American Past*, issue no. 11.

6. Make a diagrammatic map of the Erie Canal, showing its many remarkable features. See Waggoner, *Long Haul West: The Great Canal Era, 1817–1850*.

7. For reflection, discussion, investigation:

a) Why was water travel superior to overland transportation in the early nineteenth century?

b) Have the elements promoting American national patriotism changed since the period touched on in this chapter? How? And what of sectionalism?

c) "The Westerner was proud of his self-reliance and independence; . . . with equality went democracy." Is this true of Americans today?

Chapter 10

Jacksonian Democracy

*It is not impossible to conceive the surprising liberty that
the Americans enjoy; some idea may likewise be formed of their extreme
equality; but the political activity that pervades the United States
must be seen in order to be understood. No sooner do you set foot
upon American ground than you are stunned by a kind of
tumult; a confused clamor is heard on every side, and a thousand
simultaneous voices demand the satisfaction of their social wants.*
—ALEXIS DE TOCQUEVILLE

The Federalist opposition had disappeared, but the near-unanimous election of James Monroe as President in 1820 was misleading. The triumphant Republican party was itself bitterly divided. The congressional caucus that renominated Monroe for the presidency had selected him over his Secretary of the Treasury, William H. Crawford, by the slim margin of 65 to 54. In 1824, as we shall soon see, the Republicans broke up into sectional factions. The Union was in danger.

INTERSECTIONAL COMPROMISE

Of the major issues on which there was controversy between the sections, the question of the extension of slavery was the most dangerous. It was first brought to a head in 1819 when Missouri applied for admission to the Union as a slave state. As soon as the bill to allow this was presented to Congress, Representative James Tallmadge of New York proposed an amendment to the effect that slavery should be gradually abolished in Missouri and future importation of slaves into the state forbidden.

The Tallmadge Amendment passed the House of Representatives on a strictly sectional vote, but caused a violent outcry from Southerners who saw it as a violation of their equal rights in the territories of the United States. The amendment, and with it the question of Missouri's admission to the Union, was held up for over a year, while debates in Congress became increasingly bitter. "This momentous question," wrote Jefferson, "like a firebell in the night, awakened and filled me with terror. I consider it at once as the knell of the Union."

A new element in the discussion was introduced when Maine asked to be separated from Massachusetts and admitted as a free state. At this time there were eleven free and eleven slave states, thus making a balance in the Senate where each state had two members. In the House of Representatives, the North had an edge of 105 congressmen to 81. This advantage was sure to increase because conditions of life in the free states attracted more emigration from Europe. If Maine, however, were admitted as a free state and Missouri as a slave state, the balance in the Senate would continue.

The Missouri Compromise, 1820

Finally a compromise was reached. Missouri and Maine were admitted to the Union together. In the as yet unsettled portions of the vast area acquired by the Louisiana Purchase, slavery was forbidden north of the parallel 36° 30', a line running west from the southern boundary of Missouri. By these arrangements the Southerners "won the battle but lost the campaign." They had secured their immediate purpose, the admission of Missouri as a slave state. But the area closed to the future expansion of slavery was far greater than the area that might be occupied by slaveowners (see map, p. 255). The free states had been allowed this advantage partly as a result of a mistaken notion that the prairie region west of the Mississippi was unfit for human settlement. When Southerners realized that this region was not "the Great American Desert," they began to demand the annexation of Texas.

The Missouri Compromise stood untouched for over thirty years. The slavery question was so dangerous that politicians of all sections agreed that the only way to save the Union was to dodge the issue entirely.

Overlapping of Sectional Interests: the "American System"

Fortunately for the nation, the extension of slavery was the only issue on which intersectional disagreements were clear-cut. In New England, for instance, the demand of manufacturers for a protective tariff was strongly opposed by shipping interests that would lose money if the United States imported less foreign goods. In their demands for cheap land, Westerners found allies among the factory workers of the eastern cities. Even workers with no idea of ever acquiring farms of their own thought their wages would be better if others had a chance to go west. The commercial interests of southern ports such as New Orleans, Charles-

The overwhelmingly sectional nature of the vote on the Missouri Compromise explains why, for the next thirty years, politicians avoided the explosive issue of slavery whenever they could.

ton, and Baltimore made money from intersectional trade and had close ties with northern bankers and merchants. Thus conflicts within the three great sections and ties between groups in different sections blurred and softened intersectional rivalry.

Henry Clay, a strong nationalist who very much wanted to be President, saw in the overlapping of sectional interests an opportunity for compromise on a vast scale by a program of legislation that would win support from all over the country. Calling his plan the "American system," Clay proposed high tariffs that would tend to promote eastern manufactures. The revenue, however, would be used to build a transportation system needed by the West and to improve the navigation of southern rivers. Eastern textile mills would provide a domestic market for southern cotton and western wool, and eastern cities a market for

253

western foodstuffs. A national bank would supply a national currency. The "American system" eventually became the basis for legislative programs promoted by the Whig party, which Clay helped to found, and later of the second Republican party organized in 1854.

THE "FAVORITE SON" ELECTION OF 1824

The three-cornered sectional struggle broke into the open in the presidential election of 1824. Instead of one Republican presidential candidate there were four, each representing a sectional interest. Two of these "favorite sons," Henry Clay of Kentucky and Andrew Jackson of Tennessee, came from the West. John Quincy Adams found his strongest support in his native New England. William H. Crawford of Georgia represented the old South. A fifth candidate, John C. Calhoun of South Carolina, stood aside and ran for the vice-presidency.

In the election of 1824, Jefferson's Republican party broke up into factions supporting "favorite sons." Only Jackson drew support from all sections.

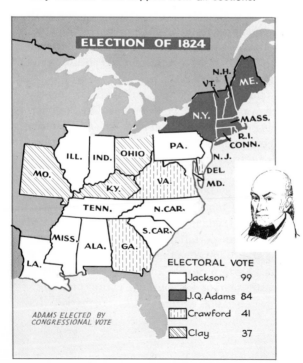

ELECTION OF 1824

ELECTORAL VOTE
☐ Jackson 99
■ J.Q. Adams 84
▤ Crawford 41
▨ Clay 37

ADAMS ELECTED BY CONGRESSIONAL VOTE

When the electoral votes were counted, it was found that Calhoun had easily been elected Vice-President; but no candidate had a majority of the presidential ballots. Jackson stood first with 99 electoral votes, Adams was second with 84, while Crawford and Clay were far in the rear with 41 and 37 votes respectively. In such a situation, the Twelfth Amendment to the Constitution provides that the President be chosen by the House of Representatives from the three men polling the highest number of electoral votes. In this case, congressmen from each state vote as a unit, with each state having one vote.

Being fourth, Clay was out of the running. But he was in a position to decide the election by throwing his weight on the side of either Adams or Jackson. The Kentuckian had strong reasons for supporting Adams, since he and the New Englander agreed on most public questions, while he and Jackson were personal enemies. Clay's influence in the House was strong enough to give the election to Adams on the first ballot. Adams won the vote of thirteen states against Jackson's seven and Crawford's four.

President John Quincy Adams, 1825–1829

No American public man has served his country with more devotion than John Quincy Adams. Few, if any, have had more ability. Yet he was a failure as President, partly because the followers of Andrew Jackson were determined that he should not succeed.

Adams's troubles began when he chose Clay for his Secretary of State—a logical appointment because of the close agreement of the two men on public questions. But in an anonymous letter to the newspapers the charge was made that Clay got the job as a result of a "corrupt bargain." Adams, so the story went, had promised to make Clay Secretary of State if the latter would swing votes to him in the House of

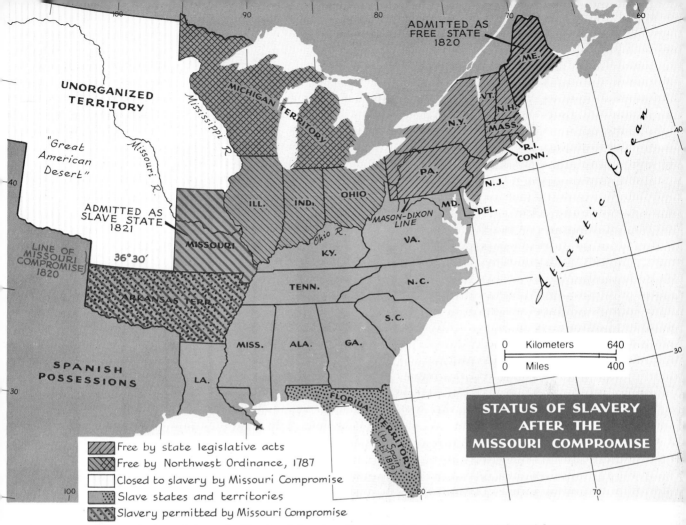

UNORGANIZED
TERRITORY

"Great
American
Desert"

ADMITTED AS
SLAVE STATE
1821

LINE OF
MISSOURI
COMPROMISE
1820

36°30′

SPANISH
POSSESSIONS

Mississippi R.

Missouri R.

MICHIGAN TERRITORY

ADMITTED AS
FREE STATE
1820

ME.

VT.
N.H.

N.Y.

MASS.

R.I.
CONN.

PA.

N.J.

MISSOURI

ILL.

IND.

OHIO

MD.

DEL.

Ohio R.

MASON-DIXON
LINE

KY.

VA.

ARKANSAS TERR.

TENN.

N.C.

MISS.

ALA.

GA.

S.C.

LA.

FLORIDA TERRITORY
(to Spain until 1819)

Atlantic Ocean

| 0 | Kilometers | 640 |
| 0 | Miles | 400 |

STATUS OF SLAVERY
AFTER THE
MISSOURI COMPROMISE

///// Free by state legislative acts
▨▨▨ Free by Northwest Ordinance, 1787
☐ Closed to slavery by Missouri Compromise
▦▦▦ Slave states and territories
▨▨▨ Slavery permitted by Missouri Compromise

By agreeing to the ban of slavery in "the Great American Desert," the South lost by the Missouri Compromise an immense region north of the 36°30′ line. This was to have far-reaching effects after the fertility of the so-called "Desert" became known.

Representatives. No trustworthy evidence in support of this smear has ever come to light. Nevertheless, the Jackson supporters kept crying "bargain and corruption" until they made many people believe them. Among those they convinced was Jackson. He had not especially wanted to be President and at first had taken his defeat calmly. But he soon became convinced that the election had been stolen, and told a Kentucky audience, "Corruption and intrigue in Washington ... defeated the will of the people."

In his first message to Congress, Adams set forth a statesmanlike program of nationalist legislation. He urged the use of federal funds not merely for roads and canals, but also for a national university, for exploration, and for scientific research. His opponents ridiculed his proposals. Adams, for instance, had suggested the building of astronomical observatories, terming them "lighthouses of the skies." How fantastic, said his enemies, to spend the taxpayers' money on such frills. When Adams and Clay proposed to send delegates to a Pan-

The presidential campaign of 1828 was a dirty one, although neither Jackson nor John Quincy Adams had any part in the mud slinging. Jackson, as this "coffin handbill" shows, was accused of being a murderous barbarian. Before the Battle of New Orleans he had six deserting militiamen executed, to encourage the rest to stay around and face the British.

American Congress called by Bolívar, Congress delayed action until it was too late for the United States to be represented.

While Adams's opponents were doing everything possible to discredit him, he refused to play politics on his own behalf. He could have strengthened his following by discharging Jackson supporters from federal jobs and filling their places with men faithful to him. This he scorned to do. He could not win support by personal charm, for it was a quality he lacked. He wrote of himself, "I am a man of reserved, cold, and forbidding manners." Observers agreed with this estimate. Adams's strict Puritan code of propriety prevented his answering opponents publicly. He let off steam by confiding his exasperations to a voluminous diary, and by going for long swims in the Potomac River, accompanied only by his Negro servant.

MUDSLINGING ELECTION OF 1828

Well before the presidential election of 1828, it was clear that John Quincy Adams and Andrew Jackson would be the only candidates. Although Adams's supporters received little or no aid from him, they built up a loosely organized following. They resembled the former Federalists in that their center of strength was in the Northeast. They tended to represent established property interests and to favor nationalist legislation. The Jackson supporters were roughly composed of the same elements that had composed the Republican party in Jefferson's time—agrarians of the South and West and those who favored limiting federal power. But there was much confusion, and support for one man or the other often depended on purely local issues, such as the rivalry of religious denominations. Party labels were confused too, although generally the Adams men called themselves National Republicans, and the Jackson followers took the name Democratic Republicans or simply Democrats. The hero of New Orleans especially attracted the rising class of professional politicians who were interested less in issues than in simply getting and holding office. Unlike Clay and Adams, the general had not made enemies by taking a strong stand on major issues. Democratic newspapers hammered on one theme above all: Andrew Jackson is the candidate of the people. The Democrats capitalized on the fact that "Old Hickory" was the first presidential candidate with a popular nickname. Hickory poles and brooms were tied on houses, steamboats, and church steeples, and hickory trees were planted at village crossroads by "Hickory Clubs."

Avoidance of Issues

Warned by the fate of Henry Clay, who had run for the presidency on the "American system" in 1824 and had come in last, the politicians avoided issues in 1828. Instead they engaged in personal attacks. The Jacksonians continued the "bargain and corruption" smear and went on to charge that Adams had allowed the federal civil service to become scandalously dishonest and had wasted the people's money on "gaming tables" (a billiard table and a chess set) for the White House. Dethrone "King John the Second," demanded Democratic editors, and put "Old Hickory" in his place with a hickory broom to clean out the "Augean Stables." Adams's followers retorted in kind. Jackson was portrayed as a headstrong barbarian who "misspelled every fourth word," a potential Julius

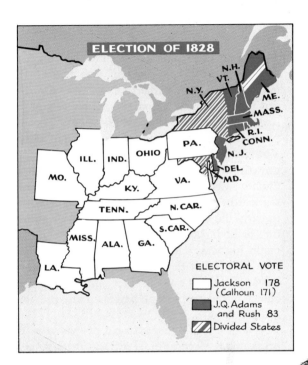

In 1828, Jackson, like Jefferson before him, carried the agrarian West and South and at the same time gained support from northern city machines. John Quincy Adams drew most of his strength from formerly Federalist New England.

Caesar who would subvert American liberties, and a "butcher" who had murdered a score of men. According to a recent historian, "There can be no question that this election splattered more filth in more different directions and on more innocent people than any other in American history." Neither of the candidates, however, engaged personally in the mudslinging.

Importance of Jackson's Election

The result of the election of 1828 was a decisive victory for Jackson over Adams by 178 electoral votes to 83. Adams was strong only in New England, where he won all but one electoral vote. Jackson swept every southern and western state except Maryland and Delaware; he also carried Pennsylvania and gained a majority of the electors in New York.

257

Although the campaign itself had been trivial and disgraceful, this election was one of the most important in American history. For the first time a candidate from the region west of the Appalachians was elected President. The six previous Presidents had all come from either Virginia or Massachusetts. Now, with the rapid growth of the West, the political center of gravity was swinging away from the eastern seaboard. All former Presidents had enjoyed in early life the advantages of wealth or education or both. Jackson, orphaned at thirteen, had made his way entirely on his own. The common people felt they had elected one of themselves. Jackson was, in fact, more truly the choice of the people than had been any previous President.

There was a higher turn-out of voters in the presidential election of 1828 than in any since 1812, when people were much worked up over continuance of the war with Britain. Now the interest was apparently in two strong candidates. Since Jackson's presidency roughly coincided with various democratic reforms, such as manhood suffrage, his election became a symbol of the growing power of the common man in politics.

ANDREW JACKSON: THE MYTH AND THE MAN

During his lifetime, Andrew Jackson was such a controversial figure that it was difficult to find the truth behind the slanders of his enemies and the extravagant praise of his admirers. According to James Parton, his first important biographer, the evidence could be so interpreted as to show Jackson to have been both "a patriot and a traitor." "He was," wrote Parton, "one of the greatest of generals and wholly ignorant of the art of war. A writer brilliant, elegant, eloquent, without being able to compose a correct sentence or spell words of four

syllables. . . . A democratic autocrat. An urbane savage. An atrocious saint." Anti-Jackson cartoons generally showed him either as a profane yokel with an ungovernable temper or as "King Andrew"—"king" then having the same impact as "tyrant" today. Jackson's friends emphasized his humble birth. Born in a log cabin on the North Carolina frontier, he had lost both parents at an early age, and had made his way to fame by his own exertions. He thus became the visible evidence that American institutions threw open "to the humblest individual the avenues of wealth and distinction." In his own time, indeed, Jackson became somewhat of a mythical figure. Thus George Bancroft, a New England historian who was also an ardent Democrat, wrote of Jackson's entrance into the presidential office:

Behold, then, the unlettered man of the West, the nursling of the wilds, the farmer of the Hermitage, little versed in books, unconnected by science[1] with the tradition of the past, raised by the will of the people to the highest pinnacle of honor, to the central post of republican freedom, to the station where all the nations of the earth would watch his actions—where his words would vibrate through the civilized world, and his spirit be the moving-star to guide the nations.

"A Gentleman and a Soldier"

The Jackson myth obscures many facts about him. His lack of education, for instance, has been much exaggerated. He could read at the age of five and by the age of eight had developed a passion for maps. Possessed of as much legal training as John Marshall, he had a successful career as a lawyer and judge in Tennessee. He bought 28 scholarly books on various aspects of law on a single trip to Philadelphia. He enjoyed reading history and subscribed to as many as twenty newspapers at one time.

---

1 "Science" here means knowledge of any kind obtained by systematic study.

Jackson's early life had been notable for violent personal quarrels. He took part in five duels, killing a man in one of them. In such actions, however, he simply reflected the violence of the frontier. As he grew older, both his temper and his actions became milder; by the time he reached the White House, he had become a person of dignity and natural courtesy. A visiting Englishwoman who saw him on the way to his inauguration wrote that "in spite of his harsh, gaunt features, he looked like a gentleman and a soldier." Jackson regarded himself as a "gentleman" and was so regarded by his Tennessee neighbors. On the frontier only gentlemen, for instance, fought duels with pistols; others used fists or knives. Jackson dressed elegantly, owned as many as 30,000 acres at one time, and kept a stable of fine horses. Although his followers referred to it as a "humble farm," the Hermitage, Jackson's home near Nashville, was as fine a mansion as Washington's Mount Vernon or Jefferson's Monticello. It had French wallpaper, and refreshments were served in imported cut glass.

Traits of Character

Without regard to education or fortune, Jackson had qualities that made him an outstanding President. A natural leader, he had been elected Tennessee's first congressman before he was thirty years old. In the War of 1812, he had been one of the few American generals who could get ill-trained militia to stand up to the British redcoats. His most obvious trait was tremendous force of will. It was related that he could instill a special desire to win even in his race horses. This characteristic was never stronger than when someone tried to defy him.

Jackson surely had no such trained mind as Jefferson or John Quincy Adams, and his political opinions were sometimes vague and

Marine Museum of the City of New York

A full-size statue of Andrew Jackson carved in wood as the figurehead of a ship. Even in his lifetime, Jackson was something of a mythical figure: the embodiment of the dream that any boy could rise from a log cabin to the White House.

changeable. Yet when questions came to him for decision, he showed quick and firm judgment. Like Washington, he habitually sought advice from several sources, and as President had a group of personal friends, called by his enemies the "kitchen cabinet," who advised him on all major decisions. "The character of his mind," wrote his friend Senator Thomas H. Benton of Missouri, "was that of judgment, with a rapid and almost intuitive perception, followed by instant and decisive action."

To will power and decisiveness, Jackson added two other virtues—honesty and loyalty. On the Tennessee frontier, he was noted for his uprightness in business matters. There is no doubting his sincerity when he said of his actions as President, "I do precisely what I think just and right." His sense of personal loyalty to family, friends, and followers was very strong. So was his loyalty to the Union. He had served the United States in the Revolutionary War at the age of thirteen and had successfully defended New Orleans against a British attack in the War of 1812. When as President he faced a threat of disunion, he was willing to take up arms again to save the nation.

JACKSONIAN DEMOCRACY

As the time for Jackson's inauguration approached, his admirers poured into Washington. Men slept five or six in a bed; when no more beds were to be had, they spent the night on sofas, billiard tables, and floors. Seized with a fear approaching panic, conservatives thought of Rome being overrun by hordes of Goths and Vandals. John Quincy Adams left Washington rather than attend the ceremony that might mean the end of the republic. A typical reaction was that of Daniel Webster, senator from Massachusetts:

Gen. J. will be here abt. 15 Feb.—
Nobody knows what he will do when he does come. . . .
My *fear* is stronger than my *hope*.

Although it was feared that Jackson would try to make political capital out of his military career, he refused a military pageant. Instead, he followed Jefferson's precedent of walking to the inaugural ceremony. His hands shook as he read a rather cautious and colorless inaugural address. What happened later, however, seemed to justify those who had gloomily predicted

that Jackson's election meant the reign of "King Mob." From the Capitol he rode on horseback to the White House, surrounded by a cheering throng. There, a reception had been prepared for invited guests and important officials only. There was no means, however, to prevent the crowd from pushing in. Chairs and china were broken; women fainted. The press around Jackson was so great that he had to be helped to escape through a back window. The crowd was induced to leave the presidential mansion only when big bowls of punch were placed on the lawn outside.

Jeffersonian and Jacksonian Democracy Compared

Like the election of 1800 that brought Jefferson to the White House, Jackson's election in 1828 has been called a "revolution." In both cases control of the federal government had been captured by men who professed belief in the goodness and wisdom of the people. The two events are directly connected because the Jacksonians regarded themselves as the political heirs of Jefferson.

Jacksonian democracy reveals its debt to Jefferson in many ways. The Jacksonians professed and practiced many Jeffersonian principles: economy in government, laissez-faire, and limitation of the sphere of federal action to powers explicitly stated in the Constitution. The Jacksonians also agreed with Jefferson that farmers were "the chosen people of God." Jackson called himself "a plain cultivator of the soil." Martin Van Buren, his successor as President, wrote in an annual message to Congress that American prosperity was "to be looked for nowhere with such sure reliance as in the industry of the agriculturalist."

In spite of their points of similarity, however, there were important differences between Jeffersonian and Jacksonian democracy. Jefferson, for instance, had a great deal to do with

Jackson on his way to Washington for his first inauguration, as drawn by Howard Pyle, a modern artist. As Jackson traveled through the country by stagecoach to Washington, D.C., great crowds cheered their hero in every town. At a session of the Senate immediately before the inaugural ceremony, he was described as "the plainest dressed man in the chamber."

founding the movement that bears his name. He and his close friend Madison organized the Republican party and led it during their sixteen years in the presidency. Both men were political philosophers, and as such they defined a fairly clear-cut Republican creed. It is not easy to define Jackson's connection with Jacksonian democracy, but one thing is certain: he did not create it. Instead, the movement found him, thrust him into office, and made him, as we have seen, a heroic symbol.

Jacksonian democracy differed from its predecessor in that it was much more far-reaching, more diverse, and more difficult to define. It stemmed from many sources and took many forms, some of them totally unrelated to Andrew Jackson. It was also, at least in its professed philosophy, more democratic. Jeffersonian democracy had been government *for* the people, but hardly *by* them. Its leaders were liberal-minded aristocrats like Madison, Gallatin, and Jefferson himself. In Jefferson's time the general feeling was that voting rights should be limited to men who had a stake in society, as shown by the possession of some property, usually land. By the time of Jackson most states, in the East as well as in the West, had adopted universal manhood suffrage. Thus a man became a full citizen not because of what he owned, but simply by virtue of being a man (a white man, that is). Among those who now gained the franchise were workingmen in eastern cities. When Jefferson had talked of "the people," he generally meant "farmers"; now the term included "mechanics" and thus acquired an urban as well as a rural dimension.

Before Jackson's time, the voters expected public officials to use their own best judgment. Now the voters came to believe that officials should act according to the direct demands of the people. One way to make government respond more directly to popular will was to increase the number of elective offices. This development did not affect the federal government, but at the state and local level positions formerly appointive—such as judges, constables, and public surveyors—were thrown open to election. Terms of office were shortened so that the people's will could be known more frequently through the process of elections.

Professional Politicians; the "Spoils System"

As new voters gained the ballot and made demands on government, they needed political organization. This was supplied by the rising group of professional politicians. And with the professional politicians came the "spoils system," which is the practice of appointing people to office on the basis of party loyalty and party service. This was not an entirely new development. George Washington had often made support of Federalist principles a test of appointment to office. When Jefferson became President, he complained of the Federalist jobholders whom he inherited. "Few die," he said,

"and none resign." He therefore only gradually replaced Federalists with Republicans.

Jackson was the first President to make wholesale removal of jobholders in order to appoint his followers to office. He based his action on the Jeffersonian principle that there should be rotation in office. "More is lost," he wrote, "by the long continuance of men in office than is generally gained by their experience." Holding that special training for the civil service was unnecessary, he said in his first inaugural that "the duties of public officers are so plain and simple that men of intelligence may readily qualify themselves for their performance." While the extent of Jackson's removal of men from office has been exaggerated, and while some of his removals were justified, his actions set a bad precedent. The spoils system lowered the efficiency and honesty of the federal government. A contemporary observer not unfriendly to Jackson noted that "office-seeking and office-getting was becoming a regular business, where impudence triumphed over worth."

Increase in Presidential Power

Another development that can be traced to Jackson personally was a great increase in the power of the presidential office. He had none of Jefferson's distrust of executive power. When he thought it necessary to carry out his policies or to crush opposition, he used the presidential office in new ways. Whereas all previous Presidents together had vetoed only nine bills passed by Congress, Jackson alone vetoed twelve. He was also the first President to use the "pocket veto." (See p. 119.)

Jefferson had found himself opposed by Chief Justice John Marshall and had come off second best. (See p. 196.) Not so Jackson. In vetoing a bill for recharter of the Bank of the United States, he went flatly against Marshall's opinion in *McCulloch v. Maryland.* When

Marshall gave a decision ordering the state of Georgia to return certain lands to the Cherokee Indians, Jackson refused to carry it out. "Marshall has made his decision," he is reported to have

QUESTION • *Does the President have the constitutional right to ignore Supreme Court decisions? Did Jackson have the right to refuse to carry out Marshall's decision regarding the Cherokee Indians?*

said. "Now let him enforce it."

In struggles with opponents in Congress and out, Jackson appealed, more than any previous President, directly to the people. His veto messages, worked over by able newspaper editors, were designed more to persuade voters than congressmen. His great power as President thus came principally from wholehearted support by the majority of the people, who regarded him as one of their own.

Situation of Blacks and Indians

Jacksonian democracy had nothing to offer two already oppressed minorities: the Negroes and the Indians. In the South, criticism of slavery became increasingly unusual, and those who made it suffered unpopularity and even physical danger. In the North, the Negro was now free, but usually as a second-class citizen. When states instituted manhood suffrage, the vote was often extended only to white men. The Missouri debates had shown that the slavery issue was so explosive that a policy was instituted that has been called "the great silence." Serious discussion of slavery as a national political issue was taboo. From 1836 to 1844 antislavery petitions to Congress were automatically "laid on the table"—that is to say, ignored. Abolitionist literature was often barred from the mails.

As to the Indians, the Jackson and Van Buren administrations ruthlessly pursued the policy begun by Jefferson: removal to territory west of the Mississippi. Twenty thousand

Cherokees, for example, were forced to move from their homes in Georgia to what is now Arkansas and Oklahoma. It is estimated that 4,000 of them died on the way because of starvation, disease, and exposure. By 1840 the few Indians still living east of the Mississippi had been herded into reservations, except for the Seminoles, some of whom managed to hold out in the swamps of Florida.

TARIFF AND NULLIFICATION CONTROVERSIES

The protective tariff of 1816 did not prove to be high enough to satisfy American manufacturers. In response to their demands, duties on imported manufactures (and on some raw materials as well) had been raised twice more, in 1824 and 1828. These laws aroused increasing resentment in the South, especially in South Carolina. That state was declining in prosperity as rich cotton lands farther west came into production. Instead of blaming natural causes, however, South Carolinians tended to attribute all their ills to the tariff. When the news of the Tariff of 1828 (called by its enemies the "Tariff of Abominations") reached Charleston, there was violent indignation. Flags were hung at half-mast; college students resolved to buy no northern goods; and there was talk of leaving the Union. But South Carolina held back from formal action against the Tariff of Abominations because John C. Calhoun, the leading politician of the state, had aligned himself with Andrew Jackson and had run for Vice-President on the Democratic Republican ticket in 1828. It was hoped that Calhoun's influence in the Jackson administration might result in tariff reduction.

Calhoun's Theory of Nullification

South Carolina did, however, make its opposition to the protective system known when in 1828 its legislature published a document known as the "South Carolina Exposition." Although unsigned, it was generally known to have been written by Calhoun. As a strong nationalist, Calhoun had supported the Tariff of 1816, calling protection "a new most powerful cement" to hold the Union together. By 1828 he had changed his point of view to that generally held in his native state: a protective tariff was "unconstitutional, oppressive, and unjust." But what could a state do to defend itself against a law passed by Congress and signed by the President? Calhoun's answer to this problem was to revive the theory of nullification that had been first suggested in the Kentucky and Virginia resolutions written by Jefferson and Madison (see p. 185). He expanded the theory, however, to a degree that the original authors never dreamed of.

Calhoun's argument may be summarized as follows: The federal government was created by a "compact" (contract) between the individual states, whereby each state gave up only such powers as were expressly granted in the Constitution (especially in Article I, Section 8). If the federal government exceeded these powers, it was no use to seek justice from the Supreme Court, because the court was itself a branch of the federal government. Instead, each individual state had the right to decide whether or not a federal law was constitutional. If the state decided in the negative, it might declare that law null and void within its own borders. Behind nullification lurked the threat to secede from the Union.

Webster-Hayne Debate

South Carolina leaders were anxious to win converts to this doctrine. They hoped for support not only in the South, but in the West,

Scene in the Senate as "Black Dan" Webster made his famous speech in reply to Hayne of South Carolina. Until 1860 the Senate met in this small semi-circular chamber; on this occasion the gallery was crowded with visitors eager to hear one of America's greatest orators.

Faneuil Hall, Boston

because both were agrarian sections and paid more for their manufactured goods as a result of the tariff. A major move toward getting western support was taken by Robert Y. Hayne of South Carolina in a senatorial debate in 1829–1830. Senator Samuel A. Foot of Connecticut, representing eastern manufacturers worried about losing their labor supply, had suggested that a limit be put on land sales. When Senator Thomas Hart Benton of Missouri angrily attacked Foot for promoting the interest of his section at the expense of the pioneer farmers of the West, Hayne supported him. In a wide-ranging, confused debate covering several days, northwestern and southern senators attempted to win Westerners to their side of various public questions. Eventually Hayne and Daniel Webster of Massachusetts engaged in a full scale discussion of nullification, with Vice-President Calhoun presiding.

Webster's political career had followed a course exactly opposite to that of Calhoun. Calhoun had been a War Hawk who had helped to bring the United States into the War of 1812; Webster had reflected the feeling of New England against the war, even to the extent of flirting with nullification of federal laws calling for raising troops. Where Calhoun had supported the nationalist legislation that followed the war, Webster had opposed it. By 1830 Calhoun had become a defender of states' rights, while Webster had come to favor a strong federal government which might promote the banking and manufacturing interests of the Northeast.

A man of imposing presence (it was said no man could be as great as Webster looked!), the senator from Massachusetts was also the greatest orator of his day. In his "Second Reply to Hayne," his greatest oration, he pointed out that in practice nullification could only mean the end of the Union. The Union, said Webster, was not a creature of the states: it was the people's government. "We the people" had forged a national government for our own welfare and meant it to endure. The greatness of Webster's speech lay in his use of American patriotism to support the idea of a Constitution flexible enough to meet the needs of a growing country. His audience was not so much the Senate as the people at large. Thousands of copies of the speech were published, and hundreds of children for the next thirty years declaimed the closing paragraph depicting the blessings of union and horrors of disunion, with the famous final words: "Liberty and Union, now and forever, one and inseparable!"

Jackson Versus Calhoun

Which side would Jackson take in the argument over nullification? Southerners hoped that the President, a slaveholder and planter himself, might favor a low tariff and nullification. Furthermore, Calhoun not only had run on the same ticket as Jackson in 1828, but had helped him choose his cabinet. The hopes of the states' rights men were raised by Jackson's first annual message to Congress in December 1829. In it the President warned Congress against "all encroachments upon the legitimate sphere of state sovereignty." He was especially opposed to the use of federal funds for roads and canals within state boundaries.

The nullifiers tried to get Jackson to show his hand at a dinner celebrating Jefferson's birthday, on April 13, 1830. Controlling the committee in charge of the banquet, they printed on the menu 24 toasts, many of them antitariff and pronullification. It was hoped that the President would fall into the mood of the occasion. But Jackson had no patience with the idea that a single state might evade the law. When his turn came, the old warrior asked everyone to rise, looked straight at Calhoun, and proposed a toast that echoed Webster: "Our Federal Union: it must be preserved."

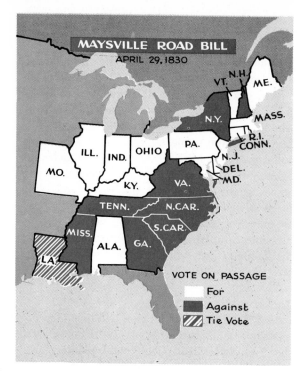

MAYSVILLE ROAD BILL
APRIL 29, 1830

VOTE ON PASSAGE
- For
- Against
- Tie Vote

Vote in Congress on a bill to have the federal government appropriate funds for a western road. The West was for it, the South generally opposed, the Northeast divided. What accounts for the sectional vote? Why did the Northeast divide?

Maysville Road Veto

The truth is that Jackson was both a nationalist and a strict constructionist. He believed in the absolute supremacy of the federal government within its sphere, but he wanted to limit that sphere. His strict constructionist point of view was shown only a fortnight after the Jefferson Day dinner by his veto of the Maysville Road bill. Congress had voted that the federal government should pay half the cost of building a turnpike from Maysville to Lexington, both of which lay within the state of Kentucky. Jackson vetoed the bill on much the same grounds as those on which Madison opposed the Bonus Bill of 1817: the Constitution did not grant the federal government power to spend the money on local transportation. Such activity was the province of the states.

"Peggy Eaton Affair"

The break between Jackson and Calhoun over nullification became personal as well as political. One point of disagreement involved a ridiculous dispute in Washington society. Mrs. Calhoun was one of the leaders of a feminine plot to exclude from official parties the wife of the Secretary of War, John H. Eaton. Jackson, whose own wife had been the object of unfair gossip, took the side of Mrs. Eaton. The extraordinary result of this "Peggy Eaton affair" was the creation of a serious division in Jackson's administration, based on whether the cabinet members and their wives were for or against the person involved. Another reason why Jackson turned against his Vice-President was his discovery that Calhoun, while Secretary of War in Monroe's cabinet, had wanted to have Jackson censured for his actions in Florida. Believing Calhoun to be disloyal, Jackson broke with him entirely. The South Carolinian resigned from the vice-presidency in 1832.

The Nullification Crisis, 1832–1833

In 1832 Congress passed a new tariff law; the rates, while lower than those of 1828, were still high. South Carolina immediately called a special convention that voted overwhelmingly for an Ordinance of Nullification. This document declared that the federal tariff laws were "null, void, and no law, nor binding upon this state, its officers, or its citizens." The ordinance went on to threaten secession. Meanwhile, the state government began to arm and drill a volunteer military force.

Jackson's response to this defiance of federal authority was to issue a "Proclamation to the People of South Carolina," in which he forcefully pointed out that nullification meant disunion and disunion meant treason. His duty as President was clear: he must enforce the law. Privately, he warned Senator Hayne that if there was bloodshed he would hang the first nullificationist he could get his hands on from the first tree he could find. He had already strengthened military forces at Charleston.

The nullification crisis was settled by a compromise. Jackson asked Congress to pass a Force Bill to give him the powers necessary to suppress disunion in South Carolina. If this passed, armed conflict might become unavoidable. While Congress debated this measure, Henry Clay presented a new tariff law. It provided for gradual scaling down of duties, over a ten-year period, to about the 1816 level. The bill was supported by both Calhoun, the nullifier, and Webster, the defender of the Union. The Tariff of 1833 and the Force Bill were passed the same day. Thus South Carolina's grievance about the tariff was removed, while at the same time its right to nullify was denied. South Carolina withdrew its Ordinance of Nullification and could claim it had won its major purpose—a lowering of the tariff.

QUESTION • Should Jackson have resisted all compromise and demanded that South Carolina back down completely, even if it meant bloodshed?

Jackson agreed to the Compromise of 1833, yet he felt it was probably a mistake to give in at all. "The nullifiers in the South intend to blow up a storm on the slave question next," he wrote a friend. "This ought to be met." The next step, predicted Jackson, would be an attempt to form a southern confederacy bounded on the north by the Potomac River.

JACKSON'S WAR ON THE BANK

At the time that the question of nullification was coming to a head, Jackson was also engaged in a dramatic struggle with the Bank of the United States. Chartered in 1816, the "B.U.S.," as it was nicknamed, was a useful institution. Its functions were the same as those of the original Bank of the United States: it performed much of the financial business of the country and controlled the supply of currency. (Be *sure* to refer back to pp. 160–161 for an explanation of these functions.)

Popular Feeling Against Banks and Monopolies

In spite of its usefulness, the Bank had many enemies who called it such names as "the Monster," "the Octopus," and "the Mammoth of the East." Opposition to it came from many sources and was motivated by different reasons. Banks chartered by state legislatures tended to be against the B.U.S. simply because it was a powerful competitor and because it undertook to prevent state banks from lending too freely or issuing too many bank notes. Another group, mostly farmers, were against all banks. They thought that the only "honest" currency was "hard money"—specie. It was the farmers, they felt, who created "real" wealth—corn, hogs, grain, cotton, tobacco—and who were somehow made to pay tribute to those who controlled "paper" wealth, such as mortgages and bank notes. "The hard earnings of the industrious farmer," said an Ohio newspaper, "are arrested [wrested] from his hands by a horde of swindlers employed by the banks."

Still another element in opposition to the Bank was a rising feeling against monopolies of every sort. Although the Bank of the United States was 80 per cent owned by private individuals, it enjoyed a monopoly of all government business. State legislatures granted somewhat similar monopolies to state banks, and also made monopoly grants to companies running toll bridges, steamship lines, and turnpikes. Feeling against this sort of exclusive privilege was especially strong in the East among workingmen and businessmen. Monopolistic charters created, it was said, "an artificial inequality of wealth" and "forced the great body of working people" to "give over hope of ever acquiring any property." It should be noted that there was no element here of opposition to capitalism or to

free enterprise as such. It was just that no artificial barrier should stand in the way of peoples'
chance to acquire wealth by their own efforts.
It was part of the creed of Jacksonian democracy that Americans should be allowed to give
free rein to their "almost *universal ambition to
get forward.*"

Jackson's Attitude Toward the B.U.S.

Jackson's personal attitude toward the B.U.S.
was typical of many Westerners. He was a
"hard money" man who distrusted all banks
and all paper money. He had once lost almost
his entire fortune and had gone into debt for
twenty years because notes accepted from a
Philadelphia merchant turned out to be worthless. The fact that the stock of the B.U.S. was
mostly owned by wealthy men of the Northeast
who had supported Adams for President surely
did not endear the institution to Jackson. For the
first three years of his presidency, however, he
took no action against the Bank save to express
the opinion that it had too much power.

Friends of the Bank finally drove Jackson
into action. In the summer of 1832, Henry Clay
presented to Congress a bill to give the Bank
a new charter, even though the old one did not
run out until 1836. Clay, a candidate for the
presidency, hoped to embarrass Jackson by
forcing him either to sign a bill he disliked or
to veto it, and so give Clay an issue for the
coming presidential campaign. The Recharter
Bill passed Congress and was sent to the President. Shortly after it reached his desk, Jackson
remarked to his closest advisor, "The Bank, Mr.
Van Buren, is trying to kill me; *but I will kill
it.*" He vetoed the recharter and with his veto
sent to Congress a message which showed little
knowledge of banking but great understanding
of why many people disliked the B.U.S. The
Bank, wrote Jackson, favored the few against
the many; it made "the rich richer and the
potent more powerful." It was un-American, be-

cause more than a quarter of its valuable stock
had been purchased by foreigners. It was an
overextension of federal power, because the
Constitution nowhere explicitly granted the federal government the right to establish a central
bank. (For a discussion of the constitutional
argument, see pp. 162–163.)

Election of 1832

In the presidential election of 1832 Jackson
ran for a second term as the candidate of the
Democratic party, a label that has remained
unchanged to the present. Clay ran as a National
Republican. There was also a strange third
party in the field, the Anti-Masonic. This short-
lived organization would now be forgotten except that it invented a new means of proposing
candidates for the presidency. Previously, nom-
inations had been made either by state legislatures or by a meeting of party members in
Congress, the so-called caucus. In neither of
these methods were the people consulted. The
Anti-Masons conceived the idea of electing a
national convention to choose their candidate.
The procedure was immediately imitated by the
Democrats and National Republicans, and has
been followed ever since.

As Clay had hoped, Jackson's veto of the
Recharter Bill made the Bank the principal
issue of the 1832 campaign. The National Republicans accused Jackson of "appealing to the
worst passions of the uninformed part of the
people and endeavoring to stir up the poor
against the rich." They produced sober arguments to show the value of the Bank to the
nation's finances. But the bank issue boomeranged. It hurt Clay and helped Jackson, whose
veto message had appeared to place him on the
side of the mass of the people against foreigners
and wealthy Easterners. The Democrats in any
case did not answer National Republican arguments but traded on Old Hickory's great popularity. When the returns were counted, they

showed that Jackson had won an overwhelming victory. He received 687,000 popular votes to Clay's 530,000, and carried the electoral college by 219 votes to 49.

Destruction of the Bank

Jackson took his re-election as a demand from the people that he destroy the power of the B.U.S. at once, even though its charter did not run out until 1836. Although by law the funds of the federal government were deposited in the Bank, Jackson resolved to remove them. This required an order from the Secretary of the Treasury. Jackson had to ask two Secretaries of the Treasury to resign before he found a third who would give the order. Federal money was then gradually withdrawn from the vaults of the B.U.S. New funds from taxation and land sales were placed in strong state banks, called by Jackson's enemies "pet banks." The removal of the deposits caused a great outcry among Jackson's opponents, who branded the action as unconstitutional. It was, said one of them, the deed of "a detestable, ignorant, restless, vain and malignant tyrant." Nicholas Biddle, president of the Bank, claimed that removal of the deposits forced him to call in its loans and stop lending. Putting this policy into effect, Biddle created such a scarcity of credit that hundreds of business people were driven into bankruptcy and scores of banks failed. Factories closed down and workers were discharged. At first all this was blamed on Jackson. Business people sent petitions urging him to save the country from depression. The President replied, "Go to Nicholas Biddle!" Eventually, Biddle's actions backfired: if one man at the head of a private institution could drive the country into depression, then Jackson was right in saying the Bank had too much power. Biddle backed down and started to lend freely again, and prosperity returned. In 1836 the the Bank charter expired. Jackson had won.

The Library of Congress

Jackson was a rich source for cartoons. Above, a cartoonist of the opposition shows him as a king, trampling on the Constitution and ruling by veto. Compare this cartoon with the cartoon on page 186.

The immediate effects of destroying the Bank of the United States were unfortunate. It had provided the country with a stable currency and had kept state banks from lending too freely. With the B.U.S. out of power, there was no check on local banks. Hundreds of new ones were chartered by state legislatures, and the number of bank notes quadrupled. The 1830's saw a period of feverish speculation in land. Land speculators had little trouble in persuading local banks to lend to them, and sales of public lands rose from 4 million acres in 1834 to 20 million acres in 1836. All this helped to cause a disastrous panic in 1837.

"Free Banking"

On the other hand, Jackson's victory over the Bank turned out to be a victory for free competitive enterprise. Before this time, state legislatures were in the habit of granting special charters to banks and business concerns, and these charters often carried with them monopoly rights and special privileges. Such arrangements denied opportunity to other business people. Jackson's success in the war on the Bank encouraged a movement toward "free banking" that had begun in New York State in 1829. Free bank laws permitted any individual or group of men to establish a state-chartered bank if certain regulations designed to protect the depositors and the public were observed. Comparable to free bank legislation were the general incorporation laws, designed to allow all business people to form corporations on the same terms. Legislatures continued, however, to pass special incorporation laws that gave privileges to favored companies.

The Laissez-Faire Philosophy

At the time of the Bank war, Jackson seemed to many conservatives to be leading the poor in an attack on the rich. Instead, he and like-minded politicians in the states were fighting to free business from government controls. The purpose was to allow business concerns to get ahead on the basis of real efficiency rather than on their ability to persuade legislators to grant them special favors.

Looking at Jackson's presidency as a whole, it should be noted that although he was a man of great personal force and dynamism, and although he greatly increased the power of the presidency, his essential mission was a negative one: to reduce the sphere of the central government. He put the "American system" in reverse. During his administration the level of the protective tariff was reduced, less and less federal money was spent on internal improve-

ments, and the central bank was destroyed. All this reflected the *laissez-faire* philosophy that the Jacksonians inherited from Thomas Jefferson. The role of government was simply "to restrain men from injuring each other" and "leave them otherwise free to regulate their own pursuits of industry and improvement."

RISE OF THE WHIGS

During Jackson's second term his opponents formed a new party called the Whigs, a loose coalition of National Republicans and a variety of other political factions opposed to Andrew Jackson. Taking their name from the English party that in the eighteenth century had resisted the power of the crown, they fought the extension of presidential power effected by "King Andrew I." Their principal leaders were Clay and Webster.

Election of 1836

As the election of 1836 approached, Jackson used his dominating position in the Democratic party to pick his successor. His choice fell upon Martin Van Buren, a New York politician whom his enemies called "the Fox," because he had a reputation of craftiness. His followers emphasized his humble birth in a small town by calling him "Old Kinderhook." Abbreviated to "O.K.," this nickname became part of American speech, meaning "all right." The Whigs were so divided they could not agree on a candidate. Instead, they nominated three "favorite sons" in the hope that among them they would get enough support to prevent Van Buren from getting a majority in the electoral college. If this happened, the election would be thrown into the Whig-controlled House of Representatives. But Jackson's continuing popularity and the general prosperity were enough to give the Democrats the election. Van Buren gained 170 electoral votes against 124 for all his opponents combined, but his majority in the popular vote was small.

Panic of 1837

Hardly had Van Buren taken office when the country was hit by one of the most severe depressions in American history, the Panic of 1837. Banks and business houses closed their doors; thousands of farmers lost their farms through mortgage foreclosures; there was almost total unemployment among eastern factory workers; and work on canals and the new-fangled railroads almost ceased.

The depression had various causes. As has already been shown, the 1830's saw tremendous land speculation. Once Jackson had crushed the Bank of the United States, there was no means to discourage banks from lending money to speculators. At the same time, the states borrowed money through bond issues to build roads and canals. By 1835 the federal government had paid off the national debt. In 1836 it started distributing surplus funds to the states as loans. This encouraged still more reckless schemes for internal improvements. The indebtedness piled up by states and individual speculators outran the power of the country to produce wealth.

QUESTION • *A curious feature of the Panic of 1837 was that so much money disappeared from circulation that it was almost impossible to transact business except by barter. Why?*

The Specie Circular

It was Jackson himself who pricked the speculative balloon by an executive order known as the Specie Circular, issued in 1836. It directed that all purchasers of public lands except actual settlers must pay for them in gold and silver coin rather than in state bank notes. This action created a demand for specie, which in turn put a strain on those banks that had

The New-York Historical Society

The panic of 1837 is depicted in this bitter cartoon. A widow and child beg, workers are barefoot, the manufactory is "closed for the present." Note the run on the bank and the auction on foreclosed property.

lent money too freely. To be sure of having specie on hand for depositors, stronger banks began to call in loans, and weaker banks failed.

Another push toward the depression came from Great Britain, whose banks at this time were the world's greatest source of credit. Attracted by high rates of interest in the United States, British investments in this country grew from $66,000,000 in 1835 to $174,000,000 in 1837. So much money was going abroad that the British became alarmed and began to call back their loans. In this way a vicious spiral began. A London bank would call on a New York bank for repayment of a loan. The New York bank might then call upon a New Orleans cotton broker for money owed, and the broker in turn on a cotton planter. The cotton planter, along with hundreds of others, would dump his cotton and slaves on an already glutted market to get cash. This in turn drove down the prices of cotton and slaves.

Partly because of the lack of a telegraph system or an Atlantic cable, the depression took some time to develop. When at last it hit, it almost completely paralyzed business. So many banks had failed that bank notes were not trusted; those who had gold and silver hoarded them. Consequently, stores closed, crops were unsold, and workers fought over the meager relief which city governments provided.

Independent Treasury System, 1840

Today, faced with such a crisis, the people would demand action by the federal government, and the federal government would take strong measures to try to pull the country out of the depression. In the 1830's, however, a depression was regarded as an act of nature like a drought or a hurricane. According to the prevailing *laissez-faire* philosophy, it was not the function of the federal government to do much about it. Van Buren emphasized this in his inaugural address in which he said that "all communities are apt to look to government for too much." His one great legislative effort was to try to get the federal government entirely out of banking. He shared Jackson's horror of a great central bank like the B.U.S., but depositing federal funds in the "pet banks" had also proved a failure. The money had often been used to promote speculation, and some of the banks had gone bankrupt in the panic.

Now Van Buren proposed the Independent Treasury System. According to this plan, the federal government would collect its taxes in gold and silver and store the specie in vaults throughout the country. Federal expenditures would also be paid in hard cash, this making federal credit literally "as good as gold." Inflation of bank notes would be discouraged because state banks would have to keep a sufficient reserve of specie to allow their depositors and those holding their notes to do business with the government. The Independent Treasury Act was finally passed in 1840.

"Log Cabin" Campaign of 1840

The Whigs looked forward to the election of 1840 with confidence, even though they were so divided on major issues that they did not even try to write a platform. Their campaign plan was simple: nominate a military hero and attack Van Buren. For their presidential candidate they passed over the real leaders of the party and chose General William Henry Harrison, whose principal attraction was that he had fought Indians at the battle of Tippecanoe. Harrison was not expected to make speeches. "Let him," said Nicholas Biddle, "say not one single word about his principles, or his creed— let him say nothing—promise nothing. Let no committee, no convention, no town meeting ever extract from him a single word about what he thinks nor what he will do hereafter. Let the use of pen and ink be wholly forbidden."

When Democrats jeered that all Harrison was fit for was to sit in front of a log cabin, drink hard cider, and draw a pension, the Whigs found a means of turning the campaign into pure ballyhoo. Against Van Buren they used the very methods the Jacksonians had used against Adams in 1828. Harrison (born to wealth and social position) was pictured as a rude frontiersman, while Van Buren (born in humble circumstances) was portrayed as a champagne-drinking aristocrat with cologne-scented whiskers. There were "log cabin" campaign songs in honor of "Tippecanoe and Tyler too," John Tyler being the vice-presidential candidate. Crowds of men and boys rolled a great ball from Kentucky to Baltimore as a symbol of the great majority that the Whigs were rolling up. Blaming Van Buren for the depression, the Whigs promised prosperity. They freely boasted that Van Buren's policy was "fifty cents a day and French soup; our policy two dollars a day and roast beef." The result of this rollicking campaign was a decisive victory for Harrison, who gained 234 electoral votes to Van Buren's 60, although the popular vote was quite close.

The Effectiveness of Party Organizations

The election of 1840 was the first to illustrate what became one of the commonplaces of American politics: that when there is a depression, the party in power gets blamed and is likely to be punished at the polls. The election returns also revealed the effectiveness of the new organizations run by professional politicians.

Whereas twelve years before, when Jackson was elected President over Adams, only a little more than 50 per cent of the eligible voters went to the polls, now the proportion was nearly 80 per cent and in some states almost reached 90 per cent. Such a high turnout revealed that the party organization had penetrated every county, village, and city precinct and had set up machinery for informing the electorate and seeing that they came to the polling places. Another significant development was the way the parties, by avoiding or compromising dangerous issues and by forming truly national organizations, had managed to damp down sectionalism. There

Robert J. Walker, Politician

Robert J. Walker, senator from Mississippi, faced an unpleasant crisis. His state had issued bonds which were to have provided a network of toll roads. The bonds had been sold widely abroad, especially to English investors. Now, the roads were not built, the company set up to build them was bankrupt, the state treasury was empty, and the payment of the bonds was overdue. Walker's recommendation, which Mississippi followed, was to repudiate the bonds.

Mississippi, although conspicuous, was not alone with her dilemma. The whole country had been ruined by the Panic of 1837. In the South, cotton growers who could not pay their debts took mules, wagons, plows, and slaves west to Texas, then an independent republic into which the debts could not follow them. Court foreclosures on abandoned mortgaged lands were so numerous that sheriffs no longer filed reports on fruitless collection attempts. They just scrawled G.T.T.—"Gone to Texas"—on the records.

Walker's political career was not ruined by the bond fiasco. Elected to the United States Senate, he influenced tariff policies during the early 1840's. When James Polk became President, Walker joined his cabinet as Secretary of the Treasury. A believer in expansionism, Walker strongly supported the Mexican War and devised means for raising the monies necessary to conduct it.

After a period of private law practice, Walker became governor of the territory of Kansas. When the Civil War broke out, Walker sided with the Union, even though much of his adult life had been spent in Mississippi. President Lincoln sent him to England on an assignment, unimportant in itself, which threw him into contact with wealthy Britishers. He constituted Lincoln's reminder to the British of their losses from the Mississippi repudiation, the President's way to cut down English investment in Confederate bonds.

MISSISSIPPI

was hardly any difference in the way the three major sections regarded the candidates. Harrison gained 56 per cent of the popular vote in the Northwest, 55 per cent in the Northeast, and 54 per cent in the slave states.

The Whig Split:
John Tyler, President, 1841–1845

It was one thing for the Whigs to win an election and another for them to run the country. While they could get into office simply by forgetting differences and attacking Van Buren, once in power they had to answer the demands of some of their followers and deny those of others. Henry Clay, now in the Senate, had worked out a program of legislation designed to appeal to as many different interests as possible. The elderly Harrison was expected to be a figurehead, while Clay and Webster ran the party. But just a month after his inauguration Harrison, worn out by visits from hundreds of office-seekers, died of pneumonia.

So John Tyler of Virginia became the first Vice-President to be elevated to the country's highest office by the death of the elected President. Placed on the Whig ticket simply to attract southern support, Tyler was opposed to most of what Clay and Webster stood for. While they were nationalists, the new President was a believer in states' rights, almost to the verge of nullification. He did, however, sign the first of several bills which went to make up Clay's program of legislation. The Tariff of 1842 pleased eastern manufacturers by raising the rates to about what they had been ten years earlier. A Pre-emption Act passed in 1841 satisfied the western demand that "squatters" on public lands have the first right to buy the lands they had settled. But when a bill re-establishing a Bank of the United States was presented to him, Tyler vetoed it. A second bill was drawn up to meet his objections, and he vetoed that too. In disgust at the President's actions, all the Whigs except Daniel Webster resigned from the cabinet, and Clay resigned from the Senate. Split wide apart, without a program or leadership, the Whigs lost heavily in the congressional elections of 1842. The Democrats now controlled the House, and the Whigs still controlled the Senate, while President Tyler was a man without a party. The federal government was at dead center.

Activities: Chapter 10

For Mastery and Review

1. Summarize the circumstances that led to a crisis between the North and South in 1820.

2. Explain Clay's American System.

3. How was John Quincy Adams elected President in 1824? What was his program as President? To what extent did it succeed or fail? Why?

4. Describe the campaign of 1828. Why was Jackson's victory important? Compare Jacksonian democracy and Jeffersonian democracy. What were some notable elements in Jackson's character?

5. Trace the development of the nullification controversy. Include: (a) the Kentucky and Virginia resolutions (see p. 185), (b) opposition to the War of 1812 (see p. 213), (c) the South Carolina Exposition, (d) the Webster-Hayne debate, (e) the Jefferson Day dinner, (f) the Maysville Road veto, (g) the South Carolina Ordinance of Nullification, (h) the Force Bill, and (i) the Compromise of 1833.

6. What is the "compact" theory of the Union? What is its ultimate threat? How did Webster

answer these arguments? In what did the effectiveness of Webster's arguments lie?

7. What had been the usefulness of the second Bank of the United States? What part did the Bank play in the election of 1832? Why did Jackson oppose the B.U.S.? Describe the contest between Nicholas Biddle and Jackson. What were the consequences of Jackson's victory over the B.U.S.?

8. Explain how Jackson's nationalism was revealed in the nullification crisis and his strict constructionist views in his veto of the Maysville Road Bill and the recharter of the Bank of the United States.

9. What sorts of people expected benefits from Jacksonian democracy? What sorts of people were left out entirely?

10. Describe the effects of the Panic of 1837. What were some of its causes? How did Van Buren react?

11. Who composed and led the Whig party? What brought about Van Buren's election in 1836? How did the Whigs campaign in 1840? Explain their failure when in control of government.

Unrolling the Map

1. On a map of the eastern half of the United States, show the states that were admitted to the Union between 1790 and 1840. Place within each its date of admission. Draw in the frontier lines of 1790, 1820, and 1840. By appropriate symbols, indicate the major products of each section as of 1840.

2. On an outline map of the United States, draw the lines of the Louisiana Purchase and those of the Missouri Compromise. By colors, indicate (a) the area opened to slavery by the Compromise, (b) the area closed, (c) the slave states, (d) the area closed to slavery by the Northwest Ordinance (1787), and (e) the other free states. Locate the Mason-Dixon Line and the "Great American Desert."

Who, What, and Why Important?

American System	election of 1828
Missouri Compromise	Old Hickory
election of 1824	Jacksonian democracy
John Quincy Adams	spoils system
South Carolina Exposition	Whig party
Webster-Hayne debate	election of 1836
Compromise of 1833	Panic of 1837
B.U.S.	Independent Treasury System
Martin Van Buren	election of 1840
Henry Clay	John Tyler
Nicholas Biddle	Tariff of 1842
general incorporation laws	Pre-emption Act

To Pursue the Matter

1. To get the feel of the financial panic that started with the Specie Circular of 1836, read "Flush Times" (pp. 161–164) and "The Panic of 1837" (pp. 167–169) in Arnof, *A Sense of the Past.*

2. Just who were the Jacksonians when Old Hickory was elected in 1828? This difficult question is discussed in a chapter entitled "Democracy and States' Rights" in Brown, *The Hero and the People: The Meaning of Jacksonian Democracy.*

3. Was Jackson more important as a man or as a myth? See Ward, *Andrew Jackson: Symbol for an Age.*

4. How did Martin Van Buren reach the White House? See "The Rise of the Little Magician," *American Heritage,* June 1962, and Remini, *Martin Van Buren.*

5. By what means did John C. Calhoun defend the South and its "peculiar institution"? See Hofstadter, *The American Political Tradition and the Men Who Made It,* Chapter 4.

6. Exactly what was new about the way Jackson treated the presidential office? See Rossiter, *The American Presidency;* James, *Andrew Jackson: Portrait of a President;* and Van Deusen, *Jacksonian Era.*

7. For discussion and investigation:

a) Does the breakup of the Republican Party in 1824 suggest that a dominant party needs an opposition force to hold it together?

b) Why did Clay throw his support to Adams in 1824? Would it have been wrong if he *had* bargained?

c) Just how democratic was Jacksonian democracy?

Chapter 11

The Spirit
of Reform

*What a fertility of projects for
the salvation of the world!*
—RALPH WALDO EMERSON

The great democratic movement of which Jackson became a symbol expressed itself in demands for all sorts of reforms. Democracy implies that people can create a better society by their own efforts. Perhaps never before or since the Jacksonian period have Americans shown such optimistic faith in creating a better world. They thought themselves isolated once and for all from the troubles of Europe. They occupied an immense area, and had as yet hardly scratched its vast wealth. Foreign travelers remarked that while other nations were proud of their past, Americans boasted of their future. Foreigners also noticed that Americans seemed always in a hurry. They never sat still; they bolted their food; and many of them could hardly wait to create a heaven on earth. While there were reform movements with a record of solid achievement, there were others of the type which Theodore Roosevelt later called "the lunatic fringe." Ralph Waldo Emerson, called "the Sage of Concord," suggested the spirit of the age when he wrote:

What a fertility of projects for the salvation of the world! One apostle taught that all men should go to farming, and another that no man should buy or sell, that the use of money was the cardinal evil; another that the mischief was in our diet and that we eat and drink damnation. . . . Others assailed particular vocations, as that of the lawyer, that of the merchant, of the manufacturer, of the clergyman, of the scholar. . . . With this din of opinion and debate there was a keener scrutiny of institutions and of domestic life than any we have known . . . .

This "keener scrutiny of institutions" largely stemmed from ideas expressed in the Declaration of Independence: that men should have equal rights to pursue happiness, that they have a duty to oppose tyranny and correct abuses. Emerson's neighbor, Henry Thoreau, made a one-man declaration of independence and went off to live by himself on the shore of Walden Pond, where he could be free of the ties of society and seek truth in nature. Generally, though, the Americans in search of a better world formed organizations to persuade others to their way of thinking.

QUESTION • *"Know all men by these presents, that I, Henry Thoreau, do not wish to be regarded as a member of any incorporated society that I have not joined." Has one the right to repudiate the government?*

Once launched, reform movements in the United States owed much of their effectiveness to the fact that Americans understood the techniques of democracy. They knew how to run meetings, select slates of officers, draw up programs, and get publicity. Reform groups often imitated the political parties and held national conventions.

ADVANCES IN EDUCATION

If our union is still to continue, to cheer the hopes and animate the efforts of the oppressed of every nation; if your fields are to be untrod by the hirelings of despotism; if long days of blessedness are to attend our country in her career of glory; if you would have the sun continue to shed his unclouded rays upon the face of freemen, then EDUCATE ALL THE CHILDREN OF THE LAND.

This passionate demand for public schools, which appeared in a western magazine in 1836, was characteristic of the period. Although the idea of universal education went back as far as the Massachusetts General School Act of 1647, public schools had grown slowly. As late as 1834, 250,000 of the 400,000 children in Pennsylvania did not attend school. In the 1830's and 1840's, however, there was a tremendous increase in the number of tax-supported schools.

Public Schools

The drive for public education had several causes. (1) Americans fervently believed that the United States should be a land of equal opportunity, a land where people "start from an humble origin and can attain to the most elevated positions." To deny a child education was to close the door of opportunity.

(2) Once all persons gained the right to vote, it was obvious that all should be educated. To leave large numbers of voters unable to read or write was to invite trouble, since true democracy demanded an informed electorate.

QUESTION • What is the connection between public education and democracy?

Furthermore, once granted the franchise, the people used their new power to vote themselves schools.

(3) Various able people devoted themselves to the cause of education. In Pennsylvania, for instance, the rising young politician Thaddeus Stevens made his reputation by eloquent speeches on behalf of free schools. In Massachusetts, Horace Mann gave up a promising political career to take a poorly paid job as secretary of the state board of education. From this post Mann successfully campaigned for a number of improvements such as establishing normal schools to train teachers and dividing students into grades, with progress from one to another. Emma Willard fought for educational opportunity for young women.

Difficulties in Establishing Public Education

The establishment of public schools was not achieved without a fight. "Why should I be taxed," ran a common opposition argument, "to educate other people's children?" Communities that declared themselves in favor of public schools were nevertheless often unwilling to raise the necessary money through taxation. Yet the arguments in favor of public schools were so convincing that by 1850 most of the free states provided free elementary education. Public schools were far less common in the South, where the plantation owners dominated society and where there were fewer cities and towns.

It was one thing to pass laws establishing schools and another to make them good. Many one-room schoolhouses were so primitive they lacked glass in the windows. Most instruction was given by untrained teachers who were paid no more than unskilled laborers. Teaching was often done by teen-age boys earning money to go to college, by single women, or by men who had failed in other professions.

Many people, especially on the frontier, saw no reason why children should learn more than the "three R's." Indeed, there was distrust of too much "book learning," which is illustrated by the following quotation from an Indiana newspaper:

> ... a dead Indian is much more to the point than a dead language. Preachers are all right: we want them in our pulpits. But a lot of training is by no means essential to good preaching. And anyway we don't have to train them here. When we want trained ones we can send back East for them. ... And as for teachers—can't any young lawyer or preacher teach the boys and girls all they need to know? Give them a little spelling, a little ciphering, and a little handwriting, with a liberal sprinkling of the rod, and they'll have more than their fathers had before them. Did Tippecanoe Harrison graduate from a seminary? Did Old Hickory Jackson know any Latin or Greek when he swung the British agents in Florida higher than Haman?

With such views widespread, it is not surprising that in the early nineteenth century secondary education was supplied not by public schools, but by private academies and seminaries supported by fees and gifts. In 1824, however, Massachusetts required all towns with 500 or more families to establish tax-supported high schools. By 1860 the other free states had generally followed suit and free high schools had displaced the private academies, although only a minority of boys and girls attended them.

Noah Webster and the American Language

Many American leaders saw in public schools a means of promoting national spirit. The man who did the most in this direction was Noah Webster, author of the famous dictionaries that bore his name. Webster, who began his career during the Revolutionary War as a schoolteacher, devoted his life to creating a uniform American speech. *"A national language,"* he wrote, *"is a band of national union."* Even more influential than his dictionary was his *American Spelling Book.* By 1837, sales of this book had

reached the amazing total of 15,000,000 copies. In 1880 the publishers reported:

> It has the largest sale of any book in the world except the Bible. We sell a million copies a year, and we have been selling it at that rate for forty years. We sell them in cases of 72 dozen, and they are bought by all the large dry goods and supply houses, and furnished by them to every crossroads store.

So it was that a New England storekeeper boasted that he sold: "Everything: whiskey, molasses, calicoes, spelling books, and patent gridirons."

The American brand of English has remained remarkably uniform. There are far greater differences between dialects spoken today in the British Isles than in the whole United States, which has more than thirty-five times the area. This uniformity of speech is in part a product of public education, but probably results still more from the fact that the American population has been continuously on the move. There has not been time for people to settle down and develop extreme local peculiarities in ways of speaking.

Higher Education

Jefferson devoted his last years to the University of Virginia, opened in 1825, where all students were free to take any course offered, and where the curriculum was broader than in other colleges. Virginia was not widely imitated, but during the Jacksonian period several pioneer institutions that greatly influenced American education were founded. The Troy Female Seminary in Troy, New York, and Mt. Holyoke College in South Hadley, Massachusetts, were the first institutions of higher education established solely for women. Oberlin College, in Ohio, was the first coeducational college, as well as one of the first to admit Negro students. The example of North Carolina in opening a state university in 1795 was widely imitated. Thus after Michigan was admitted to the Union in 1837, one of the first acts of the legislature was to charter the University of Michigan.

The Jacksonian period saw the first large-scale effort to provide adult education. This was the Lyceum movement which began in Massachusetts. A Lyceum was a voluntary organiza-tion supported by small membership fees and designed to promote "the improvement of its members in useful knowledge." The various Lyceums formed a loose federation. They provided libraries, small scientific museums, discussion groups, and lectures. To their lecture platforms came the most eminent men of the day.

Elizabeth Peabody, Schoolteacher

The Peabody sisters were at the center of the nineteenth-century educational scene. Mary married Horace Mann; Sophia, Nathaniel Hawthorne, but the third, Elizabeth, remained unmarried and a dedicated champion of every cause that excited intellectual New England during her long adult lifetime. An editor, publisher, bookseller, and confidante of the Concord literary group, she was the first woman lecturer in the United States. But she was, first, a schoolteacher.

A child when she began to teach in her mother's home in Salem, Massachusetts, she started her own school at sixteen. These "schools" for small children specialized in Latin, arithmetic, geography, and other "first things." Uneven in quality, they were necessary in a day when publicly supported education had not yet become almost universal through the United States. Early in the 1830's Miss Peabody could command about one hundred dollars per pupil per year, from which she had to pay schoolroom rent. She and her sister Mary could teach only a dozen or so pupils between them, however; and they could not hope to teach older boys, this being a matter for men.

Later, in the mid-1830's in Boston, Elizabeth was an assistant in a school run by Bronson Alcott. The unique Temple School, preserved in her *Record of a School* (1835), was a failure, but it attracted a great deal of attention. Mr. Alcott (Louisa May Alcott's father) tried to teach his pupils by "conversing with them" in his own version of the Socratic method of questioning. He led them in examinations of their souls, their "aspirations," and the discussion of such questions as, "Is it worthwhile to try to bear the cold?" Despite the topics of discussion, the Alcott method fore-shadowed the "progressive" school in its attempt to involve the students in learning by gearing the subject matter to their own immediate interests.

Elizabeth Peabody and Mary Mann were primarily responsible for the kinder-garten movement in the United States. They started the first such English-speaking school in Boston in 1860, and Miss Peabody—the "grandmother of kindergartens"—continued to champion the movement until her death at ninety in 1894.

CULTURAL ACHIEVEMENTS

In 1820 the Reverend Sydney Smith, writing in a British magazine, sneered at the low cultural level of the Americans and the lack of artistic and scientific achievement in the United States:

The Americans are a brave, industrious, and acute people; but they have hitherto given no indication of genius. During the thirty or forty years of their independence, they have done absolutely nothing for the Sciences, for the Arts, for Literature, or even for the statesman-like studies of Politics and Political Economy. . . . In the four quarters of the globe, who reads an American book? Or goes to an American play? Or looks at an American picture or statue? What does the world yet owe to American physicians and surgeons? What new substances have their chemists yet discovered? What old ones have they analysed?

Americans themselves had a sense of inferiority. People could not write poetry without "a legendary past nor a poetic present," remarked one young scholar. "Large mountains, extensive prairies, tall cataracts, long rivers [and] millions of dirty acres" did not seem suitable subjects for literature. When James Fenimore Cooper wrote his first novel, he set the scene in England and tried to attract readers by promoting the rumor that he was "a prominent Englishman." And yet almost as if in answer to Sydney Smith's taunt, the second quarter of the nineteenth century saw American authors writing books that are still read on both sides of the Atlantic and American scientists making important discoveries. It was during this period that the first American masters of fiction began to write about the American scene. Washington Irving dealt with life and legend in the Hudson River Valley, creating the immortal Rip Van Winkle. Generations of children not only here but in France and England, have pretended to be Indian warriors or wilderness scouts as a result of Cooper's novels about the New York frontier. Nathaniel Hawthorne dealt critically with the Puritan tradition of his native New England. Herman Melville's *Moby Dick* gave a fascinating account of the business of whaling, while portraying the loneliness and terror of the struggle against the elements and with human nature itself.

Poets, Essayists, and the American Scene

Like the novelists, American poets began to look at the American scene. Henry Wadsworth Longfellow immortalized the Indian hero Hiawatha; John Greenleaf Whittier in "Snowbound" described winter on a New England farm; William Cullen Bryant in "To a Waterfowl" gave a haunting picture of sunset over a lonely marsh. The finest verses of all, however, were those of Edgar Allan Poe, about a magical world no man has ever seen. Of equal rank with the poets were the essayists Emerson and Thoreau. Ralph Waldo Emerson called on people to trust themselves and to break the bonds of custom and prejudice. His friend Henry Thoreau described in *Walden* how he retired to the woods to live his own life. Another famous literary figure was the brilliant Margaret Fuller. Both by her adventurous life and her writings she proclaimed the rights of women. Poe said of her style that it was "piquant, vivid, terse, bold . . . everything a style should be."

Many American writers took active part in reform movements. Whittier, Longfellow, and James Russell Lowell joined the crusade against slavery, as did Lydia Maria Child. Thoreau went to jail rather than pay taxes to support the Mexican War. Amelia Bloomer, famous for the pantaloons she wore to protest the excesses of women's clothing, crusaded for women's rights, as did Jane Swisshelm.

Scientific Advances

About the same time as the first flowering of American literature, Americans also won fame in the field of science. Maria Mitchell taught herself astronomy while checking navigational instruments for whaling captains during her childhood in Nantucket. She discovered a new comet, which was named for her, and was the first woman elected to several learned societies. She also discovered several groups of distant stars and wrote important studies of Jupiter and Saturn. Joseph Henry, the inventor of the electromagnetic motor, headed the Smithsonian Institution, established in 1846. Research there laid the basis for predicting weather accurately.

Another who worked in a similar field was Matthew Maury, an officer of the United States Navy. After study of thousands of ships' logs, Maury developed tables that predicted winds and ocean tides at different seasons and gave directions as to shortest travel time. The tables were so accurate that the average time from New York to San Francisco by sailing ship was reduced from 180 to 133 days. His findings so aided navigation everywhere that he was honored by thirteen foreign nations. Maury was also one of the first men to make a systematic study of the ocean bottom, and he selected the route for the first transatlantic cable. He is regarded as the founder of the science of oceanography.

One of the most important events in the history of medicine occurred in the United States with the first use of ether as an anesthetic during operations. This discovery was made independently by Dr. Crawford W. Long of Georgia in 1842 and Dr. W. T. G. Morton of Boston in 1846.

The Arts

In the visual arts there was no such achievement as in literature and science, although American artists were eager to produce works which should rival those of Europe. Samuel F. B. Morse, the inventor of the telegraph, began his career as a painter who wanted to "rival the genius of a Raphael, a Michelangelo, a Titian," in order to refute the charge that America "has produced no men of genius." However, great sculptors and painters did not appear. American artists had little opportunity for the skilled training available abroad and were still dominated by European styles. For example, American sculptors were so influenced by the past that they clothed Washington and Jackson in Roman togas. Neither the public as a whole nor wealthy patrons demanded works of art. Some good work was done in painting, however, by artists who, like the novelists, turned their attention to the American scene. Such an artist was George C. Bingham, who was at his best when he painted the life he had seen on the Missouri frontier as a boy. A group of landscape painters in the East were known as the "Hudson River School" because of their romantic paintings of the Catskill Mountains at the point where they border the Hudson.

During the early part of the nineteenth century, American architects continued to use classical models developed in the Renaissance. In New England, Charles Bulfinch, influenced by English models, developed a distinctive "Federal" style that can be seen in the Massachusetts State House, the largest building in America at the time it was designed. Bulfinch later worked for fourteen years in Washington and helped to complete the design of the national Capitol. He had wide influence, especially in New England, but the style that most appealed to the American taste was known as "Greek Revival." Inspired in part by the enthusiasm for the Greeks' revolt against their Turkish oppressors, Greek Revival style was based on that of ancient temples, but was freely adapted to modern needs. It was used both in public buildings, of which the most famous is Jefferson's Virginia State Capitol, and in domestic architecture. It was often successful. "A Greek Revival town," remarks a historian of American architecture, "is a fine and handsome assembly of stately colonnades and well-turned building masses."

By the middle of the nineteenth century, American architects unfortunately abandoned the simplicity and clean lines of the Federal and Greek Revival styles and attempted to

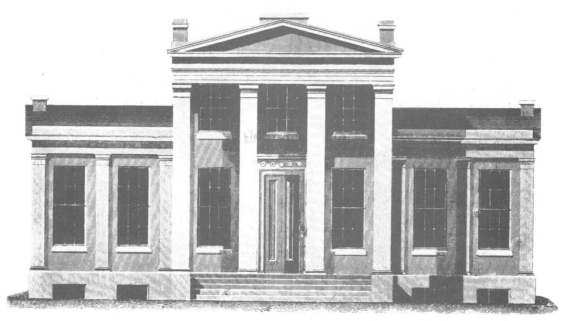

During the Jacksonian period the "Greek Revival" style, shown above, was at the height of its popularity. More original, and peculiar to the United States, were the "octagon houses," which gave maximum space and light.

imitate the Gothic style of the Middle Ages. Characterized by elaborate detail, pointed windows, and colored glass, this style was originally developed for churches and stone construction. When adapted to other purposes and to wooden buildings, it was often ridiculous. Among the few signs of real originality in American architecture were the "octagon houses," designed to give maximum light and space with a minimum of wall space and supporting rafters.

The finest American artistry did not appear so much in formal works of art as in practical objects. Some of these were, to use a phrase of Emerson's, "beautiful necessities"—especially the great sailing ships with their clean lines, gleaming spars, and carved figureheads.

WOMEN'S RIGHTS

By 1850 nearly all adult white men had gained the right to vote, but in no state had women won any active part in politics. They were second-class citizens in other ways. According to the English common law that America inherited, "the husband and wife are one and that one is the husband." When a woman married, her property passed to her husband, and children were solely under his authority. Except for the ill-paid occupation of teaching, professions were closed to women, as were most institutions of higher learning. Women were also bound by exaggerated standards of propriety, with rigid taboos about dress and behavior. The ill health and fainting spells that plagued the lives of many women were partly brought on by tight, heavy clothes.

Yet foreigners noted the deference paid to women in America and their relative freedom as compared with European women. Particularly in the West, women had a high station. The life of a frontier woman was one of endless toil, but she was a full partner in the work of settlement. In frontier regions there was such a surplus of men that women had a high scarcity value. "Guess my husband's got to look after me, and make himself agreeable to me," said a western girl. "If he don't, there's plenty will." Meanwhile, in the East, the new careers for women as factory hands and schoolteachers helped to free them from restraints and dependence. Many women of wealthy or professional families became widely read in spite of lack of opportunity for formal education, and the women's magazine, *Godey's Lady's Book*, achieved a circulation of 150,000. Since American businessmen tended to immerse themselves in work, wealthy women tended to dominate the culture of the large cities. A New York editor remarked:

> It is the women who regulate the style of living, dispense hospitalities, exclusively manage society, control clergymen and churches, regulate the schemes of benevolence, patronize and influence the Arts, and pronounce upon Operas, and it is the women ... who exercise the ultimate control over the Press.

Seneca Falls Convention, 1848

The feelings of women about their place and position in the world came to a head in 1848 when Lucretia Mott and Elizabeth Cady Stanton organized a convention to draw up a "Declaration of Sentiments and Resolutions" echoing the Declaration of Independence. Starting with the "self-evident truth" that "all men and women are created equal," the Seneca Falls declaration went on to list grievances of women against men and to demand full equality in every aspect of life.

The women's rights movement was often received with anger and ridicule. Feminists were denied the right to speak in public and were denounced as shameless or irreligious. Most politicians were indifferent or hostile, one of the exceptions being a young Whig in the frontier state of Illinois—Abraham Lincoln. The immediate results of the feminist movement were slight. Women did not gain the vote or admission to professions; most colleges continued to exclude them. They did, however, gain relief from some of their worst legal handicaps. Many states passed laws, for instance, permitting them to retain and manage their property after marriage. Above all, they drew attention to their cause, and the seriousness of their purpose.

THE ANTISLAVERY CRUSADE

The most glaring violation of democratic principles in the United States was, of course, Negro slavery. How could America claim to be "the land of the free" when human beings were bought and sold like cattle? The question became increasingly acute by 1840, as most Latin-American countries had abolished slavery, and Great Britain had banned it in her West Indian possessions. It is not surprising that the upsurge of democratic feeling in the Jacksonian period was accompanied by an increase in antislavery agitation.

The organized movement to abolish slavery began among religious groups. As early as 1776 the Quakers, in the South as well as in the North, had agreed to hold no more slaves. In Virginia in 1789 the Baptists recommended "every legal measure to extirpate this horrid evil from the land." The abolition movement at first made many converts in the

QUESTION • When an individual sees injustice being done, what should he or she do?

South. Among its early leaders were Benjamin Lundy, a New Jersey man who spent most of his active career organizing antislavery societies in southern communities, and James G. Birney, an Alabama lawyer and cotton planter, who freed his own slaves and attempted to get other owners to do the same. As late as 1831 the Virginia legislature seriously debated a bill to abolish slavery in the state. Generally, however, the increasing profitability of cotton growing and the fear of a Negro insurrection if slaves were freed tended to stifle abolitionism in the South.

Garrison and Other Abolitionists

On January 1, 1831, appeared the first edition of *The Liberator,* an antislavery newspaper edited by William Lloyd Garrison and published in Boston. Garrison's views were extreme for the time and his language violent. He denounced both Northerners who refused to be shocked by slavery and Southerners who held slaves. He demanded immediate freedom for the Negroes without compensation for the owners, whom he regarded as "not . . . within the pale of Christianity, of Republicanism, of humanity." He damned the Constitution as "a league with death and a covenant with Hell" because it protected slavery. Garrison and his followers made no attempt to win their way by political action and were willing to

divide the Union to rid the free states of the shame of being tied to the slave states.

Many abolitionists refused to follow Garrison, who had a talent for antagonizing even his own supporters. A group who proposed to abolish slavery by the use of the ballot box founded the Liberty party. It nominated James G. Birney for the presidency in 1840 and 1844, winning only a few thousand votes. Another leader who favored political activity was Frederick Douglass, a self-educated former slave, who edited an abolitionist newspaper, *The North Star.* The title suggests an important abolitionist activity, the "Underground Railroad." This secret organization, which had stations running through the northern states to Canada, brought slaves out of the South and set them free. Its agents not only took care of slaves after they had come North, but risked their lives to go into the slave states and lead Negroes to freedom. One of the most successful of these was Harriet Tubman, the "Negro Moses," who had herself been born in slavery. After making her own escape, she returned to the South again and again, liberating over three hundred of her people and always escaping arrest, even though eventually a reward of $40,000 was promised for her capture.

Southern Reaction to the Abolition Movement

It was almost certainly a mere coincidence that the first publication of *The Liberator* coincided with a slave insurrection in Virginia in 1831, led by Nat Turner, a Negro preacher who believed himself divinely inspired to lead his people from bondage. Turner's rebellion was easily quelled after about sixty whites had been killed, but it caused panic in the South. Belief that Turner had been inspired by abolitionist propaganda ended the antislavery movement in the South. From that time on, Southerners who favored abolition of slavery usually re-

Abolitionism

The Library of Congress

Part of the front page of one of the early issues of William Lloyd Garrison's *The Liberator,* a leading abolitionist paper. Note the slogan in the masthead line: "Our Country is the World — Our Countrymen, All Mankind." Harriet Tubman (left) was a leading Underground Railroad worker, who led more than 300 slaves to freedom, including her own mother in 1857.

John C. Calhoun (right) is here depicted as a modern Joshua commanding the sun (a printing press) to stand still "so that the Nation of Carolina may continue to hold Negroes . . . till the day of Judgment." This refers to Calhoun's efforts to muzzle the abolitionist press and to keep abolitionist literature out of the mails.

mained silent or left home. One of the few who did not flee was Cassius Marcellus Clay, a distant relative of Henry Clay, who edited abolitionist newspapers in Kentucky. A man of fantastic pugnacity who habitually went armed with two pistols and a bowie knife, Clay once fortified his office with two cannon and a keg of gunpowder set to go off. When he was absent one day, however, a mob seized his presses and sent them across the Ohio River to Cincinnati.

The abolitionist attacks helped to drive Southerners toward an elaborate defense of their "peculiar institution" that will be described in a later chapter (see pp. 331–334). The South began to demand the suppression of abolitionist propaganda as a price of remaining in the Union. Southern postmasters refused to deliver abolitionist newspapers, and in 1835 a bill to bar abolitionist literature from the mails passed the Senate, although it finally was abandoned. In 1836, under southern pressure, the House of Representatives passed a "gag rule" providing that all abolitionist petitions should be shelved without debate.

Despite the excitement it aroused, the anti-slavery movement at first affected politics very little. The Missouri Compromise had supposedly averted civil war by fixing for all time the boundary between slave and free territory. No prominent politician and neither major party proposed to endanger the Union by touching slavery where it was already protected by law.

THE LABOR MOVEMENT

Wherever it appeared, the industrial revolution ultimately raised the standard of living of the mass of the people by creating cheaper and more abundant goods. In several ways, however, an immediate result was to make life more difficult for workers:

(1) When machines took over the work of hand tools, many skilled crafts workers lost their jobs or were reduced to the condition of unskilled labor.

(2) There was enjoyment in skilled work and pride in good handicraft. But tending machines was monotonous, and workers gained little sense that the product was their own. Furthermore, handicraft workers worked at their own pace, factory workers at a speed set by the machine.

(3) While craft workers worked long hours, they were at liberty to begin and end the day at the time they themselves chose. If they had money in hand, and wanted to take a day off and go fishing or sleep, that was their affair. But in factories, the hours were fixed by the employer, with fines or discharge as the penalty for lateness or absence.

(4) In the small-community society before the industrial revolution, laborers often owned their own cottage, with a garden to supplement income and help tide over periods of unemployment. In the big cities created by the industrial revolution, workers were crowded into dingy, rented tenements. Periods of unemployment were more frequent than before; when they came, workers had less to fall back on.

(5) In the small shops of the earlier age, owner and employee labored side by side. They both wore homespun clothes and leather aprons. They knew each other and might have married into each other's families. The industrial revolution broke down this face-to-face relationship between employers and workers. Under the factory system, an employer often knew none of the workers, and dealt with them entirely through superintendents and overseers. Owners and workers now lived in different sections of town and moved in different social circles. Their closeness had vanished.

In brief, workers lost *security*—security of employment, security of life in small communities, and security of personal contact with employers.

Trade Societies

In such circumstances workers everywhere have organized into labor unions. In the United States the most powerful of the early unions, however, were organizations not of factory workers but of skilled crafts workers—carpenters, shoemakers, printers, and so forth. By 1830 most of the major crafts had formed what were known as "trade societies" in all the major northeastern cities. The dues collected by these trade societies paid for the funeral expenses of members and fed them and their families during strikes. The trade societies demanded higher wages, shorter hours, and the "closed shop," which meant that the employer could hire only union members.

The different crafts joined together to form city-wide federations for combined action. In 1835 the Philadelphia trade societies called a city-wide strike to force the employers to grant them a 10-hour day. The slogan of the Philadelphia workers was "6 to 6"—a working day running from 6 A.M. to 6 P.M., with an hour out for breakfast and an hour out for lunch. The trade societies from six cities also formed a National Trades Union, which was designed to promote the organization of all workers and claimed a membership of 300,000.

Factory workers were not so successful in forming unions. Since, unlike craft workers, they were unskilled, strikes among them were not so effective as among craft workers; the employers could break a strike simply by hiring other people. Many textile workers, especially in New England, were women who came to work to improve their lot in life or earn money for their dowry. To these young women from rocky farms, where little money and long hours were the rule, $2 a week was good pay and a 12- or 13-hour day not unusual. Many of the early factory owners provided the workers with educational opportunities and comfortable living conditions. But, as competition increased, conditions worsened. Some of the workers decided to organize—and met resistance. The first women's strike occurred in 1824 among the weavers of Pawtucket, Rhode Island. In 1833 there appeared a union of factory girls in Lynn, Massachusetts, followed shortly by a "Factory Girls' Association" designed to bring in all women workers. Although these early unions were generally ineffective, they were the first attempts at large-scale women's organizations in American history.

Labor's Demands

Not only did the unions make obvious demands regarding hours and wages, they also threw their weight behind many of the reforms of the Jacksonian period. No people were more interested in the founding of public schools than the trade societies. They were no less insistent than the western settlers in demanding cheap public land on easy terms. They were in the forefront of the movement to abolish imprisonment for debt. In 1830 it was estimated that 75,000 people a year were thrown into common jails for unpaid debts, often of trifling amounts. Another labor demand was for "mechanics' lien laws," which would require that the unpaid wages of workers be the first claim on the assets of a bankrupt employer. Without such protection, workers were often left holding the bag.

In order to obtain their demands, laborers went into politics. In 1829 a Workingmen's party put up candidates for local offices in New York City and polled 6,000 out of 20,000 votes. This party and others like it did not last long. Radical reformers tried to use them to promote a redivision of property ownership or to agitate for more liberal divorce laws, thus making the workers seem more revolutionary than they really were.

These parties were also torn apart by squabbles between radicals and moderates, and

The work in early factories required little skill. Long hours were the rule; daybreak to nightfall was the usual working day. Children, more nimble and more easily manageable, often replaced adults.

between representatives of different unions. Finally, professional politicians moved in and lured many workers into the major parties by including some of labor's demands in their platforms. The Democrats were especially successful in attracting workers to the support of Andrew Jackson. Van Buren revealed his debt to the labor vote when in 1840 he established a 10-hour day on all work done for the federal government, such as the construction of warships and lighthouses.

Collapse of the Labor Movement

The early trade societies faced severe legal handicaps because state courts tended to apply the English common law doctrine that forbade conspiracies in restraint of trade. In a case against shoemakers in Philadelphia, a Pennsylvania court ruled in 1806 that a combination of workingmen to force employers to raise wages was a criminal conspiracy punishable by fines or imprisonment. This became a precedent followed in other states. Thus in 1835, employers successfully prosecuted another group of shoemakers, this time in Geneva, New York. In deciding that the workers were guilty of conspiracy because their trade society demanded

that they be paid at least a dollar to make a pair of shoes, the court said:

> Competition is the life of trade. If the defendants cannot make coarse boots for less than one dollar per pair, let them refuse to do so; but let them not directly or indirectly undertake to say that others shall not do the same work for less price.

Repeated efforts by trade union lawyers to persuade judges that trade societies had a legal right to carry on collective action against employers were finally rewarded in 1842 in the case of *Commonwealth v. Hunt*. Here the highest court of Massachusetts held that a peaceful attempt by a trade society to improve the lot of its members through organized pressure such as a strike or a boycott might be legal if the methods employed were peaceful. But this rather cautious tolerance of trade societies through the principle of "virtuous ends pursued by virtuous means" came too late to help most of the early trade societies. The Panic of 1837 had already caused their collapse. Unemployment was so widespread that in order to avoid starvation workers accepted whatever wages were offered. The closed shop could not be enforced; union treasuries were emptied. It was nearly a generation before labor again tried to organize on a large scale. The labor movement of the Jacksonian period was not, however, wholly unsuccessful in securing permanent gains for workingmen. Labor influence had been a major force in promoting public schools and in making it easier for settlers to acquire public lands. Several states passed rather ineffective laws limiting the workday to 10 hours. Many states passed mechanics' lien laws, and imprisonment for debt was almost universally abandoned.

THE TEMPERANCE MOVEMENT

In addition to the reform movements designed to uplift the underprivileged groups—

Negroes, women, laborers—there were others designed to rid the country of special abuses. The most powerful of such movements was the temperance crusade which aimed to moderate or abolish the use of liquor. Its early leaders were mostly clergymen interested in doing away with the evils which they felt heavy drinking encouraged. Like other reform groups, temperance groups formed a national organization, the United States Temperance Union, founded in 1833. They started newspapers and published hundreds of thousands of pamphlets. Millions of heavy drinkers were persuaded to "take the pledge," i.e., promise to give up drinking. Temperance propaganda even included a "Cold Water Army" of children with uniforms and marching songs. The revivalist spirit of the temperance movement is revealed by a stanza from one of its songs, entitled "One More Drink":

> Stay, mortal, stay! nor heedless thus
>   Thy sure destruction seal;
> Within that cup there lurks a curse,
>   Which all who drink shall feel.
> Disease and death forever nigh,
>   Stand ready at the door,
> And eager wait to hear the cry—
>   "O give me one glass more!"

In addition to trying to persuade people not to drink, temperance societies demanded laws to put an end to the sale of liquor, and were able to convince many politicians of the justice of their cause. Abraham Lincoln, for instance, favored prohibition by state action. In urging it he argued that just as the American Revolution freed people from the tyranny of Britain, so prohibition would free people from the tyranny of alcohol. In 1851 Maine passed the first state prohibition law—an example followed by about a dozen states. Other states passed "local option" laws, which allowed towns and villages to prohibit the sale of liquor within their boundaries.

CARE FOR THE MENTALLY ILL

A relatively little publicized reform, better treatment of the mentally ill, illustrates the extraordinary influence a single determined person may exert. One of the most cruel abuses of human beings was the treatment of the mentally ill as criminals. The individual most responsible for improving this state of affairs was Dorothea Dix, a Massachusetts schoolteacher. Shocked at conditions she saw when she visited a jail in 1841, Miss Dix proceeded, entirely on her own initiative, to visit nearly all the jails and almshouses in her native state. In 1842 she wrote a report describing the conditions she found, and presented it to the legislature. "I proceed, gentlemen," she wrote in her introduction, "briefly to call your attention to the *present* state of insane persons confined within this commonwealth, in *cages, closets, cellars, stalls, pens! Chained, naked, beaten with rods,* and lashed into obedience...."

Miss Dix's findings were at once so shocking and so accurate that Massachusetts passed a law establishing asylums where the insane were to be treated as sick rather than guilty. After her success at home, Miss Dix traveled throughout the United States visiting over 800 jails and almshouses. Largely as a result of her influence, twenty states followed Massachusetts in founding insane asylums. Later she traveled abroad, helping to promote better treatment of the insane in every major European country. A friendship with a Japanese diplomat resulted in the first insane asylums in Japan.

INTERNATIONAL PEACE

While Dorothea Dix devoted herself to the sufferings of the small minority of the population who were insane, other reformers turned their attention to a problem affecting all humankind—the abolition of war. Since the formation of a federal union had apparently solved the problem of bringing independent states into combination, and since the United States was in no danger from her neighbors, it was natural for Americans to think that universal peace was attainable. In 1828 the American Peace Society was formed to promote international understanding. Its principal founder was William Ladd, who abandoned a successful career, first as ship captain and then as farmer, to devote his entire energy to the cause of peace. Ladd agitated for a Congress of Nations with courts of international justice to settle all disputes.

SOCIALISM

From Europe at this period came a new idea—socialism. This was a revolt against the poverty and inequality which socialists blamed on business competition and individual ownership of property. Socialists proposed to substitute cooperation for competition and common ownership for individual ownership. The early followers of the idea proposed to start small, voluntary communities where their ideas could be put into practice. Most of these experiments took place in the United States because land was so easy to acquire here. A famous English socialist, Robert Owen, started a cooperative venture at New Harmony, Indiana. Even more influential than he were the disciples of the Frenchman, Charles Fourier, who proposed to organize society into "phalanxes" of just 1,620 people, living in villages called "phalansteries." His converts included Horace Greeley, editor of the New York *Tribune*, the most widely read newspaper in the United States.

Since the labor movement of the 1830's had failed to get the workers better wages or more security, a few labor leaders were ready to try socialism. Many intellectuals, repelled by the ugly aspects of the factory system, were also interested. Eventually almost forty Fourierist communities were started, but most of them quickly collapsed. The "phalanxes" were too often composed of individuals without organizing ability or manual skills. There were quarrels about the division of labor. Without the profit motive, it was found difficult to get people to work hard enough to produce the goods on which life depends. Although socialism had aroused great fear among property owners, its first appearance in the United States turned out to be a failure.

RELIGIOUS MOVEMENTS

The first half of the nineteenth century saw a great variety of religious movements in the United States. In New England the Unitarians revolted against the stern Puritanism of the Congregational Church. Instead of considering people totally depraved, the Unitarians insisted that they were by nature good. Throughout the country, the immense growth of Protestant denominations, especially the Baptists and the Methodists, was marked by great revival meetings, the building of thousands of new churches, and the founding of scores of colleges and universities. In the cities, the coming of thousands of European immigrants brought a corresponding growth of the religions they professed. In Boston and New York, for instance, the Roman Catholic Church provided not only places of worship, but also schools, orphanages, and charitable organizations.

Alexis de Tocqueville, a French political scientist who made a close study of American institutions during the Jacksonian period, observed that American ministers of all faiths did "not attempt to draw or to fix all the thoughts of man upon the life to come." Life on earth was no longer a mere preparation for the hereafter; instead, people had the capacity and the duty to improve the environment in which God had placed them. Thus the new religious spirit was often intimately tied to the spirit of

Reformers and Utopians

The crusade for temperance that culminated in the passage of the 18th Amendment began with the prohibition parades of the 1830's. Another reform advocated in this early period was more humane treatment of the mentally ill, to which Dorothea Dix (right) devoted all her energies. A utopian community was planned (below) at New Harmony, Ind., to be "capable of producing permanently greater physical, moral, and intellectual advantages to every individual...," but the project failed.

reform. Indeed most of the reform movements described in this chapter were promoted by religious groups. Unitarian ministers were leaders in the abolition movement, and temperance became almost a special province of the Baptists and Methodists.

Some religious groups decided to cut themselves off from the world and found utopian communities of their own. Thus the Shakers, an offshoot of the Quakers, established scores of villages where everything was owned in common. The Shakers supported themselves by small industry, and today the furniture they made, with its fine workmanship and clean lines, is much prized by collectors. Another successful community that practiced a variety of Christian socialism was the Oneida Community in central New York, which supported itself by manufacturing efficient game traps. The Mormons, another new sect, were driven by persecution to endure the hardships of pioneering in a trek that started in western New York in 1830 and ended with the founding of Salt Lake City in 1848.

VARIETY OF REFORM; PERMANENT INFLUENCE

There is not space in this chapter to describe all the reforms advocated in the United States during the Jacksonian period. There were organizations to improve prisons, to persuade Congress to do away with flogging in the navy, to abolish meat-eating, to make contact with departed spirits, to promote a "science" called phrenology through which character could supposedly be determined by the shape of the skull. Typical of the period were the "come-outers" who "came out" in favor of every reform. There was even a "come-outer" society called the Friends of Universal Reform.

Although it may be easy to laugh at some of the "come-outers" and their odd notions, the great reform movements of the 1830's and 1840's

left behind them much solid achievement. Their influence was seen especially in state legislation dealing with such problems as prisons, the insane, child labor, liquor, mechanics' lien laws, and public schools. This illustrates one of the virtues of the federal system: it allows for vigorous action at the local level.

Some movements which had relatively little success at first, such as the feminists, formed permanent organizations which continued their agitation even into the twentieth century. The essential demands of the abolitionists, the feminists, the educational reformers, and the labor unions were all eventually fulfilled.

The motto on the front page of Garrison's paper, *The Liberator*, was, "Our Country Is the World—Our Countrymen, All Mankind." The movements here described were by no means limited to the United States. There was constant influence back and forth between Europe and the United States. The antislavery movement, for instance, achieved great strength in Great Britain before it had gone far in America. In 1833, at a time when the United States Congress would not even debate the slavery question, British abolitionists succeeded in persuading Parliament to buy out the slaveowners in the British colonies and free the slaves. The Prussian system of public schools provided Horace Mann with several of the ideas which he put into effect in Massachusetts. One of the greatest temperance lecturers was Father Theobald Matthew, an Irish priest who had persuaded over two million of the Irish to "take the pledge." Father Matthew came to New York in 1849 and was received with a great ovation. In the next two years he traveled through twenty-five states and persuaded 600,000 people to agree to give up liquor. In the other direction, the pressure of American reform on Europe, an outstanding example was Dorothea Dix. She was only one of many American reformers who had wide contacts and wide influence on both sides of the Atlantic.

Activities: Chapter 11

For Mastery and Review

1. What common purposes did Emerson see in the various reforms he described? Why were reform movements effective?

2. Summarize the reasons for starting public schools. What arguments were used against them? Describe the extent and quality of public education in 1850. What developments in colleges and in adult education came in this period? What influences in America discouraged the arts and artists? In what art form did Americans achieve the most at this time?

3. Why did the movement for women's rights start? What problems did women face campaigning? What were the immediate results?

4. Outline the development of the Abolition movement. Why did abolitionists anger people in both North and South?

5. In what ways did the industrial revolution tend to increase workers' insecurity? Why were the first labor unions in America formed? How did women workers affect the union movement? What reforms did organized labor sponsor? Account for their successes and failures.

6. Outline the reforms sought by (a) the Temperance Union, (b) Dorothea Dix, and (c) the American Peace Society. What did each achieve?

7. Why were religious and socialistic communities established? Account for the failure of some of the socialist communities. What was the connection between religious groups and reform?

8. Give instances of European reform influence on America, and vice versa.

Who, What, and Why Important?

Ralph Waldo Emerson	the Abolition movement
Horace Mann	National Trades Union
Emma Willard	Factory Girls' Association
James Fenimore Cooper	
Henry Thoreau	Lucretia Mott
Noah Webster	Elizabeth Cady Stenton
higher education	Samuel F. B. Morse
American literature	Charles Bulfinch
Matthew Maury	*Commonwealth v. Hunt*
Maria Mitchell	Temperance Union
Margaret Fuller	Dorothea Dix
Seneca Falls Convention	American Peace Society

socialism

religious revivals

Father Theobald Matthew

To Pursue the Matter

1. How did *Godey's Lady's Book* gain such a large circulation? See "Mr. Godey's Lady," *American Heritage*, October 1959.

2. What were the political activities of organized labor during the Jacksonian period and how effective were they? See Rayback, *A History of American Labor*, Chapter 7.

3. After he was President, John Quincy Adams went to Congress as a representative from Massachusetts, where he pursued an utterly independent and most dramatic course. It's worth a class report. See "Mad Old Man from Massachusetts," *American Heritage*, April 1961.

4. The Abolitionists were branded as "extremist," "impractical," "trouble-making," and "not free of racial prejudice themselves." They have been praised and defended as "men of conscience," "courageous," and "Christian." Examine the evidence. Possible sources: Filler, *The Crusade against Slavery*; Douglass, *The Life and Times of Frederick Douglass*; Donald, *Lincoln Reconsidered*; Litwack, *North of Slavery: the Negro in the Free States, 1790–1860*; and Bartlett, *Wendell Phillips: Brahmin Radical*.

5. For a description of the "lunatic fringe" of reformers in the "burned over" district of upstate New York, see Carmer, *Listen for a Lonesome Drum*.

6. Questions to investigate and discuss:

a) "The industrial revolution . . . ultimately raised the standard of living . . . (but) an immediate result was to make life harder for workingmen." (p. 286.) How do you explain this apparently contradictory statement?

b) Why were Abolitionist leaders such as Lovejoy and Garrison the objects of violence in the North?

7. Intimately connected with the reform movements of the Jacksonian period, especially in the Northeast, was an intellectual movement known as "transcendentalism." For an explanation of the philosophy of transcendentalism see Brown, *The Hero and the People: The Meaning of Jacksonian Democracy*.

PART THREE: SUMMING UP
Chapters 9–11

I. CHECKING THE FACTS

1. Which of the statements below are *main ideas* in this unit?
   a. Progress was made in some but not all areas of American society.
   b. During Jackson's administration, more people became involved in government.
   c. Labor made significant gains through the use of political power.
   d. The Monroe Doctrine established our foreign policy for several years to come.
   e. In general, women were "seen but not heard."
   f. As the economy and people's needs changed, so did attitudes toward slavery and the tariff.
   g. A conflict between nationalism and sectionalism became increasingly apparent.

2. Look at the term at the left. Then from the group at the right, select the item that is *most clearly related* to it.
   a. *internal improvements:* government reform, sectional compromise, roads and canals, boundary settlements
   b. *Jacksonian Democracy:* frequent elections, female suffrage, industrial progress, government controls
   c. *literature:* Herman Melville, Asa Gray, Matthew Maury, Maria Mitchell
   d. *Seneca Falls Convention:* labor, territory, equality, business
   e. *education:* Dorothea Dix, Henry Thoreau, Robert J. Walker, Horace Mann

II. INTERPRETING THE FACTS

1. Put the three items in each line below into *one* sentence that makes sense. (You may change the order of the words.)
   a. politics/Seneca Falls Convention/equality
   b. nationalism/loyalty/sectionalism
   c. land/slavery/expansion
   d. protection/trade/tariff
   e. compromise/democracy/adjustment

2. Tell whether each of the people or terms below was a force for *nationalism* or *sectionalism*. Give evidence to support your decision.

Bank of the United States	Rush-Bagot Treaty
Cumberland Road	Noah Webster
Maysville Road veto	John Marshall
"Log Cabin" campaign	Industrial Revolution
public schools	cotton culture

3. *Interpreting Graphs and Charts*

Examine the charts and graphs on pp. 296–97 to decide whether each statement below is *true,* *false,* or *not given* in the text.

    a. Most American workers were either farmers or factory workers.

    b. No President was free of economic problems.

    c. The rate of population growth in rural areas was consistently greater than in urban areas.

    d. A single political party dominated the American political scene.

    e. The appearance of the railroad speeded up the westward movement.

    f. The economy during this period could be described as "fluctuating."

III. APPLYING YOUR KNOWLEDGE

1. Based on your study of American history to this point, decide which of the descriptions below are *probably true* of the way in which a society changes. Give an example to support each choice.

    a. All segments of the society change at the same rate of speed.

    b. Change comes from within and without the society.

    c. Whether the change is beneficial or harmful depends on one's viewpoint.

    d. Some changes are short term, some long.

    e. A change in one part of the society is apt to affect other parts of the society.

Now, test your decisions by applying them to the world in which you live. Do your decisions hold?

2. Which of these opposing forces do you think were most crucial during the period 1820–1850? Defend your answer.

    a. Jackson v. his opponents.

    b. Tariffs v. internal improvements.

    c. Employers v. employees.

    d. Unity v. division.

    e. Poor v. rich.

    f. West v. east.

READINGS FOR PART THREE

Fiction

Baldwin, J. G. *The Flush Times of Alabama and Mississippi.* The frontier life of the old Southwest.

Stone, I. *The President's Lady.* A popular novel about Rachel Jackson.

Non-fiction

Brent, L. *Incidents in the Life of a Slave Girl.* The autobiography of a slave.

Douglass, F. *The Life and Times of Frederick Douglass.* An autobiography.

———. *Narrative of a Slave.* A most readable short version of Douglass' life under slavery and his attempt to escape.

Tocqueville, A. de. *Democracy in America.* One of the most penetrating and prophetic books ever written about the U.S., by a young Frenchman.

Ward, J. W. *Andrew Jackson: Symbol for an Age.* A fascinating study of Jackson's mass appeal in symbol, song, and myth.

AMERICAN DEVELOPMENT 1800—1850

REPUBLICANS

Jefferson

Madison

FEDERALISTS

Washington

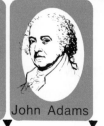
John Adams

POLITICAL DEVELOPMENTS
Presidents and Parties
(Appendix pp. 809–813)

| 1790 | 1793 | 1797 | 1801 | 1805 | 1809 | 1813 | 1817 |

TRANSPORTATION

TO TRAVEL 100 MILES (160 KILOMETERS) TOOK...

...25 hours by canalboat

...20 hours by covered wagon

...10 hours by steamboat

...5 hours by early railroad

SOCIAL DEVELOPMENTS

Change in voting requirements
Westward movement
Education
Slavery controversy
New farms from wilderness
Manifest destiny

ECONOMIC ACTIVITY

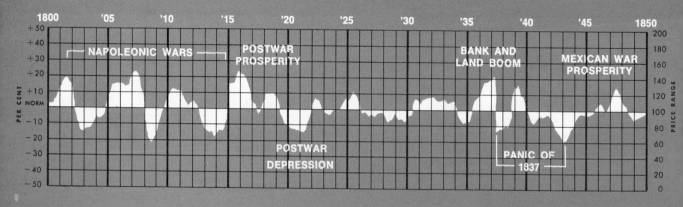

NAPOLEONIC WARS
POSTWAR PROSPERITY
POSTWAR DEPRESSION
BANK AND LAND BOOM
PANIC OF 1837
MEXICAN WAR PROSPERITY

(During Monroe's adminis-
tration the Federalists disappeared, and there was no
opposition party. See p. 224.)

DEMOCRATS

DEMOCRAT

REPUBLICAN

Monroe

**NATIONAL
REPUBLICAN**

John Quincy
Adams

Jackson

Van Buren

(At the close of Monroe's administration,
the Republicans split into the National
Republicans and Democratic Republicans, or Democrats. See pp. 256–257.)
(During Jackson's administration the National Republicans assumed the name of
Whigs.)

WHIG

William H.
Harrison   Tyler

Polk

| 1821 | 1825 | 1829 | 1833 | 1837 | 1841 | 1845 | 1849 |

Farmers Outnumber
Town Dwellers
(in millions)

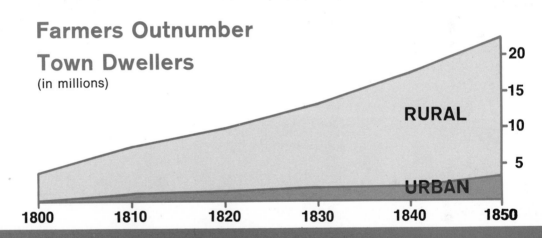

RURAL

URBAN

20
15
10
5

1800   1810   1820   1830   1840   1850

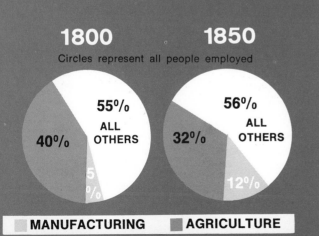

1800   **1850**

Circles represent all people employed

55%
ALL
OTHERS

40%

5%

56%
ALL
OTHERS

32%

12%

MANUFACTURING   **AGRICULTURE**

Growing Tide of Immigration*
Each symbol = 150,000 immigrants

1820–30   151,824

1831–40 599,125

1841–50 1,713,251

* No figures available before 1820.

Division
and
Reunion

Chapters in this Part

Union Forces in Battle at Cold Harbor, Virginia, 1864

AN AMERICAN TRAGEDY

During the American Civil War, hostilities were on a larger scale than the world had ever seen. The long, hard-fought contest—variously called the Great Rebellion, the War Between the States, the Brothers' War, and the Civil War—was a terrible tragedy. The losses were much higher relative to population than in any war the United States ever fought with a foreign foe. Hundreds of thousands of young men were killed, maimed, or allowed to rot in prison camps. Civilians suffered terribly. The war left a legacy of bitter feeling that lingered on well into the twentieth century.

Compromises and temporary truces for a time prevented the slavery issue from exploding. But in the end the flames of controversy between North and South were rekindled by the movement known as "manifest destiny," and in 1861 the country plunged into war.

On the eve of the Civil War, the parties ceased to serve the important function of damping down controversies before they endangered the Union. Both parties, Whigs and Democrats, broke apart. You can see the result in the map of the presidential election of 1860, on p. 341. Essentially, Southerners were demanding the right to take slaves into areas totally unsuited to slavery, and Republicans were insisting that slavery be forbidden in areas where climate and soil made its existence impossible.

Some historians say that the Civil War was brought on by a "blundering generation" of politicians too shortsighted or unskillful to arrange a compromise that would have saved the Union without bloodshed. Others suggest that the war was an "irrepressible conflict," or even a divine punishment for the terrible wrong of slavery. Or was it perhaps an inevitable consequence of rivalry between the industrial interests of the North and the planter interests of the South? Was it caused by northern invasion of southern rights, as the Confederate leaders claimed? Would it have been better to allow the seceding states to "depart in peace"?

We do not know how the tragedy could have been averted, but we can at least be thankful that there were elements that relieved the gloom: the songs, such as "Dixie" and "The Battle Hymn of the Republic"; the cheerful heroism of the defenders of Vicksburg; the magnanimity of Grant and the dignity of Lee in the surrender at Appomattox Court House; the greatness of Abraham Lincoln, who hated slavery and disunion, but who never hated his fellow Americans fighting for the "lost cause" of the Confederacy.

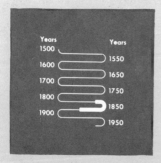

Chapter 12

Manifest Destiny

The cowards never started and the weak died on the road.
And all across the continent the endless campfires glowed.
We'd taken land and settled—but a traveler passed by—
And we're going West to-morrow—Lordy, never ask us why!
——STEPHEN VINCENT BENET

At the time the United States acquired Florida by the Transcontinental Treaty in 1819, Secretary of State John Quincy Adams remarked at a cabinet meeting that the world should be "familiarized with the idea of considering our proper dominion to be the continent of North America." This idea that the United States was bound to extend its boundaries to the Pacific Ocean, perhaps also northward to the Arctic Ocean and southward to the Isthmus of Panama, became known as "manifest destiny." It found its greatest expression in the decade of the 1840's, when the United States acquired territories even more vast than the Louisiana Purchase of 1803.

WESTWARD TO THE PACIFIC

Various elements went into the manifest destiny movement. One of them was the habitual ambition of American pioneers to move on to new land. This push westward was one of the great migrations of history. Historian James Truslow Adams described it as "a movement involving tens of millions of individuals, unthinking, collective, unmoral, akin, in all save its incredible swiftness, to the inevitable advance of a glacier." Yet, why should Americans move beyond the existing borders of the United States when most of their land was still thinly settled and most of the area between the Mississippi and the Rocky Mountains was still completely unoccupied?

The settlement of Texas was a natural westward expansion of cotton culture, which was prevented by climate from moving north. The trek to Oregon, however, was partly a result of the mistaken idea that the treeless plains from the 98th meridian to the Rockies (see map, p. 175) were unsuited to farming and could therefore be left to the Indian and the buffalo. It was, in fact, the policy of the federal government to set apart portions of this "Great American Desert" for Indian tribes expelled from their homes in the East. In 1825 the federal government declared that there was to be no further white settlement beyond a line drawn along the western boundaries of existing states and territories (see map p. 168). This was reinforced by an Indian Intercourse Act passed by Congress in 1834; it not only forbade settlement in Indian territories, but limited trade with Indians to those with special licenses. Thus if newcomers wanted available land, especially the forested and well-watered land they were used to, they had to cross the Rockies.

Manifest destiny was promoted by commercial as well as agrarian interests. Excited by the recent opening of China, eastern traders and shipowners saw the harbors of San Diego and San Francisco as necessary way stations on the route to the Far East. They also wanted the Oregon question settled in such a way that the United States would acquire Puget Sound (see map, pp. 320–321).

Patriotism as Stimulus to Expansion

A large component of manifest destiny was patriotism, flavored with the boastfulness of the frontiersman who said that he could "wade the brown Mississippi, jump the Ohio, step across the Nolachucky, ride a streak of lightning, slip without a scratch down a honey locust tree, whip my weight in wildcats, and strike a blow like a falling tree." The frontier attitude found its political reflection in "spread-eagle oratory," of which the following is a sample:

Land enough—land enough? Make way, I say, for the young American buffalo—he has not yet got land enough. . . . I tell you, we will give him Oregon for his summer shade, and the region of Texas as his winter pasture. Like all of his race he wants salt, too. Well, he shall have the use of two oceans— the mighty Pacific and the turbulent Atlantic shall be his. . . . He shall not stop his career until he slakes his throat in the frozen ocean.

Acting as a stimulus to American expansionism was the not unjustified fear that the British, who were also interested in acquiring good harbors, might seize California before the United States. But the strongest aspect of the patriotic impulse toward expansion was expressed by old Andrew Jackson, who argued that the United States had a mission to "extend the area of freedom." It was this pride in American institutions and the desire to spread them that were stressed by the New York editor who gave a name to the expansionist movement when he wrote:

Away, away with all those cobweb issues of rights of discovery, exploration, settlement, continuity, etc. Our claims are based on the right of our manifest destiny to overspread and to possess the whole continent which Providence has given us for the development of the great experiment in liberty and federative self-government entrusted to us.

A "Power Vacuum"

Since the expansion of the United States to the Pacific involved friction with the Indians, the threat of hostilities with Great Britain, and a war with Mexico, it had to be backed up by military power. Yet the United States had a weak navy and a small regular army that had to be supplemented in war by undisciplined militia. Fortunately for the United States, the vast region it set out to acquire was a "power vacuum": the inhabitants had little ability to defend themselves and no strong nation to protect them. The Plains Indians of the Missouri Valley and the Apaches of the Southwest were brave and skillful warriors, but they were divided into small bands and fought each other as readily as they did the whites. They did not know, until it was too late to act, that their entire way of life was in danger. No Pontiac or Tecumseh appeared to unite them in defense of their lands.

Although Great Britain's superior naval power would probably have enabled her to keep Oregon and take California, British political leaders had little desire to add to an empire that they thought to be already over-extended. Mexico, where a revolution occurred about once every three years, was unable to carry on war effectively. So there was little to prevent the advance of the United States to the Rio Grande and to the Pacific.

A VICTORY FOR PEACE

The first area where the advance of American settlement caused serious international friction was not in the West, as might be expected, but in the extreme Northeast. Ever since the Revolution, the northern and eastern boundaries of Maine had been uncertain, because of confusing language in the Treaty of Paris. As long as the region was unoccupied this was not a serious matter. In 1838, however, settlers from Maine, pushing into the fertile Aroostook Valley, met and clashed with lumbermen from New Brunswick. Their struggle, fought mostly with fists, is known as the Aroostook War. It nearly led to something more serious when Maine and New Brunswick called out their militias, and Congress authorized President Van Buren to call for 50,000 men in case a war with Great Britain should develop.

A general atmosphere of ill will made it seem likely that sooner or later some petty dispute would plunge the United States and Great Britain into war. Britain was considered the national enemy; orators and school textbooks kept alive the bitter memories of the Revolution and the War of 1812. On the other side of the Atlantic, American dislike was often returned with interest. The British upper class feared and scorned American democracy. British authors hurt our pride by writing books that jeered at every unpleasant feature of American life from tobacco-chewing to slavery. Many British investors were angry because they had been swindled by the frauds of American land speculators or when several states and terri-tories repudiated the debts they had incurred before the Panic of 1837. Sydney Smith, a British clergyman, wrote that a citizen from one of these states had "no more right to eat with honest men than a leper has to eat with clean men."

The Webster-Ashburton Treaty, 1842

In spite of friction and ill feeling, there were very good reasons why the United States and Great Britain should not fight, the most important being that each was the other's best customer. Great Britain was the largest foreign purchaser of American wheat, tobacco, and cotton, and the United States was Britain's biggest market for manufactured goods. Fortunately, both the British and American governments were aware of the advantages of peace. In 1842 a special British envoy, Lord Ashburton, arrived in Washington, D.C., by invitation of the United States, to attempt to settle outstanding disputes. Ashburton carried on his negotiations with Daniel Webster, then Secretary of State. Each diplomat was free of prejudice against the country of the other, Webster having traveled in England and Ashburton having married an American.

Eager to reach an agreement, the men carried on their discussions informally. They decided that it was impossible, on the basis of available evidence, to fix the correct boundary of Maine; they therefore divided the disputed territory as fairly as they could. The British got what they wanted most—enough of the northern section to make possible a direct land route from the St. Lawrence River to New Brunswick. The United States received what it wanted—the Aroostook Valley—along with other concessions on the northern boundaries of New Hampshire, Vermont, and New York. Webster and Ashburton failed to reach agreements on several other disputes, involving such matters as American ships illegally carrying slaves from Africa, the debts owed British investors, and the ownership of Oregon. Both men agreed, however, that the important thing was just to settle something. (See map, U.S. in 1850, pp. 320–321.) While the Webster-Ashburton Treaty did not remove all points of Anglo-American friction, it did clear the air and put an end to the danger of war.

THE OPENING OF OREGON

While Webster and Ashburton were settling the Maine boundary, the rivalry between Great Britain and the United States over Oregon grew acute. Ever since 1818, the two countries had agreed to disagree about possession of the region, and had carried on the curious arrangement known as "joint occupation" (see p. 235).

The interest of the United States in Oregon had started when in 1787 a Boston ship, the *Columbia,* made one of the greatest pioneer trading voyages in history. The ship left home with a supply of ginseng, the root of a common New England weed that happened to be highly prized by the Chinese as a medicine. Rounding the Horn, it sailed to the coast of Oregon to get sea otter furs, also in demand in China. After a voyage across the Pacific, the ginseng and otter furs were exchanged for Chinese tea and silk. These brought high prices when the vessel, having circumnavigated the globe, returned to the United States in 1790. The *Columbia,* which on a later voyage gave its name to Oregon's greatest river, inaugurated a regular trade. The profits were sometimes enormous: one trader got otter pelts worth $22,000 from the Indians in return for trinkets costing less than $2; another exchanged a rusty chisel for furs worth $8,000. Small wonder that in 1800, five years before the arrival of Lewis and Clark, no less than 15 New England ships cruised the coast of Oregon to get furs for the China trade.

Fur Companies and "Mountain Men"

Even more of a magnet drawing people to Oregon than the sea otter of the coast was the beaver of the inland waterways. Beaver pelts had been the chief export of French Canada before 1763, and of the British fur traders after that. By 1800, the eastern supply had been so much reduced that the discovery of beaver in the streams draining the Rockies was like a strike of gold. Fierce competition developed between three great fur companies: the British Hudson's Bay Company, the American Fur Company, headed by John Jacob Astor of New York, and the Missouri Company, owned by persons in St. Louis. The Hudson's Bay Company dominated the Oregon region itself, while the other two operated mostly at the headwaters of the streams running out of the Rockies into the Missouri River.

The struggle between the fur companies was bitter to the verge of actual warfare. They played politics in the rivalries among the Indian tribes, bribed away each other's agents, and sometimes stole each other's furs. As accessible regions were trapped out, the "mountain men," who carried on the dangerous business of trapping and trading in Indian country, penetrated farther and farther into the Rocky Mountain wilderness. It took the utmost in bravery, skill, and self-reliance to survive as a mountain man. As Bernard DeVoto wrote in *The Year of Decision, 1846:*

Woodcraft, forest craft, and river craft were his skill. To read the weather, the streams, the woods; to know the ways of animals and birds; to find food and shelter; to find the Indians when they were his customers or to battle them from stump to stump when they were on the warpath and to know which caprice was on them; to take comfort in flood or blizzard; to move safely through the wilderness, to make the wilderness his bed, his table and his tool— this was his vocation.

Narcissa Whitman, Pioneer

Many are the ornaments and statues "in front of the courthouse" throughout America. Most commemorate war. But some of them show long-skirted women, with sunbonnets pushed back, children clinging to their hands. This is the "pioneer woman" or the "pioneer mother," the carrier of civilization and domesticator of the wilderness (see History as Fable, p. 222).

One such pioneer was Narcissa Whitman. She set out for Oregon country with her husband, Marcus, in 1836. The Whitmans had a higher motive than the restlessness and land hunger that sent so many Americans west—they were missionaries, intent on bringing Christianity to the Indians. Unlike many other women, whose farm life gave them endurance for the long, hard journey, Narcissa had been reared in an upper-class Boston home. She went courageously, nonetheless. The Whitmans traveled with a band of mountain men to Fort Vancouver, spent the winter there, and in the spring of 1837 built a log home near present-day Walla Walla among the Cayuse Indians.

Here their daughter was born. Alice Clarissa Whitman was the first white child born in Oregon, and this established a bond of friendliness with the Cayuse. The Whitmans' days were busy, filled with teaching. Seeking to bring the Indians not only religion, but a whole new civilization, they taught their charges to hoe, to handle chickens, and to raise pigs and cows.

They were interrupted by tragedy. First, Alice was drowned in the river. Then, in 1847, an epidemic of measles broke out. Whitman, who had had medical training, treated whites and Indians alike. The whites, who followed his instructions, recovered; the Indians, who did not, died. The Cayuse, thinking he had planned this deliberately, struck back and murdered Marcus, Narcissa, and twelve others, a massacre long remembered.

But their enthusiasm for Oregon had had its effect, for their letters home had already started the white settlement of that country.

The heyday of the mountain men lasted only about ten years, and they did not number more than a few hundred at any one time, but they played an important part in opening overland routes to Oregon and California. They discovered the best passes through the mountains and places where rivers could be forded. They served as guides to parties of settlers crossing the mountains by wagon train. Their whiskey, as well as white people's diseases they carried with them, corrupted and weakened the Indian tribes so that they became less formidable enemies of the whites who crossed their hunting lands.

On to Oregon

Until shortly before 1840 the joint occupation of Oregon was almost entirely a British affair, with the Hudson's Bay Company acting as the government of the region. In the mid-1830's, however, American missionaries arrived to Christianize the Indians. They also began to farm and sent back glowing reports of the fertility of the country. The most famous and influential of these people were the Whitmans, the accounts of whose adventures were widely read. On a journey to Oregon in 1836, Whitman and another missionary were accompanied by their wives—the first white women to cross the continent. If women could brave the perils of such a trip, the Oregon country could be settled. In 1838 a party of American pioneers arrived there by ship; most newcomers, however, came by covered wagon over the famous Oregon Trail (see map, pp. 320–321). By 1842 there were perhaps 500 Americans in Oregon, and in the next year a single party of immigrants numbered 900.

The long, slow journey from the Missouri River to Oregon demanded courage and endurance. The heavy Conestoga wagons were usually drawn by teams of six or eight oxen which, when the going was good, moved at a pace of about two miles an hour. The necessity of fording rivers involved the chance of tipping over the wagons or drowning the oxen. Through much of the journey there was ever-present danger from Indians. To meet such difficulties, parties of immigrants had to be thoroughly organized. The members of a wagon train often chose their officers by election. One man would have charge of the cattle, another of posting sentries, another of leading the advance party which chose the way. Major decisions were reached by vote of the group as a whole.

By 1843 so many Americans had arrived in Oregon that they set up a government of their own. Following a procedure going back to the Mayflower Compact, they drew up a constitution for themselves. Its preamble, which reveals its authors' familiarity with the United States Constitution, went as follows:

We the people of Oregon territory, for the purpose of mutual protection and to secure peace and prosperity among ourselves, agree to adopt the following laws and regulations until such time as the United States of America extend their jurisdiction over us.

The last phrase shows that the Oregon settlers were determined that the United States and not Britain should rule them. A decision as to which country was to control the region could not be put off much longer.

The Mormon Migration, 1847–1849

Experience gained by the Oregon settlers was put to good use by the Mormons, who in the years 1847–1849 carried out an amazingly successful migration to the shores of Salt Lake. The Mormons, a religious group who had suffered persecution in the United States, sought a haven where they could worship as they pleased. Their leader, Brigham Young, had a genius for organization, and the migration was carried out in well-planned stages. First, scouts sought out the best routes and found sites for sawmills, flour mills, and towns. Then came small parties who built houses and fortresses and planted crops which ripened in time for the main body of immigrants. Many of the latter had no draft animals, but carried their few possessions in handcarts, singing, as they trudged the long miles, a marching song with the chorus:

Some must push and some must pull
As we go marching up the hill,
So merrily on our way we go
Until we reach the Valley, O!

In spite of hardship and disease, the Mormons soon established several flourishing settlements. They were far ahead of their time in learning the proper control of the water supply in the semi-arid regions of the far West. Around Salt Lake City, planned on a magnificent scale, irrigation transformed a desert into a garden spot.

A Mountain Man, equipped with muzzle-loading rifle, surveys his western domain. Of this hardy breed of fur-trappers an English visitor wrote in 1847: "Of laws, human or divine, they neither know nor care to know." But, "all this vast country, but for the daring enterprise of these men, would be even now a *terra incognita* to geographers . . ."

THE ANNEXATION OF TEXAS

By 1844 the question as to whether the United States would annex Texas became even more pressing than the problem of Oregon. Texas was a vast, ill-defined area extending southwest from Louisiana to the Rio Grande and west to the foothills of the Rockies. It was a natural cotton-growing region, much of it being part of the fertile coastal plain that extends across Alabama, Mississippi, and Louisiana. It had been on the northern fringe of the Spanish Empire, but Spain's hold had been limited to a few hundred settlers and a dozen Indian missions.

Texan Independence

Mexico inherited Texas after breaking away from Spain in 1821. At first the government of Mexico welcomed settlers from the United States. They were given land, provided they were of "honest, industrious" character and would join the Roman Catholic Church. By 1830 the population had mounted to 20,000. In that year, Mexico passed a law forbidding further immigration. But it was now too late to stop the flood of American settlers, and there was constant friction between the Texans and the Mexican government. This reached a climax in 1835 when the Mexican dictator General Antonio Santa Anna led an army across the Rio Grande to strengthen his rule over Texas. In February 1836, with over 2,000 troops, Santa Ana besieged 188 Texans in the Alamo, a mission station at San Antonio. After a heroic fortnight of resistance, the defenders of the Alamo were wiped out.

Meanwhile the Texans found an able general in Sam Houston, who had served under Jackson in Tennessee. In April 1836, Houston surprised

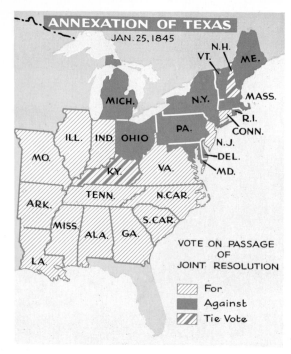

ANNEXATION OF TEXAS
JAN. 25, 1845

VOTE ON PASSAGE
OF
JOINT RESOLUTION

For
Against
Tie Vote

Many people opposed adventures in the West. The vote in Congress on the joint resolution to permit the annexation of Texas shows a clear sectional division on manifest destiny, which was also an issue of the election of 1844.

and defeated Santa Anna's army, capturing the dictator himself. After the battle, the Mexican leader agreed to accept the independence of Texas, with the Rio Grande as the boundary line. But as soon as he was free, Santa Anna refused to be bound by terms dictated at the point of the sword. Until 1845 Mexico considered Texas a rebellious province, but was unable to reduce it to submission.

The Texans had scarcely gained their independence when, in 1836, they voted overwhelmingly to join the United States. Although there was strong southern opinion in favor of annexing Texas because of its rich cotton lands into which slavery could expand, President Jackson opposed the move. He did not want to run the risk of passing on to his successor, Van Buren, a war with Mexico. Jackson went no further than to recognize Texan independence from

Mexico. Since Van Buren favored annexation even less than Jackson, the whole question was deferred.

The question was brought up again in 1843 by President John Tyler, who feared that the Republic of Texas would form too close ties with Great Britain. The British were interested in Texas as a new source of cotton and as a market for their manufactured goods. British antislavery societies hoped that the new country might be persuaded to free its slaves. The threat of Texas as a competing source of cotton and a possible haven for runaway slaves greatly alarmed Southerners, among them Calhoun, who became Secretary of State in 1844. Under his management, an annexation treaty was presented to the Senate. Calhoun was rebuffed when the Senate refused to ratify the treaty by a vote of 35 to 16. This overwhelming rejection sprang from northern opposition to adding more slave territory to the Union. Many Northerners feared that the admission of Texas was part of a great southern plot to increase the power of the slave states. In 1843 John Quincy Adams, who served eighteen years in Congress after retiring from the presidency, was one of the signers of an "Address to the People of the Free States" that said that if Texas were annexed, the free states would be justified in leaving the Union.

The Election of 1844

As the presidential election of 1844 approached, it was expected that the rival candidates would be ex-President Van Buren for the Democrats and Henry Clay for the Whigs. Texas annexation, with its threat of disunion over slavery, alarmed both men so much that they agreed to oppose it, in letters to the press published on the same day. But then the unexpected happened. While Clay was duly chosen Whig candidate for the presidency, Van Buren failed to receive the Democratic nomination. Instead, a coalition of Westerners who wanted Oregon and Southerners who wanted Texas nominated the first "dark horse" in the history of the presidency, James K. Polk of Tennessee.

The Democrats dodged the slavery aspects of the Texas problem by hitching together the demands for Texas and Oregon. Their platform called for "the reoccupation of Oregon and the reannexation of Texas." Further to minimize slavery, the Democrats put their main emphasis on taking all of Oregon, where slavery would certainly never be established, dramatizing this by the famous slogan, "Fifty-four forty or fight!" (The parallel 54°40′ was the southern boundary of Alaska.) Thus manifest destiny became the principal issue of the campaign.

To counter this unexpected challenge, the Whigs could offer only Henry Clay's great personal popularity and the slogan, "Who is James K. Polk?" calling attention to the obscurity of the Democratic candidate. Clay backed down from his earlier opposition to admitting Texas by issuing a cautious statement that he would be glad to see the region annexed, if the American people so desired and if war with Mexico could be avoided. This hedging did not save the Whig leader. Polk won the election by a slim margin. The abolitionist Liberty party candidate, James M. Birney, polled 62,000 votes and held the balance of power in Indiana, Ohio, and New York. If the Liberty party votes had been cast for Clay in New York, he would have carried the state and been elected President.

Texas Annexed, 1845

Even though the expansionist program of the Democrats had not gained support from the majority of the voters, President Tyler asserted that Polk's victory in the election of 1844 was a demand for the admission of Texas to the Union. Tyler's point of view was supported by some powerful newspaper editors and a well-organized lobby. In February 1845, both houses

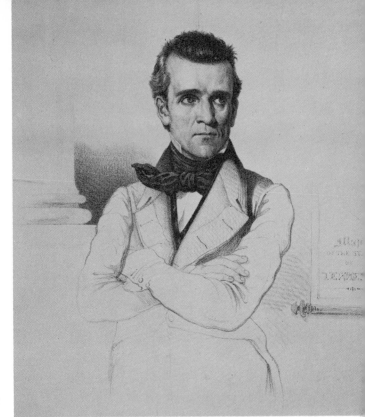

"Young Hickory," James K. Polk of Tennessee, was the first "dark horse" candidate for the presidency. He was also a most successful President, in that he accomplished the four great objectives that he intended when he entered the White House.

of Congress, by very narrow majorities, passed a resolution asking Texas to join the Union. On July 4, the Republic of Texas voted to give up its independence and become one of the United States. The Mexico-Texas boundary was still undetermined, and the Mexican government threatened war. (See U.S. in 1850, pp. 320–321.)

THE MEXICAN WAR

In 1949 many people were surprised when a poll of 55 prominent American historians listed Polk as one of the "near-great" Presidents of the United States. Although he was uncommunicative, narrow-minded, and so intensely

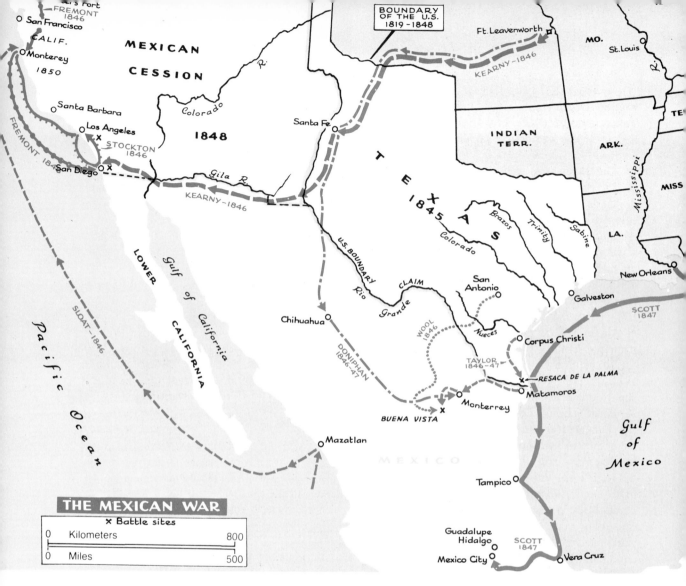

THE MEXICAN WAR

× Battle sites

| 0 | Kilometers | 800 |
| 0 | Miles | 500 |

The campaigns of the Mexican War were remarkable for the vast distances covered by United States forces and for the relatively small number of troops engaged. The Mexican armies were badly led and ill supplied, but Mexico did not surrender until forces under General Winfield Scott moved in from Vera Cruz and occupied Mexico City.

partisan that it was difficult for him to admit that a Whig could be a gentleman, few Presidents have been more successful than he. He had a strong will; he knew what he wanted; and he was a hard worker. He was a friend and disciple of his fellow Tennessean Andrew Jackson, and his followers liked to call him "Young Hickory." Polk shared both Jackson's political outlook and his belief in a strong presidency. On his first day in office he told a member of his cabinet that he had four great purposes: to lower the tariff, to re-establish the Independent Treasury System abolished by the Whigs in 1842, to annex California, and to settle the Oregon question. In 1846, under the President's urging, Congress duly voted in the Independent Treasury System and passed the Walker Tariff, which reduced duties without entirely abandoning protection. The acquisition of California and an Oregon settlement were much more difficult to achieve, but Polk was successful in these purposes too.

The Question of California

New Englanders had traded with California for fifty years and had described the region as "the richest, most beautiful, the healthiest country in the world." In the 1840's, it became apparent that the ultimate fate of the region might soon be decided. The native population had staged four rebellions against the Mexican government, which was too disorganized to govern the region effectively. As we have seen, there was fear that Great Britain, or possibly France, might annex California because of the great harbor of San Francisco, large enough to accommodate all the navies of the world.

Polk hoped to purchase California from Mexico. Meanwhile, he took measures to promote annexation. In his annual message to Congress in December 1845, he warned off Great Britain and France by repeating the "no colonization" principle of the Monroe Doctrine. He also urged the United States consul in Monterey to "arouse in the bosoms of the Californians that love of liberty so natural to the American continent"—in other words, stir up a revolution. Late in 1845 he sent John Slidell of Louisiana as envoy to Mexico to discuss the Texas question and to offer almost any amount of money for California. Slidell's mission was completely fruitless. So great was Mexican anger at the loss of Texas that any official who dared to talk with the American diplomat could have lost his position and possibly his life as well. Without having been allowed to present his case, Slidell returned to Washington.

Outbreak of War

The immediate occasion for war between Mexico and the United States was the southern boundary of Texas, where the land between the Nueces River and the Rio Grande was in dispute. Both sides sent troops to the region, but for a time they both kept out of the area. On hearing of the failure of Slidell's mission to Mexico City, Polk ordered General Zachary Taylor, commanding an American force guarding the border, to move south to the Rio Grande. Late in April 1846, Mexican soldiers crossed the river and attacked a small detachment of United States cavalry. When the news of this attack on Taylor's force reached Washington, the President asked Congress to declare war. Pointing out that his effort to negotiate peaceably with Mexico had failed, Polk argued that war had been begun "by the act of Mexico herself." On May 13, 1846, Congress declared war by overwhelming majorities in both houses.

In spite of the vote in Congress, the Mexican War was widely and bitterly attacked as a war of aggression against a weaker neighbor. It was, wrote the New England author James Russell Lowell, simply a southern scheme to steal "bigger pens to cram in slaves." Whig members of Congress, including Abraham Lincoln, then a representative from Illinois, challenged Polk's statement that he had tried to avoid war, asking why he had insisted on sending Taylor to the Rio Grande. A northern senator said that if he were a Mexican he would tell the United States: "Have you not room in your country to bury your dead men? If you come into mine, we will greet you with bloody hands and welcome you to hospitable graves."

Although attacking Polk for starting the war, the Whigs nevertheless supported it by voting supplies and men. This was not as illogical as it may seem, because it is not certain that war could have been prevented. Several months before Polk's message to Congress, the

General Winfield Scott rides a bay horse at a review of U.S. troops in Mexico City. In the difficult campaign to reach the city, Scott was greatly aided by subordinate officers trained at West Point. Among these were Lieutenant Ulysses S. Grant and Captain Robert E. Lee, both of whom were mentioned in dispatches. Many of the officers later fought in the Civil War.

Mexican government had declared itself in favor of "a necessary and glorious war." Aware of the dismal failure of American efforts to invade Canada in the War of 1812, the Mexicans did not shrink from war, but instead expected victory.

The military campaigns of the Mexican War were remarkable both for the immense distances traversed and the small size of the forces engaged. One unit, the First Missouri Regiment under Colonel A. W. Doniphan, marched and fought its way 3,500 miles in a wide crescent starting at Ft. Leavenworth on the Missouri River and eventually reaching the Gulf of Mexico by way of Santa Fe and northern Mexico. General Stephen Kearny led troops 2,500 miles from the Missouri to the Pacific. Yet no Amer-

ican commander had many more than 10,000 men under his command at any one time. Congress took no step to enlarge or improve the army and navy until after war had been declared, and the United States paid a price for unpreparedness. The volunteer regiments composing most of the American army were undisciplined and their officers often incompetent, owing their positions to political pull. But the United States Military Academy at West Point, founded in 1802 and reorganized in 1817, furnished well-trained and resourceful young officers who proved themselves invaluable in the crucial campaigns.

Second Lieutenant George Meade, a young West Pointer who later won fame in the Civil War as the victor at Gettysburg, remarked of the Mexican War, "Well may we be grateful that we are at war with Mexico! Were it any other power, our gross follies would be punished severely." Disorganized as was the war effort of the United States, it was nevertheless more efficient than that of the foe. One group after another seized power in Mexico, so that sometimes it was difficult to know who composed the government; once three different men claimed to be president! Alfonso Torro, a Mexican historian, wrote of his country's hapless condition:

Although Mexico had an enormous war budget, she really lacked an army; for hardly worthy of the name was the assemblage of drafted men, badly armed, and . . . without confidence in their leaders.

The soldiers, who were almost never paid but were maltreated and exploited by their chiefs, deserted whenever they could and even rebelled with arms in their hands when they were ordered to march. . . .

There were places where the cavalry remained dismounted because they had nothing with which to buy fodder and where the troops were almost destitute, without arms or shelter. In San Juan de Ulúa, with the American squadron already in sight, Colonel Cano was obliged to sell five cannon to a foreign vessel in order to feed the garrison.

With such a weak and demoralized enemy, it is not surprising that during the opening year of hostilities the United States easily gained control of all of California, New Mexico, and Texas. California was won as the result of a local revolt, assisted by a handful of American troops and a small fleet. Santa Fe, the principal city of New Mexico, fell to Stephen Kearny's force with hardly a shot fired in its defense. On the Texas border General Zachary Taylor penetrated nearly 300 miles into Mexico and became a national hero by winning the battle of Buena Vista against apparently overwhelming odds.

Mexico still refused to make peace, so in the spring of 1847 an expedition under General Winfield Scott was sent against Mexico City. With a force of only 10,000 men, Scott landed at Vera Cruz, and after six months of difficult campaigning occupied the capital in September 1847.

Treaty of Guadalupe Hidalgo, 1848

After the capture of Mexico City, it was some months before a Mexican government could be found to sign the peace. In the meantime ardent advocates of manifest destiny, including two members of Polk's cabinet, were urging that the United States annex all of Mexico. Before this total-annexation movement proceeded very far, a peace treaty was signed at Guadalupe Hidalgo, outside of Mexico City, in February 1848. By the treaty, the United States gained full title to Texas with the Rio Grande as a boundary, California, and all of what was then called New Mexico except the so-called Gadsden Purchase, which was acquired in 1853 (see map, pp. 320–321). The United States paid $15,000,000 outright for New Mexico and California, and agreed to pay debts of the Mexican government amounting to $3,250,000.

Although the Mexican War might have been prevented had Polk shown more patience, the map of the United States might be little different today had it not occurred. The region we acquired had never been effectively governed by Mexico, and by 1850 at least 300,000 Americans had settled there. It is probable that these people would sooner or later have insisted on joining the United States, as did Texas, and that Mexico would have been unable to prevent it.

QUESTION • If the United States had not gone to war with Mexico in 1846, do you think that California would ever have become part of the United States?

The Westward Movement

Santa Barbara Museum

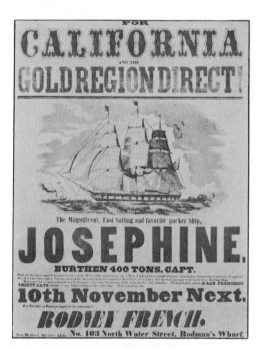

One reason that people braved the difficult voyage around Cape Horn to reach California was that those coming overland had to face those formidable warriors, the Plains Indians. The few troops at scattered posts such as Fort Laramie (right) offered no guarantee that "forty-niners" would not get scalped.

One of the principal uses of fast-sailing clipper ships was to get people to the California gold fields. But, as this remarkable photograph of abandoned ships moored in San Francisco harbor in 1850 shows, so anxious were people from all over the world to join the great gold rush that any sort of ship would do.

San Francisco Maritime Museum

Walters Art Gallery

THE UNION IN DANGER

The Mexican War and the Treaty of Guadalupe Hidalgo brought into the open the slavery issue that politicians had been trying to avoid ever since the bitter debates over the admission of Missouri to the Union. Once the United States acquired New Mexico and California, some decision had to be made regarding the status of the Negroes in the areas. Even before the war ended, the growth of antislavery sentiment in the North was revealed when the House of Representatives passed the Wilmot Proviso, an amendment to an army appropriation bill which said that all territory acquired from Mexico should be closed to slavery. This aroused an outcry from the South, and southern senators attempted to prevent the organization of Oregon as a territory because, as the people of Oregon desired, slavery was to be forbidden there. Southerners now argued that Congress had no constitutional power to forbid slavery in the territories, on the ground that to deny owners of Negroes the right to take their human property into land that belonged to the nation as a whole was to deny them their equal rights as citizens. There seemed to be no way of reconciling these two points of view. When the Polk administration left office in 1849, no steps had been taken to provide for civil government in the new territories.

The Election of 1848

In the presidential election of 1848, both sides took elaborate precautions to soft-pedal discussion of slavery. The Democrats, although controlled by their southern wing, nominated a northern senator, Lewis Cass of Michigan. Cass supported a compromise solution for the territories known as "popular sovereignty," whereby the people of the territories would decide for themselves whether or not they wanted slavery. The Whigs, whose principal strength lay in the North and the border states of Ken-

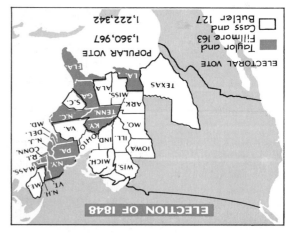

ELECTION OF 1848

ELECTORAL VOTE

- Taylor and Fillmore 163
- Cass and Butler 127

POPULAR VOTE

Taylor and Fillmore 1,360,967
Cass and Butler 1,222,342

In 1848 the slavery issue was played down, as the country tried to ease the strains of sectionalism. The Democrats, strong in the South, nominated Lewis Cass of Michigan; the Whigs, strong in the North, nominated Zachary Taylor, a Louisiana military hero and owner of 300 slaves.

Division of Oregon, 1846

The Mexican War was indirectly responsible for settlement of the Oregon boundary. It was one thing to shout, "Fifty-four forty or fight" in an election campaign, and another to take on war with the greatest sea power in the world at the same time we were fighting Mexico. Fortunately a fair compromise was possible. While by 1846 the number of American settlers in Oregon had risen to 10,000, most of them were in the fertile Willamette Valley south of the Columbia River. Neither by discovery nor by occupation had the United States a valid claim to the entire region. The British government in turn was willing to relinquish the southern half of Oregon because the Hudson's Bay Company had trapped out the beaver there and had moved its principal base from the Columbia River to Vancouver Island. In 1846, therefore, the United States and Great Britain agreed to divide Oregon along the 49th parallel (see map, pp. 320–321).

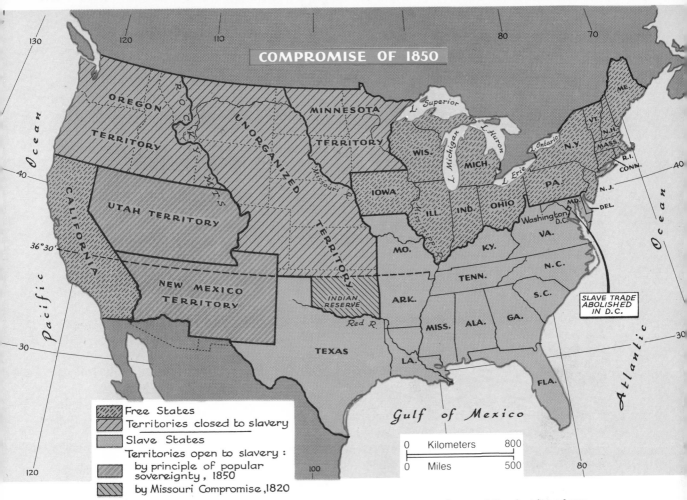

COMPROMISE OF 1850

130 | 120 | 110 | 80 | 70

OREGON TERRITORY

MINNESOTA TERRITORY

UNORGANIZED TERRITORY

CALIFORNIA

UTAH TERRITORY

36°30'

NEW MEXICO TERRITORY

WIS.

IOWA

ILL.

IND.

OHIO

MO.

KY.

ARK.

INDIAN RESERVE

Red R.

TEXAS

MISS.

ALA.

GA.

LA.

FLA.

MICH.

N.Y.

PA.

VA.

N.C.

S.C.

TENN.

ME.

VT.

N.H.

MASS.

R.I.

CONN.

N.J.

DEL.

MD.

Washington D.C.

SLAVE TRADE ABOLISHED IN D.C.

Gulf of Mexico

Pacific Ocean

Atlantic Ocean

L. Superior

L. Michigan

L. Huron

L. Erie

L. Ontario

Mississippi R.

Missouri R.

ROCKY MTS.

Legend:
- Free States
- Territories closed to slavery
- Slave States
- Territories open to slavery:
  - by principle of popular sovereignty, 1850
  - by Missouri Compromise, 1820

0 Kilometers 800
0 Miles 500

The Compromise of 1850 was only a temporary solution. Its Fugitive Slave Law and the doctrine of popular sovereignty excited conflicts — initially in Kansas — that exploded into the Civil War eleven years later.

tucky and Maryland, nominated the hero of Buena Vista, Zachary Taylor, who came from Louisiana and owned 300 slaves. This was a return to their tactics of the "hard cider" election of 1840: nominate a military hero and avoid issues. The ingenious effort to keep slavery out of the campaign failed when a group of northern Democrats united with the former Liberty party to form the Free Soil party, with former President Van Buren as its nominee. The Free Soilers gained no electoral votes, but they polled a heavier popular vote than the Democrats in New York, Vermont, and Massachusetts. They drew enough Democratic votes from Cass in New York, again as in 1844 the pivotal state, so that Taylor was elected President by an electoral vote of 163 to 127.

Discovery of Gold in California

The question of slavery in the new territories became acute after gold was discovered in California in 1848. From all over the world the "Forty-niners" crowded their way to the diggings. Ray Allen Billington described them:

In those ramshackle mining camps—appropriately labeled Poker Flat, Hangtown, Whisky Bar, Placerville, Hell's Delight, Git-up-and-git, Skunk Gulch, Dry Diggings, Red Dog, Grub Gulch, and the like—where rooms rented for $1,000 a month and eggs cost $10 a dozen, were assembled the most colorful desperadoes ever gathered in one spot. Mingling together were Missouri farmers, Yankee sailors, Georgia crackers, English shop-keepers, French peasants, Australian sheepherders, Mexican peons, "heathen Chinee," and a liberal sprinkling of "assassins manufactured in Hell."

Most of the population of California, however, were law-abiding and wanted to set up a regu-lar government; in December 1849, the Califor-nians applied for admission as a free state.

California's application for statehood touched off one of the longest and bitterest debates in the history of Congress. Some con-gressmen attended sessions armed with pistols and bowie knives. The feeling in the national legislature was a reflection of public opinion. The danger of disunion had never seemed so great. Already two of the four largest Protestant churches had split apart over the slavery issue. Every northern legislature except one had passed resolutions supporting the Wilmot Pro-viso that slavery should be excluded from the territories acquired from Mexico. Southerners threatened secession if such action were taken.

The Compromise of 1850

To deal with this alarming situation, Henry Clay, who had been in retirement since his defeat in the presidential election of 1844, re-turned to the Senate. Clay, an artist at dis-covering just where people would stand firm and where they would give in, was at first the domi-nant figure in Congress as he tried to arrange his last great intersectional compromise. This was embodied in a series of measures nicely calculated to balance northern and southern demands. The principal provisions favoring the North were that California be admitted as a free state and that the slave trade, but not slavery, be forbidden in the District of Colum-bia. The South in turn gained a stronger Fugi-tive Slave Law, designed to suppress the

Underground Railroad. The New Mexico Ces-sion was divided into two territories, Utah and New Mexico, the question of slavery to be decided by popular sovereignty when the ter-ritories were organized with territorial legisla-tures, the formula Cass proposed in the 1848 campaign. The original size of the Republic of Texas was decreased by more than 100,000 square miles, for which Texas was paid by the federal government (see map, p. 320).

Clay's measures, lumped together in an "omnibus bill," at first failed to receive sufficient support to pass, and President Taylor was known to be cool to them. Taylor died, however, in the summer of 1850 and was succeeded by Millard Fillmore, who favored the compromise. Then, while Clay was on a vacation, legislative management of the compromise proposals passed to young Senator Stephen A. Douglas of Illinois. By a skillful series of parliamentary maneuvers, Douglas put through the compro-mise as six separate bills, and they were duly signed by Fillmore. Shortly afterward Daniel Webster, who had played an impor-tant part in get-ting the Compro-mise of 1850 accepted, wrote a friend, "I can now sleep of nights. We have gone through the most important crisis that has occurred since the founding of the government, and whatever party may prevail, hereafter the Union stands firm."

QUESTION • If the slave states had seceded in 1850, would the Union have been permanently broken?

By bringing the slavery issue into the open, manifest destiny had almost broken the nation apart, but the Compromise of 1850 averted im-mediate disaster. Unhappily, it turned out to be a truce rather than a permanent peace. Eleven years later the South seceded and the Civil War broke out. By then, however, the North was more populous than in 1850, more powerful economically, and more ready to fight to save the Union.

Activities: Chapter 12

For Mastery and Review

1. Explain the rapid expansion of the boundaries of the United States between 1840 and 1850.

2. What were causes of friction between the United States and Great Britain? What made compromise desirable to both sides? What agreements were made in the Webster-Ashburton Treaty, and what matters were left unsettled?

3. What interests competed for the fur trade in the West? Who were the mountain men? What was their importance?

4. What was important about Narcissa Whitman? Describe travel on the Oregon Trail. How was the Oregon question finally settled?

5. How and why did Texas gain its independence from Mexico? Why was the treaty of annexation defeated in the Senate in 1844?

6. What were the four major objectives of the Polk administration? How was each accomplished?

7. What were the causes of the Mexican War? Why was it opposed within the United States? Explain the defeat of Mexico. What were the terms of the Treaty of Guadalupe Hidalgo?

8. Describe the gold rush of 1849 and the varied population it brought to California.

9. Why did the Mexican War reopen the controversy over slavery? Why did matters reach such a crisis in 1850? What were the terms of the Compromise of 1850, and why were they important?

Unrolling the Map

1. On a map of the western part of the United States, show the march of manifest destiny. Draw the boundaries of the United States in 1844; indicate the Rocky Mountains, the "Great American Desert," San Francisco Bay, and Puget Sound. Show the Oregon country under joint occupation and trace the boundary agreed on in 1846. Trace the Oregon, Mormon, and California trails. Locate Salt Lake City. Draw the boundaries of Texas, indicating both the Nueces River and the Rio Grande. Show the territory acquired from Mexico.

2. Study the maps showing the vote on the annexation of Texas (p. 308) and the election of 1848 (p. 316). How do you account for the sectional vote in the one and the lack of sectionalism in the other?

Who, What, and Why Important?

manifest destiny
Webster-Ashburton
  Treaty
the Whitmans
Oregon Territory
Mormons
Republic of Texas
election of 1844
Liberty party

James K. Polk
"54° 40' or fight!"
Mexican War
election of 1848
Free Soil party
forty-niners
Compromise of 1850
Stephen A. Douglas
Millard Fillmore

To Pursue the Matter

1. For the human aspects of manifest destiny—life on the Oregon Trail, the Mormons' trekking to Utah, the mountain men, the forty-niners—see Arnof, A Sense of the Past, pp. 196–210.

2. Why did the Mormons make the long trek to Utah, and why were they successful when they got there? See Billington, Westward Expansion, Chapter 26, and/or Clark, Frontier America, Chapter 22.

3. Why did Zachary Taylor become a hero? See Singletary, The Mexican War.

4. For what reasons did people seriously predict that the Union was about to break apart in 1850? See Nevins, Ordeal of the Union, vol. I, Chapter 7.

5. Why was it difficult to stop the Mexican War even after both sides were tired of fighting? See Bailey, A Diplomatic History of the American People, pp. 261–265.

6. For episodes in the fascinating story of the Texas Republic, see Tinkle, The Alamo; "The Storming of the Alamo," American Heritage, February 1961; Horgan, The Great River, vol. II.

7. Life on the Oregon Trail is described with close attention to detail in Guthrie's novel, The Way West.

8. Consider these assertions:

a) Polk was justified in the efforts he made to acquire California.

b) " 'Manifest destiny' is a fancy term meaning 'theft.' "

c) An unjust fugitive slave law was too high a price to pay for intersectional compromise in 1850.

Puget Sound

Ocean

Astoria

Portland

Columbia *R.*

Willamette *R.*

OREGON 1846

OREGON TERRITORY 1848

Vancouver

BRITISH TREATY LINE 1846

JOINT OCCUPATION U.S.-GT.BRITAIN 1818-1846

NATURAL BOUNDARY OF LOUISIANA

CEDED BY U.S., 1818

CEDED BY GT. BRITAIN, 1818

BRITISH TREATY LINE, 1818

Blackfeet *R.*

Missouri *R.*

Yellowstone *R.*

Sioux

Snake *R.*

South Pass

SPANISH TREATY LINE 1819

40

Sacramento *R.*

Sutter's Fort

San Francisco

Monterey

CALIFORNIA TRAIL

CALIFORNIA 1850

Salt Lake City

PONY EXPRESS

MORMON TRAIL

Ft. Bridger

UTAH TERRITORY 1850

TRAIL

Ft. Laramie

PONY EXPRESS

MORMON TRAIL

Platte *R.*

LOUISIANA PURCHASE

PIKES PEAK

MEXICAN CESSION

1848

Colorado *R.*

Los Angeles

San Diego

Gila *R.*

NEW MEXICO TERRITORY 1850

GADSDEN PURCHASE 1853

Santa Fe

SANTA FÉ TRAIL

TEXAS 1850

SPANISH TREATY LINE 1819

CEDED BY

NATURAL BOUNDARY OF

TEXAS 1845

30

Pacific

Rio Grande

Austin

San Antonio

Nueces *R.*

100

Lake of
the Woods

WEBSTER – ASHBURTON TREATY LINE, 1842

Quebec

MAINE
1820

Lake Superior

Montreal

St. Lawrence R.

Portland

MICHIGAN
1837

Lake Huron

VT.
1791

N.H.
1788

NNESOTA
ERRITORY
1849

WISCONSIN
1848

L. Ontario

NEW
YORK
1788

MASS.
1788

Boston

Rochester

Albany

Hartford

Providence

OUTE OF
EWIS & CLARK
1804–1806

Lake Michigan

Buffalo

New Haven

R.I.
1790

CONN.
1788

40

IOWA
1846

Detroit

Lake Erie

PENNSYLVANIA
1787

Trenton

New York

N.J.
1787

Chicago

Cleveland

Pittsburgh

Philadelphia

Council
Bluffs

ILLINOIS
1818

INDIANA
1816

OHIO
1803

Wheeling

Baltimore

DEL.
1787

Ft. Leavenworth

Washington

MD.
1788

St. Joseph

Cincinnati

Ohio R.

Westport

Richmond

VIRGINIA
1788

Norfolk

Mississippi R.

St. Louis

UNITED STATES
IN 1783

1803

MISSOURI
1821

KENTUCKY
1792

Raleigh

Nashville

NORTH CAROLINA
1789

Wilmington

TENNESSEE
1796

Memphis

Columbia

ARKANSAS
1836

Atlanta

SOUTH
CAROLINA
1788

as R.

Augusta

IANA

ed
R.

MISSISSIPPI
1817

ALABAMA
1819

GEORGIA
1788

30

Natchez

Mobile

ouston

LOUISIANA
1812

Pensacola

St. Augustine

FLORIDA
1845

New
Orleans

1810

1813

FLORIDA
PURCHASE
1819

Gulf
of
Mexico

Atlantic Ocean

UNITED STATES IN 1850

90

80

321

Chapter 13

From Compromise to Conflict

I believe this government cannot endure permanently half slave and half free.
—ABRAHAM LINCOLN, 1858

The apparent settlement of the slavery issue by the Compromise of 1850 took place during a period of remarkable prosperity. Every great interest—cotton planting, wheat farming, manufacturing, transportation—was booming. Between 1849 and 1860, California produced over two thousand times as much gold as had been mined in the United States in the previous sixty years. This flood of precious metal paid for imports and served as a circulating medium within the country. The rapid growth of the United States astonished the world: in the three decades from 1830 to 1860 the population more than doubled, climbing from 12,866,000 to 31,443,000.

"TAKE-OFF" IN THE NORTH

According to economist W. W. Rostow, the twenty years from 1840 to 1860 saw the northern United States enter a stage of economic development that he calls the "take-off." A nation enters the take-off, says Rostow, when a number of causes combine to create a situation where wealth grows relatively faster than population. Rapid and apparently self-sustaining growth becomes a dominant characteristic of the economy. In the United States, the take-off was the result of a combination of factors: new inventions, sufficient capital to build new factories, a class of business people able and willing to start new enterprises, a mobile labor supply, an increase in agricultural productivity, and a transportation system to connect farms and factories.

Although in 1850 two-thirds of the American people were engaged in agriculture, industry was catching up, partly because of a flood of new inventions. Whereas in the early years of the Republic patents had been granted at a rate of less than 100 per year, by the turn of the nineteenth century 2,500 patents were issued annually. "Would any but an American," asked an English newspaper, "have ever invented a milking machine, or a machine to beat eggs, or machines to black boots, scour knives, pare apples, and do a hundred things that all other peoples have done with their ten fingers from time immemorial?" The sewing machine, invented by Elias Howe in 1846, reduced the time for making a shirt from over fourteen hours to little more than an hour. When adapted for the purpose of sewing uppers to soles, it made possible the mass production of shoes.

Maritime Museum of San Diego

The American clipper ships that slid down the ways of builders from Maine to Maryland were perhaps the finest sailing vessels ever built. They were designed to move small cargoes such as tea and passengers at great speed. Carrying as much as an acre of sail, they required large crews. Their heyday was short because they were beaten out by steamships, which did not depend on wind and weather and so could keep more regular schedules. In what other ways were steamships more economical?

Courtesy of Essex Institute

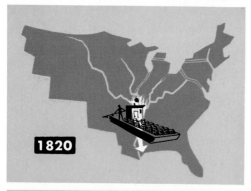

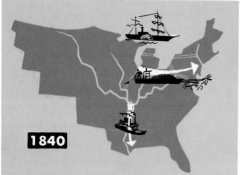

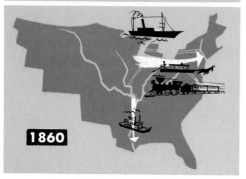

Before canals and railroads, when all midwestern produce went down the Mississippi, the West and the South were political allies. By the 1840's, the direction of commerce had begun to shift, and with it political alliances. By 1860, the West and the North had become political allies. (See the pictures and map on pages 228-229.)

The rotary press, introduced in the 1840's, allowed newspapers to publish far larger editions than ever before, so that such a paper as Horace Greeley's New York *Tribune,* with a circulation of 200,000, could exert national influence. Charles Goodyear's invention of vulcanized rubber in 1839 found innumerable uses in industry and gave the world the first cheap waterproof garments. The telegraph as a practical proposition dates from 1844, when Samuel F. B. Morse used a grant of $30,000 from Congress to build a line between Baltimore and Washington. By 1861 a telegraph line was extended across the continent, and a cable was laid across the Atlantic to Great Britain. Soon the whole world was to be linked by instantaneous communication.

Along with new inventions and new industries came further development of old industries. Thus textile factories increased in size as several operations were combined under a single roof and more efficient steam engines produced more power. The techniques invented by Eli Whitney and Simeon North of making interchangeable parts and breaking down manufacture into simple operations were now applied to the mass production of clocks, watches, farm machinery, and sewing machines. In western Pennsylvania, Brady's Bend Iron Company combined all the operations from mining to shaping the finished product and produced 15,000 tons of rails a year.

For the first time, American manufactured goods invaded world markets. At the Crystal Palace Exhibition in London in 1851, crowds were fascinated by the ingenuity of American gadgets such as mechanical churns, revolvers, and alarm clocks. Although Great Britain was still the leading manufacturing nation, the United States was in second place and had started on a period of rapid growth that would make it the industrial leader of the world by the end of the nineteenth century.

Growth of Agriculture

Agricultural productivity grew as fast as that of industry. During the 1850's, the frontier line did not advance as rapidly as in previous decades because settlers held back from the Great Plains. But in the Middle West there was ample fertile land, "as flat as a barn floor," and it attracted farmers from barren hillsides in the Northeast and immigrants from Europe. Public lands could be purchased for as little as 25 cents an acre, and the Pre-emption Act of 1841 allowed "squatters" first chance to buy. The new railroads supplemented sailing ships on the Great Lakes and the canal system in moving western grain and meat to eastern markets.

New markets at home and abroad stimulated more efficient means of food production. In Chicago and Cincinnati, meat packers began to use assembly-line methods to convey thousands of carcasses through their plants. But the most striking new development was the first large-scale use of farm machinery. There were special conditions in America that made for this. As Jefferson had pointed out, "In Europe the object is to make the most of their land, labor being abundant; here it is to make the most of our labor, land being abundant."

The first great need was for plows that could cut through the roots of recently cleared forest land or turn the tough sod of the prairies. In 1825 Jethro Wood of Scipio, New York, started to manufacture an iron plow with replaceable parts that was more efficient than any before. A much improved version, made of steel instead of iron, was developed by John Deere of Moline, Illinois; by 1850 the Deere works were turning out 10,000 plows per year.

The new plows enabled farmers to plant more land than they could later reap. Many men tried to invent a mechanical reaper to deal with the situation; the most successful was Cyrus McCormick, a Virginia blacksmith. Taking out his first patent in 1834, McCormick continually improved his machine. By 1860 over 100,000 mechanical reapers were in use. They were accompanied by still other inventions: mechanical drills to plant grain, threshing machines, and horse-drawn hay rakes.

TRANSPORTATION

With rapidly expanding domestic and foreign markets came great advances in transportation. In the decade of the 1850's the United States built the largest merchant marine in the world; inland navigation on canals and rivers reached its highest point; and the new-fangled railroads more than tripled their mileage.

Expansion of the Merchant Marine

In 1849 Great Britain repealed the Navigation Laws that had given special protection to British ships trading within her empire. The United States, however, continued to allow only its own ships to carry cargoes between American ports. Competing on even terms with British ships in British ports while enjoying an advantage in their own, American ships increased in total tonnage from 943,000 tons in 1846 to 2,226,000 tons in 1857. For a few years, vessels flying the Stars and Stripes carried more goods than those flying the Union Jack.

The greatest American triumph at sea was the clipper ship, which enjoyed its brief heyday between about 1845 and 1860. The clippers were specialized ships, built to carry cargoes of high value and small volume. Characterized by very sharp bows, an immense spread of sail, masts 200 feet high, and great length in relation to the beam, they were

QUESTION • What accounted for the speed of the clipper ships?

the fastest ocean-going sailing vessels ever built. The clipper *Lightning* once logged over 500 miles in a 24-hour period. During the 1850's,

The scene of the river at Baltimore in 1840 (above) depicts how great the traffic was along the east coast. One of the difficulties of early railroading was the development of rails (below) that would neither sag, spread, nor break. This problem was not solved until the development of steel rails after the Civil War.

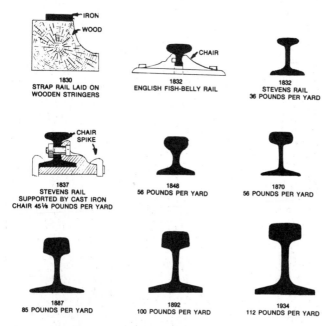

there was continuous excitement among seamen throughout the world as the American clippers broke all records for long ocean voyages. The great clippers were among the wonders of their day. Their names reflect their beauty and the pride of their builders—*Sovereign of the Seas, Sea Witch, Flying Cloud, Shooting Star, Westward Ho, Morning Light, Queen of the Pacific, Young America,* and *Great Republic.*

Alarmed by the superiority of American sailing ships, the British concentrated on the development of steamships. Between 1850 and 1860, the proportion of ocean freight carried in steam vessels went from 14 to 28 per cent, and most of this increase was British. By 1860 American shipyards were closing down for want of orders.

Inland Navigation

During this decade inland navigation reached its peak. The Erie Canal had so much traffic that it had to be widened and deepened. The Great Lakes gained such importance as a water route that 6,000 ships sailed from Chicago in a single year. Above all, this was the great period of the Mississippi River traffic. Mark Twain's *Life on the Mississippi* and *Huckleberry Finn* bear witness to the romance of the great river at this time. Remembering his boyhood in Illinois, Francis Grierson wrote as follows:

There were days when I sat for hours on this bluff [above the river]; the supreme moments came with the passing of boats, such as the *War Eagle,* the *City of Louisiana,* or the *Post Boy.* . . . When a boat made the return journey down stream it put the last touch of enchantment to the face of the waters. It filled me with visions of distant worlds as it skimmed the smooth surface, the smoke from the chimneys leaving a long, scattered trail, the white steam puffing out of the 'scape-pipes in rhythmic movements, the paddle wheels throwing out thick showers as the beautiful apparition sped like a dream southward.

The "9:45 Accommodation" by E. L. Henry (above) depicts a scene that was becoming commonplace in pre-Civil War America—the meeting of the horse and buggy and the iron horse. The water traffic on the Great Lakes in 1836 (below) moved east from Detroit to the Erie Canal, then to New York, and finally to Europe.

Some of the passenger boats were 350 feet long, although drawing only 5 feet of water; they were described as "magnificent floating palaces," with 60 or 70 staterooms and dining rooms lined with mirrors and hung with crystal chandeliers. But the great days of the river traffic were numbered. By 1860 the railroad, like the ocean-going steamship, was coming into its own and would soon make canal and river traffic obsolete.

Railroads: Early Difficulties, Later Expansion

The first successful use of the steam locomotive in the United States was on the Charleston and Hamburg Railroad in South Carolina in 1831, and other lines began operation almost simultaneously. Railroads did not, however, be-

327

A big advantage of railroads over canals was, of course, that railroads operated in winter, when canal traffic, except in the South, was tied up by ice. To the left may be seen the Chinese workers who provided much of the main muscle power for building the railroads of the West.

come an important means of transportation immediately, partly because they aroused opposition. A typical canal man's speech contained this passage:

Canals, sir, are God's own highway, operating on the soft bosom of the fluid that comes straight from nature. The railroad . . . is the Devil's own invention, compounded of fire, smoke, and dirt, spreading its infernal poison throughout the fair countryside. It will set fire to houses along its slimy tracks. . . . It will leave the land despoiled, ruined, a desert where only sable buzzards shall wing their loathsome way.

Railroads were opposed on the ground that such frightful speeds as fifteen, twenty, and even thirty miles an hour were against nature and contrary to the will of God.

Early railroads were handicapped by numerous practical problems. It was difficult, for instance, to devise suitable rails—rails which would neither spread under the weight of a train nor bend and come up through the floor of the car. A train was hard to stop: if the brake worked on the engine, the cars piled into it; if the cars were braked first, they dragged back so hard as to break the couplings. Almost everything one takes for granted on railroads today—brakes, couplings, headlights, effective lubrication of the wheels, and safe bridges—had to be worked out by painful trial and error. Furthermore, railroads were extremely expensive to build and maintain. The Panic of 1837, caused partly by overexpansion in canal and turnpike building, made both state governments and private investors wary of sinking money into a new form of transportation.

By 1850 many of the technical problems of railroading had been met, and an era of great expansion began. Before 1853 it was impossible to make a continuous journey of as much as 500 miles on any American railroad. By 1860 the Atlantic seaboard and the Mississippi River system were connected by a number of through routes. The railroad network had increased in mileage from 9,000 in 1850 to over 30,000 in 1860. The new railroads cost what then seemed colossal sums. The Erie Railroad cost about $23,000,000 to build, half again as much as the United States paid for New Mexico and California. The railroad corporations thus became the first outstanding examples of "big business."

Linking the Middle West and the Northeast

The through lines from the East to the Middle West completed a development which the Erie Canal had begun: the conquest of the Appalachian Mountain barrier. Because of the Mississippi River system, the natural economic ties of the Middle West had at first been with the South. Now, due to the railroads, the two sections drew together economically and politically. "This fact," says the historian Arthur M. Schlesinger, "far more than abolitionist agitation, was to account for northern unity when southern guns boomed out against Fort Sumter in 1861."

IMMIGRATION

One of the necessities for the take-off into sustained industrial growth is a mobile labor supply, free of attachments to long traditions of social organization or of craftsmanship, and willing to move from place to place. Many Americans had these qualities, and their numbers were supplemented by an increasing flood of immigrants. Until about 1800, immigrants to the United States were not numerous, averaging about 8,000 persons per year. But during the second quarter of the nineteenth century, a great migration began from Europe to America. Between 1840 and 1860 an average of over 200,000 immigrants reached our shores yearly; by the latter date, one out of every eight Americans was foreign-born.

Reasons for Flood of Immigration

Most of the immigrants fled poverty or oppression. In England and Germany the industrial revolution put thousands of skilled workers out of jobs. Rather than go into factories,

Samuel Morse, Artist and Inventor

On May 24, 1844, Samuel Finley Breese Morse sent a message over wires stretching 40 miles from Washington, D.C., to Baltimore. His words, "What hath God wrought!" proved to all that the telegraph was workable.

The speed of communication leaped forward. One of the first important uses of electricity, the telegraph introduced the electronic age. Morse, its inventor, was immensely honored in his day and earned a lasting place in history. Yet, untrained in science, often ignorant of the principles and theories of his field, he drew heavily on the work of others, sometimes without fitting acknowledgment. One of his biographers notes: "Morse was almost blissfully unaware of his own ignorance. . . . He lacked the mechanical skill to make his own materials with any professional finesse."

It is not hard to understand. Morse was trained in the fine arts. Born in 1791 in a Massachusetts parsonage, he early persuaded his father to send him to Europe to study painting. He wrote home that his ambition was "to rival the genius of a Raphael, a Michelangelo, or a Titian." He did, in fact, become a highly skilled artist, but the American public would buy only his portraits. They earned him some respect and a fair income, but Morse considered them mere "copying."

Spectacularly improvident, he reluctantly took a job teaching sculpture and painting at New York University. There he abandoned brush and palette for batteries and magnets, turning his rooms into a maze of wires. From his experiments came the telegraph, and, with his life more than half over, he won success—in a field he never fully understood.

many of these preferred to leave home. In 1848–1849 there were unsuccessful revolutions in Europe, especially in the German states, followed by persecution of those believing in democracy. Many German liberals fled to this country. In Scandinavia and the Netherlands there was too little soil to support rapidly growing populations. In Ireland, the greatest source of immigrants, the native population was denied home rule, and a wretched system of landholding kept them in poverty. The staple diet of Irish peasants was potatoes. When the potato crop was blighted in 1845, there was appalling suffering. It has been estimated that one million out of eight million died of starvation; in the next ten years, another million came to America.

Some immigrants actually came to this country against their will. The German city of Hamburg, for instance, found it cheaper to ship its paupers to the United States than to keep them in poorhouses or in jails. Public and private relief agencies in Britain provided money for the unemployed to take passage to America rather than go into the dreaded "workhouses," where poverty was treated as though it were a crime. Most immigrants came here, however, in high hopes of a better life. European agents of railroad companies and steamship lines described America as a land where riches could be had almost for the asking. Several states established immigration agencies to attract foreigners by such inducements as offering the right to vote to newcomers even before they became naturalized. But perhaps the most persuasive inducements to come to this country were the "America letters" written by recent immigrants to the folks back in their old homes. "The poorest families," wrote one correspondent, "adorn the tables three times a day like a wedding dinner—tea, coffee, beef, fowls, pies, eggs, pickles, good bread . . . Say, is it so in England?" The letters praised not only the prosperity of America, but its freedom

and equality. Here, they said, there were no class distinctions. No man had to tip his hat to the local squire, and workers could leave jobs if they did not like the boss. Women were not expected to do heavy work in the fields. "If you wish to be happy and independent, then come here," wrote a German farmer from his new home in Missouri.

Difficulties Faced by Immigrants

The move to America was often difficult and dangerous. On the voyage over, immigrants were packed into the steerage under conditions little better than those on board the ships that brought slaves from Africa. It is estimated that nearly 10 per cent of the steerage passengers died on the way over from malnutrition and disease. Once off the boat, their troubles were not over. They might become the prey of swindlers selling bogus railroad tickets or "farms" that later turned out to be under water. So many people made a business of cheating recent arrivals that a Swedish minister remarked, "the American competes with the mosquitoes to bleed the emigrant." Even after they had found jobs and places to live, immigrants had to deal with the settled prejudices of established Americans. Some pious folk disapproved of the way German-Americans spent Sunday afternoons listening to band concerts. American laborers resented the Irish who were forced by poverty to accept lower wages. Employers would sometimes put signs at factory gates or in windows, "No Irish need apply." The Irish workers also faced a religious prejudice so strong that it frequently broke out against them in mob violence.

Immigrants met organized opposition from a nation-wide secret society, the Order of the Star-Spangled Banner, founded in 1849. The members of this organization were called "Know Nothings," because when asked about it they replied, "I know nothing." The Know Nothings tried to keep recent immigrants from political office. They demanded that immigration be restricted and that the naturalization period be extended to twenty-one years.

The natural tendency of immigrants facing prejudice and grappling with the insecurity of a new environment was to draw together and keep to their old culture. This was reflected in the appearance of foreign-language newspapers. In New York City alone in 1851 there were seven such papers—four German, one French, one Italian, and one Spanish.

In spite of hardships, prejudice, and attempts to cling to their old ways, most immigrants adapted themselves rapidly to America. Jobs were abundant and land was cheap. Familiar with tyranny and want, the recent arrivals often appreciated American freedom and well-being more than did those whose ancestors had come over here generations earlier. Immigrants made many valuable contributions to the arts in America, to journalism, to education, and to invention. The children of foreign-born parents were quickly Americanized in the public schools, where they were taught English and learned to get along with children of different backgrounds and upbringing from their own.

Blacks in the North

There was one group of people in the North whose status resembled the immigrants in that they faced prejudice and dislike, even though their ancestors had been here for several generations—the blacks. Although they had long since been freed, northern Negroes were generally denied the right to vote and hold public office, to enter the professions and skilled crafts, and to send their children to any but segregated schools. They had to stand on the outside platform on streetcars and use only certain cars on railroad trains. Some states even forbade Negroes to enter their borders. Although the abolitionists fought these restrictions and won

a few local successes, especially in New England, northern blacks on the eve of the Civil War were second-class citizens.

THE SOUTH: "THE LAND OF COTTON" AND SLAVERY

By the 1850's, British textile machinery had become so efficient that it produced cloth cheap enough to be sold profitably to the poverty-stricken millions of Asia and Africa. The resulting demand for raw cotton brought prosperity to the deep South. In the decade of the 1850's cotton production broke all previous records. As new plantations were cleared in Mississippi, Louisiana, Arkansas, and Texas, the yield rose from less than 2,000,000 bales in 1849 to 4,540,000 bales in 1859. Seven-eighths of the world's supply came from the United States, and raw cotton comprised three-fifths of the nation's exports.

The 1850's also witnessed a revival of tobacco growing. This resulted from the discovery by Stephen, a black overseer in North Carolina, of a new method of curing that greatly improved the product. This "bright yellow" tobacco could be grown on lighter soils than had been worked formerly, and it was so much better that it sold for four times the former price. The result was a great increase in tobacco acreage.

Because it devoted most of its capital and labor force to the growing of staples, the South did not experience the industrial take-off of the North. It was also out of step with the North in other ways. On three important issues—a protective tariff, internal improvements at federal expense, and the grant of free land to homesteaders—southern opinion was opposed to the dominant sentiment among Northerners. But what most set the South apart from the North—indeed, from most of the civilized world—was its "peculiar institution," Negro slavery.

"The Peculiar Institution"

The feature of slavery that even its defenders condemned was the slave trade. Its very worst aspect, the voyage from Africa with slaves packed in like cattle and chained as well, was outlawed by international agreement in the nineteenth century. Even the Confederate Constitution, which defended slavery, forbade the importation of slaves. The domestic slave trade was less cruel, but there was nothing to prevent break-up of families.

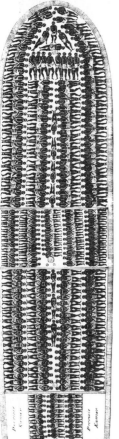

The New York Public Library

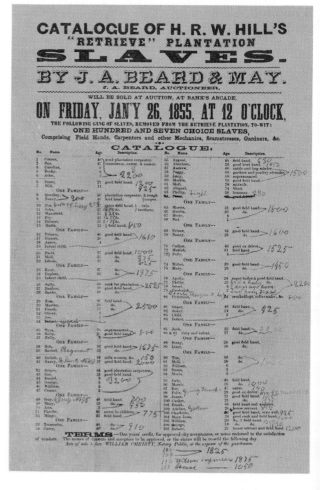

it passed two Reconstruction Acts that did away entirely with the state governments that Johnson had set up and put the South under military rule. The former Confederacy, except for Tennessee, was divided into five military districts, each under command of a major general. The officers were given the duty of setting up new governments in which black people should be guaranteed the right to vote. Those who had held office under the Confederacy or had "given aid and comfort" to enemies of the United States lost their suffrage. This meant that the majority of white southern males were disfranchised.

The Fourteenth and
Fifteenth Amendments, 1868, 1870

The Radical program was written into the Constitution by the Fourteenth and Fifteenth Amendments, which southern states were now required to ratify as a condition of readmission to the Union. The most important portion of the Fourteenth Amendment, ratified in 1868, is the first section. It specifically overrides the Dred Scott decision by making all persons born in the United States citizens of the United States and of the states where they reside. It forbids any state to deprive its citizens of equal rights under law. (For the text of the Fourteenth Amendment and explanation of its provisions see pp. 144–146.) The Fifteenth Amendment, ratified in 1870, was designed to guarantee to blacks the vote, by providing that no state might deprive any citizen of the franchise "on account of race, color, or previous condition of servitude." (See pp. 146–147.) The two amendments reveal one of the most important results of the Civil War—an immense gain in the power of the national government. Formerly, rights of citizenship and voting had been almost entirely determined by the states. Now the federal government laid down rules for the states to follow.

Andrew Johnson, a "political accident," became Vice-President because Lincoln hoped to win Democratic votes, and President because of Lincoln's death. In dealing with the Republican majority in Congress he displayed more courage than tact.

In addition to providing permanent constitutional protection for the rights of Negroes, Congress made a temporary effort to provide for their economic and educational needs. This was done through the Freedmen's Bureau, set up in March 1865, to care for former slaves. The first great federal relief agency, the bureau did useful work in providing food, clothing, and medical care. It also attempted to protect the civil rights of blacks and to see that employers treated them fairly. It spent some $5,000,000 on Negro schools. Northern missionary organizations also supported schools for freed people. The American Missionary Association, representing former abolitionists, sent hundreds of schoolteachers to the South and established nearly a score of colleges and normal schools to train black teachers.

Carpetbag Governments

Some of the leaders of the new state governments set up under the Radical program were Northerners whom the South called "carpetbaggers" (men who allegedly came seeking their fortunes with no more possessions than could be carried in a carpetbag). The epithet stuck, and as "carpetbag governments" they have been known ever since. Allied with the carpetbaggers were southern whites, who were dubbed "scalawags." Some of the carpetbaggers were respectable, honest men sincerely devoted to the public interest, but enough of them were self-seeking to give the carpetbag governments a reputation

for graft and inefficiency. Whether they were corrupt or honest, most Southerners disliked them because at the height of Radical reconstruction 700,000 Negroes possessed the franchise in the South, as against 625,000 whites. Prompted by agents of the Freedmen's Bureau and the Union League, a secret fraternal organization, black people mostly voted for Republican candidates.

But the carpetbag governments were not in truth run by and for the Negro. Even when the Negroes held a majority of the legislative seats, they were subordinate to whites. In any case, the carpetbag governments were, as a recent historian says, "an unfair test of the Negro's capacity for self-government." The conditions under which the freedmen had lived in slavery had been deliberately designed to keep them illiterate, helpless, and dependent. They could not suddenly acquire the skills needed to carry on government successfully.

Many of the carpetbag governments were corrupt. Votes in the legislatures were bought and sold like shares of stock. Most graft, however, went not to blacks but to whites at the top and to business people who received legislative handouts in the form of railway franchises, public lands, and fat government contracts. But the carpetbag governments were not unique in being graft-ridden. Unfortunately, political corruption was characteristic of politics all over the United States in the period after the Civil War. The Tweed Ring, operating only in New York City, stole more than all the carpetbag governments put together.

The period of carpetbag rule was not without achievement. The rights of women were increased, taxation was made fairer, and penal systems were reformed. Most of the new state constitutions made improvements in facilities for the care of the poor and the insane. Above all, they laid the foundations for public school systems that the South had hitherto lacked.

The Fifteenth Amendment guaranteed Negroes the right to vote in state and federal elections. Celebrations of its ratification were premature because means were found to make the amendment inoperative.

THE COLORED CITIZENS OF MARION COUNTY PROPOSE TO HAVE A GRAND MASS MEETING! AT LEBANON, KY., ON Tuesday, Feb. 22, '70, At which time they will celebrate the adoption of the XVth Amendment to the Constitution.

The following Speakers have been invited and are expected:
HON. BLAND BALLARD, HON. JAS. SPEED, COL. B. H. BRISTOW, FRED DOUGLASS, Rev. J. B. STANSBERRY, Rev. W. H. MILES, CAPT. JAS. M. FIDLER, COL. M. C. TAYLOR, A. G. DRAKE, HON. R. L. WINTERSMITH, GEN. ELI H. MURRAY, GEN. E. H. HOBSON, REV. R. MARSHALL, HON. SAM. McKEE, HON. W. C. GOODLOE, DR. J. C. MAXWELL, COL. CHAS. A. GILL, REV. J. H. HEYWOOD.

A FULL BAND OF MUSIC Will be in attendance and a GRAND TORCH-LIGHT PROCESSION, with Speeches, will be held on the night of the 22d of February. LEBANON, KY., FEB. 14th, 1870.   BY ORDER OF COMMITTEE.

A Lincoln-Douglas debate shows all the trappings of American politics at the time: two speakers, two bands, two sets of banners and placards, and an attentive, enraptured audience.

any Washington bar-room." Southerners, on the other hand, called on the North to obey the decision as the price of their remaining in the Union.

THE LINCOLN-DOUGLAS DEBATES

The question of slavery in the territories was now in almost hopeless confusion. The Dred Scott decision, supported in the South, was flatly opposed by the Republicans, dominant in the North. But what about the principle of popular sovereignty? Did the Dred Scott decision forbid the people of a territory to decide whether they wanted slavery? This was the most important issue in the Lincoln-Douglas debates of 1858.

Stephen A. Douglas and Abraham Lincoln were rival candidates for senator from Illinois, Douglas having served in the Senate for twelve years. Known to his followers as "the Little Giant" because of his small stature and great force of character, Douglas had made a national reputation by his devotion to the principle of popular sovereignty. The most prominent Democrat in Congress, he hoped to be elected President in 1860. Abraham Lincoln, his Republican opponent, was a comparative unknown. The height of his political career had been a single undistinguished term in the House of Representatives. A former Whig who had defended the Compromise of 1850, even to enforcing the Fugitive Slave Law, Lincoln was late in joining the Republican party. Yet he had a large local following and a reputation as a clever lawyer and keen debater.

The personal contrast between the two men was striking. Douglas, "a short, thick-set burly man, with a large round head, heavy hair, dark complexion, and a fierce bulldog look," radiated success. He dressed in southern plantation style, wearing a fine broadcloth suit, clean linen, and a broad-brimmed felt hat. Lincoln, "ludicrously tall, angular, and awkward in gait and gesture,"

view. Dred Scott had no right to sue in a federal court, Taney claimed, because the founders of the United States did not intend Negroes to be citizens. The Missouri Compromise ban on slavery north of the 36° 30' line was unconstitutional since Congress had no right to prohibit slavery in the territories. Such a prohibition, argued Taney, denied slaveholders their equal rights in the public domain.

Instead of settling the slavery dispute, the Dred Scott decision made it more bitter. If the decision stood, the Republican party might as well go out of existence, since its basic principle —free soil—had been declared unconstitutional. Republicans therefore claimed that the decision was not binding, but was an *obiter dictum* (an incidental opinion not called for by the circumstances of the case). Taney's decision, said a Republican newspaper, carried no more weight than "the judgment of the majority of those congregated in

QUESTION • In 1857 Northerners opposed the Supreme Court decision in the Dred Scott case. Is there, as Republicans then claimed, a higher law than the Constitution?

looked like something from the backwoods. The sleeves of his coat barely reached his bony wrists; his trousers bagged at the knees, and his stovepipe hat (inside which he kept valuable papers) emphasized his gawkiness. Yet Lincoln was a formidable opponent for Douglas. He could tell a good story and clarify his points with picturesque illustrations. Above all, he had a genius for clear, logical thinking.

Lincoln was devoted to the principles of the Declaration of Independence and opposed to slavery, but he was not an abolitionist. By the Constitution, the federal government had no right to interfere with slavery in the South. Federal interference with slavery where it already existed would give the slave states legitimate grounds for secession. Lincoln simply insisted that the institution be kept out of the territories. He thought that if the "peculiar institution" were confined to its existing area, Southerners themselves might eventually abolish it. He believed that the territories should be areas where "Hans, and Baptiste, and Patrick, and all other men from all the world, may find new homes and better themselves." To allow slave labor in the territories would make it harder for poor people to get ahead.

The Freeport Doctrine

Challenged by Lincoln to meet him face to face, Douglas debated the issues of the day with his opponent in seven Illinois towns. The two men attracted large crowds and their speeches received national publicity. Douglas attempted to show that Republicans in general and Lincoln in particular were abolitionists in disguise, bent on destroying the Union. Lincoln in turn embarrassed Douglas by asking, "Can the people of a territory in any lawful way ... exclude slavery from their limits prior to the formation of a State Constitution?" If Douglas answered "Yes," he would support the principle of popular sovereignty but would go against the Dred Scott decision. He would improve his chances for getting re-elected senator from Illinois, but would lose southern support for the presidency in 1860. If he answered "No," he would deny popular sovereignty, the principle on which he had based his political career, and might lose the senatorial election.

To wriggle out of this predicament, Douglas formulated the so-called Freeport Doctrine. According to this formula, Douglas said he accepted the Dred Scott decision that forbade Congress to bar slavery from the territories. On the other hand, he pointed out, a territorial legislature could effectively discourage slavery by failing to pass the special "police regulations" necessary to keep slaves under control. By admitting that a territorial legislature could practically nullify the Dred Scott decision, Douglas won a narrow victory in the senatorial election at the price of losing southern support for the presidency in 1860.

QUESTION • *In the Illinois senatorial election in 1858 Lincoln received more popular votes than Douglas. How, then, did it turn out that Douglas won the election?*

DRIFTING TOWARD WAR

John Brown was a fanatic who regarded himself as a heaven-sent agent to liberate slaves and punish slaveholders. In October 1859, with only eighteen followers, he seized the federal arsenal at Harpers Ferry, Virginia, intending to free and arm Negroes of the surrounding countryside. The slaves refused to follow him, and Brown was captured after ten of his men had been killed. Tried in a Virginia court for treason and murder, he was found guilty and hanged. At the trial and execution, he showed no sense of guilt nor fear of death. Southerners regarded Brown's deed with pure horror, since they feared nothing so much as a slave revolt. They were shocked to learn that Brown had been financed by some northern abolitionists. But many Northerners regarded Brown as a martyr to human freedom; Emerson said that he had "made the gallows glorious like the cross."

Southern fears were increased by the publication, in 1857, of *The Impending Crisis of the South,* by Hinton R. Helper, the son of a North Carolina blacksmith. Helper attacked slavery above all because it enriched a few "slaveocrats" at the price of dooming non-slaveholding whites to "galling poverty and ignorance." He called on small farmers to revolt against "the lords of the lash," to tax slavery out of existence, and to send all the blacks back to Africa. By its threat of internal disunion, *The Impending Crisis* alarmed leaders of the South even more than *Uncle Tom's Cabin.* Southern states banned the book from the mails, while the Republican party distributed 100,000 copies as a campaign document.

The Election of 1860

As the election of 1860 approached, the Democrats split over the issue of slavery in the territories. A northern wing of the party nominated Douglas for the presidency and backed popular sovereignty; a southern wing nominated John C. Breckinridge of Kentucky and supported the Dred Scott decision. A third group, the Constitutional Union party, especially strong in the border states, nominated John Bell of Tennessee and attempted to avoid the slavery issue. This party was composed mostly of former southern Whigs.

With such division among their opponents, the way was wide open for the Republicans. They made good use of their opportunity. Their platform was designed to attract votes from many quarters. Although continuing to demand exclusion of slavery from the territories, it an-

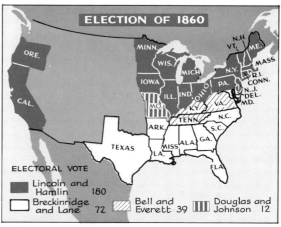

This is the momentous election over which the Union was divided. Note the severe sectional division: the North for Lincoln, the South for Breckinridge, the border states, hoping to avoid trouble, voting for Bell or for Douglas.

gled for conservative support by denying any intention to disturb slavery in the southern states and by denouncing John Brown's raid as "among the gravest of crimes." The degree to which former Whigs had moved into positions of leadership in the Republican party was shown by the way the platform emphasized an updated version of Henry Clay's American System, including a protective tariff, free homesteads for actual settlers, and federal funds for internal improvements, including a railroad to the Pacific. It sought to attract recent immigrants by denouncing Know-Nothing attempts to make naturalization more difficult.

In choosing a candidate the Republicans passed over the more prominent William H. Seward, senator from New York, and nominated Lincoln. They tried to play down the slavery issue by imitating the "Tippecanoe and Tyler too" campaign of 1840. There were torchlight parades with boys carrying rails and singing about "Honest Abe the Railsplitter," who was born in a log cabin. On his part, Lincoln was

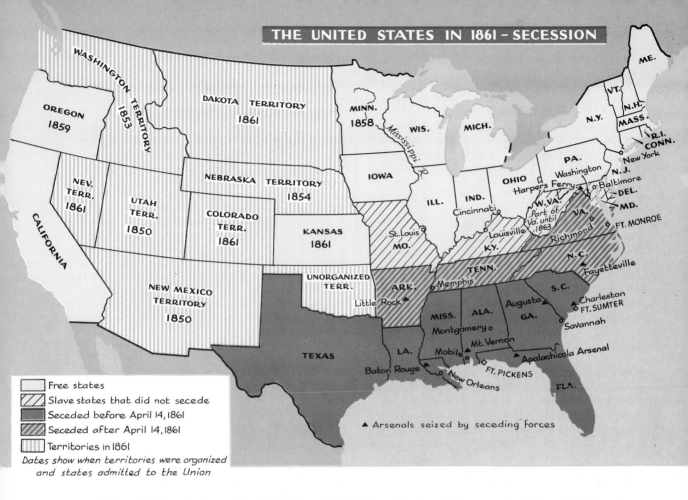

THE UNITED STATES IN 1861 - SECESSION

Legend:
- Free states
- Slave states that did not secede
- Seceded before April 14, 1861
- Seceded after April 14, 1861
- Territories in 1861

Dates show when territories were organized and states admitted to the Union

▲ Arsenals seized by seceding forces

Missouri's fears that, once free, "Kansas would infect" nearby slave states proved well-founded. Although safely within the slavery fold at the time of the Compromise of 1850 (see map page 317), Missouri and Kentucky did not secede in 1860-1861.

the only one of the candidates to make no speeches; he carried on a "front porch campaign," staying quietly at his home in Springfield, Illinois. Although the campaign was one of the most important in our history, public attention, at least in the North, was diverted from politics by events that now seem of minor importance: the launching of the "colossal" steamship *Great Eastern* (would it break in two?); the visit of the Prince of Wales (would he marry an American girl?); a delegation from Japan (would they learn American ways?).

The election turned out to be a Republican victory. Although receiving a minority of the popular vote, Lincoln gained a clear majority in the electoral college over the combined votes of all three of his opponents by carrying every free state except New Jersey, where the electoral vote was divided between him and Douglas. Breckinridge carried the deep South, while Bell and Douglas divided the border states.

Secession of the Deep South

The Republican victory caused great alarm in the deep South, the realm of "King Cotton." Leadership there passed to extremists, the so-called "fire-eaters," some of whom had long been threatening secession. They looked on Lincoln as "a baboon, a wild man from nowhere," and "a daring and reckless leader of the abolitionists." They predicted that his election meant abolition and slave insurrections. Albert Gallatin Brown, a Mississippi senator, told a southern audience:

The North is accumulating power, and it means to use that power to emancipate your slaves. When that is done, no pen can describe, no tongue depict, no pencil paint the horrors that will overspread this country. . . . Disunion is a fearful thing, but emancipation is worse. Better leave the Union in the open face of day, than be lighted from it at midnight by the incendiary's torch.

During the four-month interval between Lincoln's election in November 1860 and his inauguration in March 1861, the seven states of the deep South seceded. Their secession was based on the theory of states' rights: the Constitution was a contract between sovereign states; the free states had broken the contract by refusing to enforce the Fugitive Slave Law and by denying the southern states their equal rights in the territories; therefore the southern states were justified in resuming their "separate and equal place among nations." They did not long remain separate, but formed a new union, the Confederate States of America, calling on the other slave states to join them.

Uneasy Truce

The seceding states were able to leave the Union and to form a new federation without interference. President Buchanan was an elderly man, and his party had been repudiated at the polls. In any case he was ill-equipped to deal with the crisis; hitherto he had always deferred to the southern point of view on national issues. He denied that the southern states had a right to secede, but saw no way in which the government could force a state back into the Union.

Meanwhile there were last-minute attempts at compromise, of which the most promising was a proposal by Senator John J. Crittenden of Kentucky. The keystone of the Crittenden Compromise was the re-establishment of the 36° 30′ line in the territories, with slavery permitted south of it. Lincoln, perhaps mistakenly, refused to go along with this on the ground that he would be repudiating the most fundamental principle of the Republican party, free soil, before he had even taken office.

When Lincoln reached Washington in late February 1861, everything hung fire. While seven slave states had seceded, eight still remained in the Union (see map, p. 342). Although the North generally denied the right to leave the Union, there was apparently little desire to fight to force them back in. General Winfield Scott expressed widespread sentiment when he said, "Wayward sisters, depart in peace." Few people had confidence in Lincoln's ability to deal with the secession crisis. Even his own followers regarded him as a "crude, small-time politician." Seward, whom he appointed Secretary of State, offered to write the inaugural address for him and apparently expected to act as a sort of prime minister.

Lincoln's First Inaugural Address set forth a policy which differed little from that of Buchanan. Secession, he said, was wrong; it was a blow at the basic democratic principle that the will of the majority should prevail. Yet Lincoln suggested no active measures to force the Confederate States back into the Union. He proposed only to hold military posts not yet taken by the Confederates, to enforce federal laws where federal agents were not "obnoxious" to the local population, and to deliver the mail "unless repelled." Although refusing any concessions regarding slavery in the territories, Lincoln had no objection to a constitutional amendment forbidding federal interference with slavery in the southern states. He finally pleaded that North and South be "not enemies, but friends."

Outbreak of War

The first problem that Lincoln faced was what to do about the two southern fortresses still in federal control—Fort Pickens, in Florida, and Fort Sumter, on an island in the harbor of Charleston, South Carolina. Fort Sumter was running short of supplies, and a relief ship sent by Buchanan in January had been turned back by gunfire from shore batteries. After agonizing discussions with his cabinet, Lincoln decided to send provisions to the Fort Sumter garrison, this being in line with the policies laid down in his inaugural address. He let the Confederate authorities know in advance what he was going to do. Thus he put Jefferson Davis, the President of the Confederacy, over a barrel. If Davis allowed the fort to be provisioned, he would appear to be giving in to Lincoln. If he ordered that Fort Sumter or the relieving ships be fired on, he would be judged guilty of starting war. Davis chose the latter course, and authorized the military forces in Charleston to attack before the relief ships arrived. On April 12, 1861, shore batteries opened fire; after forty hours of bombardment Fort Sumter surrendered.

When the news of the attack reached the North, there was little more talk of letting the wayward sisters depart in peace. Instead, there was a spontaneous outbreak of patriotism such as the country had never before seen. "I never knew what popular excitement could be," wrote a Bostonian to a friend in England. "The whole population, men, women, and children, seem to be in the streets with Union flags and favors. ... Nobody holds back." When Lincoln called for 75,000 men to suppress rebellion, many more volunteered than could be organized or equipped.

There was a similar wave of feeling in the South. Faced with the prospect of obeying Lincoln's order and fighting their neighbors, many Southerners who disapproved of secession and disliked slavery nevertheless joined the Confed-

eracy. On April 4, a Virginia convention called to consider secession had voted strongly against it, but now it reversed its decision. Virginia left the Union and joined the Confederacy, along with North Carolina, Tennessee, and Arkansas (see map, p. 342).

Why a Civil War?

Ever since the Civil War broke out, people have debated why the South left the Union and embarked on the perilous experiment of war. The basic cause of the separation was probably that stated by Lincoln in his First Inaugural: "One section of our country believes that slavery is right, and ought to be extended, while the other believes that it is wrong, and ought not to be extended." But if one looks closer, one wonders about this. The actual dispute was not over slavery as such, but over slavery in the territories, where geography made the slave system unprofitable. For the Republican party to insist that slavery be banned there was (as Daniel Webster said in 1850) to "needlessly re-enact an ordinance of nature." For Southerners to demand that slavery be permitted there was to insist on a meaningless right: by secession they would probably lose all rights in the territories in any case. The fact is that both sides had come to the point where rational discussion was no longer possible. Agencies of communication had broken down with the separation of the major Protestant churches into northern and southern branches and, above all, with the disappearance of the Whig party and the split among the Democrats. Heretofore, political parties had been the principal agency in compromising sectional disputes.

Although slavery was probably the principal cause of secession, it was not the only one. The South was falling behind the North in wealth and population, and there was a tendency to blame this, as South Carolina had done at the time of the nullification crisis thirty years before, on the protective tariff. Once outside the Union, the South would no longer have to pay "tribute" to northern industrialists and bankers.

The alleged basis for secession was states' rights, as can be seen by the South's favorite name for the ensuing struggle, "the War Between the States." But the Confederacy had many aspects of a nation. Its national flag, the "Stars and Bars," and its songs, "Dixie" and "The Bonnie Blue Flag," inspired national patriotism. The "lost cause" was only officially based on the legal abstraction of state sovereignty; in fact, it was the cause of a nation struggling to be free, and the war has been called with some justice "the War for Southern Independence."

In risking war against a much stronger foe, Southerners labored under a series of misconceptions. Many of them thought that the North would not fight, and the first Confederate Secretary of War predicted that he would be able to wipe up with his pocket handkerchief every drop of blood spilled as a result of secession. Even if war came, Southerners expected to win. They believed that their men were superior to those of the North in martial virtues;

they were defending their homes and everything that they held most dear; and they expected foreign aid. In 1855 a South Carolina senator had explained why "King Cotton" would rescue the South:

Should they make war on us, we could bring the whole world to our feet. What would happen if no cotton was furnished for three years? . . . England would topple headlong and carry the whole civilized world with her. No, you dare not make war on cotton. No power on earth dares make war on it. Cotton is king.

Finally, as Lincoln's call for three-month volunteers indicates, no one foresaw the length and the bitterness of the war. If the North had realized that it was going to cost the lives of 360,000 of their young men to subdue the Confederacy, there might have been more ardent search for compromise or even acceptance of peaceable secession. If the leaders of the Confederacy had foreseen that the war would bring utter defeat, devastation, and destruction of their entire social system, they would certainly have thought twice before firing the first shot.

Activities: Chapter 13

For Mastery and Review

1. What circumstances made the 1850's a "take-off" period? What inventors and inventions of the 1840's stimulated American industry? For what reasons did the production of farm commodities increase so sensationally in the 1840's and 1850's?

2. For what reasons did American ocean commerce flourish in the 1850's? What was a clipper ship? What was the importance of the steamboat in American life?

3. Describe the handicaps faced by the early railroads. What success did "big business" meet in improving them and in linking East and West?

4. How large was the stream of immigrants reaching America between 1840 and 1860? Where did most of them come from? Why? What reception did they get?

5. By what means did the South maintain and stabilize slavery? Why did nonslaveholding whites defend the institution? What was the status of the free Negro in the South? In the North?

6. Why was the South, in the 1850's, so anxious to expand southward? What were filibusters? What was the Ostend Manifesto? Why was the United States interested in the Isthmus of Panama?

7. What part did the United States play in opening China and Japan to Western commerce?

8. For what reasons did disputes over slavery develop between 1850 and 1860 in spite of the Compromise of 1850?

9. How did the Lincoln-Douglas debates point up the slavery controversy? What was the position of each man on the question of extending slavery into the territories? What was the Freeport Doctrine? What effects did the debates have on the careers of Lincoln and Douglas?

10. How did the Democratic party split in 1860? How did the Republican platform appeal to different groups? What other party was in the field? What were the results of the election?

11. What was the situation when Lincoln was inaugurated? What policy did he propose? Why did the southern states secede?

Unrolling the Map

1. Study carefully the map on p. 229. Note how the National Road, the canals, and the railroads sought to establish communications between East and West. What was the economic and political importance of this? How do you account for the tremendous mileage of railroads built in the 1850's? Why was so much of the mileage in the East and West and so little in the South?

2. On an outline map of the world draw the lines of immigration from the European countries of origin to America. On each line (or in a key) list the main reason for immigration from each country.

Who, What, and Why Important?

"take-off"	Harriet Beecher Stowe
farm machinery	Kansas-Nebraska Act
industrial inventions	Emigrant Aid Society
clipper ship	election of 1856
"American letters"	Dred Scott decision
Know Nothings	Lincoln-Douglas debates
"peculiar institution"	*The Impending Crisis*
Ostend Manifesto	election of 1860
Gadsden Purchase	Crittenden Compromise
Clayton-Bulwer Treaty	Confederate States of
Caleb Cushing	America
Commodore Perry	Fort Sumter
Fugitive Slave Law	

To Pursue the Matter

1. Why and how are the historians still fighting the Civil War? See the last chapter of Bedford, *The Union Divides: Politics and Slavery, 1850–1861.*

2. Conduct a class poll to find out when the ancestors of each member came to America and from what countries they came. Tabulate the results. Did any come between 1840 and 1860?

3. Some towns in the 1850's refused to permit railroads to enter; others offered financial inducements. Assign roles to class members and debate the attitude of your town toward a proposed railroad through it. The following might be included: banker, stagecoach driver, canalboat skipper, steamboat pilot, merchants, manufacturers, farmers, real estate owners.

4. Why did Southerners deliberately try to keep slaves in the country rather than in the city? See Wade, *Slavery in the Cities.*

5. Compare the way the Irish and Germans adapted to the United States in the years before the Civil War. See Wittke, *We Who Built America*, Chapters 8 and 9, and Woodham-Smith, *The Great Hunger.*

6. What was it like to be a river pilot? See Mark Twain, *Life on the Mississippi.*

7. Prepare an account of the extraordinary career of Harriet Tubman, guide for the Underground Railroad. See Buckmaster, *Let My People Go: The Story of the Underground Railroad.*

8. What did Lincoln think about slavery and Negroes before 1860? See the chapter on him in Hofstadter, *The American Political Tradition and the Men Who Made It.*

9. John Brown—hero? martyr? incendiary? madman? See Nevins, *The Emergence of Lincoln*, vol. II, Chapter 3, and Benét, *John Brown's Body.*

10. According to the Confucian scheme of values, a good society gives the greatest honor to the scholar, then to the peasant, then to the crafts worker. Merchants are regarded as inferior people, and soldiers as the scum of the earth. Prepare a similar scale of American values and compare it with the Confucian one. Can you see how the Chinese regarded Westerners?

Chapter 14

The Civil War
and Reconstruction

This is essentially a people's contest.... It is a struggle for maintaining in the world that form of government whose leading object is to elevate the condition of men ... to afford all an unfettered start, and a fair chance in the race of life.
—ABRAHAM LINCOLN, 1861

The great struggle that began after the fall of Fort Sumter has been termed "the last of the old wars and the first of the new." It was the last great war in which infantry was equipped with muzzle loaders and cavalry played a major role. It was the last great war in which chivalrous respect for the enemy was a commonplace. Many officers on both sides had been personally acquainted, often as West Point cadets, and they treated each other with courtesy even after hostilities began. This attitude often extended to the enlisted men. It proved almost impossible to prevent pickets from fraternizing. When Union and Confederate armies were in contact for any length of time, there was constant exchange of "Yankee" coffee and sugar for "Rebel" tobacco.

In other aspects the Civil War was the first modern war. It was the first in which railroad lines were vital, the first in which telegraph lines, ironclad ships, and observation balloons were used as a matter of course. It foreshadowed the First World War, since the armies often dug in, and sometimes fought from elaborate trenches. It also represented a step toward the modern concept of "total war," with less and less distinction between civilians and soldiers. This was especially true of the South. The Confederacy became a "nation in arms," with men from seventeen to fifty conscripted into the army, farmers told what to plant, and women bearing a large part of the burden of keeping the troops supplied with clothing and medical supplies. In the latter years of the war, southern civilians suffered terribly as Union armies pursued a "scorched earth" policy and deliberately devastated areas through which they marched.

Before the war, the United States Army numbered only 11,000 men, mostly stationed on the western frontier. Yet North and South eventually fielded armies numbering hundreds of thousands. Although these troops often lacked discipline, no soldiers ever fought more stubbornly on the field of battle. In battles such

This is one of a fleet of blockade runners that were built in England and sailed between Bermuda and ports of the South. These highly specialized ships were built low on the water so that they could hide behind low spits of land, and with light draft so that they could navigate little used channels.

St. George's Historical Society, Bermuda

as Gettysburg and Chickamauga, 30 per cent of the soldiers were killed or wounded, yet the beaten army kept its organization.

COMPARISON WITH THE REVOLUTIONARY WAR

In the Civil War the position of the Confederacy was somewhat similar to that of the United States in the Revolution. The Southerners, fighting for independence on home soil, could win simply by holding out against northern attacks. As an agricultural region with poor communications and few big cities, the South, like the United States in 1776, could not be paralyzed by a blow at a vital center. The North enjoyed certain advantages similar to those Britain enjoyed in the Revolution. It was superior in resources of every sort—men, money, transportation facilities, food, and manufacturing (study the chart, p. 356). The federal government, like the British, was a going concern, while the government of the Confederacy had to be created overnight.

This parallel between the Revolutionary War and the Civil War is by no means complete. The Americans won the Revolutionary War partly because of aid from France, but the Confederacy had to fight alone. In the Revolution, American civil and military leadership was superior to that of Great Britain. In the Civil War, the South had better generals, especially at first, but as time passed the North found able commanders too. As to nonmilitary leadership, Lincoln proved himself more able than Jefferson Davis. Finally, the northern chances of victory

in 1861 were better than those of Britain in 1776 because in the earlier struggle America had been protected by the Atlantic Ocean. The Confederacy was open to attack by land, and its long coastline made it vulnerable by sea.

STRATEGY: NAVAL OPERATIONS

Hostilities in the Civil War extended from southern Pennsylvania to New Mexico. In scores of battles the forces engaged were more numerous than those that fought at Saratoga or Yorktown. In spite of its size, however, the basic strategy of the war was relatively simple. The Union forces set out to accomplish three great objectives: (1) blockade Confederate ports; (2) cut the South apart—first by way of the Mississippi, and then again through Tennessee and Georgia; and (3) take Richmond, the Confederate capital.

The Union Blockade

When Lincoln proclaimed a blockade of southern ports five days after Fort Sumter fell, he seemed guilty of ridiculous optimism. To patrol a coast 3,500 miles long, the United States had 40 wooden ships, manned by fewer than 1,500 men. But the North was the seafaring section of the country; the American merchant marine was near its height; and Gideon Welles, Secretary of the Navy, was one of the most energetic men in Lincoln's cabinet. Eventually the federal navy numbered over 700 ships, manned by 50,000 men. By the end of 1862, every major southern port was captured or blockaded. This reduced imports and exports to what could be carried in "blockade runners" —small, fast vessels, designed to sneak through openings in the sandbars that provide much of the South with a double coastline. Although some blockade runners were amazingly successful, they could not begin to replace the regular commerce of the South. Southern trade shrank to a fraction of what it had been before the war, and Confederate armies were deprived of adequate supplies of boots, clothing, and medicine. Furthermore, the great Union blockading fleet forced the Confederacy to keep thousands of men away from major battlefields to guard the coast. Even so, Union forces carried on successful amphibious operations against southern ports; the most notable were David Farragut's bold expeditions against New Orleans in 1862 and Mobile in 1864.

To break the blockade became a major aim of the small Confederate navy. In March 1862, a strange craft emerged from the naval station at Norfolk, Virginia. On the hull of the *Merrimac*, a former federal steam frigate now renamed the *Virginia*, the Confederates built an iron superstructure and affixed a ram. The *Virginia* easily sank two wooden ships of a Union naval squadron. While Lincoln and his cabinet were debating whether it might be necessary to evacuate Washington, Southerners predicted that the *Virginia* would "sweep the Federal fleet from off the seas" and "levy toll on every northern seaport."

When the Confederate ship reappeared, however, she was met by a new federal ironclad, the *Monitor*. The *Monitor* was easier to handle than the *Virginia*, and her guns were mounted in a revolving turret. The two ships pounded each other for four hours without inflicting serious damage, but this first battle between ironclads may be regarded as a victory

The *Monitor* was an uncomfortable ship since its hold was hot and airless. Here its crew takes advantage of pleasant weather to relax on the deck. Note the dent in the turret just to the left of the gunport. This reveals how little damage the *Virginia* inflicted on the Union ironclad.

for the North. The *Virginia* retired, never to appear again, while northern shipyards started to turn out dozens of *Monitors*.

Attempts to Break the Blockade

With few shipyards of its own, the Confederacy tried to obtain warships abroad. Efforts to buy powerful rams, designed to destroy the blockading fleet, were unsuccessful, but the Confederacy secretly purchased in England several cruisers that preyed on northern shipping. One of them, the *Alabama*, captured or destroyed 63 vessels. To avoid Confederate cruisers, hundreds of American ships were sold to foreign owners or registered under other flags. Thus the United States merchant marine suffered a blow from which it did not recover for over half a century.

THE WAR IN THE WEST

There were two major areas of land warfare: the territory west of the Appalachians, centering at first on the Mississippi, and the eastern front, centering on the area between the two capitals, Washington and Richmond. Although Union armies lost battles in the West, they won every major campaign. In little more than two years they cut the Confederacy in two, and by the end of the war had cut through it again.

In 1861 the war in the West was devoted to a struggle for control of the border states. In spite of strong pro-Confederate minorities, both Kentucky and Missouri were cleared of Confederate troops. The western counties of Virginia, soon to become the state of West Virginia, were also detached from the Confederacy. Thus the South was deprived of a strong line of defense along the Ohio River.

In the following year the Confederacy was squeezed from both north and south. The Union advance began when forces under General Ulysses S. Grant attacked Fort Henry on the Tennessee River and Fort Donelson on the Cumberland. (For the campaigns of the Civil War, study the maps on p. 352.) First taking Fort Henry, Grant surrounded Fort Donelson in February 1862. When asked on what terms he would accept surrender, Grant sent the famous answer: "No terms except unconditional surrender can be accepted. I propose to move immediately upon your works." When the fortress fell, with 12,000 Confederates and 40 cannon captured, it opened the way for a Union advance southward toward Corinth, Mississippi, and Memphis, Tennessee. This advance was marked by the bloody, two-day battle of Shiloh, or Pittsburg Landing, in April 1862. Grant's army was surprised by a Confederate force under General Albert Sidney Johnston, but escaped disaster when the Confederate general was killed, and Grant managed to bring up reinforcements. By the end of 1862, Union armies had occupied all of western Tennessee and were probing southward into the state of Mississippi. Meanwhile Admiral David Farragut had taken New Orleans, and Union armies prepared to advance northward from there.

Fall of Vicksburg and Battle of Chattanooga, 1863

As the year 1863 commenced, the Union success on the Mississippi River front depended on taking the city of Vicksburg. This town was a natural fortress, protected by high bluffs toward the river and by a maze of watercourses and swamps to the north. In late 1862 and early 1863, forces under Grant made five unsuccessful attempts to approach it.

Finally, in May 1863, Grant embarked on one of the most daring campaigns in military history. After transporting his forces down the Mississippi River to just below Vicksburg, he started inland. Against the established rules of military science and the unanimous advice of his staff, Grant cut loose from his base of supplies.

Union soldiers wait it out in the trenches. The war began as a war of movement, but dwindling southern forces eventually dug in to hold their lines. Nine months in the trenches ensued when Lee's forces met the Union army outside Richmond. Such extensive trench warfare anticipated that of World War I.

The Union soldiers were allowed only such food as they could carry or get along the way. Grant's personal baggage consisted of a toothbrush.

The Confederate commander of Vicksburg at first stayed behind his fortifications, thinking Grant was trying to trick him into taking to the open field; he then struck vainly at Grant's nonexistent line of communication. The Union forces reached Jackson, the capital of Mississippi, almost without opposition. Finally, Grant turned back and fought his way to the outskirts of Vicksburg. In 18 days his troops marched 200 miles, fought five major battles, and defeated forces larger than their own. Late in May, he laid siege to Vicksburg, and on July 4, the town fell. Five days later Port Hudson, the last Confederate post on the Mississippi River, also surrendered.

Union forces attempted now to cut through the Confederacy again by way of eastern Ten-

nessee and Georgia. Here the first key position was Chattanooga, where the Tennessee River runs near a gap southward toward Atlanta. In September 1863, General William S. Rosecrans, commanding a large Union force, maneuvered the Confederates out of the city. After Rosecrans suffered a severe defeat at the bloody battle of Chickamauga, Confederate troops besieged the Union army in Chattanooga and cut off its supplies. The Union cause was saved when Grant arrived in October. New supply routes were opened and the Confederate forces were driven from the heights around Chattanooga. By the end of 1863, the way was open for an advance into Georgia.

Sherman's March to the Sea, 1864

Early in 1864, General William T. Sherman, now in command in the West, started toward Atlanta and took the city in September. When the opposing commander struck northward to

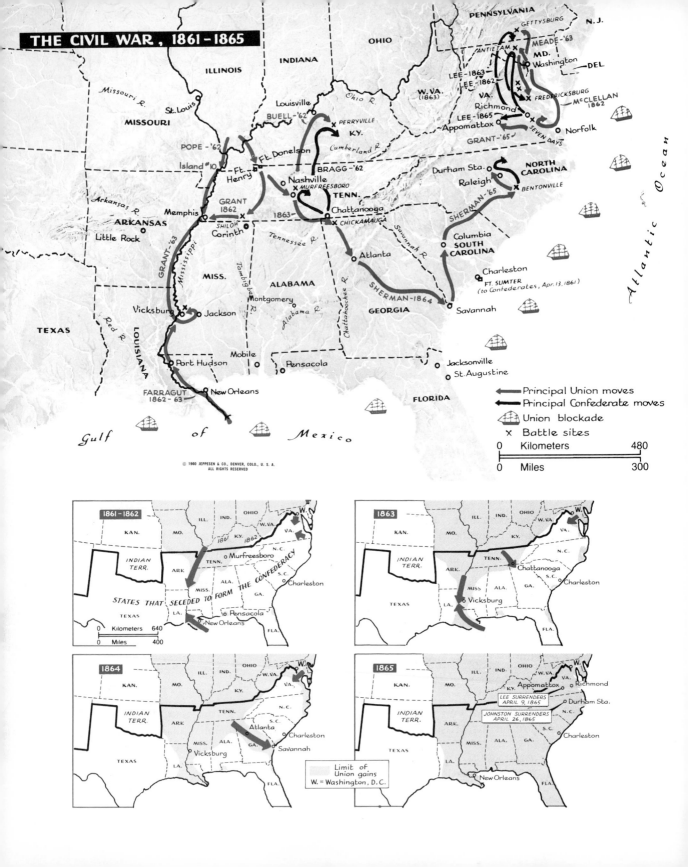

THE CIVIL WAR, 1861-1865

PENNSYLVANIA
GETTYSBURG
N.J.
MEADE - '63
OHIO
ANTIETAM
MD.
Washington
DEL.
INDIANA
W. VA.
(1863)
LEE-1863
ILLINOIS
LEE-1862
VA.
FREDERICKSBURG
McCLELLAN
Richmond
1862
Missouri R.
Ohio R.
LEE-1865
St. Louis
Louisville
Appomattox
GRANT-'65
SEVEN DAYS
Norfolk
MISSOURI
BUELL-'62
PERRYVILLE
KY.
POPE-'62
Cumberland R.
BRAGG-'62
Durham Sta.
NORTH
Island #10
Ft.
Ft. Donelson
Nashville
Raleigh
CAROLINA
Henry
MURFREESBORO
BENTONVILLE
Arkansas R.
GRANT
Chattanooga
SHERMAN-'65
Memphis
1862
1863
TENN.
ARKANSAS
SHILOH
CHICKAMAUGA
Little Rock
Corinth
Savannah R.
Columbia
Tennessee R.
SOUTH
Atlanta
CAROLINA
MISS.
Charleston
ALABAMA
FT. SUMTER
Chattahoochee R.
Vicksburg
(to Confederates, Apr.13, 1861)
Jackson
GEORGIA
SHERMAN - 1864
Montgomery
TEXAS
Alabama R.
Savannah
LOUISIANA
Mobile
Red R.
Jacksonville
Port Hudson
Pensacola
St. Augustine
FARRAGUT
New Orleans
1862-63
FLORIDA
Gulf   of   Mexico

Atlantic Ocean

Principal Union moves
Principal Confederate moves
Union blockade
x   Battle sites
0   Kilometers   480
0   Miles   300

© 1960 JEPPESEN & CO., DENVER, COLO., U. S. A.
ALL RIGHTS RESERVED

1861-1862
ILL. IND. OHIO
KAN. MO. W.VA. VA. W.
1861 KY. 1862
INDIAN TERR.
o Murfreesboro
ARK. TENN. N.C.
STATES THAT SECEDED TO FORM THE CONFEDERACY
MISS. ALA. S.C.
TEXAS
GA.
o Charleston
LA.
o Pensacola
New Orleans
FLA.
0   Kilometers   640
0   Miles   400

1863
ILL. IND. OHIO
KAN. MO. W.VA. VA. W.
KY.
INDIAN TERR. TENN.
Chattanooga
ARK. N.C.
MISS. ALA. GA. S.C.
o Charleston
Vicksburg
TEXAS
LA.
FLA.

1864
ILL. IND. OHIO
KAN. MO. W.VA. VA. W.
KY.
INDIAN TERR. TENN.
ARK. N.C.
Atlanta
o Charleston
MISS. ALA. S.C.
Vicksburg GA.
Savannah
TEXAS
LA.
FLA.
Limit of
Union gains
W. = Washington, D.C.

1865
ILL. IND. OHIO
KAN. MO. W.VA.
KY. Appomattox o Richmond
INDIAN TERR. TENN. LEE SURRENDERS
APRIL 9, 1865
ARK. JOHNSTON SURRENDERS Durham Sta.
APRIL 26, 1865 N.C.
MISS. ALA. GA. S.C.
o Charleston
TEXAS
LA.
New Orleans
FLA.

frighten him into retreat, Sherman decided to do what Grant had done before laying siege to Vicksburg—strike into enemy territory and live off the land. In November his army started southward and for nearly a month was cut off from communication with the North. It cut a path of destruction sixty miles wide through one of the richest agricultural regions of the South. Sherman's report of the campaign said, "I estimate the damage done to Georgia and its military resources at $100,000,000, at least $20,000,000 of which has inured to our advantage and the remainder is simply waste and destruction."

On December 20, 1864, Union troops marched into Savannah. In February 1865, they started northward, treating South Carolina, the state which had led the secession movement, as harshly as Georgia. When southern resistance finally collapsed in April, Sherman's force was less than a hundred miles from the Union army that had driven Lee out of Richmond.

THE WAR IN THE EAST

When Virginia joined the Confederacy, the capital was moved to Richmond. From a military point of view this may have been a blunder. The city was close to the northern border of the Confederacy and vulnerable to attack, yet it was a matter of pride to defend it at all costs. The South poured out more blood in the defense of Richmond than may have been justified. On the other hand, the success of Confederate armies in this eastern theater of war was extraordinary. Repelling one Union advance after another, they prevented the fall of the Confederate capital until the very end of the war.

Southern victories in the East were largely the result of the genius of General Robert E. Lee and his "right arm," General Thomas J. "Stonewall" Jackson. Through knowledge of the terrain, rapidity of movement, and the ability to

inspire troops to feats of endurance and heroism, these two inflicted defeats on Union forces sometimes twice as numerous as their own. Their tactics in such encounters as the second battle of Bull Run and Chancellorsville have become classic examples of brilliant generalship. In the North African campaigns of World War II, both German General Erwin Rommel and his British opponent General Harold Alexander revealed that they had profitably studied the campaigns of Lee and Jackson.

Confederate Failures: Antietam, 1862, and Gettysburg, 1863

Southern good fortune in the East did not include victories outside the Confederacy. Lee's two attempts to invade the North were both repulsed. In September 1862, his army was turned back in a campaign ending at the bloody

Nearly 200,000 blacks, both free blacks of the North and former slaves of the South, enlisted in the Union forces. Many distinguished themselves in battle.

Grant's terms at Fort Donelson earned him the nickname of "Unconditional Surrender" Grant. "Marse Robert" E. Lee (right), followed devotedly by his soldiers, emerged from the war as the hero of the South. Lee's many victories failed to overbalance northern superiority in numbers and supplies.

battle of Antietam. Caught with the Potomac at his back and facing much larger forces than his own, Lee did well to save his army.

In June 1863, he again crossed the Potomac. As he moved into southern Pennsylvania, panic seized the North. As far away as Massachusetts, governors declared a state of emergency and asked for the protection of federal troops. Lee was shadowed, however, by a Union army under General George G. Meade. An accidental clash between small units at Gettysburg developed into a great three-day battle. As it happened, Union soldiers occupied a position of great strength, the crest of a low ridge. Desperate Confederate attacks, reaching a peak in General George E. Pickett's disastrous charge, were all repulsed. On July 4, the same day that Vicksburg surrendered, Lee retreated into Virginia. From now on, many people in the Confederacy knew their cause was lost.

Grant vs. Lee, 1864–1865

In 1864 Grant assumed command in the East. Four previous generals—George McClellan, John Pope, Ambrose Burnside, and Joseph Hooker—had been put in command after victories elsewhere, only to meet defeat at the hands of Lee. In May 1864, Grant, moving southward toward Richmond, was intercepted by the Confederate army, fighting from prepared positions. But Grant kept advancing, even though in a single month of fighting he lost as many men as there were in Lee's entire force. Eventually, he laid siege to Richmond from the south, and the two armies fought nine months of trench warfare. With superior numbers Grant gradually lengthened his lines, while Union armies cut off supplies to Richmond.

Finally, Lee was forced to evacuate the Confederate capital. Union troops barred his escape westward; his men were starving. Grant urged Lee to surrender in order to prevent "further effusion of blood." The two men met at the village of Appomattox Court House in April 1865. Grant offered Lee generous terms: his soldiers might go home on giving their word not to fight again; the officers might keep their side arms and the cavalry their horses.

When Lee's army came to lay down their arms, Union troops saluted each division as it appeared. The general who ordered this mark of respect later wrote:

Before us in proud humiliation stood the embodiment of manhood: men whom neither toils and suffering, nor the fact of death, nor disaster, nor hopelessness could bend from their resolve; standing before us now, thin, worn, and famished, but erect, and with eyes looking level into ours . . . was not such manhood to be welcomed back into a Union so tested and so assured?

Within a month after Appomattox, General Joseph Johnston and the other Confederate armies surrendered. The long, bitter struggle was over.

BEHIND THE LINES

At first both North and South relied on volunteers to fill the ranks of their armies, but before long both resorted to conscription. The Confederacy, with less than a third the population of the North, started drafting men in April 1862. In March 1863, the United States Congress passed a Conscription Act that provided for an incomplete and unfair use of the draft. A draftee was permitted to avoid military service by paying $300 or by hiring a substitute. Naturally, those without money to buy their way out resented this arrangement, which made it "a rich man's war and a poor man's fight." Opposition to conscription caused the terrible draft riots in New York City in July 1863. For four days, mobs of men and boys terrorized the city, killing and plundering.

Besides the draft, the North also used a system whereby enlistees were paid a lump sum when they joined the army. Bounties offered by federal, state, and municipal governments sometimes totaled $1,500 for a single three-year enlistment. This led to the practice of "bounty-jumping," whereby a man would enlist, collect his bounty, and then desert only to re-enlist elsewhere. Nevertheless, bounties proved an effective means of luring volunteers from northern farms and factories and even from Europe.

President Lincoln at first resisted appeals to open the ranks of the Union armies to Negroes, on the grounds that such a move would be resented in the border states and might promote a slave insurrection in the South. Later the policy was changed, and nearly 200,000 Negroes, both freemen from the North and former slaves from the South, enlisted for military service. In addition, 150,000 Negroes served in the quartermaster and engineering corps. Some regiments of the "United States Colored Troops" distinguished themselves in combat, and 22 Negroes won the Congressional Medal of Honor.

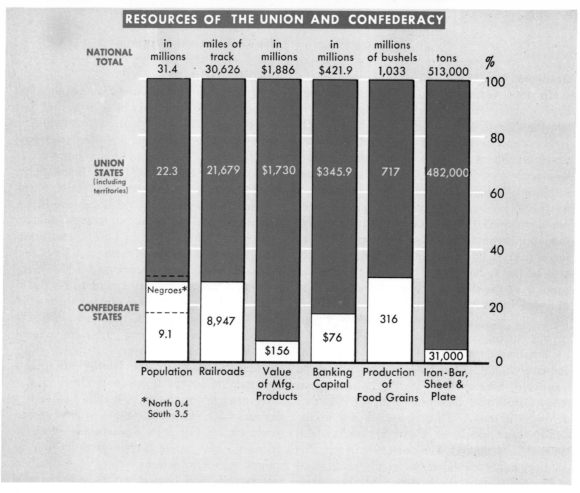

RESOURCES OF THE UNION AND CONFEDERACY							
NATIONAL TOTAL	in millions 31.4	miles of track 30,626	in millions $1,886	in millions $421.9	millions of bushels 1,033	tons 513,000	%
UNION STATES (including territories)	22.3	21,679	$1,730	$345.9	717	482,000	100 80 60 40 20 0
CONFEDERATE STATES	Negroes* 9.1	8,947	$156	$76	316	31,000	
	Population	Railroads	Value of Mfg. Products	Banking Capital	Production of Food Grains	Iron-Bar, Sheet & Plate	

*North 0.4
South 3.5

The South was greatly inferior to the North in things that make up the sinews of war: labor power and economic resources. Do these comparisons explain the southern defeat? What other statistics might help?

The Battle of Production

In a prolonged war on a vast scale, campaigns are decided as much behind the lines as on the battlefield. The Confederacy was defeated largely by its weakness in production. Through extraordinary efforts the South managed to supply its armies with sufficient arms and ammunition, but lacked the means to provide other necessities. "The great majority of desertions," says a southern historian, ". . . were caused by the hardships of military service— inferior food and clothing, a shocking lack of sanitation in the camps, the almost worthless wages the soldiers received."

The efforts of the federal government to supply the Union armies were too often marked by shocking profiteering and swindling. Army contractors sometimes supplied "clothing that would dissolve in a heavy rainstorm, sugar that would not dissolve in boiling coffee, meat that had to be swallowed in lumps, and shoes not quite so tough." But the productivity of northern factories was so great that in spite of the graft, the Union armies were usually as well equipped as any in the world. Northern farmers, using the newest farm machinery to make up for loss of labor power, not only supplied the wants of civilians and soldiers, but produced surpluses that were sold abroad. "King Wheat," it was said, defeated "King Cotton."

Finances and Taxation

The Confederacy was less able to finance a war than the North. It had intended to get money by selling cotton in Europe; when the Union blockade prevented this, bankruptcy was inevitable. The Confederate and southern state governments, like the United States in the Revolution, simply ran the printing presses. They issued billions of dollars in paper money that eventually became worthless. The Confederate government was able to keep going only by forcing civilians to accept its worthless currency in exchange for goods, and by collecting taxes in produce instead of money.

The North, with far greater resources of every kind—western mines, foreign markets, more capital to begin with—was far more successful in financing the war. About a quarter of the four billion dollars needed came from taxation, the rest from borrowing and issuing paper money. For the first time, Congress levied an income tax, which eventually amounted to 5 per cent on incomes from $600 to $5,000 and 10 per cent on incomes over that. In addition, excise taxes were levied on almost every conceivable article, such as food, tobacco, clothing, alcoholic beverages, and railroad tickets. Finally, there was a great increase in the protective tariff. The Republican platform of 1860 had promised higher duties; even before the war started, the tariff was raised by the Morrill Act of 1861. Other acts pushed duties still higher until by 1864 they averaged 47 per cent, the highest level yet. Although the wartime tariffs brought in revenue, their principal purpose was to encourage American manufacturers to greater production, so that the army would not be dependent on imports from other countries.

During the war the federal government issued over two and a half billion dollars' worth of bonds. Like the Confederacy, it also inflated the currency, but not to the same degree. This was done by issuing about four hundred million dollars' worth of "greenbacks"—paper money not backed by gold and silver. These fluctuated in value according to the success or failure of the Union armies; at their lowest point they were worth about 35 cents in gold. Such inflation was in effect a forced loan from all people who used greenbacks as currency. To encourage the sale of bonds and provide a better currency, Congress in 1863 passed the National Banking Act. This law did not get into full operation during the war and will therefore be treated later.

New Fields for Women

The importance of activity behind the lines was shown by the entrance of women into new fields. In the South they often ran plantations after the owners and overseers left for the front. They produced goods for the army, especially clothing. "Every household," wrote a southern girl, "now became a miniature factory in itself, with its cotton, cards, spinning wheels, warping-frames, looms, and so on." In the North the mechanical reaper and the "sulky" plow (in which the plowman rode the plow itself) enabled women to take the place of sons and husbands in the service.

On both sides, women took over much of the nursing, a task formerly reserved for men. Dorothea Dix turned from her work with the insane to offer her services to the federal government. As superintendent of female nurses, she fought red tape, corruption, and prejudice against her sex. Even more effective than Miss Dix in widening the sphere of women in hospital work was Clara Barton, later first president of the American Red Cross. Women also played a large part in our first great private relief organization—the United States Sanitary Commission. This organization collected millions of dollars for projects to improve the living

Clara Barton and the American Red Cross

When Clara Barton was a girl growing up in Massachusetts, her mother was so worried about her extreme shyness that she went for advice to a man who practised the new-fangled "science" of phrenology. After duly feeling the bumps and depressions on Clara Barton's head, he gave this advice: "Throw responsibility on her. As soon as her age will permit, give her a school to teach." So at the age of fifteen Clara was put to teaching school. The cure worked, and she was an immediate success.

After teaching for twenty years, Clara Barton started working for the Patent Office in Washington. Shortly after the Civil War broke out, the Sixth Massachusetts Regiment had to fight its way through Baltimore (where Confederate sympathies were strong) on the way to the capital. They arrived without most of their baggage. Clara Barton saw to it that they were supplied, and this launched her on a new career. By advertising in the newspapers, by badgering officials, and by not taking no for an answer, this small woman with slight build, prominent nose, and flashing brown eyes saw to it that medical supplies and nursing were available to the wounded. She often nursed the men herself.

Clara Barton's services to the suffering continued long after the Civil War. She alleviated the suffering of civilians in the Franco-Prussian War of 1870. She persuaded a reluctant United States Senate, fearful of "foreign entanglements," to ratify a treaty whereby the United States joined the International Red Cross. As president of the American branch, she saw that the organization helped not only victims of war, but also those of natural disasters, such as floods, epidemics, and famines. In all these activities she showed what a determined and selfless person could do, even in fields not considered "ladylike" at the time.

---

conditions of Union soldiers. Much of the money came from big sales, known as "sanitary fairs," organized almost entirely by women. It is no wonder that after the war there was a renewed demand that women, along with Negroes, be given the right to vote.

GOVERNMENT IN WARTIME

During the Civil War the authority of the central governments in both North and South was beyond anything the country had yet seen. The two Presidents, Lincoln and Davis, exerted so much power that both were accused by their own people of acting as dictators. Although founded on the principle of states' rights, the Confederate government assumed immense authority, not only in drafting men for military service, but in forcing citizens to give up mules,

slaves, wagons, and foodstuffs for the armies. The Union government controlled its people less than the Confederacy, but nevertheless exerted several new powers. Telegraph lines and railroads near the war zones, for instance, were sometimes taken over from private owners and run by the government.

Lincoln's Use of Presidential Power

Although devoted to the Constitution, Lincoln extended the power of the presidency beyond anything ever dreamed of by "King Andrew" Jackson. During the three-month interval between the fall of Fort Sumter and the opening of a special session of Congress in July 1861, he performed actions normally reserved to Congress. He called out volunteers, expanded the regular army, and spent money that had not yet been appropriated.

In 1861 there appeared to be a real danger that Maryland would secede from the Union and Washington would thereby be isolated in the midst of Confederate territory. Even in New York City there was talk of secession, led by Mayor Fernando Wood. The Lincoln administration quelled the opposition by means that clearly violated constitutional guarantees of freedom. Hundreds of suspected Confederate sympathizers were jailed without trial and without the right of *habeas corpus;* opposition newspapers were denied the use of the mails or shut down by troops; the Maryland legislature was prevented from sitting. From 1862 on, such repression was less severe, but so-called "Copperheads" were subject to arbitrary arrest and imprisonment. Forming a secret society, the Knights of the Golden Circle, the Copperheads hindered the war effort by discouraging enlistments and helping Union soldiers to desert. In dealing with alleged Copperheads, Lincoln authorized the trial of civilians by military courts and suspended the writ of *habeas corpus* in areas where pro-Confederate sympathies were strong.

QUESTION • *During the war, Georgia threatened to secede from the Confederacy. What might have been the ultimate effects of "states' rights" on the Confederacy had it survived the war?*

Ex Parte Milligan, 1866

In deciding the case *ex parte Milligan* in 1866, the Supreme Court condemned Lincoln's use of military courts to try civilians. Milligan was a Copperhead condemned to death by a military court in Indiana. The Supreme Court pointed out that Milligan had been living in a peaceful area where regular courts were operating and had been denied trial by jury. It denied that war justified the ignoring of rights guaranteed to the individual by the Constitution:

. . . it is the birthright of every American citizen when charged with crime, to be tried and punished according to law. . . . By the protection of law human rights are secured; withdraw that protection, and they are at the mercy of wicked rulers, or the clamor of an excited people.

Although Lincoln agonized over the fact that he denied citizens of the United States their rights and sometimes moderated the actions of overzealous subordinates, he defended his course of action. When federal law was being violated with the purpose of destroying the Union, the President thought that the law of survival overrode the Constitution. "Are all the laws but one to go unexecuted," he asked, "and the Government go to pieces lest that one be violated?" Must he shoot a simple-minded soldier who deserted and not touch a hair of "a wily agitator" who persuaded him? He wrote a friend in 1864:

By general law, a limb must be amputated to save a life, but a life is never wisely given to save a limb. I felt that measures, otherwise unconstitutional, might become lawful by becoming indispensable to the preservation of the Constitution through the preservation of the nation.

Lincoln found a basis for acting independently of Congress and the federal courts because, by the Constitution, the President is "Commander in Chief of the Army and Navy." The constitutional procedures of Congress and the courts are slow, yet war demands quick action. Lincoln's tendency, therefore, was to act on his own authority, although he sometimes asked Congress to approve his actions later.

It is still a matter for serious discussion as to whether it was wise or just for Lincoln to exceed his constitutional powers. He created dangerous precedents, but he certainly had no lust for power and no desire to make himself a dictator in the modern sense. He made no attempt to reduce congressmen to puppets nor to rivet himself in power by building up a

The effects of the burdens of the presidency are graphically shown in these two pictures taken just five years apart. The picture on the left shows Lincoln at the time of his nomination for the presidency in 1860, and the one on the right was taken shortly before his assassination in 1865. Most Presidents of the United States have felt the grueling pace of the demands of the office.

militaristic organization of his followers. "The Constitution was stretched," said the historian J. G. Randall, "but not subverted."

WARTIME DIPLOMACY

In no field was Lincoln apparently less fitted for the job of President than in foreign affairs. He had never been abroad and knew no foreign language; there was every reason to agree with Lord Lyons, British minister to Washington, who predicted that Lincoln would be fatally handicapped by "his ignorance of everything but Illinois village politics." Yet in diplomacy, as in other fields, he confounded those who expected him to fail.

Although the spoils system forced him to hand out diplomatic posts as political plums, Lincoln's major appointments were good.

Seward was a brilliant Secretary of State, whose occasional tendency to rashness was tempered by Lincoln's sober judgment. The key position abroad, minister to England, was held by Charles Francis Adams, the son and grandson of Presidents of the United States, both of whom had also represented this country in London. Adams knew how to be reasonable without conceding American rights, to be firm without giving offense. Understanding the importance of foreign public opinion, Lincoln sent abroad a number of unofficial "good will ambassadors." An Episcopalian bishop from Ohio worked among British clergymen; a Catholic archbishop from New York presented the case of the Union in Catholic countries; Henry Ward Beecher, a famous American preacher, addressed large audiences in England; and a former Secretary of the Treasury used his friendships with European financiers to create distrust of Confederate bonds. Above all, Lincoln succeeded in foreign affairs because he kept his head and understood how to present the cause of the Union in ways that had wide appeal. "One war at a time!" he used to say to followers who were so angry at Britain they were willing to risk hostilities.

The principal task of United States diplomacy during the Civil War was to prevent Britain from giving aid to the Confederacy. The South confidently expected such aid because of British need for her cotton. Furthermore, the British upper classes feared American democracy as a standing rebuke to their privileged position, and they would have been glad to see the disintegration of the world's largest republic. British manufacturers expected that an independent South would be a better market for their goods. Lacking industry, the new nation would be unlikely to levy protective tariffs; indeed, they were forbidden by the Confederate Constitution.

The Trent Affair

In November 1861, an incident brought Great Britain and the United States to the verge of war. A United States warship, cruising the Caribbean, stopped a British steamer, the *Trent*, and took off two Confederate diplomats, James Mason and John Slidell. The action caused rejoicing in the victory-starved North, and Congress voted the captain of the vessel a gold medal. But American joy was matched by a wave of anger in Great Britain. The British government demanded the release of Mason and Slidell; it sent troops to Canada and ordered the British fleet to prepare to go to sea. Lincoln and Seward had to choose between facing a wave of indignation in America if they let the diplomats go or the disaster of war with the strongest naval power in the world if they refused. Fortunately, the recently laid Atlantic cable broke down at this moment and so slowed communications that popular clamor on both sides of the ocean died down. Seward released Mason and Slidell. He sweetened the bitter pill by remarking that he was glad to see Britain defending the rights of neutral ships as the United States had done in 1812.

Britain and the Civil War

Charles Francis Adams compared the *Trent* affair to a sharp storm that cleared the air. It became evident that forces pushing Britain to aid the South were balanced by others making for a policy of neutrality. Although British cotton mills eventually suffered from the cotton famine caused by the blockade of the Confederacy, they carried on for some time with surpluses in British warehouses and then made up much of the deficit from other sources, such as Egypt and India. Meanwhile, the British were making money by selling war materials to the North, and during two or three bad harvests at home they became dependent on American wheat. Upper-class sympathy for the South was balanced by the fact that the middle and lower classes favored the North. Many who wished to see England become more democratic agreed with Lincoln that the war was a test of democracy. They were not wholly on the Union side, however, until it was clear that the United States was fighting to abolish slavery. Once Lincoln issued the Emancipation Proclamation (see p. 362) there was no further danger that the British government would help the South.

QUESTION • Bismarck, chancellor of the German Empire, once remarked that Europe made a serious mistake in permitting the North to preserve the Union. What did he mean?

A remaining source of friction between England and the U.S. arose from the efforts of Confederate agents to buy warships in Britain. Several cruisers were sold to the Confederate navy and left British ports for highly successful careers as commerce destroyers. An even greater threat were the "Laird rams," built in a famous British shipyard and designed for the sole purpose of breaking the Union blockade. Hearing that these ships were ready to sail, Charles Francis Adams bombarded Lord John Russell, British foreign minister, with protests, one of which contained the celebrated remark, "I need not remind your Lordship that this is war." At the last moment the British government bought the rams for its own navy.

Britain's refusal to give active aid to the Confederacy persuaded France to remain neutral. Napoleon III, the French emperor, was eager to aid the South, but not without British cooperation. Yet, as we shall see, he used the war as an opportunity to establish a government under his control in Mexico.

SLAVERY AND THE CIVIL WAR

When the Civil War began, there was surprisingly little opinion in the North that it would mean the end of slavery. Lincoln himself was, as we have seen, no abolitionist. He regarded slavery as a moral wrong and a disaster for both Negroes and whites, but as a lawyer he recognized the constitutional guarantees of the institution. He was careful to reassure the South on this point, saying that he had "no purpose, directly or indirectly, to interfere with the institution of slavery where it now exists." When Union generals freed slaves who had drifted into military posts, Lincoln overruled them. Had he not acted in this way, the northern tier of border states, especially Kentucky, might have joined the Confederacy.

Lincoln declared again and again that his "paramount object" was "to save the Union . . . *not* either to save or destroy slavery." But why pin the Union back together with bayonets at frightful cost in money and blood? One answer

is easy: patriotism. In the eighty-odd years since the Americans had declared themselves "one people," preservation of the Union had become a cause for which people were willing to give their lives. Lincoln maintained also that the struggle to save the Union was of world-wide importance as a test of whether large-scale democracy could "long endure." (Reread the quotation at the head of this chapter.)

The Emancipation Proclamation, 1863

As time passed, Lincoln came under increasing pressure to turn the war into an abolitionist crusade. There was a strong desire to punish the slaveholders of the South and an increasing conviction that the war was worth fighting only if it destroyed an institution that was a complete violation of the principles that America was supposed to stand for. Another compelling reason for emancipation was the need to win foreign support. Public opinion in Europe was so strongly opposed to slavery that if the North was fighting to abolish it, no European government would dare to aid the Confederacy. After Lee's defeat at Antietam in 1862, Lincoln announced that he would free the slaves of the Confederacy at the start of the next year. On January 1, 1863, he issued the famous Emancipation Proclamation, acting under his authority as Commander in Chief. This document did not immediately free a single slave, since it applied only to those areas behind Confederate lines. An English editor remarked that the principle behind it "is not that a human being cannot justly own another, but that he cannot own him unless he is loyal to the United States." Even so, the Emancipation Proclamation changed the entire character of the war. From that time on, Union armies were fighting to end human bondage. In a mysterious way the black people came to know of it, and whenever northern armies occupied southern territory, runaways poured into the Union lines.

Scene in the House of Representatives, January 31, 1865, on the announcement of the passage of the Thirteenth Amendment to the Constitution, abolishing slavery in the United States. The report in *The New York Daily Tribune* described the scene: "The tumult of joy that broke out was vast, thundering, and uncontrollable . . . [for] the most august and important event in American Legislation and American History since the Declaration of Independence. God Bless the XXXVIIIth Congress! . . ."

The Thirteenth Amendment, 1865

There still remained the problem of slavery in the areas where the Emancipation Proclamation did not apply—the border states and those portions of the Confederacy already conquered by Union armies. To deal with them, Lincoln recommended a policy of compensated emancipation—setting the slaves free, but paying their owners for them. This scheme was applied only in the District of Columbia. Elsewhere slavery was abolished by the Thirteenth Amendment to the Constitution, ratified in 1865. Thus a war begun simply to save the Union ended as a victory for the abolitionists.

LINCOLN FACES THE PEACE

In the presidential election of 1864, Lincoln was renominated by his party, which temporarily changed its name from Republican to Unionist to attract all who supported the war. The Democrats nominated George B. McClellan, a popular general who had twice been removed from command by Lincoln. They drew up a platform which denounced the war effort as a failure, but made no suggestion that the Confederate states be allowed to leave the Union. Although at one time Lincoln's defeat was expected, Sherman's taking of Atlanta in-

Lincoln was greatly loved and greatly hated. This cartoon shows Lincoln nonchalantly telling jokes to his cabinet, while Fessenden, Secretary of the Treasury, grinds out greenbacks, Stanton celebrates a great victory — "the capture of one prisoner and one gun," and Welles says, "They say the Tallahasse sails 24 miles an hour! . . . Well then, we'll send 4 Gunboats after her that can sail 6 miles an hour, and that will just make enough to catch her."

sured a Unionist victory. By a narrow margin the voters decided, in Lincoln's homely phrase, that "it was not best to swap horses while crossing the river."

In the four years since the untried prairie lawyer delivered his First Inaugural, his stock had risen. In spite of violent attacks in Congress and in the press, he inspired affection and trust, as shown by the nicknames "Uncle Abe" and "Father Abraham." People of judgment had begun to appreciate the ability and strength of character hidden behind Lincoln's homely exterior. One of these was the novelist Nathaniel Hawthorne, who thus recorded his impressions:

There is no describing the lengthy awkwardness nor the uncouthness of his movement; and yet it seemed as if I had been in the habit of seeing him daily, and had shaken hands with him a thousand times in some village street. . . . If put to guess his calling and livelihood, I should have taken him for a country schoolmaster as soon as anything else. He was dressed in a rusty black frockcoat and pantaloons, unbrushed, and worn so faithfully that the suit had adapted itself to the curves and angularities of his figure. . . . He had shabby slippers on his feet. His hair was black, still unmixed with gray, stiff, somewhat bushy, and had apparently been

acquainted with neither brush nor comb that morning . . . on the whole I like this sallow, queer, sagacious visage, with the homely human sympathies that warmed it; and, for my small share in the matter, would as lief have Uncle Abe for a ruler as any man whom it would have been practicable to put in his place.

Second Inaugural Address

In his Second Inaugural Address, Lincoln reviewed the causes of the war and looked forward to the peace. When he first took office, "all thoughts were anxiously directed to an impending civil war. All dreaded it, all sought to avert it." Yet war broke out. Why? Because, said the President, "One side would *make* war rather than let the nation survive, and the other would *accept* war rather than let it perish." Behind these attitudes was slavery, which the South wished to "strengthen, perpetuate, and extend," while the North wanted to restrict its spread.

Although Lincoln believed slavery wrong, he never privately or publicly expressed hatred of the slaveholders themselves. In the Second Inaugural, he pointed out that both sides "read the same Bible and pray to the same God."

Slaveowners may seem to be violating man's God-given right to freedom, "but let us judge not that we be not judged." It may be, said Lincoln, that the war was a divine vengeance on both North and South for two centuries of wrongs to the Negroes. Lincoln concluded his short address by urging that "with malice toward none, with charity for all," Americans should work to "bind up the nation's wounds," and "do all which may achieve and cherish a just and lasting peace among ourselves and with all nations."

Lincoln's charity extended to the defeated South. He directed his generals to offer Confederate armies liberal terms of surrender. When a crowd with a brass band appeared to cheer him after the fall of Richmond, he asked the musicians to strike up "Dixie," which, he said, was "now contraband of war." He had already made plans to bring the Confederate states back into the Union as soon as possible.

Lincoln's Assassination

On the night of April 14, 1865, five days after Appomattox, Lincoln was assassinated by a fanatical Confederate sympathizer, John Wilkes Booth. Booth's deed was a tragedy for both North and South because it removed the man best fitted to "bind up the nation's wounds."

After Lincoln's death, many who had scorned and ridiculed him changed their minds. One of the most dramatic of these conversions was that of the British humor magazine *Punch*, which had published cartoons showing the American President as "a bearded ruffian, vulgar charlatan, and repulsive beast." Yet after his assassination a poem in *Punch* paid him this tribute:

> Yes, he had lived to shame me from my sneer,
> To lame my pencil, and confute my pen—
> To make me own this kind of princes peer,
> This rail-splitter a true-born prince of men.

HOW TO DEAL WITH THE DEFEATED SOUTH?

When Confederate veterans—tired, ragged, and hungry—went home at the end of the Civil War, they returned to a ruined land. The region through which Sherman had marched "looked for many miles like a broad, black streak of ruin and desolation—the fences all gone; lonesome smoke stacks, surrounded by dark heaps of ashes and cinders, marking the spots where human habitations had stood." In addition to physical damage the South suffered profound dislocation of its economic life. Confederate money was worthless. Southern banks, which had done business in this currency and invested in Confederate bonds, were ruined. With the freeing of the slaves the plantation system broke down. Thousands of freedmen were on the move, possessed with the natural idea that the end of slavery meant "the day of jubilee" and no more work. Some wandered west because they heard wonderful stories of easy living out there, with hogs lying around "already baked with the knives and forks sticking in them and fritter ponds everywhere with fritters a-fryin' in them, ponds of grease and money trees." Even the many freed slaves seeking work could often not find it, because landowners had no means to pay them, and the Negroes had no means to acquire land. The disorganization of southern agriculture was so great that in 1866 the production of cotton was only half that of 1860.

Lincoln and Reconstruction

The term "reconstruction" might logically be applied to the effort to deal with such southern problems as war damage, lack of credit, and the changeover from slave labor to free. In the years 1865 to 1877, however, reconstruction referred principally to two political problems: on what terms should the southern states be readmitted to the Union, and what should be the political rights of the newly freed Negroes?

Before he died, Lincoln had turned his attention to reconstruction. As his Second Inaugural Address showed, he favored a generous policy. In order to get some sort of working arrangement as soon as possible, he proposed to readmit Confederate states to the Union when 10 per cent of the voters of 1860 signed a loyalty oath. As to the freed Negroes, Lincoln's favorite solution was the wholly impractical idea that they should be colonized in Africa and the Caribbean. He even supported an ill-starred attempt to colonize freedmen in Haiti. Meanwhile, he helped to push the Thirteenth Amendment through Congress so that all Negroes would be free. Beyond that he was willing to let Southerners work out the details of the transition from bondage to freedom, although he urged that literate freedmen and those who had served in the Union army be granted the franchise.

QUESTION • *If Lincoln had lived to complete his second term, would he enjoy as high a reputation as he does now?*

Lincoln's lenient policy toward the South was opposed by the so-called Radical Republicans, who had the support of the majority in Congress. The Radicals did not share Lincoln's belief that Southerners could immediately be trusted with defining the status of the Negroes or that effective, loyal state governments could be based on 10 per cent of the male population. In any case, they believed that it was for Congress rather than the President to determine reconstruction policies. They embodied their opinions in the Wade-Davis Bill of 1864, which provided for much more rigorous conditions for readmitting the rebellious states to the Union. When Lincoln killed the bill by a pocket veto, its authors attacked him in a widely published "manifesto." Accusing the President of a "studied outrage on the legislative authority of the people," the Wade-Davis Manifesto demanded that he "confine himself to his executive duties . . . and leave political organization to Congress." Had Lincoln lived, Congress might well have prevented him from arranging a peace based on "malice toward none" and "charity for all."

Andrew Johnson's Policies

Andrew Johnson, who succeeded to the presidency on Lincoln's death, attempted to carry out his predecessor's policies so far as he understood them, but he was seriously handicapped. As "President by accident" he commanded little popular following, and as a former Democrat he could not command the support of the Republican majority in Congress. A Tennessean who had once owned slaves, he thought that Negroes were by nature inferior to whites. Although able and courageous, Johnson was self-righteous, too apt to lose his temper, and stubborn where Lincoln had been flexible.

In the summer of 1865, Johnson encouraged the southern states to form new state governments. Each state was required to abolish slavery, repeal its ordinance of secession, and repudiate debts incurred in the war. There was general compliance with these terms. The South appeared to be heeding the advice of its most respected leader, Robert E. Lee, who said, "The war being at an end . . . I believe it the duty of every one to unite in the restoration of the country and the re-establishment of peace and harmony."

When it came to the status of the Negro, however, the new governments acted on the principle stated by the governor of Mississippi: "Ours is and ever shall be a government of white men." While Negroes were given the right to own property, to marry within their own race, and to secure protection of the laws, they were nowhere allowed to serve on juries or to vote. No state made provision for Negro schools. In addition to denying freed slaves many of the rights of citizens, southern legislatures passed special laws known as "Black Codes" to keep them under control. These laws obliged Negroes to make long-term contracts with employers; those without steady jobs might be arrested as vagrants and their labor sold to the highest bidder. Sometimes they were even bound over to work for their former masters. The new South apparently intended the Negro to be "an illiterate, unskilled, propertyless, agricultural worker."

Even some Southerners thought it a blunder to go as far as did the new state constitutions and the Black Codes in placing Negroes in an inferior caste. President Johnson was at fault, too, in not making southern leaders realize that they must accept the fact of defeat and grant more than token rights to Negroes. How little the former Confederacy had "repented" secession was revealed in the congressional elections, when most of the men chosen were former Confederate leaders. President Johnson accepted these results, but when the Republican-dominated Congress met in December 1865, it refused to seat the men elected from the South. Insisting that Congress rather than the President had the right and duty to define the terms of readmission of the southern states, congressional leaders formed a Joint Committee on Reconstruction, composed of members of both houses. The Joint Committee drew up bills providing for economic assistance to freed slaves and for federal protection of their rights. These were duly passed and presented to Johnson for his signature. The President vetoed them. He thus antagonized moderate Republicans, and leadership in reconstruction passed to the Radicals.

The Library of Congress

Richmond in ruins after Union capture. The Civil War was "total" war: civilian centers were bombarded and fired, and the countryside was pillaged and wrecked.

RADICAL RECONSTRUCTION

The Radical Republicans included men inspired by both self-interest and idealism, by desire for partisan advantage, and by genuine concern for the Negroes. Certainly, one of their motives was to keep the Republican party in power. If the southern states were readmitted to the Union immediately, and with Negroes disfranchised, they would probably support the Democratic party, as in 1856 and 1860, and enable it to regain power. To prevent this, the Radicals insisted that Negroes be given the right to vote and that former Confederate leaders be barred from politics. Supporting the Radicals in their effort to keep control of the national government were northern industrialists and

Thaddeus Stevens' harsh features suggest something of the implacable hatred he felt for the former slaveowners. He proposed to divide their land among the freed people, thus giving the blacks the economic independence that they desperately needed.

bankers, who feared that the Democrats might lower the tariff, pay off Union bonds with cheap money (by issuing large amounts of paper money, see p. 357), or destroy the national banking system that was set up during the Civil War. The cause of the Radicals was strong because they appealed to the principles of the Declaration of Independence: that people had a natural right to equality and that government must rest on consent of the governed. Senator Henry Wilson of Massachusetts said:

[Congress] must see to it that the man made free by the Constitution is a freeman indeed; that he can go where he pleases, work when and for whom he pleases . . . go into the schools and educate himself and his children; that the rights and guarantees of the common law are his, and that he walks the earth proud and erect in the conscious dignity of a free man.

Congressional Elections of 1866: The "Bloody Shirt"

In the congressional elections of 1866, the President and the Radical Republicans campaigned against each other. Johnson hurt his cause by rambling, intemperate, bitter speeches. His opponents made effective use of a technique that came to be known as "waving the bloody shirt." This consisted in deliberately stirring up war hatreds and appealing to bitter memories of carnage and of the suffering of Union prisoners in southern prison camps. There were many Northerners who felt that the South should not be readmitted to the Union until it had been further punished and had shown itself repentant for the sins of slavery and secession. "Bloody shirt" oratory equated Democrats and traitors:

Every unregenerate rebel . . . every deserter, every sneak who ran away from the draft calls himself a Democrat. . . . Every man who labored for the rebellion in the field, who murdered Union prisoners by cruelty and starvation . . . calls himself a Democrat. Every wolf in sheep's clothing who pretends to preach the gospel but proclaims the righteousness of man-selling and slavery . . . calls himself a Democrat.

The elections of 1866 resulted in a sweeping victory for the Radicals, who could now claim that they had a mandate from the people to put through their own version of reconstruction.

The principal Radical leader was Thaddeus Stevens, congressman from Pennsylvania, who insisted that the southern states were "conquered provinces." He was determined to punish the "slaveocrats" whom he held responsible for the Civil War. He would not execute them all, he said, "but surely *some* victims must propitiate the names of our starved, murdered, slaughtered martyrs." Stevens proposed that the land of former slaveholders be confiscated and parceled out among the freed people. Congress did not go all the way with Stevens, but in 1867

Radical Attacks on the Federal Courts and the Presidency

To push through their reconstruction program, the Radicals in Congress attempted to reduce both the judicial and executive departments to a subordinate position. Had they had their way, they might have destroyed the system of checks and balances and given Congress the omnipotent position enjoyed by the British Parliament. Fearing that the Supreme Court would apply the principles of *ex parte Milligan* to military courts in the South, Congress forbade appeals to that body in any cases arising under the Reconstruction Acts of 1867. To prevent Johnson from appointing justices to the Supreme Court, Congress provided that whenever a justice died or resigned he was not to be replaced. Thus the court actually dropped from nine members to eight.

Above all, the Radicals were determined to get rid of Johnson. In order to reduce the President's power of appointment, Congress in 1867 passed the Tenure of Office Act. It provided that the President might not remove important civil servants from office without senatorial permission; if he did so, he was declared guilty of a "high misdemeanor." Believing the law unconstitutional, Johnson demanded the resignation of Edwin M. Stanton, Secretary of War, in February 1868.

Immediately, the President was impeached by the House of Representatives, and brought to trial before the Senate, amid intense public excitement. After a trial lasting over two months, the Senate voted 35 to 19 that Johnson was guilty of "high crimes and misdemeanors" (see Article II, section 4, p. 128). Since this was one vote short of the two-thirds majority necessary for conviction (Article I, Section 3, clause 6), Johnson was acquitted and completed his term as President. This came about because seven Republican senators could not honestly find evidence that Johnson was guilty. Under every

The sergeant-at-arms of the Senate serving the summons of impeachment on Johnson. This was a bold attempt to remove a President for political reasons and make Congress all-powerful. This would have altered the American constitutional system of checks and balances.

sort of pressure they stood firm in refusing to put their party above the Constitution. One of them explained his actions as follows:

It is not a party question I am to decide. I must be governed by what my reason and judgment tell me is the truth and the justice and the law of this case. . . . Once set the example of impeaching a President for what, when the excitement of the hour shall have subsided, will be regarded as insufficient causes, and no future President will be safe who happens to differ with a majority of the House and two thirds of the Senate . . . what then becomes of the checks and balances of the Constitution so carefully devised and so vital to its perpetuity? They are all gone.

At one time during the Reconstruction period the majority the South Carolina legislators were black. Here Robert B. Elliot argues eloquently for laws that will protect the civil rights of black people—the right to use all public facilities, such as railroads, restaurants, and theaters on the same terms as whites.

The Election of 1868

As the presidential election of 1868 approached, the Republicans sought a candidate who could sweep the country and keep them in power. They found such a person in General Grant. Before the war Grant had been a Democrat. After Appomattox he appeared to share the Lincoln-Johnson attitude toward the South, and joined forces with the Radicals only after a quarrel with Johnson. Opposing Grant as Democratic candidate was Horatio Seymour, former governor of New York. The Democratic platform condemned the Radical reconstruction plans, reduction of the power of the federal courts, and Johnson's impeachment. Only Grant's popularity as a war hero kept the Democrats from victory. Although the vote in the electoral college stood 214 for Grant to 80 for Seymour, a small shift in the popular vote in key states would have given Seymour the election. Grant won only because he was supported by the carpetbag governments of the South and because three southern states had not yet been readmitted to the Union. It is no wonder, therefore, that throughout Grant's administration troops were stationed in the South.

RADICAL RECONSTRUCTION
ON THE WANE

Southern whites at first put up little resistance to Radical reconstruction. Weary from the war, they were preoccupied with the business of merely keeping alive amid the general poverty. But there were many "unreconstructed rebels" who were not disposed to follow General Lee's advice to let bygones be bygones. Instead, their attitude was that of a song of the period, "Good Old Rebel," of which one verse went:

> I hate that Yankee nation,
> And all they say and do.
> I hate the Declaration
> Of Independence too.

Unable to strike openly at the federal government, they organized secret, terrorist societies, of which the most important was the Ku Klux Klan. Hooded, white-robed Klansmen, riding in bands at night, intimidated carpetbaggers, teachers in the new Negro schools, and above all the Negroes themselves. The Klan was quite willing to use violence to back up its threats. Although it was finally suppressed by federal authority, it and other similar organizations frightened many Negroes away from the polls and contributed to the re-establishment of governments opposed to the Radicals. The so-called "Conservatives" gained control of one southern state after another, until by 1876 only South Carolina, Florida, and Louisiana had not been restored to "home rule."

One reason for these southern successes was that the North was becoming weary of Radical reconstruction. In 1872 a group called the "Liberal Republicans," including some of the best men in the Republican party, refused to support Grant for re-election because they thought him unfit for the presidency (see p. 448), and because they opposed Radical reconstruction policies. They nominated Horace Greeley for President and the Democrats ratified the nomination. Although Grant was re-elected, the Liberal Republican attitude toward reconstruction became more and more widespread.

Disputed Election of 1876 and Compromise of 1877

The end of Radical reconstruction resulted from the presidential election of 1876. The Democratic candidate was Samuel J. Tilden, who had gained fame as a reform governor of New York; that of the Republicans was Rutherford B. Hayes, governor of Ohio, noted for his personal honesty. The Republicans continued to wave the bloody shirt, but it was losing effectiveness. The Democrats, on the other hand, effectively attacked both Radical reconstruction and the corruption which characterized Grant's administration.

As the first election returns came in, it appeared that Tilden had won. From the three states still under carpetbag rule, however, there were two sets of returns, one favoring the Democrats and the other the Republicans. One of Oregon's electoral votes was also disputed because of a technicality. If Hayes could get *every single one* of the twenty disputed electoral votes, he would carry the election by 185 electoral votes to 184. There was nothing in the Constitution to show how to settle such a controversy. The Republicans were determined to retain the control of the presidency which they had enjoyed for sixteen years. The Democrats were determined not to be defrauded. There were threats of civil war. Northern Democrats formed "rifle clubs," and a Kentucky editor called for 100,000 Democrats to invade Washington and prevent Hayes from "usurping" the presidency.

In the end, Hayes was chosen President. The decision was left to an electoral commission, chosen from the House, Senate, and Supreme Court, composed of eight Republicans and seven Democrats. By a strict party vote the commission awarded every disputed electoral vote to Hayes, and the Democrats peacefully accepted the result. The Democrats' willingness to allow Hayes to be inaugurated was the result of a compromise between Republican leaders and southern Democrats. It differed from previous arrangements such as the Missouri Compromise and the Compromise of 1850 in that it was largely secret and was not embodied in law.

Having suffered so much from war, Southerners were repelled by the northern Democrats' talk of using violence to put Tilden in the White House. They were willing to let Hayes assume the presidency in return for concessions. The most striking of these was the end of Radical reconstruction. This came about easily when the federal troops which protected the remaining carpetbag governments were withdrawn. Without soldiers to guard them, these governments collapsed, and the South was restored to "home rule." This meant the restoration of "white supremacy." Blacks played less and less part in politics, and in some southern states, schools for them were closed down.

Less important southern demands in the Compromise of 1877 were that Hayes appoint a Southerner to his cabinet as postmaster general; that more federal funds be appropriated for southern rivers, harbors, and railroads; and that the federal government help to finance a railroad from New Orleans to the Pacific Coast. Hayes and his advisers were willing to agree to all these requests in order to get the presidency, but for reasons mostly beyond their control they were unable to carry through their bargain completely.

The significance of the Compromise of 1877 was not simply that a threat of civil war had been averted, nor that the Republicans managed to stay in power by abandoning Radical reconstruction. The Compromise was also a temporary alliance between the conservative property interests of the North and South, somewhat like the former alliance of the propertied classes in the Federalist and Whig parties.

Results of Radical Reconstruction

The results of Radical reconstruction continued for many years. One of the most obvious was the "Solid South"—a block of former slave states dominated by the Democratic party. This did not begin to break up for nearly a century. The Solid South was a reflection of the bitterness created by Radical reconstruction. Southern whites agreed with Joel Chandler Harris (famous for his stories of "Uncle Remus"), who called it "a policy of lawlessness, under the forms of law, of disfranchisement, robbery, oppression, and fraud."

Radical reconstruction was of only temporary help to the Negroes whose rights it professed to defend. Abolitionist idealism waned, and too many professed Radicals were more interested in Negro votes than in the welfare of the freed people themselves. The Radicals took no long-range steps to provide what the freed people needed most—education and the opportunity to acquire property. They closed down the Freedmen's Bureau after only five years of operation, and they failed to support or follow up promising experiments in teaching Negroes to manage cotton plantations for themselves.

And yet, as the Black Codes revealed, without federal intervention emancipation for southern Negroes meant merely a change from slavery to peonage. Although immediate efforts to aid the Negroes failed, the Fourteenth and Fifteenth Amendments wrote the principle of equality for all persons into the Constitution of the United States. For many years they remained almost a dead letter, but in the twentieth century these constitutional provisions provide the legal basis and part of the inspiration for positive efforts to bring black people at long last into full enjoyment of their rights as citizens.

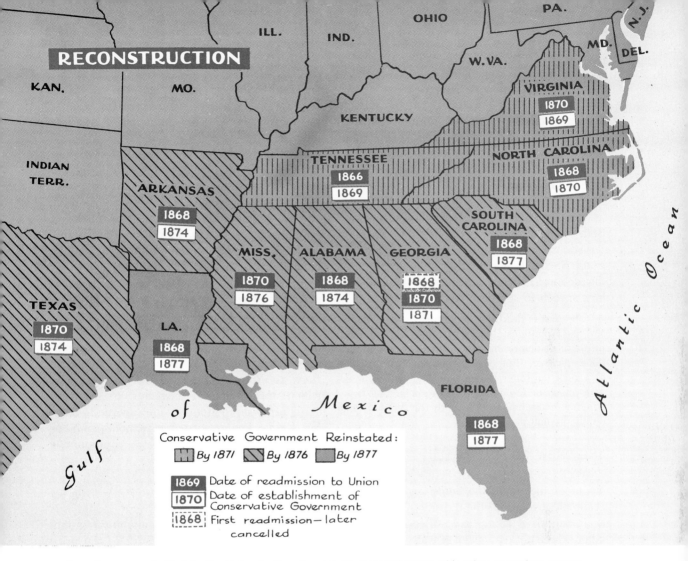

RECONSTRUCTION

KAN.

MO.

ILL.

IND.

OHIO

PA.

N.J.

MD.

DEL.

W. VA.

INDIAN
TERR.

KENTUCKY

VIRGINIA
1870
1869

ARKANSAS
1868
1874

TENNESSEE
1866
1869

NORTH CAROLINA
1868
1870

MISS.
1870
1876

ALABAMA
1868
1874

GEORGIA
1868
1870
1871

SOUTH
CAROLINA
1868
1877

TEXAS
1870
1874

LA.
1868
1877

FLORIDA
1868
1877

Atlantic Ocean

Gulf *of* *Mexico*

Conservative Government Reinstated:

| ||| By 1871 | \\\\ By 1876 | ▓ By 1877 |

1869 Date of readmission to Union

1870 Date of establishment of
Conservative Government

⌐1868¬ First readmission—later
cancelled

Georgia was readmitted to the Union in time to cast its electoral votes with other carpetbag governments for Grant. Later in 1868, military government was reimposed on the state because of irregular procedures in its new legislature. It was not readmitted until 1870, after ratifying the Fifteenth Amendment.

It is often forgotten that the South was treated more leniently than the losers in any great internal struggle of modern times. After events such as the French, Russian, and Chinese revolutions, the winning side executed many of the losers. After the Civil War the only people executed were those connected with the plot to assassinate Lincoln and the Confederate officer who ran Andersonville prison, where many Union soldiers died.

The fact that bloodshed ceased with the surrender helped to make it possible for conciliatory feeling to develop. In 1893 Woodrow Wilson, a Southerner, wrote, "The day of inevitable strife and permanent difference came to seem strangely remote." This reconciliation was promoted by a number of actions that had a profound effect on public opinion. When parts of the South were stricken by famine in 1866 and by yellow fever in 1878, large-scale relief came from the North to the stricken areas. Of more permanent importance were the gifts of northern philanthropists to promote education in the South, both Negro and white. The largest of these was made by George Peabody, a wealthy financier, who set up a permanent fund to encourage elementary school education in the South. "This I give to the suffering South," he said, "for the good of the whole country." Both General Grant and Admiral Farragut served as trustees of the Peabody Education Fund. Such acts of generosity helped to reunite the sections. The day came when Jefferson Davis in a speech to southern students said,

The past is dead; let it bury its dead, its hopes and its aspirations; before you lies the future, a future of golden promise, a future of expanding national glory.... Let me beseech you to lay aside all rancor, all bitter sectional feeling, and to make your place in the ranks of those who will bring about a consummation devoutly to be wished—a reunited country.

THE "NEW SOUTH"

While political reconstruction occupied the center of the stage, the South experienced an economic revolution—the transition from plantations and slave labor to small farms and free labor. Much of the damage of war was repaired, and the South turned again to raising cotton and tobacco.

Sharecropping and Tenancy

By 1870 the average size of southern farms was half what it had been in 1860. The large plantations were split up for a number of reasons. Their owners no longer owned slaves and lacked the money to hire day labor. Furthermore, the Negroes regarded working in gangs under any sort of continuous direction as a badge of slavery and preferred to be on their own. There were also many whites who wanted to own farms.

Few blacks or whites had the means to buy farms. Therefore many became tenants, paying for the use of the land either in cash or—more usually—by a share of the crop. This system of "sharecropping" had serious defects. The owners, often in debt themselves and anxious to get the maximum cash income from the land, put pressure on tenants not to do the wise thing and plant different kinds of crops, but to plant only cotton or tobacco. This exhausted the soil. It made the tenants more dependent on the landowners or local merchants from whom they bought—on credit—seed, fertilizer, draft animals, and food. They often ended each year deeper in debt.

In spite of its faults, tenant farming was perhaps an inevitable result of southern conditions. "Tenancy," wrote Paul H. Buck in *The Road to Reunion*, "seemed the only way by which the inefficient elements of southern agriculture—an ignorant, unpropertied labor force and a landowning class without capital or authority—could be fused into a productive combination."

Industrial Growth

In the postwar years, northern capital was of real help to the South only in providing money to build railroads; even here the price was steep. The building was often wasteful, and was over-rewarded in bonds and lands given away by corrupt carpetbag legislatures. Southern freight rates were higher than those in other parts of the country. Nevertheless, by 1890 the railroad mileage of the South was twice that of 1860, and the region had a better transportation system than ever before.

Other factors necessary for industrial "take-off" also began to appear in the South. (See p. 322.) Thoughtful Southerners had long realized that one of the great weaknesses of their region was the lack of manufacturing. By the late 1870's, however, there was increasing

The "New South"

As the southern economy recovered from the ravages of the Civil War, new industries appeared, as depicted by this steel mill in Birmingham, Alabama, and this sugar refinery in Louisiana, and people began to talk enthusiastically of the "new South." In fact, however, the region was still the least prosperous in the country and as much as ever dependent on one crop, cotton.

talk of the New South, of which a principal feature was industrial progress. Around Birmingham, Alabama, there developed a flourishing iron industry. In scores of small towns, especially along the "fall line" (see pp. 6–7), cotton mills appeared. The money for these factories was usually raised by Southerners themselves from their own slender resources of capital; such investment was often regarded as a public duty. Far from northern markets, paying high freight and interest rates, able to hire only unskilled labor, southern mills faced serious handicaps. The owners therefore felt forced to pay low wages, to hire child labor, and to work factory hands long hours.

With these developments in agriculture, transportation, and industry, the South gradually revived. By 1870 it was producing as much cotton as in 1860; by 1890 the yield had doubled again. By 1900 the manufactured products of the South were worth at least four times as much as in 1860. Great as these advances were, they did not match the agricultural and industrial growth elsewhere. The South remained the least prosperous section of the country.

FOREIGN AFFAIRS

Once the Confederacy had been defeated, the United States was brought face to face with problems in foreign affairs. Napoleon III had violated the principles of the Monroe Doctrine by setting up a monarchy in Mexico. How could he be forced out? Now that the slavery issue was buried, would the United States use its new military strength to expand its borders? The resentment which developed against Great Britain during the war remained intense. Could hostilities be avoided? It was fortunate that in meeting such problems the country had the services of two able Secretaries of State—William H. Seward, whom Johnson inherited from Lincoln, and Hamilton Fish, who served under

Grant. Their task was made easier by the respect abroad that the Union victory had gained for the United States.

Napoleon III's Intervention in Mexico, 1861–1867

One of the most serious challenges the Monroe Doctrine ever faced was an effort by Napoleon III to overthrow the Mexican Republic and replace it with a government under his influence. He desired not only to re-establish French power in the Western Hemisphere, but also to set up "an insuperable barrier" to the expansion of American democracy. French troops entered Mexico in 1861 as part of a joint expedition with Spain and Great Britain to collect debts that the Mexican government had refused to pay. The other countries withdrew, but a French army occupied Mexico City in 1863. The next year Maximilian, an Austrian prince, agreed at Napoleon's persuasion to become emperor of Mexico.

American opinion was violently opposed to Napoleon's actions, but during the Civil War there was little to do but protest. In 1864 the House of Representatives passed a unanimous resolution stating that the United States refused to recognize "any monarchical government erected on the ruins of any republican government in America under the auspices of a European power." Once the South was defeated, the United States had military power to back up its warnings; at one time 50,000 federal troops were stationed on the Rio Grande border. With such force behind him, Seward had little difficulty persuading Napoleon III to withdraw French troops early in 1867. The unfortunate Maximilian, who had trusted Napoleon's promise that "the assistance of France shall never fail the new empire," died before a Mexican firing squad. It was the Mexicans themselves, under the remarkable leadership of an Indian, Benito Juárez, who defeated Maximilian's forces, but the action of the United States probably hastened Napoleon's withdrawal. The Monroe Doctrine gained new respect abroad and popularity at home.

Alaska Purchase, 1867

Seward was a Secretary of State who believed in a policy of manifest destiny. He wanted the United States to annex Canada, Hawaii, and several Caribbean islands. His only major achievement along this line was the purchase of Alaska in 1867. This undeveloped territory, twice the size of Texas, and inhabited by only 20,000 people, was held by Russia, but was too far from Moscow for the Russian government either to rule or to protect effectively. When in 1867 the Russian minister to the United States informed Seward that the czar wished to

Purchase of Alaska was ridiculed by many as "Seward's Folly." This contemporary newspaper drawing shows Seward wheeling a large chunk of Alaskan ice to cool off hot Senate tempers.

QUESTION • Was the Alaska Purchase a better real estate bargain than the Louisiana Purchase?

sell the territory, the Secretary of State jumped at the chance. In a few hours he arranged a treaty whereby the United States bought Alaska for $7,200,000—a price of less than two cents an acre. Seward's action had little popular support, because, as has been remarked, most Americans did not know whether Alaska was "a city, an animal, or a new kind of drink." Newspapers called the area "Seward's icebox." The treaty passed the Senate, but the House of Representatives balked at voting the necessary funds until the Russian ambassador acceded to the pecuniary demands of certain needy congressmen.

Anglo-American Tension: Treaty of Washington, 1871

In the postwar period there was tension between the United States and Great Britain, as after the War of 1812 and at the time of the Aroostook War. Queen Victoria's diary reveals her fear of a war in which Britain would be

almost certain to lose Canada. The strongest American grievance involved Confederate cruisers, such as the *Alabama*, that had been allowed to slip from British ports. In 1869 Charles Sumner, chairman of the Senate Committee on Foreign Relations, made a famous speech that whipped up ill feeling. Sumner claimed that Great Britain owed us more than $2,000,000,000 in "direct" and "indirect" damages for allowing Confederate warships to sail. If the British would not pay, said the senator, the United States should take Canada.

Fortunately there were more reasonable men than Sumner in both the British and American governments. In Britain there was a realization that it had been a blunder to aid the Confederacy and thereby to risk losing Canada. It was also realized that if Britain should get involved in a war with a European power, the United States could build ships for Britain's foes and allow them to use our ports as they preyed on the British merchant marine. On the part of the United States, Hamilton Fish, Secretary of State under Grant, was willing to drop claims for indirect damages and to let an international court decide how much Britain owed in direct damages. In both governments there was a willingness to clear the books of outstanding disputes.

This mutually conciliatory attitude resulted in the Treaty of Washington, 1871. This document, containing 43 separate articles, provided for the settlement of all sorts of questions, such as a disputed boundary between the United States and Canada in Puget Sound, the rights of Americans to fish in Canadian waters, and claims of British subjects against the United States. In regard to the *Alabama* claims, the treaty contained a clause expressing "regret by Her Majesty's Government for the escape, under whatever circumstances, of the *Alabama* and other vessels from British ports."

With the British practically admitting themselves in the wrong, it did not prove too difficult to assess the amount of damages. This was done by an international court of arbitration, consisting of representatives from the United States, Great Britain, Italy, Brazil, and Switzerland. Called the Geneva Tribunal, because it met in Geneva, Switzerland, this body awarded the United States damages totaling $15,500,000, and Great Britain promptly paid. This was a remarkable victory for peace, and served to popularize the idea of arbitration instead of war to settle international disputes.

On the whole, the relations of the United States with foreign nations during the postwar years were handled with wisdom sadly lacking in the treatment of the South.

Activities: Chapter 14

For Mastery and Review

1. In parallel columns, compare the Civil War and the War of the American Revolution.

2. What were the effects of the blockade? What was the significance of the encounter between the *Virginia* and the *Monitor*? What effects did the Confederate cruisers such as the *Alabama* have upon the American merchant marine?

3. Trace the course of the war in the West. What were its purposes and how were they achieved?

4. Account for Lee's successes in Virginia. What was the importance of his defeats? Why did he finally surrender to Grant?

5. Prepare a summary comparison of northern and southern strengths.

6. How and why did the war increase the powers of the presidency?

7. Why was the British government sympathetic to the Confederacy? Why did it remain neutral?

8. Trace the changing attitude of Lincoln and of northern opinion in general toward freeing the slaves. By what steps was it accomplished and what was the immediate background of each?

9. Outline the Lincoln plan of Reconstruction. What were arguments for it? Who were the Radical Republicans? What actions did Johnson take in southern reconstruction? What were the reactions in the southern states and in Congress?

10. What self-interests did the Radical Republicans seek? What ideals? Outline the major provisions of their Reconstruction program. What were the carpetbag governments? What did they accomplish, good and bad?

11. In what ways did the Radical Republicans attack constitutional checks and balances? How did they weaken the Supreme Court? In what ways did they provide Negroes with constitutional protection of their rights as citizens?

12. How did southern whites' regain political control of their state governments? What were the terms of the Compromise of 1877? What was its principal result? What were the results of Reconstruction on the South, politically, economically, and educationally?

13. Describe postwar foreign relations, including (a) Maximilian in Mexico; (b) the purchase of Alaska; and (c) the Treaty of Washington.

Unrolling the Map

1. On an outline map of the United States, indicate the free states, the states that composed the Confederacy, and the slave states that did not secede. Indicate the lines by which the Confederacy was cut apart. Locate Vicksburg, Chattanooga, Atlanta, Savannah, and the chief Confederate ports closed by the Union blockade. Locate Richmond, Washington, and Gettysburg.

Who, What, and Why Important?

blockade
Gideon Wells
Virginia vs. *Monitor*
Alabama
Ulysses S. Grant
Vicksburg
William T. Sherman
Robert E. Lee
"Stonewall" Jackson
Gettysburg
Appomattox
conscription
greenbacks
Clara Barton
"Copperheads"
ex parte Milligan
The Emancipation
    Proclamation

Amendment XIII
Andrew Johnson
"Black Codes"
Radical Reconstruction
    program
Amendments XIV and XV
carpetbag governments
impeachment
election of 1868
Ku Klux Klan
Compromise of 1877
white supremacy
Solid South
sharecropping
Maximilian
Alaska Purchase
Treaty of Washington
Geneva Tribunal

To Pursue the Matter

1. What was the appalling price that the South had to pay for the sharecropping system, and who paid it? See Arnof, *A Sense of the Past*, pp. 266–270.

2. What were the contributions of former slaves to the Union war effort? See McPherson, *The Negro Civil War*.

3. "The Emancipation Proclamation did not free a single slave." Do you agree or disagree? See Franklin, *The Emancipation Proclamation*.

4. Make a diagrammatic map explaining how Grant took Vicksburg or one explaining how Lee won overwhelming victories with inferior forces at Second Bull Run and Chancellorsville.

5. How do you explain Lincoln's extraordinary success as a diplomat? See Bailey's *A Diplomatic History of the American People*, Chapters 22, 23.

6. Is the federal government justified in restricting freedom, even illegally, in time of crisis? See "The Case of the Copperhead Conspirator," in Garraty, *Quarrels That Have Shaped the Constitution*.

7. A most important question to consider:

In general, Southern Negroes simply exchanged a system of slavery for one of peonage after the Civil War. What would have been the elements of a program that would have prepared them for equal status? How could it have been put across?

READINGS FOR PART FOUR

Fiction

Basso, H. *The Light Infantry Ball*. Action and romance in the South before and during the Civil War.

Crane, S. *The Red Badge of Courage*. A classic narrative about a boy in battle.

Guthrie, A. B. *The Way West*. An epic trip from Missouri to Oregon in a panoramic novel.

Kantor, M. *Andersonville*. Prisoners of war, and the conditions of an infamous southern prison camp.

Mitchell, M. *Gone With the Wind*. A wonderful romance and an unforgettable story of the South in wartime.

Shaara, M. *The Killer Angels*. One of the best novels of the Civil War, portraying with great detail the battle of Gettysburg.

Non-fiction

Catton, B. *This Hallowed Ground*. A vivid history of the Civil War.

Chestnut, M. B. *A Diary from Dixie*. One of the best books on the South of this period by a pro-south but anti-slavery white southern aristocrat.

Commager, H. S. (ed.). *The Blue and the Gray*. The soldiers' own stories.

DeVoto, B. *Across the Wide Missouri*. The theme of manifest destiny, with marvelous illustrations.

Genevese, E. *Roll, Jordan, Roll*. A fascinating study of the world the slaves made on the plantations.

Sandburg, C. *Abraham Lincoln: The Prairie Years and the War Years*. A fine one-volume version of the larger six-volume work.

PART FOUR: SUMMING UP
Chapters 12–14

I. CHECKING THE FACTS

1. Which of these statements are *statements of fact* (can be proved true or false), and which are *statements of opinion?*
- a. The United States had a mission to "extend the area of freedom."
- b. Northern Negroes on the eve of the Civil War were second-class citizens.
- c. Railroads drew the West and North together economically and politically.
- d. The Compromise of 1850 was a truce rather than a permanent peace.
- e. The draft made the Civil War "a rich man's war and a poor man's fight."
- f. James K. Polk was a successful President.
- g. Abraham Lincoln freed the slaves.

2. *What and When:* Putting Things in Order
In each of the pairs of events below, tell which *occurred first.* Defend your decision orally or in writing.
- a. Emancipation Proclamation/end of the Civil War
- b. constitutional amendment defining citizenship/constitutional amendment abolishing slavery
- c. Compromise of 1850/Missouri Compromise declared unconstitutional
- d. area beyond Missouri reserved for Indians/Oregon government established by Americans
- e. annexation of Texas/Mexican War
- f. popular sovereignty in Kansas and Nebraska/popular sovereignty in Utah and New Mexico

3. Refer to the maps on p. 352 on the Civil War to *agree* or *disagree* with the conclusions given below.
- a. All major battles were fought in Confederate territory.
- b. The South was split in two by 1864.
- c. Grant led the Union Army against Vicksburg.
- d. New Orleans remained in Confederate hands until 1864.
- e. Lee was the last Confederate general to surrender.
- f. Washington fell to the Confederate Army.
- g. The Mississippi River was under Union control by 1863.

II. INTERPRETING THE FACTS

1. Where human beings are concerned, determining cause and effect is often difficult. It is, nevertheless, an important element in history. Which item in each of the pairs below would you say is the *possible cause* and which is the *possible effect?*

a. secession of southern states/victory of Republican Party in 1860
b. Mormon settlement in Salt Lake City/persecution of religious minorities
c. impeachment of Johnson/radical reconstruction
d. end of radical reconstruction/election of 1876
e. collapse of plantation system/tenant farming
f. westward expansion/popular sovereignty

2. Complete these relationships by supplying the missing term or phrase, as in this example: Hunger : food :: thirst : (*water*). More than one answer may be right if you can defend your idea.

a. Narcissa Whitman : pioneering :: Clara Barton : _____.
b. furs : Oregon :: _____ California.
c. Mexican War : _____ :: Civil War : Lincoln.
d. _____ : citizenship :: 15th Amendment : suffrage.
e. Lee : Grant :: _____ : Lincoln.
f. land : pioneer :: _____ : immigrant.

3. Each of the terms in the pairs below has a different meaning. However, they also have something in common. How are they different? How are they alike?

a. manifest destiny—imperialism
b. patriotism—nationalism
c. squatter's rights—popular sovereignty
d. cession—annexation
e. compromise—settlement
f. migration—immigration
g. doctrine—policy

III. APPLYING YOUR KNOWLEDGE

1. The first step in problem-solving is to know exactly what the problem is. When the problem is complex, the next step is to break it down into smaller elements that can be more easily handled. For example, let us say the problem is *energy*. Some elements in this problem would be the following: (1) How can the U.S. protect and preserve its future energy sources? (2) How can the American people be brought to change their habits relating to fuel consumption? (3) What should be industry's share of the available energy resources? (4) Should the government control energy resources, and if so, what means should be used (rationing, price control)?

Now, using this same method, identify some of the elements involved in rebuilding the southern economy after the Civil War. Use the model below.

Major problem	Elements of the problem
How to rebuild the southern economy.	1. _____
	2. _____
	3. _____

Part

5

The Emergence of Modern America

Chapters in this Part

PITTSBURGH, 1880

THE GILDED AGE

The period after the Civil War has received many uncomplimentary names. Mark Twain called it the Gilded Age; Lewis Mumford dubbed it the Brown Decades; Vernon Parrington described it as "a world of triumphant and unabashed vulgarity." Its immense wastefulness was symbolized by the extinction of the vast buffalo herds, its political mediocrity and corruption by the Tweed Ring in New York City. In Washington, congressmen took bribes to give away land grants to railroads, and President Grant placed seventy-five relatives on the federal payroll. In business, unabashed rascals made fortunes; Jim Fisk, after failing to corner the gold in the United States, cheerfully announced, "Nothing is lost save honor." As cities sprawled out like fungi, unplanned and ugly, pauperism, slums, and crime sprang up. In the arts, sham was everywhere, symbolized by the popular "jigsaw Gothic" architecture.

Why did all this happen? Look at the diagrams on pp. 470–471. In the period 1850–1900 manufacturing gained on agriculture, the urban population on the rural. Machinery, power, and rapid transportation were changing the environment more swiftly than ever before in history. The industrial revolution was creating brand-new political, social, economic, artistic, and moral problems faster than men could find solutions.

The unattractive features of the Gilded Age can easily blind us to its achievements. The material progress was astounding. In 1860 half the country—from Kansas to California—was practically empty of people. By 1890 this area had been so thoroughly settled that the census takers could no longer find a frontier line. Improved manufacturing processes had made scores of hitherto "luxury" products available to the ordinary consumer. In the cities there appeared such great monuments of engineering skill as the Brooklyn Bridge and such evidence of public spirit as The New York Public Library. Instruction in American universities and technical schools was on a par with that furnished by French and German universities. A new generation of architects began to design buildings with taste and imagination.

For all its faults, America, the "land of opportunity," was a mecca for immigrants. In 1886 the Statue of Liberty was dedicated, a gift of the French people in honor of the hundredth anniversary of the Declaration of Independence. The message inscribed on the base, written by poet Emma Lazarus, was addressed to the nations of Europe:

> "Give me your tired, your poor,
> Your huddled masses yearning to breathe free . . .
> Send these, the homeless, tempest-tost to me,
> I lift my lamp beside the golden door."

Chapter 15

Industrial America

> *Laughing!*
> *Laughing the stormy, husky, brawling laughter of Youth, half-naked, sweating,*
> *proud to be Hog Butcher, Tool Maker, Stacker of Wheat, Player with Railroads,*
> *and Freight Handler to the Nation.*
>
> —CARL SANDBURG

The Civil War and Reconstruction mark a sort of "great divide" in American history. The war finally settled important issues that had agitated people for many years, such as nullification and expansion of slavery, so that politics assumed quite a different character. But more important than political developments were changes in the way Americans lived. Before the Civil War the great majority of the people gained their living from agriculture and lived on isolated farms or in small towns. Although industry had begun a period of rapid growth, most manufacturing was on a small scale and was designed to supply local markets. In the thirty to forty years after the war, it expanded more rapidly in America than in any other country in the world. In 1900 American industrial production was seven times that of 1865, and the United States rose from fourth place among industrial nations to first. Agriculture also expanded with amazing speed, and the farmer was brought into and subordinated to the industrial system. According to W. W. Rostow, whose theory about stages of economic growth was mentioned in Chapter 13, the "takeoff" of the 1840's and 1850's was now followed by over half a century of self-sustaining growth, centering on expansion of railways and of heavy industry, such as the manufacture of steel.

CAUSES OF RAPID INDUSTRIAL GROWTH

It is a matter of debate whether the Civil War speeded up or slowed down the development of industry in the North. In any case, northern factories and railroads did not suffer the physical damage inflicted on those in the South. From the end of the war on there was a period of continued growth, interrupted by periods of depression in 1873–1878, 1882–1884, and 1893–1896. Industrial production doubled about every twelve to fourteen years. Although economic historians differ as to the relative importance of the causes for this explosive growth, they generally agree that the following factors were involved:

(1) *Inventions.* A flood of important inventions served to increase productive capacity

Technological problems vexed railroads from the beginning. Braking, slack control, and coupling (shown above) were a few of the many problems that had to be solved before railroads could fulfill their potential.

and to speed transportation and communication. Among these were the telephone, new methods of steel production, and the use of electricity as a source of light and power.

(2) *Vast natural resources.* The immense underground wealth of the United States had scarcely been touched. The country contained in fantastic abundance the raw materials upon which industry depended, such as coal, iron, petroleum, and copper.

(3) *Railroad building.* By 1900 the railroad mileage of the United States was greater than that of all the rest of the world. Technical improvements enabled trains to carry bulky products long distances cheaply, thus making it possible for business people to sell their goods in a nation-wide market.

(4) *Abundant capital.* The great profits to be obtained from manufacturing and transportation in the United States attracted investors. Much of the capital formerly invested in shipping was diverted to building factories and railroads. Billions of dollars came from abroad, especially from England.

(5) *A mobile labor supply.* European capitalists often had difficulty recruiting labor for new industries because workers had been brought up to traditional occupations and hated to leave their home villages. In the United States, labor was more mobile. The American tradition was to "keep moving." Laborers came to new jobs in new cities the way pioneers moved into new lands. Furthermore, the flood of immigration continued; the newcomers, already uprooted from their homes and traditions, supplied much of the "floating" labor force that industry demanded. The native American workers were noted for the ease with which they learned new processes, and the immigrants such as English textile workers, Welsh miners, and Italian farmers often brought with them important skills.

(6) *Government policies.* The Constitution gave American industrialists an advantage when it forbade the states to levy tariffs. This prohibition resulted in an immense home market—the largest free trade area in the world. Compare this with western Europe, where nearly twenty nations were levying tariffs on each others' goods.

American capitalists demanded and received special favors from Congress. A high protective tariff encouraged "infant industries" and raised manufacturers' profits by keeping out foreign goods. Liberal immigration laws insured a steady supply of cheap labor. The federal government bore about a third of the cost of building the western railroads and sold public lands containing vast mineral wealth for a small proportion of their true value.

(7) *American institutions and attitudes.* In Europe it was often difficult to change industrial methods because of continuing traditions of hand craftsmanship and the feeling that a son should follow his father's trade. But in America no such restraints existed; both laborer and industrialist felt free to abandon old techniques and try new ones.

In America more than in Europe business attracted and held people of high ability and ambition. While European capitalists often retired from business when they had acquired enough money to buy their way into the upper classes, American capitalists regarded money-making as a laudable end in itself. They had no other ambition than to be "captains of industry." At the other end of the scale Europe was plagued with an almost hereditary class of paupers who, with little hope of ever rising from poverty, lacked initiative. In the United States, on the other hand, laborers believed that hard work would be rewarded, if not by wealth for themselves, at least by wider opportunities for their children.

American law encouraged the formation of business corporations, and this form of ownership had a number of advantages over partnerships or individual proprietorships. It provided permanence of organization, so that its officers could plan far into the future. By selling bonds and stocks, a corporation could get the capital needed for its operations from the public at large, and small bits of capital could be pooled into large sums. Those with capital were attracted to corporate securities because by diversifying their investments they could spread their risks. A specialized form of corporation, the holding company, enabled capitalists to combine

The lure of freedom and higher wages drew an ever-increasing number of immigrants to America from Europe. The average influx of immigrants to the United States was over a third of a million per year between 1870 and 1900. This woodcut shows John Bull, the British counterpart of Uncle Sam, trying to hold back workers wishing to go to the United States.

Museum of the City of New York

dozens of businesses under centralized control, and it became one of the methods of forming immense business combinations.

THE GROWTH OF BIG BUSINESS

Along with the rapid industrial expansion of the United States came an immense increase in the size of the business units. By 1900 several major industries were dominated by gigantic concerns which owned scores of plants, sold products all over the country, and had hundreds of millions of dollars capital and credit behind them.

Legitimate Advantages of Big Business

The growth of big business was a natural development. Big companies could take full advantage of the nation-wide markets. They lowered production costs and improved their products by installing the newest processes. They paid high salaries to obtain the best business brains. They reduced costs by combining operations formerly carried on by separate companies, and at the same time increased efficiency by establishing separate departments for specialized functions such as purchasing, production, research, distribution, and sales.

All this was shown dramatically by the development of large-scale meat-packing. Formerly fresh meat had been slaughtered locally, and every town had at least one slaughterhouse. When the refrigerator car made it possible to ship fresh meat long distances, there appeared gigantic concerns such as Swift and Armour selling their products all over the country. The big meat-packers made such efficient use of by-products that they were often able to sell the meat for less than they paid for the animal and still make a profit out of the rest of the carcass. The Chicago humorist "Mr. Dooley" (Finley Peter Dunne) was scarcely exaggerating when he said:

A cow goes lowin' softly into Armour's an' comes out glue, gelatin, fertylizer, celooloid, joolry, sofy cushions, hair restorer, washin' sody, soap, lithrachoor an' bed springs so quick that while aft she's still cow, for'ard she may be anything fr'm buttons to pannyma hats.

Unfair Advantages of Big Business

In addition to its natural efficiency, big business was sometimes in a position to take unfair advantage of competitors or the public. It could get special discounts from transportation companies. It could sell its product in one locality at less than cost until local businesses were forced to close down or sell out. If able to get a monopoly, it could raise prices to consumers and lower those paid to producers of raw materials. It could bribe public officials to pass laws favorable to its interests or not to enforce regulations that hurt it.

The great business concerns were created by people who saw the vast possibilities for wealth in America, who were willing to take risks, and who often had few scruples when it came to driving competitors out of business, bribing legislators, or breaking labor unions. Vernon L. Parrington says of them:

These new Americans were primitive souls, ruthless, predatory, capable, single-minded men; rogues and rascals often, but never feeble, never hindered by petty scruple, never given to puling or whining. . . .

Analyze the most talked-of men of the age and one is likely to find a splendid audacity coupled with immense wastefulness. A note of toughmindedness marks them. They had stout nippers. They fought their way encased in rhinoceros hides.

Horizontal and Vertical Consolidation

Business consolidation took various forms. Sometimes there was "horizontal" consolidation of several firms engaged in a single process. Sometimes there was "vertical" consolidation of different processes all the way from extracting raw materials to selling the finished product. A horizontal combination, once established, was able to expand vertically because of the control it could exert over both producers and distributors. And a vertical combination could be so efficient that it expanded horizontally by buying out competitors or forcing them out of business.

JOHN D. ROCKEFELLER AND THE STANDARD OIL TRUST

The most successful and dramatic example of horizontal consolidation was the Standard Oil Trust, a near-monopoly of oil refineries and pipelines. Its guiding genius was John D. Rockefeller (1839–1937), who in the course of his long lifetime amassed what was reputed to be the world's largest fortune—nearly a billion dollars.

Rockefeller went to work at an early age, starting as a bookkeeper in a grocery in Cleveland. Dominated by the idea that he was "bound to be rich," he saved $800 in three years, on a salary of $15 per week. After going into business for himself, in only four years he increased his small capital until by 1865 he commanded about $100,000. Then he sank all his money in a new industry—petroleum refining.

Rise of the Oil Industry

The production and use of petroleum, like that of steel, was increasing at an almost fantastic rate. Until the 1850's, petroleum (called "rock oil") had been used only as a patent medicine. In 1855 it was discovered that when refined into kerosene it was better for lighting than whale oil and supplied a better lubricant than animal fats. The first oil well, drilled in 1859, set off a stampede to western Pennsylvania like the California gold rush of 1849. Land values in the region jumped from a few dollars an acre to hundreds of dollars a square foot. New towns appeared overnight. The demand for kerosene became world-wide. In spite of the Civil War, the petroleum industry grew so fast that by 1865 petroleum had risen to fourth place among the exports of the United States.

The petroleum business was highly speculative. Fortunes were made and lost overnight as the price of oil fluctuated wildly. Fraud was so prevalent that "oil stock" became as much a symbol for worthlessness as the continental dollars of the Revolution. It was Rockefeller's remarkable achievement to impose order on this chaotic industry.

By 1870 Rockefeller's firm, the Standard Oil Company of Ohio, with capital stock of a million dollars, was the largest of 26 refineries in Cleveland, processing 2 or 3 per cent of the crude oil produced in the United States. In nine years Rockefeller and his associates gained control of about 90 per cent of the refining business of the country. Some of their methods were so ruthless that when they were revealed Rockefeller became one of the most hated men in the business world.

Methods of Consolidation

One of Standard Oil's principal weapons was the rebate (a discount on railroad charges). In 1872 the company made a secret agreement with the railroads running out of Cleveland by which the rates on its products would be from 25 per cent to 50 per cent below those charged other companies. In order to see that the railroads were not tempted by higher rates into carrying its competitors' oil, Standard Oil had the railroads pay it a "drawback" on every barrel of competitors' oil shipped. Standard Oil was also furnished with the waybills telling the destination of competitors' oil; this provided valuable information about their business dealings.

This agreement gave Standard Oil such an advantage over all other Cleveland refineries that within three months all but five of them were forced to sell out. Once in control of oil refining in Cleveland, Standard Oil moved

The Eastman Johnson portrait of John D. Rockefeller shows him as a young man. Rockefeller dominated the oil industry by means of the great horizontal trust he organized (see chart, page 396).

rapidly toward a national monopoly. It did this by forming an alliance of the strongest companies and ablest people in the oil business, and by gaining control of the transportation of oil. In 1880 a committee of the New York legislature reported on Standard Oil as follows:

It owns and controls the pipe lines of the producing regions that connect with the railroads. It controls both ends of these roads. It ships 95 per cent of all oil. . . . It dictates terms and rates to the railroads. It has bought out and frozen out refiners all over the country. By means of the superior facilities for transportation which it thus possessed, it could overbid in the producing regions and undersell in the markets of the world.

Many of the operations in this Napoleonic campaign to conquer an entire industry were completely unknown even to Rockefeller's competitors. Companies controlled by Standard Oil continued, for instance, to do business under their former names, with "dummy directors," who were sometimes mere office boys or stenographers. In 1882, forty companies were put under one management by a secret agreement known as the Standard Oil Trust. The controlling interest in the stock of the companies was turned over to nine trustees headed by Rockefeller. This trust arrangement offered such vast possibilities for profit that it was imitated in other industries; the very word trust became a term applied to any big, monopolistic business.

Once having achieved control of most of the refining and transportation of oil in the United States, Standard Oil expanded "vertically." It gained control of oil fields, so as to have an independent source of supply, and also marketed natural gas. At the other end of the scale, it moved into the distribution of petroleum products, both in America and abroad. Eventually it controlled a fleet of ocean-going tankers and door-to-door delivery wagons in Europe. It manufactured and sold cooking stoves to increase the demand for kerosene.

Rockefeller, a devout churchgoer, never admitted that his actions in what he referred to as "systematizing" the oil industry were wrong. He pointed out that railroads customarily granted rebates to big shippers, and that rebates were not illegal when he first used them to gain advantage over his rivals. When buying out competitors, Rockefeller offered to pay them in either cash or Standard Oil stock, advising them to take the latter. Those who took his advice became rich. Much of his advantage over rivals stemmed from a passion for efficiency and hatred of waste. Standard Oil continuously improved its product. It had few labor troubles because it paid its workmen well, tried to keep

University of Chicago

The first oil well, drilled in 1859 by Edwin Drake in Titusville, Pennsylvania, began the petroleum industry. A rush to the oil fields almost as spectacular as the gold rush of '49 to California followed shortly after.

questionable legality; they ran afoul of the English common law doctrine that it is illegal to combine with others to restrain trade, a principle that was written into federal law by the Sherman Antitrust Act of 1890. Vertical consolidation, on the other hand, was not by its very nature monopolistic, and it resulted in large economies that were passed on to the consumer in the form of lower prices. It has become a common means of business combination, and can be seen today in such giant organizations as General Motors and American Telephone and Telegraph Company.

ANDREW CARNEGIE, MASTER OF STEEL

The most remarkable example of the creation of a vertical trust was the giant steel business built up by Andrew Carnegie (1835–1919). Coming to this country from Scotland at the age of thirteen, Carnegie went to work in a cotton factory, where he received $1.20 for a 72-hour week. His ability, energy, and driving ambition were so great that he rapidly worked his way upward as a telegraph operator and private secretary until by the age of twenty-two he was traffic superintendent of a branch of the Pennsylvania Railroad. By fortunate investments in a sleeping car company and in oil wells, he made a small fortune by the time he was thirty.

In the demands of the railroads for rails, bridges, cars, and locomotives, Carnegie foresaw a great future for the iron and steel industry. After seven years' experience making iron bridges, he decided in 1873 to "put all his eggs in one basket and watch the basket"—that is, to concentrate entirely on iron and steel.

Carnegie's decision followed closely on the development of two new ways of making steel—the Bessemer process and the open-hearth process. These produced steel so cheaply that it could be used for girders and rails as well as for cutlery and precision machines.

them on in times of depression, and was one of the first companies to pay old-age pensions. Rockefeller plowed much of his fortune back into society by gifts which totaled over half a billion dollars.

Standard Oil's spectacular success led to other attempts to establish horizontal combinations of companies in industries as varied as whiskey, bituminous coal, and rope. Their purpose was principally to prevent overproduction and to keep up prices. But it was difficult to control an entire industry and to keep new firms out of the market. Furthermore, efforts to suppress competition were much resented by small business people and consumers. They were also of

Andrew Carnegie, steel master. Carnegie's genius lay in his courage and in his ability to organize. His vertical empire in the steel industry (see chart, page 396) became the pattern for others to follow. After making a fortune in the early part of his life, he devoted his later years to giving it away.

Between 1866 and 1876, the production of American steel skyrocketed from 20,000 to 600,000 tons; by 1897 it was over 7,000,000 tons. Previously iron and steel had been manufactured at hundreds of small furnaces all over the country. Now almost overnight the character of the industry changed. Bessemer converters and open-hearth furnaces demanded heavy investment of capital, and needed huge amounts of coke and ore to keep them going. Small operators were soon forced out by big concerns.

Less than twenty years after Carnegie put all his eggs in one basket, he had become the greatest steel master in the world. There were a number of reasons for his success.

(1) He took a great deal of the guesswork out of making iron and steel by getting the best scientific and technological advice he could find. His chemists found out how to use by-products previously thrown away, and how to smelt ores formerly thought to be worthless.

(2) Carnegie wrote that he wanted as his epitaph: "Here lies the man who was able to surround himself with men far cleverer than

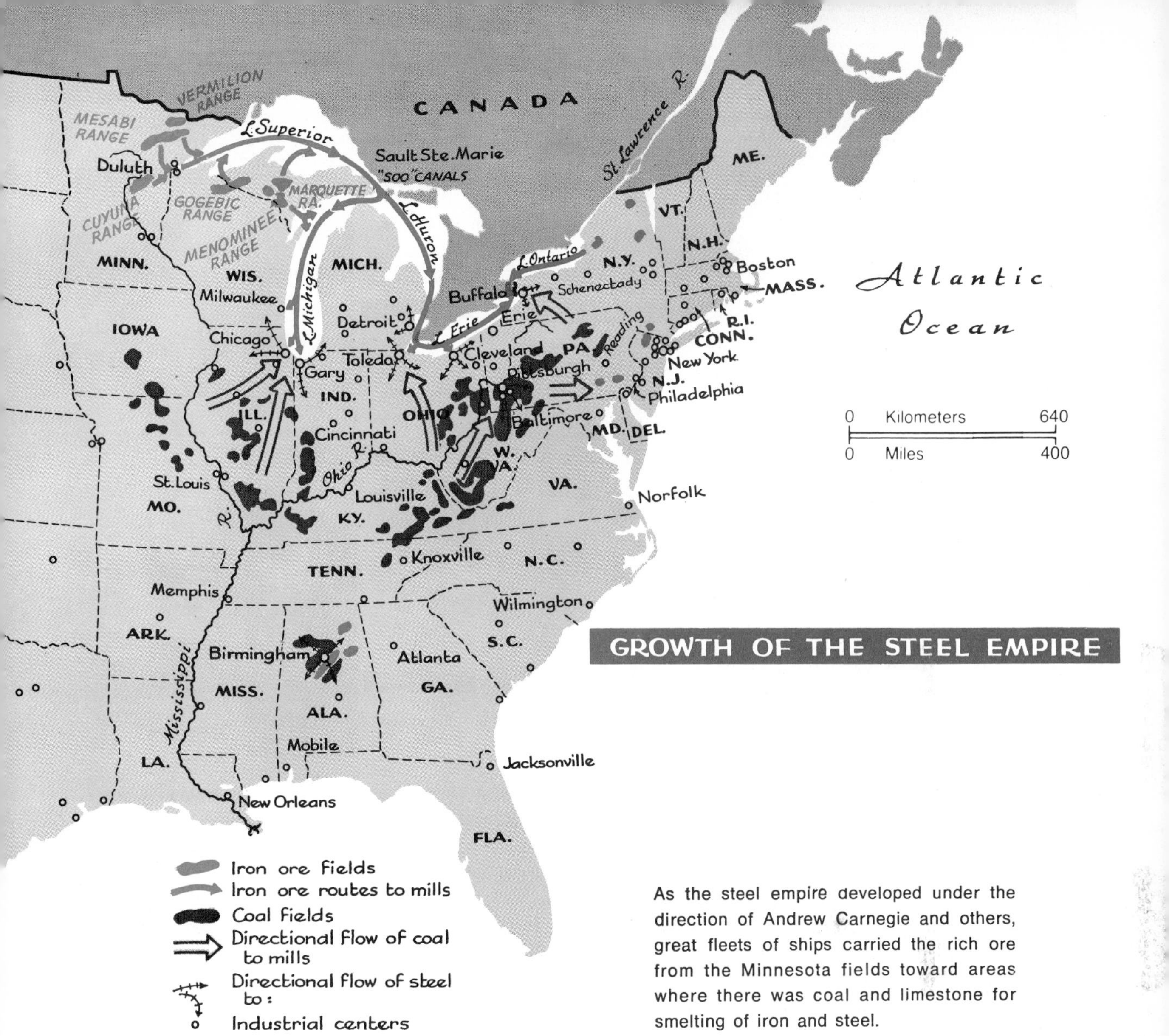

GROWTH OF THE STEEL EMPIRE

Map labels: VERMILION RANGE, MESABI RANGE, CUYUNA RANGE, GOGEBIC RANGE, MARQUETTE RA., MENOMINEE RANGE, CANADA, L. Superior, Sault Ste. Marie "SOO" CANALS, L. Huron, St. Lawrence R., Duluth, MINN., WIS., Milwaukee, MICH., L. Michigan, Detroit, L. Ontario, L. Erie, Buffalo, Schenectady, ME., VT., N.H., N.Y., MASS., Boston, Atlantic Ocean, IOWA, Chicago, Gary, Toledo, Erie, Cleveland, PA., Reading, CONN., R.I., New York, IND., Pittsburgh, N.J., Philadelphia, Cincinnati, OHIO, Baltimore, MD., DEL., St. Louis, Ohio R., W. VA., VA., Norfolk, MO., Louisville, KY., TENN., Knoxville, N.C., Memphis, Wilmington, ARK., Birmingham, S.C., Atlanta, MISS., ALA., GA., Mississippi R., Mobile, LA., Jacksonville, New Orleans, FLA.

Scale:
0 Kilometers 640
0 Miles 400

Legend:
- Iron ore fields
- Iron ore routes to mills
- Coal fields
- Directional flow of coal to mills
- Directional flow of steel to:
- ○ Industrial centers

As the steel empire developed under the direction of Andrew Carnegie and others, great fleets of ships carried the rich ore from the Minnesota fields toward areas where there was coal and limestone for smelting of iron and steel.

himself." Seeking out the ablest men in the steel industry, he took them into partnership. Always on the watch for ability in his own companies, he gave rapid promotion to young men who made good. Common laborers fared less happily. In the Homestead lockout of 1892, Carnegie's partner, Henry C. Frick, broke the steelworkers' union, driving wages down and hours up, so that the 12-hour day was standard in the industry for many years.

(3) Carnegie was a master at pricing his goods so as to make the highest profit. Sometimes he drove competitors out of business by underselling, and sometimes used protective tariffs and price agreements with other companies to keep prices at artificially high levels.

395

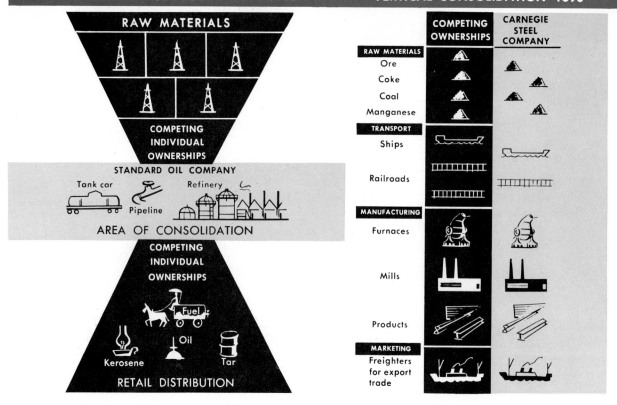

In Carnegie's empire all processes — from mines to markets — used in making steel were combined in one great vertical consolidation. The Standard Oil Company, a horizontal form of consolidation, controlled both the refining and transport stages of oil production. It was thus able to dominate the oil industry, even though it did not at first try to monopolize raw materials or markets.

(4) In time of depression, when competitors closed down and laid off their men, Carnegie rebuilt his factories and put in more efficient processes. He "gambled on the future of America," as he expressed it, "and won." When business improved, he was able to sell his products at prices which "meant vast profits for himself and absolute ruin for his competitors."

(5) Carnegie combined all the processes involved in making steel into one great vertical consolidation. In addition to blast furnaces and steel mills, his company controlled rich ore deposits near Lake Superior, fleets of ore ships on the Great Lakes, a railroad from Lake Erie to Pittsburgh, coal mines and coking ovens in Pennsylvania, plus factories for producing finished products such as wire. Carnegie summarized the result of this achievement as follows:

Two pounds of ironstone mined upon Lake Superior and transported nine hundred miles to Pittsburgh; one pound and one-half of coal, mined and manufactured into coke, and transported to Pittsburgh; one half-pound of lime, mined and transported to Pittsburgh; a small amount of manganese mined in Virginia and brought to Pittsburgh —and these four pounds of materials manufactured into one pound of steel, for which the consumer pays one cent.

Carnegie and the Gospel of Wealth

Eventually, Carnegie was making over $20,000,000 a year in a time when there was no income tax, while his workers received eight or nine dollars a week. He was producing steel so cheaply that his remaining competitors faced bankruptcy. Carnegie justified both his immense fortune and the ruthlessness of his business methods by an adaptation of the theory of evolution that had been propounded by the English naturalist Charles Darwin. Darwin maintained that in the constant struggle for existence certain species of plants and animals survive because they are more efficient, while others die out. Carnegie said that within the human race also there is a "law of competition" that decrees that only the fittest should survive. Organizing and managerial talents are so rare that men possessing them must rise to the top in a free society and must be abundantly rewarded. According to Carnegie:

We of the capitalistic persuasion put trust in the individual man. We make him a part, according to his particular skill, of a great and far-reaching industrial organization. We demote him when his ability fails, and discard him if we find a serious flaw in his character. . . . We have, then, a method, better than that of practical politics, for selecting the leaders of a democracy. By a process of pitiless testing we discover who are the strong and who are the weak. To the strong we give power in the form of the autocratic control of industry and of wealth with which the leader, who has risen by a process of natural selection, can and does do for the mass of the community what they could never do for themselves.

But to Carnegie the achievement of great power and wealth was not enough. He preached that in the latter part of a career, business people should plow their wealth back into society, and that the person who dies rich dies disgraced. In 1901 Carnegie sold his steel properties to the newly formed United States Steel Corporation for $250,000,000 and withdrew from business to devote the rest of his life to philanthropy. By the time of his death, he had donated $350,000,000 to various projects. His belief in education amounted almost to a religion, and most of the money went to such projects as building public libraries, increasing college endowments, providing pensions for college professors, and promoting research.

QUESTION • Did the large-scale benevolences of John D. Rockefeller and Andrew Carnegie justify the ruthless business methods in which they engaged?

THE GROWTH OF CITIES

In the new industrial age, the city was "the mighty heart of the body politic, sending its streams of life to the very fingertips of the whole land." Between 1860 and 1900 American urban areas grew twice as fast as the total population. Chicago, which in 1850 had been a frontier town of 30,000 people, doubled its population every ten years and became a vast metropolis approaching two million. New York became the second largest city in the world. The day dreaded by Thomas Jefferson, when Americans should abandon farming life and be piled high up on one another in cities, was clearly on the way.

Urbanization was a world-wide phenomenon associated with the industrial revolution. The new industrial cities were essentially the product of the mine, the factory, the steamship, and the railroad. New cities appeared or old ones mushroomed near coal and iron deposits (Birmingham and Pittsburgh), near sources of water power (Lowell and Lawrence, Massachusetts), at points of transshipment (Baltimore and New

Like most American cities, Albany, New York, was laid out in a rectangular gridiron design. This layout is convenient for builders and brings maximum profit to real estate owners, but it is monotonous and it makes every street a thoroughfare, dangerous for children and other pedestrians.

The Library of Congress

York City), and at railroad centers (Omaha and Chicago).

Once established, cities grew by a self-generating process. Various facilities appeared to serve industry: banks and insurance companies, docks and warehouses. These in turn attracted more industry. Immigrants, lacking agricultural skill or money to buy a farm, could often find employment only in urban areas. The recent arrivals often preferred the big cities where there were colonies of people who spoke their native language and tried to preserve old-world customs. An even greater source of supply for the growing urban population were American rural areas. Thus not merely from the rocky hillsides of New Hampshire and Vermont, but even from rich lands in Iowa and Illinois, farm boys and girls, bored with life in the country, headed for the city lights to make their fortunes. "A sort of natural selection," remarked a foreign traveler in America, "carries the more ambitious and eager spirits into the towns, for the native American dislikes the monotony and isolation of farm life with its slender prospect of wealth."

Although the modern industrial city offered many people the opportunity for a higher standard of living than they had known before, it also confronted them with a novel and often unattractive environment. Because of the pre-

vailing *laissez faire* philosophy and a lack of community sense, the new cities were built with less concern for the comforts of the inhabitants than for the profits of builders and real estate speculators. It suited the latter group to have the streets laid out in a rectangular gridiron. The result was that every street often became a dangerous thoroughfare and cities as a whole were monotonous. There was inadequate provision for parks and playgrounds, the few open spaces too often being given over to dumps and to vacant lots where a scanty growth of grass and weeds competed with cinders and tin cans. Rivers and harbors were polluted by sewage and factory wastes, and the air was made foul by smoke from thousands of chimneys. In many ways the new environment seemed a sort of prison, cutting off people from sun, air, and natural beauty.

Problems Created by Urbanization

The growth of cities created many technical and human problems. There was, for instance, a demand for new sources of water, since wells and brooks provided too scanty a supply and were often polluted. New York City was the first to make a major effort to meet this problem by building the Croton Aqueduct, twenty-five miles outside the city limits. Cities became so

398

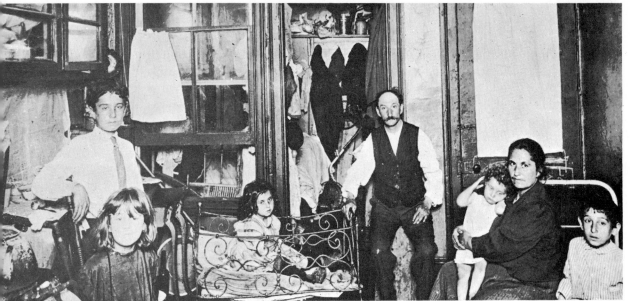

The banquet hall and its triple fireplace in Biltmore, the Vanderbilt estate in North Carolina, surpassed in grandeur royal palaces of Europe. But while the wealthy spent their money for such splendid display, city workers often lived in slums where it was impossible to keep clean or stay healthy. Such extreme contrasts in living conditions caused angry social comment, and gave rise to protest movements.

large in area that better means of transportation within them had to be devised. This need was first met by the horse car, later by the elevated railway, trolley car, and subway. The demand for space in preferred localities such as Wall Street in New York or the Loop in Chicago was answered by the skyscraper, which, in turn, added a vertical dimension to transportation in the form of the elevator.

A sinister product of urban life was an increase in crime. Until the rise of the city, there had naturally been occasional violence and theft, but never on a scale demanding an organized police force. There was, in fact, nothing resembling modern police until the formation of the Metropolitan Police of London, known as bobbies, about 1830. As American cities grew, they had to follow the British lead and provide police protection. The larger the city, the more expensive this protection was, costing five or six times as much per capita in cities with over a million people as in those with

less than thirty thousand. All this was partly the result of a breakdown in traditional morality. Whether the new city dweller came from a Connecticut village or an Italian hill town, from a farm in upstate New York or a nobleman's estate in Poland, he found it hard to follow the ways he had been brought up to consider right. It was even harder for him to train his children in the "right" way, since they found other standards in the streets where they played with children of quite different backgrounds. Law-breaking was often simply a protest against disease and monotony, against unemployment and insecurity, or against life in slums so crowded that four thousand people might occupy a single block.

Idle Poor and Idle Rich

There was probably no more poverty in the great industrial cities than in the former agricultural societies; indeed, there may have been less but poverty now became more *visible* because poor people lived in their own districts where unscrupulous building owners crowded them together in slums. Industrialism brought with it recurring periods of depression which threw millions of people out of work through no fault of their own. There also appeared a more or less permanent fringe of "unemployables"—beggars, paupers, and tramps.

The new awareness of mass poverty was coupled with another phenomenon new to American life—the appearance of a class of "idle rich." Until the industrial era there had been few very wealthy people in America. One estimate put the number of millionaires at three in 1860 as against nearly 4,000 in 1900. In the pre-industrial period, persons not needing to work for a living generally took up some other occupation—politics, literature, farming. They had been trained in the tradition that wealth carries with it duties as well as privileges. But many of the owners of new fortunes had no

time to develop such a tradition; they were bent simply on enjoying and displaying their wealth.

The newspapers of the period greedily reported the sensational doings of what was called "high society," a group of people whose one purpose in life, apparently, was pleasure. There was a dinner at Delmonico's, the finest New York restaurant, at which the guests were on horseback and "the favorite steed was fed flowers and champagne." A complete orchestra was hired to serenade a newborn child, and a diamond necklace given by a millionaire to his daughter cost $600,000.

Widespread Prosperity

The unpleasant aspects of industrialism and urbanization tend to obscure the fact that life was getting better for the mass of the people. Wherever industrialism appears, it tends to bring a rapid increase in the population. Better transportation ends famine and nutritional diseases caused by local crop failures. Improved medical service, water supply, and sewage disposal reduce mortality. A higher proportion of the population lives above a bare subsistence level. In his annual message to Congress in 1861 Lincoln said:

The prudent, penniless beginner labors for wages awhile, saves a surplus with which to buy tools or land for himself, then labors on his own account with another new beginner to help him. This is the just and generous and prosperous system which opens the way to all, gives hope to all, and consequent energy and progress and improvement of condition to all.

While Lincoln was here describing the situation of the worker in the pre-factory age when craft workers owned their own tools and worked alongside their "help," his boast that American workers had rising expectations was a true prophecy. The real wages of laboring people (what goods and services they could buy with what they were paid) more than doubled

Sports and Recreation

In the late 1800's, tennis was played enthusiastically, though gently, by both men and women (above). Baseball was also popular. Note that the players, shown below in Thomas Eakins' watercolor, did not use gloves or a catcher's mitt. "Croquet Scene" (above), by Winslow Homer, depicts a game genteel enough for the "ladies" to join in. For a time, bicycling was all the rage, as the scene below in Washington, D. C. shows.

between 1860 and 1896. Europeans traveling in this country were impressed by the high level of prosperity of the mass of the people. The English historian James Bryce wrote as follows about the lot of American workers:

In England the lot of the labourer has been hitherto a hard one, . . . with the workhouse at the end of the vista; while the misery in such cities as London, Liverpool, and Glasgow is only too well known. In France there is less pauperism, but nothing can be more pinched and sordid than the life of the bulk of the peasantry. . . . Of Russia, with her ninety millions of peasants living in half-barbarism, there is no need to speak. Contrast any one of these countries with the United States, where the working classes are as well fed, clothed, and lodged as the lower middle classes in Europe, . . . where a good education is within reach of the poorest, where the opportunities for getting on in one way or another are so abundant that no one need fear any physical ill but disease or the result of his own intemperance. Pauperism already exists in some of the larger cities, . . . But outside one sees nothing but comfort.

THE NEW LEISURE

The industrial revolution provided new leisure not merely for the very rich, but for the middle class and workmen as well. As machines more and more took over the work of hands, the labor time necessary for producing a shirt, a bucket, a pin, or a length of chain was reduced to a small fraction of what it had been formerly. Hours of work, although still long by the standards of the twentieth century, gradually responded to the fact that less labor time was now needed to meet human wants. As leisure time increased, new forms of amusement developed or were introduced from abroad by recent immigrants. City dwellers needed such distraction more than country people because their jobs were usually more monotonous. Many of the immigrants, furthermore, had a greater inclina-

tion to enjoy themselves on holidays than the older stock of Americans, for many of whom Sunday was a day of self-denial.

Sports and Amusements

To meet the new need for diversion many turned to sports. The more wealthy played golf, croquet, and lawn tennis, imported from Great Britain. College students brought in still other British sports—rowing, track, and rugby (from which the American game of football was derived). The American game of baseball was spread all over the country by college and club teams. Starting with the Cincinnati Red Stockings in 1869, more and more teams turned professional. In 1876 the National League was organized, followed shortly by others. Boxing—previously prohibited by law, like cockfighting today—began to attract public interest and to assume respectability after John L. Sullivan won the world's heavyweight championship.

The amusement which for a time outstripped all others was bicycling. After the modern safety bicycle was substituted for the dangerous "high wheeler," bicycling became a craze. There were hundreds of bicycle clubs; special trains carried cyclists into the country on Sundays; and special bicycle paths were built in parks and suburbs. There was even a demand for a bicycle path from one ocean to the other.

The cities—especially the great metropolitan centers such as New York, Philadelphia, Boston, and Chicago—became centers of a much richer cultural life than had ever existed in America. In a day when the motion picture had not yet been invented, vaudeville and the theater enjoyed their period of greatest prosperity. Opera companies and symphony orchestras were founded and halls were built to house them. In 1891 Peter Ilich Tchaikovsky, the famous Russian composer, came to America and conducted one of his own works at the new Carnegie Music Hall in New York. He wrote

The *World's* account of the "Trip Which Will Girdle the Spinning Globe" reports that "On a Four-Day Notice Miss Bly Starts Out with a Gripsack for the Longest Journey Known to Mankind — She Knows No Such Word as Fail." The map shows the route to be followed by this "veritable feminine Phineas Fogg." (*Phileas* Fogg is the hero of Jules Verne's novel *Around the World in Eighty Days* — the newspaper misspelled it!)

home that everything went wonderfully, and that he was received with even greater enthusiasm than in his native land.

The Yellow Press and Dime Novels

The increase in leisure and in literacy encouraged the development of a new form of journalism, devoted to amusing readers as well as informing them. Improvements in paper-making and printing made it possible to produce newspapers far more cheaply than ever before. At the same time there was such increased demand for advertising space that newspapers could derive support entirely from advertisers and sell copies at less than the printing cost.

The pioneer among the new penny newspapers, designed to attract the largest possible number of readers, was the New York *World*, purchased by Joseph Pulitzer in 1883. In fifteen years its circulation rose from fifteen thousand to over a million. Pulitzer, dedicating his paper "to the cause of the people rather than the purse-proud potentates," attacked unfair employers and grafting politicians with vigor. His success came less from editorial policies, however, than from new journalistic methods. Pulitzer gave his readers a regular diet of sensationalism. He was the first to use the "scare headline": "Baptized in Blood," "Death Rides the Rails." He introduced the colored Sunday supplement and the serialized comic strip. If he could not find news, he made it, as when he sent a young woman off at four days' notice to travel around the globe in less time than the hero of Jules Verne's popular novel, *Around the World in Eighty Days.*

About the same time Pulitzer bought the *World*, sports writing had its birth in Chicago when three newspapers began to print highly colored accounts of games played by the Chicago White Stockings. By the end of the century the "yellow press," furnishing its readers with daily doses of scandal, violence, comics, and sports, had become well established.

Another form of reading matter produced for a mass market was the dime novel, which was designed especially to interest boys. These were highly adventurous stories whose favorite scene was the Wild West, where heroes such as Mustang Sam and Deadwood Dick fought Indians, cattle rustlers and outlaws. These early paperbacks also portrayed the worlds of business and crime in such works as "Jay Gould's Office Boy" and "The Terrible Mystery of Car 206." Moralists suspected that dime novels would corrupt the young and they were often hidden from the eyes of alarmed parents, but their defenders pointed out that in them virtue was always triumphant and vice always received its just punishment.

QUESTION • Dime novels were accused of corrupting the young in the 19th century and were often read behind the barn. What of comic books today?

ADVANCES IN EDUCATION

One reason why newspapers could develop an immense circulation and dime novels could be published in editions of fifty thousand, was that more and better education had increased literacy. By 1900 all but two states outside the South made education for all children compulsory. The wealth of urban districts was so great that taxes could easily support the expense of better buildings, longer school terms, and graded schools that were far better than the one-room schoolhouses still prevailing in rural districts. Many cities also introduced free secondary education, and the number of public high schools increased from a few hundred in 1870 to over 6,000 in 1890. Yet public education still left great room for improvement: in 1900 the average American child received only five years of schooling, and the average expenditure per pupil was only about $25 per year.

The most striking development in American education in the latter nineteenth century was the improvement of higher education. At the start of this period, most American colleges and universities had poor equipment and libraries, and ill-trained and overworked faculties. Their fixed curriculum did not include training in modern languages, history, or science. There were no first-rate graduate schools, either in professions such as law and medicine or in the liberal arts. No American scientific school deserved to be mentioned in the same breath with the best in Europe.

By 1900 these weaknesses had been vigorously attacked. Young American scholars trained in German universities, then the best in the world, brought back higher standards of scholarship. From Germany, too, came inspiration for better scientific schools, because much of the amazing advance of German industry could be credited to the superior training of German scientists. By 1900 a number of American technical schools, such as Massachusetts Institute of Technology, California Institute of Technology, Purdue University, and Sheffield Scientific School at Yale, had been founded. These institutions supplied highly trained graduates to answer the demands of American industry for engineers, metallurgists, and chemists.

A great force for reform was a group of able college presidents, such as James McCosh of Princeton, Andrew White of Cornell, Daniel Gilman of Johns Hopkins, and William R. Harper of Chicago. The most famous of these was Charles W. Eliot, president of Harvard from 1869 to 1909. During this time Harvard's enrollment increased from 1,000 to 4,000, the teaching staff from 60 to 600, and the endowment from $2,000,000 to $20,000,000.

At the age of 14, Carey Thomas, a girl from Philadelphia, confided to her diary:

If ever I live and grow up my *one* aim and concentrated purpose *shall be* and *is* to show that women *can learn*, can reason, *can compete* with man in the grand fields of literature and science . . . that open before the 19th century.

Although a brilliant student, Carey Thomas was denied a degree at American universities. In Switzerland she gained a doctorate in literature with highest honors. Later, as dean of Bryn Mawr College (founded in 1885), she inspired young women with her high standards of scholarship and ambitions for her sex. She had a notable ability to pick able teachers: men and women. Woodrow Wilson, the future President of the United States, headed the history department.

Bryn Mawr was one of several women's colleges founded after the Civil War. Others included Vassar (1865), Smith (1875), and Radcliffe (1879). All these colleges had standards at least as high as those of all-male institutions.

But it was not through small, private women's colleges that most women got the chance for higher education. It was through co-education at the great state universities such as Ohio State, Wisconsin, and Iowa. Co-education now came into its own, having started before the Civil War at Oberlin and Antioch in Ohio. Co-education became the rule west of the Appalachians and eventually spread to the more conservative East and South.

Land Grants and Cow Colleges

In 1857 Justin Morrill of Vermont introduced a bill in the House of Representatives providing that some of the country's public lands be sold and the proceeds used to establish colleges. His measure was in line with the 1860 Republican platform: the liberal use of public lands to promote internal improvements.

Usually, internal improvements meant roads, canals, and railroads. But schooling had a long history of public backing, too. The Land Ordinance of 1785 dedicated the sixteenth section of every township to school financing (see page 86). Ordinary people used their first ballots to demand free, tax-supported schools for their children (see p. 277). Now elementary schools were not enough; colleges were needed, and the church-supported "fresh-water" colleges were not meeting the need.

Agriculture was changing; new methods had to be developed to meet new conditions in the western lands. Congressman Morrill was interested in agriculture, and his measure provided for instruction in "agriculture and the mechanic arts" in the new colleges. Still, President Buchanan vetoed the bill, doubting that Congress had the right to make the land grants.

Morrill persisted, and a new act was passed in 1862. Under it, each loyal state was allotted 30,000 acres per Congress member, and the colleges taught not only agriculture but military science and tactics as well. A second bill, passed in 1890, added further benefits. By this time, Morrill was the "grand old man of the Republican party," a senator interested chiefly in finance and the tariff. Some sixty-nine land-grant colleges were established under the terms of the two measures. No longer scorned as "cow colleges," they include many of our leading universities.

Private Gifts and Public Land Grants

Many advances in higher education resulted from gifts by wealthy men. A legacy left by Johns Hopkins of Baltimore made possible the first good graduate school for general studies and one of the world's finest medical schools. Bequests by John D. Rockefeller helped to make the University of Chicago a center of research in fields as varied as economics, biology, and Egyptology. The railroad magnate Leland Stanford established a great university in Palo Alto, California.

Along with the growth of privately endowed universities and technical schools went an expansion of state universities. Such institutions owed a great deal to the passage of the Morrill Act in 1862. This law, a landmark in American education, granted the states public lands for the endowment of colleges to teach "agriculture and the mechanic arts," but "without excluding other scientific and classical studies." Eventually the land-grant colleges received the proceeds from thirteen million acres of land.

By 1900 American college education was not only on a higher plane than ever before, but was more widely available than that provided in any other country, except possibly Scotland.

Public Libraries

For those who wished to continue their education, American cities provided opportunities which had never existed before. The most important agencies promoting adult education were improved public libraries. In 1876 the American Library Association was founded to encourage "the best reading for the largest number at the least expense." The public library, receiving support both from taxes and private donors, was by 1900 coming "to be recognized as no less important than the schoolhouse in the system of popular education."

SCIENTIFIC ADVANCE

While American universities were improving as agencies of teaching, they were also becoming centers of scientific research. Their faculties contained people whose discoveries were of worldwide importance. The Harvard faculty in President Eliot's time included Asa Gray, a botanist who made a thorough study of American plants (see p. 280); Edward Pickering, who as head of the university's astronomical laboratory directed the compilation of the first photographic record of the universe; and William James, who was equally eminent and thought-provoking as a psychologist and as a philosopher. On the Yale faculty at the same time were James Dwight Dana, one of the world's foremost geologists; Josiah Willard Gibbs, who as a mathematical physicist helped to revolutionize conceptions of matter and energy; and Othniel C. Marsh, whose studies of fossil remains resulted in the discovery of the evolution of the horse. Marsh invented the term dinosaur—from the Greek *deinos* (terrible) and *sauros* (lizard)—to describe a previously unknown kind of animal whose remains he discovered in alluvial rocks in Colorado. Scientists of equal eminence were found in new private universities such as Johns Hopkins and Chicago, and state universities such as Illinois and California. The laboratory now stood with the library as a center of university life.

The general public knew little of the university professors who extended the boundaries of pure science, but it was immensely impressed with inventors like Alexander Graham Bell. Bell, whose training was in elocution and whose great interest was in teaching deaf children to speak, figured out the principles of an effective telephone before he taught himself enough about electricity to build one. In 1876 he sent the first telephonic communication to his laboratory assistant, "Mr. Watson, come here; I want you." Only a year later he carried on telephonic conversation between Boston and New York, and his invention soon went into commercial production. Even more famous than Bell was Thomas Alva Edison, who was later erroneously given credit for inventing the electric light, the phonograph, and moving pictures.

QUESTION • Do most inventions come about because there is a technical or popular demand for them, or does the desire or need for them arise after they are invented?

Edison actually made few original discoveries. His greatness lay in his ability to turn the inventions of others into practical use. Thus the incandescent electric light had been demonstrated in England in 1840, but it was Edison who worked out cheap methods of supplying power and wire, as well as filaments that lasted more than just a few minutes. Edison had a fantastic capacity for sustained work, and he surrounded himself with highly skilled technicians. The "invention laboratory" that he founded in Menlo Park, New Jersey, was the ancestor of the great industrial research laboratories of today.

The growth of industry brought with it a host of new developments: a railroad net binding all sections into one market and one nation, the largest business concerns the world had ever seen, vast cities, some of whose populations were counted in millions, great advances in human knowledge and technology. It also brought complex problems, some of which have been touched on in this chapter and some of which will be taken up later: large-scale unemployment, crime, slums, ugliness, fraudulent business practices, violent labor disputes, and corruption in politics. There was no possibility of turning back, however, and little disposition to do so. As Franklin D. Roosevelt said later, "So manifest were the advantages of the machine age . . . that the United States fearlessly, cheerfully, and, I think, rightly accepted the bitter with the sweet. It was thought that no price was too high for the advantages we could draw from a finished industrial system."

Activities: Chapter 15

For Mastery and Review

1. Give six or seven major reasons for the rapid industrialization of the United States in the generation following the Civil War. What were the resulting effects upon the standard of living?

2. What were legitimate and unfair advantages of big business? (These might be set down in parallel columns.)

3. Study the diagrams of vertical and horizontal consolidations on p. 396, and explain each type.

4. Compare the contributions to the industrial growth of the United States of Rockefeller and Carnegie.

5. What were the problems that developed as cities grew larger? Explain each. What benefits came with industrialization and urbanization?

6. How did industrialization create leisure for great numbers of people? What amusements and new interests developed?

7. What were the characteristics of the yellow press? Explain its popularity.

8. What changes in education came with urbanization? Explain the improvements in college education during the latter years of the nineteenth century.

9. Summarize briefly advances made in science in the United States in the period between the end of the Civil War and the turn of the century.

Unrolling the Map

On an outline map of eastern United States, locate the deposits of iron in the Mesabi Range;

the coalfields of Pennsylvania, West Virginia, Ohio, and Illinois; and Pittsburgh and the steel mill cities on the Great Lakes. Study the diagram of a vertical consolidation and relate Carnegie's steel operations to your map.

Who, What, and Why Important?

mobile labor supply	urban transportation
big business	Cincinnati Red Stock-
holding company	ings
vertical consolidation	Joseph Pulitzer
horizontal consolidation	technical schools
John D. Rockefeller	Charles W. Eliot
rebates	Carey Thomas
the Standard Oil Trust	land-grant colleges
Andrew Carnegie	Alexander Graham Bell
urbanization	Thomas Alva Edison

To Pursue the Matter

1. From *The World Almanac* or *Information Please Almanac* find out the comparative sizes and populations of the continent of Europe and the United States. How many separate sovereign states are there in Europe? What are the probable economic disadvantages of this political fractionalization, compared with the United States? In what ways is western Europe seeking economic unity?

2. Find out about the methods of a modern meat-packing plant. Also read "Swift—Yankee of the Yards" in Arnof, *A Sense of the Past*, pp. 272–275. How have the great meat-packing companies changed the dietary patterns of Americans?

3. How many major products are derived from petroleum and natural gas? Next to each one you name, illustrate the product or its use.

4. Investigate the foundation and growth of your city or one near you. Why was it located where it was? What factors contributed to its growth? Make a graph, perhaps one big enough for a wall display, of population growth since 1860. Indicate, if you can, what was responsible for each major increase.

5. From "Progress in the United States," by James Bryce, and "How the Other Half Lives," by Jacob A. Riis, both in Arnof, *A Sense of the Past*, pp. 275–280, you can gain insight into social mobility in the new industrial America. Is it good for society to have people constantly moving up and down in the social scale? Does it promote democracy?

6. ". . . in 1900 the average American child received only five years of schooling, and the average expenditure per pupil was $25 per year." (p. 404.) What are the corresponding figures for your community today? How do they compare with the national average today? See *The Statistical Abstract of the United States*.

7. Report to the class on the present-day activities of one of the following: Rockefeller Foundation, General Education Board, Carnegie Corporation, Ford Foundation.

8. In Handlin, *The Uprooted*, or Chapter 11 of Wish, *Society and Thought in Modern America*, read how and why immigrants came to America in the latter half of the nineteenth century and what difficulties they had to contend with. If life in American cities was so hard, why did they come by millions?

9. In Rostow, *The Stages of Economic Growth*, you can find what he considers to be the conditions necessary for rapid economic growth. Apply his theory to the sensational growth of American industry from the 1850's on.

Chapter 16

The Opening of the Trans-Mississippi West

We primeval forests felling,
We the rivers stemming, vexing we and
piercing deep the mines within,
We the surface broad surveying, we the
virgin soil upheaving,
Pioneers! O Pioneers!

—WALT WHITMAN

At the close of the Civil War, the Great Plains (see map, p. 7) were still thought to be forever barred to white settlement. The vast Rocky Mountain plateau was equally void of white people, save for a few mining towns and Mormon communities. Yet in the ensuing twenty-five years these regions were developed with almost incredible speed. You could not tell the truth about the growth of the West, it was said, without lying.

RAILROAD BUILDING AND CONSOLIDATION

This rapid development was made possible by the railroad. As a Dakota editor wrote, "Without the railroad it would have required a century to accomplish what has been done in five years." The generation after the war saw both the great period of railroad building in the West and the consolidation of eastern lines. Steel produced by the Bessemer process (see p. 393) enabled the companies to lay heavier rails and build bridges which could carry bigger cars and more power-

ful locomotives. Other technical problems were solved. The Westinghouse air brake at last made possible the simultaneous braking of the cars and the locomotive. The invention of the kerosene lamp and later of the electric light permitted better headlights for night running. In 1860 railroads carried less than half as much freight as inland waterways; in 1890 railroads carried five times as much.

The large amounts of capital needed to build and equip railroads were obtained from various sources. The federal government gave western railroads money grants totaling over 700 million dollars and public lands whose acreage equaled that of Texas. Help came from states and municipalities and still more from private investors. The savings of New Englanders, accumulated from the West Indies and China trade, from clippers and whalers, from textile and shoe factories, helped to build thousands of miles of track across western prairies. An equally important source of private capital, however, was Europe. The value of American railroad securities owned by British investors in 1900 was two and a half billion dollars—over twice the national debt of the United States at that time.

First Transcontinental Railroad, 1869

The most dramatic achievement in railroad building was the completion of the first transcontinental line. Discussion of this project began with the discovery of gold in California in 1849. During the 1850's no less than ten routes were surveyed, and the Gadsden Purchase was acquired from Mexico principally because the Gila River Valley provided the lowest route across the western plateau. Nothing was decided before the war, however, because of intense sectional rivalry, the South wanting the eastern terminal at New Orleans, the North preferring St. Louis or Chicago. In 1862, with the South temporarily out of the Union, Congress passed an act to encourage the building of a Pacific Railroad. From Omaha the Union Pacific Company was to build westward, and from Sacramento, the Central Pacific Company was to run lines eastward. The federal government lent money to those companies at the rate of $16,000, $32,000, or $48,000 per mile, according to the terrain. They also received land grants along the right of way averaging 6,400 acres per mile.

Construction began in earnest shortly after the war and proceeded rapidly. The two railroads were competing to get more government money and public lands, as well as to secure a greater share of the trade of the interior. At the height of the struggle the Union Pacific builders employed 10,000 men. Crews of Irishmen working for the Union Pacific and of Chinese working for the Central Pacific sometimes laid as much as six miles of track a day. Once on a bet of $10,000, a Central Pacific crew laid ten miles of track between sunrise and sundown, an all-time world's record. "It is a literal fact that more ground was ironed in some days, by the two companies together, than the ox teams of 1849 averaged in a single day's journey."

The steam shovel not yet having been invented, the digging and grading were done by men and teams. Holes for blasting had to be driven by men with sledge hammers. The Union Pacific building crews had to be protected from Indian attacks and buffalo stampedes. The Central Pacific had an even more difficult time with the Sierra Nevada ranges and with snow that sometimes collected in drifts sixty feet deep. All its heavy equipment was carried from the East 19,000 miles around Cape Horn to California in a fleet of thirty ships.

The two lines met at Promontory Point, Utah, and on May 10, 1869, the "wedding of the rails" took place. The whole country was able to listen as the transcontinental telegraph reported the blow of the silver sledge hammer driving the golden spike. A magnetic ball dropped from a pole on the top of the Capitol in Washington; in Chicago a seven-mile procession paraded through the streets; everywhere the air rang with the bells of churches and firehouses. The "northwest passage" from the Atlantic Ocean to the Pacific had at last been established.

James J. Hill, Railroad Builder

The first transcontinental line was followed shortly by others—the Northern Pacific; the Atchison, Topeka, and Santa Fe; the Southern Pacific; and the Great Northern. Like other big businesses, these railroads needed at the top people of ability, imagination, and drive. The greatest of the western builders was James J. Hill (1838–1916), creator of the Great Northern. Hill was a small, short-tempered, red-bearded man of titanic energy. He foresaw that his line would tie together the whole northern tier of the United States from Lake Superior to Puget Sound. It would carry flour westward from the Dakotas and Minnesota for eventual shipment to Japan and China, and carry Pacific Coast lumber eastward for barns, silos, and homes in

The driving of the golden spike that linked the Union Pacific and Central Pacific Railroads was celebrated all over the United States. The two companies had been competing to lay the most track, and sometimes as many as eight or ten miles were laid in a single day.

the Great Plains. "We consider ourselves and the people along our lines," he said, "as co-partners in the prosperity of the country we both occupy." Believing passionately in the life of the Plains farmer, he wanted to promote maximum settlement. "Population without the Prairie," Hill wrote, "is a mob, and the Prairie without Population is a desert."

Hill started to build the Great Northern in 1879. He had neither federal subsidies nor land grants to help him, and not too much private capital either. His railroad had to pay its own way from the first. The only way to do this was to encourage settlement as soon as the rails were laid. All sorts of inducements were offered to get farmers to settle along "Jim Hill's main line"— free transportation from eastern ports, credit,

cheap tools, and farm machinery. Once established, farmers were furnished with high quality cattle, given free advice on how to improve crops, and offered prizes for the best quality produce.

Hill saw to it that his bridges and embankments were well constructed, and his grades less steep than those of competitive lines. He was constantly with the construction gangs, sometimes even seizing a pick or shovel himself. This careful construction kept maintenance costs down, enabling Hill to charge lower rates; this, in turn, meant lower prices and better markets for the grain, cattle, and lumber he shipped. Hill made mistakes, such as encouraging the planting of wheat in areas more suitable for grazing, but he showed greatness in keeping fixedly to the idea that what was good for the Northwest was good for the Great Northern.

Cornelius Vanderbilt, Railroad Consolidator

Of as much importance in the development of the country as the building of lines to the Pacific was the consolidation of existing railroads in the Middle West, East, and South into a few great systems. A highly successful railroad consolidator was Cornelius Vanderbilt (1794–1877), who built up the New York Central system. A hard-bitten former ferryboat captain, Vanderbilt had assumed the unofficial title of "commodore" because he owned a small fleet of coastal trading vessels. He did not seriously enter railroading until his late sixties, when he acquired two short lines running into New York City from the north, and then managed to buy control of the New York Central which ran as far as Buffalo. Vanderbilt was a combination of shrewd speculator, ruthless competitor, and man of vision. Much of his huge fortune came from stock market operations. He was master of the tricks whereby insiders rigged the stock market in order to force prices down or up as they pleased. In business deals the Commodore sometimes showed scant respect for either law or the public interest. On the other hand, he saw the great benefits which would come from tying the Great Lakes region to New York City by a water-level route. He extended his control over lines running all the way to Chicago, as well as stretching through Michigan and into southern Canada. In addition to bringing many lines under one management, Vanderbilt made great improvements in service. He built the Grand Central Terminal in New York City with the largest train shed in the world —600 feet long and 200 wide. He was one of the first to use the Westinghouse air brake, and the very first to lay a four-track

QUESTION • Why was it difficult to stop a railroad train? What were the advantages of the air brake?

main line (two tracks for freight, two for passenger traffic).

Consolidation proceeded rapidly in the period from the end of the Civil War to the turn of the century so that eventually most of the traffic was controlled by seven major systems with terminals in major cities and scores of branches reaching out into the countryside. A "standard" gauge (4 feet, 8½ inches) had been universally accepted and time zones established. The big systems were able to put on better rolling stock, to shunt cars from one section to another according to seasonal needs, and to speed long distance transportation. They made so many economies in operation that the average rate per mile for a ton of freight dropped from 2 cents in 1860 to three-quarters of a cent in 1900.

FATE OF THE BUFFALO AND THE INDIANS

The railroads played a part in the extermination of the buffalo which opened the western plains to cattle grazing. Buffalo formerly ranged eastward as far as Pennsylvania and the Carolinas, but their natural habitat was the Great Plains, where their numbers defied counting. It was estimated that in 1865 the herds numbered twelve to fifteen million animals. The building of the Union Pacific Railroad cut the herds in half, as a period of ruthless butchery began. Vast numbers were killed for their hides alone. Many were slaughtered by "sportsmen," who cut out the tongue or a steak to eat and left the rest of the animal for the wolves. Whole train loads of bones were shipped east for making fertilizer or charcoal. By 1883 the herds were wiped out and the buffalo was close to extinction.

This wanton slaughter meant disaster for the Plains Indians. These master horsemen and skillful warriors had been, in the words of Walter P. Webb, "the most effectual barrier ever set up by a native American population against European invaders in the temperate zone. For two

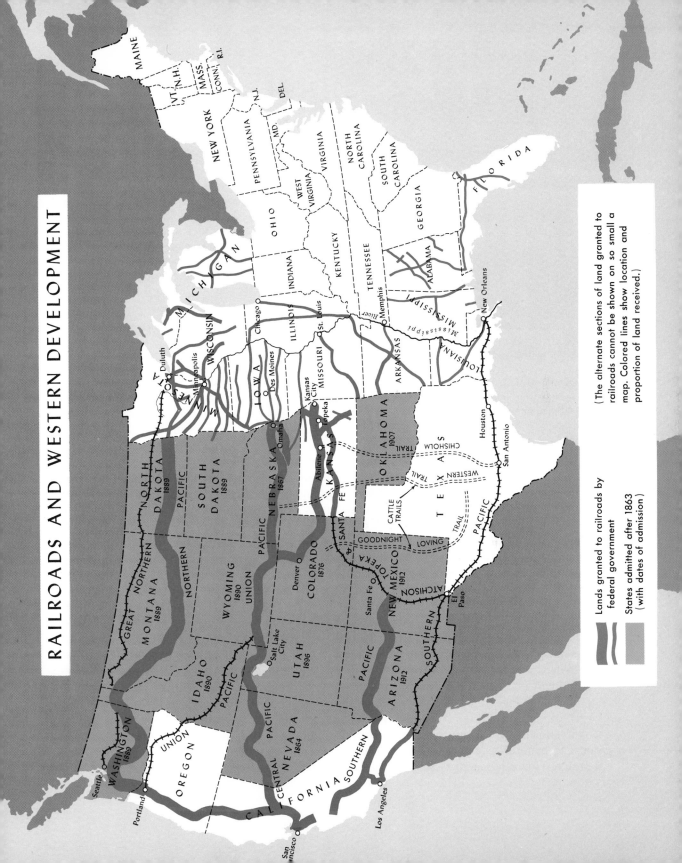

RAILROADS AND WESTERN DEVELOPMENT

MAINE

VT. N.H. MASS.
CONN. R.I.

NEW YORK

PENNSYLVANIA

N.J.
DEL.
MD.
WEST VIRGINIA
VIRGINIA
NORTH CAROLINA
SOUTH CAROLINA
GEORGIA
FLORIDA

OHIO
INDIANA
KENTUCKY
TENNESSEE
ALABAMA

MICHIGAN

WISCONSIN
Chicago
ILLINOIS
St. Louis
Mississippi River
Memphis
MISSISSIPPI
LOUISIANA
New Orleans

Duluth
Minneapolis
MINNESOTA
IOWA
Des Moines
MISSOURI
Kansas City
ARKANSAS

NORTH DAKOTA 1889
GREAT NORTHERN
MONTANA 1889
NORTHERN PACIFIC

SOUTH DAKOTA 1889
NEBRASKA 1867
UNION PACIFIC
Omaha
Topeka
Abilene
KANSAS
SANTA FE
ATCHISON TOPEKA &

OKLAHOMA 1907
CHISHOLM TRAIL
CATTLE TRAILS
WESTERN TRAIL
Houston
San Antonio
TEXAS
PACIFIC

WYOMING 1890
UNION PACIFIC

IDAHO 1890
NORTHERN PACIFIC

UTAH 1896
Salt Lake City
CENTRAL PACIFIC

NEVADA 1864

COLORADO 1876
Denver
Santa Fe
NEW MEXICO 1912
GOODNIGHT
LOVING TRAIL
El Paso

ARIZONA 1912
SOUTHERN PACIFIC

WASHINGTON 1889
Seattle
Portland
OREGON
UNION PACIFIC

CALIFORNIA
CENTRAL PACIFIC
SOUTHERN PACIFIC
San Francisco
Los Angeles

Lands granted to railroads by federal government

States admitted after 1863 (with dates of admission)

(The alternate sections of land granted to railroads cannot be shown on so small a map. Colored lines show location and proportion of land received.)

An encampment of Sioux Indians in the West. These tipis were designed not only to protect the inhabitants from wind and rain but to give a good draft to cooking fires.

and a half centuries they maintained themselves with great fortitude against the Spanish, English, French, Mexican, Texan, and American invaders, withstanding missionaries, whisky, disease, gunpowder and lead." To most of the tribes of the Great Plains, such as the Sioux, the Comanches, and the Cheyennes, fighting and horse-raiding were all-absorbing sports and prowess in battle the highest virtue. They put up such an amazing fight against troops sent against them that it has been estimated that each brave killed by the soldiers cost the federal government a million dollars. But the cause of the Indians was doomed in any case, since they were almost entirely dependent on the buffalo for food, clothing, fuel, and shelter. When the herds were wiped out, the tribes had the choice of starvation or virtual imprisonment in reservations. In spite of a few victories, such as the defeat of General George Custer on the Little Big Horn in 1876, and heroic deeds, such as the 1,500-mile march of the Nez Percés under Chief Joseph in 1877, the result was a foregone conclusion. Chief Joseph's speech at his surrender summarized the hopelessness of the Indian cause:

Our chiefs are killed. . . . The little children are freezing to death. My people . . . have no blankets, no food. . . . I want to have time to look for my children and see how many of them I can find. Maybe I shall find them among the dead. Hear me, my chiefs; I am tired; my heart is sick and sad. From where the sun now stands, I will fight no more forever.

Many Americans were ashamed of the injustice done the Indians. The report of the Secretary of the Interior to Congress in 1868 called their treatment by the United States government "revolting." In 1881 the attention of the country was focused on the matter by the publication of Helen Hunt Jackson's *A Century of Dishonor*. Mrs. Jackson pleaded that the whites stop "cheating, robbing, breaking promises." Her book led to the founding of the Indian Rights Association, devoted to improving the lot of the red men.

The early Indian reformers went on the probably mistaken assumption that the best thing for the red man would be to make him as much as possible like the white. Their attitude was reflected in the Dawes Act of 1887, which broke down Indian tribal organizations and divided some Indian reservations into 160-acre homesteads. Although the law was well intentioned, it did the Indians little or no good. They usually had little skill at farming and almost no conception of private ownership of land. They were too often at the mercy of greedy real estate speculators and grafting Indian Agents. Between 1887 and 1934, they lost an estimated 86,000,000 of 138,000,000 acres. Most of the land left in their control was almost worthless.

THE CATTLE KINGDOM

The removal of the buffalo and the Indians, as well as the opening of eastern markets by the railroad, ushered in the great days of the cattlemen. The buffalo grass of the Great Plains provided free pasturage for millions of steers, and the meat packers of Chicago bought all steers delivered at the railheads.

The Open Range and the Long Drive

The open-range cattle industry started in Texas in Spanish times, and the Spaniards developed most of its techniques—herding by mounted men, branding, roping, and the round-up. From the Spanish, too, came the distinctive dress and equipment of the cowboy—except for the six-shooter, which was so cumbersome that it was only worn occasionally. From the Texas plains came breeds of cattle able to shift for themselves, the most picturesque being the famous longhorns. In 1865 it was estimated that there were over three million cattle in Texas, but no one knew for sure because most of them were mavericks—without owners.

In Texas, cattle cost $3 or $4 a head; in St. Louis or Chicago they could be sold for $30 or $40. The "four-dollar cow" was connected with the "forty-dollar market" by means of the "long drive." As the spring turned the grasslands green, herds of steers were driven northwards to shipping centers on the railroads. The routes of the long drive were known as trails, such as the Chisholm Trail from near San Antonio to Abilene, a station on the Kansas Pacific Railroad (see map, p. 413). A single herd might number 2,500 and be attended by eight to ten cowboys, a trail boss, and wranglers to care for the horses. Cowboys had a rightful pride in their work, which demanded skill, intelligence, quick judgment, and courage. It also demanded discipline, and it is not surprising that many cowboys were veterans of the Civil War.

The profits obtained from a successful drive were enormous. On an investment of $15,000 a man might make $30,000 in less than a year. A 30 to 40 per cent return was normal. As the buffalo were cleared from the Plains, the Cattle Kingdom expanded northward until by 1885 it covered an area half as large as Europe, extending from Texas to Montana. From the East, even from Great Britain and France, men with money to invest and a taste for adventure hastened to the Plains and bought cattle.

Although offering vast profits, the industry was beset by difficulties. Steers might go blind from drought, drown in flash floods, die in stampedes, or get infected by the dreaded Texas fever. They might be stolen by rustlers or shot by angry homesteaders trying to protect their crops. Eventually, the open-range cattle industry collapsed even more rapidly than it had risen. Too many animals were put on the ranges, and overgrazing resulted. Overproduction drove prices down. Sheepherders and homesteaders competed with the cattlemen for available land.

Then in 1885–1887 disaster struck. A cold winter was followed by a summer so dry that the grass withered and streams disappeared. In the ensuing winter, that of 1886–1887, terrible blizzards covered the ground so deep with snow that the steers could not paw down to grass. Then followed an unprecedented cold spell, with temperatures ranging as low as $-60°F$. "When spring finally came," wrote Ray Allen Billington, "cattlemen saw a sight they spent the rest of their lives trying to forget. Carcass piled upon carcass in every ravine, gaunt skeletons staggering about on frozen feet, trees stripped bare of their bark—those were left as monuments to the thoughtless greed of the ranchers." The cattle industry survived this terrible blow, but the day of the open range was ended. From then on herds were raised on fenced-in ranches; English Herefords replaced longhorns; the cowboy became a ranch hand.

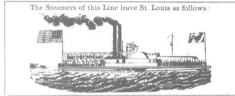

HO! FOR THE GOLD MINES!
THROUGH
BILLS LADING
GIVEN BY THE
MONTANA & IDAHO TRANSPORTATION LINE
TO
Virginia City, Bannock City, Deer Lodge
AND
ALL POINTS IN THE MINING DISTRICTS.

The Steamers of this Line leave St. Louis as follows:

The New York Historical Society

When new mining strikes were made in the West, advertisements of transportation were distributed in the East. Few travelers to the West became wealthy. Here a wagon that started out bravely, with the slogan of "Pike's Peak or Bust," returned home with the line, "Busted, by Thunder."

The New-York Historical Society

THE MINING FRONTIER

Another element in the growth of the West was the advance of the mining frontier. The finding of gold in California inspired prospectors to explore the Rocky Mountain and Great Basin regions. They were first rewarded by a gold strike in Colorado in 1858, which set off a stampede to the region the next year:

The first breath of spring started the hordes westward. Steamboats crowded to the rails poured throngs of immigrants ashore at every Missouri River town. . . . All through April, May, and June they left the jumping-off places in a regular parade of Conestoga wagons, hand carts, men on horseback, men on foot—each with "Pike's Peak or Bust" crudely printed on their packs and wagon canvas. . . . By the end of June more than 100,000 "fifty-niners" were in the Pike's Peak country.

Law and Order in the Mining Camps

The Colorado strike was followed by many others; gold was discovered in the Black Hills of Dakota, copper in Montana, silver in many places, especially in the fabulous Comstock Lode at Virginia City, Nevada. Every discovery attracted a swarm of fortune seekers, and new mining towns appeared overnight.

Human life was cheap in these communities of tents and crude houses, with their rows of saloons and gambling houses. There was a vital need for law enforcement agencies to settle disputes over mining claims, and to punish or prevent crime. Law and order were sometimes provided by self-appointed vigilance commit-tees, sometimes by mass meetings which, follow-ing a tradition going back to the Mayflower Compact, drew up their own rules and elected their own officials. Soon the different communi-ties of a region such as Colorado or Nevada would band together and demand territorial status or statehood. A foreign traveler in Colo-rado was so impressed by this American habit of self-organization that he wrote:

Making governments and building towns are the natural employments of the migratory Yankee. He takes to them as a young duck to water. Congregate a hundred Americans anywhere beyond the settlements and they immediately lay out a city, frame a state constitution and apply for admission to the Union, while twenty-five of them become candidates for the United States Senate.

With a few exceptions the actual grant of statehood did not come until the arrival of homesteaders. The miners and the cattle raisers were too roving a population to provide stable government.

The Wild West

The Wild West captured the imagination of Americans at once. Dime novels and popular ballads spread the adventures of Wild Bill Hickok, Billy the Kid, and Jesse James. A Wild West Show became part of Barnum and Bailey's famous circus; and Annie Oakley, the sharpshooter, appeared on vaudeville stages everywhere. The Wild West period lasted little more than thirty years, yet its fascination continues, as shown by Wild West storybooks and comics, dude ranches, cowboy songs and costumes, and the "Westerns" produced by Hollywood and shown on television.

QUESTION • Why was the Wild West wild?

The picturesqueness of the Wild West tends to hide its ugly features. The conquest of the Great Plains and the Rockies by the invading cattle ranchers, miners, and homesteaders was appallingly destructive of natural resources, wildlife, and human beings. Something of the "morning after" shock of their episode appeared in a speech that Charles Marion Russell, a frontier artist, made to "forward looking citizens" in Helena, Montana:

I have been called a pioneer. In my book a pioneer is a man who comes to a virgin country, traps off all the fur, kills off all the wild meat, cuts down all the trees, grazes off all the grass, plows the roots up, and strings ten million miles of wire. A pioneer destroys things and calls it civilization. I wish to God this country was just like it was when I first saw it and that none of you folks were here at all.

PEOPLING THE GREAT PLAINS

For nearly forty years after cultivation approached them, the Great Plains resisted settlement. Even allowing for the Indian conflict, the most fundamental reason for farmers' unwillingness to venture into the great ocean of grass was that it was a wholly new environment. The pioneer was used to getting water by digging a well 10 to 20 feet into the ground. In the Plains few streams ran all year round, and underground water was 30 to 300 feet down. The American pioneer was a woods dweller, dependent on trees for fuel, buildings, and fences. On the Plains, trees were found only in the bottom lands near rivers. These conditions discouraged settlers.

By 1880 the Indians were no longer to be feared. Other difficulties were overcome by the progress of the industrial revolution. Cheap iron and steel made possible the drilled well in a sheet-iron case and the iron windmill. Barbed wire made up for the lack of wooden fence rails. As has been noted, the most important factor in promoting settlement was the railroad. "You may," wrote a spectator of the Dakota boom of the early 1880's, "stand ankle deep in the short grass of uninhabited wilderness; next month a mixed train will glide over the waste and stop at some point where the railroad has decided to locate a town. Men, women, and children will jump out of the cars, and their chattels will tumble out after them. From that moment the building begins."

Meanwhile improved agricultural machinery cut the cost of raising crops. The reaper, in general use by 1865, was followed by the mechanical binder which tied the grain into sheaves as fast as it was cut. By 1880, two people and a team could harvest and bind 20 acres of wheat a day. The steam-driven threshing machine also came into general use. Other machines speeded the production of corn and hay. In addition to solving technical problems, the industrial revolution speeded the expansion of agriculture by creating a vast new urban market for food, both in America and Europe.

Homestead Act, 1862

Congress passed in 1862 the famous Homestead Act whereby a "head of a family" who was a citizen or intending to become one might acquire a 160-acre farm for ten dollars. To insure that the land went to actual settlers it provided that the owner must reside on or cultivate the land for five years. The act was passed as a result of nearly half a century of agitation by western farmers and eastern laborers. The Homestead Act did not work out as planned. An immense amount of fraud in the operation of the law enabled speculators instead of actual settlers to get the land. Requirements that a would-be homesteader put up a home and cultivate the land were met by laying down a few logs as a "foundation," and scattering a few grains of corn. People became "heads of families" by temporarily adopting neighbors' children. A more important reason for the ineffectiveness of the Homestead Act was that much of the most desirable land, near railroad lines, was usually controlled by the railroad companies themselves.

Annie, Get Your Gun

Annie Oakley was the last of one type of pioneer and the first of another. Born in 1860, she became famous only after the frontier had closed and the frontier skills of shooting, riding, and axemanship had been relegated mainly to professional exhibitions. As a performer in such exhibitions, Annie bravely invaded a man's field. She more than held her own, setting the pace for later women in business and the professions.

Too small for farm work as a child, Annie developed her marksmanship shooting rabbits and squirrels to feed her family. At fifteen, while visiting Cincinnati, she accepted the challenge of an exhibition rifleman. She shot down twenty-five glass balls to his twenty-four. She married her bested opponent, Frank Butler, the next year.

The Butlers joined the Buffalo Bill Wild West Show, and Annie became world famous. She met Queen Victoria in England, outfired the Grand Duke Michael in Russia, and neatly shot a cigarette from the lips of Prince Wilhelm in Germany. The highlights of this career form the basis for Irving Berlin's musical comedy *Annie Get Your Gun*.

High skill with a rifle no longer commands world admiration, but Annie Oakley's name still recalls a woman who achieved perfection at a man's game.

"Selling" the West

The ineffectiveness of the Homestead Act provided Westerners with a grievance, but probably did not discourage settlement. Although railroads sometimes discouraged the acquisition of free land, they actively promoted the sale of their own. They did not charge high prices because they wanted settlers to get the land into production. Land-grant railroads had "Bureaus of Immigration" to persuade farmers to settle along their lines. They maintained offices in the principal European cities, and agents in eastern seaports to meet immigrants as they left the boat. Steamship companies and western states joined the railroads in promoting the West. Advertisements described the region as so healthy that it cured all known diseases. The industrious man could expect to become wealthy; an $8,000 investment, it was claimed, might soon result in a steady income of $11,000 per year. The women were not forgotten, and the West was pictured as a happy hunting ground for unmarried ladies. "When a daughter of the East is once beyond the Missouri," said one railroad advertisement, "she rarely recrosses it except on a bridal tour."

To offset the myth of the "Great American Desert," a new myth was created to the effect that rainfall on the Great Plains would increase with cultivation; a Nebraska promoter summed it up in the catchy epigram, "Rain follows the plow." The production of wheat, centering in Minnesota, the Dakotas, and Nebraska, quadrupled. Nor did all this growth take place at the frontier. In the previously occupied "corn-hog" belt, extending from Ohio to Iowa, output increased as rapidly as in the new wheat lands. Wisconsin became a great center of cheese production. Near every great city, truck gardens were developed to provide vegetables, and a "milkshed" to supply fresh dairy products for the growing urban populations.

Difficulties of Life on the Plains

The life of a Great Plains farmer seldom approached the glowing prophecies of railroad agents. The climate supposed to cure all known diseases turned out to be severe. In the summer the temperature might go over 100°F. for days on end. In winter there were periods of great cold, and terrible blizzards drove the snow through every chink in doors and windows. Prairie fires were a constant danger in the spring and fall. Sometimes there appeared, as if from nowhere, huge swarms of grasshoppers which ate everything green, choked wells to the brim, broke the branches off fruit trees by their weight, and even devoured harnesses and tool handles. Worst of all disasters was drought. The rainfall of the Plains region is markedly less than that of the wooded East, dropping from about 30 to 40 inches along the 98th meridian to as little as 10 inches just east of the Rockies. Much of it was land suitable only for grazing; it should never have been plowed.

The greatest push westward into the Great Plains took place in the early 1880's, during a wet period which offered false promise of abundant crops. In the late 1880's drought drove thousands back east in despair. William Allen White, the famous editor of the Emporia *Gazette*, thus described a family he saw returning from western Kansas:

There came through Emporia yesterday two old-fashioned mover wagons headed east. The stock in the caravan would invoice four horses, very poor and very tired, one mule more disheartened than the horses, and one sad-eyed dog. . . . A few farm implements of the simpler sort had been loaded in the wagons, but. . . . the rest of the impedimenta had been left upon the battlefield. . . . These movers . . . had seen it stop raining for months at a time. They had heard the fury of the winter wind as it came whining across the short burned grass. . . . They have tossed through hot nights, wild with worry, and have arisen only to find their worst nightmares grazing in reality on the brown stubble in front of their sun-warped doors.

White went on to say that the family's spirits revived amid the plenty of eastern Kansas and they were ready to try again. In spite of all difficulties, however, most settlers managed to conquer their physical environment. Water from deep wells enabled them to plant gardens and trees around their homes. The railroads brought lumber and brick for houses to replace sod huts, and coal to replace cornstalks or hay as fuel.

The Literature of the Sod House Frontier

The struggle of the farmers with the Plains produced a literature quite unlike that of the Wild West. Cowboys and miners were usually young men; their lives were adventurous; they were on the move. But homesteaders took on responsibilities difficult to shed; they often pledged themselves to a bank, invested in tools and land, and started to raise a family. When misfortune hit, they had to weather it out. It is natural to find, therefore, that the literature of the Plains was realistic, sometimes bitter. This can be seen in the stories of Hamlin Garland, who was born on a Wisconsin farm in 1860. Garland's family moved west three times during his boyhood. In books such as *Main-Travelled Roads* and *A Son of the Middle Border,* he told "a tale of toil that's never done." Although describing moments of joy such as harvest time, or of beauty, as when the spring touched the Plains, Garland refused to say that "butter was always golden and biscuits invariably light and flaky." "I will not lie," he wrote, "even to be a patriot. A proper proportion of the sweat, flies, heat, dirt, and drudgery shall go in."

A principal source of settlers for the northern portion of the Great Plains was Scandinavia. So many settlers came to the wheat country that by 1890 four hundred Minnesota towns bore Scandinavian names. Letters written to relatives back home described the wonders of the new land. "Here it is not asked," wrote one, "what or who was your father, but the question is, what are you?" Another wrote of the pleasure of eating white bread every day and pork three times a week. Still another remarked that here was a country where there were no thieves or beggars. But they told of troubles too: Indian raids, prairie fires, locusts, and loneliness. Such troubles provide the subject of the greatest novel of the Great Plains, O. E. Rölvaag's *Giants in the Earth,* written in Norwegian. It describes the heroic efforts of two people, Per and Beret Hansa, to establish a farm in South Dakota. They eventually triumph, but the human cost is terrible: Beret goes slowly mad, and Per dies in a blizzard.

Frontier Women

For women, the pioneering phase of life on the Plains often meant solitude and drudgery. "Born and scrubbed, suffered and died," is the epitaph given a woman in one of Hamlin Garland's poems. Yet the settlement of the West owed more to the endless toil of frontier women than to Indian fighters, fur traders, and prospectors. A character in Edna Ferber's novel *Cimarron* pays this tribute:

You can't read the history of the United States, my friends . . . without learning the great story of those thousands of unnamed women . . . women in mud-caked boots and calico dresses and sunbonnets, crossing the prairie and the desert and the mountains enduring hardship and privation. Good women with a terrible and rigid goodness that comes of work and self-denial. Nothing picturesque or romantic about them, I suppose . . . no, their story's never really been told. But it's there just the same. And if it's ever told straight, you'll know it's the sunbonnet and not the sombrero that's settled this country.

It is not surprising that women have written some of the best accounts of Plains life, such as *Cimarron* and *My Ántonia* by Willa Cather. While not minimizing the sufferings of pioneer-

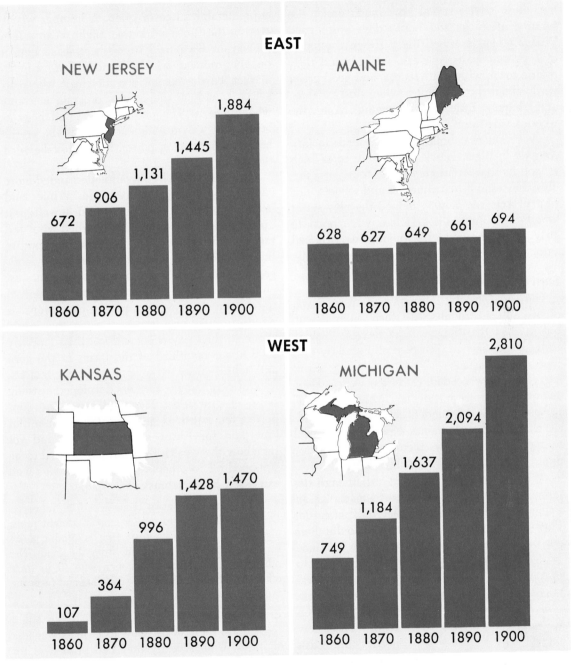

GROWTH OF POPULATION (in thousands) 1860—1900

EAST

NEW JERSEY

1860	1870	1880	1890	1900
672	906	1,131	1,445	1,884

MAINE

1860	1870	1880	1890	1900
628	627	649	661	694

WEST

KANSAS

1860	1870	1880	1890	1900
107	364	996	1,428	1,470

MICHIGAN

1860	1870	1880	1890	1900
749	1,184	1,637	2,094	2,810

Population patterns of four states, 1860-1900. In Maine there was little industry; fishing and farming were static. New Jersey had a steady growth in industry, dairying, and truck farming. Michigan's pattern was a product of the growth of lumbering, farming, and industrial cities. Kansas' growth rate accelerated because of the expansion of wheat growing, then leveled off because of drought in the late 1880's.

ing, these novels reveal how much easier life became after the sod house days were past. Willa Cather described Black Hawk, the locale of *My Antonia*, as "a clean, well-planted little prairie town, with white fences, and good green yards about the dwellings, wide, dusty streets, and shapely little trees growing along the wooden sidewalks."

A prominent building mentioned in *My Antonia* in Black Hawk was a new brick high school. As soon as farmers began to make a surplus, they established churches and schools. The Morrill Act (see p. 405) helped the new states to establish universities. These were open to girls as well as boys; the pioneer women had earned for their sex a new position of equality.

Farmers' Loss of Independence

The sorest trouble farmers had to face was often not the struggle with their environment, but the fact that they were in the grip of economic forces beyond their control. Formerly they had been subsistence farmers, producing almost everything they needed. Subsistence agriculture gave them little cash, but they were "beholden" to nobody. The independent farmer was a standard character in melodramas, especially when contrasted with unhappy factory hands, purse-proud rich people, or dishonest "city slickers."

With the opening of great urban markets, farmers tended more and more to specialize on a single cash crop, such as wheat, milk, or cattle. Their income naturally went up, but so did their expenses, since they now had to buy agricultural machinery, store clothing, and even food. The new need for cash made farmers less independent. Their prosperity, their very possession of their farms, might depend on the

QUESTION • Who enjoyed more security: the isolated subsistence farmer of the Kentucky frontier, or the wheat farmer of the Dakotas?

unpredictable price of grain. A bumper wheat crop in the Russian Ukraine might mean a lean year in the Dakotas. Farmers became dependent on the railroad which carried their crop to market, on the commission merchant who marketed it, and on the owners of grain elevators who stored it. The person who raised hogs or beef cattle was in a similar situation; he or she had little bargaining power, having to take what the packers paid.

The new type of cultivation demanded more capital investment than the old. While land itself was cheap, it cost money to drill wells, put up windmills, enclose fields in barbed wire, and buy machinery. Since few farmers could put up the cash outright, they had to borrow by mortgaging their land. Then in order to pay interest on the mortgages, they were forced to concentrate more than ever on raising cash crops. If prices dropped or a lean year came, they could not meet their payments and lost their land. By 1900 about one-third of the farms in the corn and wheat areas were cultivated by tenants.

Not surprisingly, farmers developed a strong sense of grievance. They fed the cities, supported the railroads, supplied the commodities that paid for European investments, and yet somehow the wealth they created seemed to be siphoned off to others. Their attitude was well expressed by a Nebraska newspaper:

There are three great crops raised in Nebraska. One is a crop of corn, one a crop of freight rates, and one a crop of interest. One is produced by farmers, who sweat and toil, from the land. The other two are produced by men who sit in their offices and behind their bank counters and farm the farmers.

End of a Dream

Perhaps the cruelest blow to farmers was loss of status. Until recently they had been held up as the most admirable and the happiest of people. Thus a congressman supporting free homesteads in 1851 had said:

CONQUERING THE PLAINS

These pictures show the importance of new inventions to the farmers of the "sodhouse frontier." Barbed wire, farm machinery, and steel plows all cost money, however, so that the farmers of the Great Plains were often burdened with debt before they started to wring a living from the soil.

New York City became a port of shipment for American wheat destined for the rest of the world. This busy rail yard and mammoth grain elevator were part of the shipping and marketing organization farmers came to depend on as they shifted from subsistence agriculture to producing staple crops for world markets.

The life of a farmer is peculiarly favorable to virtue; and both individuals and communities are generally happy in proportion as they are virtuous. His manners are simple, and his nature unsophisticated. . . . His life does not impose excessive toil, and yet it discourages idleness. The farmer lives in rustic plenty, remote from the contagion of popular vices, and enjoys, in their greatest fruition, the blessings of health and contentment.

But now power and prestige had shifted from the rural areas to the cities; in the new urban America, country people were regarded not as the backbone of the nation, but as "rubes," "hicks," and "hayseeds."

Along with the farmer's loss of independence and status came an event that had a profound effect on the American psychology. In 1890 the census bureau reported that settlement had been so rapid "that there can hardly be said to be a frontier line." Although in fact much land was still unoccupied and new settlement continued at a brisk pace until well into the twentieth century, the news that the frontier was closing encouraged prophets of doom, who saw the end of a "safety-valve of social discontent." Formerly the existence of unoccupied land at the frontier had promoted the idea that Americans could always make a fresh start. That was the meaning of Horace Greeley's famous advice, "Go west, young man." What was to happen now that the roles were reversed and the city had become a safety-valve of rural discontent?

424

Activities: Chapter 16

For Mastery and Review

1. What factors, technological and political, enabled railroad companies to span the Great Plains? What difficulties had to be overcome in building the first transcontinental line?

2. What were the contributions to railroading of James J. Hill and Cornelius Vanderbilt? What were the advantages of consolidating railroad systems?

3. What were the effects of the destruction of the buffalo on the Plains Indians? On the cattle industry? What change in policy toward the Indians took place at the end of the nineteenth century?

4. For what reasons did the open-range cattle industry of the West expand so rapidly and then collapse so suddenly?

5. What took the "fifty-niners" to the West? How were law and order achieved in mining communities? What imprint did the Wild West make on American life?

6. What were the obstacles to settling the Great Plains? How were they overcome? Compare the Homestead Act and the railroads as influences in peopling the Plains.

7. What difficulties did the Plains farmer encounter? How did the literature of the "sodhouse frontier" differ from that of the Wild West? Explain the role of women in the region.

8. Compare the situation of the subsistence farmer with that of the farmer specializing in a single staple crop.

Unrolling the Map

On an outline map of the United States west of the Mississippi River, show (a) the Great Plains and the area once called the "Great American Desert"; (b) the 98th meridian, labeling it "line of 20-inch average annual rainfall"; (c) the homelands of the major Plains Indian tribes; (d) the major transcontinental railroads; (e) the Chisholm Trail; (f) the most important mining communities. (See maps on pp. 7, 413).

Who, What, and Why Important?

Westinghouse air brake
Gadsden Purchase
"wedding of the rails"

James J. Hill
Cornelius Vanderbilt
Helen Hunt Jackson

Dawes Act
open range
long drive
vigilance committees
Homestead Act

agricultural mechanization
Hamlin Garland
Willa Cather
O. E. Rölvaag

To Pursue the Matter

1. Americans have variously regarded the opening of the West as dramatic, adventurous, tragic, or romantic. Six selections in Arnof, *A Sense of the Past* (pp. 283–303), may whet your appetite.

2. Graphic and accurate accounts of the opening of the Plains area are found in Webb, *The Great Plains*, and Dobie, *The Texas Longhorn*. Class talks or bulletin board displays might be worked up on such topics as the development of the six-shooter, barbed wire, the long drive, and the practical usefulness of the cowboy's dress.

3. Read Mark Twain, *Roughing It*, for gaudy details of mining camp life. Read Hutchens, *One Man's Montana*, for a view of Montana as a boy saw it a generation after it was first settled.

4. What were the differences between pioneer living in Kentucky in the 1790's and that in the Dakotas in the 1880's?

5. For a good picture of what a frontier woman's life was like, see *Down the Santa Fe Trail and into Mexico*: The Diary of Susan Shelby Magoffin, 1846–1847, edited by Stella M. Drumm, Yale, 1926.

6. Holbrook, *The Story of American Railroads*, contains fascinating chapters on the building of the transcontinental railroads, Jim Hill, great railroad disasters, and the appalling difficulties railroads had with many technical problems.

7. The last stand of the Plains Indians is well told in Clark, *Frontier America*. Is there any excuse for the way the Indians were treated? Could this chapter in American history have been prevented?

8. No textbook can give such a sense of the opening of the Great West as folk songs and stories. Look at Botkin, *A Treasury of American Folklore*. You might start with "The Lane County Bachelor," sung to the rollicking tune of "The Irish Washerwoman," with a chorus that begins:
"But hurrah for Lane County, the land of the free,
The home of the grasshopper, bedbug, and flea."

Chapter 17

Protest Movements

I'm not in a very good humor with "America" myself. It seems to me the most grotesquely illogical thing under the sun; and I suppose I love it less because it won't let me love it more. I should hardly like to trust pen and ink with all the audacity of my social ideas; but after fifty years of optimistic content with "civilization" and its ability to come out all right in the end, I now abhor it, and feel that it is coming out all wrong in the end, unless it bases itself anew on a real equality.

—WILLIAM DEAN HOWELLS

The unpleasant aspects of the new industrial America drove many thoughtful people first to questioning, then to protest. The passage above is taken from a letter to Henry James from a fellow novelist, William Dean Howells. The writer was not driven to any such critical attitude by failure to achieve wealth or reputation. On the contrary, Howells was a self-taught writer who rose from a poverty-stricken boyhood in Ohio to the enviable position of editor of the *Atlantic Monthly* when he was still in his thirties. But he came to feel that he must protest against the moral confusions and the injustices of the new industrial age. In a novel, *The Rise of Silas Lapham,* he portrayed the erosion of character that a husband and his wife undergo because of social ambition and desire for easy wealth. In *A Hazard of New Fortunes,* Howells portrayed the unfeeling attitude of the "best people" and the brutality of the police toward workers on strike against a streetcar company. An even more successful writer but no less disillusioned was Mark Twain (pen name of Samuel L. Clemens). In *The Gilded Age,* he described the personal disasters brought on a family by greed and graft. His greatest novel, *Huckleberry Finn,* is on the face of it simply an adventure story—a prolonged "chase" set on the broad Mississippi. But by setting the natural goodness of an illiterate Negro and a shiftless pauper boy against the cruelty and callousness of respectable, pious folk, Clemens questioned the justice of middle-class society.

One trouble was that the benefits of the immense new wealth created by the industrial revolution and the settling of millions of acres of virgin land were unequally divided. The rich seemed to be getting richer; the poor, poorer. The business system too often seemed a game in which the cards were stacked and the rewards went to the cheater, or at least to the person with the biggest stake. It was therefore hardly surprising that during the latter nineteenth century there appeared organizations, representing small

QUESTION • *Was this recognition of injustice a cause for pessimism or for optimism?*

business people, farmers, laborers, and reformers, to protest the dominance of the men who controlled the great corporations. Although on the whole unsuccessful, these movements won a few victories, especially in promoting legislation based on a partial abandonment of the Jeffersonian principle that the government that governs best governs least.

CURBING THE RAILROADS

Although bringing immense benefits, the railroad corporations were guilty of a variety of abuses of the public interest. Even before lines were built, railroad officials formed construction companies, in which their participation was often secret, and then pocketed immense profits by overcharging their own railroads. Railroad companies bribed state legislators for favors such as land grants and tax exemptions. They evaded laws designed to make them give services in return for privileges.

Railroad Abuses

Railroad financing was marked by a common abuse called "stock watering." Getting its name from the scheme of feeding cattle salt and getting them to drink heavily just before being weighed for market, this was the practice of increasing the number of shares of a company without adding to its assets. When Jay Gould and James J. Fisk gained control of the Erie Railroad in 1868, they issued $71,000,000 of watered stock on a property worth $20,000,000. As insiders they profited by selling watered stock to a public still ignorant of its decrease in value. On another occasion Gould gained control of the Union Pacific Railroad and induced it to buy at inflated prices the stock of other railroads that he controlled. He made $10,000,000 on this deal alone. Such action swindled other stockholders, and hurt the public because railroads that had inflated their stock issues had to keep rates high to pay dividends.

In a day when water traffic was disappearing and automobile trucking not yet dreamed of, railroads more often than not enjoyed a "natural monopoly." Railroads took advantage of this situation by charging more for short hauls, where they had a monopoly, than for long hauls, where they faced competition. Thus it cost shippers more to send certain goods from Poughkeepsie, New York, to New York City, where there was no choice but the New York Central Railroad, than all the way from Chicago, where the Pennsylvania and Erie railroads competed with it for the traffic. The New York Central also charged higher rates in winter, when the Erie Canal was frozen, than in summer, when it was open. Sometimes competing lines kept up rates artificially by a practice known as pooling, whereby companies made agreements to fix rates and divide the profits according to a prearranged formula. Still another abuse was the practice of favoring big shippers over small by granting rebates (see p. 391).

The Grange

Feeling against railroad abuses was exhibited all over the country, but was especially violent in the trans-Mississippi West, where there was practically no competition from other forms of transportation and where the lines had been favored by immense government subsidies in money and land. Although all major interests —business people, farmers, and laborers—believed themselves injured, it was a nation-wide farm organization that provided the driving force toward attempts to end railroad abuses by legislation. The Patrons of Husbandry, commonly called the Grange, was a secret organization founded in 1867. Reflecting the importance of women on the farm, it was the first fraternal organization to admit them on equal terms. Hamlin Garland remembered its rallies, with their brass bands, banners, and speechmaking, as "a most grateful relief from the sordid loneliness of the farm." By 1874, Granger lodges

In the anti-railroad cartoon above, the farmer is saying of the Iron Horse that devours his produce: "I can't afford this hired team; it takes every mite I can raise to feed him." Below, the Grange tries to arouse the sleepers. From such agitation came Granger laws, which attempted to regulate freight rates.

contained a million and a half members and had become centers of political action.

The Granger Laws

The Patrons of Husbandry agitated so successfully that in the early 1870's several states passed legislation to end or prevent railroad misdoings. These "Granger Laws" attempted to fix maximum freight and passenger rates; they forbade discrimination between places or between shippers; and they attempted to regulate other natural monopolies, such as grain elevators and warehouses.

The railroads protested violently against the Granger laws. Their principal argument was the *laissez-faire* principle that government should not interfere with private enterprise. "Can't I do what I want with my own?" asked Commodore Vanderbilt. Railroad lawyers argued that the Granger laws were unconstitutional because the Fourteenth Amendment forbade a state to "deprive any person of life, liberty, or property, without due process of law." A railroad corporation was a legal "person"; if forced to charge lower rates it was deprived of "property"; regulatory laws were an "undue" extension of state legislative power.

Defenders of the Granger laws pointed out that most railroads had received large favors from the federal and local governments. How could they now claim freedom from control in the public interest? *Laissez-faire* did not apply here. It postulates that an open market free of state control insures the public fair prices because producers compete to produce cheaper goods for sale. But as a natural monopoly, the railroad had no competitors. Its rates must therefore be controlled by government, representing the people at large.

In 1876 and 1877 the Supreme Court decided several cases in favor of the Granger laws. In the most famous case, *Munn v. Illinois,* the court supported by an 8 to 1 vote the right of an Illinois commission to fix rates for grain elevators. The court argued that since common carriers, such as railroads, and public utilities, such as grain elevators, "stand in the very gateway of commerce" and "take toll of all who pass," they exercise "a sort of public office." "Property does indeed become clothed with a public interest," said the court, "when used in a manner to make it of public consequence, and affect the community at large." Therefore the warehouse companies "must submit to being controlled by the public for the common good."

Failure of the Granger Laws

In spite of judicial support, the Granger laws were unsuccessful. The railroads fought them by cutting services or threatening to lay no more track until the acts were repealed. The laws also lost the backing of organized public opinion, as membership declined in the Grange. In attempting to reduce the profits of marketers, the Patrons of Husbandry had gone into business for themselves, setting up plow and reaper factories, grain elevators, packing plants, and banks. Bitterly fought by private companies and often inefficiently run, these businesses usually failed, and their collapse discredited the Grange. By 1880 its membership was less than a quarter of what it had been in 1874. This effort of the Grangers to undercut the marketers had one longtime result: the development of mail-order department stores, selling direct to the consumer. The first mail-order house, Montgomery Ward & Co., of Chicago, was founded in 1872 especially "to meet the wants of the Patrons of Husbandry."

Such Granger laws as remained were dealt a mortal blow in 1886. The Wabash Railway had charged shippers 25 cents a hundred pounds for carrying goods from Gilman, Illinois, to New York City, there being no other railroad into Gilman. It charged only 15 cents a hundred pounds from Peoria, Illinois, to New York; it was a longer distance, but there was competition from other lines. This violated an Illinois

statute forbidding the "long and short haul" abuse. The railroad appealed its case to the Supreme Court. While not directly attacking the principle laid down in *Munn v. Illinois*, that public utilities must submit to government control, the court held that states control only such traffic as lay entirely within their borders. Since most railroad traffic crossed the boundaries of states, the Wabash Railway decision practically wiped out state regulation of rates.

Interstate Commerce Act, 1887

The Wabash decision led to such a demand for federal regulation of railroads that Congress passed the famous Interstate Commerce Act of 1887. This law declared that railroad charges must be "reasonable and just"; it forbade pooling, rebates, and higher rates for short hauls than long. The companies were required to publish rates, give advance notice of all changes, and make annual financial reports to the federal government. Violations of these provisions were punishable by fines up to $5,000 for each offense. Enforcement of the law was placed under the Interstate Commerce Commission, a group of five men appointed by the President.

Regarding its immediate purpose, the Interstate Commerce Act was a failure. The Interstate Commerce Commission lacked power to fix rates and could only make recommendations or bring suits in the federal courts. In sixteen cases that reached the Supreme Court—a process that took four years on an average—the court held for the railroads in fifteen. In 1892, Richard Olney, a corporation lawyer who later served as Attorney General under President Cleveland wrote a railroad official urging him not to advocate repeal of the Interstate Commerce Act. "It satisfies popular clamor for government supervision of the railroads," observed Olney, "at the same time that such supervision is almost entirely nominal." Nevertheless, the Interstate Commerce Act was one of the most important laws ever passed by Congress. It established the precedent that the federal government might control large-scale private enterprise if the public good seemed to require it. It also provided a model for regulatory commissions that today oversee activities as diverse as air lines, labor relations, and television.

DEMAND FOR CHEAP MONEY

If there was anything that farmers demanded in the late nineteenth century more than the regulation of natural monopolies or the reduction of the marketers' profits, it was "cheap money." To understand this, it is necessary to explore briefly the quantity theory of money, which was widely accepted at the time, although not thoroughly understood. According to the quantity theory, the value of money, like that of any other commodity, changes according to the supply. Raise the number of dollars in circulation—in other words, *inflate* the currency—and the dollar buys less; prices go up. Restrict the amount of money in circulation—in other words, *deflate* the currency—and the dollar buys more; prices go down. This can be expressed in a simple mathematical equation:

(1) Let P stand for prices.
(2) Let M stand for amount of money in circulation.
(3) Let T stand for the total amount of goods and personal services for sale.

$$\text{Then } P = \frac{M}{T}$$

If the amount of money (M) is increased faster than the total production (T), prices will go up. This is inflation.

If the total amount of goods and services (T) increase faster than the money supply (M), prices will go down. This is deflation.

Actually, this simple form of the quantity theory of money is so incomplete as to be mis-leading. It leaves out two other factors: *velocity*—how fast money passes from hand to hand, and *credit*—which affects prices just as money and which is more abundant. But the simple equation given above is what the inflationists believed to be true in the late nineteenth century. It accorded closely with the facts of agricultural life in the three decades after the Civil War. The production of agricultural staples such as wheat and cotton (a large factor in T) nearly quadrupled, while the supply of money (M) increased very little. The prices received by farmers (P) dropped by nearly two-thirds.

Deflation and the Gold Standard

The three decades after the close of the Civil War were a period of deflation. In 1865, with the currency inflated by the wartime issuance of greenbacks, there were $31 in circulation for every person in the country. By 1895, per capita circulation had sunk to $20. This was partly the result of a world-wide movement related to wide-spread adoption of the gold standard. When a country went on the gold standard, it made all its currency convertible into gold.

Formerly most countries had been on a bi-metallic standard whereby the government coined both gold and silver and established the official value of each. In spite of official "mint prices" for gold and silver, their relative value often changed sharply. The California gold strike of 1849 so increased the amount of gold, for instance, that it became cheap in relation to silver. According to the tendency known as Gresham's Law, whereby dear money is hoarded while cheap money remains in circulation, silver went into hiding. This metal was so little used that the federal government issued 25-cent gold pieces and small bills, called "shinplasters" for denominations as low as 3 cents.

The difficulty with the gold standard in the late nineteenth century was that world production of gold did not increase as fast as the world production of goods. This restricted the currency supply and drove prices down.

Deflation was hard on farmers, who borrowed money more heavily than ever before. When a wheat farmer borrowed $1,000 in 1880, with wheat at $1 a bushel, the principal of the loan equaled 1,000 bushels of wheat. But in 1890, with wheat at 75 cents a bushel, the debt equaled 1,333 bushels. To use a homely phrase, there was "too much hog in the dollar." This state of affairs meant that thousands of farm owners lost their land and became tenants or hired people.

Greenbacks and Free Silver

As soon as greenbacks began to be called in during the late 1860's and prices began to drop, farmers started to demand inflation. They protested that bankers and bondholders lent 50-cent dollars during the war, and now wanted to be repaid in 100-cent dollars. With the slogan, "The same currency for the plowholders and the bondholder," western delegates to the Democratic Convention of 1868 were strong enough to force an inflationist plank into the party platform. In the mid-term election of 1878, a Greenback party polled over a million votes, electing fifteen congressmen.

The Greenback movement declined after 1880 as inflationists turned to free silver. In 1873, Congress decided to stop coining silver money and adopted the gold standard. Six years later, after building up a gold reserve of 200 million dollars, specie payments were resumed. These events caused a howl of protest from western silver miners because new mines, especially the famous Comstock Lode, produced a flood of silver which would no longer be coined. Denouncing what they called "the Crime of '73," silver miners demanded a policy of "free silver," meaning that the government should coin all silver brought to the mint. They were joined by debtor farmers of the West and South,

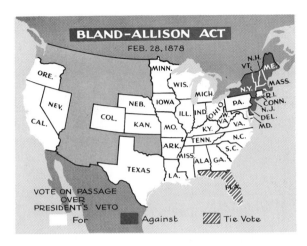

In this vote on a "cheap money" proposal, sectional interests completely overrode party lines, since debtor-agrarian sections favored inflation.

who expected that free silver would mean a cheaper dollar and higher prices.

The strength of the silver movement was shown by the Bland-Allison Act of 1878, passed over President Hayes' veto. Starting as a free silver bill in the House, this law was amended in the Senate to require that the treasury buy from $2,000,000 to $4,000,000 worth of silver a month and issue currency against it. Although adding to the money supply, the Bland-Allison Act did not halt deflation. The increase in business far exceeded that in currency. Agitation for cheap money therefore continued, reaching a peak in events to be described in the next chapter.

National Banks

As in the time of Andrew Jackson, many western farmers distrusted banks. Needing credit as never before, they could obtain it only at high rates of interest. They were especially critical of the banks created under the National Banking Act of 1863. This law provided (1) that banking associations putting at least a third of their capital into federal bonds (but not less than $30,000) might issue national bank notes up to 90 per cent of the value of the bonds; (2) that for most purposes national bank notes could be used as currency; and (3) that the national banks must submit to federal inspection.

The national bank notes were a great improvement on the wild confusion of state bank notes, issued by over two thousand institutions, many of them irresponsible and some dishonest. Federal supervision made for more stable and honest banking. The national banks failed, however, to fit the needs of farming communities since the amount of capital required for a national bank was more than most small towns could afford. The agricultural South and West were poorly served, having only one-third of the national banks and less than one-quarter of the total capitalization.

QUESTION • State bank notes, often fluctuating and sometimes fraudulent, were driven out of circulation by a 10% federal tax. Is such destruction of free enterprise justifiable?

The farmers' most fundamental objection to the national banks, however, was a feeling that they made the rich richer. Since the banks drew interest on their federal bonds and could also lend against the bank notes issued with the bonds as security, it seemed as though the government guaranteed them a double profit. Farmers' organizations therefore demanded that national banks be abolished and that the federal government provide them with cheaper credit.

ATTEMPTED REGULATION OF TRUSTS AND MONOPOLIES

In 1881 the *Atlantic Monthly* published an article entitled "The Story of a Great Monopoly," by Henry D. Lloyd, telling how the Standard Oil Company had monopolized the oil refining business. It caused such a sensation that the magazine had to print three times as many copies as usual. Throughout the next decade, as it was revealed that industry after industry was in danger of being monopolized, demands for federal regulation came from many different groups—small businessmen, farmers, consumers, and workingmen. Even officials of the great corporations themselves began to have qualms. Henry O. Havemeyer, head of the American Sugar Refining Company, which produced over 90 per cent of the sugar used in American homes, urged that producers of commodities in general use should submit to federal regulation. In the election of 1888, both parties promised action, and in 1890, Congress passed the Sherman Antitrust Act with only one dissenting vote.

The Sherman Act wrote into federal law an old principle of the English common law: that artificial restraints on trade and private monopolies are forbidden. Its core is contained in these words: "Every contract, combination, in the form of trust or otherwise, or conspiracy, in restraint of trade or commerce among the several states or with foreign nations, is hereby to be declared illegal." Any person who was found guilty of achieving a monopoly, or even of attempting to do so, might be punished by fines and imprisonment. A private individual or corporation hurt by the monopolistic activities of a rival might collect triple damages from the offender.

Early Failure of the Sherman Antitrust Act

For a number of reasons the Sherman Act was no more effective in preventing business consolidation than the Interstate Commerce Act in controlling railroad rates. It was not strictly enforced, and was so loosely worded that its meaning was doubtful. Did the act mean, for instance, that all mergers were unlawful, that all business transactions must be open to the public, that any contract whereby one company planned to take business from another was unlawful? Such decisions had to be left to the federal courts, which in the 1890's were probably more favorable to business interests than at any other time in American history. Just as the courts whittled down the powers of the Interstate Commerce Commission, they took the teeth out of the Sherman Act. In the E. C. Knight Company case of 1895 the Supreme Court ruled that an almost complete monopoly of sugar refining was not a violation of the Sherman Act, because sugar refining was manufacturing, and manufacturing was not interstate commerce.

The Supreme Court's decision that the Sherman Act applied only to transportation and telegraph companies was followed by one of the greatest periods of consolidation in American business history. In 1890 there had been 24 trusts with a total capitalization of $436 million. In 1900 there were 183 great consolidations with a capitalization of over three billion dollars. The new concentrations of power were effected through a new type of corporation known as the "holding company." A holding company did not actually engage in production or in direct services to the public, but controlled the securities of many operating companies. This new device enabled one to establish control of business concerns with less outlay of capital. Through ownership of a majority of the shares of stock, and often much less, one could put one's own people into the boards of directors of the operating companies. (See chart, p. 584.)

In spite of initial failure, the Sherman Antitrust Act, like the Interstate Commerce Act, was a most important piece of legislation. It tended to make business people more careful not to offend the public or to antagonize competitors by unfair practices. The law itself later became more effective under a less conservative Supreme Court, with more vigorous enforcement by the

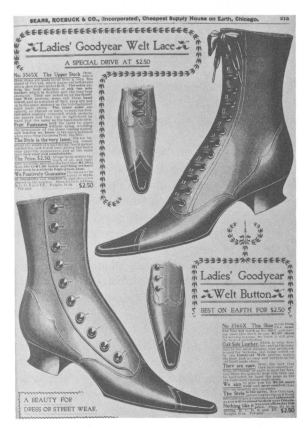

In "wishing books" — mail-order catalogs — farmers found equipment for their farms as well as fashionable wearing apparel. Here women's shoes are advertised as a specialty of Sears, Roebuck & Co.

executive department, and with strengthening amendments. Federal trust legislation remains today a "shotgun behind the door," helping to discourage monopoly and to encourage competition.

THE GROWTH OF LABOR UNIONS

The Civil War encouraged the revival of labor unions, which had dwindled because of the Panic of 1837. Workers needed higher wages to meet prices raised by the wartime inflation; with hundreds of thousands of men under arms, unions were in a strong position to demand better pay. In 1863–64, the number of local unions rose from 79 to 270. There was also organization on a national scale, since a local union was often helpless in dealing with an industrial corporation doing business throughout the country.

Difficulties Facing the Unions

In spite of rapid growth during the war and afterward, labor unions faced many difficulties:

(1) *American labor was mobile and diverse.* It was difficult to organize workmen in this country because they would not "stay hitched," but moved from job to job. Young men, who in other countries might have become labor leaders, went into business for themselves or worked up into executive positions. The inflow of immigrants, averaging over a third of a million a year between 1870 and 1900, increased the difficulties of organization. Ignorant of American wage scales and with few resources, the newcomers often accepted low pay. A Contract Labor Law, passed by Congress in 1864, allowed employers to hire foreign laborers, bring them to America, and have them work for a year to repay passage. Variety in language, religion, and customs among the immigrants made it hard to weld them into an effective organization. To discourage unionization, employers deliberately mixed nationalities. Thus a steel mill superintendent wrote:

We must be careful what class of men we collect. We must steer clear of the West, where men are accustomed to infernal high wages. We must steer clear as far as we can of Englishmen who are great sticklers for high wages, small production and strikes. My experience has shown that Germans and Irish, Swedes and what I denominate "Buckwheats"—young American country boys, judiciously mixed, make the most effective and tractable force you can find.

(2) *There was confusion of aims.* Those who wanted to bring all workers together and promote widespread reforms were opposed by others who believed that unions should work only for the short-time benefit of workers in their particular craft or industry. A small but vocal group wanted to use the power of organized labor to overthrow the capitalist system and establish socialism (see pp. 444–445). Even more radical were anarchists who preached, "All property is theft; all government is tyranny," and tried to create class hatred by bomb-throwing and assassination. Although never composing more than a small fraction of the labor movement, socialists and anarchists aroused fear and dislike which were transferred to all workers' organizations.

(3) *Unions faced strong opposition from employers.* Workers were often required to take an iron-clad oath that they would not join a union. If discharged for union activity, a worker often remained jobless, because employers combined to keep black lists of all "troublemakers." Once black-listed, a laborer could get a job only by changing residence, trade, or name. Once workers organized a plant, the employer could still fight back by a lockout (shutting the plant down) or by discharging union supporters and hiring strikebreakers (also known as "scabs"). In any strike or lockout the odds favored employers because they had the longer purse; few unions could afford to support their members through the prolonged unemployment caused by a strike.

(4) *Public opinion was distrustful of labor unions.* Laborers formed a minority group in America, and unions were an unfamiliar type of organization. Fixing wages and hours by collective bargaining between union representatives and employers was presented as violating the right of an individual to deal personally with the employer. Occasionally public opinion condemned employers when labor disputes resulted in violence. This happened during the Homestead lockout in 1892, when the Carnegie Steel

The railroad strike of 1877 resulted in the most violent upheaval in the history of American labor. In several places, such as the city of Baltimore (shown here), there were clashes between troops and strikers. Labor unions learned that violence could hurt their cause, and labor leaders thereafter tried to avoid it.

Company hired a private army of 300 Pinkerton detectives armed with repeating rifles. Generally, however, labor unions were held responsible when disorder occurred, partly because anarchists and extreme socialists loudly predicted a day when the "toiling masses" would overthrow existing society.

(5) *Law enforcement agencies usually sided with the employers.* Although employers suffered no penalties for lockouts and black lists, strikes or boycotts were judged "conspiracies in restraint of trade" for which labor leaders might be jailed or fined. Contracts between employers and unions were not usually enforceable by law. When violence occurred, or even threatened, the police and sometimes troops were arrayed on the side of the employers. Occasionally employers were permitted to hire armed guards and make them deputy sheriffs.

Labor unions survived all obstacles, although membership fluctuated according to business conditions. During the lean years following the Panic of 1873, union membership dropped from over 300,000 to 50,000. Three million men were unemployed; tramps and hoboes roamed the countryside; workers' mass meetings to demand relief were suppressed by mounted police. Such conditions created bitterness leading to violence.

This "Great Upheaval" of the 1870's culminated in the railroad strike of 1877, the most destructive labor dispute in American history.

Railroad Strike of 1877

Starting as a protest against a simultaneous wage cut by four eastern railroads, the strike spread to beyond Chicago. In city after city, strikers seized and sometimes destroyed railroad property; in Pittsburgh alone the Pennsylvania Railroad lost 2,000 cars, 25 locomotives, two roundhouses and a railroad station. Militia and workers fought pitched battles. In much of the violence railroad men themselves were less involved than teen-age boys who, unable to find employment, were on the loose. Although in fact the disorders were usually spontaneous, newspaper editors saw in them "an insurrection, a revolution, an attempt of communists and vagabonds to coerce society, and endeavour to undermine American institutions." In several cities order was restored only after President Hayes had sent federal troops, but Hayes himself was disturbed. He felt that the railroad workers had much justice on their side, and that the railroad officials had brought on the crisis by their own ruthless actions. The President confided in his diary, "Shall the railroads govern the country or shall the people govern the railroads?"

The railroad strike had complex results. There was such fear of violent revolution that state militias were reorganized and great armories were built in cities as fortresses where troops could hold out. Union leaders learned from the strike that violence hurt labor's cause. A way to prevent it was to organize unions with sufficient discipline to discourage mob action. Employers were often more resolved than ever to discourage union organization, but many of them realized that to do this they must treat their workers better. Indiscriminate wage cutting in times of depression become less common; a few companies began to take active steps to promote their workers' welfare by making provisions for old age pensions and free hospital service.

The Knights of Labor

As business improved, a new national labor organization, the Noble Order of the Knights of Labor, grew in strength. Founded in 1869 as a secret society (partly to evade the black list), the Knights of Labor came into the open in 1878 and endeavored to bring all laboring people—skilled and unskilled, blacks and whites, men and women, white collar and manual workers—into one big union. The only people excluded belonged to occupations regarded as harmful or parasitic, such as saloon keepers, gamblers, lawyers, and bankers. At the head of the Order, with the title Grand Master Workman, was Terence V. Powderly, an immigrant who rose from railway switch tender to mayor of Scranton, Pennsylvania. An eloquent speaker and tireless organizer, Powderly had great hopes for his union. "We seek and intend," he said, "to enlist the services of men of every society, of every party, and every religion, and every nation in the crusade we have inaugurated against those twin monsters, tyranny and monopoly."

Powderly persuaded the Knights to support a great variety of reforms, such as equal pay for men and women, temperance, the abolition of child labor, and above all, the establishment of cooperatively owned industrial plants. A man of peace, he opposed strikes and wished to submit labor disputes to arbitration by impartial third parties. Local assemblies of the Knights were less interested, however, in remaking society than in securing immediate gains; sometimes they started strikes which Powderly had to support to preserve his organization. In 1885 the Knights gained tremendous prestige by winning a strike against the Wabash Railway, then owned by Jay Gould. Membership soared from 100,000 to 700,000 in less than a year. Conservative newspapers feared that Powderly, the "labor czar," would become stronger than the President.

Decline of the Knights of Labor

The Knights of Labor were soon beset with troubles. Members called strikes before they had sufficient funds or discipline, and Powderly directed them badly. Like the Grangers, the Knights wasted their funds in unsuccessful attempts to set up cooperative businesses. The effort to bring all kinds of labor into one big union failed. Laborers in different crafts and industries had little interest in working for common goals. Unskilled laborers were too often undisciplined and too willing to use violence; if a strike failed, or the workers were blacklisted, they drifted into other jobs. Skilled workers, however, had more to lose and were more vulnerable to the blacklist.

The decline of the Knights was hastened by the Haymarket Square riot in Chicago on May 4, 1886. This event had its origin in a peaceful meeting of three thousand workers called to protest the shooting of striking workers by the police. Even the mayor of Chicago attended. As the meeting was beginning to disperse, someone threw a dynamite bomb into a company of policemen. Although the identity of the bomb-thrower was never established, eight known anarchist leaders were arrested and found guilty of participation in the crime. Four were executed for murder. The Haymarket riot encouraged opponents of labor organization to pin the "anarchist" label on the Knights of Labor, even though the Knights condemned the attack on the police as the work of "cowardly murderers."

From 1886 on the Knights declined as rapidly as they had grown. By 1893 their numbers had dwindled to 75,000. But their brief success was an immense stimulus to those who hoped to organize workers into an effective counterforce to the power of the corporations, and their failure taught lessons from which other labor organizations, such as the American Federation of Labor, benefited.

The American Federation of Labor

In 1886, the very year the Knights of Labor began to decline, the American Federation of Labor appeared. In principles and in structure the new organization differed greatly from the Knights. Its members were skilled laborers, organized into separate unions, each covering a particular craft. Each union managed its own affairs and fought its own battles, with only occasional help from the national organization. Initiation fees and dues were relatively high, in order to restrict membership, build up strike funds, and provide benefits to members and their families in case of sickness, unemployment, or death.

QUESTION • *If each union managed its own affairs, of what use was the AFL? Why has it survived?*

The new AFL owed much of its success to Samuel Gompers, its president for thirty-seven years. Born in London, Gompers brought to America some of the ideas of British trade unions, the best established and least revolutionary in the world. Gompers, who prided himself on being a practical man, repudiated ambitious reform schemes and was interested only in the day-to-day gains of federation members. He came to feel that socialists and radicals hurt the labor movement by frightening the public. His own personality did much to allay popular fear of labor unions and their leaders. Dressed in a Prince Albert coat, he looked and behaved much like a banker. Yet he devoted his life to the federation, and died a poor man.

So effective was the organization and leadership of the American Federation of Labor that when hard times hit again in 1893, the unions composing it not only survived but gained members, while other labor organizations declined. Between 1890 and 1900, AFL membership rose from 190,000 to 500,000.

Under the moderate guidance of Samuel Gompers, the American Federation of Labor became strong enough to hold out during the Panic of 1893. At a trade meeting in 1905 (above), Gompers is addressing a large crowd of garment workers, including many women who had by then joined unions. He aimed to organize skilled workers into horizontal unions that could monopolize certain skills (see diagram, page 638).

The American Railway Union and the Pullman Strike of 1894

The AFL failed to provide for unskilled and semi-skilled labor. To correct this and yet avoid the weakness of the "one big union" approach of the Knights, a new type of labor organization appeared. This was the industrial union, in which all classes of workers in a single industry are welded together. In some ways it resembles a vertical trust. Among those impressed by its advantages was Eugene V. Debs, an officer of the Brotherhood of Locomotive Firemen, one of several railway unions representing different kinds of jobs. He felt that the division of railwaymen into different unions weakened their power. Conductors and engineers, the "aristocracy of labor," looked down on less skilled and lower paid men, and the unskilled had no organization at all. Debs

therefore started a new organization in 1893, the American Railway Union, with headquarters in Chicago. It was not an auspicious time to found a new organization because it was a panic year. Nevertheless, the new union grew rapidly; it included all types of railway workers—switchmen, firemen, conductors, engineers, telegraph operators, station clerks, brakemen. In 1894 it was powerful enough to force James J. Hill to restore wage cuts to employees of the Great Northern Railway.

Hardly had the Great Northern strike ended than the Pullman strike began. This largest walkout the country had ever seen started in the pretty little town that George M. Pullman, the sleeping car manufacturer, had built for his workers. When the Panic of 1893 reduced demand for its cars, the Pullman Company laid off two-thirds of its employees and cut the wages of the rest. It did not reduce either its dividends or the rents charged to workers in the town of Pullman. When a delegation protested the pay cuts, its members were fired. Most Pullman workers then struck, and Pullman locked out the rest.

Pullman workers who were members of the American Railway Union called on it for help. Debs proposed that the dispute be referred to arbitration, but Pullman replied, "There is nothing to arbitrate." The American Railway Union thereupon declared a boycott, in which union members refused to work on any train which included a Pullman car. Pullman had an ally, however, in the Railway Managers Association, made up of the heads of all twenty-four railroads running into Chicago. The managers ran Pullman cars, even on trains that did not ordinarily include them. The result was that five days after the boycott began in late June 1894, 100,000 railwaymen had quit work, and railway traffic west of Chicago was almost paralyzed. Debs warned his followers not to interfere with United States mails, and appealed to them to be "orderly and law-abiding." Although a few mail trains were delayed, usually when combined with Pullman cars, there were few disturbances.

Labor and the Injunction

The Pullman strike was defeated by the federal government. Over the protests of the mayor of Chicago and governor of Illinois, who claimed they had matters in hand, President Cleveland sent federal troops to guard mail trains. Immediately rioting broke out as angry mobs, sympathetic to the strikers, taunted the soldiers. Members of the American Railway Union kept out of trouble, but nevertheless received the blame. Even before the troops appeared, the federal government also took judicial action. On application of the U.S. Attorney General, a federal judge issued an injunction (court order) forbidding any interference with transportation in interstate commerce and any attempt to persuade railway workers to quit work. The judge held that the strike was a conspiracy in restraint of trade and therefore a violation of the Sherman Antitrust Act. On refusing to obey, Debs was jailed for contempt of court. Deprived of his leadership, the Pullman strike collapsed and with it the American Railway Union.

From that time on, labor unions demanded that the use of the injunction in labor disputes be abolished. Even outside labor circles there was strong feeling that putting Debs in jail was an unfair extension of judicial power. The Springfield *Republican,* one of the most influential newspapers in the country, said, "If Debs has been violating the law, let him be indicted, tried by a jury, and punished. Let him not be made the victim of an untenable court order and deprived of his liberty entirely within the discretion of a judge."

Gains of Labor

Although labor unions lost more disputes than they won, and most workers remained entirely unorganized, laborers made genuine gains during the latter nineteenth century. The deflation, which hurt the farmer, helped the worker by lowering the cost of food. Improved technology produced better and cheaper goods. As we have seen, real wages increased, even though the average work day was reduced from 12 hours to 10 hours between 1830 and 1900.

Federal and state legislation reflected the growing political influence of labor. To keep imported labor from depressing wages, Congress passed the first laws restricting immigration. In 1882 Chinese laborers were excluded, and in 1885 it was forbidden to import workers under contract. Several states gave labor unions a new legal status by granting them the right to incorporate. Nearly all states passed laws regulating working conditions and requiring minimum standards of health and safety.

The gains won by legislation and by unions themselves were supplemented by the action of enlightened employers, motivated either by the desire to head off unionization or by genuine concern for their workers. The Standard Oil Company and the Baltimore and Ohio Railroad pioneered in providing old age pensions, and the latter firm also provided benefits in case of injury. The Pillsbury Flour Company attempted to increase its employees' sense of participation in the business by sharing profits; its example was widely copied.

REFORMERS AND RADICALS

Although commonly noted for other phenomena, such as industrial progress and agrarian discontent, the period after the Civil War, like the Jacksonian period, hatched "a fertility

John Peter Altgeld, Eagle Forgotten

He pardoned three anarchists convicted of murder. He charged a President of the United States with the "invasion of Illinois." And to many, he is known only through a poem by Vachel Lindsay.

John Peter Altgeld, son of poor German immigrants and one-time railroad laborer, was elected reform governor of Illinois in 1892. A Democrat, one of the truly progressive leaders in the politics of the 1890's, he seldom agreed with Democratic President Grover Cleveland. His single term in office severely tested his convictions.

In 1893 petitions for release of three notorious prisoners were submitted to him. Eight admitted anarchists had been convicted of murder following the Haymarket riot. Four had been hanged and one had committed suicide; only these three were still alive. In the language of Altgeld's pardon, no proof of their guilt had ever been established, so he set them free. His state and the nation heartily disagreed with him.

In 1894, when the Pullman strike crisis gripped Chicago, President Cleveland sent federal troops into the city to guard the mail trains, thus effectively breaking the strike. Governor Altgeld sent a bitter message to Washington, denouncing the "invasion" without a prior request for troops from the state government.

His position was legally correct, but the voters of Illinois did not support it. Despite his many reforms, among them the eight-hour day for women and the use of the secret ballot, they elected another man in 1897. But Altgeld remains a symbol of the courageous politicians who have advanced reform—slowly and haltingly—against heavy odds, as honored in Vachel Lindsay's lines:

"Sleep softly . . . eagle forgotten . . . under the stone.
Time has its way with you there and the clay has its own.
Sleep on, O brave-hearted, O wise man that kindled the flame—
To live in mankind is far more than to live in a name,
To live in mankind, far, far more . . . than to live in a name!"

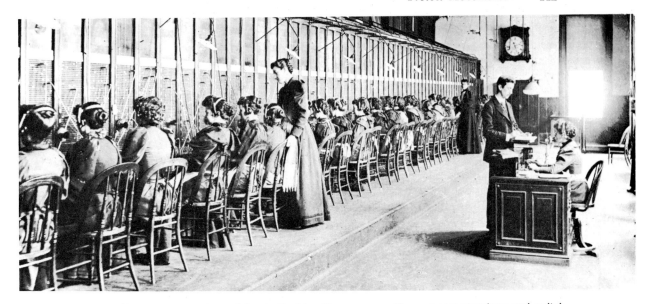

Among new opportunities for women living in the big cities were positions as stenographers and switchboard operators. Here, in a New York City office of the telephone company, many women were able to find employment and thus earn their own living.

of projects for the salvation of the world." Indeed, several reform movements of the earlier period continued their agitation. The temperance movement, for instance, was never more active. Supporters of prohibition formed a political party, and from 1872 on they ran a presidential candidate. Much more effective in promoting temperance, however, were two national organizations that waged a ceaseless campaign against the evils of liquor and the saloon: the Anti-Saloon League and the Women's Christian Temperance Union.

Women's Rights

The WCTU revealed again what the U.S. Sanitary Commission had shown during the Civil War: that women were learning the techniques of large-scale organization. The industrial cities offered women new job opportunities. The invention of the typewriter and telephone, for instance, created a need for thousands of stenographers and switchboard operators. Added to the independence gained from earning their own living was the fact that girls had the same public school education as boys. Women gained more chance for higher education with the opening of women's colleges, such as Vassar, Smith, Wellesley, and Bryn Mawr, and the advance of coeducation in state institutions.

It was no wonder that women continued to demand the right to vote, and received support from the other sex. Wendell Phillips, a former abolitionist, argued their case as follows:

> One of two things is true: either a woman is like a man—and if she is, then a ballot based on brains belongs to her as well as to him; or she is different, and then man does not know how to vote for her as well as she herself does.

Both the Knights of Labor and the American Federation of Labor supported woman suffrage. By 1900, eighteen states had given women the right to vote in school board elections; four—Colorado, Wyoming, Utah, and Idaho—had granted them full voting rights.

Grappling with New Problems: Jacob A. Riis and Jane Addams

The most all-pervasive and difficult problems to be faced were not those inherited from earlier periods, but those connected with industrialism and urbanization. The suggested solutions were as various as the problems. Some people looked back to an earlier morality for answers. Thus some pious folk sought to enforce the Puritan Sabbath as a means of regenerating the city. As a result restaurants and amusement places were closed, and there were even efforts to forbid the running of trains and streetcars. The railway strike of 1877 and the Haymarket riot of 1886 greatly alarmed those who feared immigrants carrying dangerous foreign "isms." A few politicians, notably Senator Henry Cabot Lodge of Massachusetts, professed to see a menace to America in the "new immigration" from southern and eastern Europe and advocated legislation that would discriminate against "alien races." A short-lived national organization, the American Protective Association, which had much the same philosophy as the Know Nothings of the 1850's, also sought to restrict immigration, and to bar Catholics from office as well.

Such negative and defensive reactions did not grapple with the realities of life in factories, shops, and slums. One of those who did face these realities was Jacob A. Riis, a Danish-American police reporter for New York newspapers. In the course of his work, Riis had seen again and again the connection between slums and human degradation. In 1890 he focused public attention on the slum evil in a best-selling book, *How the Other Half Lives.* By appealing to public conscience, Riis secured legislation that reduced the worst slum con-

ditions, along with other measures that improved the lives of city dwellers, such as playgrounds for schools. Among his close friends was a rising young Republican politician, Theodore Roosevelt, whom he "educated" by taking him into tenements, sweatshops, and jails.

In the year before *How the Other Half Lives* was published, Jane Addams founded Hull House, the most famous American settlement house, in a Chicago slum. Inspired by a passionate desire to put her Christian faith to work, and modeling her endeavor on Toynbee Hall, a settlement house in England, Jane Addams was determined to improve the life of the "other half." Hull House soon carried on activities as various as cooking classes, an art gallery, a gymnasium, hot lunches for factory workers, and classes in English. Above all, it was interested in children, on the principle that "a fence at the top of a precipice is better than an ambulance at the bottom." Jane Addams soon surrounded herself with young people who were glad to enlist in a war against human suffering. (See biographical sketch, p. 539.)

Religious conviction and desire to serve humanity were also the motivating forces behind the foundation of other settlement houses, such as the Henry Street Settlement in New York City, the Santa Maria Institute in Cincinnati, and South End House in Boston. In addition to their immediate services to the people in their neighborhoods, the settlement houses were schools where hundreds of men and women learned the conditions of life among the poor and then went into politics to promote reform legislation, either as lobbyists or as officeholders. "Graduates" of Hull House, for instance, were instrumental in securing the first playgrounds and public baths in Chicago, better garbage collection, and the first Illinois factory inspection law. Trained in a New York settlement house, Frances Perkins embarked on a political

The Brooklyn Bridge, longest span in the world at the time it was built, was designed by John Augustus Roebling, a German-born engineer who was killed on the job in 1869. The work was completed fourteen years later by his son, Washington Augustus Roebling.

career that reached a climax when she became the first woman in a President's cabinet (see p. 620 for biographical sketch).

Beautifying the City

Among the indictments against the sprawling industrial cities were their ugliness and their lack of provision for rest and recreation. Architects and landscape designers were among those who sought remedies. In 1876 New York City opened Central Park, designed by Frederick L. Olmstead as "a great breathing space for the toiling masses." Many other cities followed New York's example. In 1893 Chicago celebrated (a year late) the four hundredth anniversary of the discovery of America by putting on a great exposition. The country was astonished as "a rough, tangled stretch of bog and dune" along Lake Michigan was changed to a gleaming "White City," with buildings in classical style surrounded by lagoons and greenswards.

The Chicago Columbian Exposition revealed that American architecture was emerging from the period of ignorance and bad taste into which it had fallen earlier in the nineteenth century. The best American architects now thoroughly understood European styles, and adapted them for modern use. The firm of McKim, Mead, and White used Italian Renaissance style in designing the Boston Public Library. Henry Richardson adapted Romanesque style for churches, libraries, warehouses, and department stores. The Transportation Building at the Chicago Exposition, designed by Louis Sullivan, did not imitate earlier styles. Sullivan preached a new concept: "Form follows function." He meant that the architect should get rid of tradition and create buildings whose design should reveal their purposes and methods of construction. Sullivan's influence, both direct and later through the work of his famous pupil Frank Lloyd Wright, was world-wide.

The finest example of a structure whose form expressed its function was the Brooklyn Bridge, completed in 1883, some sixteen years after it was begun. Hung from great steel cables with a span half again as great as that of any previous bridge, it was designed and constructed by two German-Americans, John A. Roebling and his son Washington Augustus Roebling. The Roeblings, one of whom was killed on the job and the other crippled, succeeded in their intention of making their bridge "a great work of art," and "a great example of advanced . . . engineering" which should "forever testify to the energy, enterprise, and wealth" of New York City.

Socialism: Karl Marx and Edward Bellamy

Wherever industrialism appeared, it drove some people toward extreme solutions of the problems it created—especially toward socialism. Something seemed wrong with a system which produced both idle rich living in palaces and unemployed paupers living in slums. Some were impelled toward socialism by unjust treatment: Eugene V. Debs, for instance, became a lifelong convert after his imprisonment in a Woodstock, Ill., jail during the Pullman strike.

There are many types of socialism, but those with the most impact on the modern world stem from the writings of Karl Marx, especially *The Communist Manifesto* (1847), and *Capital* (1867–1895). Marx, who wrote with force and buttressed his opinions with great learning, predicted that capitalism was doomed. Fewer and fewer capitalists, he said, would monopolize all wealth, while the mass of the people would be pushed into the ranks of the proletariat (people without property). Eventually the proletarians, preferring the risk of death at the barricades in violent revolution to slow starvation in the factories and slums, would rise and overthrow their masters. History, said Marx, had seen continuous class struggles, but that between industrial workers and capitalists would be the last. When the workers won, they would establish a classless society which would continue happily ever after. Marx called on proletarians everywhere to join his crusade: "Workers of the world, unite!"

QUESTION • Marxian Communists have failed to gain control of highly industrialized countries, which Marx expected would be the first to fall, and yet they have succeeded in slightly industrialized countries such as Russia and China. Can you find an explanation?

Marxian socialism enlisted millions of workers in the industrial countries of Europe. In America, however, it gained only a small following, mostly among immigrant groups in big cities. Although these people talked about "the revolution" as though it were just around the corner, and published a number of newspapers with titles like *The Volcano*, they were not much of a threat to American society. Marxian socialism appeals less to the poor themselves than to intellectuals who are alienated for some reason or another from the society in which they live and who are looking for a new creed and cause. In any case, Marxism needs for its nurture widespread economic distress, which has appeared in this country only briefly during periods of severe depression.

More widely read than any of Marx's works was a socialist novel by Edward Bellamy called *Looking Backward, 2000–1887.* This told the story of a nineteenth century American who awoke from a prolonged hypnotic trance to find himself alive in a socialist paradise in the year 2000. By that time all business had been merged into one big trust run by the people themselves. There was work and leisure for all—no poverty, no crime. Bellamy's vision of a socialist utopia made such an impact that his book sold nearly half a million copies, and numerous Nationalist Clubs were founded to advance his ideas. Bellamy had no real program for promoting his ideas, however, and his following drifted into other reform movements.

Henry George and the Single Tax

A third writer with a formula for remaking society was Henry George, whose major work, *Progress and Poverty,* was published in 1879. George attacked the central problem posed by the socialists: Why should the advance of the industrial revolution, with more and more machinery for producing wealth, apparently result in more poverty? George found the answer in the tendency of people to monopolize land and hold it out of use while waiting for a rise in value. Since all wealth comes ultimately from the soil or from under it, the degree to which land is not used is also the degree to which society is poorer than it should be. Also, since land is a "limited commodity"—there being just so much of it—monopolistic landlords can charge excessive rents and thereby drive down wages and business profits.

A believer in private property, George did not propose socialism as a remedy. Instead, he urged what he called the "single tax" on land values. The rate of the single tax would be based not on existing value but on *potential* value if the land were used efficiently. Thus there would be no profit in keeping land out of use and waiting for a rise; owners would either have to develop it themselves or sell it to someone else who would do so. George argued that this would cause prosperity by promoting maximum productivity and by plowing the profits of the land monopoly back into society. His ideas had great appeal at a time when the American people were beginning to realize that the frontier was closing and when they were dismayed by the growth of monopoly.

Progress and Poverty for a time outsold all other books, including works of fiction. Henry George ran for mayor of New York City in 1886 and came close to winning, even without backing from the Republican or Democratic machines. Single-tax clubs and magazines also spread his ideas. Although the single tax idea was too radical a change to get complete acceptance, it influenced methods of taxation both in this country and abroad.

Probably the basic reason why no radical formula for altering society gained wide support was that Americans were on the whole too prosperous to want change. Even those at the bottom often felt they were better off than formerly. A New England farm boy might prefer drawing wages of a dollar a day for a 60-hour week in a factory to working from dawn to dark trying to scrabble a living from a rocky farm. A Polish immigrant might be living with his family in a single room and working in a windowless sweatshop, but for the first time in his life he was wearing shoes; he had also escaped a six-year term of conscription in the Russian army. Furthermore, the United States was so large and had so many different interests that no one idea had universal appeal. Americans wanting to promote their interests worked habitually through political parties. These tried to appeal, by a process of bargaining and compromise, to as many groups as possible.

Activities: Chapter 17

For Mastery and Review

1. Explain the elements of unfairness in each of the following railroad abuses: construction company fees, stock watering, "long and short haul" rates, rebates.

2. Who were the Patrons of Husbandry? Why were the Granger Laws passed? Why did they fail?

3. Why was the Interstate Commerce Act passed? What were its terms? Was it immediately a success or a failure? What was its long-term significance?

4. What phenomena does the quantity theory of money seek to explain? According to the theory, what is the means whereby a government may raise prices or lower them? Define the gold standard.

5. When caught by deflation, why did farmers demand the issuance of greenbacks, and later the free coinage of silver? What were the intent and the effect of the Bland-Allison Act?

6. What were the purposes and the terms of the National Bank Act of 1863? What were the virtues of the national bank system? For what reasons did farmers seek to abolish it?

7. What were the purposes and provisions of the Sherman Antitrust Act? Compare its effectiveness in regard to business organization and organized lobor. Why was the law important?

8. Why did Karl Marx predict a socialist revolution? Why did Marxian socialism have little appeal in the United States?

9. Compare, perhaps in parallel columns, the Knights of Labor, the American Federation of Labor, and the American Railway Union in regard to organization, purposes, leadership, and success.

10. What efforts were made to improve the appearances of cities and the lot of slum dwellers?

Who, What, and Why Important?

William Dean Howells
stock watering
the Grange
Montgomery Ward & Co.

Munn v. Illinois
Wabash Railroad case
Interstate Commerce Act

quantity theory
Gresham's Law
Bland-Allison Act
Sherman Antitrust Act
railroad strike of 1877
Knights of Labor
Terence V. Powderly
Haymarket Square riot
AFL
American Railway Union

Pullman strike
Jane Addams
Anti-Saloon League
woman suffrage
Jacob Riis
the Chicago Exposition
Louis Sullivan
Karl Marx
Edward Bellamy
Henry George

To Pursue the Matter

1. Study the decision of the Supreme Court in *Munn v. Illinois*, 1877, to be found in Bragdon et al., *Frame of Government*, pp. 250–257. What did this decision say about the power of government in general and of the states in particular?

2. Are railroads now natural monopolies? How have technological advances changed the situation? Were the Granger Laws fair to all concerned?

3. Read "A Great Monopoly" and "Rockefeller and the Oil Trust" in Arnof, *A Sense of the Past*, pp. 306–311. Then prepare a formal condemnation of Rockefeller's business practices and a formal defense of them. These might be presented as a debate before the class. You may want to go further and read Nevins, *John D. Rockefeller*, or Latham, *John D. Rockefeller: Robber Baron or Industrial Statesman?*

5. What factors besides the supply of money cause price inflation or deflation? By what means can each be checked or controlled?

6. What makes a locality a slum? Who is at fault? What can be done to prevent or to clean up slums?

7. Read the chapter on Karl Marx in Heilbroner, *The Worldly Philosophers*. What made Marx so persuasive and convincing to so many people?

8. Read in Merrill, *Bourbon Leader: Grover Cleveland and the Democratic party,* and in Ginger, *The Bending Cross: A Biography of Eugene V. Debs,* about the actions of the two men in the Pullman strike. Which man do you favor? Again, here is material for a debate.

Chapter 18

Parties and Politics

No period so thoroughly ordinary
had been known since Columbus
first disturbed the balance of American society.
——HENRY ADAMS

The generation following the Civil War saw American politics at their lowest ebb. The ablest men were no longer attracted to public service. It has been pointed out that if you draw up one list of Americans prominent before the war and another of those prominent after it, "You will find that your first list is made up of men engaged in politics, your second of men engaged in business."

Politics became, indeed, a business in which the first requirement was to get into office and stay there, and the principal purpose was too often private gain.

POLITICAL CORRUPTION

At every level of government—local, state, and national—corruption flourished. Many new obligations, such as police protection, water supply, and sewage disposal, were suddenly thrust on ill-paid city officials. At the same time business people were eager to get contracts for such services as paving streets, erecting public buildings, and constructing streetcar lines. The result was a corrupt alliance of business and politics. Almost every major city was dominated by a more or less dishonest political machine, riveted in power by its control over voting machinery, the courts, and the police. Occasionally the looting of city treasuries became so flagrant that angry citizens became sufficiently aroused to "throw the rascals out," and put in a reform administration. But the reformers usually did not stay long in office. They were amateurs up against professionals. Furthermore, the early municipal reformers were usually interested only in economy and honest administration. They did not grasp, as did the professional politicians, that in a large city there were thousands of people who needed help. The machines made it part of their business to take care of the poor and unfortunate. The loyalty and gratitude they

QUESTION • What do people want most, an honest government or a helpful government?

447

received in return was a large source of their strength.

The Tweed Ring

A most notorious example of municipal corruption was the Tweed Ring, which gained control of Tammany Hall, the Democratic machine in New York City, in 1868 and managed in three years to steal an amount estimated to have been anywhere from $45,000,000 to $200,000,000. Typical of the methods of "Boss" William M. Tweed and his associates was the building of a county courthouse that should have cost $250,000 and actually cost $8,000,000. Contractors were compelled to add large sums to their bills and give the extra money to the ring. Those who dared to protest were silenced by threat of higher taxes.

The Tweed Ring was attacked by *The New York Times* and by Thomas Nast of *Harper's Weekly. The Times,* resisting threats and bribes, published overwhelming evidence of the ring's dishonesty, and Nast, a great cartoonist, held it up to ridicule. So effective was Nast's attack that Tweed remarked: "I don't care a straw for your newspaper articles: my people don't know how to read, but they can't help seeing them . . . pictures." Aroused citizens, led by Samuel J. Tilden, finally drove the ring from power. Fleeing to Spain, Tweed was brought back and imprisoned.

But Tammany Hall remained in power in New York, and graft continued, although probably never again on quite such a scale as under Tweed. The "best people" held aloof from city hall because politics was "a dirty game." Meanwhile, whatever their motives, the members of the machine were in direct touch with the people. From dawn to far into the night, local leaders were at the service of the people in their neighborhoods:

By these means the Tammany district leader reaches out into the homes of his district, keeps watch not only on the men, but also on the women and children; knows their needs, their likes and dislikes, their troubles and their hopes, and places himself in a position to use his knowledge for the benefit of his organization and himself. Is it any wonder that scandals do not permanently disable Tammany and that it speedily recovers from what seems to be crushing defeat?

Dishonesty on State and Federal Levels

At the state level, politics were nearly as corrupt as in the cities. When Jay Gould controlled the Erie Railroad, he was reported to have spent $500,000 in bribes during a single session of the New York state legislature. Of the relations between the Standard Oil Company and the government of Pennsylvania an observer wrote, "The Standard has done everything with the Pennsylvania legislature except to refine it."

National politics was less corrupt, on the whole, than local, partly because public attention was focused on Washington. Nevertheless dishonesty was widespread. In 1872 it was revealed that officers of the Union Pacific Railroad, built with federal aid, had formed their own construction company, the Crédit Mobilier, and so overcharged the railroad that Crédit Mobilier dividends ran as high as 350 per cent. To forestall investigation, the company distributed shares of stock "where it would do the most good" among congressmen. Several prominent men in Congress were involved in this scandal.

By far the worst misconduct occurred during President Grant's administration. Although Grant was personally honest, he seemed unable to distinguish honest people from crooks. Dazzled by wealth, he publicly associated with such men as James J. Fisk and Jay Gould, who reaped millions of dollars from their contacts with the President and his subordinates. People close to Grant—members of his family, his personal staff, and his cabinet—peddled influence and jobs in return for cash. Thus a group of whiskey distillers were able to evade millions

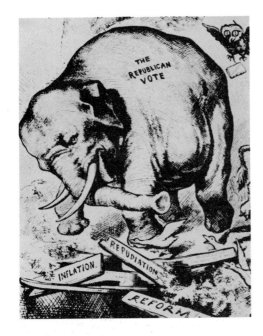

Thomas Nast, of *Harper's Weekly*, was perhaps the most effective political cartoonist in the history of the United States. The elephant as the symbol of the Republican party was his invention, and first appeared in the 1874 cartoon at left. The Democratic donkey, labeled "Copperheads Papers," is here shown kicking Secretary of War Stanton after his death in 1869. This was the first time Nast used the donkey to symbolize the Democratic party, although it had previously been used by others.

of dollars in excise taxes, and a corrupt Indian agent was able to keep his job at a cost of $40,000 in payments to the wife of a cabinet officer. Grant's brother at one time held four jobs at once, farming out the duties to other men. When the graft in his administration was finally brought to light, Grant wrote that he wanted to "let no guilty man escape," but he later protected those accused of wrongdoing from both investigation and punishment.

There was some improvement in political honesty after the Grant administration, but the spoils system was a constant source of inefficiency, and sometimes of graft. Disputes over patronage poisoned the relationship between the President and Congress and consumed an appalling amount of time. Only the assassination of President Garfield by a disappointed office seeker finally shocked Congress into taking steps to diminish the evil.

THE MAJOR POLITICAL PARTIES

In *The American Commonwealth*, James Bryce had difficulty explaining to English readers the characteristics of the major American parties. He could get no consistent answer as to how Democrats and Republicans stood on major issues such as the tariff and railroad regulation. "Neither party has, as a party, anything to say on these issues; neither party has any clean-cut principles.... All has been lost, except office or the hope of it." The hard core of each party was a group of professional politicians whose business was winning elections. Their usual tendency was either to avoid issues entirely or to try to appear all things to all people. The humorist "Mr. Dooley" described the ideal presidential candidate as follows:

Wanted: a good, active Dimmycrat, sthrong iv lung an' limb; must be . . . a sympathizer with th' crushed an' down throdden people but not be anny means hostile to vested inthrests; must advocate sthrikes, gover'mint be injunction, free silver, sound money, greenbacks, a single tax, a tariff f'r rivinoo . . . at home in Wall sthreet an' th' stock yards, in th' parlors iv th' r-rich an' th' kitchens iv th' poor.

The Republican Party

The Republican party had come into power in 1861 with the support of eastern business people and western farmers. Each group had its own demands, but they were united in opposition to the spread of slavery. Not only was slavery abolished as a result of the Civil War, but legislation passed during the war fulfilled eastern demands for a high tariff and stronger banks, as well as western demands for free land and federal aid to railroads. Thus the Republicans enjoyed the support of several groups owing it gratitude: freed slaves, manufacturers, officers and stockholders of national banks, homesteaders, owners of western railroads. In addition, the Republicans could count on the support of the powerful organization of Union veterans called the Grand Army of the Republic (GAR for short).

The Republicans had a patron saint in Abraham Lincoln, whose birthday they honored by banquets and oratory. Above all, they had immense prestige as the party that won the Civil War. "The party that saved the nation must rule it," they proclaimed. This explains why Republicans kept alive war hatreds by "waving the bloody shirt." It would not be fair, however, to dismiss the Republican party as nothing but a bundle of interest groups attempting to win elections by enmities better forgotten. Its strength came from genuine devotion to the idea of the United States as a nation rather than as a federation of states. A number of its members were inspired by the idealism that characterized the party in its early years; in 1872 and again in 1884, this reform element "bolted" to the Democrats in protest against political corruption.

The great problem of the Republican party was to keep together its eastern wing, dominated by bankers and industrialists, and its "grass roots" western wing, dominated by farmers. The two groups were likely to break into open warfare over such issues as greenbacks, free silver, tariffs, and banking. Usually, however, they managed to maintain an uneasy alliance for the purpose of winning elections. In general, the Middle West provided the presidential candidates, while the East provided the party funds.

The Democratic Party

The Democrats were so used to being out of office, according to "Mr. Dooley," that when writing their platform they forgot how to say "we commend," but automatically began to "denounce and deplore." The party strength centered in an alliance, formed in Jefferson's day, between Southerners and northern city machines, such as Tammany Hall. Both groups could "deliver the vote." From the end of Radical reconstruction until well into the twentieth century, the Solid South never wavered in its allegiance to the Democrats; New York City was almost as consistent. The Democrats had allies among western farmers, especially when prices were low, and among certain classes of business people, such as international bankers and importers who favored a lower tariff. They also attracted those doing municipal business, such as contractors and owners of street railways.

The Democratic party had two patron saints —Jefferson and Jackson. The Democrats claimed to be more concerned with the common man than their opponents, and tended to enlist more support from recent immigrants. However, the party labored under the handicap that wiped out the Federalists after the War of 1812: the charge of disloyalty. Although during the Civil

War most northern Democrats had supported the Union, the party had included a few "Copperheads." It naturally became Democratic strategy to urge that war hatreds be forgotten.

The Democratic party was perhaps more difficult to hold together than the Republican. The northern and southern wings were united in little save opposition to the Republicans. There was little in common between eastern city machines and southern farmers. At the time of the Hayes-Tilden election, conservative southern Democrats abandoned their candidate and arranged with Republican leaders the Compromise of 1877 (see pp. 373–374).

Pressure Groups and Lobbies

Although the Republican party held the upper hand, the Democrats were seldom far out of the running. In four of the eight presidential elections between 1868 and 1896, the difference in popular vote was less than 1 per cent of the total ballot. Hard times tend to hurt the party in power, and when there was a depression, Republican strength dropped. The Panic of 1873 helped to produce a "tidal wave" in the mid-term election of 1874, in which the Democrats wiped out a two-thirds Republican majority.

With the major parties so evenly divided, small changes in voting strength might decide elections. This opened the way for well-organized pressure groups. Lobbyists exerted such pressure that they were called "the third House of Congress." The great corporations regularly contributed to campaign funds, often to those of both parties, regarding such payments as "insurance" against unfavorable legislation. But business groups were not always supreme. Pressure from southern and western inflationists pushed the Bland-Allison Act through Congress in spite of opposition from bankers and bondholders (see p. 431). Similarly the strength of organized labor was seen in immigration restriction acts, passed over the opposition of shipping companies and employers. On the whole, the different interests within each party were so evenly balanced that they canceled each other out.

FLUCTUATING PARTY FORTUNES, 1877–1893

After the Reconstruction period came to an end, as a recent historian remarks, the federal government was "the epitome of lethargy. It was astonishingly idle." While the country was agitated over such matters as railroad abuses, labor conflicts, and the growth of monopoly, the two major parties spent their time fighting sham battles over petty and often irrelevant issues.

There were several reasons for this divorce between politics and reality. One was the remarkably even division of party strength; seldom was one party in control of the presidency and both houses of Congress. The power of the presidency itself was at a low ebb, so there was little opportunity for strong executive leadership. In Congress itself leadership was fragmented among committee chairmen. But perhaps the most important reason for inaction was the prevailing *laissez faire* philosophy. The federal government did not act because it was supposed to leave things alone.

The administration of President Rutherford B. Hayes (1877–1881) saw a slight but definite rise in both the tone of politics and the power of the presidency. Hayes put Carl Schurz, a noted reformer, in charge of the Department of the Interior, which heretofore had been a happy hunting ground for patronage. He also forbade the practice of "shaking down" officeholders for campaign contributions. Hayes defied congressional leaders in making major appointments and in refusing to allow Congress to use "riders" (irrelevant amendments) as a means of coercing him into accepting legislation he disapproved of. He vetoed seven appropriation bills with riders attached, and finally won a clearcut victory.

The Election of 1880

Hayes had won the resentment of a group of Republican machine politicians, calling themselves "Stalwarts," who were strongly opposed to reforming the civil service. At the Republican National Convention of 1880 an attempt by the Stalwarts to nominate Grant for a third term failed, partly because of the long-standing two-term tradition. After a prolonged deadlock, the nomination went to a "dark horse," James A. Garfield, a former Union brigadier general. To blunt the old charge of disloyalty in wartime, the Democrats nominated General Winfield S. Hancock, a hero of the battle of Gettysburg. The intellectual level of the ensuing campaign may be judged by the following excerpt from the speech of a Republican orator:

I belong to a party that believes in good crops; that is glad when a fellow finds a gold mine; that rejoices when there are forty bushels of wheat to the acre. . . . The Democratic Party is a party of famine; it is a good friend of an early frost; it believes in the Colorado beetle and in the weevil.

Garfield won the election with 214 electoral votes to Hancock's 155, but in the popular vote the margin between the candidates was only 9,564 out of over 9,000,000 votes cast.

Civil Service Reform

After a few months in the White House Garfield was shot by a half-crazy office seeker. This tragic event so excited public opinion against the spoils system that in 1883 Congress passed the Pendleton Act, which has been called (with some exaggeration) "the Magna Carta of civil service reform." This law allowed the President to place on a "classified list" federal offices that could then be filled only according to rules laid down by a bipartisan Civil Service Commission. Jobholders on the classified list were to be chosen on the basis of examinations and were not to be asked to make contributions to party funds. They could no longer be removed for political reasons. Although President Chester Arthur, who succeeded Garfield, was a veteran of machine politics, he supported the Pendleton Act and placed 16,000 officeholders (one-seventh of the total number) on the classified list. He thus initiated a shift from the spoils system to the so-called "merit system."

1884: Honesty as a Political Issue

The major theme of the presidential election of 1884 was honesty in politics. The Republican nominee, James G. Blaine, was a man of great ability and personal charm, but he had never cleared himself of charges that he made money by selling his influence in Congress on behalf of certain railroads. Blaine's nomination was such a defeat for some reformers in the Republican party that they refused to support him. These "Mugwumps" included some of the most respected and influential men in the country, such as Charles W. Eliot, president of Harvard, and George W. Curtis, editor of *Harper's Weekly*. The Democrats won Mugwump support by nominating Grover Cleveland, who as mayor of Buffalo and governor of New York had made a reputation for stubborn integrity.

The campaign of 1884 developed into one of abuse. Blaine was portrayed as a "tattooed man," with railroad stocks and bonds indelibly engraved on his skin. Cleveland was attacked because of an indiscretion in his youth. At the close of this unpleasant campaign Cleveland won the election by an extremely narrow margin. He was the first Democratic President since Buchanan. In the congressional elections the Democrats gained a majority in the House of Representatives, but the Republicans retained control of the Senate.

Cleveland in Office

Grover Cleveland was a man with little imagination and rather narrow horizons. Unskillful in political maneuvering, he often met defeat in his relations with Congress. Nevertheless, he did much to restore the prestige of the office of President. "The presidency," he said, "is the people's office." By this he meant that the chief executive alone is chosen by the whole country and can use his influence for the general good rather than for any special interest.

Cleveland's first problem was to deal with Democratic office seekers who swarmed to Washington seeking the fruits of victory after a quarter of a century in the wilderness. If he made appointments on merit alone, he would split his party wide open. If he gave in to the spoils system, he would lose the support of the Mugwumps and other independents who played a decisive part in making him President. Cleveland met this situation by compromise. While appointing so many "deserving Democrats" to office that two-thirds of 120,000 federal offices changed hands, Cleveland made every effort to see that the new appointees were qualified for their jobs. Once he wrote a Democrat who recommended an incompetent person for a federal judgeship that "such treason to the people and to the party ought to be punished by imprisonment." Such a letter did not endear Cleveland to machine politicians, but it won him public esteem.

Cleveland entered office ignorant of most national questions, but no President ever put in more study to determine what course to follow. His predecessors, for instance, had signed hundreds of private bills giving pensions to veterans unable to qualify under regular laws. Examining such bills with care, Cleveland found many of them fraudulent. One veteran asked a pension for an injury suffered while *intending* to enlist; the widow of another claimed that her husband died of apoplexy in 1882 as the result

Grover Cleveland worked hard to restore dignity to the presidential office. Although he used the spoils system, he tried to give offices only to the capable.

of a knee injury in 1863. Cleveland disapproved so many private pension bills that his vetoes totaled more than those of all previous Presidents. Seriously interested in saving the public lands for future generations, he compelled cattle ranchers and lumber companies to return land illegally taken. He also forced land grant railroads to open millions of acres to settlement or to return them to the federal government.

Cleveland and the Tariff

The public question that Cleveland studied most seriously was the tariff. During the Civil War, duties had been raised from an average of 19 per cent in 1861 to over 40 per cent in 1865. These high rates were constantly attacked by those who considered themselves hurt by them—farmers, consumers, shippers, and importers. They were joined by "free traders" who argued that a protective tariff was unwarrantable government interference with normal laws of supply and demand, and was a subsidy paid to the manufacturer out of the pocket of the consumer. Protection was defended, on the other hand, as a means of developing infant industries and protecting high wage standards of American laborers from competition with cheap foreign labor. Whenever proposals to lower the tariff appeared before Congress, they were thwarted by manufacturers' lobbies.

Shortly after taking office, Carl Schurz asked Cleveland about his ideas on the tariff question. "You know I really don't know anything about it," replied the President. "In my political career as sheriff of Buffalo County, mayor of Buffalo, and governor of New York it has, of course, not been an issue." Asking Schurz to recommend books, Cleveland investigated the problem. He became convinced that the existing tariff system was wrong, and devoted his entire 1887 congressional message to the topic.

The situation prompting action was a mounting surplus in the U.S. Treasury. It was thought inadvisable to use the extra revenues to pay off the national debt, because United States bonds were the basis for national bank notes. Offhand, one might think surplus government revenue, like business profits, a healthy sign. But, as Cleveland pointed out, the government is not in business to make money; a surplus is a sign of over-taxation. If kept in the treasury, the surplus deflated the currency by reducing the amount of money in circulation; if spent, it was an invitation to extravagance. The only cure, said the President, was to revise "our present tariff laws, the vicious, inequitable, and illogical source of unnecessary taxation." Not a free trader, Cleveland did not propose to abandon protection, but simply to remove duties on goods not produced in this country and to reduce unnecessarily high rates. The President's dramatic effort to lower the tariff utterly failed. A bill embodying his recommendations passed the House, controlled by the Democrats, but the Republican Senate ignored it.

Cleveland had presented his opponents with an issue for the presidential election of 1888. Openly avowing protection for the first time, the Republicans collected a record-breaking campaign fund. "Put all the manufacturers of Pennsylvania under the fire," said a Republican campaign manager, "and fry the fat out of them." The Republicans revived Henry Clay's name for the protective tariff as the "American system." Renominating the President, the Democrats campaigned against unnecessary taxation. As in 1880 and 1884, the result was extremely close. Although winning fewer popular votes than Cleveland, the Republican candidate Benjamin Harrison, who was the grandson of the hero of Tippecanoe, gained a majority in the electoral college.

QUESTION • How did Harrison win the election of 1888 with a minority of the popular vote?

The "Billion Dollar Congress," 1889–1891

Once in office the Republicans removed the treasury surplus by spending it. In two years the so-called "Billion-Dollar Congress" created a deficit, mostly by handouts to special interest groups. The McKinley Tariff of 1890 dried up revenue at its source by levying prohibitive rates—so high that they kept some foreign products out of the country entirely. Admitting foreign sugar duty free, the McKinley Act gave a bounty of 2 cents a pound to domestic producers. Western support for the tariff measure was won by the passage of the Sherman Silver Purchase Act, whereby the federal government undertook to buy four and a half million ounces of silver a month—practically the entire output of the United States.

Additional millions were spent on the improvement of harbors and waterways, coastal defenses, federal buildings, and sorely needed steel ships for the navy. In addition to these measures, Congress passed the Sherman Antitrust Act (p. 432) and provided for admission to the Union of North and South Dakota, Montana, Washington, Idaho, and Wyoming.

Democratic Landslides

The tariff issue that helped the Republicans to win the election of 1888 proved a boomerang two years later. A sharp rise in cost of living accompanying the McKinley Tariff caused indignation which the Democrats exploited. The congressional elections of 1890 proved a landslide, the Democrats winning 235 seats in the House of Representatives to 88 for the Republicans.

Resentment against the tariff continued in 1892. The Republican claim that high rates protected American wage scales seemed to be refuted by the Homestead lockout (see p. 434). Steel was a highly protected industry and its profits were enormous; yet the labor dispute at the Homestead plant began when the Carnegie Steel Company announced a pay cut. Cleveland and Harrison were again the nominees of their parties, but the decision of 1888 was reversed. Cleveland was elected for a second term by the largest majority since Grant's victory over Greeley in 1872. The Democrats also won control of both houses of Congress.

THE POPULIST PARTY

The election of 1892 was notable because it saw the appearance of the first third party to win electoral votes since 1860. The new organization, the People's or Populist party, was principally an expression of the grievances of the farmer. Ever since the Civil War federal policies had favored industry over agriculture, the city over the country. In spite of clamor for a cheaper dollar, the United States remained on the gold standard, to the advantage of creditors,

This cartoon of the 1890's ridiculed the way manufacturing interests brazenly demanded protective tariffs from congressmen, shown prostrating themselves before the captains of industry.

and farm prices went steadily down, to the advantage of urban consumers. The protective tariff raised the price of the goods farmers bought, to the advantage of manufacturers, but American agricultural staples were sold abroad in an unprotected market. Legislation that apparently favored the agrarian interests proved ineffective. State and federal regulation of railroads had been hamstrung by adverse judicial decisions. The Homestead Act offered free farms to settlers, but the greater part of the public lands actually went to railroads and speculators. When drought hit the Great Plains region in the late 1880's, the farmers were in a rebellious mood and were ready to fight against the discrimination of which they had been victims. "Those who could submit quietly to such outrage," said a western editor, "must be either more or less than men." According to historian Ray Ginger, "two nations" were coming into being. One of them lay east of the Mississippi and north of the Ohio, with outposts in urban areas elsewhere. Here was prosperity and growth, not only in the cities, but among the surrounding farmers who produced diversified crops for urban consumption. The other "nation" centered on the areas that produced cotton, wheat, and silver. There economic distress was widespread, and after the depression of 1893 feeling became so bitter that many thoughtful citizens feared a revolution.

The Populist party originated with two great farmers' organizations, formed after the decline of the Grange: the Southern Alliance, which covered the cotton and tobacco belt, and the Northwestern Alliance, especially strong in the Plains region. Although the two alliances failed to merge, they made similar demands—free silver, more paper money, cheaper credit, government ownership of railroads, and the restoration of railroad bounty lands to the federal government. In the elections of 1890 the

Ignatius Donnelly, Populist

It was the Fourth of July, 1892, in Omaha, Nebraska. "Cheers and yells rose . . . like a tornado from four thousand throats and raged without cessation for thirty-four minutes, during which women shrieked and wept, men embraced and kissed their neighbors . . . and leaped upon tables and chairs in the ecstasy of their delirium. . . ."

Ignatius Donnelly, the author of the Populist party platform which had aroused this response, was a short, "plump, genial Irishman who sounded like a prophet out of the Old Testament." He was at the peak of his career. He liked to strike a Napoleonic pose—right hand thrust into his vest—but his dancing brown eyes destroyed the similarity to the stern French emperor.

Born and educated in Philadelphia, Donnelly, at twenty-five, had gone west in 1856. He made a paper fortune in land speculation in Minnesota and lost it in a year. After he left the Democratic party because he hated slavery, he promptly joined the Republicans. They sent him to Congress for three terms. No reformer then, he sponsored grants to railroads in which he held stock "presented to me without solicitation on my part by the Company. . . ."

Donnelly lost his seat in Congress in 1869, and turned to writing and lecturing as a career, although he never ceased to run for political office, usually without success. He edited a newspaper, the *Anti-Monopolist,* that aired the farmers' grievances and wrote books on subjects as various as the lost continent of Atlantis and the authorship of Shakespeare's plays. He successively joined the Greenback and Populist parties. At the Omaha convention, out of his political experience, literary talent, and sense of outrage, he produced the Populist platform almost single-handedly.

He was badly defeated as Populist candidate for governor of Minnesota in 1892, but later sat in the state legislature. A biographer wrote of him, "He never attacked a small problem if a larger one was at hand; he was happiest when attempting something his contemporaries were sure couldn't be done."

Southern Alliance, working through the Democratic party, gained control of five state legislatures. In the Plains region the Northwestern Alliance organized local parties that elected six congressmen from Kansas and Nebraska. These successes encouraged the formation of a new national party. After conferences at Cincinnati in 1891 and St. Louis in February 1892, the People's (or Populist) Party held a national convention at Omaha in July 1892. Although mostly from farm organizations, delegates also represented the Knights of Labor and followers of Henry George and Edward Bellamy (see p. 445). Following the custom of the time, the convention nominated for President a Civil War veteran, General James B. Weaver. But there was nothing customary, however, about the platform. Instead of the usual resounding double talk, the Populists made clear their position and presented specific demands.

The Omaha Platform, 1892

The preamble of the Omaha platform expressed indignation at the existing political and economic conditions, which were, it claimed, bringing the nation "to the verge of moral, political, and material ruin." In the exaggerated terms usual in American party platforms, it condemned political corruption, newspapers dominated by business interests, the mortgage burden, and the condition of labor. Echoing the Declaration of Independence, it referred to the 300 Pinkerton detectives employed by the Carnegie Steel Company in the Homestead lockout as "a hireling army, unrecognized by our laws." The influence of Henry George was seen in the statements that "the land is concentrating in the hands of the capitalists," and that governmental injustice breeds "two great classes—tramps and millionaires."

Turning to money and banking, the Populists deplored the National Bank Act as a means whereby "the national power to create money" was "appropriated to enrich bondholders." World-wide adoption of the gold standard was characterized as "a vast conspiracy against mankind . . . organized on two continents." The older parties did nothing, said the Omaha platform, but carry on a "sham battle over the tariff." The new party of the "plain people" would once and for all forget war hatreds (a criticism of Republican use of the "bloody shirt"), and devote itself instead to the great task of finding means to cope with "conditions for which there is no precedent in the history of mankind."

The most radical statement in the preamble of the Omaha platform was this: "We believe that the powers of government—in other words of the people,—should be expanded . . . as rapidly and as far as the good sense of an intelligent people and the teachings of experience shall justify. . . ." In Jefferson's time it had been the agriculturalists who favored *laissez faire* and wanted to reduce the powers of the federal government, while Hamilton, supported by bankers and merchants, wanted to increase the role of government in private business. Now in the late nineteenth century the commercial interests preached the Jeffersonian doctrine, while the farmers wanted to use the power of government to restrain trusts and monopolies.

Attempted Farmer-Labor Alliance

The platform proper opened by declaring perpetual union of workers in field and factory. A farmer-labor alliance was difficult to maintain, however, because the interests of the two groups were at variance. The farmer wanted high prices for food products, the laborer wanted them low. The laborer wanted high wages, while the farmer, who was often an employer, was interested in keeping them down.

The Omaha platform revealed that it was the agriculturalists who dominated the Populist

A Fast-Growing Nation

The United States, 1860-1900

In the last four decades of the nineteenth century, the United States grew rapidly in many ways. The statistics below reveal some of these ways.

	1860	1900
Population of the United States	31,443,000	75,995,000

Ten Largest Cities

1860		1900	
1. New York	1,072,000	1. New York	3,437,000
2. Philadelphia	585,000	2. Chicago	1,850,000
3. Baltimore	212,000	3. Philadelphia	1,294,000
4. Boston	178,000	4. St. Louis	575,000
5. New Orleans	169,000	5. Boston	561,000
6. Cincinnati	161,000	6. Baltimore	509,000
7. St. Louis	161,000	7. Cleveland	381,000
8. Chicago	109,000	8. Buffalo	352,000
9. Buffalo	81,000	9. San Francisco	343,000
10. Newark	72,000	10. Cincinnati	325,000

- Which cities dropped off the list in 1900? Which were added?
- What regions of the country are represented in each list? What shift has occurred?
- Which city grew most rapidly? In what region is it?

You are aware of the great growth of manufacturing in this country from 1860 onward. Now consider the statistics below:

	1860	1880	1900
Number of Workers			
In Agriculture	5,880,000	8,920,000	11,680,000
In Manufacturing	1,530,000	3,290,000	5,895,000
In Railroads	80,000	416,000	1,040,000
Value of Farm Property	$7,890,000,000	$12,395,000,000	$20,635,000,000
Capital Invested in Manufacturing	$1,650,000,000	$ 4,821,000,000	$17,452,000,000

- What does the data on agriculture reveal? How do you explain this fact?
- What role do you think the railroads played in the growth of manufacturing, agriculture, and cities in this country during this period? Explain.

party. The major planks—concerning land, transportation, money, and credit—all reflected the interests of the farmer. The demands of organized labor, such as those for an 8-hour day on government contracts and for immigration restriction, were given a subordinate position. Not included in the platform proper, they were placed among a miscellaneous list of resolutions that were given the title "Expression of Sentiments."

The Omaha platform seems less radical in perspective than it did at the time. It approached socialism only in proposing that the government take over railroad and telegraph lines, both natural monopolies; for such action the Erie and other canals provided an American precedent. The Populists proposed not to overthrow the capitalist system, but simply to change the rules. They aimed to achieve their ends not through revolution, but through the orderly process of free elections. The Populist platform reveals an important function of American third parties—to bring to public attention measures that the major parties later adopt as their own. The majority of the Populist demands were later put into effect through either state or federal legislation.

The Populists entered the campaign of 1892 with religious fervor. They adapted revival meeting hymns as party songs. Monster rallies were addressed not only by men, but also by "women with skins tanned to parchment by the hot winds, with bony hands of toil and clad in faded calico." One of these orators, Mrs. Mary E. Lease, "the Kansas Cassandra," achieved fame by urging farmers to "raise less corn and more Hell." The balloting revealed the sectional character of the People's party. All its 22 electoral votes came from states lying west of the Missouri River. In the South, sympathy with Populist aims was widespread, but there was fear that the new party might divide the Democratic vote and let the Republicans back into power. Southern sympathizers therefore became "Popocrats"—Democrats with Populist principles.

SILVER VS. GOLD

Cleveland's second term proved difficult. Inheriting a treasury deficit from the Harrison administration, he had scarcely taken office when the Panic of 1893 burst upon the country. Although Cleveland could not have prevented this disaster, he was held somehow to blame. Furthermore, he managed to antagonize almost every element in his party.

Cleveland's Second Term

Never popular with machine politicians, Cleveland angered them further by putting 120,000 civil service jobs on the merit system. The President's hope of lowering the prohibitive duties of the McKinley Tariff faded when a few Democratic senators joined the Republicans in tacking 633 amendments on a new tariff bill, thereby keeping rates almost at former levels. Cleveland let the resulting Wilson-Gorman Tariff of 1894 become a law without his signature, but denounced the action of the rebellious senators as "a piece of party perfidy and dishonor."

QUESTION • A saying of this time was, "The tariff is political dynamite." Why?

Cleveland's use of troops in the Pullman strike was condemned by workers. Above all, he antagonized farmers by defending the gold standard. Fearful that the Sherman Silver Purchase Act would flood the U.S. Treasury with so much silver that it could not be redeemed in gold, he called a special session of Congress in 1893 and forced repeal of the law. He was able to do this only with Republican support, since most western and southern

Democrats opposed him. Even after federal buying of silver ceased, the gold standard was endangered because of the difficulty of keeping an adequate gold reserve in the treasury. To obtain the precious metal, the Treasury Department sold United States bonds. In one transaction J. Pierpont Morgan, the most powerful banker on Wall Street, obtained federal bonds so far below their market value that he and the bankers associated with him made $1,500,000. Western fury at the Morgan bond transaction was unbounded. The gold standard was bad enough, they thought, but to pay bankers to preserve it seemed almost treasonable. More and more, western Democrats turned against the President, became "Popocrats," and demanded that the Democrats favor free silver.

The Free Silver Election of 1896

Meanwhile the Republicans had become more than ever identified with business interests. A dominant figure in the party was Mark Hanna, an Ohio businessman-politician. Big, bluff, low-browed Hanna became, perhaps unjustly, a symbol of the alliance between corporate wealth and politics. Anti-Republican cartoons habitually portrayed him in a suit covered with dollar signs. In 1896 Hanna used his great organizing talents to secure the Republican nomination for his friend William McKinley, on a platform pledging high tariffs and maintenance of the gold standard.

As the election of 1896 approached, the Republicans boasted that they could "nominate a rag-baby or a yellow dog and elect it," because of divisions among their opponents. The Democratic national convention opened with such a bitter fight between Gold Democrats and Silver Democrats that it was almost impossible to keep a semblance of order. Then with dramatic suddenness, the party found a leader when a rather obscure presidential candidate, William Jennings Bryan of Nebraska, rose to speak.

The unpopular income tax of 1894 was declared unconstitutional by the Supreme Court because it was a direct tax not apportioned according to representative population.

Bryan combined a romantic devotion to free silver with a personality, voice, and presence which made him literally a spellbinder. He came before the convention, he said, to speak "in defense of a cause as holy as the cause of liberty —the cause of humanity." The Gold Democrats had expressed the fear that abandonment of the gold standard would hurt business. Bryan accused them of thinking only of *big* business; he wished to speak for a "broader class of businessmen"—small storekeepers, country lawyers, miners, factory workers, and farmers. Brought up on the Plains, Bryan spoke especially for the farm against the city:

You come to us and tell us that the great cities are in favor of the gold standard. We reply that the great cities rest upon our broad and fertile plains. Burn down your cities and leave our farms, and your cities will spring up again as if by magic; but destroy our farms, and the grass will grow in the streets of every city in the country.

He concluded with this famous passage:

You shall not press down upon the brow of labor this crown of thorns—you shall not crucify mankind upon a cross of gold!

The Cross of Gold speech contained hardly a single factual argument for a bimetallic standard, but was so charged with emotion that it made free silver a crusade, with Bryan as its peerless leader. Although only thirty-six years old, he received the Democratic nomination. The majority of the Populists also agreed to support Bryan, although they nominated a separate vice-presidential candidate. As the Nebraskan traveled 18,000 miles on the most strenuous speaking tour a candidate had ever made, it almost seemed as though he might stampede the country, as he had the convention. At least five million people heard him. Twenty years later, poet Vachel Lindsay remembered the excitement of a Bryan rally:

It was eighteen ninety-six, and I was just sixteen
And Altgeld ruled in Springfield, Illinois,
When there came from the sunset Nebraska's shout of joy:
In a coat like a deacon, with a black Stetson hat
He scourged the elephant plutocrats
With barbed wire from the Platte.

Among conservatives in the East, "the Boy Orator from the Platte" inspired something approaching terror; even from the pulpit he was denounced as "a mouthing, slobbering demagogue."

In spite of all his efforts, Bryan's cause was doomed. Most large Democratic newspapers abandoned him; the Gold Democrats deserted the party and ran a separate candidate. Collecting an immense campaign fund, Hanna hired thousands of speakers and issued an estimated

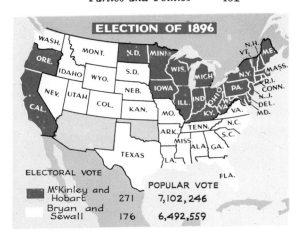

ELECTION OF 1896

ELECTORAL VOTE
McKinley and Hobart   271
Bryan and Sewall   176

POPULAR VOTE
7,102,246
6,492,559

The Solid South, the wheat-growing areas of the Great Plains, and the Rocky Mountain mining states favored Bryan and free silver, while the more prosperous farming states of the Midwest and the industrial states of the East and Midwest voted for McKinley, "the advance agent of prosperity," and the gold standard.

200,000,000 pamphlets to counter the free silver arguments. McKinley, depicted as "the advance agent of prosperity," was helped by the fact that prices of grain and cotton advanced on the eve of election day. The most serious weakness in Bryan's campaign was that free silver was a poor issue on which to base an entire campaign. No one knew what the result of free coinage of silver would be; it would not have ended fluctuation in the value of money, and might have caused a business panic. It had little appeal for industrial laborers, with whose difficulties Hanna and McKinley had genuine sympathy. Bryan had little sense of the complex problems of an industrial society, and regarded the East as "the enemy's country."

The Republicans won the election of 1896 by a decisive margin, carrying all the thickly populated states of the Northeast and Middle West. It was a victory for industry over agriculture, the city over the country, the North and East over the West and South.

This anti-Bryan cartoon suggests that "the Boy Orator of the Platte" was simply a puppet manipulated by silver mine owners, who would make fortunes out of "free silver."

McKinley in Office, 1897

The McKinley administration took office in 1897 under favorable circumstances. Prosperity was returning after three years of depression. The discovery of large gold deposits in Australia, South Africa, and the Yukon put an end to the world-wide specie famine that had been driving prices down. As an ardent believer in protection, McKinley's first important action was to call a special session of Congress to "revise" the tariff. The result was the Dingley Tariff that levied rates even higher than those of the McKinley Act of 1890. American steel companies received additional protection though they were already able to compete successfully in world markets. Duties were put on foreign paintings and sculpture, although American artists protested that they did not want to be "protected." But the American people did not react as unfavorably to the Dingley Tariff as to that of 1890, perhaps because their attention was drawn from domestic issues to foreign affairs.

FOREIGN AFFAIRS

"Our relations with foreign nations today," wrote Henry Cabot Lodge in 1889, "fill but a slight place in American politics, and excite generally only a languid interest. We have separated ourselves so completely from the affairs of other people that it is difficult to realize how large a place they occupied when the government was founded." At the time of the French Revolution and the Napoleonic Wars, the very survival of the young American republic depended on wise foreign policy. Elections turned on serious disputes over foreign affairs, and diplomacy was in the hands of the ablest men of the country.

During the long period of isolation that began about 1815, however, relations with other countries were considered so unimportant that American diplomacy was at the mercy of party politics. State Department jobs were under the spoils system, and few Secretaries of State had diplomatic experience. Foreign relations were apt to be conducted with an eye to the voters, especially in election years. A favorite maneuver, known as "twisting the lion's tail," was to appeal to the Irish vote by gestures against Great Britain.

In 1888, for instance, Republican senators, trying to discredit Cleveland as pro-English, rejected a treaty with Great Britain concerning American fishing rights in Canadian waters. To counter this move, Cleveland sent Congress a message urging strong measures against Canada unless the demands of the United States were complied with, treaty or no treaty. The President neither expected nor desired that his recommendations be carried out, but he had to appear as anti-British as his opponents.

James G. Blaine, Secretary of State

As the United States became a great industrial nation with world-wide trade, foreign relations were bound to assume more importance. James G. Blaine was one of the first men to grasp the new situation. Blaine, Secretary of State under Garfield in 1881 and under Harrison from 1889 to 1892, was especially interested in making closer commercial ties with Latin America. He presided over a Pan-American Congress, held in Washington in 1889, which set up a permanent organization that eventually became the Pan American Union. Blaine wanted to increase inter-American commerce by "reciprocity"—mutual lowering of tariff barriers. He labored without much success to get reciprocity provisions into the McKinley Tariff of 1890.

Outside the sphere of Pan-Americanism, Blaine's "spirited" diplomacy was characterized less by wisdom than by the ability to create headlines through belligerent notes to foreign nations. He engaged in a series of hot disputes with Great Britain over the protection of seals in the Bering Sea (1889), with Germany over rights in the Samoan Islands (1889), and with Chile over ill-treatment of American sailors on leave in Santiago (1891). While unimportant in themselves, these incidents dramatized the fact that American interests were expanding far beyond our borders.

Attempt to Annex Hawaiian Islands, 1893

Now that the frontier was closing, would the United States again expand its territory? This question seemed about to be answered in the affirmative when in January 1893, Americans in the Hawaiian Islands, assisted by the crew of a United States warship, overthrew the native ruler, Queen Liliuokalani. Proclaiming an independent state, they asked to be annexed. The American minister to Hawaii wrote the Department of State: "The Hawaiian pear is now fully ripe, and this is the golden hour for the United States to pluck it." President Harrison promptly sent an annexation treaty to the Senate, which did not act before Cleveland came into office in March.

Cleveland immediately withdrew the Hawaiian treaty for re-examination. Eventually he reached the conclusion that the use of American military forces to overthrow the native government as a step toward annexation was a violation of "national honesty." Braving criticism for hauling down the Stars and Stripes and "turning back the hands of civilization," Cleveland withdrew American troops from Hawaii and attempted, without success, to restore Queen Liliuokalani to her throne.

QUESTION • Was Cleveland right in refusing to annex Hawaii?

The Venezuela Boundary Crisis, 1895–1896

Cleveland's withdrawal from Hawaii implied, however, no unwillingness to assert what he considered legitimate American rights. This was revealed by the Venezuela boundary crisis of 1895–1896. The boundary between British Guiana and Venezuela had been disputed for over half a century. In 1887 and again in 1894, Cleveland suggested submitting the matter to arbitration. Great Britain, with the stronger claim to most of the disputed area, refused these requests. Finally, in July 1895, Secretary of State Richard Olney sent to London a stiff note arguing that British refusal to arbitrate was a violation of the Monroe Doctrine, and warning that "the United States is practically sovereign on this continent. . . ." After an irritating delay of several months, Lord Salisbury, British foreign minister, replied that the Monroe Doctrine had no standing in international law, and in any event it had no reference to the Venezuela situation.

Cleveland later confessed that Salisbury's note made him "mad clean through." In December 1895, he sent a vigorous message to Congress asking for $100,000 to appoint a commission to fix the Venezuela-British Guiana boundary without consulting Britain. The President wrote that he was "fully alive" to the possibility that such a course might mean war. His action met with enthusiastic support in this country while on the other side of the Atlantic it was regarded as "monstrous and insulting." For a few days war seemed imminent. The British fleet was made ready to sail, and American coastal defenses were put under repair. There was talk of invading Canada.

It was not long, however, before "sober second thought" began to prevail. In both America and Britain there was renewed consciousness of the bonds of language, trade, and common inheritance. Furthermore, Guiana was of far less importance to the British Empire than other areas, and early in January 1896, English attention was diverted from Venezuela by a dispute with Germany involving South Africa. Late in the same month Joseph Chamberlain, an English statesman, made a memorable speech in which he asserted that war between England and the United States "would be an absurdity as well as a crime." He hoped the Stars and Stripes and the Union Jack would some day float together "in defense of a common cause sanctioned by humanity and justice." The British government then agreed to arbitrate the Venezuela boundary, on terms that made it probable the verdict would favor them, as it did.

Although Alaska and a few Pacific islands had been annexed earlier, the main imperialistic thrust of the United States in the Pacific and Caribbean occurred in 1898.

U. S. AND POSSESSIONS IN 1900

The Venezuela crisis had important results. The Monroe Doctrine, which once owed its effectiveness to the British fleet, had now been successfully asserted against Britain herself. The crisis served indeed to clear the air as regards Anglo-American relations. A new realization of common traditions and common interests came to outweigh memories of the American Revolution and the War of 1812.

It was apparent that protection of the Western Hemisphere under the Monroe Doctrine demanded sea power, and the Venezuela crisis publicized the fact that the United States had only three modern battleships to pit against the vast British fleet. The crisis popularized the writings of an American naval officer, Captain Alfred T. Mahan, whose best-known work, *The Influence of Sea Power on History, 1660–1783,* was published in 1890. In this and other works Mahan argued that sea power was necessary for national greatness, and that a state which neglected its navy was courting disaster. At first Mahan had more influence abroad than in his own country. Kaiser Wilhelm II of Germany "devoured" his books and instructed his naval officers to read them. In England Mahan was showered with honors. Then he was heeded in the United States. In 1896 Congress voted to add thirteen new ships to the navy. The United States was to become a major naval power. The new fleet was shortly to go into action, not against Great Britain but against Spain.

Activities: Chapter 18

For Mastery and Review

1. What factors made for political corruption in the big cities? Explain the ineffectiveness of municipal reformers. What types of corruption appeared at the state and federal levels?

2. In what ways were the Republican and Democratic parties similar? In what ways did they differ?

3. Explain the remarkable lack of legislative achievement by the Republican administrators who held office for all but eight years between 1877 and 1901. What *did* they accomplish?

4. What were the terms and purposes of the Pendleton Act? How did succeeding Presidents extend its effectiveness?

5. Balance Cleveland's achievements against his failures during his two terms in office. What factors worked against him? Would you call him a successful President?

6. Explain what was behind the Populist revolt. What was different and radical about the Omaha platform? What were the weaknesses of Populism?

7. Why did the election of 1896 arouse passion and fear on both sides? What was the significance of the outcome?

8. What caused the Venezuela Boundary crisis, and how did it affect Anglo-American relations? What was the purpose of "twisting the lion's tail"?

9. What were the features of James G. Blaine's "spirited diplomacy"?

Unrolling the Map

Study carefully the maps showing the vote in Congress on the Bland-Allison Act and the election of 1896, pp. 431 and 461. Explain the sectional divisions in each case—what was similar and what was different? Why?

Who, What, and Why Important?

Tweed Ring
Samuel J. Tilden
Credit Mobilier
"the bloody shirt"
Solid South

lobbyists
Carl Schurz
election of 1884
Pendleton Act
Mugwumps

election of 1888
McKinley Tariff
Sherman Silver Purchase
Act
election of 1892
Omaha platform
"Popocrats"
Panic of 1893
J. Pierpont Morgan
William McKinley

Mark Hanna
William Jennings Bryan
"Cross of Gold"
election of 1896
free silver
Pan American Union
Liliuokalani
Venezuela crisis
Alfred T. Mahan

To Pursue the Matter

1. Test the idea that politics attracted men of less eminence during the generation after the Civil War than during the generation before by making your own lists of ten or a dozen men in each period. This might be done by the class as a whole.

2. Are lobbyists and pressure groups bad for the country? Are they immoral? Should they be (a) left unhampered, (b) regulated by law, or (c) declared illegal?

3. Read about William Jennings Bryan in Arnof, *A Sense of the Past*, pp. 332–333. You might go on to Vachel Lindsay's poem, "Bryan, Bryan, Bryan, Bryan"; try reading it aloud. Was "the Boy Orator of the Platte" a prophet or a shallow demagogue? See Glad, *McKinley, Bryan, and the People*.

4. Consider Bryce's conclusion (p. 449) that neither of the major political parties had "any clear-cut principles." Do you agree? Why or why not?

5. Examine the Omaha platform (pp. 805–806) in detail. How many of the reform measures proposed were substantially enacted into law within the following 25 years? Discuss the implications of the answer to this question.

6. Read the chapter in Bailey, *A Diplomatic History of the American People*, called "Cleveland and the Venezuela Crisis with Great Britain." What seems to have been Cleveland's motivation in threatening war? How was the Monroe Doctrine involved? Why did Great Britain back down?

7. Were the politics of the Gilded Age as bad as they have often been painted? See Fine and Brown, *The American Past: Conflicting Interpretations of Great Issues*, vol. II, Issue 6.

8. The dirtiest presidential election in American political history was that of 1884. It was also one of the very closest. The sorry tale is told in the August 1962 issue of *American Heritage* and in Josephson, *The Politicos*.

9. One of the fighters in the uphill battle for civil service reform was Theodore Roosevelt, who served for a time as a member of the U.S. Civil Service Commission. See Pringle, *Theodore Roosevelt*, Chapter 10.

READINGS FOR PART FIVE

Fiction

Brown, D. *Bury My Heart at Wounded Knee.* A poignant look at the famous battle from the Indian viewpoint.

Dreiser, T. *Sister Carrie. The* struggles of a young girl in Chicago at the end of the 19th century.

Ferber, E. *Cimmaron.* A fast moving novel about the last great land rush in Oklahoma.

Schaeffer, J. *Shane.* An excellent "western" about the fight between the farmers and the cattle raisers.

Vidal, G. *1876.* The year of the Centennial and a family that gets caught up in the machinations of the period.

Non-fiction

Addams, J. *Twenty Years at Hull House.* Inspiring personal testimony.

Dick, F. *The Sod-House Frontier, 1854–1890.* A good description of pioneer life.

Garland, H. *A Son of the Middle Border.* A poignant autobiographical account of growing up on a prairie farm.

Handlin, O. *The Uprooted.* A superb and moving study of how late 19th-century immigrants attempted to adjust to American life.

Josephson, M. *The Robber Barons.* A critical and highly readable study of the captains of industry.

PART FIVE: SUMMING UP
Chapters 15–18

I. CHECKING THE FACTS

1. *What and When:* Putting Things in Order
Give the letter from the time line here during which you might have been able to do each of the things described below.

	A		B		C		D	
1860		1870		1880		1890		1900

    a. Celebrated the opening of the first transcontinental railroad.
    b. Joined the Populist Party as a volunteer worker.
    c. Taken the first federal Civil Service examination.
    d. Ridden as a cowhand on the last great drive.
    e. Had first choice of a 160-acre farm for just ten dollars.
    f. Been a graduate of the first class from a land grant college.
    g. Attended the Chicago Columbian Exposition.
    h. Made the first long-distance telephone call.

2. MAP WORK
Match the items below with their numbered locations on the map. Then tell what is being described.

    a. Where Populists met to express the needs of farmers.
    b. Site of an organization to promote cooperation in the western hemisphere.
    c. Canal system used to transport iron ore.
    d. Eastern terminus of the Southern Pacific Railroad.
    e. Home of Hanna, McKinley, and the Red Stockings.
    f. Rich source of iron ore.
    g. Where fishing and farming continued to be the main industries.
    h. A major southern industrial center.
    i. City dominated by Tweed and Tammany.
    j. Site of a violent clash between police and protesters.
    k. The center of Carnegie's steel industry.

468

II. INTERPRETING THE FACTS

1. In each group below there are five items. Select *three* items you think are related, and explain why. (The two left over are also related.) Any combination is correct as long as you can explain the relationship.
   a. business, strike, wages, lockout, labor
   b. rancher, Indian, farmer, buffalo, miner
   c. investment, profits, goods, resources, production
   d. legislation, political parties, social problems, protest, lobbyists
   e. cheap money, inflation, prosperity, deflation, depression
   f. freedom, individualism, education, equality, opportunity

2. Examine the American Development chart on pages 470–471. Then, in just one sentence for each, describe the apparent trend in these areas, 1850–1900.
   a. party control of the White House
   b. farm population
   c. factory workers
   d. the economy
   e. immigration
Now, compare these graphics with those on pages 296–297. Tell how the trends during the two periods were the *same* or *different*.

III. APPLYING YOUR KNOWLEDGE

1. At any one time in a nation's history, certain groups and individuals seem to hold great amounts of power. Orally or in writing, complete this chart based on what you have learned in this unit. Then, make a similar chart based on your knowledge of the United States today.

Power Holders	Basis for Power	Evidence of Power

2. In order to think accurately about what might have happened in the past but didn't, one needs to be thoroughly grounded in a subject. However, with limited knowledge, people do have "hunches." Express your "hunches" by completing these statements:
   a. If, as Henry George suggested, the only tax the American people paid was on land, _____.
   b. If the U.S. had gone to war with Great Britain over the Venezuela dispute, _____.
   c. If labor unions were declared illegal today, ___.
   d. If businesses were not allowed to make profits, _____.
   e. If there should be a limit to government control of private enterprise, it would be _____.
   f. If all of the money in the United States today were divided equally among all citizens, _____.

469

AMERICAN DEVELOPMENT 1850 — 1900

POLITICAL DEVELOPMENTS

(By 1860 the Whig Party had disappeared, many of its northern members joining the new Republican Party. See p. 341.)

Pierce

Buchanan

WHIG

Taylor Fillmore

DEMOCRATS

REPUBLICANS

Lincoln

Johnson

Grant

| 1849 | 1853 | 1857 | 1861 | 1865 | 1869 | 1873 |

TRANSPORTATION
TO TRAVEL 100 MILES (160 KILOMETERS) TOOK...

... 13 hours by horse and buggy

... 7 hours by bicycle

... 4 hours by steamship

... less than 2 hours by 20th century train

SOCIAL DEVELOPMENTS

Civil War
Education financed
   through Morrill Act
Industrialization
Increased immigration
   result of industrial growth
External expansion
Expansion of farming
   and growth of factories

ECONOMIC ACTIVITY

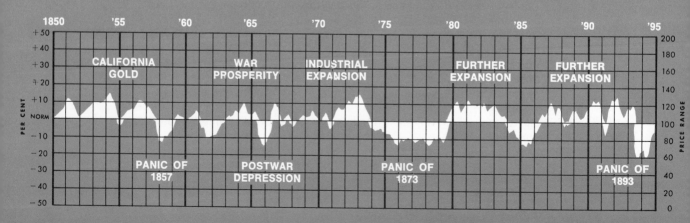

CALIFORNIA GOLD

WAR PROSPERITY

INDUSTRIAL EXPANSION

FURTHER EXPANSION

FURTHER EXPANSION

PANIC OF 1857

POSTWAR DEPRESSION

PANIC OF 1873

PANIC OF 1893

PER CENT

+50 +40 +30 +20 +10 NORM -10 -20 -30 -40 -50

PRICE RANGE

200 180 160 140 120 100 80 60 40 20 0

1850 '55 '60 '65 '70 '75 '80 '85 '90 '95

REPUBLICANS

Hayes

Garfield Arthur

DEMOCRAT

Cleveland

REPUBLICAN

Benjamin Harrison

DEMOCRAT

Cleveland

REPUBLICAN

McKinley

| 1877 | 1881 | 1885 | 1889 | 1893 | 1897 | 1901 |

Population and Immigration

(in millions)

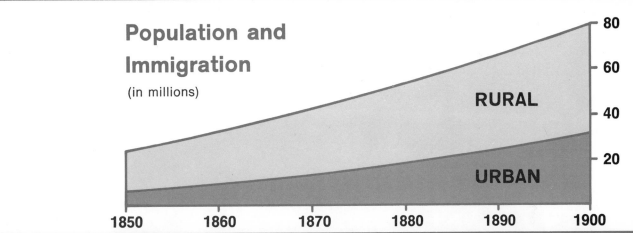

RURAL

URBAN

80
60
40
20

1850 1860 1870 1880 1890 1900

1850 1900

Circles represent all people employed

1850
56% ALL OTHERS
32%
12%

1900
59% ALL OTHERS
21%
20%

MANUFACTURING AGRICULTURE

Continuing Tide of Immigration

Each symbol = 500,000 immigrants

1851–60	2,598,214
1861–70	2,314,824
1871–80	2,812,191
1881–90	5,246,613
1891–1900	3,687,564

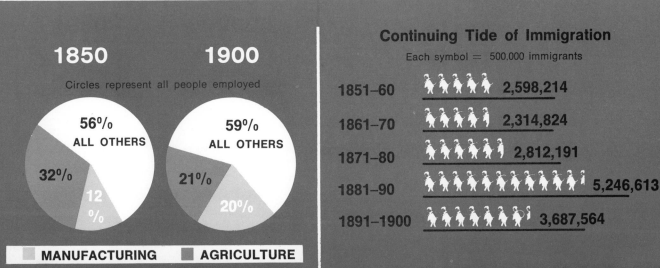

Part

6

New Horizons

Chapters in this Part

New York City's Lower East Side, about 1910

1898—MANIFEST DESTINY OR GREAT ABERRATION?

The year 1898 was a great watershed in United States history. With almost no one foreseeing what was going to happen, this country acquired an overseas empire. It started as "the War for Cuban Independence." It ended with the United States expanding into the Caribbean, extending its frontier six thousand miles across the Pacific to the Philippines, picking up Hawaii and Guam along the way. With its new possessions, the United States also acquired "commitments." Our foothold in Puerto Rico and Cuba brought a commitment to keep order in the entire Caribbean region. Possession of the Philippines gave us a new interest in the affairs of China. Eventually, we committed ourselves to defending equal trading rights in China—the Open Door—and the integrity of China itself. And this commitment ultimately led us to fight Japan in World War II.

Unquestionably, then, the Spanish-American War started a process that tremendously extended the interests and influence of the United States abroad. Was the process inevitable? Was it a new version of manifest destiny? At the time, some thought it the right and duty of the United States to expand overseas. Some historians since then have argued that a great industrial nation was bound to extend its political power to protect its growing trade and overseas investments.

There have also been those who argued that 1898 marked a great aberration —a deviation from proper American foreign policy. It was one thing to free Cuba, but it was a flat violation of the great principles of the Declaration of Independence to gain dominion over other people. And if the purpose of the Spanish-American War was to promote the economic interests of the United States, why in 1897 and 1898 were business people so opposed to our getting involved in hostilities that every war scare sent the market down? And what business did the United States have meddling in the politics of Asia, in the hope of future markets, with insufficient military power to back up its policies?

Examine the events of 1898 in detail. It may seem that the United States did not need to fight Spain in order to free Cuba and that once we were at war the annexation of the Philippines was no part of our declared purposes and was unnecessary to our military strategy. Suppose the war had not occurred and Cuba had achieved her freedom peacefully. Would that have kept United States political influence out of the Caribbean area? We doubt it. If Dewey's fleet had not been ordered to Manila Bay, would the United States have defended the Open Door and the integrity of China? Perhaps not.

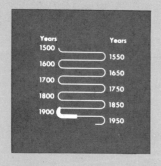

Years	Years
1500	1550
1600	1650
1700	1750
1800	1850
1900	1950

Chapter 19

Imperialism

The Philippines are ours forever: "territory belonging to the United States," as the Constitution calls them. And just beyond the Philippines are China's illimitable markets. We will not retreat from either. We will not repudiate our duty in the archipelago. We will not abandon our opportunity in the Orient. We will not renounce our part in the mission of our race, trustees under God of the civilization of the world.
—ALBERT J. BEVERIDGE

No man is good enough to govern another without that man's consent.
—ABRAHAM LINCOLN

The last quarter of the nineteenth century saw a great expansion of the power of the major European nations over "backward" areas. A principal force behind this imperialist movement was the industrial revolution. As factories increased, they produced more goods than were consumed at home and demanded raw materials obtainable only abroad. Imperialism offered new markets and new sources of raw materials. New weapons made easier the subjection of native peoples. Steamships and ocean cables tightened control over distant colonies; they also led to a race to acquire coaling stations and cable bases.

The economic elements behind nineteenth-century imperialism were combined with national patriotism and idealism. Young men were urged to "throw themselves against cannons' mouths for love of England." Many who supported imperialism held to the chauvinist notion that the white race was superior to others and therefore had a "civilizing mission." In a celebrated poem Rudyard Kipling urged the Anglo-Saxon countries to "Take up the White Man's burden."

Once launched in the 1870's, the imperialist movement resulted in a mad "scramble for empire." In the continent of Africa alone, Great Britain, France, Germany, Italy, and Belgium established claims totaling twice the area of the United States.

The United States was late in joining the race for empire. With an abundance of raw materials, an immense home market, and little surplus capital available for foreign investment, this country lacked the economic motives which operated in Europe. The tradition of isolation tended to keep America within its borders. Furthermore, the conquest of "subject" peoples seemed at variance with the fundamental idea of the Declaration of Independence—that people have the right to rule themselves. When the United States did acquire an overseas empire, most of its citizens, including the President, had no premonition of what was coming.

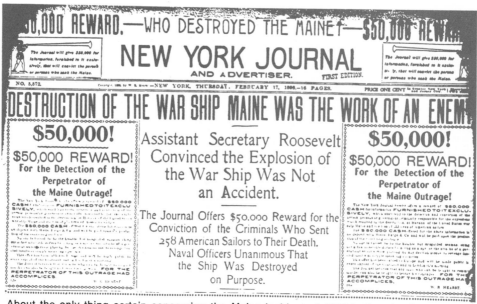

About the only thing certain concerning the *Maine* incident of 1898 is that the Spanish did not do it. But when news of the sinking reached New York, newspapers that rivaled each other in their imaginative recreations of Spanish atrocities laid the blame on Spain.

Although it may appear as though the American adventure into imperialism occurred almost by chance, voices had already been raised in favor of expansion overseas. Thus Alfred Mahan demanded not only the building of a great fleet, but the acquisition of coaling stations and strategic harbors in the Pacific and the Caribbean. A clergyman, Josiah Strong, in a book entitled *Our Country,* wrote that it was the mission of the United States to spread Christianity and civil liberty by establishing colonies. Strong, like other imperialists, borrowed the language of Darwinism to support his arguments: he maintained that the Anglo-Saxons were the "fittest to survive" in the great competition between races for the control of the globe. People of English stock, he wrote, were "destined to dispossess many weaker races, assimilate others, and mold the remainder," until they had "Anglo-Saxonized mankind." Such pseudo-Darwinian notions were preached by influential historians and political scientists. They were also held by a few important politicians, notably Senator Henry Cabot Lodge of Massachusetts and his close friend, Theodore Roosevelt, President McKinley's Assistant Secretary of the Navy. While the business community was in general opposed to foreign adventures, some American corporations were actively seeking foreign markets. If business people could be shown that by acquiring colonies the United States could expand its markets, they could be converted to imperialism. For many business people this conversion took place during the Spanish-American War.

THE SPANISH-AMERICAN WAR, 1898

The Spanish-American War had its origins in Cuba. This last important remnant of the great Spanish empire in America had long been in a chronic state of unrest. Violent rebellion broke

476

out in 1895 and developed into "one of those dreadful, tragic, hopeless situations that mark the decline or exhaustion of a colonial relationship." The insurgents were not strong enough to take the cities, but carried on bitter guerrilla warfare. They deliberately attempted to devastate the island so that the Spaniards would be glad to withdraw. Spanish attempts at suppression were inefficient and harsh. On both sides there were atrocities. President Cleveland's annual messages to Congress in 1895 and 1896 reveal the difficulties that the Cuban war caused the United States. The rebels were supplied with arms illegally sent from the United States, and it was the task of the executive department to stop this traffic.

Leaders of the Cuban independence movement were often naturalized American citizens who, when captured by Spanish authorities, demanded protection by the United States. American capitalists who had invested between 30 million and 50 million dollars in Cuba, mostly in sugar plantations, wanted the war to end. The plantation owners, doubting the capacity of the Cubans for self-government, often favored the restoration of Spanish rule, but American public opinion was overwhelmingly on the side of the right of the islanders to independence. Although Cleveland preserved strict neutrality in the Cuban struggle, he warned that if "the useless sacrifice of human life" went on, the United States might have to abandon the policy of "patient waiting."

"Remember the Maine!"

McKinley attempted to follow Cleveland's policies. He strictly enforced the neutrality laws and used his influence to prevent Congress from passing a joint resolution recognizing the belligerent rights of the Cuban rebels. The Spanish government, most unwisely, rejected McKinley's efforts to bring hostilities to an end. Meanwhile the yellow press, led by William Randolph

The Battle of Manila Bay, as idealized by an artist from descriptions received by telegraph from Manila. The ships were certainly not so close together, but otherwise it is a good picture of the fleet in action.

Hearst's New York *Journal* and Joseph Pulitzer's New York *World*, filled the front pages with exaggerated and sometimes fabricated stories of Spanish atrocities in Cuba. Finally an event occurred that led to war. On February 15, 1898, the United States battleship *Maine*, at anchor in the harbor of Havana, the capital of Cuba, was destroyed by a terrible explosion that killed 260 of her crew. To this day the cause of the disaster is unknown. It is highly improbable that the Spanish were responsible, since the last thing they wanted was American intervention. But the yellow press had no doubts. The New York *Journal* ran a headline "THE WARSHIP *MAINE* WAS SPLIT IN TWO BY AN ENEMY'S SECRET INFERNAL MACHINE," and published fake diagrams showing just how the deed was done. "Remember the *Maine!*" became the slogan of the day.

The McKinley administration and Hanna and the business interests were reluctant to go to war, and war rumors depressed the stock market. But a torrential wave of popular sympathy for the Cubans and indignation against Spain mounted until it seemed nearly certain that Congress would soon act on its own. Although at the last moment Spain offered to make almost all the concessions that McKinley asked, on April 11 the President sent a message to Congress requesting that he be empowered to use the armed forces of the United States to pacify Cuba. After a week of debate, Congress by overwhelming majorities demanded that Spain evacuate the island. When no reply to this ultimatum was received, the so-called "War for Cuban Independence" was declared on April 25. By the Teller Amendment, which was included in the ultimatum to Spain, Congress unanimously denied any designs on Cuba and promised as soon as peace was accomplished "to leave the government and control of the Island to the people."

QUESTION • *If the Teller Amendment had not been passed, would Cuba be Communist-ruled today?*

Hostilities in the Caribbean

Once hostilities started, McKinley called for 125,000 volunteers to supplement the regular army, which numbered only 28,000. In answering this call for national service, the South responded as enthusiastically as the North, and three of the four civilians appointed as major-generals were Confederate veterans. Thus the Spanish-American War revealed that "if the war cloud hovered . . . above the country, the former boys in gray would rally as proudly in defense of the Stars and Stripes as did the wearers of the blue."

In spite of incredible inefficiency, 17,000 volunteers and regulars were made ready to sail from Tampa, Florida, by the middle of June. For a campaign in the tropics they were issued heavy woolen uniforms, left over from the Indian wars; their cartridges were of an out-of-date type; and their rations included inedible meat which the soldiers nicknamed "embalmed beef."

After landing on the south coast of Cuba, the American force advanced on the city of Santiago. Even with poor equipment and confused leadership, the spirit of the American troops was much higher than that of the Spanish force barring their way. The fighting produced a popular hero in the person of Theodore Roosevelt, who had resigned from the Navy Department to serve in a volunteer regiment that he recruited himself. Against heavy fire Roosevelt personally led his "Rough Riders" in a frontal assault on San Juan Hill on the outskirts of Santiago.

Meanwhile, the American navy had not been idle. At the outbreak of hostilities, a squadron of the new White Fleet under Admiral William T. Sampson was given the task of intercepting a Spanish squadron under Admiral Pascual Cervera that was known to have left the Cape Verde Islands in April. There was such fear that Cervera would attack the undefended Atlantic Coast of the United States that eastern seaports demanded naval protection, and there was wholesale cancellation of hotel reservations at seaside resorts. Cervera's ships were finally discovered in Santiago harbor, which was immediately blockaded by Sampson's superior force. Once the American army took the heights overlooking Santiago, Cervera had the choice of surrendering or trying to break the blockade. To save the honor of Spain he took the latter course, and on July 3 his ships steamed out of Santiago harbor. In the ensuing battle all the Spanish vessels were sunk, while American losses were only one man killed and one wounded. Effective Spanish resistance in Cuba ceased with the surrender of Santiago two weeks later. American troops immediately went on to occupy another Spanish possession, the island of Puerto Rico.

"That splendid little war." Col. Theodore Roosevelt and members of the Rough Riders cavalry unit, which he organized, pose atop San Juan Hill after charging it (on foot)! For every American who died in battle in Cuba, thirteen more died of disease, most often yellow fever.

The Campaign in the Philippines

Meanwhile American forces won victories on the other side of the globe. When the war started, the McKinley administration had no notion of expanding the territories of the United States. But while he had served as Assistant Secretary of the Navy, Theodore Roosevelt had been one of a small group of influential men who favored war with Spain as a means whereby the United States might acquire an overseas empire. Whenever John D. Long, Secretary of the Navy, left Washington, Roosevelt took over. In February 1898, he ordered a Pacific squadron stationed in Hong Kong under the command of Commodore George Dewey to sail for the Philippine Islands in case war with Spain broke out. Dewey was expected to prevent a Spanish fleet in

Manila Bay from going to sea. As soon as war was declared, Dewey's fleet set sail; it penetrated Manila Bay on May 1 and soon destroyed an inferior Spanish fleet. During the battle, the cable from Manila to Hong Kong had been cut, so that at first the outside world received only a Spanish report that Dewey had been repulsed. When the truth reached the United States a week later, there was wild rejoicing. Troops were immediately dispatched to Manila, and the city was captured on August 13, a few hours after Spain had agreed on an armistice.

Representatives of the United States and Spain met to arrange peace at Paris on October 1, 1898. The only real dispute at the conference table concerned the Philippines, which Spain was unwilling to relinquish on the ground that the United States had won only the city of Manila, and that after an agreement to cease hostilities had been made.

To Annex or Not to Annex?

The decisive dispute about the future of the Philippines occurred, however, not at Paris, but in the United States. On entering the War for Cuban Independence, the American people had no idea of annexing territory, particularly a territory six thousand miles from the Pacific coast. McKinley confessed that before Dewey's victory he could not have come within two thousand miles of placing the Philippine Islands on a map. Once he said, "If old Dewey had just sailed away when he smashed that Spanish fleet, what a lot of trouble he would have saved us." Strong feeling developed against acquiring the islands. Bryan and Cleveland, the two leading Democrats, were opposed, as were many influential private citizens, among them Charles W. Eliot and Andrew Carnegie. Prominent Republicans, including Speaker of the House Thomas B. Reed and several senators, fought the annexation as a violation of American tradition.

Eventually sentiment for annexation outweighed opposition. Business interests were won over by the hope of new markets for American goods and new fields of investment. Public opinion at large was excited by the prospect of acquiring an empire over which the sun never set, or almost never. Patriotism was also involved: there was strong feeling against hauling down the Stars and Stripes, especially since some other power, such as Japan or Germany, was likely to step in and take the Philippines as soon as we left.

QUESTION • *If the United States had refused to annex the Philippines, would we have later fought Japan in World War II?*

Finally, McKinley decided that the United States must "take up the White Man's burden." As he later told a delegation of clergymen:

I walked the floor of the White House night after night until midnight. . . . And one night late it came to me this way— . . . (1) That we could not give them [the Philippines] back to Spain—that would be cowardly and dishonorable; (2) that we could not turn them over to . . . our commercial rivals in the Orient—that would be bad business and discreditable . . . ; (3) that we could not leave them to themselves—they were unfit for self-government—and . . . ; (4) that there was nothing left for us to do but to take them all, and to educate the Filipinos, and uplift and civilize and Christianize them. . . . And then I went to bed . . . and slept soundly.

New Responsibilities and Commitments

Once the McKinley administration decided to acquire the Philippines, it offered to pay for them. Therefore by the Treaty of Paris, signed in December 1898, the United States gave $20,000,000 for the islands. Spain evacuated Cuba and ceded Puerto Rico, which had been hastily occupied by American troops at the close of hostilities, and Guam, which was important as a way station to the Philippines. Anti-imperialist feeling in the Senate was so strong that the treaty was ratified by only a two-vote margin. A Senate resolution promising the Filipinos eventual independence was defeated only by the tie-breaking vote of the Vice-President.

The new sense of manifest destiny resulted in a change of policy regarding the Hawaiian Islands. As we have seen, Cleveland had opposed a move to annex them in 1893, and in 1897 the Senate rejected an annexation treaty presented by McKinley. But after Dewey won the battle of Manila Bay, the islands acquired a new importance as a stepping-stone to the Far East. They were annexed in July 1898 by a joint resolution of Congress. (See U.S. and Possessions in 1900, pp. 464–465).

The events of 1898 marked a turning point in American history. The United States was suddenly faced with the responsibility of ruling alien peoples who could not be "Americanized" by the usual process of living in the United States. It now held a commanding position in the Caribbean which soon led to a commitment to police the entire area. Possession of the Philippines in turn led to another commitment, the defense of China from external aggression.

PROBLEMS OF AN OVERSEAS EMPIRE

The new possessions acquired in 1898 posed difficult questions. How were they to be governed? Were their inhabitants American citizens? Did colonial goods enter the United States duty free? In addition to such over-all questions, each colony presented its own special problem.

The colony that had the least difficulty in attaching itself to the United States was Hawaii.

Liliuokalani, Last Monarch of Hawaii

It was a shame. They had already lived through twelve years of irresponsible monarchy, and the queen had seemed to be different—anxious to reform her playboy brother's kingdom, regal, devoted to duty. But she was about to promulgate a constitution that would put Hawaii back into the mid-nineteenth century. And what could the responsible members of society do but stop her?

Liliuokalani lived amid the faithfully reproduced splendors of the Victorian era. Her throne was red and gold; her throne room was crowded with portraits of earlier Hawaiian rulers, whose gorgeous royal feather standards lined the walls. Her home, Iolani Palace, was a remarkable structure, echoing earlier Hawaiian history. Between its windows on the outside walls were mirrors, reminders of the gifts brought by missionaries to earlier islanders, who were entranced with their own reflections in the "magic glass." Descendants of these missionaries had become prosperous business people who now saw their livelihood threatened by the strong-willed queen.

The situation was serious. Hawaii depended on its sugar industry, and the queen was unwilling to allow the planters to retain their voice in the government. Although a reciprocity treaty with the United States had brought them prosperity, the recent McKinley Tariff had made it impossible to compete with Cuban sugar in United States markets. Annexation to the United States would save the sugar industry. But the queen was interested only in restoring the authority of the monarchy.

In 1893 a Committee of Safety, secretly committed to annexation, drove Liliuokalani off the throne. President Cleveland tried to re-establish the monarchy, but the Provisional Government refused to disband, and in 1894 a republic was formed. The queen, accused of complicity in a counterrevolution in 1895, was arrested and confined to her palace. Pardoned later, she went to the mainland, where she lived on an annual pension of four thousand dollars and the income from one of her sugar plantations. Hawaii was finally annexed in 1898; in 1959 it became the fiftieth state admitted to the United States.

Between 1893 and 1898 Hawaii had been an independent republic dominated by Americans. Although the inhabitants came from many countries, especially Japan and China, English was becoming the common language. In 1900 Hawaii was made a territory, and the former president of the republic, Sanford B. Dole, was appointed its first governor. The opening of the American market to Hawaiian products such as sugar and pineapples brought great prosperity to the islands. By 1928 trade with the United States had reached the amazing total of $584 for each inhabitant of the islands.

The change of sovereignty caused more difficulties in Puerto Rico than in Hawaii. The transition from producing for the Spanish market to producing for that of the United States was difficult, and the cultural ties of Puerto Ricans were with Spain and Latin America, not with the English-speaking United States. After a brief period of military rule, Puerto Rico was given an increasing degree of self-government until by 1917 it was granted territorial status and its people were made citizens of the United States. Improved public sanitation cut the death rate in half, and public schools raised the literacy rate. The rapid increase in population, however, tended to outrun the available food supply, and Puerto Rico was far less prosperous than Hawaii. The inhabitants demanded either independence or complete self-rule under the American flag.

The Philippine Insurrection, 1899–1902

The Philippines provided the most difficult problem in colonial administration. The 7,100 islands supported a population of 7,500,000 people, divided into 43 ethnic groups, speaking 87 different languages and dialects. Culturally the Filipinos ranged from primitive peoples in the jungles to highly literate inhabitants in the cities. When Dewey reached Manila Bay, an uprising against Spain had just begun, and Filipino patriots, besieging Manila assisted the American forces. Once it became apparent, however, that the United States intended to annex the Philippines, a new uprising broke out, led by the able guerrilla chieftain Emilio Aguinaldo. It required over 60,000 troops—four times the number sent to Cuba—and three years of fighting to suppress the Filipino patriots.

Many Americans were distressed to find their country in the same position as Spain in 1895 and England in 1776—at war with a native independence movement. Former Speaker Thomas B. Reed abandoned politics in protest against imperialism and taunted a pro-expansionist by asking how much it had cost to buy Filipinos "in the bush." The poet William Vaughn Moody wrote bitter verses about expending the blood of American boys to subdue a people struggling to be free.

In 1901, even before the insurrection was suppressed, President McKinley announced that American policy toward the islands would be directed toward the good of the Filipinos. "The Philippines are ours," said the President, "not to exploit but to develop, to civilize, to educate, to train in the science of self-government." In pursuit of this ideal the President sent two commissions, composed of able and well-meaning men, to investigate the condition of the Philippines and set up a civil government.

William Howard Taft, later President of the United States, headed the second commission. Genuinely devoted to the interests of the people of the Philippine Islands, Taft started a program to prepare the Filipinos for self-government and protect them from foreign exploitation. American teachers were brought in to establish public schools. The United States bought out large foreign landowners, and introduced laws designed to keep property in the hands of the natives. Qualified Filipinos were soon brought into the governments; in 1907 an elective legislature was established; and in 1916 the United States promised the Philippines eventual independence.

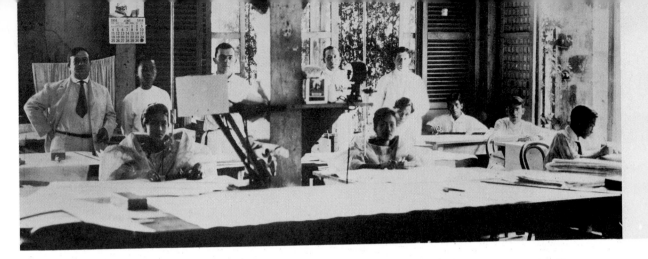

Public schools were established by American teachers in the Philippines as part of a program of educating the Filipinos in the art of self-government. Spanish-speaking children are shown being taught English.

Did the Constitution Follow the Flag?

The new overseas possessions posed constitutional problems that were summarized in the question, "Does the Constitution follow the flag?" Congress, according to the Constitution, may not levy duties on goods carried from one part of the United States to another. Did this mean that no tariff duties might be laid on goods from American colonies? The Constitution guarantees to all American citizens certain civil rights. Did this guarantee extend to the inhabitants of the new colonies who had no conception of the principles or practices of Anglo-Saxon justice? Did the head-hunting Igorots of the Philippine rain-forest, for instance, have the right to trial by a jury of their peers?

Such questions were appealed to the Supreme Court, which in the "insular cases" decided that the Constitution did not completely apply to overseas possessions. In a confused 5 to 4 decision (*Downes v. Bidwell*, 1901), the court ruled that Puerto Rico was not strictly speaking part of the United States, but was a dependency; therefore Congress might levy tariffs on Puerto Rican products. Other decisions held that inhabitants of dependencies enjoyed full civil rights only if granted them by congressional legislation. Since 1903, however, Congress has granted independence to the Philippines, as well as free trade and an increas-

ing measure of civil rights to other dependencies. Today, therefore, the problem of whether or not the Constitution follows the flag is no longer an important issue.

Cuba and the Platt Amendment

By the Teller Amendment, passed on the eve of the Spanish-American War, the United States pledged itself to withdraw from Cuba as soon as order was restored. After three years of civil war, however, the island was in terrible condition. For the sake of the Cuban people themselves, the United States felt duty-bound to remain and help in reconstruction. For nearly four years Cuba was under military rule directed by General Leonard Wood. The most dramatic achievement of Wood's able and energetic administration was the suppression of yellow fever. An American medical mission under Dr. Walter Reed proved the accuracy of the theory held by a Cuban physician, Carlos J. Finlay: that yellow fever was transmitted by the stegomyia mosquito. In the course of the investigation, American doctors and volunteers deliberately allowed themselves to be bitten by mosquitoes, and some of them died as martyrs to medical progress. A successful campaign to eliminate mosquitoes from Havana was carried on under the direction of Major William C. Gorgas, an army medical officer. By 1901, for the first time in centuries, there was no yellow fever in the Cuban capital.

Meanwhile the Cubans made progress toward self-government. They held municipal elections in 1900, and in 1901 adopted a constitution modeled on that of the United States. In 1902 American military authority came to an end. Cuban independence was not complete, but was limited by the so-called Platt Amendment which Congress tacked on to an army appropriation bill in 1901. The Platt Amendment governed the relations between Cuba and the United States for thirty-three years. Its most important provisions were: (1) Cuba should not make any treaty with a foreign nation which weakened its independence; (2) it should allow the United States the right to buy or lease naval stations; (3) its public debt should not exceed its capacity to pay; and (4) the United States should have the right to intervene to protect Cuban independence and keep order. These provisions, written into the Cuban constitution and into a treaty with the United States, made Cuba an American protectorate. In 1903 the United States granted Cuba special tariff favors, especially a 20 per cent reduction of the duty on sugar imported by the United States. This so encouraged sugar production that by 1920 Americans had invested over a billion dollars in the island.

NEW COMMITMENTS IN CHINA

Although American missionary enterprise in China had continued, Chinese-American commerce had slackened since the great days of the tea clippers; in 1898 only 2 per cent of China's trade was with the United States. The acquisition of the Philippines revived interest in business opportunities in China. Manila, it was predicted, would become as important a center for commerce with China as the great British port of Hong Kong.

At the close of the nineteenth century, it looked as though the "Celestial Empire" was to go the way of Africa and be partitioned among stronger powers. The hopeless inefficiency of the imperial government was revealed

The emergence of Japan as an imperial power is satirized by this cartoon in Puck. Little did the world know then that in less than forty years Japan would become the greatest power in the Far East. Note the cartoonist's characterization of the various other powers.

The striking way in which the Spanish-American War seemed to commit the United States to action in the Far East is suggested by the detachment of U.S. cavalry to help rescue Europeans in Peking during the Boxer Rebellion. The troops are at the Great Wall. The U.S. tried to prevent China's division among foreign powers.

in 1895 when the recently Westernized Japanese easily defeated the Chinese, annexing Formosa and the Pescadores Islands (see map, p. 704). In 1898 and 1899, Russia, Germany, France, and Great Britain "leased" Chinese ports, some of them for ninety-nine years. It was expected that each "leasehold" would become the center of a "sphere of influence" so that through holding Port Arthur, Russia would dominate Manchuria; through Kiaochow, Germany would control the Shantung Peninsula, and so forth.

Two powers were opposed to parceling out Chinese territory—the United States and Great Britain. The United States feared that it would be unable to cash in on the possession of Manila by enlarging its share of China trade. Great Britain, controlling 80 per cent of the trade,

feared that some of her profits would be diverted to other countries. Early in 1898 the British government sounded out the United States on a joint declaration in favor of the "Open Door"—the preservation of equal trading opportunities in China for all foreign nations. At that time the United States was cool to the idea, but the annexation of the Philippines changed the American attitude.

John Hay's "Open Door" Notes, 1899

John Hay, Secretary of State, was one of the first well-qualified men to hold the position since Hamilton Fish had served under Grant. Hay, who had begun his political career as one of Lincoln's private secretaries, was aware of the importance of foreign policy, and thought that the days of isolationism must end. He favored a policy of cooperation with Great Britain, and defended the acquisition of an overseas empire. It was therefore natural that he should become interested in defending the Open Door. In September 1899, he sent notes to the major countries having leaseholds in China asking that they keep the ports open to the vessels of all nations on equal terms, levy equal tariffs on imports, and charge equal railroad rates within their spheres of influence. Since none of the nations involved wished to state publicly that it intended to discriminate against the trade of other countries, none chose to dispute these points. Hay immediately announced that the Open Door had been "guaranteed." He was credited in the United States with having achieved a great diplomatic victory.

Hay's achievement was less important than it seemed at the time. His request was "like asking all persons in a room who were not thieves to stand up." The polite but evasive replies to Hay's notes hardly amounted to a guarantee. Furthermore, the notes did not protect China from being carved into spheres of influence where foreign powers had exclusive rights to build railroads and exploit natural resources. Hay's skillful and well-publicized actions were principally designed to popularize the expansionist policies of the McKinley administration; in this they were successful.

The Boxer Rebellion and Second Open Door Notes, 1900

In 1900 a group of Chinese patriots, calling themselves "Fists of Universal Harmony," were so bitterly resentful of foreign interference that they started an uprising with the intention of wiping out the "foreign devils" and their Christian converts. The Chinese government lent secret aid to what came to be called the Boxer movement. The Boxers killed over two hundred foreigners, mostly missionaries and their families, and attempted to slaughter the foreign diplomats in Peking. For seven weeks nine hundred foreigners, cut off from the outside world, held out in the Chinese capital. They were rescued by a joint military expedition to which the United States contributed 2,500 troops.

During this crisis, Hay labored successfully to prevent full-scale war against China and to persuade the powers not to use the Boxer Rebellion as an excuse to partition the unhappy country. In July 1900, he again sent identical notes to countries with important interests in China. In these second Open Door notes, Hay went far beyond the first in that he not only urged equal commercial opportunity, but declared it to be the policy of the United

QUESTION • *Were the actions of the Boxers defensible?*

States to seek a solution that would "preserve Chinese territorial and administrative entity." Hay did not ask the other powers to commit themselves, and he gave no guarantee that the United States would back up the policy with force. But later the idea developed that the United States was committed both morally and militarily to defending Chinese integrity, and this ultimately led to war with Japan forty-odd years later.

Hay also used his influence toward scaling down the large indemnity that the Chinese government was forced to pay as punishment for encouraging the Boxers. The American share of the $333,000,000 that China paid foreign countries was 25 million dollars, an amount that proved more than enough to satisfy all Americans who claimed to have suffered in the rebellion. In 1907, the United States as a gesture of good will toward China returned $11,000,000, and in 1924, $6,000,000 more. The Chinese government used the money to educate Chinese youths at American universities.

Roosevelt, rushing back from a camping trip, arrived at McKinley's bedside too late to see him alive. The Vice-President's assumption of power was not greeted happily by all members of his own party. Mark Hanna, who had opposed his nomination on the 1900 ticket, feared what the "damned cowboy in the White House" would do. Not yet 43 years old, Roosevelt was the youngest man ever to serve as President. Above, he passes through police lines to reach the house where McKinley's body lay in state.

IMPERIALISM AS A POLITICAL ISSUE

For a few years after the Spanish-American War, imperialism was one of the major issues of national politics. In October 1899, an anti-imperialist congress met at Chicago, attended by delegates from all over the country. The anti-imperialists drew up a platform denouncing the attempt to subdue the Philippines as "open disloyalty to the distinctive principles of our government." They quoted what Abraham Lincoln said about slavery: "No man is good enough to govern another man without that man's consent. When the white man governs himself, that is self-government, but when he governs himself and also governs another man, that is more than self-government—that is despotism."

The Election of 1900

So widespread was opposition to imperialism that in 1900 Bryan, again the Democratic candidate, attempted to make it "the paramount issue" of the presidential campaign. He weakened his case, however, by continuing to demand free silver, which had become a dead issue. The Republicans renominated McKinley for President and for Vice-President proposed Theodore Roosevelt, who, since leading the Rough Riders, had become governor of New York. As far as possible, the Republicans avoided discussion of imperialism, a question on which they themselves were divided. Adopting for their slogan "the full dinner pail," they claimed credit for the prosperity the country had enjoyed during McKinley's administration, and predicted a depression if Bryan were elected. The result of the election was a more decisive Republican victory than that of 1896.

McKinley's Last Speech

In September 1901, six months after his second inauguration, McKinley attended an exposition in Buffalo and made a speech which revealed an intense awareness of America's new position in the world. Heretofore, the President had been considered the "high priest of protective tariffs," but at Buffalo he announced a change of heart, saying:

Isolation is no longer possible or desirable. God and man have linked the nations together. No nation can longer be indifferent to any other. . . .

Our capacity to produce has developed so enormously, and our products have so multiplied, that the problem of more markets requires our urgent and immediate attention. . . .

We must not repose in fancied security that we can forever sell everything and buy little or nothing. If such a thing were possible, it would not be best for us or for those with whom we deal. We must take from our customers such of their products as we can use without harm to our industry and labor.

To meet the new situation the President proposed reciprocity treaties with foreign nations, providing for mutual lowering of tariffs.

McKinley did not live to put his new policy into effect. The day after delivering his speech on reciprocity he was shot by an anarchist, and died a week later. In the newspaper headlines the news of the President's death had to compete with the Vice-President's efforts to reach his bedside. When it was known that the President was dying, Roosevelt was summoned to Buffalo. He was on a camping trip deep in the Adirondack wilderness, and a guide had to be sent out to find him. In order to reach a railroad, Roosevelt drove thirty miles at night by wagon over rough and dangerous roads. When he reached the station, he learned that McKinley was already dead. Just short of forty-three years old, he was the youngest President who had ever entered the White House.

Activities: Chapter 19

For Mastery and Review

1. Explain the forces behind imperialism in the latter part of the nineteenth century.

2. What circumstances led to the Spanish-American War? What were the terms of settlement?

3. In parallel columns, list the arguments for and against annexation of the Philippines, Puerto Rico, and Hawaii. What problems were encountered in each place?

4. What was the reaction to imperialism as expressed in American politics? What was McKinley's view on America's new position in the world?

5. Why did the United States hold Cuba under military rule? What was accomplished? What were the terms of the Platt Amendment?

6. What is a sphere of influence? Why was the Open Door policy established? How was it developed? What was the Boxer Rebellion? What was the role of the United States in it?

Unrolling the Map

1. On an outline map of the world, show places connected with (1) *the Spanish-American War*, including Cuba, Santiago, Puerto Rico, the Philippines, Manila Bay, Guam; (2) *the Open Door Policy:* Peking, Port Arthur, Kiaochow, Formosa, Shantung Peninsula, Hong Kong, Korea, Manchuria. (See maps, pp. 465, 550.)

2. Study the map on pp. 464 and 465. To what extent had the United States become a world power on whose empire the sun never set?

Who, What, and Why Important?

Cuba	Emilio Aguinaldo
the *Maine*	William Howard Taft
yellow press	"insular cases"
Teller Amendment	Platt Amendment
Rough Riders	Leonard Wood
Battle of Santiago Bay	Carlos J. Finlay
Commodore Dewey	Walter Reed
Battle of Manila Bay	sphere of influence
"White Man's Burden"	John Hay
Treaty of Paris, 1898	Open Door
Hawaii	Boxer Rebellion
Puerto Rico	election of 1900

To Pursue the Matter

1. Prepare an outline map of the world to show (a) European colonial possessions acquired by 1815; (b) those acquired between 1815 and 1914; and (c) American colonial holdings in 1914. How many of these are still colonies?

2. Irreverent accounts of the Spanish-American War and of Roosevelt's part in it are found in Millis, *The Martial Spirit*, and Pringle, *Theodore Roosevelt*.

3. Can you reconcile the Teller Amendment with the Platt Amendment?

4. See if "Mr. Dooley's" type of humor appeals to you. Try his account of "Tiddy Rosenfelt's" adventures in Cuba in Arnof, *A Sense of the Past*, pp. 344–345. If you want to go on, there are two paperback anthologies of Dooley in print: Filler, *The World of Mr. Dooley*, and Hutchinson, *Mr. Dooley on Ivrything and Ivrybody*.

5. The medical research on yellow fever makes a dramatic story. Study it in De Kruif, *Men Against Death*.

6. Re-study the Northwest Ordinance (see pp. 86–88) to see how America provided for governing land and people beyond the original thirteen states. Its text is found in Bragdon *et al.*, *Frame of Government*, pp. 65–87. Why was the precedent set up in 1787 not applied overseas?

7. Using historical examples, clarify the distinctions between (a) colony, (b) protectorate, (c) sphere of influence, (d) mandate, and (e) trusteeship.

8. Come-to-life color can be found in "Prisoners in Peking," in Arnof, *A Sense of the Past*, pp. 352–354; for a change of pace, try the excerpt just before: "The Jovial Mr. Taft," pp. 349–351.

9. For an interesting exposition of the tide of imperialism that flowed from the war with Spain, see May, *From Imperialism to Isolationism, 1898–1919*, pp. 1–32.

Chapter 20

Theodore Roosevelt and Foreign Affairs

No nation can claim rights without acknowledging the duties that go with the rights.
—THEODORE ROOSEVELT

It was thoroughly characteristic of Theodore Roosevelt to try to reach McKinley's bedside by a dangerous ride through a wilderness. No other President has had such a genius for the dramatic gesture. He preached what he called "the strenuous life." He told young men, "Don't flinch, don't foul, hit the line hard!" He practiced what he preached.

Theodore Roosevelt's interests seemed universal, his energy inexhaustible. Even as President he found time to read prodigiously in many different fields; to play tennis, box, hunt grizzlies, ride horseback, and go on rugged hikes through the woods; to engage in public discussion of such diverse matters as "race suicide" (the declining birth rate), "nature fakers" (writers who told improbable tales about wild animals), simplified spelling (he was a poor speller himself), and changes in the football rules. He continued to be a devoted father to his six children, quite willing to hold up a state dinner for a pillow fight with his sons.

Roosevelt had the magnetism of the true leader. One of his Rough Riders said of him, "If he and I were crossing Brooklyn Bridge and he ordered me to jump over, I'd do it without asking why." An author who had been to lunch at the White House wrote of his experience: "You go into Roosevelt's presence, you feel his eyes upon you, you listen to him, and you go home and wring the personality out of your clothes." He was the darling of reporters because everything he did was news, and of cartoonists because his big teeth, eyeglasses, moustache, and Rough Rider uniform made him easy to caricature.

Roosevelt's public nickname, "Teddy," suggested a certain childlike quality, and it was true that he had a childish desire not to miss anything, a childish enjoyment of showing off, and sometimes a childish insistence on having his own way. "You must always remember," wrote a friend, "that the President is about six."

ROOSEVELT: THE MAN AND HIS CAREER

The picturesque and sometimes ridiculous aspects of Roosevelt's character tend to obscure his genuine abilities and solid achievement. Although sickly and timid as a small boy, he courageously overcame his handicaps, at first through hunting trips in the Maine woods, later by boxing, playing polo, and riding the cattle ranges in North Dakota. He started to collect birds and animals as a child, and became a serious naturalist who contributed to scientific journals. His vigorous outdoor life did not prevent him from writing several books and scores of magazine articles on a variety of subjects. Inspired by Francis Parkman (see p. 35), he produced a six-volume work, *The Winning of the West,* which glorified "the hard, energetic, practical men who do the pioneer work of civilization." His eagerness for experience brought him into contact with all kinds of people. Although born to a wealthy and socially prominent New York family, he learned to appreciate and make friends with persons in every walk of life.

Less than a year after he graduated from college, Roosevelt announced that he intended to join the local Republican club and run for office. His friends were shocked and warned that he would have to rub shoulders with his social inferiors, with "saloon-keepers, horse-car conductors, and the like." Roosevelt replied that the people he knew did not belong to the governing class, and the others did; he intended to be one of the governing class. In 1881 he was elected to the New York legislature, and was twice re-elected. In ensuing years he was Republican candidate for mayor of New York City, a member of the United States Civil Service Commission under Harrison and Cleveland, and a New York City police commissioner. McKinley appointed him Assistant Secretary of the Navy. He resigned from this position to help organize the Rough Riders. His popularity as a military hero made him governor of New York in 1898.

Throughout his political career, Roosevelt steered a course somewhat between being a "Muldoon" (straight party man) on the one hand, and a "Mugwump" (an independent) on the other. In the New York legislature he opposed machine politicians and cooperated with

governor Grover Cleveland to promote civil service reform, even though Cleveland was a Democrat. In the 1884 presidential campaign, however, he refused to desert the Republican party, even though he thoroughly disapproved of its candidate, James G. Blaine. "A man cannot act without and within the party," Roosevelt said at the time. "He can do either, but he cannot possibly do both. . . . It is impossible to combine the functions of a guerrilla chief with those of a colonel in the regular army; one has greater independence of action, the other is able to make what action he does vastly more effective." This remark also illustrates Roosevelt's attitude toward reform. He wanted clean government that should be responsive to the people's needs, but distrusted what he called the "lunatic fringe" of reformers who were impatient to make over society at once. He could do good, he felt, only by not attempting the impossible.

QUESTION • Who decides what is "impossible"? or "possible"?

Use of Presidential Power

Such was the force of Roosevelt's personality that, although faced with no great crisis, he much increased the scope and power of the office of President. Acting on what he called the Jackson-Lincoln theory of the presidency, he claimed the right to do practically anything he thought would benefit the people. "I did not usurp power," he said in his autobiography, "but I did greatly broaden the use of executive power. I . . . caused to be done many things not previously done by the President and head of the departments. In other words, I acted for the public welfare . . . whenever and in whatever manner was necessary, unless prevented by direct constitutional or legislative prohibition. . . ."

There was hardly any method of exerting power that Roosevelt did not attempt. Con-

The Library of Congress

"Far better it is to dare mighty things, to win glorious triumphs, even though checkered by failure, than to take rank with those poor spirits who neither enjoy much nor suffer much, because they live in the gray twilight that knows not victory nor defeat." —Theodore Roosevelt, 1910.

stantly urging reform legislation, he "built prairie fires" behind reluctant congressmen by rallying public support for his measures. His speeches, letters, and off-the-cuff remarks to newspapermen made headlines, partly because he was a talented phrase-maker who talked of "race suicide," "the big stick," and "malefactors of great wealth." He made any cause in which he was engaged as dramatic as storming San Juan Hill. "Roosevelt," ruefully admitted one of his critics, "has the knack of doing things, and doing them noisily, clamorously; while he is in the neighborhood the public can no more look the other way than the small boy can turn his head away from a circus parade followed by a steam calliope."

When Roosevelt could not get Congress to act, he often went ahead on his own. When he wanted to send a fleet around the world and Congress would not vote funds, he pointed out that as commander in chief he had the power to order the fleet anywhere on the globe. If Congress wanted to get it back home, it would have to appropriate the money. When the Senate refused to ratify a treaty with the Dominican Republic, Roosevelt simply continued the arrangement as an "executive agreement." Although unable to persuade Congress to pass legislation to put trusts under new controls, Roosevelt made a name for himself as "Teddy the Trust Buster" by reviving and enforcing the Sherman Act.

Prestige and Politics

When existing powers of the presidency were inadequate, Roosevelt often achieved his ends by using the great prestige of the office. He forced a settlement of the great coal strike of 1902 by persuading miners and owners to arbitrate their differences. He had no legal right to intervene in the strike, but neither owners nor workers could ultimately refuse to heed the President's plea that the public welfare demanded a settlement. To promote cooperation between the federal government and the states in the field of conservation, Roosevelt called a Conference of Governors at the White House in 1908. The governors were under no compulsion to come, but few persons turn down a presidential invitation, so the governors of all the states either came themselves or sent representatives.

Roosevelt owed much of his power to his mastery of practical politics. In the opinion of Grover Cleveland, he was "the most perfectly equipped and the most effective politician thus far seen in the presidency." He did not make Cleveland's mistake of breaking with his party followers. Although sometimes he pushed legislation through Congress by enlisting public opinion, at other times he achieved his ends by personal conferences or logrolling. While he promoted civil service reform, he also consulted party leaders about many appointments and used patronage to promote both his own political fortunes and measures he favored.

Finally, Roosevelt could rightly ascribe his effectiveness and his immense popularity to the fact that he was doing his best to promote "the common welfare of all our people." His great activity sometimes produced small results, and he sometimes seemed to be charging up the wrong hill, but Teddy won the people's love because they felt he was fighting on their side.

Roosevelt and Foreign Affairs

Although not a trained diplomat, Roosevelt had more knowledge of the outside world than any President since John Quincy Adams. He had crossed the Atlantic several times, spoke French and German, and was informed about foreign countries and their politics. He had numerous acquaintances and friends abroad. Above all, Roosevelt had what he called "large ideas" about the position of the United States in the world. He was resolved that the United

The Battle of Santiago de Cuba saw the end of Spanish naval power in the Americas. The American fleet, bottled up Cervera's fleet in Santiago harbor, defeating the Spaniards as they attempted to leave.

States should be treated like a great power and act like one. His actions were sometimes impulsive, sometimes unwise, but he firmly believed that power imposed responsibility. In the Western Hemisphere, he enlarged the scope of the Monroe Doctrine and secured United States domination of the Caribbean. In the Pacific and Far East, he attempted to keep a balance of power and restrain first Russian, then Japanese, ambitions. He was the first President to interest himself in the peace of Europe.

THE "BIG STICK" IN THE CARIBBEAN

One of Roosevelt's mottoes in foreign policy was, "Speak softly and carry a big stick." The Big Stick was most in evidence in the Caribbean. The acquisition of Puerto Rico and the establishment of a protectorate over Cuba gave the United States new interest in this region. The Spanish-American War revealed the need for a canal through Panama or Nicaragua to connect the Atlantic and Pacific oceans. As Alfred Mahan had foreseen, the building of an isthmian canal would change the Caribbean from a "comparatively deserted nook of the ocean" to one of great strategic importance.

Second Venezuelan Affair, 1902

Roosevelt, like Cleveland, defended Venezuela from possible European aggression and strengthened the Monroe Doctrine in doing so. (See p. 463.) In 1901 Venezuela owed money to citizens of several European countries, and Cipriano Castro, the dictator-president, refused either to pay the debts or submit them to arbitration. Roosevelt had little sympathy for Castro. In his annual message of 1901, the President said the Monroe Doctrine did not protect American nations against punishment for misbehavior, but only against loss of territory. Acting on this, Great Britain and Germany, the two principal creditors, blockaded Vene-

zuelan ports in an effort to force payment. This action had been taken after consultation with the State Department, and there was no threat of annexing territory. Nevertheless, the blockade became intensely unpopular in the United States, because the Monroe Doctrine seemed in danger of violation. Feeling was intensified when Venezuelan gunboats were sunk and Venezuelan ports bombarded. The public reaction prompted Roosevelt to urge an end of the blockade and the submission of the dispute to arbitration. Great Britain was quicker to heed the President's warning than Germany. Roosevelt's personal letters reveal that he distrusted the rising German empire, which had the best army in the world and was building a modern navy. The saber rattling utterances of Kaiser (Emperor) William II made German policy appear more bellicose than it was in fact, and Roosevelt had written his friend Senator Lodge that the Germans might take some step in the West Indies or South America "which will make us either put up or shut up on the Monroe Doctrine."

Several years later, Roosevelt told a picturesque story of how he had delivered an ultimatum to the German government in regard to Venezuela: either the emperor accepted arbitration at once or an American fleet under Admiral Dewey would attack the German blockading force. Later research fails to support this dramatic account, which has been called "a product of the Rough Rider's imagination rather than his memory," but apparently Roosevelt did deliver some kind of informal warning. In any case, both the British and the Germans withdrew their fleets. An English newspaper remarked, "the Monroe Doctrine emerges with an immensely increased authority."

The Roosevelt Corollary, 1904

In 1903, Luis Drago, Argentine foreign minister, urged that the use of force in collect-

THE COUP d'ETAT.

Among Roosevelt's severest critics was the New York *World,* whose continuing criticism of the Big-Stick policy (left) drove him to prosecute the newspaper for criminal libel—the first time a President had tried this since 1798. (The Supreme Court ruled unanimously in favor of the newspaper.) Below, "A Quiet Day" in the life of Teddy as seen by John T. McCutcheon in the *Chicago Tribune* criticizes Roosevelt's love of game hunting.

ing debts from bankrupt countries be declared contrary to international law. This so-called Drago Doctrine posed a problem for the United States. If the United States opposed Drago and allowed foreign nations to blockade the coasts and bombard the cities of defaulting Latin-American nations, the door was left ajar to further aggression. If the United States followed Drago and forbade forcible collection of debts, it might be pushed into defending financial dishonesty. The United States' reply to the Drago Doctrine was the Roosevelt Corollary to the Monroe Doctrine. Whenever, said the President in 1904, an American republic was guilty of "chronic wrongdoing," the United States might have to assume an "international police power." To put the Corollary in another way: if the United States forbade European nations the right to collect debts by force, it might have to intervene itself.

The Roosevelt Corollary was first applied in the Dominican Republic. The country was in debt to both European and American creditors, but governmental inefficiency and corruption prevented payment. In 1905, the United States took over the collection of Dominican customs, paying 45 per cent of the proceeds to the

Dominican government and 55 per cent to foreign bondholders. In answer to the charge of imperialism, Roosevelt formally renounced aggressive designs on the island republic. The United States had no more desire for Dominican territory, he remarked, than "a gorged boa constrictor might have to swallow a porcupine wrong-end-to."

According to the Platt Amendment (pp. 483–484), the United States already had the right to intervene in Cuba in order to protect that country from foreign aggression or to preserve life, liberty, and property. In 1906 bitter party rivalry in Cuba threatened to erupt into civil war. In contrast to his attitude in 1898, Roosevelt had little wish to get involved, but was persuaded to intervene by the threat of anarchy. He established a provisional government under William Howard Taft, with American troops to back him, but urged that interference with Cuban rights of self-government be as gentle as possible. After re-establishing order, the United States withdrew early in 1909.

The Panama Canal Zone, 1903

Roosevelt's most dramatic and debated action in the Caribbean was his acquisition of the Panama Canal Zone in 1903. The United

Gorgas Defeats the Mosquito

Even though they hired Ferdinand de Lesseps, the great engineer of Suez, the French failed to dig a canal across the Isthmus of Panama. Yellow fever and malaria made it impossible.

The Americans had learned a lesson. One of the first major assignments went to William C. Gorgas, who was named chief sanitary officer in 1904. He had taken part in the successful Havana battle against yellow fever waged by Carlos Finlay and Walter Reed (see p. 483). Gorgas fought inertia, bureaucratic inefficiency, and confused control among his superiors for three years. Not until 1907 did he get the full support he needed, when George W. Goethals became chief engineer of the entire Panama Canal project.

With Goethals' help, Dr. Gorgas provided a complete health program for a great community of workers, nearly all of whom had to acclimate themselves to the foods, habits, and insect threats of the tropics. Immune himself to yellow fever because he had once had it in Texas, Gorgas threw himself into a fight against three diseases: the plague, yellow fever, and malaria.

With quarantine, fumigation, and extermination of rats and fleas, he defeated the plague. He attacked yellow fever and malaria with a war on mosquitoes. All buildings, houses, and tents were screened. Stricken patients were segregated. Cities, villages, and farms were cleaned up; streets were paved, sewage systems installed, and drinking-water cisterns covered. All standing water, whether in swamps or gutters, was sprayed with an oil containing carbolic acid, resin, and alkali.

The statistics tell of Gorgas' victory. In 1906, 82.1 per cent of all employees in the Canal Zone were hospitalized for malaria at some time during the year. By 1913, the percentage had dropped to 7.6. The lesson taught by Finlay and Reed had been well-learned.

States and Great Britain had become interested in an isthmian canal in the mid-nineteenth century, as shown by the Clayton-Bulwer Treaty (see pp. 334–335). No move was made to dig a canal, however, until the 1880's, when a French company made a vain and costly effort to cut through Panama. Early in the 1890's, an American company started to dig a canal through Nicaragua, but they soon abandoned the attempt.

An incident in the Spanish-American War made Americans aware of the strategic need for a canal for shuttling warships between the Atlantic and Pacific. The battleship *Oregon*, ordered from Puget Sound to Cuban waters, was forced to steam 14,000 miles around Cape Horn —three times as far as if there had been a shortcut. If an isthmian canal were to be useful to the American navy, the United States would have to fortify it, but the Clayton-Bulwer Treaty stood in the way. In 1901 the British government agreed to the Hay-Pauncefote Treaty whereby the United States might build, control, and fortify a canal, so long as ships of all nations were charged equal tolls.

Immediately, Secretary of State John Hay negotiated a treaty with Colombia for a canal through the Isthmus of Panama. The resulting Hay-Herran Treaty provided for the lease of a zone six miles wide at the cost of a down payment of $10,000,000 and rent of $250,000 a year. In August 1903, however, the Colombian Senate unanimously refused to ratify this agreement. The Colombians argued with justification that the payment offered them was too small, since the bankrupt French canal company was to receive $40,000,000 for a temporary lease and some rusting machinery.

Roosevelt was furious at what he called an attempt by "inefficient bandits" to extort money from the United States. He even considered seizing Panama without a treaty, but that proved unnecessary. On November 3, 1903, a revolution (financed by agents of the French canal company) broke out on the isthmus, and an independent Republic of Panama was proclaimed. The United States cruiser *Nashville*, which had appeared on the scene the previous day, aided the revolutionaries. On November 6 the United States recognized Panamanian independence. Less than two weeks later the United States and Panama signed the Hay-Bunau-Varilla Treaty, which was similar to the previous Hay-Herran Treaty except that in the new treaty the Canal Zone was enlarged.

Roosevelt defended his Big Stick diplomacy in Panama on the ground that he advanced "the needs of collective civilization" by hastening the building of an inter-ocean canal. But he also said on one occasion, "I took the canal zone and let Congress debate." His action was quite widely condemned in the United States as a piece of unjustifiable aggression. In Latin America it aroused dislike and distrust of the "Colossus of the North." There was no reason to insist on the Panama route in any case, since it would have been possible to cut a sea-level canal through Nicaragua that would have provided a shorter route between the Atlantic and Pacific ports of the United States.

QUESTION • If the Canal had been dug across Nicaragua instead of Panama, what would be the difference today?

Building the Canal: Goethals and Gorgas

Once the Canal Zone was acquired, Roosevelt was determined, as he expressed it, "to make the dirt fly." The engineering difficulties involved in cutting through the Isthmus of Panama were enormous, and the public health problem even greater. In 1885 an Englishman wrote of Panama:

"In all the world there is not perhaps now concentrated in any single spot so much foul disease, such ... physical and moral abomination. The Isthmus is a damp, tropical jungle, intensely hot, swarming with mosquitoes ... the home, even as Nature made it, of yellow fever, typhus, and dysentery."

Roosevelt eventually put the digging of the canal under the direction of George W. Goethals, a colonel in the Corps of Engineers, and the direction of public health under the same Dr. Gorgas who had cleaned up Havana. Both men succeeded brilliantly. The canal was completed in 1914, by which time Gorgas had made the Canal Zone one of the most healthful places in the world. In the United States at that time the death rate was 14.1 per thousand; in the Canal Zone, the rate was 6 per thousand.

"Dollar Diplomacy"

Roosevelt's successor, President William Howard Taft (1909–1913), continued his policies, but with a shift of emphasis. Taft's Secretary of State, Philander C. Knox, was interested in active promotion of American business interests abroad, with the slogan, "Every diplomat a salesman." In Latin America this so-called "dollar diplomacy" resulted in increased promotion of United States manufactures (including warships), and in active efforts to increase the investments of American financiers in the area. In furtherance of this policy the United States intervened in Nicaragua in 1911 to put in a government acceptable to the United States, to force it to accept a loan from New York bankers, and to put the customs office under a former United States colonel. Knox declared that the United States did not covet an inch of territory south of the Rio Grande and wished only to exercise "a measure of benevolent supervision over Latin American countries." But the economic imperialism and armed intervention that he fostered increased the unpopularity of the United States in Latin America.

BALANCE OF POWER IN THE FAR EAST

Roosevelt's most perplexing problems in foreign affairs concerned the Far East, an area out of reach of the Big Stick. In the Caribbean his diplomacy was supported by overwhelming force, but the position of the United States in the Far East was weak. Roosevelt called the Philippines the "Achilles heel" of American defense; they were easily vulnerable to attack by Japan. In China, the United States lacked sufficient military power to back up the policies set forth in Hay's Open Door notes of 1899 and 1900. The only real defense of equal trading opportunities in China or of Chinese integrity lay in keeping a "balance of power" between the nations with territorial ambitions in the Far East. "The Open Door Policy," wrote Roosevelt, "completely disappears as soon as a powerful nation determines to disregard it, and is willing to run the risk of war rather than forego its intention."

The Russo-Japanese War, 1904–1905

China's two closest neighbors were especially threatening. The Japanese, already in possession of the string of islands off China's north coast, thought it their manifest destiny to expand on the Asian mainland. They established a protectorate over the independent kingdom of Korea and had designs on the rich Chinese province of Manchuria. Russia was already established in Manchuria, with a leasehold at Port Arthur and control over Manchurian railroads. The Russians also hoped to move into Korea. (See map, p. 465.) This clash of interests led to the Russo-Japanese War in 1904. In this contest American opinion was at first overwhelmingly pro-Japanese. The czarist government was unpopular here because of its tyranny and persecution of subject peoples. America regarded the Japanese with an almost paternal air because of Commodore Perry's exploits, and it admired their rapid westernization. Roosevelt himself thought a Japanese victory would keep the balance of power in the Orient. "Japan," he wrote his son, "is playing our game."

To the astonishment of the world, Japan won overwhelming victories over Russia both on land and sea. By the summer of 1905 both countries were ready to make peace, Japan because she was nearing the end of her resources, Russia because of fear of revolution at home. Neither country wished to approach the other directly, but the Japanese secretly asked Roosevelt if he would serve as go-between. After consulting the czar, Roosevelt formally offered to help the warring nations make peace. They accepted the President's proposals, and sent diplomats to a peace conference which met at Portsmouth, New Hampshire, in August 1905.

Roosevelt, as he expressed it, had brought the horses to water, but was not sure he could make them drink. Although not present at the peace table, the President indirectly affected the negotiations by persuading the powers to withdraw extreme demands. He induced Japan to give up claims for a money indemnity and Russia to give up the southern half of the island of Sakhalin. By the Treaty of Portsmouth, Japan also took over Russian interests in southern Manchuria.

Difficulties with Japan

Although Roosevelt won a personal triumph and was awarded the Nobel Peace Prize for his success in bringing hostilities to an end, the Treaty of Portsmouth had unhappy results. By siding with the Russians on the indemnity question, he caused such ill feeling in Japan that anti-American riots broke out in Tokyo and the American embassy had to be guarded with troops. The ease of the Japanese victory caused fear in America and Europe that the "white race" would be overwhelmed by the "yellow race"; this notion of the "yellow peril"

was played up by the yellow press. On the Pacific Coast, feeling began to rise against Japanese immigration, resulting in discrimination against Japanese children in the public schools. Japan regarded this as an insult. More significant than the tide of ill will, which subsided, was the fact that the recent war altered the balance of power in the Orient. Now it was no longer Russian expansion that was most to be feared, but Japanese. Roosevelt himself feared that there was serious danger of war.

In a rather complicated series of maneuvers, Roosevelt attempted at the same time to soothe Japanese anger, satisfy Japanese ambition, save the Philippines from Japanese aggression, and show the Japanese that he was not afraid of them. Although the federal government had no power to force a city or state to change its education laws, the President persuaded the Californians to stop discriminating against Japanese school children. Japan in turn agreed to halt the emigration of laborers to America. This compromise, arranged in 1907 and 1908, was known as the Gentlemen's Agreement.

QUESTION • Which of these purposes were accomplished for the time being? Which permanently?

Regarding the balance of power in the Far East, Roosevelt attempted to avert danger of Japanese expansion toward the Philippines by agreeing to recognize the predominant position of Japan in Korea and Manchuria. At least this is what seems to be the substance of two rather vaguely worded executive agreements, the Taft-Katsura "agreed memorandum" of 1905, and the Root-Takahira Agreement of 1908. At the same time, in a truly Rooseveltian gesture, the President attempted to impress Japan with American naval power by sending an American fleet to Tokyo during its journey around the world in 1908.

Japan stunned the world when she beat the Russians in the Russo-Japanese war. She was now a world power. But war took its toll. Here a wounded soldier undergoes an operation. Note the Western nurse on the right.

The "dollar diplomacy" of the Taft administration found its reflection in the Far East in efforts by Secretary of State Knox to promote American railroad and financial interests in Manchuria. Finding that American businessmen were being discriminated against in Manchuria, Knox proposed that the railroads in the province be put under international control. Russia and Japan, recent enemies, joined forces to reject this idea. Knox's action was criticized by Roosevelt in a letter to Taft that revealed the basic weakness of the American position in the Far East:

I utterly disbelieve in the policy of bluff . . . or in any violation of the old frontier maxim, "Never draw unless you mean to shoot." I do not believe in our taking any position anywhere unless we can make it good; and as regards Manchuria, if the Japanese choose to follow a course of conduct to which we are adverse, we cannot stop it unless we are prepared to go to war, and a successful war about Manchuria would require a fleet as good as that of England, plus an army as good as that of Germany.

OTHER ROOSEVELTIAN DIPLOMACY

Roosevelt's appreciation of the fact that the United States was "no longer isolated but a member of the family of nations" was shown by his unprecedented effort to avert a European war over Morocco. American attention had been drawn to this turbulent North African state in 1904, when an alleged American citizen Perdicaris and his wife were kidnapped by a bandit named Raisuli. Secretary of State Hay demanded that the Moroccan government return Perdicaris and punish Raisuli. "We want Perdicaris alive or Raisuli dead," he telegraphed. Eventually the Moroccan government produced Perdicaris alive by paying his ransom.

The Algeciras Conference, 1906

The next year American diplomacy became involved in a complicated international crisis. In spite of open door treaties guaranteeing Morocco's independence and equal commercial opportunities for foreign merchants, French influence was increasing and it was obvious that the country might soon become a French protectorate. This threatened to violate an international "Open Door" agreement, to which Germany was a party, that guaranteed foreign nations equal trading rights in Morocco. In March 1905, Kaiser William II disembarked from his yacht at Tangier and declared that he would do all in his power to preserve Moroccan independence. His action was motivated less by concern for German trading rights than by a desire to weaken French international prestige and the alliances that France was making in an effort to "encircle" Germany. War seemed imminent, and it threatened to engulf most of Europe, since Germany was allied to Austria-Hungary and Italy, while France was allied to Russia and closely linked to Great Britain. The situation was relieved when the German emperor appealed to Roosevelt to lend his support to an international conference on Morocco; the emperor even agreed in advance to accept whatever solution Roosevelt thought fair. Roosevelt was hesitant to break a precedent going back to George Washington's time in order to engage in diplomacy that dealt with a purely European affair. He decided, however, that as a great power the United States had an interest in preserving the peace so long as it did not involve commitment to the use of military power.

At the resulting Algeciras Conference of 1906, the United States, represented by the able diplomat Henry White, proposed an arrangement which was agreed upon by the powers and which possibly averted war. Although the Senate ratified the Algeciras agreement regarding Morocco, it expressed distrust of Roosevelt's rather risky involvement in European politics. The senators passed a resolution saying that ratification was "without purpose to depart from the traditional American foreign policy which forbids participation by the United States in the settlement of political questions which are entirely European. . . ."

International Arbitration

In spite of his reputation for belligerency, Roosevelt supported arbitration as a peaceful means of settling international controversies. International conferences in 1899 and 1907 at The Hague in the Netherlands established a permanent arbitration court and defined the means whereby nations could appeal to it to settle disputes. The United States, which had previously arbitrated more questions than any other nation except Great Britain, was ably represented at both Hague Conferences. During Roosevelt's presidency, two disputes with Canada, one over the Alaskan boundary and the other over American fishing rights at the mouth of the St. Lawrence River, were successfully submitted to arbitration. In the Alaskan matter, however, the President aroused Canadian ill will

by making it clear that he would accept no judgment that did not coincide with the claims of the United States, and by appointing as United States representatives to the arbitration commission two noted expansionists, one of whom had often proposed that Canada be annexed.

In 1908 Secretary of State Elihu Root negotiated treaties with twenty-five nations whereby both sides agreed in advance to arbitrate disputes. These agreements were less important than they might have been because either nation could refuse the way of peace if it thought its vital interests, independence, or honor were involved. The Senate also insisted, over Roosevelt's protest, that it must agree in advance whether or not a dispute should be referred to arbitration.

Improvement of the Army and Navy

Military affairs were one of Roosevelt's main interests; one of his friends called him "a perpetual volunteer." Roosevelt argued that diplomacy, even with peaceful purpose, had to be backed by force. On no matter did he press Congress harder than in demanding appropriations for annual additions to our fleet, and he personally directed how the money was spent. Learning that the gunnery methods of the navy were obsolete, he saw to it that the whole system of training was changed. He later claimed that, gun for gun, the fleet was three times as efficient when he left office as when he came in.

There appeared to be less reason to enlarge the army than the navy. It was reduced in size by a quarter between 1901 and 1909, but its efficiency was greatly increased. Elihu Root, who served both McKinley and Roosevelt as Secretary of War, was among the ablest cabinet members in the history of the United States. Under his leadership many weaknesses revealed in the Spanish-American War were removed. Root centralized authority, improved promotions, and tried to arrange for better army-navy cooperation. He introduced the General Staff for over-all planning and the Army War College to provide officers with further training. Newton D. Baker, Secretary of War in World War I, called Root the best Secretary of War in American history, and said that without his work "the participation of the United States in the World War would necessarily have been a confused, ineffective and discreditable episode."

A Better Foreign Service

Throughout his political career, Roosevelt had favored civil service reform, and as President he greatly advanced the efficiency of the executive department. He was especially interested in improving the diplomatic corps. During the long period of nineteenth century isolation, the State Department had become a happy hunting ground of the spoilsmen. Diplomatic posts were given as a reward for party service, and wholesale removals followed every change of party fortunes. The foreign service was in such low repute that in 1889 the New York *Sun* suggested it be abolished. But when foreign affairs assumed increasing importance, the United States could not afford such an inefficient system.

On the death of John Hay in 1905, Roosevelt appointed Elihu Root Secretary of State, and Root attempted to improve the efficiency of the State Department as he had improved that of the army. Root had to fight an attitude toward the foreign service that was reflected in a letter he received from a friend: "If there are any nice berths like the Consulate at Bordeaux, France, or at Buenos Aires lying around loose, I might make application for one. I need a rest." Working in cooperation, Roosevelt and Root provided that future appointments to the lower ranks of the diplomatic service be based on examinations set by the Civil Service Commission. Regular promotion was established. Although salaries were low, and the top posts were still under the spoils system, the groundwork was laid for a professional, nonpolitical foreign service.

Roosevelt's unprecedented and sometimes highhanded actions in the fields of foreign relations have often been criticized. Nevertheless, as Walter Lippmann wrote, Roosevelt "grasped the elements of a genuine foreign policy." He tried to make American military power and foreign service adequate for its position in the world, and used diplomacy to advance peace and discourage aggression.

Activities: Chapter 20

For Mastery and Review

1. Prepare a brief character sketch of Theodore Roosevelt, emphasizing elements that made him an unusual man. What effects did his personality have upon politics?

2. What is meant by the Big Stick? Trace the logical sequence from the Second Venezuelan Affair through the Drago Doctrine and the Roosevelt Corollary to the interventions in Santo Domingo in 1905 and in Cuba in 1906.

3. By what steps did the United States acquire the Panama Canal Zone? What treaty negotiations were involved? What was the reaction in Latin America to American methods?

4. In what respects was our diplomatic position in the Orient weak? How did the balance of power affect the Open Door policy? What were the factors that led to the Russo-Japanese War? On which side did American sympathies lie? Why? What were the terms of the Treaty of Portsmouth? How did this treaty affect the balance of power in the Orient?

5. What were the Gentlemen's Agreement and the Root-Takahira Agreement? What was the Knox proposal concerning Manchuria? What was Roosevelt's criticism of that proposal?

6. What were the events leading to the Algeciras Conference? What part did Roosevelt play in the conference? What was the Senate's reaction to Roosevelt's participation in European diplomacy?

7. Summarize Elihu Root's importance as a diplomat. What arbitration machinery was established to settle international disputes? What cabinet posts did Root hold? With what success?

Unrolling the Map

1. On an outline map of the Caribbean area, locate the following: Cuba, Puerto Rico, Santo Domingo, Venezuela, Nicaragua, Colombia, Panama, the Canal Zone, and the Panama Canal. With the completed map before you, discuss in class the strategic relation of the countries listed above to the Panama Canal.

2. On an outline map of the eastern part of the Orient, locate the following: the Philippine Islands, China, Korea, Manchuria, Port Arthur, Sakhalin, the Japanese Islands, Shanghai, Hong Kong, Singapore, French Indochina, and Vladivostok. Use the completed map when you discuss the balance of power in Asia, the Russo-Japanese War, and the Treaty of Portsmouth.

Who, What, and Why Important?

"lunatic fringe"
Conference of Governors
"Big Stick"
Second Venezuelan Affair
Drago Doctrine
Roosevelt Corollary
Santo Domingo
intervention in Cuba
Panama Canal Zone

the *Oregon*
Hay-Pauncefote Treaty
Hay-Herran Treaty
Republic of Panama
George W. Goethals
William C. Gorgas
dollar diplomacy
balance of power
Russo-Japanese War
Treaty of Portsmouth
"yellow peril"

Gentlemen's Agreement
Root-Takahira Agreement

Algeciras Conference
international arbitration
Elihu Root

To Pursue the Matter

1. The quotation on p. 491, ". . . I intended to be one of the governing class," was taken from *The Autobiography of Theodore Roosevelt*. For a longer excerpt, telling of his entry into New York politics, see Arnof, *A Sense of the Past*, pp. 355–357.

2. With a classmate, plan and present an informal debate on the relative merits of the Drago Doctrine and the Roosevelt Corollary. You might set up the class as a meeting of the Pan-American Union, and assume that the defender of the Drago Doctrine is a Latin-American diplomat, while the defender of the Roosevelt Corollary is the U. S. Secretary of State. You might then open a general debate. Sources: Perkins, *The Monroe Doctrine*, and Bailey, *A Diplomatic History of the American People*.

3. Study the history of the diplomacy which led to the leasing by the United States of the Panama Canal Zone, with a view to finding answers to such questions as: Was Colombia justified in holding out for a higher price? What do you make of the activities of the French? Were Roosevelt's actions justifiable? What mysteries remain? Sources: Pringle, *Theodore Roosevelt*, and Bailey, *A Diplomatic History of the American People*.

4. Do you agree with Roosevelt's statement about the relation of force to diplomacy (p. 494)?

5. Discuss arbitration as a means for settling international disputes. Is it feasible? How successful has it been?

6. Was Roosevelt really imperialistic? See May, *From Imperialism to Isolationism*, pp. 26 ff.

7. Was "dollar diplomacy" a paying proposition? Possible sources: Bailey, *A Diplomatic History of the American People*, and Perkins, *The Monroe Doctrine*.

8. Was Roosevelt wise in acting as peacemaker in the Russo-Japanese War?

Chapter 21

The Square Deal and the New Freedom

A man who is good enough to shed his blood
for his country is good enough to be given a square
deal afterward. More than that no man is entitled
to, and less than that no man should have.
——THEODORE ROOSEVELT, 1903

The forces of the Nation are asserting themselves against
every form of special privilege and private control, and
are seeking bigger things than they have heretofore
achieved. They are sweeping away what is unrighteous
in order to vindicate once more the essential rights of
human life ...
——WOODROW WILSON, 1912

Theodore Roosevelt's entrance into the presidential office roughly coincided with the beginning of a ferment of reform known as progressivism, or the progressive movement. We will defer until the next chapter an attempt to define this development in detail. Suffice it for now to explain that progressivism operated at both the local and the national level, and that —like Populism—it proposed government control of business in the public interest. Two Presidents were outstanding progressive leaders: Theodore Roosevelt and Woodrow Wilson.

ROOSEVELT'S DOMESTIC POLICIES

When Roosevelt was under consideration as Republican candidate for Vice-President in 1900, Mark Hanna warned that there was only one life between "that cowboy" and the White House. McKinley's death made the cowboy President, and there was fear in conservative business circles as to how he would behave. Roosevelt began to fulfill their worst expectations in his first message to Congress. He urged federal legislation to deal with the "tremendous and highly complex industrial developments which went on with ever accelerated rapidity during the latter half of the nineteenth century." In a speaking tour in 1902, he said that he stood for such regulation of business as would insure a "square deal" for capital, labor, and the public at large. Roosevelt thought that the Republican party must move with the times or popular feeling would destroy it, as it destroyed the Whig party in the 1850's. He argued that the only way to preserve the capitalist system, with which he had no fundamental quarrel, was the way of "conservative reform."

For a time, however, Roosevelt pursued a rather cautious course. He had promised "to continue absolutely unbroken the policy of President McKinley," and he was warned by Mark Hanna to "go slow." As "President by accident" he felt he had no call to push a general program of reform. But even before being elected President in his own right, Roosevelt showed his hand by attempting to enforce the Sherman Antitrust Act and by intervening in the coal strike of 1902.

The Trust Buster

Roosevelt was disturbed by the power of "the mighty industrial overlords" and their immunity from government control. As we have seen (see p. 432), the Sherman Antitrust Law was a dead letter. A period of rapid concentration of industry reached a climax with the formation of the United States Steel Corporation in 1901. This vast holding company was formed when a syndicate of bankers, headed by J. Pierpont Morgan, bought out Andrew Carnegie at a price of $250 million and then combined the Carnegie iron and steel properties with others they controlled. Capitalized at nearly one and a half billion dollars, United States Steel controlled more than half the steel production of the United States and was by far the biggest industrial combination the world had ever seen. The American public was appalled by the size of the new venture and by the kind of power that it gave to one person. "Mr. Dooley" expressed the attitude of the times when he described Morgan's ordering an office boy to take some change out of the cash register and run over and buy Europe for him.

Roosevelt was not opposed to big business as such, since he thought it was an inevitable de-

velopment, but he wanted to put it under law. He repeatedly urged Congress to pass laws regulating trusts more strictly. He favored legislation, for instance, that would require full disclosure of corporate financing, with a view especially to preventing stock watering. In response to his pleading, Congress did establish a Department of Commerce and Labor in 1903, but with little power, and an Expedition Act to give precedence in the courts to cases involving the Interstate Commerce Act or the Sherman Antitrust Act; but that was all.

Roosevelt made a reputation as a trust buster by reviving the Sherman Act. In 1902 his attorney general brought suit to dissolve the Northern Securities Corporation, a holding company (see chart, p. 584) formed by railroad magnates and bankers (including J. Pierpont Morgan) to control the three railroad systems of the Northwest. In 1904 the Supreme Court decided that the Northern Securities Corporation violated the Sherman Act and ordered it dissolved. After this success the Department of Justice started more trust-busting suits against corporations than had been brought under the three previous Presidents. In most of these cases the government won. Although trust busting was popular with the public, Roosevelt himself recognized that it was not a particularly effective means of regulating business. It did not prevent monopolies, but only attempted to break them up after they had already been formed. The President was actually less interested in the economic effects of enforcing anti-monopoly laws than in the symbolic effect of making even the most powerful businessmen publicly obey the law.

The Coal Strike of 1902

One of the most prolonged strikes in American history started in May 1902, when nearly 150,000 men walked out of the anthracite mines of eastern Pennsylvania. The strikers had such real grievances that public opinion tended to be on their side. Wages were low and layoffs frequent; average earnings were less than $300 per year. Living in cheaply built company towns, the miners were obliged to trade at company stores that charged high prices. They had been organized into an industrial union, the United Mine Workers, by John Mitchell, who had started work in the mines as a boy of twelve. Opposed to revolutionary violence, Mitchell had worked with Mark Hanna, Samuel Gompers, and Grover Cleveland to found the National Civic Federation, an organization devoted to promoting peaceful labor relations. In the strike of 1902, Mitchell offered to submit to two prominent clergymen and a third man of their choice the question of whether the miners' wages were "sufficient to enable them to live, maintain and educate their families in a manner conformable to established American standards and consistent with American citizenship."

The coal operators hurt their case by extreme unwillingness even to discuss the miners' demands. George F. Baer, principal spokesman for the employers, answered Mitchell's suggestion that religious leaders decide miners' wages by pointing out that "anthracite mining is a business and not a religious, sentimental or academic proposition." Since the operators held such an attitude and the miners were almost 100 per cent behind Mitchell, the strike dragged on with no prospect of settlement. By October the retail price of anthracite had risen from $5

John Mitchell, Miner

Most labor leaders come up through the ranks, bringing to their office firsthand knowledge of work in mines and factories. Modern leaders have the help of staffs of technical advisers, economists, and statisticians. Unseen, but sitting with the union group at every bargaining session, is the history of labor's defeats: strikes lost through violence and by court injunction, families starving, men killed by lack of safety measures. John Mitchell took this history with him to the White House in 1902.

Against him were all the well-organized anthracite-mine operators. Their mines were located in a small area in Pennsylvania. Relatively few, they had been able to set up agreements on quotas of coal to be mined by each, on wages to be paid, and on prices to be charged the public. Their cozy arrangement benefited from the monopoly on coal transportation maintained by a half-dozen railroads, which also owned coal lands in the area. They believed, as one of them said: "The rights of laboring men would be protected, not by agitators, but by the Christian men to whom God in His infinite wisdom had given control of the property interests in this country."

To such a man, a coal mine was property. To John Mitchell, coal mining was a way of life. He knew the mines. Tall, brawny from backbreaking work with pick and shovel, Mitchell had developed patience. His self-control could resist bitter provocation. Of the angry scene in the White House, President Roosevelt said: "There was only one man who behaved like a gentleman, and it wasn't I."

to $30 a ton. With the threat of a coal famine during the winter months, the public interest demanded that the strike be ended. Appeals for action poured in to the President.

Roosevelt had no power, either by law or by precedent, for forcing the operators and miners to come to an agreement, but he resolved to use the influence of his office to the full. As he later wrote his sister,

I could no more see misery and death come to the great masses of the people in our large cities and sit by idly, because under ordinary conditions, a strike is not a subject of interference by the President, than I could sit by idly and see one man kill another without interference because there is no statutory duty imposed upon the President to interfere in such cases.

On October 1, Roosevelt invited representatives of the operators to meet Mitchell at the White House. In a stormy session nothing was accomplished, but public opinion turned even more against the employers, who called Mitchell an "outlaw" and denounced the President for not using the Sherman Antitrust Act against the union. At this point, Roosevelt considered a questionably legal seizure of the mines by federal troops. Before he took such drastic action, a compromise was reached. Elihu Root, the President's representative, and J. Pierpont Morgan, whose banking firm indirectly controlled most of the anthracite mines, held a conference. After it, Morgan put enough pressure on the operators to force them to back down. Morgan's action was apparently prompted by the fear that the unreasonableness of the coal operators, added to the sufferings of a coal-less winter, would create popular hostility to business in general. The operators finally

QUESTION • *What should be the powers of government in labor-management disputes where the public interest is affected?*

The New York Public Library

A 1900 cartoon shows Roosevelt as a new playmate for President McKinley, the "little boy" of the Trusts. When Roosevelt became President he attacked monopolies, and was called "Teddy the Trust Buster."

agreed to submit the miners' demands to arbitration by a five-man commission appointed by the President. Roosevelt's action in using the prestige of his office and his personal influence on Morgan to settle the strike was recognized in this country and abroad as an important precedent. The London *Times* commented that "the President has done a very big and entirely new thing. We are witnessing not merely the ending of the coal strike, but the definite entry of a powerful government on a novel sphere of operation."

Roosevelt Re-elected, 1904

As the presidential election of 1904 approached, the conservative "Old Guard" of the Republican party was unhappy at the prospect of four more years of the Rough Rider in the White House. The New York *Sun* accused him

A 1904 cartoon, "The Mysterious Stranger," by John T. McCutcheon, pointed up Missouri's break with the Solid South. Roosevelt won the election by the largest margin obtained since the Civil War. He attributed his success to the "plain people," to whom he promised a "square deal." The election strengthened his hand over Congress, enabling him to get some progressive legislation through that conservatively led body.

of "out-Bryaning Bryan" by "harrying trusts," "bringing wealth to its knees," and "putting labor unions above the law." It seemed possible that Mark Hanna might try to block Roosevelt's renomination, but Hanna died in February 1904. Roosevelt had popular opinion behind him and was, as even his enemies admitted, the ablest politician of the day. Through the use of patronage the President had built up a personal machine within his party. He received the unanimous nomination from the Republican national convention.

Meanwhile the Democrats turned a somersault. They cast Bryan aside and angled for conservative votes by nominating Alton B. Parker, a wealthy New York judge. Parker had no popular following, and antagonized former Bryan followers by defending the gold standard. Roosevelt won by the largest margin since the Civil War. He immediately announced that he would abide by "the wise custom which limits the President to two terms." He attributed his triumph to the "plain people . . . the folk who work hard on farm, in shop, or on the railroads, or who own little businesses which they run themselves."

Roosevelt's Progressive Legislation

Now President in his own right, Roosevelt strongly urged Congress to pass a number of reform measures. Although failing to pass the more severe antitrust law which Roosevelt demanded, Congress in 1906 enacted the Hepburn Act which provided stricter control of railroads. Popular demand for more effective regulation than that provided by the Interstate Commerce Act of 1887 was almost universal. William Allen White expressed prevailing sentiment in a letter to a railroad official: "The railroads cannot name senators, pack state conventions, run legislatures and boss politics generally . . . and then successfully maintain that they are private carriers doing a private business." Some prominent people, including Bryan, proposed that the railroads be owned and operated by the government. Thinking such a step would lead to far-reaching disaster, Roosevelt urged tighter regulation as an alternative.

In 1905 the House of Representatives, by a vote of 346 to 7, passed a bill going beyond the President's recommendations. The Senate, however, was dominated by a clique of wealthy men who were frankly the representatives of the great corporations. On the other hand, Roosevelt also had allies in the Senate, of whom the most well-known was Robert La Follette, a former reform governor of Wisconsin. Many Democrats, under the leadership of "Pitchfork Ben" Tillman, a former "Popocrat" (see p. 459), also favored stricter railroad regulation. As a result of popular support, clever politics, and willingness to compromise, Roosevelt was able to push the Hepburn bill through the Senate 18 months after he urged Congress to act.

The Hepburn Act strengthened the Interstate Commerce Act of 1887 in several ways. It abolished the "free pass," which railroads

granted to politicians and other influential people such as newspaper editors. It widened the jurisdiction of the Interstate Commerce Commission to include express companies, pipe lines, ferries, and sleeping-car companies. Railroad corporations were restrained from operating other businesses (such as coal mining). Most important of all, the Interstate Commerce Commission was granted power to fix rates, although its decisions might be appealed to the courts. Complaints to the commission soon multiplied forty times and a great many rates were lowered.

In 1906, at Roosevelt's urging, Congress passed two laws that protected consumers—the Pure Food and Drug Act and an act providing for federal inspection of meat. The public agitation that was behind this legislation will be described in the next chapter (see p. 533).

Where Roosevelt Failed to Act

In spite of such laws, the legislative achievement of Congress under Roosevelt's leadership was so unimpressive that he was accused of producing "more noise than accomplishment." Although he favored revision of the tariff, he regarded the issue as "political dynamite." He never tried to force action on it, although he occasionally threatened to bring it up unless congressional leaders would agree to support legislative measures in which he had a special interest. With little knowledge of money and banking, Roosevelt never seriously supported long-overdue efforts to make the banking system more stable and the currency system more flexible.

One reason for the failure to produce much-needed reform legislation was Roosevelt's feeling that politics was "the art of the possible." His philosophy of reform was one of gradualism; he was willing to accept half a loaf if he could not get the whole. Furthermore, the Republican leaders in Congress, carry-overs from the McKinley-Hanna period, were unsympathetic to progressive legislation. The President could persuade them to act only when he had overwhelming public opinion behind him.

Although Roosevelt accomplished less than he seemed to promise, he restored the people's faith in the power of the federal government to serve their interests. By preaching the Square Deal, he promoted the idea that the cure for the evils of unrestrained individualism was not socialism, but moderate reform. Above all, he created a demand for reform. According to a recent historian, "Roosevelt was the best publicity man progressivism ever had."

Roosevelt and Conservation

No cause was nearer Roosevelt's heart than the effort to conserve natural resources. Perhaps his earliest and deepest enthusiasm was for the wilderness. The former national policy, based on the idea that natural resources were inexhaustible, had resulted in colossal waste. Forests had been cut without thought of erosion or future timber needs, cattle ranchers and sheepherders had been allowed to overgraze grasslands; homesteaders had plowed land that should have remained in grass. Wild life had suffered from such slaughter as wiped out the buffalo herds and the passenger pigeon.

Existing laws designed to preserve the public lands, forests, and mineral deposits were usually not strictly enforced. Nevertheless, a policy of conservation instead of exploitation had begun long before Roosevelt took office. It can be seen in such measures as the establishment of Yellowstone Park in 1872 and in the act passed during Benjamin Harrison's administration giving the President power to withdraw lands from sale and make them National Forests. But no one did as much for conservation as Roosevelt. He encouraged legislation such as the Newlands Act of 1902 which provided for federal aid to irrigation projects. He enforced laws against illegal occupation of public lands. He more than tripled the area of the National Forests, and his able chief forester, Gifford Pinchot, saw that they were honestly and efficiently administered. Above all, Roosevelt *made conservation popular.* He stimulated interest by his writings, by his vacations in the West, by his constant demand for better conservation laws, and by willingness to use the power and prestige of the presidential office.

When Congress blocked his efforts, Roosevelt enlisted private individuals and promoted state action. In May 1908, he called a national conference on conservation at the White House. It included the governors of all states or their representatives, government foresters, congressmen (including some who opposed the President), and the officers of private associations of naturalists and sports lovers. Results of this conference included the creation of over forty state conservation commissions and of a National Conservation Commission which prepared an inventory of the natural resources of the United States.

Just before leaving office Roosevelt held a North American Conservation Conference, and he even contemplated a world conference. Senator La Follette, often critical of Roosevelt, paid tribute to the "high statesmanship" the President showed in "dinning into the Nation" the idea of conservation. La Follette predicted that future historians would say that Roosevelt's greatest achievement was not the Square Deal, but his leadership in the movement to preserve natural resources for the benefit of the people at large.

The Election of 1908

Like Andrew Jackson (see p. 270), Roosevelt named his successor: His choice fell upon his intimate friend William Howard Taft, who had a distinguished public career as a federal judge, governor of the Philippines, and Secretary of War. With his control of the party machinery and his mastery of publicity, Roosevelt easily headed off other candidates and arranged for Taft to receive the Republican nomination in 1908. The Democrats, who had fared badly in 1904 with the conservative Parker, went back to Bryan. The Nebraskan made little headway against the man who had Roosevelt's endorsement; he ruefully complained that the Square Deal had stolen his thunder. Taft had little difficulty in winning, although he did not defeat Bryan as decisively as Roosevelt had beaten Parker.

TAFT IN OFFICE, 1909–1913

While Roosevelt set off for a year's hunting trip in Africa, Taft called a special session of Congress to deal with the tariff. This was an issue Roosevelt had avoided, but the Republican platform of 1908 had pledged "revision" of the tariff, and Taft said that this meant revision downwards. Since passage of the Dingley Tariff of 1897, prices had advanced more rapidly than wages, and the resulting "HCL" (high cost of living) was blamed on unduly high rates. There was a common idea, shared by Taft, that high rates encouraged monopoly and increased the profits of monopolistic trusts.

The Payne-Aldrich Tariff, 1909

Congress met in March 1909, and within less than a month the House of Representatives passed a measure providing for substantial reductions in the tariff, without abandoning the principle of protection. Twice before, in 1888 and 1894, the Senate had killed attempts to lower the tariff, and in 1909 it did it again. Under the leadership of Senator Nelson W. Aldrich, over 600 amendments were tacked on to the House bill. Many of these amendments contained jokers designed to conceal higher rates, such as changing a duty on certain small articles from so much "per hundred-weight" to so much "per hundred."

"Taft has the most lovable personality," Roosevelt once said, "I have ever come in contact with . . ." But their beautiful friendship was wrecked on the realities of politics and ambition.

When Aldrich attempted to railroad the amended bill through the Senate, he was met by revolt in his own party. Several Republican senators, nicknamed the "insurgents," used their privilege of unlimited debate to reveal the way Aldrich and his allies carried out the demands of high-tariff lobbyists instead of the popular will. Too late, Taft attempted to persuade the Old Guard leaders to reduce the rates, but they made only slight concessions. The average level of the Payne-Aldrich Tariff was actually higher than that of the Dingley Tariff, but Taft signed the bill. He feared a split in his party, and

Ha ha! you are making up your Cabinet. I in a

light-hearted way have spent the morning testing the

rifles for my African trip. Life has compensations!

Ever yours,

ϡ, R.

When he wrote this light-hearted note to his hand-picked successor, Roosevelt had little inkling of the difficulties Taft would face as President, and still less any thought that he and Taft would one day become political and personal enemies.

thought the new tariff an improvement. It contained a corporation tax, established a tariff commission to make a scientific study of rates, and provided for some flexibility in rates at the discretion of the President. Taft's action, however, was widely regarded as a betrayal of his campaign promise, especially in the Middle West.

Taft in Difficulty

Taft lost popularity still more after the Ballinger-Pinchot controversy. The Secretary of the Interior, Richard A. Ballinger, had reopened to private purchase certain waterpower sites and coal land that had been withdrawn while Roosevelt was President. His action was protested by Chief Forester Pinchot, who gave his charges to the press. Ballinger was publicly accused of fraud, but Taft was convinced of his innocence (which has since been established). When he dismissed Pinchot for insubordination, the President was thought an enemy of conservation.

Immediately following the Ballinger-Pinchot controversy came an outbreak of insurgent Republicanism in the House of Representatives; it took the form of an attack on the speaker of the House, "Uncle Joe" Cannon. The speaker had come to enjoy a power over legislation greater in some ways than that of the President. He appointed all committees; he decided what bills should be referred to which committees; by almost absolute control over debate he could push some measures through without discussion and see that others never reached the floor. Cannon had used these powers to hold up progressive legislation. He had cooperated with Aldrich to raise the tariff rates in 1909, and had long been an opponent of conservation. With the motto "Not one cent for scenery," he had prevented the creation of National Parks and Forests. Finally, in March 1910, a coalition of Democrats and insurgents forced a change in the rules of the House that stripped the Speaker of much of his power.

The attack on Cannon hurt Taft, who in order to keep party harmony had been almost forced to align himself with the Speaker. By signing the Payne-Aldrich Tariff, supporting Ballinger against Pinchot, and backing Cannon, Taft gave the impression that he had "sold the Square Deal down the river." He was described

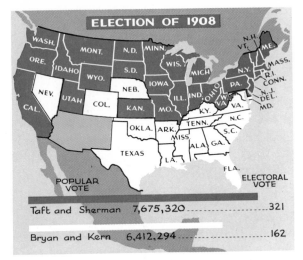

ELECTION OF 1908

POPULAR VOTE / ELECTORAL VOTE

Taft and Sherman   7,675,320 321

Bryan and Kern   6,412,294 162

Although he was but 49 years old, Roosevelt felt he had to keep his promise not to run in 1908. He called in his secretary and said, "We must have a candidate. We better run Taft . . . see Taft and tell him." Taft easily won.

by an insurgent senator as "a large good-natured body entirely surrounded by people who know exactly what they want." Popular indignation was so great that the congressional elections of 1910 resulted in a sweeping Democratic victory.

There was an element of unfairness in the attacks on Taft. He was a man of ability and integrity, and he had genuinely supported Roosevelt. But he lacked his predecessor's gift of dramatizing issues and enlisting public opinion. Furthermore, his theory of the presidency allowed him less freedom of action than his predecessor had assumed. Trained as a lawyer, he was unwilling to break precedents. While Roosevelt claimed the right to do anything not forbidden, Taft used "only those powers expressly authorized by law."

To some degree, however, Taft brought his troubles on himself. He had a very different temperament from other politicians, and he had a hard time keeping up with the incessant work of the presidential office. He did not really want to be President; his greatest ambition—later fulfilled—was to sit on the Supreme Court. Worst of all, he did not enjoy politics, and it is there-

fore not surprising that he was not a success as a politician.

Progressive Legislation under Taft

In spite of his difficulties, Taft could boast of considerable achievement. He was a vigorous trust buster, who initiated almost twice as many suits against monopolistic business combinations as Roosevelt. During his presidency, Congress passed much progressive legislation, nearly all of it with the backing of the President. In 1910 the Mann-Elkins Act both extended the jurisdiction of the Interstate Commerce Commission to include telegraph and telephone lines and increased the ICC's powers.

In 1913 a Railroad Valuation Act empowered the ICC to assess the value of American railroads as a basis for fixing fair rates. Congress established postal savings banks (a former Populist demand) to protect the small depositor, and established the parcel post to help the small shipper. Conservation was promoted by the establishment of the first National Forests in the Appalachians and by a law empowering the President to withdraw valuable mineral deposits from sale. During Taft's presidency, Congress proposed the Sixteenth and Seventeenth Amendments, legalizing a federal income tax and providing for popular election of senators. Both were ratified in 1913. (See pp. 146–147).

QUESTION • With so much progressive legislation while he was President, why was Taft considered conservative?

Roosevelt and the "New Nationalism"

Meanwhile, Roosevelt re-entered the political arena. In spite of his intention to remain out of politics, he was soon drawn in. With his natural feeling for what the people wanted at any given time, Roosevelt aligned himself with the insurgent wing of the Republican party, who had started to call themselves "Progressive Republicans" or simply "Progressives." In a speech at Osawatomie, Kansas, during the congressional election of 1910, he preached what he called the "New Nationalism." In words that recalled the Populist platform of the 1890's and foreshadowed the New Deal of the 1930's, Roosevelt said:

We are face to face with new conceptions of the relations of property to human welfare.... The man who wrongly holds that every human right is secondary to his profit must now give way to the advocate of human welfare, who rightly maintains that every man holds his property subject to the general right of the community to regulate its use to whatever degree the public welfare may require it.

In the New Nationalism speech, Roosevelt outlined a much more radical program of action than he had ever proposed as President. He favored both state and federal legislation which would actively promote human welfare. Attacking the courts for declaring progressive legislation unconstitutional, he suggested that state judges be subject to recall (see p. 530), and that Supreme Court decisions be subject to reversal by popular vote. Expressing distrust of legislative bodies, he said he regarded "the executive as the steward of human welfare." By taking such a stand, Roosevelt became almost in spite of himself the natural leader of the Progressive Republicans.

The Election of 1912

The great question in American politics on the eve of the election of 1912 was whether Roosevelt would run for the presidency. He had said he was out of politics, and this was re-enforced by his no-third-term pledge of 1904. On the other hand, he had convinced himself that Taft was unfit; and it was against his nature to sit on the side lines. Senator La Follette, a man of great ability and courage, had the support of many Progressive Republicans, but when

he suffered a temporary nervous collapse, scores of progressives beat a path to Roosevelt's door. In February 1912, on the prearranged petition of seven progressive governors, the former President announced his candidacy. "My hat is in the ring," he said, explaining that his promise not to run for a third term referred to a third *consecutive* term.

There followed a struggle for control of the Republican party that reached its climax at the national convention in June. Conservatives and most of the professional politicians rallied behind Taft. So did many former supporters of the Square Deal who thought Roosevelt too radical or who disliked his running for a third term. Except for some devoted followers of La Follette, the Progressive Republicans lined up for Roosevelt. In states where convention delegates were chosen or instructed in primary elections, Roosevelt was generally the choice of the voters.

The Taft forces had the immense advantage of controlling the party machinery. Of 241 convention seats disputed by Taft and Roosevelt, the convention's Credentials Committee gave 233 to Taft. Elihu Root, chairman of the convention, kept such a tight hold on proceedings that he was accused of driving a steam roller over the Roosevelt forces. When Taft was chosen on the first ballot, Roosevelt charged the Republican party leaders with stealing the nomination. He stood ready, he said, to carry on the battle for progressive principles outside the party.

Formation of the Progressive Party

In August a convention met in Chicago to found a new party, which took the name Progressive. The delegates were a curious mixture —college professors, social workers, newspaper editors, former Rough Riders, wealthy men pricked with social conscience, and a few professional politicians who were "getting on the bandwagon" for their own purposes. The prevailing mood was one of exaltation; the delegates chanted "Onward, Christian Soldiers" and "The Battle Hymn of the Republic." Senator Albert J. Beveridge, who had followed Roosevelt out of the Republican party, made the keynote address which has been compared to Bryan's Cross of Gold speech (see p. 461). He called on the new party, sprung from the grass roots, to work for a nobler America. The Progressives, said Beveridge, stood for "social brotherhood" as against "savage individualism," for "a representative government that represents the people," as against invisible government by the corrupt boss and the "robber interest."

The Progressive platform demanded reforms typical of the period—more direct democracy through such means as the initiative and referendum; conservation of natural resources for the general welfare; woman suffrage and the prohibition of child labor; a revised currency system and the introduction of an inheritance tax; and protection of wage workers through safety laws, limitation of hours of labor, and workers compensation. The party nominated Roosevelt for the presidency. It immediately acquired a symbol when the former President announced that he felt like a "bull moose."

The Progressive party had ample enthusiasm and a presidential candidate who was the most popular man in public life since Andrew Jackson. It also had abundant campaign funds, supplied by wealthy business people who believed that capitalism could survive only if it reformed. But the Bull Moose crusade was a forlorn hope. Most of the Progressives were amateurs with little or no knowledge of practical politics. Party machinery could not be set up in thousands of election districts overnight. All that Roosevelt accomplished by bolting his party was to turn control of the Republican party over to the Old Guard and to insure the election of a Democratic President.

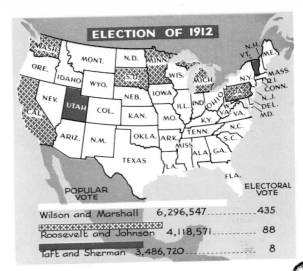

ELECTION OF 1912

POPULAR VOTE		ELECTORAL VOTE
Wilson and Marshall	6,296,547	435
Roosevelt and Johnson	4,118,571	88
Taft and Sherman	3,486,720	8

After the defeat of 1912, Roosevelt realized that there was no hope for the Bull Moose party. "There is only one thing to do," he said, ". . . go back to the Republican party."

WOODROW WILSON AND THE "NEW FREEDOM"

When the Democratic convention met at Baltimore in June 1912, there was discord between a progressive wing, of which Bryan was a member, and delegates representing conservative city political machines. Although disclaiming any desire for a fourth nomination, Bryan was influential in seeing that the Democratic platform was as progressive as that of the Bull Moose party itself. After a protracted struggle, Woodrow Wilson, who had won national fame as a reform governor of New Jersey, was nominated on the 46th ballot, partly through the help of Bryan.

In the ensuing campaign Taft was not active, privately expressing the opinion that Wilson was sure to win. The real battle was between Roosevelt and Wilson. Both men supported progressivism, although under different labels. Wilson countered Roosevelt's New Nationalism with what he called the "New Freedom." Although it was remarked that there was as much distinction between the philosophies of the two candidates as between Tweedledum and Tweedledee, they did in fact differ. The

Both in informal speeches, such as this one under a willow tree in New Jersey, and in more formal addresses, Wilson was able to impress listeners with his sincerity and eloquence. It was said of him that although he could not establish easy communication with individuals, he could be "confidential in a crowd."

New Nationalism was consciously Hamiltonian in outlook. It accepted big business as a fact of life and proposed a more powerful federal government and a strong executive to keep it under control. It proposed to extend federal power in the direction of human welfare. The New Freedom was Jeffersonian in that it advocated use of federal power simply to insure equal opportunities, but not to provide active assistance to individuals.

Roosevelt and Wilson

The personal contrast between the two men was striking. Roosevelt had long been the most prominent political figure in the country. Wilson had been in active politics only three years. Roosevelt, the former Rough Rider, was typed in the popular mind as a fighter, who called on men to enlist in a war on privilege. Wilson, the former professor, appealed to cool reason. Roosevelt enjoyed mixing with all sorts of people. Wilson was aloof; he once confessed that he would as soon slap a man in the face as slap him on the back. Someone likened Roosevelt to a great national spectacle, like Niagara Falls; people jammed the halls where he spoke, but it is not certain that they came so much to listen as to gape. While lacking his rival's personal magnetism, Wilson proved a most effective campaigner. On the platform his tall, angular figure displayed an ease of manner and his homely face exhibited a warmth frequently lacking in personal relations. From his early teens he had dreamed of swaying people to great purposes by the power of eloquence, and even his enemies admitted that once on his feet he could be irresistibly persuasive. He somehow knew how to both touch people's conscience and appeal to their reason.

An attempt to assassinate Roosevelt gave him an opportunity to demonstrate extraordinary courage and self-possession. On his way to give a speech in Milwaukee he was shot in the chest by a no-third-term fanatic. Pausing long enough to make sure that his assailant received police protection, Roosevelt insisted on delivering his speech before receiving medical attention. Not seriously wounded, he was later able to resume his vigorous campaigning.

The result of the election fulfilled Taft's prediction. With the Republican party split, Wilson won a large majority in the electoral college, although gaining only a minority of the popular vote. Roosevelt's popularity and the great demand for reform put him ahead of Taft. Even Debs, the Socialist, polled more than a quarter as many votes as the Republican candidate.

QUESTION • *Would Wilson have been elected if Taft had been his only opponent? If Roosevelt had been the Republican nominee?*

Wilson's Previous Career

Woodrow Wilson had gained national prominence as a foe of privilege and as a person with extraordinary powers of leadership. During eight years as president of Princeton University, he not only raised standards and improved teaching, but also fought social privilege as represented by snobbish undergraduate clubs. As governor of New Jersey he successfully fought the bosses who represented special interests, not the interest of the people as a whole. Under his leadership, the New Jersey legislature enacted an elaborate program of progressive measures.

The extraordinary successes gained by the "scholar in politics" can be explained partly by the fact that from boyhood he had been ambitious to hold high office. Not only had he trained himself in public speaking, but he had also devoted much of his life to studying the techniques of effective political leadership. A longtime admirer of the British government, he developed the theory that the President, like the British prime minister, should take the initiative in guiding and promoting legislation. The President alone, in his opinion, stood for the interests of the whole nation.

In addition to books on government, Wilson had written a history of the United States and innumerable articles, mostly on political topics. He was well informed on domestic issues, especially the tariff. A Southerner who had lived his adult life in the North, a Democrat who admired Hamilton as well as Jefferson, a scholar who knew the past as well as the present, Wilson was able to see public questions in perspective. As befitted the son and grandson of clergymen, he approached public questions with high idealism.

Wilson's inauguration, like that of Jefferson and Jackson, represented a peaceful revolution on behalf of the common people. As the President rose to deliver his inaugural address, the audience broke through fencing which had been set up to keep them away from the rostrum. Wilson forbade the police to drive them back. He said instead, "Let the people come forward."

Wilson's First Inaugural

Wilson's First Inaugural Address was one of the shortest and most eloquent ever delivered. Few previous Presidents had been more a master of English prose, and few who succeeded him were as skillful with our language.

Wilson began by asking the meaning of the Democratic triumph at the polls. His answer was that it was "much more than the mere success of a party. The success of a party means little except when the Nation is using that party for a large and definite purpose." This purpose was clear: it was to do away with the evils which, along with many blessings, industrialism had brought. These evils the President listed as follows: "inexcusable waste" of natural resources, the "human cost" of unrestrained individualism, and the use of government "for private and selfish purposes."

Wilson made clear that he would concentrate on three major reforms: a lower tariff, a new system of banking and credit, and better regulation of business. He also proposed better credit facilities for agriculture, increased conservation, greater protection of the consumer, and social legislation as a matter of "justice, not pity." The President revealed himself as "a progressive with the brakes on" by warning that property and personal rights must be respected. Ridiculing extremists who could take "excursions whither they cannot tell," he said that economic problems would be approached cautiously, "in the spirit of those who question their own wisdom."

Wilson closed by repudiating partisanship and calling on all Americans to join him in bringing about reform:

This is not a day of triumph: it is a day of dedication. Here muster, not the forces of party, but the forces of humanity. . . . I summon all honest men, all patriotic, all forward-looking men to my side. God helping me, I will not fail them, if they will but counsel and sustain me!

Wilson and Congress

The new President entered office under handicaps. He was a minority President, chosen by only 42 per cent of the voters. Without experience in national politics, he had so little acquaintance with party leaders that he had not met some of the members of his cabinet until he came to Washington for the inauguration. The Democratic party was a loose alliance of local interests not expected to work well in harness; long out of office, the Democrats lacked men with experience in government.

On the other hand, Wilson enjoyed certain advantages. The election of 1912 showed that most of the people demanded progressive legislation. If the Democrats did not support the President, warned a Congressman, they would "be turned into the wilderness for forty years more." No prominent Democratic leaders opposed Wilson, as Cannon and Aldrich had thwarted Taft. On the contrary, Wilson enjoyed the loyal support of Bryan, the most influential man in the Democratic party, whom he appointed Secretary of State. Above all, Wilson provided consistent, effective leadership. No President before or after him entered office "with clearer ideas of what he wished to do, and how he proposed to do it." He told his cabinet, "Having been chosen the leader of my party, I feel it my duty to lead."

REFORMS IN TARIFFS, BANKING, AND TRUST BUSTING

The President lost no time in embarking on his reform program. Like Taft, Wilson at once called Congress into special session. Breaking a precedent which had stood since Jefferson's time, he appeared in person before Congress and delivered a special message on the tariff. This dramatic action was an example of Wilson's long-standing belief that the President's greatest power lay in focusing public attention on important issues. This "speech from the throne" made the headlines. As Wilson and his wife drove back to the White House, she remarked that Roosevelt probably wished he had thought of it. "Yes," he replied, "I think I put one over on Teddy."

Wilson's message charged that high tariffs had built up "a set of privileges and exemptions from competition behind which it was easy . . . to organize monopoly." Lower rates, he claimed,

What's Wrong In America?

Wilson's First Inaugural Address, 1913

The shortcomings of industrial America were widely recognized when Woodrow Wilson became President in March 1913, so it was no surprise that his brief and eloquent inaugural address was devoted to domestic reform. Here he details aspects of contemporary America that he wants to see changed:

We have been proud of our industrial achievements, but we have not hitherto stopped thoughtfully to count the human cost, the cost of lives snuffed out, of energies overtaxed and broken, the fearful physical and spiritual cost to the men and women and children on whom the dead weight and burden of it all has fallen pitilessly . . . .

There has been something crude and heartless and unfeeling in our haste to succeed and be great. Our thought has been, "Let every man look out for himself, let every generation look out for itself. . . ."

We have itemized with some degree of particularity the things that ought to be altered and here are some of the chief items: a tariff which cuts us off from our proper part in the commerce of the world, violates the just principles of taxation, and makes the Government a facile instrument in the hands of private interests; a banking and currency system . . . perfectly adapted to concentrating cash and restricting credit; an industrial system which . . . holds capital in leading strings, restricts the liberties and limits the opportunities of labor, and exploits without renewing or conserving the natural resources of the country; a body of agricultural activities never yet . . . afforded the facilities of credit best suited to its practical needs; . . . forests untended, fast disappearing without plan or prospect of renewal, unregarded waste heaps at every mine. . . .

There can be no equality of opportunity, the first essential of justice in the body politic, if men and women and children are not shielded in their lives, their very vitality, from the consequences of great industrial and social processes which they can not control, or singly cope with. Society must see to it that it does not itself crush or weaken or damage its own constitutent parts.

•What specific laws did Wilson propose to deal with the ills he mentions? How far was he successful in persuading Congress to pass them? See pages 518-524.

•How did Wilson's analysis of the troubles of America resemble that of the Populists and how did it differ? See pages 455-459.

•If you were in Wilson's shoes today, what items would you put on a list of "things that ought to be altered?"

would help business by putting business people under "constant necessity to be efficient, economical and enterprising." Opening the American market to foreign products would at the same time open foreign markets to American goods. Wilson warned, however, against undue haste, making clear that he did not favor removing protective duties entirely.

* The Underwood-Simmons Tariff, 1913

The House of Representatives soon passed a bill embodying the President's recommendations. The real fight took place in the Senate, where previous attempts to lower the tariff had foundered (see pp. 453–454, 459, 511), and where the Democrats had only a three-vote majority. Lobbyists swarmed to Washington, and senators were bombarded with letters and telegrams from their home states. Before senatorial opposition had time to crystallize, Wilson made another appeal to the people. In a statement to the press he denounced the "insidious" lobbyists who attempted "to overcome the interests of the public for their private profit." He asked an aroused public opinion to insist that Congress put an end to "this unbearable situation."

The President followed this by personal conferences with Democratic senators and by letters to those who threatened to oppose him. Wilson had once written that the use of patronage to influence Congressmen was "immoral," but he now allowed Bryan and Albert S. Burleson, his Postmaster General, to satisfy congressmen's demands that federal jobs be filled by "deserving Democrats." Office seekers recommended by senators who voted against tariff reduction obviously would not be "deserving." Under such varied pressure from the executive the Senate voted to accept the House bill with little change.

The Underwood-Simmons Tariff was the first substantial lowering of import duties since 1857. It attempted to fix duties at a level where costs of production in the United States and abroad would be equalized. It removed protection entirely from industries no longer needing it. Thus steel ingots and barbed wire were put on the free list, since American steel companies had long competed successfully with foreign producers.

A most important section of the Underwood-Simmons Act was the provision for levying an income tax, now legalized by the Sixteenth Amendment. Rates varied from 1 per cent on incomes over $3,000 to 6 per cent on those over $500,000. Originally introduced merely to make up for losses in revenue caused by lowering the tariff, the income tax became in a very few years the federal government's chief source of revenue.

QUESTION • How do these income tax rates compare with the present pattern?

Weaknesses of the Banking System

While the tariff debate was at its height, Wilson appeared before Congress to introduce the second major item in his reform program: a revision of the banking and currency system designed to provide businessmen with more abundant and more available credit. Like the tariff message, Wilson's speech was so brief and readable that many newspapers published the entire text.

In 1907 a sharp panic had revealed that the American banking and currency system needed overhauling. The collapse of a few business houses and a sudden calling in of loans caused money to "go into hiding" and banks to stop lending. In 1908 Congress set up a National Monetary Commission, headed by conservative Senator Aldrich, to investigate the situation and propose change. After four years of study, the Aldrich Commission reported that the financial organization of the United States was faulty in the following respects:

A short, sharp panic in 1907 caused widespread bank failures and unemployment in the cities. Here workers without jobs stand in line to get bread and soup, which was all that kept them from outright starvation in an age before unemployment insurance or other forms of social security.

(1) *American banking lacked stability in time of crisis.* There were insufficient monetary reserves and insufficient cooperation between banks.

(2) *The currency was inflexible.* The amount of money in circulation was based on the amount of gold and silver in the treasury, plus the bonds held by the national banks. There was no means of increasing or decreasing the supply of money according to the needs of the country.

(3) *There was no over-all, central control of banking practices.* In other modern, industrial-ized countries there were central banks, such as the Bank of England and the Bank of France, which directed banking policy. The United States had had nothing of the sort since Jackson destroyed the second Bank of the United States.

(4) *There was too much concentration of bank capital in New York City.* A dispropor-tionate amount of bank capital was centered in Wall Street. Meanwhile other parts of the country, especially isolated rural districts, often suffered from a lack of adequate banking fa-cilities and credit.

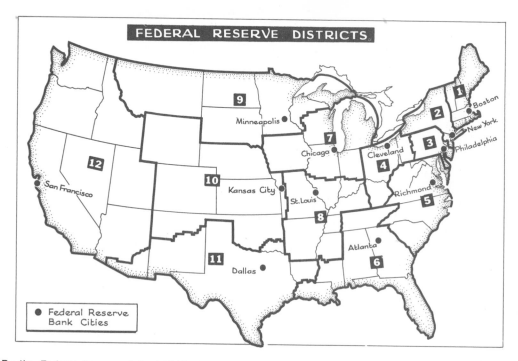

FEDERAL RESERVE DISTRICTS

By the Federal Reserve Act of 1913, the country was divided into twelve districts, each served by a single "bank for bankers". This arrangement made the banking system more responsive to local needs and less dominated by Wall Street. The Federal Reserve system is designed to check deflation and inflation, by so adjusting the rediscount rate that credit is made cheaper or more costly. Another major function of the reserve banks is to expand and contract the amount of currency in circulation. When business people borrow from a bank, the bank rediscounts these notes at the district Federal Reserve Bank, which in turn issues new currency backed by the business people's notes. Similarly, when the notes are paid off, the currency is withdrawn from circulation. By what criteria do you think the twelve districts were chosen?

The Federal Reserve Act, 1913

While there was little doubt about the ills of the banking and currency system, there was dispute about the cure. Wilson himself complained, "There are almost as many judgments as there are men." Bankers favored a great central bank, privately controlled, like the first and second Banks of the United States. Many progressives, especially Bryan, feared that this would make the "money trust" (as they called it) even stronger. They wanted strict federal control of banking and credit. The bankers, in turn, intensely distrusted Bryan as a "wild man." It was Wilson's difficult task to select a plan which would work and at the same time win

support from both bankers and Bryanites. The plan finally developed by several able congressmen, with Wilson's backing, was called the Federal Reserve Act. Under constant pressure from the President, Congress enacted this into law in December 1913. It was one of the most important and useful pieces of legislation in the history of the United States.

The new system provided for twelve Federal Reserve Banks situated throughout the country (see map, above). All national banks were required to join them and other banks might also do so. The Federal Reserve Banks did not deal directly with individuals but instead serviced member banks. These "banks for bankers" concentrated reserves, so that individual banks could be supported in time of temporary difficulty such as a "run." They provided for local needs and made it easier to move funds from one part of the country to another.

Local banks had frequently lacked funds to provide for perfectly sound loans to business people and farmers. Stores and factories had closed, and crops had rotted for lack of funds to pay for harvesting. The Federal Reserve Act greatly improved this situation by providing for a new form of "flexible" currency known as Federal Reserve notes, issued in response to business needs. The new money was put into circulation when local banks needing cash brought business people's promissory notes to Federal Reserve Banks and received Federal Reserve notes in return. For this service the Federal Reserve Banks charged a small fee called a "rediscount."

When a Federal Reserve Bank thus bought promissory notes, it could print and issue more paper money, with those notes as part of the security, or collateral, protecting the value of the currency. When the notes were paid up and the money came back to the Bank, it would retire the currency. The amount of money in circulation was also controlled by raising or lowering the rediscount rate. Raising the rate discouraged banks from lending and "contracted" the currency; lowering the rate encouraged lending and "expanded" the currency. Thus currency and credit in any Federal Reserve district expanded or contracted according to the economic needs of each region.

The Federal Reserve Act provided for a compromise between private and public control. The Federal Reserve Banks themselves were privately owned, and a majority of their directors were elected by the member banks. Over-all control of the Federal Reserve Banks was in the hands, however, of a seven-man Federal Reserve Board appointed by the President. Thus the center of financial power was moved from Wall Street to Washington.

On the whole, the Federal Reserve Act was successful in providing the United States with a banking system responsive to the needs of a great industrial nation. It succeeded in its first great test during World War I when it assisted industry to expand and helped the federal government to finance the war effort.

The Clayton Act, 1914

Less than a month after signing the Federal Reserve Act, Wilson asked Congress to pass a more effective antitrust law than the Sherman Act. Denying any desire to interfere with legitimate business activities, the message proposed various methods of preventing "the indefensible and intolerable" abuses of private monopoly. Late in 1914 Congress passed the Clayton Act which forbade the following practices that destroyed competition or closed the door to new business concerns:

(1) *Ruinous price-cutting,* such as when a large company deliberately sold goods at a loss to drive weaker competitors out of business.

(2) *"Tying" contracts,* whereby a purchaser of goods from a particular company had to agree not to trade with its competitors.

(3) *Inter-corporate investment,* by which a company bought part ownership in a rival concern.

(4) *"Interlocking" directorates between large corporations and banks,* whereby the same people acted as directors in many different companies. (In 1913 a congressional investigation revealed that the eleven partners of the firm of J. Pierpont Morgan held over sixty directorships in banks and business concerns.)

The Clayton Act contained two sections apparently favorable to trade unions. As has been noted, the Sherman Act, by forbidding conspiracies in restraint of trade, had proved more effective against labor unions than against business monopolies. In the Danbury Hatters' case, fought out in the federal courts from 1903 to 1915, a union had been ruined financially by being forced to pay triple damages to a business concern whose product had been boycotted. To discourage such use of antitrust laws the Clayton Act stated that "nothing in the antitrust laws shall be construed to forbid the existence and operation of labor . . . organizations." Ever since Debs had been jailed for contempt in the Pullman strike (see p. 439), labor unions had protested the use of court injunctions forbidding strikes and boycotts. In answer to their protests, the Clayton Act forbade federal courts to issue injunctions against peaceful strikes, picketing, boycotts, or union meetings.

Because of loose wording and unfavorable interpretation by the federal courts the Clayton Act was not effective. Thus the protection of labor unions from suits under the Sherman Act was limited only to unions when pursuing their "legitimate" purposes. It was up to the courts to define "legitimate." And injunctions might still be issued when "necessary to prevent irreparable damage to property or to a property right," which again left a large loophole for conservative judges.

Wilson's Changing Philosophy

With the passage of the Clayton Act the legislative program that Wilson had originally promoted was complete. In accordance with the principles of the New Freedom, he had changed the rules and attempted to see that the rules of competition were made more fair. He had resisted such efforts to go farther as the passage of a federal child labor law or the establishment of federal credit agencies to provide farmers with cheap loans.

But after the passage of the Clayton Act, Wilson approved a law that revealed that he was being pushed toward more active intervention of government in the economy. This was an act establishing a Federal Trade Commission to investigate and regulate business practices. The commission was given power to order companies to "cease and desist" from unfair conduct. Although in practice the activities of the commission were mild, the idea of establishing such a regulatory commission was borrowed from Roosevelt's New Nationalism.

Other legislation revealing a shift toward the more active role for government that Roosevelt had advocated was passed during the latter part of Wilson's first term. Twelve regional Federal Farm Loan Banks were established and endowed with public funds in order to provide loans for agriculture at rates not to exceed 6 per cent. A Federal Highways Act gave federal funds to states for road building; the law, which revealed the growing importance of the automobile, was designed to help farmers get their produce to market. Reversing his earlier stand, Wilson supported the Keating-Owen Child Labor Act that prohibited the employment of children under fourteen in factories producing goods for interstate commerce. The Adamson Act, passed under threat of a nation-wide tie-up in transportation, established an 8-hour day for railroad workers.

Not since Hamilton's financial program in the opening years of the Republic had so much constructive legislation been passed so quickly. Sometimes keeping Congress in session through hot summer months, Wilson had supplied a skillful and dynamic leadership not previously surpassed by any President in time of peace. Chauncey Depew, a noted conservative Republican, said that for a man regarded as a mere theorist, Wilson had accomplished "the most astonishing practical results."

Wilson's achievement as an architect and promoter of progressive legislation was later all but forgotten. It was obscured by adventures in foreign affairs that ended in tragedy for him and for the world.

Activities: Chapter 21

For Mastery and Review

1. Concisely describe the major elements in Roosevelt's Square Deal program.

2. Why did Roosevelt select Taft as his successor? What problems did Taft encounter as President?

3. What did Roosevelt mean by New Nationalism?

4. Why did Roosevelt decide to run for office again in 1912? Why did he not receive the Republican nomination? Who composed the Progressive party?

5. What were Wilson's qualifications for the presidency? Describe his personality. What were the major points of his inaugural address? On entering office, what were his handicaps and advantages?

6. What was Wilson's position on the tariff? By what techniques did he force his views on Congress? What did the Underwood-Simmons Tariff do?

7. What were the faults of American financial organization in 1913? Summarize the structure and operation of the Federal Reserve System. What was done to provide cheaper credit for farmers?

8. What were the purposes and provisions of the Clayton Act? What other legislation of the Wilson administration aided labor and farmers?

9. What shift in Wilson's political philosophy occurred during his first term in the White House?

Who, What, and Why Important?

trust-busting	Progressives
Department of Commerce and Labor	election of 1912
	Underwood-Simmons
Northern Securities	Tariff
Corporation	income tax
coal strike of 1902	National Monetary
Hepburn Act	Commission
Pure Food and Drug	Federal Reserve Act
Law	Clayton Act
Meat Inspection Act	Federal Trade Commission
conservation	sion
election of 1908	Danbury Hatters' Case
Payne-Aldrich Tariff	Federal Highways Act
"Uncle Joe" Cannon	Keating-Owen Act
Mann-Elkins Act	Adamson Act

To Pursue the Matter

1. No President has ever provided the country with such fun as did "Teddy." To find out why this was so read about him in *Our Times*, by Mark Sullivan, a newspaperman who knew Roosevelt well. A few especially recommended chapters are: in vol. II, "A Dude Enters Politics"; in vol. III, "Teddy"; and in vol. IV, "Thru!" *Our Times* also portrays Roosevelt, the master politician in action, as, for instance, when he dealt with the coal operators in the strike of 1902 (vol. II, Chapter 24) or battled for federal meat inspection and pure food laws (vol. II, Chapter 27).

2. Assess Roosevelt's successes and failures in the field of conservation. See Harbaugh, *Power and Responsibility: The Life and Times of Theodore Roosevelt*, Chapter 19.

3. One of the most disputed actions in Roosevelt's career was his bolting the Republican party in 1912. Possible ways of bringing out the drama of his action: (a) A debate on the topic, "*Resolved:* That Theodore Roosevelt stands condemned before the bar of history for wrecking the Republican party"; (b) Turn the class into a mock 1912 Republican Convention, with all members delegates and some playing special roles, such as Roosevelt himself, the presiding officer, Elihu Root, Robert La Follette, and so forth. There is an abundance of material on this convention in biographies of Roosevelt; see Kelly, *Fight for the White House*, and White, *Autobiography*.

4. How did the progressivism of Theodore Roosevelt differ from that of Woodrow Wilson? See the chapters on the two men in Ganley, *The Progressive Movement*.

5. Compare the birth of an unsuccessful crusade with "A Day of Dedication" in Arnof, *A Sense of the Past*, pp. 379–381.

6. What were the causes and circumstances of the Panic of 1907? Would the Federal Reserve System have prevented the panic? Some light is shed on this question in "J. P. Morgan, 'One-Man Federal Reserve,'" in Arnof, *A Sense of the Past*, pp. 384–387.

7. Why were so few laws enacted during Roosevelt's presidency?

Chapter 22

The Progressive Movement

*In this widespread political agitation that at first
seems so incoherent and chaotic, there may be distinguished
upon examination and analysis three tendencies. The first
is found in the insistence by the best men in all political
parties that special, minority, and corrupt influence
in government—national, state, and city—be removed;
the second tendency is found in the demand that the structure
or machinery of government, which has hitherto been
admirably adapted to control by the few, be so changed and
modified that it will be more difficult for the few, and
easier for the many, to control; and, finally, the third
tendency is found in the rapidly growing conviction
that the functions of government at present are
too restricted and that they must be increased and extended
to relieve social and economic distress.*
—BENJAMIN PARKE DE WITT, 1915

The reform legislation passed during the Roosevelt, Taft, and Wilson administrations was a manifestation at the national level of a widespread feeling that many aspects of American society were in crying need of improvement. For all of America's wealth and progress, many thoughtful observers saw much that alarmed them.

CAUSES FOR ALARM

Millions of American laborers were underpaid and overworked. Wages of industrial workers averaged $10 to $12 for a 60-hour week, with recurring periods of unemployment. Women garment workers sometimes received as little as 50 cents for a twelve-hour day. The accident rate in factories and on the railroads was appalling, and there was no provision for compensating the men, women, and children who were injured. According to an estimate made in 1904, 10 million people were "underfed, underclothed, and poorly housed." Systems of relief for the poor were meager and unsystematic.

At the other end of the scale were people rich beyond the dreams of avarice, who thought nothing of asking forty guests to a dinner that cost $250 per plate, people who owned great yachts, baronial palaces, private railroad cars, and summer retreats covering thousands of acres. But it was not so much the wealth of the new plutocrats that was alarming as their power. Not only were the great corporations beyond the reach of government, but they dominated it. At every level—federal, state, and municipal—could be seen what the Kansas editor, William Allen White, called "the alliance between government and business to the benefit of business."

The spectacle of insolent wealth at one extreme and sullen poverty at the other made many people fear revolution. This feeling was dramatized by one of the most widely read poems ever written by an American, "The Man with the Hoe," by Edwin Markham, published in 1899. In describing Jean François Millet's famous painting of a desperately tired peasant resting on his hoe in the fields, Markham uttered a bitter protest against those who brutalized others by exploiting them. By asking two rhetorical questions the poet issued a solemn warning:

O masters, lords and rulers in all lands,
How will the Future reckon with this Man?
How answer his brute question in that hour
When whirlwinds of rebellion shake the world?

SOURCES OF THE PROGRESSIVE MOVEMENT

As if in answer to Markham's warning, much that was wrong with American society was righted by the progressive movement [1] that was at its height during the first fifteen years of the twentieth century. This was misnamed because there was not one movement, but many. Progressivism had so many sources and ran through so many channels that there was hardly an aspect of American life not touched by it. Its leaders included former Populists and Grangers, labor union officials, settlement house workers, crusading authors and editors, prohibitionists, naturalists and foresters, municipal and civil service reformers, and politicians. Some were enlightened businessmen, including two partners of J. Pierpont Morgan. In general, progressivism, like the earlier Jeffersonian and

Jacksonian agitation, was inspired by the basic principle of the Declaration of Independence: the preservation or creation of equal opportunity. The progressives aimed to destroy privilege, by which they were apt to mean the corrupt partnership of private interests and political bosses.

Relation to Populism

Progressivism owed a good deal to the Populist movement; indeed, William Allen White said that the progressives "caught the Populists in swimming and stole all their clothes except the frayed undergarments of free silver." Most of the demands found in the Omaha platform of 1892 (a very liberal one), were enacted into law during the progressive period. But Populism had been an agrarian movement that rather ineffectively sought allies in the cities. The Populists had not asked for active help from government (except in regard to ownership of railroads and telegraph lines) so much as for changes in the rules to give farmers an even break. But now in the cities there was a strong sense that government must play a more active role:

A philosophy that called for "leaving things alone" . . . seemed either unreal or hypocritical in the cities. . . . The wage earner had to look to the government to make sure that the milk bought for his baby was not watered or tubercular; he had to look to government to regulate the construction of tenements so all sunlight was not blocked out. If only God could make a tree, only the government could make a park.

The progressive leadership was different from that of the Populists, in that it was not drawn so much from victims of existing conditions as from people in comfortable circumstances

---

[1] *Note* that "progressive" and "progressive movement" are not capitalized here. "Progressive" with a capital "P" refers to several minor political parties that have taken this label, especially to the Progressive party that nominated Theodore Roosevelt for the presidency in 1912.

who sympathized with the sufferings. of others. This could be seen in the way many Catholic priests, Jewish rabbis, and Protestant ministers preached the new "social gospel": that religious bodies should devote themselves to improving society as well as to ministering to the spiritual needs of their congregations. As was pointed out (see p. 442), men and women of various religious faiths had started settlement houses in city slums. In the progressive period they were pioneers in such activities as slum clearance and agitation for legislation limiting hours of employment and forbidding child labor. The National Council of the Churches of Christ, representing 32 denominations, was founded in 1905 and pledged itself to support a program of social reform. In every large city the Salvation Army, which had been founded in England, provided food, lodging, and hope for the despairing and destitute. How broad was the appeal of the social gospel was shown by the success of *In His Steps*, written by Charles M. Sheldon, a Kansas minister. This novel, which in dramatic terms asks the question, "What would Jesus have done about it?", was published in 1896 and eventually sold over 20 million copies.

QUESTION • Should religious leaders take an active, militant part in reform movements?

Pragmatism

The universities provided another breeding ground for reformers. Many people, both in and out of academic life, were profoundly influenced by the philosophy known as pragmatism, especially connected with the name of William James of Harvard. Pragmatism can perhaps be summarized as follows: "For human purposes, whatever promotes human welfare is true enough." It was in the spirit of pragmatism that those in the social sciences such as economics, sociology, and public law studied human institutions with the idea that they might be improved. Henry B. Adams, head of the famous department of history, politics, and economics at Johns Hopkins University, told his graduate students, "By the instrumentality of scholars great improvement of society is to be made." From Johns Hopkins came such notable men as Woodrow Wilson and Newton D. Baker, a reform mayor of Cleveland, who later served as Wilson's Secretary of War.

An academic figure who attained great influence and high position was Oliver Wendell Holmes, Jr., son of a well-known literary figure and a veteran of the Civil War. Early in his career, while a lecturer at the Harvard Law School, Holmes applied the pragmatic method in a book entitled *The Common Law*. Human law, he claimed, was not a sacred set of principles, never to be changed, but a social instrument that must be adapted to changing needs. When Theodore Roosevelt later appointed him to the Supreme Court, Holmes helped to write his legal views into the Constitution, often by his famous dissenting opinions which were followed by a majority of the justices only after he had retired.

During the progressive era the greatest victory for the view that in deciding a case justices should consult present facts as well as ancient precedents was that of *Muller v. Oregon* (1908), involving an Oregon law limiting the number of hours women might be employed. Previously the Supreme Court had declared similar legislation to be unconstitutional under the Fourteenth Amendment, on the ground that it interfered with workers' "liberty" (see p. 144). Louis D. Brandeis won the case for the state by preparing a brief that produced abundant evidence that long hours had evil effects on women's health. During Wilson's administration, Brandeis joined Holmes on the Supreme Court. The famous phrase "Brandeis and Holmes dissenting" often revealed their differences of opinion with their more conservative colleagues.

The Muckrakers

Victories over "the system," or "invisible government," as progressives called the business-boss alliance, were possible only because an indignant public insisted, and continued to insist, that it was "time for a change." A group of authors whom Roosevelt nicknamed "muckrakers" helped to inspire this indignation and to keep it alive. Although the muckrakers wrote for popular magazines with very wide circulation, they were usually not hack writers, but intelligent men and women profoundly disturbed by the abuses they discovered. In her *History of the Standard Oil Company,* Ida Tarbell described how that company obtained special favors from railroad companies and politici. ns. In *Following the Color Line,* Ray Stannard Baker revealed the patterns of discrimination in both the North and the South. Lincoln Steffens revealed shocking graft in city after city. Steffens decided that the people most responsible for corruption in politics were not the politicians themselves, but those who wanted special favors from government. These favors might be franchises, persuading enforcement officers to "look the other way," or "pull" with judges or police; they all involved the idea of privilege for "insiders."

Some muckrakers were novelists who put their criticisms of existing conditions into fictional form. In *The Octopus,* Frank Norris told how railroads lorded it over wheat farmers in a rich western valley. *Coniston* and *Mr. Crewe's Career* by Winston Churchill (the American novelist) described political corruption in New England. Booth Tarkington's *The Gentleman from Indiana* recounted an honest man's struggle with a political boss and with organized crime.

The pure food and meat inspection laws passed in 1906 during Theodore Roosevelt's

By revealing horribly unsanitary conditions in meat-packing plants Roosevelt raised such a clamor for reform that a reluctant Congress passed a meat inspection law to end the abuses.

administration demonstrated the effectiveness of the muckrakers. Articles in *The Ladies' Home Journal* and *Collier's Weekly* revealed that so-called patent medicines were generally useless and sometimes contained dangerous drugs. The American Medical Association joined the crusade against such preparations, as well as against the adulteration of food by preservative chemicals. Federal regulation was opposed by some senators, who declared it unconstitutional to interfere with the "liberty" of citizens to poison themselves. Nevertheless, a combination of presidential pressure and widespread demand proved irresistible, and the Pure Food and Drug Law was enacted. A similar law was inspired by the best-selling novel *The Jungle,* by Upton Sinclair, which portrayed horribly unsanitary conditions in slaughterhouses. When Roosevelt learned that many of Sinclair's charges were true, he became, as Mark Sullivan has written, "all act." He overwhelmed opposition to federal inspection of meat by threatening to publish the most sensational findings of a committee which had secretly investigated the abuses. Within a short time Congress passed a Meat Inspection Act.

The findings of the muckrakers were borne out by sober investigations. The most famous of these occurred in 1905 when Charles Evans Hughes, a brilliant young lawyer, probed life insurance companies in New York. Hughes revealed that officers and directors of some of the largest insurance companies in the country ran a sort of spoils system, voting themselves huge salaries, appointing members of their own families to well-paid positions, buying securities from firms in which they had an interest, paying a United States senator (who was also a director) $20,000 a year for "legal services," and spending hundreds of thousands of dollars a year to influence state legislators. As a result of this investigation, New York passed laws to control the activities of insurance company officials and to protect the interests of the policyholders. Hughes gained such popularity that he was elected governor of New York and was launched on a distinguished political career.

DIRECT DEMOCRACY

The achievements of progressivism at the national level that were described in the last chapter were less far-reaching than those at the local level. It was more difficult to create nationwide demands for reform than to organize effective campaigns on a smaller scale. The federal government was also difficult to prod into action. The Senate, chosen by boss-dominated state legislatures until 1913, was a highly conservative body. In the House of Representatives the dominating figures such as the committee chairmen and the speaker were usually men highly resistant to change. The Supreme Court was somewhat less conservative than in the 1890's, but it was usually suspicious of the extension of federal power into new areas, as it demonstrated when it declared unconstitu-

tional a federal law providing workmen's compensation for railroad workers in 1908 and a federal child labor law in 1918. Partly because of the attitude of the courts, most of the evils described by the muckrakers—child labor, municipal corruption, and industrial accidents, for instance—were outside the constitutional sphere of the federal government.

At the local level the variety of reform during the progressive period was so extraordinary that we can only indicate its general character. The progressives had an optimistic faith in the intelligence and good will of the people at large. "The cure for the evils of democracy," they said, "is more democracy." A number of arrangements were introduced to reduce the power of political bosses and provide for direct democracy.

(1) **The direct primary.** Progressives claimed that the prevailing system of nominating candidates for office by boss-ridden party conventions allowed voters only to choose between Tweedledum and Tweedledee. The direct primary, first used in Wisconsin, took the nomination of party candidates away from conventions and gave it to the voters in a special election held in advance of the regular election.

(2) **The initiative, referendum, and recall.** The initiative and referendum, which originated in Switzerland, were both designed to give the people a direct voice in legislation. The initiative permitted a certain proportion of the voters, say 15 per cent, to force action on a particular issue. The referendum was a means of submitting political issues to a yes-or-no vote of the people. By the recall, voters gained the right to remove from office an elected official who no longer enjoyed their confidence by holding a special election.

(3) **Corrupt practices laws.** These laws limited the amount of money that candidates and their supporters might spend in elections, and also regulated campaign contributions,

Two suffragists demonstrate before an audience of indifferent males in New York City. The Nineteenth Amendment, passed in 1920, gave all women the right to vote. Theirs' was a hard-won victory.

especially by corporations. Elihu Root, who himself had made a fortune as a Wall Street lawyer, explained the need for such legislation in a speech to a New York State Constitutional Convention:

Great moneyed interests are becoming more and more necessary to the support of political parties, and political parties are every year contracting greater debts to the men who can furnish the money to perform the necessary functions of party warfare ... [we must] prevent ... the great aggregations of wealth from using their corporate funds, directly or indirectly, to send members of the legislature to these halls in order to vote for their protection and the advancement of their interests as against those of the public.

(4) New types of municipal government. In many cities, elective offices were so numerous that the voter could not exercise intelligent choice, nor could he fix responsibility for graft, extravagance, and inefficiency. The structure of municipal government was often so unwieldy that it required a boss to provide unified direction. A flood that nearly wiped out Galveston,

Texas, in 1900 helped to start a new type of city government. In the crisis the citizens of Galveston gave the job of running the city to a commission of five men, elected by the voters at large. This commission plan proved so successful that it was widely copied. From it developed the city-manager plan, whereby an elected city council employs a trained manager to run the government, just as in private industry company directors hire a superintendent to run a factory. The early city managers were often engineers, because much of the business of running a modern city—such as sewage disposal, water supply, and paving streets—was technical in nature. By 1912 over two hundred cities had adopted commission or city-manager plans.

QUESTION • Do more elective offices and more frequent elections mean more real democracy?

(5) Women's suffrage. The progressive movement advanced the cause of women's suffrage. It was difficult to argue that the people should have a wider say in the government and

One reason why women had reason to demand the right to vote was that more of them were taking jobs in offices and factories. Above left, a woman serves as art editor of a magazine. Right, women wrap tins of baked beans.

not count women as people, especially since they were taking more and more jobs in industry, office work, and education, as well as playing a prominent role in reform movements. By 1914 eleven states, all west of the Mississippi, had granted women full suffrage. In the East the suffragettes were successful in publicizing their cause by holding dramatic parades and circulating monster petitions.

(6) **Direct election of senators.** The United States Senate had long been known as a "rich men's club." James Bryce remarked in the 1880's that some men became senators because they were rich, while a few were rich because they were senators. Chosen by state legislatures for six-year terms, the senators could often ignore public opinion. The constitutional arrangement often handicapped local government, because whenever there was a senatorial election coming up, state legislators were apt to be chosen on the basis of which candidate they favored rather than on how they stood on local issues. As early as 1892 the Populists demanded election of senators by direct popular vote. During the progressive period the demand became so great that in 1913 the Seventeenth Amendment to the Constitution provided for direct election of senators (see pp. 146–147).

CONTROL OF PRIVATE ENTERPRISE

As Theodore Roosevelt's career as a "trust-buster" revealed, progressives were resolved to put business under the law and to regulate it for the public welfare. At all levels of government they pushed through legislation toward this end.

Equalization of Taxation

Through their control over lawmaking agencies, great corporations had often been able to evade their share of taxation. Robert La Follette, governor of Wisconsin from 1900 to 1905, found that, in terms of market value of their property, railroads paid the state less than half as much as did other businesses. He forced through laws to tax railroad property on an equal basis, and his example was followed elsewhere. Theodore Roosevelt, when governor of New York, had led a similar movement to tax public service corporations on the value of their franchises. The movement toward more equal taxation reached the federal sphere when in 1909 Congress first taxed corporation profits. In 1895 the Supreme Court in a 5-to-4 decision had declared the income tax unconstitutional, but the Sixteenth Amendment (see p. 146), ratified in 1913, empowered the federal government to levy such a tax.

Regulation of Public Utilities

The progressive period saw the passage of a great deal of state legislation, along the lines of the former Granger laws, to regulate public utilities such as street-car lines and electric-light companies. Many states set up public service commissions with the power to control the rates charged by public utilities and sometimes to regulate the way they were financed. Doubtful of the effectiveness of regulation, some cities bought out private owners and ran public utilities directly; by 1915 all but one of the thirty-six largest cities owned or operated their own waterworks. At the national level, the progressives, as we have seen, urged stricter regulation of trusts, railroads, and banks.

Protection of Consumers

A basic principle of common law that Americans inherited from England was *caveat emptor* (let the buyer beware). This meant that if purchasers bought worthless oil stock, a spavined horse, bread made of sawdust, or patent medicine consisting of coloring matter and water, they had no one but themselves to blame. During the progressive period, a new attitude began to make itself felt. It was argued that consumers

had no means of knowing when food was adulterated, meat prepared under unsanitary conditions, children's soothing syrup dosed with opium, or medicine mislabeled. Such frauds not only injured consumers, but also penalized those who produced honest products and marketed them honestly. Therefore laws were passed at both the federal and local levels to provide for inspection of food, penalize fraudulent producers, forbid the use of certain drugs in patent medicines, and insist on accurate labeling. Still another protection for consumers were city building codes which forbade some of the worst features of the former tenement houses by providing for legal minimums regarding light and air, fire escapes, size of rooms, and sanitation.

Protection of Wage Earners

A grim feature of the advance of industrialism was the employment of children in factories. Although children started to work on farms almost as soon as they could walk, the work itself was often varied and healthful, as well as being part of normal family life. In factories, however, the work was monotonous, the conditions were often unhealthy or dangerous, and the children were under the unfeeling discipline of strangers. Factory children were often denied the opportunity for schooling.

A National Child Labor Committee was formed in 1904 to promote the legal abolition of child labor. A book by John Spargo, *The Cry of the Children,* revealed "conditions which might well shame a civilized people into action." In the textile industry more than one-eighth of the employees were less than sixteen years old, and some children entered cotton factories at the age of seven or eight. In the anthracite industry thousands of "breaker boys" were hired at the age of nine or ten to pick slag out of coal, being paid 60 cents for a ten-hour day. The nature of the work was such that breaker boys acquired permanently bent backs, and often crippled hands as well. Public opinion was so stirred that by 1914 every state but one had fixed a minimum age for employment; most of them had established other controls as well. In 1916 and again in 1919 Congress passed laws seeking to forbid child labor in factories producing goods for interstate commerce, but both were declared unconstitutional by the Supreme Court. Meantime Congress had established the Children's Bureau as a branch of the Department of Labor. The Children's Bureau has little or no power, but by investigation, persuasion, and the publication of excellent pamphlets it has helped immensely to improve the well-being of American children.

Until the twentieth century, the victims of industrial accidents had little or no protection. They often could not afford doctors' bills and could seldom save enough to tide themselves over a period of convalescence without great deprivation. During the late nineteenth century, countries as far removed as Germany and New Zealand had introduced workmen's compensation, also called employers' liability. Such legislation required employers to insure their workers against accidents. If workers were injured, they received medical and hospital care plus compensation for lost wages. In the United States, agitation for workers compensation was so great that forty-two states had provided for it by 1921. Such legislation not only helped workers after they had been injured, but also reduced industrial hazards. Since employers paid lower insurance premiums if they lowered their accident rate, it was to their self-interest to introduce safety devices and to train their laborers to be careful.

Child labor and workers compensation laws were only two of the many types of legislation designed to reduce the hazards and insecurity of employment. Other legislation provided for better factory inspection, for regulation of working conditions for women,

for limiting the hours of labor, and for the abolition of crowded, unsanitary sweatshops. The frontier tradition of self-reliance was so strong, however, that the United States did not go so far in the direction of social security legislation as many European countries which had already passed laws providing for unemployment insurance and old-age pensions.

OTHER REFORM MOVEMENTS

The spirit of reform expressed itself in many other ways. It resulted in playgrounds and dental clinics for children; in the founding of the Boy Scouts, the Campfire Girls, and the Girl Scouts; in juvenile courts and reform schools to care for young delinquents. Americans began to have second thoughts about looting their land, with the result that both the states and the federal government passed laws providing for conservation of natural resources and for great public recreation areas. Private charities multiplied and increased their usefulness. One of the greatest medical feats in history was the successful campaign by the Rockefeller Foundation to eradicate hookworm in the rural districts of the South.

Educational Advances

The early twentieth century was a period of such advance in education that a European observer remarked that "children reign supreme in the United States." In elementary grades the school year was lengthened and the curriculum enriched by the introduction of music, drawing, and manual training. The number of students in high schools doubled; on the average, a new high school building was completed every day in the year. Under the influence of the philosopher John Dewey, a few schools began to abandon a rigid, traditional curriculum and rote learning in favor of studies that related to modern society and methods designed to enlist the natural inquisitiveness and creativity of the individual child. At the college level, Columbia built up a great school of education; Wisconsin was a leader in making universities serve a wider public through extension courses and traveling lecturers; Princeton, under Woodrow Wilson, introduced the "preceptorial system" which supplemented lectures with small informal discussion groups.

In the field of adult education, a picturesque and important development was the growth of "Chautauqua." It started as a summer lyceum by the shores of Chautauqua Lake in western New York. It became so popular that it was copied all over the country, often by traveling tent shows playing one-week stands. Millions of people crowded the circus tents in thousands of small towns to hear a variety of cultural offerings—Shakespearean readings, choruses, orchestras, preachers, lecturers, and politicians. "Chautauqua Week" was a great event to men, women, and children in isolated rural communities. Still another contribution toward alleviating the loneliness of farmers' lives was the institution by the Post Office Department of rural free delivery service. In the days before radio and television it meant much to farm people that at last they could get magazines and daily papers delivered to their door.

Farm Cooperatives

The agricultural prosperity of the early twentieth century was promoted not merely by high agricultural prices, but by various ways in which farmers learned to conduct their business more efficiently. The Granger and Populist movements had taught farmers useful techniques of organization. These were put to direct practical use in the development of producers' cooperatives that undertook functions previously performed by farmers themselves or by people engaged in farming—food processing, storing, transporting, and marketing. In dairying for in-

stance, cooperative creameries pasteurized milk, made butter and cheese, and carried the products to city wholesalers in refrigerator cars. Cooperatives both increased the efficiency of farming and returned to the farmer a larger share of what the consumer paid for his product.

The Advance of Temperance

The temperance movement made great gains during the progressive era. The Woman's Christian Temperance Union and the American Anti-Saloon League, both well-financed by voluntary contributions, carried on unremitting propaganda against the evils of alcohol and of the saloon. The Anti-Saloon League became a force in politics by throwing support to candidates on the basis of their attitude toward prohibition. The position of the opponents of prohibition was weakened by the admitted evils of the saloon and the notorious tie-up between saloonkeepers and corrupt politicians. The temperance forces won so many local victories that by 1914 nearly half the people of the United States lived in "dry" territory. Twelve states had passed statewide prohibition laws and nearly all the rest had provided for local option (see p. 289).

The Socialist Movement

During the progressive period the socialist movement gained strength. In 1912 Eugene V. Debs polled over 900,000 votes. Even at this high point the Socialist party gained less than one-sixteenth of the total ballot. But for several reasons, the socialist movement had an importance greater than its numbers might seem to warrant. Socialist ideas were widely circulated by popular authors such as the Americans Jack London and Upton Sinclair, and the Britishers H. G. Wells and George Bernard Shaw. Although very few of the progressives were socialists, they owed much of their success to the widespread feeling that reforming capitalism was the only alternative to abolishing it.

Eugene V. Debs was again Socialist candidate for the presidency in 1912. The nearly one million votes he received were still only 6 per cent of all votes cast.

Edward Bellamy's novel *Looking Backward* (see p. 445) had made socialism seem an attractive alternative to the existing industrial society, and his influence was reinforced by other writers, of whom the greatest was the Russian novelist and Christian Socialist, Leo Tolstoy. An influential American Christian Socialist was Walter Rauschenbusch, whose widely read book, *Christianity and the Social Crisis* (1907), argued that the Kingdom of God on earth would come only when a socialist society based on love of one's neighbors had taken the place of *laissez-faire* capitalism based on competitive desire for gain.

The organized socialist movement was not based as much on the teachings of the Bible as on the works of Karl Marx. By the twentieth century, Marxian socialists were active in all western countries. They tended to divide into two groups. Some Marxists believed that socialism could be introduced gradually into capitalistic society through piecemeal reforms finally gained through the ballot box. Others thought the only way to cure capitalism was to abolish it.

When the American socialists split at the close of the nineteenth century, the majority joined the moderate faction led by Debs. He argued that in a free country the socialists could abolish capitalism and establish a "cooperative commonwealth" by voting themselves into control of the government. Pending the time when they gained power, the moderate socialists favored many reforms supported by the Populists or progressives, such as a graduated income tax, women's suffrage and public relief for unemployed persons.

QUESTION • *How do you account for the small popularity of socialism in America?*

Radical Socialism

Opposed to the Debs following was a radical group led by Daniel De Leon, a brilliant, intolerant Marxist revolutionary. He preached that gradual, piecemeal reform was worse than useless because it would make capitalism tolerable and workers would never be driven to rebellion. De Leon denounced reformers as sentimentalists, moderate socialists as "traitors to the working class," and Samuel Gompers as a tool of Wall Street. He repudiated existing trade unions as agencies of compromise with capitalists. Instead, he proposed to organize all workers into great industrial unions that would eventually take over the means of production. Yet, paradoxically, he was against violence.

Debs and De Leon briefly cooperated in the founding of a new labor organization, the Industrial Workers of the World in 1905. The IWW repudiated both of them, however, and instead followed leaders who preached "revolutionary activity" in the form of violence and sabotage. The IWW first gained strength in western mining towns and lumber camps, where the frontier tradition of lawlessness still

The shocking conditions of tenements, as shown in the picture at left taken by Jacob Riis in the 1890's, and growing awareness of the ill effects of child labor, as suggested in the picture of the "Breaker Boys," caused many to turn to organized efforts to do away with child labor and slum conditions.

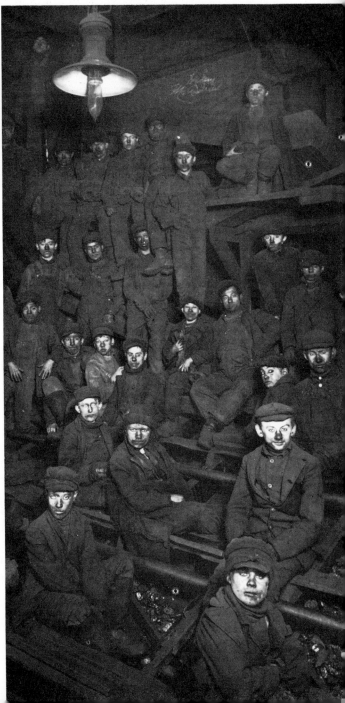

Social Problems that Stirred the American Conscience

The growing awareness of the plight of black people led to the formation of the NAACP in the early 20th century. The NAACP New York office is shown below.

persisted. It went on to attempt to organize those outside the protection of existing labor unions: migrants, immigrants, and unskilled workers. Wherever the IWW appeared, there were strikes, and often violence, which were repaid in kind by deputy sheriffs, company police, and private vigilante groups. Yet although the "Wobblies," as they were called, made headlines and actually won a few strikes, their membership never began to approach that of the non-revolutionary unions. The movement lost ground when its leaders opposed American participation in World War I and disintegrated during the "red scare" that followed the war.

FAILURES OF PROGRESSIVISM

Eventually any wave of popular emotion subsides; so it was with progressivism. Muckraking became a journalistic formula, and the public grew tired of scandals. Many of the democratic reforms did not work out as planned, partly because the advocates of direct democracy had too optimistic a faith in the public's continuing interest in politics. Too frequent elections promoted voter indifference. Sometimes as few as 10 per cent of the eligible voters took part in primary elections. In any case, primary elections were apt to weaken party discipline and responsibility by taking the selection of candidates out of the control of the party organization. The new machinery for centralizing control of municipal government was no insurance against boss rule. After "throwing the rascals out" and setting up a commission or city-manager plan, the citizens of a town often lost interest and let the rascals back into power again. Public ownership of public utilities sometimes proved inefficient, as well as a fruitful source of patronage and graft.

Furthermore, the benefits of progressivism were unequally distributed. The middle class leaders of the movement feared labor unions scarcely less than trusts, and manufacturers organized effectively to prevent unionization, often with the active cooperation of local courts and police. The principal advance of labor during this period was among the minority of skilled workers. The real wages of unskilled workers actually dropped, since it was a period when the prices they paid for commodities increased more rapidly than their rates of pay.

Treatment of the "New Immigrants"

A factor that depressed the wage scale was a great flood of immigrants, averaging a million a year, the majority from southern and eastern Europe. This "new immigration" caused alarm not merely among native laborers, who saw it as a threat to their livelihood, but among those who feared them simply as aliens. The new immigrants were more strange to established American custom than were the "old immigrants" from northern and western Europe, and they had to face discrimination, both by law and by custom. This even reached such ridiculous lengths as the passage of state legislation forbidding the teaching of foreign languages in schools. Pressure from labor union leaders and organizations such as an Immigration Restriction League induced Congress in 1897, 1913, and 1915 to pass laws requiring a literacy test of immigrants. Presidents Cleveland, Taft, and Wilson vetoed all three, always on the ground that illiteracy was a reflection of lack of opportunity rather than lack of ability. Finally, however, such a law was passed over President Wilson's veto in 1917.

QUESTION • Where do immigrants come from today? Are they subjected to similar discrimination?

Frustration for the Black

The most conspicuous failure of progressivism was in regard to the Negro. Since the close of Radical Reconstruction in 1877, the place of the Negro in the South had evolved into a pattern of settled inferiority—in other words, of "white supremacy." This development did not take place at once. During the 1880's, visitors to the South from the North and from Europe were impressed by the way blacks and whites mingled in public facilities such as streetcars, theaters, and soda fountains. A Negro newspaperman, returning from the North to his birthplace in South Carolina in 1885, found less discrimination in traveling and eating arrangements than in New England. The conservative whites, often former planters, who dominated southern politics for a time were quite ready to give Negroes a dignified, although subordinate, place in southern life. In return, the Negroes generally voted for the "quality folk" in elections. But in the decades before and after 1900, there were successful efforts, varying in degree from state to state, to segregate Negroes both by law and by custom and to deprive them of political rights. Segregation extended to "virtually all forms of public transportation, to sports and recreations, to hospitals, orphanages, prisons, and asylums, and ultimately to funeral homes, morgues, and

Jane Addams, Social Reformer

While on vacation in Madrid in the spring of 1888, a frail, small, well-to-do young American woman suddenly hit on a strange plan. Taking her inspiration from Toynbee House, a social settlement house in the East End of London, she decided that she would go to a large city, find a place in the middle of the poorest district, and begin to live as a neighbor and friend to the very poor. By doing this, Jane Addams hoped to find a way to broaden the applications of democracy. She believed that to limit the concept of democracy to the eighteenth-century idea of political equality would not answer the growing needs of late nineteenth-century industrial America.

Returning to the United States, she founded Hull-House, on South Halsted Street in the immigrant section of Chicago. There she blazed a trail of social responsibility to the community. Out of the experiences of Hull-House came the first juvenile court in the United States, the first public playground in Chicago, pensions for mothers, the start of industrial medicine, and the union label. Jane Addams' interests extended far beyond Hull-House to gaining suffrage for women, ending child labor, and establishing collective bargaining in labor disputes. She helped found the National Association for the Advancement of Colored People. From 1914 on, she was prominent in the movement to end war, winning the Nobel Prize for Peace in 1931. Perhaps her greatest achievement was the fact that thousands of women were moved by her example of moral leadership to enter actively into the life of the community. Three years before her death in 1935, she summed up her goals: "To marshal the moral forces capable of breaking what must be broken and building what must be built; to reconstruct our social relationships through a regeneration of the heart; to repair a world shattered by war and sodden self-seeking; to establish moral control over a mass of mechanical achievements."

cemeteries." At the same time, blacks were not only deprived of the franchise by various devices, but were also barred from holding office, sitting on juries, and serving in the police. They were even forbidden to reside or as much as spend the night in some counties in the deep South. The practice of white supremacy was enforced not only by law but by intimidation, which took its most extreme form in lynching and other forms of mob violence.

The subordination of Negroes in the South was accomplished with little protest from the North. Average whites in the North were ready to accede to the southern "solution" for the race problem, partly through indifference, partly because it seemed the price of reunion of the sections, and partly because they were inclined to be affected by the pseudo-Darwinism of the day and to believe that Negroes were racially inferior. While the cruder forms of keeping blacks "in their place" were not practiced in the North, black people were generally restricted to ill-paid occupations and an inferior social status. Their children were often sent to segregated schools, where they often received inferior education.

The Supreme Court reflected prevailing opinion by refusing to hold that segregation by state law was a violation of the Fourteenth Amendment. In the case of *Plessy v. Ferguson* (1896), the court held, with only one judge dissenting, that a Louisiana law that required railroads to provide "separate but equal" railroad accommodations for Negroes was constitutional. The "separate but equal" doctrine was later upheld with regard to schools and other enterprises serving the public.

Founding of the NAACP

These unhappy experiences explain a shift in Negro leadership during the progressive era. At the turn of the century, the most influential black leader was Booker T. Washington, a former slave who had worked his way up from abject poverty and had founded Tuskegee Institute in eastern Alabama in 1881 to train Negroes in agricultural and industrial skills. Washington thought blacks should accept the idea that they could not make the jump to equality with whites at once. They must first undergo a period of subordination while they learned skills, acquired property, and developed habits of thrift and industry. Washington was even willing to accept segregation of Negroes during this tutelage. But as the Negroes' lot not only failed to improve but often got worse, some turned from the counsels of the head of Tuskegee to that of others.

The most prominent new leader was W.E.B. DuBois, a brilliant, highly-educated black born in Massachusetts. He insisted that Washington was doing the Negroes harm by acquiescing in injustice. Instead of training for industrial jobs as "hewers of wood and drawers of water," DuBois proposed to give the ablest Negro children, the "Talented Tenth," the finest possible education so that they might better lead their fellow Negroes from bondage. Where Washington was willing to wait, DuBois wanted immediate action now. He was one of the organizers, along with John Dewey, Jane Addams, and others, of the National Association for the Advancement of Colored People (NAACP), founded in 1909 and dedicated to the proposition that all Negroes should gain the rights guaranteed them by the Constitution of the United States.

The progressive era closed with the entrance of the United States into World War I, and Americans turned from reforming their own society to a fruitless crusade "to make the world safe for democracy." For all its shortcomings, the progressive movement had protected the weak, curbed the strong, enriched people's lives, promoted equality, and averted revolution by restoring faith in the processes of democracy.

Activities: Chapter 22

For Mastery and Review

1. For what reasons did thoughtful men fear a social revolution in the early years of the twentieth century?

2. From what sources did the progressive movement grow? Who furnished the leadership? How was it like Populism? How different? What was the "social gospel"? How do you define pragmatism? How did it affect progressivism?

3. Who were the muckrakers? List seven (include John Spargo) and the area on which each concentrated.

4. Summarize each of the six applications of direct democracy enumerated in this chapter.

5. In what ways did the progressives seek to regulate business for the public welfare? Explain each. How did progressivism affect (a) the use of natural resources, (b) education, and (c) agriculture?

6. Assess the benefits and failures of progressivism.

7. Trace the development of "white supremacy" in the South from 1877 to 1914.

8. What were the bases of socialism in America? Why did it fail?

Who, What, and Why Important?

U.S. Steel Corporation	public utilities
"The Man with the Hoe"	city building codes
progressivism	child labor
William James	workers compensation
Muller v. Oregon	temperance movement
Oliver Wendell	John Dewey
Holmes, Jr.	Chautauqua
muckrakers	Immigration Restriction
Charles Evans Hughes	League
direct democracy	*Plessy v. Ferguson*
initiative, referendum,	NAACP
and recall	William DuBois
corrupt practices laws	Booker T. Washington
city managers	moderate socialism
Sixteenth Amendment	Daniel De Leon
Seventeenth Amendment	IWW

To Pursue the Matter

1. Ganley, *The Progressive Movement*, offers you greater length and depth than this chapter is permitted. Why does Ganley use the term "traditional reform"?

2. Many of the muckraker volumes have been reissued in paperback; many may also be found in public libraries. Weinberg and Weinberg, *The Muckrakers*, is a useful anthology. Individuals might report on the findings of any of the great muckrakers. They might also ask themselves this question: How far, if at all, are conditions better now? If better, why? If not, why not?

3. What elements of direct democracy have survived? Which ones are visible in your community? Are they effective? How do you account for the successes and the failures?

4. Investigate democracy in Switzerland, New Zealand, and Australia, and summarize the democratic practices found there and borrowed by America.

5. Investigate the work of the Rockefeller Foundation in its fight against disease. You might also examine efforts of the Rosenwald Foundation.

6. Were the failures of progressivism due basically to (a) lack of adequate leadership, (b) lack of enough education, (c) human nature, or (d) other causes?

7. Walter Lippmann, one of the nation's leading political commentators, examined the progressive movement in *Drift and Mastery*, published in 1914. An interesting excerpt from that book, entitled "The Muckrakers," may be found in Arnof, *A Sense of the Past*, pp. 364–366.

8. Westin, "The Case of the Prejudiced Doorkeeper," and Woodward, "The Case of the Arkansas Traveler," in Garraty, *Quarrels That Have Shaped the Constitution*, are fast-paced accounts of what was behind the Supreme Court cases that upheld the segregation of Negroes. The lone dissenter, Justice John Marshall Harlan, was a former slaveholder. On what grounds did he base his dissent? What is the position of the Supreme Court today?

PART SIX: SUMMING UP
Chapters 19–22

I. CHECKING THE FACTS

1. *What and When:* Putting Things in Order

Put the events in each group below in chronological order, numbered 1–3.

Related to Cuba:
sinking of the *Maine*
Platt Amendment
Teller Amendment

Related to China:
Open Door Policy
foreign intervention
Boxer Rebellion

Related to Panama:
opening of the Canal
Panamian Revolt
Clayton-Bulwer Treaty

Related to the U.S.:
populism
New Freedom
Square Deal

2. *Judging Sources*

Examine these items from the text related to foreign affairs. Then decide whether each is a *primary* or a *secondary* source.

    a. front page of the New York *Journal,* p. 476
    b. scene of the Battle of Manila Bay, p. 477
    c. picture of the Rough Riders, p. 479
    d. caption under the picture, p. 479
    e. author's description of the *Maine* incident, p. 477
    f. McKinley quote: "I walked the floor . . . ," p. 480

II. INTERPRETING THE FACTS

1. A premise is a statement that is given and accepted. In each of the statements below, a *premise* is followed (after the slash) by a *reason* why the premise is valid. For each statement, decide whether:

    1. The premise is *valid,* and the reason is also *valid;* or
    2. the premise is *valid,* but the reason is *invalid;* or
    3. the premise itself is *invalid.*

    a. Women's suffrage made gains during the progressive period/because of its influence on eastern legislatures.
    b. W.E.B. DuBois opposed Booker T. Washington/because he believed blacks had waited too long for equal rights and opportunities.
    c. Progressive achievements came through federal actions/because of the liberal nature of the Supreme Court.
    d. "New" immigrants had difficulty assimilating/because their cultural backgrounds were so different from what they found in America.
    e. In the U.S. today, "muckraking" does not exist/because major problems have been eliminated.
    f. Socialism still has advocates in the United States/because the goal of individual enterprise has not yet been reached.

2. Examine the illustrations and their captions in this unit, and decide whether each of these descriptions is *probably true* or *probably false*. Tell which picture you used to make your decision.

    a. Newspapers cost a penny apiece.

    b. Queen Liliuokalani of Hawaii was typical of islanders untouched by western ways.

    c. Yellow fever killed more Americans in Cuba than did the Spanish.

    d. Japan's rise to the status of world power was no surprise to the rest of the world.

    e. Theodore Roosevelt enjoyed the complete support of the American press.

    f. Filipinos refused to accept any part of American culture after the U.S. gained control.

    g. The reason blacks did not attain equality during the progressive era was that they did not organize to help themselves.

    h. The one group of Americans that was always protected from harm was the children.

III. APPLYING YOUR KNOWLEDGE

1. Summarize the main ideas of this unit.

    Rule 1: You must use all of the terms below.

    Rule 2: You must not use more than 5 sentences.

• imperialism	• foreign policy	• future
• hostilities	• progressivism	• nation
• annexation	• minorities	• equality
• empire	• reform	• leaders
• responsibilities	• consumer	• America

READINGS FOR PART SIX

Fiction

Allen, H. *San Juan Hill.* The story of a young man who joins TR's Rough Riders.

Norris, F. *The Octopus.* A muckraking novel dealing with railroad companies.

Sinclair, U. *The Jungle.* The novel about Chicago meatpacking that led Theodore Roosevelt to establish the Food and Drug Commission.

Non-fiction

Howe, I. *World of Our Fathers.* The eastern European background, and life in New York City during the later 19th and early 20th centuries for Jewish immigrants.

Pringle, H. F. *Theodore Roosevelt.* An excellent biography of the flamboyant President.

Riis, J. *How the Other Half Lives.* A classic study, with photos, of tenement life in New York City during the late 19th century.

Riordan, W. *Plunkitt of Tammany Hall: A Series of Very Plain Talks on Very Practical Politics.* An amusing yet serious defense of machine politics by its master practitioner.

Steffens, L. *The Autobiography of Lincoln Steffens.* The life and times of a crusading muckraker whose work was widely read.

Crusade
and
Disillusion

PRESIDENT WILSON IN PARIS, 1918.

MOODS

Perhaps there is no more vivid experience in life than the sudden remembrance of things past. What brings this on is hard to say—sometimes a sound, such as a distant train whistle or the song of a bird; sometimes a smell, such as the scent of lilacs or a wood fire. For a moment you remember what it was like to be three years old and reaching up for the hand of a grown-up, or six and getting water up your nose at your first swimming lesson.

In the history of nations, as in the lives of individuals, different periods have characteristic moods. The progressive period of the early twentieth century was one of high purpose. The delegates to the Bull Moose convention in 1912 chanted "Onward Christian Soldiers," and Woodrow Wilson called his inaugural "a day of dedication." The spirit carried on into the World War: America was joining in a crusade to "make the world safe for democracy." And there was the poignant gaiety of the doughboys singing "Over There" as they marched to the ghastly slaughter on the Western Front.

With the coming of the twenties, there was an abrupt change. A new mood of disillusionment was reflected in two war plays, "No More Parades" and "What Price Glory?" The cynics' prophet, magazine editor H. L. Mencken, never tired of ridiculing the great American "booboisie." Crazes came and went: flagpole sitting, marathon dances, Florida real estate, mah-jongg. The United States had emerged from the World War the wealthiest nation on earth, caught up in an ever-rising spiral of prosperity, and "two cars in every garage" was a 1928 campaign slogan. This was the "jazz age," its pursuit of pleasure evoked by its popular songs "Fascinating Rhythm," "I Want to Be Happy," "Ain't We Got Fun."

But the mood changed again, from "Just Around the Corner" (there's a rainbow in the sky) to "Brother Can You Spare a Dime?" With the Great Depression, the light-heartedness of the twenties shifted to something the country as a whole had never experienced before—bleak fear and despair. Thousands of people stood in lines for a bowl of soup and a crust of bread—while farmers were burning unsalable surpluses of wheat and corn. Self-respecting persons, with no jobs and savings gone, sold apples on street corners. Life had a nightmarish quality—as though the country were under a spell, or had been attacked by Invisible Martians.

And then there was "Happy Days Are Here Again," the Democratic campaign song in 1932. It conjures up one of the most loved and most hated figures in American political history, Franklin D. Roosevelt, with his New Deal and his "firm belief that the only thing we have to fear is fear itself."

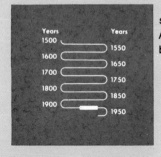

Years
1500
1600
1700
1800
1900

Years
1550
1650
1750
1850
1950

Chapter 23

The First World War

Governments and individuals conformed to the rhythm of the tragedy, swayed and staggered forward in helpless violence, slaughtering and squandering on ever-increasing scales, till injuries were wrought to the structure of human society which a century will not efface, and which may conceivably prove fatal to the present civilization.
—WINSTON CHURCHILL

As Wilson's First Inaugural Address showed, his attention on taking office was focused entirely on domestic issues. About such matters as the tariff and banking he was well informed; he also had the assistance of experts such as Senator Carter Glass of Virginia, principal author of the Federal Reserve Act. In foreign affairs, however, he was personally less well equipped, and he had few experienced advisers. William Jennings Bryan, his Secretary of State, had no training in diplomacy. The permanent staff of the State Department was composed largely of Republican appointees whom Wilson suspected, with some reason, of lack of sympathy for his policies. The top diplomatic posts were filled, as usual, with political appointees; Bryan also appointed scores of untrained "deserving Democrats" to lesser posts.

WILSON'S FOREIGN POLICY

On the day he took office Wilson remarked to a friend that it would be the irony of fate if his administration had to deal much with foreign affairs. As it turned out, he was soon confronted with difficult and complex foreign problems that involved the fate of the whole world.

"A New Note in International Affairs"

Whatever his handicaps, Wilson was resolved, as one of his biographers has written, to "strike a new note in international affairs" and to see that "sheer honesty and even unselfishness . . . should prevail over nationalistic self-seeking in American foreign policy." Both he and Bryan were opposed to imperialism, to the Big Stick, and to war. They believed that the United States should exert leadership in the world by the force of moral example.

Wilson repudiated dollar diplomacy during his first fortnight in office. During the Taft administration, a group of American bankers had been urged to join those of other countries in making a loan to the new Chinese republic. To insure repayment it was proposed that the finances of the Chinese government be put under the supervision of foreign "advisers." In March 1913, representatives of the American bankers came to Washington and asked whether the government would give them support. Wilson refused on the ground that such interference with Chinese sovereignty was "obnoxious to the principles upon which the government of our people rests."

Bryan's principal activity as Secretary of State was the negotiation of "cooling-off" treaties between the United States and more than a score of foreign nations. Countries signing these agreed not to go to war for a year after a matter of dispute was referred to a fact-finding commission. There was no requirement that the findings of the commission be accepted; the idea was simply to give time for war fever to subside.

In a dispute with Great Britain over tolls on ships using the Panama Canal, Wilson revealed his determination that the United States should scrupulously observe its international obligations. As the Canal approached completion, Congress passed a law in 1912 exempting United States coastwise shipping from tolls. Great Britain protested that this was a violation of the Hay-Pauncefote Treaty which guaranteed equal rates for ships of all nations. In 1914 Wilson appeared before Congress and in a very short message urged that exemption for American ships be repealed. His principal argument was that out of self-respect the United States should act in such a way as to "deserve our reputation for generosity and for the redemption of every obligation without quibble or hesitation." Congress followed Wilson's advice, even though his opponents accused him of "cringing before the British throne."

"Moral Imperialism" in Mexico

On entering the White House, Wilson faced a diplomatic crisis in regard to Mexico. In 1911 the Mexicans overthrew Profirio Díaz, a dictator who had repressed his people for thirty years, while granting to foreign investors the right to exploit his country's rich mineral resources. Díaz was succeeded by Francisco Madero, an idealist sincerely devoted to the interests of the people of Mexico. But shortly before Wilson's inauguration Victoriano Huerta, a "strong man," seized power, and the deposed Madero was murdered, presumably on Huerta's orders. Now the question was: should the United States recognize

a murderous usurper as lawful ruler of Mexico? It had generally been our policy to recognize any established government without passing judgment on how it gained power. American capitalists, who had invested a billion dollars in Mexico, favored Huerta because, like Díaz, he would keep order. Other nations with large Mexican investments, notably Great Britain, lost little time in recognizing the new ruler.

In devising a Mexican policy, Wilson again repudiated dollar diplomacy. He intended to favor "the submerged eighty-five per cent" of the Mexican people, "struggling toward liberty," over the privileges of foreign investors. Convinced that without support by the United States "the unspeakable Huerta" would be overthrown, Wilson refused him recognition and attempted to prevent him from obtaining arms. The President called this line of action "watchful waiting."

This policy ran into all sorts of difficulties. Mexico had plunged into civil war. Scores of American lives were lost in the resulting disorder, and millions of dollars' worth of American property was destroyed. Wilson's policy was distrusted in Latin America as an unwarranted interference in Mexican affairs. In April 1914, United States naval forces, attempting to enforce the arms embargo, clashed with Mexican troops and seized the city of Vera Cruz. War seemed imminent.

At this point Wilson made a gesture that temporarily lessened Latin-American distrust of the "Colossus of the North." Resisting clamor for war, the President accepted an offer from the ABC Powers (Argentina, Brazil, and Chile) to mediate the dispute between the United States and Mexico. At a conference at Niagara Falls, the ABC Powers supported Wilson in advising that Huerta must go. He soon went into exile, and Venustiano Carranza, the candidate favored by the United States, was recognized as lawful ruler.

A meeting between Pancho Villa (center) and General Pershing (right) at a time when it appeared that Villa had no ill will toward the United States. Later he raided the United States and Pershing chased him fruitlessly in Mexico.

Mexico's troubles were still not over. Peasant armies under the guerrilla leaders Emiliano Zapata and Pancho Villa ravaged large areas; robbery and banditry were commonplace. In 1916 Villa raided the United States, murdering innocent citizens in Columbus, New Mexico. Immediately Wilson sent 6,000 United States troops under General John J. Pershing across the border in pursuit. The expedition not only failed to catch the Mexican chieftain, but was resented by Mexicans of all parties. War threatened again, but fortunately, neither Carranza nor Wilson wanted it. Eventually the American troops were withdrawn, and Mexico was left to her own devices. Although Wilson's Mexican policy was well intentioned, it won the United States no friends. The English ridiculed his attempt to "shoot the Mexicans into self-government." Latin Americans regarded his "moral imperialism" with no more favor than the Big Stick diplomacy of Theodore Roosevelt.

Although Bryan and Wilson were opposed in principle to dollar diplomacy, their Latin-American policy, outside of Mexico, differed little from that of the previous Republican administrations. Following the example set by Roosevelt, the United States exercised an "international police power" in the Caribbean.

United States marines were sent to preserve order and set up stable government in Nicaragua, Haiti, and the Dominican Republic. In 1917 the United States expanded its naval control over the Caribbean area by purchasing Denmark's strategically valuable Virgin Islands.

OUTBREAK OF WAR IN EUROPE

By 1914 there had not been a general European war for nearly a century and none between major powers since 1870. Many people thought that Western nations had abandoned war, save for skirmishes between whites and "natives" on the fringes of empire. Yet suddenly, between July 28 and August 4, 1914, Europe plunged into one of the bloodiest and most costly struggles in all its long history.

How did this appalling event occur? We cannot answer with certainty. It is generally agreed, however, that two basic forces bringing about the First World War were *nationalism* and *imperialism*. The basic morality in nationalism was "my country right or wrong." There was no higher political authority than the nation; there was no higher object of earthly devotion. A nation had to be prepared to defend both its territory and its "honor." In the late

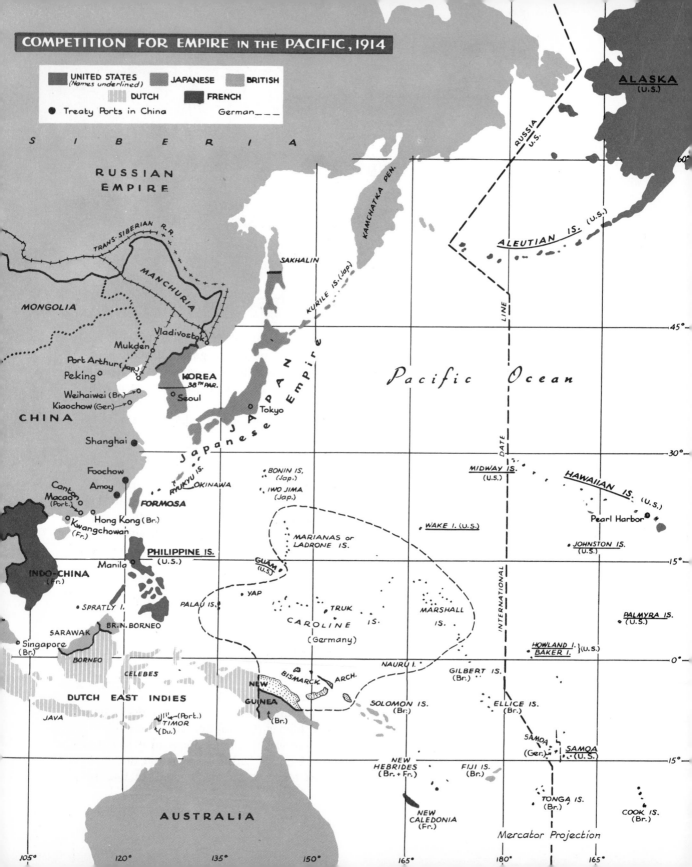

COMPETITION FOR EMPIRE IN THE PACIFIC, 1914

UNITED STATES (Names underlined) JAPANESE BRITISH
DUTCH FRENCH
● Treaty Ports in China   German _ _ _ _

S I B E R I A

RUSSIAN EMPIRE

MONGOLIA

TRANS-SIBERIAN R.R.

MANCHURIA

Vladivostok
Mukden
Port Arthur (Jap.)
Peking
Weihaiwei (Br.)
Kiaochow (Ger.)

CHINA

Shanghai

Foochow
Amoy
Canton
Macao (Port.)
Kwangchowan (Fr.)
Hong Kong (Br.)

INDO-CHINA (Fr.)

Manila

SPRATLY I.

SARAWAK
BR. N. BORNEO

Singapore (Br.)

BORNEO

DUTCH EAST INDIES

CELEBES

JAVA

TIMOR (Port.)
(Du.)

AUSTRALIA

KAMCHATKA PEN.

SAKHALIN

KURILE IS. (Jap.)

KOREA
38TH PAR.
Seoul

J A P A N
Tokyo

Japanese Empire

RYUKYU IS.
OKINAWA
FORMOSA

PHILIPPINE IS. (U.S.)

PALAU IS.

YAP

BONIN IS. (Jap.)

IWO JIMA (Jap.)

MARIANAS or LADRONE IS.

GUAM (U.S.)

TRUK

CAROLINE IS. (Germany)

NEW GUINEA (Br.)

BISMARCK ARCH.

NAURU I.

SOLOMON IS. (Br.)

NEW HEBRIDES (Br. + Fr.)

NEW CALEDONIA (Fr.)

RUSSIA
U.S.

ALASKA (U.S.)

ALEUTIAN IS. (U.S.)

Pacific Ocean

DATE LINE

INTERNATIONAL

MIDWAY IS. (U.S.)

HAWAIIAN IS. (U.S.)

Pearl Harbor

WAKE I. (U.S.)

JOHNSTON IS. (U.S.)

MARSHALL IS.

PALMYRA IS. (U.S.)

HOWLAND I.
BAKER I. } (U.S.)

GILBERT IS. (Br.)

ELLICE IS. (Br.)

SAMOA (Ger.)
SAMOA (U.S.)

FIJI IS. (Br.)

TONGA IS. (Br.)

COOK IS. (Br.)

Mercator Projection

60°
45°
30°
15°
0°
15°

105°   120°   135°   150°   165°   180°   165°

nineteenth century the major European countries also felt impelled to express their national virility by joining the "scramble for empire." (See p. 550.) They rapidly extended their power into less developed areas, especially Asia and Africa. Out of this process developed bitter international rivalries. Thus, for many years Great Britain attempted to "contain" Russian aggression along a great arc extending from Turkey through Persia, Afghanistan, Tibet, and northern China. During the same period, the expansion of the French empire in Africa brought risk of war with Italy over Tunis, with Great Britain over the Sudan, and with Germany over Morocco.

Added to the tension over these imperial rivalries was the long-standing French desire for *revanche* (revenge) against Germany for the defeat suffered in the Franco-Prussian War of 1870. There was also a complicated situation in the Balkan peninsula, the "tinderbox of Europe," where newborn nations such as Serbia and Bulgaria clashed with each other and with the decaying Ottoman and Austrian empires.

Although the foregoing rivalries failed to produce a major European war between 1870 and 1914, they created great fear. And fear produced a great armament race, as each country strove to increase its powers of "self-defense." The armament race in turn produced not only more fear, but a situation in which the military leaders, who thought in terms of how best to fight a war, tended to take over from the diplomats, who generally hoped to prevent it.

Perhaps the principal reason why the First World War came when it did, as well as why it came so suddenly, was a system of rival alliances. The Triple Alliance, created by the German statesman Otto von Bismarck, drew together Germany, Austria-Hungary, and Italy. France became alarmed at her diplomatic isolation. The British feared growing German competition for trade, colonies, and naval supremacy. Therefore, France and Britain arranged a partnership known as the Entente Cordiale (cordial understanding). The defeat of Russia in the Russo-Japanese War removed most of Britain's fear of Russian rivalry. Gradually there emerged the Triple Entente that grew into an alliance between France, Russia, and Great Britain. The great powers attracted smaller countries as "satellites." Thus, Germany and Austria had Bulgaria and Turkey on their side, while Serbia was tied to Russia.

The danger of this situation was that in any international dispute, no matter how trivial, opposing governments might call on allies for support and bring on a general war. This happened in 1914. When a fanatical Serb patriot assassinated Austrian Archduke Ferdinand at Sarajevo, Austria demanded reparation from Serbia and was backed by her ally Germany. Serbia was backed by Russia, and Russia by France. The British government was too closely tied to France and Russia to be effective in its efforts for peace. Quickly the military leaders took over from the diplomats, and each army strove to strike first. As Austrian troops invaded Serbia, German armies advanced on Paris through defenseless Belgium, and the "Russian steamroller" headed slowly for Berlin. Great Britain at once joined France and Russia. In 1915 Italy joined the Allies (France, Russia, Great Britain) against the Central Powers (Germany, Austria, Turkey).

NEUTRALITY

As Europe plunged into the abyss, Americans rejoiced in their traditional isolation and in the protection of the Atlantic Ocean. President Wilson said that this was "a war with which we had nothing to do." Besides issuing the customary Neutrality Proclamation, he warned Americans to be "impartial in thought as well as in action." But people inevitably took sides. Many of the eight million Americans of German descent supported their former fatherland. Many Irish-Americans, motivated by traditional hatred for Britain, also favored the Central Powers. In general, however, American opinion was on the side of the Allies. This stemmed partly from a sense of common heritage with Great Britain. There was also strong sentiment for France, reflected in the lines:

> Forget us, Lord, if we forget
> The sacred sword of Lafayette.

Even stronger than sentiment for either Britain or France was that *against* Germany. This feeling had been stimulated by various incidents, by the sabre-rattling statements of Kaiser William II, and by a movement known as Pan-Germanism. The Pan-Germans preached that the Germans were to dominate the world; they glorified war. The vague anti-German sentiment that existed in America even before the war was crystallized by Germany's unprovoked invasion of Belgium in August 1914, and by the harsh treatment of the Belgians after that event.

Partiality for the Allies was strengthened by propaganda. Both sides used it, but German propaganda was clumsy and unconvincing, while that of the British was extremely skillful, especially in accusing the Germans of wholesale atrocities in Belgium.

Violations of American Neutral Rights

In the early years of World War I, as in the period before the War of 1812, the United States had the largest share of neutral trade and suffered serious violations of its neutral rights. The British were the first to break established international law as they clamped a tight blockade on the Central Powers. They planted mines in the North Sea, forced American ships into English ports for inspection, limited trade with neutral countries such as Denmark, opened American mail, and put food on the list of contraband materials not to be exported to Germany. The British blockade was so effective that trade between the United States and the Central Powers shrank to less than 1 per cent of its prewar level. Meanwhile exports to the Allies nearly quadrupled. For their very survival the Allies needed American war materials and food. The prosperity of the United States in turn came to depend on war orders. The economic tie with the Allies became even closer when American citizens bought over two billion dollars' worth of French and British bonds.

Serious as British violations of American neutral rights were, they were less maddening than those of Germany. To meet the challenge of the British blockade and to starve Britain into submission, the Germans relied on a new weapon, the ocean-going submarine. The so-called "U-boats" were deadly when they attacked without warning, but they broke long-established rules of warfare which provided that unarmed ships should not be sunk without providing for the safety of passengers and crews. In the years 1914–1917, approximately 200 Americans lost their lives on Allied ships torpedoed by U-boats.

"Waging Neutrality"

In meeting violations of our neutral rights, Wilson took much the same position as had Jefferson during the Napoleonic wars. Like Jefferson, he detested war, yet was not a pacifist. He attempted both to avoid hostilities and to "wage neutrality" by insisting on American rights. During the early months of the war, most of his protests were directed against England. These were not particularly effective, partly because Walter H. Page, the American ambassador in London, was strongly pro-British, as were some of Wilson's closest advisers, and partly because submarine warfare soon created tension with Germany.

Although American lives were lost when the British liner *Lusitania* was sunk by the Germans, some Americans insisted that "Real Patriots Keep Cool." Wilson himself said that the United States was "too proud to fight," a statement for which he was ridiculed.

The first difficulties over U-boats occurred in February 1915, when the German government announced that ships approaching Britain and France might be torpedoed without warning. Immediately, Wilson said he would hold Germany to "strict accountability" for loss of American lives or property. The full horror of unrestricted submarine warfare was brought home in May 1915, when the British liner *Lusitania* was torpedoed off the coast of Ireland. The Americans who were drowned numbered 128: 37 women, 70 men, and 21 children. Many along the eastern seaboard, including Theodore Roosevelt, thought that America should go to war, or at least break off relations with Germany. But many others thought that Americans taking passage on ships of nations at war did so at their own risk. Wilson steered a middle course. He refused to take extreme measures against Germany and incurred ridicule by saying that the United States was "too proud to fight." On the other hand, he sent note after note insisting that the German government safeguard the lives of non-combatants in the war zones. During the *Lusitania* crisis, Bryan resigned as Secretary of State, because he thought Wilson's firm insist-

ence on neutral rights would lead to war. Bryan's point of view was so widely shared that early in 1916 Congress was on the point of forbidding Americans to travel on the ships of belligerent nations. Wilson managed to prevent this move, arguing that if we gave up any rights, "many other humiliations would certainly follow."

Late in March 1916, Wilson's policy was severely tested when a U-boat torpedoed the French passenger ship *Sussex,* with resulting injury to several Americans. Although his closest advisers favored breaking off relations with Germany at once, Wilson chose to issue one last warning. He demanded that the German government immediately promise to abandon its methods of U-boat warfare or risk war with the United States. At this time Germany hoped for a great victory at Verdun that would defeat France in a few months; on the eastern front German arms were already close to victory. Germany therefore gave in to Wilson's demands, promising, with certain conditions, to sink no more merchant ships without warning, and offering compensation to Americans injured on the *Sussex.* This *Sussex* pledge enabled a Democratic senator to boast that Wilson had "wrung from the most militant spirit that ever brooded over battlefield an acknowledgment of American rights and agreement to American demands."

The Election of 1916

As the presidential election of 1916 approached, there were strenuous efforts to reunite the Republican party. Roosevelt was not happy in the Progressive party. It included too many impractical reformers of the type he had nicknamed the "lunatic fringe"; it had even less chance of winning in 1916 than four years earlier. Roosevelt hoped that the Republicans might heal the feud of 1912 by nominating him; instead they chose Charles Evans Hughes, who resigned from the Supreme Court to run. Roosevelt nevertheless refused to run as a Progressive, thus killing the party he had founded. The question still remained whether those who had voted for the Progressive ticket in 1912 would return to the Republican fold or whether they would vote for Wilson.

The Democrats enthusiastically renominated Wilson. In the ensuing campaign they pointed with pride to their candidate's extraordinary suc-

Compare this map to that of the Bryan-McKinley presidential race of 1896 (see page 461). What was similar and what was different in the two elections? Why did Bryan lose and Wilson win?

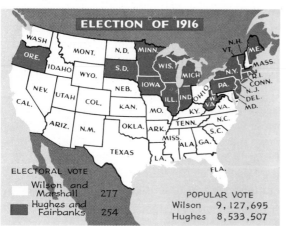

ELECTION OF 1916

ELECTORAL VOTE

Wilson and Marshall   277

Hughes and Fairbanks   254

POPULAR VOTE
Wilson   9,127,695
Hughes   8,533,507

cess as a legislative leader; they also coined the effective slogan, "He kept us out of war." On domestic policy the Republicans were divided between the Old Guard, who opposed reform, and former Progressives, who favored it. In foreign affairs the Republicans "played both ends against the middle": some denounced Wilson for being too easy on Germany, while others rebuked him for being too friendly with Britain.

The election was one of the closest in history. On the night of election day even the Democratic *New York Times* conceded a Republican victory. But later it became apparent that Wilson had performed a political miracle by gaining a majority in the electoral college without the support of the three most populous states, New York, Pennsylvania, and Illinois. The Republicans could have won by carrying California, but lack of cooperation between Old Guard and Progressive Republicans lost Hughes the majority by a small margin. Wilson swept rural America even more completely than Bryan had in 1896, and by adding the vote of just one important industrial state, Ohio, he was able to gain re-election.

AMERICA ENTERS THE WAR

During the 1916 election campaign Wilson never personally claimed that he could guarantee to keep the United States neutral. By repeatedly holding Germany to "strict accountability" for the loss of American lives caused by submarines, he left himself small margin of choice should the German government decide to resume unrestricted submarine warfare. "Any little German lieutenant," he told his Secretary of the Navy, "can put us into war at any time by some calculated outrage." The only sure way to keep America out of the war was to end it. As head of the only great power still at peace, Wilson felt it his responsibility to bring the warring nations together. On December 18, 1916, he asked them to state their peace terms.

Los Angeles Examiner

CHARACTER QUALITY · ENTERPRISE ACCURACY

AN AMERICAN PAPER FOR THE AMERICAN PEOPLE · THE GREAT NEWSPAPER OF THE GREAT SOUTHWEST

VOL. XIV—NO. 113 · Official Forecast—Cloudy · TUESDAY · LOS ANGELES, APRIL 3, 1917 · PRICE TWO CENTS · TELEPHONES—MAIN 8300, HOME 10195

WAR! SAYS WILSON; BIG ARMY WANTED

FIRST OF U.S. ARMED SHIPS IS 'U' VICTIM

LATEST EARLY MORNING NEWS

(By International News Service)
PASSAIC, N. J., April 2.—A Jewish volunteer regiment of 1000 members is being recruited here. They are preparing to offer their services to the President at the first call for volunteers.

* * *

(By International News Service)
PANAMA CITY, April 2.—Officials here have received a report of a German mobilization at Tampico on the east coast of Mexico.

* * *

500,000 MEN NEEDED AT ONCE; AID TO ALLIES WITHOUT LIMIT

President Calls on Congress to Throw All Nation's Resources Against German Autocracy

(BY INTERNATIONAL NEWS SERVICE)
WASHINGTON, April 2.—The address of the President follows:

"Gentlemen of the Congress:

"I have called the Congress into extraordinary session because there are serious, very serious choices of policy to be

Here Is American Congress War Declaration Resolution

(BY ASSOCIATED PRESS)
WASHINGTON, April 2.—Immediately after the President left the Capitol, the Senate and House reconvened and an identic joint resolution was introduced in both Houses declaring the existence of a state of war. The resolution follows:

"Joint resolution declaring that a state of war exists between the Imperial German Government

CONGRESS RALLIES TO STIRRING PLEA OF NATION'S CHIEF

Amid Scenes of Wild Enthusiasm

An effective Democratic slogan in the Wilson-Hughes presidential race of 1916 had been, "He kept us out of war." Yet only five months after election day, here was Wilson calling for war on Germany "amid scenes of wild enthusiasm." What had happened in the meantime?

Both sides answered with demands that their opponents would accept only if completely defeated. After receiving these replies, Wilson gave a notable speech to the Senate on January 22, 1917, arguing for "peace without victory." A victor's peace, he said, "would leave a sting, a resentment, a bitter memory upon which terms of peace would rest only as upon quicksand. Only a peace between equals can last."

German Declaration of Unrestricted Submarine Warfare

The Germans soon destroyed Wilson's hope of acting as mediator. During the previous year, German armies had failed to win victory at Verdun, and had later suffered heavy losses in the four-month battle of the Somme. Time was running out, as the British blockade began to cause severe shortages, even starvation. To answer this, the submarine fleet was increased. The leaders of the German navy promised to starve England into submission in five months if U-boats were allowed to sink on sight. Even

if this violation of the Sussex pledge drew America into the war, it was assumed that the United States could not raise an army and transport it to Europe before the Allies collapsed. Therefore, on January 31, 1917, the German government announced that vessels in waters near Great Britain, France, and Italy might be sunk without warning.

Wilson now felt he had no choice; on February 3, 1917, he broke off diplomatic relations with Germany. When goods piled up in Atlantic ports because ships feared to sail, he asked Congress for power to arm American merchant ships. This measure passed the House by 403 votes to 13, but was blocked in the Senate by a filibuster of twelve senators. The President refused to be bound by the effort of "a little group of wilful men" to make "the great government of the United States helpless and contemptible." Acting under a law of 1797, he armed merchant ships with guns manned by navy crews ordered to shoot submarines on sight.

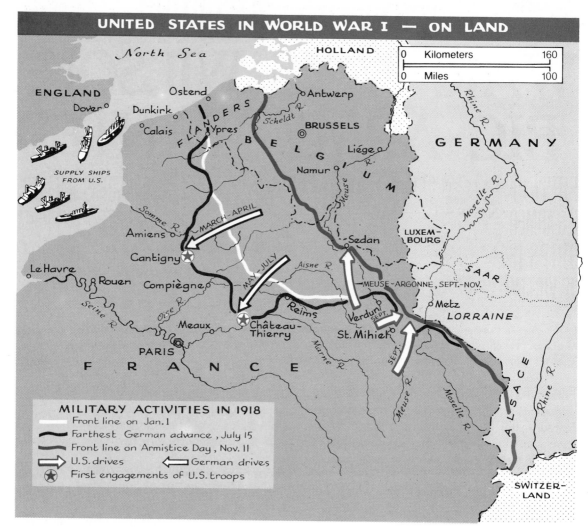

UNITED STATES IN WORLD WAR I — ON LAND

North Sea

HOLLAND

| 0 | Kilometers | 160 |
| 0 | Miles | 100 |

ENGLAND

Dover

Ostend

Antwerp

Dunkirk

FLANDERS

Calais

Ypres

Scheldt R.

BRUSSELS

B E L G I U M

Liége

Namur

Meuse R.

GERMANY

Rhine R.

Moselle R.

SUPPLY SHIPS
FROM U.S.

Somme R.

MARCH–APRIL

Amiens

Cantigny

LUXEM-
BOURG

Sedan

SAAR

Le Havre

Rouen

Compiègne

Aisne R.

MAY–JULY

Reims

MEUSE–ARGONNE, SEPT.–NOV.

Metz

LORRAINE

Seine R.

Oise R.

Meaux

Château-
Thierry

Marne R.

Verdun
SEPT.

St. Mihiel

SEPT.

Meuse R.

Moselle R.

PARIS

F R A N C E

ALSACE

Rhine R.

SWITZER-
LAND

MILITARY ACTIVITIES IN 1918

— Front line on Jan. 1
— Farthest German advance, July 15
— Front line on Armistice Day, Nov. 11
⟹ U.S. drives   ⟸ German drives
★ First engagements of U.S. troops

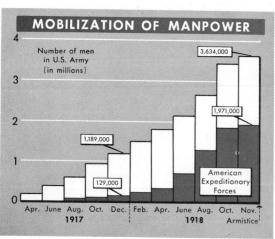

MOBILIZATION OF MANPOWER

Number of men
in U.S. Army
(in millions)

3,634,000

1,971,000

1,189,000

129,000

American
Expeditionary
Forces

| Apr. | June | Aug. | Oct. | Dec. | Feb. | Apr. | June | Aug. | Oct. | Nov. |
1917   **1918**   Armistice

The United States army under General Pershing played a minor role in stopping the German drives of 1918, but went fully into action only in the last months of the war. The very existence, however, of two million fresh American troops in France, and more to come, helped to kill the German will to continue hostilities. Neither the Germans nor the Allies had expected that the United States could create an army so rapidly or that it would fight so well.

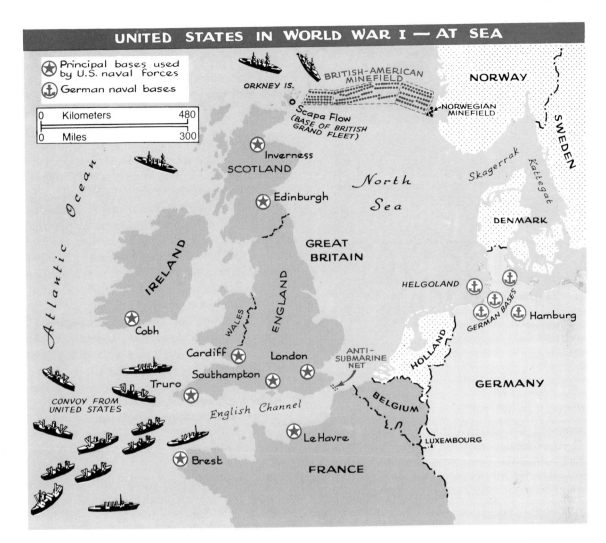

When the Germans declared unrestricted submarine warfare in January 1917, they knew that they might goad the United States into war. But they expected that the U-boats could prevent American supplies and troops from reaching Europe. So effective, however, were anti-submarine measures that not a single troopship was lost on the way to Europe. In addition to the activities shown on these pages, about 14,000 American troops were sent to Russia in 1918-1919.

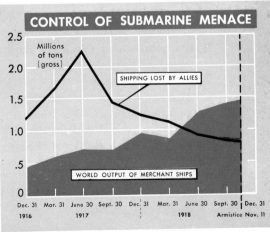

557

Anti-German feeling in World War I, whipped up by propaganda agencies, went to such ridiculous lengths as banning Beethoven from symphony concerts.

Meanwhile, antagonism toward Germany mounted. On March 1 it was revealed that the German foreign minister Arthur Zimmermann had cabled the German minister to Mexico instructing him in the event of war to arrange an alliance, holding out to Mexico the hope of recovering Texas, Arizona, and New Mexico. On March 12 an unarmed American merchant ship was sunk without warning, followed by three more on March 19. Two days later Wilson called for a special session of Congress to consider "grave questions of national policy."

Wilson's War Message

At one o'clock of the morning Congress was to meet, Wilson asked his friend Frank Cobb, of the New York *World,* to the White House. He said that he had "never been so uncertain about anything in his life" as about going to war. "Is there anything else I can do?" he asked. Cobb answered that Germany had thrust war

upon us. The President agreed, but said he feared the effects of war on American life. "Once lead this people into war," the President predicted, "and they'll forget there ever was such a thing as tolerance." It was with a heavy heart that on April 2 he addressed Congress.

In one of the most eloquent speeches ever delivered in the Capitol, Wilson asked Congress to declare war on the German Empire. He distinguished between violation of our neutrality rights by the Allies and by Germany, pointing out, "Property can be paid for; the lives of peaceful and innocent people cannot be. . . . The present German submarine warfare is a warfare against all mankind." The President insisted, however, that our quarrel was only with the "military masters" of Germany; he expressed "sincere friendship" toward the German people.

QUESTION • Did Wilson have any honorable alternative to the agonizing decision to war on Germany?

Maintaining that the United States had "no selfish ends to serve," Wilson enlisted the American people in a crusade for a better world. We were glad to fight, he said, to make the world "safe for democracy," to insure "the rights and liberties of small nations," and to promote a world organization of free countries that would "bring peace and safety to all nations."

Four days after Wilson's message, Congress declared war on Germany by the overwhelming margins of 82 votes to 6 in the Senate and 273 to 50 in the House.

THE WAR ABROAD

When the United States entered the war, the Allies seemed in danger of defeat. In April 1917, John Jellicoe, first lord of the admiralty, said that Britain's outlook was desperate. U-boats were sinking ships at a rate that threatened to wipe out the entire merchant tonnage of the world; the British Isles had only a two-month supply of food. Late in 1917 the Italians suffered a severe defeat at Caporetto. After the Russians overthrew the Czarist government in March 1917, their military effort slackened. When the Bolsheviks seized power in November, Russia stopped fighting entirely, thus releasing German armies for service on the western front. By the severe Treaty of Brest-Litovsk in March 1918, Russia was forced to give up immense areas, in which the Germans set up puppet governments. The conquered territory included the Ukraine, one of the richest grain-growing areas in the world; from it the Germans hoped to obtain food to relieve the severe shortages caused by the British blockade.

The Allies did not expect that the United States would give much help in the actual fighting. Not until 1916 had Wilson been persuaded to support plans for military preparedness, and by the spring of 1917 these had not been developed very far. Including both regulars and

The Doughboys

On April 6, 1917, the Congress of the United States declared war on the German empire.

Nearly twenty years later congressional investigating committees tried to find out why. Did the makers of munitions press war to increase their profits? Did international bankers promote American intervention to protect their investment in government bonds issued by the Allies? Was Wilson carried along by the pro-English sympathies that he shared with some of his closest advisers? Or was the whole thing a result of the decision to insist on outmoded "rights of neutrals" on the high seas?

At the grass-roots level there was enthusiasm for the war, if little understanding of just how the United States got in. Americans became convinced that they were on the side of good, destined to destroy evil and somehow to create a better world.

The four million "doughboys" (the GI's of World War I) were suddenly torn from civilian life and sent to training camps that consisted of flimsy barracks set in seas of mud in winter and dust in summer. They were issued uniforms and shoes that seldom fitted, two scratchy blankets each, and a mess kit. At first there was a shortage of weapons, and infantrymen drilled with wooden guns, while artillerymen used logs.

A million doughboys were packed into the ill-smelling holds of transports and shipped to France, often before their training was completed. In France there was apt to be more training, and then at last men were moved up toward the front lines in the famous French "40 and 8" boxcars (40 men and 8 horses). Finally they marched into the hell of trench warfare, singing as they went, for these were the last American armies that regularly sang on the march. The songs they sang—"Over There," "K-k-k-katy," "Pack Up Your Troubles," "Keep the Home Fires Burning," and "Mademoiselle from Armentières"—bring back a poignant memory of young men who somehow kept their spirit and sense of humor in unhappy situations.

Soon after U.S. entry into the war, a citizen army was trained and moved to French battlefields. The American Expeditionary Force was assigned its own sector of the Allied front. "Over the top" from the trenches meant a plunge into enemy fire and into a tangle of barbed wire strung across "no man's land."

National Guardsmen, the United States had only 200,000 soldiers; of these less than 25,000 were ready to take the field. The army possessed only 1,500 machine guns, 55 obsolete airplanes, and no heavy artillery whatever.

Forging an Army

In the face of this discouraging outlook, the United States mobilized at a speed which astonished both friends and foes. Supported by his able Secretary of War, Newton D. Baker, Wilson insisted that troops should be raised by a draft on the democratic principle of "a universal obligation to serve." Opponents of conscription said that it was "un-American" and that it would "Prussianize" the country. Champ Clark, speaker of the House of Representatives, remarked that in Missouri, where he came from, people thought there was "precious little difference between a conscript and a convict."

Nevertheless, the President's will prevailed, and in May 1917, Congress passed the Selective Service Act that made all men between twenty-one and thirty liable for military service. In June, nearly 10 million young men quietly registered for the draft. There was no such resistance to conscription as occurred during the Civil War; this was perhaps because the registration was carried on entirely by civilians at ordinary centers of civilian life such as schools and town halls. Draft liability was eventually extended to all men between eighteen and forty-five, and 2,800,000 were chosen for service. Another million were supplied by volunteers.

Housing and training this vast number of men required the building of 32 camps, each able to shelter over 40,000 men. In spite of great difficulties in equipping them, the camps soon came to resemble small cities, with running water, electric light, amusement centers, libraries, and hospitals. After preliminary training averaging six months, the troops went abroad for further instruction before being sent into battle. Nearly two million men reached France before hostilities ended. This vast new reservoir of manpower was in itself an important cause of victory; it lowered German morale and raised that of the Allies. In *Testament of Youth*, Vera Brittain, who served as a nurse behind the British lines, described her first sight of American troops as follows:

I was leaving quarters to go back to my ward, when I had to wait to let a large contingent of troops march past . . . though the sight of soldiers marching was now too familiar to arouse curiosity, an unusual quality of bold vigour in their swift stride caused me to stare at them with puzzled interest.

They looked larger than ordinary men; their tall, straight figures were in vivid contrast to the undersized armies of pale recruits to which we had become accustomed. . . . Had yet another regiment been conjured out of our depleted Dominions?

Then I heard an excited exclamation from a group of Sisters behind me.

"Look! Look! Here are the Americans!" . . .

The coming of relief made me realize how long and how intolerable had been the tension, and with the knowledge that we were not, after all, defeated I found myself beginning to cry.

Victory on Land and Sea

In the spring and early summer of 1918, Germany made a last desperate attempt to win victory in the West and came uncomfortably close to success. A drive starting in March nearly drove through the British lines; another in June threatened Paris. American troops helped to stop the advance. They especially distinguished themselves in a counterattack at Château-Thierry, less than fifty miles from the French capital. The tide turned in mid-July as Marshal Ferdinand Foch, supreme commander of all Allied armies, ordered a great counter-offensive. General John J. Pershing, leader of the American Expeditionary Force, insisted on a separate American army with its own sector of the front. The Americans were assigned the sector north and east of Verdun. In mid-September, 550,000 "doughboys" won an overwhelming victory in wiping out the St. Mihiel salient. Then a still larger force drove toward the key city of Sedan through the best defended portions of the German lines. By early November, the Americans had almost reached their objectives and were preparing to advance into Germany. British and French forces met with even greater success. When the Armistice was signed on November 11, the Allies were advancing everywhere.

Meanwhile, American naval forces practically merged with the British in war against the submarines. The invention of the depth charge provided a new weapon. Its effective use demanded hundreds of patrol vessels in the sea lanes to watch for U-boats and to convoy ships. In addition to 79 destroyers, the United States sent abroad 170 small "sub-chasers," plus a variety of former yachts, tugs, and fishing boats. "Almost any craft which could carry a wireless, a gun, and depth charges was boldly sent to sea." By the end of 1917 the number of U-boat victims was cut in half. Not a single loaded troop transport was sunk on the way from America to Europe. In 1918 the United States navy took the principal part in laying an anti-submarine mine barrage nearly three hundred miles across the North Sea. This went far toward bottling up the U-boats entirely.

THE HOME FRONT

To raise and equip vast armies, to increase the size of the navy elevenfold, to keep munitions and food flowing to the Allies required a profound reorganization of American life. "It is not an army that we must shape and train for

A poster put out by the Food Administration urges citizens to conserve food. The self-denying frame of mind was one of the reasons why it was easy to push through the Eighteenth Amendment establishing national prohibition in 1918.

war," said the President, "it is a nation." In preparing for "total war" the United States enlisted not only fighting men, but industries, labor unions, railroads, farmers, and housewives.

Mobilization of Industry, Labor, and Agriculture

Since modern war is a battle of production, the most obvious need was to gear American industry to the war machine. Soon the entire economic life of the country was under the control of various federal agencies. The most powerful of these was the War Industries Board, which had charge of purchasing for both the Allies and the United States. Under the driving leadership of Bernard Baruch, a Wall Street speculator, the War Industries Board attempted "to operate the whole United States as a single factory dominated by one management." Enlisting the ablest business brains in America as "dollar-a-year men," Baruch set up an organization that converted factories to war production, determined priorities of raw materials, and fixed prices.

Cooperating with the War Industries Board were several agencies that took over especially critical areas of American economy. The Fuel Administration conserved coal and oil by means as diverse as introducing daylight saving time and reducing the work week of factories not in war production. The Railroad Administration took over the railroads from private management and ran them as a single system. Former President Taft served as co-chairman of the War Labor Board (WLB), which sought to prevent labor disputes. In return for the promise of labor leaders not to call strikes, the WLB raised wages to a point where they would "insure the subsistence of the worker and his family in health and reasonable comfort," insisted on equal pay for men and women, and guaranteed unions the right to organize.

Job opportunities and high wages during the war served as a magnet to draw perhaps half a million black workers from southern farms to northern factories. Most of them held unskilled or semi-skilled jobs, but by 1920, 150,000 blacks were skilled workers or foremen.

The war agency that most affected civilian lives was the Food Administration, directed by Herbert Hoover, who had achieved fame in organizing relief for Belgium. With the slogan "food will win the war," extraordinary efforts were made to reduce consumption and increase production. Housewives were urged to "Hooverize" by "serving just enough" and planning for Wheatless Wednesdays or Meatless Mondays. To increase wheat production a federally financed Grain Corporation guaranteed farmers first $2.00, then $2.26 per bushel, and in 1918 bought the entire American wheat crop.

Financing the War

The World War was costly beyond all expectation. By 1919 the federal government had spent about 33 billion dollars, of which 10 billion went to the Allies as loans. About a third of the money was raised by taxation, the rest by borrowing. The income tax was increased to a basic 12 per cent on incomes of $4,000 or more, with rates running up to 77 per cent on incomes over $1,000,000. Heavier burdens on corporations included an "excess profits" tax, designed to return war profits to the government. Excise duties were levied on items as varied as theatre tickets, chewing gum, and phonograph records.

To borrow over twenty billion dollars, the government sold four issues of Liberty Bonds, plus a postwar issue of Victory Bonds, direct to the people. Bonds were issued in denominations as low as $25, with War Savings Stamps for as little as 10¢. Through posters, rallies, volunteer sales people, "Liberty Loan sermons," and persuasion by employers, the purchase of bonds was made a test of patriotism. Even children were enlisted and urged to put their pennies in War Savings Stamps. Twenty-one million people, more than a fifth of the nation's population, subscribed to the Fourth Liberty Loan.

Control of Opinion

Since so much depended on voluntary civilian cooperation, the government undertook to "sell" the war. A Committee on Public Information was set up under George Creel, who described his job as "the world's greatest adventure in advertising." Creel mobilized advertising people, commercial artists, authors, songwriters, actors, orators, and motion picture companies. Millions of pamphlets explained such matters as the causes of the war and American war aims. The effect of this flood of propaganda was to reinforce Wilson's idea that the war was a crusade. While this probably heightened the war effort, it also helped to produce the very intolerance that Wilson dreaded. Congress passed the Espionage and Sedition Acts, designed to prevent spying and disloyalty. These were so severe that they silenced opposition to the war. The Postmaster General was given authority to ban newspapers, magazines, and pamphlets from the mails at his discretion. Under these laws hundreds of people were imprisoned, sometimes even for opinions expressed in private conversations. People were even jailed for criticizing the Red Cross or the YMCA.

Although they were enforced with unnecessary vigor, the Supreme Court upheld the principle of the Espionage and Sedition Acts in a decision written by Justice Holmes. "When a nation is at war," said Holmes, "many things that might be said in time of peace are such a hindrance to the effort that their utterance will not be endured. . . ." Holmes refused, however, to support punishment when there was no "clear and present danger" of hurting the United States, or when the accused were apparently being jailed for unpopular political beliefs.

An unhappy result of enthusiasm for the war was persecution of Americans of German ancestry. Wilson's insistence that we were "the sincere friends of the German people" could not stand against posters displaying Germans as bloody-handed "Huns." Anti-German feeling went to such ridiculous lengths as banning the teaching of the German language in schools and abandoning public performance of music by Beethoven, Schubert, and Wagner. There were super-patriots who even insisted that sauerkraut should be called "Liberty cabbage."

Increase in Presidential Power

As in the Civil War, there was a huge increase in the power of the President. Instead of acting independently of Congress, as did Lincoln (see pp. 358–360), Wilson insisted that Congress formally grant him whatever emergency powers he thought necessary. By a series of laws, notably the Lever Act of 1917 and the Overman Act of 1918, the President was not only given control over agriculture and industry, but allowed to set up or reorganize government agencies at his discretion. Such bodies as the War Labor Board were created by him without even senatorial ratification of their top officers. Thus Wilson had greater authority than any previous President. It was understood, however, that these extraordinary powers were granted only "for the duration," and that with the return of peace the President and Congress should resume their normal constitutional relations.

The entrance of the United States into World War I has often been condemned as an unwise departure from the isolationist tradition of the Founding Fathers. It would have required, however, almost superhuman restraint on the part of the American government and American people to remain neutral; had they done so, a German victory might have imperiled national safety. The war effort has been deplored because it vastly increased the power of government and led to a spirit of intolerance. All sacrifices in money and blood, all restrictions on personal freedom, might have been justifiable if victory had led to a just and enduring peace. But such was not to be the case.

WILSON'S PEACE PROGRAM

Although Wilson did all in his power to crush Germany, he never ceased to think ahead to the peace that would follow victory. His peace program was crystallized in the Fourteen Points, published in January 1918. The President hoped to enlist public opinion everywhere in support of this charter for a new world order. The Fourteen Points may be summarized under three headings:

(1) *Abolition of general causes of war* (points 1–5). This section advocated open instead of secret diplomacy; freedom of the seas; reduction of trade barriers; disarmament; and an impartial adjustment of colonial claims, giving consideration to the needs of native peoples.

(2) *"Self-determination" for Europe* (points 6–13). This upheld the right of peoples to live under a government of their own choice. Thus Poland was to be an independent state; France was to get back Alsace-Lorraine; and in the Balkans new boundary lines were to be drawn on the basis of nationality.

(3) *"A general association of nations"* (point 14). The idea of an international organization to prevent war was centuries old, and it now had an immense appeal because of the obvious failure of the balance of power. Wilson made it the cornerstone of his program.

Although based on "the principle of justice to all peoples and nationalities," the Fourteen Points bristled with practical difficulties. Some of the questions raised were: Would nations agree to disarm? How was it possible to be "impartial" in assigning colonies? How to draw boundaries in areas that contained people of different nationalities? Would nations surrender enough sovereignty to a world organization to make it effective?

Words as Weapons

Whatever the objections to Wilson's program, it helped to shorten the war. Using words as weapons, the President deliberately drove a wedge between the German people and their government. He offered "a place of equality among the nations of the world" to Germany once it had thrown off the yoke of its "military masters." His promise of "self-determination" stimulated revolts among the subject peoples of the Austrian Empire. His speeches, showered behind enemy lines from airplanes, weakened the will to fight. When the German gov-

When strong opposition to the Versailles Treaty developed, Wilson went on tour to appeal to the American people. The cartoonist shows him "going to talk to the boss." Had radio broadcasting then been possible, the President would have reached more citizens from his desk in the White House.

ernment realized that victory was impossible and approached Wilson about arranging peace, he questioned its right to speak for the German people. By so doing he helped to bring on revolution. On November 9 the Kaiser abdicated and fled to Holland. Two days later Germany signed an armistice on terms so severe that there was no chance of renewing hostilities.

Obstacles to Wilson's Program

Wilson could not get the Allies to agree to his peace program until the very last moment. When he did so, British officials gave notice that they had reservations about "freedom of the seas," while the French insisted that Germany must pay reparations for war damage. Wilson also failed to reckon with war hatreds. The French wanted revenge against the nation that had devastated their "sacred soil" and destroyed a generation of young men. In parliamentary elections held in Britain immediately after the Armistice, David Lloyd George, the prime minister, promised to squeeze Germany "until the pips squeak."

Wilson also faced difficulties at home. Although he had directed the war on a nonparti-san basis, he made the mistake of injecting politics into the postwar settlement. In the midterm elections of November 1918, he asked voters to show support for his peace program by returning Democrats to Congress. Instead, the people elected Republican majorities in both houses. Theodore Roosevelt immediately proclaimed that "our allies and our enemies and Mr. Wilson himself should all understand that Mr. Wilson has no authority whatever to speak for the American people at this time." Shortly after the election, Wilson announced his intention to go in person to the Peace Conference. The wisdom of this decision is disputed, but in any case the President should certainly have asked a prominent Republican to accompany him. Henry White, sole Republican member of the peace delegation, was a retired career diplomat without political influence.

In December 1918, Wilson reached Europe and made a triumphal tour of the Allied nations. Everywhere huge throngs greeted him like a new messiah bringing "peace on earth, good will to men." Small wonder if he thought he could overcome those who doubted or opposed him.

Wilson's Fourteen Points demanded "open covenants openly arrived at," but the Treaty of Versailles was actually hatched in secret by the "Big Four," who are shown here in a moment of relaxation. They are, from left to right, David Lloyd George of Great Britain, Vittorio Orlando of Italy, Georges Clemenceau of France, and Woodrow Wilson.

The Peace Conference

The Peace Conference opened at the palace of Versailles in January 1919, but most of the sessions were held in Paris. It was attended by delegates from twenty-seven nations, but the defeated countries were not represented. Dominating the proceedings were the leaders of the three most powerful nations—Wilson, the idealist; Lloyd George, the brilliant but unstable British prime minister; Georges Clemenceau,

"the Tiger," whose indomitable will had helped to steel France to resist the German onslaught. With Vittorio Orlando, the Italian premier, these men formed "the Big Four" who met in secret to arrange the treaty terms. Secret meetings may have been necessary to speed up the work of the conference, but they hurt Wilson. They robbed him of his most effective weapon, direct appeal to popular opinion, and they seemed a violation of the first of the Fourteen

Points that had pledged "open covenants openly arrived at." Nevertheless, the President scored an immediate triumph by forcing plans for a League of Nations into the peace treaty. In mid-February the covenant (charter) of the League, written by Wilson himself, was accepted by the conference. The President then returned to the United States for a month.

During Wilson's absence his political influence in the United States had weakened alarmingly. There was widespread sentiment that while the country was readjusting to peace, the President should be "here, not there." It was apparent that the entire peace program was in danger when 39 Republican senators and senators-elect—far more than enough to defeat a treaty—signed a statement opposing American entrance into the League in the form proposed by Wilson. In this situation the President would have been well advised to stay home and "mend his fences." Instead, he publicly denounced the "narrow, selfish, provincial purposes" of his opponents, and insisted that the League must be part of the peace treaty. He then returned to Paris for three more months. At the peace table, he made some concession to his critics by insisting on changes in the treaty to protect American interests. For instance, the League Covenant now recognized the right of the United States to maintain the Monroe Doctrine. To persuade the Allies to accept such changes, Wilson was obliged to make concessions in their favor.

When completed, the Treaty of Versailles was a victor's peace. Germany was much reduced in territory, stripped of her colonies, and required to pay heavy reparations. Self-determination was violated where it suited the interests of the Allies, and some of the Fourteen Points were entirely ignored. Nevertheless, Wilson had put across much of his program, and trusted the League to right injustices after war hatreds had subsided. Paul Birdsall in *Versailles Twenty Years After* concludes that

whatever Wilson's mistakes, he "emerged as the only man of real stature in Paris."

Defeat of the Versailles Treaty

In June 1919, the President returned to America to face his foes. Those who still hated the "Hun" thought the treaty too "soft"; liberal editors thought it too harsh, various national groups thought it unjust to their former native lands; some Republicans were opposed simply because Wilson was a Democrat. There was fear that the League was an "entangling alliance" against which Americans had been warned by Washington, Jefferson, and Monroe. In the Senate a small group of "irreconcilables" branded the League as a "treacherous and treasonable scheme" that should be "buried in Hell." A much larger group, the "reservationists," would have been content if the Senate had ratified the Versailles Treaty with reservations to protect American freedom of action.

Instead of compromising with his critics, as he had compromised with representatives of other nations at Paris, Wilson insisted on unconditional ratification of the treaty. Convinced that he could overwhelm the opposition by enlisting public opinion, he resolved to make a direct appeal to the people. Starting in Ohio in September, he traveled 8,000 miles, making 37 formal speeches on behalf of the treaty in 22 days. Almost everywhere his reception was enthusiastic; he seemed to be regaining popular support. Most of the "vocal classes" of the country—editors, the clergy, college professors —were already strongly on his side. Had his strength held out, he might have won the battle. But the strain of the presidential years had been too great for Wilson's rather frail physique. His health collapsed and he had to abandon his speaking tour. Shortly after returning to the White House, he suffered a stroke that half paralyzed him and impaired his speech. He was bedridden for months, isolated from even his closest advisers.

In November 1919, and again in March 1920, the Senate failed to ratify the Versailles Treaty. In both cases most Republican senators insisted on reservations written by Henry Cabot Lodge, a bitter foe of Wilson. A majority of the Democrats followed the President, who insisted that the United States either enter the League unconditionally, or stay out. Had Wilson seen the necessity for compromise, the United States would have joined the League.

Wilson's greatness was that he tried to lead the world toward a lasting peace and his country toward service to humanity. His tragedy was not merely that he failed in this great endeavor, but that his failure stemmed partly from his own errors of judgment. He was un-

QUESTION • *Would Wilson have won his fight for United States membership in the League if he had been able to speak to the people by radio?*

fortunate not to die while on his speaking tour. He would then have lived on in popular memory as a martyr to the cause of world peace. Instead, he survived to see his party repudiated at the polls in the presidential election of 1920 and his country turn to a policy of narrow isolationism. In 1923, shortly before he died, he warned, "I can predict with absolute certainty that within another generation there will be another world war if the nations of the world do not concert the method by which to prevent it."

AFTERMATH OF THE WAR

The United States began to demobilize as soon as hostilities ended. Within a short time, the army was reduced to less than half a million men; the navy disbanded its vast patrol fleet; economic controls were lifted; the "dollar-a-year" men left Washington; and industry reconverted to peacetime production. This rapid demobilization resembled on a vast scale a band of frontiersmen returning to the plow after repelling an Indian raid. With Wilson first preoccupied with the peace treaty and then incapacitated, there was little over-all direction. Congress did, however, pass important legislation dealing with the railroads.

Resisting demands that government operation be continued, Congress turned the railroads back to their owners by the Esch-Cummins Act of 1920. This statute gave the Interstate Commerce Commission almost complete power to fix rates as well as to regulate railroad financing, but the commission's function was now less to restrain railroad companies than to help them. Many railroad companies were in danger of bankruptcy, partly as a result of competition from the automobile. The ICC was therefore given power to consolidate smaller railroad lines into a few great systems, and was required to fix rates high enough to guarantee that railroad companies received a "fair return" on investment.

The sudden transition from war to peace created many difficulties. Industry enjoyed a brief postwar boom resulting from deferred demand for consumer goods, but prices rose to a point where many consumers could not afford to pay them. The cost of living had approximately doubled from 1914 to 1919. High prices helped to create labor unrest. Once the War Labor Board disbanded, the truce between employers and organized labor ended. The year 1919 saw a record number of strikes, some of them marked by violence. In most cases the strikes were unsuccessful. Notable defeats occurred in the coal and steel industries. In steel, 350,000 men remained off the job for four months without winning a single important demand. When John L. Lewis, head of the United Mine Workers, called over 400,000 men out of the pits, the government revived its wartime powers and ordered the men back to work.

After a "buyers' strike" in 1920, business activity slackened, and by 1921 the country was

||||| Germany, 1914

/// Austria-Hungary, 1914

1914 boundaries where changes were made

Nations formed after World War I

CHANGES IN THE MAP OF EUROPE BY THE TREATY OF VERSAILLES

Defeat in World War I meant the end of three monarchies, those of the Romanovs in Russia, of the Hohenzollerns in Germany, and of the Hapsburgs in Austria-Hungary. Germany lost all her colonies and much territory in Europe. Russia lost territories to the West held since Peter the Great. The Austro-Hungarian Empire simply disintegrated and was divided among seven countries.

in the grip of a depression. The farmers were especially hard hit. With the slackening of wartime demands for food and the end of government price guarantees, agricultural prices dropped so rapidly that many farmers faced bankruptcy.

The "Red Scare"

One reason for the lack of success of labor unions after the war was fear of communism. When the Bolsheviks (Communists) seized control in Russia in 1917, they called on workers everywhere to revolt. A conspiratorial organization, the Third International, was created specifically to promote world revolution. In 1919 Bolshevism seemed on the point of overrunning all eastern and central Europe. Several strikes in America were led by IWW leaders who had joined the Third International. Although the overwhelming majority of labor leaders and most American Socialists refused to ally with the Communists, they were nevertheless suspected of planning violent revolution. The same laws and the same private vigilantism that had been used against suspected pacifists or pro-Germans during the war were now turned against radicals. During the period of the "red scare," measures taken to suppress radicalism were so extreme that they endangered traditional American freedoms. Aliens as a group were suspect, especially if they had Russian names. Attorney General A. Mitchell

Palmer rounded up some 6,000 alleged Communist aliens and deported nearly 600 of them, sometimes without trial. By a vote of 140 to 6, the New York legislature excluded five Socialists over the protests of Governor Alfred E. Smith and of the state bar association, led by Charles Evans Hughes. The "red scare" was accompanied by a wave of feeling against Negroes, who had come to northern cities lured by the full employment of the war years. During the "red summer" of 1919 there were severe race riots in which whites were the aggressors. In Chicago nearly forty people were killed and over 500 injured. Eventually the "red scare" subsided, but it left an evil legacy of intolerance and violence that lived on in such organizations as the Klu Klux Klan, which attracted nation-wide membership in the 1920's.

Prohibition and Women's Suffrage

The First World War helped to add two amendments to the Constitution, both the culmination of century-old reform movements. The Prohibitionists had made great gains before 1914, and once the United States entered the war, their cause was still further advanced. "Hooverizing" put the country in a self-denying mood, and war needs impelled the government to forbid the use of grain for the manufacture of liquor. By January 1919, two-thirds of the states ratified the Eighteenth Amendment, which prohibited "the manufacture, sale, or transportation" of intoxicating beverages. War conditions also advanced the cause of woman's rights. It was difficult to deny the suffragists' demand that women be allowed to vote after they had done men's work in factories and fields and had served with courage and devotion behind the lines in Europe. After many years effort and much labor, women won the Nineteenth Amendment, which granted them the franchise on the eve of the 1920 election.

During the last year and a half of Wilson's term of office, the country was virtually leaderless. Although the President recovered his health sufficiently to transact routine business, he was only a husk of his former self. His "single track mind" and what remained of his powerful personality were both still concentrated on getting the United States into the League of Nations. Retaining a belief that the American people would not retreat from world leadership, he urged that the presidential election of 1920 be a "great and solemn referendum" on the League issue.

Activities: Chapter 23

For Mastery and Review

1. What problems faced Wilson in Mexico, and by what means did he attempt to solve them?

2. What were major causes of World War I? What brought it on suddenly in 1914? How were the sympathies of Americans involved?

3. How were the neutral rights of the United States violated by Great Britain? By Germany? Why did Bryan resign as Secretary of State? What was the *Sussex* pledge, and of what value was it?

4. On what grounds did the United State break off relations with Germany? Why did she declare war?

5. What was the military situation in 1917? What were the major contributions of the United States to victory over the Central Powers?

6. What federal agencies were created to direct the war effort? Explain the role of each. By what means did the federal government raise troops? Raise money? Control public opinion?

7. What were the major elements in Wilson's peace program? What obstacles did it encounter abroad and at home? What were Wilson's errors in tactics in promoting his program, both abroad and at home?

8. How was demobilization accomplished? What was done for railroads and shipping? What

caused labor disturbances in 1919 and 1920? What were the immediate and longtime results of the "red scares"?

9. To what degree were the Eighteenth and Nineteenth Amendments results of the situation during World War I?

Unrolling the Map

1. On an outline map of the Caribbean area, locate the places with which the Wilson administration was especially concerned: the Panama Canal, Nicaragua, Haiti, the Virgin Islands, Mexico, and the Dominican Republic. How much was strategic defense of the Panama Canal involved?

2. On an outline map of Europe, locate the two sets of belligerent powers and the neutrals in World War I. How did the basic geographical situation favor the Allies? How did it favor the Central Powers?

Who, What, and Why Important?

"cooling off" treaties
Panama Canal tolls
Mexican Revolution
Victoriano Huerta
"Pancho" Villa
ABC Powers
armed merchant ships
War Industries Board
War Labor Board
Bernard Baruch
Herbert Hoover
excess profits tax
Selective Service Act
Liberty Bonds
George Creel

Fourteen Points
Triple Alliance
Triple Entente
propaganda
U-boats
Sussex pledge
Versailles Conference
League of Nations
Henry Cabot Lodge
Esch-Cummins Act
"red scare"
John L. Lewis
Eighteenth Amendment
Nineteenth Amendment

To Pursue the Matter

1. Would Wilson have done better to allow "the unspeakable Huerta" to retain the presidency of Mexico, which he apparently obtained by fraud and murder? See Perkins, *The Monroe Doctrine.* Does the United States face similar problems today?

2. In World War I there was far less swift movement of troops than in previous wars, as the

armies settled into prolonged and incredibly bloody trench warfare. Why? What uses were made of airplanes and tanks? Source: Baldwin, *World War I.*

3. William Jennings Bryan resigned as Secretary of State because he felt that by insisting on defense of neutral rights (including the right of American citizens to travel on belligerent ships) and by lending money to the Allies the United States was heading for an unnecessary war with Germany. Prepare a debate on the topic: "*Resolved:* That Bryan was right." Two readily available sources of material on both sides are Bailey, *A Diplomatic History of the American People,* and May, *From Imperialism to Isolationism.*

4. If there are members of the class who can sing or play instruments, prepare a program of war songs. Bring the class in on the choruses of "Tipperary," "Keep the Home Fires Burning," "Over There," "K-k-k-katy," "Oh, How I Hate to Get Up in the Morning," and so forth.

5. Fredericks, *The Great American Adventure: America in the First World War,* is a highly readable account of the American war effort. Its chapters on the submarine menace, on airmen, and on the Meuse-Argonne offensive provide excellent material for class reports.

6. Individuals or committees might investigate the background and explain—with maps—each of the Fourteen Points.

7. How far to blame Wilson for the failure of the United States to join the League of Nations, and how far to blame his enemies? Possible sources: Garraty, *Woodrow Wilson,* and Bailey, *A Diplomatic History of the American People.*

8. The materials for a dramatic sketch for a school assembly with some such title as "Cast Down" or "The Tragic Collapse" are found in three glimpses of Woodrow Wilson—abroad, stricken as he campaigned for the League, and after—in the chapter on World War I in Arnof, *A Sense of the Past.*

9. An eminent historian has included Wilson among the three great failures in American history (the other two, he said, were Jefferson and Lincoln), because by his actions he defeated his own program and contradicted his own ideals. Do you agree?

Chapter 24

Normalcy

The business of America is business.
—CALVIN COOLIDGE

Several men of prominence sought the Republican nomination in 1920, but after a convention deadlock the prize went to a "dark horse," Senator Warren G. Harding of Ohio. This unexpected choice revealed the backstage influence of a powerful group of Old Guard senators, as well as the foresight of Harding's campaign manager who predicted that the Republican nominee would be chosen in a "smoke-filled room" at "2:11 A.M."

THE ELECTION OF 1920

As Frederick L. Allen pointed out in *Only Yesterday*, the Ohio senator was an ideal candidate for people who were tired of Woodrow Wilson. Wilson was cold and unapproachable; Harding "was an affable small-town man, at ease with 'folks.'" Wilson favored government regulation of business; Harding wanted to leave it alone. "Wilson thought in terms of the whole world; Harding was for America first.... Wilson wanted America to exert itself nobly; Harding wanted to give it a rest."

To oppose Harding the Democrats chose another Ohioan, Governor James M. Cox, who loyally supported Wilson's ideals. By campaigning for the League of Nations, Cox attempted to make the election of 1920 a "great and solemn referendum."

The Republicans did not debate the League, partly because they themselves were divided on the issue. Harding, conducting a front porch campaign in the style of McKinley, said he favored "a society of free nations" to keep peace. Thirty-one prominent Republicans, including Herbert Hoover, Elihu Root, and Charles Evans Hughes, said this meant that Harding agreed with them that the United States should join the League, with reservations. But several irreconcilable senators seemed certain that Harding was on their side. Thus, as Walter Lippmann pointed out, the Republican candidate received support from "men and women who thought a Republican victory would kill the League, plus those who thought it was the most practical way to procure the League...."

The election was an overwhelming Republican victory. "It was not a landslide," said Wilson's secretary Joseph P. Tumulty, "it was an earthquake." Harding carried every northern and western state and even broke the Solid South by carrying Tennessee. A key to the result may be found in an unusual word, "normalcy," which Harding used during the campaign; it suggested return to the "good old days" that never were, but for which many longed. To quote again from Frederick Allen's *Only Yesterday:*

The nation was spiritually tired. Wearied by the excitements of the war and the nervous tension of the Big Red Scare, they hoped for quiet and healing. Sick of Wilson and his talk of America's duty to humanity, they hoped for a chance to pursue their private affairs without governmental interference and to forget about public affairs. There might be no such word in the dictionary as normalcy, but normalcy was what they wanted.

A peculiarity of the election of 1920 was that both vice-presidential candidates eventually became President. Second place on the Democratic ticket went to Franklin D. Roosevelt, who, like his distant cousin Theodore, had served as Assistant Secretary of the Navy after an apprenticeship in New York politics. Harding's running mate was Governor Calvin Coolidge of Massachusetts. Coolidge made a nation-wide reputation during a strike of the Boston police in September 1919, by the statement, "There is no right to strike against the public safety by anybody, any time, anywhere!" He succeeded to the presidency when Harding died suddenly in 1923.

FOREIGN AFFAIRS

After his election, Harding announced that the League issue was "dead as slavery." His administration, he said, would not lead America into the League of Nations "by the side door, back door, or cellar door." Nevertheless, the administrations of Harding and Coolidge were driven by force of circumstances to become involved in many of the problems of the postwar world. The United States was simply too powerful and too widely involved in world affairs to retreat to nineteenth-century isolationism.

European Affairs

Failure to ratify the Versailles Treaty left the United States still technically at war with

Republican statements on the League of Nations were so contradictory that both enemies and friends of the League were encouraged by them.

Germany. In July 1921, a congressional resolution formally declared hostilities at an end, and shortly thereafter a treaty was signed. By this agreement Germany paid damages for unrestricted submarine warfare, and the United States paid German owners for certain property seized during the war. The United States, however, had nothing to do with enforcing the Versailles peace terms regarding Germany or any other part of Europe. In an Armistice Day address in 1923, Woodrow Wilson denounced American policy as a retreat into "sullen and selfish isolation."

One postwar international problem that demanded a solution, in spite of the intention to keep out of European affairs, was that of the war debts owed to the United States by the Allies. These amounted in all to $10,350,000,000. Most of this money had been spent in the United States for food and war materials. The debtor nations, already saddled with the heavy costs of the war, had difficulty in meeting their payments. They argued that they could not pay in gold because there was hardly enough of the precious metal in existence, and that they could not pay by building up credits through the sale of goods in the United States because high tariffs closed the American market to foreign products. There was also the argument that since we had lost fewer people than the Allies, we should be willing to assume an extra financial burden. The United States government took the position that it could not ask its taxpayers to assume the debts; that the Allies had gained territory and reparations payments as a result of victory while America had claimed no reward; and that to cancel debts would be to destroy faith in international agreements. The war debt dispute caused hard feeling and charges of ingratitude on both sides of the Atlantic.

Following a policy set forth by Congress in 1922, the Harding and Coolidge administrations scaled down the debts on the basis of apparent ability to pay. Eventually, the United States made agreements with seventeen of the twenty debtor nations, reducing the debts by 30 to 80 per cent. Most of the money America received ultimately came from Germany in the form of reparation payments to the Allies. And to help pay reparations Germany got private loans from other countries—especially from the United States!

The World Court and the League

Although abandoning all intention of entering the League, Harding and his three successors—Coolidge, Hoover, and Franklin Roosevelt—urged that the United States join the permanent Court of International Justice, commonly called the World Court. This separate agency of the League was designed to settle disputes between countries according to international law. Its purpose and methods were in line with American diplomacy, and Elihu Root helped to draw up its charter. American public opinion favored joining the Court, but the isolationist minority in the Senate always managed to prevent it.

Although the United States took no formal part in the affairs of the League and World Court, American "observers" cooperated with useful League agencies such as the commission to prevent traffic in opium. Two former American Secretaries of State served as judges of the Court, and prominent American bankers offered help with European financial arrangements. Jeremiah Smith, Jr., worked out a reorganization of Hungarian finances; Charles G. Dawes and Owen D. Young acted as chairmen of international conferences that made plans for German reparation payments to the Allies.

The Washington Conference, 1921–1922

Although withdrawing almost completely from European politics, the Harding administration cooperated with Japan and major European powers in arranging a series of important treaties dealing with the Pacific and Asia. These were the product of an international conference that met at Washington in 1921.

The Washington Conference was called principally because of friction between the United States and Japan. The Japanese had used the First World War as an opportunity to expand. They reaped a rich harvest at Versailles by acquiring all Germany's Pacific islands north of the equator and the German leasehold of Kiaochow. They treated as their own the rest of the Chinese province of Shantung (see map, p. 550). A dispute between the United States and Japan developed over the island of Yap, a cable station between Guam and the Philippines. America also distrusted Japanese intentions regarding the easternmost provinces of Russia. In 1918 the Allied nations and the United States had sent troops to keep the Trans-Siberian Railroad out of Bolshevik control. The Japanese forces were more numerous than all the others combined, and they stayed in Siberia after the other troops had withdrawn. As tension mounted, there was talk of war on both sides of the Pacific.

The situation was further complicated by the fact that Japan was allied to Great Britain. The British were anxious to break this tie: it was unpopular in Canada, Australia, and New Zealand, and it might lead to friction with the United States. The British also wanted to halt an expensive naval building program into which they were pushed by the expansion of the American and Japanese navies. When, therefore, the U.S. State Department suggested a conference on Far Eastern affairs and naval disarmament, it received full support from Britain.

The Washington Conference was attended by the principal naval powers of the world, those with Pacific possessions, and those with a stake in China. After negotiations lasting from November 1921, to February 1922, three important treaties were drawn up.

(1) *Four-Power Treaty* (United States, France, Great Britain, Japan). This treaty terminated the Anglo-Japanese Alliance and was also intended to protect the Philippines from Japanese aggression. The four powers with island possessions in the Pacific agreed to respect each other's holdings, and in the event of controversy to try to arrange a peaceable solution.

(2) *Five-Power Treaty* (United States, France, Great Britain, Italy, Japan). This provided for disarmament, naval limitation, and a ten-year "building holiday" among the principal naval powers. At the very beginning of the Washington Conference, Charles Evans Hughes, American Secretary of State, caused a sensation by proposing that the nations either scrap or abandon plans for building sixty-six capital ships totaling nearly two million tons.

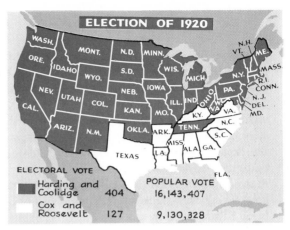

ELECTION OF 1920

ELECTORAL VOTE
Harding and Coolidge — 404
Cox and Roosevelt — 127

POPULAR VOTE
16,143,407
9,130,328

The leadership of the Democratic party in 1920 was faltering, and the public was disillusioned with the results of World War I. The end result was a landslide for Harding, who had campaigned for a "return to normalcy."

Hughes's proposals were accepted. Great Britain, the United States, and Japan agreed on a 5–5–3 ratio for first-class ships, while France and Italy were assigned ratios of 1.75 each. These proportions were intended to "freeze" the relative strength of the five navies as they existed in 1921. "Secretary Hughes," said a British observer, "sunk in 35 minutes more ships than all the admirals of the world have sunk in a cycle of centuries."

A little-noticed feature of the Five-Power Treaty was an agreement by the United States and Great Britain not to build new fortifications or naval bases in the western Pacific. This was designed to persuade Japan to accept an inferior naval ratio by giving her control of waters near her. The agreement pushed the American naval frontier back to Pearl Harbor, leaving the Philippines and Guam virtually defenseless.

(3) *Nine-Power Treaty* (United States, Belgium, China, France, Great Britain, Italy, Japan, the Netherlands, Portugal). This put the China policies of John Hay (see pp. 485–486) in treaty form. The powers signing it agreed to preserve equal commercial rights in China and promised to refrain "from taking advantage of

conditions in China to seek special rights or privileges." Following out this policy, Japan soon withdrew from the province of Shantung.

The Washington Conference seemed a great victory for American diplomacy. Except for the Rush-Bagot Agreement (see p. 235), this was the first time in history that nations had mutually agreed to beat their swords into plough-shares. The Anglo-Japanese Alliance was broken; Japan drew back and promised to refrain from future aggression. But the disarmament agreement did not touch land forces, and at sea it did not prevent unlimited construction of ships under 10,000 tons, such as submarines, destroyers, and light cruisers. The United States Senate weakened the effectiveness of the Four-Power Treaty by insisting on a reservation to the effect that the United States had no commitment to mutual defense of Pacific possessions. The barriers to Japanese aggression were thus purely verbal. The Senate reservation and the American and British pledge not to

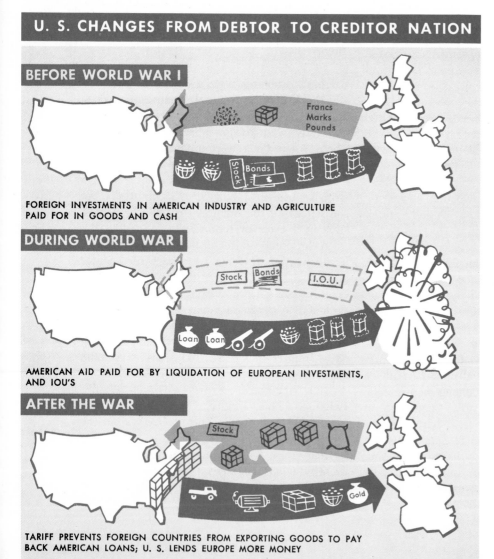

U. S. CHANGES FROM DEBTOR TO CREDITOR NATION

BEFORE WORLD WAR I

Francs
Marks
Pounds

Stock
Bonds

FOREIGN INVESTMENTS IN AMERICAN INDUSTRY AND AGRICULTURE PAID FOR IN GOODS AND CASH

DURING WORLD WAR I

Stock   Bonds   I.O.U.

Loan   Loan

AMERICAN AID PAID FOR BY LIQUIDATION OF EUROPEAN INVESTMENTS, AND IOU'S

AFTER THE WAR

Stock

Gold

TARIFF PREVENTS FOREIGN COUNTRIES FROM EXPORTING GOODS TO PAY BACK AMERICAN LOANS; U. S. LENDS EUROPE MORE MONEY

During World War I, European countries borrowed from the United States. After the war, America's high tariff wall prevented these nations from selling their goods here to pay back the loans. They were forced to borrow even more from the United States to repair extensive war damage.

build naval bases near China meant that the only defense of China, Hong Kong, and the Philippines was Japan's promise to be good.

On the other hand, the immediate results of the Washington Conference were encouraging. The treaties cleared the air as regards danger of war in the Pacific; they gave hope that nations could be persuaded to disarm.

The Kellogg-Briand Treaty, 1928

Another disarmament conference at Geneva in 1927 proved a failure, but in 1928 France and the United States took the lead in promoting the Kellogg-Briand Treaty (Pact of Paris), which attempted to "outlaw war." Sixty-three nations eventually ratified this document, whereby they all solemnly agreed to abandon war "as an instrument of national policy" and to settle disputes by peaceful means. The Pact of Paris was hailed as a great victory for peace and a sign that the United States was willing to assume responsibilities in keeping with its place in the world. Skeptics pointed out, however, that the treaty contained no enforcement machinery, nor did it prohibit wars in "self-defense."

QUESTION • The Kellogg-Briand Pact seemed a simple, forthright way to end the threat of war. Why did it not work?

Shifting Policies in Latin America

The Harding and Coolidge administrations followed the Roosevelt Corollary to the Monroe Doctrine and occasionally intervened to preserve order in Caribbean countries. But there was increasing awareness that such intervention was acutely resented throughout Latin America. Although not willing to give up the right of intervention, Secretary of State Hughes believed that it should be used with caution and only to promote stability, not to assist United States investors. In the mid-1920's, United States marines were withdrawn from the Dominican Republic and Nicaragua. But in 1926 a revolt broke out in Nicaragua against President Adolfo Diaz, who had been put in power with the assistance of American financial interests. Coolidge sent 5,000 marines to the assistance of Diaz, an action that aroused a storm of protest both within this country and without. Coolidge was accused of carrying on a "private war" and of fighting to "make the world safe for American bankers." Criticism somewhat subsided when the President sent Henry L. Stimson, one of the ablest and most trusted men in American politics, to arrange a truce between the warring factions. Stimson was successful in arranging new elections under United States supervision, although revolutionary disturbances continued well into the 1930's.

Mexico continued to present the United States with difficult problems. A new constitution, ratified in 1917, stated that all mineral resources belonged to the Mexican government. This seemed to violate the rights of United States investors who had bought Mexican mineral deposits, especially oil lands, in good faith. For a time there was danger of war, particularly since Mexico and the United States were backing rival factions in Nicaragua.

Fortunately the governments of both countries acted with moderation. In 1927 Coolidge appointed Dwight Morrow as ambassador to Mexico. Morrow understood and sympathized with the difficult problems facing the Mexican government in attempting to raise the standards of its people. For its part the Mexican government satisfied, at least temporarily, the claims of United States investors. Morrow's friendliness and tact were in pleasing contrast to the unpopularity of armed intervention in Nicaragua. They foreshadowed a new policy on the part of the United States toward its Latin-American neighbors.

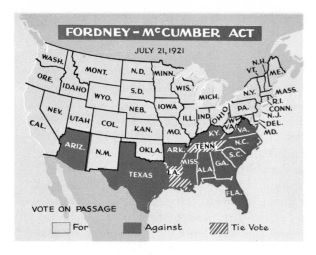

A protective tariff was one result of the Republican landslide of 1920. Opposition from agrarian states was reduced by the imposition of high duties on imported farm products.

DOMESTIC POLICIES AND POLITICS

In their domestic policies the administrations of Harding and Coolidge made it apparent that "normalcy" meant a general retreat from government regulation of business. Although the federal government actively aided business people by levying protective tariffs, promoting foreign trade, and breaking strikes, its policy in other matters was one of *laissez-faire*. There was little effort to enforce the antitrust laws against business combinations. The regulatory agencies such as the Interstate Commerce Commission and Federal Trade Commission were rendered ineffective by packing them with members who had little sympathy with curbing private enterprise. Senator George Norris, a former Progressive, called this "the nullification of federal law by the process of boring from within."

These policies accorded with the dominant feeling of the time. The 1920's were a period of prosperity characterized by remarkable achievements in the field of business enterprise. "The business of America," said Coolidge, "is business." Politics reflected this attitude.

Fordney-McCumber Tariff, 1922

The new trend was immediately seen in the tariff laws. In 1922 Congress passed the Fordney-McCumber Act, which raised import duties to high levels. During the war, industry had begun to spread into the South and the West, so there was increased sentiment for protection in these agricultural areas. Agriculturalists themselves supported the Fordney-McCumber Tariff because it placed high duties on food products. During the war the United States had seized German patents, especially in the fields of optical glass and chemical products. "Infant industries" based on these patents demanded special protection. The return to protection was also part of the general retreat to isolationism. The Fordney-McCumber Act was designed to be "flexible"; it therefore set up a Tariff Commission to study costs of production here and abroad. On recommendation of the Tariff Commission, the President might raise or lower duties up to 50 per cent. In practice, this meant that rates often went still higher.

Federal Finances

World War I had raised the national debt from less than $10 per capita to over $200. The Harding and Coolidge administrations attempted to lower this burden by greater economy. In 1921 Congress created a Budget Bureau in the Treasury Department to introduce more system into federal finances. Until this time, income and outgo had never been coordinated. The efforts of the Budget Bureau to introduce savings were especially supported by Coolidge, with whom economy amounted to such a passion that he devoted serious attention to federal expenditures on lead pencils and typewriter ribbons. After the Washington Conference there was no threat of war on the horizon, and military expenditures were greatly lowered. At one time the War Department was hard put to it to find money for six light tanks.

Andrew Mellon, Secretary of the Treasury from 1921 to 1932 and an immensely wealthy man in his own right, believed that heavy taxes on excess profits, inheritances, and large incomes "penalized success" and discouraged investment in productive enterprise. At Mellon's insistence Congress abolished the wartime excise and excess-profits taxes and reduced tax rates on incomes by nearly two-thirds. Nevertheless, so great was the prosperity of the United States, with resulting high tax collections, that the national debt was reduced by eight billion dollars between 1921 and 1929.

Immigration Restriction

Immigration in the decade before World War I averaged a million persons a year, and by 1914 over two-thirds of the immigrants were coming from southern and eastern Europe, regions where living standards were low and opportunities for education were limited. The movement to restrict the "new immigration" was successful in pushing a literacy test through Congress in 1917.

The "new immigrants" were inclined to congregate in cities, where there was the greatest chance for employment. They often formed compact communities of the same national origin, so that every great metropolis had a "little Italy," a "little Poland," a "little Greece," and so forth. This in turn gave rise to the charge that they were resistant to "Americanization." Americans of older stock resented the new immigrants' increasing political power, which was expressed through the political machines of the big cities. They feared even more that the newcomers would overthrow traditional values. Conservative labor unions disliked the new immigrants because they threatened to lower wage scales. Employers, who had previously favored unrestricted immigration as a means of hiring cheap labor, now came to fear that the new immigrants brought with them the seeds of revolution.

Hester Street in New York City, with its tenement houses looking down on crowded streets and sidewalks, shows the conditions that awaited many of the "new immigrants" who poured into the United States by the millions before World War I. Usually people of the same national origin stayed together, both because of discrimination and because they felt happier with other people who shared "the old ways."

During and after World War I, feeling against "hyphenated-Americans" was stimulated by the anti-German hysteria, by the "red scare," and by a sinister "native American" organization, the Ku Klux Klan. When immigrants, to escape the hardships that the postwar European situation imposed on them, started to pour into the United States, Congress took quick action. In 1920 Woodrow Wilson vetoed a bill to restrict immigration, but in 1921 Harding signed the Emergency Quota Act, which cut the number admitted from any country in a single year to 3 per cent of the number of that nationality residing in the United States in 1910. Three years later the Immigration Quota Law made restriction a permanent policy. This law of 1924 temporarily reduced the quota still further, setting it at 2 per cent of those resident in this country in 1890. It also provided that after 1927 the total number of immigrants admitted to the United States per year was to be 150,000, their nationalities apportioned on the basis of the census of 1920. This meant that over 85 per cent were to be admitted from northern and western Europe. The blatant racialism behind the law was further revealed when immigrants from Asia and Africa were either assigned very small quotas or barred entirely. A most unfortunate feature of the bill was total exclusion of Japanese immigration, even though the Gentlemen's Agreement of 1907–1908 had been faithfully observed. Secretary of State Hughes wrote that Japanese exclusion undid all the good accomplished by the Washington Conference. The Japanese regarded the law as a national insult and the day it went into effect was a day of public mourning and humiliation. The incident discredited moderate Japanese politicians who sought cooperation with the United States and advanced the cause of reactionary militarists who were planning to assassinate their way to power and to embark on a path of conquest.

Death of President Harding

Those who had arranged Harding's nomination in 1920 neither expected nor desired him to be a strong President. He fulfilled their expectations. With his massive head and fine presence, he "looked like a President," and he genuinely wanted to do well. He lacked, however, sufficient knowledge, intellectual discipline, or will power to direct policies effectively. Had he carried out his expressed intention of surrounding himself with the "best minds," he might still have avoided failure. Some appointments were commendable, such as that of former President Taft as Chief Justice and future President Hoover as Secretary of Commerce. But other jobs went to incompetent or dishonest personal friends. Corruption was more widespread and on an even larger scale than under Grant. The head of the Veterans Bureau, for instance, arranged fraudulent contracts that cost the taxpayers an estimated 200 million dollars. The Secretary of the Interior eventually went to prison for secretly leasing to private interests oil lands reserved for the navy at Elk Hills, California, and Teapot Dome, Wyoming, in return for bribes totaling over $300,000. When Harding began to learn what was going on, he complained privately that he had been betrayed. In the summer of 1923 he suddenly died in San Francisco, on his return from a trip to Alaska.

Calvin Coolidge: Conservative

When awakened to hear that Harding's death had made him President, Vice-President Coolidge was at his boyhood home in Vermont. He took the oath of office, administered by his father, in the flickering light of a kerosene lamp. This homely scene typified the relation of the new President to his time. Coolidge had many of the traits associated with rural, small-town America. He was intensely conservative, cautious, given to few words. "I have not been hurt," he once remarked, "by what I have not said." In occasional public speeches and magazine articles he preached the old-fashioned virtues of honesty, thrift, and hard work. His philosophy of government was simple: economy and *laissez-faire*. To take as little action as possible was with Coolidge almost a principle of life; he once said, "Four-fifths of all our troubles in this life would disappear if we would only sit down and keep still." He is said to have been the only President who slept ten hours every night and took a nap in the afternoon.

The 1924 Campaign

By 1924 the scandals of the Harding administration had been brought to light, thus presenting the Democratic party with a ready-made issue in the presidential campaign. But the Democrats' chances for victory were thrown away at its national convention. Ever since Reconstruction days, the strength of the Democrats had rested on an alliance between agricultural interests of the South and the West and city machines of the North and the East. In 1924 the two groups split, partly over Prohibition, which the rural regions favored and the cities opposed, and even more over the Ku Klux Klan. This secret society, which took its name and mumbo-jumbo ritual from the southern organization of Reconstruction times, resembled the Know-Nothings of the 1850's in that it was not only designed to intimidate the blacks, but was also the enemy of the Catholics, Jews, immigrants, and "foreign ideas" such as the League of Nations. In carrying out their aims, Klansmen were willing to use terror and violence. By the mid-1920's they had become a major force in politics, mostly in the South and the Middle West, but also in other states including Maine and Oregon.

At the 1924 Democratic Convention, Bryan made his last great political move by supporting a resolution to denounce the Klan as un-American. The motion was defeated by a single vote after angry debate. In the balloting for the presidential nominee, William G. McAdoo of California, generally supported by the West and South, opposed Governor Alfred E. Smith of New York, a Roman Catholic, whose following came mostly from urban areas of the East. A deadlock between the two candidates lasted so long that the cowboy-humorist Will Rogers suggested that the eventual nominee might be born in the convention. By the time a compromise candidate, John W. Davis of West Virginia, was nominated on the 103rd ballot, the Democrats had lost all chance of winning the election.

An unusual aspect of the 1924 election was the attempt by Senator La Follette of Wisconsin to start a new Progressive party. Like the Populists, the new organization was an attempt to form a farmer-labor alliance. The Progressive platform favored such measures as government ownership of water power, abolition of business monopolies, protection of the right of workers to form unions, and higher taxes on inheritances. Its foreign policy was isolationist.

The Republicans campaigned on the slogan "Keep cool with Coolidge"; the way to keep business thriving, they said, was not to "rock the boat" but to keep in power the party that favored business. This strategy was successful. In an election that attracted only half the eligible voters to the polls, Coolidge won easily. The Democrats carried only the states of the former Confederacy, and the Progressives carried only La Follette's own state.

THE GOLDEN TWENTIES

During the 1920's the United States went almost dizzy with prosperity. New industries appeared overnight; the production of goods rose to unprecedented heights; former luxuries became necessities. A combination of increased leisure for both men and women, new gadgets, new amusements, and more money to spend resulted in something approaching glorification of wealth and of the material comforts that went with it.

Growth of the Automobile Industry

The outstanding symbol of the new age was the automobile. In the early twentieth century, when the manufacture of automobiles in the United States was just beginning, driving cars was a sport, like playing polo or racing yachts. By 1928, when 26,500,000 motor vehicles were registered, it was no exaggeration to talk of a "nation on wheels."

The person most responsible for changing the automobile from a rich person's toy to everybody's necessity was Henry Ford. Ford's famous "Model T," affectionately known as "tin Lizzie," was so simple in operation that anyone could learn to drive, and so cheap that even families with modest incomes could afford it. Ford applied many familiar techniques of successful industrialists, such as the use of standardized parts and the formation of a vertical trust to combine different operations and eliminate middlemen's profits. His greatest achievement was the assembly line, in which conveyors brought the parts to the workers, and in which operations were broken down into such simple tasks that most of the work could be done by unskilled labor. The speed of production was such that the Ford Company "boasted that raw iron ore at the docks at eight Monday morning could be marketed as a complete Ford car on Wednesday noon, allowing fifteen hours for shipment."

Ford's economies so reduced costs that while the average price of American automobiles in 1907 was $2,123, Ford offered a model for $850 in 1908, $540 in 1914, and $290 in 1924. Other employers called Ford a Bolshevist because his pay scale was so high that it created discontent among those who worked elsewhere. It was his belief that high wages combined with mass production methods and low prices would produce an immense market for goods. By the mid-1920's other great vertical trusts, notably General Motors and Chrysler, were competing with Ford.

The impact of the automobile on American life was revolutionary. Railroads lost revenue as pleasure cars and buses cut passenger traffic, and trucks competed for freight. New fields for small enterprise appeared—garages, gas stations, diners, tourist homes. Draft animals disappeared from farms as tractors took their place. The isolation of rural areas lessened as cars put towns within easy reach of many farmers. City dwellers went to the country on holidays in such numbers that it was said, "If all the cars in America were placed end to end, it would be Sunday."

Radio and Motion Pictures

An invention which burst on the country even more rapidly than the automobile was the radio. In 1920 station KDKA in Pittsburgh issued the first commercial broadcast in history at the time of Harding's election; six years later, when the Federal Radio Commission was established to regulate them, broadcasting stations numbered 732. Between 1921 and 1929, the sales of radio equipment skyrocketed from $13,000 to $338,000,000. The fantastic expansion of radio stimulated an immense increase in the sale of other goods because broadcasting stations were supported by advertising revenues. The young motion picture industry also mushroomed; by 1929 it was estimated that there were 100,000,000 paid admissions in movie theatres every week. Here were two more great "blotting paper" industries that created prosperity by soaking up raw materials and employing great numbers of workers.

Sinclair Lewis and his wife ride in a Model T Ford. In quite different ways, both Sinclair Lewis and the mass-produced automobile came to symbolize the period of the 1920's.

Radio and motion pictures made it possible for the general public to "attend" sporting events—through the running commentaries of "sportscasters" and through newsreels. The two inventions helped to make the 1920's a golden age of sport. Sports previously little known, such as golf and tennis, and well-established sports, such as football, boxing, and baseball, reached new heights of popularity. Notre Dame's famous backfield, the "Four Horsemen," were better known than cabinet members, and Babe Ruth became a national hero. Gertrude Ederle swam the English Channel.

QUESTION • What was the "national game" of the 1920's? How are things different today?

A New Formula for Wealth

It seemed as though Americans had discovered a magic formula for producing wealth and fulfilling human wants on a scale never before thought possible. Its ingredients were high wages, mass production, standardized products, and a nation-wide market. This formula tended to favor big business over small, because only big business could set up assembly lines, do the research necessary for constant development of new products, and afford nation-wide advertising. It was natural, then, that the 1920's should be a period of concentration of industry. Concentration was effected partly by mergers, in which two or more companies combined as one, and partly by holding companies, which bought voting control of operating companies. Big business also entered the field of retail selling by the expansion of chain stores, soon familiar sights on many Main Streets. By 1929 they had captured a quarter of the grocery business of the country.

Whereas average Americans formerly regarded the "trusts" as enemies, they now relied on big business to create new opportunities. Never before had business people stood so high in public esteem. Striking evidence of the new attitude was seen in the behavior of the stock

METHODS OF CORPORATE CONTROL

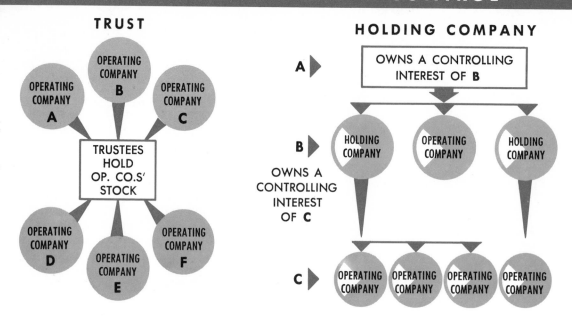

Business in America has grown bigger in the twentieth century as more efficient organizations have expanded and absorbed competitors. Varying methods of organization have been used, such as the trust and the holding company. In the latter, control may be exercised with as little as 15 or 20 per cent of the stock of a subsidiary, if the remainder is widely spread among investors.

market. For the first time in history, members of the general public began to buy securities. The prices of shares of stock, especially those connected with new industries, mounted to dizzy heights. More and more purchasers "invested in the future."

Ownership of securities became more widely distributed than ever before; thus millions of people gained a direct stake in capitalism. But this development was not accompanied by a corresponding diffusion of control over business enterprise. On the contrary, new devices for concentrating financial power were invented. One of these was the so-called "pyramiding" of holding companies, whereby it was possible with a relatively small outlay of capital for men to gain control of immense industrial properties. Another quite open-and-aboveboard method whereby promoters gained the use of "other people's money" without surrendering

control was the issuance of non-voting preferred stock. Both of these devices led to such abuses that they were later forbidden by law.

Labor and Labor Unions

In 1927 André Siegfried, a French sociologist, wrote, "A worker is far better paid in America than anywhere else in the world." Between 1921 and 1928, the average annual wage rose from $1,171 to $1,408. Workers bought automobiles and radios by the millions, usually on the installment plan. Mass production of clothing made garments of good cut so cheap that a visiting Englishman remarked that American shopgirls "dressed like duchesses."

The benefits of the new industrialization did not extend to all labor. The greatest rewards went to skilled workers in powerful unions, especially in the building trades, and to the unskilled in the new, highly mechanized industries. In certain "sick industries," such as textiles and coal mining, wages actually declined. Blacks in the South were still mostly confined to poorly paid agricultural work. The unprecedented demand for new sources of labor during World War I started a mass migration of blacks from the South to northern and western cities, which continued during the 1920's, partially stimulated by the decline of immigration. They found greater opportunity, to be sure, but they were usually able to obtain only unskilled or menial jobs, and most trade unions denied them membership.

The new processes of manufacture caused constant technological unemployment. Although people replaced by machines usually found jobs elsewhere, the transition was sometimes difficult. Not only were they often forced to leave home to find employment, but they also frequently lost the benefit of long training in a particular skill. An extreme example of the latter situation was unemployment among musicians caused by the introduction of juke boxes and sound films. Although the assembly line lowered immensely the costs of production, many laborers could not stand the monotony

---

Electrical Genius—Charles Steinmetz

In 1893 the General Electric Company bought the small company which Rudolf Eickemeyer had set up to carry out electrical experiments. They acquired some equipment and a few patents, but the prize they were after was Charles Steinmetz.

Steinmetz had emigrated from Germany in 1889, fleeing German officials angered by an editorial he had written advocating socialism. A hunchback from birth, frail, sickly, and threadbare, he knew no English. He would have been denied admission to the United States as a pauper if a Danish friend, a fellow immigrant, had not lent him money and agreed to sponsor him.

His first American employer was Eickemeyer, to whom Steinmetz developed a strong loyalty. He gained recognition in electrical science with his work on the law of hysteresis, which governs the loss of power by alternating magnetism. General Electric offered him a job with an excellent salary and superb research facilities. But Steinmetz would not leave Eickemeyer while the latter could use him.

He did join General Electric in 1893 and, as the "Electrical Genius of GE," made contributions to science and science engineering which sped the nation into an Age of Electricity. More than two hundred patents flowed from his work, which included the study, explanation, and harnessing of alternating current. Before Steinmetz, it had been impossible to transmit electricity more than 3 miles without using multiple generators.

With all this, he remained a Socialist. In 1916 he published *America and the New Epoch,* advocating government ownership, but private management, of industry. In 1922 he even ran for the office of state engineer of New York on the Socialist ticket. He was decisively defeated; America would permit him to be a Socialist but would not encourage him by electing him to office.

and nervous tension of working at a speed set by the machine. This was particularly true of middle-aged workers, and "old at forty" became a bitter slogan to them.

The "prosperity decade" saw labor unions declining in numbers and strength. The American Federation of Labor, a craft workers' organization with little ability or desire to enroll the unskilled, had difficulty enough holding its own members in the face of the anti-union activities of employers' associations. Employers joined to promote the open shop, labeled "the American plan"; in actual practice the open shop often meant a "shop closed to union members." Although Herbert Hoover, Secretary of Commerce, persuaded President Harding to make a successful personal appeal to the leaders of the steel industry to abandon the 12-hour day, the federal government was usually on the side of the employers. Thus Attorney General Harry M. Daugherty helped to break railroad and coal strikes in 1922 by obtaining injunctions that prohibited every conceivable union activity, including picketing, making public statements to the press, and jeering at strikebreakers. During the 1920's a series of Supreme Court decisions whittled away the protections that unions thought they had secured by the Clayton Act of 1914. Injunctions were again freely used to stop strikes and boycotts, and unions were punished under the Sherman Antitrust Act for "conspiracies in restraint of trade."

There was relatively little labor unrest. This was partly because of the spread of "welfare capitalism." Companies tried to make workers "partners in production" by enabling them to buy shares of stock, by profit-sharing, and by providing medical care, old-age pensions, and recreational facilities. But the principal reason why the number of workers involved in strikes dropped sharply was that workers shared the general confidence in business leadership. It was typical of the period that the president of the American Federation of Labor was hired by a Wall Street broker to broadcast advice on investments.

THE PLIGHT OF AGRICULTURE

The farmers were the one great economic group that did not share in Coolidge prosperity. Their average income in 1929 was less than a third of that of the rest of the country. As in the period after the Civil War (see pp. 422, 430), they were squeezed between rising costs and declining income. As one account puts it, "Freight rates, wages, taxes, farm implements, and the like, all of which went into the farmers' cost of production, remained high or came down via the stairway, while farm prices took the elevator."

Farm prices did not recover from the disastrous toboggan slide of 1920–1921 (see graph, p. 626). The foreign market dwindled because the United States had changed from a debtor to a creditor nation. Before the First World War, foreign investments in America exceeded American investments abroad; the principal means of making up this unfavorable credit balance was for the United States to export agricultural staples, such as wheat and cotton. During the war the balance shifted the other way, principally because of American loans to the Allies. With the return of peace, countries owing the United States money preferred not to buy products. Great Britain, for instance, often bought wheat from the Argentine or Canada rather than from the United States, especially since the Fordney-McCumber Tariff reduced the American market for British manufactured goods.

The domestic market also diminished. The use of new fabrics such as rayon lessened the demand for cotton; Prohibition curtailed the market for grain; the substitution of tractors and trucks for draft animals reduced the need for fodder. Eating habits too were changing. Americans consumed more fruit, vegetables, and milk, less bread and meat.

Faced with decreasing demands for the traditional staples, farmers might have been expected to shift to other products, but that was easier said than done. A southern tenant farmer usually had no skill at anything but raising cotton; a Dakota wheat farmer usually lacked the capital, let alone the knowledge, to change over, say, to dairy farming. Moreover, credit and marketing facilities were usually available only for the staple crops of each region. Many farmers had borrowed heavily during the war to buy new acreage at inflated prices. The only obvious way to pay off the debt was to raise more crops. More crops meant unsaleable surpluses. Unsaleable surpluses meant low prices. Low prices meant that the debt burden was heavier.

The Farm Bloc and the McNary-Haugen Bill

As at the time of the Grangers and the Populists (see pp. 427 and 455), farmers organized for political action. Early in Harding's administration, Congress members from the Middle West and the Plains region formed what was known as the "Farm Bloc." Although predominantly Republican, it was drawn from both parties, and included about 25 senators and 100 representatives. Strong enough to hold a balance of power, it was able to force through several laws favoring farmers. The Packers and Stockyards Act, passed in 1921, subjected meat packers and marketers handling livestock to federal regulation. The Capper-Volstead Act of 1922 entirely exempted farm cooperatives from antitrust laws. In 1923 an Intermediate Credits Act established federal banks to make loans especially helpful to farm cooperatives. None of these measures dealt, however, with the staple farmers' fundamental problem: the unmarketable surpluses. If wheat farmers, for instance, were to get the benefit of the 42-cents-a-bushel protective tariff which priced foreign wheat out of the domestic market, they somehow had to limit the amount of wheat available to American consumers.

Some farm experts proposed to "put a price tag on a bushel of wheat" by forming a great national farmers' organization to restrict production to the amount that could be sold. The Farm Bloc, however, supported the McNary-Haugen bill, which was presented to Congress every year from 1924 to 1928. The essential idea behind the proposed laws was that the federal government should buy up surpluses and sell them abroad. This would immediately raise the domestic price. Whatever losses the government suffered would be covered by an "equalization fee"—a tax charged against producers. Supporters of the McNary-Haugen bill claimed that it would give farmers benefits that manufacturers got from the tariff and would raise farm incomes by as much as a third. The bill twice passed Congress, but on both occasions President Coolidge roused himself from his habitual inertia and vetoed it. In vigorous prose Coolidge argued that the proposed law was unworkable, that it subjected farmers to "bureaucratic legislation and control," and that it favored a special interest. The counter-argument that the protective tariff and Secretary of the Treasury Andrew Mellon's tax policies also favored special interests did not sway the man who believed that the business of America was business.

NEW DIRECTIONS

The rapid changes induced by the progress of technology during this period caused serious problems. In the hands of careless or incompetent drivers, automobiles were so dangerous that in 1928 and 1929 they killed as many Americans as lost their lives in World War I.

Cities began to "rot at the center" as automobiles enabled homes, factories, and shops to move to the suburbs. The "canned entertainment" of radio and motion pictures seemed to be destroying the ability of Americans to amuse themselves.

A distressing aspect of the 1920's was that crime itself became big business, partly as a result of the failure to enforce Prohibition. After the ratification of the Eighteenth Amendment in 1919, Congress passed the Volstead Act, which defined intoxicating beverages as those containing over ½ of 1 per cent of alcohol. The Prohibition Bureau set up to enforce the law was understaffed, underpaid, graft-ridden, and ineffective. Illegal drinking provided millions of customers for a billion-dollar industry that was taken over by criminal elements. The "big shots" in the liquor "racket" became wealthy enough to buy mansions in Florida and powerful enough to corrupt and even to dominate local governments. Bootlegging and gangsterism were confined for the most part to urban areas: Rural districts and small towns remained predominantly dry, both in sentiment and in practice.

The 1920's brought not only great material prosperity, but a "slump in idealism." A postwar letdown in moral standards was reflected in the corruption of the Harding administration and in the lawbreaking that made it almost impossible to enforce Prohibition. The moral fervor of the progressive period and the World War turned sour with the failure of the crusade to make the world safe for democracy. "We are tired of causes," wrote F. Scott Fitzgerald, whose novels described the antics of a disillusioned "lost generation" of young people. The older generation deplored the way the young "ran wild"—at least that was what it was called when "flappers," with short skirts and bobbed hair, danced the foxtrot and the Charleston, and drank bathtub gin.

Cultural Achievements

Fitzgerald was only one of several authors whose sense of change and of the challenge to old values made the 1920's a vital and important period for literature. Some writers, such as the novelist Willa Cather and the poet Robert Frost, attempted to recapture the philosophy and life of rural America that the machine was destroying. Others, such as the poet Carl Sandburg, tried to interpret the industrial city. In Eugene O'Neill the United States produced its finest playwright, who found material for drama in many aspects of the modern scene, ranging from the rage of a stoker in the hold of a steamer to family tensions in a decaying New England town. Ernest Hemingway, who had driven an ambulance on the Italian front in the First World War, reflected the meaningless violence of war in "hard-boiled" fiction that created a new literary style. The poet T. S. Eliot saw the world filled with "hollow men" and predicted that everything would end "not with a bang but a whimper."

The postwar disillusion was often expressed in criticism of the American scene. Taking their cue from a statement attributed to Henry Ford, "History is bunk," a school of "debunking" historians attempted to show that American history was nothing to be proud of. In his novels *Main Street* and *Babbitt*, Sinclair Lewis satirized the life of the small-town middle class. H. L. Mencken, successively editor of *Smart Set* and *The American Mercury*, made fun of the "vast, undifferentiated herd of good-natured animals" who composed the bulk of machine-age society. Mencken saw no hope for betterment. "If I am convinced of anything," he wrote, "it is that Doing Good is in bad taste."

Achievements in literature were matched in the arts. The building of city skyscrapers and suburban homes provided architects with abundant opportunities. Frank Lloyd Wright, a pupil of Louis Sullivan, achieved world fame for

One of the greatest of modern musicians was Louis Armstrong, who learned to play his magic trumpet in the cradle of jazz, New Orleans. Here he is shown (standing left of Lil Hardin at the piano) when he was a member of the King Oliver band in the 1920's. That this group was in existence early in the age of jazz is suggested by the banjoist at the right and by the absence of saxophones.

his bold use of new materials and for designs completely free of traditional influence. In jazz, which came north with Negro Dixieland bands from New Orleans during the First World War and was carried to Europe by Negro soldiers, America produced a new form of music. At first regarded with horror as a contribution to corrupting the morals of the young, jazz was soon accepted as an important art form—as was shown by George Gershwin's "Rhapsody in Blue." Never had the American scene been better portrayed in pigment than by those artists who displayed the life of the people, such as Reginald Marsh, Thomas Hart Benton, and George Bellows, or by those who portrayed its inanimate forms, such as Edward Hopper, John Marin, and Charles Burchfield. In the new art of photogra-

QUESTION • *What was new about jazz?*

phy, Alfred Stieglitz made a world-wide reputation. At his famous gallery, "An American Place," in New York, Stieglitz provided a display place and a rendezvous for artists from all corners of the earth.

Much of the new wealth of the 1920's went into education, both through the expansion of tax-supported public schools and through private donations to colleges and universities. No previous decade in the history of American education saw such a rise in school attendance or such increase in teachers' salaries. The introduction of the school bus made possible the gradual replacement of barren, one-room schoolhouses by large, well-equipped central schools. The curriculum was enriched by new subjects. Not only did high school enrollment increase, but many more students went on to college, and the enrollment in junior colleges quadrupled.

World War I had been a liberating experience for many black Americans. Especially was this true of those who went abroad and were freed for a time from the second-class citizenship that blacks suffered in the United States. The postwar years saw the appearance of a new black, a person "who had pride in heritage and self and who, through poetry, music, dance, and the theater, was able to create works of beauty out of travail and sufferings as well as out of the more humorous facts of life." A striking manifestation of this new spirit among black people was the "Harlem Renaissance." In New York City, the intellectual capital of the United States, a number of highly talented people rose to prominence. Some were in the performing arts: the actors Charles Gilipin and Richard B. Harrison; the singers Roland Hayes and Ethel Waters; the dancer Bill Robinson and the singer-actor Paul Robeson. Others were scholars: the sociologist E. Franklin Frazier and the economist Abram L. Harris. Still others were authors —the poets Countee Cullen and Langston Hughes; the novelists Jessie H. Faucet and Walter White.

Among black people themselves a more influential figure than the intellectuals and artists was a dynamic leader from Jamaica, Marcus Garvey. His Universal Negro Improvement Society had a million members. Garvey told his followers they would never find justice in America and proposed to lead them back to Africa. People were not interested, but Garvey had stimulated the pride of blacks in their history and their African heritage.

After the Vote: The Status of Women

The 1920's and '30's were a period when women gained greater personal freedom. Heavy duties at home were made lighter by new household equipment, commercial laundries, and canned foods. The automobile gave women more chance to escape supervision and to claim the freedom of deciding when to go where. These new developments were reflected by the emergence of the "flapper"—a flamboyant, self-assertive woman who smoked cigarettes in public, drank hard liquor when she felt like it, and dressed in a way her mother and grandmother would not have conceived possible. Her new bobbed hair style was the finishing statement to newly won freedoms that would permanently change American society.

These gains, though clearly observable, were not matched by gains on other fronts. Women no longer perceived a political cause around which to rally. Women did not emerge as a significant bloc, either in legislatures or at the polls, that influenced legislation. In the working world, the overall percentage of women who worked remained at about 25% until 1940. Most women who worked did so out of necessity rather than choice. Those who did were often domestics or garment workers, whose wages were low and hours long. Most Americans, both women and men, believed that women who could afford to should remain at home. In a poll taken in 1936, 75% of women agreed.

Thus, in spite of new personal freedoms, women were trapped by the belief that their role was different from that of men, that they were to be only wives and mothers. Women who did work suffered severe discrimination. They received 50 to 60% as much as men for the same work, and they were not considered suitable physically or emotionally for many jobs.

Individual women, however, did manage to achieve under these difficult conditions. Amelia Earhart decided to fly planes, and in 1932 she became the first woman to complete a solo flight across the Atlantic. Dorothy Thompson became a famous journalist. Mary McLeod Bethune, though black and born into poverty, studied teaching and founded her own school. She became a vice-president of the NAACP and was named a special consultant on black affairs by President Roosevelt. Many women gained prominence in music, the arts, and literature.

Activities: Chapter 24

For Mastery and Review

1. Who were the presidential candidates in 1920? Explain the nomination of Harding. What did the election decide?

2. How did the United States make peace with Germany? What were the war debts? Why did they cause disputes?

3. For what reasons was the Washington Conference called? Summarize its accomplishments and results. What were the terms of the Kellogg-Briand Treaty?

4. What was Stimson's problem in Nicaragua? Morrow's in Mexico?

5. Describe the chief features of the Fordney-McCumber Tariff. Study the map on p. 578, and describe the geographical pattern of the vote. How, and with what success, were taxes reduced in the 1920's?

6. Why was U.S. immigration policy changed? Describe the Immigration Quota of 1924.

7. What were the scandals of the Harding administration? Why did they so little affect the 1924 election? Who was elected?

8. Summarize Henry Ford's contribution to America. What basic changes has the automobile made in our way of living? The radio? The motion picture? Professional sports?

9. Outline the new formula for wealth of the 1920's. What were its effects? Who benefited? What happened to organized labor? To farmers?

10. What new problems arose in the 1920's? How was the slump in idealism reflected in literature? Discuss cultural achievements of the era.

Unrolling the Map

On a map of the world, indicate (a) the nations signing the Four-Power, Five-Power, and Nine-Power Treaties; (b) the points of friction between the United States and Japan: Shantung, Yap, and eastern Siberia (see the map on p. 550); (c) American Pacific holdings: Guam, the Philippines, and the Hawaiian Islands; (d) European holdings in the Pacific in the 1920's.

Who, What, and Why Important?

election of 1920	election of 1924
war debts	Robert La Follette
World Court	Henry Ford
Washington Conference	KDKA
5-5-3 ratio	Marcus Garvey
Kellogg-Briand Treaty	open shop
Henry L. Stimson	welfare capitalism
Dwight Morrow	Gertrude Ederle
Fordney-McCumber Tariff	Prohibition
Budget Bureau	Amelia Earhart
Immigration Quota Law	Mary McLeod Bethune
Teapot Dome	Frank Lloyd Wright
Ku Klux Klan	Harlem Renaissance
	Alfred Stieglitz

To Pursue the Matter

1. Did the Washington Conference result in gain or loss for the United States? For China? For Japan?

2. What forces and what American attitudes were behind the demands for severe restriction of immigration in the 1920's? What were the consequences of such restriction? Useful source: Jones, *American Immigration.*

3. Allen, *Only Yesterday,* gives a wonderful portrait of the twenties. Separate chapters on such topics as "Harding and the Scandals," "Alcohol and Al Capone," and "The Big Bull Market" could be sources for class reports.

4. A black page in American history was the intolerance displayed in the 1920's. What were its sources, how was it displayed, and why did it subside? Possible sources: Hofstadter, *The Twenties;* Chalmers, *Hooded Americanism: The First Century of the Ku Klux Klan.*

5. Did Henry Ford "save capitalism" and refute Marx? Read what a French observer thought in Bruckberger, *The Image of America,* Chs. 18 and 19.

6. How did jazz come to take over in the 1920's? How was the jazz of the 1920's different from the jazz of today?

7. The 1920's have been called the golden age of American sports. Who were the great performers and champions of the era? Find pictures of them. Get them reproduced, for a wall display.

Chapter 25

Crash

The United States is the only nation that ever drove to the poorhouse in an automobile.
—WILL ROGERS

After Coolidge had ruled himself out of the presidential race by a characteristically brief pronouncement, "I do not choose to run in 1928," the way was cleared for the choice of Herbert Hoover as Republican nominee. Previously known as a practical humanitarian, Hoover had now captured the imagination of the country as an "engineer in politics." While Secretary of Commerce under Harding and Coolidge, he used the influence and facilities of the federal government to promote better business practices and eliminate waste. In the interest of efficiency he encouraged standardization of everything from the threading of nuts and bolts to accounting methods. He promoted research in fields as diverse as fish propagation and automobile accidents. He favored the formation of "trade associations" composed of all the companies in a single business and persuaded them to reduce the need for government regulation by drawing up voluntary "codes" of "fair trade." These agreements outlawed practices such as misbranding and selling at a loss to force a competitor out of business.

To oppose Hoover, the Democrats nominated one of the most competent and colorful figures in public life, Alfred E. Smith. His nomination had been blocked by the influence of the Ku Klux Klan in 1924 because he was a Roman Catholic and the grandson of immigrants, but in the intervening four years the Klan had declined as people reacted against its lawless methods and vicious intolerance. Four times governor of New York, Smith had been brilliantly successful both in promoting social legislation and in improving the efficiency of state government.

THE ELECTION OF 1928

The only issue of consequence in the election was Prohibition. Both candidates promised to enforce it, but Smith urged that at the very least the Volstead Act be amended to permit individual states to sell light wines and beer. Hoover supported Prohibition in rather guarded terms, calling it "a great social and economic experiment, noble in motive and far-reaching in purpose." An unpleasant development during the electioneering was a smear campaign against Smith because of his religion. Wild tales circulated that Catholics had surrounded Washington with alleged church sites that were really gun emplacements and that the Pope would move to the American capital if Smith were elected. Although Hoover publicly deplored such tactics, they undoubtedly hurt the Democratic candidate, especially in rural districts.

It is doubtful, however, if the Democrats ever had a chance. The Republicans campaigned on such slogans as "Two cars in every garage." Again, as in 1924, the electorate voted for prosperity. Hoover carried the electoral college by a vote of 444 to 87 and broke the Solid South by carrying five states of the former Confederacy. But Smith's defeat was not as hopeless as it appeared: he polled twice as many votes as Davis in 1924 and carried the twelve largest cities.

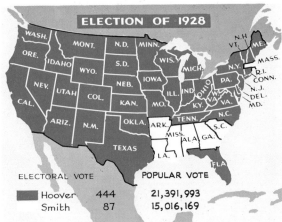

ELECTORAL VOTE		POPULAR VOTE
Hoover	444	21,391,993
Smith	87	15,016,169

The Republicans promised the "end of the poorhouse" and "two cars in every garage" as the great tide of prosperity carried Herbert Hoover to victory over Alfred Smith in the 1928 election.

Hoover's Political Philosophy

In the closing days of the 1928 campaign, Hoover made a speech explaining his idea of the proper relation of government to business, and his belief in what he called "the American system of rugged individualism." The great prosperity of America, he said, was based on three factors: *self-government,* as far as possible through local agencies; *individual freedom* to encourage initiative; and *equality of opportunity.* This was in contrast to the European doctrines of "paternalism" (in which the government attempts to provide for individual security) and "state socialism" (in which basic industries are run by government). In the emergency presented by the First World War, it had been necessary to regiment "the whole people temporarily into a socialistic state," but such regimentation was wholly out of place in peacetime.

The true role of government, Hoover argued, was that of "an umpire instead of a player in the economic game." It was a false liberalism that favored such "liberal" legislation as government operation of electric power plants. Once the federal government invaded the field of business, democracy would be threatened, since it depended on decentralization, and personal liberty would be endangered, because it depended on economic freedom. Hoover made clear, however, that his idea was not one of "devil take the hindmost." "It is," he said, "no system of *laissez-faire.*" Within its proper sphere, the federal government had a part to play in helping to provide "economic justice as well as political and social justice."

Hoover mentioned conservation of natural resources, flood control, and scientific research as legitimate activities of government. Occasionally it might sell power or commodities as a by-product. But if government went further than that, it would undermine "the very instincts which carry our people forward to progress." As an example, Hoover pointed to Russia, whose natural resources equaled America's and whose people worked as hard, but which was far behind America in wealth because it lacked the benefits of 150 years of freedom and self-government.

"Our experiment in human welfare," Hoover maintained, "has yielded a degree of well-being

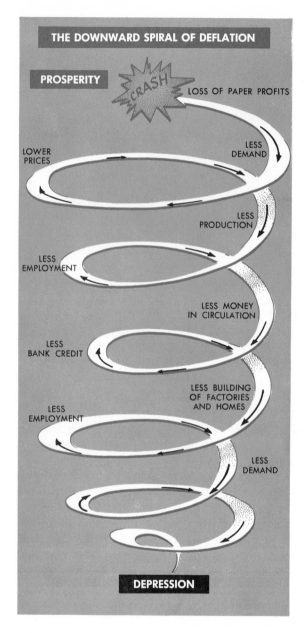

THE DOWNWARD SPIRAL OF DEFLATION

PROSPERITY

CRASH

LOSS OF PAPER PROFITS

LOWER PRICES

LESS DEMAND

LESS PRODUCTION

LESS EMPLOYMENT

LESS MONEY IN CIRCULATION

LESS BANK CREDIT

LESS BUILDING OF FACTORIES AND HOMES

LESS EMPLOYMENT

LESS DEMAND

DEPRESSION

The fear of a crash of the stock market has continuously plagued economists. Following the work of Lord Keynes, many economists now believe that there are stabilizers in the economic system that can prevent a major depression.

unparalleled in the world.... We are nearer to the ideal of abolition of poverty and fear from the lives of men and women than ever before in any land."

HOOVER IN OFFICE

When he entered the White House in March 1929, Herbert Hoover radiated optimism. In his inaugural address the new President predicted that, "given a chance to go forward with the policies of the last eight years," the United States would soon "be in sight of the day when poverty will be banished from this nation." Unlike Coolidge, Hoover did not propose to sit back and let matters take their course. As he had said during the recent campaign, he believed that the federal government should help people to help themselves.

An engineer, a thorough and competent administrator, Hoover wanted facts as a basis for action. To get the facts he appointed commissions to investigate problems as diverse as better housing, old-age pensions, unemployment insurance, child welfare, and conservation. The most famous was that headed by former Attorney General George W. Wickersham, which devoted two years to investigating Prohibition enforcement. The eleven members of the Wickersham Commission were unable to agree either on the success of the "noble experiment" or on what should be done about it. In general, they saw that it was ineffective and promoted crime, but proposed its continuance. Their report was satirized by the humorist Franklin P. Adams:

Prohibition is an awful flop.
   We like it.
It can't stop what it's meant to stop.
   We like it.
It's left a trail of graft and slime,
It don't prohibit worth a dime,
It's filled our land with vice and crime,
   Nevertheless, we're for it.

Agricultural Marketing Act, 1929

One problem that could not wait for the slow process of a committee investigation but demanded immediate action was the plight of agriculture. In their 1928 campaign platforms both Democrats and Republicans had promised farm relief. Hoover therefore called Congress into special session in April 1929 to pass legislation on behalf of agriculture. The Farm Bloc again demanded legislation that would enlist the federal government in buying surplus farm products and selling them abroad. Hoover opposed this on the ground that "no Government Agency should engage in buying and selling and price-fixing of products." The President proposed instead that the federal government help farmers to set up their own organizations to market produce more efficiently and adjust supply to demand. Following this recommendation, Congress passed the Agricultural Market Act of 1929. This law created an eight-man Federal Farm Board which was furnished with 500 million dollars to help existing farm organizations and to create new ones. Under the terms of the law, the Farm Board established great national cooperatives such as the National Livestock Marketing Association and the American Cotton Cooperative Association. The Farm Board loaned these cooperatives money to keep prices stable by buying and selling in the open market. In spite of these efforts American farmers were soon worse off than ever because the rest of the country and world plunged into the worst depression in history.

THE GREAT DEPRESSION

Between 1925 and 1929 the market value of securities on the New York Stock Exchange more than tripled, increasing from $27,000,000,000 to $87,000,000,000. Most of this fantastic rise was the result of a wave of speculation similar to that in land in the 1830's (see p. 269). Many who were gambling in the great bull market bought "on margin," which meant that they might be wiped out if prices dropped. The fever was supported by billions of dollars in loans made by brokers, mostly "call money" that the borrower was obliged to repay on demand. As the fever mounted, securities sold for as much as fifty times their earning power; stock in a company that never paid a dividend rose to as much as $40 to $50 per share; speculators' paper profits went up accordingly.

QUESTION • *How does buying on margin increase both profits and risks?*

Although some bankers, brokers, and economists saw danger, many others were swept along in a tide of optimism. If miracles were possible in the automobile and radio industry, why not in finance? Even President Coolidge abandoned his usual cautious silence to say that he saw nothing wrong with a great increase in brokers' loans. With this official blessing the market went on a dizzy climb. The Federal Reserve Board made belated efforts to stop the ascent by advising member banks not to loan money which might be used for margin buying of stocks, but its warnings were ignored. Although security prices occasionally sagged, the market always recovered under pressure of new investors who hoped to get "something for nothing" by buying stock and waiting for it to rise.

When the market started to weaken in September 1929, few people really expected that security prices would slip from their "permanently high plateau." But late in October disaster struck. During the most agonizing days in American financial history, an avalanche of selling caused such a collapse that by mid-November the average price of securities had been cut nearly in half and investors had lost about 30 billion dollars, a sum almost equal to the entire cost of American participation in World War I.

Thousands of small investors lost the savings of a lifetime; people who had accounted themselves rich in October were heavily in debt three weeks later; almost every newspaper contained news of suicides. A columnist advised people to look up as they walked down Wall Street for fear of falling bankers.

What Caused the Depression?

The collapse of the stock market was only a prelude to a catastrophic economic decline from which the United States did not entirely recover for twelve years. The causes of the Great Depression were so complex that econo-

mists have debated them ever since, but the following conditions surely helped either to produce or to intensify it:

(1) **Direct and indirect effects of World War I.** The Great Depression was world-wide. The First World War had not only destroyed productive capacity but had built up a great load of government debts, both domestic and international. These debts not only put heavy tax burdens on people everywhere, but also clogged the channels of international trade. Each debtor nation, attempting to sell as much and buy as little as possible, raised tariffs and set up limits on imports (import quotas). For

The stock market bubble burst on October 24, 1929, when a sudden flurry of selling caused pandemonium to break loose on the floor of the New York Stock Exchange, "Black Thursday" was followed by an even blacker Tuesday when, as *The Sun* indicates, 16 million shares of stock were dumped on the market.

a time American investors kept the machinery of international trade going by lending abroad with great freedom. But when borrowers reached the end of their capacity to pay, American loans ceased. And when lending stopped, United States' foreign trade dwindled rapidly.

(2) **The depressed condition of agriculture.** The prolonged slump in agriculture was like a cancer sapping the economic life of the entire country. The shrinkage of farmers' purchasing power cut down the market for manufactured goods and so kept factories from producing to capacity and workers from finding employment. The declining value of farms made it harder for farmers to get credit and imperiled banks that had invested in farm mortgages.

(3) **Overproduction—or underconsumption.** The rapid introduction of labor-saving machinery greatly increased the productive capacity of American industry so that it produced more goods than the market could absorb. For a time this was concealed by the widespread practice of installment buying, whereby the purchaser made a down payment and promised to pay the rest in installments spread over months or years. Carried to extremes, as it was in the late 1920's, installment buying was dangerous because it created a heavy load of private debt and dried up future purchasing power.

Looked at another way, the trouble was underconsumption. In the 1920's the rich got richer much faster than the rest of the people. Some 30,000 families at the top of the economic pyramid received as much as about 11 million families at the bottom. Manufacturers hired no more workers in 1929 than in 1923, and wages went up at a far slower rate than executive salaries or corporation profits. The Brookings Institution estimated that in 1929 over two-thirds of American families received less than $2,500 per year, a sum said to be a minimum decent living. About a fifth of the nation was living at a bare subsistence level. Thus there was insufficient purchasing power to support mass production industry.

(4) **Stock market speculation.** While in itself stock gambling was not one of the primary causes of the depression, it made it more severe. Billions of dollars that, according to the Mellon theory of wealth, should have gone into new products were diverted into speculation. The fantastic demand for securities encouraged unsound and even dishonest practices. When the market finally broke, the demand of investors for money to cover their losses was so great that it caused a credit squeeze throughout the entire country and even in Europe. Above all, the suddenness and violence of the stock market crash helped to change the mood of the country from one of optimism to one of fear.

(5) **Unwise governmental policies.** The economic policies of the federal government during the 1920's, while perhaps not a primary cause of the depression, surely contributed to it. The prohibitively high Fordney-McCumber tariff, combined with the insistence of the Harding and Coolidge administrations on collecting war debts, interfered with world trade and destroyed the American farmers' foreign markets. The Mellon tax policies and the indifference to the plight of agriculture contributed to the maldistribution of wealth. Failure to curb or discourage the stock market boom made the ultimate crash more severe. Finally, antipathy to government regulation of private enterprise meant failure to halt business abuses or to institute needed reforms in the financial system of the country.

(6) **The self-generating effects of the depression itself.** Once launched, the depression had a sort of momentum of its own that helped to create a vicious downward spiral. This can be seen by examining what happened to a man whom we shall call James Kelley, and how

what happened to him affected other people. In 1929 Mr. Kelley, a salesman for a clothing manufacturing firm, lived in his own home (which he had bought with the help of a mortgage from the bank), had a car (which he was buying on an "easy payment" plan), and had laid by some money for a rainy day in a savings bank. On the advice of a broker friend, he also was "taking a flyer" on the stock market, buying on margin. His immediate plans included the purchase of an expensive cabinet radio, and his long-term ambitions included sending his two teen-age children to college. But when the stock market crashed in the autumn of 1929, Mr. Kelley lost every cent he had put into the stock market, since his margins were wiped out.

So Mr. Kelley and thousands of others who had "lost their shirts" stopped buying such luxuries as new radios. Radio companies therefore closed down plants or ran them only part time, laying off thousands of workers and cancelling orders for copper, wood veneer, and glass tubes. Thus Montana copper miners, Minnesota lumberjacks, and Ohio glassworkers lost their jobs. So many men decided to mend their old suits instead of buying new ones that Mr. Kelley's company eventually closed down and he was laid off. He was lucky enough to find work elsewhere, but at such low pay that in order to continue mortgage payments on his house he stopped paying installments on his car, which therefore became the property of a finance company. His savings bank failed and so he lost the money with which he had intended to send his children to college. They hung around street corners because business people, hard put to it to take care of their older workers, were not hiring young people. Multiply Mr. Kelley by millions and one can see how there developed a chain reaction that closed down more factories, drove more firms into bankruptcy, and put more men out of work.

ATTEMPTS TO STEM THE DEPRESSION

Before 1929 Americans had regarded a depression in much the same light as a hurricane or a blizzard; it was something to be weathered. The Great Depression was the first for which the federal government seriously sought remedies. No sooner had the stock market collapsed than President Hoover asked leaders of industry, finance, and labor to the White House. He called on labor leaders to abandon wage demands, on leaders of industry to keep up employment, and on bankers to continue lending. As the crisis deepened, the President worked fourteen and sixteen hours a day to find means of checking the ever-downward spiral of business activity.

Believing that "90 per cent of our difficulty in depressions is caused by fear," Hoover tried to restore confidence by optimistic statements that better days were ahead. In this he was joined by other leaders of politics and industry. So many rosy predictions were contradicted by worsening conditions that the phrase "prosperity is just around the corner" became a joke. The President's position was made all the more difficult because he was blamed for the depression. This might be unfair, but it was nothing new; blame for hard times had always been pinned on the administration in power.

In dealing with Congress and the public, Hoover was handicapped by political inexperience. A man of great ability with a sincere desire to serve the country, he unfortunately lacked the political education that comes from being a state legislator, congressman, or governor. He had learned neither the technique of appealing to popular opinion nor that of arranging compromises between different interests and factions. Even had he possessed such skills, the President's position would have been difficult. Within his own party, the "regulars" never gave him wholehearted support, and members

The Great Depression and The New Deal
A Challenge for Economic Recovery

The Great Depression was the most severe that the United States has ever experienced. Beginning with the stock market crash in 1929, it reached its lowest point in 1932-1933 (see "Rock Bottom," pp. 605-608). The figures given below present some of the economic aspects of the disaster. Study these, and find out how the New Deal affected unemployment, bank failures, and farm income. Then ask yourself or discuss in class this question:

- How successful was the New Deal in pulling the country out of the Great Depression?

	Number of Unemployed Workers (including per cent of the labor force unemployed)	Failures of National Banks	Consumer Expenditures (in millions of dollars)	Farm Income (in millions of dollars)
1929	1,550,000 (3.2%)	89	$77,222	$11,941
1933	12,830,000 (25.2%)	1,101	45,795	6,401
1935	10,610,000 (20.3%)	4	55,699	7,615
1937	7,700,000 (14.3%)	4	66,507	9,176
1939	9,480,000 (17.2%)	4	66,834	8,658

Use your imagination and try to think what the figures shown above meant in the lives of individual people. What was the impact of high unemployment among young people? How did bank failures affect older people? What did it mean to farmers when they had to sell wheat or corn or milk at a price less than the cost of production?

The following statistics may help you to put the depression into human terms (1929 = 100%):

	1929	1932
Marriages in the United States	100%	78%
Suicides	100	130
Admissions to mental hospitals	100	260

of the Farm Bloc were in open revolt. In the mid-term elections of 1930 the Democrats won control of the House of Representatives and made gains in the Senate, so that during his last two years in office Hoover had to deal with a hostile Congress.

Hawley-Smoot Tariff, 1930

Like President Taft in 1909, Hoover was unable to control Congress on the tariff issue. At the beginning of his term he suggested minor tariff increases, mostly on agricultural products, but the Republican majority in Congress, joined by a number of Democrats, undertook to increase duties on all sorts of goods. Almost any interest demanding protection from foreign competition got it.

When the highly protective Hawley-Smoot bill reached the President's desk in 1930, over a thousand leading economists signed a letter urging him to veto it. They argued that it would be a subsidy to inefficient producers, would raise consumer prices, would reduce American foreign markets, and would cause ill feeling toward the United States in other countries. The economists were joined by many conservative newspapers, by the American Bankers Association, even by some manufacturers. Yet if Hoover used his veto he would isolate himself politically by repudiating leaders of his own party. Furthermore, at the President's insistence, the new bill provided for a revised Tariff Commission with power to raise and lower rates; he hoped that this would "take tariff-making out of Congressional log-rolling." He therefore signed the bill.

QUESTION • *If high tariff rates can be expected to cut down exports as well as imports, why did manufacturers demand increased duties?*

Within a year of the passage of the Hawley-Smoot Tariff twenty-five foreign nations made laws to restrict purchases of American goods. The foreign trade of the United States dropped more rapidly than international trade in general. Some American corporations hurdled foreign barriers only by establishing factories in foreign countries. Thus an act designed to promote business activity within the United States instead created employment abroad.

Failure of the Federal Farm Board

American agriculture, already in difficulties, was hit harder than ever by the depression. Farmers' income was more than cut in half between 1929 and 1932; their heavy burden of debt became almost insupportable. Although at first Hoover opposed governmental price-fixing, in the crisis the Farm Board tried to maintain the price of wheat and cotton by buying surpluses off the market. The Farm Board also attempted, but without success, to persuade farmers to stop surpluses at their source by reducing the amount of land planted. Eventually the immense quantities of wheat and cotton held by the federal government drove prices down because buyers feared that the government would sell as soon as there was a rise. Finally, in 1931, the Farm Board acknowledged defeat and stopped its purchases after suffering a loss of nearly 200 million dollars. Thereupon prices dropped even lower. By 1932 farmers were receiving only 38 cents for wheat that in 1929 had sold at $1.04; cotton had dropped from 17 cents to 5; in the "corn-hog belt" farmers used unsaleable corn for fuel.

Federal Spending

Once it was clear that this depression was worse than any other, Hoover tried to restore prosperity by use of federal credit. He supported increased appropriations for roads, land reclamation, and dams, all of which provided employment. Residential building was one of the industries which suffered most from the

Herbert Hoover, Humanitarian

The first savage impact of depression wreaked terrible personal havoc. Good jobs, life savings, mortgaged homes—all disappeared overnight. Around many an American city grew up a fringe of shacks, built of orange crates and tin cans hammered flat. These impromptu slums were often named "Hoovervilles."

It was natural that desperate men should make President Hoover their scapegoat, but it was hardly fair. His philosophy of government did not permit direct federal relief to the suffering and unfortunate, but he was not a "do-nothing" President. Lacking the warmth and informal friendliness of more successful political leaders, he yet did more to try to stem a depression than any previous chief executive.

Not even a superficial student of his career could question his humanitarianism. In 1914 Hoover was a mining engineer, important in his field and wealthy by his own efforts, but almost unknown to the American public. Without any official status, he set up an organization to feed and care for the civilian population of Belgium and northern France. He devoted all his energies to this work until the United States' entry into World War I ended his neutral standing. The hostilities over, he directed a similar effort in Russia until Soviet suspicions forced him and his staff to leave. Again, in 1927, when a disastrous flood hit Mississippi, he directed a program of relief for the homeless and destitute.

In 1931, at the depth of the depression, that reputation was forgotten. Not for fifteen years were his skills called on again. But in 1946 he toured Europe and South America, assessing food needs for the American government. In 1947–1951 and 1953–1955 he headed a commission studying United States government operations. And to the world, it was again apparent that he had not lost his Quaker "concern" for his fellow human beings.

depression; in 1932 less than one-tenth as many homes were built as in 1929. At the President's suggestion, Congress therefore established twelve Federal Home Loan Banks to provide cheap credit for builders and homeowners.

It was also at Hoover's urging that in 1932 Congress established the immense Reconstruction Finance Corporation (RFC). With two billion dollars in resources, the RFC lent to banks, business concerns, and local government agencies. The idea was that the machinery of commerce could be stimulated into activity by credit poured in from the top. Projects favored by the RFC under Hoover were designed to be "self-liquidating." That is, they were supposed to pay their way so that the government would eventually get back its money. Thus projects such as toll bridges and dams producing electric power were favored over those which might be

socially useful but brought in no revenue, such as playgrounds, schools, and city halls.

There was a point beyond which Hoover refused to use the power and resources of the federal government. He feared that too much reliance on federal action would result in the very "paternalism" and "state socialism" against which he had warned in the 1928 campaign. He opposed direct federal relief for the unemployed on the grounds that it would weaken the self-respect of those who received it, that it would undercut the efforts of private charity, and that it would destroy the tradition of local responsibility for the unfortunate. When Congress passed the Garner-Wagner bill in 1932 to provide direct aid to the unemployed and a large increase in public works, Hoover vetoed it. He also vetoed the Norris bill, which provided that the federal government should go into the business of producing electricity and making fertilizer in the Tennessee Valley. He said that this was a socialistic measure which would "break down the initiative and enterprise of the American people."

All along, Hoover hoped that the national economy would right itself, as had always happened in previous depressions. He was like a physician who prefers to trust the natural recuperative powers of the patient, assisted by a few safe medicines, rather than try new drugs. In this case, however, the patient began to demand more drastic remedies.

"A DEEP PASSION FOR PEACE"

Hoover was the most widely traveled man ever to occupy the White House. In many years spent abroad he had visited every continent and had developed a wide acquaintance with foreign leaders. As administrator of Belgian relief between 1914 and 1917, he had seen the devastation of World War I at first hand; as a Quaker, he believed that war was wicked. On accepting the presidential nomination in 1928 he declared:

I think I may say that I have witnessed as much of the horror and suffering of war as any other American. From it I have derived a deep passion for peace. Our foreign policy has one primary object, and that is peace. We have no hates; we wish no further possessions; we harbor no military threats.

Friendliness Toward Latin America

As Secretary of Commerce, Hoover had learned how much distrust of the "Colossus of the North" hurt the trade of the United States with Latin America. To allay this ill feeling, he used the interim between his election in November 1928, and his inauguration in March 1929, to make a good-will tour of ten Latin-American countries. In twenty-five formal addresses, published in English, Portuguese, and Spanish, Hoover constantly stressed the idea that the United States wished to act as a "good neighbor" to the other republics of the Western Hemisphere.

The policies of the United States toward Latin America during the Hoover administration carried out ideas expressed in his good-will tour. The President successfully arbitrated a long-standing boundary dispute between Chile and Peru. He sent more skillful diplomats to Latin America. Most important of all, the United States abandoned military invervention in Latin-American countries. In 1930 the State Department published a study of the Monroe Doctrine made by a career diplomat, J. Reuben Clark, who held that the Roosevelt Corollary (see p. 494) had no historical basis. "The Monroe Doctrine," said the Clark Memorandum, "states a case of the United States vs. Europe, not of the United States vs. Latin America." It therefore provided no excuse for intervention in the internal affairs of American republics. Acting in accordance with this principle, Hoover withdrew troops from Nicaragua. He also refrained from intervention in several countries that were in a state of disorder and that repudiated debts to the United States. His forbearance won him little good will south of the border, however, because the Hawley-Smoot tariff hurt the Latin-American economy, already hit by the world-wide depression.

Disarmament

Hoover strongly favored disarmament, not merely because he was a man of peace, but also because armaments increased tax burdens and were a wasteful use of productive capacity. On taking office, he began arrangements for a conference on naval disarmament. During preliminary negotiations, Ramsay MacDonald, British prime minister, visited the United States. He

1ˢᵗ REPRESENTATIVE OF CIVILISED STATE:
"DON'T YOU THINK, AFTER ALL THERE MAY BE
SOMETHING IN THE IDEA OF HAVING A POLICE FORCE?"

2ⁿᵈ DITTO:
"TUT TUT! TOO RISKY! MUCH WISER AND CHEAPER
TO WAIT UNTIL WE'RE ALL MURDERED IN OUR BEDS."

"Let's call off this endurance contest." The United States and England promoted the London Naval Conference of 1930. Left, a cartoonist ridicules five countries that protested verbally when Japan violated previous pacts by seizing Manchuria in 1931. United States Secretary of State Stimson wanted forceful action.

and Hoover carried on some of their business while sitting on a log at the President's summer camp at Rapidan, Virginia. Such personal diplomacy led to a naval disarmament conference that met in London early in 1930, attended by the same countries that signed the Five-Power Treaty of 1922. Its purpose was to extend to other naval craft the limitations already fixed for battleships.

After four months of discussion, the London Naval Conference produced a treaty fixing ratios for submarines, cruisers, and destroyers for the American, British, and Japanese navies. Italy and France refused to sign, however, partly because they could not agree on proper ratios of strength. Fearing future aggression from Germany and Italy, the French government said that it favored disarmament only if other powers would make an agreement to protect France from invasion.

Ever since 1927, a disarmament conference under the auspices of the League of Nations had been sitting at Geneva. Its work was ham-

pered by the fact that too many of the delegates were professional military men, by the activities of lobbyists for armament manufacturers, and by mutual distrust. During sessions lasting on and off for five years, the delegates fruitlessly discussed air bombing of primitive villages, the influence of fog on war, and methods of counting hogs in estimating a country's war potential.

604 Crusade and Disillusion

Finally in 1932 President Hoover brought the Geneva Conference briefly to life with sensational proposals that the nations of the world either entirely abandon aggressive weapons or cut existing armaments by a third. No action resulted. With Adolf Hitler rising to power in Germany, and Japan beginning to invade the continent of Asia, disarmament seemed an invitation to aggression. Hoover's appeal could have had a chance for success only if the United States was willing to join "collective security" arrangements whereby nations agreed to use economic boycotts or military power against aggressors. The Senate, reflecting American public opinion, would have prevented Hoover from making any such agreements, even had he desired to do so.

The Hoover Moratorium, 1931

By 1931 the depression had hit Germany so hard that if the Germans attempted to pay reparations to the Allies, they would have to default on their debts to American private investors. Furthermore, Germany's unemployment and heavy debt burdens caused acute discontent that was reflected in the rapid growth of two mass anti-democratic parties—the Communist and the Nazi. German reparations could not be canceled without the consent of America's former Allies. They relied on German payments to furnish the money to pay off war debts to the United States.

Although Hoover, like Harding and Coolidge before him, had said that reparations were "wholly a European problem," the force of events now drove him to attempt some kind of settlement. In 1931 he arranged an international moratorium providing that both war debts and reparations should be suspended for a year. This wise measure was designed to protect American investments in Germany, to save the German Republic from collapse, and to stimulate international trade. Unfortunately it

came too late to do much good. Hoover's Secretary of State, Henry L. Stimson, urged that war debts and reparations be canceled once and for all, but this the President refused to do. It would have been a highly unpopular measure in this country and would have worsened Hoover's already poor relations with Congress.

The Hoover-Stimson Doctrine

The Hoover administration encountered its most difficult diplomatic problem in the Far East. In September 1931, Japanese army leaders took advantage of the depression that weakened the Western powers and of civil war that weakened China to seize control of the rich Chinese province of Manchuria. This was a brutal violation of the Nine-Power Treaty of 1922, which guaranteed China against aggression, as well as of the Kellogg-Briand Pact, which outlawed wars of aggression. It was also a breach of the Charter of the League of Nations, to which both China and Japan belonged.

In this crisis the Council of the League of Nations asked the United States, although not a League member, to send a representative to sit with it. The United States thereupon appointed an observer who attended meetings of the council. An American army officer also served on a League commission to investigate Japanese actions in Manchuria.

Even before the League finished its investigation, Secretary Stimson denounced Japanese aggression. In January 1932, he sent identical notes to Japan and China that said that the United States would refuse to recognize the legality of any territorial arrangement which violated the Kellogg-Briand Pact. This Stimson Doctrine of nonrecognition was designed to enlist world opinion against aggressor nations. The League of Nations followed Stimson's lead and passed a similar nonrecognition declaration.

Although the nonrecognition policy had been worked out by Hoover and Stimson to-

With ten or twelve million people out of work at the height of the Depression, men and women turned to selling apples or whatever possessions still remained to them. Here people are selling apples on the sidewalks of New York.

gether, it meant different things to each man. Stimson wanted it to be a warning which might later be backed up by action, such as an embargo, and perhaps the threat of military action. But according to Hoover, the statement itself was action enough. He told his cabinet that economic sanctions might lead to war and that Japanese aggression in Asia did "not imperil the freedom of the American people." Should we be obliged to "arm and train Chinese," we would "find ourselves involved in China in a fashion that would excite the suspicions of the whole world." The British and French governments were also unwilling to apply sanctions. The Japanese militarists thus learned that the Western power would put up only verbal barriers against their designs for the conquest of China and Southeast Asia.

It is highly doubtful if American public opinion would have supported any effort to halt Japanese aggression that would have threatened to involve the United States in war. This was seen early in 1933 when Congress by large majorities overrode Hoover's veto and voted that the Philippine Islands should be given independence after a ten-year period. This measure was in accordance with the demands of Filipino leaders, and was partly motivated by pressure from domestic interests that wanted to keep out Philippine competition, but a major reason for its passage was that the American people wanted to shed the burden of defending the islands.

ROCK BOTTOM

By the summer of 1932 the American economy was close to rock bottom. National income had dropped from $81,000,000,000 to $41,000,000,000. The steel industry was working at 22 per cent of capacity. Thousands of business concerns had gone into bankruptcy and thousands of banks had closed their doors. A quarter to a third of the industrial laborers of the country were unemployed and many others worked only part time. In every large city there were bread lines, soup kitchens, people selling apples on street corners, and people so hungry they raided garbage cans. A popular song, "Brother, Can You Spare a Dime?" reflected the frequency of begging. Local governments, faced by dwindling tax receipts and mounting relief costs, were so near bankruptcy that fire fighters, police, and schoolteachers sometimes went unpaid for months at a time.

The depression was uneven in its impact. It tended to have the harshest effects on those who could least bear it. Thus the wages paid industrial workers and the income received by farmers fell more rapidly than dividends and interests from stocks and bonds. Those with fixed incomes, such as college professors, were actually better off because prices declined. Although the bottom dropped out of the new car market, enough people managed to hold on to their old ones so that the use of gasoline did not decrease. Cigarette sales rose steadily.

Want in the Land of Plenty

As the depression deepened, the buoyant optimism of the prosperity decade was replaced by fear. "I'm afraid," said Charles M. Schwab, the steel magnate. "Every man is afraid. I don't know, we don't know, whether the values we have are going to be real next month or not." Loss of confidence affected all sorts of people. Some men who lost their jobs suffered such shock that they became unemployable; business people hesitated to build new factories or bring out new products; banks were unwilling to lend money, even to borrowers with good character and ample collateral. How far faith in the future had been replaced by pessimism was reflected in the stock market, where security prices dropped to levels almost as ridiculously low as those of 1928–1929 had been absurdly high. Stock in Radio Corporation of America, for instance, dropped from a high of $101 per share in 1929 to a low of $2.50 in 1932.

The puzzling thing about the depression was the starvation in the midst of plenty. There was no slackening of the productive capacity of farms and factories. On the contrary, farmers' problems were that they grew far more food than they were able to sell. Throughout the depression, manufacturers continued to increase productive capacity by introducing new labor-saving machinery even though effective demand for their goods declined steadily. It just didn't seem to make sense. One economist wrote, "Depression shows [people] a senseless cog in a senselessly whirling machine which is beyond human understanding and [which] has ceased to serve any purpose but its own."

QUESTION • *Why were there starvation and want at a time when there were immense surpluses of food?*

In earlier depressions there had been opportunity to go back to the farm or go West, but now few people had roots in the soil, and there was no longer any frontier. The popularity of regional and historical fiction, such as Walter Edmonds' fine stories of life along the Erie Canal or Marjorie Kinnan Rawlings' novels about the back country in Florida, perhaps stemmed from a desire to escape to the past. This may also help to explain the wide audience accorded *John Brown's Body,* Stephen Vincent Benét's great narrative poem about the Civil War.

Fear of Revolution

In this time of suffering and bewilderment there was fear of revolution. Lloyd's of London, the great British insurance organization, began to write riot insurance policies in the United States. In rural areas farmers were in a rebellious mood. They organized armed bands to prevent sheriffs from taking the farms of those unable to pay interest on their mortgages. They protested the low prices of farm products by declaring "farmers' holidays" and preventing shipments of food to the cities.

In May 1932, some 1,500 veterans of World War I moved on Washington to demand immediate payment of the bonus not due until 1944. By June, the "army" grew to about 17,000. Given fare home, most left, but about 1,500 refused and were dispersed by troops using bayonets and tear gas. In and near big cities, fear of insurrection made some wealthy people buy places of refuge—such as Vermont farms or Caribbean islands. Looking for scapegoats, people were apt to blame the depression on the very people whom they had willingly followed a few years earlier—the industrialists and bankers. This tendency increased when the public learned that a few of these people were guilty of trying to evade taxes on huge incomes and of immoral business practices designed to produce quick profits for insiders.

Prophets and Their Cures

In the circumstances it was probably inevitable that various prophets would appear, offering to lead the American people out of the wilderness of poverty and stagnation into a promised land of plenty and full employment. Huey Long, the near-dictator of Louisiana, promised to "share the wealth" and "make every man a king" with a $5,000-a-year income. An engineer, Howard Scott, preached Technocracy —a society run by scientists and engineers, in which units of energy called "ergs" would somehow take the place of money.

The depression offered hope to both socialists and communists that capitalism was in its "death throes" and would soon be replaced by a society in which goods would be distributed more fairly. "Production for use," based on human needs would replace "production for profit," based on greed. Both groups proposed that the government take control of the means of production and distribution. Both promised abundance for all when a planned economy would replace free competition. But socialists and communists were bitterly opposed to each other. The socialists proposed to gain power by persuasion and the ballot box. The Communist party line varied according to instructions from Moscow. At this time, although they put up candidates for office, the official doctrine was that capitalism could be overthrown only by violent revolution. This was what Earl Browder, the general secretary of the party, called the "omelet theory"—just as it is impossible to make an omelet without breaking eggs, it is impossible to make a revolution without breaking heads.

During the early 1930's the Communists made much of the fact that there was no unemployment in Russia. On the contrary, there was actually a labor shortage as the Bolshevik government undertook a vast "Five-Year Plan" to increase heavy industry, transportation, and power production. What the defenders of Russian Communism did not know or did not tell, however, was the terrible price in human suffering that went with the Five-Year Plan. In 1931, for instance, several million farmers in the Ukraine, the richest agricultural region in Russia, were allowed to starve to death because they resisted the Soviet government's efforts to force them to give up their land and their livestock.

Blind to the character of the Soviet regime and genuinely sympathetic with the suffering caused by the depression here, several well-known literary figures endorsed the Communist cause, and a number of young Americans, some of them idealistic and intelligent, joined the Communist party. This organization operated on two levels. On the surface it was a minor political party seeking to win support at the ballot box. But it also included a secret "inner circle," closely linked to Moscow, which was engaged in constant conspiracy, looking to the eventual overthrow of capitalist society. The party never numbered more than a few thou-

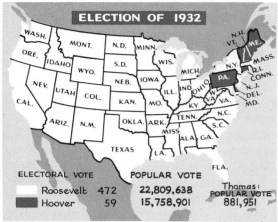

ELECTION OF 1932

ELECTORAL VOTE		POPULAR VOTE	
Roosevelt	472	22,809,638	Thomas: POPULAR VOTE
Hoover	59	15,758,901	881,951

In 1924 and 1928 the Republicans won overwhelming victories at the polls by capitalizing on the general prosperity. "We in America," President Hoover declared in 1928, "are nearer to the final triumph over poverty than ever before in the history of any land." The issue boomeranged in 1932 as voters blamed Hoover for the Depression and their dashed hopes.

sands, because the turnover was rapid. New members were often quickly disillusioned by the rigid discipline enforced and by constant internal bickering.

Both those who feared a revolution in the United States and those who hoped for one proved to be mistaken. Although many Americans were suffering, although many were angry and wanted a change, there was never any danger of a great uprising like the French Revolution of 1789 or the Russian Revolution of 1917. One reason was that there was little consciousness of class distinctions in America. Another reason was the ballot box. As *Time* magazine observed:

Doubtless the most potent factor in keeping the country steady and averting even the threat of an armed uprising has been the certainty—such as exists in no other large country—that November, 1932, would in due constitutional order bring a presidential and congressional election.

THE PROMISE OF A NEW DEAL

As the presidential election of 1932 approached, the Democrats scented victory for the first time since 1916. The Democratic national convention refused Al Smith's bid for renomination and instead chose Franklin D. Roosevelt, who had succeeded Smith as governor of New York. By carrying New York in the race for governor in 1928 while Smith was losing it in the presidential election, Roosevelt proved himself a remarkable vote-getter. He had been reelected in 1930 by an immense majority. The Democratic platform of 1932, the shortest in American political history, was a forthright document which urged the repeal of the Prohibition Amendment and blueprinted much of the later New Deal legislation. The Democrats' most effective asset, however, was Roosevelt himself. Although crippled by infantile paralysis, he put on a whirlwind campaign, making twenty-seven major speeches and many minor ones. The tone was set when he took the unprecedented step of flying to the Democratic convention to make his acceptance speech. In his address he pledged "a new deal for the American people." In later addresses he described the New Deal in rather vague terms, but it was clear that he intended to take action that would help "the forgotten man at the bottom of the economic pyramid."

The Election of 1932:
Rugged Individualism Repudiated

Meanwhile the Republicans renominated Hoover, who suffered under the severe handicap of having to argue away the depression. He maintained that hard times were the result of economic collapse abroad, for which his administration could not be held responsible, and that without his relief measures the disaster might have been worse. He attacked the Democrats as dangerous radicals. In his last speech of the campaign Hoover predicted that if Roosevelt were elected, "the grass will grow in the streets of a hundred cities, a thousand towns; the weeds will overrun the fields of a million farms." He flatly rejected his rival's statement that "the national government has a positive duty to see that no citizen shall starve." "You cannot," said Hoover, "extend the mastery of government over the daily life of a people without somewhere making it master of people's souls and thoughts."

On election day, the great Republican victories of the 1920's were completely reversed, as Roosevelt carried 42 of the 48 states. This landslide revealed a willingness to blame the Republicans for the depression and also, according to the veteran editor William Allen White, a general desire "to use government as an agency for human welfare." Yet even at the depth of the worst depression in history, few American voters favored socialism or communism. The Socialists polled 900,000 votes and the Communists only 100,000; their combined share was a little more than 2 per cent of the total vote.

The Country Leaderless

In the intervening period between Roosevelt's election in November and his inauguration in March, the Twentieth Amendment (pp. 148–150) was added to the Constitution. Among its provisions was one which changed the date of the presidential inauguration from March 4 to January 20. Had this amendment gone into effect sooner, it would have been better for the country. The country was virtually leaderless, as it had been during the four months before Lincoln came into office in 1861 (p. 343). Hoover had been repudiated; Roosevelt was without power to act. Hoover attempted to get his successor's cooperation in dealing with such matters as war debts and saving the banking system, but the President-elect refused to commit himself to specific policies until actually in office.

During the interval between the election and the inauguration, the economic machine ground almost to a standstill when the banking system collapsed. Although thousands of smaller banks, especially in the rural regions, had failed, most of the larger banks had stood firm. Early in 1933, however, the entire country was seized by a banking panic. Thousands of depositors withdrew their money and hoarded gold. In such a situation even the soundest institutions were bound to stop payment eventually, because there was not enough gold to cover all deposits. As the situation deteriorated, state governors issued proclamations closing the banks of their states until confidence should be restored. By March 4, inauguration day, every private bank in the country was closed.

QUESTION • Was it right or wrong for Franklin Roosevelt to refuse to commit himself to certain policies at Hoover's request during the period before he was actually inaugurated?

Roosevelt's Inaugural Address

No President had ever before been inaugurated at a time of such crisis. As D. W. Brogan remarked, "It was as if Sumter had been fired on the day before Lincoln became President." It was a cold, gray day as Roosevelt delivered his inaugural address and the crowd shivered as they stood around the Capitol. Many millions sat by their radios. A President's voice had never reached so many people.

The new leader rose to the solemn occasion. "This is a day of national consecration," he began, in words reminiscent of Woodrow Wilson's First Inaugural twenty years earlier. "This is preeminently a time to speak the truth, the whole truth, frankly and boldly," he continued. His

During the ride to Roosevelt's inauguration, Hoover was silent and glum. He feared the new administration would embark on dangerous experiments. The incoming President, in spite of the grim situation, seemed confident of his ability to meet the crisis into which the country was plunged.

voice, always clear and well-controlled, seemed to have a new quality of confidence and courage. One writer described it as the "patroon voice, the headmaster's voice, the bedside doctor's voice that spoke to each man and to all of us."

"The only thing we have to fear is fear itself," the voice went on, "nameless, unreasoning, unjustified terror which paralyzes needed efforts to convert retreat into advance." This was nothing new; this was what Hoover and other leaders had been saying all along. Why was it now effective? First, Roosevelt really admitted that this was a "dark hour of our national life," that "only a foolish optimist" could "doubt the dark realities of the moment." Secondly, he reflected the popular mood of the country in blaming the "money changers" for allowing starvation in the midst of plenty. He promised vigorous leadership and bold action.

The new President urged that the government treat the crisis as it would "the emergency of war." "This nation," he said, "wants action, and action now." Sketching the need for various relief and reform measures, he called for im-

mediate legislation. If Congress proved unable or unwilling to act quickly, he would ask for such emergency powers as would be given him "if we were in fact invaded by a foreign foe." He called for discipline and cooperation, and expressed faith in the future of "essential democracy." Finally, he asked divine protection and guidance.

Although this address had an electric effect on the country, it was also disturbing. Did Roosevelt's attack on the "money changers" mean he intended to do away with private banking? Did criticism of relief efforts carried on "in the pattern of an outworn tradition" mean he might turn to socialism? Was there a threat of dictatorship when he asked the people to "move as a trained and loyal army willing to sacrifice for the good of a common discipline"? Only the future could give the answer to such disturbing questions. Meanwhile the immediate effect of the inaugural address was to lift as if by magic the clouds of gloom and fear that hung over the country. Congress and the people were ready and eager to take whatever course the new leader should recommend.

610

Activities: Chapter 25

For Mastery and Review

1. Explain why Hoover beat Smith in the 1928 election. Define Hoover's attitude on the relationship of government and business. What was Hoover's farm program? How did it work out?

2. Explain the reasons for the speculative boom in the stock market. What appear to be the causes of the Great Depression? Briefly explain each.

3. By what methods and agencies did Hoover attempt to stem the depression? Where did he draw the line? Why?

4. In what respects did Hoover's policies toward Latin America mark an important change? Why were his efforts at disarmament unproductive? What was behind the Hoover-Stimson Doctrine in regard to Manchuria? Estimate its effectiveness.

5. Describe various effects of the Great Depression on American society.

Unrolling the Map

Study the election maps of 1928 and 1932 (pp. 593, 608). Which were the areas of enduring strength for each party? Which ones shifted? To go deeper into the question of traditional voting patterns and analysis of what happened in the Republican landslide of 1928 and the Democratic landslide of 1932, go back to the map of the last previous Democratic triumph, the election of 1916 (p. 554), and Harding's victory in 1920 (p. 575). In what areas did the "New Deal" reveal more strength in 1932 than did the "New Freedom" in 1916? Why? Explain differences between the Harding landslide in 1920 and that of Hoover in 1928.

Who, What, and Why Important?

election of 1928
rugged individualism
Wickersham Commission
Agricultural Marketing Act
brokers' loans
stock market speculation
market crash
the Great Depression
Hawley-Smoot Tariff

Federal Farm Board
Reconstruction Finance Corporation
Good Neighbor
London Conference
Geneva Conference
Hoover Moratorium
Hoover-Stimson Doctrine
Philippine independence
Bonus Army

Huey Long
Socialists and Communists

election of 1932
Twentieth Amendment

To Pursue the Matter

1. When prices of farm products are high, a farmer tends to cultivate more land and to produce more, in order to make more money. When prices of farm products fall, a farmer tends to cultivate more land and to produce more, in an attempt to maintain his income; but the more the farmer produces, the lower prices go. What is the solution?

2. In less than a month in 1929, "investors had lost about 30 billion dollars" (p. 595). "By 1932 farmers were receiving only 38 cents for wheat that in 1929 had sold at $1.04" (p. 600). Where did these values go? Did any people get the money that so many lost?

3. By what means did Roosevelt, who appeared to many to have few qualifications for the office of President except that he wanted it, get the Democratic nomination in 1932 against strong opposition? Sources: Freidel, *Franklin D. Roosevelt: The Triumph*, or Schlesinger, *The Crisis of the Old Order*.

4. How far is it fair to blame the Great Crash on the policies of successive Republican administrations? See Leuchtenberg, *The Perils of Prosperity*, Chapters 5 and 13; Galbraith, *The Great Crash*, especially Chapters 2, 3, and 10; and Hoover's defense of himself in the second volume of his autobiography. This could be turned into a debate on the topic, "*Resolved:* That Republican economic policies from 1921 to 1933 were disastrous for the United States," or, "*Resolved:* That the Great Depression was a result of causes beyond the control of the Coolidge and Hoover administrations."

5. It takes an effort of will and imagination to conceive of the feeling of senseless despair that seized millions of people during the depression years. Shannon, *The Great Depression*, gives over fifty accounts of how the depression affected different people. It could be the basis for an effective series of brief sketches, played rapidly one after another before a class or school assembly. A briefer account is found in Davies, *The New Deal: Interpretations*, Chapter 1.

PART SEVEN: SUMMING UP
Chapters 23–25

I. CHECKING THE FACTS

1. Another title for this Part might be:
- THE BEST OF TIMES, THE WORST OF TIMES
- THE ROAD TO PROSPERITY
- THE GOLDEN YEARS

Defend your choice.

2. Put the items in each group in chronological order numbered 1–3.

a. U.S. declaration of war
Sussex Pledge
Sinking of the Luisitania

b. Suffrage movement
19th amendment
Women in World War I

c. Russian Revolution
"Red Scare"
End of World War I

d. Hoover's Administration
Assistance to business
Roosevelt

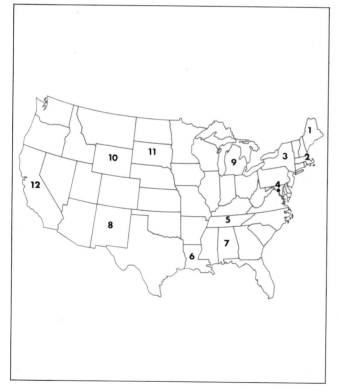

3. MAP WORK.

Match the items below with their numbered locations on the map.

a. Where guerilla border raids and retaliation by American troops resulted in the threat of war.

b. Where at an international conference agreement was reached on a ten-year naval "holiday" and trade relations with China.

c. Where the secret leasing of navy oil reserves to private companies caused a national scandal.

d. Where federally owned and operated power plants changed the economy of a rural region.

e. Where the Republican party carried the state in every election from 1916–1932.

f. Where farmers felt the impact of the depression long before workers in industrial areas.

g. Where new American musical art form was birthed—dixieland jazz.

h. Where Wall Street, the heartbeat of the national economy, was the first to feel the effects of the "crash."

II. INTERPRETING THE FACTS

1. Cartoonists tend to use certain techniques to convey their messages. Look at the cartoons on pages 565, 573, and 603 in this Part, plus any others in the text. Then indicate by *yes* or *no* which of the factors below *seem to be common* to most cartoons.

    a. labels and symbols
    b. controversial issues
    c. exaggeration of detail
    d. action

    e. humor
    f. comparisons or opposites
    g. neutrality of opinion
    h. political viewpoint

From what you have decided about the characteristics of cartoons, compose a set of questions that a person might use to interpret a cartoon. Use this question as a start. Then continue on your own.

    (1) What does each figure represent?
    (2) _____

III. APPLYING YOUR KNOWLEDGE

1. After drawing a chart like the one on the left, list the qualities that you feel distinguish "heroes" from "villains." Making a chart like the one on the right, list the heroes and villains of the World War I period as implied or stated in the text. Now, how are your two charts the *same* and *different?* And, how do you explain the similarities and differences?

MY	
HEROES	VILLAINS

THE TEXT's	
HEROES	VILLAINS

Take the next step by applying your qualities for hero and villain to the world as you see it *today.*

    Name the heroes you have.
    Name the villains.

In one sentence, state an hypothesis (intelligent guess) about what makes "heroes" and "villains."

READINGS FOR PART SEVEN

Fiction

Cather, W. *One of Ours.* The effect of World War I on a young Nebraska farmer.

Cobb, H. *Paths of Glory.* A moving story of French soldiers in World War I by an American writer.

Fitzgerald, F. S. *The Great Gatsby.* The rich and how they played in the 1920's.

Lewis, S. *Main Street; Babbitt; Dodsworth.* Three novels about small town life and small town people of the 1920's and '30's.

Non-fiction

Allen, F. L. *Only Yesterday.* A light, bright, social history of the Jazz Age.

Leighton, I. (ed.). *The Aspirin Age.* Engaging essays on the '20's and '30's.

Lindbergh, C. A. *The Spirit of St. Louis.* A thrilling and moving account of the author's epic solo flight across the Atlantic Ocean.

Mowry, G. F. (ed.). *The Twenties: Fords, Flappers, and Fanatics.* An entertaining and varied collection of primary sources.

Part
8

The Roosevelt Years

Roosevelt and Churchill

WPA Artists at Work

VOICES AND POWER

The development of radio meant that for the first time political leaders could talk directly to their people. All Germany could hear Hitler's strident voice of destruction, as he whipped up his shouting followers to a frenzy of hate against the Jews, the Czechs, the Poles, and the "decadent democracies." Similarly, all Italy could hear Mussolini as he stood on a balcony high above a crowded square and called on his Fascist legions to carve out a new Roman empire. In England at the time of the Battle of Britain Winston Churchill galvanized the British people as he told the Germans, who were poised to invade his seemingly helpless country, "We will fight; we will never surrender." According to the weary fighter pilots whose victory over the German air force saved England, Churchill's voice over the loud-speakers was like a drug that instilled in them new energy and new courage.

In America, as his First Inaugural Address revealed, the radio immensely enhanced Roosevelt's power. He was the first President to make full use of the instrument, and no President since has equaled his ability to reach the people. This may have been an effect of his personality, but it may also be that the disembodied voice of radio is more effective than television, in which attention to the message is diverted by the visual image of the speaker. In any case, Roosevelt's addresses to Congress, "fireside chats," and hard-hitting campaign speeches persuaded the American people to elect him President four times.

Of course, he was more than a voice. It was a time that demanded action, and the President was a man of action. One political scientist estimated that in a given period Roosevelt made 37 times as many decisions as that master of inertia, Calvin Coolidge. Indeed, he so expanded the sphere of presidential action that there was a genuine fear he would become a dictator, like Hitler or Stalin.

But Roosevelt was no dictator. Once a group of young people came to the White House and complained to him that his administration had done too little for housing, for education, for civil rights, for old people. One of them told the President he was sick and angry at the way the New Deal had failed. Roosevelt said to him, "Maybe you would make a much better President than I have. Maybe you will some day. If you ever sit here, you will learn that you cannot, just by shouting from the housetops, get what you want all the time."

The following Part is called "The Roosevelt Years" because he was the most prominent feature on the political horizon. But it is well to remember always that he was more often a follower than a director of events, and that ultimately he could lead the American people only in directions they wanted to go.

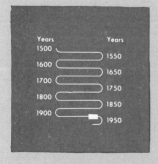

Chapter 26:

The New Deal:
First Phase

*The country needs and, unless I mistake its temper,
the country demands bold, persistent experimentation.
It is common sense to take a method and try it. If it
fails, admit it frankly and try another. But above all, try
something.*
—FRANKLIN D. ROOSEVELT

President Roosevelt fulfilled his promise to provide "action now." On Sunday, March 5, 1933, the day after his inauguration, he called Congress into special session. On Monday, acting under a forgotten statute of World War I, he declared a nationwide "bank holiday" to allow examination of individual banks before reopening. On Thursday Congress met and passed the Emergency Banking Act. On Sunday, March 12, the President gave his first "fireside chat" over the radio. He explained to the American people what had been done, how the banks would be reopened, why it would be "safer to keep your money in a reopened bank than under the mattress." The next day most banks began to do business. The panic was ended.

This was just a beginning. In the "Hundred Days" between March 9 and June 16, Congress passed more laws than had ever appeared on the statute books in such a short time. Most of this was "must" legislation drawn up by the executive department, presented to Congress for its approval, and passed with little debate. Never had a President enjoyed more support. As Will Rogers wrote, "The whole country is

with him. Even if what he does is wrong, they are with him. Just so he does something. If he burned down the Capitol, we would cheer and say, 'Well, at least we got a fire started, anyhow.'"

F.D.R.—A COMPLEX PERSONALITY

Before taking office, Franklin Roosevelt had given little evidence of the qualities of leadership he displayed during twelve years in the White House. As late as 1932 Walter Lippmann had called him "an amiable man ... who, without any important qualifications for the office, would very much like to be President." Good fortune seemed his outstanding attribute. The only son of wealthy parents, he inherited a name that his distant cousin Theodore made "the best trade name in American politics." Once, however, he had experienced calamity. In 1921 he suffered an attack of infantile paralysis so severe that only after a long struggle was he able to walk, and even then only with great difficulty, heavy braces on his shrunken legs. Yet this blow may have been good fortune in

In his first inaugural, President Roosevelt summoned the country to fight the depression. "Our greatest primary task is to put the people to work."

disguise. The experience gave Roosevelt genuine sympathy for the unfortunate and distressed. After his long and painful battle toward recovery, no opposition, no obstacle, no misfortune could dismay him. Indeed, he seemed to thrive on crisis.

Like Andrew Jackson, who occupied the White House a century before him, Roosevelt aroused both bitter hatred and passionate devotion. Like Jackson, he was regarded by his enemies as a dictator and by his followers as a savior of democracy. He, too, gave his name to an age, and received credit (or blame) for much that he had little to do with, or that would have happened whether or not he had been President.

It is difficult to assess Roosevelt because he was a complex person. Robert Sherwood, his close associate for five years, wrote of the apparent contradictions in his character:

Being a writer by trade, I tried continually to study him, to try to look beyond his charming and amusing and warmly affectionate surface into his heavily forested interior. But I never really understood what was going on in there. . . . He could be a ruthless politician, but he was the champion of friends and associates who for him were political liabilities . . . and of causes which apparently competent observers assured him would be political suicide. He could appear to be utterly cynical, worldly, illusionless, and yet his religious faith was the strongest and most mysterious force that was in him. . . . He liked to fancy himself as a practical, down-to-earth, horse-sense realist . . . and yet his idealism was actually no less . . . than Woodrow Wilson's. Probably the supreme contradiction in Roosevelt's character was the fact that . . . he achieved a grand simplicity. . . . Roosevelt wrote himself by word and deed in large and plain letters which all can read and in terms which all can understand.

Master of the Art of Politics

Both friends and foes agreed on one thing: that Roosevelt was a master of the art of politics. Few Presidents had such varied political training. In the New York legislature, he learned about government at the local level. As Assistant Secretary of the Navy during World War I, he had an inside view of the federal government in time of crisis. As a candidate for Vice-President during the campaign of 1920, he met people in all parts of the country. As governor of New York, he dealt with many of the same problems he later faced as President.

Roosevelt's greatest strength lay in the warmth and understanding of his approach to people. Countless numbers who heard his compelling voice over the radio felt he was talking directly to them. After a fireside chat he sometimes received as many as fifty thousand letters a day. He also knew how to handle the press. In frequent press conferences Roosevelt submitted to such a barrage of questions from reporters as no other President had ever been willing to face. Thus he supplied the newspapers with information and comment that "made news" and focused attention on Washington.

On the face of it Roosevelt was a careless administrator. He sometimes appointed two, three, or four people with differing opinions to do the same job. He could be ruthless with anyone he thought disloyal, and yet he sometimes kept an incompetent in office because he was too soft-hearted to dismiss him. He often undercut subordinates by changing policies without consulting them. It could be a frustrating, even infuriating, business to work under FDR, but it was also exciting. If effective administration means the ability to enlist and keep the services of persons of ability, Roosevelt must be rated highly. In spite of the "built-in confusion" of his methods, he was flexible and prompt in action. He got things done.

Roosevelt's Advisers

A special feature of the Roosevelt administration was that he drew many of his closest advisers from the academic world. Even before receiving the Democratic nomination for President, he gathered a group of professors from Columbia University, who acquired the nickname of the "brain trust." He kept them around him after he entered office. More by conversation with these people than by reading, he acquired necessary information about the economy and ideas for policies. Although fear was expressed that the federal government was falling under the domination of "mere theorists," the fact was that the President made his own decisions, usually with a strong sense of what was practically and politically possible. The brain trust was invaluable to him because it provided Roosevelt with expert knowledge and disinterested advice.

One of the President's most trusted aides was his wife, who became almost as well known —also as much loved and hated—as he himself. Eleanor Roosevelt had been painfully shy and

unsure of herself as a girl and young woman. But as time went on, and especially after her husband's attack of polio, she became increasingly active in politics. She forced herself to overcome fear of crowds and learned to speak in public. She became Roosevelt's eyes and ears. During the first year of the New Deal, she traveled 40,000 miles and seemed to be everywhere in the country at once. He trusted the accuracy of the information she brought him, and would tell his cabinet, "My Missus says that people are working for wages well below the minimum set by NRA in the town she visited last week." Mrs. Roosevelt shared to the full her husband's concern for the less fortunate and his optimistic faith that something could be done to right the ills of the world. Indeed, those who knew the Roosevelts well thought that her concern for the disadvantaged was more profound than his. (See the vignette, p. 660.)

FIRST PHASE OF THE NEW DEAL: "TRY SOMETHING"

Roosevelt came into office with no very clear idea of how he was going to deal with the economic crisis. This did not dismay him. "There is nothing to do," he said, "but meet each day's troubles as they come." Some laws were passed against the President's wishes, but he signed them to head off something he liked even less, or to avoid holding up other legislation. His principal contribution to the New Deal, in addition to dynamic leadership and political skill, was his "try something" philosophy. He likened himself to a quarterback on a football team who calls plays, and if one does not work, tries another. In any case, he felt, action was better than inaction.

The New Deal was thus no carefully worked out program, like that of Alexander Hamilton in the Washington administration, or that proposed by Woodrow Wilson when he took office in 1913. Instead, it reflected the haste which went with trying to attack the depression on many fronts at once. It reflected the special demands of pressure groups. Some New Deal measures would have been enacted sooner or later in any case, because they embodied long-standing demands for change. Thus Congress repealed the Volstead Act and permitted the sale of light wines and beer. In December 1933 came the Twenty-first Amendment, which repealed the Prohibition amendment once and for all.

Despite the apparent confusion, the New Deal had three obvious aims: *recovery* from the depression, *relief* for its victims, and *reform* of the economic system. Much legislation reflected all three of these purposes.

During the first phase of the Roosevelt administration, 1933 to early 1935, the dominant purposes were recovery and relief. During this period, the President and his advisers had the idea that through a series of temporary expedients they could get the economy into high gear again, and then let it carry on by its own momentum. This "first New Deal" was therefore not much different in purpose and philosophy from Hoover's efforts to stem the depression. During this early period, too, Roosevelt re-

Madam Secretary: Frances Perkins

The President-elect came right to the point: "I've been thinking things over and I've decided I want you to be Secretary of Labor." Frances Perkins was sitting in Franklin Roosevelt's study in February 1933. No woman until then had held a cabinet post, but Roosevelt believed that the time had come to recognize their importance in the political world. Frances Perkins was a good choice for this purpose.

She had left college a progressive and an ardent admirer of Theodore Roosevelt. She had become a professional social worker because of her "concern" —in the Quaker sense—for social justice. Realizing that social justice for the twentieth century would require new laws and legal machinery, she had spent much time in the New York capital, Albany. There she had lobbied for social legislation, seeking to improve working conditions for women and to limit child labor. She had served as chairwoman of the Industrial Board under Governor Al Smith and as industrial commissioner under Governor Roosevelt.

But now she argued with Roosevelt. A woman in the cabinet, yes; but the Department of Labor should go to someone identified with organized labor. Roosevelt replied that her work as industrial commissioner was enough. She told him of her stand: the need for federal aid for direct unemployment relief, for a program of public works, for federal laws dealing with minimum wages, maximum hours, old age insurance, abolition of child labor. Roosevelt agreed that these were desirable. As to the constitutionality of such laws, "Well, that's a problem," he said, "but we can work out something when the time comes."

On March 5, 1933, Frances Perkins took the oath of office as Secretary of Labor. She and Harold Ickes were the only persons to serve in the Roosevelt cabinet from its first to its last day.

sembled Hoover in seeking the support of the business community. He spoke of an alliance of "business and banking, agriculture and industry, and labor and capital." His purpose throughout his entire presidency was to save the capitalist system. The difference from the previous administration was in the magnitude and variety of legislation and in a much greater willingness to call on the full powers of the federal government.

Although opponents charged that the New Deal was inspired by alien "isms," its origins were mostly to be found in earlier American protest movements, such as those of the Populists and the progressives. FDR put into effect several measures first proposed by Teddy Roosevelt. New Deal laws dealing with banking, the tariff, and child labor were further developments of legislation passed under Woodrow Wilson. The New Deal was, however, so much more far-reaching than anything achieved or proposed by Theodore Roosevelt or Wilson that it had the aspects of a revolution.

BANKING, SECURITIES, CURRENCY

As has already been indicated, Roosevelt's first concern was the banking crisis. There were those who urged him to make major reforms. "The banking system," wrote Ernest K. Lindley, "lay unconscious on the table and the temptation to operate on it was strong." Some midwestern senators, reflecting the traditional agrarian distrust of bankers, demanded that all banks be taken over by the federal government. The control of credit, they argued, was as much a responsibility of government as control of currency. Furthermore, the banks had contributed to the boom-bust cycle by lending too freely in the 1920's and then refusing to lend as the depression deepened. But Roosevelt chose to save the existing system by providing it with federal aid and restoring public confidence.

Through the issuance of new currency and Reconstruction Finance Corporation loans, sound banks were soon enabled to reopen. Others were put under temporary federal control and reopened later. A few hopelessly unsound banks closed their doors for good.

In June 1933, Congress passed the Glass-Steagall Act, which provided for several reforms in the banking system. A Senate investigation had revealed that one of the serious malpractices of the 1920's had been the way the banks that financed corporations also peddled their own securities to those who sought their advice on investments. The Glass-Steagall Act therefore forced commercial banks to have nothing more to do with financing corporations or selling securities. The law also provided for a Federal Deposit Insurance Corporation (FDIC) to insure private deposits in member banks of the Federal Reserve system up to $5,000. The American Bankers' Association fought this provision "to the last ditch," calling it "unsound, unscientific, unjust, and dangerous." Roosevelt himself thought it an over-expansion of federal responsibility and only accepted it because it had overwhelming support in Congress. As it turned out, the FDIC brought great benefits: it both protected the savings of small depositors and promoted the stability of the banking system by increasing public confidence. Runs on banks became almost unheard of.

Securities Exchange Commission

Congress responded to widespread demand that the federal government prevent fraud and speculation in the issuance and marketing of stock. The Federal Securities Act of 1933 changed the principle of selling securities from "let the buyer beware" to "let the seller beware." Under threat of heavy penalties, companies that issued or marketed securities were obliged to make available to investors complete and truthful information. The Securities Exchange Commission (SEC), created in 1934, oversaw and regulated the issuance of all new securities. It also set up rules for stock market operation to discourage wild speculation and to stop practices whereby "insiders" manipulated stock market prices. Roosevelt shocked a good many of his supporters by appointing a shrewd Wall Street speculator, Joseph P. Kennedy, as first chairman of the SEC. The President said he wanted someone in the job who knew the tricks of the trade.

Abandonment of the Gold Standard

When Roosevelt came into office, he faced strong pressure to inflate the currency. A number of congressmen proposed to "run the printing presses" and issue billions of dollars in paper money; others favored a revival of Bryan's almost forgotten solution for all economic ills—free silver. Some of Roosevelt's advisers proposed a "commodity dollar," which should be so managed as to keep prices of commodities stable—rather like the old Populist demand for a dollar based on wheat and corn. Furthermore, in 1931 Great Britain had decided to go off the gold standard, and many other countries had followed suit. This

QUESTION • Why did going off the gold standard give a nation a competitive advantage in world trade?

reduced their cost of producing goods and gave them a competitive advantage in world trade against countries still on the gold standard, such as the United States.

The Roosevelt administration pursued a course somewhere between those who favored extreme inflation and those who wanted to retain the gold standard. It reduced the gold content of the dollar so that the new dollar was only worth 59¢ in relation to the old. It forbade all private hoarding of gold and called in all gold coins except those with sentimental or historical value. Under pressure from Congress the Treasury bought vast quantities of silver. Such measures did not cause runaway inflation, because the President did not use powers granted him by Congress to issue more currency.

The Federal Budget

Roosevelt revealed a conservative approach to finance in early efforts to balance the budget. His first action after reopening the banks was to demand that Congress cut $400,000,000 from payments to veterans and $100,000,000 out of the ordinary expenditures of the federal government. In spite of strong opposition in his own party, Congress passed an Economy Act in response to the President's demands. But the expenses of the New Deal program soon began to create bigger deficits than those of the Hoover administration. For a time the Roosevelt administration carried two budgets: a regular budget that was balanced and an unbalanced "emergency budget," supposedly temporary. Only hesitatingly and unwillingly did Roosevelt come to the opinion that deficit spending was the price that must be paid if relief agencies were not to close down, leaving millions to starve.

Pump-Priming

One idea behind New Deal relief spending was "pump-priming"—pouring government credit into the channels of trade to stimulate recovery. The Hoover administration had tried very mild pump-priming through public works and RFC loans to banks, big corporations, and municipalities. The pump-priming under Roosevelt was on a much larger scale. The idea behind it was that the depression frightened banks and business concerns into "over-saving," and therefore the government should create purchasing power by giving money to those who would certainly spend it. It was claimed that a single dollar given a relief worker produced several dollars in the national income. Since workers had too few resources to save dollars, they would immediately spend it, say at the corner grocery. The grocer would pass the dollar on to a farmer, the farmer to a manufacturer of tractors, the manufacturer to a worker, and so on. Critics of pump-priming have questioned whether in the long run it does lead to more private spending and have expressed fear that the federal deficits that it creates are inflationary.

AID TO AGRICULTURE

By 1933 many farmers were in a rebellious mood. During the previous five years, one farmer in ten had lost his land as banks foreclosed mortgages. In parts of the Midwest, farmers banded together to prevent judges and sheriffs from foreclosing mortgages. In April 1933, a group of enraged men dragged an Iowa judge from the bench and beat him up. In several parts of the country, a Farm Holiday Association proposed a national farm strike unless the debt burden was eased and agricultural prices rose.

The New Deal attempted to raise commodity prices by controlled inflation of the currency. It also provided relief for debt-burdened farmers through the Frazier-Lemke Farm Bankruptcy Act, which provided for a five-year moratorium on mortgage foreclosures. A new agency, the Farm Credit Administration, refinanced mortgages at lower rates of interest and provided short-term loans on commodities.

Above all, the Roosevelt Administration sought a solution to the question that had plagued American agriculture since the end of World War I—what to do about unsaleable surpluses? In the 1920's agrarian demands that the federal government buy surpluses and sell them abroad had been thwarted by Coolidge's vetoes

of the McNary-Haugen bill and Hoover's opposition to a similar proposition. The efforts of the Federal Farm Board to buy surpluses in 1930–1931 had ended in disaster. Now an entirely new approach was attempted: stop the surplus at its source by paying farmers to take land out of cultivation.

Agricultural Adjustment Act, 1933

In May 1933, Congress passed the Agricultural Adjustment Act (AAA), which had the purpose of giving farmers the same relative purchasing power they had enjoyed during five prosperous years (1909–1914) before World War I. To restore what were known as "parity prices" for farm products, the federal government paid "benefit payments" to those who agreed to reduce production of basic crops like cotton, wheat, tobacco, hogs, and corn. Money for these payments was obtained by a tax on "processors," such as flour millers and meat packers, who passed the cost on to the consumer. The AAA got under way in 1933 when cotton farmers plowed under a quarter of their acreage and hog producers killed six million pigs instead of fattening them for market. In 1934 and 1935, farmers withdrew 30 million acres from cultivation in staple crops and received over a billion dollars in benefit payments. Farm surpluses were greatly reduced, although this was perhaps less the result of the AAA program than of widespread drought. In any event, total farm income rose by more than 50 per cent between 1932 and 1936 and prices of farm products rose from an index figure of 65 in 1932 (1909=100) to 115 in 1936.

In spite of the New Deal measures, over-all farm income still lagged behind that of the rest of the country. Furthermore, the benefits were unequally distributed. AAA payments went to owners rather than to tenants or to hired men; the big one-crop farmers received greater benefits than the smaller farmer who raised several

Franklin D. Roosevelt Promises Bold Leadership
Roosevelt's First Inaugural Address, 1933

Franklin D. Roosevelt took office as President in the darkest days of the Great Depression. In the closing paragraphs of his Inaugural Address he promised vigorous leadership to pull the country out of the depression:

It is to be hoped that the normal balance of executive and legislative authority may be wholly adequate to meet the unprecedented task before us. But it may be that an unprecedented demand and need for undelayed action may call for temporary departure from that normal balance. . . .

I am prepared under my constitutional authority to recommend the measures that a stricken nation in the midst of a stricken world may require.

These measures, or such other measures as the Congress may build out of its experience and wisdom, I shall seek within my constitutional authority to bring to a speedy adoption.

But in the event that the Congress shall fail to take one of these two courses, and in the event that the national emergency is still critical, I shall not evade the clear course of duty that will then confront me.

I shall ask Congress for the one remaining instrument to meet the crisis—broad executive power to wage a war against an emergency as great as the power that would be given me if we were in fact invaded by a foreign foe. . . .

We do not distrust the future of essential democracy. The people of the United States have not failed. In their need they have registered a mandate that they want direct, vigorous action.

They have asked for discipline and direction under leadership. They have made me the present instrument of their wishes. In the spirit of the gift I take it.

In this dedication of a nation we humbly ask the blessing of God. May He protect and guide every one of us. May He guide me in the days to come!

- What specific statements in the address might people have found threatening?

- In what ways did President Roosevelt contribute to upsetting the "normal balance of executive and legislative authority?" Look back to the discussion of "Separation of Powers" and "Checks and Balances," pages 117, 119, and 121, and ahead to the discussion of "The Imperial Presidency" of Richard Nixon, pages 765-792.

- Is a "temporary departure" from the normal constitutional balance possible? If Congress once gives up power, can it get it back? If so, how?

crops. In many cases the AAA actually created distress, since by reducing acreage it lessened the demand for agricultural labor and for tenants. AAA payments, for instance, enabled owners of cotton plantations to buy new farm machinery, with the result that tenants were "tractored off the land."

Dust Bowl

The New Deal had to cope with a terrible disaster that struck the Great Plains in 1934 and 1935. During World War I, prices had tempted farmers to grow wheat and cotton in the former grazing lands west of 98° longitude (see map, p. 7). Plows and harrows broke up the deep, tough sod that had previously prevented erosion and conserved moisture in this semi-arid region. When the years 1933–1935 proved unusually dry, there was danger that the region would become a desert. Terrible dust storms carried away topsoil in such quantities that even on the Atlantic seaboard the sun was obscured by a yellow haze. The water table of parts of the Plains region sank so low that deep wells ran dry. Between 1934 and 1939 an estimated 350,000 farmers emigrated from the "dust bowl." To take care of immediate distress, Congress provided funds so that dust bowl farmers could get new seed and livestock. On a long-term basis, the Department of Agriculture dealt with the dust bowl by helping farmers to plant 190 million trees in shelter belts, which cut wind velocity and retained moisture. Farmers were also encouraged to restore the Plains to what they had been in the days of the cattle kingdom and earlier—a grazing region.

There was much criticism of the New Deal farm program. Many farmers did not like being told how much they could plant. Deliberately creating scarcity when people were hungry seemed immoral. The benefits of the AAA were unequal. On the whole, though, the New Deal provided more direct assistance to farmers than to any other group in the population. Hundreds of thousands of families were saved from bleak poverty and despair.

INDUSTRY AND LABOR

The principal measure whereby the New Deal tried to promote the recovery of industry was the National Industry Recovery Act of June 1933, which Roosevelt hailed as "probably ... the most important and far-reaching law ever passed by the American Congress." It proposed a partnership of business, labor, and government to attack the emergency of hard times. Much of its inspiration came from the United States Chamber of Commerce which in 1931 proposed a "national economic council" to balance production with consumption and to prevent cut-throat competition. If permitted to combine to control standards and prices, asserted the Chamber of Commerce, industry could keep up wages and insure workers against accidents, sickness, and old age.

The law provided that representatives of management and labor draw up "codes of fair competition." These were based on the notion that one of the primary causes of the depression was overproduction. The United States was a "mature economy," it was argued, with a productive capacity greater than its needs. What was demanded of industry as of agriculture was controlled production, with equitable arrangements to divide the proceeds among different business firms and their employees. Codes were established to spread employment by reducing the length of the work week, to put a floor under wages, to allow industries to fix "fair" prices, and to punish "chiselers." To spread business among as many firms as possible, factories were usually limited to two shifts a day. Every code was supposed to have the force of law and was enforced by a "code authority" appointed by the President. The various codes

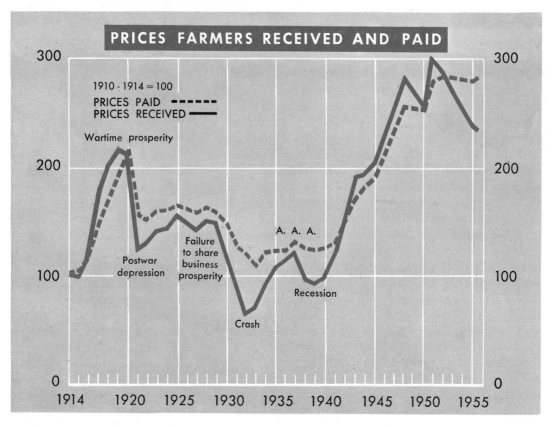

PRICES FARMERS RECEIVED AND PAID

1910 - 1914 = 100
PRICES PAID ------
PRICES RECEIVED ——

Wartime prosperity

Postwar depression

Failure to share business prosperity

A. A. A.

Recession

Crash

Using the years 1910-1914 as the base year, this chart of the prices of farm products and of goods bought by farmers helps to explain why the farmer was weighed down by debts between the two World Wars.

and code authorities were under the over-all direction of a National Recovery Administration (NRA). As head of the NRA, Roosevelt appointed a colorful, energetic ex-army officer, General Hugh S. Johnson, formerly Bernard Baruch's right-hand man in the War Industries Board.

The NRA was launched with parades, fireworks, and speeches. Business firms signing code agreements were allowed to display a blue eagle with the words "We Do Our Part." The beginning of the experiment was accompanied by a revival of business confidence; production rose temporarily to 93 per cent of the 1929 figure. Soon about 600 codes had been

drawn up, covering 22 million workers and nine-tenths of American business concerns.

NRA in Difficulties

It was not long, however, before the NRA ran into difficulties. It was easy to see that the steel and textile industries should have codes, but did the fly-swatter, dish-mop, and armored-car manufacturers each need one? Were rubber balls subject to the code for toys or to that for athletic supplies? Even more serious than confusion caused by trying to draw up rules for all American industry was the fact that the NRA did not work out as planned. Prices increased more rapidly than wages. While a few businessmen were prosecuted for violations of NRA codes, many successful "chiselers" escaped notice. Henry Ford, the country's greatest industrialist, refused to have anything to do with the NRA. In trying to promote cooperation between business concerns, the NRA relaxed the antitrust laws. According to competent observers the result was a great increase in monopolistic practices and the growth of big business at the expense of small concerns. (For New Deal efforts to regulate business and control monopoly, see pp. 637, 644.)

Revival of Trade Unionism

No group suffered more during the depression than wage workers. In 1932 a third of the country's laborers were unemployed, and the pay envelopes of the rest had shrunk. Some women earned as little as $3 a week. Many of the benefits of "welfare capitalism" were also withdrawn: companies running at a loss could not afford pensions, health plans, or vacations with pay; they could not continue profit-sharing when there were no profits to share. At the same time, labor union membership declined to its lowest point since before American entrance into World War I.

When cooperative efforts by employer groups failed to keep wages up, there was widespread feeling, even outside the ranks of labor, that a way to prevent wage cuts and preserve purchasing power might be to strengthen labor unions. This trend was apparent even before Roosevelt came into office. In March 1932, President Hoover had signed the Norris-La Guardia Act, which improved the legal position of labor unions. The law declared that "the public policy of the United States" was that a worker should have "full freedom" to join a union and empower it to represent him in bargaining with his employer. This law went beyond the Clayton Act in limiting the right of federal courts to issue injunctions against labor unions. It also declared that "yellow-dog contracts," whereby a worker promised his employer not to join a union, were not enforceable at law.

Section 7-a

Once the New Deal was launched, labor's right to organize received further protection. Section 7-a of the National Recovery Act provided that every NRA code should guarantee the workers' right of collective bargaining and forbid employers to interfere with the formation of labor unions. Section 7-a encouraged a revival of unionism. Between May and October 1933, the American Federation of Labor gained 1,500,000 new members.

After a first wave of success, the new effort to enlist workers in unions stalled. The American Federation of Labor, composed mostly of skilled workers, was not well suited to the task of organizing labor in the mass production industries. Employers were generally opposed to unionization of their plants. In some cases they headed off effective organization and technically complied with the Norris-La Guardia Act and Section 7-a by forming company unions of their own workers. Company unions lacked bargaining power because they had no support from outside.

In 1934 the struggle to organize erupted into violence in every section of the country. Laborers struck, demanding the right to organize as essential to their security and dignity; employers, usually with the local police and militia on their side, opposed unionization of their plants as an interference with their right to run their own affairs. More often than not strikes resulted in defeat for the workers. In spite of sympathy for organized labor, the Roosevelt administration could do little. A National Labor Relations Board had been set up to enforce Section 7-a, but its only weapon was to take away the blue eagle emblem. Em-

Men thronged the employment agencies looking in vain for work. To take care of the younger men, a Civilian Conservation Corps was established; it did such useful work as planting trees. Women suffered equally from unemployment.

ployers ignored it with impunity. Union people began to say that NRA stood for "National Run Around." They demanded of Congress more **vigorous protection of the right to organize** that had been guaranteed them by law.

Death of NRA

So strong was criticism of the NRA that in 1934 General Johnson resigned "under a hail of dead cats," as he expressed it. Roosevelt attempted to keep the organization going under a National Recovery Board composed of representatives of industry, labor, and consumers, but the elaborate codes and code administrations were obviously breaking down. Of an alleged 155,000 cases of code violations only 400 were prosecuted in the courts. It is quite possible that the NRA would have died a natural death when the act creating it expired in the summer of 1935, but

QUESTION • How was the NRA like the Hoover-sponsored trade associations of the 1920's? How was it different?

before then the Supreme Court put an end to it by declaring it unconstitutional. In a case that involved the wholesale poultry code in New York City *(Schechter Poultry Corp. v. United States),* the court found that "codes of fair competition" were unlawful because Congress had no right to delegate lawmaking powers to the President and code authorities. Although Roosevelt remarked that the justices seemed to want the country to return to the horse-and-buggy era, he made no serious attempt to revive the NRA. As the next chapter will show, however, many of its features were carried on by later legislation.

RELIEF MEASURES

In 1933 those most in need of immediate aid were the twelve to fifteen million unemployed, many on the verge of starvation. At first Roosevelt, like Hoover, thought that relief was primarily the task of local agencies, and expected them to provide it until industry and agriculture recovered enough to provide jobs. It was soon apparent, however, that many states, municipalities, and local charities had reached the end of their resources. In May 1933, Congress therefore established a Federal Emergency Relief Administration (FERA), the first of several great New Deal relief agencies. FERA made loans and outright gifts to states and municipalities, which distributed the money as they chose. They generally provided a "dole"—either outright payments in money or handouts of clothing and food.

The dole was the cheapest form of relief, but those receiving it for any length of time lost self-respect and technical skills. Thus it tended to make the unemployed unemployable. Partly because of the influence of Harry Hopkins, a former social worker who eventually became Roosevelt's most intimate adviser, the New Deal turned in autumn of 1933 to a great

628

work relief program, the Civil Works Administration (CWA). At its height the CWA employed more than 4,000,000 people. It built or improved 1,000 airports, 500,000 miles of roads, and 40,000 school buildings. Because of the very speed of the operation and Hopkins' desperate desire to get relief to people in distress, some of the CWA projects were simply "make work" of little usefulness, to which its critics applied the term "boondoggling." In 1934 Roosevelt gave in to fierce criticism from conservatives and called off the program.

The CCC and PWA

The most generally admired New Deal agency reflected the fact that Franklin Roosevelt, like Theodore Roosevelt before him, was an ardent conservationist. This was the Civilian Conservation Corps (CCC), which offered outdoor work to unemployed, single men between 18 and 25 years of age. The basic wage was $30 a month, of which $22 went back to the boy's family. By the midsummer of 1933, the CCC had established 1,500 camps and put 300,000 young men into wilderness areas. They planted trees, cleaned beaches, fought blights, made reservoirs, and checked erosion. But the most important work of the CCC was to check human erosion. The average CCC boy returned to his home after six months or a year ten or fifteen pounds heavier, better disciplined, improved in health, and with a heightened sense of self-respect.

A section of the National Industrial Recovery Act of 1933 established a Public Works Administration (PWA), which Roosevelt put under the direction of his able Secretary of the Interior, Harold Ickes. A cautious, scrupulously honest man who wanted to make sure that not a dollar was wasted, Ickes tried to see that all projects undertaken by PWA were useful, well planned, and efficiently administered. It was therefore some time before PWA had much

The appalling human wastage of the depression, with a third of the working men of the country unable to find employment and dependent on inadequate relief, is suggested by this picture of a despairing man in a San Francisco breadline in 1933.

effect on employment, but eventually it engaged in projects in 99 per cent of the counties of the country. It built great dams, sewer systems, waterworks, even cruisers and aircraft carriers. Generally PWA worked through private contractors, rather than hiring workers directly.

Help for Home Owners

The depression saw many families lose their homes when mortgages were foreclosed. A Home Owners' Loan Corporation was therefore set up by Congress in 1933 to refinance small mortgages at lower rates of interest. Within three years it lent over $300,000,000

629

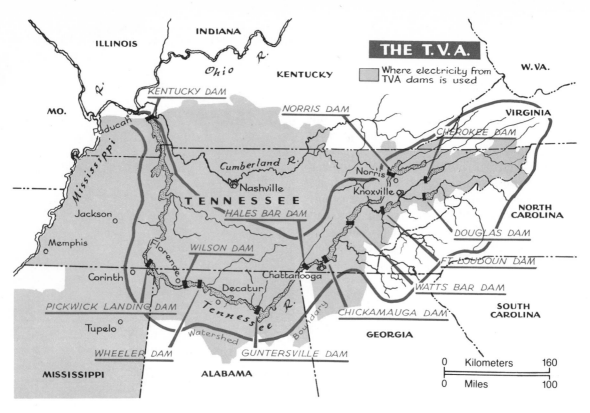

THE T.V.A.

Where electricity from TVA dams is used

ILLINOIS
INDIANA
KENTUCKY
W. VA.
MO.
KENTUCKY DAM
NORRIS DAM
VIRGINIA
CHEROKEE DAM
Paducah
Cumberland R.
Norris
Nashville
Knoxville
TENNESSEE
NORTH CAROLINA
Jackson
HALES BAR DAM
DOUGLAS DAM
Memphis
WILSON DAM
FT. LOUDOUN DAM
Florence
Chattanooga
Corinth
Decatur
WATTS BAR DAM
PICKWICK LANDING DAM
Tennessee R.
CHICKAMAUGA DAM
SOUTH CAROLINA
Tupelo
Watershed
Boundary
GEORGIA
WHEELER DAM
GUNTERSVILLE DAM
MISSISSIPPI
ALABAMA

0 Kilometers 160
0 Miles 100

The Tennessee Valley Authority, set up in 1933, has been both hailed as an outstanding example of social planning and damned as a radical interference with private enterprise. Its purposes include control of floods, production of cheap electrical power, improvement of land use, better navigation of the Tennessee River, and the establishment of recreation areas.

to more than a million people threatened with losing their homes. A Federal Housing Agency, established in 1934, also helped to revive the hard-hit construction industry by guaranteeing bank loans to pay for new housing and home repairs. These agencies promoted much-needed reform in methods of writing and repaying mortgages so that borrowers were protected from excessive rates of interest and were enabled to pay off the principal in a reasonable period of time.

SOCIAL PLANNING: THE TVA

While most early New Deal laws were stop-gap emergency measures, the Roosevelt administration also engaged in one dramatic adven-

ture in longtime social and economic planning. In May 1933, Congress, under Roosevelt's prodding, established a Tennessee Valley Authority (TVA) designed to promote the well-being of the immense area drained by the Tennessee and Cumberland rivers. The authority itself was a new type of federal agency; as the President described it to Congress, it was to be "a corporation clothed with the power of government but possessed of the initiative and flexibility of a private enterprise." It was given immense powers and endowed with ample funds.

The most notable fact about the Tennessee Valley area before the TVA was the way its natural resources had been exploited or wasted. Forests had been cut off, and most of the farmers eked out a bare living on exhausted land. Heavy rainfalls contributed to erosion and caused disastrous floods. Over half the people of the Valley were on relief in 1933.

Under a three-person board of directors, the TVA set about with vigor to change all this. Employing as many as 40,000 men at a time, it built or improved 25 great dams, moved farmers from marginal lands, reforested millions of acres, established power plants and fertilizer factories, and even built new towns. The Tennessee River became a great inland waterway, over 600 miles long, carrying a heavy freight of barges. The new man-made lakes and public parks provided recreation areas. Perhaps the most notable changes resulted from the immense amount of cheap electricity that TVA produced. In 1933 only two of every hundred farms in the Valley had electricity; by 1960 practically all had it. This improved agriculture by enabling farmers to install refrigerators, milking machines, and cream separators. It reduced the back-breaking toil of housework by enabling people to buy washing machines and electric stoves. It attracted heavy industry to the Valley.

Criticism of TVA

The TVA received a barrage of criticism. It was denounced as a communist measure, as a gigantic pork barrel, as a robbery of the rest of the country to benefit a particular section. Above all, it was attacked by private power companies. One purpose of TVA was to provide a "yardstick" whereby it might be possible to assess fair rates for electricity all over the country. In the Valley itself rates charged to consumers were cut by two-thirds. But representatives of private utilities argued that the TVA yardstick was unfair, and was arrived at only by writing off part of the costs of producing electricity to flood control and navigation. The private utilities were even more alarmed by TVA as a threat to their very existence, in the Valley at once and perhaps eventually in

the country as a whole. For the federal government to socialize production of private power was, they argued, a form of robbery.

Defenders of TVA argued that promotion of a single region helped the country as a whole: prosperity is indivisible. They argued that the yardstick worked. Utility rates all over the country were reduced in the 1930's and 1940's, yet power companies made more money than ever, because lower rates meant more varied use of electricity. As to the charge that TVA was a communistic measure, its proponents pointed to American precedents for the socialization of natural monopolies. Like the Erie Canal, TVA was action by government that stimulated private enterprise.

Opponents of TVA were persuasive and powerful enough to see that no other river authorities were granted such great powers as it enjoyed. The federal government did, however, build other power plants. The most famous of these was the Grand Coulee Dam on the Columbia River, the largest structure ever made by people except for the Great Wall of China.

SHIFT IN INDIAN POLICY

With the close of the Indian Wars in the 1880's (the last skirmish took place in 1890), the federal government at long last abandoned a policy that could fairly be summarized as expulsion and extermination. The Indian Rights Association, organized to promote justice for the Indians, persuaded Congress to pass the General Allotment Act (the Dawes Act—see p. 414) in 1887. The law provided that after a period of tutelage the lands of Indian reservations were to be divided into plots of 40, 80, or 160 acres and granted to individual Indians. This arrangement was based on the idea that the best thing for native Americans was to make them as much like other Americans as possible.

It was reinforced by the education system: children were taken from home at an early age, crowded into boarding schools, and given some "book learning" before being sent back to the reservation. They acquired little knowledge of, but possibly scorn for, the culture of their ancestors. Meanwhile, older people received just enough food to sustain life and clothing to cover their nakedness.

However well meaning, the new policy was scarcely better than the old. By 1934 the Indians held only 48 million of the 133 million acres they had possessed in 1887. Although all were citizens of the United States, state laws often discriminated against them, and the federal government treated them like children, running their affairs for them.

Change for the Better

Improvement began in the Coolidge administration with a reorganization of health services for Indians. President Hoover appointed two able and dedicated people as commissioner and deputy commissioner of Indian Affairs. They began a reform of the Service.

A real revolution in Indian policy occurred during the New Deal years. Acting on the advice of anthropologists who had studied Indian culture, the Roosevelt administration promoted a new approach that was made law in the Indian Reorganization Act (1934). According to John Collier, a new commissioner of Indian Affairs, the purpose of the act was to enable the Indians "to earn a decent livelihood and lead self-respecting, organized lives in harmony with their own aims and ideals." Instead of promoting individual ownership, the federal government now encouraged Indians to revert to their own traditions, which usually regarded land as something like air and water accessible to all within the tribe on equal terms. Instead of being weakened, tribal organization was strengthened. Indians were encouraged to become members of the federal Indian Service. Children were now taught the traditions of their own people in school. Indian handicrafts, art forms, and ceremonies were revived.

That the new arrangements brought benefit could be seen in the reversal of two unhappy trends: Indian landholdings increased after 1934, and the population of the reservations, which had dwindled to just over 200,000 in 1928, had increased by 1940 to 380,000.

As with the blacks, the troubles of the Indians were not over. Most of them were still desperately poor, still ill equipped to deal with an alien civilization, still subject to bias. But the trend had now turned in their favor.

Activities: Chapter 26

For Mastery and Review

1. What were the purposes and origins of the New Deal? Just what did Franklin D. Roosevelt contribute to it?

2. What steps were taken by the New Deal in the areas of banking, securities, and currency? To what extent were these aimed at recovery? To what extent at reform?

3. What was the basic problem plaguing American agriculture? What farm legislation did the New Deal enact? With what success?

4. What was the NRA? What were its purposes and plan of operation? What problems did it encounter? What happened to it?

5. Distinguish among the relief agencies established during the first year of the New Deal as to purposes and methods. On what grounds were they criticized?

6. Explain the purposes of TVA and its program. How was it criticized? How defended?

7. Who opposed the New Deal in 1934? Explain the results of the midterm elections of that year.

Unrolling the Map

On a map of the United States locate (a) the "dust bowl" and (b) the TVA, locating major dams and labeling states in which TVA power is used.

Who, What, and Why Important?

Emergency Banking Act	AAA
fireside chats	dust bowl
the "Hundred Days"	NRA
"brain trust"	Norris-LaGuardia Act
Eleanor Roosevelt	*Schechter v. United*
Twenty-first Amend-	*States*
ment	CCC
Glass-Steagall Act	PWA
FDIC	HOLC
SEC	TVA
pump-priming	Liberty League
Frazier-Lemke Act	Frances Perkins

To Pursue the Matter

1. To what previous period, in European history, was the term "the hundred days" applied? Is there an analogy to the beginning of the New Deal?

2. Compare major features of the New Deal with the Populists, the Square Deal, and the New Freedom, showing connections, contrasts, and differences, both in philosophy and in specific proposals or acts. This might be made into a wall chart, with different committees taking different topics, such as treatment of labor, agriculture, the government and business, and banking and currency.

3. Why had European nations gone off the gold standard? Who in America demanded currency inflation, and by what means? Compare nineteenth century demands for cheap money (see pp. 430–432, 459–461).

4. What made Franklin Roosevelt tick? Clues are found in the second chapter of Davies, *The New Deal: Interpretations.*

5. Why did Franklin Roosevelt promote the TVA? President Dwight D. Eisenhower once called the TVA "creeping socialism." Do you agree or disagree with this characterization? See Lilienthal, *TVA: Democracy on the March.*

6. What was the importance of the New Deal to the South? See Ezell, *The South Since 1865,* Chapter 22.

7. How did Roosevelt deal with the disaster of his attack of polio? Would he have become President if he had not had it? Best source: Friedel, *Franklin D. Roosevelt: The Ordeal.* See also Perkins, *The Roosevelt I Knew,* and Burns, *Roosevelt: The Lion and the Fox.*

8. In many ways the AAA was a shocking piece of legislation, since it reduced the supply of food when many people all over the world were going hungry. Given the circumstances of the time, can you figure out any alternatives? See Schlesinger, *The Coming of the New Deal,* Part II, Chapters 2–5.

9. Authoritative pictures of Roosevelt as a politician, dealing with Congress, public opinion, and party politics, are found in Burns, *Roosevelt: The Lion and the Fox,* Chapter 10, and in Schlesinger, *The Coming of the New Deal,* Part VIII, Chapters 32–34. Comparisons with Theodore Roosevelt and Woodrow Wilson would give added depth.

Chapter 27

The New Deal: Second Phase

*We are determined to make every American citizen the
subject of his country's interest and concern; and we
will never regard any faithful, law-abiding group within
our borders as superfluous. The test of our progress
is not whether we add more to the abundance of those
who have much; it is whether we provide enough for
those who have too little.*

—FRANKLIN D. ROOSEVELT

As the last chapter suggested, the New Deal failed to stem a mounting tide of unrest among the underprivileged. Ten million people were still unemployed as the year 1935 began. They received just enough relief to keep them and their families alive. The circumstances under which they received their miserable dole were usually humiliating. In rural districts, small farmers and tenants were being driven off the land. Everywhere, millions of elderly people faced stark misery, without savings, pensions, medical care, or hope. Here was an explosive mixture of suffering and discontent.

"THUNDER ON THE LEFT"

Much more of a threat to the Roosevelt administration than the prostrate Republican Party or the Liberty League was "thunder on the left" from radical critics of the New Deal. There was a rising demand for drastic action to deal with the fact, as Roosevelt later ex-

pressed it himself, that one-third of the nation was "ill-housed, ill-clad, ill-nourished." Upton Sinclair, the former muckraking novelist, nearly won the governorship of California in 1934 by advocating a plan to "End Poverty in California" through setting up cooperative colonies of the unemployed. Dr. Francis Townsend, a former public health officer shocked by the plight of older people, proposed that the federal government give every retired person over sixty a pension of $200 per month, to be paid for by a national sales tax. He won a fanatical following numbering millions, organized into thousands of Townsend clubs, who sang "Onward Townsend Soldiers" and insisted that Congress act at once. Another pied piper of the distressed was Father Charles E. Coughlin, the "Radio Priest," whose broadcasts were heard by an audience said to reach the amazing total of 40,000,000 people. Although originally a supporter of Roosevelt, Coughlin charged that the New Deal had sold out to the bankers. His

National Union for Social Justice demanded heavy taxation of wealth and a guaranteed wage for everyone.

The most dangerous left-wing foe of the New Deal appeared to be Huey Long, senator from Louisiana. With the fervid backing of the rural poor, he had become a dictator in his own state. He was now bidding for national power; he even wrote a book entitled *My First Days in the White House*. With a folksy, humorous manner and a gift for pungent expression, Long knew how to win audiences. He proposed to make "Every Man a King" by confiscating the property of the wealthy and giving every family a home and $2,000 a year, with free college education for the children. His followers were organized in "Share Our Wealth" clubs. Postmaster James A. Farley, Roosevelt's campaign manager, conducted a secret poll which indicated that if the senator ran for President on a third-party ticket in 1936, he might receive three or four million votes, possibly enough to give him the balance of power between the Democratic and Republican parties. The threat never materialized, because in September 1935, Long was assassinated by a political opponent.

Shift to the Left

Roosevelt did not engage in public debate with his left-wing critics, but in his annual message to Congress in January 1935, he indicated that he was prepared to put the New Deal on a new tack. He admitted that in spite of all efforts, "we have not weeded out the overprivileged and we have not effectively lifted up the underprivileged." He proposed that the federal government dedicate itself to providing greater security for its citizens. Under pressure both from the President and from a large segment of the public, Congress headed off the extreme demands of share-the-wealth advocates by a new program of legislation.

The second phase of the New Deal had the same over-all objectives as the first—recovery, relief, and reform. But now the emphasis was more on reform, less on short-term, emergency measures. There was greater concern for the less fortunate members of society, and at the same time the attempt to enlist the support of the business community was abandoned. Like the Populists and progressives before them, the New Dealers now tried to restrain business through tighter controls and attacks on monopoly. In government finance, the New Deal drifted from its earlier conservatism. Efforts to balance the budget became weaker and were finally discarded entirely. New taxes were frankly designed to redistribute wealth, although not to the degree demanded by Father Coughlin or Huey Long.

The political alignment behind the New Deal was also altered. In 1932 Roosevelt had received support from all segments of the population, including the business community. Partisanship was played down, as he sought the votes of moderate and progressive Republicans. Now there was greater emphasis on the Democratic party organization. The traditional basis of Democratic strength—the Solid South and northern city machines—was reinforced by a coalition of organized labor and organized farmers: the alliance that the Populists attempted in the 1890's. In addition, the Democratic party now received more backing than ever from the underprivileged.

Work Relief: WPA and Other Agencies

The most immediate result of the shift in attitude that marked the new trend was the President's demand for large-scale work relief. The unemployables would continue to live on doles administered by local agencies, but the federal government would provide useful employment for all who were able and willing to work. "We must," Roosevelt told Congress, "preserve not only the bodies of the unemployed from destitution, but also their self-respect, their self-reliance and courage and determination."

Responding to the President's request, Congress appropriated $5,000,000,000 in April 1935 for "work relief and to increase employment by providing useful projects." An immense new agency, the Works Progress Administration (WPA) was set up under Harry Hopkins. The WPA embodied Hopkins' conviction that the first purpose of relief was to "help men keep their chins up and their hands in." He attempted to see that no matter what skills a man or woman possessed, the WPA would provide a chance to use them in a way that would benefit society. And so, in addition to the more obvious work relief projects, such as building schools and making roads, the WPA found employment for "white collar" workers—librarians, writers, teachers, musicians, actors, and artists. WPA projects included theatrical performances, symphony concerts, state guide books, traveling libraries, and mural paintings in post offices. There was inevitable inefficiency and "boondoggling," but on balance the WPA produced social benefits for the rest of the country as well as for those it rescued from bread lines.

The WPA was supplemented by other new relief agencies. A Resettlement Administration (RA) attempted, without much success, to re-establish poverty-stricken farmers on the land. A Rural Electrification Administration (REA) extended power lines into farming areas not reached by private utilities. A "junior WPA," the National Youth Administration (NYA), helped high school and college students to continue their education by providing part-time work, such as typing and library cataloguing.

Meanwhile, previously established agencies continued to operate. The Reconstruction Finance Corporation lent large sums to business and to local governments. The CCC put twice

as many young men as before to work in the open air. The PWA now rolled into high gear and provided employment for hundreds of thousands of people on great public works.

Social Security

Life in the pre-industrial village society had been marked by unremitting toil, by high mortality from disease, and sometimes—when crops failed—by desperate want. But there had been no unemployment, and no business cycles of alternating prosperity and depression. Old people and orphans had been taken care of, because on farms there was usually "room for one more." But even in good times the modern city worker was subject to unpredictable loss of employment. When too old to work, he often had no place to go but the poorhouse. To deal with this fundamental problem of insecurity, Congress passed the Social Security Act of 1935. This was the one New Deal measure clearly inspired by foreign examples. Social security measures, first tried in Germany in the 1880's, had spread through western Europe, as well as to Australia and New Zealand. They had also been tried out in the United States by state governments and private employers.

The Social Security Act was a complex measure. It furnished the states with money grants to assist them in caring for dependent children, cripples, "unemployables," and the blind. The federal government financed state programs of unemployment insurance through a payroll tax paid by employers. The act set up a national system of old age and survivors pensions varying from $15 to $85 per month; the money came partly from pay deductions, partly from employer contributions.

The Social Security Act had many flaws. Some of the provisions for financing it were unworkable; the benefits it provided were meager and insufficient. The act specifically excluded protection for some who needed it most, such as agricultural laborers, domestic help, and sailors in the merchant marine. Nevertheless, the establishment of the social security system was a landmark in the history of the United States. It established the principle that an industrial society has a responsibility toward those it casts out of employment and those too old to work. Eventually, many of the injustices and omissions of the original law were repaired.

Extension of Federal Control over Business

Several pieces of legislation passed in 1935 revealed that the New Deal's earlier efforts to win the support of the business community had been abandoned. Federal regulation of private enterprise was extended; new efforts were made to curb monopoly; and heavier taxes were levied on wealth.

By the earlier banking legislation of 1933, ultimate control of banking practices remained with private bankers, especially those who were directors of the nine Federal Reserve Banks, and among the Federal Reserve Banks especially that of New York. The Banking Act of 1935 centered control of the Federal Reserve system in a seven-person Board of Governors appointed by the President. Now such fundamental decisions as whether to expand or contract currency and credit by raising or lowering the rediscount rate (see p. 523) were made in Washington rather than on Wall Street. Another expansion of federal regulation was the Motor Carrier Act which put interstate bus and truck lines under the Interstate Commerce Commission.

One of the major agencies of monopolistic control of industry was the holding company (see text and diagram, pp. 583–584). Some of the worst abuses of the device were found in the field of public utilities. In 1935 an estimated three-quarters of the electric light and power companies of the United States were

"Three Little Pigs" was a favorite Walt Disney animated cartoon. The little pigs, threatened by the wolf who would "blow their house down," sing triumphantly, "Who's afraid of the big bad wolf?"

controlled by thirteen holding company groups. They were used not merely to centralize control, but to siphon off immense profits and to conceal serious breaches of business ethics. "A holding company," remarked Will Rogers, "is a thing where you hand an accomplice the goods while the policeman searches you." There was, however, a wholly legitimate use for holding companies in the utilities field. They promoted efficiency by coordinating the functions of local operating companies, and effected economies through centralized purchasing, auditing, and engineering. In the summer of 1935, Roosevelt had a bill introduced into Congress which provided for a "death sentence" on holding companies. After a prolonged and bitter fight, a law was passed that essentially embodied the President's wishes. Over a period of years, holding companies in the utilities field were to be abolished save where, in the opinion of the Federal Power Commission and the Securities Exchange Commission, they were useful in promoting efficiency.

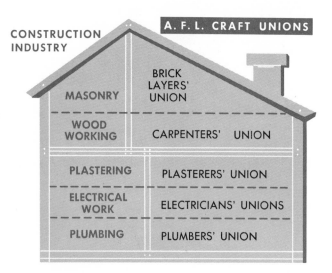

CONSTRUCTION INDUSTRY

MASONRY | BRICK LAYERS' UNION
WOOD WORKING | CARPENTERS' UNION
PLASTERING | PLASTERERS' UNION
ELECTRICAL WORK | ELECTRICIANS' UNIONS
PLUMBING | PLUMBERS' UNION

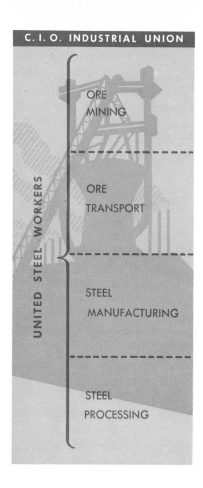

C. I. O. INDUSTRIAL UNION

UNITED STEEL WORKERS

ORE MINING
ORE TRANSPORT
STEEL MANUFACTURING
STEEL PROCESSING

In the "horizontal" organization, represented by the American Federation of Labor (AFL), workers belong to unions representing crafts, and several unions may work on the same project. In the "vertical" organization of the Congress for Industrial Organization (CIO), all workers in an industry belong to the same union.

Throughout the first years of the New Deal, income and corporation taxes remained at the modest levels fixed when Andrew Mellon was Secretary of the Treasury (see p. 579). Now Roosevelt proposed new taxes that would fall with special weight on large accumulations of wealth. The President was apparently not especially interested in increasing federal revenues. Instead, he intended to head off the various "share the wealth" schemes that had attracted large public support. He also hoped to reduce concentration of economic power. The Revenue Act of 1935 which finally emerged from Congress laid new surtaxes on incomes over $50,000. Inheritance taxes were also imposed, with a top of 70 per cent. Moderate corporation taxes were levied, higher rates being laid on large corporations, on those that made excessive profits, and on those that passed profits on to holding companies. Although the law was attacked as communistic and confiscatory, it actually did little to redistribute wealth, while at the same time it quieted the clamor of the followers of Father Coughlin and Huey Long.

THE ADVANCE OF LABOR

In 1935 Congress enacted an important and lasting piece of legislation—the National Labor Relations Act. It was called the Wagner Act, after Senator Robert F. Wagner, who introduced it. Roosevelt was cool to the bill at first, and only lent it his support when the Supreme Court killed the National Industrial Recovery Act and with it Section 7-a which affirmed labor's right to organize.

On the theory that labor was handicapped in dealings with management, the Wagner Act put restraints on employers without corresponding checks on unions. It set up a National Labor Relations Board (NLRB), which had power to hold secret elections in factories to find out whether workers wanted to join a union. It could order employers to stop anti-union activities, arbitrate grievances, and reinstate workers dismissed for union activities. For a time, employers resisted the National Labor Relations Act as an interference with their right to run their plants as they chose and as a violation of the worker's right to "freedom of contract." But after the Supreme Court upheld the law in 1937 in a decision written by Chief Justice Charles Evans Hughes, the NLRB became generally effective.

The Wagner Act stimulated a burst of labor union activity, marked by the appearance of a new national labor organization. As has already been suggested, the American Federation of Labor was ill equipped both in philosophy and in structure to organize the great mass production industries, such as radio, steel, automobile, and textile. Soon there arose within the AFL a group of energetic labor leaders who called themselves the Committee for Industrial Organization (CIO). Its principal figure was John L. Lewis, president of the United Mine Workers, one of the most aggressive, colorful, and controversial figures in the history of American labor. Lewis proposed that all workers, skilled and unskilled, be organized in industrial or vertical unions in place of the craft or horizontal organization of the AFL (study the diagram on p. 638). The rise of the CIO caused a bitter dispute as old-line leaders of the AFL, led by President William Green, foresaw that the type of organization demanded by Lewis would disrupt existing craft unions. Eventually, the CIO seceded from the AFL to form its own national organization with the same initials but a different title, the Congress of Industrial Organizations.

Success of the CIO

In 1936 the CIO attacked the strongest citadel of the open shop—the steel industry. Under the leadership of Philip Murray, four hundred organizers went through the steel towns distributing pamphlets, holding meetings, and buttonholing workers. Within a few months, they signed up enough members to threaten a nation-wide strike. The strike never occurred, because in March 1937, John L. Lewis, now president of the CIO, and Myron C. Taylor, chairman of the board of the United States Steel Corporation, announced that they had settled their differences. To the amazement of the country, "Big Steel" granted a wage increase, reduced the work week to 40 hours, and recognized the CIO steel union as bargaining agent for its members. By 1941 the CIO had signed contracts with the entire steel industry. Its attempt to organize the "Little Steel" companies was achieved, however, only after a struggle so bitter that it resulted in bloodshed.

Meanwhile, the CIO had moved into the automobile industry. Although hourly rates in the industry were high, seasonal layoffs reduced the average wage to less than $1,000 per year. Workers also had a strong sense of grievance against the speed-up which occurred when management increased the rate at which cars moved along the assembly line. The auto workers were difficult to organize. Mostly unskilled, they tended to change jobs when dissatisfied rather than to try for better conditions. The employers actively discouraged union membership, partly by exploiting racial and religious antagonisms between blacks, southern Protestant whites, and Roman Catholics of Polish and Bohemian descent. In 1936, however, the CIO granted a charter to the United Auto Workers Union (UAW). Under the leadership of Homer S. Martin, a former preacher, the UAW enrolled thousands of workers.

CIO leaders did not want to challenge the automobile industry until the struggle with the steel companies ended, but locals of the UAW forced their hand early in 1937 by starting sit-down strikes in several General Motors plants. The workers stopped work but remained in the factories, being careful not to destroy any property. The sit-downs caused great controversy and also great difficulties for the law enforcement agencies. They were peaceful, yet they were an il-

QUESTION • One assumption underlying sit-down strikes was that the job is property belonging to the worker. Is a job truly property? Is one's labor the equivalent of property?

legal occupation of employers' property, and the workers made it plain that they would leave only if forced out by troops. Finally, to avoid violence, General Motors gave in and signed a contract with the UAW. By 1941 the other automobile companies also recognized the union. Sit-downs were abandoned, however, both because they were against the law and because they caused public resentment.

As a result of the foregoing developments, the number of workers in labor unions increased from less than 3 million in 1933 to nearly 9 million in 1939. Never in American history had the economic and political power of a large section of the population grown so rapidly.

THE NEW DEAL ON TRIAL

As we have seen, the New Deal came under constant attack, both from those who thought it did not go far enough and from those who thought that it went too far. To homegrown radicals, such as Upton Sinclair, Huey Long, and Father Coughlin, the New Deal relief and social security measures were mere "crumbs from the rich man's table." To Socialists, such as the perennial presidential candidate Norman Thomas, the New Deal was simply an attempt to patch up capitalism and to "plan scarcity." Thomas could find a good word to say only for the TVA—"a beautiful flower in a garden of weeds." The Communists at first denounced Roosevelt as a "fascist" who pretended to be a friend of the toilers, but was really a tool of the bankers and trusts. The Communist party was opposed to all New Deal efforts at recovery and reform because it feared they would satisfy the masses and put back the day when the workers would rise and overthrow their capitalist masters. In 1935, however, orders came from Moscow for a change in the "party line": Communists were now ordered to align themselves with all "progressive" forces against fascists and reactionaries. The party, therefore, switched to support of the New Deal. Party members attempted to infiltrate trade unions, youth groups, and federal agencies.

The second phase of the New Deal, with its concern for those afflicted with poverty, weakened its left wing critics, and the assassination of Huey Long removed their most effective leader. But the new "hard line" against big business and the "soak the rich" taxes stimulated opposition from the right. The majority of the newspapers of the country turned against the Roosevelt administration, as did most business people and many professionals, such as lawyers, doctors, and engineers. Many Roosevelt opponents worked themselves into fury at "That Man in the White House" (or simply "That Man"). They convinced themselves that he was a Socialist or Communist in disguise, a would-be dictator as dangerous to American liberties as a Mussolini, a Stalin, or a Hitler. Eleanor Roosevelt was denounced with equal fervor.

The Election of 1936

On the eve of the 1936 presidential election, the Democrats renominated Roosevelt by acclamation and enthusiastically endorsed the New Deal. The President set the tone of his campaign in his acceptance speech in which he said that he was engaged in a war to free the country from the "economic royalists" who had sought to enslave its people. The shift in support for him since 1932 was revealed by the fact that business people contributed only about a fifth or a sixth as much proportionately in 1936 as in 1932. But the CIO contributed three-quarters of a million dollars. In spite of the prediction of his campaign manager, James Farley, that he would carry every state except Maine and Vermont, Roosevelt took no chances and campaigned vigorously. He rang constant changes on the theme that the common people were far better off than in the dark days when he took office in 1933.

The Republicans, up against the most popular Democrat since Andrew Jackson, faced a bleak prospect. Their candidate for President was Alfred M. Landon, a popular and moderately progressive governor of Kansas. They denounced Roosevelt for "usurping" power, endangering "the American system of free

Fiorello H. LaGuardia, Municipal Reformer

"When I make a mistake, it's a beaut!" Few politicians have had the courage or the good sense to make such a statement. But then, "the Little Flower" was no ordinary politician. An Episcopalian of Italian ancestry with a Jewish mother, LaGuardia symbolizes the coalition politics that have developed in many American cities in an effort to find answers to the problems of urban life.

LaGuardia was a congressman from East Harlem for more than a decade, during which time he made an enviable record in the fights against prohibition and child labor. He is best known for the Norris-LaGuardia Act, which regulates the use of the injunction in labor disputes. But his greatest achievements came as mayor of New York City from 1933 to 1945.

A roly-poly, five-foot-two dynamo, he galvanized the city and brought it out of the doldrums of the depression. He fought against the gangsters, unified the subway system, restored the city's credit, reorganized the civil service, established a city planning commission, and led the fight for greater democracy in city government by reform of the city's charter. At the same time, he chased fire engines and read the comics over the city-owned radio station during a newspaper strike so the "kids" would not miss Dick Tracy. During his administration the city led the country in building massive complexes of low-cost housing, as well as parks, playgrounds, bridges, airports, and highways.

Although a life-long Republican in a solidly Democratic city, LaGuardia outmaneuvered Tammany Hall and was elected for three four-year terms. He claimed, "I could run on a laundry ticket and beat these bums." He added style and verve to politics, at the same time bringing honesty and good government. As he summed up his work, "Our theory of municipal government is an experiment to try to prove that nonpartisan, nonpolitical local government is possible. . . ."

enterprise," and sending out "swarms of inspectors to harass our people." Their platform supported, however, most of the essential features of the New Deal, such as relief for the unemployed, protection of labor's right to organize, and subsidies for agriculture. Landon enjoyed the support of a number of conservative Democrats, including Al Smith, and most of the press. The *Literary Digest* poll, which had correctly predicted the winner of every presidential election since 1916, foretold a Republican victory.

When the returns came in on November 3, Farley's prediction as to the result proved to be right. The Republicans carried only Maine and Vermont, as Roosevelt won by the largest margin since Monroe's all-but-unanimous election in 1820. A Union party with William Lemke, a radical farm leader from North Dakota as its candidate, and with the endorsement of Father Coughlin and Dr. Townsend, polled close to a million votes. The Socialists and Communists won only negligible support. The Congressional elections were almost as one-sided. Only 17 of 96 senators and 89 of 435 members of the House were Republicans.

Why had the *Literary Digest* poll gone wrong? The answer to this question explains the nature of the new political coalition that supported Roosevelt. The *Literary Digest* based its prediction on replies to postcards sent to a random sampling of names in the telephone book. Thus it was weighted in favor of the upper-income levels of the population. A large proportion of those who voted for Roosevelt, especially in the cities, did not have telephones. An element in the result, although not a decisive one, was that for the first time the black vote was cast for a Democratic candidate. Four years earlier, Republican politicians in black city wards noted, "They're getting tired of Lincoln." Blacks, who were too apt to be "first fired, last hired," owed much to the New

Deal relief policies. Their gratitude was shown at the election booths.

The Supreme Court Fight

The 1936 elections apparently gave Roosevelt and the immense Democratic majority in Congress a mandate from the people to expand the New Deal. Roosevelt indicated in his Second Inaugural Address that he intended to propose new legislation to aid the "one-third of a nation" that suffered from want. But before the New Deal could go on, it had first to reckon with the Supreme Court.

During 1935 and 1936, the Supreme Court had declared unconstitutional a number of major New Deal laws. The destruction of NRA, which has already been mentioned, was followed by a decision (*United States v. Butler*) that invalidated the Agricultural Adjustment Act. In declaring the AAA unconstitutional the majority of the court made the amazing assertion that the production of great staple crops, such as wheat and cotton, which were sold all over the country, was "a purely local activity." The court denied both to the states and to the federal government the right to set minimum wages, leaving a "no man's land" wholly outside the sphere of governmental action. Laws designed to ease the debt burden and to save municipalities from bankruptcy were declared to deprive creditors of property "without due process of law." Never had the Supreme Court invalidated so much legislation. Furthermore, laws that had not yet come before the justices were widely disobeyed. Thus employers openly defied the National Labor Relations Board, trusting that the Supreme Court would strike down the Wagner Act.

During Roosevelt's first term, no Supreme Court justice had died or resigned, so that for the first time since Madison's second term in office the President had no opportunity to make new appointments. Of the "nine old men" on the court, seven had been appointed by Republican Presidents. The court was divided between four extreme conservatives, three liberals, and two "swing men" who voted sometimes one way and sometimes another. The country was presented with the spectacle of laws that affected millions of people, passed by large majorities in Congress, being supported or rejected by margins of 6 justices to 3 or 5 to 4. The unpredictable opinion of one or two men overweighed the collective judgment of the President and Congress.

Much as Old Hickory considered the election of 1832 a command to destroy the Bank of the United States, Roosevelt apparently thought his sweeping victory in 1936 justified him in curbing the Supreme Court. In February 1937, without prior consultation with most of his close advisers or with Democratic leaders in Congress, the President presented legislation to reorganize the entire federal judicial system. Along with useful schemes for reform of the lower courts was a provision that the President might appoint one extra member to the Supreme Court for every justice over seventy years of age. This meant that the court might be increased from nine to fifteen members. In presenting this plan, the President argued that the court needed "younger blood" to enable it "to recognize and apply the essential concepts of justice in the light of the needs and facts of an ever-changing world." The "court-packing" bill caused a revolt in the President's own party. Alarmed by the threat to the independence of the judiciary, enough Democrats joined the Republicans in Congress to defeat the President's proposal, after a legislative battle that went on for more

QUESTION • Should changes in the composition of the Supreme Court be left to the chance of justices dying or resigning?

When Roosevelt attacked the Supreme Court, he provoked such violent criticism that his "court-packing" proposal was defeated. This cartoon suggests that the proposed new justices would have been mere "rubber stamps."

than five months. The President thus suffered a major defeat; he also lost the confidence of many who had up to now given him wholehearted support. He claimed, however, that he had lost the battle but won the campaign. Even before the court-packing bill was defeated, the court had apparently reversed itself. In two 5-to-4 decisions, it supported the constitutionality of the Social Security and National Labor Relations acts. In any event, the character of the court soon changed, as older justices retired and were replaced by other men.

Recession, 1937–1938

By 1937 the economy had recovered so far that it was close to the level of 1929, although the gnawing problem of widespread unemployment still remained. Roosevelt's financial advisers feared another period of wild lending such as marked the 1920's; they also advised a cutback in spending in order to bring the federal budget into balance. The Federal Reserve banks therefore tightened credit, and the WPA cut the number it employed by half. Bumper crops brought huge farm surpluses and a collapse in agricultural prices. The economy soon plummeted down into what the New Dealers called a "recession", and their opponents, a "Roosevelt depression." Industrial production dropped by one-third, almost down to the levels of 1932.

The President blamed the slump on business people who, he claimed, had sabotaged recovery by failure to invest in new productive capacity, and by monopolistic practices that kept prices at artificially high levels. Business people naturally blamed the President, saying that the extravagance and experimentation of the New Deal had destroyed confidence.

To meet the new economic crisis the President called Congress into special session, and it voted to pump new billions into work relief programs and subsidies to agriculture. The new flood of pump-priming brought a quick revival of business activity at the cost of a greater federal deficit.

Last New Deal Measures

In 1938 Congress passed a number of New Deal measures that carried out earlier policies. A Fair Labor Standards Act abolished child labor and provided for a ceiling on hours and a floor under wages, at least for most workers engaged in businesses classified as "interstate commerce." A new Farm Settlement Administration was established to promote the well-being of poverty-stricken farmers and was more effective than the earlier Resettlement Administration in doing so. A new AAA attempted to cope with the ever-present difficulty of surpluses by paying farmers not merely to take land out of production but also to improve the soil and control erosion. It also provided facilities so that surpluses could be stored from year to year, with the purpose of providing an "ever normal granary." A food stamp plan helped to end the scandal of hunger in the midst of plenty by distributing without charge surplus agricultural products among those on relief.

The anti-monopoly philosophy of the second phase of the New Deal was seen when Congress established a Temporary National Economic Committee (TNEC) to conduct an exhaustive investigation of American business practices. The committee collected mountains of testimony, and some of it revealed that business concerns engaged in price-fixing, in deliberate creation of scarcity, in agreements not to compete, and in abuse of patent laws. By the time its reports came out, however, the United States was at war, and there was little interest in enacting new anti-monopoly legislation. During 1938 and 1939, Thurman Arnold, the vigorous head of the Antitrust Division of the Department of Justice, did, however, conduct over 200 investigations of monopolistic practices. He brought nearly 100 cases of alleged violations of the Sherman and Clayton acts into court. He was able to get a number of industries to agree to abandon practices that destroyed competition and hurt the consumer.

End of the New Deal

The legislation described in the foregoing section was by no means all that Roosevelt asked for. A congressional coalition of Republicans and conservative southern Democrats was increasingly effective in thwarting New Deal measures. In 1938, therefore, Roosevelt threw his weight in primary elections against the "copperheads" in his party and in favor of liberal Democrats. This attempted "purge" ended in defeat. The President's interference in local politics was resented, and in most cases the conservative Democrats won. In the midterm elections, furthermore, the Republicans staged a modest comeback, picking up eight seats in the Senate and 81 seats in the House. The Republican-southern Democratic coalition was now more powerful than ever, and was able to veto further extension of the New Deal.

An example of the work of the Public Works Administration is the Grand Coulee Dam on the Columbia River. The largest structure of its kind in the world (4,173 feet long and 550 feet high), it harnesses the river to provide water power, irrigation of arid land, and flood control.

Roosevelt accepted the judgment of the voters. In his annual message to Congress in January 1939, he announced that at least for the time being he would urge no new programs of reform. Instead, he turned his attention to the ominous world situation and the imminent threat of World War II.

AN ESTIMATE OF THE NEW DEAL

The New Deal was a movement of bewildering complexity and contradiction; it spelled no more sense, it was charged, than alphabet soup. And yet certain patterns emerged. It was clear, for instance, that the power and sphere of action of the President were greatly enlarged. Congress could thwart the President and occasionally act independently of him, but the initiative in law-making had moved down Pennsylvania Avenue from the Capitol to the White House. It was even more clear that the scope of federal power had increased enormously, as the central government assumed many functions previously reserved for states and municipalities, such as the regulation of conditions of labor and the provision of relief for the poor.

In its day-to-day attempts to deal with the economic crisis, the New Deal operated on no consistent economic theory. It was damned with equal fervor by *laissez-faire* economists and by socialists. Yet in retrospect we can see that something in between traditional capitalism and socialism had emerged, combining features of both. The essential structure of private ownership was disturbed only in the area of the production and distribution of electricity, and even there only marginally. Elsewhere, the ownership of the means of production and distribution of goods and services continued in private hands. Profit remained the dominant motive. On the other hand, the federal government became the "senior partner" in the economic system, with power to intervene in the interest of stability and individual welfare. According to Mario Einaudi, who saw America with the perspective of a profound knowledge of European politics, the New Deal had found a middle way:

It demonstrated that a strong public hand did not mean exclusion of private efforts. It viewed under a fresh light the old disputes about property rights and, against the Marxist doctrine, it made clear the possibility of bringing to private property a sense of its duty to the community at large, without interfering at all with its formal structure. Property could be chastised and yet left alive.

Shortcomings and Successes

As has been pointed out, the great failure of the New Deal was that it never pulled the country out of the depression. It moved by fits and starts, and there was some justice in the complaint of business people that its unpredictability made for lack of confidence. For all its genuine concern with the unfortunate, its relief efforts were spotty and sometimes unfair. Little was done, for instance, for one of the poorest and most exploited segments of the population —farm labor, especially in the South. Those who benefited most from the New Deal were those best able to exert political pressure, especially organized labor and the farm organizations. So the most powerful got the handouts rather than the most in need.

QUESTION • *Under conditions like those of the 1930's, would you vote in favor of a program such as the New Deal?*

For all its shortcomings, the New Deal accomplished much. In the field of conservation, it made a determined attack on the terrible exploitation and waste of natural resources that had been characteristic of the United States from the first. Of equal importance was the conservation of human resources effected by the Fair Labor Standards Act, the Social Security Act, and the great relief agencies. Above all, the Roosevelt administration preserved faith in democratic processes at a time when democracy in the western world was on the defensive or in retreat. As the next chapter will explain in more detail, the existence of free governments in all Europe, indeed in the whole world, was threatened by the rise of the fascist dictators, Mussolini and Hitler. The 1930's saw one country after another succumb to their agents, their allies, or their imitators. The New Deal showed that it was not necessary to sacrifice liberty to achieve economic security or effective government. Roosevelt was fully aware of the world-wide significance of what he was attempting. In 1936 he said:

In this world of ours in other lands, there are some people, who, in times past, have lived and fought for freedom, and seem to have grown too weary to carry on the fight. They have sold their heritage of freedom for the illusion of a living. They have yielded their democracy.

I believe in my heart that only our success can stir their ancient hope. They begin to know that here in America we are waging a great and successful war. It is not alone a war against want and destitution and economic demoralization. It is more than that; it is a war for the survival of democracy. We are fighting to save a great and precious form of government for ourselves and for the world.

NEW ADVANCES

During the New Deal the federal government was only one agency of reform. Like the earlier progressive period, this was an era of reform at every level. In education the most important advance was that, although total school enrollment declined, students in high school increased by 50 per cent. This was partly because teen-agers, unable to find jobs, went to school in order to occupy themselves. Secondary education had become the rule rather than the exception—a situation which existed nowhere else in the world. Private enterprise as well as government agencies cleared slums and erected better housing. In 1938, for instance, the Metropolitan Life Insurance Company started a 50-million-dollar housing project in New York City. The TVA was not alone in planning for improved use of land. The state of Ohio built the Muskingum River Project, which ended floods, prevented erosion, and de-

The political oppression in Europe in the 1920's and 1930's forced many scientists and artists to flee to the United States. A representative of this group who enriched American life was Arturo Toscanini, "Il Maestro," who led the New York Philharmonic Orchestra. Its Sunday afternoon concerts brought classical music to millions of radio listeners.

veloped recreation areas. In several industrial states there were "little New Deals"—programs of legislation designed to improve labor standards, control corporations, and extend social services.

The great strain on local government caused by the depression encouraged municipal reform. The 1930's saw a great expansion of the city-manager plan (see p. 531), which attempted to put local government into the hands of nonpolitical experts. New York City's vigorous little mayor, Fiorello H. LaGuardia, showed what could be done to free city government from corruption. Robert Moses, LaGuardia's park commissioner, made New York a better place to live in by building playgrounds, improving parks, and cleaning polluted waters.

The prolonged depression apparently did not impede technological advance. During the 1930's commercial aviation came of age. By 1940, air lines were carrying millions of travelers and had extended their services to Europe and the Far East. Industrial laboratories continued to produce new wonders. The Du Pont Corporation easily weathered the depression by manufacturing two new materials—cellophane, which answered the need for a cheap, transparent, nonporous wrapping material; and nylon, a fabric that soon displaced silk.

Amusements, the Arts

In the field of amusement, the 1930's saw the universal introduction of the sound picture. Although Hollywood often presented a distorted or unreal picture of American life, there were more film plays of real merit than ever before. As a result of the inspired imagination of Walt Disney, the animated cartoon created a new world of fantasy, peopled with figures who gained world-wide affection—Mickey Mouse, Donald Duck, and Pluto. The motion picture also gained as a means of education. Every month *The March of Time* produced a film presenting in dramatic form some important modern problem or development. The depression brought only a temporary halt to the expansion of radio, and by 1940 possession of radio sets was almost universal. This was one explanation of Roosevelt's success in winning support of the electorate when most of the press was against him. Although many radio broadcasts were designed for the lowest common denominator of intelligence, there was an increasing demand for more serious programs, such as the news analyses of commentators like Lowell Thomas and H. V. Kaltenborn, or the concerts of the New York Philharmonic Orchestra, directed by Arturo Toscanini.

Artists and writers seem to find the crisis-ridden America of the 1930's more congenial than the prosperous America of the 1920's. In any case, there was a marked return to the native scene. A dominant school of painting portrayed the countryside and the life of the people, its most well-known members being Grant Wood, John Steuart Curry, and Thomas Hart Benton. The WPA art projects, especially the murals in public buildings, gave the disciples of this school such an opportunity to get their work directly before the public as had never existed before. In the field of the novel two important new writers confined themselves to the American scene: Thomas Wolfe, who fictionalized his youth in North Carolina in *Of Time and the River,* and John Steinbeck, whose best-seller *The Grapes of Wrath* told of the trek of a family of displaced tenant farmers from Oklahoma to California. In the theatre, playwrights turned to the life around them; whether in the light-hearted musical, *Of Thee I Sing,* which spoofed the American political scene; Thornton Wilder's *Our Town,* which conjured up the day-to-day life of a New England community; or Clifford Odets' *Waiting for Lefty,* which dealt with a taxi drivers' strike.

A climax of the LaGuardia administration was the New York World's Fair of 1939–1940, the greatest exhibition of its kind in history. In a dreary area of swamp and city dumps in Flushing, Long Island, was erected a great wonderland where foreign countries, American states, and private corporations vied to erect buildings and fabulous exhibits. The most popular feature at the World's Fair was the General Motors building, where the theatrical designer Norman Bel Geddes built what he called a "Futurama." This showed "the world of tomorrow" that technical advance and intelligent planning would make possible. Even after ten years of depression and near-depression, Americans had not lost the optimistic feeling that new frontiers still lay ahead.

Activities: Chapter 27

For Mastery and Review

1. What left-wing organizations sprang up in the 1930's? Who were the leaders? What was the New Deal response? How did Roosevelt strengthen the Democratic party?

2. What were the intentions of the new relief program? For each agency, summarize its assignments and, in general, its accomplishments.

3. What were the antecedents of the Social Security Act of 1935? What did it accomplish? What flaws became apparent?

4. By what measures was federal regulation of business increased? What was the outcome of each?

5. What were the provisions of the National Labor Relations Act? What were its effects in stimulating union activities? Why was the CIO organized? What did it achieve?

6. Who were the major and minor presidential candidates in 1936? What groups supported each man? Why? Explain the presidential and congressional election results.

7. What was the attitude of the Supreme Court toward the New Deal? How did Roosevelt propose to deal with the Supreme Court? Did he win or lose?

8. What steps were taken to deal with the recession of 1937–1938? With what results?

9. What further legislation came from the New Deal? Why did the New Deal come to an end? Summarize the successes and the shortcomings of the program (parallel columns would be useful).

Who, What, and Why Important?

Dr. Francis Townsend	"court-packing" bill
Huey Long	recession
Father Coughlin	new AAA
WPA	TNEC
Social Security Act	elections of 1938
Banking Act of 1935	Muskingum River
Revenue Act of 1935	Project
Wagner Act	Fiorello LaGuardia
CIO	Grant Wood
Communist party line	Thomas Wolfe
election of 1936	

To Pursue the Matter

1. Investigate Huey Long's career, then write an essay or story entitled, "If Huey Long Had Lived."

2. Compare the interest groups that composed the Democratic party in 1936 with the party when it elected Andrew Jackson, James Buchanan, Grover Cleveland, and Woodrow Wilson. This might be illustrated with maps. Why was the New Deal able to cement an effective alliance between farmers and organized labor when the Populists failed in the 1890's?

3. How does social security work today? What people are covered and what people excluded? Who pays? How much? What benefits are rendered by the system?

4. Why did the Supreme Court, hostile to so much of the New Deal, approve the Wagner Act? Study the decision, and the annotations, of *National Labor Relations Board v. Jones & Laughlin Steel Corporation*, 1937, in Bragdon *et al.*, *Frame of Government*, pp. 258–265.

5. The Constitution does not prescribe the number of Supreme Court justices. What has been the history of the changes in its size?

6. What is meant by the "business cycle"? Was the recession of 1937–1938 part of such a cycle? What others can you identify? Do we still have them? Why or why not?

7. Davies, *The New Deal: Interpretations*, has an excellent chapter called, "What Was the New Deal?" How far does it agree with this book?

8. Members of the class might make up a questionnaire to find out how older people of their acquaintance voted in 1932 and 1936, and their reasons. Then pool the results. Do they agree or disagree with explanations in this text?

9. Do you agree with Roosevelt's court-packing plan of 1937? If so, why? If not, why not, and what do you think he should have done? Possible sources: Burns, *Roosevelt: The Lion and the Fox,* Chapter 15; Schlesinger, *The Politics of Upheaval,* Part III, Chapters 24–26.

Chapter 28

The Good Neighbor and the Axis Threat

Because the people of this nation have come to a realization that time and distance no longer exist in the older sense, they understand that what harms one segment of humanity harms the rest.
—FRANKLIN D. ROOSEVELT

Like his distant cousin Theodore, Franklin Roosevelt was acquainted with the world beyond the shores of the United States. He had made thirteen trips to Europe; he had first-hand knowledge of the Caribbean area; through family connections with the China trade he had acquired an interest in Asia. He resembled Theodore Roosevelt, too, in realizing that as a world power the United States had a commitment to help preserve the peace of the world. As a former associate and disciple of Woodrow Wilson, he believed in world organization to promote international cooperation and allay disputes. But when he entered the White House in 1933, Roosevelt's attention was focussed almost entirely on domestic affairs. The affairs of Europe and Asia were no immediate concern. Furthermore, the dominant mood of the country was strongly isolationist, and this mood was reflected in Congress. Even when it appeared that Europe might be conquered by Nazi Germany, a far more dangerous threat to the world than the former German empire, the overwhelming desire of the American people was to avoid another Wilsonian crusade to make the world safe for democracy. Even when

Roosevelt came to feel that the expansion of Germany was a mortal threat to the United States, his efforts to alert the United States to the danger were marked by caution and lack of candor. Only when dealing with foreign affairs in this hemisphere did he act with the directness and boldness that usually characterized his political style.

THE GOOD NEIGHBOR POLICY IN LATIN AMERICA

In his First Inaugural Address, Franklin Roosevelt pledged that the United States would be a "good neighbor" in the family of nations. In Latin America this pious phrase meant that the President and his Secretary of State, Cordell Hull, pursued with vigor the efforts to improve relations with our southern neighbors that Coolidge and Hoover had begun. At a Pan-American Conference at Montevideo, Uruguay, in 1933 the United States joined in over a hundred resolutions and recommendations for fostering cooperation between the countries of the Western Hemisphere. The most important of these said that "No state has the right to intervene in the internal and external affairs of another." Thus the Franklin Roosevelt administration formally abandoned the right of intervention introduced by Theodore Roosevelt as a corollary of the Monroe Doctrine.

The words of this nonintervention agreement were soon translated into deeds. The United States withdrew the marines from Haiti, wrote a new treaty with Cuba which put an end to the Platt Amendment (pp. 483–484), and gave up the right to police the government of Panama. Later it abandoned control of the finances of the Dominican Republic. Even when the Mexican government took over, at a fraction of their value, oil and farming lands owned by citizens of the United States, the Roosevelt administration made only mild protests.

Pan-Americanism

In pursuing the Good Neighbor Policy, the Roosevelt administration promoted the ideal of Pan-Americanism whereby the countries of the Western Hemisphere are joined *as equals.* In 1936 a Pan-American Conference at Buenos Aires, Argentina, drew up an important "Declaration of Principles of Inter-American Solidarity and Cooperation." By this statement, the American nations agreed to forego territorial conquest or the use of force in collecting debts, to refrain from interfering in the affairs of one another, and to settle all disputes by peaceful means. What gave this real force was that the United States, by all odds the most powerful country, was willing to deny itself the privilege of dominating weaker neighbors.

QUESTION • Has the United States succeeded in treating its Latin American neighbors as equals? Do you think that it should do so, or that another policy would be more successful?

The Roosevelt administration continued to treat Latin-American countries with the kind of courtesy shown by Dwight Morrow's mission to Mexico and by Hoover's trip to Latin America before his inauguration. At the Montevideo Conference, Secretary Hull broke precedent and made calls on the other delegates before they had opportunity to call on him. Henry Wallace, Secretary of Agriculture, learned enough Spanish to talk to Latin Americans about their agricultural problems in their own language. Roosevelt himself attended the Buenos Aires Conference; this was only the second time a President had left the shores of the United States. Roosevelt's warmth and charm undoubtedly won friends for this country.

Closer Cultural Relations with Latin America

More important than official courtesy, and probably as important as resolutions or treaties, was the effort to advance closer cultural relations among the nations of the Western Hemisphere. The cultural ties of Latin-American countries had always been with Europe, especially with Spain, France, and Portugal. People in the United States tended to dismiss Latin America as a backward area inhabited by lazy peons, guitar-playing *caballeros,* beautiful *señoritas,* and small-time dictators. Latin Americans had an equally unflattering opinion of us. Luis Quintillana thus describes the Latin-American notion of the typical *gringo* (citizen of the United States):

He is always in a hurry, pushing people around for no reason at all. His tastes are very simple: baseball, automobiles, and cocktails. When he is not chewing gum, smoking cigars, or gulping Coca-Cola, he is eating ice cream.

Intellectually, this creature, so successful in business, is rather slow and limited. . . .

The business office is the natural habitat of a gringo. When he works—and the poor devil must work incessantly because "his wife spends all the money"—he always does so in shirt sleeves, propped back in a swivel chair, with feet on the desk. He seldom takes off his hat, and once seated never gets up, even to greet callers.

During the 1930's, deliberate efforts were made to correct wrong impressions and create better feelings on both sides of the Rio Grande. The Montevideo Conference provided for revision of school textbooks to eliminate misunderstandings, and the Buenos Aires Conference set up a committee to promote closer cultural relations. A division of the State Department under Nelson A. Rockefeller brought Latin-American artists, musicians, and students to the United States, and in exchange sent students and professors from the United States to learn and to teach. These activities were supplemented by local and private agencies. American public schools introduced courses and units in Latin-American history, geography, and civilization. In Hollywood the moving picture companies agreed to eliminate from films, especially from Westerns, anything that would give offense to Latin Americans. The Mexican painter José Clemente Orozco was commissioned to paint murals in the Dartmouth College Library, and the Brazilian singer Carmen Miranda took leading parts in Broadway reviews and Hollywood musicals. Magazines such as *Time* provided editions in Spanish and Portuguese for readers in Central and South America.

Although mutual ignorance and distrust were not abolished overnight, there was little doubt that the various aspects of the Good Neighbor Policy created new friendliness for the United States in the countries "south of the border." This paid dividends when the United States attempted to organize the Americas against the threat of German and Italian aggression.

RELATIONS WITH EUROPE

During Roosevelt's first years in office, the United States seemed no more disposed to pursue a policy of cooperation with European nations than when Harding and Coolidge had been in the White House. During the campaign of 1932, Roosevelt made a public statement that he no longer believed that the United States should join the League of Nations. Like Coolidge and Hoover before him, he urged American membership in the World Court, but was thwarted by the opposition of isolationist senators.

When the Hoover Moratorium on war debts and reparations ran out in November 1932, most of our former Allies refused to resume payment. Previously, German reparations had furnished them the funds with which to pay. But in the summer of 1932 reparations were cut to a small fraction of their former amount, and after Adolf Hitler gained power in Germany in 1933, they ceased entirely. Roosevelt, like his predecessors, insisted that reparations were none of our business, and that he expected the Allies to continue payment of the war debts. After 1933, however, no country except Finland paid in full. Congress responded to this by passing the Johnson Act of 1934, which forbade future loans to any nation failing to pay its debts to the United States.

Wrecking the International Economic Conference, 1933

During the first year of the New Deal, the Roosevelt Administration pursued a policy of economic isolation. Not only were NRA and AAA attempts to advance recovery within the United States without reference to the rest of the world, but the President was empowered to raise the already high rates of the Hawley-Smoot Tariff. In the summer of 1933, represent-

LATIN AMERICA AND THE GOOD NEIGHBOR POLICY

Boxes show major exports to U.S.

★ Pan American Conference site, with date of meeting.

| 0 | Kilometers | 1600 |
| 0 | Miles | 1000 |

UNITED STATES

MEXICO

Havana (1928)(1940)

CUBA

SUGAR

Mexico City (1901-02)(1945)

LEAD
PETROLEUM
COPPER
ANTIMONY
SUGAR

COFFEE

BR. HONDURAS

HONDURAS

GUATEMALA
EL SALVADOR

NICARAGUA

COSTA RICA

Panama (1939)

PANAMA

PETROLEUM

Caracas

VENEZUELA

Georgetown
Paramaribo
Cayenne

GUIANAS
(Br.) (Neth.) (Fr.)

COFFEE
PETROLEUM

Bogotá (1948)

COLOMBIA

Quito

ECUADOR

Pacific Ocean

PERU

LEAD
COPPER
ANTIMONY

Lima (1938)

La Paz

BOLIVIA

BRAZIL

COFFEE
SUGAR

ANTIMONY
LEAD

PARAGUAY

Asuncion

Rio de Janeiro (1906)(1947)

CHILE

ARGENTINA

URUGUAY

Santiago (1923)

Buenos Aires (1910)(1936)

Montevideo (1933)

COPPER

Ocean

Atlantic

INTER-AMERICAN PACT AREAS

ATLANTIC PACT AREA

Atlantic Pact signed Aug. 28, 1949

AREA OF RIO PACT

Rio Pact signed Aug. 30, 1947

Miles
0   3000

⚓ Destroyer Deal bases (Leased from Gt. Britain, 1940)

atives of 66 nations met at an International Economic Conference in London. It had been called at the urging of former President Hoover, and its purpose was to discuss measures that would promote international cooperation, such as mutual lowering of tariff barriers and stabilization of currencies. Whether or not the conference had much chance of success is debatable, but there is no doubt that Roosevelt wrecked it by publicly forbidding agreements that would peg the value of the dollar to that of any other currency. He feared that such action would hurt his efforts to raise American farm prices. His action had the unfortunate effect of increasing European dislike and distrust of the United States.

Reciprocal Trade Agreements Act, 1934

Once the United States had achieved some measure of recovery, Roosevelt was willing to consider measures of economic cooperation with other countries. In 1934 the Democrats returned to the traditional low-tariff position of their party. An important influence in inducing Congress to abandon the policy of high protection was Secretary of State Cordell Hull. A disciple of Woodrow Wilson, Hull believed that international prosperity and good will could be promoted by reducing tariff barriers.

In 1934 Congress passed the Reciprocal Trade Agreements Act, which has been periodically renewed. This law empowered the executive department to make treaties with foreign nations providing for mutual lowering of duties on imports. By the act of 1934, the rates of the Hawley-Smoot Tariff could be reduced as much as 50 per cent in return for concessions from other countries.

This law had several practical advantages over previous attempts to lower the tariff. It prevented logrolling in the halls of Congress and relieved individual Congress members from pressure to see that products of the home district

received protection. It also enabled the State Department to use American concessions as a lever for persuading foreign countries to open their markets to the products of the United States. Within six years of the passage of the first Reciprocal Trade Agreement Act, the State Department wrote treaties with over twenty nations, covering more than 60 per cent of American foreign trade. The effects of the Reciprocal Trade Agreements are difficult to assess, but they surely did not bring the great benefits Hull predicted. On balance, however, they have tended to promote prosperity in the United States and in the world at large and have also generated good will.

Recognition of the USSR, 1933

Another change in American policy took place when the United States recognized the government of Russia in 1933. Although the Bolsheviks had ruled Russia ever since 1917, the United States had refused to grant them recognition, departing from its usual practice of recognizing any effective government, no matter how it gained power. American policy reflected two considerations: (1) the Bolsheviks refused to pay debts or individual claims incurred by previous Russian governments; (2) they preached and plotted world revolution. In 1920 they had founded the Third International, a world-wide organization whose purpose was to undermine capitalism and overthrow existing "bourgeois" governments. But with the rise of Stalin after Lenin's death in 1924, the Bolsheviks had apparently abandoned hope of inciting world revolution and instead were concentrating on the industrial development of Russia itself. By 1933 most other countries had recognized the Bolshevik government. Thus the Soviet Union seemed less of a threat to the established order. Russia's great need for industrial equipment seemed to promise a profitable market for American goods at a time

Adolf Hitler, whom many did not regard as a serious threat in the early 1930's, leads a march of his brown-shirted Nazis through a German city street. Hermann Goering, who told the Germans that they must have "guns before butter," is at his right. By 1946 most of the Nazi leaders were either dead or in prison, convicted of war crimes.

when our foreign trade had been cruelly hit by the depression. "The United States would probably recognize the Devil," remarked Will Rogers, "if it could sell him pitchforks." Japanese aggression in Manchuria provided another argument for recognizing the USSR, since the United States and Russia had a common interest in halting Japan's advance.

In 1933, therefore, the Soviet diplomat Maxim Litvinov came to Washington and arranged with Roosevelt an agreement whereby the United States recognized the Soviet Union in return for certain concessions. The Soviet government promised, for instance, to negotiate a debt settlement and to refrain from subversive activity, either directly or through its puppet, the American Communist Party. In 1934 normal diplomatic relations were resumed. The Roosevelt-Litvinov pact proved disappointing. The Russian government bought little in the United States; it never offered a debt settlement satisfactory to American negotiators; it

continued to support subversive agents in this country. On the other hand, the agreement gave the United States government a "window" in Russia and opportunity to gain valuable information concerning a country about which it was dangerous to be ignorant.

AGGRESSION, ISOLATION, APPEASEMENT

During the New Deal period, the threat of a second world war came ever closer. In Japan fanatical militarists assassinated their way to power and planned to establish domination of the Far East and the Pacific. The Italian dictator Benito Mussolini made plans to realize his dream of controlling the Mediterranean and the Near East. On March 5, 1933, the day after Roosevelt was inaugurated, the German parliament voted dictator Adolf Hitler the power to carry out a program for the conquest of central and eastern Europe and the acquisition of overseas colonies.

Fascism

Mussolini and Hitler preached and practiced a new political doctrine known as fascism. The fascists repudiated democracy; Mussolini called it a "rotting corpse." Instead of the idea that the government exists to preserve individual rights, they favored the "totalitarian" state which controls the total life of its people. The citizen (or rather, the subject) exists only to serve and to obey. Instead of using the democratic machinery of voluntary parties competing in free elections, the dictators imitated the Bolsheviks and set up all-powerful official parties: the Fascists in Italy and the National Socialists (Nazis) in Germany. Elections in these one-party countries were not intended as a means of selecting officials, but as a demonstration of civic loyalty. The voter was given the choice of voting "yes"—that he accepted the officials chosen for him by the party—or "no." Voting "no" was not only futile, but dangerous, since it put the individual *and* his family in peril of punishment for "disloyalty."

Both dictators demanded absolute obedience. Mussolini wrote, for instance, that a state must culminate in a "pinpoint"—meaning himself. Finally, both men—and here they were joined by the Japanese militarists—believed that their countries had a divine right to expand at the expense of neighboring peoples. The Nazis preached that the Germans were a master race of "blond beasts," with a mission to conquer Europe and establish a "thousand-year empire." In the course of this conquest, "lesser breeds"—Poles, Ukrainians, the French—would be reduced to serfdom or slavery. The Nazis revealed new dimensions of the human capacity for evil in

QUESTION • If Mussolini and Hitler used high-pressure indoctrination successfully to sell fascism to their people, why not teach democracy the same way? Or do we?

their treatment of the Jews. Years later, the horrors of concentration camps, and their infamous gas extermination chambers, continued to shock the world. The "final solution of the Jewish problem" was almost reached: six million Jews perished in 1939–1945.

Conquest

By the mid-1930's, it was already evident that Italian, German, and Japanese glorification of war was no idle talk. In 1935 Mussolini climaxed years of sabre-rattling by an unprovoked attack on Ethiopia, followed by conquest and annexation of the entire country. In 1936 Japan exercised her right to withdraw from the disarmament provisions of the Treaties of Washington and London (pp. 574–577 and 602) and started to increase her navy. In 1937 Japanese armies poured into China and soon controlled the northern and central plains. Meanwhile Hitler, disregarding the Treaty of Versailles, began to build a great army, navy, and air force. Nazi agents disguised as students, tourists, and business people carried on subversive activity, not only throughout Europe, but even in Asia, Africa, and the Americas. An attempted Nazi takeover of Austria failed in 1934, but in March 1938, Hitler embarked on a career of aggression by annexing the Austrian republic.

Meanwhile in 1936 the two European dictators formed an alliance that became known as the "Rome-Berlin Axis." This partnership went into business together when it supported the rebellion of General Francisco Franco against the left-wing government of Spain in 1936. For almost three years, Spain was torn by bitter civil war in which Italian and German weapons and troops contributed greatly to Franco's eventual victory. Spain provided a proving ground for German and Italian tanks and bombers and a school for troops. It was obvious that Hitler and Mussolini were planning future aggression.

Neutrality Legislation, 1935–1937

The response of the majority of the American people to the Axis threat and to the possibility of a new world war was a determination not to get involved. They were disillusioned with the former great crusade to "make the world safe for democracy," which had left only a greatly increased domestic debt and billions of dollars lost in uncollectible foreign debts. Nor had it brought a stable peace. In 1934 and 1935, a committee headed by Senator Gerald P. Nye of North Dakota made an investigation of the munitions industry which revealed that American armament manufacturers had made large profits by supplying arms and credit to the Allies during the years 1914–1917. This led to the notion that American participation in World War I had been arranged by "merchants of death," assisted by British propagandists. The attempt to defend neutral rights had also been a decisive element in bringing the United States to war, as it had helped to bring on the War of 1812. There was increasing feeling that Bryan had been right in 1914–1915 (see p. 553) in urging that the United States supply no arms to the belligerents, make them no loans, and abandon defense of neutral rights on the high seas. Wide acceptance of what may be called the "sucker theory" of World War I led to a great increase in pacifism, especially among young people. An expression of this attitude was a short-lived organization in colleges, the Veterans of Future Wars, which ridiculed military service and demanded their veterans' bonus in advance.

In 1935, 1936, and 1937, Congress passed three Neutrality Acts designed to keep the United States from getting involved in wars overseas, even if this meant allowing aggression to go unchecked. The laws varied in detail, but in general they (1) put an embargo on the sale or transportation of munitions to belligerents, (2) forbade loans to nations at war outside of this hemisphere, (3) insisted that raw materials to belligerents be paid for in advance and be carried in belligerent ships (this was called "cash and carry"), and (4) ordered American ships to stay out of war zones and American citizens to refrain from traveling on belligerent ships. When the Spanish civil war broke out, Congress with only one dissenting vote forbade shipments of war materials to either side.

Appeasement

The response of the two great European democracies, Great Britain and France, to the threat of Axis aggression was somewhat similar to that of the United States. Their people had suffered far more severely than the Americans in World War I. Like the Americans, they were disillusioned with the results of that struggle. Much as they disliked Italian, German, or Japanese expansion, they disliked the thought of war even more. Pacifism reached new heights: a majority of the students in the famous debating union at Oxford University voted that on no account would they go to war for king or country. Reflecting such sentiments, the British and French governments pursued a policy known as "appeasement." This consisted in making concessions to the aggressor nations in the hope of satisfying their demand for "room to live." It reached its height at the Munich Conference of September 1938, when British and French statesmen allowed Germany to annex part of Czechoslovakia in return for Hitler's promise to make no further demands.

The appeasement policies of France and Britain, combined with the American neutrality laws, confirmed the Axis powers in their opinion that they had nothing to fear from the "decadent," "soft," peace-loving democracies. Italy followed up the conquest of Ethiopia with the annexation of Albania in 1939. Hitler soon broke his solemn promise at Munich and swallowed up the rest of Czechoslovakia.

Roosevelt Overborne by Isolationist Sentiment

Roosevelt had signed the Neutrality Acts without protest, although he would have preferred to have been allowed some discretion in distinguishing between aggressors and their victims. Secret information revealed that the Axis powers were bent on war. American isolation simply reinforced the Anglo-French appeasement policies. The President became convinced that "storm cellar neutrality" was more dangerous than resistance to the dictators. (In England Winston Churchill reached the same opinion, but he was not in office.) Roosevelt first showed his hand in a speech delivered at Chicago in October 1937. He warned his audi-

ence that if aggression continued unchecked, there was no reason to suppose the Western Hemisphere and America would be spared. He suggested that the United States should help to cure "the epidemic of world lawlessness" by joining with other powers to "quarantine" aggressors.

Just what the President meant by his "quarantine" speech was never clear because public opinion forced him to abandon for a time any attempt to organize collective action against the aggressors. Two months later Japanese planes bombed and sank the United States gunboat *Panay* on a Chinese river. It was an attack as deliberate as the British assault on the *Chesapeake* in 1807, infinitely worse than the sinking of the *Maine*, but American opinion remained unmoved. The majority of those questioned by a Gallup poll a week after the *Panay* was at-

"England's new defense" satirizes the appeasement policy of British Minister Neville Chamberlain. Chamberlain is shown here with Sir John Simon, British Foreign Minister, and Lord Halifax, putting his trust in Hitler's worthless promises.

tacked thought that the United States should withdraw from China entirely. The principal effect of the *Panay* crisis was to speed congressional action on the so-called Ludlow Resolution, which would have provided that the United States, unless actually invaded, could declare war only after a popular referendum. The resolution was opposed by the President, who sent a strongly worded message to Congress saying that it would cripple his conduct of foreign relations and encourage other nations to violate American rights with impunity. Nevertheless, it was voted down in the House of Representatives by a margin of only 21 votes, 209–188.

By 1939 Japan controlled the richest areas of China, and the Chinese government had been driven back into the hinterland. President Roosevelt found means of getting some supplies to the Chinese, in spite of the Neutrality Act, because of the technicality that the Japanese had not declared war when they invaded China. But materials went in vast amounts from the United States to Japan—including 90 per cent of the copper and metal scrap used to feed its war machine—because the Japanese, with a large merchant marine and far more money, could "cash and carry." That the militarists planned further conquest was seen when, in 1939, Japan seized the Spratley Islands in the South China Sea, only 400 miles from the Philippines.

In the spring of 1939, German annexation of Czechoslovakia revealed that Hitler was bent on unlimited conquest. France and Great Britain at last decided that appeasement had failed and that Hitler must be stopped, by arms if necessary. Yet Congress refused to lift the arms embargo so that the two great democracies could buy weapons to arm themselves against the Nazis. It was small wonder that when, in April 1939, Roosevelt attempted to extract from Mussolini and Hitler a promise not to attack 31 countries, the dictators answered him with

ridicule. They had nothing to fear, they thought, from the isolationist, peace-loving American republic.

Organizing the Western Hemisphere Against the Axis

Only in the Western Hemisphere did Roosevelt have any success in getting nations to cooperate against possible Axis aggression. Several Latin-American countries contained large German and Italian minorities. Among them appeared organizations to spread the anti-democratic doctrines of fascism and prepare the way for Axis penetration of South America. German "tourists" and "commercial agents" appeared in such numbers that it was hard to believe they were interested merely in natural beauties or business opportunities. The Nazi government also bought South American air lines and manned them with German pilots. Since these lines ran at a loss, it was suspected that their purpose was military rather than commercial.

At the 1938 Pan-American Conference in Lima, Peru, Cordell Hull attempted to line up the Latin-American countries against the Axis. The Declaration of Lima, which came out of this meeting, proclaimed that the American republics were bound together in "continental solidarity." It said that the nations composing the Pan American Union would collaborate "against all foreign intervention or activity." On the face of it this was a victory for "Pan-Americanism," the idea that all American states, large and small, work together. It also appeared that at last the Monroe Doctrine was made "multilateral" rather than "unilateral"—that is, it was no longer a case of the United States defending Latin America for its own self-interest, but instead a case in which the United States joined with its sister republics to the south in common defense. There was no machinery, however, to force Pan-American cooperation. The resounding phrases of the Lima Declaration revealed that Latin Americans had lost some distrust of the United States and feared European aggression. But the United States was still free to act as it pleased in defense of its own self-interest; it was still a "colossus," although a more friendly one than in the days when Theodore Roosevelt chastised Caribbean republics for "misdoing."

The Declaration of Lima was followed up by positive help to Latin-American governments that wanted to reduce Nazi influence. Thus the State Department helped Colombia to buy out a German air line that operated within easy striking distance of the Panama Canal. The War and Navy departments also worked out better means of defending the Americas and of lending assistance to any Latin-American nation that requested arms or military advice.

Relations with Canada

The Good Neighbor Policy was applied to Canada. In 1931 Canada had become a fully independent nation, tied to Great Britain by sentiment and traditional loyalty to the British crown. This opened the way for more direct cooperation between Canada and the United States, which faced each other across the longest unfortified boundary in the world. Both Hoover and Roosevelt favored the St. Lawrence

Eleanor Roosevelt, First Lady

When Eleanor and Franklin Roosevelt were first engaged, she took him to the slums of New York City, where she worked in a settlement house. Under her guidance he saw for the first time "how the other half lived" (see p. 442) and it shocked him. This incident typified their relationship. Eleanor was a full partner in her husband's political career. Indeed, when he was crippled by infantile paralysis, it was she who insisted that he take up politics again. In doing so she had to fight Franklin's charming, domineering mother who wanted her boy to retire as a country gentleman.

When Roosevelt entered the White House, Eleanor became the most active First Lady in the history of the presidency. A person of insatiable curiosity, abounding energy, and deep concern for social justice, she traveled to every corner of the land. A cartoon of the time portrayed a coal miner deep in the earth exclaiming to his companion, "Good Lord, here comes Mrs. Roosevelt!" Eleanor aroused disapproval for unconventional actions such as writing "My Day," a syndicated newspaper column, and serving hot dogs to the King and Queen of England.

When Franklin died, his widow expected to retire and devote herself to her numerous family. Instead, she became a major political figure in her own right. President Truman appointed her a delegate to the United Nations. There she headed the Human Rights Commission. During this international phase of her life she traveled more widely than ever—to India, the Soviet Union, the Far East. Everywhere she made friends, especially among the young, because of her warmth, her directness, and her genuine interest in making people's lives better.

She was busy right up to her death in November 1962. Her last magazine article detailed things she liked to do on Christmas. One of them was to ask a stranger from a foreign country to dine with the family. She had treated all humanity as her family. Her friend Adlai Stevenson paid her this tribute: "She would rather light a candle than curse the darkness, and her glow has warmed the world."

Seaway project, whereby the United States and Canada would jointly build a great waterway which would enable ocean-going ships to enter the Great Lakes and would produce hydroelectric power for both countries.

When the Seaway Treaty came before the United States Senate in 1934, however, it failed to be ratified. Nevertheless, Canada and the United States were already cooperating, through "joint commissions" in many matters of common interest, such as offshore fisheries, protection of wildlife, and navigation of the Great Lakes. Canadian disappointment at the failure of plans for the Seaway was somewhat reduced when, in 1936, the United States arranged a Reciprocal Trade Agreement that opened our markets to Canadian products. A private agency that improved relations was the Carnegie Endowment for International Peace. In 1935 it started a series of conferences to improve understanding. Attended by scholars, journalists, and diplomats, these meetings proposed several practical ways of breaking down the barriers of ignorance and misunderstanding.

When the shadow of Hitler's ambition began to touch the Americas, Roosevelt assured Canada that it enjoyed the protection of the Monroe Doctrine. While on a visit to Kingston, Ontario, in 1938, the President promised that "the people of the United States will not stand idly by" should Canadian soil be threatened by foreign invasion.

EUROPE AT WAR AGAIN

The nightmare that haunted Hitler in planning his career of conquest was the fear of having to fight a two-front war such as Germany had waged in World War I. The Nazi dictator scored one of the great diplomatic victories of modern times when, in August 1939, he removed the danger from the east by making a nonaggression treaty with the USSR. This cleared the way for a Nazi attack on Poland.

Ever since the Treaty of Versailles, Germans had denounced the arrangements that granted Poland a "corridor" to the Baltic Sea, cutting Germany in two, and which put the German city of Danzig under control of the League of Nations. Late in August 1939, Hitler demanded that Danzig be reunited with Germany and that Poland grant Germany the right to build a road across the corridor. He accused Poland of atrocities against its citizens of German ancestry. On August 31 he delivered an ultimatum and, before the Polish government had time to reply, sent his armies into Poland without declaring war.

Conquest of Poland: "Blitzkrieg"

Poland was a country almost the size of France; its army was large; its people were patriotic. The Poles expected to hold out at least until winter, when "General Mud" would come to their aid and slow up the invaders. Long before winter set in, however, the German armies won a complete victory. They moved so fast, in fact, that they created a new word— *blitzkrieg*, meaning "lightning war." As German armored divisions cut behind the Polish defenders in a series of pincer movements, the German air force ruthlessly bombed not only Polish cities but also refugees fleeing the war zones. This was a deliberate attempt to terrorize the civilian population. Within three weeks Warsaw, the Polish capital, had fallen, and in little more than a month the Nazis were totally victorious. Meanwhile Russia, as part of its bargain with Hitler, seized eastern Poland.

Two days after Hitler's armies went to war, Great Britain and France, having agreed to defend Poland, declared war on Nazi Germany. The British and French were unable, however, to aid the Poles. They had neither enough land forces to invade Germany, nor enough bombers

The Axis: Early Victory

By June 1940, the Axis was in control of most of western Europe. Here mounted units of the Wehrmacht march through the Arc de Triomphe in Paris and down the Champs-Elysées. The devastating effect of this on the French is indicated by the expressions on the faces of some people watching the Germans enter their beloved country.

to attack from the air. Their only possible move was to blockade Germany by sea.

Lifting the Arms Embargo, November 1939

The Nazi blitzkrieg against Poland confirmed the American people both in their intense dislike of Hitler and in their determination to keep out of war. Roosevelt accurately reflected this mood when he issued a public declaration calling on Americans to be neutral in deed, even though he could not ask them to be neutral in thought. After war broke out, it was apparent that American neutrality legislation favored Germany. The embargo on sale of arms or munitions to the warring powers prevented Great Britain and France from using their command of the sea to obtain arms. The German government, which had put "guns before butter" for several years, had little need to import weapons. Roosevelt's sympathies, like those of the majority of Americans, were so strongly with the Allies that in September 1939, he urged Congress to repeal the arms embargo. There was bitter opposition to this measure, and Congress members were bombarded with thousands of telegrams imploring them to "keep America out of the blood business." After six weeks of impassioned debate Congress followed the President's recommendations. France and Britain could now get arms from the United States as long as they could pay cash and supply the ships. Other features of the neutrality legislation were retained and even strengthened, such as the ban on sending United States shipping into war zones.

Russian Attack on Finland

The collapse of Poland in September 1939 was followed by a curious lull in hostilities, nicknamed the "phony war" or "sitzkrieg." Great Britain and France, desperately attempting to rearm, made no offensive move against Germany. Hitler was equally quiet. The only major event to disturb the calm was a war between Russia and Finland. After the USSR occupied eastern Poland in September 1939, it also asked "permission" to occupy all or part of the four countries that lie along the eastern shore of the Baltic Sea—Lithuania, Latvia, Estonia, and Finland. The governments of all the states but Finland thought it hopeless to refuse Russian demands and allowed Soviet troops to move in and "protect" them.

But Finland, blessed with better natural defenses and inspired by a long history of resistance to Russian aggression, refused to give in. On November 30, five Russian armies attacked Finland. All were defeated. For over three months the Finns carried on a heroic defense that won the intense sympathy of the people of the Western democracies. Nowhere was this sympathy more intense than in the United States, but the determination to keep out of hostilities was equally strong. The only gesture that Congress was willing to make in support of Finland was to vote $30,000,000 for non-military supplies. Forced to fight alone against a power that had fifty times as many troops, Finland surrendered in March 1940.

Germany Sweeps On

The "phony war" came to an end in the spring of 1940 with a series of Nazi attacks that were even more surprisingly successful and more terrifying than the blitzkrieg against Poland. On April 9, Hitler sent his forces northward against Denmark and Norway, again without declaration of war. Denmark surrendered at once, since its situation was clearly hopeless. The Norwegians, who had more chance to defend themselves because of the rugged terrain of their country, were at first too stunned by the suddenness and ruthlessness of the attack to put up much resistance. The Norwegians fought bravely, but resistance was crushed and two British landings in the north at Trondheim and Narvik were repulsed. What made the conquest of Norway even more frightening was the report—now known to be exaggerated—that the Norwegian defeat had been arranged beforehand by Nazi agents in the Norwegian army under the direction of Vidkun Quisling. So now "quisling" was added to "blitzkrieg" as the symbol of a new and diabolical Nazi tactic.

Even before the Norwegian campaign was complete, Hitler struck again and once more revealed novel and fearful tactics. On May 9, 1940, he attacked the Netherlands and Belgium simultaneously. In spite of opening the dikes, and of desperate resistance in the course of which a quarter of the Dutch army was killed or wounded, Holland was forced to surrender in five days. In the course of the fighting, Nazi bombers destroyed the defenseless city of Rotterdam. Belgium surrendered in eighteen days; the Belgian fortress of Eben Emael, considered impregnable, was taken in a few hours by a handful of gliderborne soldiers, who suffered very few casualties.

In Belgium, the Nazis finally collided with major British and French forces. To the amazement and horror of the free world, the Nazi blitzkrieg was as effective against them as against the Poles, Norwegians, Dutch, and Belgians. German armored divisions first cut through to the sea, driving a wedge between the British and main French armies. After Belgium suddenly surrendered on May 28, a force of over 300,000 men, two-thirds British, was trapped at Dunkirk on the French side of the English Channel. By mobilizing planes, warships, and an amazing armada of over 600 private craft ranging from tugs to private yachts, Britain managed to perform the "miracle of Dunkirk" and evacuate 90 per cent of its army. But the evacuation was only a moral victory, as vast amounts of supplies and arms were left behind.

The Fall of France, June 1940

After Dunkirk, the German armies turned south and east and in three weeks had overrun more than half of France. The French surrendered on June 22, 1940. By the terms of the armistice, Germany kept over a million prisoners of war as hostages, and occupied nearly two-thirds of France, including Paris. The rest of the country was ruled by an authoritarian government under Marshal Henri Philippe Pétain. Once the heroic defender of Verdun in World War I, Pétain was now willing to collaborate with Hitler. General Charles de Gaulle, however, organized the "Free French" movement, which enlisted French people overseas and organized resistance in France.

Meanwhile Hitler's ally, Mussolini, had entered the war. When it was clear that France had been defeated, the Italian dictator announced that he was coming to the aid of his German allies, and Fascist troops invaded France in mid-June. On the day of the attack President Roosevelt, speaking at Charlottesville, Virginia, remarked, "On this 10 day of June, 1940, the hand that held the dagger has struck it into the back of its neighbor."

Once France was knocked out of the war, Nazi soldiers sang a new song, "We sail against England." Britain was clearly marked as Hitler's next victim. Her army was far smaller than that of Germany and had been stripped of its equipment in the French disaster. All southern England was within easy range of the superior German air force. It would be a matter of hours for German transports to cross the Channel.

Threat to the United States

The fall of France and the threat to Britain shook many Americans out of the comfortable feeling that events outside the Western Hemisphere were none of our affair. The possibility that Hitler and Mussolini might add the French and British fleets to their own suddenly

Nationwide debate over aid to Britain in 1940 evoked the talents of William Allen White (right), editor of the widely-circulated *Emporia Gazette*. White headed a pro-intervention citizens' group, which argued that adherence to traditional isolationism could only postpone U.S. confrontation with the forces of Hitler.

made the Atlantic Ocean seem narrower. If Hitler conquered Britain, the United States might have to fight the Axis powers without a single powerful ally.

An immediate effect of the disastrous situation in Europe was a speed-up in American rearmament. Up to now Congress had been reluctant to heed Roosevelt's warnings that the United States must greatly expand its military force, especially airplanes. But between June and September 1940, it appropriated thirteen billion dollars for defense and voted to raise taxes, even though it was an election year. To mobilize industry, finance, and labor, the President created a seven-man National Defense Advisory Commission. A National Defense Research Committee enlisted American scientists in a race against time to overcome the lead the Germans had gained in military technology.

An even more drastic step toward total defense was the passage of the Selective Service Act in September 1940. Under the operation of this first peacetime draft in the history of the United States, 800,000 young men were immediately conscripted into the army for a year of military service.

Debate over Foreign Policy

The fall of France and the Battle of Britain triggered an impassioned debate over foreign policy. On one side were the interventionists who favored aid to all who fought the Axis. Opposing them were the isolationists, or noninterventionists as they preferred to be called, who insisted that the United States should limit itself to defense of the Western Hemisphere.

The interventionists formed a national organization, the Committee to Defend America by Aiding the Allies. At its head was the veteran Republican editor, William Allen White, who, in June 1940, explained the practical argument for intervention:

If we do not help the allies, if we turn our backs on them, they will see no reason for helping us by giving us their fleets . . . if these fleets go to Hitler, he will have power to take British possessions in the West Indies. These islands control the Panama Canal. . . . He will not move without the British or French fleets. But he will move in then, and war will be certain.

The interventionists furthermore maintained that the defeat of Nazism was necessary to save Europe from a return to the Dark Ages when barbarian conquerors all but destroyed western civilization.

Those who opposed intervention included a few frankly pro-fascist people and also many who had no love for Great Britain. It included others who believed that fascism, for all its ugliness, was the "wave of the future" and therefore certain to win. Most non-interventionists, however, simply took the traditional line that Europe's quarrels were no business of the United States and that it was dangerous for us to meddle in them. They organized a national organization, the America First Committee.

QUESTION • At what exact point, in your opinion, did the United States abandon neutrality?

Their most prominent spokesman was Charles A. Lindbergh, whose solo flight across the Atlantic in 1927 had made him a national idol. Lindbergh, who had inspected the German air force, argued that Hitler was unbeatable and that he was a threat to the United States only if we unwisely stripped our defenses to aid Britain. Senator Arthur Vandenberg said that aid to the Allies meant war. "You cannot," he said, "become the arsenal of one belligerent without becoming the target of the others."

Activities: Chapter 28

For Mastery and Review

1. What were the principal features of the Good Neighbor policy toward Latin America as evolved by Franklin Roosevelt and Cordell Hull? Consider both general principles and specific actions that evolved from them.

2. How did early New Deal policies toward Europe reflect economic isolationism? Why was the Johnson Act passed? What change of policy was reflected in the International Trade Agreements? Assess their results.

3. Why did the United States not recognize the Bolshevik government of Russia before 1933? Why was recognition then arranged? With what success?

4. What are the principal features of fascism? What nations composed the Axis, and why were they a threat to the peace of the world and to civilization?

5. What sentiment was behind the Neutrality Acts? What were their terms? What was Roosevelt's position? Why did Great Britain and France adopt a policy of appeasement? With what results?

6. How did Axis aggression threaten Latin America? What was the Declaration of Lima? Describe United States-Canadian relations in the 1930's. What was the Declaration of Panama, and what did it accomplish?

7. Trace the course of war in Europe in 1939 and 1940, and the influence of events on American public opinion.

Unrolling the Map

1. On an outline map of the Western Hemisphere, locate the Latin-American nations. Locate also the sites of important conferences: Montevideo, Buenos Aires, Lima, Panama. Indicate the leading United States imports from Latin America.

2. Locate the countries of Europe as they were in 1938. Locate the Rhineland, Sudetenland, Memel, Danzig, and the Polish Corridor. On the basis of this map, discuss the Axis program of conquest.

Who, What, and Why Important?

Good Neighbor Policy
Montevideo Conference
Cordell Hull
Nelson Rockefeller
Buenos Aires Conference
Johnson Act
London Economic Conference
Reciprocal Trade Agreements Act
Roosevelt-Litvinov Pact
fascism
Nazis
Axis
Nye investigation
Veterans of Future Wars

Neutrality Acts
appeasement
quarantine of aggressors
Panay
Declaration of Lima
St. Lawrence Seaway
blitzkrieg
"phony war"
Finland
Dunkirk
Selective Service Act
Committee to Defend America by Aiding the Allies
America First Committee

To Pursue the Matter

1. What was the interrelationship between reparations, war debts, and high tariffs? Are the Reciprocal Trade Agreements a permanent solution to the tariff controversies that used to be charac-teristic of American politics and to the question of America's position in world trade?

2. "The Monroe Doctrine is a one-sided state-ment of the interests of the United States and has always been interpreted as such." Did the Good Neighbor Policy refute this judgment? See Perkins, *The United States and Latin America,* or the chapter on the Good Neighbor Policy in Bailey, *A Diplomatic History of the American People.*

3. What are the differences between commu-nism and fascism? Consult Lee *et al., Contemporary Social Issues,* problem 5.

4. Could Hitler have been stopped before em-barking on his career of conquest? Could Roosevelt have done anything to help France and Britain stand up to the Axis? See Divine, *The Reluctant Belligerent,* and Sherwood, *Roosevelt and Hopkins.*

5. What accounted for the extraordinary mili-tary successes of the Nazis in 1939 and 1940? See any history of World War II, such as Davis, *Ex-perience of War: The United States in World War II.*

6. Should the United States have stood up to Japan earlier? Possible sources: Feis, *The Road to Pearl Harbor,* and Divine, *The Reluctant Belliger-ent.*

7. For a contemporary account of "The Miracle of Dunkirk" see Arnof, *A Sense of the Past.* What would have been the effect on America and on Europe had Great Britain been conquered by Germany in 1940?

Chapter 29

The Second World War

The New World, with all its power and might, steps forth to the rescue and liberation of the Old.
——WINSTON CHURCHILL

When France fell, President Roosevelt ranged himself clearly on the side of intervention. In the speech at Charlottesville in which he damned Mussolini's attack on France, he said it was a "delusion" to believe that the United States could become "a lone island in a world dominated by the philosophy of force." He pledged that America would send to the foes of fascism "the material resources of this nation." In the summer of 1940 this meant that the United States would furnish aid to Britain.

THE BATTLE OF BRITAIN

In mid-July, less than three weeks after France surrendered, the Battle of Britain began in earnest. Nazi bombers attacked southern England to prepare the way for invasion by German armies across the English Channel. The troops defending Britain had been largely stripped of equipment in escaping from France; some Home Guard units were armed only with pitchforks and shotguns. England seemed doomed to go the way of Poland and France. But in her dark hour she had found a great leader, Winston Churchill. Offering his people only "blood, tears, sweat, and toil," Churchill pledged that Britain would resist to the uttermost.

> ...we shall defend our island, whatever the cost may be, we shall fight on the beaches, we shall fight on the landing-grounds, we shall fight on the fields and in the streets, we shall fight in the hills; we shall never surrender, and even if, which I do not for a moment believe, this island, or a large part of it were subjugated and starving, then our Empire beyond the seas, armed and guarded by the British fleet, would carry on the struggle, until, in God's good time, the New World, with all its power and might, steps forth to the rescue and liberation of the Old.

To Roosevelt, America's first line of defense was now the English Channel. In the summer of 1940 he overruled the advice of some of his military advisers and "scraped the bottom of the barrel" to send American rifles, machine guns, and artillery to Great Britain.

In addition to the threat of invasion, Britain faced starvation. Nazi submarines in the Atlantic had greater cruising range than the U-boats of World War I. They hunted in "wolf packs," making it harder for merchant ships, once sighted, to escape. By midsummer, 1940, British ships were being sunk at a rate nearly four

668

times as fast as new ships could be launched. Already half the ships in the British fleet had been damaged or sunk. In this crisis, Churchill and Roosevelt arranged an extraordinary deal. On September 2, the President announced that he had given Britain fifty overage destroyers and had received in exchange, by gift or 99-year lease, sites for eight naval and air bases extending from Newfoundland to British Guiana (see map, p. 653). It was evidence of his country's desperate plight that Churchill was willing to make a bargain so favorable to the United States.

The destroyer deal was an act of war against Germany on the part of the United States, yet the majority of Americans supported the measure as an act of self-defense. And the British justified Roosevelt's confidence. Londoners stood up under daily bombing by hundreds of planes with calm and even cheerful courage. In the sky a handful of British fighter pilots inflicted such heavy losses on the German air force that the Nazi plan to invade England, "Operation Sea Lion," was abandoned. "Never in the field of human conflict," said Churchill, "was so much owed by so many to so few."

Protection of the Western Hemisphere

Hitler's victories aroused fear that the Nazis might take over the American colonies of conquered countries in the Western Hemisphere. The most important of these were Dutch Guiana, the French and Dutch West Indies, and the Danish colony of Greenland (see map, p. 758). A Pan-American Congress at Havana, Cuba, in July 1940, dealt with this threat. It drew up the Act of Havana which forbade the transfer of colonies from one non-American nation to another. If there was danger of such a change of control, or if a colony proved unable to govern itself, it might be taken over by "trustees" representing the twenty-one American republics. An individual American nation

These ships were among the fifty sent Britain according to the "destroyer deal" of 1940. The Lend-Lease Act of 1941 provided for much greater aid to the Allies, on terms which "would promote the safety of the United States."

(meaning the United States) was empowerd to take emergency action if necessary. The Act of Havana provided evidence that the Monroe Doctrine might evolve toward multilateral cooperation of all the American republics rather than unilateral action by the United States.

THE ELECTION OF 1940

The issue of intervention cut across party lines. Many Democrats who favored Roosevelt's domestic politics were isolationists, while many anti-New Deal Republicans favored all-out aid to Britain. In a gesture designed to put foreign policy above politics, Roosevelt appointed two Republican interventionists to his cabinet in June, 1940. Frank Knox, Republican vice-presidential candidate in 1936, became Secretary of the Navy, and Henry L. Stimson, who had served in the cabinets of Taft and Hoover, became Secretary of War.

As the presidential election of 1940 approached, the battle between interventionists and isolationists was fought out in both major parties. In June the Republicans nominated a newcomer to politics, Wendell L. Willkie. A successful businessman, Willkie had won fame for his intelligent criticism of New Deal policies, and admiration, even from those who disagreed with him, for his forthright and attractive personality. Since he was sympathetic with the aims of the Committee to Defend America by Aiding the Allies, his nomination was a victory for the interventionists.

The great question on the eve of the Democratic convention was whether Roosevelt would break the precedent that went back to Washington and Jefferson and seek a third term. If war had not broken out, he probably would not have run; his party indeed might have refused to nominate him. But in the face of the Nazi menace he felt his experience was needed, although he refused to say whether he would run until the Democrats actually met in convention. He then announced that he was willing to accept the presidential nomination if he were drafted. He was renominated with only scattered opposition.

In the ensuing campaign, the great issue before the country—abandoning neutrality to aid Britain—received surprisingly little attention, because both candidates were on the same side. Roosevelt even informed Willkie in advance about the destroyer deal. Yet Willkie carried on a vigorous campaign. He attacked the abandonment of the two-term tradition, accused Roosevelt of thinking himself indispensable, and

pointed out the failure of the New Deal to end unemployment. Roosevelt attempted to keep aloof from obvious campaigning, but he was drawn into the battle when Willkie began to predict that Roosevelt's re-election would mean war. If the President's promise to keep American boys out of foreign war, he said, were no better than his promise to balance the budget, "they're already almost on the transports." Roosevelt's response, delivered in a speech in Boston, was one that later hurt him: "I have said before, but I shall say it again and again and again. Your boys are not going to be sent into any foreign wars." The President surely did not intend or want to send American troops abroad, but if this country were attacked, there might be no choice.

QUESTION • Would you have favored the interventionists in 1940 or have been on the side of the isolationists?

In November, Roosevelt was re-elected, even though Willkie polled the largest Republican vote up to that time. In a world in crisis the majority of the American people were unwilling to gamble on a change in leadership.

Lend-Lease Act, March 1941

At the end of 1940 it appeared that England would survive the Nazi threat, and Churchill even began to talk of victory. "Give us the tools," he said, "and we will finish the job." But the British government was running desperately short of funds to pay for the tools. To meet this situation President Roosevelt proposed late in December 1940, that the United States become "the great arsenal of democracy." America must, he said, furnish arms to Hitler's enemies on the same principle that a person lends "a length of garden hose" when a neighbor's house is on fire.

The President's recommendation touched off two months of furious debate. Senator Burton

A. Wheeler of Montana called it "the New Deal's Triple A, for it will plow under every fourth American boy." But Wendell Willkie helped to remove the so-called Lend-Lease bill from partisanship by coming to its support, and public opinion was strongly in its favor. In March 1941, it was enacted into law by large majorities in both houses of Congress. The President was empowered to send American supplies and weapons to foreign nations on whatever terms he thought would promote the safety of the United States. The only limitations were that Congress had to appropriate the money and that the President had to consult with both the army chief of staff and the chief of naval operations.

Battle of the Atlantic

It was one thing to vote funds for lend-lease and another to get goods across the Atlantic in time to help. When Hitler attacked Yugoslavia and Greece in the spring of 1941, lend-lease aid was promised, but the Nazis overran these countries before it could reach them. While German bombers had failed to knock out Britain, German submarines might still starve her into submission. In trying to see that lend-lease supplies reached their destination, the United States was drawn step by step into the critical battle of the Atlantic.

By agreement with the Danish minister in Washington, the United States temporarily took over Greenland in April 1941, partly to prevent its use as a weather station by the Nazis. The same month American naval vessels, patrolling the western Atlantic, began to "trail" Axis submarines, but not attack them. In July, United States marines occupied Iceland to help protect the "bridge of ships" to Britain. By September, after Nazi submarines had sunk American merchant vessels without providing for the safety of crews or passengers, American naval vessels began to convoy ships as far as Iceland. In Oc-

tober, two American destroyers on convoy duty were torpedoed; one of them, the *Reuben James,* was sunk. Congress in November abandoned the last important provision of the neutrality laws by voting to allow American merchant ships to enter combat zones. These ships were armed, and their guns manned with navy crews.

To try to keep the Nazi menace from its shores, the United States had become engaged in a "shooting war." This was, however, a limited war: the United States sent arms to the enemies of Hitler and used force to guarantee their delivery, but it sent no troops. Public opinion polls revealed again and again that the American people wanted to defeat the Axis and at the same time keep our young people from foreign battlefields. This attitude was strikingly illustrated when in the summer of 1941 the President urged Congress to extend by eighteen months the terms of service of men drafted into the armed forces. The necessary legislation passed the House by only a single vote, 203–202, and the extension was limited to six months.

Japanese Aggression in the Far East

While the attention of the American public was focused on the Atlantic and Europe, events were taking place in the Pacific and Asia that eventually plunged the United States into total war.

The war in Europe had presented Japanese war leaders with a golden opportunity for conquest. The four European powers with the greatest stakes in the Far East were France, the Netherlands, Great Britain, and Russia. France and the Netherlands had been conquered by Hitler in 1940, and Great Britain was wholly involved with resisting the Nazis. Japan signed a five-year neutrality pact with Russia in April 1941, and Hitler's armies invaded Russia in June. Already in control of most of China, Japanese forces occupied French Indochina in

1940 and 1941. They were poised to strike the Philippines, Malaya, Burma, and the Dutch East Indies. It was an area containing in abundance raw materials needed by Japan's growing population and expanding industry: rice, rubber, tin, zinc, and petroleum. The only barrier remaining was the United States. In accordance with the Stimson Doctrine, the United States had refused to recognize the Japanese conquest of Manchuria because it violated both the Nine-Power Treaty of 1922 and the Kellogg-Briand Peace Pact. The United States had protested the Japanese invasion of China as violations of these treaties.

In September 1940, Japan formally entered into alliance with the Axis powers, Germany and Italy. Thus resistance to aggression in Europe and Asia became part of the same struggle. Understandably, United States policy toward the Japanese stiffened. It hardly made sense to provide vital war materials both to Hitler's enemy, Britain, and his ally, Japan. The federal government first cut down exports of vital war materials, such as aviation gasoline. Then in July 1941, the Japanese were denied the use of their credit to make purchases in the United States. In August an American lend-lease mission was sent to China. On the other hand, Secretary Hull attempted month after month to persuade the Japanese to abandon their career of conquest. He baited his arguments by offering wider commercial opportunities in the United States. The Japanese diplomats who conferred with Hull assured him that they in turn would like to arrange a peaceful settlement with the United States. But they never offered to abandon Japanese conquests in Manchuria and China.

In November 1941, the Japanese government still seemed interested in peace, since it sent a special envoy to Washington to arrange a Far East settlement. But the militarists who dominated Japan had already decided to attack the United States without a declaration of war.

Attack on Pearl Harbor

The Roosevelt administration had secret information of the possibility of new Japanese aggression, but expected it to be in the direction of the East Indies. The military authorities had been alerted to the possibility of efforts to cripple the Pearl Harbor naval base, but they expected sabotage rather than a military attack. And on the morning of December 7, 1941, the average American had no intimation that a sudden change was to take place in life. In recalling the mood of that Sunday morning, Jonathan Daniels wrote:

The Matson Line was advertising vacation cruises to Hawaii. The upswept hair-do was receiving early attention. Traffic accidents in the country were already up sixteen per cent above ... 1940. John L. Lewis was about to win a decision in his contention that miners in the captive mines of the steel companies must join his United Mine Workers of America. A New York gambling house had been raided. . . .

President Roosevelt, suffering from a slight cold, had just had lunch in his bedroom in the White House when he received a telephone call from Frank Knox, Secretary of the Navy. A wire had just been received from Hawaii:

AIR RAID ON PEARL HARBOR
THIS IS NO DRILL

GLOBAL WARFARE

Soon after it reached the White House, news of the Japanese attack on Pearl Harbor was broadcast to the American people. Many will never forget hearing newscasters breaking in on symphony concerts, football games, and children's programs to tell of the awful event. The next day the President asked Congress to accept the "state of war" that Japan's "unprovoked and dastardly attack" had "thrust upon the United States." Congress declared war with only one opposing vote. Three days later, Ger-

When the Japanese struck at Pearl Harbor, besides inflicting heavy losses in human life, they burned 164 American planes. America recovered from that blow to line up as many as 1,000 superfortresses at its base on Guam, within easy striking distance of Japan.

many and Italy declared war on the United States; Congress again accepted the challenge, this time without dissent.

Although a brilliant military feat, the attack on Pearl Harbor eventually proved to be a colossal blunder on the part of the Japanese. To be sure, it cleared the way for an easy conquest of the Philippines and the East Indies by crippling the American naval forces in the Pacific. But the unprovoked attack united the American people as almost nothing else could have done. In their anger they forgot the bitter partisan quarrels over foreign policies and thought only how to best win a war that no one had wanted.

Axis Victories

However determined to defeat the Axis the American people may have been, the immediate outlook was bleak. For six months the Japanese carried all before them. They took American outposts at Guam and Wake Island, easily conquered the British colony of Hong Kong, and overran the independent Kingdom of Thailand. In February 1942, the great British fortress of Singapore, designed to resist attack by sea, fell before a land attack from the Malay Peninsula. In April came the surrender of the heroic United States-Filipino force that had been holding out on the peninsula of Bataan west of Manila in the Philippines. Under orders from President Roosevelt, General Douglas MacArthur, the commander at Bataan, was sent to organize the defense of Australia. "I shall return," he vowed.

Meanwhile, the Japanese occupied most of Burma and the East Indies. In the extreme north, they seized Kiska and Attu, two of the Aleutian Islands. The total population of the areas occupied by Japan in mid-1942 was over 600 million. If the Japanese war lords could have held out, they would have ruled the most populous empire the world had ever seen.

The year 1941 had been a victorious one for the Axis in Europe and North Africa. In March and again in June, General Rommel, "the Desert Fox," commanding an Italian-German force, launched drives toward the Suez Canal that pushed the British to the borders of Egypt. In April Nazi armies overran Yugoslavia and Greece in three weeks. In May the Nazis staged the first airborne invasion in history and took the island of Crete from a British force.

In June Hitler launched a massive attack against his recent ally, Russia. It seemed for a time as though the 180 Nazi divisions engaged in this invasion would "go through Russia like a hot knife through butter." By December the Germans had occupied an area twice the size of France, including most of the Ukraine, one of the richest agricultural regions in the world. Only with the onset of winter had they been checked at the very gates of Moscow and Leningrad. It was generally predicted that Russia would be crushed in 1942. After that, German armies might sweep through the Middle East and join forces with their Japanese allies in India.

In the face of these grim prospects the two war leaders, Churchill and Roosevelt, never lost their courage or their confidence in ultimate victory. Pictures of the smiling Churchill, with his billy-cock hat, big cigar, and "V for Victory" salute, seemed a sort of guarantee that Britain would not go under. In his annual message to Congress, delivered in the midst of disasters, Roosevelt told Congress:

> We cannot wage this war in a defensive spirit. As our power and our resources are fully mobilized, we shall carry the attack against the enemy—we shall hit him and hit him again wherever and whenever we can reach him.

Difficult Military Problems

In World War I, the United States had simply to guard the sea lanes to Europe and send enough troops to break the stalemate on the western front. In World War II, America had to carry on global warfare in the Atlantic and Pacific, in Europe, in Africa, and in Asia. There was little time to lose. Germany and Japan were so close to dominating the great "heartland" of Europe and Asia that it seemed almost as though nothing could dislodge them.

President Roosevelt as commander in chief was immediately faced with a vital decision: should the United States strike harder against Japan or against Germany? American anger was directed most strongly against the Japanese, since it was they who had attacked us. But the President followed the advice of his military counselors who considered Germany the more dangerous foe. Although Japan was not allowed to rest secure in the Pacific, the main weight of American military might was thrown against Hitler.

The Russian Front

Success or failure of the war in Europe hinged on whether Russia could hold out until the United States and Britain could strike from the west. Although Nazi armies had suffered heavily from the Russian winter after the campaign of 1941, they were still strong enough to launch a second great offensive in the spring of 1942. Worry as to whether Communist Russia might some day prove a more dangerous foe than Nazi Germany was silenced by Churchill at the time Hitler's invasion of Russia began. "I have only one purpose," he said, "the destruction of Hitler. . . . If Hitler invaded Hell, I would make at least a favorable reference to the Devil in the House of Commons." It followed, therefore, that the western Allies must give what aid they could. The three possible routes by which supplies might be sent to Russia were long and difficult: across the Pacific to Vladivostok and then across Siberia, around Africa to the Persian Gulf and then north through Iran, or through submarine-infested waters around Norway to the port of Murmansk.

American Allies: World War II

The events of late 1942 constituted a turning point in the Second World War. British offensive in North Africa kept pace with American victories in the Pacific. Above, British tanks in the Sahara helped rout Axis forces under Rommel. A Soviet counteroffensive begun in November 1942 forced German surrender of Stalingrad in February 1943. Russian troops advanced westward, taking Berlin (right) two years later.

Before Allied aid could reach the eastern front, the Nazi steam roller was again under way, striking toward the rich oil fields near the Caspian Sea. By midsummer the Germans were more than halfway to their goal. But at Stalingrad (since renamed Volgograd) on the Volga River the Russians made a heroic defense which held up Hitler's armies month after month. Meanwhile, thousands of British tanks and American trucks and hundreds of thousands of tons of American supplies had reached Russia. In November the Russians were strong enough to strike back. The besiegers of Stalingrad were themselves besieged. Late in January 1943, the tattered remnants of a Nazi army which once numbered 330,000, surrendered. The Russian armies then started an advance to the west which ended at Berlin over two years later. They kept two-thirds of the Nazi troops engaged and, in the words of Churchill, "tore the guts out of the German army."

Attack from the West

Meanwhile, American forces concentrated in the British Isles for a blow against the Axis. In November 1942, a British-American army landed in Morocco and Algeria to attack the Germans and Italians in North Africa. Rommel, defeated by a British army in the battle of El Alamein in October, was retreating westward from Egypt. Pressed from two sides, Axis armies were bottled up in Tunisia and, in May 1943, they surrendered.

The way was now open for an advance on what Churchill optimistically called "the soft underbelly" of Europe. In July and August 1943, British and American forces took Sicily, and in September they landed in Italy. Although Mussolini had by this time been overthrown, German armies still occupied Italy. The country was mountainous and German resistance fierce; progress up the Italian boot was slow. Not until

June 1944, did the Allies enter Rome, only halfway to the Alps.

One reason for the limited success of the Italian offensive was that the United States and Britain were building up strength for a direct attack on western Europe. Although the American and British air forces were engaged in "round the clock" bombing of German industry and transportation, German armies could be defeated only on the ground. On June 6, 1944 (D-Day), the greatest amphibious force in history, carried in 9,000 vessels, landed in Normandy on the coast of France. Planning for this risky attack on "Fortress Europe" had been under way for over two years.

Within a month after D-Day, a million men had crossed the English Channel. In August the Americans and British broke out of Normandy and struck rapidly eastward. By September they reached the western border of Germany. The Russians meanwhile closed in from the east. The Nazis fought to the last. In June 1944 they had started to bomb Britain from the coast of Europe with V-1's and V-2's (jet-propelled and rocket-propelled bombs). In December twenty German divisions drove a "bulge" into the Allied lines in Belgium. But in March 1945, the western Allies were able to cross the Rhine and penetrate the heart of Germany. Meanwhile, the Russians pushed westward, taking Berlin in April. The great Nazi machine that had brutalized human beings by glorifying war, by its purges of "non-Aryans," by its mass executions and concentration camps, collapsed in ruins. Late in April, Hitler committed suicide in his underground shelter in Berlin. On May 7, German military leaders agreed to unconditional surrender.

In his history of the Second World War, Churchill wrote that many Europeans, on both the Axis and Allied sides, thought that the Americans would prove soft and undisciplined.

In World War II, as in World War I, the immense productive capacity of the United States astonished us and confounded our enemies. After Japanese torpedo planes attacked and sank the carrier *Wasp* in September 1942, only one U.S. carrier remained afloat in the Pacific. By 1944 the United States had produced ships enough to land great armies in Europe and to turn the tide in the Pacific. The picture below shows carriers and attendant craft poised for a strike at Japanese positions in the last year of the war.

General Dwight D. Eisenhower, known as "Ike" among the troops, seldom missed an opportunity to talk to soldiers face to face. His warmth and sincerity went a long way to win the affection of the men in the army, just as his ability won their respect.

Churchill never shared this doubt. He had studied, he wrote, "the American Civil War fought out to the last desperate inch." On the night he heard that the United States had entered the war, he knew Hitler would be defeated. "I went to bed," he said, "and slept the sleep of the saved and thankful." The achievements of American soldiers, sailors, and airmen justified Churchill's confidence.

Dwight D. Eisenhower—Early Career

The commander of the armies that landed in Africa and Sicily in 1942 and 1943, as well as of the great force which established the second front and drove deep into Germany, was an American general, Dwight D. Eisenhower. Few men have ever met more difficult tasks with more success.

Born in Denison, Texas, in 1890, Eisenhower spent most of his boyhood in Abilene, Kansas, which had been a brawling "cow town" only a few years before. It was unlikely that he would become a professional soldier, because his family, of Pennsylvania Dutch stock, were pacifists. Nevertheless he competed for and won an appointment to the United States Military Academy. His parents were poor, and this was a chance to get a free higher education. From the time he entered West Point in 1911 until he emerged from obscurity thirty years later, Eisenhower worked hard to make himself a competent officer.

It was not all easy going. Older than most of the cadets, he had difficulty adjusting to the strict discipline of the military academy. In World War I he was disappointed in his ambition to command troops in France. Between the two world wars, there was a period when he gained no promotion for sixteen years. Yet within the rather small circle of regular army officers Eisenhower gained a high reputation. He stood first in his class in the Army War College, a specialized training school for the ablest officers. He served as aide to General MacArthur, and at MacArthur's request went to the Philippines to help organize the Filipino army. He had read widely in the history of warfare, and made a special study of two problems with which he had to deal later: (1) how to get unified command in an alliance of several nations, and (2) how to make most effective use of motorized vehicles and airplanes.

When World War II broke out, Eisenhower was still only a lieutenant colonel whose great ambition was to command a regiment. But senior officers recognized his ability, and after a brilliant performance in war games in Louisiana in 1941, he was called to serve on the General Staff in Washington. Reporting to Chief of Staff General George C. Marshall a week after Pearl Harbor, he was asked to prepare reports on the best over-all strategy for both the Pacific and European theaters of war. The chief of staff was impressed by Eisenhower's grasp of the war as a whole, as well as by his qualities of leadership. Within a few months Roosevelt, on Marshall's advice, appointed Eisenhower to command the American forces in Europe. Later he became supreme commander of all the forces of the Allies in the west.

Eisenhower's Abilities

Eisenhower justified his superiors' faith in him. Over and above military competence, his task demanded a variety of qualities. He needed the ability to compromise between military representatives of different countries, and between different branches of the military services. Yet he had to be stubborn when it came to insisting that he, and he alone, must make the final military decisions. He had to be cautious about putting military forces in the field before they were sufficiently trained or equipped, yet to gain time he had to take enormous risks, such as when he ordered the D-Day attack on the day planned in spite of appalling weather. He had to be flexible enough to permit changes of plans in the face of sudden difficulties, such as the German breakthrough in the Battle of the Bulge, or of sudden opportunities, such as a German failure to destroy a Rhine River bridge.

As this map suggests, it was the Russians who, in Churchill's phrase, "clawed the guts" out of the German army. The first Anglo-American attack on "fortress Europe," by way of Italy, stalled south of Rome. After the Normandy landing on "D-Day," June 6, 1942, the Americans and English finally established a "second front" and engaged the main German forces.

Eisenhower had the ability to inspire not only the respect but the affection of his troops, of his allies, and of the people back home. His charm, his modesty, his genuine devotion to the cause of democracy against Naziism, all helped to make him one of the most popular military men in history.

Turn of the Tide in the Pacific

The Japanese were unable to organize their vast conquests before the tide of war began to turn against them. In May 1942, an American naval force narrowly defeated a Japanese fleet in the battle of the Coral Sea. A month later an immense Japanese flotilla was turned back with heavy losses in the three-day battle of Midway. These engagements were the first in modern naval history in which surface ships did not exchange a single shot. All damage was inflicted by planes or submarines.

In August 1942, American forces took the first step on the long and bloody road to Tokyo when marines landed on Guadalcanal in the Solomon Islands. The struggle to hold Guadalcanal, fought out on the ground, at sea, and in the air, lasted six months and several times seemed close to failure. Not until 1943 did Japanese resistance there cease.

Conquest of the Pacific Islands, 1943–1945

In risking war with the United States, the Japanese had failed to reckon with the industrial strength of America and its ability to mobilize that strength rapidly. By December 1942, 17 of the 19 ships damaged at Pearl Harbor were again in commission, and new units were constantly being added. In the autumn of 1942 only one American aircraft carrier remained afloat in the entire Pacific; by 1945 over a hundred carriers were in service. The United States Navy developed entirely new techniques of fueling and repairing ships at sea. Fleets were thus able to operate for long periods without returning to their bases.

During 1943 and 1944, American forces engaged in "island hopping" toward the Philippines and Japan. A southern thrust, commanded by General MacArthur, moved along the north shore of New Guinea until it was possible to strike northwest toward the Philippines. In October 1944, MacArthur fulfilled his promise to return to the Philippines when he landed on Leyte. MacArthur's advance was matched by amphibious operations, directed by Admiral Chester Nimitz, against Japanese-held islands in the Central Pacific.

In 1945 the last of the island outposts of Japan fell with the taking of Iwo Jima in March and Okinawa in June. The Japanese defended these islands with almost unbelievable bravery; although Iwo Jima has an area of only eight square miles, American marines suffered over 20,000 casualties in capturing it. The Japanese now began to use "Kamikaze" pilots who flew bomb-laden planes into American ships even though it meant suicide. The Kamikazes scored 279 hits on United States naval vessels off the island of Okinawa.

By midsummer 1945, Hitler had been defeated and all the forces of the Allies could be concentrated against Japan. American forces were expected to suffer appalling losses in overcoming the fanatical resistance of Japanese armies fighting on the sacred soil of their own country. The Russians were expected to dispose of Japanese troops in Manchuria.

The Atom Bomb and Japanese Surrender, 1945

The most terrible weapon the world had ever known made it unnecessary to invade Japan or to count on the Russians for help. In complete secrecy American and European scientists had developed an atomic bomb. The first of these was exploded in New Mexico on July

16, 1945; its destructive power was equal to 20,000 tons of TNT. On July 26 the President urged Japan to surrender at the risk of destruction, but the Japanese prime minister said the warning was "unworthy of public notice." On August 6 an atomic bomb nearly wiped out the Japanese city of Hiroshima and killed over

QUESTION • Should the atomic bombs have been dropped on Hiroshima and Nagasaki? Would the United States have used them on Berlin and Nuremberg?

seventy thousand inhabitants. Two days later Russia entered the war and invaded Manchuria. After a second bomb was dropped on the city of Nagasaki on August 9, the Japanese government agreed to end the war. The surrender took place on September 2 on the battleship *Missouri* anchored in Tokyo Bay.

THE HOME FRONT

To fight the Axis, the United States had to mobilize manpower and resources more quickly and completely than ever before. By 1944 more

At the time of its greatest extent, late in 1942, the Japanese empire was, in terms of population, the largest the world had ever seen, and it contained immense resources. But British and American military and naval forces defeated Japan before it had time to consolidate the immense conquests the Japanese militarists had made in Asia, the East Indies, and the Pacific.

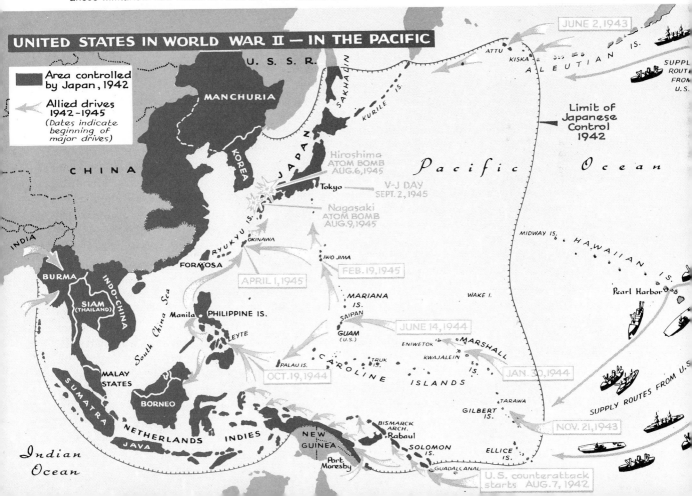

UNITED STATES IN WORLD WAR II — IN THE PACIFIC

Area controlled by Japan, 1942

Allied drives 1942–1945 (Dates indicate beginning of major drives)

With so many men fighting in the armed forces, women moved in ever greater numbers into factory jobs previously held by men. At the same time, job opportunities for black people expanded.

than eleven million men were in uniform. Thousands of women joined the armed forces, performing noncombatant services. Civilians spotted airplanes and trained themselves to deal with possible air raids. Even with so many men under arms, the total number of those employed in industry rose to new heights.

The immense demand for labor during World War II speeded the shift of blacks from agriculture to manufacturing and improved their economic status. In response to the threat of a march on Washington to protest discrimination in defense industries, President Roosevelt in 1941 established a Fair Employment Practices Committee (FEPC). The purpose of the FEPC was to eliminate discrimination against blacks in defense plants and government service. It opened some factory doors and helped black men and women to move into white collar and supervisory jobs previously closed to them.

This was total war, enlisting all the energies of the nation.

The Battle of Production

Despite the skill and bravery of American military men, it is fair to say that victory over the Axis powers was made possible only by the immense productivity of American industry. Americans themselves were amazed at the speed with which industry shifted to turning out war materials. For example, when President Roosevelt in May 1940, talked of making 50,000 airplanes a year, some people thought he had gone out of his mind. Yet by 1944 plane production rose to 120,000. Mass production methods were so effectively applied in the shipping industry that the average time to construct a freighter dropped from a year to less than two months. Within four years American shipyards launched tonnage equal to the entire merchant fleets of the other countries of the world.

As in 1917–1918, federal agencies assumed over-all direction of private companies engaged in war work. The major agencies for control were a War Production Board headed by Donald Nelson and later an Office of War Mobilization under James F. Byrnes. Their functions included letting contracts, fixing priorities of scarce materials, and assisting industry to build new plants or convert old ones. Since the powers and jurisdiction of some agencies overlapped others, and since the armed services could seldom agree on what they wanted, there were abundant red tape, confusion, and waste. Nevertheless, by 1944 close to 50 per cent of American production went into war materials. Total output of all goods nearly doubled. Stalin paid this tribute: "Without American production the United Nations could never have won the war."

Since one of the major elements in production is keeping labor on the job, a National War Labor Board was set up, with powers similar to those of the War Labor Board of 1917. The work of the agency was made easier by the fact that after Pearl Harbor both the CIO and the AFL made a no-strike pledge. Although there were numerous small wildcat (unauthorized) strikes, and two major strikes of the coal workers, the no-strike pledge was on the whole well kept. Work stoppages amounted to a small fraction of one per cent of working time.

In June 1941, Roosevelt reorganized the scientific research program by creating the Office of Scientific Research under the direction of Vannevar Bush. This organization had almost as much to do with winning the war as the army, navy, or air force. It developed radar-controlled artillery, more accurate bomb sights, a proximity fuse that immensely increased the effectiveness of antiaircraft fire, and the bazooka, with which infantrymen could knock out tanks. It helped to make jungles habitable by developing insect-destroying DDT, and to save lives through the use of penicillin and blood plasma. The most dramatic and fateful achievement of all was the harnessing of nuclear energy for military purposes.

Attempts to Control Inflation

The expansion of war industries caused a corresponding increase in employment. Individual take-home pay also increased, because the work week was longer and workers received time-and-a-half pay for hours worked overtime. Thus more people had more to spend. At the same time the shift of industries to war production reduced the availability of consumer goods. Runaway inflation threatened. The danger was attacked in a variety of ways. Wages were stabilized at an increase of about 15 per cent and rents were "frozen." An Office of Price Administration (OPA) attempted to fix the prices of consumer goods and rationed products in short supply, such as meat, sugar, gasoline, shoes, and canned goods. The federal government reduced civilian purchasing power by taxes on small incomes as well as large, taken directly out of payrolls. There was a determined effort to persuade people to buy war bonds, which would defer purchasing power until later. This many-sided attack on inflation was not completely successful, but it undoubtedly did immense good. The cost of living rose 29 per cent between 1939 and 1945 as compared with 63 per cent during the First World War (1914–1918).

In the Second World War there was greater effort than in the first to limit profiteering. In addition to heavier corporation and excess profits taxes there were surtaxes on high incomes that reached the almost confiscatory figure of 94 per cent. Far more than the earlier "soak-the-rich" taxes, the war taxes tended to redistribute the wealth.

Civil Liberties

World War II did not inspire the enthusiasm or idealism of either the Civil War or World War I. The prevailing attitude was that beating the Axis was a dirty job that simply had to be done. There were few war songs, and none to compare with "John Brown's Body," "Dixie," or "Over There." At the same time there was little effective opposition to the war. There was on the whole less invasion of civil liberties during this war than in earlier ones. Conscientious objectors were treated leniently. The press and radio agreed to voluntary censorship and were in turn freed from much direct control. Government propaganda was on no such mammoth scale as in 1917–1918. But on one important occasion the rights of civilians were violated by the federal government on a scale never before seen. In the excitement following the attack on Pearl Harbor, over a hundred thousand Japanese-Americans, most of them citizens, were routed from their homes and herded into detention camps. It is estimated that they lost nearly half their property. That this forced "relocation" was unnecessary was revealed by the loyalty of Japanese-Americans in Hawaii during the war, as well as by the fine fighting record of Nisei (Japanese-American) troops.

The Election of 1944

In spite of occasional dire predictions that once at war the United States would throw the Constitution overboard, elections were held as usual. The Republicans made heavy gains in the congressional elections of 1942, when the war was going badly. There were hopes, therefore, of a Republican victory in the presidential election of 1944. The Republican nominee was Thomas E. Dewey, governor of New York, who had achieved nation-wide fame as a district attorney prosecuting racketeers in New York City. The Democrats renominated Roosevelt for a fourth term. Dewey chose not to attack the New Deal. He was unable to criticize effectively the conduct of the war, since victory was in sight. He promised, however, to provide new and vigorous administration to replace the "tired old men" of the Democratic administration. The Democrats maintained that the great problems of war and peace must be kept in experienced hands. Once again the voters agreed with this argument. Although Dewey faired slightly better than Wilkie in 1940, Roosevelt again won the presidency by a wide margin.

WARTIME DIPLOMACY

The problems faced by the United States in the field of foreign affairs in World War II all centered, naturally, on achieving victory over the Axis. As one historian has written, the aims of the United States were:

. . . to sustain and fortify the tottering British Empire; to keep alive the defeated French nation, almost inanimate under Hitler's heel but still alive and stirring in North Africa; to arm . . . the swarming Russian legions; and to prevent the remaining neutrals, Spain, Portugal, Sweden, Switzerland, and Turkey, from falling prey to the enemy: in short, to win the war in Europe, then with Russia's hoped-for aid to knock out Japan in Asia: first VE Day, then VJ Day.

Closely tied to the problems of fighting the war was the job of making arrangements for the peace which should follow.

The Atlantic Charter, 1941

The most novel feature of the conduct of foreign affairs during World War II was the way heads of state journeyed vast distances, often by air, to confer in person. President Roosevelt, especially, liked to make direct confrontation with rulers of other states. He had a somewhat exaggerated belief in his ability to arrive at effective agreements through persuasiveness and charm, as he had dealt with Congress members or members of his cabinet.

The first great meeting of heads of state occurred before American entrance into the war when, in August 1941, Roosevelt and Churchill met on shipboard off the coast of Newfoundland and jointly issued the Atlantic Charter. This was a statement of the "common principles" on which depended "hopes for a better future for the world." It was somewhat similar, in both intention and content, to Wilson's Fourteen Points. It looked to a world in which aggression should cease, in which peoples should have the right to choose their form of government, in which natural resources should be shared to provide a better life for all, and in which the burden and fear of armaments should be removed. It suggested, without specifying any of the details, a new world organization to keep the peace.

The United Nations Declaration, 1942

After Pearl Harbor, Roosevelt turned his attention to promoting an effective alliance among the nations opposed to Hitler. On January 1, 1942, representatives of the twenty-four countries at war with the Axis met in Washington and signed the Declaration of the United Nations. Each member of the United Nations agreed to abide by the Atlantic Charter, pledged full economic and military support of the war against the Axis, and promised not to make a separate peace. These provisions were written into the lend-lease agreements whereby the United States furnished aid to its allies.

In holding the great alliance together, Roosevelt and Churchill were in constant touch. Although they frequently differed on strategy, neither wavered in admiration for the other. Making close working arrangements with other major allies was more difficult. The Chinese government had been pushed back into the hinterland of China, and Generalissimo Chiang Kai-shek was naturally unhappy because the European theater of war got priority. General Charles de Gaulle, leader of the Free French, disapproved of the way the United States continued to recognize the Pétain government (see p. 664). The United States hoped by this policy to keep Hitler from seizing the French fleet and from occupying Algeria and Morocco. Even after the Allied North African campaign, Roosevelt and Churchill failed to make De Gaulle a full partner in their discussions because of uncertainty as to whether he really represented France.

Cooperation with the USSR presented the greatest difficulty. Both Roosevelt and Churchill had publicly denounced the Soviet government at the time of the Finnish War in 1939–1940. Churchill said that Soviet policy was impossible to understand; Russia, he remarked, was "a riddle wrapped in a mystery inside an enigma." Stalin, who had almost never been outside his country, was intensely suspicious of the capitalistic democracies. Nevertheless, the "strange alliance" between the two great democracies and totalitarian government of Russia continued to the end of the war. Germany apparently could not be beaten without Russian aid, and the Russian war effort in turn depended on supplies from Britain and the United States. Admiration for the heroism of the Russian people, whose losses on the bloodiest front of the war were heavier than those of any other nation, lulled distrust of their government.

Wartime Conferences

Cooperation in plans for war and peace was worked out at a series of international conferences. At Casablanca, Morocco, in January 1943, Roosevelt and Churchill agreed to demand "unconditional surrender" from the Axis powers. At Quebec, Canada, in August 1943, the two men agreed on peace terms for Italy, while their military advisers developed plans for the second front in western Europe. At Cairo, Egypt, in November 1943, Roosevelt and Churchill met Chiang Kai-shek and arranged that Japan should be stripped of her Pacific empire. Korea was also promised independence. From Cairo Roosevelt and Churchill flew to Teheran, capital of Iran, to meet with Stalin. There the three men discussed postwar arrangements, the possibility of Russia entering the war against Japan, and plans for the D-Day attack in the west.

In February 1945, Churchill, Roosevelt, and Stalin met again at the Crimean Conference at Yalta. Publicly they agreed that their nations, along with France, should occupy Germany after the war, that Naziism should be rooted out, that a conference should meet at San Francisco in April to create a new world organization, and that the peoples of Europe should have democratic governments based on free elections. Secret clauses of Yalta agreements dealt with the terms on which Russia should enter

A jovial Roosevelt, flanked by Stalin and Churchill at the Teheran Conference. The apparent good will of this meeting was rapidly dissipated as it became clear that the Russian dictator would not keep promises of free elections in Central European countries.

the war against Japan after Germany was defeated. The USSR was promised the Kurile Islands and the southern half of Sakhalin, both Japanese territories. In China the USSR was expected to keep control over Outer Mongolia, to join with the Chinese government in controlling Manchurian railroads, and to obtain an ice-free naval base and port. Stalin in turn agreed to support the Nationalist government of Chiang Kai-shek as the legitimate ruler of China.

The Yalta agreements later came under violent attack as a "sell-out" to Russia. This charge ignored several facts. In the first place, it seemed vital to keep Russia in the war against Germany at a time when American forces had hardly recovered from the Battle of the Bulge

and, even more important, to bring Russia into the war against Japan. It was expected that the defeat of Japan would cost from half a million to a million American lives and would take eighteen months. Secondly, no territorial concession was made to Stalin that the United States and Britain were in a position to prevent, except the Kurile Islands. Thirdly, Stalin on his part made concessions. The main trouble with Yalta was not the agreements themselves, but that Russia later broke them. Central European nations were never granted free elections, and Stalin failed to fulfill his promise to support Chiang Kai-shek. Churchill's judgment of Yalta was this: "Our hopeful assumptions were soon to be falsified. Still, they were the only ones possible at the time."

QUESTION • Would Russia have entered the war against Japan if no promises had been made to her at Yalta?

Death of Roosevelt

On the afternoon of April 12, 1945, President Roosevelt suddenly died at Warm Springs, Georgia. His death was perhaps mourned more widely than that of any other man in history. According to Henry L. Stimson, his Secretary of War, who served him loyally yet observed him critically, Roosevelt had been a great war President. While he made mistakes in picking subordinates and in failing to give them clear responsibility, he had shown, according to Stimson, a clear grasp of world strategy, "courage and determination . . . in time of threatened disaster," and "very strong faith in the future of our country and of freedom, democracy, and humanitarianism throughout the world."

Before his death, with victory in sight, Roosevelt was thinking ahead to peace. On his desk was a draft of a speech for a Jefferson Day Dinner. It contained these words:

Today we are faced with the preeminent fact that, if civilization is to survive, we must cultivate the science of human relationships—the ability of all peoples, of all kinds, to live together and work together in the same world, at peace.

BIRTH OF THE UNITED NATIONS

On April 25, 1945, representatives of about fifty anti-Axis nations met at San Francisco, California, to make plans for a world union. The groundwork had been carefully laid. In October 1943, foreign ministers of the United States, China, Great Britain, and the USSR met at Moscow and agreed to establish "a general international organization" to maintain "peace and security." In the next month the United States Senate passed the Connally Resolution favoring American membership in the proposed league. From August to October 1944, diplomats of the great powers met at Dumbarton Oaks, a mansion near Washington, to make detailed plans. At Yalta, Russian objections were temporarily quieted when the United States and Britain agreed that seats in the proposed United Nations Assembly be given to two additional republics of the USSR—the Ukraine and Byelorussia.

Charles Drew, Life Saver

Classmates remember Charles Drew as the best all-around athlete at Amherst College. They also remember him as "a perfectly wonderful guy" and "the most admired man on campus." But he was not elected to a fraternity nor to Scarab, the senior honor society. He was black.

Aided by a loan from Amherst classmates, Drew went on to medical school at McGill University, in Canada, and graduated second in his class in 1933. At McGill he began to do research in blood transfusion. This culminated in a pioneering book, *Banked Blood: A Study in Blood Preservation,* published in 1940.

In the same year British doctors appealed to the United States to send blood for victims of German air raids. In response, the American Red Cross set up a blood bank in New York City, and asked Charles Drew to be its director. Dr. Drew enlisted medical teams in hospitals. He persuaded priests, rabbis, and ministers to urge their congregations to give blood. Under Drew's influence, "Blood for Britain" concentrated on producing dried blood plasma. This was easily transported and could be quickly reconstituted with the addition of sterile water. As good as whole blood for most purposes, plasma could be given to people of all blood types.

Drew later headed the blood bank program for the armed forces. Blood plasma, often injected right on the battlefield, saved the lives of thousands of wounded men suffering from hemorrhage and shock.

When the War Department, giving in to race prejudice, ordered that blood from black donors and white donors be segregated, Drew resigned in protest. He returned to Washington, his home town, to teach surgery at Howard University. He also traveled through the South demonstrating surgical techniques, sometimes on kitchen tables in poverty-stricken all black schools. In 1950, at the age of 45, he was killed in an auto accident while driving to Tuskegee Institute to give a lecture to black doctors.

In planning for the San Francisco Conference, Roosevelt had tried to avoid mistakes made by Woodrow Wilson in 1918–1919. He slighted neither the opposition party nor Congress when choosing the United States delegation. The House and Senate each sent one Republican and one Democratic member. The President also selected Commander Harold E. Stassen, former Republican governor of Minnesota, and Virginia C. Gildersleeve, dean of Barnard College, whose presence symbolized the increasing political importance of women. The diplomats at Versailles had tried to form a world organization and to arrange detailed peace terms at the same time. The idea behind the timing of the San Francisco Conference was to form the world organization first, while the nations were still united in a wartime alliance, and write the peace treaties later.

San Francisco Conference, 1945

Negotiations at San Francisco were made difficult by growing suspicion, on the part of her Allies, of Russia's intentions. Already it appeared that the agreements made at Yalta were being broken, both in regard to Russian treatment of Poland and in regard to the extent to which one of the great powers could prevent action by the United Nations. Nevertheless, the San Francisco Conference managed to produce in two months the constitution for an international league similar to the former League of Nations. The eloquent preamble of the UN Charter pledged all the countries signing it to "faith in fundamental human rights," to "justice and respect for obligations arising from peace treaties," to efforts to "live together as good neighbors," and to the maintenance of "international peace and security." All nations great and small were equally represented in a General Assembly, which had the right to debate world affairs but little power to direct them. The principal responsibility for keeping the peace

was to rest with the Security Council of eleven members which would always be in session. The United States, China, France, Great Britain, and the USSR each had a permanent council seat, the other six places being rotated. Decisions of the Security Council required a vote of seven members, including all five of the permanent members. Thus each permanent member had the right to veto any major action, and the Security Council would be effective only so long as the wartime cooperation of the "big five" continued. In other words, the UN was powerless to act if a single major power decided to prevent it.

UN Agencies

The charter provided for an International Court of Justice, but it had no power to compel obedience to its decisions. It planned for a number of international agencies, such as a Trusteeship Council to oversee certain "backward areas," an Economic and Social Council to promote international economic co-operation and raise living standards, and a Military Staff Committee to organize a peace-keeping UN military force. UN agencies were to be staffed by a permanent civil service, the Secretariat, selected and paid by the organization itself. The Security Council might ask UN members to punish aggression by either economic boycott or military action.

The action of the United States regarding the UN Charter contrasted with that in 1919 when a minority of the Senate blocked American membership in the League of Nations. In 1945 the United States was the first to take action, when the Senate ratified the Charter by a vote of 89 to 2. The first use of the atom bomb nine days later reinforced the feeling that "it must not happen again." Trusting the new organization, in which they hoped to take a full part, and blind to its weaknesses, Americans hoped to return forever to the path of peace.

For Mastery and Review

1. What aid was given by the United States to Great Britain prior to December 1941? What was the Battle of the Atlantic, and what part was taken in it by the United States?

2. Trace the growing tension between Japan and the United States from 1931 (Stimson Doctrine) to 1941 (Pearl Harbor).

3. How extensive were Axis victories at the height of their conquests? Be specific for each area.

4. Trace the African and European campaigns in which American military forces took part. Describe the invasion and defeat of Germany by the Allied armies.

5. What were the key battles that led to the defeat of Japan? Why the sudden surrender?

6. What effects did the war have on the home front? Describe the American battle of production. What efforts were made to control inflation?

7. Trace the conferences and agreements that led to the United Nations, beginning with the Atlantic Charter in 1941. What was the basic framework provided for the United Nations?

Unrolling the Map

1. On a map of the world today, locate Japanese and German conquests at their greatest extent. Estimate the population of each empire were it still in existence.

2. Make maps of the Pacific and Afro-European theaters of war, noting major battles, especially turning points such as the battles of Midway, Stalingrad, and D Day.

Who, What, and Why Important?

Battle of Britain	Bataan
destroyer deal	Stalingrad
Act of Havana	Dwight D. Eisenhower
interventionists	African campaign
election of 1940	"soft underbelly"
Winston Churchill	D Day
Lend-Lease Act	Battle of Midway
Battle of the Atlantic	Leyte Gulf
Iceland	Charles Drew
Pearl Harbor	atomic bomb
Douglas MacArthur	battle of production

OPA	Yalta
"relocation" of Japanese Americans	United Nations: Security Council,
election of 1944	General Assembly,
Atlantic Charter	specialized agencies,
Chiang Kai-shek	veto

To Pursue the Matter

1. The selections in Arnof, *A Sense of the Past*, pp. 452–474, present high points of World War II. Read them to capture the changing moods of the period.

2. How did the New Deal and World War II affect American Negroes? See Ginsberg and Eichner, *The Troublesome Presence*, Chapter 11.

3. In 1940 German planes were bombing London every night. By 1943, British and American planes were bombing German cities "around the clock." Find out how this "battle for the air" was won.

4. Make up a questionnaire with which members of the class can ask their parents and other elders about their memories of the attack on Pearl Harbor. Did the news change their attitude toward the advisability of war with the Axis powers? Collate and analyze the results.

5. What was the importance of the Russian victory at Stalingrad? Was Churchill wise in deciding: "...we shall give whatever help we can to Russia and the Russian people"?

6. Study further the "consumers' front" during the war; learn about shortages and the rationing system. Find out why taxes and the sale of bonds helped to control inflation. If wage controls, price ceilings, and rationing are justifiable during war, should they be continued permanently?

7. Winks, *The Cold War: From Yalta to Cuba*, has a chapter, "The Beginnings of the Cold War, 1941–1945," that gives a somewhat different interpretation of the Yalta Conference and its effects from the one given in this text. What do other authors say?

8. For a readable account of the decision to make and drop atomic bombs, see Davis, *Experience of War*. And for the appalling story of what it was like to suffer an atomic bombing attack, read Hersey, *Hiroshima*.

PART EIGHT: SUMMING UP
Chapters 26–29

I. CHECKING THE FACTS

1. In each group below, look at the term at the left. Then, from the group at the right, select the item that is *most clearly related* to it.
   a. *pump priming:* stock watering, irrigating western lands, government loans and handouts, increasing aid to Britain
   b. *brain trust:* industrial leaders, intellectual advisors, financial experts, professional politicians
   c. *dust bowl:* Great Plains, Arizona desert, Tennessee Valley, cotton belt
   d. *Section 7-A:* child labor, pensions, tariffs, unionism

Now, once again, look at the term at the left. This time select the item at the right that is *least related* to it
   a. *Fascism, 1940:* Czechoslovakia, Spain, Germany, Italy
   b. *reciprocal tariff:* two-way, mutual, agreed, protective
   c. *PWA:* dams, ships, sewer systems, private homes
   d. *TVA:* Grand Coulee Dam, Norris Dam, Wilson Dam, Wheeler Dam
   e. *Schecter v. United States:* chickens, presidential power, Congressional power, AAA
   f. *writers:* Steinbeck, Toscanini, Wolfe, Wilder

2. *What and When:* Putting Events in Order
List in their correct order the events on this list.
   Italy conquers Ethiopia
   Munich and appeasement
   Hitler takes control of Germany
   Annexation of Czechoslovakia by Germany
   Fall of Poland
   England and France at war

II. INTERPRETING THE FACTS

1. In two or three sentences, explain how the items in the pairs below were in conflict with each other during the period you have just studied.
   a. New Deal, 1st phase—New Deal, 2nd phase
   b. individualism—government controls
   c. reform—radicalism
   d. democracy—dictatorship
   e. minorities—majorities
   f. isolationism—internationalism

2. Three of the items in each of these groups have something in common. One does not. Tell which item does not belong. Then, suggest a title for the three that are related.

Title _____	*Title* _____	*Title* _____
a. Huey Long	b. Security Council	c. Munich
Fiorello LaGuardia	veto	Casablanca
Dr. Francis Townsend	Big 5	Teheran
Father Coughlin	Atlantic Charter	Yalta

III. APPLYING YOUR KNOWLEDGE

1. When individuals or nations decide that one course of action has more advantages and fewer disadvantages than another, they have decided on the basis of *comparative advantage*. What were the comparative advantages of the first course of action over the second in each of these pairs?

    a. government intervention—laissez-faire.

    b. reform—revolution.

    c. war—peace.

During the period of this unit, would you have made the same choices? Can you cite some examples of decisions being made *today* based on comparative advantage?

2. Take a stand on each of these statements of opinion, and defend it, orally or in writing.

    a. "Yesterday's radicals are today's conservatives."

    b. "The United Nations was doomed to be just a debating society from the start."

    c. "Of all of the Presidents to date, Franklin D. Roosevelt did the most for the country."

READINGS FOR PART EIGHT

Fiction and Drama

Clurman, H. (ed.). *Famous American Plays of the 1930's.* Much of the flavor of the '30's is caught in these works by Steinbeck, Odets, and others.

Hersey, J. *A Bell for Adano.* Military government in Italy during the war, Americans, villagers, and the intent to help—an entertaining story.

Steinbeck, J. *The Grapes of Wrath.* The dramatic story of a family forced to leave Oklahoma in the '30's; a classic.

Warren, R. P. *All the King's Men.* A gripping, thinly veiled account of Huey Long of Louisiana.

Non-fiction

Agee, J. and Evans, W. *Let Us Now Praise Famous Men.* A sensitive and beautifully written essay with photo-graphs, on the barren lives of a southern tenant farm family.

Bird, C. *The Invisible Scar.* A fascinating study, if a bit uneven, of the social effects of the Great Depression.

Burns, J. M. *Roosevelt: The Lion and the Fox.* A penetrating and highly readable biography of FDR.

Hersey, J. *Hiroshima.* A short and devastating account of the impact on the city on which the first atomic bomb was dropped.

Lingeman, R. R. *Don't You Know There's A War On? The American Home Front, 1941–1945.* A highly readable account of life on the home front and the social changes brought by the war.

Roosevelt, E. *This I Remember.* Mrs. Roosevelt's excellent memoir of the New Deal.

691

Part

9

An Age of Anxiety

Chapters in this Part

Bathers on Lake Michigan, in View of Gary, Indiana, Steel Mills

A NEW AWARENESS

Americans of today are in general far better off than their predecessors of the early 1900's. They are more healthy, and their life expectancy has risen from about 50 to over 70 years. They are better clothed, better fed, better educated. They work shorter hours and expect vacations with pay. They are far less subject to discrimination on account of race, religion, or sex. Yet the dominant mood of Americans today is one of anxiety, while at the opening of the twentieth century it was one of optimism. Why?

Certainly one reason for the shift in mood has been the impact of incredibly rapid technological changes. These have profoundly altered people's lives. Mechanization of agriculture has all but destroyed the family farm. The automobile has ringed every city with endless suburbs and at the same time has caused the central cities to decay. The American family structure has weakened. Individuals have less of a framework for their lives. Many resort to acts destructive of self, such as drug-taking, or destructive of society, such as crime.

Technological progress has made warfare infinitely more horrible. Heavy artillery and the machine-gun turned World War I into a blood-bath for the soldiers at the front. In World War II the bomber made life a nightmare for civilians in great cities such as London, Hamburg, and Tokyo. In the event of a third world war, nuclear weapons threaten the end of civilization, even of the human species.

The consciousness of imminent disaster created by the atomic bomb has penetrated even the minds of children. Consider the following poem written by an eight-year-old boy in 1972:

PRETTY SOON YA KNOW
Something about our world?
It's gonna crack pretty soon,
It'll be gone about half past noon—pretty soon,
Are you aware, or do you not care
About this . . . aware?

In the forefront of people's minds is a new awareness that there are limits to material growth and prosperity. Americans have had the feeling that natural resources are unlimited, an illusion not seriously shaken until the Arab oil embargo of 1973–1974. When car owners had to line up for gas before dawn on winter mornings, Americans began to realize that petroleum is a limited resource. And petroleum is only one resource in short supply. How long, for instance, can we go on throwing away so many metal containers and junking so many cars that twenty-odd tons of ore must be mined per person every year?

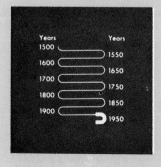

So—there is good reason to call this an age of anxiety. But awareness of our difficulties is a necessary prelude to dealing with them. Conscious efforts are at last being made to conserve our dwindling resources and to preserve the fragile environment. Positive legal steps have enlarged opportunities for racial minorities and for women so that they are on their way to achieving the equality due them as American citizens. A broader world viewpoint is developing that recognizes the common needs of all passengers on space-ship Earth.

Chapter 30

The Cold War Begins

I suppose that history will remember my term of office as the years when the Cold War began to overshadow our lives. I have had hardly a day in office that has not been dominated by this all-embracing struggle . . . And always in the background there has been the atomic bomb.

—HARRY S. TRUMAN

Late in the afternoon of April 12, 1945, Vice-President Truman was called to the White House. There Eleanor Roosevelt met him and said, "Harry, the President is dead." For a moment Truman could not speak. Then he said, "Is there anything I can do for you?" Mrs. Roosevelt replied, "Is there anything *I* can do for *you?* You're the one in trouble now." Next day the new President met reporters. He told them he felt as though the moon, the stars, and all the planets had fallen on him. He asked them to pray for him.

On the face of it Harry S. Truman was ill prepared for the presidency. His previous political career had been that of a machine politician in Missouri, followed by two terms in the United States Senate. His one notable achievement had been the chairmanship of a Senate War Investigation Committee that had uncovered waste and profiteering in war industries during World War II. It had saved the taxpayer hundreds of millions of dollars.

Franklin Roosevelt had met the new Vice-President only three times since the inauguration in January. He had not briefed him on major matters of foreign policy or military strategy. Truman thus knew nothing of the atomic bomb or Russia's secret agreement to enter the war against Japan.

At the time he was suddenly pushed into the limelight, the new President seemed to be the most average of average men. *The New Yorker* magazine wrote of him:

There's one thing about President Truman—he is made in the image of the people. You go into a men's shop to buy a pair of pajamas, President Truman waits on you. You go to have a tooth x-rayed, Truman takes the picture. You board a downtown bus, Truman is at the wheel. Probably it's those glasses he wears, but whatever it is, we rather like having a President who always seems to be around. President Roosevelt was *for* the people, but Harry Truman *is* the people.

The public later discovered that Truman sometimes lost his temper over minor matters. At first he made mistakes by being in a hurry. For instance, he signed without reading it an order

Clement Attlee, Prime Minister of Great Britain; Harry Truman, President of the United States; and Joseph Stalin, Premier of Russia, meet at Potsdam, near Berlin, in July 1945, accompanied by their foreign ministers. They agreed on "three D's" for Germany: demilitarization, de-Nazification, and democratization.

cutting off lend-lease shipments abroad right after Germany's defeat. This action made our allies think the United States was willing to let them starve. The President discovered his mistake and resumed shipments, but the incident cast doubt on his judgment.

As time went on, it became clear that President Truman was no ordinary man. He worked hard and efficiently. He mastered the details of his job. He learned how to delegate action and at the same time assume responsibility. An outstanding trait was indicated by a sign on his desk: "The buck stops here." He was at his best when great crises arose, such as the Russian attempt to cut off Berlin or the Communist invasion of southern Korea. At such times the President displayed an extraordinary capacity for quick, effective, and yet restrained action.

THE COLD WAR

At the close of World War II, Winston Churchill exclaimed, "America stands at this moment at the summit of the world." When the war began only six years before, the United States had an army smaller than that of Portugal. Now the American armed forces were probably the most numerous and certainly the best equipped

in the history of warfare. They also possessed the ultimate weapon—the atomic bomb.

The war years saw a change in American attitudes as striking as the sudden increase in military might. In 1939 the dominant mood of the country had been isolationist. A Gallup poll revealed that only 39 percent of the people favored American membership in an international organization such as the League of Nations. By 1945, 81 percent favored joining the United Nations. This time the American people did not intend to retreat into what Woodrow Wilson called "sullen and selfish isolation." Instead, they were prepared to work with their wartime allies in trying to create a prosperous and peaceful world. They had high hopes for the United Nations as an agency for the peaceful settlement of disputes between countries.

But scarcely had the shooting stopped than Americans found themselves engaged in a struggle that became known as the Cold War—"cold," or non-shooting war, as opposed to a "hot," or shooting war. Aligned with the United States on one side of the struggle were many countries of the free world. On the other side was Soviet Russia, with its satellite countries. The rivalry could be foreseen even before the end of World War II, when Stalin and Truman disagreed about the promise Russia had made at Yalta to allow free elections in Poland. Within two years the Cold War was fully under way when the United States helped Greece and Turkey to resist Communist aggression with varying degrees of intensity over the years. It has hardly stopped since, and our distrust of the Communist nations has been a factor in the foreign policy of every President since Truman.

The Cold War has been a struggle like no other in which the United States has ever been engaged. Twice, in Korea and Southeast Asia, it became a shooting war. It has meant also a constant state of military preparedness and military support for countries threatened by Communist aggression. Both sides have attempted to "buy" allies with gifts ranging from food to steel mills. Above all, it has been a struggle for the minds of people.

The "Iron Curtain"

As early as 1946 Joseph Stalin, the Soviet dictator, had apparently decided that no lasting peace was possible between the capitalist and Communist worlds. He said so publicly, and his actions fitted his words. In the countries of Central Europe that Russian armies had liberated from the Nazis, the Communists set up one-party governments that took orders from Moscow.

These governments ruthlessly suppressed all opposition, dissent, and free expression of opinion.

In a speech delivered at Fulton, Missouri, with President Truman on the platform, Winston Churchill declared: "From Stettin on the Baltic to Trieste on the Adriatic an iron curtain has descended across the continent." The West, said the former British prime minister, must meet the challenge. It must use force if necessary, because the Communists had contempt for weakness. Truman and his advisers came to agree with Churchill that a "get tough" policy had been forced upon them.

The Strength of Communism

The new antagonists were in some ways more dangerous that the Axis. The Communists held no such military superiority as Nazi Germany and imperial Japan enjoyed early in World War II, but they had more effective psychological weapons. The Nazis' glorification of Germans as a master race, their scorn of Slavic peoples, and their persecution of Jews made them hated and feared even before their armies conquered neighboring countries. In Asia, the "divine mission" of the Mikado to rule China and Southeast Asia had no appeal except to the Japanese.

In contrast to Fascists, the Communists proclaim a message with wide appeal. Most people

"From Stettin on the Baltic to Trieste on the Adriatic an iron curtain has descended across the continent," warned Churchill in a Fulton, Missouri, speech in 1946.

in the world live in poverty; the Communists promise work and a decent living for all. Millions suffer discrimination because of race, religion, or sex; the Communists declare that all people (at least all workers) are comrades. Many people, especially the young, want to find identity by dedicating themselves to a cause; the Communists call all men and women of good will to join in a crusade against poverty and oppression. The Communists profess belief in government by the people and call the states they control "people's democracies." It has often been only after the Communists take over a country that its people learn that the bright promises of Communism are false.

The strength of Communism rests not merely on its military strength or its message, but also on supporters all over the world. Communist Party members are will-

QUESTION • Compare and contrast the meaning of the word "party" (Republican Party, Communist Party) in the U.S. and the USSR.

ing to engage in spying, sabotage, and the promotion of unrest. Sometimes they have won enough support to organize guerrilla forces and to gain power through civil war. Such tactics have been used, with varying success, in Greece, Malaysia, Indochina, the Philippines, Mozambique, and Angola.

The Communists see the world as a battleground between themselves, representing the forces of progress, and the imperialistic capitalists, defending reaction and oppression. In the long run, they believe, no real agreement, no meeting of minds, is possible. But both the Communist and non-Communist worlds realize that if the cold war turns to hot, there may be mutual annihilation by nuclear weapons. Therefore both sides seem gradually to be learning to live with each other.

THE WEST ORGANIZES

To meet the threat of Communist aggression, the Truman administration developed policies that were to be carried on with no major change by Presidents Eisenhower, Kennedy, and Lyndon Johnson. Truman would have been helpless, however, without the support of Congress, Republicans as well as Democrats. A high proportion of Republican representatives and senators were bitterly opposed to the President's domestic measures, but nevertheless backed him in his dealings with foreign nations. In particular, Arthur H. Vandenberg, ranking Republican member of the Senate Foreign Relations Committee, worked closely with Truman in forming policies and winning support for them. The President, in turn, publicly thanked Republicans for support.

The Policy of Containment

Truman's methods of meeting the Communist threat did not command universal support. Indeed, they often caused bitter debate both in Congress and among the public at large. Different groups attacked them as too stingy, too expensive, too aggressive, too soft. In spite of incessant discussion and occasional inconsistency, a fairly clear line of action emerged. It was known as "containment." The essential purpose of containment was to keep Communism within its existing boundaries. It said to Moscow, and later to Peking as well, "Thus far you have gone and no farther!"

The Truman Doctrine, 1947

Containment began in Europe. Early in 1947, the British government secretly informed Washington that it must soon withdraw its troops from Greece. American diplomats in Greece sent word that this would mean a Communist take-over.

Already, guerrillas, with military support from behind the Iron Curtain, controlled much of the country. It was feared that if Greece fell to the Communists, Turkey would go next, then perhaps Italy or the Middle East. At once Truman decided that the United States must act. In March 1947 he told Congress that it must be the policy of the United States "to support free peoples who are resisting attempted subjugation by armed minorities or by outside pressures." Congress immediately voted military and economic aid to both Greece and Turkey, and the Greek government eventually suppressed the Communist rebellion.

All this was in direct contrast to what happened in 1823 when Americans were urged to help Greek rebels to defend themselves against the Turks. Then President Monroe stated in the Monroe Doctrine that the United States would not interfere in the affairs of Europe. The Tru-

George C. Marshall, Soldier and Statesman

George C. Marshall has been called the "architect of victory" in World War II, although he spent little time on the battlefield.

A "man's man," with an unexpectedly salty sense of humor, he disliked his position in the rear echelon. But as Army Chief of Staff from 1939 until November 1945, he organized the American effort. Well before Pearl Harbor, in December 1941, he had begun to raise, train, and equip a citizen army of ninety divisions.

Marshall opposed the British plan to carry the invasion of Europe northward from Italy, fighting successfully for the direct cross-Channel assault on the Continent. During the war he helped to plan strategy at all the important conferences—Washington, Casablanca, Quebec, Teheran, Cairo, Malta, Yalta, and Potsdam.

After World War II, President Truman sent Marshall to China to attempt to arrange a truce in the civil war between the Nationalists, led by Chiang Kai-shek, and the Communists, led by Mao Tse-tung. He failed in this endeavor, as was probably inevitable. Once hostilities had been resumed, Marshall used his influence against all-out support of the Nationalists, on the ground that the United States had neither the will nor the power to make a large enough commitment in China to defeat the Communists. No one knows whether or not this was true, but Marshall inevitably received blame when the Communists took over all of China except Taiwan and a few small islands in 1949.

In January 1947 Truman named Marshall Secretary of State. Europe was close to economic collapse, and it looked as though the Communists would pick up the pieces. On June 5, at the Harvard University commencement exercises, Marshall announced the plan for American aid to Europe which has become known as the Marshall Plan. It was enthusiastically approved in London, and the French ministry called a special meeting to discuss French participation. In the same year, basic planning began on what became the North Atlantic Treaty Organization. The Western world, which—through lack of imaginative leadership—had nearly defaulted to communism, again moved forward.

man Doctrine was a dramatic example of the shift from the isolation of the United States in the nineteenth century to its sense of world-wide responsibility in the twentieth.

The Marshall Plan, 1947–1952

Immediately after World War II, the United States saved Europe from starvation. It contributed three-quarters of the total support of the United Nations Relief and Rehabilitation Agency (UNRRA) that supplied food, shelter, clothing, and medicines to millions of people made destitute by war. But "soup kitchen" relief offered no permanent solution. The economy of most of Europe was shattered. In France alone, railroad bridges totaling 600 miles in length had been destroyed. People almost starved to death because crops could not be moved to market. In the American and British zones of Germany, food rations provided little more than a thousand calories per day. American cigarettes passed as currency.

One pack was said to equal a worker's monthly wage. During the severe winter of 1946–1947 in Great Britain, electricity was turned on for only three hours a day. Such a situation provided a seedbed for Communism. The Communist Party in France attracted more voters than any other. In Italy it received the support of a third of the electorate.

In June 1947, Secretary of State George C. Marshall proposed that the United States help European nations in a common effort to raise production. Marshall included Russia and the countries behind the Iron Curtain in his offer. But the USSR denounced the whole scheme as "Yankee imperialism." Western nations cooperated gladly, however. They drew up detailed plans for restoring production and controlling inflation. They also agreed to break down trade barriers, such as tariffs and quotas, that interfered with the flow of commerce.

In four years, Congress voted almost as much

When the Russians closed off the routes from the West to Berlin in 1949, American and British cargo planes carried on an around-the-clock air lift. Here Berliners, standing in the rubble of their shattered city, watch an American bomber flying in with supplies.

money for the Marshall Plan as was used to pay the entire expenses of the federal government in 1937 and 1938. The plan proved to be an almost unbelievably successful attack on poverty and despair. By 1950 industrial production in countries receiving Marshall Plan aid had risen 64 percent. It continued to rise at a rate faster than that of the United States or the USSR. The prosperity of Western Europe came to exceed all former levels. The appeal of Communism diminished.

The Berlin Air Lift, 1948–1949

In 1945, Russia was granted control of eastern Germany except for Berlin. The former German capital, located well within Communist Germany, was divided into four sections under American, British, French, and Russian rule. In the summer of 1948, the USSR tried to drive the western powers out of Berlin by stopping all automobile and railroad traffic from western Germany. Overruling advisers who feared the outbreak of a shooting war, President Truman insisted that Berlin be supplied by air. He ordered an "air lift" that supplied the needs of a city of two million people. Night and day for ten months, British and American cargo planes carried in food, medical supplies, clothing, raw materials for manufacturing, even coal. In May 1949, the Russians backed down and lifted the blockade. "When we refused to be forced out of Berlin," wrote Truman, "we demonstrated to the people of Europe that with their cooperation we would act, and act resolutely, when their freedom was threatened."

The North Atlantic Treaty Organization, 1949

To rebuild Western Europe's economy without increasing its military strength might simply invite Russian aggression. Therefore in April 1949, nine European countries, plus Iceland, Canada, and the United States, formed a military alliance, the so-called North Atlantic Treaty Or-

ganization (NATO). By the NATO agreement each country was bound to treat an attack on one as an attack on all. The members promised to build up their military strength. The United States helped with money, arms, and troops. General Eisenhower became the first commander of the NATO forces (see map, "Areas of Tension," p. 702).

For the first time in its history the United States had made an alliance in peacetime. Indeed, NATO was exactly the kind of "permanent alliance" that George Washington had long ago warned Americans to avoid (see pp. 176, 189). Nevertheless the United States Senate ratified the North Atlantic Treaty without reservations by a vote of 69 to 13. Europe was now America's first line of defense.

COMMITMENTS IN ASIA

At the close of World War II the purposes of the United States in Asia were simply to restore peace and to assist, where possible, the desire of Asian peoples to be free of foreign rule. The United States felt it had a special commitment to three countries: the Philippines, Japan, and China. In the first two countries, American policies were largely successful. In the last, it suffered a severe defeat.

The Philippine Republic

In 1934, the United States had promised independence to the Philippines. On July 4, 1946, that promise was fulfilled, and the Stars and Stripes were hauled down from the flagpoles of public buildings. The United States granted the new Philippine Republic tariff concessions in American markets and gave it $600,000,000 to repair war damage. In return, the Filipinos granted the United States special commercial privileges and the lease of military bases. Later, when the Philippine Republic was threatened by the Hukbalahaps, a Communist-led guerrilla movement, the United States sent funds and weapons to

AREAS OF TENSION
EUROPE and MIDDLE EAST
About 1950

- Communist bloc
- NATO countries
- Under military occupation
- Non-aligned

assist in their suppression. Although the new republic had difficult economic and political problems, the transition from colony to nation was on the whole successful.

Occupation of Japan, 1945–1951

In July 1945, shortly before atom bombs fell on Hiroshima and Nagasaki, the heads of the British, American, and Russian governments met at a conference in Potsdam, outside Berlin. There they made plans for treatment of postwar Germany and Japan. The essential arrangements for Japan were: 1) militarists should be punished and Japan disarmed; 2) Japanese rule should be restricted to the home islands; and 3) the people should be educated in democracy. Troops were to occupy Japan until these aims were accomplished. To carry out this Potsdam Declaration, General Douglas MacArthur was appointed Supreme Commander of the Allied Powers (SCAP).

Although inter-Allied commissions were appointed to advise him, MacArthur in fact wielded dictatorial power. Under his able leadership, Japan underwent a notable period of reform. Its armies and navy were disbanded, its war industries dismantled. A few militarists were tried and convicted of war crimes; many more were purged from government jobs. Political democracy was advanced by abolition of the secret police, by a new constitution, and by women's suffrage. The emperor remained as a symbol of national unity, but was no longer worshipped as a god. Economic opportunity was promoted by attempts to break up the great trusts owned by a few families, by encouragement of trade unions, and by more equal division of land among the peasants. A reorganized educational system attempted to instill democratic values instead of national myths and blind obedience. At first, the intention had been to make Japan pay reparations, but the Japanese lacked the resources to pay them. Instead, they received nearly two billion dollars in aid from the United States. Never had a victorious nation treated a defeated foe with more generosity.

The Japanese showed courtesy, even friendliness, toward their conquerors. They willingly accepted most of the SCAP reforms. When MacArthur finished his rule, the Japanese were heading toward remarkable prosperity and an honored place among the nations. In a treaty signed at San Francisco in 1951, the country regained its independence.

In some ways, the Japanese conquered their conquerors. In America, as a result of close exposure to their culture, there developed a growing appreciation of the achievements of the Japanese in architecture, gardening, philosophy, physical culture, and art.

Communist Triumph in China

Few peoples have undergone such suffering as did the Chinese in the twentieth century.

For half a century the country was seldom free of foreign invasion, civil war, or both. By the end of World War II, the Chinese were profoundly war-weary, but new troubles were in store.

Throughout the twentieth century the United States had generally favored an independent, unified China. American missionaries and educators had devoted their lives to the welfare of the Chinese people. It was the flat refusal of the United States to accept the Japanese conquest of China that led to the Pearl Harbor attack in 1941 (see p. 672). And yet there had been a large measure of unreality in American policy. Until the Pearl Harbor attack, American leaders had been willing to preach the Open Door policy and the integrity of China, but not to back up their words with force.

In planning for the peace, Roosevelt had insisted that China should be treated as a great power. It gained a permanent seat on the UN Security Council in spite of the doubts of Churchill and Stalin. When hostilities came to an end in 1945, the United States helped the Nationalist armies of Chiang Kai-shek to reoccupy territory that had been held by the Japanese. American engineers helped to rebuild Chinese railways.

Since the early 1930's there had been civil war in China between the Nationalist government and the Communists led by Mao Tse-tung. The struggle against Japan provided the Communists with a golden opportunity. Mao extended the territory under his control from 35,000 square miles containing a million and a half people to over 200,000 square miles containing some 65 million. Mao's well-disciplined troops befriended the peasants. His policies at this time were so moderate that many American observers did not think him a true Communist but merely an "agrarian reformer." Meanwhile, the war had immensely weakened the Nationalists. The Japanese controlled the cities, where the Nationalists had most of their popular support. During its exile in the western provinces, the government

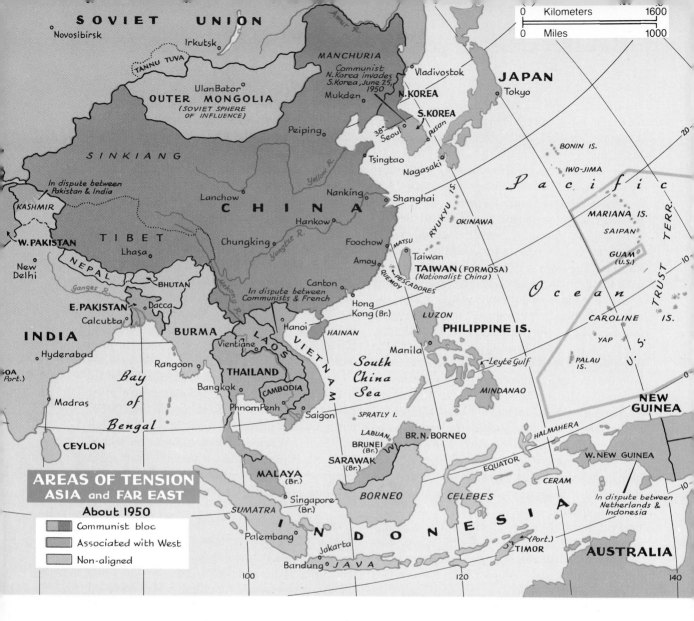

led by Chiang Kai-shek had become inefficient and corrupt. Its one-party organization, the Kuomintang (pronounced "Gwomindong"), was undemocratic and oppressive.

In 1946 General Marshall went to China to try to arrange a peace between the Nationalists and Communists. He was unsuccessful, and full-scale war broke out in 1947. As Mao's forces gained ground, Truman was urged to send massive military support to Chiang, including military "advisers." But Marshall, now Secretary of State, thought it was more important to save Western Europe from Stalin than China from Mao. He opposed the use of troops to support Chiang's tottering regime. The United States did send aid to the Nationalists, but that was not enough to prevent their collapse. The Communist armies swept all before them. By 1950 Chiang's forces held only the island of Taiwan and a few offshore islands (see map, p. 704).

Once in power, the Chinese Communists slaughtered or silenced all opponents. They attempted to weaken the intense family loyalty that had been the basis of the Chinese social system. They preached bitter hatred of the United States.

The China policy of the Truman administration came under violent attack and became a bitter political issue. Critics insisted that a more accurate estimate of Communist purposes and strength, plus all-out aid to the Nationalists, would have saved the situation. Others argued that the time to save China had been in the 1930's, when Japan first attacked. The probabilities are, however, that the United States was never in a position to save China. It is highly unlikely that American public opinion would have supported risk of war with Japan in the 1930's or large-scale military intervention in the late 1940's.

Divided Korea

Korea had been promised "freedom and independence" at the Cairo Conference in 1943. Yet it suffered a tragic fate after liberation from 35 years of Japanese rule. When Japan surrendered in 1945, Russian troops occupied Korea north of the 38th parallel of latitude. Aided by native Communists, they set up a "people's republic." Like other satellite states, North Korea was cut off from the outside world. In 1947 a UN fact-finding commission was not allowed to set foot north of the 38th parallel.

Meanwhile, in the south the United States fostered a Republic of Korea under Syngman Rhee, who had spent much of his life in exile in this country. In 1948 the UN recognized the southern republic as the lawful government of the peninsula. The next year the United States withdrew troops. American military experts advised that Korea should be regarded as outside the "defense perimeter" of the United States, since it could be defended only at great cost. As we shall see later in this chapter, this withdrawal proved to be an invitation to Communist aggression.

THE UNITED NATIONS

No country had done more to promote the formation of the United Nations than the United States. No country had higher hopes for it as a means of ridding the world of the scourge of war. It was fitting that the magnificent capitol buildings of the UN should be in this country. American hopes were, indeed, somewhat exaggerated. The UN lacked power to enforce its decisions and in some situations even lacked the power to make a decision. The United States itself was partly to blame for the weakness of the UN. The Americans were fully as responsible as the Russians for writing the big-power veto into the UN Charter. In 1946 the United States Senate further weakened the international organization. It voted the crippling Connally Amendment to American acceptance of membership in the International Court of Justice. The Connally Amendment stated that the United States would decide for itself whether or not it would accept the decision of the World Court in any particular case. When the most powerful nation in the world refused to grant the judicial branch of the UN independent power, it postponed indefinitely the hope that international disputes might be decided by rule of law.

UN Failures

An obvious reason why the UN did not live up to the bright hopes that surrounded its birth was the Cold War. "To the Communists," wrote a close observer, "the UN is no more than an instrument of conflict." Meetings of UN bodies were often paralyzed because diplomats from both sides of the Iron Curtain spent their time denouncing each other, or because action was blocked by Russian vetoes.

It had been expected that the UN would have a peace-keeping army of its own, as provided by the charter. This idea was soon abandoned because the Russian and American positions were so far apart. Efforts at disarmament by interna-

ALIGNMENT IN THE UNITED NATIONS, 1945

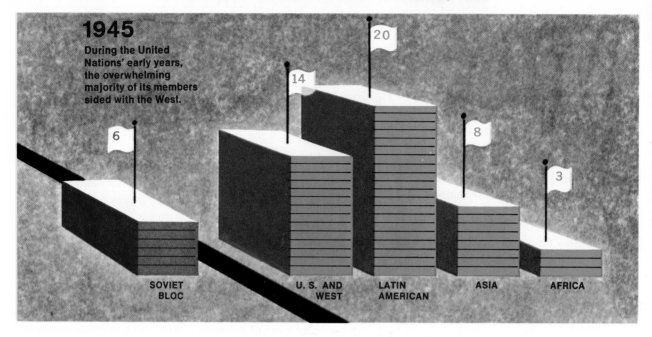

1945

During the United Nations' early years, the overwhelming majority of its members sided with the West.

SOVIET BLOC — 6
U. S. AND WEST — 14
LATIN AMERICAN — 20
ASIA — 8
AFRICA — 3

The Cold War prevented the United Nations from becoming a peaceful agency of international cooperation. Instead, the Communist nations lined up behind the USSR and the non-Communist nations behind the U.S. Later a group of Asian and African nations took a middle ground. See "Neutralism," p. 732.

tional agreement failed for the same reason. The most appalling failure in this area came with the collapse of efforts to outlaw atomic warfare.

The tragic result of failure to put atomic energy under international control was a race to produce new weapons. The USSR had manufactured an atomic bomb by 1949, the British by 1952. Meanwhile, the United States developed the even more terrible hydrogen bomb. The radioactive "fallout" from a single explosion could destroy or endanger the lives of all people living in an area as large as New Jersey. According to the great scientist Albert Einstein, the destruction of all life on Earth was now "within the range of technical possibilities."

UN Achievements

Although failing to bring peace in the Cold War, the UN has done much to avert or halt armed conflicts. During the first five years of its ex-

istence, it had arranged an uneasy truce between Israel and Arab states and another between India and Pakistan in the disputed province of Kashmir. It had brought war to an end in the Dutch East Indies and fixed terms under which the Republic of Indonesia came into existence.

Keeping the peace has not been the UN's only function. Its "specialized agencies," such as the World Health Organization, the International Bank for Reconstruction and Development, and the Food and Agriculture Organization, do vital work in widely varying fields. They combat epidemics, stabilize currencies, and supply loans to promote industry in developing countries.

Still, it is as a peace-making agency that the UN is judged. Here its one undeniable value has been that it is a bridge between the Communist and non-Communist worlds. It has been a place where both sides can appeal to world opinion. According to John Foster Dulles, secretary of state from 1963 to 1959:

The United Nations . . . is, in its own right, weak; but its power to expose gives it influence. If the spotlight is turned on one who is perpetrating a theft, he will often drop his booty. The power to turn on a light so bright that all the world can see is itself an enormous power.

Perhaps the greatest value of the UN as a peace-keeping mechanism is the least spectacular. It does not reach the headlines. The UN provides a channel constantly open for communication between the nations of the world. Many international disputes have been settled by quiet, informal discussion among UN delegates. It is often easier to compromise differences by "corridor diplomacy" than by making speeches or by passing resolutions.

PROSPERITY AND WIDENING OPPORTUNITIES

During the war years, the American economy had climbed out of the depression to a new pinnacle of prosperity. National income had more than doubled. Unemployment almost disappeared. No longer needed, the New Deal relief agencies closed down. With twelve million people in the armed forces, there was a desperate shortage of labor. Thus millions of people who had never before punched a time clock were employed in factories. The number of blacks in defense industries more than tripled. Six million women joined the labor force, an increase of nearly 60 percent. Many of these were married women with children. People who were formerly used to poverty had lifted their sights. "Times have changed," remarked a labor leader. "People have become accustomed to new conditions, new wage scales, new ways of being treated."

Victory over the Axis made people proud, but also fearful. The same newspapers that carried news of Japan's surrender predicted that six to ten million people would soon be unemployed. After all, previous major wars had been followed by depressions (see charts, pp. 296–297, 470–471,

and 802–803). And even if the factories kept running, what about the recently hired blacks and women? Would they be laid off? After all, thought many, was not the "natural" place for blacks picking cotton, washing dirty dishes, or mopping floors? And, in the same vein, was not the home the "natural" place for married women?

Continuing Prosperity

The fears of those who expected a postwar depression proved groundless. There was only a slight downturn in business activity and none in the total of people employed. Indeed, within three or four years wartime totals of employment were exceeded.

The continuing boom apparently had a number of causes. As the United States continued to feed not only its own people but millions abroad, farm income remained high. During the war years individuals had saved an estimated thirty billion dollars. These savings provided a reserve of buying power. Although sharply cut back, military expenditures remained high by prewar standards and poured money into the economy. The Marshall Plan restored European markets for American goods. Perhaps the most important preventive of a postwar depression was full employment, which provided an immense reservoir of purchasing power.

More Women in Jobs, But . . .

When the veterans came back from the war, they displaced many women in factories. In the automobile industry, for instance, the proportion of women on assembly lines dropped from 25 percent in 1944 to 7.5 percent in 1946. The head of the Women's Bureau, a federal agency supposed to protect women's rights, remarked that "women ought to be delighted to give up any job and return to their proper sphere in the kitchen." Federal and state support of child care centers in factories was stopped. But while women lost some jobs, they did not disappear from the labor market. Instead, continuing prosperity opened new places to them. By 1952 two million more women were employed than at the end of the war in 1945 and three times as many as before World War II began in 1939. A high proportion of the new female labor force was married; many were in their 40's or 50's.

Not only did women gain in employment, but they also moved out of confining, ill-paid work as house servants to jobs with shorter hours and more freedom. Indeed, the increasing scarcity of domestic servants resulted in a new feature of American life, the "baby sitter." The shift in type of employment was dramatically shown by the experience of black women. Between 1940 and 1950 the percentage of black women employed as servants dropped from 72 to 48 percent, and the number of those working as farm laborers from 20 to 7 percent. Meanwhile the percentage hired by factories rose from 7 to 18 percent.

The rise in female employment did not mean that women had gained economic equality. Women in industries earned less than two-thirds as much as men. They tended to be assigned dull, repetitive jobs. Only a trickle of women were allowed to enter professional schools of law and medicine. During the 1940's the percentage of women in well-paid supervisory and professional jobs actually declined.

Thus the situation of American women during the 1940's presented surprising contrasts. On the one hand, an unprecedented number of women moved into the labor force. On the other hand, little progress was made in areas of great concern to women—professional employment, child-care centers, and equal pay.

Gains by Black Americans, But . . .

Largely because of general prosperity, black Americans, like American women, not only kept the gains they had made during the war years but made further progress. Indeed, during the decade of the 1940's blacks made the greatest economic advance since Reconstruction. There

was a massive shift of blacks from farming to manufacturing, from rural areas to urban, from the southern states to the rest of the country. The number of blacks in white collar, skilled, and supervisory jobs nearly tripled, from about 300,000 to nearly 900,000. Blacks at least got a foot in the door in occupations as diverse as the law, nursing, and professional sports. Their average income, even allowing for inflation, about doubled.

To some degree these advances were the result of changing white attitudes. The war against the Axis and the Cold War both played a part. The brutal racism of the Nazis helped to make Americans sensitive to racism in their own country. In the Cold War the struggle for the minds of the people of the world, most of them nonwhite, revealed the United States as handicapped by discrimination not only against blacks, but also against people of Asian and of Latin-American origin. A notable book, *An American Dilemma*, by the Swedish sociologist, Gunnar Myrdal, helped to allay racism in this country. To Myrdal, the American dilemma was the conflict between our professed belief in liberty and justice for all and our denial of liberty and justice to black citizens. Myrdal argued that for their own welfare and peace of mind, as well as for the sake of their relations with other nations, Americans must learn to practice what they preach.

Meanwhile blacks were organizing to gain their rights as never before. It had been the threat of scores of thousands of blacks marching through Washington that induced President Roosevelt to establish the Fair Employment Practices Commission (FEPC). During the war years membership in the National Association for the Advancement of Colored People (NAACP) increased from 100,000 to half a million. Teams of able lawyers hired by the NAACP brought a series of suits in federal courts to put an end to violations of the constitutional rights of blacks.

But blacks, like women, fell far short of gaining full equality in the 1940's. In the North, they were crowded into city ghettos. Black wages averaged about 60 percent of those paid whites. Blacks were still apt to be "last hired, first fired." In the South, traditional patterns of segregation still held. It was a continuous personal humiliation for blacks that they had to sit in the back of the bus, to use separate entrances and separate facilities in public buildings, or to

Jackie Robinson Breaks the Color Barrier

Behind a big desk sat one of the master minds of baseball, Branch Rickey, general manager of the Brooklyn Dodgers. Facing him stood a rookie player, Jackie Robinson. Rickey was telling Robinson what it would be like to be the first black player in major league baseball. He played the part of a hotel clerk refusing Robinson a room in a hotel because he was black. He imitated a fan shouting racist epithets. Rickey told Robinson he would have to "wear the armor of humility" and submit to insults without fighting back. Robinson said he could do it.

Rickey had been seeking just the right man to break the color barrier in professional baseball. Jackie Robinson filled the bill. He was a superb athlete, the only man who had ever won letters in four sports at the University of California at Los Angeles. He was used to playing on teams with whites. He had a good war record. Above all, he had self-control: he could keep his temper.

In the spring of 1947, Robinson started playing first base for the Dodgers. Often it was as bad as Rickey had predicted. In one southern town police ordered Robinson off the field. In northern cities hotels refused to admit him. Opposing players shouted obscenities. Teammates refused to speak to him. But Robinson kept cool. He replied to his tormentors by playing brilliant baseball. In his first year with the Dodgers he led the National League in stolen bases and was voted Rookie of the Year.

In time Jackie's fellow players accepted him and asked him to join their card games. He became a favorite with fans, white as well as black. Gradually he threw off "the armor of humility." He revealed himself for what he really was—"a fiery, quick-boiling competitor." And the fans loved it.

Jackie Robinson fulfilled Branch Rickey's hopes. He opened the door for other black athletes—in other sports as well as baseball, in the South as well as in the North. Black players could now be elected to Baseball's Hall of Fame. They could be national heroes.

In 1949 Robinson appeared before a congressional Committee on Un-American Activities. The Congressmen had heard that black people were so disgruntled at their treatment in this country that in another war they would fight for Russian Communism rather than for this country. Robinson was called to testify, along with other prominent black Americans. He said he was not an expert on Communism, but he was an expert on what it was like to be a black person in the United States. "Every black worth his salt," he said, "resents racial slurs." "I am a religious man," he told the Committee. "Therefore I cherish America where I can be free to worship as I please. . . . But that does not mean that colored Americans are going to stop fighting racial discrimination in this country until we've got it licked. It means that we are going to fight all the harder because our stake in the future is so big."

stand outside to be served at a drugstore. Most southern blacks were still kept from voting, either by custom or by law. Almost none held political office.

The "GI Bill of Rights"

In 1944 Congress passed a law, the Servicemen's Readjustment Act, that ultimately had great effects in promoting equality of opportunity. Known as the "GI Bill of Rights," it helped returning veterans finance homes, buy farms, and start small businesses. Above all, it provided for higher education. The bill made it possible for millions of former GI's to gain college degrees. Many of these would never have thought of returning to school. The GI Bill was revolutionary in the way it opened doors for young people from low-income families who had never had a chance for much education. The law had a continuing effect. Younger brothers and sisters and cousins of the original GI's followed their footsteps to college. Meanwhile colleges and universities expanded their facilities and sought out students from all levels of society.

Inflation

The government spending that had created war prosperity carried with it the danger of inflation. Inflation is characterized by an increase in the amount of currency in circulation and a sharp rise in prices. In spite of much higher taxes and higher income, the federal government ran a huge deficit during the years of World War II. The national debt increased from fifty billion dollars to nearly two hundred and seventy billion. The federal government borrowed much of the sum from Federal Reserve Banks. The banks in turn issued new money with federal bonds as security. The result was currency inflation. There was four times as

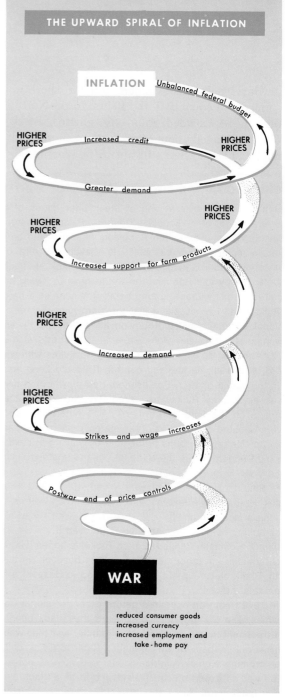

THE UPWARD SPIRAL OF INFLATION

INFLATION

Unbalanced federal budget

HIGHER PRICES

Increased credit

HIGHER PRICES

Greater demand

HIGHER PRICES

HIGHER PRICES

Increased support for farm products

HIGHER PRICES

Increased demand

HIGHER PRICES

Strikes and wage increases

Postwar end of price controls

WAR

reduced consumer goods
increased currency
increased employment and
take-home pay

A constant difficulty since the first years of World War II has been the ever-rising spiral of inflation that raises prices and wipes out savings.

much money in circulation in 1945 as in 1938. (See explanation of the "quantity theory of money," p. 430.)

Another force producing inflation was the immense backlog of demand for consumer goods that had been rationed during the war. When wartime rationing and price controls came to an end in 1946, prices immediately jumped by 25 percent or more. In the words of a headline in a tabloid:

PRICES SOAR
BUYERS SORE
STEERS JUMP OVER THE MOON.

While prices went up, pay checks shrank when factories returned to a 40-hour week and employers stopped paying overtime. Workers demanded higher wages. If these were not granted, they struck. In 1946 there were five thousand strikes, an all-time high. Nearly 4,600,000 people were involved. Most alarming were strikes involving basic industries, such as steel, automobiles, and coal. These threatened to paralyze the whole economy. Even President Truman, who generally favored labor, asked Congress to drive striking railroad workers into the army. A United Mine Workers strike was halted by order of a federal court. On an appeal, the Supreme Court held that the Norris-LaGuardia anti-injunction law (see p. 627) did not forbid the government to order laborers back to work, to prevent "a public calamity."

QUESTION • Does anyone gain from inflation? If so, who? Who gets hurt most? Why?

POLITICS IN THE TRUMAN YEARS

Labor unions and their activities were a central issue in the midterm congressional elections of 1946. The fear inspired by the big strikes induced voters to favor conservative candidates. The Republicans showed new vigor as they campaigned on the slogan, "Had enough?" For the first time in sixteen years they gained control of both the Senate and the House.

The Taft-Hartley Act, 1947

An immediate result of the swing toward conservatism was the Taft-Hartley Act, passed over President Truman's veto in 1947. This complicated measure was designed to prevent labor unions from abusing their power. Among practices it forbade were the closed shop (which forced employers to hire only union members), jurisdictional strikes (designed to force an employer to recognize one union instead of another), "featherbedding" (the practice of limiting workers' output to provide more jobs), and high initiation fees. Union officers were required to take an oath that they were not members of the Communist Party. The use of union funds in political campaigns was forbidden. If a strike threatened to cripple the national economy, the President had the right to get a court order to enforce an eighty-day "cooling off" period.

The Taft-Hartley Act was one of the most controversial measures ever passed by Congress. Its defenders argued that the act merely controlled irresponsible labor unions the way the Wagner Act (see pp. 638–639) restrained anti-union activities of employers. Labor leaders denounced the act as a "slave labor law," erasing the gains unions had made since 1933. They resented the non-Communist oath as an affront to their loyalty.

Truman and Civil Rights

Truman came from a former slave state. Members of his mother's family had been ardent supporters of the Confederacy. But in his early career he had fought the Ku Klux Klan. As

Harry Truman gleefully displays a copy of a newspaper that had jumped to the conclusion that Dewey's early lead on election day, 1948, assured him victory.

President, he defended no cause more strongly than equal rights for black Americans. When Congress refused to pass a law continuing the wartime Fair Employment Practices Commission, Truman resorted to executive action. In 1946 he appointed a fact-finding Commission on Civil Rights. He told its members that he wanted to make the Bill of Rights apply equally to every American. In 1947, the Commission published an eloquent report, *To Secure These Rights*. It made recommendations designed "to guarantee the same rights to every person regardless of who he is, where he lives, or what his racial, religous, or national origins are." The commission's recommendations went beyond erasing discriminations against blacks. It urged, for instance, that immigration quotas be abolished and that West Coast Japanese-Americans who had been deprived of freedom and property in

World War II be repaid for their losses.

Congress refused to pass the laws recommended by the Commission on Civil Rights, but Truman took a major step in his role as Commander-in-Chief. In 1948 he issued an order that there should be equality of opportunity for all members of the armed forces. The most important result of this order was the rapid elimination of segregated units. By the time Truman left office in 1953, segregation in the army, navy, and air force was greatly reduced. For the first time in the history of the United States, large numbers of blacks and whites lived together on a basis of equality.

Election of 1948: A Political Miracle

One reason for the deadlock between the President and the Republican leaders of the

Eightieth Congress was that both sides were jockeying for political advantage. For instance, in the summer of 1948 Truman called Congress into special session and urged it to pass laws promoting public housing, price controls, subsidies to farmers, and civil rights for blacks. When no action was taken, Truman blamed the country's ills on the "do-nothing Congress."

The 1948 Republican Convention again nominated Thomas E. Dewey. The New York Governor campaigned as though he were certain to win. He avoided discussion of issues and called on Americans to join him in promoting "unity."

The Democrats renominated Truman, but only after party leaders had failed to persuade General Eisenhower to run. The party was badly split. Many southern members resented Truman's efforts to promote racial equality. Some of these formed a separate States' Rights Party, nicknamed "Dixiecrats," which nominated Governor J. Strom Thurmond of South Carolina for President. In the North, Henry A. Wallace, former secretary of agriculture and Vice-President, bolted the Democrats and ran under the label Progressive.

Nearly all political experts and public opinion polls predicted a Dewey victory. Betting odds ran 15 to 1 in his favor. One of the few Democrats who did not privately concede the election was Truman himself. Traveling over 30,000 miles by train, the President made over 350 speeches to people gathered in ball parks, city squares, and "whistle stops." He made his target the "do-nothing" Eightieth Congress, saying it was for the "privileged few" and that he was for "the common, everyday man." Especially, Truman called on farmers and industrial workers to protect the gains they had made under the New Deal.

Although he lost four southern states to Thurmond and a million northern votes to Wallace, Truman was returned to office. Explanations for this unexpected result were Republican overconfidence, the continuing strength of the New Deal, and successful Democratic efforts to get voters to the polls. The three-way Democratic split that looked disastrous may have been a blessing in disguise. The Dixiecrat rebellion helped Truman's cause with black voters in the North. Wallace's campaign blunted efforts to pin the Communist label on the President. Professional pollsters failed to note a last-minute swing of undecided voters toward the Democrats. In any case, the result was a personal triumph for Truman. His whistle-stop campaign had turned the tide.

The "Fair Deal"

In January 1949, Truman proposed a "Fair Deal," which meant a continuation and expansion of the New Deal. The President urged slum clearance, federal subsidies for public schools, government-fostered medical insurance, aid to agriculture and higher minimum wages. Although the new Congress was Demo-

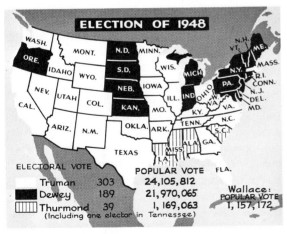

ELECTION OF 1948

ELECTORAL VOTE

POPULAR VOTE

	Electoral Vote	Popular Vote
Truman	303	24,105,812
Dewey	189	21,970,065
Thurmond	39	1,169,063
(Including one elector in Tennessee)

Wallace: POPULAR VOTE 1,157,172

The 1948 election results surprised the nation. Even the most careful political observers had underestimated the effectiveness of Truman's one-man campaign and the New Deal's continuing appeal.

The Korean War brought great suffering to the inhabitants. At its close, the fighting resembled that in France in World War I, as is suggested by this sketch of infantrymen coming back from the front as American artillery lays down a barrage.

cratic, it was controlled by an unofficial alliance of Republicans and conservative southern Democrats. They blocked most of Truman's proposals.

In 1949 there was a halt in postwar prosperity. But the situation was never as bad as in any year during the 1930's. There was no panic or serious need for large-scale relief. The New Deal had brought various "built-in stabilizers" that operated almost automatically against a downward plunge in the economy. These included price supports for agricultural products, unemployment insurance, increased social security benefits, and minimum wage laws. The Full Employment Act also helped to create confidence because the federal government was now committed to action to stop a catastrophic drop like that of 1929–1932. Private enterprise contributed to economic stability by such measures as company pension plans.

The Korean War, beginning in 1950, changed the economic picture sharply, as a rearmament program competed with the demand for consumer goods.

THE KOREAN WAR, 1950–1953

By 1950 the USSR had lost prestige after having been checked in Europe by the Truman Doctrine in Greece, the Berlin Air Lift, and the Marshall Plan. Withdrawal of American troops in South Korea apparently led to hopes of a cheap Communist victory in South Korea. On June 24, 1950, North Korean armies, trained and equipped by the Russians, invaded South Korea without warning. This action provided a vital test for the UN. If it backed down in the face of unprovoked aggression, it would be powerless in the future. On the day after the invasion, the Security Council met, found North Korea guilty of a "breach of the peace," and called on UN members to aid South Korea. Russia was boycotting the Security Council at the time and so was unable to use its veto. The next day, without waiting for action by Congress, Truman ordered American military forces into action. Several other UN countries also sent military, medical, and naval units to aid South Korea. General MacArthur was placed in command of all the UN forces.

After early Communist successes, MacArthur made a brilliant surprise landing at Inchon, behind the Communist lines. He then swept northward toward the Yalu River, the boundary between Korea and Manchuria. But in November the tide turned again, as Chinese Communist "volunteers" poured across the Yalu and drove the UN forces back almost to the 38th parallel (see map, p. 715).

UN policy in Korea was to fight a limited war. Thus UN planes were forbidden to bomb Chinese bases in Manchuria. General MacArthur resented such limitations. In April 1951, he criticized the Truman administration's refusal to use Chiang Kai-shek's Nationalist Chinese troops in Korea. MacArthur's letter was a deliberate challenge to the principle that the civilian power of the President must be superior to that of the military. Truman felt he had no choice but to remove MacArthur from command, and proceeded to do so.

The "Great Debate," 1951

When MacArthur came home in 1951 to receive a hero's welcome, there was a great debate on foreign and military policy. The general's demand that the war be extended into Red China was countered by the Joint Chiefs of Staff. According to General Omar N. Bradley, a full-scale attack on Red China would involve the United States "in the wrong war at the wrong time in the wrong place with the wrong enemy." MacArthur argued that the United States should act independently of the UN if that body tried to limit the use of American military might. "There is no substitute," he declared,

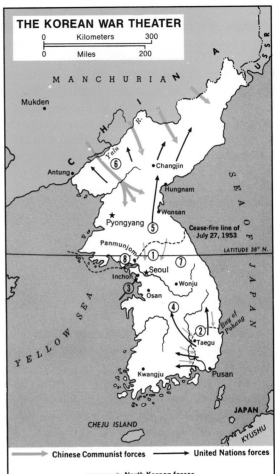

THE KOREAN WAR THEATER

Chinese Communist forces ——→ United Nations forces ——→

North Korean forces ——→

1. North Koreans make initial attack, June 25, 1950.

2. Farthest advance of North Koreans; United Nations forces make stand at Pusan perimeter, June to September 1950.

3. United Nations forces land at Inchon, Sept. 15, 1950.

4. Following Inchon landing, United Nations forces drive north from Pusan perimeter.

5. United Nations forces cross 38th parallel and drive north to Yalu River.

6. Chinese Communists cross Manchurian border, Oct. 16, 1950.

7. United Nations forces retreat to positions south of 38th parallel, December 1950 to January 1951.

8. Truce talks begin at Kaesong, July 10, 1951. Cease-fire agreement finally signed at nearby Panmunjom, July 27, 1953

"for victory." He further argued that Asia was of more strategic importance to the United States than Europe. Administration supporters insisted that to weaken the UN would ultimately weaken the United States, and that Western Europe, the second greatest industrial region in the world, must be defended at all costs.

The great debate failed to alter American policy, except that there was a stiffening in attitude toward Red China. American naval forces were sent to defend Taiwan. The United States flatly opposed admission of Red China to the UN. Secretary of State Dean Acheson remarked, "We cannot allow governments that want to get into the United Nations to shoot their way in."

The Korean War settled down to a prolonged stalemate. When Eisenhower was elected President in 1952, he declared that a Korean settlement would be one of his first tasks. Finally, after seemingly endless negotiations, a ceasefire was arranged in July 1953. It left Korea a divided country, much as it had been before the war began.

The Korean struggle was frustrating and costly for the United States. But Communist hopes for a quick victory had proved fruitless, and Communist aggression drove neutral nations closer to the United States. Furthermore, the attack on Korea stimulated non-Communist nations to rearm in order to defend themselves.

FEARS OF INTERNAL SUBVERSION

The Cold War and the Korean War caused great fear of Communists operating within this country. The question arose: could Communists claim the constitutional rights of freedom of speech and association? In 1949, twelve members of the Communist Party in the United States were convicted of conspiracy. The federal courts held that it was not a denial of the First Amendment to punish membership in an organization whose purpose was "to overthrow the government of the United States by force."

In the face of the Communist threat, there was a tendency to take extreme precautions against conspiracy. These often hurt innocent people and narrowed the liberties of Americans. Many people were required to take loyalty oaths before being hired for jobs. Security checks of government officials went to such lengths that they hurt morale and lowered efficiency. There was a tendency to confuse criticism of American institutions with disloyalty. As Judge Harold Medina told the jury that convicted the twelve Communists, denial of the right to criticize does not strengthen the country but weakens it by allowing abuses to go unchecked. In a unanimous decision in 1952, the Supreme Court declared state loyalty oaths unconstitutional. The Court observed that laws directed against Communists may make it dangerous for others "to think, speak, or write critically."

QUESTION • Should anyone be required to take an oath of loyalty to the U.S.?

The China disaster and the frustrating Korean stalemate helped to produce a mood in this country not unlike the "red scare" that followed World War I. The public looked for scapegoats, and opponents of the Truman administration found them. The President had "lost" China, said his critics, because his close advisers were Communists or Communist dupes. Robert A. Taft, Republican leader in the Senate, charged that the State Department was riddled with subversives who had "surrendered to every demand of Russia . . . and promoted at every opportunity the Communist cause in China." In fact, one former State Department official, Alger Hiss, had been jailed in connection with charges that he had passed secret department documents to a Communist spy ring.

Far more reckless in his charges than Taft was Senator Joseph R. McCarthy of Wisconsin. He declared that the Democratic Party had been guilty of "twenty years of treason," in the course of which Roosevelt had deliberately sacrificed the fleet at Pearl Harbor and had sold out to Russia at Yalta. McCarthy claimed to have lists of 205, or 57, or 81 "card-carrying Communists" in the State Department. Not one of these was ever discovered, and a Senate committee declared that McCarthy's charges were "a fraud and a hoax." But in the atmosphere of the time the senator gained an ever-increasing following.

The new witch-hunting went far beyond the federal government. Private vigilante groups pinned the Communist label on liberal and reformist people in every walk of life. They drove allegedly "pink" professors out of colleges. They got supposedly subversive textbooks banned from schools. They succeeded in getting broadcasters and entertainers barred from television, and actors from the stage and films.

ESTIMATE OF HARRY TRUMAN

When he left office, President Truman's stock was low. He was blamed for the frustrations of what was called "Mr. Truman's War" in Korea. Conservatives suspected him of being "soft on Communism." Liberals thought that his loyalty checks in the executive department had hurt innocent people. Furthermore, it was revealed that there had been corruption in high places. Men close to the President had received valuable gifts in return for political favors. The President was not personally involved, and dishonesty was on no such scale as during the Grant and Harding administrations. But the "Truman scandals" provided Republicans with a ready-made political issue for the 1952 presidential elections.

Truman's reputation rose after he left the White House. He has become a rather popular folk hero, as was shown by the success of a TV series in 1976 entitled "Give 'em Hell, Harry." His career appeared to show that any "common, everyday man" could be a successful President if he were honest, decisive, and fearless. When Gerald Ford was suddenly elevated to the presidency in 1974, he said he found Truman an example and an inspiration.

It is evidence of Truman's stature that most of the Fair Deal measures he recommended have since been made into law. And the essential foreign policies of the United States have been those begun during his administration. In the foreign sphere especially, the wonder is not that there were failures, but that serious mistakes were so few. The problems the President and his advisers faced were new and complex. The public was weary of foreign adventures. Congress was often suspicious or hostile. And yet Truman managed to lead the country from isolationism into responsibility.

Truman did not do it alone. Ultimately he could act only with public support. He succeeded because the people of the United States had reached a fundamental decision: their responsibilities and commitments must match their wealth and power. In 1952 a group of scholars from Oxford University in England paid America this tribute:

The faults and shortcomings of America—which, unlike those of the Soviet Union, are wide open to the world and freely discussed by the Americans themselves—have led too many people to ignore the plain fact that the U.S.A. has been the best "top nation" since Rome. It establishes order, resists the aggressor, defends the attacked, strengthens the weak, and succors the poor. The U.S.A. is the first world power to give money away, to tax itself for the foreigner in peacetime. We are too little astonished at the unprecedented virtuousness of the U.S. foreign policy and at its good sense.

Activities: Chapter 30

For Mastery and Review

1. What was the general estimate of Harry Truman in 1945?—in 1953, when he left office? What is it today? How do you explain the changes in his reputation?

2. Explain the strengths of Communism. Explain the origins and continuance of the Cold War. In general, what has been American policy toward the Communist powers?

3. Summarize the achievements of Truman in organizing the West against Communism. To what extent was he successful?

4. In what areas of the Far East did the United States actively concern itself after World War II? Estimate the success of American activities in each area.

5. What were some United Nations failures? —some achievements?

6. How did the shift to a peacetime economy affect prosperity? What caused inflation? Why was labor dissatisfied? What were the purpose and main features of the Taft-Hartley Law?

7. How did women fare during the postwar period? What were the gains of blacks? What were the activities of the Truman administration on behalf of blacks?

8. How do you explain Truman's surprising victory in the election of 1948? Why were political forecasts inaccurate?

9. How did General MacArthur disagree with the Truman administration as to how to conduct the Korean War?

10. What were the effects of the Cold War within the United States?

Unrolling the Map

1. On an outline map of Europe, indicate the countries for which the Truman Doctrine was directly formulated, the nations members of NATO, the nations cut off from the West by the Iron Curtain, and the division of Germany into zones of occupation.

2. On an outline map of Asia indicate areas of tension between the Communist world and the West.

Who, What, and Why Important?

"Iron Curtain"
"containment"
Truman Doctrine
Marshall Plan
Berlin Air Lift
NATO
SCAP
Connally Amendment
Gunnar Myrdal
GI Bill of Rights

Taft-Hartley Act
Commission on Civil Rights
election of 1948
Thomas E. Dewey
States Rights Party ("Dixiecrats")
"Fair Deal"
Douglas MacArthur
Joseph R. McCarthy

To Pursue the Matter

1. Examine the charge that the Truman administration "lost" China, or that Truman ought not to have settled for less than total victory in Korea. Sources: Winks and Yergin, *The Cold War*, pp. 38–51; Spanier, *American Foreign Policy Since World War II*, Chapter 4; Latourette, *The American Record in the Far East, 1945–1961;* and Feis, *The China Tangle.*

2. Could the United States have "saved" China from Communist domination? If so, how and when? If not, why not?

3. Allocate credit for the origin of the Marshall Plan. See Arnof, *A Sense of the Past*, pp. 482–486.

4. A lively account of the whistle-stop campaign by Truman himself is found in Arnof, *A Sense of the Past*, pp. 479–481. Has TV made such a political maneuver obsolete?

5. Compare and contrast ideological bases of "Americanism" and Communism. For an excellent treatment of this vital topic see Winks and Yergin, *The Cold War.*

6. On balance, has Russia won the Cold War, or the United States? Or has it been a stand-off? Is the Cold War over? How has the Cold War affected American freedoms? —the American presidency?

Chapter 31

Complacency
and Confrontation

America has a notable record of responding to challenges and making the most of opportunities. With our growing population, our extraordinary record of rising productivity, the inherent dynamism of our free enterprise economy, there is every reason to face the future with all confidence.
—ROCKEFELLER BROTHERS PANEL, 1958

Dwight D. Eisenhower, who succeeded Harry Truman in the White House, proved to be one of the most popular Presidents in modern times. He was also one of the least disposed to lead. In effect, he gave the country a rest after twenty strenuous years. The national mood during the 1950's has often been described as complacent. Many Americans seemed ready to settle down and enjoy the remarkable prosperity that had begun in World War II.

But the 1950's were not the 1920's. Americans could no longer turn their backs on the rest of the world. Although Eisenhower soon brought the Korean War to an end, the Cold War continued. It was accompanied by the menace of nuclear weapons that threatened the very existence of humanity. There were new confrontations between the Communists and the free world in Indochina, the Middle East, Africa, Europe, and the Americas. Although Eisenhower's tendency in domestic matters was to let sleeping dogs lie, in foreign affairs his administration vigorously pursued the policy of containment initiated by Truman.

A GENERAL IN THE WHITE HOUSE

When asked to run for the presidency in 1948, Eisenhower had flatly refused. He then said that "the necessary and wise subordination of the military to civil power" was best maintained when professional soldiers stayed out of politics. In 1952, he reluctantly gave in. The Democrats nominated Adlai E. Stevenson, whose record as a vigorous and popular governor of Illinois made him an attractive candidate.

The ensuing campaign was exciting. The candidates traveled widely—Eisenhower by train, like presidential candidates before him, and Stevenson by plane, like candidates from this time on. Stevenson labored under the burden of having to defend the Truman administration that had lost the confidence of the country.

Republicans campaigned effectively on the slogan "It is time for a change!" and "Communism, Corruption, Korea." Above all, they capitalized on Eisenhower's popularity with the motto, "I like Ike."

As running mate for Eisenhower, the Republicans chose Richard M. Nixon, a 39-year-old senator from California. He had made a reputation pursuing alleged Communists in government and the film industry. It looked as though Nixon might be dropped from the Republican ticket when it was revealed that he had received gifts totaling $18,000 (more than his salary as senator) from wealthy Californians. But Nixon defended himself in a nationwide radio-TV broadcast. The fund, he insisted, had been used for legitimate political expenses. He did admit that his family had kept one gift, a cocker spaniel puppy named "Checkers." The Checkers speech saved Nixon.

It is doubtful if Stevenson ever had a chance in 1952. Certainly Eisenhower clinched victory when a fortnight before election day he promised to make a trip to Korea to make peace.

Far more people voted in 1952 than in any previous presidential election. The result was a personal triumph for Eisenhower. He gained over six million more popular votes than Stevenson and carried the electoral college, 442 to 89.

Eisenhower's Theory of the Presidency

Once in the White House, Eisenhower revealed that his long career as an army officer did not mean that he expected simply to give orders. On the contrary, he thought the President's sphere of action and authority should be limited. He should not attempt to dominate Congress, or even to exert strong influence upon it. Instead, he should share leadership with the legislative body.

Within the executive department itself, Eisenhower tried to decentralize decision-making. His top officials, he said, should be a "team." The cabinet assumed new importance and became a genuine advisory body. For the first time in history it had a full-time secretary, an agenda, and regularly kept minutes. Eisenhower made Sherman Adams, former governor of New Hampshire, his "chief of staff." Adams exerted great power through his ability to decide what information got through to the President and which people saw him.

The advantages of Eisenhower's orderly arrangements for sharing and delegating authority were seen when he was three times stricken with illness. In each case the White House staff carried on the government without serious diffi-

Eisenhower campaigns in California in 1952.   Earl Warren is in the car in front seated at his left, and Richard Nixon, the Vice- Presidential candidate, is in the second car.

culty. But by insisting that he receive advice and information only "through channels," the President isolated himself. At crucial times he seemed to be in the dark about decisions made by subordinates.

"The Straight Road Down the Middle"

At the time he accepted the Republican nomination, Eisenhower declared that in economic matters he would "travel the straight road down the middle" between conservatism on one side and radicalism on the other.

It pleased the business community that Eisenhower ended the wage and price controls that Truman had imposed during the Korean War. It pleased the oil interests that at the President's urging Congress passed a law granting to the states control of offshore petroleum fields. This reversed a Supreme Court decision that had placed them under federal control.

Eisenhower's attitudes toward the budget and toward government ownership of public utilities were close to those of Herbert Hoover (see pp. 593–594). Throughout his presidency he attempted, usually without success, to balance the budget by cutting government services. He insisted that a balanced budget would strengthen the nation by halting inflation. He condemned the TVA as "creeping socialism" and tried unsuccessfully to arrange for private industry to provide new power plants in the TVA region.

In spite of conservative actions, the new Republican administration was often closer to Franklin Roosevelt than to Herbert Hoover. Repeatedly Eisenhower insisted that his administration was friendly to "the little fellow." With his encouragement, Congress extended social security to ten million people not previously covered, and increased the benefits. Eisenhower advocated slum clearance. Without success, he tried to persuade Congress to enact a program of health insurance partly underwritten by the federal government.

An achievement in which Eisenhower took genuine pride was the building of the St. Lawrence Seaway. Presidents Hoover, Roosevelt, and Truman had failed to persuade Congress to join with Canada in the project. Eisenhower insisted that the Seaway was necessary for defense, for the economic well-being of the United States, and for friendly relations with our northern neighbor. Congress passed the necessary legislation in 1954. In 1959 the President and Queen Elizabeth of Great Britain formally opened the Seaway. This great engineering feat opened the Great Lakes to ocean-going ships. It created a second Mediterranean Sea.

Eisenhower and Senator Joseph McCarthy

It had been predicted that the election of a Republican President would put an end to Senator Joseph McCarthy's charges that the federal government was honeycombed with Commu-

nists (see pp. 716). But McCarthy continued his crusade. He subjected the Eisenhower administration to a series of humiliating investigations. He accused the Secretary of the Army of "coddling Communists." He arranged a private "treaty" whereby certain Greek shipowners agreed not to trade with Red China.

For a time McCarthy was successful in giving the impression that he was saving the country from Communism. A public opinion poll early in 1954 reported that 50 percent of those questioned were favorable to him and less than 20 percent opposed. Opposition in the Senate subsided after he used his influence with the public to drive out of office four or five senators who had spoken against him.

President Eisenhower privately detested McCarthy and thought his methods were "un-American," but he refused to come to the public defense of himself or of his subordinates. He felt that ultimately the senator would destroy himself. In 1954 the tide turned. In a series of televised hearings of McCarthy's subcommittee, the public had an opportunity to see his disregard of law and decency. After the hearings were over, a Senate resolution to condemn him for his conduct was passed by a vote of 67 to 22. From this time on, the senator's influence rapidly declined and with it the widespread witch-hunting movement known as "McCarthyism."

McCarthyism had done great harm to this country. It had injured the reputation of the United States in the free world. It had lowered the morale and efficiency of the State Department. It had ruined the careers of scores of patriotic Americans, not only in government but in the professions, education, the theater, and the movies. These men and women lost their jobs and were often blackballed from further employment on the basis of flimsy evidence, perjured testimony, "guilt by association," or mere suspicion.

The Warren Court

During his first year in office, Eisenhower appointed as Chief Justice, Earl Warren, former governor of California and Republican candidate for Vice-President in 1948. During the ensuing fifteen years, the "Warren Court" interpreted the Constitution in such a way as to expand civil rights and liberties. It curbed the investigative powers of congressional and state legislative committees by insisting that witnesses have some of the protections they would have in a court of law. It extended the freedom of speech, press, and assembly. It protected suspected criminals from forced confessions, guaranteed them the right to counsel, and restricted police rights of search, seizure, and interrogation. Reviving the original purpose of the framers of the Fourteenth and Fifteenth Amendments, the Supreme Court protected the rights of black Americans. The most famous decision in this area was *Brown v. Board of Education,* which declared it illegal to segregate school children by race (see p. 726).

These decisions provoked criticism, much of it violent. The Court was accused of "coddling criminals." It was blamed for aiding the Communist conspiracy, and of encroaching on the powers of the states, of Congress, and of the President. Critics of the Chief Justice put up billboards and distributed bumper stickers that read, "Impeach Earl Warren." In 1959, even the American Bar Association formally urged the Court to use more restraint.

Eisenhower's Illness: The Question of Presidential Disability

As the presidential election of 1956 approached, Republican chances rested on Eisenhower's willingness to run. In September 1955, the President suffered a heart attack. The shock to business confidence was great. The stock market dropped more sharply than at any time since 1929. The President, however, recovered rapidly. Given "a parole, if not a pardon" by his doctors, he announced in February 1956 that he would run again.

The President's illness focussed attention on the question of presidential succession. The Constitution provided that the Vice-President should succeed to the presidential office in case the President should be unable to discharge the duties of his office. It did not say who was to decide

QUESTION • Has the public the right to know if the President is suffering from illness?

Here Senator McCarthy testifies in a highly publicized series of hearings that resulted from his charge that the United States Army was "coddling Communists." Joseph Welch, lawyer for the Army, at the table on the left, appears supremely unimpressed.

when the President was incompetent to do so.

When Eisenhower was stricken with ill health, there was little difficulty. His chief aide, Sherman Adams, managed domestic affairs, and his Secretary of State, John Foster Dulles, directed foreign affairs. But after the Kennedy assassination in 1963, Congress at last proposed, and the states ratified, the Twenty-Fifth Amendment to the Constitution. The Twenty-Fifth Amendment (see p. 152) provides for regular procedures in case the President is unable to perform the duties of office. It deals with the difficult situation that might arise if a President felt able to discharge the duties of office, but others thought not. The amendment also provided for replacement of the Vice-President in case he or she were called to the White House by the death or resignation of the President.

Eisenhower's Second Term

Renominated unanimously as Republican candidate, Eisenhower again ran against Adlai

---

"Mr. Sam"

It is often not realized that the speaker of the House of Representatives wields a power in domestic affairs close to that of the President. Since he is head of the majority party in the House, his position is like that of prime minister in a parliamentary system such as Great Britain's. Few laws are passed without his approval.

Some speakers, such as the fabled "Czar" Reed and the anti-progressive "Uncle Joe" Cannon, have been autocrats. "Cactus Jack" Garner, who was speaker before serving two terms as Vice-President under Franklin Roosevelt, remarked, "You can't run the House without getting your knuckles bloody." Sam Rayburn, who was speaker for seventeen years—more than twice as long as any other man—did not agree. Although he could be stern and had been known to break a gavel trying to silence opponents, he preferred persuasion and compromise. His methods usually worked, and he was regarded as one of the most effective presiding officers in the history of Congress.

One reason for Rayburn's success was that he liked people. "I haven't time to hate," he said, and also, "The way to get along is to go along." His colleagues affectionately called him "Mr. Sam." He was short, stubby, and wholly bald, with "a voice like a turkey gobbler." Although intensely partisan and always mindful of political advantage, he was also fair-minded and a man of his word. Mr. Sam was respected and trusted by Republican opponents as well as by fellow Democrats. His office door was always open to representatives seeking advice and help.

Born in 1882, Rayburn was one of the last "frontier politicians." The eighth of eleven children of a small cotton farmer in Texas, he heard his elders talk of Indian raids and the deeds of Davy Crockett. He gained "book larnin' " by sweeping floors and milking cows to pay his way at East Texas Normal College. Later, the five dollars a day he earned as a state legislator enabled him to go through law school at the University of Texas.

He had dreamed of being speaker of the House since he was twelve years old, and he had immense pride in having achieved his ambition. He would rather be speaker, he said, than be ten Senators. Once he was asked about Presidents under whom he had served. "Don't use that word 'under,' " he snapped. "I've never served under anybody. I've served with them."

Stevenson in 1956. As in 1952, there were no serious issues dividing the candidates. The Republicans claimed that the administration had brought peace and prosperity—"everything is booming except the guns." Capitalizing on fears about the President's health, the Democrats concentrated their fire on Nixon, again candidate for the vice-presidency.

When radio and TV brought the election results into millions of homes on the night of November 6, they revealed an extraordinary result: Eisenhower was elected by an even greater margin than in 1952. But the President's popularity did not rub off on his party. Republican congressional candidates ran so far behind him that the Democrats controlled both the Senate and the House of Representatives.

In his second term, Eisenhower was more independent of party than any other President in modern times. In his own party he had followers, the so-called "modern Republicans," but many of the "Old Guard" regarded him as dangerously tainted with New Deal philosophy and with internationalism. The President found allies, however, among Democrats. The two

chief Democratic leaders in Congress—House Speaker Sam Rayburn and Senate Majority Leader Lyndon Johnson, both Texans—were as much followers of the "middle way" as the President himself. Thus there was formed a rather shaky alliance of "modern Republicans" and moderate to liberal Democrats. These were opposed by Old Guard Republicans and conservative southern Democrats. The most striking achievement of the liberal coalition was passage of the Civil Rights Acts of 1957 and 1960, both designed to guarantee black Americans the right to vote.

THE WORKING WORLD; CIVIL RIGHTS

During the 1950's the prosperity of the late 1940's continued. There were two brief recessions in 1953–54 and in 1957–58. In both cases the Eisenhower administration resisted demands for a public works program on the New Deal model. Instead, the President and his advisers trusted the "built-in stabilizers" mentioned in the last chapter (see p. 714). By 1960 business activity reached new heights.

More Jobs for Women

The general prosperity opened more jobs for women. Indeed, female employment increased four times faster than that of men during the decade. Previously, more wives of men with low incomes worked than those married to men with higher salaries. It was a matter of necessity. Now there was a striking increase in employment among well-educated women married to men in middle and upper income brackets. Such women often went into the job market less because of need, than because they found personal satisfaction outside the home. Women actually lost ground, however, in the 1950's. They were paid less than men and did not have access to higher positions such as school principals, full professors in colleges, and supervising jobs in industry.

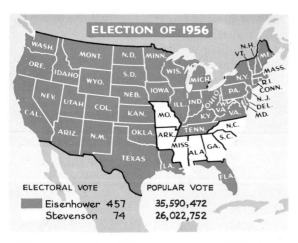

ELECTION OF 1956

ELECTORAL VOTE	POPULAR VOTE
Eisenhower 457	35,590,472
Stevenson 74	26,022,752

Eisenhower won more electoral votes in 1956 than he did when first elected in 1952. In spite of his personal popularity, the Democrats won control of Congress.

One of the very few women who held high positions in American industry during the 1950's was Virginia Sink, an engineer for the Chrysler Corporation.

Gains of Organized Labor

During the 1950's, organized labor was less militant than in the 1940's. This was principally because workers were better off. Wages had gone up so much that workers felt more and more that they were members of the middle class. Industrial peace also resulted from new attitudes on the part of management and union leaders.

"Scientific management" was once a term that referred only to the mechanical efficiency of workers, eliminating waste motion, putting in more machinery, improving lighting and safety devices. Now a new philosophy of management stressed the idea that workers were human beings first and machine tenders second. With considerate treatment, a worker produced more.

On the other side of the bargaining table, unions no longer had to fight for their right to exist. Labor peace was also advanced when the American Federation of Labor and the CIO settled their old feud (see p. 639). In 1955 they merged into a vast new "union of unions," the AFL-CIO. The merger greatly reduced the nuisance of jurisdictional disputes that had occurred when two unions were struggling to organize workers in the same plant.

Strikes continued, but on no such scale as right after World War II. Most disputes were settled by direct bargaining. "Welfare capitalism" in the form of pension plans, vacations with pay, and free or inexpensive medical care became the rule rather than the exception.

The number of workers in organized labor increased from less than four million on the eve of the New Deal to over eighteen million in the mid-1950's. Then it started to decline. This was partly the result of resistance to unions expressed in state "right to work" laws. Even more, it probably resulted from the fact that higher wage scales made unions seem less useful.

Farm Problems and Policies

Most farmers did not share in "Eisenhower prosperity." Between 1948 and 1956 the farmers' share of the national income dropped from 9 to 4 percent. In Eisenhower's first term, perhaps half a million farmers gave up and left the soil.

The agricultural policies of the Eisenhower administration hastened the decline of the small family farm with diversified crops. Farm policy favored efficiency. Large, one-crop farms were more efficient. Only the farmers with large capital could purchase the latest machinery, use the latest scientific methods, and buy or lease the best lands. Even in a falling market, they could reduce their costs so much that they could still make a profit. By 1959 half the farmland in this country belonged to the one farmer in 25 who owned 1000 acres or more. Signifying the change in American agriculture, the term "agribusiness" (agriculture + business) came into the language.

The forgotten people in agriculture were the seasonal farm workers who followed the harvests around the country. Many of the migrants were Mexican-Americans from the Southwest. Probably even more came from Mexico itself. Under an agreement (1942) and a law (1951),

Many farm workers were Mexican-Americans who migrated through the United States, following the crops. Here they pick tomatoes in Florida.

as many as 400,000 *braceros* (transient Mexican laborers) were admitted each year on temporary visas. There were also large numbers (an estimated million in 1954) of "wetbacks"—Mexicans who came into the United States illegally. These migrant workers worked long hours for low pay. They were protected neither by the National Labor Relations Act nor by federal minimum wage laws. Their living conditions were often deplorable and their children grew up with little, if any, schooling.

Slow Progress for Blacks

The rapid economic advance of blacks during and after World War II slowed down in the 1950's. Especially in the South, blacks were victims of advancing technology. A mechanical cotton picker that only large-scale farmers could afford drove many black farmers off the land and greatly reduced the demand for farm labor. The introduction of automation cut the demand for unskilled and semi-skilled workers in a great variety of businesses.

There was some progress in putting an end to the humiliating practice of forced segregation of black people. President Eisenhower picked up where Truman had left off and completed integration of the armed forces. By persuasion and by discreet use of executive power, Eisenhower managed to integrate public facilities such as swimming pools and private facilities such as hotels, theaters, and restaurants in the District of Columbia.

The Supreme Court joined the fight against racial discrimination. As we have seen, in the case of *Brown v. Board of Education,* May 1954, the Court declared that local laws establishing separate schools for black and white children were a violation of the equal protection clause of the Fourteenth Amendment. This was a complete reversal of *Plessy v. Ferguson* (1896), which had supported the right of a state to supply "separate but equal" public accommodations.

The desegregation decision was generally obeyed by school authorities in the North, in some of the border states, and in the District of Columbia. In the South, school desegregation was to come more slowly. President Eisenhower did not take vigorous action to enforce the desegregation decision in the South. It was not until Governor Orval Faubus of Arkansas defied a court order to allow black students into a school at Little Rock, Arkansas, that the President acted. Calling out federal troops, Eisenhower forced the Little Rock authorities to accept nine black high school students.

The Supreme Court had struck down various legal methods whereby southern states kept black citizens from voting. But custom and intimidation kept most blacks from registering to vote or going to the polls. Congress passed Civil Rights Acts in 1957 and 1959 to protect the blacks' right to vote. Here too the Eisenhower administration was cautious. In the years 1957-1960, the Department of Justice brought only ten suits to secure voting rights for black persons. Only 25 percent of adult blacks voted in the states of the Deep South, and only 5 percent in Mississippi.

Black Protests: A New Leader

Black impatience with their slow progress toward equality led to organized demonstrations. In 1955, Rosa Parks, a black seamstress, refused to move to the rear of a bus in Montgomery, Alabama, as was customary in the South. She said her feet hurt. She was arrested and charged with violating a city ordinance. Local blacks thereupon organized an almost complete boycott of the entire city bus system. This was the first time the masses of black people had ever joined together in an organized protest in the South. The boycott lasted nearly a

Protected by federal troops, a black girl quietly faces a jeering mob as, in response to a court order, a high school is desegregated in Little Rock, Arkansas, in 1957.

year, and nearly drove the bus company into bankruptcy. Eventually the Supreme Court declared that discriminatory seating on buses was illegal.

The principal leader of the Montgomery bus boycott was a 27-year-old black minister, the Reverend Martin Luther King, Jr. He adapted the non-violent techniques of the great Indian leader, Mahatma Gandhi. King insisted that his followers disobey unjust laws, but at the same time try to love their oppressors and never strike back. In the wake of the Montgomery victory, King founded the Southern Christian Leadership Conference (SCLC) to fight discrimination in public facilities throughout the South. Schooled in non-violence, thousands of black high school and college students staged "sit-ins" in lunch counters and stores. Sometimes they were joined by white sympathizers. They willingly submitted to arrest, jail sentences, and fines. And generally they won. Soon there was partial or total integration of public accommodations in most cities of the South.

"THE AFFLUENT SOCIETY"

In 1958, the economist John Kenneth Galbraith published *The Affluent Society,* a book in which he declared that the recent American prosperity was something new in the world. All previous societies had been based on an "economy of scarcity." In them, productivity was so low that most people could expect nothing but back-breaking toil and poverty. Most countries in Asia, Africa, and South America are in this category today. In the United States and a few other highly industrialized countries, said Galbraith, there had developed an "economy of abundance." In them, advanced technology produced more goods than human beings could consume. Thus poverty was limited to certain classes of people, like the physically handicapped, those living in depressed areas (where

Starting in the 1950's, American children have spent more time with eyes glued to television screens than they have spent in school. Whether this immersion has done them harm or good has been a matter of continual controversy.

a mine or factory had closed down, for instance), or among social groups adapting to a new environment (like Puerto Ricans in New York City).

Galbraith was accused by some of having overstated the case for affluence (see p. 750), but statistics in general bore out his positive picture of post-World War II American society. Not only did American productivity run ahead of increase in population, but the greater wealth produced was also more evenly distributed. During the "golden twenties" the wealthiest 5 percent of the people had received 35 percent of the nation's income. By 1960 this had shrunk to 18 percent, even before taxes. Most Americans now earned enough not merely for necessities like food and housing, but for luxuries such as automobiles and electrical appliances. The percent of those owning their own homes increased from 40 to 60 percent between 1940 and 1960. So many Americans could now afford automobiles that new super-highways were overcrowded as soon as completed. There was more leisure than ever before as hours of work were shortened and millions of workers for the first time enjoyed vacations with pay. Combine an automobile for almost every family with an-

nual vacations, and the result was a new business: the motels that lined highways from Maine to California.

Not only were Americans better off, but they were more secure. Unemployment insurance and social security now covered the majority of job holders. These were supplemented by a great variety of private pension plans. Subsidies protected farmers against sudden declines in market prices. Bank depositors, investors, and mortgage holders were all protected from loss by the federal government.

The Impact of Television

The prosperity of the 1920's had been characterized by the meteoric rise of three new industries—automobile, radio, and motion picture. The corresponding symbol of the period following World War II was television. In 1945 there were only six television broadcasting stations, and less than one receiving set for every 20,000 people. Within a few years TV sets were as common as telephones.

Television brought political events into living rooms. With the election of 1952, television arrived politically. TV cameras invaded party conventions, recording not merely speeches from the floor but even committee debates in "smoke-filled rooms." During the campaign, both parties spent millions on broadcasts costing as much as $2000 a minute. As we have seen, Nixon's "Checkers" speech rescued his political career.

Although TV brought vivid awareness ·of politics and heightened the interest of the voters, it also raised disturbing questions. Would TV favor the candidate who was the best actor, or the one who could afford to buy most time on the air? Would televising congressional investigations promote the search for truth and justice?

Some people also feared that television would lower the level of American culture. Supported as they were by a mass audience, TV programs often appealed to the lowest common denominator of public taste. In order not to offend potential customers, they tended to avoid controversial issues. Instead, they furnished entertainment designed "to fix the attention but not engage the mind." TV was accused of destroying the desire to read, of allowing people "to remain stupid without finding it dull."

QUESTION • Should there be any legal restrictions on the portrayal of violence on TV?

Yet there were counter currents that at least partially contradicted the prophets of doom. There were TV programs that certainly did "engage the mind." Educational TV, still in its infancy, promised to be unexpectedly successful in stimulating children's imagination as well as in extending the influence of master teachers.

Technological Progress: Automation, Computers

The decade after World War II saw spectacular advances in science. With more money to spend, more university-trained scientists, and perhaps more faith in science than any other country, the United States was the leader in this development. Among 64 Nobel Prize winners in physics and chemistry between 1946 and 1964, there were 28 Americans, 14 British, 6 Germans, and 4 Russians. No other country had more than two.

Striking advances in both the productivity of industry and in uniformity of quality were made possible by automation. Automation consists in having a machine run a machine. The secret is "feedback." The operating machine tells the controlling machine what is going on (temperature change, increased flow, alteration in speed, and so forth). The controlling machine in turn changes its directions to the operating machine to keep the process going the way it should. A simple example is that of a thermostat and an oil-burning furnace. In far more complicated fashion, an oil refinery, a flour mill, or a paint factory can be automated so that all processes from raw materials to finished product may be carried on without human intervention.

A woman reading a "print-out" from a computer. These complex machines can solve almost instantaneously problems formerly beyond human capacity.

Computers are an American development made possible by modern electronics. They can perform the most complex mathematical operations in a fraction of a second. Their "memories" can store large amounts of information and report it back on demand. Computers can be programmed to reason logically and even to translate foreign languages. They are used today for a great variety of purposes. They make hotel reservations, sort bank checks, guide satellites, do scientific computations, predict election results, forecast weather conditions, identify fingerprints, and set type for printing.

Both automation and computers have caused dislocation in the job market. Automation has tended to displace unskilled workers like elevator operators. Computers have taken over from white collar workers such as auditors and clerks. In the long run, computers and automation create more jobs than they do away with, but the new openings tend to demand at least a high school education and special training.

Progress in Medicine

During the twentieth century, human beings have made more progress in medicine than during all previous history. World War II showed how rapidly medicine was advancing. In the Spanish-American War, fought in 1898, far more men died of disease than of wounds. In World War II, the death rate of the fighting men was no higher than it would have been at home. The threat of malaria in Pacific islands and Burmese jungles was met by the use of a new, synthetic drug, atabrine, to replace quinine. Penicillin and sulfa drugs dramatically reduced wound infection.

In April 1955, the country heard of one of the most dramatic advances in the history of medicine—the development of the Salk vaccine for preventing infantile paralysis, or poliomyelitis. This was the climax of many years of research supported in part by millions of small donations to the annual March of Dimes. After a gigantic trial run on 440,000 children, Salk vaccine was declared effective. It was soon available to all, and today polio has practically disappeared.

In similar fashion other diseases have been wiped out or the danger from them greatly reduced. In the United States in 1900 the great killers were pneumonia, tuberculosis, and diphtheria. Now these have been almost eliminated. Today, normal life expectancy in this and other industrialized countries runs beyond the Biblical definition of old age, three score years and ten. Today, of the three great killers, two—cancer and heart disease—mostly affect older people. The third is a product of affluence and especially affects young people—automobile accidents.

Suburbs and Central Cities

The automobile changed the face of America. Its greatest effect was to cause rapid growth of the suburbs. It was the automobile that made possible a mass migration of city dwellers, seeking light, fresh air, greenery, and a place of their own. In the decades after World War II, cities were ringed by seemingly endless housing developments carved out of rural landscapes. Shopping centers with vast parking lots were created to serve the new residential areas. Industries began to follow population out of the cities.

Meanwhile the central cities deteriorated. To accommodate floods of traffic, new "arteries" were cut through them, often destroying whole neighborhoods. The middle class and more prosperous workers left them for the suburbs. With a stationary or declining population, consisting more and more of poor minority groups, there were increasing financial problems. Taxes could no longer support the mounting demands for services such as public transportation, police protection, and education.

DULLES-EISENHOWER POLICIES IN ASIA AND THE MIDDLE EAST

President Eisenhower delegated much of the conduct of foreign affairs to his secretary of state, John Foster Dulles. Grandson of one secretary of state, nephew of another, Dulles had long experience in high-level diplomacy.

Secretary Dulles preached a vigorous foreign policy. During the presidential campaign of 1952 he denounced mere "containment" of Communism. Instead he advocated "liberation" of the subject peoples behind the Iron Curtain. He threatened that renewal of Communist aggression would be met with "massive retaliation." The Department of Defense adapted its military strategy to this concept. It cut down conventional military forces, such as those used in Korea. Instead it developed nuclear weapons and airplanes to deliver them to their targets. This was said to promise "more bang for a buck."

In actual practice, the foreign policy of the Eisenhower administration was more cautious than Secretary Dulles' sword-rattling would suggest. President Eisenhower insisted "there is no alternative to peace." A nuclear war was unthinkable—it might well mean the end of civilization. He and Dulles therefore continued the Truman policy of containment. They made no effort to dislodge Communists from any area where they were already established.

Peace in Korea; War in Southeast Asia; Truce with China

In July 1953, a settlement ended the Korean War. Unhappy Korea was still divided along a line held by the opposing armies when hostilities ceased. The struggle had been frustrating and costly for the United States. It had accomplished, however, its primary aim of repelling Communist aggression.

Hardly had the fighting ended in Korea than the United States was faced with the problem of Communist expansion in another Asian peninsula. After Japan surrendered Indochina in 1945, the French attempted to resume their prewar position as rulers. But Japanese victories early in World War II had destroyed the prestige of Europeans and had whetted the appetite of Asians to rule themselves. In Indochina there were three different nationalities, each wishing a state of its own: the Cambodians, the Laotians, and the Vietnamese (see map, p. 757). To complicate matters further, the strongest leader of the Vietnamese independence movement, Ho Chi Minh, was a dedicated Communist, trained in Soviet Russia and China. He headed a movement called the Vietminh that began a war in 1946 to drive the French from Indochina. The United States was not directly involved, but it supplied more than a third of the war materials used by the French from 1950 on.

In 1954 a French army was besieged by the Communists in the key fortress of Dienbienphu. A military disaster threatened. The question arose: should the United States enter the war? A French defeat might lead to Communist domination of all Southeast Asia. As President Eisenhower explained at a press conference:

You have a row of dominoes set up, and you knock over the first one, and what will happen to the last one is the certainty that it will go over very quickly.

To save the first domino, the French urged that American planes bomb Communist positions. Dulles favored such action. But when Eisenhower discovered that he could get no support from other nations or from leaders of Congress, he refused to get drawn into a "hot" war. Dienbienphu fell in May 1954, and the Vietminh took over northern Vietnam. A truce arranged at Geneva, Switzerland, in July, kept southern Vietnam under French control.

France soon pulled out, but did not leave the South open to the Vietminh. The United States moved into the vacuum and supported a shaky government headed by an anti-Communist, Ngo Dinh Diem. Diem's regime was inefficient, dictatorial, and unpopular, but American economic and military support enabled him to survive.

During the Korean War, President Truman had ordered the United States Seventh Fleet to patrol the waters between Taiwan, held by Chiang Kai-shek, and mainland China, held by the Communists. The Eisenhower administration continued this policy. It refused to recognize the Communist government of Mao Tsetung and opposed its entrance into the UN. Thus during the Eisenhower years the China problem remained exactly where it was when he came in.

Bandung Conference: Neutralism

In May 1955 representatives from 29 Asian and African states met at Bandung, Indonesia. The two thousand delegates came from countries containing more than half the people on earth. Most of them had recently won freedom from Western rule. Resentment of their former white masters continued.

In such an atmosphere Chou En-lai, China's able foreign minister, might have been expected to gain a diplomatic victory by harping on the familiar theme that the Communists were the enemies of "colonialism." To the relief of the West, many African and Asian leaders proved as fearful of future Communist aggression as they were of former Western imperialism.

Bandung thus focused attention on a point of view known as "neutralism." It was especially connected with Prime Minister Nehru of India. Nehru insisted that India was an "uncommitted nation." He held that it was degrading for African or Asian nations to become "camp followers" of either side in the Cold War. He im-

partially denounced Russia for suppression of Hungarian freedom and for aggression in Korea; Red China for the invasion of Tibet; Britain and France for their war on Egypt; and the United States for supplying arms to India's uneasy neighbor Pakistan.

Neutralism was hotly debated in the United States. Some observers compared neutralism to the early isolationist policy of the United States —necessary for a new, comparatively weak nation. Others, Secretary of State Dulles among them, denounced neutralism. They took the view that no person or nation has a right to be neutral in a struggle between tyranny and freedom.

The Middle East—A Powder Keg

For several reasons the United States was drawn into the Middle East, an area extending from the Mediterranean to the boundaries of India. Before World War II, American capital had entered the Middle East to develop its rich oil deposits. During the war, American lend-lease supplies reached the Soviet Union from the Persian Gulf through Iran. After the war, many Americans were intensely interested in the state of Israel that had been set up in 1948 in the original Jewish homeland of Palestine.

The Middle East was a "powder keg ready to explode." The Arab States detested Israel and hoped eventually to destroy it. The Arabs distrusted each other. In many areas there was poverty and discontent. Finally there was always the threat of a Russian thrust southward toward the oil fields and warm water ports.

QUESTION • For what reasons should the U.S. be interested in peace in the Middle East?

In 1955 the Russians were obviously thinking of a move into the Middle East. Powerful radios in the southern USSR broadcast anti-Western propaganda to the Arab world. In the

UN the Russians blocked action to promote peace between Israel and her neighbors. Russia arranged a "commercial treaty" with Gamal Abdel Nasser, ruler of Egypt. By its terms, Egypt sent Russia cotton and in return received tanks and guns.

Suez Crisis, 1956

Even after the arms deal between Egypt and the USSR, Dulles promised to lend Nasser American funds to start construction of a new irrigation dam at Aswan on the Nile. When Nassar set about making a deal with Red China, Dulles changed his tack. Without warning, he cancelled the American loan. Nasser replied to this humiliation by seizing the Suez Canal from its French and British owners in July 1956.

Dulles' blunt tactics infuriated the British, the French, and the Israelis. The three nations decided to act independently of the United States. On October 25, 1956, Israeli troops invaded Egypt and seized the Sinai Peninsula. Five days later British and French paratroopers seized the northern portions of the Suez Canal.

This sudden attack threatened a general war. During a frenzied UN debate, the world saw the extraordinary spectacle of the United States voting with the USSR to condemn the actions of Israel, France, and Britain. Under UN pressure the three nations agreed to withdraw from Egypt, and a hastily-organized UN force moved in to keep the peace.

The crisis had been highly embarrassing to the United States. Israel had been established with American economic and diplomatic assistance. Britain and France were America's closest allies. Yet the three countries had gone to war without consulting America beforehand. The whole affair might have shattered the Western alliance. But the Soviet suppression of the Hungarian Revolution, which took place at this time, persuaded the Western powers to close ranks against Russia.

The Eisenhower Doctrine

The Suez crisis weakened the prestige of the United States and its allies. It appeared to open the door to Communist penetration of the Middle East. To forestall such an event, President Eisenhower in January 1957 asked Congress for power to use American military forces to defend the Middle East. This new application of the containment policy was known as the Eisenhower Doctrine. It told the world that the Middle East was "out of bounds" to Communist aggression.

The Eisenhower Doctrine was put into effect with dramatic suddenness in mid-1958. On July 14, the pro-Western monarch of Iraq, King Faisal II, was assassinated by army officers who were in league both with Colonel Nasser and with the USSR. Their action threatened the two small states of Lebanon and Jordan. The next day Eisenhower landed American Marines in Lebanon and two days later 2000 British paratroopers landed in Jordan.

Again the United Nations convened to consider a Middle East crisis, and again a compromise was reached. In return for guarantees that Lebanon and Jordan would be safe from subversion or invasion, the American and British forces were withdrawn. So for the fourth time the UN patched up a truce. But the powder keg was still explosive. The basic problems of the Middle East—poverty, misgovernment, inter-Arab rivalry, Arab-Israeli strife, and the threat of Communist aggression—still defied solution.

TENSIONS IN EUROPE AND LATIN AMERICA

On entering office in 1953, Eisenhower attempted to strengthen the North Atlantic Treaty Organization. He favored the formation of a single army under unified command. But the French, fearful of Germany, were opposed. The defense of the West was somewhat strengthened, however, when Germany was allowed limited rearmament and membership in NATO.

The NATO alliance faced other difficulties besides coordinating military power. Within Europe itself there were age-old divisions and fears. Furthermore, many Europeans had little love for America. Socialists as well as Communists regarded the U.S. as a dollar-crazy land where workers were exploited in order to swell the profits of a few great trusts, a land where all values were based on the simple question: "Will it sell?" Conservatives saw Europe as in danger of being "Coca-colonized," as their young people took to wearing blue jeans, reading comic strips, and listening to jazz. Many Britishers thought the United States to blame for Britain's loss of power and prestige in the Middle and Far East. In France, the U.S. received blame for the loss of Indochina.

Fortunately for the Western alliance, the USSR could be depended on to create fears that persuaded Western Europe and the United States to maintain a common front.

Unrest behind the Iron Curtain

The Soviet answer to the Marshall Plan had been a Council for Economic Aid, supposedly designed to help the satellite countries. The counterpart of NATO was a military alliance, the Warsaw Pact. But both these organizations helped create unrest behind the Iron Curtain. It became clear that the Council for Economic Aid was an agency for subordinating the economies of the "people's democracies" to the needs of Russia, and the Warsaw Pact a means of keeping Soviet troops on their backs.

In October 1956, two satellite countries rose against their Soviet overlords. In Poland there were anti-Soviet riots in the cities, and Polish soldiers exchanged shots with the Russians. The USSR backed down and granted concessions, among them a reduction in the number of troops in Poland. A new Polish premier granted more freedom of worship to Roman Catholics and permitted limited freedom of speech and press. The Polish government was still Communist, but no longer a puppet with all the strings pulled by Moscow. In 1957 it even asked for and received loans from the United States to purchase food and machinery.

Revolution in Hungary, 1956

A rebellion in Hungary had tragically different results. It started with peaceful protests against Soviet domination. When Communist leaders attempted to suppress the unrest, they stirred up a hornet's nest. Overnight the Hungarian people rose against the police state that oppressed them. On October 29, after less than a week of fighting, the Budapest radio jubilantly told the Hungarians, "You have won!" Russia had agreed to allow Hungary a large measure of independence. For five days Hungary had a taste of freedom. Former political leaders came out of jail or hiding. Suppressed newspapers reappeared. A new government was set up. But on November 3, Russian tanks and troops suddenly attacked Budapest and overcame its gallant defenders.

As these events unfolded, the United Nations tried to aid the Hungarians. The General Assembly demanded that Soviet forces withdraw from Hungary. But the USSR refused even to allow UN observers into Budapest. Great as was American sympathy for Hungary, President Eisenhower made no attempt to rescue that unhappy country for fear that to do so would result in a war with Russia.

Emerging Africa

Until recently, the great continent of Africa was controlled by European nations. As late as 1955 there were only five independent countries. By January 1961, this number had increased to 27.

A statue of Stalin was pulled down from its pedestal when the Hungarians in Budapest drove out their Communist masters in 1956 and for a brief period enjoyed the heady wine of freedom. Russian tanks soon put an end to the uprising. In spite of Dulles' talk of "liberation," the United States took no action to prevent the reimposition of Russian control of Hungary, since hostilities might lead to nuclear war.

Until the close of the Eisenhower administration, the United States took little active interest in African affairs. Americans were traditionally sympathetic to anti-colonial movements. But there was a reluctance to take an active part on the side of the emerging African nations against America's European allies, France and Great Britain.

The Belgian Congo (later renamed Zaïre) was granted independence in 1960, but with no preparation for self-rule. There were said to be only 17 native university graduates in an area three times the size of Texas. The first local governing council met only three weeks before the Belgians pulled out. Immediately there were outbreaks of intertribal warfare. The province of Katanga (later known as Shaba), rich in minerals, attempted to secede. To make the situation worse, two Congolese leaders called for Russian military aid, and the Soviet leader,

Nikita Khrushchev, assured them that the USSR would supply it.

The threat that the Congo might become a battleground of the Cold War was averted by the United Nations. Under the skillful leadership of Secretary-General Dag Hammarskjöld the UN slowly took charge. Hammarskjöld himself was killed in a plane crash while trying to arrange a cease-fire between rival Congolese factions. A UN army kept order; UN technological and economic assistance averted starvation and helped to reorganize the economy.

There was fear of Soviet intervention in other African states, but even the Republic of Guinea, which had the closest ties with Russia, expelled the Soviet ambassador in 1961 and suppressed a local Communist party. The new African nations were, in fact, strongly neutralist. They were too weak militarily and had too many problems of their own to takes sides in the

Cold War. "When the bull elephants fight," re- marked the Ghanaian leader Kwame Nkrumah, "the grass gets trampled down."

Trouble in the Americas

The Western Hemisphere did not escape the world-wide Communist drive for power. In 1954 it appeared that Communists had large in- fluence in the government of Guatemala. The Guatemalan authorities proposed to take over the lands of the United Fruit Company, a United States corporation, and distribute them among poor peasants. Denied the right to pur- chase arms in the United States, Guatemala re- ceived them from behind the Iron Curtain.

Secretary Dulles saw the Guatemalan situa- tion as a dangerous threat. If the United States acted on its own, however, to overthrow the Guatemalan government, it would reawaken Latin-American fears of the "Colossus of the North." Nevertheless, joint action with other Latin-American countries was possible. In March, an Inter-American Conference that met at Caracas, Venezuela, resolved that extension of the Communist system in this hemisphere would be considered a threat to the Americas. In June the regime in Guatemala was over- thrown by anti-Communist forces that had been secretly armed and trained by the United States.

On the surface, the Latin-American coun- tries and the United States were members of a partnership. But Latin Americans had good cause to believe that they were "forgotten neigh- bors." They saw billions of dollars being poured into remaking Europe's economy and shoring up weak governments in Asia, while they received about 3 percent of U.S. foreign aid. In 1960 South Korea received more aid than all Latin- American countries put together.

It took a visit to Latin America by Vice- President Nixon in 1958 to make this country realize the results of such neglect. In most of the eight countries he visited, Nixon faced hos-

tile demonstrations. In Peru and Venezuela he was in actual danger from angry mobs.

Re-Examination of Latin-American Policy

Nixon's unpleasant experience led to re- examination of our Latin-American policy. A special report by Milton S. Eisenhower, the President's brother, made three major criticisms: 1) the United States failed to inform Latin America about this country; 2) it neglected Latin America as a field for investment and economic assistance; 3) in dealings with Latin- American countries, the United States did not distinguish between relatively democratic gov- ernments and brutal dictatorships.

Milton Eisenhower proposed more cultural interchanges between this country and its south- ern neighbors and the establishment of means whereby Latin America could obtain easier credit. As to the dictators, he pointed out that our declared policy of non-intervention pre- vented us from taking active measures to over- throw them. He agreed, however, with Vice- President Nixon, who had suggested we reserve our *abrazo* (embrace) for democratic leaders and give dictators "a cool handshake."

The new policy toward Latin-American dic- tators had its first test in Cuba. There the cor- rupt and ruthless government of General Ful- gencio Batista faced a rebellion headed by the radical Fidel Castro. The United States stopped all aid to Batista, an action that helped Castro and his followers toward victory. They entered Havana on January 1, 1959. Castro was popular in the United States. But enthusiasm for the Cuban leader waned as he announced himself a Communist, denounced the United States, con- fiscated private property, and sought the friend- ship and military support of Russia and Red China. President Eisenhower barred Cuba from the great United States sugar market and even- tually broke off relations with the Castro gov- ernment. These actions provided no answer to

Chapter 32

Charisma and Catastrophe:
The Kennedy-Johnson Years

This is a dangerous and uncertain world. . . . No one expects our lives to be easy, not in this decade, not in this century.
—JOHN FITZGERALD KENNEDY

In the 1960 presidential campaign, the Republicans ran Vice-President Richard M. Nixon, and the Democrats, Senator John F. Kennedy. The backgrounds of the two men presented striking contrasts. Kennedy, a Roman Catholic from Massachusetts, was the son of a wealthy man who had served as chairman of the Securities Exchange Commission and as United States ambassador to Great Britain. Nixon, born a Quaker in California, worked his way up from relative poverty. But both men were young: Nixon was forty-seven years old; Kennedy, forty-three. Both were "cold warriors," who saw the United States as engaged in a long and dangerous struggle against the forces of Communism all over the globe. Both were shrewd and experienced politicians. Nixon, with UN Ambassador Henry Cabot Lodge as his running mate, was able to retain the support of the right wing of his party. Meanwhile, Kennedy headed off a possible southern revolt by persuading his principal rival for the nomination, Senator Lyndon B. Johnson of Texas, to join his ticket.

At the start of the campaign the Gallup poll showed Nixon in the lead. Later the tide turned, apparently as a result of four TV debates. The debates aided Kennedy. He had been less in

the public eye than Nixon and now revealed that he was highly informed and poised under fire. Toward the end of the campaign Kennedy assured himself of the black vote by telephoning the wife of Martin Luther King, Jr., who had been jailed for protesting segregation in a southern city. As election day approached, the polls showed Kennedy in the lead. But a great ques-

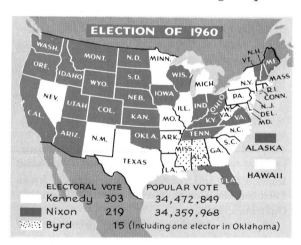

In the 1960 presidential election, Democrat John F. Kennedy won a slim victory. Senator Byrd polled 8 electoral votes in Mississippi, 6 in Alabama, 1 in Oklahoma. How could Nixon have won?

tion mark was the religious issue. Would prejudice against a Roman Catholic hurt Kennedy, as it had hurt Al Smith in the election of 1928?

Kennedy carried the election by one of the narrowest margins in the history of American politics. He won in the electoral college, 303-219, but in several states a difference of only a few thousand votes would have swung the electoral votes the other way. Kennedy generally ran behind Democratic candidates in Congress, but he laid to rest the idea that a Roman Catholic could not be elected to the Presidency.

"THE NEW FRONTIER"

Kennedy's brief and eloquent inaugural address was full of echoes from American political literature and from the Bible. He devoted himself entirely to defining the position of America in a hungry and divided world. The torch, he said, had been passed on to "a new generation of Americans," who had been disciplined by war and a bitter peace. This generation was committed, said Kennedy, to the rights for which America had stood since the Revolution. He warned the Communist world that the United States would remain strong. But he also urged that both sides renew the search for peace. They should join forces against the common enemies of man: "tyranny, poverty, disease, and war itself."

To his fellow citizens as well as to the peoples of the world, Kennedy pleaded, "Ask not what America will do for you, but what together we can do for the freedom of man."

Kennedy's Charisma

The Kennedy administration acquired as a label the "New Frontier." Its style was certainly new. For the first time, the destiny of the United States was in the hands of Americans born in the twentieth century. The President and his closest advisers were brilliant, articulate, and tough-

Mrs. Kennedy and outgoing President Eisenhower look on as incoming **John** Kennedy delivers his inaugural address on a cold January day in 1961.

minded. Several of them were from university faculties. They were people who were confident of their ability to make this country and the world a better place to live in. The social life of the White House was more than ever the subject of attention, as beautiful Jacqueline Kennedy, the President's wife, sought to make it a center of art, music, and literature.

In his public appearances the new President combined idealism with realism and informality with dignity. Above all, he possessed "charisma," the gift of leadership that inspires trust and devotion. Kennedy's charisma was effective not only in this country, especially among the young, but among people all over the world, even behind the Iron Curtain.

Kennedy's Domestic Program

When it came to domestic policy there was not much that was new about the New Frontier. Essentially the Kennedy administration proposed a continuation of Franklin Roosevelt's New Deal and Truman's Fair Deal.

Although the Democrats enjoyed large majorities in both houses of Congress, Kennedy was not able to persuade Congress to turn much of his domestic program into law. Congress was dominated by conservatives. Southern Democrats, most of them elderly, headed ten of sixteen committees in the Senate and twelve out of twenty in the House. In alliance with Republicans, they killed many New Frontier measures, as formerly they had dealt with Truman's Fair Deal program.

Following a pattern set by the Truman administration, Kennedy was generally successful in legislation relating to foreign affairs. The Congress voted funds to support the Peace Corps and the Alliance for Progress (both to be described here shortly). It responded favorably to requests for increased appropriations for defense. In the Trade Expansion Act of 1962 Congress authorized the President to lower tariffs on foreign goods or to eliminate them entirely in return for trade concessions by other nations.

Perhaps the President's most publicized legislative victory was the establishment of a National Aeronautics and Space Administration (NASA), which had the stated goal of "a man on the moon by 1970." There were those who ridiculed the idea of spending an estimated twenty billion dollars for manned space flights. But to Kennedy exploration of space was a great adventure and American prestige was at stake. In 1957, the Russians had gained immense publicity by sending up "Sputnik," the first missile to go around the earth. Sputnik was followed by the first manned flights. The Kennedy space program was the answer to these achievements of the USSR.

The country was generally prosperous during the Kennedy years. Like Eisenhower before him, Kennedy was determined to control inflation and on the whole succeeded. The administration urged labor unions to moderate their demands for higher wages. Prodded by Secretary of Labor Arthur J. Goldberg, the steel in-

dustry signed the first contract with its workers since 1945 that did not contain such a wage increase that higher prices were a foregone conclusion. When in April 1962 several steel companies announced a simultaneous rise in prices, the President revealed one of his rare flashes of anger. Using all the resources of his position, he forced the steel companies to back down and lower their prices.

Kennedy and Civil Rights

During the Kennedy administration black Americans demanded more insistently that they receive the rights that are supposedly the birthright of every American. In the South, "sit-ins" in 1960 were followed by freedom rides in 1961. Blacks, or mixed groups of blacks and whites, challenged segregation, especially in interstate buses and bus stations. The "riders" quietly submitted to violence at the hands of mobs and to jail sentences for "loitering" and "vagrancy" and "inciting to riot."

The Kennedy administration was sympathetic to black aspirations. Kennedy himself had insisted on a strong civil rights plank in the Democratic platform of 1961. But during his first two years in office he disappointed liberal followers and black leaders by moving cautiously in regard to new civil rights laws. His administration did, however, make strong and varied use of executive power. During the years 1961–1963, the Department of Justice brought six times as many suits to protect black voting rights as the Eisenhower administration in 1958–1960. The result was that by the election of 1964 the percentage of black citizens registered in the deep South had risen from 25 to 40 percent. The Interstate Commerce Commission, under pressure from members of the Kennedy administration, forbade segregation on railroads and interstate buses.

In education, the Department of Justice backed suits for desegregation of schools. In

A feature of the early civil rights movement was the use of techniques of non-violent resistance first developed by Mahatma Gandhi in India. The method was first used successfully in the Montgomery, Alabama, bus strike of 1955. Here black civil rights workers chain themselves together in protest against job discrimination.

September 1962, a black Air Force veteran, James Meredith, supported by a court order, sought entrance to the University of Mississippi. When Governor Ross Barnett refused to admit him, Kennedy sent four hundred United States marshals, followed by federal troops. Meredith was admitted, but only after two people had been killed in mob action. After this incident blacks were admitted to other formerly all-white southern colleges and universities.

But progress was slow. In 1963, nine years after *Brown v. Board of Education*, only one half of one percent of black public school children in the eleven former Confederate states had been admitted to desegregated schools. Although many southern communities desegregated public facilities after boycotts and "sit-ins," others not only refused but also used violence to intimidate blacks. In Birmingham, Alabama, police dogs and electric cattle prods were used against black demonstrators. Black homes and churches were bombed. In Birmingham in May 1963 southern blacks fought back for the first time. Abandoning Gandhian techniques, they met violence with violence.

"March on Washington," 1963

In June 1963, President Kennedy finally abandoned his cautious stand on civil rights legislation. In a powerful address over television, he urged Congress to pass laws that would end all aspects of racial discrimination. Lending weight to the President's program was a great "March on Washington" in August. Over 200,000 people, blacks and whites together, converged on the capital. They were led by priests, rabbis, ministers, and civic leaders. Singing hymns and spirituals, they marched toward the Lincoln Memorial in testimony of all humans' rights to be free and equal. The mood was exalted and joyful. As a fifteen-year old black girl described it:

All around, in the faces of everyone, there was this sense of hope for the future—the belief that this march was the *big* step in the right direction. It could be heard in the voices of the people singing and seen in the way they walked. It poured out into smiles.

At the Lincoln Memorial, the marchers heard eloquent addresses, especially one by Martin Luther King, Jr. Then the crowds slipped quietly away. It had been the largest and most peaceful protest in the history of our country.

A NEW TACK IN FOREIGN POLICY

As his inaugural address revealed, foreign policy was Kennedy's principal concern. Few

President Kennedy accompanied by President and Mrs. Lleras of Venezuela leaving a housing project made possible by Alliance for Progress funds.

Presidents have entered the White House better prepared in this area. He had traveled widely and had written two books on foreign affairs. His essential aims did not differ from those of the Truman and Eisenhower administrations. There was no relaxation of efforts to contain Communism, but beyond that Kennedy steered a new tack. There was greater willingness to seek relaxation of tensions if it could be done without sacrificing American interests. There was less insistence that all who are not with us are against us, and therefore greater tolerance of neutralism.

In his inaugural address Kennedy had pledged American help to "those people in the huts and villages across the globe struggling to break the bonds of misery." He was genuinely sympathetic to the concerns of the less devel-oped and recently independent nations. He formed sincere friendships with some African leaders.

The Peace Corps

Kennedy's concern for the problems of less fortunate nations was revealed in a new approach to foreign aid—the Peace Corps. This body was composed of American men and women who volunteered for service to humanity. Its members submitted to rigorous training, lived with the people to whom they were sent, ate the same food, spoke the local language. They laid out sewage systems in Bolivia, trained medical technicians in Chad, and built a model town in Pakistan. A high proportion taught English and practical skills. They received only a living wage and a small vacation allowance. Although volunteers were of all ages—some even in their seventies—most of them were young. They sought opportunities to help others, to be on their own, and to test themselves in difficult situations.

Peace Corps volunteers went only to countries which asked for them. Twelve nations welcomed them in 1961, the first year. Communists attacked Peace Corps members as spies. Some Americans nicknamed the corps "the Children's Crusade" and ridiculed the "starry-eyed do-gooders" who composed it. But the Peace Corps was a success. Selectivity was high; only two of the first seven hundred had to be sent home. A previously skeptical Congress voted increased appropriations. All the original twelve countries requested more volunteers. By 1968, 47 more countries had asked for them.

QUESTION • If you had the chance today, would you join the Peace Corps?

The Bay of Pigs Disaster

During the Eisenhower administration, it had become clear that the Castro government in

Cuba was an ally of Communist Russia. Seeing this Communist bridgehead as a threat to the Western Hemisphere, Eisenhower authorized support of an anti-Castro revolution. The United States Central Intelligence Agency (CIA) enlisted a force of Cuban refugees and trained them in Guatemala. The CIA believed that a landing in Cuba would touch off an uprising against Castro. Kennedy's highest military advisers, the Joint Chiefs of Staff, approved the project. Newly in office, trusting the experts, the President agreed that the project should go forward.

On April 17, 1961, therefore, American planes flown by Cuban exiles bombed Cuban air fields and a force of 1500 men waded ashore at a place called the Bay of Pigs. The prediction that the landing would trigger a revolution was not fulfilled. Instead, nearly the entire force was killed or captured. The appalling failure of this "invasion by proxy" was a heavy blow to the prestige of the new Kennedy administration abroad. Castro was strengthened in power. The Soviet leader, Khrushchev, posed as the defender of Latin America against "the Colossus of the North."

Kennedy took the entire blame for the Bay of Pigs disaster. From then on he distrusted military experts. Curiously, his rating in American public opinion polls went up. "The worse I do, the more popular I get," he observed wryly.

The Alliance for Progress

The Castro movement, known as "Fidelismo," threatened to spread to other countries in Latin America. Promoted by Cuban agents, it often found ready support among the poverty-stricken and discontented. Partly to meet this threat, Kennedy proposed a long-term effort to build up the Latin-American standard of living. In August 1961, an Inter-American Economic and Social Council drew up plans for an "Alliance for Progress" somewhat on the lines of the Marshall Plan. Over a ten-year period the United States proposed to help Latin-American countries help themselves in such projects as better schools, housing and public health, fairer methods of taxation, and the distribution of large landholdings to small farmers. Even though American aid to Latin America quadrupled, the chances of success were by no means certain. Communists regarded the Alliance as a front for American imperialism. Wealthy Latin Americans saw it as a revolutionary force and a threat to their property. In some countries, notably Chile, Colombia, Venezuela, and the Central American republics, the Alliance promoted reforms. In others, opposition from the right, the left, or both sides at once, prevented it from doing much good.

Second Cuban Crisis—"Eyeball to Eyeball"

In the summer of 1962, it became apparent that the Russians were sending military aid to Cuba. They were training and supplying the Cuban army and building a "fishing port" on the coast that could double as a submarine base. But so long as Kennedy was convinced that the military preparations in Cuba were defensive, he made no move.

In mid-October, however, aerial photographs revealed that the Russians were building launching sites in Cuba and equipping them with missiles. These could deliver nuclear weapons to American cities, including Washington, in a matter of minutes. The Joint Chiefs of Staff urged a full-scale invasion of Cuba by the United States. Other advisers urged heavy bombing of the missile sites. The President's brother Robert told him that if he did not act he would deserve to be impeached. Kennedy acted, but with restraint. Keeping his intentions secret until the last moment, he told the nation over TV that he had declared a naval "quarantine" of Cuban waters. This meant that American naval vessels would halt and search all

Khrushchev meets Kennedy at Vienna in June 1961. Although the two leaders treated each other with wary politeness, they could not pierce the Iron Curtain that separated the Communist and capitalist worlds.

ships approaching Cuba. Kennedy also demanded a prompt dismantling of the missile sites. Behind his action was the unspoken threat of nuclear war between the United States and the Soviet Union.

For five agonizing days the world appeared to be on the brink of nuclear disaster. During this period, Kennedy was rewarded for his earlier restraint. The Organization of American States supported his action by a vote of 19-0. The *New York Times* termed this "the clearest show of hemisphere unity since World War II." Finally, Soviet leader Khrushchev backed down, accepted the blockade, and promised to send the missiles back home. Kennedy was careful not to humiliate his opponent. Instead, he praised him for "his statesman-like decision" and "welcome contribution to peace". The two men, it was remarked, had stood eyeball to eyeball, and the other man had blinked first. But the risk had been appalling.

Confrontation and Negotiation

Although holding to the containment policy, Kennedy sought means of relieving the tensions of the Cold War. In his inaugural address he had said, "Let us never negotiate out of fear, but let us never fear to negotiate." In June 1961, he flew to Europe and met Khrushchev in the Austrian capital city, Vienna. The President later reported to the American people that his meeting with the Russian premier was "a very sober two days". The two men treated each other with wary politeness, but could find no area of agreement. Khrushchev may have thought that he could intimidate the young, untried President who had recently been hurt by the Bay of Pigs disaster. The Russian leader handed Kennedy a near-ultimatum on East Germany and Berlin. He insisted that the Western powers recognize the German puppet state and that the four-power occupation of Berlin come to an end. When the President refused, the Communist answer was to build a wall across Berlin, blocking free movement between their section of Berlin and the rest of the city. This weakened the economy of West Berlin, which had drawn much of its labor from the Russian sector. The wall also closed off the flight of refugees from East Germany. Those attempting to escape were ruthlessly shot down by East German police.

In June 1963, Kennedy visited West Berlin. A vast cheering crowd gathered to hear him at the City Hall. The President told them:

Freedom has many difficulties and democracy is not perfect, but we have never had to put up a wall to keep our people in. . . . All free men, wherever they may live, are citizens of Berlin, and therefore, as a free man I take pride in the words, *"Ich bin ein Berliner."* [I am a Berliner.]

Even more alarming than tension over Berlin was the fact that during Kennedy's administration the Russians resumed testing of atomic weapons in the atmosphere. They exploded over forty bombs, one with 3,000 times the power of that which destroyed Hiroshima. Kennedy attempted to persuade the Russians to ban above-ground testing, which polluted the atmosphere of the entire world. Russia would agree to no satisfactory method of inspection. However, the inspection issue became less important as means were found to monitor explosions from outside the USSR. Demands for on-site inspection were abandoned, and in August 1963 the United States, Great Britain, and the USSR signed a test-ban treaty. The agreement prohibited atomic tests in the atmosphere, outer space, and under water. It provided that other nations could join. It did not reduce the power or number of atomic weapons, but in defense of the treaty, Kennedy quoted a Chinese proverb: "A journey of a thousand miles begins with a single step."

Neutralist Laos

The landlocked Indochinese state of Laos had been declared neutral by the Geneva Agreement of 1954. But when Kennedy came into office it was in danger of being overrun by Communist forces. The day before he left the White House, Eisenhower warned his successor, "You might have to go in there and fight." The CIA

Khrushchev had said that atomic war would be so horrible that if it took place, "the living would envy the dead." Although they agreed on little else, he and Kennedy made a beginning on atomic disarmament.

and the Joint Chiefs of Staff advised a strong defense of Laos, even the use of nuclear weapons. But when Kennedy learned that the Russians were willing to compromise on support of a neutralist Laotian government, he accepted. He did not consider Laos vital to the United States, at least not so vital as to risk war.

Deepening Involvement in Vietnam

In 1954, while he was a senator, Kennedy had strongly opposed American involvement in Vietnam, saying:

To pour money, material, and men into the jungles of Indochina would be dangerously futile and self-destructive—I am frankly of the opinion that no amount of military assistance can conquer an enemy which is everywhere, and at the same time nowhere, an enemy which has the sympathy and covert support of the people.

Once in the White House, however, he saw

matters differently. Learning that the Viet Cong (Communist guerrilla forces) were gradually winning control of more territory in South Vietnam, the President gradually raised the number of American military advisers in Vietnam from less than 700 to over 15,000. These forces were not supposed to engage in combat, but only in "support," such as aerial reconnaissance or instruction in military tactics. The line between support and combat, however, was hard to draw.

Meanwhile the government of Ngo Dinh Diem in South Vietnam (see p. 732) became increasingly corrupt, tyrannical, and unpopular. Finally, in November 1963, Diem was assassinated in a coup led by South Vietnamese officers. Henry Cabot Lodge, the American ambassador, and American military leaders had advance knowledge of the plot. More than ever, the United States was running South Vietnam. There is some evidence that Kennedy had decided that the situation in Vietnam was hopeless and had made up his mind to pull American troops out of the country.

TRAGEDY AND A NEW PRESIDENT

Kennedy's years in office came to a sudden and appalling end when he was assassinated while visiting Dallas, Texas, on November 22, 1963. Throughout the world, men and women felt a sickening sense of loss. Never was a death so widely mourned. In Italy, women brought flowers to the gates of the American embassy in Rome. In India, crowds wept on the streets of New Delhi. In Africa, President Sékou Touré of Guinea said, "I have lost my only true friend in the outside world." In America, millions of people were in a state bordering on shock. Something of the sense of this tragic time was caught by a conversation between the newspaper columnist, Mary McCrory, and a member of Kennedy's staff, Daniel Moynihan. In response to Ms. McCrory's remark that "we'll never laugh

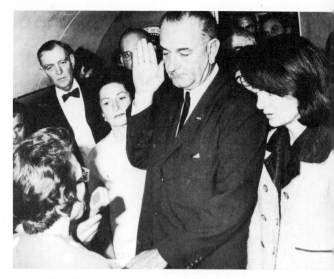

Lyndon B. Johnson took the oath of office a few hours after the assassination of President Kennedy in Dallas. The shock and grief on the faces of those present reflected the feeling of the stunned nation. In this solemn atmosphere, Johnson assumed his heavy duties.

again," Moynihan replied, "Heavens, Mary, we'll laugh again. It's just that we'll never be young again."

It was the feeling of youth snuffed out, of promise unfulfilled that made Kennedy's death peculiarly tragic. We can never know whether he would have achieved greatness. What we do know is that this first President born in the twentieth century brought to the White House an infectious zest for life, a sense of humor, and a sense of mission. He did not have time to achieve his purposes; perhaps he never could have achieved them. But he had the ability to inspire his fellow Americans, especially the young, with a sense that they could make the American dream come true.

The actual circumstances of Kennedy's assassination have been shrouded in mystery. His apparent assassin, Lee Harvey Oswald, was himself killed only two days after Kennedy's death, so we do not know his story. A commission headed by Chief Justice Warren investigated the tragic event and issued a report of over 800 pages, along with 26 volumes of testimony. The Warren Commission concluded that Oswald was the assassin and that he acted alone. But later investigators have found loopholes in the commission's conclusions.

Lyndon B. Johnson, Texan

Kennedy was succeeded in office by Lyndon B. Johnson, who had been Kennedy's rival for the presidential nomination in 1960 and then his running mate. Johnson took the oath of office on the plane that carried Kennedy's body from Dallas to Washington. Beside him stood Jacqueline Kennedy, her dress still spattered with blood.

Johnson had qualities that the public mind associates with Texas, his native state. He was a big man, possessed with immense energy, drive, and ambition. Almost fanatically gregarious, he liked nothing better than to entertain hundreds of people at a barbecue on his 4000-acre cattle ranch.

Although in personality and style Johnson was very different from Kennedy, he shared the same essential purpose: to combine Cold War containment abroad with New Deal liberalism at home. But where Kennedy by preference and training was more interested in foreign affairs, Johnson was the reverse. He had had little experience in dealing with foreign countries, but as majority leader of the Senate he had become skilled in the legislative arts. Indeed, he was regarded as perhaps the most effective legislator since Henry Clay (see pp. 253-254, 318).

Civil Rights Act of 1964

Johnson's first great legislative achievement was a civil rights act along lines that Kennedy had proposed on the eve of his death. Although a southerner, Johnson had become completely dedicated to the cause of equal rights for black citizens.

On July 2, 1964, President Johnson had the satisfaction of signing the strongest civil rights act since Reconstruction. Passed by large majorities in both houses of Congress, it provided that all citizens should have equal access to public facilities such as parks and libraries, and to private businesses serving the public, such as restaurants and theaters. It forbade discrimination in employment or education. It strengthened the right to vote. A few months after the Civil Rights Act of 1964 was passed, the Department of Justice reported general compliance throughout the South. All twelve southern legislators who voted for the law were re-elected in 1964.

The Landslide of 1964

The Democrats inevitably selected Johnson as their candidate in the presidential campaign of 1964. The GOP convention at San Francisco was controlled by members of the right wing of the party. Determined, they said, to give voters "a choice, not an echo," they nominated the highly conservative Senator Barry Goldwater of Arizona. His opposition to civil rights legislation

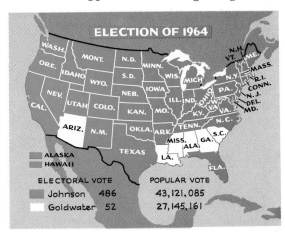

Lyndon Johnson won a landslide victory over Barry Goldwater, his conservative Republican opponent. Paradoxically, the only states Goldwater carried, except his own state, Arizona, were in what was formerly the solidly Democratic South.

One front in the "war on poverty" waged by the Johnson administration was in Appalachia, a vast neglected area where farmers scratched a poor living from worn-out soil.

repelled black voters. His coolness toward social security made older people fearful. His support of the open shop hurt him with organized labor. Above all, Goldwater's talk of winning victory over Communism created fear. This fear was not lessened by the senator's opposition to the nuclear test ban, and his suggestion that military commanders should be allowed to decide for themselves whether or not to use nuclear weapons.

Johnson meanwhile promised a "Great Society" in which no one was poor, every boy and girl had an equal chance for education, and every slum had disappeared. He preached peace on earth and promised not to escalate the war in Vietnam.

Long before election day, polls correctly predicted that Johnson would win by a landslide. He became the second President in modern history to win more than 60 percent of the popular vote. In the electoral college Goldwater carried only Arizona, his own state, and five southern states where former "Dixiecrats" (see p. 713) switched to the Republican Party.

"THE ROAD TO THE GREAT SOCIETY"

In his State of the Union message to Congress in January 1965, Johnson spelled out what he thought was needed to put America "on the road to the Great Society." He sought legislation that would "open opportunity to all our people" and would "improve the quality of American life." In the ensuing ten months Congress passed a series of laws matched in volume and importance only by those enacted during the hectic first months of the New Deal. The legislation was designed to complete much of the unfinished business left over from Johnson's Democratic predecessors, Franklin Roosevelt, Truman, and Kennedy.

"The Other America": Poverty in the Midst of Plenty

Behind the Great Society program was a new awareness that many Americans did not share in the general prosperity. Contributing to this awareness was a short book entitled *The Other America,* by Michael Harrington, published in 1962. It was essentially an answer to

John K. Galbraith's *The Affluent Society* (see p. 727). Harrington agreed with Galbraith that the productive capacity of America was so great that all people should be able to live well. He disagreed, however, with Galbraith's claim that only "pockets" of poverty remained. Instead, he insisted that perhaps forty million Americans, a quarter of the population, were poor. He thought this a disgrace.

Harrington said that the public was unaware of this vast mass of human misery because in various ways the poor were invisible. In the cities, they were concentrated in slums hidden from the eyes of those who lived in prosperous suburbs. In rural areas they were found especially in Appalachia and the deep South, far from the highways traveled by tourists. Many poor were elderly people leading "lives of quiet desperation" in secluded rooms.

According to *The Other America,* much of the poverty afflicting this country was caused by the very technology that created its vast wealth. Automation killed the jobs of many unskilled and semiskilled workers, who were then unable to find steady employment. Small farmers could no longer make a decent living in competition with the big landowners who could afford the latest agricultural machinery.

QUESTION • *Should the federal government help out small farmers so they can stay on the land?*

Harrington insisted that poor people were often trapped in circumstances from which they could not escape. Lyndon Johnson's Great Society program was designed to change such life patterns.

Help for the Poor and Neglected

The Great Society laws extended federal influence into areas previously reserved for local government or private enterprise. It was directed especially toward help for the poor and neglected. Both aspects of the program were displayed by the Elementary and Secondary Education Act of 1965. For the first time, the federal government gave direct, massive aid to public and parochial schools. The money was to be spent in ways that would especially benefit children of low-income families. A parallel act to aid colleges provided scholarships for needy students. Still a third law established a Job Corps to train unskilled workers, especially school dropouts.

Another cluster of laws supplied direct assistance to the poor. A new agency, the Office of Economic Opportunity (OEO), was put in charge of a vast Anti-Poverty Program. It was granted power in some cases to overrule local governments. The purpose was not simply to provide relief, but to help the poor to help themselves. Thus the OEO promoted "Community Action Programs" (CAP) that taught the poor methods of working together for purposes as diverse as establishing nursery schools and cleaning up parks. The CAP also taught people how to organize protests and how to put pressure on landlords, employers, and government agencies.

After nearly twenty years of controversy, Congress finally passed a "Medicare" Act that provided people over sixty-five with hospital and nursing home care. Medical centers were to be established where medical facilities were scarce. Medical schools received funds to increase enrollments and so to avert a shortage of doctors.

Fairer Immigration Policy

For over forty years, the immigration policy of the United States had discriminated in favor of people from northwestern Europe. A system of national quotas was both unjust and ridiculous. Thus, out of a total of 157,000 immigrants admitted per year, Great Britain and Ireland were allotted 83,000. India, with a population of 450,000,000, and Andorra, with 6,400, each had the minimum quota of 100. Truman, Eisenhower, and Kennedy had all assailed the racist aspects of the quota system, but without persuading Congress to make changes. By the Immigration Act of 1965 national quotas were abolished. The law established a "global" quota and favored people with special skills.

"Consensus"

Lyndon Johnson owed some of his success as a legislator to his belief in "consensus." In terms of practical politics consensus meant something for everybody. Businesspeople were pleased when Congress, at Johnson's urging, abandoned excise taxes on hundred of items—furs, jewelry, TV sets, theater tickets. Business gained by the poverty program. Not only did it increase purchasing power, but corporations were hired to run Job Corps centers. Johnson's program included the now almost traditional subsidies to farmers. To aid labor unions, the President urged repeal of Section 14-b of the Taft-Hartley Act that allowed states to pass "right to work" laws outlawing the union shop. The farm bill went through Congress, but the repeal of Section 14-b failed to pass the Senate.

The President had reason to boast that the 89th Congress produced "the greatest outpouring of creative legislation in the history of this nation." But to translate the legislative blueprint for the Great Society into effective legislation required large sums of money. It was therefore necessary to reduce or at least keep in check the even vaster amounts demanded by the Department of Defense. Full-scale domestic reform demanded peace abroad.

Equalizing the Right to Vote

In March 1965, Martin Luther King, Jr. organized a "March of Freedom" from Selma, Alabama, to Montgomery, the state capital, fifty

"I have a dream today . . . " Martin Luther King addressing the great "March on Washington" of 1963. (See p. 743.)

miles away. King's purpose was to dramatize the fact that many blacks were still denied the right to vote in states of the deep South. In Selma, black citizens outnumbered whites, but they composed only three percent of the voters. Over 400 white members of the clergy joined the demonstration. The marchers were harassed by police and by unruly mobs. One white minister was killed. The march was able to reach Montgomery only after President Johnson had sent federal troops and FBI agents to provide protection.

Meanwhile, Johnson appeared before a joint session of Congress to demand that at long last all black citizens should be guaranteed the right to vote. In response to the President's plea, Congress passed the Voting Rights Act of 1965. It empowered the federal government to register voters in any district where less than 50 percent of adults were on the voting lists, or where it appeared that local officials were discriminating against blacks seeking to register as voters. Johnson ordered scores of "examiners" to sign up voters in the deep South. In a single year, they registered over 400,000 people.

The Voting Rights Act of 1965 also aided other minorities. It rendered illegal a New York State law that required voters to be able to read English. Now Puerto Ricans who read only Spanish were allowed to vote. Similarly Spanish-speaking Mexican-Americans in Southwestern states gained the franchise.

In 1964, the Twenty-Fourth Amendment to the Constitution

QUESTION • *What re-strictions, if any, should be placed on the right to vote?*

(see pp. 152-153) abolished payment of a poll tax as a qualification for voting in federal elections. The poll tax requirement had been a means whereby states kept poor people from the polls.

During the 1960's, equal voting rights were also promoted by a notable series of decisions handed down by the Supreme Court, headed by Earl Warren. The Court forbade states to define the boundaries of election districts in such a way as to discriminate against blacks. It forbade states to set up districts with unequal population for electing members of state legislatures and of the United States House of Representatives. Up to this time the number of people in congressional districts had varied greatly. In Michigan, for example, it took six or seven times as many people to elect a representative in Detroit as in country districts. The population of voting districts for state legislatures had varied even more wildly. In California a single state senator represented over six million people in Los Angeles, and another represented only fourteen thousand in a rural district. To remedy these injustices, the Supreme Court applied the so-called "one man, one vote" principle. This meant that voting districts for a legislative body should contain the same number of people. Thus one person's vote is worth as much as another's.

THE BLACK REVOLUTION

The Selma March of Freedom that helped to produce the Voting Rights Act of 1965 was the last great triumph for Martin Luther King, Jr. It was also the last victory for what King stood for: blacks and whites working together in non-violent demonstrations. King's insistence on Christian love and turning the other cheek seemed to many blacks a form of "Uncle Tomism." Although blacks had gained rights that would have seemed surprising ten years earlier, they still had not gained equality. The improvement in economic status of blacks in comparison with that of whites, begun during World War II, had by now practically ceased.

This glacial progress created in blacks a mood of frustration and a new militance. Many felt that black Americans must no longer wait for whites to bestow rights on them but must seize them for themselves. The goal now, as preached by radical leaders such as Stokely Carmichael of SNCC (Students Non-Violent Coordinating Committee), was "black power."

Black power certainly meant political action. Carmichael defined this as "the coming together of black people to elect representatives and *to force these representatives to speak to their needs.*" For the first time since Reconstruction, blacks began to be a force in southern politics. In the 1964 presidential election, black votes supplied Johnson's winning margin over Goldwater in Arkansas, Florida, Texas, and Virginia. Blacks elected increasing numbers of local and state officials in the South. In the North, in 1967, blacks were elected mayors of Cleveland, Ohio, and Gary, Indiana.

Perhaps inevitably, given what blacks had suffered for three centuries, some black leaders preached violence. Much of the assault was verbal—bitter denunciations of "whitey" in black literature, in the black theater, at rallies of blacks. But some blacks deliberately armed themselves and organized for a civil war. It would be a struggle in which they might lose, but they would at least assert their willingness to die rather than to accept inferiority.

The changed black attitude revealed itself in a variety of ways. There was new interest in African culture. This in turn was reflected in "Afro" haircuts and clothes based on African styles. Heroes of black history now included Nat Turner, who led a bloody slave rebellion in 1831 (see p. 284).

Riots in Black Ghettos

In August 1965, the country was shocked by a riot that took place in Watts, a predominantly black section of Los Angeles. For four days, mobs looted, burned, and fought the police. Order was restored only after 12,500 members of the National Guard had been called out.

Those who investigated the Watts riot made the chilling prediction: "So serious and explosive is the situation that . . . the August riots may seem by comparison to be only a curtain raiser to what could blow up one day in the future." So it proved. There was somewhat of a lull in 1966, but in the "long hot summer" of 1967 there were outbreaks in over sixty cities. Those in Newark, New Jersey, and in Detroit, Michigan, were even worse than the Watts outbreak.

Most of the riots took place outside the South, in parts of the country where blacks supposedly enjoyed equal rights. Adam Clayton Powell, Jr., a black member of Congress from New York City, had an explanation for this striking phenomenon. In the South, he said, what blacks wanted was relatively easy for whites to give—the right to sit at a drugstore counter or in the front of a bus. In the North,

blacks had long been able to sit where they pleased. Now they wanted "a bigger piece of the pie"—better jobs, more money, better places to live. White jobholders and property owners felt threatened.

There was, in truth, no easy answer to what caused the riots or how to avert them. They showed that moderate black leadership, such as that which organized the magnificently disciplined March on Washington of 1963, had not reached down to the poor in the ghettos. They showed that mere attainment of paper rights was not enough to erase the blacks' sense of rejection and injustice.

The riots were especially difficult to comprehend or to deal with because once under way, the outbreaks became irrational, almost suicidal. Always more blacks got hurt than whites and more blacks suffered loss of property. Every outbreak tended to harden white prejudice. The latter aspect was the most difficult of all. President Johnson's commission to study the disasters reported:

What white Americans have never fully understood—but what the Negro can never forget—is that white society is deeply implicated in the ghetto. White institutions created it, white institutions maintained it, and white society condones it.

Progress, But —

The brutality of those who attacked "Freedom Riders" and bombed black churches, the polite but hardly less deadly race prejudice of suburban dwellers, the black youths breaking store windows, and the burning cities tended to obscure the fact that immense progress had been made during the "Second Reconstruction." A good many legal disabilities had been erased and humiliating customs abandoned. In the presidential election of 1940, only 100,000 blacks had voted in the entire South. In 1968, as many as that voted for a black candidate for governor of Georgia. In 1940, practically the

BLACK AMERICANS ON THE MOVE

What does the data on this map indicate about possible opportunities for blacks in various regions of the U.S.?

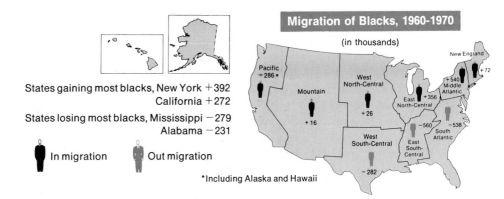

States gaining most blacks, New York +392
California +272
States losing most blacks, Mississippi −279
Alabama −231

In migration   Out migration

Migration of Blacks, 1960-1970
(in thousands)

Pacific +286*
Mountain +16
West North-Central +26
East North-Central +356
West South-Central −282
East South-Central −560
South Atlantic −538
Middle Atlantic +540
New England +72

*Including Alaska and Hawaii

Why at this period did blacks want to leave the South? What were the attractions of other parts of the country?
Why did this outward movement from the South slow down, and in some cases even reverse itself, in the 1970's?

Black Registered Voters in the South and Selected States

	1960 NUMBER	1960 PER CENT OF ALL REGISTERED VOTERS	1970 NUMBER	1970 PER CENT OF ALL REGISTERED VOTERS
South (11 states)	1,463,333	10.7	3,357,000	16.5
Virginia	100,100	10.4	269,000	15.2
South Carolina	58,122	10.8	221,000	24.9
Mississippi	22,000	4.4	286,000	29.3
Texas	226,815	9.8	550,000	13.5

High School Graduates Aged 25-29
(in per cent)

All races*
Blacks

1940: 38.1 / 11.6
1960: 60.7 / 38.6
1970: 75.4 / 56.2

*Including blacks

What federal legislation encouraged the increase in black participation in politics in the South? What were some of the effects?
To what causes do you attribute the rapid advances of blacks in number of years in school?

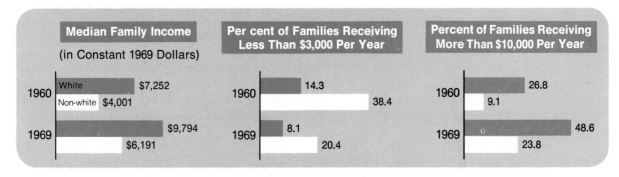

Median Family Income
(in Constant 1969 Dollars)

1960: White $7,252 / Non-white $4,001
1969: $9,794 / $6,191

Per cent of Families Receiving Less Than $3,000 Per Year

1960: 14.3 / 38.4
1969: 8.1 / 20.4

Percent of Families Receiving More Than $10,000 Per Year

1960: 26.8 / 9.1
1969: 48.6 / 23.8

Do these figures show that non-white people are overcoming their economic handicaps relative to whites?
Did the gap between whites and non-whites narrow in the 1970's?

only field where blacks in any numbers achieved eminence was entertainment, even there only to a limited extent. By the late sixties, blacks were stars in professional baseball, basketball, and football. There were black ambassadors, bishops, and judges (one a member of the United States Supreme Court). But large as the gains had been, blacks still had a long way to go before they gained the equality the United States promises to all its people. As the explosions in the cities revealed, patience was wearing thin. In the words of the black writer James Baldwin, "The Negroes in this country may never be able to rise to power, but they are very well placed to precipitate chaos and to ring down the curtain on the American dream."

JOHNSON AND FOREIGN AFFAIRS

In his dealings with foreign countries Johnson retained two of Kennedy's principal advisers —Presidential Assistant McGeorge Bundy and Secretary of State Dean Rusk. Thus the essential policies of the Kennedy administration continued. The fall of Nikita Khrushchev in 1964 produced little change in dealings with Russia. The policy of coexistence and limited cultural exchange continued. In June 1967 the Six Days War in the Middle East saw Israel win an amazing victory over its three hostile neighbors, Egypt, Syria, and Jordan. Although Russia had backed and armed the Arab states and the United States was behind the Israelis, the very suddenness of the Israeli victory averted danger of a major clash. President Johnson had an informal meeting with Soviet Premier Aleksei Kosygin at Glassboro, New Jersey, later in 1967. The men exchanged views, but no cessation of the Cold War seemed possible.

Dominican Intervention, 1965

In the Americas, Johnson continued support for the Alliance for Progress and the Cuban boycott. The President aroused fear in Latin America, however, and controversy in the United States by armed intervention in the Dominican Republic. In April 1965, a rebellion broke out against a rightist government that had seized power in the island country. Fearing that the rebels were controlled by Communists, Johnson ordered 20,000 Marines to the Dominican Republic. This intervention was the first of its kind since 1927.

The Dominican situation revealed difficulties in the policies of the United States toward Latin America in the Cold War period. When a Communist revolution threatened, the United States might prevent it, but not without arousing Latin-American opinion against the "Colossus of the North". If the United States did nothing, another Castro might come to power. Fear of "Fidelismo" also persuaded the United States to support reactionary governments whose oppressive policies drove people to revolt.

Deepening Involvement in Vietnam

In June 1971, the *New York Times*, followed by other newspapers, published hitherto secret intelligence reports entitled *History of the United States Decision-Making Process in Vietnam Policy*. These so-called Pentagon Papers revealed a shocking fact. For two decades the Presidents of the United States, acting in secret and without consulting Congress, had waged war, either directly or by proxy, in Indochina. And under every President—Truman, Eisenhower, Kennedy, Johnson—the situation had deteriorated.

When Johnson entered the White House, Diem had just been assassinated. Within three months there was another palace revolution, followed by a series of "revolving door" governments as one military clique after another gained power in Saigon. The military situation got worse. The United States was faced with three disagreeable choices:

(1) *Admit defeat and pull out.* If the "domino theory" (see p. 731) was true, this meant that the rest of Southeast Asia would soon fall to the Communists.

(2) *Continue support of South Vietnamese regimes in their struggle with the Communist Viet Cong.* These regimes were so unstable and unpopular that this policy meant defeat eventually.

(3) *Actively enter the war and attack North Vietnam.* This would mean not only loss of lives and vast expense, but the possibility of war with Red China.

By the summer of 1964 the Johnson administration began to move cautiously toward the third alternative. In secrecy, the United States began limited bombing of Viet Cong positions and supported commando raids on the North Vietnamese coast. In reprisal for one of the latter, North Vietnamese torpedo boats unsuccessfully attacked two United States destroyers in the Tonkin Gulf (see

QUESTION • *Under what circumstances, if any, should Congress give over its war powers to the President?*

map). President Johnson then went to Congress and asked for authorization to bomb the North. Told that the attacks on the American warships had been unprovoked, Congress responded with the Tonkin Gulf Resolution. Passed in August 1964, it authorized the President to defend any state in Southeast Asia in any way he chose. In effect, Congress handed over its war powers to the President.

"Escalation" of the Vietnam War

Now that Johnson had obtained a blank check from Congress, his military advisers urged him to cash it by bombing North Vietnam. During the presidential election he held off doing so, for he presented himself as the peace candidate against Goldwater, the militant anti-Com-

VIETNAM WAR THEATER

0   Kilometers   300

0   Miles   200

THE WORLD: POLITICAL AND MILITARY ALIGNMENTS — 1968

Militarily allied with the West
Politically allied with the West
Communist bloc:
Soviet sphere of influence
Chinese sphere of influence
Independent communist
Non-aligned countries

munist. Even after the election he continued to hold off. A commentator wrote that the Pentagon Papers revealed "a desperately troubled man resisting the awful pressure to plunge deeper into the Vietnam quagmire—resisting his advisers as instinctively as an old horse resists being led to slaughter. The President backs, whinnies, and shies away, but always in the end the reins tighten—the pressures are too much for him."

Finally, in February 1965, after a Viet Cong attack on an American base, Johnson authorized "escalation" of the war by massive bombing. In April, Johnson made the fateful decision that American ground forces should engage in combat.

The situation of the United States in the Vietnam War was far more difficult than it had been in Korea. The United States fought in Korea as an agent of the United Nations, with widespread support outside the Communist world. Now the United States was intervening in a civil war. Most non-Communist South Vietnamese were indifferent or hostile to the local government, no matter what group happened to be in power. The United States had few allies in the struggle. World opinion was generally hostile to American policy in Vietnam.

The military operations themselves have been described as a "dirty, ruthless, wandering war." There was no battlefront, as in Korea. Instead, the enemy, using hit-and-run tactics, was hard to find. The Viet Cong, employing terrorism against civilians, controlled much of the countryside. The United States, dropping bombs and napalm on areas supposedly controlled by the Viet Cong, killed thousands of non-combatants. Meanwhile, defoliants turned farm lands and forests into deserts.

Johnson's military advisers had grossly underestimated the will and the ability of the Viet Cong to continue fighting. As a result, the United States poured increasing numbers of troops into

Vietnam, reaching a total of over a half million. American casualty lists mounted.

Defense Secretary Robert S. McNamara began to have doubts. In a memorandum to Johnson in May 1967, he wrote:

The picture of the world's greatest superpower killing or seriously injuring 1000 noncombatants a week, while trying to pound a tiny backward nation into submission on an issue whose merits are hotly disputed is not a pretty one. It could conceivably produce a costly distortion in the American national consciousness and in the world image of the United States—especially if the damage to North Vietnam is complete enough to be "successful."

The Vietnam War had damaging results at home. Johnson talked bravely about the ability of the United States to afford "both guns and butter." But increasing military demands took money that might have gone to poor people in such projects as slum clearance, job training, and education. Thus, indirectly, the poor paid for the war.

The Vietnam War produced controversy in the United States between the "hawks" who supported the war and the "doves" who opposed it. Until early in 1968 public opinion polls revealed that the hawks represented the dominant opinion among the American people. Some hawks were militant anti-Communists who seriously believed that if the United States did not crush the Viet Cong, they would soon be fighting them on the beaches of California. More generally, the hawks were those who instinctively supported their country in war and trusted the President of the United States.

The doves included respected journalists such as Walter Lippmann, staid newspapers such as the *New York Times,* and even some military men, such as General James M. Gavin, who had served as Kennedy's ambassador to France. Highly vocal opposition to the Vietnam War at first centered on college campuses, where it often took the form of massive student

Three U.S. Marines carry a wounded fellow soldier from the ruins of Hué, South Vietnam.

demonstrations. A way-out fringe of the doves resorted to illegal or bizarre forms of protest, such as burning draft cards or American flags. As the war dragged on, the feeling between hawks and doves became increasingly bitter— so bitter indeed that it threatened to tear this country apart.

1968—A YEAR OF DISASTER

In January 1968, *Newsweek* magazine remarked that America was "divided and confused as never since the Great Depression." At home it was freely predicted that the summer would bring more racial violence and that more cities would burn. Abroad, the Vietnam War continued.

The year turned out to be worse than anticipated. The first rude shock came in February. General Westmoreland, the American commander in Vietnam, had assured the country that the Viet Cong had all but lost the war. But in February its supposedly exhausted forces attacked scores of South Vietnamese towns during Tet, the Vietnamese New Year. Eventually the attacks were repelled with heavy losses, but

they had revealed that the enemy forces still had the will and ability to fight. Westmoreland asked for 200,000 more American troops.

The Tet offensive of the Viet Cong was a turning point. Public opinion polls now showed that the majority of Americans opposed the war. Johnson had become so distrusted and so unpopular that for fear of hostile crowds he seldom appeared in public. In the New Hampshire presidential primary, Senator Eugene McCarthy, running as a dove, challenged Johnson. McCarthy "shook every corner of the political landscape" by a near victory. Four days later, Senator Robert Kennedy, the late President's brother, threw his hat in the ring. He too had become a dove.

In a TV talk to the country on the last day of March, Johnson stunned the nation by announcing that he would not seek re-election as President. In the same address Johnson announced that he would halt 90 percent of the bombing, and that he would seek to negotiate a peace in Vietnam. In the relief that greeted this news, the stock market made a huge upward jump of 20 points.

The mood of the country soon changed to dismay when on April 4 a sniper's bullet killed Martin Luther King, Jr., in Memphis, Tennessee. A bitterly ironic reaction to the murder of the great preacher of non-violence was a week of rioting, arson, and looting in 125 cities. Washington, D.C., suffered more grieviously than when it was captured by the British in the War of 1812. At one time forty fires were burning in the nation's capital. Over 50,000 troops were needed to suppress the disorders.

Johnson's withdrawal left the race for the Democratic presidential nomination wide open. By early June, Robert Kennedy appeared to be challenging Vice-President Hubert Humphrey. Then another shocking tragedy occurred. Kennedy was assassinated by an Arab nationalist, furious at American support of Israel.

The year 1968 saw student protests in foreign countries as well as in the U.S. Some were violent, while others, such as this demonstration against the Vietnam War, were peaceful.

Robert Kennedy's death removed from American politics a young man who had an extraordinary sympathy for and ability to communicate with those most alienated from American society—the poor, the blacks, many of the young, the Chicanos, and the American Indians.

Late in April, another form of violence had jolted the public. Hundreds of radical students seized buildings of Columbia University in New York City. They were evicted only after an attack by a thousand police armed with nightsticks. The Columbia riot touched off a wave of turmoil in a score or more institutions of higher learning throughout the country. Student violence was not limited to the United States. In the previous year there had been student riots, some of them more serious than any in the United States, in Rio de Janeiro, London, Rome, Madrid, as well as beyond the Iron Curtain in Warsaw and Prague. The same week as the Columbia outbreak, French students battled police in the streets of Paris and were joined by millions of workers in a great general strike.

The world outlook was further darkened by events in Czechoslovakia. There in the spring of 1968 student protests triggered a rebellion. The Czechs overthrew the repressive Stalinist regime that had been imposed on the country in 1948. A new premier restored freedom of speech and press, freer contact with the West, and a measure of democracy. The men of the Kremlin could not tolerate such freedoms. In late August, 200,000 Russian troops with tanks and machineguns overran Czechoslovakia. Unable to resist, the Czechs unhappily submitted.

Meanwhile, prospects for restoring peace in Vietnam grew dim. Diplomats from the United States and North Vietnam met in Paris in May. But they could not agree on a formula for ending hostilities. After a lull, the war continued unabated, and the number of American troops in Vietnam reached a new high.

PRESIDENTIAL ELECTION, 1968

Early in August, the Republican National Convention, meeting in the South for the first time, convened at Miami Beach, Florida.

Richard M. Nixon was nominated on the first ballot. As his running mate, Nixon chose Spiro T. Agnew, governor of Maryland, a political unknown.

The Democratic Convention, meeting in Chicago in late August, was a disaster. TV cameras inside the hall gave millions of viewers the picture of an angry, disunited party. Outside, they showed confrontations between thousands of jeering, blue-jeaned, long-haired anti-war demonstrators and police who freely used nightsticks and tear gas. In the midst of near-chaos, Vice-President Hubert Humphrey easily won the Democratic nomination.

A third candidate was George C. Wallace, who as governor of Alabama had promised "segregation forever." Wallace aspired to be more than a southern candidate, and his name appeared on the ballot in all fifty states. He appealed especially to those who felt threatened by the black revolution and by city violence. He promised to back local police in enforcing "law and order."

At first, the campaign was dull. Nixon, backed by a unified party and a full campaign chest, seemed sure to win. As a member of Johnson's administration, Humphrey felt that he had to support the President's Vietnam policies, an insurmountable handicap. Humphrey gained, however, when he took a stand for peace in Vietnam. A week before the election, President Johnson aided him by announcing that the bombing of North Vietnam had been halted and that a cease-fire would soon follow. The polls, which in September had predicted a Republican landslide, now called the race a toss-up.

The pollsters were right. The vote in the presidential race was so close that it was not until the morning after the voting booths closed that it was certain Nixon had won. Although his margin in the popular vote was slight, he carried the electoral college by 301 votes to Humphrey's 191 and Wallace's 45. In the Congressional races the Democrats easily kept control of both houses.

A PROMISE FOR THE FUTURE

When the Kennedy-Johnson administration came into office in January 1961, it had been a time of youth and optimism, a time when Americans had confidence that they could face and solve their problems, a time when they believed in their mission in the world. Now race riots had turned inner cities into asphalt jungles given over to arson and violence. Heroes of the New Frontier—John F. Kennedy, Martin Luther King, Jr., and Robert Kennedy—had been assassinated. Tens of thousands of young Americans had been killed or maimed in the most unpopular war the United States had ever fought. A casualty of the war had been the New Frontier and Great Society programs designed to make life better for the poor. But there had been dark times in America before. The country looked to the promise of new leadership, as it had in the depths of the Great Depression in 1932, to rescue it from despair.

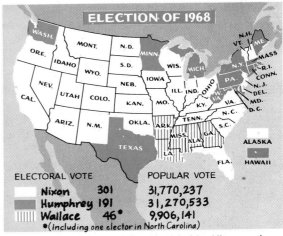

Compare the pattern of states carried by Nixon and Humphrey with the pattern of Kennedy and Nixon states in the 1960 election map on page 740.

Activities: Chapter 32

For Mastery and Review

1. Compare and explain Richard Nixon's defeat in the presidential campaign of 1960 and his victory in 1968.

2. Explain the gap between Kennedy's intentions in the New Frontier program and congressional action in carrying it out.

3. How far were Kennedy's foreign policies a new departure and how far a continuation of earlier policies? Which actions would you praise and which would you condemn? Why?

4. Account for Johnson's landslide victory in 1964.

5. What were the purposes of Johnson's "Great Society" program and what legislation resulted from it?

6. Account for the change in character of the black revolution during the Kennedy-Johnson years. Compare the purposes and the achievements of the Kennedy and Johnson administrations in promoting civil rights.

7. What steps did Johnson take to escalate the war in Vietnam and what were the results for America?

Unrolling the Map

1. Compare the maps of three landslide elections—Johnson over Goldwater, 1964 (p. 749); Roosevelt over Hoover, 1932 (p. 608); Harding over Cox, 1920 (p. 575). Briefly explain why in each case the landslide occurred, and note the geographical base of the winning and the defeated candidates.

2. Compare the map of Nixon's victory in 1968 (p. 763) with that of Wilson's equally narrow victory in 1917 (p. 554). How do you account for the remarkable turn-around of the geographical bases of Democratic and Republican strength?

Who, What, and Why Important?

election of 1960
"New Froniter"
"Sputnik"
NASA
"freedom riders"

OEO
Medicare
Immigration Act, 1965
"consensus"
Voting Rights Act, 1965

James Meredith
March on Washington
Peace Corps
Bay of Pigs
Alliance for Progress
Cuban missile crisis, 1962
Berlin Wall
test-ban treaty
Laos
Ngo Dinh Diem
Lee Harvey Oswald
Civil Rights Act, 1964
election of 1964
Barry Goldwater
"Great Society"
Michael Harrington
Elementary and Secondary Education Act, 1965

Twenty-fourth Amendment
"one man, one vote"
Watts
"black power"
Dominican Intervention, 1965
Pentagon Papers
Tonkin Gulf Resolution
escalation
"Hawks" and "Doves"
Tet offensive
Eugene McCarthy
Robert F. Kennedy
Martin Luther King, Jr.
election of 1968
Hubert H. Humphrey
George C. Wallace

To Pursue the Matter

1. In 1960, Richard M. Nixon lost and in 1968 won, both times by the narrowest of margins. What turned him from a loser into a winner? See the two volumes by T. H. White, *The Making of a President, 1960,* and *1968.*

2. What would have happened, do you think, if John Kennedy had lived? Would he have been reelected? Would he have seen his New Frontiers program enacted into legislation? Would he have kept the United States out of the Vietnam quagmire?

3. President Kennedy and his wife Jacqueline forged a new relationship between the White House and the arts that sent people back to Thomas Jefferson for parallels. See "The Arts and Thomas Jefferson," in Peterson (ed.) *Thomas Jefferson: A Profile;* chapter 15 of Sorenson, *Kennedy;* and chapter 27, parts 3-5, of Schlesinger *A Thousand Days.*

4. What was the impact of the war on Vietnamese society? What was it in their country's past that gave the Vietnamese extraordinary will to resist? See Fitzgerald, *Fire in the Lake.*

5. Find and play to the class a record of Martin Luther King, Jr.'s address at the Lincoln Memorial at the climax of the 1964 March on Washington, entitled "I have a dream today."

Chapter 33

An Imperial Presidency

Power always corrupts, and absolute power corrupts absolutely.
—LORD ACTON

Richard M. Nixon was the first President in modern times to be elected after having lost on a previous try, in 1960. During the 1968 election campaign he had changed his public image. The "old Nixon" had been intensely partisan, willing to use ruthless tactics on occasion. When he ran for Congress from California in 1946 as a newly discharged naval officer, he was merciless against his opponent, suggesting that he was tied to the Communists. He employed similar tactics when he ran for Senate in 1950. As a member of Congress, he had been one of the most vocal anti-Communists in the House. Political opponents called him opportunistic and self-serving. When he lost the election for governor of California in 1962, his political career seemed to be at an end. He held the press responsible for his defeat. He told reporters that they would not have Richard Nixon "to kick around any more!"

But Nixon made a remarkable comeback. During the years out of office in the 1960's he read widely, especially in foreign affairs. He traveled abroad to acquaint himself with foreign countries and their leaders. He kept in touch with rank-and-file Republicans all over the country.

A "new Nixon" had apparently emerged. He now impressed competent observers as calm, broad-minded, statesman-like. He promised that his administration would be "open to new ideas, open to men and women of both parties, open to the critics as well as those who support us."

"We want to bring America together," he said.

James Michener, the author, a Democrat not disposed to admire Nixon, described a meeting with the President as follows:

In one meeting with President Nixon topics came up that he could not have possibly anticipated, and he proved himself amazingly well informed and completely accurate even in small details. He was crisp, quick, well organized and able to absorb jokes at his own expense. That he was warm I would not claim, but that he was attentive to his job and schooled in its ramifications no one could deny.

A NEW STYLE IN FOREIGN AFFAIRS: SECRECY, SURPRISE, SUMMITRY

Like Woodrow Wilson before him, Richard Nixon took almost sole charge of foreign affairs. And as Wilson had used Edward M. House as a personal adviser in foreign affairs, so Nixon employed Henry A. Kissinger, a brilliant Harvard political scientist. He acted first as a member of the National Security Council, later as Secretary of State. Stationed in a basement office in the White House, Kissinger constantly examined the international situation. His job was to present the President with "options"—choices of policy and possible consequences. He also went on missions abroad, often unknown to the public. Nixon and Kissinger between them developed a unique style in foreign affairs, characterized by summitry, surprise, and secrecy.

Détente with Russia and China

Nixon, like Wilson, aimed to be a peacemaker. In his Inaugural Address he proclaimed, "After a period of confrontation, we are entering into a period of negotiation. Let all nations know that during this administration our lines of communication will be open."

As one means of communication Nixon made elaborately staged visits to leaders of foreign countries. Within a month of his inauguration, he visited heads of state in western Europe. In the summer of 1969 he traveled around the world, visiting six Asian countries, and—here was a surprise—Rumania. This was the first time an American President had gone behind the Iron Curtain. In Rumania, Nixon declared, "We seek normal relations with all countries, regardless of their domestic policies."

Heretofore Nixon had been regarded as almost a professional anti-Communist. He had seen the world as a battleground, with the Communist bloc of nations arrayed against the Free World. Now in regard to the Communist powers he pursued a policy of relaxation of tensions known as "détente." He held that it would be "a safer world and a better world if we have a strong, healthy United States, Europe, China, Russia, and Japan, each balancing the other." This was a return on a global scale to the balance of power concept that dominated European diplomacy during the eighteenth and nineteenth centuries. It was a rejection of the idea that peace could best be kept by an international organization such as the UN.

QUESTION • *According to the balance of power theory, with which nations should the U.S. ally itself in Asia? in Europe?*

Since diplomatic channels to Russia were open, it was not difficult to begin negotiation with that country. Nixon initiated talks with the Soviet Union about the possibility of ending the Arab-Israeli conflict. He sent Americans to meet Russians at Helsinki, Finland, in the so-called Strategic Arms Limitation Talks (SALT), designed to halt the atomic arms race. He reached an agreement with the USSR to ban biological warfare.

Before entering office, Nixon had written in a magazine article, "We cannot afford to leave China forever outside the family of nations." Once in power, he sent "signals" to the People's Republic of China to suggest that the United States might be willing to end its boycott of the Chinese Communists. Prohibitions that prevented Americans from trading with or traveling in China were lifted. The President withdrew the Seventh Fleet from the defense of Taiwan.

For a time China sent no answering signal. Chinese newspapers continued to denounce the United States. Gaudy posters portrayed Uncle Sam as a "foreign devil," a "capitalist-imperialist aggressor" against the peace-loving Chinese people. But in April 1971 the barriers dropped slightly, and in a curious fashion. An American ping-pong team traveling in Japan received and accepted an invitation to visit China. There the players were treated with great courtesy.

As a response to "ping-pong diplomacy" Nixon made the sensational announcement in July 1971 that he would visit Peking. Later that same year the People's Republic of China was admitted to the UN. At the same time, the Nationalist Chinese regime on Taiwan was expelled from the organization. The United States protested these moves, but did not exercise its veto power to prevent them.

The Peking and Moscow Summits

In February 1972 President Nixon's plane, "Air Force One," flew him to China. Americans glued their eyes to TV screens to watch Mr. and Mrs. Nixon using chopsticks at formal dinners, attending the opera, visiting the Great Wall,

President Nixon and Secretary of State William Rogers chat with Chinese Premier Chou En-lai during Nixon's dramatic visit to China in May 1972.

and toasting their hosts in rice wine.

Meanwhile the President and his aides talked behind closed doors with Chinese leaders. Both countries agreed to seek "more normal" relations. But major political difficulties remained, including the Vietnam War and the status of the Nationalist Chinese regime on Taiwan. Still, the Peking summit meetings cleared the air. It was a great diplomatic coup for Kissinger and Nixon, a step toward world peace.

A Moscow summit followed in May 1972. The Moscow summit produced more tangible results than that at Peking. The United States and Russia brought the first round of SALT talks to an end with a treaty that at least slowed down the arms race. There were also agreements to increase trade, to exchange scientific information, and to cooperate in battling pollution.

Although détente with China and Russia had notably advanced world peace, the Nixon-Kissinger foreign policies did not escape criticism. The emphasis on secrecy and surprise sometimes meant failure to consult allies. Notably Nixon failed to consult with Japanese statesmen prior to reversal of American policy toward China. The President was also censured for sacrificing the friendship of India by support of Pakistan in a war between India and Pakistan in 1971. Nixon was condemned above all for his failure to extricate the United States from Vietnam.

War in Southeast Asia: "Credibility," "Vietnamization"

During the 1968 presidential campaign, Nixon, without revealing how, had declared that he planned to end American participation in the Vietnam War. Had he not made such a declaration, he probably would not have been elected. Once in office, he resumed the peace negotiations with the North Vietnamese in Paris, but without success.

The President was faced with a most difficult decision. Would he continue American participation in the Vietnam War against mounting public opposition? Or would he get out and admit defeat? He could not bring himself to take the latter course. If the United States failed to display willingness to use force, our allies would not trust us. Our enemies might be tempted to test our will to repel aggression. The containment policy would be in danger.

In order to maintain credibility, the United States not only continued to fight but extended the war. In March 1969, the President ordered bombing of Communist positions inside Cambodia —this was done in such secrecy that even the Secretary of the Air Force did not know of it. In April 1970, Nixon, without prior consultation with Congress, ordered a joint American and South Vietnamese invasion of Cambodia to attack Communist "sanctuaries" in that country. Although the President asserted that this move

QUESTION • Is there ever a justification for a secret military operation? If so, when?

THE VIETNAM WAR

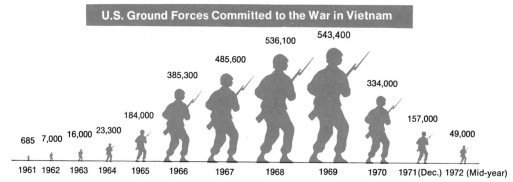

How do the charts above and below (right) reflect the results of Johnson's policies in Vietnam?—of Nixon's policies in Vietnam?

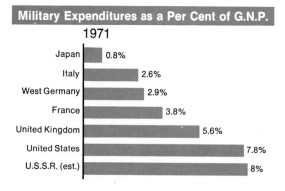

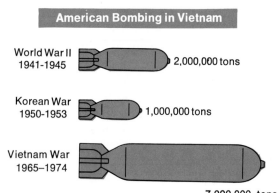

Which country was spending more on armaments in 1971—the U.S. or the USSR? Did the close of the Vietnam War bring reduced American military expenditures? How to account for Japan's extremely low military expenditures?

would shorten the war, many Americans felt that he was, on the contrary, expanding the conflict.

At the same time he extended the American war effort into Cambodia, the President was withdrawing American troops from Vietnam. To replace the American forces that were brought home, the United States pursued the policy of "Vietnamization," whereby the Americans armed and trained the Army of the Republic of Vietnam (ARVN). Nevertheless, American desire to see a quick end to the war was not stilled. Massive demonstrations for peace took place in October and November, 1969 (see pp. 779–780).

To make up for the troops that had been sent back home, the Americans resorted to heavy bombing of Communist areas. By 1972 the tonnage of bombs dropped during the Nixon administration was greater than that during Lyndon Johnson's presidency. Indeed, by the end of the war, the total tonnage of bombs dropped by the Americans on Vietnam was more than twice that dropped by Americans on all targets in World War II and the Korean War combined (see graph on opposite page).

Finally, in January 1973, the United States and North Vietnam agreed on a ceasefire. American troops entirely withdrew from South Vietnam. They left a continuing civil war behind them.

DOMESTIC AFFAIRS UNDER NIXON

The Nixon administration was not a time of major domestic legislation. There was an inevitable deadlock between a Republican President and a Democratic Congress. Nixon's major interest was in foreign affairs. The President's purposes were sometimes confused and contradictory. For instance, he proposed a radical and expensive system of direct money grants to the poor. When it was not enacted, however, he cut down funds for existing programs of aid to education, housing, job training, and welfare assistance. The President expressed sympathy for the economic handicaps of blacks and talked about promoting "black capitalism," but made no specific proposals. He spoke strongly in favor of cutting federal spending in order to balance the budget, and at the same time urged greater military appropriations.

One of Nixon's favorite ideas was what he called "the new federalism." By this he meant that government should be decentralized, with greater responsibilities assumed by states and municipalities. In a message to Congress he declared:

> I reject the patronizing idea that government in Washington, D.C., is inevitably more wise and more efficient than government at the local or state level. . . . The idea that a bureaucratic elite in Washington knows what is best for people . . . is really a contention that people cannot govern themselves.

Following the President's lead, Congress passed a series of revenue-sharing bills that granted federal funds to local agencies to use as they saw fit.

In line with his "law and order" promises, the President secured additional funds for crime control. Largely on his initiative, Congress passed legislation designed to combat crime in the District of Columbia. The anti-crime bill included controversial provisions that reduced traditional protection of those in the hands of the law. Habitual criminals, for instance, might be held in "preventive detention" without right to bail, and in some circumstances police might make searches without a warrant.

The Changing Supreme Court

Nixon's most severe rebuff from Congress was in relation to the Supreme Court. During the 1968 campaign he had attacked the record of the Warren Court for its "permissive" attitude toward the rights of those suspected of crime (see p. 722). He deplored Supreme Court decisions that curtailed the powers of the police in interrogating suspects, that gave alleged criminals the right to counsel almost from the moment of arrest, and that forbade the use of electronic "bugging" equipment in gathering evidence. Such decisions, Nixon maintained, violated "the first civil right of every American, to be free of domestic violence." He promised to fill vacancies on the Supreme Court with "strict constructionist" judges who would not "weaken the peace forces as against the criminal forces."

Earl Warren resigned as Chief Justice shortly after Nixon took office. In his place the President nominated Warren Burger, a highly respected conservative judge. When vacancies again appeared, the Senate successively defeated the nomination to the Supreme Court of two southern lower court judges, Clement Haynsworth and C. Harrold Carswell. Opponents of these men charged that they lacked the stature needed for the highest court in the land. Despite the rejection of these two nominees, Nixon lost the battle only to win the campaign. He was eventually able to fill four vacancies with conservative judges, one from the South. The Burger Court, also known as the "Nixon Court," did not abolish the protections of criminal suspects set up by the Warren Court. It did, however, whittle them down. Its harder line against criminals was dramatically revealed when it reversed the opinion of the Warren Court that capital punishment was a violation of the Bill of Rights.

The "Southern Strategy"

Nixon's effort to put a southern judge on the Supreme Court was just one move in the so-called "Southern Strategy." This was an effort on his part to woo the South, especially the millions of voters in the region who had voted for George Wallace in 1968.

The most publicized aspect of the southern strategy lay in the realm of school desegregation. In the latter years of the Johnson administration the Department of Health, Education, and Welfare (HEW) cut off federal funds from school systems that deliberately kept white and black students apart. Its efforts were reenforced by a Supreme Court decision, *Green v. County School Board*, in 1968. In this case a unanimous court declared that school boards must immediately eliminate racial discrimination "root and branch." Flying in the face of this decision, the Nixon administration attempted a slow-down in efforts to integrate black and white students. The Justice Department took the side of school boards attempting to preserve racial separation. HEW was less strict in demanding desegregation as a condition of receiving federal subsidies.

The Nixon administration and the Supreme Court—now headed by the President's own appointee, Chief Justice Burger—were now on a collision course. The Court refused to change its stand in favor of immediate integration. Furthermore, it insisted that often the only way to achieve integration was by busing. This might mean transporting black children from inner city neighborhoods to formerly all-white schools and white children from their neighborhoods to formerly all-black schools.

Busing children away from the traditional neighborhoods would have met with opposition in any case, but now it aroused racial prejudices and fears. Thus busing became an intensely controversial issue and one that soon extended far beyond the South.

"Nixonomics"

The Nixon administration inherited a difficult economic situation. The combined cost of Lyndon Johnson's war on poverty and the Vietnam War had caused a greatly unbalanced federal budget and mounting inflation. In the years from 1964 to 1969 the dollar lost a fifth of its purchasing power.

THE U.S. ECONOMY—
PROBLEMS OF AN AFFLUENT SOCIETY

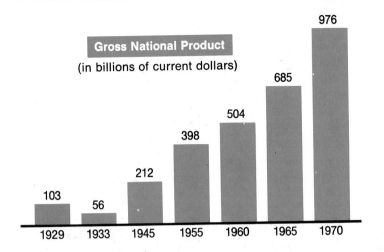

Gross National Product
(in billions of current dollars)

1929	1933	1945	1955	1960	1965	1970
103	56	212	398	504	685	976

Estimated Per Capita Income in Selected Countries c. 1970

(in U.S. dollars)

U.S.	3,910
Sweden	3,553
Canada	3,092
France	2,783
Argentina	871
Mexico	600
Egypt	102
India	72

Has personal income in the U.S. increased more rapidly than population?
How is the impact of the depression shown in the graph at the left?
What problems of the U.S. economy are suggested by the graphs below?

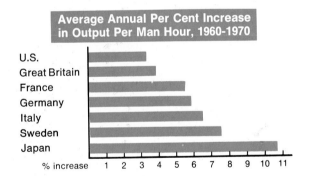

Average Annual Per Cent Increase in Output Per Man Hour, 1960-1970

U.S.
Great Britain
France
Germany
Italy
Sweden
Japan

% increase 1 2 3 4 5 6 7 8 9 10 11

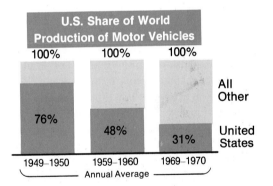

U.S. Share of World Production of Motor Vehicles

1949–1950	1959–1960	1969–1970
100%	100%	100%
76%	48%	31%

All Other

United States

Annual Average

Consider together the graph of increase in worker output of Sweden and France with the figures at top right of per capita income.

Is the gap between the U.S. per capita income and that of other industrialized nations closing or widening?

Is the gap between the U.S. and poor nations such as India closing or widening?

How to account for the relative decline in U.S. production of motor vehicles?

Do the inflation figures at the right weaken or strengthen the impact of the graph of increasing GNP at top left?

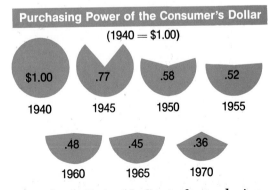

Purchasing Power of the Consumer's Dollar
(1940 = $1.00)

1940	1945	1950	1955
$1.00	.77	.58	.52

1960	1965	1970
.48	.45	.36

How does inflation (decline in the purchasing power of the dollar) affect different groups?

On entering the White House, Nixon—who often used the vocabulary of football—announced an economic "game plan." It had two major features: reducing expenditures and curtailing the supply of money. By the end of 1970 it was apparent that the game plan (nicknamed "Nixonomics" by a columnist) had failed. Drying up the money supply drove up interest rates, and higher interest rates in turn discouraged investment in new enterprises. Unemployment mounted. The stock market declined. The slowdown in business reduced federal revenues. Prices and wages continued to spiral upward.

In 1971 there developed a dangerous situation in American economic relations with other countries. For a number of years the United States had been running a deficit in payments with the rest of the world. It had been sending abroad many billions of dollars in tourist expenditures, in business investments, in military costs for the defense of Western Europe. Heretofore these outgoing dollars had been almost matched by income because the United States exported more goods than it imported. In 1971, however, for the first time in nearly a century, Americans bought more than they sold. The balance of payments deficit jumped from four billion dollars in 1970 to twenty-two billion in 1971.

The deficit revealed that the United States was no longer dominant in world markets. Between 1950 and 1970, for example, the American share of world automobile production dropped from 76 to 31 percent. Hundreds of thousands of German Volkswagens, Japanese Toyotas, Swedish Volvos undersold American cars in the American market every year. The same phenomenon could be seen in textiles, shoes, and electrical equipment.

The most serious effect of the payments was that it weakened faith in the value of the dollar. Since world trade depends on stable money and since the dollar was the major currency of the world, the dollar crisis threatened to disrupt international commerce. Another worldwide depression threatened.

Thus President Nixon was confronted with a domestic recession, erosion of the world economic position of the United States, and a dollar crisis, all at the same time. Suddenly and unexpectedly he acted. On August 15, 1971, he announced a 90-day freeze on prices and wages. To discourage imports, he placed a 10 percent additional duty on all goods from abroad. He allowed the dollar to decline in value in relation to foreign currencies. This made it more difficult to buy abroad and therefore cut down imports. It also made American goods cheaper in relation to foreign currencies and encouraged exports.

These measures brought at least temporary relief, although they caused ill feeling in countries that depended on the American market, such as Japan. The basic difficulties remained, however, and during the Nixon years the country continued to be plagued by mounting prices and chronic unemployment.

"SPACE-SHIP EARTH": ECOLOGY

The grim year 1968 ended with a bright and glorious event. At Christmas time three astronauts in the space ship *Apollo 8* voyaged round the moon and made a safe return with a phenomenally accurate splashdown in the Pacific Ocean. The space program reached a climax on July 20, 1969, when, as the whole world watched the event on television, two American astronauts became the first human beings to set foot on the moon. By 1971 astronauts from *Apollo 15* were cruising the lunar surface in an electric car.

There was worldwide admiration for such triumphs of human intelligence and cooperation. There were also sober second thoughts.

QUESTION • Was the U.S. wise to have spent billions on the space program? If not, how should the money have been used? If so, why so?

The flights created awareness that all human beings are astronauts on "Spaceship Earth," endowed with limited resources and dependent on each other. The poet Archibald MacLeish remarked of the astronauts' view of the earth from afar:

To see the earth as it truly is, small and blue and beautiful in that eternal silence where it floats, is to see ourselves as riders on the earth together, brothers in that bright loveliness and eternal cold—brothers who know they are truly brothers.

"The Quiet Crisis"

There were people who deplored the billions of dollars and thousands of top-flight minds employed in sending men into space. All this effort might have been devoted to what Stuart Udall, Kennedy's Secretary of the Interior, called "the quiet crisis." Americans fouled their environment with sewage, junkyards, dumps, and strip mines, while phosphates and detergents, along with industrial wastes, contaminated their water. Udall urged that modern Americans learn something of "the land wisdom of the Indians," who regarded their hunting grounds as a sacred trust to be transmitted unspoiled to their descendants.

Most former pollution—sewage, garbage, paper, and iron junk—was biodegradable. That is,

Rachel Carson, Quiet Crusader

Rachel Carson did not appear to be a crusader. A quiet, shy, scholarly person, she worked as an obscure biologist in a federal agency. But in 1951, *The Sea Around Us,* a fascinating book about life in the oceans, brought her fame. A later work, *The Edge of the Sea,* was almost as successful.

A quality that shines from Rachel Carson's writings is reverence for all forms of life—from sea urchins clinging to rocks on the coast of Maine to the cats that kept her company in the lonely business of writing. With other scientists, she became increasingly aware that many kinds of life were threatened by new pesticides, especially chlorinated hydrocarbons such as DDT. Even in minute amounts these poisons kill not merely insects but also beneficent bacteria, algae, and earthworms. Indestructible, they remain in the soil and have cumulative effects. They have threatened several species of birds with destruction, including the American Eagle.

Rachel Carson felt a sense of outrage. It was urgent to give warning. For five years she worked on a book to tell the public of the new danger. It was a heroic task. She was suffering from illness that would soon end her life. She knew she would be publicly attacked.

Silent Spring appeared in 1962. Powerful interests damned it. *Time* magazine branded it as "unfair, one-sided, and hysterically over-emphatic." But the book was widely read. Within a year it was translated into fifteen languages.

Rachel Carson died in 1964, but her influence lived on. She had made "ecology" a household word. She had promoted a new awareness that "man is part of nature and his war against nature is inevitably a war against himself."

As the garbage dump above suggests, a special problem today is that many containers do not rust or decay. To the right: a stream of industrial waste pollutes the headwaters of the Hudson River.

it could be broken down by bacterial action or oxidation and absorbed back into the chain of life. But an alarming fact about new forms of pollution—cellophane, plastic containers, aluminum cans, and lethal hydrocarbons such as DDT—is that they are absorbed with difficulty, if at all. The messes they cause get worse and worse. Furthermore, DDT is a slow poison that is passed on from one organism to another, as Rachel Carson made clear in *Silent Spring* (see previous page). Nor are there barriers to pollution. DDT is now found even in penguins in remote Antarctica.

There is increasing awareness that human beings, especially affluent human beings like the Americans, threaten to make the earth unlivable. Ecology, a formerly rare scientific term, became a household word in the 1960's. It is the science of the mutual relationship between organisms and their environment. Ecological awareness in turn began to create a new set of values. These values cast doubt on hitherto un-

examined American assumptions such as that technological progress is automatically good, or that economic growth ("two cars in every garage") should be the major goal of the economy.

Environmental Action

Concern about the environment led to a variety of governmental actions. In 1970 Congress passed a Clean Air Act to compel automobile manufacturers to make cars that would emit less poisonous exhaust. In order to make ecology a continuing concern of the federal government, Nixon created an Environmental Protection Agency (EPA). William D. Ruckelshaus, head of EPA, ordered a ban on nearly all domestic uses of DDT, in spite of opposition from powerful agricultural interests. Rachel Carson had won a posthumous victory.

In 1971 the United States Senate had to decide whether or not to continue construction of a Supersonic Air Transport (SST). Strongly in favor of the huge high altitude plane were the airplane industry, the Department of Defense, the CIO-AFL, and the Nixon administration. Opponents of SST objected to its noise and to the danger that it would deplete the ozone in the high atmosphere. Such depletion threatened an increase in skin cancer and even a change in the world's climate. After a dramatic and prolonged debate the Senate decided by a vote of 51 to 46 to discontinue the SST. It was a notable victory for the environmentalists.

"Consumerism"; Ralph Nader

In 1971 a new word entered the dictionary—"consumerism." It means organized political action on behalf of the buying public. The movement is sometimes called "Naderism" after Ralph Nader, who became a folk hero almost overnight in 1966. He had written a book, *Unsafe at Any Speed*, which detailed the failure of automobile manufacturers to design cars for safety. Nader so aroused public feeling that Congress promptly passed a Motor Vehicle Safety Act with a federal commission to enforce its provisions.

Nader was a young lawyer possessed of incredible energy, dedication, and capacity for sustained indignation. He resembled the muckrakers of the early 1900's (see pp. 529–530) in his ability to ferret out facts, his willingness to name names, and his sensationalism.

Drawing by F.B. Modell; © 1966 The New Yorker Magazine, Inc.

"I happen to know Ralph Nader's mother drives this model."

In response to the consumerism pressure, Congress passed several laws to protect the public. They included stricter federal inspection of meat and the prohibition of too frequent use of x-rays. Permanent agencies were established, such as a Bureau of Consumer Protection under the Federal Trade Commission.

The Oil Crisis, 1973–1974

In October 1973, nine Arab oil-producing states suddenly imposed an embargo on shipments of crude oil to the United States. Their purpose was to force this country to cease favoring Israel in the chronic Arab-Israeli hostilities. The action produced a crisis and near-panic in this country. Prices of petroleum products shot up. There were shortages of gasoline for cars and oil for heating homes, schools, offices, and factories.

The oil crisis was met by various stopgap measures. A 55-mile-an-hour speed limit was imposed on highways. Oil and gasoline supplies to wholesalers were curtailed 10 to 20 percent. But there was no rationing, and Americans were not compelled to give up their wasteful habits.

The oil crisis made the public suddenly aware that world supplies of petroleum were running out. Unless a new source of cheap energy could be found, the automobile era was approaching its end. It was a time for serious long-range planning but little was done. The Arab states called off the boycott in March 1974.

The oil issue had another serious effect. By forcing a sharp increase in the price of petroleum products, the oil shortage added to the already high cost of living and fueled the fires of worldwide inflation.

DEMANDS FOR EQUALITY

During the years of the Johnson and Nixon presidencies, social movements that had been

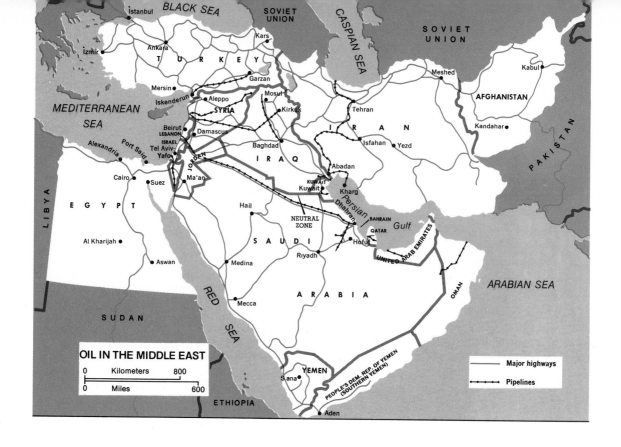

OIL IN THE MIDDLE EAST

| 0 | Kilometers | 800 |
| 0 | Miles | 600 |

——— Major highways

•—•—•—• Pipelines

at work since the end of World War II continued at an accelerated pace to reshape the American social landscape. The Black Revolution had the effect of making other minority groups in the country more aware of inferior status and more determined to demand equality. Other groups could—and did—effectively employ the techniques of protest developed by black leaders—sit-ins, marches, political organization, lobbying, threatened and actual violence.

Chicanos

Next to blacks, the largest minority group in the country are the Hispanos, or Spanish-speaking people. They number over 11,000,000. New York City contains perhaps 2,000,000 Hispanos, mostly from Puerto Rico. Part of Miami, Florida, is a "Little Havana," inhabited by hundreds of thousands of Cuban immigrants.

The largest group of Hispanos are the Mexican-Americans or Chicanos, who are mostly to be found in the southwestern states. Some Chicanos are descendants of people who settled in the region in the seventeenth and eighteenth centuries. Many more came in the twentieth century. The latter include an unknown number of "wetbacks," who entered the United States illegally. Although the Chicanos have faced less legal discrimination than black Americans, they have nevertheless suffered from prejudice. A report on the status of Chicanos in Texas in 1959 observed:

Social discrimination manifests itself in a variety of ways: refusing service in barbershops, soda fountains, cafés, drive-ins, beauty parlors, hotels, bars, and recreation centers; segregation in housing, movies, schools, churches, and cemeteries . . ., reluctant service in hospitals, social welfare offices, and courts; and even refusing to permit Mexican-American hostesses in USO's. Sometimes there are signs, "No Mexicans allowed," "Mexicans will be served in kitchen only."

A high proportion of Mexican-Americans have worked as seasonal farm workers. As such they were unprotected by federal minimum wage laws, unemployment insurance, or social security. The education of migrant children was often scanty and was frequently interrupted. Chicano children living in settled communities and able to go to school were handicapped. They were often taught in English, a foreign language to the children, by teachers who knew no Spanish.

Recently matters have changed for the better. Chicanos have found job opportunities in many parts of the country. They have organized to promote their interests. Similar to the blacks' National Association for the Advance-

Cesar Estrada Chavez, Gandhian Chicano

Cesar Estrada Chavez was born in 1927. When he was ten years old, he started working in the field with his parents. They earned a precarious living as laborers, following the crops from southern Arizona to northern California. Cesar received so little schooling that at the age of twenty-one he could barely read. Powerfully built, of medium height, his coal-black hair and brown skin reveal Indian ancestors.

From young manhood Chavez was determined to improve the lives of his fellow Chicanos. In 1965 he embarked on what seemed to be a hopeless cause: the creation of an effective labor union among seasonal workers. As head of the AFL-CIO United Farm Workers Organizing Committee, Chavez was master of customary trade union tactics—picketing, strikes, and boycotts. He was also a devoted follower of Mahatma Gandhi and Martin Luther King, Jr. He preached and practiced what he called "militant nonviolence." Like Gandhi he led a life of extreme austerity. He lived on as little as $5.00 a week. When members of his union engaged in violence, Chavez—like the Hindu leader in similar circumstances—fasted for twenty-three days. Like Gandhi and King, Chavez is profoundly religious. A devout Catholic, he attends mass daily.

Chavez had displayed remarkable ability to work with others. He insists that he works on behalf of all laborers, not merely Chicanos. He threatened to quit his union if it discriminated against Filipinos. He organized an unlikely nationwide coalition of labor union members, housewives, college students, Protestant ministers, and Catholic bishops to boycott California grapes picked by non-union labor. The boycott was so effective that it cut grape sales in New York City by a third. Finally, after five years of agitation, most California grape growers gave in and signed a contract with Chavez' union.

Chavez has not been wholly successful. Against his wishes, members of his union have engaged in violence and intimidation. He was far less effective in organizing workers in Florida, Texas, and Arizona than in California. His United Farm Workers' Union had a ten-year struggle with a rival union organized by the Teamsters. Finally, in 1977, the Teamsters gave in and agreed that Chavez alone might organize those who labored in the fields.

Chavez is a man who, to quote his own words, has tried "to 'overcome' with love and compassion, with hard work and long hours, with stamina and patient tenacity, with truth and public appeal, with mobility and discipline, with politics and law, with prayer and fasting." Just before his assassination in 1968, Robert Kennedy called Chavez "one of the greatest of living Americans."

ment of Colored People (NAACP) is the League of United Latin-American Citizens (LULAC). This organization has won suits in federal courts to guarantee Chicanos the right to serve on juries, to send their children to unsegregated schools, and to receive instruction in Spanish as well as English.

The Chicanos are also beginning to be active in politics. Chicanos have been elected to local and state offices in the Southwest. They have sent their first members to the House of Representatives and the Senate.

Like the blacks, Mexican-Americans have developed a new pride in their identity. They welcome the term "Chicano," formerly a badge of inferiority.

Puerto Ricans

Puerto Ricans, as residents of a commonwealth of the United States, are free to enter the United States proper without restriction. Beginning after World War II, thousands of islanders sought to escape the poverty of their homeland by flocking to the cities of the Northeast such as New York and Newark and later to Midwestern cities.

Like many immigrants of the early 1900's, they were rural in background and had difficulty adjusting to the complicated ways of American cities. Their problem was compounded by the fact that they were faced with almost as much discrimination as American blacks. The jobs they could get were low paying. They often had to settle for inadequate housing.

But their status gradually improved. They were able to find better jobs, many started their own businesses, and they began to become a political force in the cities in which they lived. In 1970 the first representative to Congress of Puerto Rican origin, Herman Badillo, was elected from New York City.

The Lot of American Indians: "Red Power"

At the close of the nineteenth century, American Indians were a vanishing race. Now that is no longer true. Of all racial minorities, however, they share least in the benefits of American life. A study made in 1966 revealed that Indians suffered so much from malnutrition and disease that their life expectancy was 46 years, compared with a national average approaching 70 years. They had less formal schooling than any other minority group. Family income was less than half the national average. Most Indian reservations, where about half the Indians lived as wards of the federal government, were on arid, worn-out lands.

During the 1960's the Indians displayed a new militancy. In the state of Washington, men from over fifty Indian tribes joined a "fish-in." They deliberately broke game laws and risked imprisonment to protest loss of their former fishing and hunting rights. In South Dakota, Sioux tribes organized a statewide referendum against a law to give the state direct control over their reservations. The law was defeated by a four-to-one vote, and the Sioux celebrated with traditional war dances. A National Congress of American Indians proclaimed "Red Power." It demanded that the paternalistic policies of the federal Bureau of Indian Affairs be abandoned. "We simply want to run our lives our own way," said a young leader of the Congress. "Our own way" meant that many Indians wanted to retain or return to their ancient cultures, their rituals, their dances, their tribal organizations, their languages.

In 1973, a more militant Indian group, the American Indian Movement (AIM), seized the Indian reservation settlement of Wounded Knee, South Dakota, by force of arms to dramatize the Indian cause. They demanded that lands taken from Indians in violation of treaties be returned to them and that development programs on reservations be managed by tribal governments.

There was evidence that at long last white Americans might try to deal justly with Indians. In 1970 the Pueblo Indians of Taos, New Mexico, regained the Sacred Blue Lake, a place vital to their religious life. In 1972 millions of acres of land in Alaska were guaranteed to Indians and Eskimos. In 1975 a federal court decided that the Passamaquoddy and Penobscot Indians had a valid legal claim to over half the state of Maine, along with $25 billion in damages and unpaid rents. Lawyers of the Interior and Justice Departments argued on their behalf. Indians in Massachusetts, Connecticut, New York, and North Carolina also brought suit to recover tribal lands.

Rebellion on the Campus

In the 1960's and early 1970's young people were leaders in every movement to promote social justice. Their activities centered above all on college campuses. Revolutionary activity had long been a tradition of universities in countries as diverse as France, Argentina, Japan, and Czarist Russia. American college students, however, had generally been indifferent to movements seeking to alter the existing order. In the United States, so-called "college life" centered on having a good time—on proms, football weekends, fraternities and sororities. Observers of American college students in the 1950's described them as an apathetic generation. All they wanted, it appeared, was to prepare for jobs in an affluent society. At this time Clark Kerr, president of the University of California at Berkeley, observed: "The employers will love this generation; they are not going to press any grievances. They are going to be easy to handle. There aren't going to be any riots."

But suddenly a striking change of mood occurred. It first appeared, ironically enough, at Clark Kerr's own Berkeley campus, where in 1964 there was a riot involving thousands of students. Agitation for redress of student grievances spread to hundreds of institutions of higher learning. Conservatives insisted that parents, schools, and colleges had become too permissive. They regarded campus rebellions as the temper tantrums of spoiled children on a large scale. Those who took the side of the students argued that college students were more intelligent and better educated than ever, more disposed to question established beliefs, more eager to play a role in society. They were shocked by the contrasts between ugly facts of American life and the ideals of a society that claimed to provide "liberty and justice for all."

Certainly a large element in bringing on the new mood was a "generation gap" between students and their elders. This was summed up in the slogan, "Trust no one over thirty." Students developed a distinct culture, with characteristic styles of dress and behavior that dismayed older people. The new campus generation professed to be indifferent to vocational advancement and material success. Instead, they were interested in self-realization, in "doing their own thing."

A principal target of the students was the colleges and universities themselves. Demands made on hundreds of campuses included: abolition of codes of dress, attendance, and behavior; a more flexible curriculum, relevant to "the real world"; less rigid marking systems; participation in the decision-making process of institutions.

It was the Vietnam War that fanned rebellion to massive proportions. In fact, opposition to the war originated on the campuses of the country. Sit-ins and demonstrations marked each step in the escalation of the war. Hundreds of students publicly burned their draft cards to show their distaste for the war. There were widespread demands that universities terminate research supported by the Department of Defense and that units of the Reserve Officers Training Corps (ROTC) be discontinued.

When incidents inflamed campus opinion, students could exert influence beyond their numbers. Such a time occurred in the spring of 1970. On May 1 came news that President Nixon had ordered the invasion of Cambodia. Immediately there were protests, some of them violent, on scores of campuses. At Kent State University, at Kent, Ohio, rioting reached such proportions that an ROTC building was burned. The Governor sent in the National Guard. On May 4 a contingent of National Guardsmen, harassed by students, fired into the crowd, killing four students and wounding ten. On May 14 in a riot at Jackson State University, an all-black institution, at Jackson, Mississippi, student protest was suppressed by state police who fired at random into a dormitory. They killed two students and wounded nine.

The news from Kent and Jackson State, added to that from Cambodia, brought on a nationwide student strike. Over seven hundred colleges and universities either called off classes for a time or closed down completely. Professors often sided with the students.

For a time American society seemed dangerously polarized between those who considered the action of the guardsmen and the police a crime and those who defended it as a necessary action to preserve "law and order."

In the mid-1970's the atmosphere on campuses changed again. Violence of speech and action subsided. There was renewed interest in traditional studies. College libraries reported an increase of books in circulation. The change of temper is difficult to explain. Certainly the end of the Vietnam War in 1973, with its threat of compulsory military service, had something to do with it. The talk of violent revolution had

been somewhat of a fad with no relation to reality. What the students wanted on the campuses they themselves had won—notably a great relaxation of rules and a much more flexible curriculum. They had also acquired full citizenship with the passage of the Twenty-sixth Amendment to the Constitution. This granted the right of voting in federal and state elections to anyone over eighteen years of age. When they first acquired this right in 1971, many students plunged into politics. They had a great deal to do with nominating George McGovern for Democratic candidate for President in 1972. After his defeat, there was much less political activity among young voters.

The Women's Liberation Movement

Women compose over 50 percent of the American population, but their political, economic, legal and social situation resembles that of a disadvantaged minority. In 1920, the Nineteenth Amendment to the Constitution (see pp. 148–149) granted women the right to vote. Relatively few, however, have held political office, especially high political office. In 1977, women held less than five percent of the elective offices in the United States. No woman was a United States senator or a justice of the Supreme Court, or mayor of a major city. Only one was a state governor, two were Cabinet members. Of the 435 members of the House of Representatives, 18 were women. In her lively biography, *Unbought, Unbossed,* Shirley Chisholm, the first black woman to serve in the House of Representatives, wrote:

In the political world I have been far oftener discriminated against because I am a woman than because I am black. When I decided to run for Congress, I knew I would encounter both anti-black and anti-feminist sentiments. What surprised me was the much greater virulence of the sex discrimination.

WOMEN IN AMERICA

Note the striking difference in the pattern of the average women's life since the opening of the 20th century. Not only, as shown here, is the child-bearing and rearing period shorter, but women have fewer children and live far longer.

Women Live Longer Than Men
EXPECTATION OF LIFE AT BIRTH

1901-1910
Male — 49.3
Female — 52.6 (↑21.8 Probable child-bearing period)

1968
Male — 66.6
Female — 74.4 (↑20.8)

↑ Median age at first marriage

/// Probable child-bearing period

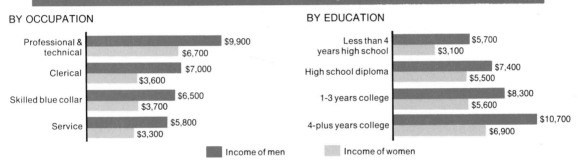

Median Incomes of Men and Women Workers, Same Age, Same Number of Years on Job, Same Number of Years of Education, Holding Same Type of Job, c. 1971.

BY OCCUPATION

	Income of men	Income of women
Professional & technical	$9,900	$6,700
Clerical	$7,000	$3,600
Skilled blue collar	$6,500	$3,700
Service	$5,800	$3,300

BY EDUCATION

	Income of men	Income of women
Less than 4 years high school	$5,700	$3,100
High school diploma	$7,400	$5,500
1-3 years college	$8,300	$5,600
4-plus years college	$10,700	$6,900

Income of men   Income of women

Compare the above figures with those of the graph of income of whites and non-whites (p. 755). Does the comparison agree with Shirley Chisholm's statement that she had found more discrimination as a woman than as a black?

As we have seen (see p. 707), World War II brought women into the job market as never before. Ever since, the number of women in the labor force has increased. In the mid-1970's they composed about 40 percent of those employed. In a report published in 1976 the United States Department of Labor revealed that full-time working men received on the average 75 percent more pay than full-time working women. Men held 95 percent of jobs paying $15,000 and up. The Labor Department noted that women received as many years of schooling as men, but the kind of education and counseling they received "directed them into traditional and low-paying jobs." Even when women do exactly the same work as men they tend to receive lower pay (see graph above).

The life expectancy of women has risen to over seventy years. The average mother has more than half her adult life ahead of her after her child-rearing days are over (see graph, p. 781). Women were asking what they were to do if not to take a job. And why not a good one?

Recently there had been a remarkable resurgence of feminism, known in its modern phase as "women's liberation." One might date its beginning to 1963, with the publication of *The Feminine Mystique* by Betty Friedan. This book attacked the concept that the destiny of women was to be wives and mothers, devoting their lives to child-rearing and washing dishes. Ms. Friedan described in acid terms how women's magazines, news media, and advertisers created an image of women designed to imprison them in the household. "The image of women that emerges," she wrote, ". . . is young

Militant feminists demonstrate for the proposed Equal Rights Amendment to the Constitution.

and frivolous, almost childlike; feminine; passive; gaily content in a world of bedroom and kitchen, sex, babies and home." When such a person did work, it was only to gain "pin money." She was not to be considered a serious competitor in the labor market.

In 1966, Ms. Friedan headed a group who founded the National Organization for Women (NOW). NOW grew rapidly from 300 members in a single chapter to several thousand in scores of chapters scattered throughout the country. NOW proved an effective lobby against various forms of discrimination, such as separate want-ads for male and female job opportunities, and airline rules that women flight attendants must retire at 32 years of age. The task of NOW was greatly assisted by the fact that the Civil Rights Act of 1964 prohibited discrimination against women in employment.

QUESTION • In what ways does the English language reveal former male domination of society?

In the short time it has been in existence, the modern women's rights movement has scored notable triumphs. To cite only a few: Women have entered areas formerly reserved entirely for men, such as the priesthood of the Episcopal Church and the armed service academies at West Point and Annapolis. The impact of the women's movement can be seen in schools, with the admission of girls to shop courses and the great increase in funds for girls' athletics. Many formerly all-male colleges admitted women as students. Women entered the professions—law, medicine, engineering, and others—in greater numbers.

In 1972, Congress voted by overwhelming majorities in both houses to submit to the states for ratification an Equal Rights Amendment (ERA) to the Constitution. It forbade the United States or any state to abridge "equal rights under the law" on account of sex. For ERA to become law, 38 states had to ratify it by 1979. By mid-1977, 35 states had done so.

NIXON LANDSLIDE, 1972

There was no doubt that Nixon would run again as Republican candidate in the presidential election of 1972. He ran against Senator George McGovern of South Dakota, who won the Democratic nomination with the support of a coalition of young people, blacks, and women. The McGovern campaign never got off the ground. The Democratic Vice-Presidential candidate, Senator Thomas Eagleton, was forced to resign when it was discovered that he had been three times hospitalized for mental illness. Democratic party regulars and labor union leaders were cool toward McGovern, if not hostile.

Meanwhile, President Nixon conducted an astute campaign. He made sure of the support of right-wing Republicans by choosing Vice-President Spiro Agnew to run again. The removal of ground troops from Vietnam had defused the war issue. The recent Peking and Moscow summits seemed to signal the end of the Cold War. The President appealed to "middle Americans" by his praise of the virtue of hard work, by his stand against busing, and by appeals to patriotism.

During the last month of the 1972 campaign,

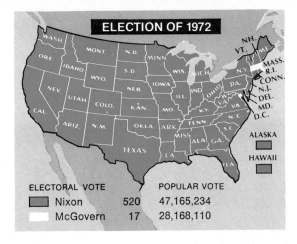

ELECTION OF 1972

ELECTORAL VOTE		POPULAR VOTE
Nixon	520	47,165,234
McGovern	17	28,168,110

President Nixon justified the prediction of political pollsters by gaining a victory even greater than that of Johnson over Goldwater in 1964 (see map, p. 749).

Henry Kissinger announced that a Vietnam ceasefire was imminent. Although hostilities had not ended by election day, belief that the unpopular war was coming to an end increased Nixon's already immense lead over McGovern. The final result was predictable. On election day the President received 61 percent of the popular vote and gained every electoral vote except those of Massachusetts and the District of Columbia.

Richard Nixon had won an immense victory, but never had the coatttails of a victorious candidate been so short. In spite of his huge majority, the President failed to carry Republican congressional candidates with him. The Democrats easily kept control of both houses of Congress. This strange result had a possible explanation. The political advisers of the President had organized a Committee to Reelect the President (CREEP), which collected a campaign fund of over fifty million dollars. But the immense sum was devoted entirely to promoting Nixon's candidacy. CREEP refused to cooperate with the Republican National Committee in assisting Republican candidates for Congress.

Nixon's campaign managers were guilty not merely of failing to cooperate with fellow Republicans. It later turned out that much of the campaign fund had been illegally contributed by corporations and that "dirty tricks" used by agents of CREEP against the Democrats went beyond the limits of decency. Furthermore, a group employed by CREEP had been arrested while breaking into the office of the Democratic National Committee in the Watergate Office Building in Washington. The President's press secretary dismissed the affair as a "third-rate burglary." This incident, seemingly trivial at the time, was to have tragic consequences for the President.

"THE IMPERIAL PRESIDENCY"

In 1973, Arthur M. Schlesinger, Jr., published *The Imperial Presidency*, a book that warned the American people that they were in danger of tyranny. Schlesinger's book was only one among several that expressed alarm at the immense increase in the power of the American chief executive.

A Product of World War II and the Cold War

The imperial presidency was a product of World War II and the Cold War. One can see its origins when Franklin Roosevelt on his own authority carried on a naval war against Nazi submarines during the Battle of Britain. From Roosevelt on, every President used his power as Commander-in-Chief to carry on war without a congressional declaration: Truman in Korea, Eisenhower in Guatemala, Kennedy in the Bay of Pigs, Johnson in Vietnam. Furthermore, conduct of foreign affairs became almost the exclusive concern of the executive department. Formal treaties, which, according to the Constitution, are made with the "advice and consent" of the Senate, have given way to "executive agreements," in which the Senate plays no part.

With these developments has come a great increase in the power of the "military-industrial complex" against which President Eisenhower gave warning in his farewell address (see p. 738). This power is often exercised through the National Security Council (NSC), which, rather